HANDBOOK ON CONTEMPORARY EDUCATION

HANDBOOK ON CONTEMPORARY EDUCATION

Compiled and Edited by
Dr. Steven E. Goodman
in association with
Reference Development Corporation

R. R. BOWKER COMPANY
A Xerox Education Company
NEW YORK & LONDON, 1976

Published by R. R. Bowker Co. (A Xerox Education Company)
1180 Avenue of the Americas
New York, N.Y. 10036

Printed and bound in the United States of America.

Reference Development Corporation creates and compiles
specialized information resources, and is located at Princeton
Station Office Park, Box 2331, Princeton, New Jersey 08540.

Library of Congress Cataloging in Publication Data

Main entry under title:

Handbook on contemporary education.

   1. Education——1965—   ——Handbooks, manuals,
etc. 2. Education——United States——1965—
——Handbooks, manuals, etc. 3. Education——1965—
——Addresses, essays, lectures. I. Goodman,
Steven E. II. Reference Development Corporation.
LB17.H27   370   75-26744
ISBN 0-8352-0640-8

CONTENTS

PREFACE

This Handbook has been created to provide access to information about contemporary topics in education. Practitioners and students at all levels in education have a need to know what is happening today, in addition to historical treatments within the literature.

Each paper within the Handbook is designed to provide the user with needed "state-of-the-art" information as well as further sources of information. One of the significant features of each paper is the inclusion of specific programs, projects and activities so that the researcher can locate *human resources* as well as the literature.

The handbook will be of use to graduate and undergraduate students in education and to practicing teachers, administrators, librarians and planners. The papers and the further sources of information cited in each paper should lead the reader to thousands of people and documents for either research or program planning purposes.

A thorough review of *Research in Education,* a monthly U.S. Government publication, indicates that there are few papers, articles or reports that attempt to summarize the current state of affairs on specific topics in education. This handbook should allow the user to spend more time in the analysis of what is found instead of spending endless hours trying to locate information.

The Handbook is indexed by subject field using the terminology provided by the Educational Researches Information Centers (ERIC) system. Some of the references cited at the end of the papers include an "ED" number. This refers to the number cited in *Research in Education,* which can be found in most libraries.

The editor wishes to thank the authors, as well as those organizations that gave permission to reprint significant papers.

Dr. Steven E. Goodman
Associate Professor
St. John's University, New York

PART I

EDUCATIONAL CHANGE AND PLANNING

1

EDUCATIONAL FUTURISM

by Walter G. Hack
Professor of Educational Administration
Ohio State University
Columbus, Ohio

The nature of man as a rational being suggests a concern for the future. The ends sought and the means used in the meeting of this concern have evolved in a pattern not dissimilar to man's cultural evolution. The earliest written history of such concern has been identified (Hencley and Yates, 1974) as the *Book of the Dead* from Egypt sometime around 3500 B.C. This early concern for the future evolved toward speculation of what the future would be like. Utopian or doomsday concepts are examples of this response. Superstition provided an early vehicle for envisioning the future. Oracles, seers, witches and crystal balls became means of forward glimpses. Early rational approaches employed historical perspectives as bases for simple projection and anticipation of the future. As technology has broadened the data base and extended the ability to order, store, retrieve and process data, complex forecasting has been developed.

A universal concern for the future is taken for granted; and in recent years an interest has emerged in both ascertaining the nature of the future and means to influence or determine it (Hack et al., 1971). These notions are embraced in the concept of futurism. The scientific study of the future has been defined (Hencley and Yates, 1974) as a systematic process for identifying trends and alternatives that point to the issues of the future; the process also identifies the opportunities as well as the problems which are likely to be a part of the future.

Futurism as an area of both study and concern has shown several faces. The basic concept is generic, as it can be considered as a generalized phenomenon, e.g., the nature of the future. It frequently displays a more particularistic character when one considers the nature of a specialized area, e.g., the future of education. However, basic tenets of futurism must be considered before one can profitably explore a specific topic such as that of educational futurism.

The major dimensions of the examination of this specific topic are related to (a) the purposes, or the "why," of educational futurism; (b) the methodology, or the "how," of educational futurism; (c) the substantive findings, products, or the "what," of educational futurism; and (d) the emerging controversies or issues in educational futurism.

REVIEW OF THE LITERATURE

The literature of futurism is varied, and, with its relatively recent emphasis toward applications in discrete areas of human endeavor, it is difficult to describe in a comprehensive and systematic fashion. As a consequence, the following review will be limited to a representative selection of recent literature dealing with futurism as a general concept and with educational futurism in particular.

Perhaps the major impetus for the current interest in the systematic study of the future was provided by the Commission on the Year 2000 of the American Academy of Arts and Sciences (Bell, 1967). This Commission of outstanding scholars from many disciplines and interests developed the idea of alternate futures accommodating the interaction of four sources of change in society. These included technology, diffusion, structural developments in the society, and the relationship of the United States to the rest of the world. The commission reported both futuristic methodologies and substantive alternative futures.

Kahn and Wiener (1967) expanded on certain aspects of the Commission on the Year 2000. Their major emphasis was on speculation regarding international politics, the supporting multifold trends, and implications for policy research to operationalize futurology.

Operational models of futuristic studies were developed (Armytage, 1968) which provided a linkage between the early intuitive and speculative work and a systematic methodology.

In 1968 an anthology (Baier and Rescher, 1968) was published which explored the interface of values and technology on the future with the thesis that social change could be affected in ways that would not be incompatible with primary social values. Futuristic perspectives which emphasized new processes and methods of determining "value impact forecasting" were proposed and prototypes were proposed.

Futurism from a generalist perspective received its greatest popular impetus from *Future Shock* (Toffler, 1970). In describing the symptoms of future shock in terms understood by nearly all (and experienced by most), Toffler attributed a mass neurosis to the shock of the premature arrival of the future on today's society. Factors responsible for future shock grew out of a new society characterized by (a) the temporal rather than the permanent, (b) pace which is rapid rather than moderate, and (c) change which is characterized by a system-break rather than a sequential development. Toffler proposed ways for the future society to cope with such shock. These range from crisis counseling through technological control and social futurism. Considerable emphasis was given to Councils of the Future for schools and lifelong educational capabilities.

Educational futurism as a discrete area of interest seemed to develop in a pattern similar to that of futurism in a general perspective. There have been many intuitive and speculative statements regarding education, e.g., what schools ought to be and what authors would like them to be. An early departure from the former was *Inventing Education for the Future* (Hirsch, ed. 1967). Hirsch and his associates considered ways to study the future, and determined the future's impact on education. They considered specific educational innovations that seem to be called for, then developed a systematic way to relate changes, needs, and strategies in educational futures.

Work at the Educational Policy Research Center of Syracuse University (Ziegler and Marien, 1970) provided approaches to define educational futures. In a macrosystem where education is only one part, five planning models were developed: the future as the present; the future as an extrapolation of the past; the single alternative future; the technological future; and the comprehensive future.

A committee of the National Conference of Professors of Educational Administration (Hack et al., 1971) used the alternative futures approaches in *Educational Futurism: 1985.* The authors used a comprehensivist approach by assembling the results of specialists working on complex problems and issues of specialization. In this context alternate educational futures were developed in terms of program, governance, organization, the administrators, and educational planning.

A learning systems perspective (Barnes, 1972) has been developed as an important consideration in educational futurism. Based on the assumption of the closing of the industrial age and the coming of a new age, a living-learning system was designed around a Disorientation/Orientation/Reorientation center. The center was to orient the learner to the new learning system and at the same time gain fresh insight into himself and his environment.

Speculation about the future as defined by contemporary educational issues (Shane, 1973) has established a useful link between today and the future. Since the issues relate to major educational policies, future concerns in these areas provided some policy targets. Shane spoke to contemporary issues including educational objectives, changing needs, educational control, curriculum content and organization, ethnic minority needs, professionalism, accountability, legal status, and school finance.

An example of the aggregation of knowledge about educational futurism and its impact is the work of the University Council of Educational Administration. In a recent book (Hencley and Yates, 1974) a sophisticated and comprehensive treatment of both methodology and substance of educational futurism is provided. Authors from many disciplines speak to concerns which include a rationale for and an historical evolution of, forecasting techniques, a number of techniques, the interrelationships between and among the techniques, and underlying philosophical issues of forecasting.

Futuristic studies applied to the purposes and processes of educational institutions are best illustrated by *The Future: Create or Inherit* (Case and Olson, 1974). The book, a product of the Study Commission of Undergraduate Education and the Education of Teachers, reflects varying perspectives on educational futurism as establishment—or revolutionary—oriented, as technologically—or value—related, and as requiring a legalistic or a poetic approach.

It has been estimated by Joseph (Hencley and Yates, 1974) that university courses in forecasting the future have expanded rapidly—from less than 100 in 1969 to "thousands" by 1973. Examples of such courses de-

voted to educational futurism include a seminar offered by New York University, an inquiry seminar in educational administration at the University of Vermont, and courses offered by the University of Wisconsin, Bowling Green State University, and Miami University.

Conferences on educational futurism designed for educational practitioners have been offered by professional organizations. Two examples are "Alternative Futures for Education Symposium '73" (Research for Better Schools, Inc., 1973) and "The Uses of Futurist Techniques in Long Range Educational Planning" (American Association of School Administrators, 1973).

Contemporary literature is a rich source of insight into the bases of educational futurism. A major theme in the rationale for the study of futurism is that of the necessity for the control of social problems which are growing in magnitude as a result of modern technology (Baier and Rescher, 1969). Futurism provides a vehicle for such control within the context of the dominant values of the persons affected.

The necessity for a comprehensive new world view, as well as social invention, provides a rationale for futurism (North, 1970). An aggressive reform movement is called for at both individual and system levels.

Joseph (Hencley and Yates, 1974) presented a most comprehensive, yet cogent, basis for educational futurism. He cited the need for such forecasting in order to avoid the inevitable devastation if present trends were perpetuated. He also cited the utilization of futurism in avoiding future shock and in responding to current negativism and possible panic.

The how, or methodology, of educational futurism reflects one dimension of the problem of technology— the rapid proliferation of scientific literature which results in an information blizzard, making it almost impossible to know and understand all the alternatives. Items in the review of the literature reflect several methodologies. However, the most up-to-date taxonomy of techniques for forecasting the future is found in the work of Earl C. Joseph (Hencley and Yates, 1974). He describes thirteen techniques:

- *Trend extrapolation forecasting.* Extrapolated future based on plots of the past
- *Delphi forecasting.* A multistep process of intuitive forecasts of alternative possible futures by "experts." The experts are polled and repolled to arrive at a consensus.
- *Scenario forecasting.* A description about a future in a systematic and developmental form with emphasis on how events transpired to get from today into the future.
- *Matrix forecasting.* Includes several varieties (cross-impact, decision, mission and cross-correlation matrices) which break down the future into discrete components. This allows each component to be compared separately with each of the others, and thus show interaction.
- *Relevance tree and contextual map forecasting.* Trees or networks of alternative pathways to future

goals. These maps depict time flow, the hierarchy of events and their interconnectivity.

- *Simulation forecasting.* Models which simulate the future can predict future probables. These models, utilizing computer gaming, depict the structure and interactions in forecasting possible futures.
- *Monte Carlo analysis forecasting.* Relates probabilities of occurrence. It is based on "constrained randomness" and usually used with other methods of forecasting.
- *Morphological forecasting.* A systematic process which identifies or formulates solutions through the analysis of present or future problems. The alternative solutions become the goals, or the alternative futures.
- *Alternative futures.* Conceptions of the future which differ from projections of current trends. These narrative descriptions are derived from many different systematic techniques.
- *Bayesian statistical forecasting.* Utilizes available relevant information in order to draw statistical inferences about the uncertain future.
- *Force analysis forecasting.* The identification, analysis and forecasting of the future impact of forces (sets of events, pressures, problems, social reactions, etc.) on the area of study. It describes the environment of change and the future of the given area.
- *Markov chain forecasting.* Applies probability theory to a mathematical model for describing processes in a sequence of steps through a set of states. The technique is used to analyze current movements for the purpose of forecasting future movements.
- *Precursor forecasting.* Involves the analysis of multiple forecasts which together yield patterns of change in one discrete field.

The what, or substantive product, of exercises in educational futurism is in many ways both common and unique. From their specific forecasts, it is apparent that the futurists do not agree as to what the future will hold, but they do agree it will be far different from today. There is some consensus among the educational futurists about the character of several dimensions of education, and the following are somewhat representative conclusions.

In terms of purposes of education, most of the conventional purposes will be retained, but new technological pressures will sharpen concern for increased mutual interdependency in a more fragile environment (Shane, 1973; Hencley and Yates, 1974; Case and Olson, 1974).

Educational programs will be more individualized and open, and will utilize a wide variety of institutions, technology, and resources (O'Toole, 1968; Barnes, 1973; Case and Olson, 1974).

The organization of a school or its future counterpart will be nonbureaucratic. Instead it will reflect the differentiation of its program and will use concepts such as an open information processing system (Frymier, 1973; Hack et al., 1971; Case and Olson, 1974).

The governance base of educational institutions will be broadened. A wide variety of groups in a broadened concept of community will participate in educational decision making (Shane, 1973). Furthermore, governance roles and structures are likely to be changed as the concept of representativeness changes, e.g., teachers serving on policy boards. The locus of governance will shift more decisions to higher levels of government (Hack et al., 1971).

The administrator of a school organization will have a new role and will function in a different fashion. He will assume many functions which today are identified as legislative, simply because of the complexity of policy issues and his technical competency to understand the overall picture (Cleveland, 1973). One of the major functions of the future administrator will be that of leading his staff in understanding the nature and dynamics of the school as a complex organization (Hack et al., 1971).

CURRENT ISSUES

In any new field of interest which has not yet established the parameters of a recognized discipline, there are many disparate issues. A large number of these deal with the nature, scope, and character of the field, and so are definitional in nature, e.g., what constitutes educational futurism? Of more substance are issues in educational futurism which fall into three general categories. (It is granted that many sub-issues spin off each of these major concerns, and no attempt will be made to elaborate on such spinoffs.)

The first issue in educational futurism concerns itself with the relationship(s) among speculation, projection, and forecasting. There is considerable controversy regarding the appropriateness of each of these approaches to the study of futurism, and the nature of the contribution each can make. Speculation is supported by those who value creative approaches to designing the future, whereas projection is favored by those who rely on moving from the present to the future by logic and empirical data. Forecasting involves multiple futures and alternative means to respond to them. It is somewhat eclectic in both content and methodology. Thus, the major issue involves the questions of what emphasis and what purposes are served by each of the three approaches. There is also the related question of the relationship of the approaches to bring about complementarity, wherein each approach supports the others.

A second major issue involves the selection of the appropriate methodology to achieve a given objective. The taxonomy of thirteen methodologies described earlier provides a wide range of alternatives. The nature of the available data base has much to do with appropriate methodology. Projection would be very difficult and of questionable validity if historical data were incomplete or inaccurate. The Delphi technique is dependent on the capability of experts in the given field of the exercise.

The third major issue deals with values. Simply stated, the issue asks, "Is it appropriate for futurists to intervene in the modification of human values by inventing a future?" Some futurists take the position that work should be done within the context of present dominant values, whereas others accept both the inevitability of change in values and the responsibility of value change in the direction of rational futurism rather than evolutionary chance.

REFERENCES

Baier, Kurt and Rescher, Nicholas. *Values and the Future: The Impact of Technological Change on American Values.* New York: The Free Press, 1969.

Barnes, Ron. *Learning Systems for the Future.* Bloomington, Indiana: Phi Delta Kappa Educational Foundation, 1972.

Bell, Daniel. *Toward the Year 2000: Work in Progress. Daedleus,* Summer, 1967, 96.

Case, Charles W. and Olson, Paul A. *The Future: Create or Inherit.* Lincoln, Nebraska: Study Commission on Undergraduate Education and the Education of Teachers, 1974.

Hack, Walter G. et al. *Educational Futurism: 1985.* Berkeley, Calif.: McCutchan, 1971.

Hencley, Stephen P. and Yates, James R. *Futurism in Education.* Berkeley, Calif.: McCutchan, 1974.

Hirsch, Werner, ed., *Inventing Education for the Future.* San Francisco: Chandler, 1967.

Kahn, Herman and Wiener, Anthony J. *The Year 2000, a Framework for Speculation.* New York: Macmillan, 1967.

North, Robert C. *Alternative Futures for Society: Certain Variables and Parameters.* Paper presented at the annual meetings, American Orthopsychiatric Association, San Francisco, March 24, 1970.

O'Toole, John F. *Education in the 1980's: An Overview.* Santa Monica, Calif.: System Development Corporation, 1968.

Shane, Harold G. *Looking to the Future: Reassessment of Educational Issues of the 1970's. Phi Delta Kappan,* 1973, 54, 326-337.

Toffler, Alvin, *Future Shock.* New York: Random House, 1970.

Ziegler, Warren L., with the assistance of Michael Marien. *An Approach to the Futures–Perspective in American Education.* Syracuse: Educational Policy Research Center, 1970.

ADDITIONAL RESOURCES

Bibliographic

Anderson, Robert H., Almy, Millie, Shane, Harold G., and Tyler, Ralph. *Education in Anticipation of Tomorrow.* Worthington, Ohio: Charles A. Jones, 1973.

Armytage, W. H. G. *Yesterday's Tomorrows: A Historical Survey of Future Societies.* Toronto: University of Toronto Press, 1968.

Baier, Kurt, and Rescher, Nicolas, eds., *Values and the Future: The Impact of Technological Change on American Values.* New York: The Free Press, 1969.

Bell, Daniel, ed. *Toward the Year 2000: Work in Progress.* New York: Houghton-Mifflin, 1968.

Bennis, Warren G., and Slater, Philip E. *The Temporary Society.* New York: Harper & Row, 1968.

deBrigard, Paul, and Helmer, Olaf. *Some Potential Societal Developments–1970-2000.* Middletown, Conn.: Institute for the Future, 1970.

Fuller, R. Buckminster. *Utopia or Oblivion? The Prospects for Humanity.* New York: Bantam Books, 1969.

Gross, Bertram M., ed. *Social Intelligence for America's Future: Explorations in Societal Problems.* Boston: Allyn and Bacon, Inc., 1969.

Harman, Willis W. *Alternative Futures and Educational Policy.*

Menlo Park, Calif.: Stanford Research Institute, 1970.

Hirsch, Werner Z. and Colleagues. *Inventing Education for the Future.* San Francisco: Chandler, 1967.

Kahn, Herman, and Wiener, Anthony J. *The Year 2000: A Framework for Speculation on the Next Thirty-Three Years.* New York: Macmillan, 1967.

Marien, Michael, comp. *Alternative Futures for Learning: An Annotated Bibliography of Educational Trends, Forecasts and Proposals.* Syracuse: Educational Policy Research Center, 1971.

Marty, Martin E. *The Search for a Usable Future.* New York: Harper & Row, 1969.

McHale, John. *The Future of the Future.* New York: George Braziller, 1969.

———. *Typological Survey of Futures Research in the U.S.* Binghamton: State University of New York, Center for Integrative Studies, 1970.

Michael, Donald N. *The Unprepared Society: Planning for a Precarious Future.* New York: Basic Books, 1968.

Rochberg, Richard, Gordon, Theodore J., and Helmer, Olaf. *The Use of Cross-Impact Matrices for Forecasting and Planning.* Middletown, Conn.: Institute for the Future, IFF Report R-10, April 1970.

Theobald, Robert, ed. *An Alternative Future for America II.* Revised and Enlarged Edition. Chicago: Swallow, 1970

Toffler, Alvin. *Future Shock.* New York: Random House, 1970.

Weaver, W. Timothy. *The Delphi Method.* Syracuse: Educational Policy Research Center. Working Draft, June 1970.

Ziegler, Warren L., with the assistance of Michael Marien. *An Approach to the Futures–Perspective in American Education.* Syracuse: Educational Policy Research Center, 1970.

Futurist Organizations and Journals

Futures. The Journal of Forecasting and Planning. Guildford, Surrey, England: Iliffe Science and Technology Publications, Ltd., 32 High Street.

Notes on the Future of Education. Published by the Educational Policy Research Center at Syracuse, 1206 Harrison Street, Syracuse, N.Y. 13210.

Policy Sciences: An International Journal for the Policy Sciences. American Elsevier Publications, 52 Vanderbilt Avenue, New York, N.Y. 10017.

Technological Forecasting: An International Journal. American Elsevier Publications, 52 Vanderbilt Avenue, New York, N.Y. 10017.

The Futurist. *A Journal of Forecasts, Trends and Ideas About the Future.* Washington: World Future Society, P.O. Box 19285, Twentieth Street Station, Washington, D.C. 20036.

2

PLANNING CHANGE IN EDUCATION

by Sam D. Sieber
Educational Consultant
Red Hook, St. Thomas, United States Virgin Islands

The term "change agent" has enjoyed a vogue since its introduction in 1958 by Lippitt, Watson and Westley in a book entitled *The Dynamics of Planned Change.* At that time the term referred to outside agents whose help was enlisted by any groups, organizations or communities (the "client system") involved in a deliberate effort to improve themselves, their relationships or their setting, or to agents who themselves initiated a "change effort." Subsequently, the term was expanded to cover a wider array of tasks and personnel than envisioned in this original conception. Further, the introduction of alternative terms to sharpen the concept and to avoid the negative connotations of "change agent" has created some terminological confusion. It becomes important, therefore, to understand the major, distinctive *types* of change agents in education—their activities, their contributions and their possible limitations. The types discussed here are the Advocate, the Conveyor (or Information Specialist), the Organizational Development Trainer, the New Style Consultant, the Quality Controller, the Political Change Agent, and the Academic Trainer. (See also Havelock, 1969, Chapter 7.)

In seeking to delineate the typical problems faced by change agents and the best means of overcoming them, Lippitt, Watson and Westley (1958) drew upon experiences in a wide range of settings, including business and industrial firms, government bureaus, and total communities. Taking a cue from medical practice and psychological counseling, they placed special emphasis on the "diagnosis" of the client system's "problem," an approach which persists in certain definitions of the change agent's responsibilities (see below). Other major tasks of the change agent in this original conception were to assess the client system's motivation and capacity to change; to assess his own motivation and resources; to select appropriate change objectives; to establish and maintain a clear-cut relationship with the client system (or subparts of the system); to choose the appropriate helping role to recognize and guide the phases of change; and to choose appropriate specific techniques and modes of behavior to effect change. While the authors admitted that disagreement existed among professional change agents about how to perform these tasks, an essential point of agreement seemed to be that successful change efforts required a knowledge of how to deal with complex and sensitive human relationships under stressful circumstances.

It is clear that the original definition of the change agent covered a wide range of activities. In recent years the term has been expanded to cover an even wider array of tasks. In a review of research on innovation, Rodgers (1962) applied the term to the county agent of the U.S. Department of Agriculture whose major role was conveying new ideas and practices to farmers. Further, the possibility of change agents operating as members of the client system is now widely accepted. In the field of education in particular, the change agent concept has been expanded to include virtually every professional position. Thus, a recent catalogue of a graduate training program in the diffusion and adoption of instructional innovations (Indiana University, School of Education, 1972) lists the following positions among those which "might involve change agent roles":

State Department curriculum consultants
Directors or coordinators of federal programs
School district administrators
Public school principals and department
    chairmen
Public school teachers
Curriculum coordinators
Audiovisual coordinators and media specialists
Managers of learning resources centers
College and university administrators
College and university faculty members
Staff members of urban education and poverty
    programs
Personnel of continuing education and extension
    programs
ERIC Clearinghouse personnel
R&D Center personnel
Regional educational laboratory personnel
Curriculum development center personnel
Educational renewal center personnel

And a project at the University of Michigan has sought to train students in public schools as change agents. In short, anyone participating in the field of education, regardless of how humble or exalted his position, is now deemed a potential change agent.

This expansion of the concept to cover every conceivable effort to improve educational practice has converted the term into a catch-all phrase. Moreover, it appears that the term has acquired certain connotations that antagonize clients. As Havelock and Havelock (1973) point out:

> The descriptive term "change agent" has wide currency, but is probably offensive to a number of educators because it implies a "know-it-all" expert who pushes change for the sake of change. Such connotations are misleading and destructive for the man who is trying to establish a new position. (p. 171)

Accordingly, Havelock and Havelock list a number of alternative titles to avoid the change agent stigma, for example, "innovation process consultant," "knowledge utilization coordinator," or "problem-solving process agent" (p. 170).

The introduction of competing terms, however, has created additional confusion, since different persons may understand these terms in different ways. Sometimes there would even seem to be confusion in the mind of a single expert. For example, in one publication Havelock (1969) views change agents as one kind of "knowledge linking role"; but in a later publication (Havelock and Havelock, 1973) he views "resource linkers" as one kind of change agent.

These remarks on the way in which the meaning of the term has been stretched should not be taken to imply that specialization in the improvement of educational systems is not a worthwhile endeavor. The original conception of Lippitt, Watson and Westley afforded both rationale and legitimation in an area of work that was sorely needed in education. (See also Bennis, Benne and Chin, 1969, for an important collection of papers that gave further impetus to this movement.) But today, owing to the many new roles that are emerging in educational planning, it is impossible to describe the goals and functions of the definitive change agent in education. Rather, we must devote attention to several major types of change agents that have appeared in recent years.

THE ADVOCATE

The advocate represents a type of change agent whose job is to promote a particular program or practice, such as team teaching, the new math, individually prescribed instruction (IPI), flexible scheduling, open schools, instructional resource centers, middle schools, a new textbook by a commercial publisher, and so on. In short, the Advocate is best understood as a kind of salesman of educational innovations. Owing to the pressures on the R&D Centers, Regional Laboratories, and other developmental agencies to demonstrate the success of their new products, the advocacy of particular practices and programs has reached a floodtide in recent years.

Advocates may be found either inside or outside the school system. The insider has been called a "leader" by Havelock (1969), a term which includes formal leaders such as C&I Supervisors, "gatekeepers," who provide outsiders with access to the system, and opinion leaders, who influence other members to try out a particular innovation. Still another type of inside change agent is the innovator himself, who by word or deed advocates a new practice. Sometimes an informal leader is given formal authority to supervise the installation of a new program in which he has a keen interest. (For an outline of how this might operate, see Sieber, 1968, pp. 381-382.) Since innovators are often perceived as mavericks by the school staff, it is sometimes advisable to encourage the more prestigious or conservative leaders to become innovators so that the rest of the staff are favorably impressed. (For a study that identifies innovators in contrast to opinion leaders, see Herlig, 1971.) Frequently, "home-grown" innovations are diffused to other schools through School Study Councils, although these councils also transmit the products and ideas of university-based personnel and other R&D experts (Danenburg, 1970, Kohl, 1973).

Outside Advocates are of many kinds, and do not necessarily meet with educators on their home grounds. The proponents of "basic education" who captured the nation's attention in the late 1950s were Advocates who resorted to the mass media. Directors of federal programs and other top-level managers who are "pushing" a specific practice or program by means of planning, supervision or publicity may also be regarded as Advocates.

Clearly, the Advocate is a familiar personage in the educational scene and needs no further introduction. His significance to the present discussion resides mainly in his frequent failure to effect widespread or enduring change, a failure which has given rise to a variety of alternative change agent roles (to be discussed below). (For evidence of the failure of major innovations to be adopted, see Gideonse, 1970; Goodlad, Klein, et al.,

1970.) There are probably several reasons for the failure of advocacy. In the first place, because the Advocate tends to specialize in a particular innovation, there is a dual tendency to neglect the suitability of the innovation to a specific client system and to exaggerate the claims of the innovation. This tendency arouses skepticism and promotes ultimate failure. A second problem with the Advocate is his neglect of the organizational, cultural, and interpersonal barriers to adoption or change. Typically, an Advocate rests his case on rational appeals, such as research evidence or a particular philosophy of education, while paying scant attention to the nonrational incentives for change (or for conservatism) or to the bureaucratic barriers to innovation. (For a discussion of organization and community influences that affect the adoption of innovations, see Sieber, 1968; for criticisms of the "Rational Man" strategy of change, see Sieber, 1972.) A third reason for failure is that Advocates are seldom concerned with the "institutionalization," or continued maintenance, of an innovation. Hence, even when a new practice is adopted, its lifespan is generally short. For these reasons, educational planners have sought to develop a number of alternative change agent approaches.

THE CONVEYOR (OR INFORMATION SPECIALIST)

Few trends in planned educational change have been more dramatic in recent years than the emergence of a host of specialties and agencies devoted to the collection, abstracting, storage, retrieval and dissemination of educational information. Here we use the title of Conveyor to refer to individuals engaged in any of these activities at any level of the educational structure. (For the frequency with which different information functions are performed by local and state agencies, see York, 1968.) Information transmitted by the Conveyor may consist of research reports, state-of-the-art summaries, packages of how-to-do-it materials, bibliographies on a particular topic, curriculum guides and proposal guidelines. The format of these materials may vary from microfiche (up to 90 pages can be reproduced on a thin film) to hard-cover books, while the methods of retrieval may range from the latest computerized programs to conventional library research. Unlike the Advocate, the Conveyor typically waits until the client requests his assistance with a particular need or problem; thus, he is more "user-oriented" than the Advocate. Also, rather than promoting a particular practice, the Conveyor affords access to an enormous reservoir of alternative resources.

Realizing that the voluminous resources of educational research and development that had been generated in recent decades were not reaching administrators and teachers, educational planners in the 1960s began searching for methods of expediting the flow of valuable information to local and state agencies. Now, according to a review of the field by Hood (1973):

There are literally hundreds of examples of organizational arrangements and training programs designed to promote more effective use of educational R&D information. Byers (1971) provides an analysis of 83 degree training programs and 55 non-degree programs. York (1968) provides a description and analysis of 40 organizational arrangements and 24 training programs. (p. 103)

According to Burchinal (1973), the "largest and most effective centers" providing information and retrieval services at an intermediate educational level are the Merrimack Education Center, Chelmsford, Massachusetts; Research Information Services for Education, King of Prussia, Pennsylvania; and the Board of Cooperative Educational Services, Boulder, Colorado. An even larger operation, with an annual budget exceeding one million dollars, is the Educational Resources Center at San Mateo, California. State agencies with major information centers and outreach services supported by the National Institute of Education are Iowa, Kansas, Massachusetts, Rhode Island and Florida. (Also see Miller's *Guide to State Information Sources,* 1973.) Stanford University's Institute of Communication Research is currently working on an evaluation design for educational information linkage programs of all kinds.

All of the educational information agencies make some use of a documentation and retrieval system known as ERIC (Educational Resources Information Center), founded by the U.S. Office of Education in the mid-1960s. Twenty ERIC clearinghouses have been set up to screen the abstract documents in particular areas of interest, such as disadvantaged education, rural education, higher education, etc. (All U.S. Office and N.I.E. sponsored reports are automatically included in ERIC.) In addition to expediting the retrieval of individual documents, the ERIC clearinghouses provide reviews, bibliographies and state-of-the-art papers. PREP packets (Putting Research into Educational Practice) are monthly interpretative summaries of current knowledge on selected topics, and are available through the Government Printing Office. (PREP publication No. 29, August 1972, reports "New Products in Education" together with the names and addresses of the developers.) For information about how to use ERIC, write the National Institute of Education, Code 401, Washington, D.C. 20202.

Since ERIC was restricted to the unpublished literature, an indexing and abstracting system for published literature was also founded by the U.S. Office (CIJE, or Current Index to Journals in Education, available from CCM Information Corporation, 866 Third Avenue, New York, N.Y. 10022). Further, in fiscal 1970 several projects were funded under a new "targeted communications" program to prepare summaries and interpretations of research for a variety of specific, nonresearch audiences who need to make decisions about educational change. In addition, an information service containing exemplary programs, known as ALERT, is operated by the Far West Lab for Educational R&D. (The interim version, available from the Government Printing Office, Washington, D.C. 20402 for $5.75, Stock No. 1780-1072, is a *Sourcebook of Elementary Curricula, Programs and Projects.* This report covers 300 programs in a number of fields and topics in elementary education.

Also, for an exhaustive overview of the dissemination efforts sponsored by the U.S. Office and the National Institute of Education, See Burchinal, 1973; for an appraisal of ERIC's strengths and weaknesses, see Paisley, 1973; for a study of the utilization of ERIC, see Fry, 1972.) Federal responsibility for diffusion of educational information is now mainly carried out by the Dissemination Task Force, National Institute of Education, Code 600, Washington, D.C. 20208.

Perhaps the most elaborate organizational development in the field of educational dissemination is the special education network. As described by Hood (1973):

> The network is actually a federation involving: (1) the ERIC network, through the ERIC Clearinghouse on Exceptional Children; (2) the Council for Exceptional Children (CED), which provides a comprehensive program, a program of conventions and exhibits, and working relationships with other organizations and agencies; and (3) the Special Education Network, consisting of a coordinating office, the ERIC-CEC Clearinghouse, the National Center for Educational Media and Materials, 4 Regional Media Centers, 13 Instructional Materials Centers, and approximately 310 associate centers. The network, in turn, links with special education departments in colleges, special education directors/consultants in state departments of education, and with a variety of organizations and individuals concerned with exceptional children. (See the December 1968 issue of *Exceptional Children* for the operations of the network.) (p. 105)

There is also a vocational-technical education network that is similar in structure, although not in magnitude, to the special education network.

A major drawback of the Conveyor strategy is that it depends heavily on the initiative of clients to learn about available resources, to seek the most suitable resources, and to adapt these resources to their particular situation. Thus, there is a tendency for only the most up-to-date, energetic, and innovative practitioners to take advantage of the Conveyor's offerings. (For research on who utilizes information sources, see Fry, 1972; Sieber, Louis and Metzger, 1972.) Educational planners have therefore begun to experiment with "linkage" roles, extension systems and other outreach services. A highly promising development was a recent tryout by the U.S. Office of an educational extension system operated jointly by three state education agencies, six intermediate service centers and a number of local districts. The tryout was known as the Pilot State Dissemination Program (Sieber, Louis and Metzger, 1972). There were three key elements of the system: (1) computerized access to the national pool of research and exemplary practices; (2) extension agents who were able to help clients determine their needs, order pertinent information from the state agency, and assist clients in using the information that was acquired; and (3) the opportunity for clients to define their needs and to choose from an array of options or alternative solutions. (Because the change agents in this program were performing activities beyond the mere conveyance of information, we shall return to them in a later section.) Evaluation of this program demonstrated its success in reaching many teachers and administrators who ordinarily would not request specialized information for problem-solving, and also in effecting a variety of changes in educational practices at the local school or district level. Moreover, the vast majority of teachers and administrators served by the system indicated a desire to use its services again. (For a thorough documentation of the program, together with forms and guidelines, see Sieber, Louis and Metzger, 1972. For information from the state agencies that participated in the program, contact the state education agencies of South Carolina, Oregon and Utah.)

State and local agencies may set up their own information retrieval facilities, of course, with or without joining in any of the networks or programs mentioned above. Several guidelines for establishing such facilities exist or are in process of development. A very useful set of guidelines for setting up an information retrieval office has been prepared by Coulson (1972). Brickley (1972) has developed instructions for establishing and using an ERIC collection; and Magisos (1971) demonstrates how to interpret target audience needs in designing an information system for vocational-technical education. In addition, the Educational Reference Center of the National Institute of Education in Washington, D.C., offers technical assistance to directors of information centers upon request. Finally, an information center might wish to avail itself of Wagner's *Directory of Educational Information Resources* (1971) or the newsletter published by the Research Information Section of the South Carolina Department of Education entitled *The Information Dissemination Report,* which covers national developments in the field.

THE ORGANIZATIONAL DEVELOPMENT TRAINER

Organizational development training (sometimes called OD) grew out of the tradition of T-group or sensitivity training of the National Training Lab (Schein and Bennis, 1965). Sensitivity training seeks to increase the individual's receptiveness to new ideas, self-awareness, interpersonal trust and sensitivity to the concerns of others. Owing to the emphasis on personality change, sensitivity training was originally given to individuals who came from a variety of organizations for training purposes. This circumstance gave rise to the program of transferring interpersonal skills to the home organization. Later, sensitivity training was applied to members of the same organization, but it appeared that this type of training alone was not sufficient for increased efficiency, effectiveness, and organizational growth (see Campbell and Bunnette, 1968; Friedlander, 1968; Lansky, et al., 1969). Accordingly, organizational training was developed to provide skills in specific organizational roles, and particularly in roles requiring teamwork. These skills are joint decision-making and problem-solving, and effective communication. Miles states the rationale for this approach in succinct terms:

> . . . it had become more and more apparent that school district innovativeness really depends on "organization health," rather than on the efforts of isolated "hero innovators" as such. Intelligent innovation and its adoption are much more

dependent on systems than on persons. (Miles, 1965, p. 114)

An organizational development training program is normally conducted within a school or district by experts in human relations. A major goal of training, however, is the creation of "self-renewing" structures among the school staff so that the program will continue after the experts have withdrawn. The objective of training is to teach a "systematic, adaptive, and flexible problem-solving sequence" (Langmeyer, Schmuck and Runke, 1969, p. 3). In general, this sequence consists of (1) clarifying the problem-area or end-states that are desirable; (2) evaluating the forces acting to keep problems from moving toward solution (force-field analysis); (3) setting priorities on the forces to be increased or decreased; (4) making action-plans; and (5) evaluating the effects of the action taken. A number of specific techniques are employed in a training program, including paraphrasing to improve communication, simulation of problem-solving through game-playing, and various procedures for improving meetings, such as feedback through "buzz groups" and the "link-pin fishbowl."

A more elaborate technique is known as "survey feedback," which was developed by Mann and his associates (1957). This procedure entails a survey of staff or student attitudes, administrator-teacher relationships, goals of the district, classroom practices or work motivations. Data collected in the survey are then relayed to the staff by a special consultant, in an effort to sharpen skills in the identification and diagnosis of school problems and in the invention of solutions. Shared decision-making among all staff members, regardless of formal position or rank, is a major goal of this procedure. (For a useful model of this approach, see McElvaney and Miles, 1971. For specific applications, see Benedict et al., 1967.)

In general, the overarching goal of the Organizational Development Trainer is to "unfreeze" the client system so that new ideas, new educational practices, and new modes of staff relationships can emerge. Thus, a generalized capacity for change ("openness"), rather than the adoption of specific innovations, is the intended outcome of this highly client-centered approach. These features sharply differentiate the Organizational Development Trainer from both the Advocate and the Conveyor. (For a critique of the assumptions underlying OD, see Pomfret, 1972, p. 126.)

Research on organizational training suggests that the program has moderately long-term effects on organizational behavior, including teachers' interactions with students. (For evaluations and overviews, see Schmuck, Runkel and Langmeyer, 1969; Schmuck, 1968; Schmuck and Runkel, 1968; Schmuck and Runkel, 1970; Schmuck and Miles, 1971.) Two major research and development centers where guidelines for organizational development are being evolved are the Center for the Advanced Study of Educational Administration, University of Oregon; and the Ontario Institute for Studies in Education, 252 Bloor Street West, Toronto 5, Ontario, Canada.

THE NEW STYLE CONSULTANT

The New Style Consultant is reminiscent of the change agent as originally conceived by Lippitt, Watson and Westley (1958). In contrast with the Advocate's belief that his own program or practice is the best of its kind, and should therefore be adopted without further delay, it is the responsibility of the New Style Consultant to understand the client's need or problem as a prelude to determining what resources are necessary and what kind of help should be given. In contrast to the one-way communication of the Conveyor, there is a dialogue between consultant and client that may continue through several stages of problem-solving. And while there are certain similarities to the Organizational Development Trainer, the New Style Consultant places less emphasis on readying the system for change and more emphasis on acquiring resources and helping with particular innovations. As defined by Havelock (1969), the Consultant is "a facilitator, helper, objective observer, and specialist in how to diagnose needs, how to identify resources, and how to retrieve from expert resources" (pp. 6-7). This role would seem to be the key element in what Havelock calls the "linkage model" of planned change. (See Havelock, 1973, pp. 23-32, for a description of this model and the opinions of experts concerning its basic propositions.)

It should be noted that this definition of the consultant departs from common usage both in specificity and in scope. Hence, our reference to the "new style" consultant. Traditionally, a consultant is anyone with substantive or procedural expertise who is called upon to convey his knowledge or to offer advice. But following the lead of mental health consultation, collaborative diagnosis is emphasized. Further, in recognition of the phenomenal increase in the magnitude and variety of educational resources, the ability to link up the practitioner with the right resources, wherever or whatever they may be, becomes an important aspect of the Consultant's role. And because educational resources are frequently couched in language that is either incomprehensible to practitioners or fails to offer implications or guidelines for action, the Consultant is obliged to synthesize and to translate resources into a form that may serve as a basis for action.

Finally, some form of facilitation or "process helping" seems also to be a desirable part of the role. In the first place, the client might request the consultant to help with an innovation that have evolved from his consultative work; and in the second place, the client might simply be unable to take appropriate action by himself, especially if it is necessary to involve other staff members. This role demand raises the specter of the consultant's time being totally preempted by certain clients, of course. Accordingly, some form of flexible specialization within a consultant team might be advisable with certain team members concentrating on the process of installation and tryout.

Earlier we referred briefly to the extension agents of the Pilot State Dissemination Program (Sieber, Louis, Metzger, 1972) as Conveyors, but noted that pressures to assume additional responsibilities carried them beyond the mere conveyance of information. Thus, this project afforded the first major test of the New Style Consultant role as a joint function of state, intermediate and local educational agencies. The first task of the extension agent was to gain acceptance and credibility, which often was not forthcoming until resources and assistance had already been given to clients. Other tasks were to identify the need or problem of the client, and then to define this need for the retrieval staff in the stage agency. After the information was received from the state agency, the agent evaluated its relevance and highlighted the most pertinent points; otherwise, clients tended to be confused or overwhelmed by the materials. Further, he often suggested how the client might manage a change process, and offered evaluative advice and moral support as time went by. Finally, he tried to set up self-renewing structures, such as research and development committees and in-house information officers. In performing these tasks it was often necessary to convene staff members, and in particular to bring together teachers and administrators, into a common decision-making enterprise.

In sum, this pilot project demonstrated that the role of a successful change agent at the local level must not only combine a number of responsibilities, but that the agent must be able to shift from one set of skills to another. Significantly, the same conclusion has been reached about the county agent of the agricultural extension system (Stone, 1952; Wilkening, 1956). With regard to client load, it is recommended that on the average one extension agent be hired for every 300 potential clients. Geographical distance between client systems is, of course, an important constraint in rural areas.

This research also revealed that several assumptions about the New Style Consultant role are unwarranted. Some of these assumptions are: (1) the client is willing to undergo diagnosis of his initially stated need; (2) the felt need of the client for resources or assistance usually requires diagnosis; (3) resources to help the client always exist; (4) resources are undifferentiated by quality, so that the only real job is to decide about type of resource rather than about quality; (5) accurate communication of the client's need from the agent to the retrieval staff, and from the retrieval staff to the computer or other information source, is unproblematical; and (6) there is a desired sequence of change agent activities—acceptance, diagnosis, retrieval, interpretation and facilitation—when in fact there may be reversals and omissions in this sequence depending upon the individual client. Because these assumptions were not borne out in practice, it would seem that much greater emphasis should be placed on the consultant's own flexibility and resourcefulness in deciding how to interact with each client. (For some guidelines, see Sieber, Louis and Metzger, 1972, especially Appendix G, "Developing a Strategy Based on Particular Clients and Their Setting.") This brings out a critical lesson. The key to the success of an extension and retrieval system utilizing the New Style Consultant is the opportunity for clients to define their own needs and to choose from an array of options or alternative solutions. (For arguments in favor of non-interventionist, user-oriented approaches to educational change, see Fullan, 1972, and Sieber, 1973.)

This principle is gradually being adopted on a wide scale. Thus, the research and Development Center for Teacher Education, University of Texas, has been working on a "Concerns-Based Adoption Model" which advocates

> ... attending to the expressed concerns and observed level of use and making sure that intervention strategies are related to the present state of the individual's (and the change agent's) use of the innovation. (personal communication from Dr. Gene E. Hall, November 12, 1973)

The Office of Fiend Development, Ontario Institute for Studies in Education, Toronto, has likewise adopted this principle in the operation of its regional centers.

Owing to the complexity of the New Style Consultant's role, several training programs and manuals have been devised to prepare individuals as "educational consultants" or "extension agents." (See Paisley and Coulson, 1972; Havelock, 1973; Havelock and Havelock, 1973; Watson, 1967; Banathy et al., Far West Laboratory for R&D, 1973, Jung, 1970.) But it would also seem that certain personal traits are prerequisites for success in the role. As delineated by Sieber, Louis and Metzger (1972), an extension agent should be:

> non-authoritarian, patient with clients who have trouble articulating their need or using information, able to tolerate delay and ultimate frustration in obtaining results, have low need for ego-aggrandizement, and enjoy performing a variety of activities without a sense of being "hassled." When the situation demands, he should be able to exercise leadership among school personnel. Further, he should be capable of thinking and speaking clearly with a minimum of jargon and aura of expertise. ... Finally, he should be orderly and able to maintain records and reporting systems. (Although we have adopted the patriarchal "he," whether the agent is male or female seems to be irrelevant.) (p. 592)

For a number of concrete recommendations for the establishment and management of a retrieval and extension system in state and intermediate agencies, see Sieber, Louis and Metzger, 1972, Chapter 14; for case studies of the work of extension agents, see volume 2 of their report.

THE QUALITY CONTROLLER

Specialists who are concerned with the objective measurement of the operation and impact of educational practices in order to ascertain their quality are an important type of change agent today. Here we discuss two major kinds of Quality Controllers: the Systems Analyst and the Evaluator.

The Systems Analyst evolved from experience in the defense industries and entered education via the example of the Pentagon during the administration of Defense Secretary McNamara. The major objective of the Systems Analyst is to measure the relationships between inputs and outputs on the one hand, and outputs and goals on the other, so that the least cost, commensurate with quality of performance, is achieved. Some of the practices associated with this strategy are "management by objectives," "accountability," the use of "behavioral objectives," and the "planning, programming and bud-

geting system" (PPBS). In the words of one observer (Fullan, 1972),

> PPBS is designed to aid school systems in a deliberative process of defining goals in measurable ways, identifying alternative means, selecting means in light of resources and other constraints, and evaluating achievement of goals. (p. 29)

By means of this process, it is hoped that administrators will be impelled to seek information and other resources to achieve the goals they have specified. (See Bushnell and Rappaport, 1971; Hartley, 1968, 1972; Lawless, 1972.)

Although the logic of this approach seems unimpeachable, it has been criticized for its centralizing tendency in decision-making, its emphasis on the most easily measured learning outcomes, its inattention to the need for continuous diagnosis of the learning process, and its external character (Fullan, 1972). Regarding the last point, Fullan argues that "the achievement of complex educational goals can come only as a result of *internalized* accountability—that is, the individual learner must be fundamentally involved in defining objectives for himself and in evaluating what he does in this regard" (p. 29). The same point, of course, applies to teachers as learners.

An additional criticism that might be levelled against systems analysis concerns its sociological naiveté as a research model. The statement of goals which is elicited by the traditional Systems Analyst rests on the assumptions that clear-cut goals do exist or should exist; that they are not subject to continual change; that they are unrelated to one another in a complex network of contingency; that "official" goals are the real "operative" goals of an organization; and that they are shared by everyone. (For criticisms of the "goal attainment" model of evaluation, see Schulberg and Baker, 1968.) In sum, it would seem that the traditional Systems Analyst subtly imposes a set of restrictions on educational planning that prohibits a continuous adjustment of resources and goals through joint diagnoses and decision-making within the school or classroom. For this reason, it is regarded by its critics as being insufficiently "user-oriented." Clearly, in contrast with the Organizational Trainer, it does not provide individuals with problem-solving skills; and in contrast with the New Style Consultant, it does not assist the client in diagnosis of needs and in the retrieval, synthesis, and transformation of resources.

Despite these shortcomings, the traditional Systems Analyst might render a useful service in achieving limited managerial goals which are not directly related to teaching and learning. Moreover, in recent years efforts have been made to modify the traditional PPBS system in the direction of greater flexibility and participation by the school staff. The process of planning, programming and management (PP&M) being developed by Hood (1973) at the Far West Laboratory includes "continually redetermining the relevance to redefined goals" among its eight functions. Since Hood proposes that PP&M serve the purpose of "self-renewal" in schools, he advises training all school personnel "rather than a select cadre of change agents" (p. 113). In effect, then, he proposes that school practitioners become their own Systems Analysts.

The Center for Advanced Study of Educational Administration, University of Oregon, has undertaken to install another version of PPBS in a number of school districts. Dale Lake, at the State University of New York in Albany, is building a model that combines problem-solving processes with management systems; a similar effort is being made by Jung at the Northwest Regional Laboratory, in collaboration with R. E. Corrigan Associates.

Three self-contained packages for training in the PP&M process are:

Operation PEP (Dr. Russell Kent, 590 Hamilton St., Redwood City, California 94063)

SAFE (Dr. Robert E. Corrigan, 8701 Adah Street, Garden Grove, California 92641)

Educational Management Training Program (Far West Laboratory, Hotel Claremont, Berkeley, California 94705)

For a useful "Innovations Evaluation Guide" to assist in determining costs and benefits of new practices, write the Center for Vocational and Technical Education, Ohio State University, Columbus, Ohio 43210.

The Evaluator is another type of quality control specialist. Unlike the Systems Analyst, he normally focuses on a particular practice or program rather than on total organizational effectiveness. Also, he is more flexible in his choice of procedures, drawing on a wide array of social research methods to suit the particular situation and practice to be evaluated. (For an overview of evaluation research in education, see Stufflebeam et al., 1971.) The emergence of "formative evaluation," which provides continuous assessment and recurrent feedback to the staff engaged in developing or trying out a new practice, has demonstrated that a strong user-orientation can be applied to the systems approach (Scriven, 1967; Sieber, Louis and Metzger, 1972, Appendix J). Clearly, this client-oriented type of evaluation will appeal to many practitioners who are weary or wary of traditional evaluation techniques. Since there are many problems in the conduct of formative evaluation, however, the reader should refer to the literature cited above, as well as to standard texts on research methods in the social sciences. In addition, a 30-hour self-instructional curriculum package entitled "Evaluating the Process of Educational Change" has been developed by Dr. Virgil Blanke and associates at the School of Education, Ohio State University.

It should be emphasized that a key function of evaluation of any kind is to prevent the adoption of practices which are fashionable but useless, or which are not applicable to a particular school or district. Clearly, in the absence of controlled development and tryout, many practices of doubtful merit are likely to be adopted. (See Clark and Hopkins, 1966, on the developmental and field testing roles of specialists in educational R&D.) Owing to the availability of evaluation personnel in universities, independent research agencies, state departments of education and many urban school districts, there can be little excuse for not availing oneself of assistance in evaluating new practices.

THE POLITICAL CHANGE AGENT

A strategy of change which is usually neglected in the literature on educational innovation is the manipulation of power. (See Sieber, 1972, on the practitioner as a "Powerless Functionary.") It seems that experts on planned change shy away from this strategy, despite the fact that a major inhibitor of change is the existing distribution of power within educational systems and between these systems and the community. How to alter power and decision-making structures in order to effect change, therefore, is the concern of the Political Change Agent. Recently, two models have been proposed: the "political linkage agent" (Tye, 1973) and the "change-through-crisis" model (Chesler et al., 1973).

The political linkage agent seeks to avert crises and conflict by developing new modes for sharing power between the board of education and administrators on the one hand, and the community, students, and teachers on the other, in the formulation of educational policy. The tasks of this change agent are to help improve the quality of communication between the "political subsystem" and the "user groups"; to overcome status barriers to group interaction; to help identify problems and focus on major issues; to link the client to resources for problem-solving; and to assist in the selection of alternatives. To our knowledge, this conception of a political change agent has not been systematically installed and tested. (For training guidelines, selection criteria, and so forth, see Tye, 1973.) Of course, there are similarities between this approach and organizational development training (discussed above), but the emphasis of the Political Linkage Agent is on the distribution of political power rather than on decision-making about normal school problems.

The "change-through-crisis" model utilizes a crisis situation to restructure the system (Chesler et al., 1973). Two kinds of change agents are envisaged in this model: the "advocator-organizer-agitator" and the "social architect." The former helps to clarify the problem that has caused the crisis, a procedure which might entail "helping it to surface or escalate"; while the latter "insures that the crisis be used constructively rather than being reacted to simply for purposes of restoring the status quo" (p. 151). A project conducted by Chesler at the University of Michigan, entitled "Alternative Responses to School Crisis," tried out three programs in different schools. One program provided the high school principal with an "expanded repertoire of managerial strategies"; another trained students as change agents and developed student-teacher collaboration in planning school change; and another focused on the community and school board by helping to organize forces to alter decision-making processes. More recently, the "Educational Change Team" project at the University of Michigan has been working on a *Resource Manual* to serve as a guide in the use of techniques for advocacy of oppressed interest groups (particularly students) and for the constructive utilization of conflict. The manual also includes annotated lists of organizations offering action, research, or financial resources. (For additional information, write to Educational Change Team, 201 Catherine Street,

Ann Arbor, Michigan 48108.)

The possibility of enlisting parents as political change agents has been thrust upon education by the "community control" movement of the inner cities and the "alternative school" movement in middle-class areas. The demands of lower income groups for a greater share in educational decision-making is a reflection of the widespread revolt of disadvantaged groups against many forms of institutional injustice in America. As Pomfret (1972) points out:

> In the United States the community-control movement is premised partly upon the recognition by many black ghetto parents and white academics that systematic social discrimination rather than individual inadequacy accounts for the failure of schools to act as avenues of upward social mobility for poor children. Locating the responsibility for this failure in bureaucratic intransigence, institutionalized racism, and a systematically induced sense of powerlessness, parents are demanding that control over school affairs be returned to the local community or neighborhood. (p. 116)

Despite this political motivation, greater parental involvement may offer opportunities and pressures for improvement of educational practices, or for greater motivation to remain in school and to exert more academic effort. On the other hand, parents might need to be directly involved in their children's education for the latter to benefit (Cohen, 1969). Moreover, it is sometimes argued that community control will tend to provincialize and debase the educational program.

The pros and cons of community control and alternative schools have generated a sizable literature. For a critical review and for techniques intended to ensure that "parents from the neighborhood served by the school participate in a sustained and systematic way as an organized distinct instructional and decision-making group within the school," see Pomfret (1972). This article also provides a good bibliography for the reader who is interested in the role of parents as change agents.[1]

THE ACADEMIC TRAINER

Owing to the wide array of arrangements and activities in schools or departments of education, we can do little more here than concede an important role to the Academic Trainer as a change agent. Three major organizational arrangements, however, deserve mention.

The first arrangement is the University Council for Educational Administration (UCEA). This is an association of some 54 universities devoted to updating the knowledge of professors of administration through career seminars, creation of instructional materials, pooling of resources for graduate students, performing research on preparatory programs, and bringing the knowledge of the social sciences to bear on educational administration. The *UCEA Newsletter* provides information about innovations in preparatory programs, new instructional materials and emergent publications. *Educational Administration Abstracts* and *Educational Administration Quarterly* are other publications of UCEA'

The second arrangement is the Inter-Institutional Program established by the Research and Development Center for Teacher Education, University of Texas. As part of this program the Center has been working closely with approximately 25 teacher training institutions and less closely with another 25 to 30 training institutions. Experts in program development help these institutions to use the innovations they have adopted. These innovations consist of new materials, products and procedures for operating a "personalized teacher education program" developed at the Center. The network also facilitates the flow of resources among these institutions.

A third arrangement utilizes academic personnel as change agents in direct contact with practicing school personnel. This arrangement is the School Study (or Development) Council. Ordinarily these councils are sponsored by a local institution of higher education, a provision which involves Academic Trainers as part-time consultants. According to a recent survey, the three activities regarded as most important by study councils are inservice training, dissemination, and development, in that order. (Danenburg, 1970). Ideas and practices are shared among council members by means of meetings, workshops, newsletters, conference proceedings and journals.

Since the founding of the first school study council by Paul Mort in 1942, the number of councils has grown to 81, most of which were set up in the 1960s. (Some possible reasons for the popularity of these councils are given by Kohl, 1973). Today there is great variation in the structure and size of membership. According to Kohl (1973):

> Some councils encompass large geographical areas; others are quite small, for example, the Associated Public School System includes public school systems across the entire nation, whereas the Western New York School Study Council has members in one region of New York state. The New England School Development Council has member schools in six New England states. The Tri-State School Study Council has member systems from Pennsylvania, Ohio, and West Virginia, whereas the Public Schools for Cooperative Research Council includes only certain schools in the eastern portion of Tennessee. School study councils also vary in size. The largest regional study council, the New England School Development Council, reports a membership of 249 public school systems. The smallest, the Fox Valley School Study Council, reported 13 public school systems on its membership roster. (pp. 2-3)

For additional information about school study councils, see Danenburg, 1970; or write The National School Development Council, Inc., University Park, Pa.

Because the school study councils involve groups of teachers and administrators from the same district, they are able to avoid the frustrations of the faculty member who is preparing individual teachers and administrators. Brickell (1961), among others, reports that college faculty experience "utter futility in equipping teachers with skills which were not needed or not wanted in the elementary and secondary schools in which those teachers subsequently went to work" (p. 49). An additional advantage of councils is that the governing boards are composed entirely of school personnel, a condition that undoubtedly ensures a high degree of "client orientation."

It seems unlikely, however, that a school study council will be successful in encouraging the adoption and maintenance of worthy innovations unless they utilize some of the change agent techniques mentioned in the preceding portions of this study. As noted earlier, advocacy is not enough. In particular, the councils need to resist the appeal of "home-grown" practices from neighboring districts, and instead to draw upon the national pool of research and exemplary practices. Further, council members should keep themselves informed of the different change strategies and procedures which are being developed around the country. Indeed, one of the major responsibilities of the Academic Trainer who is working with a school study council should be to encourage tryouts of the different change agent activities reviewed here.

CONCLUDING REMARKS

In this attempt to delineate the major types of change agents, we have stressed the differences among them while understating the similarities. Also, we have not explored the possibilities of synthesizing several approaches. The intelligent administrator will discern these possibilities for himself. It would be unfortunate indeed if the different types of change agents were viewed as competing with one another for the prize of educational immortality. The future will undoubtedly produce entirely new strains as well as hybrid roles in the planning of educational change.

In addition to the work referred to in our review, the reader might wish to explore any or all of the following bibliographies on educational change and innovation.

NOTES

[1] See also *Bibliography on Decentralization of Decisionmaking,* Educational Resources Center, 333 Main Street, Redwood City, California 94063, January 1973.

BIBLIOGRAPHIES

Havelock, R., Huber, J., and Zimmerman, S. *Major Works on Change in Education.* Ann Arbor, Michigan: Center for Research on Scientific Knowledge, Institute for Social Research, University of Michigan, 1969.

Kurland, N., and Miller, R. *Selected and Annotated Bibliography on the Processes of Change.* New York State Education Department and the University of Kentucky, 1966.

Rogers, E. M. *Bibliography on the Diffusion of Innovations.* East Lansing, Michigan: Department of Communication, Michigan State University, July 1967 (Supplement to the Bibliography, September 1968).

Skelton, G. J., and Hensel, J. W. *A Selected and Annotated Bibliography: The Change Process in Education.* Columbus, Ohio: ERIC Clearinghouse on Vocational and Technical Education, Center for Vocational and Technical Education, Ohio State University, 1970.

Spitzer, W. K. *A Bibliography on the Process of Change.* Melbourne, Florida: Institute for Development of Educational Activities, Inc., 1968.

Stuart, M., and Dudley, C., eds. *Bibliography on Organization and Innovation.* Eugene, Oregon: Center for Advanced Study of Educational Administration, University of Oregon, 1967.

_____. *Bibliography on Administration Evaluation.* Redwood City, California: Educational Resources Center, 1972.

REFERENCES

Banthy, B. et al. *The Educational Information Consultant: Skills in Disseminating Educational Information.* San Francisco: Far West Laboratory, 1972.

Benedict, B., et al. The Clinical-Experimental Approach to Assessing Organizational Change Efforts. *Journal of Applied Behavioral Science,* 1967, 3, 347-380.

Bennis, W. G., Benne, D. D., and Chin, R., eds. *The Planning of Change* (second edition). New York: Holt, Rinehart and Winston, 1969.

Bigelow, R. C. *The Effects of Organizational Development on Classroom Climate.* Eugene, Oregon: Center for the Advanced Study of Educational Administration, University of Oregon, 1969.

Brickell, H. *Organizing New York State for Educational Change.* Albany, New York: New York State Education Department, 1961.

Brickley, R. *How to Establish and Use an ERIC Collection.* King of Prussia, Pennsylvania: Research and Information Services for Education, August, 1972.

Burchinal, L. G. Influence of Federal Initiative upon Communication in Education. *Journal of Research and Development in Education,* 1973, 6, 116-131.

Bushnell, D., and Rappaport, D., eds. *Planned Change in Education.* New York: Harcourt-Brace-Jovanovich, 1971.

Byers, M. L. *A Survey of Existing Training Opportunities in Educational Research and Research-Related Areas.* AERA Task Force, Technical Paper #24. Washington, D.C.: U.S. Government Printing Office, 1971.

Campbell, J. P., and Dunnette, M. C. Effectiveness of T-Group Experiences in Managerial Training and Development. *Psychological Bulletin,* 1968, 70, 73-104.

Chesler, M. A., and Lohman, J. E. Changing Schools Through Student Advocacy. In Schmuck, R. A. and Miles, M. B., eds. *Organization Development in Schools.* Palo Alto, California: National Press Books, 1971, 185-211.

Chesler, M. et al. Change-Through-Crisis Model. In Havelock, R. G. and Havelock, M. C., et al., *Training for Change Agents.* Ann Arbor, Michigan: Center for Research on Utilization of Scientific Knowledge, 1973, 150-155.

Clark, D. L., and Hopkins, J. E. Roles for Research, Development, and Diffusion Personnel in Education: Project Memorandum #1, CRP Project no. X-022, April 1966. School of Education, Indiana University.

Cohen, D. K. The Price of Community Control. *Commentary,* 1969, 48, 23-32.

Coulson, J. M. Toward Establishing an Educational Information Dissemination Center. Washington D.C.: Dissemination Task Force, National Institute of Education, code 600, 1972.

Danenburg, W. *Characteristics of School Study and Development Councils.* University Park, Pennsylvania: The National School Development Council, Inc., 1970.

Friedlander, F. A Comparative Study of Consulting Processes and Group Development. *Journal of Applied Behavioral Science,* 1968, 4, 377-399.

Fry, B. M. *Evaluation Study of ERIC Products and Services.* (Summary volume) Graduate Library School, Indiana University. Final Report, Project No. BR 00375, Grant No. OEC-0-70-3271, U.S. Department of Health, Education and Welfare, Office of Education, March 1972.

Fullan, M. Overview of the Innovative Process and the User. *Interchange,* 1972, 3, 1-46.

Gideonse, H. *Educational Research and Development in the United States.* Washington, D.C.: U.S. Government Printing Office, 1970.

Goodlad, J., Klein, M. F., et al. *Behind the Classroom Door.* Worthington, Ohio: Jones, 1970.

Hartley, H. *Educational Planning-Programming-Budgeting.* Englewood Cliffs, New Jersey: Prentice-Hall, 1968.

———. PPBS: Status and Implications. *Educational Leadership,* 1972, 29, 658-661.

Havelock, R. G. Dissemination and Translation Roles. In Eidell, T. L. and Kitchel, J. M., eds., *Knowledge Production and Utilization in Educational Administration.* Columbus, Ohio: University Council for Educational Administration, 1968, 64-119.

——— (in collaboration with Guskin, A., et al.). *Planning for Innovation through Dissemination and Utilization of Knowledge.* Ann Arbor, Michigan: Center for Research on Utilization of Scientific Knowledge, 1969.

——— (in collaboration with Guskin, A., et al.). *The Change Agent's Guide to Innovation.* Englewood Cliffs, New Jersey: Educational Technology Publications, Inc., 1973.

——— and Havelock, M. C. *Training for Change Agents.* Ann Arbor, Michigan: Institute for Social Research, University of Michigan, 1973.

Herlig, R. K. *Identifying Latent Innovators in Education,* Doctoral thesis, University of Missouri, 1971.

Hood, P. D. How Research and Development on Educational Roles and Institutional Structures can Facilitate Communication. *Journal of Research and Development in Education,* 1973, 6, 96–113.

Hutchins, C. L., et al. *Conceptualization and Plans: ALERT: Alternatives for Learning Through Educational Research and Technology.* Berkeley, California: Far West Laboratory, 1970.

Indiana University, School of Education, Division of Instructional Systems Technology. *Diffusion and Adoption of Instructional Innovations Training Program.* Bloomington, Indiana: Indiana University, 1972.

Jung, C., Pino, R., and Emory, R. *RUPS: Research Utilization and Problem Solving; Classroom Version; Leader's Manual.* Portland, Oregon: Northwest Regional Educational Laboratory, 1970.

Kohl, J. W. *The Viability of the Development Council: A Voluntary Educational Change Agency.* Paper delivered at the meeting of the American Educational Research Association, New Orleans, Feb. 25-March 1, 1973. National School Development Council, Inc., University Park, Pennsylvania.

Langmeyer, D., Schmuck, R., and Runkel, P. *Technology for Organizational Training in Schools.* Eugene, Oregon: Center for the Advanced Study of Educational Administration, University of Oregon. (no date)

Lansky, L., et al. *The Effects of Human Relations Training on Diagnosing Skills and Planning for Change.* Eugene, Oregon: Center for the Advanced Study of Educational Administration, 1969.

Lawless, D. Educational Resources Allocation System Task Force: An Initial Statement. Unpublished paper, Task Force of Ministry of Education, Ontario, 1972.

Magisos, J. *Interpretation of Target Audience Needs in the Design of Information Dissemination Systems for Vocational-Technical Education.* Ohio State University: Center for Vocational and Technical Education, 1971.

McElvaney, C. T. and Miles, M. B. Using Survey Feedback and Consultation. In Schmuck, R. A. and Miles, M. B., eds., *Organizational Development in Schools.* Palo Alto: National Press, 1971, 113-138.

Mann, Floyd C. Studying and Creating Change: A Means to Understanding Social Organization. *Research in Industrial Human Relations,* 1957, 17, 146-167.

Miles, M. B. Planned Change and Organizational Health. In Carlson, R. A., et al., eds., *Change Processes in the Public Schools.* Eugene, Oregon: Center for the Advanced Study of Educational Administration, 1965, 11-36.

Miller, D. H. *Guide to State Information Sources.* ERIC Clearinghouse, 1973.

Paisley, W. J. Improving a Field-Based "ERIC-Like" Information System. *Journal of the American Society for Information Science,* 1971.

——— and Coulson, J. *Development of Training Resources for Educational Extension Services Personnel,* Report on Extension Models, Personnel Functions, and Selection Criteria. Stanford, California: Institute of Communication Research, Stanford University. Unpublished First Draft, September 1972.

Pomfret, A. Involving Parents in Schools: Toward Developing a Social Intervention Technology. *Interchange,* 1972, 3, 114-130.

Rogers, E. M. *Diffusion of Innovations.* New York: Free Press of Glencoe, 1962.

——— and Shoemaker, F. F. *Communication of Innovations: A Cross Cultural Approach.* New York: The Free Press of Glencoe, 1971.

Schein, E. H. and Bennis, W. G. *Personal and Organizational Change Through Group Methods: The Laboratory Approach.* New York: John Wiley and Sons, 1965.

Schmuck, R. A. Helping Teachers Improve Classroom Group Processes. *Journal of Applied Behavioral Science,* 1968, 4, 401-435.

——— and Miles, M. B. *Organizational Development in Schools.* Palo Alto, California: National Book Press, 1971.

———, Runkel, P. J., and Langmeyer, D. Improving Organizational Problem-Solving in a School Faculty. *Journal of Applied Behavioral Science,* 1969, 5.

——— and Runkel, P. J. *Organizational Training for a School Faculty.* Eugene, Oregon: Center for the Advanced Study of Educational Administration, University of Oregon, 1970.

——— et al. Handbook of Organizational Development in Schools. Palo Alto, California: National Press Books, in press.

Scriven, M. The Methodology of Evaluation. In Tyler, R. W., et al., eds., *Perspectives of Curriculum Evaluation.* Chicago: Rand McNally and Company, 1967.

Sieber, S. D. Organizational Influences on Innovative Roles. In Eidell, T. L., and Kitchel, J. M., eds., *Knowledge Production and Utilization in Educational Administration.* Columbus, Ohio: University Council for Educational Administration, 1968, 120-142.

———. Formative Evaluation: An Exploration with Case Materials, Appendix J in Sieber, S. D., Louis, K. S., and Metzger, L. *The Use of Educational Knowledge.* New York: Bureau of Applied Social Research, Columbia University, 1972.

———. Images of the Practitioner and Strategies of Educational Change. *Sociology of Education,* 1972, 45, 362-385.

———. The Pilot State Dissemination Program. *Journal of Research and Development in Education,* 1973, 6, 88-95.

———. Research on Knowledge Utilization: The Pilot State Dissemination Program. *Bulletin of the School of Education,* Indiana University, in press.

———. Federal Support for Research and Development in Education and Its Effects. *Yearbook of the National Society for the Study of Education.* Chicago National Society for the Study of Education, in press.

———, Louis, K. S., and Metzger, L. *The Use of Educational Knowledge: Evaluation of the Pilot State Dissemination Program.* New York: Bureau of Applied Social Research, Columbia University, 1972.

Stone, J. T. How County Agricultural Agents Teach. East Lansing: Michigan Agricultural Extension Service Mimeo Bulletin, 1952.

Stufflebeam, D. L., et al. Educational Evaluation and Decision-

Making. Itasca, Illinois: Peacock Publishers, 1971.

System Development Corporation. *Reference Manual for Educational Information Service Centers, Technical Memorandum.* Falls Church, Virginia: System Development Corporation, June 1968.

Tye, K. The Political Linkage Agent. In Havelock, R. G. and Havelock, M. C. *Training for Change Agents.* Ann Arbor, Michigan: Center for Research on Utilization of Scientific Knowledge, 1973, 143-150.

Wagner, J. *Directory of Educational Information Resources.* New York: CCM Information Corporation, 1971.

Watson, G., ed. *Change in School Systems.* Cooperative Project for Educational Development. Washington, D.C.: NTL Institute for Applied Behavioral Science, 1967.

———. Using Research for Change. Project under NIMH Contract No. HSM-42-69-1 entitled "Review of Literature on Research Implementation." Los Angeles, California: Human Interaction Research Institute, 1969.

Wilkening, E. A. Roles of Communicating Agents in Technological Change in Agriculture. *Social Forces,* 1956, 34, 361-367.

York, L. J. *Arrangements and Training for Effective Use of Educational R & D Information: A Literature Survey.* Berkeley, California: Far West Laboratory, 1968.

3

COLLEGE FACULTY AS CHANGE AGENTS

by David P. Butts
Professor of Science Education and
Chairman, Department of Science Education
The University of Georgia
Athens, Georgia

To make an idea live, wrap it up in a person. Implementation of changes in education today is being done by tapping a tremendous resource—college faculty members. Because this slumbering resource is becoming alive to how they can help change to occur, varieties of fresh and exciting educational experiments are in progress both on campus and in schools.

Much has been said and done to improve the learning experiences of students in American schools. Large amounts of money have been invested in the development and refinement of curricula in many subject areas. With this developmental effort completed, one could expect to pause and listen to the exciting hum of children engrossed in their pursuit of learning. But when some observers (Coleman, Jackson and Silberman) listen, they find that schools in the 1960s are very similar to the established routines of schools of the 1920s. In effect, they have found that programs without people result in little or no change. College faculty are becoming one source of assistance for classroom teachers. Because they can bridge the gap between the theoretically desirable and the present reality, the college educator can

widen the horizon of what can be, while strengthening the depths of meaning in what is.

College educators are demonstrating their ability as change agents on more than half of our college campuses. To a lesser extent, this enthusiasm and insight is reaching away from the college campus to the public schools. As an example most school districts tap the shoulder of an "expert" college educator for a brief one-shot innoculation. It is estimated that fewer than ten percent of the nation's schools have joined in partnership with college educators in a mutual cooperative effort toward change. Such efforts are illustrated in the National Science Foundation's Cooperative College-School Programs. Through these programs of joint investment of resources and people, the college educator works in the school setting helping teachers cope with problems they see as relevant.

In our recent past, college educators have been awakened to the potential of change agents through a variety of efforts. For many years, they have said that:

- We should be more specific about what we are trying to do;
- We should identify objectives in relation to the requirements of particular professional roles;
- We should plan learning experiences in direct relation to these objectives;
- We should give more attention to the individualization of instruction;
- We should involve the schools more directly in the training program; and
- We should evaluate the results of what we are doing— the outcomes and products.

In brief, what is now happening is that college faculty are becoming involved rather than resting on their ability to talk and to serve as critics.

COLLEGE FACULTY INVOLVED AS CHANGE AGENTS

College faculty are becoming involved through specific programs to enable them to serve as leaders and resource personnel to schools. The Leadership Resource Personnel program of the National Science Foundation illustrates this dynamic interaction of college faculty working with other college faculty to secure the knowledge of new programs, to demonstrate the personal competencies needed to work with others in ways consistent with the rationale of the change, and to generate a personal commitment to implement the desired change. Through such programs, college faculty are becoming awakened to ways of working in schools and how their own program on campus needs rethinking.

A second major influence in involving college faculty as change agents has been the development of newer strategies of instruction and organization. The Keller Plan for Personalizing System of Instructions (PSI) has been enthusiastically shared between individuals on many American and foreign campuses. In this widespread movement to rethink the organization of college instruction, college faculty are serving as stimuli to others in the challenge to find more relevant ways to guide students.

A third major influence has been the dual emphasis on competency-based certification for teachers and performance-based teacher education. Although independent from the PSI movement (indeed, on some campuses both PSI and PBTE have occurred at the same time but unknown to each other) PBTE has emerged as a lighthouse effort of teams of college faculty to make the professional preparation of teachers more effective. To some, it represents a way for college faculty to hold themselves more accountable for the performance of their products.

Related to the second and third major influences on college faculty involvement is the interdisciplinary sharing essential in the development of instructional modules. To some college faculty, instruction is an art best achieved by an insightful teacher who knows both the structure of what is to be taught and the promise and pitfalls of individual learners. To other college faculty some validity in the "art" viewpoint is acknowledged, but they also recognize that it can serve as a justification for fuzzy thinking and superficial workmanship. They see designing instructional modules as an applied science in which elements of "art" are placed within a systematic framework. This framework is resulting in the fertile cross-communication between systematic analysis programmers, subject matter expertise, and multimedia instruction specialists. Thus, as college faculty have become involved in changing their instruction (in courses as in PSI), or in programs as in CBE, they serve as mutual stimulants to change in educational practices on the college campus.

A fifth major influence in involving college faculty is concern of some for the mechanical, impersonal, nonhumanness that some find to be characteristic of education both in college and public schools. Searching for ways to make the interaction between learner and teacher more personal has resulted in the development of such programs as Personalizing Teacher Education, and its related Personalizing School Programs of the Research and Development Center for Teacher Education at The University of Texas at Austin. A key assumption of these programs is if learners are to gain from their learning opportunities they must see a link between their personal lives and the learning opportunity. Learning is assumed to be at its best when the learner himself initiates the action and interprets the results of his actions within his personal concerns. With expanded freedom to initiate and to interpret, the learner becomes less dependent on the instructor. He has greater responsibility in initiating a task, asking questions, and seeking answers, because the task represents his personal activity. To enable a learner to have access to this freedom, he must first confront himself with what he can or cannot do. Through this confrontation or assessment phase, he knows about himself. Through the sharing of what he knows about himself and what the instructor knows about him, an awareness then exists that is a personal and mutual knowledge of what "we" (instructor and learner) know about "me." A third phase is essential, in which through the instructor's knowledge of the interest and ability and values of the learner is used to shape the nature of the tasks. This arousal then is an extension

of what we know about me, to what *I* want to do. In personalizing learning, the learner is now ready to embark on the achieving phase—strategies for becoming involved in a challenge that has personal meaning. As college faculty become involved in personalizing learning, they rapidly become key change agents both with colleagues on campus and in classrooms in schools. They find the challenge of being open equally meaningful in both contexts.

TWO ILLUSTRATIONS

At The University of Texas College of Education's Institute for Teacher Education there is an active illustration of teams of college faculty and public school teachers cooperating together as change agents. The Personalizing Teacher Education Program, PTEP, is based on the entire faculty team accepting the assumption that they, as individuals, and that their college students and the children with whom these college students will work, are unique human beings. They also believe that all the team faculty and student members, or at least nearly all in this group, can develop adequacy and effectiveness in coping with learning if given proper instruction and time to learn. The team also assumes that growth will be enhanced if individual self-esteem is not negated through insidious comparisons with others. Thus, the main goal of this program is to maximize the potential of all—the faculty, the student, and the children, within a framework of competency-based education.

In describing the Personalized Teacher Education Program it is appropriate first to define how, as an example of a personalized program, it is different from a nonpersonalized program. Personalization is an approach in which the instructional activities or competencies are provided only when the need for them has been clearly aroused in the individual learner. A key to this arousal of need is the initial diagnostic assessment, in which the learner confronts himself with a task that reveals specific knowledge of what he can or is not able to do. Assessment is followed by an awareness phase, in which what the learner knows about himself and what the instructor knows about the learner is shared, so that they mutually know where the learner is with respect to desired goals. However, because the learner needs to learn does not automatically mean that he wants to learn specific skills. Only if the both of these conditions are present will there be arousal—need plus want-to. If not, here is the opportunity for the professional staff to look at specific goals through the eyes of the individual learner (a personal approach) and search for ways to translate the task needs into personal needs. The achieving phase follows as enabling activities are provided. This cycle of assessment, awareness, arousal, achievement thus is an individual experience, a personal interaction between learner and faculty team.

The focus of PTEP is the personal development of each participant with a framework of CBTE. Basic to this development is the provision of learning experiences that are consistent with the concern level of the participant. The well-documented sequence of teacher concerns, from immature concerns about self to more mature concerns about what impact the teacher is having on the learner, is a basic dimension of PTEPs rationale. Thus, by diagnosing the prospective teacher's concern level, and then providing developmental experiences in a field-based context, the resolution of early concerns and the initiation of later or more mature concerns are facilitated. Concerns do have a substantial focus. In PTEP the field-based setting provides the key to keeping each participant's focus on the main object of teaching—the child. Through the vehicle of continuous interaction with children, it is possible for the faculty team to use the process of personalizing learning to enable each prospective teacher to acquire the competency-based products assumed to be part of an effective teacher, but these competencies are sequence-based on the readiness of the individual. Especially through the interdisciplinary program with mathematics-science, the model used with the prospective teacher is consciously applied to learning experiences of children; i.e., through personalizing learning strategies, children are helped to acquire specific competencies in a sequence based on their individual readiness. A significant common element of this combination of competency-based instruction within a concerns (or personalized) context is that it is the responsibility of the instructor to both diagnose and utilize information gained from the individual learner in selecting and sequencing learning instruction. Thus this competency-based instructional program cannot be conducted equally well with or without learners present.

A second illustration of college faculty as change agents, especially within their campus and between campuses elsewhere, is the CBTE of the University of Houston.

The Houston program is competency-based, personalized, designed through systematic procedures, regenerative, field- and campus-centered, and operated by a consortium, and it synthesizes a number of programmatic and organizational innovations in a preparation program for prospective elementary and secondary teachers.

Competencies are stipulated with three levels of criteria: cognitive, performance, and consequence; however, the major program emphasis focuses on the latter two. It seems far more relevant in a teacher education program to emphasize what a teacher can do and what he can accomplish as a result of his actions, than simply what he knows. The program emphasizes development of prospective teachers who are effective students of human behavior, who can demonstrate a wide range of teaching styles, and who are rational decision-makers with competencies designed around these attributes.

The Learning Module—composed of specific objectives, a prospectus, alternate enabling activities (with student-identified activity as one option), pre-assessment, and post-assessment—is the instructional unit in the program, rather than courses. The program has designed a training package for faculty, *Developing Learning Modules,* which is composed of a work text and 5 slide tapes, and which models modules that are developed for prospective teachers.

Self-pacing through the program, coupled with student-advisor selection of competencies to be demon-

strated, combine to make the program individualized. In addition, personal-professional counseling is provided students by counselor educators. A personal assessment inventory provided initial data for a series of individual conferences. A one-week retreat at the beginning of the program emphasized personal assessment and team building. Micro-teaching lessons are critiqued by a curriculum specialist and a counselor, who consider teaching content, strategies, and interaction.

Systematic procedures were employed in program development. A comprehensive study of problems of teachers in multi-ethnic settings was completed as part of a needs assessment which also included interviews with parents, pupils, teachers, and administrators. Library searches generated data which were employed to test proposed program models.

An evaluation unit assesses the viability of each module and of the program focus. These procedures are designed to lead to an improved regenerative program.

A third illustration of college faculty as change agents in public schools is the Leadership Resource Personnel Workshops. One series of these, at the Science Education Center of The University of Texas at Austin, was planned to involve college science educators in activities that would enable them to serve as change agents in school districts near their institution. The plan of the project was based on the assumption that a change agent will be most effective if he has, first, a knowledge of the change desired, second, a competence in interacting with people in a way consistent with the philosophy and intent of the change, and third, a personal commitment to implementing the change. Subsequent studies on the impact of this type of programmed development of change agents demonstrated that the goals were indeed realized. College faculty viewed strategies and ideas gained in the conference as useful for both preservice and inservice teachers. They found that individually they had a greater insight into the needs and interests of the preservice students—especially with respect to preservice teachers' dislike for lectures. While fewer than half of the college faculty had had direct contact with public schools, each of them were able to establish cooperative working activities with school districts during the year after the conference. College faculty want to and can be awakened to the challenge of being change agents.

ISSUES

The active involvement of college faculty as change agents is not viewed by everyone as unmitigated bliss. Some controversial aspects of this development are as follows.

Within the administrative structure of many colleges, there persists the idea that professors belong on the college campus involved in both teaching and research that helps generate new knowledge. They should not be participants in activities that involve them in the real world of public schools. Especially in teacher education, this viewpoint, sincerely held by many administrators, does not recognize that new knowledge may be generated through naturalistic *or* empirical research. Thus the issue: is it appropriate for a college teacher educator to be involved as a change agent in public schools?

A second issue relates to the concern many have clearly defined as a conflict of interest. Can a professor who should be concerned with critical evaluation of ideas at the same time serve as an advocate or change agent for the idea? Is it possible to actively work for change and simultaneously be critical of the implications of the change? An illustration of this issue is the CBTE movement. Is it appropriate for a professor to actively encourage the adoption of this change when its research base is still being developed?

A third issue related to college faculty's involvement as change agents centers in the development of modules as in PSI, CBTE, or PTE. In each of these cases, individuals claim that the modules serve as vehicles to dehumanize education. Empirical evidence is needed to further define this issue, to establish its validity, and to offer possible alternatives.

In conclusion, college faculty are demonstrating in a variety of ways their ability to serve as change agents on their own campuses, in other colleges, and in public schools.

> It must be remembered that there is nothing more difficult to plan, more doubtful of success, nor more dangerous to manage, than the creation of a new system. For the initiator has the enmity of all who would profit by the preservation of the old institutions and merely lukewarm defenders in those who would gain by the new ones. The hesitation of the latter arises in part from the fear of their adversaries, who have the laws on their side, and in part from the general skepticism of mankind which does not really believe in an innovation until experience proves its value.
>
> —Niccolo Machiavelli

Tapping this resource has been a key way to facilitate change. But all do not view this type of behavior as consistent with the role of a college educator as an impartial searcher after knowledge. Ideas wrapped up in people are most likely to move, and moving targets are more noticeable than stationary ones.

ADDITIONAL RESOURCES

Bown, O. L., and Menaker, S. L. *Personalization Impact on Students and Faculty*. Austin: Research & Development Center for Teacher Education Report Series #65.

Butts, David P. *Manpower Development*. Austin: Science Education Center, The University of Texas at Austin.

_____. The Classroom Experience Model in Designs for Inservice Education. Research and Development Center for Teacher Education Monograph. Austin: The University of Texas at Austin.

_____. Widening Vistas in Science Education. *Science Education*, March 1970, 130-133.

_____. and Gibb, Glenadine. *Teacher Renewal Through Interdisciplinary Mathematics-Science*. Austin: Research & Development Center for Teacher Education Report Series #80.

_____, Hall, G. E., and Koran, J. J. *College Teachers: A Resource for Implementing Change*. Austin: Research & Development Center for Teacher Education Report Series #55.

Houston, R., and Howsam, R. *Competency-Based Teacher Education*. Chicago: Science Research Associates, 1972.

The National Science Foundation. *Instruction Improvement*

Implementation. August 1973, E-74-4.

The PBTE Series—A basic series of publications on performance-based teacher education, its accomplishments and its prospects. Individual titles can be secured from: American Association of Colleges for Teacher Education, One Dupont Circle, N.W., Washington, D.C. 20036. Currently this group is focusing on a comprehensive analysis of our national effort in research and development of basic instructional and evaluation materials. More information on this can be secured from: The National Commission on Performance-Based Education, Fredrick McDonald, Director, Educational Testing Service, Princeton, New Jersey 08540.

4

INNOVATION

by James W. Kolka
Associate Professor and Senior Budget Planner
University of Wisconsin
Madison, Wisconsin

About fifteen years ago, a popular joke told of a man who was walking on a sidewalk when he suddenly came upon a person who had just been thrown against a curb by an automobile collision. Injured, but still able to muster his strength, he shouted to the pedestrian, "Help, call me an ambulance, please call me an ambulance!" to which the pedestrian replied, "OK, you're an ambulance."

While the joke may reflect the paucity of wit in the late 1950s, it does point to a difficulty which occurs when we consider the term "innovation." A tabulation of new academic ventures in higher education seems to indicate that a great many universities have said of a program, "OK, you're an innovation." Given the diversity in shape, size, academic mission, academic quality and academic capability of the vast array of colleges and universities which comprise the American academy, there may be considerable justification for allowing a university to independently declare that a program is "innovative." After all, the introduction of a "great books" program could constitute a significant innovation for a university which, up to now, has emphasized a professional engineering curriculum with little regard for the broader liberal arts. By this definition, innovation is system-specific, relative to the idiosyncratic experiences of a particular institution.

However, if a definition is accepted which states that innovation is relative to each institution, we could find ourselves heir to the same type of criticism that was levied at William James when he implied that the philosophy of pragmatism accepted truth as a matter of individual taste. To counter such a critique, it would be necessary to arrive at a more universal definition. Rather than promulgate a new orthodoxy, this analysis will adopt the methodology originally used by English jurists to articulate the common law: observe and record activities which have been identified as innovative in the contemporary academic marketplace. The attempt to find uniformities will be reserved for the conclusion of this study.

HISTORICAL ANTECEDENTS

In order to evaluate contemporary views of innovation, it is necessary to establish the time and space coordinates from which the observation is made. The time is the latter third of the twentieth century, and the coordinates American higher education. Since the American academy owes a considerable debt to its institutional forebears, a genealogical identification is in order.

Beginning with the founding of Harvard College in 1636, the academy has experienced a profound metamorphosis, from a colonial period when a few private colleges trained young men for the ministry and public service, to a period of super industrialization when vast public university systems attempt to provide mass education, serve the needs of society and accommodate the disparate professional interests of a "community of scholars." The passing of the Morrill Act by the United States Congress, the emergence of new academic disciplines, the appearance of the "department," the growth of graduate education and the use of the case method for legal and business instruction are but a few of the developments in the academy which historically could be considered "innovative."

That the academy has institutional tendrils rooted in a dynamic past is evident. In order to examine conditions which have stimulated contemporary efforts at innovation, it is necessary to focus on the present and the recent past. The post-World War II period witnessed unparalleled growth in American higher education, which reached a frantic zenith in the late 1960s. It was during this period when public infatuation with higher education reached its height. More people went to college than ever before, both in gross numbers and net distribution across the socio-economic spectrum. University education became the "new frontier," the great equalizer, the ticket to upward social mobility. To a considerable extent, the effect was circular: a college education was sought, therefore, a college education was important; therefore, a college degree was essential. (In spite of the sequential nature of this description, each of these stimuli appeared at approximately the same time and tended to be mutually reinforcing.)

Just when the future seemed brightest, and public and private largess was at its peak, new winds began to blow. The disarming quietude of the post-Korean War period germinated seeds of social change. A growing concern for racial equality, President Eisenhower's indictment of the "military industrial complex," and the Cold War were legacies of the 1950s. As the student apathy of that generation was replaced by a growing number of student activists in the early 1960s, the society first seemed to express interest, but this subsequently turned into alarm. In the same manner that "a boy is forever a part of the farm," so, too, the student cannot be separated from changes occurring within the society.

The growing "multiversity" came under criticism that it was a monolithic enterprise wedded to non-academic (military) research, uninterested in quality instruction, and contemptuous of free expression. Perhaps these elements of discontent would never have fused in a peaceful setting but we are deprived of quiet speculation, since a vaguely justified Asian land war burst into the consciousness of the university, conscripted male students, and provided the catalyst which polarized many students into a core of opposition. The academy found itself walking a hazy line between those who would pull it in the direction of service for the State and those who would make it a vehicle for opposition to the State. The rational world of the university, and many of its idealistic constituents, clashed head-on with a society which preferred the hard, unswerving emotions of patriotism. Action became more important than thinking, and winning (ends) became more important than how or why to get there (means). To society, the university had become a living necklace rather than a mute physical adornment; the elegant coach of earlier days revealed its true identity —it was a talking pumpkin.

This whirl of events provided the stage for a renewed interest in innovation. The pleas for relevance and improved undergraduate instruction were born in a period when education seemed in need of change and money was available for its support. Yet, just when the spirit of a mini-reformation began to emerge, the public began to show anger with the much-publicized student violence on campus. While the initial response was to cut support for higher education, the public backlash obscured another unrelated dynamic: the population pool of eighteen-year-old adults began to stabilize in the United States, resulting in the decline of new enrollments. The period of great expansion was over, and the absence of "growth dollars" began to affect all public programs. Even though legislators meted out fiscal punishment to the rebellious university sector, they were also faced with a need to reallocate dwindling public resources to new areas of public concern. In other words, disenchantment with the university occurred at the same time that university expansion was subsiding and public resources were stretched to the breaking point. The financial crunch set the tone for higher education in the 1970s.

CONTEMPORARY EFFORTS AT INNOVATION

This brief historical summary is particularly important if one is to understand the fate of many innovative programs. Even though new efforts at innovation continue to appear, most of the innovative programs were originated during the period of expansion. Programs born in a period of affluence were forced to attain puberty in a period of recession. Their fate was soon evident—they became the most likely candidates for cutbacks, employing the time-honored "last hired, first fired" ethic of the labor market. A list of such programs follows:

1. New Universities with Institution-Wide Innovative Missions

This general category refers to those institutions which were created with an institution-wide academic mission. The period of expansion granted an opportunity for state Boards of Regents and Private Boards of Trustees to create institutions which provided alternative models to more traditional university structures.

a. Non-Fixed-Location Innovative Institutions

This subcategory refers to those instances where support was given for the creation of institutions which did not possess a fixed physical location. Public state supported examples of this sort of venture are Empire State University in New York. Private examples are Antioch West in Los Angeles and the University Without Walls of the Union of Experimenting Colleges and Universities (UWW has both public and private institutional sponsors). They are called innovative not so much for the content of their academic programs (which are frequently quite traditional) as for the method of delivery; credit for experience, decentralized instructional programs, instruction in non-fixed instructional settings (storefront or home), and the use of self-regulated learning units. The objective of these programs is to make education available to groups of students previously left outside of the mainstream of higher education due to the time requirements of jobs and other comparable responsibilities. (The success of the British Open University provided a significant stimulus for the use of this model in the United States.) While the cutting of costs is still an unresolved question for such programs, they appear to be popular with state officials. (These types of efforts are not entirely new; an historical antecedent can be found in the correspondence courses of an earlier era.)

b. Fixed-Location State-Created Innovative Institutions

This subcategory describes those colleges and universities with unique academic missions which were created by state education administrators (Boards of Regents, Boards of Trustees and Boards of Higher Education), and which are situated in a specific physical setting (a campus). Examples are Governor's State University and Sangamon State University in Illinois, the University of California-Santa Cruz and the State University of New York at Purchase. (A private example would be Prescott College in Arizona.) These institutions have been given a mandate to concentrate on a specific problem area such as public affairs, social problems or environmental problems. The implementation of the program is left to the administration and faculty of each campus. The range of innovation varies from the creation of new learning environments—unstructured classrooms and work experience; to new ways to approach knowledge—interdisciplinary studies and problem-oriented learning; to new ways to teach traditional subjects—individual instruction contracts, audio-tutorial instruction, community-oriented field research, tutorial and dynamic instruction. The critical point to remember is that these institutions have been created and supported at a state level.

c. Fixed-Location State-Tolerated Innovative Institutions

This subcategory refers to those institutions which received tacit approval for existence by state level administrators, but where the impetus for an innovative mission sprang from the campus. This is true of the environmental interdisciplinary mission of the University of Wisconsin-Green Bay, and the contract learning, individualized study mission of Evergreen State College. While these institutions closely resemble their counterparts in the preceding category, they differ in that they began not because of system support, but in spite of a lack of support. Not having been given programmatic sanction at the state level, these institutions have expended a considerable amount of administrative energy justifying their unique missions. The type of innovation is comparable to that described in the preceding subcategory—problem orientation, individual contracts, interdisciplinary studies and so forth. Because the support for innovation has been generated by campus-level administrators, these universities are particularly vulnerable. They survive only so long as campus administrators and faculty grasp the tenuous nature of their institution's existence and are willing to expend energies justifying the institution's survival to state level administrators. Continual vigilance is a major concern for this category of innovative institution. The question is whether this level of energy can be maintained over time.

2. The Transformation of Existing Colleges to Institution-Wide Missions

This category refers to those colleges and universities which have undertaken an institutional analysis and as a consequence of that effort have decided to support an innovative academic mission. Examples of such institutions are Ottawa University in Kansas and Ferris State College in Michigan. The type of innovation adopted is comparable to that described in the previous sections. It ranges from new ways to approach knowledge (substantive changes) to new methods of approaching traditional subjects (procedural changes).

3. The Creation of Innovative Colleges Within Traditional Structures

Since the preponderant majority of American Institutions of higher education adhere to traditional methods of instruction and approaches to knowledge, this response to innovation has achieved considerable popularity. Examples of innovative colleges are New College, University of Alabama; Johnston College, University of Redlands; Cook College, Rutgers University; College Within a College, University of Kansas; and Para College, St. Olaf College. The range of innovation from procedure to substance and traditional to non-traditional is as varied as that related in the previous sections. What is different is the inheritance of traditional faculty departments with traditional reward structures. Since departments possess budgets and judge faculty performance, faculty activities in new colleges will be acceptable only insofar as they conform to the ambitions of the department. While a few departments may take a benevolent view of what constitutes legitimate scholarship, most will judge their peers on traditional criteria. Consequently, efforts expended on innovative programs will, at best, be viewed as secondary and frequently will be seen as illegitimate by faculty peers.

4. The Creation of Innovative Programs Within Traditional University Structures

Of all approaches to innovation, this has proven to be the most popular, both because it is less expensive and because it poses the lowest level of threat to the departmental structure.

a. Institutes

This device is one of the time-honored mechanisms used by universities to deal with new developments. Traditionally, institutes have been created in order to seek research money and address special problems. Because such institutes are built of soft money and shaped around the existing university structure, their acceptance is not in question. But when an institute is given a budget and faculty and told to develop a curriculum, the matter is quite different—this type of institute competes directly with existing departments. (Some universities have created interdisciplinary institutes such as the Institute for Environmental Studies at the University of Wisconsin-Madison, and have given them the right to decide questions of faculty promotion and tenure.) In sum, innovative institutes have fared better when they accommodated the existing faculty structure. This is particularly true in smaller universities where institutes are more visible, and consequently more exposed to scrutiny.

b. Special Programs

Innovative programs have many of the same characteristics described for innovative institutes. The difference is the instructional emphasis of programs such as area studies or urban studies. Traditionally, these programs have been geared to drawing together scholars from several disciplines who share a common interest, such as Latin America. Essentially, these programs utilize existing resources to create a new curricular option for students, and at the same time provide an opportunity for scholars to communicate across disciplinary lines. This type of program is not a threat to departments because it links existing disciplinary courses, offers students a program alternative, and complements the efforts of the traditional discipline.

The success of this type of activity takes a different turn when innovative programs attempt to obtain an independent budget, develop their own curriculum and compete for dollars with existing programs. Two liabilities inhere to such efforts: (1) programs which deviate from traditional norms are automatically suspect for their academic legitimacy; and (2) in a period of economic retrenchment, new programs survive at the expense of ongoing programs. For example, the new popularity of programs such as black studies, women's studies, Chicano studies and Native American studies makes these sorts of activities suspect when popularity is taken as prima facie evidence of illegitimacy. Where such programs have achieved independent status, they have generally experienced a hostile reception from their peers. Such hostility can result in ostracization by the university faculty and be transmogrified into rejection, due to a lack of traditional scholarship.

c. Miscellaneous

This catchall category is used to identify innovative approaches to traditional subjects. Even though these programs are primarily involved with new methods of delivery, the nature of the program can produce substantive changes in the educational programs of individual students. Examples of this approach are credit for experience, audio and video tutorial self-programmed instruction, lifetime learning, senior citizen free enrollment, off-campus instruction, individual learning contracts, degree by committee and so forth. The primary objective is to reach a new student clientele and reduce the inflexibility of traditional in-class instruction. These programs are frequently geared to individualizing instruction for students. Where the instruction is mechanized, the cost per student is relatively low. However, where the instruction is individually tailored and requires a high degree of instructor-student interaction, cost per student frequently is quite high. Many of these programs have attained considerable popularity, so it is reasonable to anticipate future innovations of this nature.

CONCLUSIONS

It is now time to return again to the question posed in the introduction, "What is meant by the term innovation in higher education?" Because innovation literally means "the initiation of something new," there is validity for accepting the notion that a program is innovative if it introduces a significant new dimension to the academic program of a specific university. Yet, meaningful though such a program may be, it may also constitute an insignificant contribution to contemporary American higher education. With this in mind, contemporary attempts to innovate may be classified according to the magnitude of their contribution to the academy:

Campus-Specific Innovations. This category has been adequately identified. It refers to new programs which provide significant educational alternatives to students and faculty on a specific campus. The primary purpose of such programs is to expand the quality of education in a college or university. This may vary from a great books program to an ethnic studies center. Whatever the innovation, it is oriented to a specific campus.

Procedural Innovation. While this type of innovation can also be specific to a particular campus, this category is directed to efforts of greater magnitude which are presently found throughout American higher education, such as credit for experience, credit by examination, self-instruction packages, audio and video tutorial learning programs, on-site instructional programs, independent study, pass/no credit courses, and so forth. The primary concern of such programs are variations and improvements in methods of delivery. Also, these types of efforts attempt to tailor programs to the background of the students, with the underlying premise that students should not have to relearn what they already know. Pedagogically, such programs have made significant inroads in the oft-criticized inflexibility of American higher education. Given their initial success and popularity, it is reasonable to expect additional strategies for making learning more mobile and flexible. The primary concern for this type of innovative thrust will be to make certain that flexibility doesn't abrogate intellectual substance.

Substantive Innovation. In order of magnitude, this is probably the most significant contribution that innovation makes to contemporary higher education. (Procedural innovation is significant for making the educational process more meaningful to students, while substantive innovation is significant for expanding the realm of human inquiry.) Innovative programs have stimulated conditions for the development of new intellectual paradigms, attempting to move inquiry beyond its present intellectual boundaries. In this regard, two developments are particularly significant:

(a) *Problem-Solving Instruction.* Again not a new contribution—the use of the case method in legal education and land grant research are problem-solving approaches of an earlier time. However, what is new is the magnitude of the problems chosen for study and our technical capacity to deal with them. Consequently, the study of urban problems need not be confined to the study of a single disciplinary perspective, but can simultaneously incorporate several dimensions: social, environmental, technical, spatial and aesthetic. The theme need not be the accommodation of fragmented urban planning, but the quality of life in contemporary urban settings.

(b) *Interdisciplinary Analysis.* It is evident that this category is closely related to problem-solving. More specifically, this approach refers to recent efforts to create conditions where the disciplines can integrate, both to solve problems and to intellectually formulate new methods for inquiry. Because contemporary problems require a broader intellectual construct, the problems exceed the boundaries of a single discipline. The need for interdisciplinarity is evident.

The final point to be considered is, where are we now and where are we going? Campus-specific and procedural innovation are well under way. However, substantive innovation is in its formative stages. What may have been an evolutionary step in human inquiry (the institutionalization of learning and the development of the disciplines) has now been writ in stone through the mechanism of the university department and its control over hiring, promotion and tenure. The creation of an open climate which accommodates and encourages new interdisciplinary formulations is not particularly strong in contemporary colleges and universities. Professional careers and legitimate research are still bound rather tightly to the departmental model. (After all, professional socialization and security were learned in this context.) In consequence, significant efforts in interdisciplinary teaching and research have fared poorly in academe.

One other aspect must be considered in this regard. Over the past ten years, public college and university financing has shifted beyond Boards of Regents and Boards of Higher education to Bureaus of the Budget and State Departments of Administration. Well-intended efforts to maintain accountability and control have created funding formulas which feed tax dollars to the university by level (freshman-sophomore, junior-senior, graduate), by general subject matter area (life sciences, social sciences, etc.), and in some instances by cost per student credit hour in specific disciplines. In many respects, this procedure is the epitome of the Western rational model, allowing for tight accounting within a university and lateral program audits across universities. (English departments can be compared on unit costs in universities x, y and z.)

Tidy though this process may be, it freezes the institutional shape of the university at the time the funding strategy was adopted. Consequently, the institutional structure of contemporary universities, with the department as the primary unit, has been "writ in stone" by two dynamics. For the academy, it means that the shape of higher education in the mid 1960s has provided an institutional exoskeleton which will persist much longer than might have been true in times past. The creation of new intellectual approaches which defy the power base of the department, and do not conform to existing funding formulas, will find a difficult reception. For contemporary higher education, it means that innovations will continue to appear which are campus-specific and/or procedural in context. Even though the most significant contribution to knowledge will come from substantive innovation, it will evolve at a much slower rate.

REFERENCES

Axelrod, J., Freedman, M. B., Hatch, W., Katz, J., and Sanford N. *Search for Relevance: The Campus in Crisis.* San Francisco: Jossey-Bass, Inc., 1969.

Baskin, S., ed. *Higher Education: Some Newer Developments.* New York: McGraw-Hill, 1965.

———. *New Approaches to the Open University.* Union for Research and Experimentation in Higher Education. Yellow Springs, Ohio: Antioch College, 1970.

Baskin, Samuel. *The University Without Walls: A Proposal for a Degree Program in Undergraduate Education.* Union of Experimenting Colleges and Universities, Yellow Springs, Ohio: Antioch College, 1970.

Ben-David, Joseph. *American Higher Education: Directions Old and New.* Berkeley: The Carnegie Commission on Higher Education, 1973.

Brick, M., and McGrath, E. *Innovations in Liberal Arts Colleges.* New York: Columbia University Press, 1969.

Carlson, E. *Learning Through Games.* Washington, D.C.: Public Affairs Press, 1969.

Cheit, Earl. *The New Depression in Higher Education.* New

York: McGraw-Hill, 1971.

First Report: University Without Walls. Union for Experimenting Colleges and Universities, Yellow Springs, Ohio: Antioch College, 1972.

Gould, S. B., and Cross, K. P., eds. *Explorations in Non-Traditional Study.* San Francisco: Jossey-Bass, 1972.

Heiss, Ann. *An Inventory of Academic Innovation and Reform.* Berkeley: The Carnegie Commission on Higher Education, 1973.

Hodgkinson, Harold L. *Institutions in Transition.* The Carnegie Commission on Higher Education. New York: McGraw-Hill.

Ikenberry, S. O., and Friedman, R. C. *Beyond Academic Departments.* San Francisco: Jossey-Bass, 1972.

Kolka, James W. Administrative Strategies to Stimulate Innovation in Higher Education. Paper presented at the spring seminar of the American Council on Education, Academic Administration Internship Program, Washington, D.C., May 26, 1973.

_____. Una Experiencia De Universidad Interdisciplinaria, in *Interdisciplinaridad De La Enseñanza e Investigación.* Madrid: EsPES' 2000 y La Universidad Santiago de Compostela, 1973.

Lee, C. B. T., ed. *Improving College Teaching.* Washington, D.C.: American Council on Education, 1967.

Levien, R. E., ed. *The Emerging Technology: Instructional Uses of the Computer in Higher Education.* New York: McGraw-Hill, 1972.

Mahew, Lewis. *Colleges Today and Tomorrow.* San Francisco: Jossey-Bass, 1969.

Marien, Michael, ed. *An Annotated Bibliography of Trends, Forecasts and Proposals for Alternate Futures for Learning.* Policy Research Center, Syracuse University, Syracuse, New York, 1971.

Newman, Frank. *Report on Higher Education.* Washington, D.C.: U.S. Department of Health, Education and Welfare, 1971.

Noonan, J. F. The Impact of Curricular Change on Faculty Behavior. *Liberal Education* 57 (October, 1971), 344-348.

Ohmer, Milton. *Alternatives to the Traditional.* San Francisco: Jossey-Bass, 1972.

Sticker, Hugh. *Experimental Colleges: Their Role in American Higher Education.* Tallahassee: Florida State University Press, 1964.

Tubbs, Walter E. Jr., ed. *Toward a Community of Seekers.* Lincoln, Nebraska: Nebraska Curriculum Development Center, University of Nebraska, 1972.

Vermilye, Dyckman, ed. *The Expanded Campus.* San Francisco: Jossey-Bass, 1972.

Walker, Charles U., ed. *Elements Involved in Academic Change.* Washington, D.C.: Association of American Colleges, 1972.

5

DISSEMINATION OF INFORMATION IN EDUCATION

by C. L. Hutchins
Formerly, Associate Director
Far West Laboratory for Educational Research
and Development
San Francisco, California

The dissemination of information in education is a process by which awareness, trial, and use of innovations or practices is brought about by messages conveyed through mediated or interpersonal channels. Examples include information systems such as ERIC, information or resource centers, and change-agent programs. Other examples would include educational journals, workshops, conferences, meetings of professional organizations, and the activities of such people as the educational field representatives of commercial organizations.

If the effect of the dissemination of information were studied in the manner that the effects of the mass media have been studied (Klapper, 1960), it is probable that the bulk of the effect would be found to reinforce existing beliefs and practices. As an area of formal study and programmatic development, however, the dissemination of information is usually viewed in the context of facilitating educational change. As a result, this paper reviews the status of projects that focus on the creation of printed or audiovisual products for identifying or describing educational innovations; projects that disseminate these products through formal systems; and projects that support the use of information products by deploying resource personnel, change agents, or other interpersonal linkages that facilitate change.

REVIEW OF THE LITERATURE

The study of the role of information in education practice grows out of the larger study of organizational change in education. This field is traditionally traced to the work of Mort and his students, who were responsible for a large number of studies between the 1920s and the 1950s. This work did not emphasize the role of communication or the dissemination of information as a major factor in the change process. Expenditure per pupil seemed to be the major variable that accounted for school adaptability, according to Mort and his students (Ross, 1958). It was not until the 1960s that the dissemination of information began to emerge as a major variable worthy of independent study. This came about largely through the cross-fertilization of research on innovation adoption outside the field of education with the advent of the post-Sputnik interest in curriculum development and use. Within a period of about five years, major works by Carlson (1965), Miles (1964), and others focused at least in some way on the role information played in the diffusion of educational innovations. Much of this work was directly drawn from theories of mass communication (Klapper, 1960), organizational change (Bennis et al., 1961), rural sociology (Rogers, 1962, 1971; Ryan and Gross, 1943; Deutschmann and Fals Borda, 1962), anthropology (Spicer, 1952), and the diffusion of innovation in the medical profession (Coleman, 1957).

Rogers' (1962, 1971) work is perhaps best known. Among the characteristics of an innovation that account for its rate of diffusion, he identified the concept of "communicability"—the degree to which information about an innovation may be disseminated to others. Rogers also identified five critical stages in the adoption process: awareness, interest, trial, evaluation, and adoption. In practice, the study and use of information to facilitate diffusion is usually directed to the awareness and interest stages. Little attention has been given the role of information in the final three stages.

Carlson's (1965) work has been specific to education. Much of his study of the spread of selected innovations among schools was based upon the communication channels among school superintendents. The role of information in these channels was not studied carefully, however. It was presumed that advice was the major form for most of the communications.

Most existing literature relevant to the study of the role of information in the educational change process is summarized by Havelock (1969). The contribution of his work is to focus on the linkage role that information plays, and to provide a framework for reviewing the great bulk of the existing literature. Of particular note is the fact that Havelock separates findings based on the study of individuals, interpersonal linkages, organizations, and social systems. The seven factors Havelock uses to explain the dissemination and utilization process are: linkage, structure, openness, capacity, reward, proximity, and synergy.

One of the most recent works of significance has been the evaluation study of the "pilot state dissemination" program sponsored by the National Center for Educational Communications (NCEC). The study was conducted by Sieber (1972). It documents in great detail the interrelationship between field agents and information services in three different states. Among many other points, the report discusses the utility of linkage systems in meeting the needs of educators as they plan or implement changes in school practice. The report is quite long, and deserves more attention than it has thus far received.

If any conclusion can be drawn from the current research, it is simply that the dissemination of information is an important element in the change process, but that its utility is derived from its relationship to other elements involved in the total change process. The research suggests that information is a necessary but not sufficient cause for change. However, we know very little about what functions information serves in the change process. We do not know which types of information serve which functions in which contexts. We do not know how information can be manipulated to produce alternative outcomes. What little knowledge we have tends to come from psychological research, and ignores

the complexities of social organizations. For example, it is likely that at any point in time varying numbers of different individuals within a single school system might be at each of the points along Rogers' linear adoption scale (awareness, interest, etc.). At what point is an institution "aware"? There is a clear need for strong conceptual models and research that can increase our knowledge of the role of information in the educational change process.

SPECIFIC PROGRAMS AND/OR APPLICATIONS

A great burst of programs and activities based on the dissemination of information in education followed passage of the Elementary and Secondary Education Act of 1965. Of course, these programs were not without precedent: the National Defense Education Act, the Cooperative Research Act, and the legislation supporting the National Science Foundation had led to specific activities that recognized the importance of information as a mechanism for facilitating change. Nor should we ignore the traditional activities of professional associations, foundations, and commercial enterprises. But, clearly, the scope of the programmatic effort increased in 1965. A brief description of some of the efforts that emerged at this time should be helpful in understanding what happened between 1965 and 1972.

By far the largest group of activities emerged under the sponsorship of an organization that eventually became known as the National Center for Educational Communications. NCEC, as it was called, was part of the Office of Education. The leadership for that organization came from Lee Burchinal and Thomas Clemmons. Among the programs they helped put in place were these:

ERIC (Educational Resources Information Center). ERIC is a formal information system designed to search, screen, organize, and disseminate what would otherwise be fugitive materials: research and theory articles, technical reviews of developments, curriculum guides, and other educational information. Much of the actual processing of documents is done at a dozen or more subject-oriented clearinghouses located across the nation. Through its major indices, *Research In Education* and *Current Index to Journals in Education,* users can gain access to a wide range of materials available in microfiche, hard copy, or computer tape. ERIC is now sponsored by the National Institute of Education.

During its life, NCEC also sponsored a series of reviews of current trends in educational theory and practice. These were called PREPs (Putting Research into Educational Practice). Each issue was contracted to an authority in a given field and, after printing, was released through state education agencies and through the Superintendent of Public Documents.

NCEC also sponsored several major dissemination programs to increase the use of products that had been Federally sponsored. For example, a large scale installation-support program was dedicated to the diffusion of the "Multi-Unit School" developed by the Wisconsin

Research and Development Center for Cognitive Learning. The "Minicourses" and "Parent/Child Toy Library" developed by the Far West Laboratory for Educational Research and Development also received large-scale dissemination support under NCEC auspices. The "First Year Reading Skills Program" developed by the Southwest Regional Educational Laboratory also received a contract to encourage utilization through dissemination of information and demonstration.

Other Federal projects are also worth noting:

Under the sponsorship of the National Center for Educational Research, several of the regional laboratories set up programs for the dissemination of information. At the Far West Laboratory for Educational Research and Development, an information system was established that eventually became known as ALERT (Alternatives for Learning through Educational Research and Technology). In addition to several information units that reviewed innovations in such areas as elementary science, social studies, and early childhood education, the Laboratory produced a catalog of well-developed innovations for elementary schools (Henrie, 1972).

Title III of the Elementary and Secondary Act funded a very large number of local and regional resource centers that were designed to provide services to local schools, including information about programs designed to change educational practice. An illustration of a center that was originally started with Title III funding, but is now funded locally, is the San Mateo County (California) Educational Resources Center. This agency undertakes searches and produces indices and reviews in selected fields. The Northern Colorado Educational Board of Cooperative Services, Boulder, Colorado, is another example of an agency that was originally funded through Federal resources but now utilizes local funds and charges for services. They provide program development and evaluation services to schools in their areas, as well as information retrieval and dissemination services to a larger area.

Private and professional efforts include:

EPIE (Educational Products Information Exchange) Institute was created to catalog and evaluate educational products. The EPIE Institute is a nonprofit agency utilizing subscriptions and contracts for support. It has produced a number of reviews of products, curricula, and other educational innovations.

SRIS (School Research Information Service) is a research service of Phi Delta Kappa. It provides bibliographies and searches, and publishes a quarterly journal on current thinking on research and innovation in education.

The Institute for the Development of Educational Activities, Inc. (IDEA) distributes information about selected innovations. This information includes a large number of films. From time to time IDEA, through the support of its parent organization, the Kettering Foundation, also provides additional implementation support for selected innovations.

Of course, the National Education Association (NEA) continues to publish a large number of documents that review various aspects of educational practice. Numerous other professional associations are also active in trying to promote educational change and development through the dissemination of information.

From the commercial world a host of services and publications have been established in many formats and media—from directories to microfiche to on-line data services.

CURRENT CONTROVERSIES

In the early 70s the promising role which the dissemination of information appeared to be developing seemed to decline. Though the literature does not yet reflect this decline, it can clearly be seen in termination of many of the projects listed in the previous section. With the exception of the commercial and professional programs, ERIC alone survives among the government programs. And there is even significant talk of a new role for ERIC, as the National Institute of Education reviews its future.

One could attribute this turn of events to the vagaries of Federal policy. But there seem to be more fundamental issues at stake. First, from the perspective of some observers the information projects that emerged after 1965 did not bring about the educational change that had been hoped for; many Title III information projects, etc., never were able to produce evidence that they were successful in changing educational practice. Some argue that expectations were too high, and others argue that the results were there but were never well documented. At even a more fundamental level, the controversy seesaws between those who believe we do not have enough knowledge of how to bring about change, and of how to use information in that process, and those who believe that although knowledge might be improved, we nevertheless have sufficient experience on which to base new efforts to bring about change. Usually the latter position is supported by citing the utility of "extension agents" in the field of agriculture, noting the communication research on the role of opinion leaders and interpersonal channels of secondary diffusion, and citing anecdotal or other data from projects such as the three-state pilot project evaluated by Sieber.

The controversy is real, and the outcome will probably be signaled by the course of action taken by the National Institute of Education (NIE) as it struggles with deciding whether to start putting a large-scale dissemination program in place or undertake a large-scale research program.

Whatever course the NIE takes, it is likely that the future of the dissemination of information in education will be influenced to a greater or lesser degree by some of the following forces. Marketing research in business and industry is becoming increasingly sophisticated (Kotler, 1971). As time goes on, it is unlikely that education will remain unaffected by this movement; cost-effectiveness, improvement of marketing programming techniques, and new tactics for bringing about behavioral change are all likely to have an impact on the field. The concept of social marketing is also expanding (Zaltman, 1972). More and more, students of this field are beginning to recognize the relationships that exist between efforts to change social behavior in such fields as birth control, consumer practices, etc., and similar efforts in education. Research on organizational and institutional behavior is also growing, and is likely to form an important base for increasing knowledge and practice in the dissemination of educational information.

One other controversy should be noted here, though it cannot be discussed in any detail. The issue of copyright is becoming increasingly important to educational dissemination. The landmark case of *Williams & Wilkins v. United States* signals the growing conflict between the producers of educational information, particularly the commercial publishing industry, and the consumers of that information. As copying equipment has improved and proliferated, more and more students, professors, and libraries have promoted the dissemination of educational information through photocopying. Naturally, this poses a major threat to the industries that depend on the sale of books, journals, etc., to support their efforts to create, transform, and disseminate new information. The outcome of this case, appealed to the Supreme Court late in 1974, or similar ones should provide a major key to direction which the field of dissemination of information in education takes.

REFERENCES

Bennis, W. G., Benne, K. D., and Chin, R. *The Planning of Change.* New York: Holt, Rinehart and Winston, Inc., 1961.

Carlson, R. O. *Adoption of Educational Innovations.* Eugene, Ore.: The Center for the Advanced Study of Educational Administration, University of Oregon, 1965.

Coleman, J., Menzel, H., and Katz, E. "The Diffusion of an Innovation Among Physicians." *Sociometry,* December 1957, Vol. 20, pp. 253-270.

Deutschmann, P. J., and Fals Borda, O. *Communication and Adoption Patterns in an Andean Village.* San Jose, Costa Rica: Programa Interamericano de Information Popular and Facultad de Sociologia, Universidad Nacional de Columbia, 1962.

Havelock, R. G. *Planning for Innovation through Dissemination and Utilization of Knowledge.* Final Report, Contract OEC-3-7-070028-2143, Ann Arbor, Michigan: Center for Research on Utilization of Scientific Knowledge, Institute for Social Research, July 1969.

Henrie, S. N. *A Sourcebook of Elementary Curricula Programs and Projects.* San Francisco: Far West Laboratory for Educational Research and Development, 1972.

Klapper, J. T. *The Effects of Mass Communication.* New York: The Free Press of Glencoe, 1960.

Kotler, P. *Marketing Decision-Making: A Model Building Approach.* New York: Holt, Rinehart and Winston, Inc., 1971.

Miles, M. B., ed. *Innovations in Education.* New York: Teachers College Press, Teachers College, Columbia University, 1964.

Rogers, E. M. *Diffusion of Innovations.* New York: The Free Press of Glencoe, 1962.

_____ and Shoemaker, F. *Communication of Innovations.* New York: The Free Press, 1971.

Ross, D. H. *Administration for Adaptability: A Source Book Drawing Together the Results of More than 150 Individual Studies Related to the Question of Why and How Schools Improve.* New York, Metropolitan School Study Council, 1958.

Ryan, B., and Gross, N. C. The Diffusion of Hybrid Seed Corn in Two Iowa Communities. *Rural Sociology,* March 1943, Vol. 8, pp. 15-24.

Sieber, S. D. et al. *The Use of Educational Knowledge; Evaluation of the Pilot State Dissemination Program.* Final Report, Contract OEC-0-70-4930, September 1972, Vol. 1 and 2. (ERIC ED 065). 740.

Spicer, E. H., ed. *Human Problems in Technological Change.* New York: Russel Sage, 1952.

Zaltman, G., Kotler, P., and Kaufman, I., eds. *Creating Social Change.* New York: Holt, Rinehart and Winston, Inc., 1972.

ADDITIONAL RESOURCES

Carlson, R. O. *Adoption of Educational Innovations.* Eugene, Ore.: The Center for the Advanced Study of Educational Administration, University of Oregon, 1965.

Havelock, R. G. *Planning for Innovation through Dissemination and Utilization of Knowledge.* Final Report, Contract OEC-3-7-070028-2143, Ann Arbor, Michigan: Center for Research on Utilization of Scientific Knowledge, Institute for Social Research, July 1969.

Lionberger, H. F. *Adoption of New Ideas and Practices.* Iowa State University Press, 1961.

Maguire, L. M., Temkin, S., and Cummings, C. P. *An Annotated Bibliography on Administering for Change.* Philadelphia, Administering for Change Program; Research for Better Schools, Inc., October 1971.

Miles, M. B., ed. *Innovations in Education.* New York: Teachers College Press, Teachers College, Columbia University, 1964.

Rogers, E. M. *Diffusion of Innovations.* New York: The Free Press of Glencoe, 1962.

_____ and Shoemaker, F. *Communication of Innovations.* New York: The Free Press, 1971.

Sieber, S. D. et al. *The Use of Educational Knowledge; Evaluation of the Pilot State Dissemination Program.* Final Report, Contract OEC-0-70-4930, September 1972, Vol. 1 and 2. (ERIC ED 065). 740.

6

THE SCHOOLS AND PROPERTY TAX

by Alan C. Stauffer
Research Associate
Research and Information Services
Education Commission of the States
Denver, Colorado

Traditionally, public education in the United States has been financed from a combination of state, local and federal revenues. By far the most important school revenue producer has been the local tax on real property. The amount of money school districts have been able to spend on each student has depended on the amount of taxable real property within the school district boundaries. Wealthy school districts have abundant and valuable taxable properties within their boundaries. They usually do not have to levy as high a tax rate as poor districts (those that lack taxable wealth).

This system of finance has been challenged in state and federal courts on the basis that local disparities in taxable wealth produces unequal educational opportunities and inequitable tax burdens. The court challenges have focused national attention on the property tax system, causing many to criticize other weaknesses in it: inherent problems, such as alleged regressivity (requiring the poor to pay a greater percentage of income than the rich), and administrative problems, such as unequal property assessments. If the property tax is to remain a major producer of educational revenue, the system needs to be reformed to answer these major criticisms. At least nine states took major steps in 1973 to correct the problem of unequal taxable wealth in school districts. All states have enacted some form of property tax relief to aid the poor and elderly. Only a handful of states have made significant reforms in the actual administration of the tax.

THE PROPERTY TAX AS A REVENUE PRODUCER

Property taxes produce much more local revenue than any other tax. In the fiscal year ending in September 1972, the tax produced $36.7 billion in local revenue. This amounted to 84.6 percent of all local revenue (Census of Governments, 1972). Most local government services compete for the use of the property funds generated. Police and fire protection, streets, sewers, and hospitals are generally financed by the tax. In most states the largest single consumer of the revenue is the local school district. About 95 percent of all local school revenues are generated by property taxation. This takes 50 percent of the revenue produced by the tax. With the spiraling costs of both school and municipal services, the competition for property tax revenues becomes more keen. Many large urban school districts (areas that require more municipal services) have found it difficult to compete.

THE SCHOOL PROPERTY TAX AND THE COURTS

The problems caused by local property tax use in school finance formulas received national attention in August 1971 in the now famous *Serrano v. Priest* California case. Serrano argued that poor school districts (those that lack taxable wealth) are discriminated against, since they cannot raise sufficient revenues even with tax rates much higher than wealthy districts. Serrano pointed to the Beverly Hills School District (assessed property valuation of $94,700 per pupil) which levied a tax of $3.16 per $100 of assessed valuation in order to provide $1,516 per year for each school child. In Serrano's Baldwin Park District there was an assessed valuation of only $5,600 per pupil, and residents paid $5.74 per $100 to provide $691 per pupil per year. The California Supreme Court ruled that a school system where the quality of education is a function of local wealth was not constitional. The litigation was returned to the trial court to determine the facts in the case.

The Serrano case served as an impetus for cases in other states. Only Hawaii (one state-wide school district financed by the state) was not suspect. By August 1972, 52 similar cases had been identified in 31 states (Intrastate School Finance Court Cases, 1972). One of these cases, *San Antonio Independent School District v. Rodriquez,* eventually was heard by the Supreme Court of the United States, to see if the "Serrano Condition" was outlawed federally by the equal protection clause of the Fourteenth Amendment. The court held that the Texas system did not violate the U.S. Constitution. But the court did point out the inequities of the system, and challenged state legislatures to correct the situation.

Since the Rodriquez decision, the New Jersey Supreme Court held in *Robinson v. Cahill* that New Jersey's school finance system was unconstitutional, under a provision in the state constitution dealing explicitly with education rather than equal protection of the law. Thirty-four of the current cases have been filed on both state and federal grounds, with 16 of them (like New Jersey) appealing to explicit provisions on education in state constitutions. None of the cases have challenged the constitutionality of the property tax per se. They have challenged the way states allocate property tax revenue to finance schools.

THE PROPERTY TAX AND OTHER EDUCATIONAL PROBLEMS

The Serrano-type cases have called national attention to the problem of unequal local taxable wealth and the quality of education. There are other educational problems associated with the tax which need to be mentioned: the effects of unequal property assessments on school bonding and taxing limitations; the effects of unequal assessments on the distribution of state aid; the effects of property taxation on community development; and the effects of taxpayer disaffection on school bond and budget elections.

Most states have written into law, or into their constitutions, certain bonding and taxing limitations for local school districts. These limitations usually keep the school districts from taxing more than a set percentage of local assessed valuation. (Local assessed valuation is the value of local taxable property set by the local assessor.) Assessed value is seldom equal to actual market value of property. The assessment level, or ratio, is the ratio between the value set by the assessor and actual market value. This ratio usually varies in every school district. In some school districts assessed value will be expressed in a lower ratio than in other districts. This distorts the true picture of local wealth. Such districts cannot tax or bond themselves as much as they could if their value were stated correctly. Overassessed districts are not limited to the extent intended by law. The assessor can change a school district's revenue raising ability simply by raising or dropping the assessed value/market value ratio.

Unequal assessment/market value ratios also have an effect on the equitable distribution of state aid to local education. Many states distribute state aid in inverse proportion to local assessed valuation. Districts where property is underassessed are overpaid in state aid. The reverse is true for overassessed districts.

The property tax system has lead to problems with orderly community development. School districts with abundant taxable wealth and small student populations have a unique tax advantage. Zoning powers have been used to create or to preserve such districts, often at the expense of rational community development patterns. Families desiring to locate in "desirable" school districts may be prevented from doing so because of unavailability of housing in the price category they can afford. Racial and economic segregation is often a result.

One way local governments and school districts can increase the taxable wealth in their jurisdiction is through annexation. An annexation means a loss of taxable wealth to the government from which the land was annexed. In the scramble for taxable property, competing local governments often become engaged in "annexation wars." An annexation by one government leads to one or two annexations by a competing government. Needless to say, the political and school district boundaries are constantly changing, sometimes four or five times a year. This condition makes school planning very difficult, if not next to impossible. Some school districts feel they must turn to annexation in order to survive and preserve racial balance. This is true in large cities where the middle class has fled to the suburbs and eroded the core city tax base.

Finally, the property tax is reported to be the most disliked tax in the country (Public Appraisal of Major Taxes, 1972), which may have something to do with taxpayer resistance to school budget and bond elections. People dislike the tax for several reasons. Property taxes usually become due in one or two lump sums a year. This makes tax payments very painful in relation to other taxes, hidden in sales prices or withheld from paychecks. Property taxes have an adverse affect on low-income families on fixed incomes. Rapidly increasing school costs have brought about property tax rate inflation, and forced many elderly taxpayers to sell their homes. People are also unhappy about the property tax because of the way it is administered. Untrained elected assessors are often susceptible to intense political pressure. Many assessors in most states are unsupervised, and have only the crudest tools to keep up with rapidly inflating market values of real estate. In 1963 the Advisory Commission of Intergovernmental Relations (ACIR) made an in-depth study of the inadequacies of property tax administration in the states, and specific reforms were recommended (ACIR, 1963). Ten years later, two independent studies (Stauffer, 1973; Subcommittee on Intergovernmental Relations, 1973) have shown that very little progress has been made since 1963. All these conditions cause taxpayer resentment against the tax that supplies the greatest amount of local school revenue.

WHAT STATES ARE DOING TO REFORM THE SCHOOL TAX SYSTEM

Reform of the property tax and school finance in 1973 took place on three fronts: (1) reform of school revenue distribution formulas; (2) property tax relief; and (3) reform of property tax administration. Spurred on by court pressures, state policymakers and finance theoriticians have worked feverishly to devise systems of school finance where local taxable wealth does not affect school district spending levels. By June 1, 1972, state study groups were organized in all 50 states (Pipho, 1972). By Autumn 1973, basic changes were made in school finance structures in at least nine states. The states have opted to keep the local property tax and devise mechanisms for equalizing the inequities caused by disparities in the taxable wealth of school districts. The technique used to accomplish this is called "district power equalizing." The major alternative of full state funding of education has not caught on. The Oregon State Legislature passed a school finance package that would be substantially the same as full state funding, but the proposal was solidly defeated in a vote of referendum.

District power equalizing is a technique devised to keep the local property tax while negating the problem of unequal taxable wealth among school districts (Coons, 1970). The technique is aimed to eliminating the court objections raised in the Serrano and Rodriguez cases. Power equalizing has not yet been tested in the courts.

Under a power equalizing plan all school districts have the same "power" to spend at whatever level they choose, providing they exert the required tax effort. Theoretically, in an ideal power equalizing system the state would guarantee an equal assessed property valuation behind every student. If the yield of a uniform local tax rate in a given district does not produce the amount that would be produced if the district actually had the guaranteed valuation, the state makes up the difference. The state takes away, or "recaptures," revenues from wealthy districts where the uniform school tax produces more than the guaranteed amount. Many states seem willing to guarantee the property tax yield, but few seem willing to recapture the excesses of wealthy districts.

All the major state school finance changes in 1973 have elements of power equalizing in them. Colorado guarantees that each mill ($.001) levied for school purposes will produce $25 per student. Kansas requires certain tax efforts in order for the districts to be guaranteed the ability to spend at various levels. Utah requires a uniform mill levy in all districts, and makes up the difference between what the tax raises and a pre-set support level. Maine requires a uniform rate to pay for 40 percent of all school costs, and then guarantees the yield of additional optional local leeway mills (extra taxes then can be levied by the district in addition to the required taxes). Florida mandates a seven-mill tax and pays the school districts the difference between the yield and a legislatively set support level. Montana, Illinois, Wisconsin and Michigan have similar new laws. In Maine, Utah, Montana, and Wisconsin, recapture of excess funds is possible. The other states do not recapture excess funds for some mill levies, such as local leeway.

These states have, in essence, legislated a statewide property tax. The property in the state is taxed on the basis of local assessments. The revenue is spread across the state as if the state had levied a tax, collected the proceeds, and then distributed it to the school districts. The major problem with the system is that most states have different assessment ratios in each school district. Some districts are underassessed while others are over-assessed. Few are assessed at the ratio prescribed by law (some states do not prescribe a ratio). Since the states pay extra aid to those districts with low valuations, an underassessed jurisdiction stands to gain extra unearned dollars. Overassessed districts are unjustly penalized. This condition can be compensated for by equalizing (adjusting for differences in ratios) district assessed values before determining how much state aid is due. Another cure is to base district valuation on state assessments rather than on local assessments. Reform of assessment practices, including establishing strong state controls over assessment and appraisal functions, will help cure the problem on a more lasting basis.

Power equalizing has been criticized as being incompatible with the concept of education as a fundamental right under state government (Fleischmann Report, 1973). If education is so important that local wealth cannot determine its quality, why should local educational policymakers, or local voters, be able to decide what the level of spending should be? Proponents of this view hold that the state should decide what an adequate education is and provide the resources to bring it about.

There was much state action to bring about property tax relief in 1973. Many states had budget surpluses for the first time. Federal revenue sharing was also available. The result was that now every state in the union enacted some kind of property tax relief program for the elderly and/or low-income families. One of the most popular forms of property tax relief is called the "circuit-breaker." When total taxes paid exceed a legislatively set percentage of one's income the "circuit-breaker" goes into action: the state refunds the taxpayer part of his tax payment or reduces his income tax bill. "Circuit-breakers" are popular, since they give property tax relief only to those who need it. In addition, local tax bases are not eroded. In other forms of relief the state often requires local governments to grant exemptions, but the state does not reimburse the local governments for tax revenue lost. Wisconsin was the leader in the "circuit-breaker" movement. Now at least 21 states have adopted some form of the concept.

Reform of the administration of the property tax is coming slowly. People often associate reform with an increased valuation on their home. States have been hesitant to superimpose controls on locally elected assessors. But without substantial reform in assessment administration the property tax will never be really fair or well accepted. Some of the long-overdue reforms include:

Requiring that assessors, whether elected or appointed, meet minimum professional standards;

Consolidating assessment jurisdictions for economy and reducing the cost of computer applications;

Establishing state agencies with power to supervise local property tax administration;

Publicly disclosing assessment ratios in all jurisdictions;

Publicly disclosing the value of all exempt properties.

In 1973, Maryland, Montana, and Florida took major steps to improve property tax administration. In Maryland and Montana, assessors are now state employees. In Maryland, assessors must meet minimum standards under the state merit system. In Florida, an agency was created with the power to supervise local assessments. The agency will also establish a loan fund for local assessors to improve their own administrations. In other years Oregon, California, and New York also made substantial improvements in the administration of the property tax.

CONCLUSION

The property tax is the major producer of local school revenue. Because of the reliance on the tax, schools suffer from unequal tax burdens and unequal spending levels. State courts have held that this condition is not tolerable. It appears the states are turning to the concept of power equalizing to preserve the local property tax while equalizing disparities in local wealth. The success of this approach may depend on how well the states will be able to cope with unequal assessments among school districts. The states have made progress in relieving the excess burden the tax has on the poor and the elderly. Very little progress has been made in upgrading the administration of the tax.

REFERENCES

Advisory Commission on Intergovernmental Relations. *The Role of the States in Strengthening the Property Tax,* 2 Volumes. Washington, D.C.: U.S. Government Printing Office, June 1963.

Coons, John E., Clunne, William H. III, and Sugarman, Stephen D. *Private Wealth and Public Education.* Cambridge, Massachusetts: Belknap Press of Harvard University, 1970, 201-242.

Intrastate School Finance Court Cases: States and Cases as of August 1972. Washington, D.C.: Lawyers' Committee for Civil Rights Under Law, 1972.

The New York State Commission on the Quality, Cost, and Financing of Elementary and Secondary Education. *The Fleischmann Report on the Quality, Cost, and Financing of Elementary and Secondary Education in New York State, Vol. 1.* New York: The Viking Press, 1973, 88-89.

Pipho, Chris. *Survey of School Finance Study Commissions and Committees.* Denver: Education Commission of the States, Research Brief No. 3, March 1973.

Public Appraisal of Major Types of Taxes. Research Park, Princeton, N.J.: Caravan Surveys, Inc., Research Finding Prepared for Advisory Commission on Intergovernmental Relations, March 1972.

Stauffer, Alan C. *Property Assessment and Exemptions: They Need Reform.* Denver: Education Commission of the States, Research Brief No. 3, March 1973.

Subcommittee on Intergovernmental Relations of the Committee on Government Operations, United States Senate. *Status of Property Tax Administration in the States: Compilation of State Responses to Survey.* Washington, D.C.: U.S. Government Printing Office, March 23, 1973.

U.S. Bureau of the Census, Census of Governments, 1972, Vol. 2. *Taxable Property Values and Assessment-Sales Price Ratios Part 1: Taxable and Other Property Values.* Washington, D.C.: U.S. Government Printing Office, 1973, 1-2.

ADDITIONAL RESOURCES

Books

Advisory Commission on Intergovernmental Relations. *State-Local Revenue Systems and Educational Finance.* Washington, D.C.: The President's Commission on School Finance, 1971.

Dochterman, Clifford L. *Understanding Education's Financial Dilemma: The Impact of Serrano-type Court Decisions on American Education.* Denver: Education Commission of the States, 1972.

Johns, Roe L., Alexander, Kern, and Stollar, Dewey H., eds. *Status and Impact of Educational Finance Programs.* Gainsville, Florida: The National Educational Finance Project. 1971.

Morley, Anthony and others. *A Legislator's Guide to School Finance.* Denver: The Education Commission of the States, August 1972, reprinted February 1973.

Netzer, Dick. *The Economics of the Property Tax.* Washington, D.C.: The Brookings Institution, 1966.

Stauffer, Alan C. *Major School Finance Changes in 1973* (Preliminary Paper) Denver: Education Commission of the States, June 8, 1973.

Wise, Arthur E. *Rich Schools, Poor Schools: The Promise of Equal Educational Opportunity.* Chicago: The University of Chicago Press, 1972.

Organizations

Finance Project
Education Commission of the States
1860 Lincoln Street, Suite 300
Denver, Colorado 80203
(303) 893-5200

International Association of Assessing Officers
1313 East 60th Street
Chicago, Illinois 60637
(312) 324-3400

Lawyers' Committee for Civil Rights Under Law
733 Fifteenth Street, N.W.
Suite 520
Washington, D.C. 20005
(202) 628-6700

National Educational Finance Project
1212 S.W. 5th Avenue
Gainesville, Florida 32601
(904) 378-1479

Court Cases

Bradley v. Milliken, 345 F. Supp. 914 (1972).
Brown v. Board of Education, 349 U.S. 294 (1955).
Davis v. School District of the City of Pontiac, 313 F. Supp. 734 (1970).
Green v. County School Board of New Kent County, 391 U.S. 430 (1968).
Griggs v. Duke Power Co., 401 U.S. 424 (1971).
Hobson v. Hansen, 269 F. Supp. 401 (1967).
Keyes v. School District No. 1, Denver, Colorado, 313 F. Supp. 61 (1970), 131 F. Supp. 90 (1970).
Keyes v. School District No. 1, Denver, Colorado, 93 S. Ct., 2686.
Plessey v. Ferguson, 163 U.S. 544 (1896).
Stuart v. School District No. 1 of the Village of Kalamazoo, 30 Mich. 69 (1874).
Swann v. Charlotte-Mecklenburg Board of Education, 402 U.S. 1 (1971).

7

ACCREDITATION AND HIGHER EDUCATION

by Robert Kirkwood
Special Consultant to the Regional Accrediting Commissions;
Formerly Executive Director
Federation of Regional Accrediting Commissions
Washington, D.C.

Accreditation is a process of recognizing educational institutions whose performance and integrity entitle them to the confidence of the educational community and the public. In the United States, this recognition is extended largely through nongovernmental or voluntary agencies which have responsibility for establishing criteria, visiting and evaluating institutions at their request, and approving those institutions which meet their criteria.

Institutional accreditation at the postsecondary level is a means used by regional accrediting commissions for purposes of:

Fostering excellence in postsecondary education through the development of criteria and guidelines for assessing educational effectiveness;

Encouraging institutional improvement of educational endeavors through continuous self-study and evaluation;

Assuring the educational community, the general public, and other agencies or organizations that an institution has clearly defined and appropriate educational objectives; has established conditions under which their achievement can reasonably be expected; appears in fact to be accomplishing them substantially; and is so organized, staffed, and supported that it can be expected to continue to do so;

Providing counsel and assistance to established and developing institutions;

Protecting institutions against encroachments which might jeopardize their educational effectiveness or academic freedom.

In American Higher education accreditation performs a number of important functions. For one, it helps intensify each institution's efforts toward maximum educational effectiveness. The accrediting process requires each institution to examine its own goals, operations, and achievements, followed by the expert criticism and suggestions of a visiting team, and later by the recommendations of the accrediting agency. Since the accredited status of an institution is reviewed periodically, the institution is encouraged toward continual self-study and improvement.

Institutional accreditation is granted by the accrediting commissions of regional associations of schools and colleges, which together include more than 2200 institutions in the United States and its possessions, Mexico, and France. In addition, there are many developing institutions which receive the benefit of consulting and other services as they work toward accreditation. The regional commissions accredit total institutions only—not parts of them.

While operating procedures of the accrediting commissions differ somewhat in detail, to allow for and even encourage regional variations, their rules of eligibility, basic policies, and levels of expectation are similar. These similarities are further developed through the Federation of Regional Accrediting Commissions of Higher Education, to which they all belong.

Institutional accreditation does not imply similarity of aims, uniformity of process, or comparability of institutions. Instead, it indicates that, in the judgment of the responsible agents of the academic community, an institution's own goals are soundly conceived; that its educational programs have been intelligently devised, are competently conducted, are capable of fulfilling the institution's goals, and are, in fact, accomplishing them substantially. It also stresses that the institution should be organized, staffed, and supported so as to continue to merit such confidence in the foreseeable future.

SPECIALIZED PROGRAM ACCREDITATION

In contrast to institutional accreditation, specialized accreditation of professional schools and programs is granted by a number of national organizations, each representing a single professional area such as architecture, law, medicine, or social work. Though each of these organizations has its distinctive definitions of eligibility, criteria for accreditation, and operating procedures, most of them have undertaken accreditation as one means of protecting the public against professional incompetence. Their emphasis, therefore, is on assuring that the purposes and accomplishments of professional programs meet the needs of society and of the professions. Because of the differing emphases, institutional accreditation is not, and should not be interpreted as being, equivalent to specialized accreditation of each of the several parts or programs of institutions. This distinction must be clearly understood, for in several professions—principally the health professions—states require that students graduate from a program accredited by an appropriate professional agency before they can be admitted to licensure examination.

Many of the specialized accrediting agencies in the professional fields require that a college or university be accredited by a regional commission before its professional programs are eligible for specialized accreditation. Several professional accrediting agencies, however, have accredited professional programs at institutions not otherwise accredited. In some cases, there are free-standing professional schools unrelated to universities or other educational complexes or consortia. Law, medical schools, and theological seminaries are the most typical, and these are accredited by the appropriate professional agency.

While the Federation of Regional Accrediting Commissions of Higher Education coordinates the work of the regional institutional accrediting commissions, the National Commission on Accrediting fulfills a similar function for the specialized and professional agencies. Both organizations are supported by the educational institutions they serve, and both include lay members representing the public interest on their governing boards. They work closely together in efforts to coordinate accrediting activities and to strengthen the value and effectiveness of independent accreditation.

ACCREDITATION OF PROPRIETARY EDUCATION

As the role of proprietary education gains increased recognition in the total educational scene, the work of several agencies dealing primarily with institutions in this sector grows in importance. The National Association of Trade and Technical Schools, the Association of Independent Schools and Colleges (formerly the United Business Schools Association), and the National Home Study Council each have accrediting commissions which work with schools in largely specialized fields and are largely of a proprietary nature.

GOVERNMENT AND ACCREDITATION

Although educational accreditation at the postsecondary level has been independent of any governmental control during its half-century of activity, the growing investment of the federal government in higher education has brought some changes. In 1968, the Accreditation and Institutional Eligibility Staff (AIES) was established in the Bureau of Higher Education of the United States Office of Education (USOE). Among its responsibilities is the primary one of recognizing and reviewing accrediting agencies to determine whether their policies and procedures are in accord with the criteria for recognition set forth by the U.S. Commissioner of Education. Any agency—institutional, specialized, or professional—whose accreditation is in any way related to a federal funding program, must now be reviewed by the AIES before it will be included in the list of agencies recognized by USOE.

To some, this development has raised the spectre of governmental takeover of accreditation. Others see it as a logical step in the evolution of a complex system of postsecondary education unique to the United States. As the triangular pattern has emerged, the states play their role through the chartering of postsecondary institutions having specific authorization to grant certificates and degrees. Then the independent accrediting agencies take over, providing incentives to the institutions to achieve high levels of quality in their educational programs, and assuring the public and the academic community that they are indeed doing so. The AIES forms the third side of the triangle, reviewing the work of the accrediting agencies and holding them accountable to the criteria for recognition established by the U.S. Commissioner of Education. In many respects, practical and applied as well as theoretical, this is one of the better examples of checks and balances inherent in the democratic process. Nevertheless, there is continued wariness among many educators about the government's becoming too great a controlling force in higher education.

This is especially true with respect to the rising involvement of state and local governments in higher educational affairs. Until the 1950s, the extent of their involvement was limited to funding state universities and teachers' colleges and not much else. Quickly through the fifties, and at an accelerated pace in the sixties, states, counties, and even municipalities established hundreds of new institutions and transformed normal schools into general-purpose colleges or universities. While much of this happened without plan or design, it soon became apparent that central planning and structure were needed to organize all the elements into a more coherent whole. Gradually, state systems, boards of higher education, coordinating councils, and other forms of centralized supervision began to emerge. At first these affected only public institutions, but eventually some states began to subsidize private colleges and universities as well, and to varying degrees these institutions also began to incur obligations to the state agencies.

NEW PRESSURES ON ACCREDITATION

All of which leads to the point that the accrediting process has been complicated by these developments. Traditionally, the regional accrediting commissions have worked in direct relationship with each individual institution, public and private. They intend to continue to do so, but in a number of states where budgeting and other forms of control have been centralized (at least for public institutions) it will be necessary to look at the central organization, to the extent that its activities can be determined to affect the educational quality of individual campuses.

Other forces are also impinging on accreditation in ways that will inevitably affect traditional patterns. One example is the rising demand for consumer protection currently being translated into federal and state laws, some of which will undoubtedly affect educational institutions. Accreditation is being looked to as a guarantor that a college or university is indeed providing the educational opportunities described in its catalog or otherwise advertised. After years of low-profile activity, when many even within the academic community were not especially aware of the meaning or importance of accreditation, the accrediting agencies are now assuming a more public role, and accreditation is receiving wider attention both within and outside of academic circles.

FRACHE

The regional accrediting commissions anticipated some of these developments several years ago, and have been actively updating their operations. Through the Federation of Regional Accrediting Commissions of Higher Education (FRACHE), they have achieved a notably high level of national consistency in policies and procedures. At the same time, the regionals are striving to preserve and promote institutional diversity and to counteract the homogenizing tendencies of centralized planning and controls. Each regional commission has developed useful materials to assist institutions in internal self-study and planning, activities which are viewed as absolutely essential to the accrediting process.

To this end, the Federation is engaged in a long-range research effort to develop new approaches to self-study and evaluation. Particular attention is being focused on ways in which institutions measure the outcomes of the educational opportunities they promise or provide. Some fear has been expressed that a shift of emphasis in this direction will result in a return to simple quantification as a means of measuring quality. However, the long experience of the regionals in assessing the whole spectrum of types of higher educational institutions precludes any such oversimplification of the accrediting process.

A further step has been taken toward strengthening nongovernmental accreditation and assuring its independence through the cooperative efforts of the regional and specialized accrediting commissions fostered by FRACHE and the National Commission on Accrediting. Attention is being concentrated on more effective coordination of self-study and evaluation activities, in the interests of reducing unnecessary duplication and relieving institutions of excessive costs or other burdensome aspects of accreditation. Despite some criticism from the larger and more complex universities and community colleges about accreditation's demands on their resources, however, there is virtually unanimous support among educational administrators for continuation of accreditation as a non-governmental activity. To the extent that the various accrediting agencies maintain their credibility and responsibility, and demonstrate their responsiveness to the changing educational scene, to that extent is accreditation likely to remain as a unique system for assuring the quality of American postsecondary education and stimulating its further improvement.

REGIONAL AND SPECIALIZED ACCREDITING AGENCIES

Commission on Higher Education
Middle States Association of Colleges and Secondary Schools

Commission on Institutions of Higher Education
Commission on Vocational-Technical Institutions
New England Association of Schools and Colleges

Commission on Institutions of Higher Education
North Central Association of Colleges and Secondary Schools

Commission on Higher Schools
Northwest Association of Secondary and Higher Schools

Commission on Colleges
Commission on Occupational Education Institutions
Southern Association of Colleges and Schools

Accrediting Commission for Senior Colleges and Universities
Accrediting Commission for Junior Colleges
Western Association of Schools and Colleges

AGENCIES ACCREDITING PRIMARILY PROPRIETARY INSTITUTIONS

Accrediting Commission
Association of Independent Colleges and Schools

Accrediting Commission
National Association of Trade and Technical Schools

Accrediting Commission
National Home Study Council

SPECIALIZED AND PROFESSIONAL ACCREDITING AGENCIES

Architecture—National Architectural Accrediting Board
Art—National Association of Schools of Art
Business—American Association of Collegiate Schools of Business
Chemistry—American Chemical Society
Community Health Education—American Public Health Association
Dental Hygiene—American Dental Association
Dentistry—American Dental Association
Engineering—Engineers' Council for Professional Development
Engineering Technology—Engineers' Council for Professional Development
Forestry—Society of American Foresters
Home Economics—American Home Economics Association
Hospital Administration—Accrediting Commission on Graduate Education
Industrial Technology—National Association for Industrial Technology
Journalism—American Council on Education for Journalism
Landscape Architecture—American Society of Landscape Architects
Law—American Bar Association
　　Association of American Law Schools
Librarianship—American Library Association
Medical Record Administration—American Medical Association in collaboration with the American Medical Record Assn.
Medical Technology—American Medical Association, in collaboration with the Board of Schools of Medical Technology
Medicine—Liaison Committee on Medical Education
Music—National Association of Schools of Music
Nursing—National League for Nursing
Occupational Therapy—American Medical Association, in collaboration with the American Occupational Therapy Association
Optometry—American Optometric Association
Osteopathy—American Osteopathic Association
Pharmacy—American Council on Pharmaceutical Education
Physical Therapy—American Medical Association, in collaboration with the American Physical Therapy Association
Podiatry—American Podiatry Association
Psychology—American Psychological Association
Public Health—American Public Health Association
Social Work—Council on Social Work Education
Speech Pathology and Audiology—American Speech and Hearing Association
Teacher Education—National Council for Accreditation of Teacher Education
Theology—American Association of Theological Schools in the United States and Canada
Veterinary Medicine—American Veterinary Medical Association

ASSOCIATIONS RECOGNIZED TO GRANT PROGRAM ACCREDITATION AT THE ASSOCIATE DEGREE LEVEL

Dental Assisting—American Dental Association
Dental Hygiene—American Dental Association
Dental Technology—American Dental Association
Engineering Technology—Engineers' Council for Professional Development
Nursing—National League for Nursing

BIBLIOGRAPHY

Dickey, F.G., and Miller, J. W. *A Current Perspective on Accreditation,* Washington: American Association for Higher Education, 1972.

Hartnett, R. T. *Accountability in Higher Education.* Princeton: Educational Testing Service, 1971.

Kells, H. R. Institutional Accreditation: New Forms of Self-Study. *Educational Record,* 1972, 53, 143-148.

Kirkwood, R. The Myths of Accreditation. *Educational Record,* 1973, 54, 211-215.

Pace, C. R. *Thoughts on Evaluation in Higher Education.* Iowa City, Iowa: American College Testing Program.

Puffer, C. E. *Report on Institutional Accreditation in Higher Education.* Chicago: Federation of Regional Accrediting Commissions of Higher Education, 1970.

Study of Accreditation of Selected Health Educational Programs. Washington: Commission report, National Commission on Accrediting, 1972.

Van Antwerp, Eugene I. *Accreditation in Postsecondary Education.* Washington: Council on Postsecondary Accreditation, 1974.

8

HIGHER AND POST SECONDARY EDUCATION—AN OVERVIEW

by Carl J. Lange
Vice President for Administration and Research
The George Washington University
Washington, D.C.

This study considers the topics of higher and post-secondary education. Recently, the term postsecondary education has been used to refer to the broad spectrum of educational activities beyond high school. The meaning of the term and the implications for future developments in higher education institutions is becoming an issue of major current importance. Intended as a broad overview, this study considers major trends and issues which reflect the current status of developments and emerging directions.

There are approximately 2600 institutions of postsecondary education in the United States, including about 950 community and junior colleges. On the order of 1000 are public; 1500 are private. If one adds proprietary and private nonprofit career schools, the number would increase by 11,000. While there are forces pressing toward bringing all these types of institutions under the umbrella term of postsecondary education, this overview will be primarily concerned with the more traditionally identified institutions, numbering 2600.

The period of the fifties through the mid-sixties was one of substantial growth and generous support for higher education. Enrollments grew at a steady pace and funds for support of higher education, both federal and state, were plentiful. A period of turmoil and near chaos began in the late sixties, with radical activism and challenges to the traditional modes of approach in higher education prevailing. This period of radical activism and disruption has subsided, and higher education is now in a period of searching self-examination and self-renewal under conditions of financial constraint. The no-growth theme now appears to be a dominant one, with enrollments leveling off and costs rising.

This shift to no or limited growth has occurred more rapidly than anticipated by many, and is seen as placing new demands on educational leaders. The requirements now are for choice, as Cheit (1972) describes it, among divergent goals. In an analysis of the financial constraint besetting higher education, he states that "if his analysis is correct, in the coming months and years public policy will be shaped by efforts (1) to move public systems closer to full cost pricing; (2) to have high quality institutions both public and private; and (3) to extend access" (p. 16). He sees the formal resolution of these divergent goals as becoming a major policy issue in many, perhaps most, states. In contrast to the recent past, when leadership was seen during the growth period as mediating conflicts between ambitious departments, and then keeping the peace during the period of campus disturbance, it is now to be identified through the choices it makes.

Heyns (1973), in his first presidential address to the American Council on Education's annual meeting, urged vigorous public debate about policy issues, and described three major tasks which encompass many of the specific problems before higher education. These three tasks reflect many major issues that appear in recent literature. The first is "to develop within our instituions the mechanisms and the attitudes that nourish continuous self-renewal. . . . Improvements in performance and in the satisfactions of higher education are more likely to come from small incremental gains than from quantum leaps" (p. 34). A theory about financing higher education is the second large task. "We must achieve some general agreement about which sources of support should provide for particular educational functions" (p. 35). He sees the need for consensus as especially urgent if controversy between public and private institutions is to be avoided. The third task is "to develop and strengthen mechanisms for collective planning, coordination, and control. Involved is the whole range of regional and state commissions and councils, both statutory and voluntary, advisory and decision-making" (p. 36).

Thus, the current atmosphere is one of careful study, analysis and debate by educational leaders and scholars, relative to finance, coordination among an increasingly complex set of educational enterprises, and self-renewal to meet educational needs and maintain quality.

Of particular relevance to these issues are questions relating to the goals of higher education. There have been numerous studies of goals spanning the period from 1947 to the present. Stimulated by diverse concerns, these various studies reveal considerable consistency in their evolutionary development. Trivett (1973), in a comprehensive review of the major literature related to goals, provides a synthesis of major studies beginning with the Truman Commission report *Higher Education for American Democracy* (1947) and extending through such studies as the *Assembly on University Goals and Governance,*

22 reports by the Carnegie Commission on Higher Education, and the Newman *Report on Higher Education.* He cites the goal of extending access, or equality of opportunity for higher education, as central to all goal statements since 1947, and postulates a change in the meaning of the phrase from "equality of access," through expansion, to "equality through diversity of acceptable offerings." Now universal access is the unifying goal, with the added condition that attendance be successful. Related is an emphasis on the role of the learner and differentiated response to the individual student.

This goal of extending access is reflected in open admissions policies, lifelong learning with development of external degree and non-traditional degree programs, and extension of the range of educational institutions eligible for student loans. Debate and studies related to all these developments are prevalent in recent literature, and are likely to become increasingly so in the coming decade. Many of these current developments have a long history in higher education, but recent emphasis may be moving concerns that were peripheral in the past to a more central position.

Open admissions has been the subject of much discussion and debate. The City University of New York (CUNY) planned open admissions for the mid-seventies. Student pressure during the late sixties led to an earlier decision. In 1969, the New York City Board of Higher Education decided to initiate an open admissions policy in CUNY and, at the time, contracted with the American Council on Education's Office of Research to evaluate the first year of the program. Astin and Rossman (1973), in a status report, concluded that though many issues and questions were still unresolved, and some questions were impervious to empirical analysis, results of the first year "must be viewed as providing strong support for the Board of Higher Education's 1969 decision" (p. 37). The Astin and Rossman evaluation focused on two kinds of outcomes: those related to cognitive and academic achievement and those related to motivation and attitude. Interestingly, the level of degree to which a student aspired was particularly important in predicting persistence and achievement, regardless of his past achievements.

Other, more impressionistic and less quantitative, evaluations have been made. Observations of the impact of open admissions on educational experiences in the classroom which relate more to process than outcome suggest that new dimensions are added to class discussions in ways that could not be specifically anticipated. Some feel that higher education can be enriched by the experiences brought by students admitted through open admissions. At the same time, a new emphasis is being placed on the learning process and educational theory, in order to provide successful learning experience. The issues involved in open admissions are complex, and are likely to be the subject of continuing research, discussion, and debate.

The goal of universal access to higher education extends beyond open admissions to traditional academic programs. Flexibility in degree programs has been a major trend. Lifelong learning has emerged as a priority objective, with external degree and non-traditional degree programs developing considerable prominence in the literature of the past several years. The Open University in Great Britain has been used as a model for development of similar programs in the United States. The external degree programs offered by New York State and the University Without Walls are among the more prominent early developments in the United States. A Commission on Non-traditional Study sponsored by the Educational Testing Service has recently examined the issues involved in these new types of programs. As with most new developments, definitions are not clear, and there is need for clarification related to these programs. The movement is essentially oriented toward providing the types of education beyond high school desired or needed by citizens of all ages and in situations accessible to them. Use is made of television, tape cassettes, and other products of educational technology, to provide learning experiences for students in locations remote from the sponsoring institution. Another important aspect of non-traditional degree programs is allowing credit for off-campus experience, including field experience and work experience. Critical and still unresolved questions relating to evaluating such experiences for awarding academic credit are under investigation and discussion.

The community college movement has been a development of major importance in increasing access to education beyond high school. Many community colleges in effect practice open admissions, and tuition costs are typically very low with heavy state and local support. These colleges have been struggling to clarify their mission, with perhaps the major issue being between a vocational/career orientation, as contrasted to academic preparation for transfer to four-year degree programs. This issue has produced the concept of the comprehensive community college, and the current trend is to serve both sets of objectives.

A significant development in extending the concept of postsecondary education is the action of the Ninety-Second Congress. The Educational Amendments of 1972 gave legal and monetary force to a broadened concept of postsecondary education. This legislation makes Basic Educational Opportunity Grants available to students on the basis of financial need, and allows the student a relatively free choice of institution. As a result of this legislation, and other forces at work both nationally and internationally, postsecondary education is acquiring a new meaning. Trivett (1973) provides a discussion of these developments. The implications of this trend to broaden the range of educational experience beyond high school, as well as the trend to modify traditional higher education offerings, may well be the dominant themes of the coming decade.

In the past, forces in higher education have tended to work toward homogenization. Lesser institutions would set as their overriding goal the acquisition of characteristics of elite institutions. Now it would appear that forces are at work which will stimulate greater diversity of function, with a variety of educational needs and desires served by a variety of institutions.

The UNESCO report *Learning to Be* (1972), produced by the International Commission on the Development of Education, and the Carnegie Commission Report *The*

Purpose and the Performance of Higher Education (1973), are examples of reports considering the many issues related to these future developments in higher education.

There are many other concerns and developments in higher education which can only be alluded to in a brief overview. In the governance area, the issues related to centralization of control and planning by state governing boards, as opposed to preserving autonomy of individual institutions, will become increasingly important with the need for coordination of diverse functions. At the individual institutions level the period of the late sixties saw an increase in student and faculty participation in governance. In many colleges and universities students are named to committees formerly reserved for faculty and administrative officers. Collective bargaining by faculty has emerged rapidly as a new trend, sharply reversing historical views of faculty that unionizing is counter to professional interests. Most faculties that have formal unions are in public institutions. While a sizable number of institutions have moved to collective bargaining, some have voted against it. The issue of collective bargaining is one that will be discussed widely in the years ahead. Tenure has been under scrutiny for a variety of reasons—the increased emphasis on accountability, legal implications of collective bargaining, and financial constraints all have served to stimulate discussion of tenure. While there have been some moves to introduce relatively novel practices for dealing with tenure, few major shifts have been made.

A major trend has been the interest in the development and use of modern management techniques in higher education, including computerized management in-information systems, simulation models for analysis of cost-benefits related to decision alternatives, and various accounting devices. The popularity of these approaches has been stimulated by financial constraints and pressure for accountability. Related to this development is the use of empirical techniques, such as the Delphi Technique, in the identification and definition of objectives for colleges. These techniques provide for collection of information from the college community concerning objectives and, through iterative application, consensus on priority of objectives can be evaluated. (Peterson, 1970).

There has been a recent surge of interest in faculty development and faculty evaluation. The interest in faculty evaluation is oriented toward use of evaluation techniques for improving faculty performance. The interest in faculty development is related to development of modifications in learning experiences. A major development in this area is personalized instruction systems, which identify objectives for courses and provide instruction at the student's own pace. Other developments include service learning, experience-based learning, and a wider use of internships.

The recent past has seen the development of programs of study and courses for various ethnic minority groups (e.g., black students). More recently, programs of women's studies and courses have been introduced. These changes have been stimulated by the civil rights movement and the feminist movement, and are again symptomatic of the response of higher education to demands of equal opportunity.

There are many additional areas of concern, development, and issues in the field of higher education that have not been mentioned, much less considered in this overview. A major concern, for example, is how higher education can be responsive to social and domestic problems in the research and public service areas. Questions relating to liaison with urban communities, and organizational problems within universities that permit problem-oriented responses, as opposed to discipline-oriented, are at issue. Related to this are issues concerning graduate and professional education. These and many other topics of importance have not been considered. In addition, the many developments in more traditional education have not been discussed. Rather, an effort has been made to deal with issues and developments that point to major new directions in higher education. As a closing note, it should be pointed out that there is substantial evidence that the public and students hold positive views of higher education, and moves to new structures and enterprise should be approached with a strong disposition to preserve the many strengths of our current system. The papers which follow deal in detail with many of the topics and issues included in this overview.

REFERENCES

Assembly on University Goals and Governance: *A First Report.* Cambridge, Massachusetts: The American Academy of Arts and Sciences, January 1971.

Astin, A. W., and Rossman, J. E. The Case of Open Admissions: A Status Report. *Change, 1973, 5,* 35-37.

Carnegie Commission on Higher Education. *Campus and the City: Maximizing Assets and Reducing Liabilities.* New York: McGraw-Hill, 1972.

_____. *The Capitol and the Campus: State Responsibility for Postsecondary Education.* New York: McGraw-Hill, 1971.

_____. *A Chance to Learn: An Action Agenda for Equal Opportunity in Higher Education.* New York: McGraw-Hill, 1970.

_____. *College Graduates and Jobs: Adjusting to a New Labor Market Situation.* New York: McGraw-Hill, 1973.

_____. *Continuity and Discontinuity: Higher Education and the Schools.* New York: McGraw-Hill, 1973.

_____. *Dissent and Disruption: Proposals for Consideration by the Campus.* New York: McGraw-Hill, 1971.

_____. *The Fourth Revolution: Instructional Technology in Higher Education.* New York: McGraw-Hill, 1972.

_____. *From Isolation to Mainstream: Problems of the Colleges Founded for Negroes.* New York: McGraw-Hill, 1971.

_____. *Governance of Higher Education: Six Priority Problems.* New York: McGraw-Hill, 1973.

_____. *Higher Education and the Nation's Health: Policies for Medical and Dental Education.* New York: McGraw-Hill, 1970.

_____. *Higher Education: Who Pays? Who Benefits? Who Should Pay?* New York: McGraw-Hill, 1973.

_____. *Institutional Aid: Federal Support to Colleges and Universities.* New York: McGraw-Hill, 1972.

_____. *Less Time, More Options: Education Beyond the High School.* New York: McGraw-Hill, 1970.

_____. *The More Effective Use of Resources: An Imperative for Higher Education.* New York: McGraw-Hill, 1972.

_____. *New Students and New Places: Policies for the Future Growth and Development of American Higher Education.*

New York: McGraw-Hill, 1971.

_____. *The Open-Door Colleges: Policies for Community Colleges.* New York: McGraw-Hill, 1970.

_____. *Opportunities for Women in Higher Education: Their Current Participation, Prospects for the Future, and Recommendations for Action.* New York: McGraw-Hill, 1973.

_____. *Priorities for Action: Final Report of the Carnegie Commission on Higher Education.* New York: McGraw-Hill, 1973.

_____. *The Purposes and the Performance of Higher Education in the United States: Approaching the Year 2000.* New York: McGraw-Hill, 1973.

_____. *Quality and Equality: New Levels of Federal Responsibility for Higher Education, and Quality and Equality, Revised Recommendations.* New York: McGraw-Hill, 1968 and 1970.

_____. *Reform on Campus: Changing Students, Changing Academic Programs.* New York: McGraw-Hill, 1972.

_____. *Toward a Learning Society: Alternative Channels to Life, Work, and Service.* New York: McGraw-Hill, 1973.

Cheit, E. F. *Coming of Middle Age in Higher Education, Address to Joint Session.* A.A.S.C.U., N.A.S.U.L.G.C., 1972.

Heyns, R. W. Renewal, Financing, Cooperation: Tasks for Today. *Educational Record,* 1973, 54, 32-37.

Peterson, R. E. *The Crisis of Purpose: Definition and Uses of Institutional Goals.* ERIC Higher Education Report No. 5, 1970.

International Commission on the Development of Education. *Learning to Be. The World of Education Today and Tomorrow.* Paris: UNESCO, 1972.

Trivett, D. A. *Goals for Higher Education: Definitions and Directions.* ERIC Higher Education Research Report No. 6. Washington, D.C.: American Association for Higher Education, 1973.

U.S. Office of Education. *Report on Higher Education [Newman Report].* Washington, D.C.: U.S. Government Printing Office, March 1971.

U.S. President's Commission on Higher Education. *Higher Education for American Democracy.* New York: Harper and Brothers Publishers, 1947.

9

GRADUATE EDUCATION IN TRANSITION

by David W. Breneman and Sharon C. Bush
National Board on Graduate Education
Washington, D.C.

Graduate education has been most commonly defined as postbaccalaureate programs leading to the master's or doctorate degree in the arts and sciences disciplines and in some professional fields, but excluding first professional degrees in such fields as law, medicine, and theology. Programs which lead to first professional degrees have been excluded on the premise that research is the unifying core of the educational process designed to prepare individuals for research-oriented careers. However, the growth of practice-oriented graduate programs, which emphasize preparation for professional practice and the application of existing knowledge (similar to study in law or medicine), has reduced the significance of the distinction between graduate and professional education.

The above definition of graduate education also reflects an organizational logic from the perspective of the individual institution. Graduate degree programs are generally under the broad supervision of a graduate dean, with departmental faculties involved in teaching both undergraduate and graduate students, while self-contained professional programs such as law and medicine have little or no linkage with undergraduate curricula. But this organizational distinction of graduate vis-à-vis professional becomes ambiguous and situational when considering other types of professional schools such as library science and social work, which may or may not offer undergraduate programs.

Thus, careful consideration of the commonly accepted definition of graduate education suggests that it does not represent a consistent taxonomy based on either educational or structural characteristics, nor is it a true definition in the sense of conveying the essential meaning of graduate education.

Rather than attempt a single, comprehensive (and elusive) definition, it is more meaningful to discuss graduate education in terms of its fundamental purposes and functions. One enduring function of graduate education is the development and education of highly trained manpower. A second broad purpose is the creation of new knowledge through research. Preserving, structuring, and disseminating knowledge is a third function, with graduate education responsible for the training of future college and university teachers. Finally, graduate education sustains critical inquiry into the basic values and beliefs of society itself, contributing to reform and renewal. The relative emphasis and particular form of these primary purposes of graduate education are constantly evolving, both in response to cultural and social needs and from dynamics internal to the university.

It has been claimed that "the gravest single problem facing American higher education is . . . (the) . . . alarming disintegration of consensus about purpose" (Ashby, 1971). Graduate education, too, must balance its own integrity and capabilities to fulfill its fundamental purposes, with a sensitivity to the increasingly diverse demands of a pluralistic society.

To understand graduate education today and how it might evolve in the future, we must first review its past. Prior to 1876, advanced education in America was dominated by the college, which offered a traditional, classical curriculum designed to "shape the character of the student according to a rigid model of a pious, righteous and educated gentleman" (Ben-David, 1972). A master's degree was awarded to college alumni, frequently with no formal study required. But beginning in 1861, when Yale University awarded the first Ph.D., and followed by the successful establishment of the Johns Hopkins University in 1876, patterned after the German model, an educational revolution was precipitated which ended in the creation of the modern American university. The graduate school infused all of American higher education with a spirit of scientific inquiry and professionalism, culminating in the Ph.D.

More recently, in the decade of the 1960s, graduate education entered what many call the "golden years," in terms of prestige, affluence, and public support. During this period the number of institutions offering graduate degree programs increased from 605 in 1960 to 808 by 1970 (U.S. Office of Education, 1963; U.S. Office of Education, 1971). In 1960, 9,829 Ph.D. degrees and 74,455 master's degrees were awarded by institutions of higher education, but ten years later these figures had nearly tripled to 29,866 and 208,291 degrees respectively (U.S. Office of Education, 1962; U.S. Office of Education, 1970). First-time graduate enrollments expanded at an average annual rate of 11 percent during the period from 1960 to 1968.

One factor affecting the character of graduate education has been the rapid growth of research activities in colleges and universities. The National Science Foundation estimates that Federal Expenditures for basic and applied research in colleges and universities increased from $766 million in 1959-1960 to $2,005 million in 1969-1970, representing a real increase of more than 250 percent[1] (National Science Foundation, 1972).

Graduate student fellowships and traineeships supported by the federal government grew from $35.3 million in 1960-1961 to $212.4 million in 1967-1968[2] (Federal Interagency Committee on Education, 1970). Interest in strengthening the academic science capabilities of the nation was embodied in such programs as the National Science Foundation Science Development Program, which provided over $230 million directly to selected universities with the aim of increasing "the number of institutions of recognized excellence in research and education in the sciences."

What we see is a major expansion of higher education in general and graduate education in particular. More students than ever before participated in graduate education, and universities were deeply involved in research activities. But by 1970 the "golden years" had begun to wane. Undergraduate enrollments, which had increased the demand for graduate student teaching assistants and new faculty, began to slow; total Federal research and development expenditures levelled off (National Science Foundation, *National Patterns*, 1973), and public support for colleges and universities dimmed in the wake of student upheavals. First time graduate enrollments rose only 0.1 percent from Fall 1970 to Fall 1971. The number of doctoral students receiving Federal fellowship and traineeship support declined by more than 85 percent from a high of 51,289 in 1967-1968 to an estimated 6,600 students for fiscal 1974 (Federal Interagency Committee on Education, unpublished preliminary estimates for 1974). Rising costs in colleges and universities became a subject of urgent concern to individual institutions, students, and state governments providing support to higher education. The high costs of graduate education in particular were widely articulated, and this reinforced the determination of emerging statewide coordinating agencies to seek control over the expansion of new and existing graduate programs. An apparent oversupply of doctorates in many fields surfaced in the public consciousness. The projected levelling-off and ultimate declines in undergraduate enrollments for the 1980s because of demographic factors weakened another rationale for the high rates of Ph.D. production which had been deemed necessary in the 1960s to meet the staffing needs of colleges and universities.

Graduate education today faces not only changes in its past environment but, moreover, is pressed with new demands. The surge of public concern about societal problems (such as environmental and urban ills) has dramatized a need for professional (and interdisciplinary) graduate programs designed to train highly-skilled persons in these areas. The Federal government has placed increasing emphasis on applied and mission-oriented research in contrast to basic research, a development that may redefine the role of research in graduate student training. Statewide planning agencies are continuing to take a strong interest in the management of graduate education (including both private and public institutions). More efforts are underway to try to identify and reduce the costs of graduate education. Efficiency is a slogan of the 1970s.

The trend toward universal access to higher education, which has stimulated demands for pluralism at the undergraduate level, is also affecting the character of graduate education. Graduate education is no longer a privilege of the elite (whether financial or intellectual); a recent survey of college seniors reported that nearly 50 percent aspire to an advanced degree at some time in the future (Bayer, Royer and Webb, 1973). Increasing emphasis on credentialism for employment opportunities and promotion has motivated many persons to return to graduate school to seek advanced degrees; and nontraditional forms of graduate education are springing up. Demands of minority students and women, who in the past have not participated fully in graduate education and now aspire to educational equality, come at a time when some Federal and state agencies are urging stabilization or decreases in financial support of graduate institutions and students— premised on the belief that more graduate degree-holders are being produced than the economy can absorb.

What we see emerging is a set of different, more strident attitudes toward graduate education, and a consequent shifting of decision-making authority, both overtly and implicitly. With the advent of increasing public recognition of the financial requirements of graduate education, greater demands for accountability arose. The past perception of graduate education as a kind of uniform good has been punctured, with students, faculty, employers, government, and the general public making demands on the system, voicing their views of what graduate education should be and should do. This, then, is the crux of the problem. How can graduate education moderate and meet a multitude of demands (often competing), yet maintain a viable integrity to move to the future?

We may now turn to a number of specific issued in light of these concerns.

THE LABOR MARKET FOR PH.D.'s

This issue currently enjoys considerable public visibility since the unemployment (or underemployment) problems of some Ph.D.'s, although often exaggerated, have received national attention. Earliest forecasts of a supply-demand imbalance in academic employment for Ph.D.'s were made by Allan Cartter (1965). Subsequent projections of a bleak academic employment for doctorates (Balderston and Radner, 1971; Wolfle and Kidd, 1971; National Science Foundation, 1971) are based largely on reduced growth rates and even absolute declines in undergraduate enrollments by the early 1980s.

A major value judgment surrounding labor-market projections for highly educated manpower involves the wisdom of rationing access to graduate education on the basis of labor market forecasts, as opposed to allowing individuals free choice to develop maximum potential (Bowen, 1973). Whether graduate schools should respond only to current labor market demands or seek to develop new skills that may benefit society in the future, although effective market demand may not currently exist, is a further subject of debate. On the technical side, controversy surrounds the efficacy of projection techniques used by various investigators. It is argued that most projection techniques ignore relevant economic variables and are too mechanical in extrapolating future trends from the past (Freeman and Breneman, 1974).

COSTS AND FINANCING OF GRADUATE INSTITUTIONS

Universities are complex organizations that engage in four separately identifiable, but jointly produced activities—undergraduate education, graduate education, research, and public service. Determining and imputing costs to separate activities in such situations is extremely difficult. Furthermore, university programs are supported financially in varying proportions by Federal, state and local governments, endowment earnings, philanthropy, and student tuition and fees (O'Neill, 1973; Carnegie Commission, 1973). The combination of complex cost patterns and multiple-source funding virtually assures a continuing debate over the "proper" sharing of the costs of university activities, including graduate education and research.

Public demands for greater efficiency and increased accountability in higher education have challenged traditional patterns of university governance, and have given rise to new management techniques designed to improve university administration (Weathersby and Balderston, 1972; Schroeder, 1973). Graduate education has not been ignored, as economists have attempted to determine graduate cost patterns (Powel and Lamson, 1972). The financing of graduate education inevitably leads to questions of university governance. The recent report of the Newman Task Force on graduate education (Department of Health, Education and Welfare, 1973) argued that it is a major Federal responsibility to encourage internal reform of graduate education by providing portable fellowship grants, awarded directly to the student and freely transferable across programs and institutions. Much of the current debate on the financing of higher education is couched in terms of institutional vs. student support, with one underlying issue being decision-making authority.

GRADUATE STUDENT FINANCIAL SUPPORT

Students finance the costs of graduate education through a mixture of fellowships, research and teaching assistantships, loans, and self-support, including family resources, with the mix varying by field, by level, by university, and over time (Creager, 1971; National Science Foundation, *Graduate Student Support,* 1973). Income foregone while in school must be considered as a private cost incurred by students for their graduate education.

Federal fellowship and traineeship support has plummeted from a high of 51,289 students supported in 1967–1968 to an estimated 6,600 in fiscal year 1975 (Federal Interagency Committee on Education, 1970, and preliminary figures for 1974). The implicit rationale for this strong action rests in the Federal government's belief that while graduate education may indeed serve several valuable functions, the Federal government's prime responsibility (in providing graduate student support) is to insure an adequate supply of highly trained manpower. The economist might point out, however, that since graduate education is part of a complex production process, withdrawal of graduate student support may adversely affect the university's capabilities to fulfill its other functions (Dresch, 1974). The disadvantaged student may argue that to deprive him of financial support, and perhaps an opportunity to obtain an advanced degree, may prevent him from developing his full intellectual and professional potential.

The degree to which graduate students should be expected to draw upon parental sources of income to finance their graduate education is also controversial, as is the suggestion that long-term, income-contingent loans should be a major mechanism for graduate student support. The Graduate and Professional School Financial Aid Service (GAPSFAS) incorporates a mechanism for calculating parental contributions (Educational Testing Service, 1973), while alternative mechanisms for implementing income-contingent loan programs have been proposed (Johnstone, 1972).

TEACHING

Since two of the fundamental purposes of graduate education are education of highly skilled professionals and the training of future generations of college and university teachers, teaching has remained a topic of long-standing debate. The Ph.D., with its emphasis on scholarly research, has traditionally been considered the appropriate degree for college and university teaching, but this has come under increased questioning with the rise of mass education and an increasing pluralism in student needs and desires.

Surveys of community and junior college faculty and administrators reveal that for the most part, the research-oriented Ph.D. degree is considered to be inappropriate preparation for teaching community and junior college students (Dressel and DeLisle, 1972; Martorana, et al., 1975; Change, 1972). Individuals with broad disciplinary backgrounds, training and experience in the art of teaching, and a strong commitment to the ethos of the community college are desirable faculty.

Dissatisfaction in many quarters with the preparation of college teachers has led to interest in reorientation of existing degree programs and implementation of new degrees such as the Doctor of Arts degree and Master of Arts in Teaching. Those who advocate retaining the traditional, research-oriented Ph.D. as the prerequisite for all undergraduate teaching stress that the scholarly research experience enables the teacher to evaluate and convey to students the intellectual dynamic of the subject. Proponents of the D.A. degree and modifications of other degrees argue that the narrow research component and disciplinary specialization are inappropriate preparation for the bulk of undergraduate teaching responsibilities. All agree, however, that the most basic problem rests with the nature of the incentive structure for faculty promotion and academic prestige that rewards research and independent scholarly contributions above teaching excellence.

THE QUALITY OF GRADUATE EDUCATION

During the 1960s most institutions expanded their graduate programs, and many schools were encouraged to enter graduate education for the first time. Questions were raised about the effects of this rapid growth on the overall quality of graduate education. A survey ranking the quality of doctoral programs in selected disciplines reported that 75 percent of the departments surveyed showed an increase in the quality ratings of their graduate faculty during the period from 1964 to 1969 (Roose and Andersen, 1970; Cartter, 1966). However reassuring this may appear to be, there is concern about the nature of these ratings themselves (Blackburn & Lingenfelter, 1973). A major criticism of these surveys is that they employ a unidimensional quality rating, based on subjective peer evaluation of the reputation of the graduate faculty, e.g., "gossip". But quality is a multidimensional attribute. Moreover, quality in relation to what? Differences in program mission and objectives must be recognized, and then appropriate criteria for assessing excellence can be developed. A high-quality program oriented toward training research-oriented Ph.D.'s is very different from a high-quality program aimed at producing highly-skilled professionals or practitioners at the doctoral level.

Moreover, these particular ratings tell us little about the quality of the student experience. Complaints about curricular and program requirements are not new, but the fact is that many students, particularly those in doctoral programs, do not complete their graduate programs (Stanford University, 1972; Heiss, 1970). Attrition and prolonged time-to-degree are serious problems (Mooney, 1968). Breneman (1970) found extreme variations in these measures among 28 departments at one university and developed a theory of departmental behavior, focusing on internal budgetary processes and external market forces, to explain these differences.

Currently, many individual institutions, multicampus systems, and state coordinating agencies are undertaking systematic reviews of existing and proposed graduate programs, with the aim of identifying and eliminating redundant, inefficient and low-quality programs.

THE MASTER'S DEGREE

Although the number of master's degrees awarded each year has increased from 74,500 in 1960 to 209,400 in 1971, and is almost ten-fold greater than doctorates awarded, the meaning of a master's degree continues to be ambiguous and variable (Mayville, 1972; The University of the State of New York, 1972). The economic significance of the master's degree is not well understood, nor are student motivations for obtaining the degree. Disaggregation and more meaningful classification of various types of master's degree programs are needed. For example, certain professional programs, such as a master's in business administration or social work, are aimed specifically at training practitioners in specialized subjects, while the significance of a master's degree in French literature or political science is less clear. Moreover, there is little consensus as to appropriate curricula for the various degree programs, as well as wide variance in standards of quality. It has been suggested that teacher certification requirements stimulate much of the motivation for master's study, and in some cases, marginal programs have been implemented as expedient responses to credential requirements.

NONTRADITIONAL GRADUATE EDUCATION

Demands for more flexible dimensions in education, curricular relevance, innovative learning environments, and opportunities for occupational renewal have all been loosely grouped under the rubric of alternative forms of "nontraditional" education. A more useful taxonomy of nontraditional forms of education has been suggested by the work of the Commission on Nontraditional Study, and delineates the following categories: (1) educational programs that extend traditional curricula through new means to new student bodies, such as the University of California Extended University; (2) programs that extend new curricula through new means to both new and traditional student bodies, such as The Union Graduate School, Goddard College; (3) programs that provide a new time dimension in education (the three-year baccalaureate); and (4) programs that offer credit for previous work and/or life experience, such as the New York State Regent's Degree. Nontraditional forms have found their greatest initial support in undergraduate education, although a number of nontraditional graduate programs and institutions have recently been initiated (Panel on Alternative Approaches, 1973). And a survey of undergraduate students at the University of California revealed a greater interest in nontraditional education at the graduate level than at the undergraduate level (Gardner and Zelan, 1973).

But nontraditional education is confronted with an additional concern specific to the graduate level—standards of quality. Since undergraduate curricula are generally less specialized and more diverse than graduate programs, they are inherently more compatible with the program innovations and flexibility characteristic of nontraditional forms. Graduate education, however, is responsible for certification of highly skilled specialists for academic and professional careers. Can an external degree program suitable for training a Ph.D. in chemistry be developed? How can the quality of a "university without walls" be evaluated in terms of preparation for a career in public administration? If the process of graduate education is radically changed in nontraditional forms of education in order to meet student learning needs and desires, how may this mesh with society's demands for highly trained professionals?

Although most graduate education takes place within traditional colleges and universities, there is a strong movement toward development of single-purpose graduate institutions such as Rosemead Graduate School of Psychology and the Wright Institute. These institutions, which offer doctoral programs in psychology, as well as graduate programs initiated by A. D. Little Co. and the Rand Corporation, present an interesting example for, and challenge to, traditional institutions of higher education. This broadened perspective, exemplified by the recent change in terminology from "higher education" to "post secondary" education (thereby including proprietary institutions), supports the diversity of educational opportunities at all levels.

NOTES

[1]Research expenditures are given in constant 1958 dollars; the GNP implicit deflator was used to allow comparison in real terms.

[2]Expenditure figures for graduate student support are given in constant 1967 dollars; the consumer price index was used to convert current to constant dollars.

REFERENCES

Ashby, E. *Any Person, Any Study.* New York: McGraw-Hill, 1971.

Balderston, F. E., and Radner, R. *Academic Demand for New Ph.D.'s, 1970-90: Its Sensitivity to Alternate Policies.* Ford Foundation Program for Research in University Administration, Paper P-26. Berkeley: Office of the Vice President—Planning and Analysis, University of California, 1971.

Bayer, A. E., Royer, J. T., and Webb, R. M. *Four Years After College Entry.* Washington, D.C.: American Council on Education, 1973.

Ben-David, J. *American Higher Education: Directions Old and New.* New York: McGraw-Hill, 1972.

Blackburn, R. T., and Lingenfelter, P. E. *Assessing Quality in Doctoral Programs: Criteria and Correlates of Excellence.* Center for the Study of Higher Education, 1973.

Bowen, H. R. Manpower Management and Higher Education. *Educational Record.* Winter 1973, 54, 5-14.

Breneman, D. W. *An Economic Theory of Ph.D. Production: The Case at Berkeley.* Ford Foundation Program for Research in University Administration, Paper P-8. Berkeley: Office of the Vice President—Planning and Analysis, University of California, 1970.

_____. *Graduate School Adjustments to the "New Depression" in Higher Education.* With a *Commentary* by the National Board on Graduate Education. Washington, D.C.: National Board on Graduate Education, 1974.

Carnegie Commission on Higher Education. *Higher Education: Who Pays? Who Benefits? Who Should Pay?* New York: McGraw-Hill, 1973.

Cartter, A. A New Look at the Supply of College Teachers. *Educational Record,* Summer 1965, 44.

_____. *An Assessment of Quality in Graduate Education.* Washington, D.C.: American Council on Education, 1966.

Chance, C. W., and Youra, D. G. *The Doctor of Arts Degree in Washington—An Attitudinal Survey.* Council on Higher Education, 1972.

Creager, J. A. *The American Graduate Student: A Normative Description.* Washington, D.C.: American Council on Education, 1971

Department of Health, Education and Welfare. *Report on Higher Education: The Federal Role—Graduate Education.* (Frank Newman, Chairman). Washington, D.C.: Department of HEW, 1973.

Dresch, S. D. *An Economic Perspective on the Evolution of Graduate Education.* Washington, D.C.: National Board on Graduate Education, 1974.

Dressel, P. L., and DeLisle, F. H. *Blueprint for Change: Doctoral Programs for College Teachers.* The American College Testing Program, 1972.

Drew, D. E. *Science Development: An Evaluation Study.* Washington, D.C.: National Board on Graduate Education, 1975.

Educational Testing Service. *Graduate and Professional School Financial Aid Service.* Princeton: Educational Testing Service, 1973.

Federal Interagency Committee on Education. Report on Federal Predoctoral Student Support. Washington, D.C.: Department of Health, Education and Welfare, 1970; and preliminary figures provided by FICE on predoctoral student support for fiscal year 1974.

Freeman, R., and Breneman, D. W. *Doctorate Manpower Problems, Forecasts and Policy.* Washington, D.C.: Technical Report, National Board on Graduate Education, 1974.

Gardner, D. P., and Zelan, J. *A Strategy for Change in Higher Education: The Extended University of California.* Prepared for Organization for Economic Cooperation and Development, 1973.

Heiss, A. M. *Challenges to Graduate Schools.* San Francisco: Jossey-Bass, 1970.

Johnston, D. B. *New Patterns for College Lending: Income Contingent Loans.* New York: Columbia University Press, 1972.

Martorana, S. V., Toombs, W., and Breneman, D. W., eds. *Graduate Education and Community Colleges; Cooperative Approaches to Community College Staff Development.* Washington, D.C.: National Board on Graduate Education, 1975.

Mayville, W. V. *A Matter of Degree: The Setting for Contemporary Master's Programs.* Washington, D.C.: American Association for Higher Education, 1972.

Mooney, J. Attrition Among Ph.D. Candidates: An Analysis of a Cohort of Recent Woodrow Wilson Fellows. *Journal of Human Resources,* Winter 1968.

National Board on Graduate Education. *Graduate Education: Purposes, Problems, and Potential.* Washington, D.C.: National Board on Graduate Education, 1972.

———. *Comment on the Newman Task Force Report on the Federal Role in Graduate Education.* Washington, D.C.: National Board on Graduate Education, 1973.

———. *Federal Policy Alternatives Toward Graduate Education.* Washington, D.C.: National Board on Graduate Education, 1974.

———. *Science Development, University Development and the Federal Government.* Washington, D.C.; National Board on Graduate Education, 1975.

National Science Foundation. *1969 & 1980 Science & Engineering Doctorate Supply & Utilization.* Washington, D.C.: U.S. Government Printing Office, 1971.

———. *Resources for Scientific Activities at Universities and Colleges, 1971.* Washington, D.C.: U.S. Government Printing Office, 1972.

———. *National Patterns of R&D Resources: Funds & Manpower in the United States—1953-73.* Washington, D.C.: U.S. Government Printing Office, 1973.

———. *Graduate Student Support and Manpower Resources in Graduate Science Education, Fall 1971.* Washington, D.C.: U.S. Government Printing Office, 1973.

O'Neill, J. A. *Sources of Funds to Colleges and Universities.* New York: McGraw-Hill, 1973.

Panel on Alternative Approaches to Graduate Education. *Scholarship for Society.* Princeton: Educational Testing Service, 1973.

Powel, J. H., and Lamson, R. D. *Elements Related to the Determination of Costs and Benefits of Graduate Education.* Washington, D.C.: Council of Graduate Schools, 1972.

Roose, K. D., and Andersen, C. J. *A Rating of Graduate Programs.* Washington, D.C.: American Council on Education, 1970.

Schroeder, R. G. A Survey of Management Science in University Operations. *Management Science,* 1973, 19, 895-906.

Stanford University. *The Study of Graduate Education at Stanford—Report to the Senate of the Academic Council.* Stanford University Press, 1972.

The University of the State of New York. *Master's Degrees in the State of New York.* Albany: The State Education Department, 1972.

U.S. Congress, Senate. *Education Amendments of 1972.* Washington, D.C.: House Documents Office, 1972.

U.S. Office of Education. *Earned Degrees Conferred—1959-60.* Washington, D.C.: U.S. Government Printing Office, 1962.

———. *Enrollment for Advanced Degrees, Fall 1960.* Washington, D.C.: U.S. Government Printing Office, 1963.

———. *Students Enrolled for Advanced Degrees: Fall 1968.* Washington, D.C.: U.S. Government Printing Office, 1970.

———. *Earned Degrees Conferred—1969-70.* Washington, D.C.: U.S. Government Printing Office, 1970.

———. *Students Enrolled for Advanced Degrees: Fall 1970.* Washington, D.C.: U.S. Government Printing Office, 1971, and preliminary figures provided by the U.S. Office of Education on enrollment for advanced degrees, Fall 1971.

Weathersby, B. G., and Balderston, F. E. *PPBS in Higher Education Planning and Management.* Ford Foundation Program for Research in University Administration, Paper P-31. Berkeley: Office of the Vice President—Planning and Analysis, University of California, 1972.

Wolfle, D., and Kidd, C. V. The Future Market for Ph.D.'s. *Science,* 1971, 173, 784-793.

ADDITIONAL RESOURCES

Berelson, B. *Graduate Education in the United States.* New York: McGraw-Hill, 1960.

McCarthy, J. L. and Lamson, R. D. *The Costs and Benefits of Graduate Education: A Commentary with Recommendations.* Washington, D.C.: The Council of Graduate Schools, 1972.

Mayhew, L. B. *Reform in Graduate Education.* Atlanta: Southern Regional Educational Board, 1972.

National Board on Graduate Education. *An Annotated Bibliography on Graduate Education.* Washington, D.C.: National Board on Graduate Education, 1972.

National Research Council. Summary Report: *Doctorate Recipients from United States Universities.* Washington, D.C.: National Research Council, a series published yearly from 1967.

———. *Profiles of Ph.D.'s in the Sciences.* Washington, D.C.: National Academy of Sciences, 1965.

———. *Careers of Ph.D.'s—Academic versus Nonacademic.* Washington, D.C.: National Academy of Sciences, 1968.

———. *Mobility of Ph.D.'s—Before and After the Doctorate.* Washington, D.C.: National Academy of Sciences, 1971.

National Science Board. *Graduate Education: Parameters for Public Policy.* Washington, D.C.: U.S. Government Printing Office, 1969.

———. *Science Indicators—1972.* Washington, D.C.: U.S. Government Printing Office, 1973.

Storr, R. F. *The Beginning of the Future: A Historical Approach to Graduate Education.* New York: McGraw-Hill, 1973.

10

THE STATE AND LAND-GRANT UNIVERSITIES

Prepared by the Office of Research and Information
The National Association of State Universities
and Land-Grant Universities

A special segment of public higher education in the United States consists of the principal public universities of the 50 states and the 71 land-grant colleges and universities. These institutions are committed to the expansion of educational opportunity for masses of American young people and dedicated to research as a solution to many of the world's problems. They have a history of service to their states through all-encompassing extension and continuing education programs.

The institutions covered in this article are the 128 state and land grant universities listed below. Today they enroll approximately 30 percent of all students in higher education, although they represent less than five percent of the nation's more than 2,500 colleges and universities.

Together they enrolled approximately 2,702,442 of the 9,025,032 students enrolled in all higher education institutions in the nation for the 1972 academic year. These institutions award about 36 percent of all bachelor's and first professional degrees, 42 percent of all master's degrees and 64 percent of all doctorates.

Among the alumni of state and land-grant institutions are more than half of the nation's governors, senators and congressmen. More than half of all living American Nobel Prize winners are also alumni of these institutions, and one-third of the members of the National Academy of Sciences are on the faculties of state and land-grant colleges and universities.

In addition, state and land-grant universities conduct more than half the research underway at the universities in the nation. From state and land-grant universities have come such wide-ranging discoveries as streptomycin and neomycin, helium, the first sound-on-film motion picture, hybrid corn, the isolation of the first enzyme, and the first complete laboratory synthesis of a gene.

THE STATE AND *LAND-GRANT UNIVERSITIES

Alabama
*Alabama A&M University
*Auburn University
University of Alabama
Alaska
*University of Alaska
Arizona
Arizona State University
*University of Arizona
Arkansas
*University of Arkansas
*University of Arkansas, Pine Bluff
California
*University of California

University of California, Berkeley
University of California, Davis
University of California, Irvine
University of California, Los Angeles
University of California, Riverside
University of California, San Diego
University of California, Santa Barbara
Colorado
*Colorado State University
University of Colorado
Connecticut
*Connecticut Agriculture Experiment Station
*University of Connecticut
Delaware
*Delaware State College
*University of Delaware
District of Columbia
*Federal City College
Florida
*Florida A&M University
Florida State University
*University of Florida
Georgia
*Fort Valley State College
Georgia Institute of Technology
*University of Georgia
Guam
*University of Guam
Hawaii
*University of Hawaii
Idaho
*University of Idaho
Illinois
Southern Illinois University
*University of Illinois
University of Illinois, Chicago Circle
University of Illinois, Urbana-Champaign
Indiana
Indiana University
Indiana University, Bloomington
*Purdue University
Iowa
*Iowa State University
University of Iowa
Kansas
*Kansas State University
University of Kansas
Kentucky
*Kentucky State University
*University of Kentucky
Louisiana
*Louisiana State University
*Southern University
Maine
*University of Maine
University of Maine, Orono
Maryland
*University of Maryland
University of Maryland, College Park
Massachusetts
*Massachusetts Institute of Technology
*University of Massachusetts
University of Massachusetts, Amherst

Michigan
   *Michigan State University
   University of Michigan
   Wayne State University
Minnesota
   *University of Minnesota
Mississippi
   *Alcorn A&M College
   *Mississippi State University
   University of Mississippi
Missouri
   *Lincoln University
   *University of Missouri
   University of Missouri, Columbia
Montana
   *Montana State University
   University of Montana
Nebraska
   *University of Nebraska
   University of Nebraska, Lincoln
Nevada
   *University of Nevada, Reno
New Hampshire
   *University of New Hampshire
New Jersey
   *Rutgers, The State University of New Jersey
New Mexico
   *New Mexico State University
   University of New Mexico
New York
   City University of New York
   *Cornell University
   State University of New York
   State University of New York, Albany
   State University of New York, Binghamton
   State University of New York, Buffalo
   State University of New York, Stony Brook
North Carolina
   *North Carolina A&T State University
   *North Carolina State University
   University of North Carolina
   University of North Carolina, Chapel Hill
North Dakota
   *North Dakota State University
   University of North Dakota
Ohio
   Kent State University
   Miami University
   *Ohio State University
Oklahoma
   *Langston University
   *Oklahoma State University
   University of Oklahoma
Oregon
   *Oregon State University
   University of Oregon
Pennsylvania
   *Pennsylvania State University
   Temple University
   University of Pittsburgh
Puerto Rico
   *University of Puerto Rico

Rhode Island
   *University of Rhode Island
South Carolina
   *Clemson University
   *South Carolina State College
   University of South Carolina
South Dakota
   *South Dakota State University
   University of South Dakota
Tennessee
   *Tennessee State University
   University of Tennessee
   University of Tennessee, Knoxville
Texas
   *Prairie View A&M University
   *Texas A&M University System
   Texas Southern University
   Texas Tech University
   University of Houston
   University of Texas System
   University of Texas, Austin
Utah
   University of Utah
   *Utah State University
Vermont
   *University of Vermont
Virgin Islands
   *College of the Virgin Islands
Virginia
   University of Virginia
   *Virginia Polytechnic Institute and State University
   *Virginia State College
Washington
   University of Washington
   *Washington State University
West Virginia
   *West Virginia University
Wisconsin
   *University of Wisconsin
   University of Wisconsin, Madison
   University of Wisconsin, Milwaukee
Wyoming
   *University of Wyoming

THE PUBLIC UNIVERSITY CONCEPT

The state and land-grant universities have accepted a responsibility to the public from the start. They developed from the great chartered state universities of the 18th Century, planned and established in the infancy of the Republic. They are the direct outgrowths of a public hostility to purely denominational education which sprang up in the United States on the heels of the Revolutionary War. They include among their numbers the 20th-Century manifestations of the Jeffersonian and Jacksonian ideals embodied in the landmark 1862 Land-Grant Act, which vastly expanded educational opportunities for the youth of a westward-looking nation.

The oldest state universities are the University of Georgia, chartered as the nation's first state-supported university in 1785, a scant nine years after the Declaration of Independence; the University of North Carolina, which was chartered in 1789; The University of Vermont, chartered in 1791; the University of Tennessee, established in 1794; and the University of South Carolina, founded in 1801.

Two other universities, which eventually became the land-grant universities for their respective states, were established as private institutions earlier than the first state universities. They were the University of Delaware, established in 1744 as an academy by the Presbyterian Synod of Philadelphia, and Rutgers, founded as Queens College in the colony of New Jersey by royal charter in 1766.

The number of state universities grew rapidly in the 19th Century, including in their ranks the Universities of Michigan, Minnesota and Wisconsin—institutions which achieved for public universities a new and special identity.

From their inception, the major state universities of the country contested the emphasis in American higher education on an exclusive classics-oriented curriculum. Their models were the emerging universities in Germany and the democratic idealism of the University of London.

THE MORRILL LANDMARK

The rising tide of democratic idealism reached a high point in the midst of savage civil strife. On July 2, 1862, Abraham Lincoln signed a bill far less famed than the Emancipation Act to which he had affixed his signature six months earlier, but one which achieved such an impact that the benefits it has brought the United States have been called beyond measure.

This was the Land-Grant Act, written and shepherded through Congress by Vermont's Senator Justin S. Morrill. The bill provided for "the endowment, support and maintenance of at least one college in each state where the leading object shall be, without excluding other scientific and classical studies, and including military tactics, to teach such branches of learning as are related to agriculture and the mechanic arts . . . in order to promote the liberal and practical education of the industrial classes."

Land grants were made to states on the basis of 30,000 acres for each member of Congress. The income from the sale of the land would endow the colleges and the states were to be the administrators. Altogether, the federal government gave almost 11,383,000 acres of land for the establishment of land-grant colleges and universities. Today there is at least one land-grant college in each of the 50 states, plus the District of Columbia, Puerto Rico, Guam and the Virgin Islands.

THE 1890 COLLEGES

Seventeen Southern states established predominantly black colleges or designated existing institutions to receive land-grant funds under authority of the Second Morrill Act, passed by Congress in 1890. The Act contained a historic provision barring money from colleges which did not offer admission to blacks, although the funds were to be granted to segregated colleges in states where there were separate schools for blacks and whites. The black land-grant colleges established under this bill were far from being "equal" institutions of educational opportunity. But they did supply opportunity for many who otherwise would have had none. Despite many problems and setbacks, these colleges today have developed into viable institutions of higher education, which play a major role in educating minority students for full and productive participation in American life.

Research and experimentation at land-grant colleges proved so successful that in 1887 Congress passed the Hatch Act, which established an agricultural experiment station in every state in connection with the land-grant college. Today these stations are considered to be among the best tools of agricultural scientific inquiry in the world. The results of their research, from new strains of seed and fodder, and the control of disease and insects, to food rating and testing, have been an incalculable boon to the state and national economies.

To transfer the results of research to those who needed it most, the land-grant colleges arranged to establish "extension" courses for farmers unable to come to the campus. Demonstration farming showed how to use improved methods of agriculture to raise better crops. Home economics departments wrote pamphlets, and helped women to improve rural home life through instruction in meal planning, the use of labor-saving devices, and interior decorating.

In 1914 Congress passed the Smith-Lever Act, which gave recognition to these early successes and the funds to the land-grant institutions to carry them on, by establishing extension programs in every state. Thus the triumvirate of teaching, research and extension was formed. It is at the heart of the land-grant philosophy.

CURRICULUM REFORM

The state and land-grant universities today are utilizing curricula innovations which were undreamed of even a decade ago. They have sought to utilize new teaching techniques, to speed up the educational process, and to meet the particular needs of a rapidly changing society. The effort has not been 100 percent successful. But the recognition of the requirement to respond to public needs has been especially acute.

Besides changing the emphasis and enlarging the scope in agricultural and engineering schools, the state and land-grant universities have responded to student demands for relevancy and involvement by adding new courses and degrees, and by changing requirements in nearly all disciplines.

The same major state universities and land-grant colleges which normally graduate more than half the nation's Ph.D.'s in agriculture, business, and engineering also are making significant contributions to the fields of painting, sculpture, poetry, literature, theater, music, film, photography, and dance. For example, since 1964 Indiana University has granted more doctorates in music than any other university in the United States. In addition, Indiana has the nation's largest student body majoring in musical arts.

State and land-grant institutions also have pioneered

in establishing programs which provide degrees without majors. The Bachelor of General Studies degree program at the University of Michigan, in existence since April 1969, is probably the largest no-major degree program in operation at any American university. The 1971-72 enrollment in the program, for example, included approximately 900 freshmen and sophomores and 500 upperclassmen. The University of Minnesota also has established a Bachelor of Elected Studies (B.E.S.) degree, which is similar to the Michigan degree.

Open universities, or "colleges without walls," represent further efforts on the part of today's educators to find new approaches to undergraduate education. In 1971, the State University of New York created Empire State College as a no-campus institution to provide students with an alternative to the traditional classroom experience. Empire State draws on the resources of the entire state university system to offer programs leading to a B.A. degree to students who may never see a traditional university campus.

"LEARNING CENTERS"

An administrative staff located in Saratoga, New York directs various "learning centers" scattered throughout the state, which serve as convenience points where students periodically meet with faculty. Long-range plans call for the establishment of eight area learning centers and a maximum enrollment of 4,000 students.

The first American test of the innovative Open University Program, developed in England in 1969, was launched in 1972 by four public institutions, including three state universities. The British program allows students to study on their own with the aid of radio, tape cassettes, television and the printed word. A degree can be earned entirely in this manner. Institutions participating in the U.S. experiment are Rutgers University, the University of Houston, the University of Maryland, and California State College at San Diego. During the experiment each university offers two or three foundation courses for credit in the area of the humanities, science, and mathematics.

State and land-grant universities are among the leaders in training both doctors and lawyers. The total enrollment of law degree candidates at approved American Bar Association law schools, as of the beginning of 1972, was 103,382. Of this total, 38,884, or 37.2 percent, were enrolled at institutions holding membership in the National Association of State Universities and Land-Grant Colleges.

PROFESSIONAL TRAINING

In the area of medicine, state and land-grant universities enrolled 23,914 students in their medical schools in 1971-1972—55.1 percent of the total medical school enrollment of 43,399 in the entire United States.

Medical schools at state and land-grant universities, moreover, are responding in a variety of ways to the crisis in medical education in this country. From increasing enrollments to shortening the period of training and making substantive curriculum changes, these instituions

have shown concern not only about producing more doctors, but also about maintaining and improving the quality of the medical education which students receive.

Increases in enrollments of entering classes, ranging from 10 to 67 percent, are being made by some of these medical schools. The University of Colorado, for example, increased the enrollment of entering medical students nearly 50 percent between 1967 and 1970. The number of first-year medical students at Michigan State University increased 65 percent between 1970 and 1971. Indiana University, which already boasted the largest medical school in the country, forecast in 1967 a 50 percent increase in enrollment of new medical students by the autumn of 1973. Other institutions planning substantial medical student increases are the Universities of Kansas, Iowa, Missouri and Vermont.

Research—the search for new knowledge—is a major function of state and land-grant universities. In fact, there is probably no person in the United States whose life has not been touched in some way by a research accomplishment of a state and land-grant university. Here is just a sampling of ways this kind of research has affected modern American life:

The wonder drugs streptomycin and neomycin, which have helped save literally thousands of lives, were developed at Rutgers University.

The first sound-on-film motion pictures were developed at the University of Illinois. Early research in television transmission was carried out at Purdue University.

A simple and effective heat sterilization technique for canned foods was developed by Dr. Karl F. Meyer of the University of California's Hooper Foundation. The discovery virtually eliminated the threat of botulism, the deadliest form of food poisoning, and gave birth to the modern American canning industry with its annual dollar volume of more than $5 billion.

Dr. William Dock of the University of Michigan, while involved in research during the first part of the century, was the first to recognize heart attacks. Pioneer work in the development of the electrocardiograph, used in diagnosing abnormalities of heart action, was also done at Michigan.

When America's first satellite roared into space, the first communication this country received from outer space came from miniature instruments designed and built under the direction of Dr. James Van Allen of the University of Iowa.

RETURN FOR TAX DOLLARS

The cumulative benefits of state and land-grant university research has more than repaid the public for tax dollars spent in support of these institutions. The first isolation of a human cancer virus was accomplished by a medical team at the University of Texas M. D. Anderson Hospital and Tumor Institute. The team then succeeded in growing the virus in human lymph cells in the laboratory. This could open the way to learning causes and possible prevention techniques of many cancers.

Two Ohio State University professors reported the effective use of the drug L-Dopa in relieving the bone pain in a portion of patients with advanced breast cancer. Also, findings which offer the hope of eventually stimulating the human defense mechanism to fight cancer have been reported by the University of Minnesota. A test which may reduce from five years to one month the time required to determine the success or failure of a cancer patient's surgery has been developed by scientists at the University of Tennessee. The test will alert physicians to begin immediate treatment of surgical patients whose cancer has not been eliminated, possibly saving their lives.

SOME AREAS OF CONTROVERSY

Societal benefits of medical and scientific research are easy to document. However, in at least one area universities have faced growing criticism that has caused them to re-evaluate research policies. This is in the area of defense research, much of which has been classified.

The controversy reached its most tragic manifestation in August 1970, when a bomb smashed the University of Wisconsin's Mathematics Research Center, killing one person. As an aftermath of the Wisconsin tragedy, there has been a re-thinking of official policies regarding defense sponsored and classified research on most U.S. campuses. An example is the following list of restrictions applying to classified research developed by the University of Michigan. Restricted are:

Research which "limits open publication of information about the research beyond approximately one year."

Research which restricts the publication of information about the research sponsors or "the purpose and scope of proposed research."

"Research, the clearly foreseeable and probable result of which, the direct application of which, or any specific purpose of which is to destroy human life or to incapacitate human beings."

Another area of some controversy has surrounded the charge by some critics that the land-grant university has become the "handmaiden of agribusiness." According to these critics, the great food conglomerates have taken over the farms and have driven the little farmer out of business and caused a great rural migration to the cities.

A RESPONSE

In response, one distinguished educator, Chancellor John T. Caldwell of North Carolina State University, has said, "One would think it would be better for the tractor and the combine not to have been invented." The fact is that Americans have taken for granted the dazzling array of abundant foods that has been available to the public, and there has been a vast ignorance on the part of many about today's agriculture. "There is little romance in going broke, or in not knowing from one crop to the next that the mortgage can be paid," Chancellor Caldwell has noted. "There is little romance in not having enough to afford minimum family transportation. There is little romance in not having good schools for the children, or in not having a doctor somewhere around."

Chancellor Caldwell, along with other land-grant college educators, believes it is the duty of the land-grant colleges to do whatever they can to make farms, big and small, profitable, to make rural life more agreeable, and to mitigate the hardships of rural transformation:

For thousands of years men have used their intelligence to try to free humanity from drudgery and burdens that sustained only poverty for all but a few. Man has sought to release himself, his body and his time and his mind for a higher quality of life. The goal of the land-grant colleges has been to further man's accomplishments on behalf of the human spirit. Nowhere has this success been more apparent and brought more blessings than in the agricultural enterprise and the homes of rural America.

Public colleges and universities were created, and exist today, to serve public purposes. In the mid-19th Century flowering, two purposes predominated. One was to provide the skills and brains required for the explosive development of an industrial economy. Sciences and professional disciplines were fashioned literally from scratch. The other was to expand opportunity for advanced education to thousands of young people who were not served by elitist institutions, which prepared students only for teaching and preaching, medicine and law.

Yet as Dr. Ralph Huitt, Executive Director of the National Association of State Universities and Land-Grant Colleges, has said, the record of yesterday will not serve the needs of tomorrow. University people, Dr. Huitt suggests, must never forget that their function is to serve the community and its government.

REFERENCES

The following material is published by:
The Office of Research and Information
National Association of State Universities and Land-Grant Colleges
One Dupont Circle, N.W., Suite 710
Washington, D.C. 20036

Appropriations of State Tax Funds for Operating Expenses of Higher Education.
The Case for Educational Support.
International Development Assistance.
People to People—The Role of State and Land-Grant Universities in Modern America. Beale, Lucrece.
Problems in Graduate Education.
Proceedings of Annual Meetings, National Association of State Universities and Land-Grant Colleges.
Public Negro Colleges, A Fact Book.
Recommendations for National Action Affecting Higher Education.

11

COMMUNITY AND JUNIOR COLLEGES

by Collins W. Burnett
Chairman, Department of Higher Education
University of Kentucky
Lexington, Kentucky

The community college, which is the major growth area in the junior college classification, is probably the most significant development in American higher education thus far in the 20th century. Referred to sometimes as a modern social invention or phenomenon, the community college is "the people's college" in the sense that it reflects the egalitarian philosophy of the 1970s; moreover, programs are determined by and are constantly adjusted to the needs of people in the local community, which may be an urban center, a rural center, a county, or several counties. It is a part of the people rather than apart from the people.

Consisting of programs which include terminal one-year or two-year options, and the transfer program for those students who want to continue at a four-year institution to earn the baccalaureate degree, according to Fields (1962) the truly comprehensive community college must have the following five characteristics: it must be democratic, comprehensive, community-centered, adaptable, and provide life-long education.

The term "junior college," in a generic sense, includes all organized patterns of learning experiences on a two-year basis (freshman and sophomore years) beyond high school which are accredited by one of the six regional accrediting associations in the United States. Included in this broad term are many types of junior colleges, such as church-related, private, public, Federal, proprietary, community, and county. The area vocational school, technical institute, and university branch center are not included within this term. For the purpose of this article, the term community college will refer to all public two-year institutions, and particularly the comprehensive community college. Private junior college will refer to all two-year institutions at the lower division level.

According to Blocker, et al. (1965), the first private junior college was Monticello College, founded in 1835. Vincennes University in Indiana, which is now a community college, traces its origin to 1801. Some think that Decatur Baptist College in Texas, established in 1897, may be the oldest junior college in continuous existence (Burnett, 1968). The first public junior college was started in 1902 in Joliet, Illinois, through the influence of William Rainey Harper, the first president of the University of Chicago. Harper may have known about junior colleges, but the concept developed from his perception that the greatness of the University of Chicago would be determined by a strong upper division program and an outstanding graduate school (Storr, 1966). The lower division, or junior college, should be eliminated from the University program by establishing a system of feeder institutions which would provide transfer students to the senior division, or college (junior and senior years), at the University. Harper's plan included the strategy of attempting to persuade some four-year colleges, e.g., Muskingum College, his alma mater at New Concord, Ohio, to convert to a two-year program (Burnett, 1968).

In spite of some problems and weaknesses, the community college has made a significant impact on American higher education. Monroe (1972) pointed out that community colleges, or some form of the public two-year junior college, were operating in all but one of the 50 states, enrolling about 30 percent of all undergraduate students. According to *The Chronicle of Higher Education* (1974), the total enrollment in all public and private junior colleges for the fall of 1974 was about 3,275,974, which was an 11.9 percent increase over 1973-1974, while the total enrollment in all of higher education for the fall of 1974 showed only a 5.5 percent increase over the previous year.

According to the American Association of Community and Junior Colleges (1973), in the fall of 1972 there were 1,141 community and private junior colleges with an enrollment of 2,866,062. About 234 of these were private junior colleges. In 1930, there were 469 institutions with an enrollment of 77,014.

Parker (1973) found no significant enrollment change over 1972 in the church-related junior colleges, but there was a loss of .6 percent for independent private junior colleges. There was an increase of 6.2 percent in the public junior college area.

The enrollment within a single two-year institution varies from about 200 students in a small private junior college to approximately 38,000 at a large institution such as Miami-Dade in Florida. Most of the private junior colleges have small enrollments.

Since the trend in enrollment seems irreversible in favor of public higher education, continued increases in the number of community colleges, and in enrollment, can be expected. Medsker and Tillery (1971), in a study done for the Carnegie Commission on Higher Education, recommended that 230 to 280 new community colleges be created by 1980. Thompson (1970) showed that in 1950 about 50 percent of all college enrollment was in the public sector. By 1985 he projected that about 85 percent of all college enrollment will be in the public sector.

One other way to test the importance of the community college is to determine to what extent the 50 states have developed a state agency to coordinate or control the community college. Wattanbarger and Sakaguchi (1971) reported that this development had occurred in 43 states.

The concept and influence of the junior college has been noticeable for some time in other countries of the world, particularly in Japan, Canada, Jordan, Ceylon, Brazil, Chile, Colombia, and Peru (Yarrington, 1970).

That until recently there has been very little sophisticated research about junior colleges or their students, either on a regional or a national basis, is a valid criticism. Cross (1968), in her study of the characteristics of the junior college student, mentioned that this type of research was a new phenomenon. About half of her references were dated 1966 or 1967; she did not even bother with sporadic research efforts prior to 1960. Her major contribution was the interpretation of data from the SCOPE (School to College: Opportunities for Postsecondary Education) study which followed 90,000 high school graduates as they moved into jobs, marriage, and postsecondary education.

Richards, Rand, and Rand (1965) made a major contribution to the study of junior college environments in their factor analysis of 36 measures of junior college characteristics. Panos (1966) studied nearly 7,000 entering freshmen in a sample of junior colleges, to report on such variables as parents' educational and racial backgrounds, high school academic achievement, and educational aspirations. Hoyt and Munday (1966) studied the academic potential and college grades of junior college freshmen, reported the predicted validity of American College Testing data, and compared the results for 85 junior colleges with those of 205 four-year colleges. Another research report dealt with a national emphasis which considered institutional characteristics, student characteristics, and prediction of success in junior colleges (*The Two-Year College and Its Students: An Empirical Report*, 1969).

A significant study by Knoell and Medsker (1965), which should be a part of the repertoire of both high school and college counselors, dealt with 7,243 junior college students who transferred in 1960 to 43 four-year colleges and universities in 10 states. Trent and Medsker (1967) did a comprehensive five-year study of a sample of 10,000 students, to determine their patterns of employment and college attendance following graduation from high school.

Since 1970 a number of significant research studies and scholarly books have been published. The importance of the community college and the private junior college has caught the attention of researchers and writers. Rodgers (1972) developed a separate set of standardized factor scores for each of the 621 community colleges and the 151 private junior colleges listed in *American Junior Colleges* (Gleazer, 1971). From his analysis of the two sets of standardized factor scores he developed two sets of factor labels. He arrived at two important findings: (1) there is enough difference between private and public junior colleges to warrant the conclusion that these two sectors cannot be grouped together, and (2) there was no difference between colleges supported by state appropriations, local taxes, and student fees, and those supported by state appropriations and student fees only.

Elton (1971) is one of the few researchers of junior college characteristics who became interested in non-intellective measures. Using the Omnibus Personality Inventory and American College Testing standard scores, he found that the ACT Mathematics score was the most significant variable differentiating female educational outcomes. The ACT Social Studies score was the most significant variable differentiating male outcomes. Although the personality variables (OPI) did not predict educational outcomes at any significant level, the direction of the scores reflected some important possible behavior outcomes.

As far as significant general books are concerned, four should be mentioned. Blocker, Plummer, and Richardson (1965) interpreted the social synthesis of the two-year college. More recently, Richardson, Blocker, and Bender (1972) have published the best treatment of governance for the two-year institution. Cohen and Associates (1971) treated the community college as a constant variable in a critical analysis of the institution, students, faculty, and programs. Monroe (1972) developed a profile of the major aspects of the community college, which can be used as a reference or as a textbook for graduate students.

Two national study groups have produced notable publications which have a focus on the community college. The Carnegie Commission on Higher Education, which was formed in 1967, has published three volumes that are noteworthy. *The Open-Door Colleges: Policies for Community Colleges* (1971) was a special report, with recommendations which emphasized the comprehensive community college with the full range of program options and an "open-door" access to all qualified individuals. Although *Less Time, More Options* (1971) did not deal directly with the junior college, many of its recommendations and comments do relate to this area. For example, the point is made that the Federal government has the responsibility of "assisting the spread of community colleges across the 50 states" (p. 25). One of the goals for the future is that by 1980 community colleges be available to most people in all of the states. Medsker and Tillery (1971) made a strong recommendation in *Breaking the Access Barriers* that from 230 to 280 new community colleges be developed by 1980. Although the major attention is to community colleges (as it should be), Chapter 8 deals specifically with the nature, problems, and future of the private junior college.

The second national study group, the Newman Committee, has published two reports, one for Phase I and one for Phase II. *Report on Higher Education* (1971), which was the publication for Phase I, devoted only one short chapter to the community college, with a closing admonition that community colleges need to produce and live up to the term, "community" in meeting the specific needs of students.

The second report of the Newman Committee, as presented in *The Chronicle of Higher Education* (1973), did not relate directly to the community college, but in several of its recommendations the open admissions, program options, and flexibility of combining work and study reflected aspects of this type of institution.

As was noted previously, all but one of the states had community colleges operating by 1972, according to Monroe (1972). It should be made very clear, however, that this statement needs careful consideration. In some states, for example, there is only one community college. In other states the set of community colleges may be inadequate in meeting the needs in the state, due to a narrow philosophy or restricted budgets. In still other states, the lack of effective programs may be due to poor leadership on the part of the several community college presidents, or perhaps the lack of leadership in the state coordinating board for public higher education.

Too often excellent programs in community colleges seem to be identified with those states that have the largest systems of community colleges, viz., California, Texas, Michigan, New York, and Florida. For all anyone knows, the best programs may be in Ohio, Kansas, Illinois, or Kentucky.

Typically the comprehensive community college, as described by Fields (1962), has the following pattern of programs: (1) one-year and two-year terminal programs in the technical and semiprofessional areas, such as data processing technician, technical illustrator, soils technician, civil engineering technician, nursing, and dental technology; (2) general education; (3) liberal arts for those who plan to transfer to a four-year institution; (4) developmental, which not only includes such remedial areas as reading skills, study skills, and writing skills, but also pre-college freshman-level courses in chemistry, mathematics, and physics for those who want to enroll in programs which require one or more high school units in a particular content area; (5) student services which include counseling, testing, orientation, and extra-class activities; (6) community services, which include dozens of short-term workshops, seminars, and institutes involving citizens of the community in the gamut of such programs.

A variation of this program arrangement is illustrated by the Community College System (13 units), which is under the aegis of the University of Kentucky. In order to avoid any caste system the terminology of general education, liberal arts, and technical and semiprofessional areas has been replaced by four divisions which constitute the academic organization in each college. These divisions are: biological science and related teaching fields; physical science and related teaching fields; social science and related teaching fields; and arts and humanities and related teaching fields.

One major emphasis in the community college which amazes many persons is that of continuing education (or, a more appropriate term, continuing learning). The community college has become the symbol of lifelong learning. Programs are available to recent high school enrollees, to people in the professions, business, industry, to housewives who may or may not have one or more college degrees, and to the more mature adult who may be in his 60s or 70s. Cuyahoga Community College in Cleveland has Golden Age Scholarships; the University of Kentucky has the Donovan Scholarships. These kinds of student aid are intended for senior citizens, and usually mean free tuition.

Another dimension of community college programs is that of flexibility. If citizens in Louisville, Kentucky, request a new program in hotel and restaurant management, faculty at Jefferson Community College, with the help of a lay advisory committee, can determine the need, cost, resources, and other components in such a terminal program, and announce it for student registration within the semester. Likewise, if such a program were started in 1975 to meet a need in Jefferson County, the same program could be terminated five years later when the need was met.

There are at least five current controversies, or issues, which hang like the sword of Damocles over the community colleges. Since there seems to be only one major issue facing private junior colleges, this area can be considered first. The 234 junior colleges which are private or

church-related face the issue of whether to change the traditional liberal arts preparation for students who plan to transfer to a baccalaureate degree college, or struggle to hold on to the edge of the cliff with the hope that more students and more financial support will drop from somewhere. Although some of the nonpublic junior colleges are shifting in program emphasis from liberal arts to meeting needs of the local community, even as some private four-year colleges are doing, the future does look bleak. Moreover, changing to non-liberal arts programs is opposed by some faculty and board members on the basis that such a change is a departure from the traditional transfer program.

The first of the five major issues facing community colleges is that in attempting to meet the educational needs of all adults in the community, the institution seems like the headless horseman trying to ride in all directions at the same time. On the other hand, if the community college does not implement the concept of the people's college, some new social device may be developed to meet the need. In this regard, Boyer (1972) has suggested a "third wedge" philosophy which is both terminal and transfer, but neither, which would permit more flexibility for learners to move in and out of college and work experience.

Second, the issue of terminal versus transfer programs has never been buried. Rather than accept the fact that both can co-exist and even reinforce each other, the proponents of each argue the exclusive merit of one over the other. In reality, many programs are still out of balance in favor of the transfer emphasis. In the Kentucky System, only 38 percent of the students are enrolled in terminal programs.

A third issue, which has a relationship to the two points mentioned already, is that of the Trojan Horse phenomenon (Burnett, 1971). Too often the prestige of the Ph.D. degree causes the administrator to employ faculty who have backgrounds in the discipline with no orientation to the philosophy and programs of the community college. The result is a constant pressure from a group of unhappy, frustrated faculty who want to emphasize the liberal arts program, or who want to convert the institution into a four-year liberal arts college. The other side of the coin, which suggests only a small number of doctorates, brings forth the criticism that the faculty without the Ph.D. are incompetent and lack the scholarly background which is necessary in any college situation.

A fourth issue is that of reinforcing the stance of the access (or open-door) concept with appropriate program options and adequate personnel resources to provide accommodation. Cross (1971) pointed out that the institution cannot implement accommodation (adjusting to the individual learner) without program options and a strong developmental program. Too often the open door becomes a revolving door. To meet the challenge of programs for all, without any qualifications on the admissions process, requires strong financial resources, and adequately prepared faculty, administrators, and student personnel specialists. Some critics point out that this cost does not justify the effort.

Finally, the fifth issue—that of quality, with all of its

relationships to other issues—is a constant debate. Critics claim that the community college is a spastic leap toward higher education that never arrives. Learners are coddled in a public school environment; learning is only surface deep; students and faculty are inferior to their counterparts in four-year colleges; programs are started without any serious effort at evaluation. Proponents of the community college admit the need for carefully designed programs of evaluation and research. These advocates point out, however, that evaluation, at least, must be done within the context of the philosophy of the college, and not on the basis of some National Merit Scholar approach. The wide diversity of ability, motivation, interest, and age represented by the learners requires a different model for determining quality.

REFERENCES

American Association of Community and Junior Colleges. *1973 Community and Junior College Directory*. Washington, D.C., 1973.

Blocker, C. E., Plummer, R. H., and Richardson, R.C., Jr. *The Two-Year College: A Social Synthesis*. Englewood Cliffs, N.J.: Prentice-Hall, 1965.

Boyer, E. L. Neither Transfer nor Terminal: The Next Step for Two-Year Colleges. *Intellect*, 1972, *101*, 110–112.

Burnett, C. W., ed. *The Community Junior College: An Annotated Bibliography*. Columbus, Ohio: The Ohio State University Press, 1968.

Burnett, C. W. The Trojan Horse Phenomenon. In Bennett, C. W., ed., The Two-Year Institution in American Higher Education. Lexington, Ky.: Bureau of School Service, College of Education, University of Kentucky, 1971.

Cohen, A. M., and Associates. *A Constant Variable*. San Francisco: Jossey-Bass, 1971.

Cross, K. P. *The Junior College Student: A Research Description*. In cooperation with the Center for Research and Development in Higher Education, University of California, Berkeley, and the American Association of Junior Colleges. Princeton: Educational Testing Service, 1968.

_____. Access and Accommodation in Higher Education. *The Research Reporter*, 1971, *6*, 6-8.

Elton, C. F. Prediction of Educational Outcomes among Junior College Students. *The Journal of College Student Personnel*, 1969, *10*, 44-46.

Fields, R. R. *The Community College Movement*. New York: McGraw-Hill, 1962.

Gleazer, E. J., Jr., ed. *American Junior Colleges*. Washington, D.C.: American Council on Education, 1971.

Hoyt, D. P., and Munday, L. *Academic Description and Prediction in Junior Colleges*. ACT Research Reports, No. 10. Iowa City: American College Testing Program, 1966.

Knoell, D. M., and Medsker, L. L. *From Junior to Senior College: A National Study of the Transfer Student*. Washington, D.C.: American Council on Education, 1965.

Less Time, More Options. Education Beyond the High School. A special report and recommendations by the Carnegie Commission on Higher Education. New York: McGraw-Hill, 1971.

Medsker, L. L., and Tillery, D. *Breaking the Access Barriers*. The Carnegie Commission on Higher Education. New York: McGraw-Hill, 1971.

Monroe, C. R. *Profile of the Community College*. San Francisco: Jossey-Bass, 1972.

Panos, R. J. *Some Characteristics of Junior College Students*. ACE Research Reports, Vol. *1*, No. 2. Washington, D.C.: American Council on Education, 1966.

Parker, G. G. Enrollments in American Two-Year Colleges,

1971-73: Statistics, Interpretation, and Trends. *Intellect*, 1973, *101*, 457-474.

Report on Higher Education. Newman, F. B., chairman. Washington, D.C.: U.S. Government Printing Office, 1971.

Richards, J. M., Jr., Rand, L. P., and Rand, L. M. *Regional Differences in Junior Colleges*. ACT Research Reports, No. 9. Iowa City: American College Testing Program, 1965.

Richardson, R. C., Jr., Blocker, C. E., and Bender, L. W. *Governance for the Two-Year College*. Englewood Cliffs, N.J.: Prentice-Hall, 1972.

Rodgers, S. A. A Comparative Analysis of All Accredited Two-Year Colleges. Unpublished dissertation, University of Kentucky, Lexington, 1972.

Storr, R. J. *Harper's University: The Beginnings*. Chicago: University of Chicago Press, 1966.

The Chronicle of Higher Education, 1974, *9* (13), 8.

_____, 1973, *7*, 22-25.

The Open-Door Colleges. A special report and recommendations by the Carnegie Commission on Higher Education. New York: McGraw-Hill, 1970.

The Two-Year College and Its Students: An Empirical Report. Monograph Two. Iowa City: The American College Testing Program, 1969.

Thompson, R. B. Trend Toward Public Higher Education Continues—Peak Enrollments Still Twelve Years Away. Unpublished manuscript. The Ohio State University, Columbus, 1970.

Trent, J. W., and Medsker, L. L. *Beyond High School*. Berkeley, California: Center for Research and Development in Higher Education, 1967.

Wattenbarger, J. L., and Sakaguchi, M. *State Level Boards for Community Junior Colleges: Patterns of Control and Coordination*. Institute of Higher Education, University of Florida. Gainesville: University of Florida, 1971.

Yarrington, R. W., ed. *International Development of the College Idea*. Washington, D.C.: American Association of Junior Colleges, 1970.

ADDITIONAL RESOURCES

American Council on Education Research Reports
Office of Research
One Dupont Circle
Washington, D.C. 20036

American Junior Colleges
Gleazer, Edmund J., Jr., ed.
American Council on Education
One Dupont Circle
Washington, D.C. 20036

Barron's Handbook of Junior and Community College Financial Aid
Proia, Nicholas C., and DiGaspari, Vincent M.
Barron's Education Series, Inc.
Woodbury, New York

Change Magazine
Box 2450
Boulder, Colorado 80302

The Chronicle of Higher Education
1717 Massachusetts Avenue, N.W.
Washington, D. C. 20036

College and University Business
P.O. Box 667
Hightstown, New Jersey 08520

College Mangement
CCM Professional Magazines, Inc.
22 West Putnam Avenue
Greenwich, Connecticut 06830

Community College Review
Segner, K. B., ed.
310 Poe Hall
North Carolina State University
Raleigh, North Carolina 27607

Community College Social Science Quarterly
Grossmont College
El Cajon, California 92020

Community and Junior College Journal
Harper, W. A., ed.
American Association of Community and Junior Colleges
One Dupont Circle N.W.
Washington, D.C. 20036

Current Index to Journal in Education
Macmillan Information
886 Third Avenue
New York, New York 10022

Dissertation Abstract International
A continuation of *Dissertation Abstracts*
(Volumes 1-29, July, 1969)
University of Michigan
Ann Arbor, Michigan 48104

Encyclopedia of Educational Research, Fourth Edition
Ebel, R. L., ed.
A project of the American Educational Research Association
Toronto: The Macmillan Co., Collier-Macmillan Ltd., 1969

ERIC Clearinghouse for Junior Colleges
University of California
Los Angeles, California 90024

Intellect
Brickman, W. W., ed.
Society for the Advancement of Education, Inc.
1860 Broadway
New York, New York 10023

Junior College Directory
American Association of Community and Junior Colleges
Washington, D.C.

New Directions for Community Colleges
Jossey-Bass, Inc.
615 Montgomery Street
San Francisco, California 94111

*Research Studies in Education: A Subject-Author Index and
    Research Methods Bibliography*
Phi Delta Kappa, Inc.
Bloomington, Indiana 47401

Psychological Abstracts
The American Psychological Association, Inc.
1200 Seventeenth Street, N.W.
Washington, D.C. 20036

Research in Higher Education
Elton, C. F., ed.
College of Education

University of Kentucky
Lexington, Kentucky 40506

Simon, K. A., and Grant, W. V.
Digest of Educational Statistics, 1972 Edition
U.S. Department of Health, Education and Welfare
Washington, D.C.

12

PRIVATE VOCATIONAL SCHOOLS

by A. Harvey Belitsky
Senior Professional
National Planning Association
Washington, D.C.

FROM NEGLECT TO RECOGNITION

Private vocational schools provide short and intensive training aimed at preparing their postsecondary students for direct entrance into employment. The schools are usually proprietary in nature, but some private nonprofit schools also provide training similar to that offered by the profit-seeking schools. Like any other schools, the private vocational schools ought to be evaluated largely on the basis of their performance in achieving their established training objectives. Yet throughout most of their history, the proprietary nature of most of the schools has cast doubts on the credibility of their objectives and hindered their evaluation. Perhaps it is more accurate to say that the schools have generally been ignored.

Despite neglect by researchers, educators and counselors, the schools have expanded in number and been profitable. In part this can be attributed to the fact that the public schools could not always accommodate all of the available students within their communities. But, more important, the course offerings have often differed significantly from those in the public institutions, and hence have been able to fill unique student needs. Although the private vocational schools have received considerable recognition during the last 10 years, the growth in volume and breadth of public vocational education at the postsecondary level could generate substantial direct competition from tax supported schools.

ESTIMATED NUMBER OF SCHOOLS

The limited attention to the operations of the private vocational schools helps to explain why estimates of the number of such schools have only recently been made. Belitsky (1969) estimated the number of schools to be approximately 7,000 for the year 1966. A later survey by the National Center for Educational Statistics (*Directory of Postsecondary Schools, 1973*) estimated that nearly 6,500 private schools were offering occupational programs for the 1970-1971 school year. Although the estimates were remarkably close, the surveys differed in the categories of schools included. For example, the government study contained over 100 correspondence schools, while Belitsky left such schools out of his estimate. Despite other differences, there was agreement in both studies to include schools in these categories: trade, technical, business, cosmetology, and barbering. It was estimated that more than 80 percent of the students in 1966 were enrolled in the trade, technical, or business fields (Belitsky, 1969). However, the cosmetology and barber schools remain quantitatively important because they, rather than the public schools, train most of the persons entering these occupations.

EXAMPLES OF RECOGNITION

Most recently, growing recognition has been accorded the schools by organizations and individuals who previously had little direct contact with, and hence meager information about, the schools' objectives and operations. Professional associations—including but not confined to those in the medical and dental fields—have acknowledged that private vocational schools, which are also called specialty schools, often perform a service in spite of, and perhaps because of, the fact that their programs aim to achieve limited objectives. Educators and career counselors, even while favoring occupational training that deals with a cluster of occupations, rather than a single occupation, also seem to be much more willing to recognize that the highly specialized training found in the typical private school is appropriate for certain individuals—for example, students who must see progress at frequent intervals during their training period; or students who, out of financial consideration or personal preference, desire training that can be completed in a matter of months. For full-time students, the annual tuition in a trade and technical school averages about $1600; the yearly tuition averages about $1200 for a business school student.

Numerous corporations—including, among others, Bell and Howell, Control Data, International Telephone and Telegraph, Ryder Systems, and the Columbia Broadcasting System—have expressed their ultimate recognition through their decisions to invest in private vocational education, usually by purchasing existing schools and later expanding their operations. Corporations would of course not undertake the ownership and management of these schools unless they expected the demands for the training provided in the schools to generate acceptable profits.

The recognition of private vocational schools by community colleges and the non-degree-granting public institutions at the postsecondary level has been through the indirect art of emulation. The rapidly growing community colleges, traditionally concerned with preparing and encouraging students to transfer to colleges and universities after two years of study, have been adding more terminal vocational training of less than two years' duration to their programs.

More states have decided to give the private vocational schools consideration as qualified degree-granting institutions, and a growing number of the schools have applied for and received recognition as two-year and four-year colleges. However, such growth affects only a minority of all schools; and the distinctive character of the schools is likely to place limits upon such growth unless, of course, the receipt of a degree becomes a fetish for even a greater number of occupations.

There is a growing trend both on the local and national scene toward exploring and taking advantage of the unique kinds of training provided by the private vocational schools. The National Association of Trade and Technical Schools (NATTS) has been receiving a substantially larger number of requests for its directory of member schools from college counseling departments, which, in turn, distribute the directories to those college students who are considering transferring to a private vocational school; and the Council on Postsecondary Accreditation has accepted NATTS as a member. Under several government programs—including Basic Opportunity Grants and veterans education—it is the accredited private schools which have received special recognition from the Federal government and numerous states, respectively; the United States Information Agency's guidance film for foreign students planning to enroll in U.S. schools also advises attendance at accredited schools. Finally, pilot programs are underway to provide advance rating and bonuses for graduates of private vocational schools who enroll in the U.S. Navy; and training in the schools on a contract basis is also being considered.

DISTINCTIVE ROLE

What is the distinctive nature of the training programs in private vocational schools that has finally resulted in their growing recognition? The specific programs within the schools cannot be described in any standard sense, because the programs are virtually as varied as the numerous occupations for which they train. Among the trade and technical schools, at least 250 different occupational courses are offered in such well-known fields as electronics, drafting, automobile maintenance, radio-TV repair, photography, tool and die design, welding, various forms of transportation and traffic management, etc. However, several operating procedures can be described which are distinctive to the schools, and which make it possible for the schools to adapt readily to the needs of students and employers.

The demand for the training provided by the private schools can be attributed to the frequent absence of training both on the job and in other schools. A surprisingly large portion of the training that is available for already employed persons involved only informal on-the-job training. Many high school graduates (and non-graduates, too) who do not enroll in a two- or a four-year college are almost totally unprepared for any specialized work. As a result, employers can often offer only meager opportunities to inexperienced job applicants. These applicants have good cause for trying to secure some training in advance.

FLEXIBILITY AND ADAPTABILITY

Because of the schools' job-oriented training programs, and their concern with student placement, the schools maintain close contacts with those types of private concerns which will employ the schools' graduates. The schools are therefore in a good position to keep up with changing technology; and their proprietary structure enables the schools to follow through much more rapidly on curriculum changes than can most public institutions, which require approval of a local school board or state legislature. Even a new industry that is unlikely itself to train all of its needed personnel may rely heavily upon school owners who can foresee a profitable undertaking, and decide to invest in the instructors, facilities, and equipment required to provide the new training. Examples of such fields include data processing, waste reconversion, and the various medical occupations that became vital after passage of Federal legislation.

The flexibility and adaptability of private schools are useful in attracting and serving a variety of students with a variety of needs. Students are admitted at frequent intervals; hence, a majority of surveyed trade and technical schools accepted new students no less than once every two months (Belitsky, p. 36). This is possible because a) the courses are of short duration or b) students proceed at their own rate of progress, because most learning takes place within a shop or laboratory setting. Once a student is enrolled, he can, if he wishes, attend on a year-round basis, thereby assuring the fastest possible completion of an occupational program. Since most students must hold outside jobs while attending school, classes are offered on a full or part-time basis, which usually means day and evening sessions respectively. Students may complete their courses at frequent intervals during the year, and their periods of entering the labor market will match such frequency.

PUBLIC CONTRACTS

Despite broad recognition for their distinctive courses and operations, private vocational schools have generally failed to benefit under the 1968 Amendments to the Vocational Education Act. While the Amendments provide state boards of education authority to contract for training with accredited schools in general, only some schools with courses in cosmetology and the flight portion of aviation training have been awarded contracts.

The private vocational schools have, however, been more extensively utilized under the Comprehensive Employment and Training Act of 1974 (CETA). In some cases, public schools with CETA contracts have even subcontracted for training with private schools that are able to enroll students at frequent intervals.

There are several reasons in favor of greater contractual usage of the private schools at both the secondary and postsecondary levels of education. Enrollments in the schools could be easily expanded, because they operate well below capacity (Belitsky, pp. 44-46). The schools would, moreover, be unlikely to grow to unmanageable size. The average enrollment for a business school is less than 350 students; a typical trade and technical school has about 200 students; and the cosmetology and barbering schools have even smaller enrollments.

The private schools, rather than the public schools, could assume the expense of keeping the contents of a curriculum current. Of course, in broad economic terms the costs might not differ whether the private or public schools tried to remain up-to-date. However, many private school administrators are convinced they can accomplish this with lower costs; and this is an important consideration, because of the administrative and financial difficulties that are involved in increasing the number of occupational courses in most public school systems.

Numerous students who are unable to enroll in short courses, because they are unavailable in their public school systems, could be enrolled in the adaptable private schools in a part time basis. These students, given the freedom to select vocational courses which they find interesting, may find themselves increasingly stimulated by their academic courses, too—especially if there are cooperative attempts to provide some integration between the academic studies in the public schools and the occupational training of the private schools.

IMPROVING SCHOOL PERFORMANCE

It should not be supposed that all private vocational schools are successful in meeting their training objectives and, further, that all these objectives are even worthy of being fulfilled. Certain schools have made extravagant promises about their training programs to prospective and enrolled students, and some schools continue to do so. An interest in distinguishing the superior schools from the shoddy ones was a principal reason for the formation of NATTS in 1965. It was hoped that the Association would soon qualify as a recognized agency of accreditation of trade and technical schools, in much the same way that the Accrediting Commission of the Association of Independent Colleges and Schools had been designated several years earlier to accredit private business schools; the U.S. Office of Education did designate this function to NATTS in 1967.

Although an increasing percentage of all schools have applied for and received accreditation, the majority of schools remain unaccredited, and the process of formally recognizing the schools through accreditation can itself be further improved. Through its regulatory powers, the Federal Trade Commission has attempted to protect students against the malpractices of certain schools; and considerable attention has been given to dealing with misleading practices in the recruitment of students. Through the use of special written materials, other information media, and visits to public secondary schools, the Commission has also instituted a campaign to assist prospective students in choosing private vocational schools of good quality.

Efforts to enhance the accrediting process have been made by several private and public organizations. SASHEP (Study of Accreditation of Selected Health Educational Programs) has recommended a decrease in the number of accrediting groups in the health field; and at least some progress has been made regarding consolidation of the diverse groups involved. A report by the American Vocational Association has dealt with securing single accrediting standards for private and public postsecondary schools; and standardization has taken place in some major areas.

It is widely agreed that accountability should be given greater emphasis in the accrediting process. Unfortunately, however, little action has been taken to apply those means that measure the actual performances of schools; and clearly any measure of accountability ought to be applied to both private and public vocational schools.

REFERENCES

Ash, L. C. et al., *Instruments and Procedures for the Evaluation of Vocational Technical Education Institutions and Programs.* Washington: American Vocational Association (under USOE Grant), 1971.

Belitsky, A. H. *Private Vocational Schools and Their Students.* Cambridge, Mass: Schenkman Publishing Co., 1969.

_____. *Private Vocational Schools: Their Emerging Role in Postsecondary Education.* Kalamazoo, Mich.: The W. E. Upjohn Institute for Employment Research, June 1970; also reprinted in *Trends in Postsecondary Education.* OE-50063, Washington: GPO, Oct. 1970.

_____. Vocational Schools, Private. *The Encyclopedia of Education,* The Macmillan Co., 1971.

Clark, H. F., and Sloan, H. S. *Classrooms on Main Street.* New York: Teachers College Press, 1966.

Directory of Postsecondary Schools with Occupational Programs, 1971. DHEW Publication No. (OE) 73-11410, Washington: GPO, 1973.

Hoyt, K. B. *An Introduction to the Specially Oriented Student Research Program at the State University of Iowa.* Iowa City: State University of Iowa, 1962.

Johnson, E. L. *A Descriptive Survey of Teachers of Private Trade and Technical Schools Associated with the National Association of Trade and Technical Schools.* Doctor of Education dissertation submitted at the George Washington University, Feb. 1967.

Kincaid, H. V., and Podesta, E. A. "An Exploratory Survey of Proprietary Vocational Schools", in Quirk and Sheehan, eds., *Research in Vocational Education: Proceedings of a Conference,* June 1966, Madison: The University of Wisconsin, 1967.

Wilms, W. W. *Proprietary Versus Public Vocational Training,* Berkeley: Center for Research and Development in Higher Education, 1973.

13

RELIGION AND GOVERNMENT IN EDUCATIONAL ARENAS

by Michael Robert Smith
Assistant Professor of Education
Pfeiffer College
Misenheimer, North Carolina

Three educational arenas in which church and state battles are continuously waged include: parental attempts to guide the religious education of their children, countered by the police power of the state as *parens patriae* to supersede the wishes of parents; efforts to amend the Constitution, or circumvent its interpretation by the Supreme Court, and establish prayer and religion in the public schools; endeavors to secure public tax monies with which to support elementary and secondary parochial schools and church-affiliated colleges and universities.

The three topics have been treated separately, though each is inextricably intertwined with the others. Each subject was structured with the intent of producing a sort of matrix within which would be embedded sufficient history, recent developments, and careful predictions.

PARENTS, STATES, AND THE EDUCATION OF CHILDREN

In America parents have a time-honored right to direct the course and process of the education of their children. Our highest court has, on three occasions, graced this precious principle with judicial dignity. The parental right over education is, however, balanced by the state's acknowledged responsibility to educate its citizens. Thus, parents may not substitute their views for that of boards of education and legislators, nor may the latter by their actions unnecessarily limit the constitutionally guaranteed freedoms of parents.

Yet parental rights have been transgressed. In a 1972 Supreme Court case (*Wisconsin v. Yoder*) the infringement involved the duration of education mandated by a state. Parents were prosecuted for violating the compulsory education law by not sending their children to high schools. To do so would have meant sacrificing their religious beliefs, and relinquishing their First Amendment religious freedoms. One half century ago (*Meyer v. Nebraska,* 1923), the encroachment centered about the very nature of education, as parents were denied the liberty of engaging instructors to teach their children foreign languages per se, or to teach their children subjects in languages other than English. To have forgone such freedoms would have demanded a deprivation of the exact types of liberties promised by our Fourteenth Amendment. And in 1925 (*Pierce v. Society of Sisters*) the trespass was upon the process of fulfilling the educational stipulations of the state. Parents were required to send their children to public schools, and attendance at private schools, secular or sectarian, would have resulted in prosecution. Although religious beliefs were at stake, the Supreme Court granted relief under the Fourteenth Amendment, for not until 1940 (*Cantwell v. Connecticut*) was the First Amendment held to bind the states. Still, a charter for all time was struck in the name of parental freedom, as the Court thought it

> entirely plain that the Act of 1922 unreasonably [interfered] with the liberty of parents and guardians to direct the upbringing and education of children under their control.... The child is not the mere creature of the state; those who nurture him and direct his destiny have the right, coupled with the high duty, to recognize and prepare him for additional obligations (*Pierce* at 535)

Redress for such grievances was not easily won, for the state has a duty as well to enhance and preserve public safety, peace, and social order. And it is well established that children should be safeguarded from labor which would threaten their health and safety. Further, who can deny Thomas Jefferson's argument that an informed citizen is a better citizen? Nor is there any way to gainsay the fact that the state's citizens should be self-sustaining, in order that they may be productive and no burden upon society. Certainly education is a key ingredient for each of those worthy tasks, making its regulation and control incumbent upon the state.

Therefore, where laws in pursuit of the state's educational obligations are clearly essential in fact, the state's control over the child will be paramount. Laws, however, may be merely essential in theory, and where that is the case parental rights will reign supreme. In *Meyer* (at 398) the state sought to insulate its children, saying the "legislature [has] seen the baneful effects of permitting foreigners who had taken residence in this country, to rear and educate their children in the language of their native land." But the Court held (*Meyer* at 401) that the Constitution is not limited "to those born with English on the tongue." In *Pierce* the law would have molded all children in the image of the state, but the Court would not hear of it, saying that:

> The fundamental theory of liberty upon which all governments in this Union repose excludes any general power of the State to standardize its children by forcing them to accept instruction from public teachers only. (*Pierce* at 534-535)

And in *Yoder*, the requirement of high school was based on the assumption that children must be prepared for the culture of the majority, which is the "right" culture. But such coercion would have frustrated the timeless Amish practice of educating their adolescents in their own way, and for their own culture. Furthermore, our Supreme Court held (*Yoder* at 30) that "there [could] be no assumption that today's majority is 'right' and the Amish and others like them are 'wrong'."

Pleas of parents for exemptions to the state's educational laws have often gone unheard, for the courts are slow in overturning rules of state or local boards of education, the educational legislators use strong arguments in defense of their laws. One such argument is that the Constitution only mandates freedom for religious beliefs, and that religious actions may be limited for the good of the state. Indeed, the Court itself has often curbed religious actions, and for proof one is not required to look past the first monogamous Mormon. But the trend of the Court's decisions suggests that religious practices are now constitutionally protectible, and the burden of proof is on the state to show how they diminish health, safety, or general welfare.

Another of the state's arguments is that since its laws apply uniformly to all, how can it be that any single parent or group is singled out for religious persecution? But the Court, looking past the face to the effect of legislation, said in *Yoder* (at 28):

> A regulation neutral on its face may, in its application, nonetheless offend the constitutional requirement for governmental neutrality if it unduly burdens the free exercise of religion.

In the regulation of education, the effect of most laws applies to the parent, not the child; the parent is liable, as he is thought to control and choose for the child. It might be assumed that children grow old enough to choose for themselves, and that their choices could differ from those of their parents. Even so, the state has curiously argued that the child's protection would still be found in a law which exempts no parent. For example, if a parent could not be prosecuted for failing to send his child to school, but the child in fact wanted to attend, the child's wishes would be transgressed, and the state would be an unwilling partner in the transgression. But if the parent's and child's wishes were reversed, the latter opting to abstain from school, the state would happily ignore his choice. Apparently the child must choose as the state thinks best, if the sanctity of his wishes is to be considered.

Mr. Justice Douglas was the sole dissenter in *Yoder*. There he pointed out that psychological research now has established that the modern adolescent is mature enough to make his own moral and intellectual decisions. Further, the Court has on numerous occasions acknowledged that adolescents are persons, no less than their parents, to be protected by our Constitution. In fact, very few years have passed since high school students (*Tinker v. Des Moines,* 1969) were assured of all the freedom of expression offered by the First Amendment. Surely the day is approaching when the state will no longer be able to reach through the parent and manipulate the constitutional freedoms of the adolescent. The next great struggle between the state and the religiously persecuted may well involve the adolescent in his own search for educational autonomy.

PRAYER IN THE PUBLIC SCHOOLS: ANOTHER PARENTAL RIGHT?

Perhaps the most remarkable feature of our Constitution is its relatively unaltered state in the wake of a thousand-plus attempts to alter it. Yet, surely no feature of that resilient document has withstood more shocks than the First Amendment. The offending passages require Congress to "make no law respecting an establishment of religion or prohibiting the free exercise thereof. ..." A mandate for governmental neutrality, those simple clauses stand today like impregnable fortresses, battered from countless salvos but fundamentally unaltered.

From this viewpoint the count was a close one when, on November 8, 1971, the House of Representatives fell only 28 votes short of the two-thirds majority needed to approve this innocuous-sounding proposal:

> Nothing contined in this Constitution shall abridge the right of persons lawfully assembled, in any public building which is supported in whole or in part through the expenditure of public funds, to participate in voluntary prayer. (Congressional Record, H10691)

The "Wylie Amendment," as H. J. 191 came to be known, was the culmination of almost eight years of reaction to two decisions which stamped the Supreme Court's imprimatur upon the First Amendment. In 1962 (*Engel v. Vitale*) the voluntary observance by public school students of a state-structured, non-denominational prayer was held unconstitutional, and the following year, in *Abington v. Schempp,* the Court decided against state-prescribed Bible-reading and recitation of the Lord's Prayer in the public schools, saying (at 222):

> The test may be stated as follows: what are the purpose and
> the primary effect of the enactment? If either is the advance-
> ment or inhibition of religion then the enactment exceeds the
> scope of legislative power as circumscribed by the Constitu-
> tion. That is to say that to withstand the strictures of the Es-
> tablishment Clause there must be a secular legislative purpose
> and a primary effect that neither advances nor inhibits re-
> ligion.

Those favoring the proscribed religious activities saw
them as falling within the ambit of parental rights, but
knew well that they failed the Court's latest test. Clearly,
supplications to God in schools partly financed with ag-
nostic and atheistic taxes *advanced* religion.

Since those landmark decisions, the standard-bearer
for citizens seeking to alter the First Amendment has
been the Reverend Robert G. Howes of Arlington, Virginia, leader of a National Coalition called Citizens for
Public Prayer. Reverend Howes is not easily discouraged.
In fact, his efforts led the issue back to the Senate Constitutional Amendments Sub-Committee for fresh consideration in 1973.

The philosophical rift between pro- and anti-amend-
ment forces runs deep. Advocates of amendment see the
Court's 1962 and 1963 decisions as religious restrictions,
denials of voluntary prayer, and tortuous misreadings of
the First Amendment's religious clauses. Those against
say the Court has restricted nothing except governmental
control of the personal practice of religion, therefore true
voluntary prayer has been safeguarded. Opponents point
to Representative Wylie, the 1971 prayer amendment's
sponsor, who, when asked "who would be responsible
for deciding or controlling the nature of the prayers to
be uttered in the schools," simply replied "the composition or selection of the prayer would be the function of
the local school authorities (Congressional Record,
H10489)."

The latest twist in the struggle is lent by 1975 bills in
the Senate and House of Representatives (S.283, and
H.R.1678) which would limit the jurisdiction of all Federal courts over controversies concerning "voluntary
prayer" in the public schools. Presumably, the thinking
of the sponsors of the bills (Senator Jesse Helms and
Representative Daniel Flood) is that where voluntarism
and governmental sponsorship coexist in peace, the
courts ought not to interfere.

PAROCHIAL SCHOOLS AND THE PUBLIC PURSE

The Arguments for Tax Support

From the early 1800s until 1925, parents of nonpub-
lic-sectarian school schildren argued that they were forced
to pay school taxes in addition to the tuition costs of the
nonpublic schools; they claimed "double taxation." With
Pierce v. Society of Sisters a second argument was born:
if parents have the right to send their children to sectarian schools, and wish but cannot afford to do so, the
State prohibits their free exercise of religion if it does
not financially underwrite their choice. Over the recent
past a third argument, given rise by the confluence of

many factors, took this shape: the cost of operating re-
ligiously-affiliated schools is prohibitive without state
financial assistance; if such aid is not forthcoming private
schools will close, and overburdened public schools will
have to absorb the additional cost. Together these arguments have stimulated a spate of legislative schemes aimed
at securing some type of public tax aid, mainly for Roman
Catholic elementary and secondary schools.

Tax Aid and Judicial Response

The efforts of parochial school parents have yielded a
limited number of fringe-type concessions. No doubt
these benefits have proven valuable, but they do not approach the parity sought. Further, recent intensified activities of legislatures in states heavily populated by Cath-
olics may have fatally damaged future opportunities for
any type of meaningful aid. In 1971 (*Lemon v. Kurtzman*) the Supreme Court frowned on an attempt to
"purchase the services," or literally to pay for a portion
of salaries of religious school teachers teaching secular
subjects in sectarian schools. In 1972 (*Brusca v. State
Board of Education*) one of the prime arguments for
aid was brushed aside with the Court's approval of a
lower court's holding (*Brusca*, 332 F. Supp. 275 at 278)
that since *Pierce*, parents indeed have the right to choose
their children's schools, but "tax-raised funds to assist
parents in the free exercise of their religion would necessarily be to support religion," a thing denied by the Establishment Clause. In 1973 (*Committee for Public Education and Religious Liberty v. Nyquist*) a number of
schemes were squelched. There a state contended that
since it mandated certain services (particularly testing)
in nonpublic schools, it should be able to pay for them.
But that proved too much, so the Court countered that
to sustain such a law would free the state to mandate and
pay for everything. Other state statutes sought to pay
for the maintenance and repair of nonpublic school facilities (including overhead costs), but the Court pointed
out (Nyquist at 2967) that what could not be erected at
public expense could not be maintained by tax dollars.
Finally, the state contended that it should be allowed
to reimburse parochial school parents for tuition costs,
or to allow income-tax credits for expenses parents incurred; i.e., that aiding parents is not the same as aiding
religious schools. At this point the coup de grace fell.
Mr. Justice Powell (Nyquist at 2972) said, "whether the
grant is labeled a reimbursement, a reward or a subsidy,
its substantive impact is still the same." A new test was
created: does a statute have the "substantive impact" of
aiding religion?

Supreme Court opinions, 1973 through 1975, did not
vary from precedents set in earlier opinions. The Court
has insisted, heretofore (Nyquist at 2965), that a law in
question, in order to pass muster under the Establishment
Clause . . . reflect a clearly secular legislative purpose . . .
have a primary effect that neither advances nor inhibits
religion, and . . . avoid excessive government entanglement with religion." Parochial-aid statutes that have
"passed muster" have been few in number and narrowly
structured in nature. Textbooks (*Board of Education v.
Allen*, 1968) for elementary and secondary schools;

federal construction grants (*Tilton v. Richardson*, 1971) for colleges; and the usage of the state's borrowing powers, for college support purposes—where no cost to the state ensued (*Hunt v. McNair*, 1973)—have passed all three tests. Prior to the evolution of the tests, a statute survived a Fourteenth Amendment challenge (*Everson v. Board of Education*, 1947) where it provided for reimbursement to parents for the cost of transporting their children to schools.

SOME CAUTIOUS PREDICTIONS

Presumably one could pattern a statute after those that have been approved by the Court. In each case the benefits were released to all recipients with an interest in them. Just as the Court, in *Wisconsin v. Yoder*, refused to allow any group of parents to be singled out for persecution, it has also allowed none to be isolated for special benefits. In each case approved, the benefits were of a non-ideological nature. Buses and state-approved secular textbooks are at great variance from teachers' salaries and tuition costs. Beyond this the going gets tougher. Ways must be found to ensure the secular usage of tax funds, for if an institution is permeated with religion to receive a benefit (*Hunt v. McNair* at 2875) government and religion necessarily entangle.

The question now is, which new plans would confer benefits on all, be ideologically neutral, avoid entanglement, and not have the substantive impact of aiding religion? Any predictions would require speculation, but the hazards are not that grave. Some rational guidelines attenuate the risks. The next concerted effort at the elementary and secondary level may focus on "shared time." This is an arrangement where parochial students take at public schools courses not offered by their own schools, thereby saving on expensive equipment required by certain curricula. There is precedent for this, in that the Federal government has financed shared time plans under the Elementary and Secondary Education Act since 1965. In addition, no court rulings have decided the legality of Federal expenditures for parochial elementary and secondary schools, though the right to challenge such practices does now exist (*Flast v. Cohen*, 1968). Another possibility is the voucher system, a scheme which would grant vouchers to parents, redeemable at any school. This plan is favored by the national Office of Education. Proponents of it may also find encouragement in the words of the Court (Nyquist at 2966): "we fully recognize the validity of the State's interest in promoting pluralism and diversity among its public and nonpublic schools." A likely possibility, though, is that emphasis will switch from the elementary and secondary to the college level. At this plane the burden of proving that the school is permeated with religion is difficult. The "entanglement hurdle" has been easily surmounted in the only two Supreme Court decisions to date. This way holds promise for those who would travel it.

If these predictions prove wide of the mark, the inaccuracy will lie in their form, not substance. The public purse has been attractive enough to perennially sustain the efforts of parochial-aid lobbyists, and there is no reason to suspect a change. The latest dissenting opinions offer evidence that the timeless arguments used in favor of tax support have left their marks, and that the day may yet come when the public will pay for part or all of religiously affiliated school expenses.

But the public always exacts a price for its support; indeed, the form of its price is even now found in the fabric of recent opinions. It is called governmental instrumentalism, and means essentially that to the extent something is publicly financed, it may be publicly controlled. The exclusion of prayer, Bible reading, and state-imposed discrimination was premised upon the fact that the schools are publicly financed. Is it unreasonable to ask whether a citizen might not sue for an end to the same practices in publicly-financed "private" schools? In *Hunt v. McNair* (at 2878) the state of South Carolina was given authority by statute, approved by the highest Court, to almost totally regulate the affairs of a Baptist-controlled college if, for any reason, the college could not meet its financial obligations to the state:

> The Authority [State's agent] is also empowered, inter alia, to determine the location and character of any project financed under the act; to construct, maintain, manage, operate, lease as lessor or lessee, and regulate the same; to enter into contracts for the management and operation of such project; to establish rules and regulations for the use of the project or any portion thereof; and to fix and revise from time to time rates, rents, fees, and charges for the use of a project and for the services furnished or to be furnished by a project or any portion thereof. In other words, the College turns over to the State Authority control of substantial parts of the fiscal operation of the school—its very life's blood.

The public purse, then, is open only to colleges willing to expel their close religious ties, willing to jeopardize their religious practices, willing even to forego their autonomous nature, if necessary. At what point do the private and the public blend indistinguishably into one?

REFERENCES

Bradfield v. Roberts, 175 U.S. 291 (1899). Public funds were allowed to be used for the support of a hospital chartered by Congress, where such charter, if abused, was subject to amendment and termination. The fact that members of the hospital's governing board were all of one faith had no bearing on the decision.

Speer v. Colbert, 200 U.S. 130 (1906). Georgetown University, a Jesuit-controlled institution, was chartered as a nonsectarian institution by an act of Congress. Simple religious control of the governing board could not make the school sectarian, or different from its original charter.

Quick Bear v. Leupp, 210 U.S. 50 (1908). Private funds, held in trust by Congress, were allowed to be used for support of a sectarian school for Sioux Indians.

Meyer v. Nebraska, 262 U.S. 390 (1923). States were not allowed to ban foreign languages in public and private schools, thereby infringing upon constitutionally guaranteed liberties by which parents guide their children's education.

Frothingham v. Mellon, 262 U.S. 447 (1923). A taxpayer's interest in the moneys of the treasury was held to be too small and indeterminable to allow for court challenge of a federal spending program.

Pierce v. Society of Sisters, 268 U.S. 510 (1925). States could not enforce laws requiring attendance at public schools only.

Parents were held to have the right to direct their children's education. Private schools were unequivocally guaranteed the right to exist and operate.

Cochran v. Louisiana State Board of Education, 281 U.S. 370 (1930). The "child-benefit" theory was established by this decision. The taxing power of the state was held to have been exerted for the public purpose where all school children (public and private) were provided free textbooks by the state. The case involved the Fourteenth Amendment.

Cantwell v. Connecticut, 310 U.S. 296 (1940). The Fourteenth Amendment was declared to embrace the liberties guaranteed by the First Amendment, rendering the states, as well as Congress, powerless to advance or restrain religion. Individual liberty to publicly practice religion could not be inhibited without due process.

Murdock v. Pennsylvania, 319 U.S. 105 (1943). Public distribution of religious literature, a First Amendment right, could not be conditioned upon payment of a tax, nondiscriminatory though it was.

West Virginia State Board of Education v. Barnette, 319 U.S. 624 (1943). Public school officials could not compel patriotic or religious orthodoxy. Specifically, they were barred here from forcing children to salute the flag and recite the pledge of allegiance.

Everson v. Board of Education, 330 U.S. 1 (1947). This was the first challenge to the use of public funds for the support of private schools, as determined by the First Amendment. By a five-to-four margin, a state was allowed to reimburse all parents for the cost of transporting their children safely to public or private schools. The decision was based on child benefit and general welfare doctrines, as the Court said that "No tax in any amount, large or small, can be levied to support any religious activities or institutions, whatever they may be called, or whatever form they may adopt to teach or practice religion." (15)

Illinois ex rel. McCollum v. Board of Education, 333 U.S. 203 (1948). Tax-supported schools could not be used for instruction in religious faiths (as opposed to teaching *about* various religions), even where salaries of instructors were financed by the religions involved. Such practices violated the First Amendment.

Zorach v. Clausen, 343 U.S. 306 (1952). Tax-supported schools could (without violating the First or Fourteenth Amendments) manipulate their schedules to release students for off campus religious instruction—where such instruction was wholly at the expense of participating religions.

McGowan v. Maryland, 366 U.S. 420 (1961). Sunday closing laws were upheld, in that they provided a uniform day of rest; notwithstanding the incidental side-effect of encouraging church attendance. The Court said, "If the primary purpose [as contradistinguished from an incidental one] of the state action is to promote religion, that action is in violation of the Amendment, but if [the operative effect of] a statute furthers both secular and religious ends, an examination of the means used is necessary to determine whether the state could reasonably have attained the secular end by means which do not further the promotion of religion." (466, 467)

Engel v. Vitale, 370 U.S. 421 (1962). A state could not formulate a prayer for daily recitation in its schools. "When the power, prestige and financial support of government is placed behind a particular religious belief, the indirect coercive pressure upon religious minorities to conform to the prevailing officially approved religion is plain." (437)

Equally significant was a comment made here by Justice Douglas about the earlier *Everson* case. Justice Douglas was then one of the five in the five-to-four opinion. Here, though, he said, "The Everson Case seems in retrospect to be out of line with the First Amendment." (443)

Abington School District v. Schempp, 374 U.S. 203 (1963). The First Amendment was held to be transgressed by government-sanctioned Bible reading, and recitation of the Lord's Prayer in the schools. A test for state statutes was established: "That is to say that to withstand the strictures of the Establishment Clause there must be a secular legislative purpose and a primary effect that neither advances nor inhibits religion." (222)

Justice Douglas made these oft-quoted remarks: "What may not be done directly may not be done indirectly lest the Establishment Clause become a mockery." (229-230)

Board of Education v. Allen, 392 U.S. 236 (1968). The *Schempp* test of a neutral purpose and primary effect was applied, and a state's practice of loaning secular textbooks to private/ parochial schools was upheld.

Flast v. Cohen, 392 U.S. 83 (1968). The 1923 ban on challenges to Federal spending programs (established in *Frothingham*) was removed for citizens who can confirm a connection between a Congressional Program and a violation of their constitutional rights.

Walz v. Tax Commission of City of New York, 397 U.S. 677 (1970). Tax exemptions to churches were found neither to be required nor prohibited by the First Amendment. Exemptions do not amount to government sponsorship; they simply constitute abstention from seeking church support of the state. The test fashioned here was that of "excessive entanglement of government and religion," calling for continuing surveillance. Exemption calls for less involvement than would taxation.

Lemon v. Kurtzman, 403 U.S. 602 (1971). The Walz test of excessive entanglement barred states from purchasing ("contracting") secular educational services from church-related schools; and from paying salary supplements to teachers of secular subjects in church-related schools. The statutes failed the *Walz* test because of the surveillance required to ensure continued secular use of the funds. Further, one statute called for continuing financial aid, and created potential for political division along religious lines.

Tilton v. Richardson, 403 U.S. 672 (1971). By a five-to-four decision, private colleges were allowed to construct facilities with federal grants. The buildings could never be used for religious activities. The grants were non-renewing in nature.

Wisconsin v. Yoder, 92 S. Ct. 1526 (1972). Where a religion historically, continuously opposed compulsory secondary education; and where the state failed to show how its interest in educating its citizens would be endangered by accommodating the religious group; continued compulsory education was violative of First Amendment rights.

Brusca v. State of Missouri, 405 U.S. 1050 (1972). Parents have a right to send their children to church-related schools, but the free exercise of their religion was not violated where the state did not assist the parents. The Court, in affirming this lower court decision (332 F. Supp. 275) addressed a long-standing contention that states, by their refusal to provide aid to religions, violate the Free Exercise Clause of the First Amendment.

Wolman v. Essex, 406 U.S. 912 (1972). A lower court decision (342 F. Supp. 399) proscribing reimbursements to parents for parochial school tuition was upheld. Payment to the parent for transmittal to the church-related school (as opposed to payment to the school) had no mitigating effect on the court's decision.

Committee for Public Education and Religious Liberty v. Nyquist, 93 S. Ct. 2955 (1973). Direct money grants for maintenance and repair costs to parochial schools; tuition reimbursement to parents of parochial school students; tax credits to parents who failed to qualify for tuition reimbursements—all failed the *Schempp* test, in that each had the primary effect of advancing religion. Tuition reimbursements to parents (rather than the school) offered a select group an incentive to send their children to sectarian schools. (2972) Tax credits could not be justified by the *Walz* case. The credits have no historical foundation, would increase involvement between church and state, and would be restricted to one class of citizens for one purpose. (2975-2976)

Sloan v. Lemon, 93 S. Ct. 2982 (1973). Tuition reimbursement to parents of all private school children (sectarian and secular) violated the First Amendment since the primary effect of the Act advanced religion. The Court also said that the benefits to the "secular side of religion," thus far allowed under the child-benefit theory, were indirect and incidental; but these nonetheless "approached the 'verge' of the constitutionally impermissible." (2987)

———

14

COMMUNICATIONS SATELLITES IN EDUCATION

by Robert P. Morgan
Director, Center for Development Technology
Washington University
St. Louis, Missouri
and
Jai P. Singh
Formerly, Associate Director for Communications
Center for Development Technology
Washington University
St. Louis, Missouri 63130

Planning studies and experiments are underway to explore the use of communications satellites in education, both in the United States and in other countries and regions. These studies and experiments seek to take advantage of the ability of satellites to deliver educational radio, television, digital data, and other signals over wide areas, to reach remote areas, and to tie together people and institutions to share resources, experiences, and ideas. (Morgan and Margolin, 1971; Morgan and Singh, 1972, 1973; Singh and Morgan, 1972; Grayson et al., 1972).

Applications Technology Satellites (ATS) I and III, developed by NASA, have been and are being used in the U.S. for educational communications experiments of limited scope (Morgan and Singh, 1973). More extensive educational television distribution, and instructional broadcasting experiments involving inexpensive, community-reception-type receivers, are planned during 1974-1976 in the U.S. and India, using the ATS-6 satellite (Morgan and Singh, 1973; and Singh and Jamison, 1973). A number of educational experiments or demonstrations during 1975-1977, using a joint U.S.-Canada Communication Technology Satellite (CTS), have been proposed by U.S. and Canadian educational institutions and other agencies. Major planning efforts for operational satellite systems which serve education are underway within large countries like India, Brazil, In-

donesia, and Iran. UNESCO has supported studies of regional satellite systems for Africa, Latin America, and the Arab countries.

Communications satellites are one of many technologies of current or potential interest to educational technologists and planners. The extent to which satellites will be used depends upon the extent to which educational and communications technology proves responsive to educational needs, the extent to which "cost-effectiveness" can be demonstrated, and the extent to which technology in general finds future use in education. In particular, satellites have the potential for providing relatively low cost (on a per-pupil basis) educational services—computer-aided instruction, radio, one-way and talk-back television, library and computer resource sharing, etc.—to large numbers of people and institutions, provided that economies of scale can be achieved. Such services may prove to be responsive to calls for greater access, individualization, and productivity in U.S. education, as well as the need to extend education and literacy to greater numbers of individuals in developing countries. However, to achieve this potential suitable organizational arrangements and structures must be devised which respond to the particular educational setting of the country or region.

COMMUNICATIONS SATELLITES

Use of satellites for communications was first outlined by the radio engineer and science fiction writer Arthur C. Clarke in 1945. Just 18 years later, after a series of experiments with low and medium altitude satellites which required large and complex earth-stations, the stationary satellite Syncom-II was successfully placed in geo-synchronous orbit. In such an orbit the satellite is some 23,000 miles over the equator, and stays in one fixed position relative to points on earth. Three of these satellites in the proper position could beam signals which cover almost the entire surface of the earth.

The demonstration of the feasibility of using a stationary satellite in geo-synchronous orbit for communications paved the way for commercial communications satellites.[1] Since the orbiting of the Early Bird (Intelsat-I) satellite, launched for the International Telecommunications Satellite Consortium (INTELSAT) in 1965, communications satellite technology has come a long way and has acquired a high degree of sophistication. Intelsat has launched four generations of satellites; investment costs per circuit year of satellite capacity dropped from $15,000 for Early Bird to $500 for Intelsat IV (Pritchard, 1969); earth-stations have increasingly become less complex and less expensive; and satellites have moved from international to domestic communications. Canada has a full-fledged domestic communications satellite system of its own, and a small number of commercial domestic communications satellite systems have begun operating or are being planned for the U.S.A.

It is important to recognize that satellites in use for international telecommunications today, and the present generation of domestic satellites coming into being, have relatively low power transmitters which provide "fixed-satellite services," to connect relatively large and expensive earth stations. However, the satellite technology has reached a point where relatively inexpensive, rooftop type receivers for receiving radio and television programs or broadcasts over a wide area from relatively high-power satellites will be feasible shortly. In recognition of this possibility, the 1971 World Administrative Radio Conference (WARC), held in Geneva, defined and allocated radio frequencies for a "broadcasting satellite service" in which signals transmitted or retransmitted by satellites are intended for direct reception by the general public. Two distinct categories exist in this service: systems that allow individual reception by simple receiving units in homes, and systems that are designed for community reception, either by a group of the general public at one location or through a distribution system covering a limited area. However, it should be pointed out that WARC regulations for broadcasting satellite service do not permit direct reception by unaugmented conventional TV receivers of the type in use today.

EDUCATIONAL USES OF SATELLITES

The applications currently contemplated for communications satellites in education are indeed diverse (Morgan and Margolin, 1971; Morgan and Singh, 1972), reflecting the differences in educational systems and needs of the nations or regions where uses of communications satellites have been proposed. In the U.S., formal systems of education have been serving large portions of the school-age population, and higher education is becoming more widespread with the inception of the community college. According to Koerner (1973), three current educational demands center on greater access to education by those not served, greater individualization of education, and greater economy. There is also current emphasis on nontraditional forms of study (Commission on Non-Traditional Study, 1973). These movements may provide clues as to opportunities for satellite utilization in the U.S. In a developing nation like India, higher priority may be given to building a system of basic education and an infrastructure, almost from scratch, to communication skills and attitudes necessary for the economic and social development of the nation, with particular emphasis on rural areas (Singh and Jamison, 1973).

In the U.S., with its relatively well developed telecommunications infrastructure, including considerable investment in educational telecommunications facilities (Morgan et al., 1973), the rationale for utilizing satellites for educational communications differs from that in countries which may not have well developed telecommunications plants. The key to satellite utilization, as opposed to other communications technologies, lies in provision of significantly new services that existing terrestrial facilities are unable to accommodate or provide, and provision of services similar to those provided by existing technologies but at significantly reduced cost (Morgan and Singh, 1973). Educational satellite planners are emphasizing educational networking for sharing of library, computer, and human resources; educational services which are not adequately provided by the existing formal system; direct delivery of high-quality educational material and resources to small and remote institutions; and educational television and ratio networking.

In developing nations like India, the emphasis is on taking advantage of the wide-area coverage and broadcast capabilities of the satellite to provide a quantum jump in the mass-communication capabilities of those nations, and to expand and improve their basic education system quickly. Brazil's extensive satellite planning effort emphasizes educational radio and television programming, to be used in formal education in the remote, less developed areas of the Northeast.[2]

Figure 1 illustrates possible educational satellite services in the U.S., and Table 1 summarizes primary roles in Education which satellites may provide. If and when educational services are implemented, they are likely to be developed in conjunction with local distribution facilities such as cable-television systems, Instructional Television Fixed Service (ITFS) systems, regional terrestrial networks, and broadcast facilities. The use of satellites for direct delivery of services to rooftops of schools and learning centers is of interest in areas where

TABLE 1. PRIMARY ROLES FOR SATELLITES TOWARDS THE DELIVERY OF CERTAIN EDUCATIONAL COMMUNICATIONS MEDIA AND SERVICES

Service	Primary Roles for Satellites
Instructional Television	Direct delivery to schools and learning centers, to broadcast stations, ITFS and cable headends for further redistribution.
Computer-Assisted Instruction	Delivery of CAI to small, remote institutions, particularly those 70-80 miles or more away from a major metropolitan area.
Computing Resources Multi-Access Interactive Computing	Delivery of interactive computing to remote institutions for the purposes of problem solving and implementation of regional EIS.
Remote Batch Processing	Delivery of raw computing power to small, remote institutions for instructional computing and administrative data processing.
Computer Interconnection	Interconnection of the computer facilities of institutions of higher education and regional computer networks for resource sharing.
Information Resource Sharing Interlibrary Communication	Interconnection of major libraries for bibliographic search and interlibrary loans, etc.
Automated Remote Information Retrieval	Interconnection of institutional and/or CATV headends with major information storage centers.
Teleconferencing	Interconnection of educational institutions for information exchange without physical movement of the participants, and for gaining access to specialists.

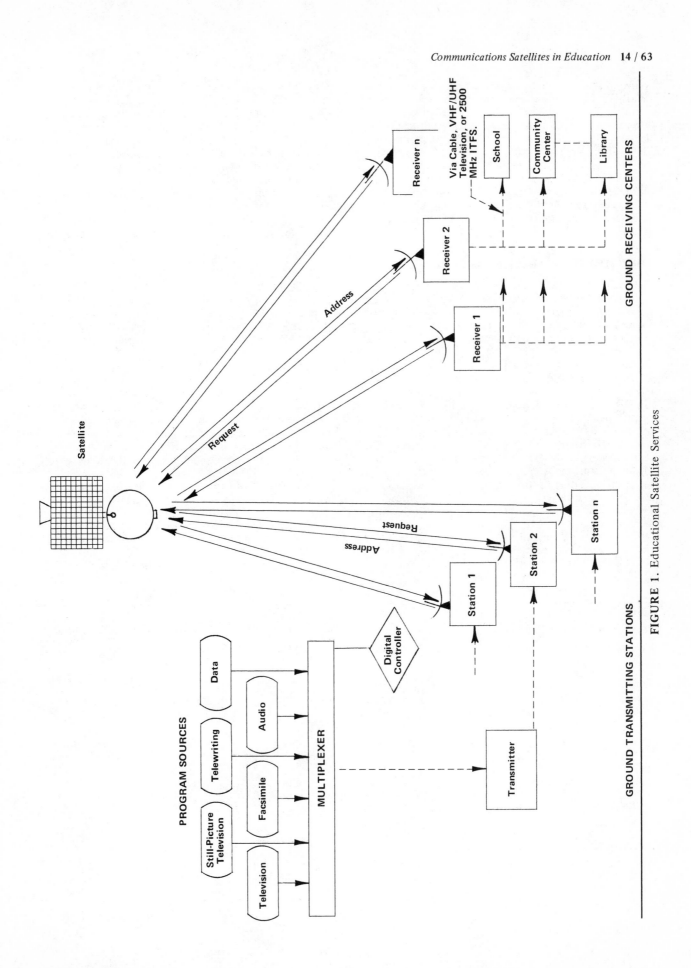

FIGURE 1. Educational Satellite Services

topographical and/or demographic conditions make local distribution and interconnection systems less attractive economically—areas such as Alaska, the Rocky Mountains, and parts of Appalachia. Satellites look promising for delivery of educational services to wide but sparsely populated areas, and for interconnection of cable systems, but the cable-television headend interconnection is not necessarily promising unless educational interests can make greater inroads into local cable systems. Cable systems tied together by satellite could conceivably provide a second interconnection for public television programs.

EDUCATIONAL SATELLITE EXPERIMENTS

In 1969, after two years of studying the application of communications satellites for mass communication, education, and telecommunications, India became the first country to commit herself to a large-scale experiment in satellite delivery of instructional television to rural areas. This experiment, scheduled for 1975-1976, will be conducted in cooperation with NASA by the Indian Space Organization (ISRO), using NASA's Applications Technology Satellite (ATS)-6. In this experiment, the ATS-6 satellite will be used to broadcast directly to 2500 rural community receivers. Some 2000 additional receivers will be served by rebroadcast through low-power VHF transmitters interconnected by ATS-6. The primary instructional objectives of the experiment involve family planning, improved agricultural practices, and national integration. Certain portions of the programming will also be devoted to general school education and teacher training (for details see Chitnis et al., 1971; Singh and Jamison, 1973).

The history of experiments with satellites for educational communications in the U.S. dates back to January 4, 1970, when the Corporation for Public Broadcast-

ing (CPB) initiated an experiment in transcontinental interconnection employing NASA's Applications Technology Satellites 1 and 3. Since then a number of educational communications demonstrations and experiments using ATS-1 and 3 satellites have been completed or are continuing (see Table 2). With the sole exception of the CPB transcontinental interconnection experiments conducted using C-band (4 and 6 GHz) transponders, experiments continuing or completed to date have employed Very High Frequency (VHF) transponders onboard ATS-1 and 3—using frequencies that are not assigned for operational services, and that are incapable of accommodating wideband or high data-rate communications such as television relay/distribution.

The Health-Education Telecommunications (HET) experiment, jointly sponsored by NASA, the department of Health, Education and Welfare (DHEW), and the Corporation for Public Broadcasting (CPB), involves educational experiments in Alaska, Appalachia, and the Rocky Mountains. This experiment, which began in late spring of 1974, employs the ATS-6 satellite to distribute health and educational material to public broadcasting stations, cable television headends, translators and community centers in S-band (2500 MHz) using low-cost/receive terminals ($3,300-3,500 per unit in quantities of 100 or so). It also was designed to use VHF transponders onboard the ATS-1 and 3 spacecrafts to accommodate limited narrowband interaction (voice or low-speed data/facsimile) from selected remote installations (Potter and Janky, 1973).

In addition to demonstrating the feasibility of distributing ETV signals to low-cost terminals, the HET experiments were planned to explore the three dimensions of educational delivery arrangements—the hardware, software, and human-support elements. These were to be weighted in different ways to assess the impact of different combinations on the learning, participation, and opin-

TABLE 2. APPLICATION TECHNOLOGY SATELLITE EDUCATIONAL COMMUNICATIONS EXPERIMENTS

Completed	Concluded	Spacecraft	Purposes
Corporation for Public Broadcasting	March 1970	ATS 1, 3	Transcontinental Interconnection
Stanford University	June 1972	ATS-3	Computer-Assisted Instruction Delivery to Rural Areas
Continuing	*Started*		
State of Alaska (National Library of Medicine, National Public Radio, and U.S. Office of Education)	June 1970	ATS-1	Educational/Instructional Radio; Teacher Training
University of Hawaii	March 1971	ATS-1	Pacific Interconnection of Institutions of Higher Learning
DHEW/CPB/NASA (Alaska, Appalachia, and Rocky Mountain States)	June 1974	ATS-6 ATS 1, 3	ETV Distribution and Limited Interactive Services
Approved	*Estimated Start*		
India/NASA	Summer 1975	ATS-6	ITV Broadcasting
Conditionally Approved			
A Number of Proposals for Experiments Using CTS	Winter 1975	CTS	Dental education; Intercollege Resource Sharing; Document Delivery; Library Resource Sharing

ions of the program-receiving audience. The programming has focused upon career education and inservice teacher development. The total cost of the entire experiment, exclusive of the space segment, is estimated to be in the range of $10-13 million. The scale, duration and funding support of HET experiments, and the technology involved, with particular respect to ETV distribution in S-band to low-cost terminals, make it the first true demonstration of the capabilities offered by high-power satellites, even if it touches upon only few of the opportunities that satellites potentially may provide.[3]

Communications Technology Satellite (CTS), a Canadian program in cooperation with NASA, is to be launched in the winter of 1975. Like ATS-6, it contains a high-power transponder which allows use of inexpensive and small earth terminals, but in the Ku-band (12 to 14 GHz). A number of proposals for user experiments with CTS have been submitted by a variety of U.S. organizations and institutions to NASA. These include experiments in dental education, inter-institutional and inter-regional resource sharing of library services and documents, and experiments with new arrangements for the delivery of educational services, both within and outside the framework of the traditional college/university setting.

EMERGING U.S. DOMESTIC SATELLITE SYSTEMS

The first phase of the domestic satellite proceedings of the Federal Communications Commission is now over (FCC, 1972-1973), leading to the emergence of a small number of commercial domestic satellite systems in the mid-1970s. Among those organizations which either operate or are planning to operate such systems are Western Union, RCA, and American Satellite Corporation.

The Federal Communications Commission (FCC), in its Report and Order in Docket 16495, adopted on March 10, 1970, declared that applicants proposing multipurpose domestic communications satellite systems should discuss the terms and conditions under which satellite services would be made available for noncommercial broadcast networks, and for data and computer usage in meeting the instructional, educational, and administrative requirements of educational institutions. There has been relatively little movement since then in terms of actual educational participation in such systems. In early 1975, the Public Broadcasting Service was involved in discussions concerning the possible use of commercial domestic satellites for interconnecting public television stations. It may be that switching to a satellite-based operation will provide a technically and economically attractive alternative to the current terrestrial AT&T interconnection.

At the end of 1974 a Public Service Satellite Consortium was formed, consisting of potential users from the education and health sectors. This organization is exploring a number of possible satellite options, and has been concerned initially with developing a sufficiently strong user base, articulating its requirements, and seeking financial support. The outcome of the efforts of the Consortium, and of the planning studies being carried out by public broadcasting agencies, will be important

factors in determining the future of educational satellite utilization in the U.S. Other important factors include the outcomes of the ATS-6 and CTS experiments.

CURRENT ISSUES

Many of the factors which will determine whether or not communications satellites are used extensively in education are administrative, economic, and political in nature, rather than technical. In the U.S., fixed/broadcast communications satellites are one of a number of information transfer technologies competing in a sector, namely education, which until now has not made extensive use of technology. Moreover, no operational satellite systems with relatively high-power transponders for directly interconnecting inexpensive earth-terminals are in sight. Much depends on the initiatives that Federal agencies concerned with educational and communications technology, the communications industry, and educational interests take to further the development of such systems. It should be kept in mind, however, that much of U.S. education is of a decentralized nature, whereas operational communications satellite systems for education are only feasible for large-scale utilization and wide-area coverage. Thus, organizational, legal, social, and political issues, as well as economic issues, become paramount. Some of these issues have begun to be analyzed (Walkmeyer, 1973; Morgan et al., 1975; Walkmeyer et al., 1975). The outcome of satellite initiatives by public broadcasting and by the Public Service Satellite Consortium may prove to be of importance in the future.

On the international scene, some interesting administrative and political issues arise, particularly with respect to the development of broadcasting satellite systems (Chayes et al., 1973). To what extent will countries participate in regional satellite systems involving new forms of technical, economic and political cooperation? To what extent and under what conditions can one country use a satellite to broadcast messages into the territory of another, messages which could possibly include hostile propaganda and advertising, and programs which disturb religious, cultural or social life under the disguise of educational programs? While the U.S. takes the position that its participation in an internationally agreed code of program content for broadcasting satellites is not possible, because the First Amendment to the U.S. Constitution provides that "Congress shall make no law ... abridging the freedom of speech, or of the press," the majority of the nations are pressing for such a code.

There are also a host of other issues which need resolution before cooperative regional or international educational satellite systems become a reality. These include issues related to copyright protection for the authors and performers of broadcast programs, protection of individuals from false statements through right of reply, and the costs versus the benefits associated with the large investments required for the deployment of such systems. The decade of the 70s may be crucial in determining whether such issues can be resolved, and whether communications satellites can truly live up to their visionary promise in the field of education.

NOTES

[1]The Soviet Union was the first nation to deploy a domestic communications satellite system, Molniya. The satellites are in an inclined, non-stationary orbit designed to provide complete coverage of the country's northernmost areas.

[2]During the spring of 1975, Brazil was involved in utilizing the ATS-6 satellite.

[3]An evaluation of the HET experiment is being carried out by the Syracuse University Research Corporation under National Institute of Education Sponsorship.

REFERENCES

Chayes, A. et al. *Satellite Broadcasting.* London: Oxford University Press, 1973.

Chitnis, E. V. et al. Indian Project: Satellite Instructional Television Experiment (SITE), *Proceedings of the Collogue International—Les Satellites d'Education,* Centre National d'Etudes Spatiales, Nice, France, May 1971.

Clarke, Arthur C. Extraterrestrial Relays. *Wireless World,* Vol. 51 No. 10, October 1945, pp. 305-328.

Commission on Non-Traditional Study. Diversity by Design. San Francisco: Jossey-Bass, 1973.

Federal Communications Commission. Docket 16495 in the Matter of Domestic Communciations Satellite Facilities. Rules and Orders dated March 20, 1970, June 16, 1972, and December 12, 1972, Washington, D.C.

Grayson, L. P., Norwood, F. W., and Wigren, H. E. Man-Made Moons: Satellite Communications for Schools. National Educational Association, Washington, D.C., 1972.

Koerner, J. Educational Technology: Does It have a Future in the Classroom? *Saturday Review,* 1973, Vol. 1, No. 4, 43-46.

Morgan, R. P., and Margolin, J. B. Systems for Emerging Nations: An Overview, in *Communication Satellites for the 70's: Systems* (N. E. Feldman and C. M. Kelly, eds.), Cambridge, Massachusetts: MIT Press, 1971, pp. 89-99.

_____, and Singh, J. P. A Guide to the Literature on Application of Communications Satellites to Educational Development. An ERIC Paper, ERIC Clearinghouse on Media and Technology, Stanford University, California, April 1972.

_____. Satellite Utilization for Educational Communications in the United States. AAS Paper No. 73-150, 19th Annual Meeting, American Astronautical Society, Dallas, Texas, June 1973.

_____, Anderson, B. C., and Greenberg, E. Satellites for U.S. Education: Needs, Opportunities and Systems. *Communications Satellites: Systems and Advanced Concepts* (P. L. Bargellini, ed.), Cambridge, Massachusetts: MIT Press, 1974, pp. 441-480.

_____, Singh, J. P., Rothenberg, D., and Robinson, B. E. Large-Scale Educational Telecommunications Systems for the U.S.: An Analysis of Educational Needs and Technological Opportunities. Memorandum No. CG-75/1, Center for Development Technology, Washington University, St. Louis, Mo., April 1975.

Pierce, John R. *The Beginning of Satellite Communications.* San Francisco: San Francisco Press, 1968.

Potter, J. G., and Janky, J. M. The ATS-F Health-Education Technology Communications Systems. *Proceedings of 1973 International Conference on Communications,* Seattle, Washington, June 1973.

Pritchard, N. L. Communications Satellite Technology, Present and Future. Symposium on *Long-Term Prospects for Satellite Communications,* Instituto Internazionale Delle Comunicazioni, Genoa, Italy, June 1971.

Singh, J. P., Morgan, R. P., and Rosenbaum, F. J. Satellite Networks for Education. *Proceedings of the 1972 International Telemetering Conference,* Los Angeles, California, October 1972, pp. 419-439.

Singh, J. P., and Jamison, D. T. The Satellite Instructional Television Experiment in India: A Case History. Center for Development Technology, Washington University, St. Louis, Missouri, September 1973.

Walkmeyer, J. E. Jr. Planning Alternative Organizational Frameworks for a Large Scale Educational Telecommunications System Served by Fixed/Broadcast Satellites. Memorandum No. 73/3, Center for Development Technology, Washington University, St. Louis, June 1973.

_____, Morgan, R. P., and Singh, J. P. Market Scenarios and Alternative Administrative Frameworks for U.S. Educational Satellite Systems. Memorandum No. CG-75/2, Center for Development Technology, Washington University, St. Louis, Mo., April 1975.

ADDITIONAL RESOURCES

ERIC Clearinghouse on Media and Technology at Stanford University, Stanford, California 94305, has published a paper, "A Guide to the Literature on Application of Communications Satellites to Educational Development," by Morgan and Singh, which is a good first source in this area for non-specialists. In addition to introducing pertinent literature, it also describes concerned U.S. organizations, agencies, and information services.

The Center for Development Technology of Washington University (St. Louis, Missouri 63130) has been conducting a research program on application of communications satellites to educational development. This program, sponsored by the National Aeronautics and Space Administration (NASA) since 1969, is another source for up-to-date information on the subject.

MAJOR INTEREST GROUPS, ASSOCIATIONS, AND ORGANIZATIONS IN THE AREA OF EDUCATIONAL APPLICATION OF COMMUNICATIONS SATELLITES

Center for Development Technology
Box 1106, Washington University
St. Louis, Missouri 63130

Commissioner for Education
Federal Communications Commission
1919 M. Street, N.W.
Washington, D.C. 20554

Joint Council on Educational Telecommunications
1126 Sixteenth Street, N.W.
Washington, D.C. 20036

National Aeronautics and Space Administration
Communication Programs
Office of Applications
Washington, D.C. 20546

National Education Association
Division of Educational Technology
1201 Sixteenth Street, N.W.
Washington, D.C. 20036

Office of Telecommunications Policy
Department of Health, Education, and Welfare
Washington, D.C. 20201

National Institute of Education
Division of Technology and Productivity
Washington, D.C. 20208

15

EDUCATION IN LESS DEVELOPED COUNTRIES

by Philip J. Foster
Director, Comparative Education Center
Professor, Education and Sociology
University of Chicago
Chicago, Illinois

THE QUANTITATIVE DEVELOPMENT OF SCHOOLING

Problems of definition hinder efforts to make meaningful generalizations about education in the less developed nations. Formally, the latter are frequently regarded as a residual category that excludes Europe, the USSR, North America, the Antipodes, Japan, and South Africa (Unesco, 1972). This classification, however, obscures massive differences in levels of socio-economic development among the LDCs, and in this context Harbison and Myers (1964) made a pioneer attempt to develop a more useful taxonomy employing explicitly educational criteria. Their classification of LDCs, based on percentage enrollments at different school levels combined with other selected indices of stocks of trained manpower, can be faulted for its arbitrary weighting of scale items, but it highlights the risks involved in generalizing about educational issues over a wide range of countries that are extraordinarily heterogeneous in terms of any index of development.

Given this caveat, some indication of the recent expansion of schooling at all levels in the LDCs provides a useful background for the examination of substantive educational issues. Current data (Unesco, 1972) suggest that primary school enrollments over the two decades (1950/1960 and 1960/1970) rose by 84 and 64 percent respectively; the increase in secondary level enrollments for the same two decades was 143 and 122 percent, while higher education accelerated its rate of decennial expansion from 123 to 165 percent. These figures indicate that the rate of growth in primary schooling in many countries has now peaked, although numerical enrollments continue to rise. At the same time, higher education is growing exponentially, largely in response to great expansion in primary and secondary enrollments in the late 50s and 60s. While recognizing the existence of substantial accounting errors and serious problems connected with the development of meaningful systems of cross-national classification, it is likely that current enrollment ratios for the appropriate age categories in all LDCs now broadly stand at about 50 percent at the primary, 5 percent at the secondary and about 1 percent at the tertiary level, but with immense cross-national and regional variation. Thus in sub-Saharan Africa, for example (still the least formally educated of the continents), enrollment ratios for the appropriate age levels range from 14 percent (primary), 1 percent (secondary), and zero (tertiary) in Niger up to virtually full primary enrollment in the Cameroun, with ratios of 8 percent and 0.4 percent at the secondary and tertiary levels in that country. Such differences are equally apparent in the other less developed continents.

Moreover, current enrollment trends cannot be usefully extrapolated: numerical enrollments at all levels may increase, but in the very least developed nations rapid population growth, plus escalating educational costs (Jolly, 1969), make it unlikely that current lower-level enrollment ratios can be maintained—let alone rapidly expanded. In Ghana, for example, primary school ratios have declined from the middle 60s, while in Nigeria gross numerical enrollments at the primary level have fallen in the last decade. This situation may become more general in the poorest of the LDCs, with the consequence that universal primary schooling (or the achievement of general literacy) becomes an increasingly remote goal, while post-primary education of all types will remain inaccessible to all but a tiny minority of the relevant age cohorts.

EDUCATION AND SOCIAL CHANGE

Given such constraints upon quantitative expansion, the thrust of educational research and policy in the LDCs has taken a new direction in the last decade. Preoccupation with the achievement of quantitative targets has been replaced by attempts at more substantive analyses of the contribution of education to development. Three major issues present themselves: (1) the question of the relationship between education and economic growth, conceived both in terms of income-per-capita and income distribution; (2) the possible nexus between education and political development (in this case the notion of "development" is difficult to handle empirically, but is often conceived of in terms of "political stability"; the development of a sense of "national identity," particularly in those nations that have recently emerged from a period of colonial overrule, and "citizen participation" in the political process); (3) the theme of social equity, and equality of educational opportunity, constitutes an issue that underlies current economic and political dilemmas. In what measure does schooling contribute to a diminution or increase in social, economic, and cultural differentials as between subgroups in the LDCs, and to what extent does it provide enhanced opportunities for occupational and social mobility for the less privileged segments of national populations?

These broad sets of issues are in some measure amenable to empirical inquiry, but issues 2 and 3, in particular, are undergirded by broad normative questions that must be addressed if meaningful educational planning for development is to occur. Further, it is only too infrequently recognized that insofar as broad educational goals can be meaningfully ranked, policies concerned with pursuing either economic, political, or egalitarian objectives may be essentially in conflict: an educational system designed, for example, to maximize the economic contribution of schooling would probably look very different from one structured with primarily egalitarian considerations in mind.

EDUCATION AND ECONOMIC DEVELOPMENT

In an early study, Bowman and Anderson (1963) undertook a cross-national exploration of the relation between income-per-capita and various measures of education. Correlations between levels of economic development and schooling were high at both upper and lower ends of the development continuum, but relationships were much more indeterminate over the middle range. Inferentially, formal education was seen to be of varying significance at different levels of development, although the data suggested that widespread primary schooling, and a literacy threshold of about 20 percent, was particularly crucial at the very earliest stages of development.

1. The Manpower Planning Approach

Bowman and Anderson's conclusions had little impact in the middle and later 60s, when research and policy in the LDCs tended to focus on the provision of high- and middle-level manpower as a principal key to economic growth. The stock of such manpower was conceived to be dependent on the size of the secondary and tertiary educational sectors and, correspondingly, resources were proportionately directed to the postprimary levels.

However, lacking adequate data and resting upon questionable assumptions about the relations between schooling and development, early attempts at manpower forecasting were of questionable utility (Ahmad and Blaug, 1973).

2. The Rate of Return Approach

Apart from the difficulty of converting forecasts into educational equivalents, it was apparent that projections of educational needs in the LDCs could not be made without reference to notions of "price" and "productivity." Thus, as manpower planning has declined as an instrument of formal educational policy, there has been a more recent development of attempts to assess the contribution of education in terms of costs and benefits, with particular concentration on the calculation of private and social rates of return to different types and levels of schooling in the LDCs. This literature is now fairly extensive, and examples include Blaug et al., 1969; Bowles, 1967; Carnoy, 1967; Clark and Fong, 1970; Hinchcliffe, 1971; Rogers, 1972; Smyth and Bennett, 1967.

In a summary of research in this tradition, Psacharopoulos (1973) concludes that the most profitable level of investment is generally at the primary level, with only a modest social payoff to secondary and particularly higher education. Moreover, the returns to investment in schooling are normally above those accruing to those in physical capital. The evidence thus far makes a strong case for increased investment in lower level schooling in the LDCs, and suggests that, in view of high rates of substitution in production between different types of educated manpower, cost-benefit analysis provides a more cogent basis for making educational planning decisions than do manpower forecasts. A major development in the next decade may well consist of attempts to build cost-benefit considerations into manpower planning models that have thus far been based on essentially demographic-type data.

3. Education and the Social Psychology of Development

Both manpower and cost-benefit approaches, however, do not consider a series of intervening variables through which educational "inputs" are transformed into economic "outputs." In other words, to what extent does schooling contribute to the acquisition of economically relevant skills—or, perhaps more important, to the development of new attitudes and dispositions that are, in turn, manifested in changed patterns of behavior that enhance productivity? This latter line of investigation lies within the sociological and social-psychological tradition, and is best exemplified in the work of Inkeles (1969), Kahl (1968), and McClelland (1961, 1966). The latter has attempted to establish that development is correlated with the existence of a high level of "need for achievement," and that the achievement syndrome is related to schooling. Moreover, he has suggested that the need for achievement can be raised as a result of deliberately designed instruction (McClelland, 1969).

A second body of cross-national research in the same broad tradition, by Inkeles et al., related development to the existence of "modern men" in national populations. Modern attitudinal orientations (other things being equal) are conceived to be potentially significant for development, and it is empirically demonstrable that level of formal education is uniformly the strongest predictor of scores on modernization scales.

Criticism of the social-psychological approach to the problem of education and economic development takes several forms. First, it has been argued (Stephenson, 1968) that modernization scales are ethnocentric in nature and have little relevance for the LDCs, though, in fact, such scales exhibit a high degree of cross-national validity and reliability. Second, such research may have little relevance to educational planning decisions that of necessity must be made on the basis of manpower or cost-benefit types of analysis. Third, although correlations between education and economically significant attitudes are empirically demonstrable, it is difficult to factor out true "school effects" as distinct from attitudinal maturation that may be correlated with, but not consequent upon, schooling. Armer and Youtz (1969) argue that school effects depend in large measure on the curriculum of educational institutions, but Holsinger (1973) has suggested more convincingly that the modernization potential of schools stems more from their general structural attributes than their formal curriculum.

EDUCATION AND POLITICAL DEVELOPMENT

In structural terms the more educated nations can be regarded as politically developed, insofar as their political institutions exhibit a higher level of differentiation, along with the existence of integrative mechanisms for the effective incorporation of diverse interests into the general polity. However, other more normatively-based conceptions of political development hinge upon such notions as "citizen participation" and "stability," defined largely in terms of the orderly transfer of authority within the context of a competitive political process. Lipset (1959, 1963) has shown, for example, that the existence of Western-type democracy is substantially correlated with widespread diffusion of formal schooling and literacy. A fuller treatment of these themes has since been made by Cutright (1963) and McCrone and Cnudde (1967), who examined the relationship between democratic political development, education, urbanization, and mass communication. Moreover, it is generally demonstrable that in terms of individual political attitudes, level of formal education is correlated with "liberalism," "tolerance," and a higher sense of political efficacy (Lipset, 1963; Almond and Verba, 1963). On the basis of this kind of evidence it is not surprising that many LDCs have regarded educational investment as justified in terms of the political socialization effects of schooling and its presumed contribution to national integration, particularly in countries with ethnically and culturally diverse populations. In short, the schools are expected to contribute to the creation of a common national "political culture."

Other investigations have suggested, however, that the rapid diffusion of schooling in the LDCs can (at least in the short run) enhance rather than diminish overt conflict, and perhaps lead to increased political instability (Foster, 1962; Abernethy, 1969; Coleman, 1965). Where education is in limited supply, and largely controls access to mobility opportunities and political power, then inequalities in educational provision (particularly when these are linked to ethnic or regional differentials) become a focus of political dissent. Moreover, the educational system itself becomes politicized, and constitutes an arena wherein traditional hostilities obtain focus (S. and L. Rudolph, 1972). Again, insofar as formal schooling is assumed to generate higher levels of occupational and social aspiration that cannot be met within the context of existing resources, then education indirectly becomes a contributory factor to political conflict along class lines. It is necessary, therefore, to distinguish between schooling as a potential agency of general political socialization and its role as a structural element contributing to political conflict between cultural and ethnic groups or emergent class interests.

In this context, a good deal of commentary on education in the LDCs has been focused on the "school leaver problem" (Callaway, 1963; Gutkind, 1970; Hunter, 1962). It is suggested that increased educational outputs (initially at the primary, but subsequently at secondary and even higher levels) tend to outstrip job opportunities in the modern sector of less developed economies. Consequent widespread unemployment among youth, it is averred, linked with massive integration to urban centers, will create a massively unstable political situation. However, empirical research (Brownstein, 1972; Dubbeldam, 1970; McQueen, 1969) suggests that in Africa, at least, these conclusions are hardly justified: school leavers do not migrate on the scale that has been assumed, and movement to the towns is usually temporary. Further, although access to full-time paid wage employ-

ment becomes increasingly difficult to obtain by those with lower educational qualifications, it is demonstrable that most of the latter are productively absorbed into a range of economic activities marginal to both the modern and traditional sectors. In short, the "school leaver problem" may turn out to be more an artifact of a certain tradition of social research, rather than a substantive political issue, in many of the LDCs.

EDUCATION AND SOCIAL EQUALITY

The governments of most LDCs, particularly those of the postcolonial nations, are eommitted to raising levels of social welfare, and within this general rubric the provision of equality of educational opportunity becomes a salient theme. Insofar as schooling is probably a more significant means of occupational mobility and status acquisition than it was in the developed nations at earlier periods in their history, it follows that governments in the LDCs are under massive pressure to provide increased access to formal education for their citizens.

It is evident, however, that most LDCs are still characterized by major inequalities in the distribution of schooling, in terms of region, social origin, and ethnicity (Clignet and Foster, 1966; Foster, 1965; Olson, 1972; Havighurst and Gouveia, 1969). Such differentials have often initially resulted from uneven internal patterns of economic change, since expansion in the demand for schooling is typically correlated with the growth of an exchange, rather than a subsistence, economy. However, although there may be clear historical reasons for patterns of inequality, such explanations do not serve to stem pressures for equity from substantial minorities who perceive themselves to be left behind in the development process.

Unfortunately, it is demonstrable that at some stages of educational development relative imparities in educational access may increase rather than diminish, even when enrollments are expanding at all levels. This paradoxical, if sometimes short-term, consequence demonstrates that mere quantitative growth in schooling does not lead to the "democratization" of educational opportunity, since available resources may be disproportionately devoted to urban centers or other more economically advanced regions, or to those students whose superior academic performance is correlated with higher levels of socio-economic background. This is not to suggest that educational opportunities are monopolized by more privileged strata or regions, since it may still be the case that the vast majority of students come from less privileged sectors within which the bulk of national populations are to be found (Foster, 1969). Nonetheless, marked imparities exist and are extraordinarily difficult to eradicate, even where major resources are devoted to the task of creating equality of opportunity. Moreover, given limited resources and a high rate of growth where child population exceeds the rate of expansion in available school places at all levels, it is possible in some areas that the profile of student populations may become more exclusive. In short, far from being effective instruments of mobility for underprivileged groups, the schools (particularly at postprimary levels) could function largely as "status maintenance" institutions for the offspring of minorities whose initial status and levels of educational attainment distinguish them from the general population (Reimer, 1972). This is only a contingent possibility, but it is quite evident that concern over the "elitist" implications of educational development has led to major reappraisals of educational strategies in several LDCs in recent years. Undoubtedly, the most major transformations of educational structures have been effected in the socialist nations of Cuba, China, and Tanzania (Paulston, 1973; Lee, 1973; Odia, 1971). However, even where other LDCs have not attempted such radical solutions to their educational problems, it is not unusual to find the explicit or implicit use of regional or ethnic "quotas" as a policy tool designed to achieve greater equity in the distribution of schooling (Takei, Bock, and Saunders, 1973).

SOME CURRICULAR ISSUES

The preceding discussion of salient problems of education in the LDCs has been concerned with the supply and distribution of schooling rather than the question of educational content. However, a substantial proportion of literature on education in the LDCs has dealt with problems of curricular change, and, in the case of the postcolonial states, this focuses upon effort to adapt metropolitan curricula to local conditions and needs. Unfortunately, most of this writing is vague and prescriptive in nature, and in the absence of reliable evaluative research, is of questionable utility. To give an example, it is not clear in the context of rural development that agriculturally oriented curricula in lower-level schools have any significant effect on the attitude of youth toward farming or rural life in general (Foster, 1965(b)). Likewise, in the political sphere it is by no means evident that curriculum has much to do with the creation of new political commitments and dispositions. It is possible to point to a number of concrete issues of this kind in the LDCs and conclude that it is doubtful whether major curriculum change can be effected in the short run (Beeby, 1966). Indeed, the whole question of whether curriculum reform plays any significant role in more general processes of social and economic change is still moot. There is one area of curriculum, however, in which the schools do play a major role, and that is in the provision of basic literacy. Insofar as literacy leads to major changes in patterns of communication behavior, it can be safely said that schooling stands at the heart of the whole development process.

REFERENCES

Abernethy, D. *The Political Dilemma of Popular Education.* Stanford: Stanford University Press, 1969.

Ahamad, B., and Blaug M., eds. *The Practice of Manpower Forecasting.* Washington, D.C.: Jossey-Bass/Elsevier, 1973.

Almond, G. A., and Verba, S. *The Civic Culture.* Princeton: Princeton University Press, 1963.

Armer, M., and Youtz, R. Formal Education and Individual Modernity in an African Society. *American Journal of Sociology,* 1971, *76,* 604-626.

Beeby, C. E. *The Quality of Education in Developing Countries.* Cambridge: Harvard University Press, 1966.

Blaug, M., Layard, P. R. G., and Woodhall, M. *The Causes of Graduate Unemployment in India.* London: Allen Lane, the Penguin Press, 1969.

Bowles, S. The Efficient Allocation of Resources in Education. *Quarterly Journal of Economics,* 1967, *31,* 189-219.

Bowman, M. J., and Anderson, C. A. Concerning the Role of Education in Development. *Old Societies and New States,* ed. Geertz, C. Glencoe: Free Press, 1963, 247-279.

Brownstein, L. *Education and Development in Rural Kenya.* New York: Praeger, 1972.

Callaway, A. Unemployment Among African School Leavers. *Journal of Modern African Studies,* 1963, *1,* 351-371.

Carnoy, M. Rates of Return to Schooling in Latin America. *Journal of Human Resources,* 1967, *2,* 359-374.

Clark, D. H., and Fong, P. E. Returns to Schooling and Training in Singapore. *Malayan Economic Review,* 1970. 15.

Clignet, R., and Foster, P. *The Fortunate Few: A Study of Secondary Schools and Students in the Ivory Coast.* Evanston: Northwestern University Press, 1966.

Coleman, J. S. *Education and Political Development.* Princeton: Princeton University Press, 1965.

Cutright, P. National Political Development, *Politics and Social Life,* ed. N. Polsby. Boston: Houghton-Mifflin, pp. 569-582.

Dubbeldam, L. F. B. *The Primary School and the Community in Mwanza District, Tanzania.* Groningen, Holland: Wolters-Noordhoff, 1970.

Foster, P. Ethnicity and the Schools in Ghana, *Comparative Education Review,* 1962, *6,* 127-135.

_____. *Education and Social Change in Ghana.* Chicago: University of Chicago Press, 1965 (a).

_____. The Vocational School Fallacy in Development Planning. *Education and Economic Development,* ed. Anderson, C. A., and Bowman, M. J., Chicago: Aldine Press, 1965 (b), 142-166.

_____. Education, Economy and Equality. *Interchange,* 1971, *2,* 51-61.

Gutkind, P. G. W. *The Energy of Despair: the Social Organization of the Unemployed in Two African Cities.* Montreal: Centre for Developing Area Studies, McGill University, 1970.

Harbison, F., and Myers, C. A. *Education, Manpower and Economic Growth.* New York: McGraw-Hill, 1964.

Havighurst, R. J., and Gouveia, A. J. *Brazilian Secondary Education and Socioeconomic Development.* New York: Praeger, 1969.

Hinchcliffe, K. The Rate of Return to Education in Ghana. *Economic Bulletin of Ghana,* 1971, 15.

Holsinger, D. The Elementary School as Modernizer: A Brazilian Study. *International Journal of Comparative Sociology,* 1973, 14.

Hunter, G. *The New Societies of Tropical Africa.* Oxford: Oxford University Press, 1962.

Inkeles, A. Making Men Modern: On the Causes and Consequences of Individual Change in Six Developing Countries. *American Journal of Sociology,* 1969, *75,* 208-225.

Jolly, R. Costs and Confusions in African Education: Some Implications of Recent Trends. *Education in Africa,* ed. Jolly, R. Nairobi: East African Publishing House, 1969, 47-62.

Kahl, J. A. *The Measurement of Modernism: A Study of Values in Brazil and Mexico.* Austin: University of Texas Press, 1968.

Lee, H. P. Education and Rural Development in China Today. *Education and Rural Development.* London: Evans Bros., 1973, 209-233.

Lipset, S. M. Some Social Requisites of Democracy: Economic Development and Political Legitimacy. *American Political Science Review,* 1959, *53,* 99-105.

_____. *Political Man.* New York: Doubleday, Anchor Edition, 1963.

McClelland, D. C. *The Achieving Society*. Princeton: Van Nostrand Co., 1961.

_____. Does Education Accelerate Economic Growth? *Economic Development and Cultural Change*, 1966, *14*, 257-278.

_____, and Winter, D. G. *Motivating Economic Achievement*. New York: Free Press, 1969.

McCrone, D. J., and Cnudde, C. F. Toward a Communications Theory of Democratic Development: A Causal Model. *American Political Science Review*, 1967, *61*, 72-79.

McQueen, A. J. Unemployment and the Future Orientations of Nigerian School-Leavers. *Canadian Journal of African Studies*, 1969, *3*.

Odia, S. Rural Education and Training in Tanzania. *International Labour Review*, 1971, *103*, 13-28.

Olson, J. B. Secondary Schools and Elites in Kenya, *Comparative Education Review*, 1972, *16*, 44-53.

Paulston, R. Cuban Rural Education: A Strategy for Revolutionary Development. *Education and Rural Development*. London: Evans Bros., 1973, 234-260.

Psacharopoulos, G. *Returns to Education*. San Francisco and Amsterdam: Jossey-Bass/Elsevier, 1973.

Reimer, E. *School is Dead*. New York: Doubleday, 1972.

Rogers, D. C. Student Loan Programs and the Returns to Investment in Higher Levels of Education in Kenya. *Economic Development and Cultural Change*, 1972, *20*, 243-259.

Rudolph, S. H., and L. I. *Education and Politics in India*. Cambridge: Harvard University Press, 1972.

Smyth, J. A., and Bennett, N. L. Rates of Return on Investment in Education: A Tool for Short-term Educational Planning Illustrated with Ugandan Data. *World Yearbook of Education*. London: Evans Bros., 1967, 299-322.

Stephenson, J. B. Is Everyone Going Modern? A Critique and a Suggestion for Measuring Modernism. *American Journal of Sociology*, 1968, *74*, 265-275.

Takei, Y., Bock, J. C., and Saunders, B. *Educational Sponsorship by Ethnicity*. Oxford, Ohio: Ohio University Papers in International Studies, South East Asia Series, No. 28, 1973.

Unesco, *Statistical Yearbook, 1971*. Paris: Unesco, 1972.

16

RURAL EDUCATION

Everett D. Edington, Director
Educational Resources Information Center
Clearinghouse for Rural Education and Small Schools
Las Cruces, New Mexico

One of the real problems concerning the small rural school today is the fact that a great many important decisions which relate to the future are based not upon fact and knowledge, but on opinion and emotion. This is true both for those persons in favor of the small schools and also for those who are opposed to their existence, and want to enlarge them into larger units. There is little doubt that a number of small schools in the United States today should not continue to exist in their present form. Their students would get much better educational programs if they were consolidated or merged into larger units. On the other hand, a great many students may

have been severely handicapped by losing some of the advantages of the smallness and closeness of the rural school when moved into a larger unit. There is also the problem of isolation. Large numbers of schools cannot consolidate or merge with other school districts because of the distances involved and the terrain in the areas in which they are located.

There is a misconception by many today that there are a very small percentage of school-age youth in rural America. This is not true, as approximately 25% of the population live in the country and in towns of 2500 or less, while over 35% live in nonmetropolitan areas of 50,000 or less. Roughly one-third of the population do not live in urban or suburban areas (Tamblyn, 1971).

Let us first look briefly at some of the characteristics of rural America and its schools. Most of the research does not paint a happy picture for education of children in rural areas. Frieda Gehlen (1969), in her presentation at the National Working Conference on Solving Education Problems in Sparsely Populated Areas, in Denver, painted a bleak picture for a great many rural schools. She classified them as having a limited curriculum, conservative tax picture, conservative faculty and staff, and a student population homogeneous in background and values. She indicated that controversial areas in which conflict would be likely to arise are usually either eliminated or not faced squarely. Gehlen did indicate, however, that change could come as a result of the will of the small rural community to improve educational opportunities.

Edward Breathitt (1967), in his presentation at the National Outlook Conference on Rural Youth, painted a similar bleak picture. He indicated that the youth of rural America are not afforded an equal educational opportunity. The disadvantages are general in nature and are not confined to any single area of the country, but are widespread enough so that they constitute a national problem. He indicated that probably the greatest need would be to change the migration stream from rural to urban America. There is some indication that these streams of migration have leveled off. Some even feel that the migration has reversed and we are seeing more people going to rural areas. This may be true of the suburban areas surrounding the cities, but is not necessarily true of the isolated rural communities.

Nels Ackerson (1967), also at the National Outlook Conference on Rural Youth, indicated that rural youth are confronted with a serious paradox of opportunities and frustrations. Opportunities are plentiful for those who possess skills and abilities necessary for competing in our technologically advanced society, but limited for those who are unable to compete in our society in either job competition or in social processes. He felt it was necessary to accept three challenges: (1) to take full advantage of available rural opportunities; (2) to realize limitations of rural life, recognizing that opportunities exist elsewhere; and (3) to be aware of our responsibilities, not only to rural America but to an America where there are no divisions between rural and urban communities.

Probably the worst thing that can be done is to bemoan the fact that there are disadvantages in rural

America. What is needed is to recognize the advantages and opportunities, and capitalize on these in our educational programs.

William Clement's 1970 report, *Ideal High School Size, a Mirage in the Desert,* points out a number of advantages of the small school. These are as follows:

Better pupil-teacher ratios;

Varied assignments for the high school teachers, which aid them in not becoming too specialized in broader inner concepts;

Individualized guidance and counseling. He here stresses the fact that in smaller schools, the administrators and teachers have a much better opportunity to know the child and to provide better guidance; and

Working conditions of teachers are usually more acceptable in smaller schools and rural communities. These conditions also provide a more wholesome atmosphere for students.

Many of the things which he points out have not necessarily been proven, but are widely advocated by those persons favoring the small schools.

Paul Ford (1967), in his study of remote high schools in the northwestern part of the United States, found that a large number of daily preparations did not seem to trouble teachers in small high schools. The teachers from both large and small schools acquired a great deal of job satisfaction from the personal relationships with students, and teachers in the small schools are considerably more involved with student activities than teachers in large high schools. This helps give the closer contact of the teachers with their students. He also found that students from smaller high schools tend to participate in more high school activities, particularly student government and athletics, than did their peers in large high schools. The variety of such activities was quite limited in the small high schools, and the students in these schools did not believe these activities to be as important to their future life as did their peers from the larger schools. He also reported the lack of cultural-type activities for the rural school student. Ford also found that in the Northwest the teachers from the larger schools used more innovations than those from the small schools.

A great many of these types of disadvantages can be overcome, however, with proper planning. He also stated (Ford, 1967) that it appeared that neither administrators nor teachers in small high schools have availed themselves of the educational potential offered by very small classes or frequent student-teacher contact. Activities could be planned that would take the students away from their small rural area into larger urban settings. This could be done not only during the school year, but also during the summer-time activities. An excellent example of this type of summer program is the one developed in Cochise County, Arizona, in which students travel to a large Army base in the area to obtain various skills. This travel to a different environment also provides the opportunity to obtain needed social skills.

The major conclusion of Ford's report was that the small remote high school does not take advantage of its small size. Frequent contacts among teachers, students, and parents are not utilized to offer imaginative programs for the education of rural youth. Rather than taking advantage of the potential that exists, small high schools appear to be imitating traditional patterns of program organization and staff utilization. Some of Ford's major recommendations for those schools which were remote and necessary were as follows:

The Division of Curriculum Instruction of the State Department of Public Instruction should be responsible for planning and development. This responsibility would include developing appropriate types of curriculum activities for the school.

An advisory panel made up of teachers and administrators representing the small schools should meet with State Department's instruction personnel and university educators in planning their programs. Each panel should probe deeply into the potential problems of such a school, and serve in an advisory capacity as the Division carried forth arrangements to improve education in the small school districts.

A series of inservice training sessions and summer institutes for teachers and administrators of the small schools should be conducted by the State Department of Education.

The State Department of Education and Universities and Colleges should provide consultants to work with the problems of the rural schools.

As soon as possible the State Department should establish at least one demonstration project in the state to illustrate the latest effective practices in curriculum design and staff organization appropriate to remote schools.

FINANCES

Generally, research has shown that the per-pupil cost in small schools is much higher than in the large schools. This may be due to the much lower pupil-teacher ratios than are found in the larger schools. This enables teachers to have much looser contacts with the students. The study done by the Massachusetts State Board of Education (1968) did not find the cost difference to be true. In a comparison of regional and small high schools, they found that the regional schools cost approximately one hundred dollars per student more to educate than the small rural high schools. The explanation given for this was that the regional schools provided a much more comprehensive program than did the small schools, and provided more opportunities in areas such as vocational education, language laboratories, and other more expensive curriculum areas. The Massachusetts Study was, however, unique in its findings concerning the costs per pupil in the rural versus the larger schools.

Most of those states having large rural populations have fewer fiscal resources per child to support educational programs than the average state. When personal income per child of school age is used as an index of wealth, 29 of the 34 states falling below the national average are states with large rural populations (Tamblyn, 1971). The inability to support educational programs in rural states is often reflected in poorer facilities and equipment, less curriculum material, and less qualified teachers. This has resulted in high dropout rates and less qualified graduates than from other schools. The latter is debatable and difficult for many people to accept, but evidence tends to show them having less success in college and more poorly equipped to enter employment. Rural areas have also not fared well in receiving their share of the Federal dollar for human resources-type programs. Tamblyn (1973) reported the following:

> Federal spending for human resources, for example, has greatly favored metropolitan counties. This is illustrated by the following comparisons for counties experiencing pronounced population declines: (a) per capita Federal welfare payments were roughly four times greater in metropolitan than in nonmetropolitan counties, (b) per capita outlays for health services were four times greater in metropolitan counties, and (c) per capita Federal outlays for manpower training and development were three times greater in metropolitan counties. Despite a greater incidence of substandard housing in nonmetropolitan counties, per capita Federal outlays there were only half as large as in metropolitan counties. While nonmetropolitan counties accounted for two-thirds of all substandard housing units in 1968, they received only 16 percent of all housing assistance. (p. 14)

> Though nonmetropolitan areas account for about half of all children between the ages of 6 to 17 years in families with income below the poverty level, these areas received only 41 percent of the outlays for Title I of the Elementary and Secondary Education Act, 36 percent of Headstart and Headstart Follow-through, 24 percent of Aid to Families With Dependent Children, and 20 percent of all Child Welfare Services funds. (p. 16)

CURRICULUM

Traditionally speaking, the small school is far behind when compared to the larger school in the number and types of programs offered to the students. Some interesting facts come to light, however, when one observes some things that are happening today in our more innovative schools. Many aspects of the open classroom are very little different from those that have existed for many years in the old one-room schools. Students progress at their own rate in a completely ungraded situation, with the teacher working with individual students and the students helping each other. Many courses can be developed which fit better into the flexible scheduling programs possible in small schools.

In Oregon, educators reported the implementation of a program which divided the high school language arts program into sixteen quarter credits needed for graduation (Blaser, 1970). The classes were grouped by student ability and interests. They also developed an optional vocational math course, as well as laboratory oriented science courses for ninth graders which the students could use in discovering methods in the physical science program.

In the Dilingham High School District, Dilingham City School District, Alaska (The Nongraded Trimester, 1971), in high school grades 7 through 12 a scheduled

curriculum was established which provided students and teachers with an active voice in determining their educational experiences. The result was a group of over 200 one-half credit minicourses offering a variety of time arrangements. All courses were nongraded through the ninth grade level. Junior high level students were given the opportunity to schedule into regular high school level courses. The school year was divided into 60-day trimesters and 63-minute time blocks, consisting of 3 twenty-one-minute modules. Reaction to the new schedule in curriculum appeared to be thoroughly favorable from students, teachers, and others.

One of the most comprehensive programs in the development of curricula for the rural schools is that carried out by the Northwest Laboratory in Portland, Oregon. At the present time, the program has been funded to develop a community approach to the problems of the small rural schools. This will be carried on for a minimum of at least three years, with possible funding for two additional years. The major purpose will be a concerted effort to determine how total community involvement can provide for better educational programs for rural students.

An excellent example of the curriculum innovation is the Art-by-Telephone Program as reported by Michael J. Clarke (1970). This program, funded under Title III of the Elementary and Secondary Education Act, involved rural high schools in Nevada, Oregon, Idaho, and Utah. The program was designed to offer art instruction from a master teacher to students enrolled in high schools with limited resources. Instruction in art was provided by joining a number of widely separated small rural high schools into a conference situation in which all units of the system, including the instructor, were served by common two-way communications-amplified telephone service. Each school was equipped with the telephone amplifier, receiver, and transmitter so that the student in the classroom could hear all conversation and also initiate oral response. The problem with this and other similar types of programs is that as soon as funding is gone the program is dropped. State Departments of Education need to take greater responsibility for providing such curriculum innovations to the small rural schools within their states.

One of the greatest criticisms of the rural schools in the area of curriculum has been their lack of adequate vocational and occupational training programs for the students. This did not need to be so, as was pointed out by Gordon Swanson (1970) in his paper presented at the National Training Institute for Vocational Related Personnel in Rural Areas, in Auburn, Alabama. He states that organizational and administrative programs in vocational education in rural areas can be strengthened to better meet the needs of the students. Other examples of programs in rural areas are the Utah Integrated Shop Programs and Mobile Office Education Programs in Southern Utah (Loveless, 1971), and The Fort Benton Trades and Industry Curriculum Outlines in Fort Benton, Montana (Fort Benton Trades, 1971). Each of these programs shows that industrial and occupational-type programs can be initiated in rural schools. Rural school administrators can take better advantage of their limited work stations for co-op programs and extend the boundaries of their schools into neighboring cities in order to develop better cooperative programs. In some cases, excellent cooperation has been obtained with large military establishments, thus providing work stations for students in the rural areas. A recent set of guidelines for establishing cooperative programs in small schools is found in Cooperative Vocational Programs in Small Schools, a suggested guide for program planning, which is published by the ERIC Clearinghouse on Rural Education and Small Schools, (1972) in conjunction with the University of Nebraska.

ROLE OF INTERMEDIATE UNIT

A major breakthrough in the broadening and more efficient use of educational resources in rural areas is the broadened role of the Intermediate Unit, wherein those types of services that smaller districts are unable to afford are provided over a larger area. This requires that each small district need assume only a portion of the costs.

Types of services vary widely, and may include guidance services; special instructional programs; computer services; school health services; and services of consultants, coordinators, and supervisors. Growing very steadily in this area are programs that are transported from one school to another. For example, audiovisual services have been supplied to many small schools on a cooperative basis.

Another type of program that may be shared is the inservice training program for teachers, wherein an intermediate unit (county, service center, or other type of unit) may provide inservice programs for teachers in the area. Many states—such as Texas, Nebraska, South Carolina, Michigan, and New York—have made these types of units legal by appropriate legislation. The units are organized in different ways in the various states, and may or may not have taxing power. In some the policy-making boards are lay people, where in others they are composed of professional representatives of the districts involved.

A very effective resource that these units have been able to provide is that of information. Many of the units serve as resource centers and have ERIC files as well as other types of materials available for use by students and teachers.

Another concept within the realm of shared services is that of sharing the students. For example, students may travel from one district to another in order to receive certain types of programs. This is reciprocal, in that one small district may have one type of program and another district may have another type of program, with students switching districts to attend those schools offering programs to meet the students' needs.

IMPROVEMENT OF TEACHER QUALITY AND PERFORMANCE

Possibly the most rewarding of all types of practices and techniques for improvement of the small school are those responsive to improvement of teacher quality and performance. Teacher quality may be linked to two factors beyond the immediate control of the school administrator: (1) program deficiencies in the institutions involved in preparation of teachers, and (2) shortcomings in the local socioeconomic environment which preclude the recruitment and retention of high-quality teachers. While the first of these problems may be solved by bringing pressure to bear upon the teacher-training institutions, the second may require considerable effort, including financial, to permit small schools to compete for quality teachers. This may tend to take care of itself, however, if the adequate supply of teachers continues.

The most immediate returns, however, can be gained from inservice programs for practicing teachers and administrators. In a great many cases, the first change that must take place relates to pointing out the need for inservice training to the local educators and the lay leadership. In this area small amounts of resources, if managed wisely, can be quite effective. This may be done at the county level, or even in a larger district, since a number of teachers and administrators may share the individuals or materials providing the inservice training. Some financial assistance from state or Federal levels may be necessary to aid the rural school districts in implementing such programs. The "problem districts" could be identified, and then massive programs could be initiated in working with the educational personnel to bring about the necessary improvement.

A good example of an inservice program for improving instructional performance of teachers in rural schools was conducted by the Southern Association of Colleges and Schools (Codwell, 1969). The purpose of the program was to determine the effects of microteaching on the instructional behavior of rural school teachers. As a result of teachers having had the opportunity to observe and analyze their teaching behavior on videotape, there were significant indications of improvement in instructional skill, teacher attitude, and teacher-pupil interaction.

USE OF TECHNOLOGY

One of the real possibilities in improving instruction in the rural schools is that of improving the use of technology. The use of radio, television, telephone and other media could greatly broaden the educational opportunities for rural youth.

A major program which will soon be in operation is a satellite which will be orbited above the Rocky Mountain states to beam television programs on a number of different channels to schools within this area. A major concern of the project will be that of beaming adequate curriculum education programs to the students in the rural areas in the Rocky Mountain states. Television has long been used in these areas, but for those schools that are too remote or too far removed from educational television, this satellite would be a real advantage. Videotape materials, too, could be used more extensively in the rural schools. As was mentioned earlier, the use of amplified telephones now coming into use is a quite inexpensive method to bring a speaker or expert to the classroom by telephone.

GUIDANCE SERVICES IN THE RURAL SCHOOLS

Guidance services in the rural schools many times do not have a person designated as a full-time guidance counselor, but can take advantage of the closeness of the teacher to the student, parent, and community and provide an excellent guidance program by utilizing those resources that are available. The guidance services in such a situation are not isolated, but an integral part of the classroom activities. Any program of improvement with rural schools must provide an extensive program of in-service education to the teachers. Many of the teachers have roots in the communities, are important members of the communities, and are well respected. State Departments of Education and intermediate units need to develop extensive inservice programs to take advantage of these characteristics of the teachers and to bring them up-to-date in modern technology.

CONCLUSION

In no way is it advocated that the small rural school is the best school in all situations. There are still many instances where consolidation would help meet some of the problems. However, in many isolated situations it is impossible for consolidation to take place. Also, in many situations the student would lose contact with his home community, and thus break ties which would be very beneficial to him. There are certain characteristics of the small school that can be taken advantage of to provide a more adequate educational program. The most important of these characteristics is the smallness itself, which can provide for more individualized instruction. The closeness that the student, teacher, parent, and community share also aids in developing the student in this setting. Care should be taken, however, not to let emotions get in the way of better educational programs; this should be done in both the large consolidated school and the small isolated school.

REFERENCES

Ackerson, Nels J. Rural Youth in a Changing World. October, 1967, 6 pp. ED 016 549.

Blaser, John W. *The Corbett Report on Non-Graded Language Arts, Functional Mathematics Option, and Introductory Physical Science.* Corbett High School, Oregon, January, 1970. 43 pp. ED 041 645.

Breathitt, Edward T. The Status of Rural America. October, 1967, 6 pp. ED 015 075.

Clark, Michael J., Allan, Blaine W., and Anderson, David N. *Art-by-Telephone: Design and Evaluation.* Clark County School District, Las Vegas, Nevada, 1970, 31 pp. ED 044 222.

Clements, William H. Ideal High School Size: A Mirage in the Desert. 1970, 24 pp. ED 055 689.

Codwell, John E. *A Demonstration of the Effect of an Adaptation of Microteaching on the Instructional Behavior of Rural School Teachers. Final Report.* Southern Association of Colleges and Schools, Atlanta, Georgia, October, 1969, 78 pp. ED 034 620.

Data Comparisons of Regional and Small High Schools. Massachusetts State Board of Education, Division of Research and Development, Woburn, Massachusetts, January, 1968, 3 pp. ED 052 879.

Ford, Paul, Hite, Herbert, and Koch, Norman. *Remote High Schools–The Realities.* Northwest Regional Educational Laboratory, Portland, Oregon, April, 1967, 73 pp. ED 012 208.

Fort Benton Trades & Industry Curriculum Outline. Fort Benton Public Schools, Montana, 1971, 66 pp. ED 062 030.

Gehlen, Frieda L. *The Political Aspects of Small Town and Rural Schools.* Paper presented at National Working Conference on Solving Educational Proglrmas in Sparsely Populated Areas, Denver, Colorado, March 17-19, 1969, New Mexico State University, University Park. ERIC Clearinghouse on Rural Education and Small Schools, May, 1969, 42 pp. ED 030 502.

Jongeward, Ray, and Heesacker, Frank. *Sharing Educational Services. PREP-XIII.* Northwest Regional Educational Laboratory, Portland, Oregon, 1969, 89 pp. ED 036 666.

Loveless, Austin G. *Utah Integrated Shop Program. Final Report.* Utah Research Coordinating Unit for Vocational and Technical Education, Salt Lake City, Utah, July, 1971, 27 pp. ED 056 793.

The Nongraded-Trimester-Minicourse Concept: Report to Date. Dilingham City School District, Alaska, May, 1971, 51 pp. ED 050 863.

Purpose and Potentials, Part One: Basic Program Plans. Annual Report to the United States Office of Education. Northwest Regional Educational Laboratory, Portland, Oregon, September, 1968, 194 pp. ED 050 854.

Swanson, Gordon. *Organization and Administration of Vocational Education for Rural Areas.* Paper presented at National Training Institute for Vocational and Related Personnel, Auburn, Alabama, April 7, 1970. National Center for Occupational Education, Raleigh, North Carolina, April, 1970, 13 pp. ED 040 801.

Tamblyn, Lewis R. *Rural Education in the United States.* Rural Education Associates, Washington, D.C., 1971. ED 054 884.

_____. *Inequality–A Portrait of Rural America.* Rural Education Associates, Washington D.C., 1973. ED 073 878.

University of Nebraska. *Cooperative Vocational Education in Small Schools: Suggested Guide for Program Planning.* Educational Resources Information Center, Clearinghouse on Rural Education and Small Schools, New Mexico State University, Las Cruces, New Mexico, March 1972.

17

COMMUNITY EDUCATION

by Jack D. Minzey, Director
Center for Community Education
Eastern Michigan University
Ypsilanti, Michigan

Community Education is a philosophical concept which serves the entire community by providing for all of the educational needs of all of its community members. It uses the local school to serve as the catalyst for bringing community resources to bear on community problems in an effort to develop a positive sense of community, improve community living, and develop the community process toward the end of self-actualization.

—Minzey, LeTarte, 1972, p. 19

This philosophy, while not new as a concept, is a relatively modern movement which has seen phenomenal growth in the past decade. There are currently 810 school districts with community education programs involving 3,867 buildings, 2,292 full- and part-time directors, and serving 5,236,480 people as either enrollees or participants. Expenditures for community education in 1973-1974 amounted to 55 million dollars. There are 53 Centers for Community Education located at institutions of higher education across the nation, and plans have been developed to increase that number to a minimum of 120. Seven hundred and fifty highly selected persons have been trained in community education through a one-year intern program offered by a consortium of universities, and another 3,000 persons have been trained in short-term training or graduate degrees in community education at various universities throughout the country.

There are six states which have passed legislation for community education, providing funds for the support of such programs, and six other states have legislation pending. Twenty-four states either have employed or are seeking community education consultants for their State Departments of Education. There has also been national interest in the community education movement, and in 1974 the Congress passed a Federal Community Education bill, employed a community education staff to implement the legislation, and appointed a National Community Education Advisory Council.

An organization called the National Community Education Association was begun in 1966, and currently boasts a membership of 2,000 persons. This organization provides various services for members, including an information clearinghouse and data bank. There are also 14 state or regional community education associations.

Several foundations and business organizations have shown interest in this concept and have provided assistance through funding. The *Phi Delta Kappan* devoted its November 1972 issue to this topic, and numerous other magazines have carried articles or complete issues on this subject. *The Community Education Journal* was introduced in February 1971 as a publication to report and promote the development of this concept. The National Congress of Parents and Teachers adopted community education as a part of their national platform in September 1971, and the Junior Chamber of Commerce did the same in March 1972. Several other national organizations have since endorsed this concept. In addition, there have been numerous supportive examples, such as the creation of a special community education committee by the North Central Association of Colleges and Secondary Schools, and a special study to determine the effects of community education on the design of educational facilities by the Council of Educational Facility Planners.

It is interesting to speculate on the reasons for this sudden interest in community education. Some people would attribute it to the growth and complexity of our modern-day society. These persons would generalize that the nature of our current social structure demands new roles for our institutions, and that community education is a necessary role which the public schools must

assume. Other people feel that community education is a role which schools used to carry out and have now slipped away from. They feel that schools no longer do all the things they are capable of doing, and that community education is not only the appropriate role of the school but that it makes good economic, educational, and social sense.

Another group thinks that community education is really the answer to the hypocrisies of education. They point out that community education addresses itself to such issues as relevancy of curriculum, interaction with the community, dealing with the child as a gestalt, education as a lifetime process, and community control of schools—issues which educators claim to believe in, but do not carry out in the discharge of their responsibilities. Still others feel that community education is a technique for restoring participatory democracy to our communities. And finally there are those who believe that community education is growing as a response to the demands being made by members of our society. These include demands for greater use of our school facilities, for more educational accountability, for serving adult educational needs, for attacking community problems, for attention to senior citizen concerns, for better communication, for coordination of resources, and for community involvement in decision-making.

Since community education has been in existence as a concept for a long time, there still remains the question of why the idea has not engendered similar excitement in the past. This may be partially explained by the fact that community education today is not the same as it had been conceived in the past, and this change in perception is at least partially responsible for the current receptivity. In the historical development of community education, the early promoters of this idea tended to stress the program aspect of community education. There were, to be sure, some pioneers who conceptualized a community development aspect of community education, but the publicity given to the movement went to those who emphasized program. Consequently, for many years community education was associated with recreation programs for youth, and adult-education programs covering such things as adult basic education, high school completion, vocational education, avocational programs and recreation.

The components of community education have expanded in recent years, however, and it has become a far more encompassing idea. The transition has actually gone from viewing community education as a set of add-on programs to one of developing a concept which affects the total philosophy of a school system and describes a major role expansion for education.

In order to get a better perception of community education, it is best to look at this concept by analyzing its ingredients. It should be pointed out that these ingredients are in addition to the traditional role which the school plays.

EXTENDED USE OF COMMUNITY FACILITIES

Professional educators and community members are well aware of the potential for expanded use of school facilities. Most school districts have great investments in land and buildings which lie idle for large portions of the school year. Many school buildings are in use less than 15 percent of the actual hours of the year. In a school district which practices community education, school facilities would be available for use by all community groups for all hours of the day, week, or year. In addition, coordination of all community facilities, along with those of the school, would assist in making maximum use of the total physical resources of the community.

MAKING CURRICULUM MORE RELEVANT

In considering the term relevancy, one must ask, relevant to what? In the case of curriculum, we are implying relevancy to the community. Many American schools of today are as separated from their communities as if a moat existed between them and the rest of the environment. In order to develop an appropriate curriculum, schools must know the community they serve and provide a program which more adequately serves community purposes. The community must be brought into the school and the school must be taken into the community. This interweaving of school and community will tend to enhance both, and result in a relationship which more effectively meets the goals of education.

MEETING THE EDUCATIONAL NEEDS OF THE ENTIRE COMMUNITY

When we look at the educational needs and the school's responsibilities in a community, we tend to focus on a small portion of the population and only a few years of the lives of that group that is to be served. Yet there are many educational needs which are being neglected. For the regular school-aged child, community education means extended activities of a remedial, enrichment, or recreation nature. Such activities would take place before and after school, week-ends, and summers.

For adults there should be the same educational opportunities as offered to the traditional students, and on an equal priority basis. The student body of the school would become all persons who live in that community. Such programs would include basic education, high school completion, recreation, avocational programs, and vocational training. There would also be other adult offerings such as dances, dinners, socials, public service meetings, cultural programs, and any other activities which the adult population might need or want.

EFFECTIVE USE OF SOCIAL AND GOVERNMENTAL RESOURCES

If one looks closely at most communities, it becomes apparent that there are many formal organizations, institutions, and agencies established to deal with community needs. Unfortunately, the services of these groups are not effectively delivered to most of those who qualify for such services. In fact, such services are rarely delivered to as many as 10 percent of those who could benefit. The problem generally encountered in providing such services is one of coordination and delivering the services to where it is convenient for recipients to take advantage of them.

In Community Education the community school becomes the delivery system to help solve this problem. The community school, which has the advantage of being a neighborhood facility, is in a position to know the problems of the community and the resources available. The community school director and his staff can coordinate the bringing together of problems with existing resources and develop resources where none previously existed.

DEVELOPMENT OF COMMUNITY PROCESS

This aspect of community education deals with the recapturing of the true sense of community through participatory democracy. In order to achieve this component of community education, community councils would be developed in each neighborhood served by an elementary school. These councils would be selected on the basis of community representation and ability to provide two-way communication. These councils would identify community problems, establish priorities, and work out solutions through community action. The community school director would serve to encourage and assist these groups until they effectively become self-energizing.

While community education in its total capability has only been achieved in a few communities, there are many school districts which have portions of the concept and support the philosophy of community education. The fact that community education has not been totally accomplished is probably due to several factors. In some cases communities do not understand the ramifications of community education and implement only a portion of it. In others, community education is seen as a developmental concept and districts start with programs, anticipating to move to community development at a later time. Finally, the goals of community education are difficult to attain. In a sense, they require a restructuring of educational philosophy and a new relationship between school and community. Both are extremely difficult to achieve. One important characteristic of community education is that there is no one plan which fits every community. Each community must identify and develop those community education components which they feel they need, and implement them in the order which they believe most appropriate.

Thus, while varying in many ways and existing at different stages of development, it is possible to identify community education programs in communities of all sizes. The examples run the gamut from very large cities of over a million in population to small districts of 5,000 people. There are urban, suburban, and rural types of districts with community education, including areas of high density population as well as consolidated school districts which necessitate an enormous amount of busing. The districts vary also from very poor communities to those which are very affluent.

There are many good examples of communities with outstanding community education programs. To cite specific examples, however, would be unfair to those which are omitted. Persons interested in information about exemplary programs could obtain such information by contacting either the National Community School Education Association or one of the University Community Education Centers.

It would be unfair also to fail to point out that community education does have its share of controversy. One of the problems facing Community Education is that there is not unanimous agreement as to its definition, and consequently it suffers from being identified in many ways. It is perceived by different groups as being synonymous with adult education, recreation, neighborhood schools, social work, poverty programs, and community control, and thus it not only garners all of the enemies of these ideas, but in many communities the full potential of community education is never realized due to its limited interpretation.

A second problem is the resistance which comes from the traditional school hierarchy. School people have a very good idea of what the role of the public schools should be. They resent being given a greater responsibility, and are opposed to outsiders using their buildings and their equipment. Boards of education, administrators, teachers, and custodians are often threatened by such suggested change as that implied by community education, and either actively or passively resist its implementation.

In a similar fashion, other agencies, organizations, and institutions are threatened by what they perceive community education to be, and they too oppose its development. These groups frequently have created a sphere of interest which they have staked as theirs, and they fear that by allowing others to provide similar services they will lose their own identity and become expendable.

Still another area of controversy for community education is how it is to be financed. While much lip service is given to the legitimacy of community education, there is still a reluctance to use public dollars to pay for it. Community education is allowed to exist if it is able to generate its own funding. Consequently, community educators must spend a substantial amount of their time as fund raisers, at the expense of providing services to their community.

Another problem has to do with staffing. Many communities want to start community education without additional staff. Without additional staff, however, it is impossible to develop a quality program. In addition, when communities do add staff they do not make allowances for growth in the program. Sometime after the community education is implemented, the program will plateau. This is usually because the staff will become so busy with programs that they are unable to supply the energy necessary to develop the ultimate in community education. As a result, communities tend to settle for that portion of community education which a limited staff can supply.

Regardless of the problems, however, interest in community education is continuing to grow rapidly. The rate of development, in fact, while still affecting less than three percent of the school districts in the country, has still outstripped the ability of the current resources to implement and train in relation to the concept. The transition of community education from add-on programs to a philosophy of education suggests an enormous change in the role of the public schools. The degree of promise, for not only educational change but for community development and involvement, which is offered by the concept of community education, has stirred an excitement in our communities. The growth in the concept and the increase in the numbers supporting and promoting it would indicate that community education has arrived in many communities and may be on its way to becoming the underlying philosophy of American education.

REFERENCES

Minzey, Jack D., and LeTarte, Clyde. *Community Education: From Program to Process.* Midland, Michigan: Pendell Publishing Company, 1972. The statistics in this report are taken from data collected by the Mott Foundation and the National Community Education Association as of March 1975.

ADDITIONAL RESOURCES

Biddle, William. *The Community Development Process.* Chicago: Holt, Rinehart, and Winston, Inc., 1966.

Burns, F. J., and Manley, Reed. *The Community School in Action. Community Education Journal.* Midland, Michigan: Pendell Publishing Company, Vol. 1 No. 1; Vol. 3 No. 4, February 1971 through July 1973.

Decker, Larry E. *Foundations of Community Education.* Midland, Michigan: Pendell Publishing Company, 1972.

44th Yearbook, Part I, NSSE. *The Community School Emphasis in Postwar Education.*

Henry, Nelson B. *The Community School.* 52nd Yearbook, Part II, NSSE. Chicago: University of Chicago Press, 1953.

Hiemstra, Roger. *The Educative Community.* Lincoln, Nebraska: Professional Educators Publications, Inc., 1972.

Manley, Frank J., and Totten, Fred W. *The Community School.* Galien, Michigan: Allied Education Council, 1969.

Melby, Ernest O. *Administering Community Education.* New York: Prentice-Hall, 1955.

Minzey, Jack D., and LeTarte, Clyde E. *Community Education: From Program to Process.* Midland, Michigan: Pendell Publishing Company, 1972.

National Center for Community Education, 1017 Avon Street, Flint, Michigan 48503.

National Community School Education Assocation, 1017 Avon Street, Flint, Michigan 48503.

Olsen, Edward. *Modern Community School.* New York: Appleton-Century-Crofts, Inc., 1953.

_____. *The School and Community Reader.* New York: Macmillan, 1963.

Phi Delta Kappan. Midland, Michigan: Pendell Publishing Co., November 1972.

Role of the School in Community Education. Associated Educational Services Ford Press, Midland, Michigan, 1968.

REGIONAL CENTERS

University of Alabama
 Center for Community Education
 School of Education
 University Station
 Birmingham, Alabama 35294
 (205) 934-5208

Alma College
Center for Community Education
614 W. Superior
Alma, Michigan 48801
(517) 463-2141, Ext. 366

Arizona State University
Southwest Regional Center for Community School
Development
415 Farmer Education Building
Tempe, Arizona 85281
(802) 965-6186

Ball State University
Institute for Community Education Development
222 N. College
Muncie, Indiana 47306
(317) 285-5033

Brigham Young University
Dr. Israel Heaton, Director
Rocky Mountain Regional Center for Community School
Development
281 Richards Building
Provo, Utah 84801
(801) 374-1211, Ext. 3813

California State University—San Jose
California Center for Community Education Development
School of Education, Room 219
San Jose, California 95114
(408) 277-3313 or 277-3101

University of Connecticut
Northeast Community Education Development Center
U-142
Storrs, Connecticut 06268
(203) 486-2738 or 486-2242

Eastern Michigan University
Center for Community Education
101 Boone Hall
Ypsilanti, Michigan 48197
(313) 487-2137 or 487-2335

Florida Atlantic University
Southeastern Regional Center for Community Education
College of Education
Boca Raton, Florida 33432
(305) 395-5100, Ext. 2825

University of Missouri
Midwest Community Education Development Center
801 Natural Bridge Road
543 Lucas
St. Louis, Missouri 63121
(314) 453-5746

Northern Michigan University
Center for Community Education
Learning Resources 2-A
Marquette, Michigan 49855
(906) 227-2176 or 227-2181

University of Oregon
Northwest Community Education Development Center
1736 Moss Street
Eugene, Oregon 97403
(503) 686-3895 or 686-3996

Texas A&M University
Center for Community Education
College of Education
204 New Office Building
College Station, Texas 77843
(713) 845-2820 or 845-1429

University of Virginia
Mid-Atlantic Center for Community Education
College of Education
Charlottesville, Virginia 22903
(804) 924-3625 or 924-3898

Western Michigan University
Community School Development Center
3314 Sangren Hall
Kalamazoo, Michigan 49001
(616) 383-0047

COOPERATING CENTERS

Appalachian State University
Community Education Center
College of Education
Duncan Hall
Boone, N.C. 28607
(704) 282-2288

University of Arkansas
Community Education Development and Training Center
Graduate Education Building, Room 214
Fayetteville, Arkansas 72701
(501) 575-4407

California State University—Los Angeles
California Center for Community Education Development
5151 State University Drive
School of Education
Los Angeles, Calif. 90032
(213) 224-3784

Central Michigan University
Cooperating Center for Community Education
Department of Educational Administration
Ronan 109
Mt. Pleasant, Michigan 48858
(517) 774-3541

Colorado State University
Community Education Center
Fort Collins, Colorado 80521
(303) 491-6474

University of Delaware
Center for Community Education
College of Education
Newark, Delaware 19711

Drake University
Center for CED
College of Education
Des Moines, Iowa 50311
(515) 271-3196

University of Florida
Center for Community Education
260 Norman Hall
Gainesville, Florida 32611
(904) 392-0895

Gallaudet College
Gallaudet Center for Community Education
Washington, D.C. 20002
(202) 447-0575

Georgia Southern College
Center for Community Education
Box 8132
School of Education
Statesboro, Georgia 30458
(912) 764-6611, Ext. 200 or 577

Idaho State University
Idaho Center for Community Education
P.O. Box 59 – Campus
College of Education
Pocatallo, Idaho 83201
(208) 236-2689

Illinois Community College Board
Center for Community Education
Illinois Park Place
Springfield, Illinois 62701
(217) 782-2495

Kansas State University
Center for Community Education
Department of Administration & Foundations
Manhattan, Kansas 66508
(913) 532-5910

Kent State University
Center for Community Education
College of Education
Kent, Ohio 44240
(216) 672-2808

University of Maine
Shibbles Hall
Orono, Maine 04473
(207) 581-7020

Miami University
Cooperating Center for Community Education Development
McGuffey Hall
Oxford, Ohio 35056
(513) 529-6826

Michigan State University
Cooperating Center for Community Education
Erickson Hall
East Lansing, Michigan 48824
(517) 353-6453

Montclair State College
Community Education Development Center
14 Normal Avenue
Upper Montclair, New Jersey 07043
(201) 893-4296

University of Nebraska
Center for Community Education
Education Administration Department
Lincoln, Nebraska 68508
(402) 472-2235

Nevada Community College System
Community Education Center
405 Marsh Avenue
Reno, Nevada 89502
(702) 784-4021

New Mexico State University—Las Cruces
Community Education Center
Las Cruces, New Mexico 88003
(505) 646-1328

New Mexico State University—San Juan
Center for Community Education
Farmington, New Mexico 87401

Oklahoma State University—Stillwater
Community Education Center
309 Gunderson Hall
Stillwater, Oklahoma 74074
(405) 372-6211, Ext. 7257

College of St. Thomas
Community Education Center
2115 Summit Avenue
St. Paul, Minnesota 55105
(612) 647-5352

Shippensburg State College
Educational Development Center
Shippensburg, Pennsylvania 17257
(717) 532-9121

University of South Carolina
Center for Community Education
College of Education
Columbia, South Carolina 29208
(803) 777-6400

Southeastern Louisiana University
Louisiana Center for Community Education
P.O. Box 792
University Station
Hammond, Louisiana 70401
(504) 549-2217

Southern Illinois University
Center for Community Education
Educational Administration
Carbondale, Illinois 62901
(618) 453-2418

University of Southern Mississippi
Department of Educational Administration
Southern Station
Hattiesburg, Mississippi 39401

Syracuse University
Center for Community Education
Area of Educational Administration and Supervision
103 Waverly
Syracuse, New York 13210
(315) 423-4696

University of Tennessee
Center for Community Education
Division of Education
323 McLemore Street
Nashville, Tennessee 37203
(615) 254-5681

University of Vermont
Community Education Development Center
College of Education
Burlington, Vermont 05401
(802) 656-2030

Virginia Polytechnic Institute
Center for Community Education Development
4078 Derring Hall
Blacksburg, Virginia 24061
(703) 951-5106

University of West Florida
Center for Community Education
Pensacola, Florida 32504
(904) 476-9500, Ext. 395

West Virginia College of Graduate Studies
Center for Community Education
Kanawha County Schools
200 Elizabeth St.
Charleston, West Virginia 25311
(304) 348-7770

Worcester State College
Community Education Development Center
486 Chandler St.
Worcester, Massachusetts 01602
(617) 754-6861

Wright State University
Center for Community Education
Office of Continuing Education
Dayton, Ohio 45221
(513) 426-6650

University of Wyoming
Wyoming Center for Community Education Development
Evanston Jr. High Office of the Field Coordinator
Evanston, Wyoming 82930
(307) 789-3749

18

COMMUNITY ACTION PROGRAMS AND PUBLIC EDUCATION

by James J. Vanecko
Associate Professor of Urban Studies and Sociology
Brown University
Providence, Rhode Island

The phrase "community action" is a Rorschach test for the political ideology and policy preferences of most people active in urban politics, as well as for scholars of the topic. Not only can it mean a wide variety of things to different people, but the phrase can provoke an equally wide range of emotional responses, from enthusiastic endorsement to utter disgust.

Given that the topic is so volatile, is it possible to define and describe community action programs? It does seem possible. However, such definition and description must be done through a careful juxtaposition of the interplay—indeed the contradictions—between ideal definitions and practical reality. To do less would only result in one more addition to the long list of definitions extant without facilitating syntyesis. Hopefully, this article will facilitate synthesis, though the completion of

extant without facilitating synthesis. Hopefully, this article will facilitate synthesis, though the completion of scale national evaluation of the Community Action Program, of which the author was a director (Vanecko, 1969 and 1970; Jacobs and Vanecko, 1970). Thus, this article focuses on the Community Action Program of the Office of Economic Opportunity—a national program including approximately 1,000 local agencies begun in 1965 and continuing, at least nominally, through the present. Before reporting on the empirical investigation of community action, some definitional issues must be clarified.

We begin with a discussion of the idea of community action. Secondly, we discuss how this idea relates to public education, since this is a volume concerned with education. Third, we report on empirical research. Finally, an attempt is made to resolve some of the contradictions between the theory and practice, and thus to aid synthesis.

The Community Action Program is one of the very few, if not the only, major domestic program undertaken by the U.S. Government which has its roots in, and even owes its existence to, social science theory—more specifically, to structural-functional theory in sociology. It is possible to trace the origins back into the 19th Century, but it is sufficient for an adequate understanding to trace it as far back as the development of sociological theory in the post-World War II U.S.

The most concise statement of the general theoretical framework is Merton's statement (1957) concerning the structure of opportunity and the goals-means paradigm. Merton suggests that societies structure opportunities by prescribing both a set of goals for personal achievement and self-esteem, and a set of means to those goals. In the case of the United States, as well as western post-Reformation societies generally, the goals are economic affluence and the means are hard work, formal education, and deferral of gratification. Merton uses this paradigm to analyze how the lack of equilibrium in this opportunity structure creates institutional barriers to the achievement of prescribed goals for some groups, and results in a variety of adaptative mechanisms being developed by those groups.

It was no accident that both the most direct application of Mertonian theory and the roots of the "War on Poverty" were in the study and effort to cope with juvenile delinquency. Richrd Cloward and Lloyd Ohlin not only wrote a book on juveniles which became a very young classic (1960), but they also tried to put the ideas of that book into practice. Cloward's and Ohlin's ideas were applied during the late fifties and early sixties in the "Grey Areas" projects of the Ford Foundation, and in "Mobilization for Youth" in New York City. Essentially their ideas, and these programs, were formed around the notion that dropping out of school and juvenile delinquency could not be understood or alleviated in terms of some pathology of the juveniles, but rather had to be understood as a response to the opportunity structure which was not open to poor youth of large cities. Delinquency was seen not simply as a response to the lack of opportunity, but just as importantly to the lack of opportunity in a society which so strongly taught the success goals and then deprived some of the opportunity to achieve success. The response was conceptualized as "innovative." The goal was internalized but the means were denied, so new means were created. More important, though, than the interpretation of delinquent behavior itself, was the notion that opportunity was organized and structured. This meant that in order to solve the delinquency problem one must change the structure of society, or at least communities. One could change the structure through its concrete manifestation in institutions which affected and served people.

Robert F. Kennedy, then Attorney Genral of the United States, took a keen interest in juvenile delinquency in the early 1960s, and thus so did the entire Kennedy Administration. This interest led to the formation of the President's Committee on Juvenile Delinquency and the employment of Lloyd Ohlin as a central planner of its programs. The history of the committee, and its rapid evolution into a task force to develop a program to combat poverty, is a matter of quite extensive description and discussion (Sundquist, 1969; Moynihan, 1969a and 1969b; Donovan, 1967). Indeed, it seems that every participant on or near that task force has written at least an article, and often a book, describing and analyzing its deliberations. This article, then, won't re-review that history. Suffice it to state that the task force itself represents the most significant redirection of national policy away from alleviation of juvenile delinquency— a sympton of deeper ills—and towards the restructuring of communities in an effort to open opportunities and eliminate poverty.

As the theory of structured inequality and denial of opportunity—a sociological theory parallel to the economic theory of structural unemployment—meshed with the thresher of policy-making at the Presidential level, a set of loosely organized, frequently competing, and sometimes conflicting programs called "community action" were harvested.

At the most general and comprehensive level, the notion of community action is conceived of as both redistributive and a zero sum game, and as non-redistributive and nonzero sum. On the one hand community action was thought of as a program or programs designed to give the poor access to resources to which they did not have access. If resources are scarce, this implies others having less access than formerly. On the other hand, community action was thought of as designed to organize and coordinate resources which formerly were disorganized, and thus to make these resources more useful and effective.

At another level, the dilemma of community action was whether institutional change could be accomplished through the restructuring of economic resources alone, or whether the restructuring of political power was also required. The former conception involves the creation or provision of jobs, of human capital resources—education, job training, and access to services. The latter involves the development of tactics and strategies to gain access to institutions and the organization of the poor.

A final dilemma in the definition of community action was concerned with the question of how deep institutionalized denial of opportunity was. One approach was that there was simply a disequilibrium between the location of jobs and economic resources on the one hand

and people's access to them on the other hand. The personal services provided by political machines for generations of European immigrants had been replaced by the bureaucratic services of the post-New Deal age. These routes of access through services available were forbidding in their impersonality, and often badly organized. Reorganization and a familiarity that made them more personal would solve the problem. The other horn of this dilemma was the view that it wasn't simply the gap between where jobs were and where people were—whether geographically or in some larger personal sense—that was the problem, but that there had been a basic transformation of society because of the mechanization of agriculture, the shift from industrial production to service provision, and automation. This transformation was creating a permanent poverty, that required a basic reorganization of resources and redefinition of economic justice.

It is on the horns of these dilemmas that the community action program was defined and enacted into law as part of the Economic Opportunity Act of 1964. It was not that everyone was unaware of these dilemmas, for a similar analysis had appeared early in the program (Marris and Rein, 1967). It was simply that the enthusiasm for the possibilities and varied promises carried the day.

The definition of community action contains the contradictions and the dilemmas. Community action is an effort on the part of all segments of the community to harness all of the resources available within that community in order to restructure the organization of opportunity.

What, then, has community action been over the course of the ten years that it has been the policy of the Federal government? The remainder of this article reports on empirical research into that question. It does so in the context of community action and public education. Public education was one of the institution at both the heart of the theory of community action and of its practical application. New educational programs, and changes in the existing programs, were among the most universal primary goals of the program.

The research described below is part of a larger study of the Community Action Program conducted for the Office of Economic Opportunity by several organizations and scholars. Since it is described more fully elsewhere (Vanecko, 1969a and b; Greenberg, 1974), the description here will be very brief. The research was an evaluation of why some community action programs were more effective than others in bringing about institutional change. It was not an evaluation of whether the Community Action Program was an effective alternative to some other program, or to no program, nor did it evaluate the ultimate objective of moving people out of poverty. Institutional change was assumed to be a means to poverty reduction, if not elimination. The unit of analysis was a city. Specifically, a probability sample of 100 cities of 50,000 or greater population, stratified according to size, and all with Community Action Programs, was studied. In each of these cities, survey interviews were conducted with officials of the Community Action Programs and with informed people outside of the programs.

The creation of a local community action program and its operation involved the resolution of the dilemmas cited above in a very practical policy decision. Community Action Programs could choose to intervene in the service sector directly, or they could organize the poor. Apparently none found a way to emphasize both.

Table 1 illustrates the most important result of this research. It shows the relationship between the policy choice made by the boards and staffs of Community Action Programs—how much to emphasize organizing the poor—and the amount of institutional change which took place in a city.

TABLE 1. CAA COMMUNITY ORGANIZATION GOAL ORIENTATION AND GENERAL INSTITUTIONAL CHANGE (Percent)

General Institutional Change	CAA Community Organization Goal Orientation			N
	No Emphasis	Some Emphasis	Most Emphasis	
1st quartile (lowest)	57	31	–	13
	(8)	(5)	(0)	
2nd quartile	14	25	25	12
	(2)	(4)	(5)	
3rd quartile	29	13	35	12
	(4)	(2)	(7)	
4th quartile (highest)	–	31	40	13
	(0)	(5)	(8)	
Total	100	100	100	50
	(14)	(16)	(20)	

gamma	=	.59
tau	=	.47
$Z\tau(.05)$	=	.19
$Z\tau(.01)$	=	.25
$Z\tau(.001)$	=	.30
χ^2	=	18.16
df	=	6
significance level	=	<.01

Table 2 shows that even holding constant these characteristics of cities, the effects of an organization policy on the part of Community Action Agencies (CAAs) is to produce more institutional change than other policies. There are some differences when these variables are held constant between the two partial correlation coefficients, but this only indicates the types of cities in which this policy is most effective. For example, in the fifth row we see that when political activity in poor neighborhoods is low, the effect of a CAA which has an organization policy is greater than when political activity is high; Q = .81 versus Q = 0.3. However what is most important about Table 2 is that all of the net partial Q coefficients are high.

Table 1 indicates that the greater the emphasis by the Community Action Program on organizing the poor, the higher the level of institutional change. Among those cities in which the Community Action Agency had most emphasis on organization, 40% also had a high level of change, whereas among the CAAs with the least emphasis on organization none also had a high level of change. This

TABLE 2. CAA COMMUNITY ORGANIZATION GOAL ORIENTATION AND GENERAL INSTITUTIONAL CHANGE, CONTROLLING FOR CITY CHARACTERISTICS (O Coefficients of Association)

Zero order	.71	Partial Q When Control Variable Is–	
City Characteristics	Net Partial Q	Low	High
City size	.71	.83	.50
Percent nonwhite	.65	.84	.39
Percent poor	.64	.91	.38
Region	.64	–	–
Level of political activity	.58	.81	.03
CAP expenditures	.70	.14	.80

relationship could take place by change less than one time in 100 comparisons. Since the measurement of institutional change incorporates 38 different single measures, which range from very concrete items, such as the student/teacher ratio in a public school, to vaguer items, such as increased participation in the PTAs in poor neighborhoods, we are confident that the statistical correlation is not a matter of happenstance or measurement error. It is possible, though, that some third factor—such as the civil rights movement and the general climate of change during this time period (1964-1968)—could account for both the change taking place and the decision to emphasize community organization. In order to test this possibility, many characteristics were statistically controlled and this relationship reexamined.

Table 2 once again shows the relationship between CAAs' policy toward organization and away from service provision as it related to institutional change. This time the most important (statistically) characteristics of cities are held constant.

Since we now know that Community Action Programs were caught in the middle between the dilemma of organizing the poor and harnessing resources, and since we have seen that local CAAs made the choice between service provision and organization goals, we ask two questions. First and most important, how does this empirical reality alter the ideal definitions of community action? Second, how does the policy choice represented above relate to public education? The second question will be addressed first. In discussing that question, we can illustrate or give evidence to support our answer to the former question.

One of the four institutions which served and affected the poor which we included in the research discussed here was the public schools. Crucial in the debate at the time of the formation of the Community Action Program, and certainly crucial in the succeeding ten years of debate on the causes of poverty, has been the question of whether the schools have any effect on poverty. The answer has mostly been "no." The response has been varied, both with regard to what should be changed about the schools and whether schools are at all relevant. The Community Action Program was formulated under the assumption that schools are relevant and crucial. Thus, the CAAs were not only involved in running educational programs, but also in trying to change

TABLE 3. CAA EMPHASIS ON COMMUNITY ORGANIZATION, BY CHANGE IN THE PUBLIC SCHOOL SECTOR

School Change Variable	Q Coefficients of Association
	CAA Emphasis on Community Organization
Change within schools:	
Hiring minority groups	−.53
Decrease in student-teacher ratio	.33
Decreased crowding	−.01
Auxiliary staff	.27
Innovations	.33
Cooperation with programs	.48
Mean Q	.15
Mean Q (excluding hiring of minority groups)	.28
Change in school-community relations:	
Appraisal:	
Assessment	.13
Responsiveness	−.17
Interaction:	
PTA interaction with community groups	.27
Resident participation	.09
School promotes participation	.30
Mean Q: Appraisal	−.02
Interaction	.22
Total	.12
Change in PTA:	
Membership[a]	.26
Attendance	.52
Mean Q	.39
Total mean Q	.17

[a]These coefficients are gammas, not Qs.

the schools, the question we ask is did the CAAs change the schools, and if so, how?

Table 3 shows the association between CAA goal orientations, or policy positions, and all of the measures of change pertaining to public schools. In very general terms, the findings are the same as in the first two tables. A policy supporting community organization rather than service provision leads to institutional change or, in this case, change in the public schools serving the poor. However, overall the effect is much weaker. The mean Q coefficient of .17 is much less than the coefficient of .59 in Table 1 and the mean coefficient of .65 in Table 2. Thus, the effects which CAAs had on public schools was less than the effects they had on other institutions. It is probably more important to note what specific items account for this lower effect.

The change variables in Table 3 are divided into three general groupings: change within schools, change in school-community relations, and change in the PTA.

The overall differences between these three groups is not great, but that is the effect of wide variation within the groups. For the sake of brevity, the pattern must be summarized. First, with the exception of minority hiring, concrete changes within the schools are effected by an organization policy. Second, poor people's assessment of the schools, and their interaction with the schools, are not very much affected by an organization policy. Finally, parent activity—measured by PTA membership, attendance, and contact with other community—groups is most affected by an organization policy.

The above findings add up to the following picture. When CAAs decide to organize the poor, their effect is both to activate poor parents and to bring about changes within the school, but they probably also make poor people more critical, skeptical, and aggressive. In short, they both induce small changes within the schools and begin a potential cycle of increasing demands and change.

What then does the above analysis tell us about the definition of community action and its current status? It tells us that without some unforeseen infusion of new political resources, some deux ex machina, community action is likely to be a compromise between the entrenched interest groups and the demands of the newly enfranchised poor. It is likely to add an organized voice to where once there was dissonance, but that this voice will have to compete with the existing choirs. For example, a change least likely to occur is for there to be a substantial increase in the hiring of minority group members, probably because the hiring of teachers is a capability most dear to one of the best organized and most active choirs—the teachers' associations and unions. This, of course, is not unlike the process of enfranchisement of any group or interest. The system bends and doesn't break, gives in on some issues and adjusts.

Thus, it seems that community action and the Community Action Program organized people so that their common stake in the institutional structures of a community became apparent and encouraged their participation. It did not change the opportunity structure of communities in any comprehensive or even extensive way. It did promise, perhaps hesitantly, an escalating cycle of change.

What of the present, though? The Community Action Program exists in name only, and soon probably not even in name. There is not much continuing demand for change, because the organization of those demands rested on a fragile foundation shored up by the legitimating presence of distinguished boards and official titles, and the implicit backing of the Federal government. The demands have turned to disillusionment. The educators and administrators who care find it difficult to hear a melody to which they can apply any lyric derived from their experience and knowledge. In a time when the criticism of education's relevance to the poor is most severe, the dialogue between the poor and the educators has ceased. Though only a beginning, community action was a forum for dialogue between the poor and the educational establishment. Today, community action is not. The voice of the poor is silent.

REFERENCES

Braber, George, and Purcell, Frances, eds. *Community Action Against Poverty.* New Haven: College and University Press, 1967.

Cloward, Richard, and Ohlin, Lloyd. *Delinquency and Opportunity.* New York: The Free Press, 1960.

Donovan, John C. *The Politics of Poverty.* New York: Pegasus, 1967.

Greenberg, Stanley. *Politics and Poverty.* New York: John Wiley & Sons, 1973.

Greenstone, J. David, and Peterson, Paul E. *Race and Authority in Urban Politics.* New York: Russell Sage Foundation, 1973.

Jacobs, Bruce, and Vanecko, James J. *The Impact of the Community Action Program on Institutional Change.* Chicago and Cambridge, Mass.: National Opinion Research Center and Barrs, Reitzel and Associates, 1970.

Levine, Robert A. *The Poor Ye Need Not Have With You.* Cambridge, Mass.: The MIT Press, 1970.

Marris, Peter, and Rein, Martin. *Dilemmas of Social Reform.* Chicago: Aldine, 1967, 1973.

Merton, Robert M. *Social Theory and Social Structure.* New York: The Free Press, 1957.

Moynihan, Daniel Patrick. *On Understanding Poverty.* New York: Basic Books, 1969a.

_____. *Maximum Feasible Misunderstanding.* New York: The Free Press, 1969b.

Sundquist, James L. *On Fighting Poverty.* New York: Basic Books, 1969.

Vanecko, James J. Community Mobilization and Institutional Change. *Social Science Quarterly.* 1969, *50,* 609-630.

_____. *Community Organization Efforts, Political and Institutional Change.* Chicago: National Opinion Research Center, 1970.

19

THE ROLE OF THE SCHOOL AS A SITE FOR SOCIAL SERVICES

by Susan J. Baillie, Research Staff
and
Laurence B. DeWitt, Director
Educational Policy Research Center
Syracuse, New York

In recent years there have been a number of experiments with locating public schools and social services on a common site. These enterprises were established with several different objectives in mind. First, there was the expectation that costs could be reduced through the sharing of facilities. Second, it was hoped that these services could be made more efficient through the cooperation and interaction of the social service and school staffs. Third, it was known that clients of social services frequently utilize more than one service, and it was assumed that the services could therefore be made more accessible to users by locating them at a common location. Finally, there was usually the hope that these school-social service centers would become community centers; that they would serve as community focal points for personal and community development and interaction.

REVIEW OF RECENT DEVELOPMENTS AND PROGRAMS

A number of communities are currently experimenting with various ways to integrate social services. To assess the opportunities and drawbacks of using schools as the central site, a number of school-social service programs have been examined. These programs have been initiated in deteriorating inner-city neighborhoods where community revitalization was a major objective, as well as in the most modern new towns. The concept appears to be attractive in a wide variety of social settings and lends itself to a diversity of approaches.

Our primary approach to consideration of school-social service centers has been the study of individual cases. These centers are a relatively new phenomenon, and there exists only a very limited literature on the subject.

The integration of social services with the school represents a basic attempt to redefine the function of the school, enlarging and rendering it less parochial. This is manifest in at least three areas: (1) attempting to use the school-community centers to redefine and enlarge the concept of neighborhood; (2) involving the community in decision-making; and (3) redefining whom the public school facility serves and what services are offered.

A number of the community service centers involve schools in low-income areas and attempt to revitalize the quality of life in these declining neighborhoods. A number of the schools are in new communities. The school-social service centers planned, under construction, or newly opened in these areas are meant to give the neighborhood positive focus and to bring the residents together for the purpose of common self-betterment.

The centers located in deteriorating inner-city areas face problems entirely different from new town centers. These neighborhoods were at one time unified by religion or race or class status. They were enclaves that in one way or another met the basic needs of the families residing there. The public school was a respected institution believed capable of transforming lower-class and immigrant children into middle-class adults, and was the primary service demanded of the government. Other kinds of institutions served other kinds of needs reasonably well, as measured against the expectations of the time.

The current residents of low-income urban neighborhoods are entering the economy and making an attempt to achieve social mobility under very different circumstances. Low-skilled, low-paying jobs that might at least allow heads of families the hope of better lives for their children, are not readily available. The faith in the process of mobility that once characterized low-income neighborhoods has been replaced by a greater degree of resignation and resentment.

This chart of school-social service centers gives an overall picture of the nature of individual centers:

Name of School/ Location	Level/Number of Students	Racial Composition	Current Operating Status	Services Offered
Quincy School Boston, Mass.	Elementary 800 students	over 70% non-white, primarily Chinese with blacks, Puerto Ricans, Cubans, and Armenians	planning stages completed	recreation, health and day care services
Williams Community Education Center Flint, Michigan	Elementary 800 students	52% white 42% black 6% Spanish	operating	comprehensive social services
Welfare Island (new community will include a number of small schools integrated into the community) New York	Elementary and Secondary Schools	25% low-to-moderate income 25% middle income 15% upper income 15% low-income elderly 20% public housing racially mixed	under construction	comprehensive social services
Buffalo, New York Waterfront (new community for 10,000 people)	Elementary and Secondary Schools 1,440	racially mixed	first housing units occupied; planning for school and town center ongoing	health, recreation, and day care services
New Haven Community Schools New Haven, Conn.	10 Schools 21,000 students	57% black 9% Puerto Rican 34% white	program began in 1962	neighborhood centers for cultural and recreational life
John F. Kennedy School and Community Center Atlanta, Georgia	Middle Schools 1,000 students	99% black	opened March 1971	comprehensive social services
Human Resources Center Pontiac, Michigan	Elementary 1971-1972 1,400 planned 2,000	38% black 62% white	operating	comprehensive social services
Florence Lehmann Multi-Educational Center Minneapolis, Minn.	Adults	racially mixed	operating	comprehensive social services
George Washington School No. 1 Elizabeth City, New Jersey	Elementary	33% Spanish 55% black 12% mixed	operating	comprehensive
Port Charlotte Cultural Center Port Charlotte, Florida	Adults 7,000	primarily white	operating	adult education, recreation, cultural activities, public library, V.A. Office, Social Securities Office
Brockton High School Brockton, Mass.	High School 5,600 students 9,000 adults	racially mixed	operating	adult education, recreation, cultural activities, skill training, adult civic education

Multi-faceted service delivery complexes are being planned, with the hope of disrupting the process of human decline that characterizes many inner-city neighborhoods. For example, the Superintendent of the Pontiac, Michigan, school system, when faced with the need to replace a half dozen inner-city elementary schools, responded by saying that inner-city schools should do more than provide "warm, attractive housing for school children in segregated neighborhoods." (Chase, 1970) He thought that if "white and black children could be brought together in one setting with fully enriched educational, social, and recreational programs, there should be a potential environment to improve the total living of residents in that quadrant of the inner city." (Chase, 1970)

George Washington Community School No. 1 was built for the transient and racially mixed population of Elizabeth City, New Jersey. The area served by the facility has the highest concentration of disadvantaged persons in the city. The new community school was built in the neighborhood as an attempt to serve the needs of the entire community, providing the rather transient neighborhood with a common place to which they might turn.

The Williams Community Education Center, in Flint, Michigan, represents an attempt to address the educational, health, recreational, and social service needs of the entire community surrounding an elementary school. The Center began with the consolidation of two elementary school communities (one white, one black) into a central area, and the reconstitution of the previously segregated communities through a single focus for common self-improvement.

Other experiments with social service integration give further evidence of the concept's flexibility with respect to racial integration. The Quincy School Complex in Boston's South Cove area is another attempt to ease racial integration of a school, while providing a focal point of neighborhood activities and of service delivery for the larger surrounding community.

On the other hand, the John F. Kennedy Center in Atlanta and the New Haven Community Schools have not tried to racially integrate their constituencies. Rather, they have focused on improving the quality of life of the neighborhood's residents.

The Welfare Island and Buffalo Waterfront projects involve the creation of entirely new communities and, as such, will begin with a "new" population residing in a community designed to meet comprehensively the many needs of a socially, economically, and racially mixed constituency.

The value of community involvement in making decisions about the school and community centers was recognized, and is an integral component of all the projects observed. The project planners, school department officials, and administrators all indicated that members of the communities responded positively to the creation of integrated delivery systems.

For instance, planning for the Human Resources Center at Pontiac involved setting up a committee of 30 community members charged with the task of making community interests and attitudes known to the planners. The committee came up with 33 specific recommendations for the proposed center; 32 were incorporated into the plan. The members of this citizens' advisory committee were chosen by the PTAs of those elementary schools which were merged to form the Center.

However, in Atlanta a neighborhood resident who owned property on the proposed site refused to sell his land to the developers, because he believed that homeowners were being displaced unnecessarily, and that the school should be built in a neighborhood where it could be racially integrated. A group of blacks in Atlanta was organized to fight the construction of the school. They filed suit in Federal court with the support of the NAACP. The case was lost, and today the school is located on the planned site and is 99.9% black.

A similar problem arose at the Quincy School Complex, where planners decided that the school would initially be part of a joint-occupancy facility shared by married student housing for the Tufts/New England Medical Center. The community's Chinese residents were opposed to the construction of closed occupancy apartments. They were also opposed to the state-mandated creation of racial balance in their school. The opposition of the Chinese community has delayed construction to the point where the plan itself is a stalemate. However, no longer are there plans for university housing, although racial balance is still state-mandated.

In all of the cases we examined there appeared to be some element of community involvement. But in no case was there community control of either the facility or the planning; in all instances community members worked with professionals, rather than having the professionals obligated to carry out decisions by the community.

Most of the school-social service centers we examined emphasized total community participation, including students, in the various services offered. However, the Lehmann Multieducational Center's services are primarily for the diverse student body actually at the center. The Port Charlotte Cultural Center had focused its activities almost exclusively on older citizens; now, however, they are beginning to change this orientation to a wider age range.

In the course of our investigation, we found it necessary to make distinctions between the kinds of services offered by school-social service centers. The provision of adult education and recreational opportunities for the community differs substantially from the delivery of "hard-core" social services such as health, public welfare, and employment assistance. Many school systems offer some form of adult education. Extending the program so that it involves a larger segment of the community costs more money, and demands a considerable investment of time and energy on the part of those involved. The Kennedy School, the Williams School, the Human Resources Center in Pontiac, the Lehmann Center, and George Washington School No. 1 are all operating with "hard" social services at present, while the Quincy School, Welfare Island, and the Buffalo Waterfront projects are planning to offer these services.

Secondly, the integration of social services, with or without education, has great potential. Since an individual's needs are interrelated, it makes sense to interrelate services aimed at meeting these needs. Education can and should play a vital role in the fully integrated social services program. Virtually every community has reasonably accessible educational facilities, which are used almost exclusively during the daytime from nine to three. Further, educational services are social services; that is, they address a very important felt need of a large number of individuals. Aside from the core educational program of kindergarten through twelfth grade, there are a number of educational services which are intimately related to other social needs; day-care, early childhood education, vocational education, health care, job training and retraining, and many others.

It is expected that the school children will benefit by having other kinds of services available to them and by having their parents involved in the school milieu, to the extent that negative attitudes about the school are somewhat overcome and parent's as well as children's needs are met. Many parents had educational experiences which left them fearful, suspicious, and hostile toward the school. Involving these persons in a positive environment, where they are treated like human beings with important contributions to make to the school/community center, can be one way of providing an environment where children see daily that the school, and thus learning, can be an integral and fulfilling part of their lives.

The John F. Kennedy Community Center attempts to provide complementary interaction of social services for the convenience of its constituents and as an enabling mechanism for their self-improvement. For example, night care centers are provided for the children of parents taking evening classes. At the Minneapolis Lehmann Center, an interlocking set of job training classes, job placement, and social betterment programs are offered to help the "whole" student in his attempt at personal self-improvement.

A third justification often cited as a reason for integration of social services are the cost factors. The integration of social services with education offers an obvious potential for improving the quality and nature of the services provided. At the same time, it also appears to present some possibilities for reducing costs. Increased efficiency and avoidance of duplication have allowed some communities to construct facilities they would have been unable to afford otherwise. In developing the Williams Community Center, a variety of public departments combined resources to provide a community center site with a recreation-education area, indoor-outdoor community swimming pool, and ice skating facilities. Only through the cooperation of the school and recreation officials were the residents of Arlington, Virginia able to have at their disposal a junior high school and community center offering community educational and recreational facilities. It should be pointed out that most of the cases we examined which incorporated "hard" social services or new recreational facilities in their programs did this in conjunction with new school buildings, where additional space could be provided for these services.

There has been increasing Federal and state interest in the development of school-social service centers. Currently, seven states—Michigan, Florida, Utah, Washington, New Jersey, Minnesota, and Maryland—have passed legislation authorizing the use of school facilities for instructional, recreational, and/or service programs for community members. Eight other states have introduced similar legislation. At the Federal level, the Congress is considering several bills, primarily those identified with community education in the schools, which would encourage and lend support to the increased use of the schools for delivery of social services to their communities.

CURRENT CONTROVERSIES

A broad range of potential problems confront school-social service centers. We do not consider them insurmountable, but they do reinforce what is now commonly known: there are no easy answers to hard social problems. However, we must always search for new approaches which offer the possibility of substantial improvement in the organization and provision of human services. Integrating various social services in a common site with public educational activities will not prove advantageous in all circumstances. The following constitutes a brief summary of the major areas of uncertainty and potential problems.

First, there may be serious objections from various quarters concerning the mixing of particular kinds of social services in a common site. Take, for example, the case of a community whose schools have been beset by student violence during school hours. Both the administrators and the clients of some of the social services, such as welfare or social security, might be very reluctant to locate their offices in the same facility with these schools. Similarly, it is not difficult to imagine groups of parents strenuously objecting to the location of drug and alcoholic addict rehabilitation centers within the schools.

We do not claim that these and other "hard" social services cannot be combined with public schools—we know that there are cases where they have been. But they do represent a potential for serious problems for the development of joint facilities involving schools and other social services.

Second, the cost considerations concerning such facilities are somewhat unclear. It appears that integration of schools with *some* social services offers an opportunity for sizeable dollar cost savings. These savings are based on the more efficient utilization of planned or existing public facilities, with a resultant saving of public funds, or, possibly, the leasing of only partially used public facilities to private organizations, with a resultant increase in public revenue. Recreational facilities, auditoriums, libraries, and the use of schools by adult education and community organizations are examples.

There seems to be reason to doubt that substantial dollars savings can be realized by locating daytime social services in the same building with schools. If such integration were to be based on physically decentralizing these services—increasing the number of social service branches—it would probably result in some marginal cost increases in terms of administrative and staff efficiency.

But the major cost factor associated with integrating such daytime social services as health and welfare with schools involves the question of access and availability. If these services were made more accessible and amenable to current and potential clients, it would surely result in a very considerable increase in the use of these services. There seem to be no reliable estimates of the number of individuals who are legally entitled to existing social services but who are not receiving them, due to unawareness or timidity and embarrassment. But we would be surprised if they were less than 20% of those now receiving them.

Third, the whole notion of creating school-social service centers runs into enormous problems concerning racial integration. Such centers could inherit all of the racial problems with which schools are currently plagued, and then some. Alternatively, such centers might possess the potential for ameliorating racial tensions. The fundamental problems appear to rest with the definition of the community to be served. Would there be separate centers for whites and blacks—following the lines of the current racial composition of existing schools? Would this be a socially desirable development? Would it not lead to even greater separation and, perhaps, polarization of the races? On the other hand, does busing of either students or social service clients essentially contradict the whole principle upon which school-social service centers are based: a neighborhood or community orientation?

There are no ready-made answers to these questions. They involve very fundamental and personal concepts in the area of human values and ethics. These are problems with which our society has been grappling for over a century. And the notion of integrating schools with other social services raises these issues, once again, in exceedingly stark terms.

Finally, administrative and bureaucratic pitfalls in social service integration schemes are legion. An advocate or group of advocates, preferably armed with political clout and money, and possessing unusual degrees of patience and perseverance, seem almost necessary if a school-social service center is to be "pushed through." Even then, creation of such a center does not in any way guarantee success in terms of realizing the goals of such centers: i.e., improved services delivery, broadly defined. The key operational issues revolve around the personal and working relationships between professionals working in different service areas, and between the professionals and the community. One should not underestimate the potential of existing and entrenched social service bureaucracies to resist the fundamental reconstituting required for physical and functionally integrating schools and social services.

CONCLUSIONS

We do not concur in full with the Petronius Principle, though the bulk of historical evidence seems to weigh heavily on its side:

> We trained hard, but it seemed that every time we were beginning to form up into teams we would be reorganized. I was to learn later in life that we tend to meet any new situation by reorganizing; and a wonderful method it can be for creating the illusion of progress while producing confusion, inefficiency, and demoralization. (Petronius Arbiter, ca. 60 A.D.)

There are a number of financial, legal, administrative, and racial obstacles to full physical integration. There are equally perplexing obstacles to the development of administrative cooperation in the provision of these services. Finally, even a well-meshed system of interrelated social services with a high degree of inter-professional cooperation can appear to potential clients to be well-intentioned, but nonetheless it can be a foreign and manipulative institution which still does not address what they perceive as their most pressing needs.

Mere relocation of social services under one roof does not in any automatic way mean that social service delivery will be qualitatively or quantitatively different. Unless the physical integration of the schools and social services is accompanied by something more than relocation, neither schools nor social services will necessarily be any better than they were before.

REFERENCES

Abt Associates Incorporated. *Comprehensive Neighborhood Programs: A Synthesis of Research Findings.* (Prepared for the Office of Economic Opportunity, Evaluation Branch) Cambridge, Massachusetts: Abt Associates, Inc., November 1970.
———. *A Study of Neighborhood Action.* (Prepared for the Office of Economic Opportunity, Office of Program Development, Evaluation Branch) Cambridge, Massachusetts: Abt Associates, Inc., October 15, 1971.
Baillie, Susan, DeWitt, Laurence, and O'Leary, Linda. *The Potential Role of the School as a Site for Integrating Social Services.* Syracuse, New York: Educational Policy Research Center, October 1972.
Chase, William W. *Design for Regenerating a City.* U.S. Department of Health, Education and Welfare, Office of Education, American Education. March 1970.
Clinchy, Evans. *Joint Occupancy: Profiles of Significant Schools.* New York: Education Facilities Laboratory, 1970.
Community Education Journal. All issues.
Guide to Alternative for Financing School Buildings. New York: Educational Facilities Laboratory, 1971.
Kenney, James B. The Community School: A Base for Coordinating the Delivery of Human Services. *Minnesota Health,* Winter, 1973, pp. 10-12.
Kriesberg, Louis. Organizations and Inter-Professional Cooperation. *Comparative Organizations,* W. Heydegrand, ed. New York: Prentice-Hall.

20

EDUCATIONAL COOPERATIVES AND REGIONAL EDUCATION SERVICE

by Larry W. Hughes
Professor of Educational Administration
and
Charles M. Achilles
Associate Professor of Educational Administration
Coordinator of Field Services
The University of Tennessee
Knoxville, Tennessee

The terms educational cooperative (Ed. Coop.) and Regional Education Service Agency (RESA) are not in and of themselves definitive. For purposes of this study the terms will be treated basically as synonyms. An educational cooperative entails a joint effort of two or more education organizations to enlarge the scope, quality, and accessibility of educational programs and services. Cooperation, change, innovation, and expansion of alternatives are key elements of the definition. RESA is a more generic term that may include Ed. Coops. but also includes agencies which focus less on innovation and more on simple pooling of resources and sharing services.

For consideration in this study, the cooperative endeavor must satisfy these criteria:

Have a definable board of control and/or formal organizational structure, but not be the fundamental school operational unit.

Include a formally established public educational organization (although it would not have to be exclusively made of public schools; there are some cooperatives which also include agencies from the private sector of the economy).

Have some history of existence and promise of continuation (not wholly dependent upon grants and gifts).

Require some degree of constituent contribution.

Thus, for example, such operations as Title III ESEA activities, and the common regular meetings of superintendents in geographic proximity to each other, are excluded. Also excluded are those cooperative endeavors which are simply "shared operations," such as special vocational-technical and community college districts. This article is concerned, then, with those cooperative arrangements which influence elementary and secondary education and have emergent, change-incubating functions.

TYPES OF COOPERATIVES

In name and form educational cooperatives, or RESAs, can be categorized as follows: intermediate educational units, voluntary educational cooperatives, school study or development councils, and school-industry cooperatives. Although it deserves some mention, one long-standing form of school district cooperation—the traditional intermediate or county unit—has been excluded from the cooperative designation, since its primary focus was that of communication and administration, rather than to serve as a change inducer or to enlarge the scope, quality, and accessibility of programs.

In recent years educators have identified the restructuring of educational patterns for both general and vocational education programs as a priority problem area. A continuing concern is that of developing means whereby children located in small, sometimes impoverished, school districts may be provided a quality education. School consolidation has provided some answers. Yet, the act of physically bringing together larger and larger groups of students is geographically unfeasible in some places, and impractical in others, and is without "magic" to necessarily create quality education by itself.

The technological capability exists to permit school districts, regardless of location and size, to participate in joint efforts to improve curriculum, recruit and utilize instructional and special personnel more efficiently, and provide for sound and efficient school business and purchasing practices; while still maintaining their independence and close psychological relationships with the school communities and neighborhoods they were initially established to serve.

The concept of the educational cooperative is, then, the result of educational need, technological possibilities, geographic realities, and sociological precepts. It provides efficient and effective deployment of educational resources and professional expertise. Generally, an educational cooperative is a system containing a number of contiguous (although not necessarily so) independent school districts within a defined region that develop and share educational resources through communications media, mobile facilities, inservice training, joint research and development, and computer and data processing technology. Cooperatives can be found in urban, suburban, and rural settings.

Probably every school district has entered into some cooperative arrangement of a more or less formal nature. Cooperation between educational agencies can be found in every state, although various forms of cooperative endeavors are more prevalent than others in some sections of the nation. One type of cooperative—the school study council, of which there are over 80—has more often been found in the Northeast and Midwest. Some states have mandated new regional units (e.g., Texas, Pennsylvania). Other states have legally designated voluntary, but statewide, organizations (e.g., Oregon); and still other states have fully voluntary cooperative activities with permissive legislation only (e.g., Tennessee).

MODES OF ORGANIZING

There are different modes of organizing for cooperative endeavors between school systems. Eligibility for membership, voluntary or mandated participation, funding sources, and budgetary restrictions, among other characteristics, serve to differentiate among various kinds of educational cooperatives or regional educational service agencies.

Regional education agencies are called by many overlapping and synonymous terms, such as Board of Cooperative Educational Services, Educational Service Agency, Cooperative Educational Service Agency, Intermediate District, Regional Service Agency, Educational Cooperative, etc.

Isenberg (*Regional Education Service Agency Prototypes . . .*, 1967) suggested a rationale for classifying regional organizations according to the degree of completeness or perfection each has as an autonomous public corporation, ranging from the most complete and autonomous to the nonprofit, purely voluntary corporation. Figure 1 depicts this classification for RESAs, including representatives of each type. Furthermore, Isenberg and Hoyt (1970) suggested that any plan to organize, develop, or identify RESAs include a substantial number of optional arrangements, but that there are four broad areas of concern: (1) the board of control or governance; (2) responsibilities and opportunities of that board; (3) financial arrangements; and (4) required and/or permissive features of the program of services to be operated.

REGIONAL EDUCATION AGENCIES*

Autonomous ⟶	*Semi-autonomous* ⟶		*Dependent*
Public Corporation ⟶	*With Line Function* ⟶	*Without Line Function* ⟶	*Non-Profit Corporation or Confederation*
Type:			
I	II	III	IV**
Examples:			
Michigan: Intermediate Unit	New York: BOCES	Texas: Regional Educational Service Centers	School Study and Development Councils
Muscatine-Scott County School System (Iowa)	Pennsylvania: Intermediate Unit	Oregon: Intermediate Education District	School-Industry Cooperatives
Minnesota: Proposed MESA			Voluntary Cooperatives

*All arrangements are multi-district; some are single county and some are multi-county.
**These units are not technically a second-echelon of a three echelon system since they are creations of the local districts and, thus, below the local districts in the hierarchy of organization. In fact, however, they sometimes act between the state and local agencies.

FIGURE 1. Classification Scheme for Cooperative Types
(Adapted from Hughes and Achilles, 1971: *16*)

The Voluntary Cooperative

The organization of voluntary educational cooperatives varies, but in the main a pattern is followed which could be described as quasi-legal and quasi-hierarchical (Hughes and Achilles, 1971). Most commonly they do not occur in the traditional line authority from the state education agency to the local district, but rather are controlled by the constituent districts, with a governing board composed of administrators from member districts. It is not usual to have representatives from other social agencies or institutions serving ex officio on such boards. The primary function of voluntary cooperatives seems to be to provide programmatic and instructional services to children; less so, to provide administrative services, although these are important, especially where the cooperative includes data processing services.

Voluntary cooperatives are not mandated or established by formal regulations. Most exist in states with permissive legislation that allows school districts to collaborate.

In some states the permissive legislation facilities school cooperation; in others legislation impedes it. For example, in Minnesota there are provisions whereby local schools can cooperate and develop a mechanism for taxation. Local districts in Virginia can be penalized by the Aid Reimbursement Formula for spending local money for regional educational cooperation. Districts generally can contract between and/or among themselves for cooperative action. (Hughes and Achilles, 1971, p. 88)

Voluntary cooperatives receive financial support from a variety of sources, often from a combination of local district funds, state funds, federal grants, and private foundation grants and gifts. Some have a legal option to seek permission to levy taxes to support their activities, but this is not common. The basic funding source is the local school district, and costs are often computed on a per-pupil basis, or prorated based upon services received. Some cooperatives receive income from sales of publications or contracted services.

An array of services is provided for constituents. These services can be classified generally as developmental activities, direct service to pupils and professional and nonprofessional employees, administrator assistance, inservice education, cooperative operation of schools for exceptional children, and operation of experimental or developmental programs. Some voluntary cooperatives engage in research, although this is usually action research and field studies. Long-range planning and educational communication are emerging RESA services.

Industry/Education Cooperation

A review of the literature (Hughes and Achilles, 1971) suggests that industry/education cooperatives may be generally classified in one of three ways: *industry to school*—i.e., "adopt-a-school," or for the performance of a specific job-training program with a total school system; *industry/education councils*—usually operating on a regional basis with orientation primarily toward business and industries, but with assistance to schools where possible; and *educational councils or research centers*— usually operating on a multi-school system basis, but receiving financial support from both industry and education.

One study (Weatherby, Allen, and Blackner, 1970) identified six different and emerging types of industry/ education partnerships. They are: (1) consortiums involving a school system and a university-based, semi-private organization; (2) cooperation involving an industry and a school or schools; (3) consortium between a school system and several businesses; (4) industry/ education consultative arrangements; (5) industry/ education performance contracts; and (6) industry/ education regional councils.

Interest in cooperative endeavors between business/industry and education is becoming increasingly widespread. Educators realize that the job of educating America's youth is not the sacred domain of the schools; other facets of the community cannot be ignored. Business, industry, and labor are becoming more conscious of their social responsibilities, triggered in part by social problems (e.g., environmental pollution) which invariably lead to involvement in some type of educational endeavors. Examples of industry/education cooperatives include the Educational Research Council of America, the Greater Wilmington Development Council, the Institute for Educational Research, and the Joint Council on Economic Education.

Studies and reports providing more comprehensive information on industry/education cooperation include Sovde, 1970; Banta and Towne, 1969; and two publications of the Educational Research Council of America, 1969 and 1970.

School Study Councils

School Study Councils were initiated in 1944 by Paul Mort, of Teachers College, Columbia University. By 1973 there were over 80 operating councils, and the year 1970 saw the development of ten councils. A school study council is a group of local school systems working together, usually under the sponsorship of an institution of higher education, to solve common problems of member districts and/or to expand services to administrators, faculty, and pupils. Two other studies (Danenberg, 1970; Babel, 1970) have made comprehensive reviews of school study councils and their functions.

Intermediate Education Service Agencies

Intermediate Education Service Agencies are more formalized than voluntary cooperatives. Some of these RESAs are arms of the state education agency, or serve functions for local districts as designated by the state agency. One predominant feature of this type of cooperative endeavor is state sponsorship, or legitimation, of the organization. Two of the three predominant trends in educational regionalism (Stephens and Ellena, 1973) pertain directly to this type of RESA.

> In state school systems historically having a three echelon structure—state education agency, county school system, local school district—the establishment of a new, middle-echelon, multi-county regional service unit.
> In state school systems historically having a two echelon structure—state education agency and local school district—the establishment and promotion of a cooperative arrangement between and among local school districts. (p. 19)

The trend is for the continuing development of the Intermediate Education Service Agency, as more and more states consider regionalism, as one way to meet the growing demands upon education.

Current trends in RESA development might be considered the fourth generation of development (Of course not every state which has RESAs has gone through the total process, or has progressed through all four stages.)

The four stages or generations might be identified as follows:

1. The traditional county or intermediate superintendency.
2. The initial formal regional cooperative agency, which usually was limited to only a few school districts and a relatively small geographic area.
3. The combining of several small regional agencies into a larger Regional Education Service Agency, or the planned reorganization of small but single-purpose cooperatives.
4. The development of Regional Education Service Agencies whose major purpose is comprehensive planning, not only for education, but also for other social services and purposes such as health, land use, recreation, planning, etc.

The second and third generations held quite strictly to planning for and providing services to education only. The fourth generation is marked not only by larger geographic regions, but also by an expansion into services other than those designed specifically for education.

States which have initiated action toward the development of the larger regional agencies include New York State, with plans for 14 such units; Michigan, with plans for approximately 14; and Minnesota, which seems to be thinking in terms of 10 or 11 such agencies.

TRENDS AND CONCERNS: THE MYTHOLOGY OF EDUCATIONAL COOPERATIVES

Educational cooperatives are not free from controversies; the literature lacks "hard" data relating to the success of such endeavors. Some local districts fear that educational cooperatives or RESAs will infringe on local control, especially where the cooperative arrangement is encouraged by the state education agency and may be viewed as an administrative arm of it. Some states do not encourage educational cooperative development, and may even penalize a local education agency for belonging to such a cooperative by not permitting state funds to be used in the support of those cooperatives. Other states encourage local funds to be used for cooperative endeavors, and provide financial incentives for this. Several myths have developed with respect to RESAs. Three of the more common myths are discussed here.

Educational Cooperatives Reduce the Cost of Education

Few data substantiate this statement. Basically the RESA provides a new and expanded service. Although usually provided at a per-unit cost which would be less than if the individual districts were to provide them, the addition of new services increases costs. Over time some economies should be realized, however.

Educational Cooperatives as a New Organizational Form will Insure Better Individual Performance

Changes in administrative or teaching behavior are not caused simply by reorganizing. Practicing educators must be retrained, because persons will need to be prepared for the new responsibilities and positions implied by educational cooperatives.

The Educational Cooperative is an Intermediate Step Between the Local Educational Agency and the State Education Agency, and thus is a Link is the Chain of Command between State and Local Levels

This statement need not be true, except in those states where specific line responsibility is designated to the RESA as an arm of the state education agency. As long as the RESA is controlled by, and receives funding and support from, the local districts, it will be an agency of the local level. This remains true even if the state department provides funds and/or incentives available to local districts for cooperative endeavors.

SUMMARY

The concept of the educational cooperative is new in some places, and its role and responsibility, advantages and disadvantages, must be understood. In some areas where intermediate units have been located, many school people and lay people may have misconceptions about this cooperative, and see it as an administrative unit which will superimpose itself on the local education agency. Other people may be fearful of forced consolidation. Some of these concerns may be justifiable, but in the last analysis the educational cooperative, if it functions as a voluntary service agency, is responsible to and controlled by member districts.

One feature of the schools which continues to be highly valued in many areas of this nation is local control of its institutions. There is evidence that this is highly valued in both urban and rural groups and may account, in part, for the hue and cry in urban areas for "decentralization." Hughes and Spence (1971) point out that:

Developing out of the desire to continue local control while at the same time achieving some of the obvious benefits of the services of a larger school unit has been the recent move toward the educational cooperative. It seems to promise hope for the improvement of rural educational systems with less locally perceived threat than the 'consolidated school." (p. 44)

They go on to suggest that such organizations as a permissive, unmandated educational cooperative now developing in Appalachia, the semi-voluntary educational service centers of Nebraska, and the mandated regional service centers of Texas, do represent attempts to improve education in rural areas through shared leadership and services, while at the same time maintaining local autonomy.

Currently there is a continuing trend toward cooperation and regional approaches in education. This same trend can be found in other government agencies, and the country abounds with regional planning services, regional social service agencies, regional transportation agencies, etc., so that the trend to more regionalism and cooperation between heretofore totally independent school districts is consistent with the temper of the times.

Although forms of informal cooperation between and among local districts have been in evidence for some time, the growth of this cooperation and the legitimacy of it through permissive or mandated legislation is causing educators to look more closely at the problems and benefits of cooperative efforts. While the 1940s to the 1950s could be thought of as a period of consolidation of schools—and much consolidation remains to be done—and the late 1960s may be remembered for decentralization, as large districts attempted to become more responsive to local needs, the 1970s may well be remembered as the time of the Educational Cooperative. The Educational Cooperative, or the Regional Educational Service Agency, provides much of the economy and service capability of large districts, while also providing more flexibility and local autonomy. Things best done on a large scale can be conducted through the educational cooperative; activities best accomplished by individual districts are placed there. Furthermore, demonstration, development, innovation, expansion of opportunities, and new ways of solving problems emerge from the educational cooperative.

REFERENCES

Babel, John. An Investigation of the Operational Functions of School Study Councils with Recommendations for the Improvement of these Functions in Ohio Councils. Unpublished doctoral dissertation, The Ohio State University, 1970.

Banta, Trudy W., and Towne, Douglas C. *Interpretive Study of Cooperative Efforts of Private Industry and the Schools to Provide Job Oriented Education Programs for the Disadvantaged.* Washington, D.C.: USOE Bureau of Research, U.S. Department of Health, Education and Welfare, March 20, 1969.

Danenburg, William. Perceptual Analysis of a Model Regional School Development Council. Unpublished doctoral dissertation, The University of Tennessee, 1970.

Hoyt, Eugene. *Regional Education Agency,* Title V Elementary and Secondary Education Act Proposal, Washington, D.C.: Appalachian Regional Commission, 1970. (Mimeographed).

Hughes, Larry W., and Spence, Dolphus L. *Attitudes and Orientations of Rural Groups and Effects on Educational Decision Making and Innovation in Rural School Districts.* Las Cruces, New Mexico: ERIC/CRESS, 1971.

Hughes, Larry W., Achilles, Charles M., Leonard, James, and Spence, Dolphus L. *Interpretive Study of Research and Development Relative to Educational Cooperatives.* Washington, D.C.: U.S. Office of Education Bureau of Research, 1971 (ERIC: ED 059-544).

Regional Education Service Agency Prototypes, Optional Statutory Arrangements and Suggestions for Implementation. Prepared for Program Development Section, Bureau of Elementary and Secondary Education, U.S. Office of Education. Washington, D.C.: Department of Rural Education, National Education Association, 1967 (Isenberg, Robert).

Sovde, Richard D. *The Potential for Industry/Education Collaboration in New England.* Cambridge, Massachusetts: New England School Development Council (NESDEC), 1970.

Stephens, Robert E., and Ellena, W. J. Regionalism in Education: Forms, Trends and Benefits. *The School Administrator.* Arlington, Va: AASA, June, 1973.

Ten Years of Accomplishment (Annua. Report, 1969). Cleveland, Ohio: Educational Research Council of America, 1969.

Weathersby, Rita E., Allen, Patricia R., and Blackaer, Alan R., Jr. *New Roles for Educators: A Sourcebook for Career Education.* Cambridge, Mass.: Harvard Graduate School of Education, 1970.

What is ERC? A Monograph. Cleveland, Ohio: Educational Research Council of America, May 11, 1970.

ADDITIONAL RESOURCES

Two interpretive studies of research and development focusing on educational cooperatives funded by the U.S. Office of Education have been produced in recent years; both provide comprehensive information. They are:

Northwest Regional Educational Laboratory. *Project Report* (Identification, Synthesis, Evaluation and Packaging of "Shared Service" Research and Developmental Efforts in Rural Areas). Portland, Oregon: Northwest Regional Educational Laboratory, 1969. (ED 028 885) Prep Series #13, USOE.

Hughes, L., Achilles, C. M., Leonard, J., and Spence, D. *Interpretative Study of Research and Development Relative to Educational Cooperatives,* 173 pages, ERIC (ED 059-544), 1971. Prep Series #23, USOE.

Planning and Changing, a journal for school administrators, includes articles on regionalism and annually devotes one issue to regionalism.

The Catalyst for Change, the Journal of the National School Development Council, discusses programs of a cooperative nature which are conducted by study councils and their constituent districts.

Hughes, L., Achilles, C. M., Leonard, J. R., and Spence, D., *Bibliography: Educational Cooperation and Regional Education Agencies.* January 1971. 50 pages, ERIC Document Reproduction Service (ED 059-544).

Kohl, J. W., and Achilles, C. M. *A Basic Planning and Evaluation Model for Cooperation in Providing Regional Education Sources.* Monograph, Center for Cooperative Research with Schools, College of Education, The Pennsylvania State University (ED 053 827), 1970.

Descriptive Design for the Education Cooperative, Appalachian Education Laboratory, Charleston, West Virginia (ED 25 325), October 1971; and other working papers of the AEL, as well as articles in AEL's publication, *Appalachian Advance,* especially 1968-1972.

Appalachia, the magazine of the Appalachian Regional Commission, 1966 Connecticut Avenue, Washington, D.C. 20035, has featured articles on Regional Educational Service Agencies periodically since 1968.

Shared Services and Cooperatives: Schools Combine Resources to Improve Education. National School Public Relations Association, Washington, D.C. (#411-12798), 1971, 60 pp.

Major interest groups and associations concerned with educational cooperatives include the following: the Regional Education Association of the NEA, 1201 Sixteenth Street, N.W., Washington, D.C. 20026; National School Development Council, 249 Reid Hall, Montana State University, Bozeman, Montana 59715; Appalachian Regional Commission, 1666 Connecticut Avenue, N.W., Washington, D.C. 20235; Appalachia Education Laboratory, Box 1348, Charleston, West Virginia 25325. A new organization, the Association of Rural Education Associations (AREA), is attempting to improve the development, operation, and planning of RESAs and to increase communication among RESAs. The National School Development Council (NSDC) has similar functions for executive secretaries of school study councils. The Rural Education Association of the National Education Association has interest in the development of improved educational programs through cooperation. Both the Appalachian Regional Commission (ARC) and the Appalachia Education Laboratory

(AEL) have encouraged the development of regional approaches to improve and expand education in Appalachia.

21

INDUSTRY-EDUCATION COOPERATION

by Samuel M. Burt, Consultant
School of Business Administration
The American University
Washington, D.C.

Hardly a textbook concerning public school administration, or a school superintendent's speech to a civic organization, neglects to pay homage to the constantly available volunteer cooperation of industry and business representatives in the service of the public schools. If the practice was as stirring and pervasive as the rhetoric, our schools would be the most relevant, responsive, and respected of the nation's public institutions. That public schools do not enjoy such a reputation cannot be disputed. That industry involvement in public education is not the norm is well-recognized. Nevertheless, a considerable body of literature, and numerous case studies of industry-education cooperation in local school systems, do demonstrate that such cooperation is taking place in a number of schools and is helping to improve, enrich, expand, equalize, and make relevant public education for all students—youth as well as adults. With all facets of American society insisting that our public schools respond positively and continuously to the multiple needs of students preparing or attempting to cope in a rapidly changing technological world, there is assurance that the near future will see many more educators and school administrators seeking the assistance, involvement, participation, and cooperation of industry in the public schools.

DEFINITIONS AND LIMITATIONS

For purposes of this essay, the terms "industry" and "industry people" will be used as a matter of convenience for inclusive reference to representatives of business, manufacturing, labor, agriculture, the professions, and private and public employers other than those in public education. Industry involvement, cooperation, and participation in public education is defined as including those services, activities, money, literature, supplies, etc., provided at no charge by industry, either voluntarily at its own initiative or at the request of school people. Participation and cooperation by industry in education resulting from, or as a by-product of, selling equipment, books, furniture, supplies, etc. (estimated at $55 billion per year), while of considerable assistance and importance to school administration and classroom instruction, is not discussed here. The related topics of community involvement, community control, citizen participation, volunteer aides, etc., is also left to other writers.

HISTORICAL DEVELOPMENT HIGHLIGHTS

In vocational education, the involvement of industry has been an accepted practice from its earliest days. Recognition of the interdependence of industry and vocational education was reflected in the regulations issued by the U.S. Office of Education as far back as 1922. The description of duties of supervisors of trade and industrial education, then and now, still include cooperation with industry. Today every state, either by legislation or by regulations of the state department of education, encourages (with some states requiring) local school system vocational and technical education officials to establish advisory committees of industry people for each occupational education program offered in each secondary and postsecondary school. Furthermore, a number of states require that each local school system within the state appoint an advisory committee on vocational education for the entire system. In addition, in accordance with requirements of the 1968 amendments to the Vocational Education Act of 1963 (P.L. 90-570), each state must appoint a State Advisory Council on Vocational Education which shall include a number of industry representatives. This same law requires the establishment of a National Advisory Council on Vocational Education, which also includes a number of industry representatives.

It is estimated that, in toto, more than 100,000 industry people are more or less involved in serving on vocational education advisory committees at the federal, state, and local school levels. Notwithstanding these numbers, there are more vocational and technical education programs in local schools throughout the United States which do not have the benefit of formally organized advisory committees than those which do. However, the instructors for many programs which do not utilize committees do maintain informal and personal relationships with one or more industry people, on whom they occasionally call for advice and assistance. Furthermore, the fact that a school program reports the existence of an advisory committee does not necessarily mean the committee is being utilized effectively, or even used at all. To improve and expand the use of industry advisory committees in vocational and technical education, the American Vocational Association (the major professional organization of vocational and technical educators) and its state-affiliated organizations have, for a number of years, engaged in a variety of promotional and educational activities addressed to their members. More recently, the National and State Advisory Councils on Vocational Education have joined in campaigns urging school officials to establish local school system and occupational program advisory committees.

Other than in vocational education, meaningful industry involvement and cooperation in general education first flowered on a major scale throughout the United States in 1957, when our nation embarked on an all-out program to expand its scientific manpower to overtake Russia in the "space-age" competition. The public hue and cry which arose in the United States from Russia's leadership in space flight led to a national examination of curricula for our nation's school programs in science and related fields. Since a number of the companies involved in the space age industries were both among the largest corporations of our nation, and had long maintained cooperative relations with schools in their communities, they immediately expanded their cooperative activities to include assistance in developing the new science, mathematics, and engineering curricula. The overriding concern was to persuade schools to improve their science-related courses, so as to attract more young people into courses leading to careers in the sciences.

In pursuing this overall objective, a new industry-education cooperation organizational movement was initiated in several parts of the United States—the formation of regional and local school system industry-education councils. The councils were funded mostly through company membership dues or contributions, although school systems and individuals also paid membership dues. For example, in California, where this new movement originated, all major business and manufacturing organizations were members of either the Southern or the Northern California Industry-Education Councils, as was almost every local school system and many junior colleges. Both of these regional councils employed full-time executive directors and staff. The Central New Jersey Industry-Education Council, in addition to membership dues, also received funds from the Federal Government for its staff services and operational programs.

A number of other local and regional industry-education cooperation groups were formed during the late 1950s and the decade of the 1960s, as a result of the activities of the National Association for Industry-Education Cooperation, the National Community Resources Workshops Association, the U.S. Chamber of Commerce, and the National Association of Manufacturers.

The last two organizations, through their national education committee efforts, for over 50 years had encouraged their local affiliates to be actively involved in a variety of cooperative activities with their local public schools. In providing guidance and leadership to their locals, both national organizations issue case studies of industry-education cooperation, and periodically hold regional and national meetings to support, improve, and expand such programs at the local, state, regional, and national levels. The NAIEC, established early in the 1940s, is the only national organization in the United States whose sole mission is to promote industry-education cooperation at all levels of the educational system. The NCRW (now merged with NAIEC) was organized early in the 1950s to help local educators and school officials become intimately acquainted with industry, business, and other resources in their communities which could be utilized for enriching school instructional programs.

The activities and experiences of the above-mentioned national organizations and the local affiliates, plus the vocational and technical education advisory committees, served to acquaint many thousands of executives of numerous large and small national and local companies, trade associations, and labor unions with the variety of problems affecting public education during the 1950s and the early 1960s. This knowledge was further enhanced during the middle 1960s, as industry became involved in providing remedial education and training programs for the disadvantaged and the hard-core unemployed, as part of our nation's "war on poverty." Industry soon learned that a major deficiency of many of the "disadvantaged" was a combination of lack of basic education, retention skills, and a job. Industry also soon learned that remedying these deficiencies was extremely expensive after youth and adults had left school, and that it would make much more sense if these basic "coping" skills were provided while individuals were elementary and secondary school students.

This realization was brought into sharp focus by the riots and destruction which took place in many communities during the summer of 1967. Assessments of the causes of these riots resulted in the decision by many industry leaders throughout the United States to make improvement of the schools of our ghettoes the first line of attack in curing the malaise of our large cities. In concluding that they must become deeply involved in helping improve public education, a number of companies became engaged in a new strategy for industry-education cooperation—educational partnerships. Initiated by Michigan Bell Company and the Chrysler Corporation in Detroit, this strategy consisted of a company and a school "adopting" each other, whereby a company (or several companies) concentrated all the volunteer cooperative educational efforts of its executives and staff to the benefit of the "adopted" school. The thesis for this strategy was that each school would be able to call on its industry "partner(s)" for a variety of available services and assistance designed to help improve, enrich, and expand educational opportunities for its students.

The National Alliance of Businessmen and the Urban Coalition, both organized in the late 1960s, also are sponsoring programs of industry-education cooperation to help youth and adults obtain appropriate education and training to become gainfully employed and enter the mainstream of the American economic and social system.

VARIETY OF INDUSTRY-EDUCATION COOPERATIVE ACTIVITIES AND SERVICES

By 1969, the variety of volunteer cooperative activities and services available from industry to public schools upon request of teachers and school administrators had become quite extensive, as indicated below.

A Composite Listing of Volunteer Industry Services to Public Education and Improving School Management and Administration

1. Participating in campaigns for bond issues and special tax levies.
2. Helping to plan school building programs, including land acquisition and building designing.
3. Providing advice on budgeting, accounting, and school financing.
4. Providing advice concerning purchasing policies and procedures.
5. Helping to plan systems of transportation.
6. Providing advice on school insurance policies and programs.
7. Providing advice in planning and administering cafeteria services.
8. Assisting in planning safety campaigns, fire protection programs, etc.
9. Testifying in support of school organizational and financial needs at meetings of local, state, and federal agencies and legislative bodies.
10. Helping to develop maintenance programs for buildings, equipment, and grounds.
11. Assisting in developing systems of educational accountability, including the use of performance contracts.
12. Helping to develop manuals of organization and administration.
13. Helping to plan personnel practices and procedures, labor negotiations procedures, and contracts with school personnel.
14. Assisting in the preparation and review of budget requests for laboratory and shop equipment and supplies.

Upgrading Professional Staff

1. Providing research and work-experience opportunities for teachers and other school officials during school holidays and summers.
2. Arranging plant and office visits for teachers and counselors.
3. Offering industry and business experience workshops, conferences, and seminars for teachers and guidance counselors.
4. Providing funds to assist teachers when they attend regional and national meetings of teacher and industry organizations.
5. Inviting teachers and guidance counselors to attend local industry meetings, and offering free memberships in local industry associations.
6. Conducting clinics on utilizing new industrial equipment, supplies, and techniques for possible application to school programs.
7. Providing awards and prizes to teachers and guidance counselors for outstanding service, etc.
8. Financing college-credit community resources study courses.

Improving Instructional Programs

1. Helping to determine educational policies and objectives of the school system as well as individual school programs.
2. Arranging for student field trips to offices and plants.
3. Providing classroom and assembly speakers.
4. Providing industry people as resource teachers.
5. Sponsoring and participating in student club programs.

6. Providing on-the-job opportunities in cooperative education programs.
7. Helping to develop relevant curricula for a variety of school courses, particularly in industrial arts and in vocational and technical education.
8. Providing industrial equipment, free or on loan, and free expendable supplies for use in chemistry, physics, and other laboratories, as well as for vocational and technical education programs.
9. Providing books and magazines on specialized business and industry subjects.
10. Sponsoring citywide and statewide student contests in a variety of subject areas.
11. Providing information to teachers and counselors concerning desirable aptitudes and educational and experience background which applicants for entry-level jobs should have, so that educators may properly plan their student recruitment, educational training, and job-placement programs.
12. Assisting and participating in surveys of local industry manpower needs to assist curriculum and program planners.
13. Helping to develop, and participating in, student occupational achievement-testing programs.
14. Evaluating physical conditions, adequacy of equipment, and layout of laboratories and shops.
15. Assisting in the development and evaluation of course content to assure its currency in meeting the changing skill and knowledge needs of industry and business.
16. Providing free audio-visual aids for use in a variety of instructional programs.
17. Assisting in the development of evening school skill improvement and technical courses for employed plant personnel.
18. Assisting in the development of apprenticeship and on-the-job training related to educational courses.
19. Providing sample kits of raw materials, finished products, charts, posters, etc., for exhibit and instructional purposes in classrooms and shops.
20. Compiling and publishing directories of community resources and personnel available to teachers, schools, and the school system for various volunteer services.

Improving Public Relations

1. Helping to plan, and participating in, community public relations programs.
2. Providing speakers to address civic and trade groups concerning school programs and problems.
3. Arranging for the publication of articles in local and national industry trade magazines concerning the school system's vocational and technical education programs.
4. Arranging for the publication of articles in local newspapers concerning school programs.
5. Attending meetings of local, state, and federal agency and legislative bodies in support of local school system program meeds.
6. Participating in radio and television programs designed to "sell" various school programs to the public.
7. Contributing funds to advertise specific school program offerings in local newspapers.
8. Helping to organize, and participating in, citizen advisory committees for local schools, for individual school programs, and for the school system.
9. Advising industry and business employees and their families concerning school programs by means of bulletin boards, news stories in company publications, and enclosures in pay envelopes.
10. Advising the general public about school programs and problems by means of enclosures with invoices mailed to customers.

Helping Students

1. Helping to plan pupil personnel services.
2. Serving as tutors to individual students and groups of students.
3. Providing prizes, awards, and scholarship grants to worthy and outstanding students.
4. Providing career and job-placement counseling and guidance services to students applying for admission to vocational and technical courses.
5. Providing paid on-the-job experience opportunities in cooperative education programs.
6. Providing vocational guidance and career literature to teachers and counselors for use by students.
7. Providing jobs for school dropouts, as well as graduates, through special arrangements with teachers and counselors.
8. Serving as speakers at career-day meetings and during student assemblies on career opportunities in business and industry.
9. Participating in the development of aptitude tests for selection of students for vocational and technical education programs.
10. Sponsoring student research projects and providing plant, laboratory, and staff assistance in the conduct of the research project.

ATTITUDES OF EDUCATORS TO INDUSTRY-COOPERATION EFFORTS

With such a storehouse of volunteer services available from industry organizations and people, it might be assumed that most public education officials at all levels would invite and welcome industry to participate and become involved in school programs and the resolution of school problems. The fact is that, generally speaking, there is a minimal effort on the part of school administrators to initiate or encourage industry-cooperative efforts. And since school officials are responsible for administering the schools, no outsider can become involved or participate in school affairs unless invited to do so by the appropriate officials.

Many educators resent what they consider layman interference in their area of professional competence and responsibility. Some of this negative reaction stems from one or more unfortunate experiences with industry involvement. Much of the resentment, however, stems from the distrust of school people who know very little about industry, its people, and their motivations for wanting to become involved in public school matters. Some of the reasons for this xenophobic attitude (Burt, 1971) are:

Lack of knowledge as to how industry is organized, how it functions, and how its multiple goals are achieved.

Suspicion of industry motivations for becoming involved in public education.

Fear that industry groups will become special-interest pressure groups within the schools, and may even be seeking to control the schools.

Jealousy on the part of administrative and managerial staff concerning their prerogatives and responsibilities, which might be invaded by laymen with expertise in business management.

Concern of professional staff that industry training techniques may replace broader-based educational programs and goals.

Confusion as to what services can best be provided by industry, who should be approached, and when.

Insistence that laymen—individuals as well as committees—serve only in an advisory capacity, despite industry's desire and ability to provide many types of volunteer cooperative services desperately needed by the schools, and for which the schools have no funds.

Lack of coordination of existing industry-education cooperative programs in individual schools of the school system.

Unwillingness to develop regional programs of industry-education cooperation embracing several separate school systems, despite the fact that industry people are drawn from a metropolitan area composed of a number of separate communities.

ATTITUDES OF INDUSTRY REGARDING INDUSTRY-EDUCATION COOPERATION

The negative attitudes, lack of knowledge, and confusion on the part of educators concerning industry's reasons for wanting to become involved in helping improve public education is particularly frustrating to industry, since most industry representatives are quite sincere in their desire to be of public service. It has been observed that the American industry executive

is first and foremost a human being, and as such has many needs—economic, personal and social—which must be fulfilled. It is a peculiar attribute of many industry executives that their personal lives are so intertwined and identified with their occupations and industry organizations that they can conduct business and pursue profits—at the same time satisfying their self-fulfillment needs through business-associated and business-supported voluntarism in public and societal service. (Burt and Lessinger, 1971)

Even more to the point, Patrick and Eells (1969), writing about businessmen and education, reported:

Few business people are neutral or unmoved by the educational establishment. If they do not distrust it or attack it, they are likely to be challenged by it, flattered to be involved in some of its problems and eager to suggest improvements. Seldom does the church, the YMCA, the local hospital or the community chest kindle the same attitudes or create comparable urges to participate and cooperate.

Among the reasons why volunteer service to public education has such universal appeal for industry people are the following:

Desire to fulfill a civic responsibility by becoming involved in a traditionally important public service activity such as public education.

Desire to enhance personal prestige among their business associates, friends, customers, and family circle through recognition of public service.

Desire to be known as philanthropic and altruistic.

Desire to help youth.

Additionally, many companies, large and small, in their recognition of the need to become constructively involved in helping ameliorate the societal problems of our nation and its communities, are encouraging their employees to participate in civic, community, and governmental affairs. They see voluntary involvement of their people in public service, particularly in public education, as serving both the public interest and their own self-interest, in terms of helping to meet industry needs for, among other things:

Qualified manpower.

Conserving public tax monies.

Providing a credible public relations image.

Assuring viable communities in which to conduct business.

Returning to the schools the responsibility for remedial education, which industry had undertaken as a part of its involvement in the "war on poverty" during the late 1960s.

Of these major corporate motivations, the need for a continuing supply of well-educated, well-trained manpower has always been of primary significance to industry. When employers in the late 1950s and 1960s perceived that the schools were providing them with a large body of manpower without appropriate economic attitudes and a sufficiently high level of basic skills in reading, computing, and "producing," many more employers than in previous years felt the need to assist the schools to achieve the goals of public education, particularly those dealing with the world of work. It was no surprise, then, that when in 1971 the Health, Education, and Welfare Assistant Secretary Sidney J. Marland (then Commissioner of Education) called on public education to concentrate on the concept and goals of career education, industry wholeheartedly and universally supported him. During 1972 and 1973, a number of regional and national conferences were sponsored by the U.S. Office of Education and the Chamber of Commerce of the United States to bring educators and industry people together to discuss cooperative efforts for implementing career education; and the National Association of Manufacturers issued several new publications dealing with industry-education cooperation. At the local school system level, however, little progress was made, as reported late in 1973 in an analysis of four Federally-funded career education demonstration projects for bringing the community into the schools:

> . . . relatively little attention has been paid thus far to improving and expanding the mechanisms for bringing the community into the school facility for educational purposes. (Raizen, 1973)

Even those Federally-funded projects designed as Employer-Based Career Education models (as differentiated from School-Based Education models) were reported as achieving minimal success. The major reason, in the opinion of many students of industry-education cooperation, is the lack of knowledge on the part of educators as to what can be reasonably expected from, and how to work with, employers and other community resource organizations, institutions, and people. Given this lack of knowledge, and continuing misunderstanding and suspicision of industry motivations for seeking to be involved in public education, there is still much to be done before industry-education cooperation moves from rhetoric to reality in most public school systems.

THE FUTURE

A recent report by a national industry and business-oriented research organization concerning industry-education cooperation described the current status as "a fragile partnership" (The Conference Board, 1973). This author believes it is not so much fragile as it is fractionalized, leaderless, and directionless. In short, what is now needed to give form to the proven substance of industry-education cooperation is a national organization with sufficient funds and staff so that the case-study experiences throughout our nation can be welded into effective, replicable programs at the regional, state, and local community levels. Furthermore, with the establishment of such an organization closer and more effective working relationships between educators and businessmen will become possible. The need for such collaborative relationships was highlighted by Willard Wirtz (1973), former Secretary of the U.S. Department of Labor and now President of The Manpower Institute, when he spoke to the National Academy of School Executives:

> Educators and businessmen have lived pretty far apart, for reasons deeply engrained and in the traditions of the society. And if there are significant signs now of a larger recognition of a commonality of interests and responsibilities here, there remain elements of the relationship between the Butcher and the Beaver in Lewis Carroll's *Hunting of the Snark:*
> > The valley grew narrower and narrower still
> > And the evening grew darker and colder,
> > Til (merely from nervousness, not from goodwill)
> > They marched along shoulder to shoulder.

While fear of the consequences of noncollaboration may be an excellent motivation for cooperation, there are a number of other hopeful signs that progress is being made in achieving the beneficial potential of industry-education cooperation for our nation's public schools:

Recognition on the part of both educators and industry that long-term commitments to industry-education cooperation must be made by assignment of full-time staff to develop and implement such cooperation at the local, state, regional, and national levels. The U.S. Office of Education and several state departments of education have already made such appointments.

The National Association for Industry-Education Cooperation is currently seeking funds from both industry and education to employ full-time staff, to expand its national services, and to establish self-supporting regional and state affiliates.

Continued funding by the U.S. Office of Education of the research and demonstration projects for Employer-Based Career Education models, so that educators will learn how to more effectively involve employers in public education.

Continuing efforts of the U.S. Chamber of Commerce, the National Association of Manufacturers, the American Vocational Association, the American Association of Community and Junior Colleges, and other national, regional, and local industry and educational organizations, to promote meaningful industry-education cooperation.

Recognition by State Advisory Councils on Vocational Education that local school system and school occupational education advisory committees must be established and supported to the fullest possible extent; also that both the State Councils and local committees must be involved in all areas of public education, instead of restricting their concerns to vocational and technical education alone.

Restructuring of a number of university graduate school curricula in school administration to include studies dealing with the involvement of citizens, industry, and community resources in public education, as evidenced by a growing number of doctoral dissertations on these subjects.

Growing recognition and acceptance by many school administrators that their school systems have the responsibility for helping students obtain employment, as well as continuing education at the postsecondary level. This "school-to-work" as well as "school-to-college" responsibility will require the development of close working relationships between educators and employers.

All of these forces, coming together at this moment in time, augur well for the imminent creation of what must be the first move, and the sine qua non, for effective industry-education cooperation—a properly funded and staffed national organization. Given this organization, the "tillers of the soil" in the field of industry-education cooperation will become the major force they can and should be, in helping improve, expand, enrich, and equalize our nation's system of public education.

REFERENCES

Books

Burt, Samuel M. *Industry and Vocational-Technical Education.* New York: McGraw-Hill, 1967. A study of local advisory (cooperating) committees.
_____, and Lessinger, Leon M. *Volunteer Industry Involvement in Public Education.* D. C. Heath, 1970.
Chamberlain, Neil W., ed. *Business and the Cities.* Basic Books, 1970.
Corson, John J. *Business in the Humane Society.* New York: McGraw-Hill, 1971.
Patrick, Kenneth G., and Eells, Richard. *Education and the Business Dollar.* New York: Macmillan, 1969.

Chapters in Books

Banta, Trudy W. "An Interim Report on the Interpretive Study of Cooperative Efforts of Private Industry and the Schools to Provide Job Oriented Programs for the Disadvantaged." *Notes and Working Papers from the National Conference on Cooperative Vocational Education.* University of Minnesota, Minneapolis, 1969. The complete study by Trudy W. Banta and Douglas C. Towne is available from ERIC, ED 027 442.
Burt, Samuel M. "Involving Industry and Business in Education." Gordon F. Law, ed., *Contemporary Concepts in Vocational Education.* American Vocational Association, 1971.
_____. "Industry Involvement in Vocational Education." Roman Pucinski, ed., *The Courage to Change.* New York: Prentice-Hall, 1971.
_____. "Changing Relationships Between Schools and Industry." Gerald Somers, ed., *Vocational and Technical Education Today.* University of Wisconsin Press, 1971.
_____. "The Vocational Education Advisory Committee." *Encyclopedia of Education.* New York: Macmillan, 1971.
Kurzman, Stephen. "Private Enterprise Participation in Antipoverty Programs." *Examination of the War on Poverty,* Vol. 1. Senate Committee on Labor and Public Welfare, Subcommittee on Employment, Manpower and Poverty, 1967.

Monographs and Reports

The Advisory Committee and Vocational Education. The American Vocational Association, 1510 H Street, N.W., Washington, D.C. 20005, 1969.
Riendeau, Albert J. *The Role of the Advisory Committee in Occupational Education in the Junior Colleges.* American Association of Junior and Community Colleges, One Dupont Circle, N.W., Washington, D.C. 20006
Burt, Samuel M. *Strengthening Volunteer Industry Service to Public Education,* 1971. *State Advisory Councils on Vocational Education,* 1969. *Toward Greater Industry and Government Involvement in Manpower Development* (co-author, Herbert E. Striner), 1968. Upjohn Institute for Employment Research, 300 S. Westnedge Avenue, Kalamazoo, Michigan 49007.
Private Industry and Public Education. Advisory Council for Occupational Education, Board of Education, New York City.
National Association of Manufacturers, Education Department, 227 Park Avenue, New York City 10017:
    Industry-Education Councils

    Industry-Education Coordinator
    Community Resources Workshops
    Student-Industry Plan for Action
    Also case study reports of effective industry-education cooperative programs.
Resource Book for Members of State Advisory Councils. Washington, D.C.: The National Advisory Council on Vocational Education, 1973.
Operating Plans for the Employer-Based Career Education Model. Philadelphia: Research for Better Schools, Inc., July 20, 1973.
Detrick, R. L. *Youth Employment and Industry-Education Cooperation in the Greater Long Beach Labor Market.* Doctoral dissertation, University of California, 1972, published on demand by University Microfilms, Ann Arbor, Michigan.
Clary, Joseph Ray. *State Advisory Councils on Vocational Education.* Information Series No. 22, ERIC Clearinghouse on Vocational and Technical Education, Ohio State University, Columbus, Ohio 43210, 1970.
Hamburger, Martin, and Wolfson, Harry E. *1000 Employers Look at Occupational Education.* Board of Education, New York City, 1969.
Jobe, Max E. *Administrative Aspects of State Advisory Councils on Vocational Education.* Unpublished doctoral dissertation, University of Georgia, Athens, Ga., 1972. (Note: A limited number of copies are available by writing to the author at State Advisory Council on Vocational Education, 1123 North Eutah Street, Baltimore, Maryland 21201.)
A Handbook for Members of Advisory Councils for Occupational Education. State Department of Education, Albany, New York.
Robertson, J. Marvin. *An Evaluation System for State Advisory Councils of Vocational Education.* University of Georgia, Athens, Ga., 1972.
Raizen, Senta A. et al. *Career Education: An R and D Plan* Santa Monica, Cal.: The Rand Corporation, May 1973.

ADDITIONAL RESOURCES

Chamber of Commerce of the United States, Education Department, 1615 H Street, N.W., Washington, D.C. 20006 Position papers, reports, and case studies concerning industry assistance and involvement in public education.
National Association for Industry-Education Cooperation, Suite 600, 1000 Sixteenth Street, N.W., Washington, D.C. 20036. Case studies, reports, and literature concerning community resource workshops, industry-education councils, etc.
Institute for Development of Education Activities, P.O. Box 446, Melbourne, Florida 32901. Reports of several conferences dealing with industry and community involvement in education. Latest report title is *Toward More Effective Involvement of the Community in the School,* August 1972.
Institute for Educational Development, 52 Vanderbilt Avenue, New York, N.Y. 10017. Several case study reports of industry assistance to public schools.
National School Public Relations Association, 1801 North Moore Street, Arlington, Virginia 22209. Case study reports of industry assistance to public schools.
National Center for Voluntary Action, 1735 Eye Street, N.W., Washington, D.C. Monthly free publication, *Voluntary Action News,* occasionally carries stories of volunteer industry assistance to schools.
Educators Progress Service, Inc., Randolph, Wisconsin 53956. Publishes lists and descriptions of free teaching materials, films, filmstrips, etc., available from industry, business, and other sources. Special volumes on social studies, health, counseling, and other areas of study.
The Conference Board, New York, N.Y. Over the years has conducted studies and published reports on various aspects

of industry and business involvement in education. Latest publication is *Business and Education: A Fragile Partnership,* 1973.

22

MULTIAXIAL PHYSICIAN-EDUCATOR CHILD DEVELOPMENT TEAM

by Victor Cogen
Director, Educational IMPACT
Cherry Hill, New Jersey

Medicine, education, and psychology, the three major disciplines most important to a child with learning disabilities, are joined in a new cooperative relationship using the theories of Jean Piaget as a cohesive force. Encouraged by the results of programs initiated in Pennsylvania (Child Development Center, Norristown; Geneva Academy, Levittown; Bristol Township School District, Bucks County), a newly formed medical-educational partnership intends to effect an important impact on child development sciences at both state and national levels.

The author's Piaget-Based Early Learning Program emphasizes early identification of the child who has a learning disability. It then attempts to build an adequate foundation for children who need the mental structures necessary to learn. The children engage in a set of tasks that correspond to the specific levels of development which Piaget has identified. Many of the tasks are presented to the children in the form of games, wherein they may learn by play and imitation.

REVIEW OF DEVELOPMENTS

The new cooperative effort inaugurates a change from the traditional team by eliminating some of its shortcomings and providing a means of tapping the true potential of skilled professionals grouped together in a common effort. The team approach is not to be belittled. On the contrary, it is a significant improvement over some other methods that are still prevalent. One of these, still utilized extensively, is a restricted diagnosis; restricted, that is, to an examination by one discipline. The diagnostician may be a psychologist, for instance, who will administer a psychological battery to a child and forward his conclusions and recommendations to an educator. The results of his study may or may not include an instructional prescription. Frequently he merely classifies the child in some manner, such as placing the pupil in a category, i.e., learning-disabled, educable-retarded, emotionally disturbed, etc. Almost invariably, the data are accompanied by an I.Q. score. The administrator, armed with this justification, then places the child in "an appropriate setting" for educational purposes.

Another approach is to add a diagnosis made by the representative of a second discipline to the initial study. A child suspected of being disturbed may be examined by a psychiatrist, while a neurologist must be consulted if the youngster is earmarked for the category of brain injury or neurologically impaired. Audiologists and opthomologists may be consulted for those children with hearing and visual impairments, and other specialists become involved as they are thought to be needed. This procedure is, obviously, an improvement over the single-disciplinary examination, but falls short of the effectiveness of the team. The team brings in a variety of specialists and attempts to broaden the picture of the child's difficulties, and to prescribe a suitable remedial program.

What may be witnessed is a steady growth in attempts to help children with problems, including those with learning disabilities, with more and more sophisticated methods. While still in practice, the unidisciplinary approach, whether it is education, psychology, or medicine, is at the bottom of the growth pattern. The involvement of more than one discipline to shed additional light on the child provides an improvement, but even this approach leaves many gaps.

A team of professionals, exchanging information and views, would appear to be much more desirable, and is gaining acceptance across the nation's school districts. However, this approach, while desirable in concept, is still inadequate in performance. The interdisciplinary team varies from agency to agency, and a given criticism may not apply to any specific instance. However, in general there are major weaknesses that do pertain.

Frequently the group does not have a physician, as if the physiological development of the child were of no consequence in determining the etiology of his impairment, the remedial measures necessary, and the instructional techniques to be employed. In fact, a leading text in pupil personnel services, and another in school guidance services, do not take into account the role of the physician at all. Some teams rely on reports submitted by physicians who are not team members. The child is sent to them for an examination and the results are forwarded to the requesting authorities. This is equivalent to the independent diagnosis state of affairs mentioned earlier. The medical practitioner looks at the child from the restricted viewpoint of his own discipline. This approach presupposes that the child can be segmented, that each segment is an entity, and that each entity is independent of all others and may be treated without consideration of the whole.

Many physicians, dealing with handicapped children, have behaved as if the field of medicine were the only one that should concern doctors. Professionals in other endeavors have had similar feelings. Thus, this philosophy seems to advise that we should keep the physicians out of education, the educator out of medicine, and the psychologist out of both. However, those involved with the child are not only concluding that this arrangement makes a poor team, but that this philosophy reduces the effectiveness of the total service to the subject. Any group that attempts to remedy the effects of a child's handicap without direct medical representation, in the author's view, has omitted an essential team component.

The mere inclusion of a doctor of medicine in the group, however, is insufficient. The structure of the team must be considered. A hierarchical child services construct often leads to discontent, uncooperativeness, and a breakdown in effectiveness. In some cases, those at the top merely lecture to those below, and fail to profit from the possibilities of a totally interacting team membership. Sometimes a pecking order develops which precludes the development of optimum contributions by each participant. This arrangement is not interdisciplinary, as it purports to be, but is rather a multidisciplinary representation with each field acting as an entity.

The author and his colleagues, working with learning disabled and neurologically impaired children, have found that placing a physician on the team with an active role, and operating in a horizontal fashion, is still insufficient. Medical training and experience, including a specialty, are still not adequate for the type of team envisioned. Needed for the concept being espoused are additional specialties. Medical representation must be more extensive than one physician, and must encompass several subdisciplinary specialties. In the field of learning disabilities, the determination has been that the team must include a pediatrician, a neurologist, and a psychiatrist. These three are basic, and constitute a medical core; other specialties must be available on an on-call basis.

Earlier, reference was made to the necessity of involving those with expertise in the physiological development of the child, or medical practitioners. Now, a psychiatrist is listed as being part of a central core of professionals. There are two points to be made regarding this specialty. First, the affective evolvement of the youngster cannot be overlooked. This is, of course, the realm of the psychiatrist. The affect also properly belongs with the physiological classification, since an overwhelming amount of research has related behavior to the nervous system, the endocrine system, and certainly, if one should want to consider it separately, brain chemistry. Secondly, the Piagetian notions being used confirm the interaction of these systems with the development of cognition and the ability to learn. Piaget perceives the cognitive and affective spheres to be interfaced.

The weakness of an interdisciplinary team must be erased by the inclusion of not only medical representation, but also of broadened medical participation. The design utilized must be arranged horizontally, so that all may contribute and all contributions may be utilized in assessing the needs of a child. However, even with these factors accounted for, experience demonstrates that communication among the disciplines is difficult. This problem exists because the individual fields are not adequately familiar with each other's language. In addition, they are unknowledgeable about each other's strengths and limitations. A breakdown in understanding is quite possible in the team approach, and actually happens frequently.

Sometimes the objectives of individuals from different disciplines vary; sometimes their priorities differ, and frequently misunderstanding occurs because the participants are each operating from a different theoretical base. Unfortunately, some team members also are defensive about their fields, feel others are encroaching, and have their performances hampered by sensitive egos. The multidisciplinary team is better than no team at all, but there is a next step.

Reference to such a development was made at a meeting called by Henry W. Baird, M.D., for the staff at St. Christopher's Hospital, Philadelphia, on May 30, 1973. A series of reports were presented which reviewed the Piagetian-based program for mentally handicapped youngsters at the Child Development Center in Norristown, to study the medical implications of the success of the program. The conclusion, after discussion, was that the curriculum had been highly effective; the children had undergone remarkable and favorable change. These views were based on observations and examinations by physicians representing various subdivisions of medicine, i.e., neurology, pediatrics, and psychiatry. The same views were held by educators and psychologists.

Interest and enthusiasm were directed not only at the program, but at the team of professionals who had interacted in an unusual way to execute the plan of the program. The nomenclature applied to this newly designed, cooperative system of working is "multiaxial," a term supplied by H. Allen Handford, M.D., after the World Health Organization model to indicate the equality of importance of each represented profession.

A third feature of the endeavor was recognized at the conference. The author had supplied the curriculum, Dr. Handford had contributed the mode of operation, but Frank W. Shaffer, M.D., offered the guidelines and objectives for the participants themselves, who are now regarded as "child developmentalists." Although the term child development has had frequent usage, Dr. Shaffer sees it in a somewhat different light. He envisions special training by physicians, educators, psychologists, and others in the disciplines of their colleagues on the team. This approach would help in dissolving professional language barriers, lead to an understanding of the possible contributions of each field (along with the recognizing of its limitations), and developing shared goals and responsibilities.

The purpose of this approach, then, is to have distinct specialties coalesce into a single, effective effort, now called the multiaxial team. The outworn vertical effort is discarded in favor of true cooperation, wherein each member is familiar to some reasonable degree with the other member's field. This lends itself to ready acceptance in verbal philosophy, but is difficult to achieve in practice. Members are frequently faced with situations requiring their admission that (1) a given set of knowledge is unknown to their respective disciplines; and (2), even more horrendous, the information is available but that they are unfamiliar with it. In addition, they must acknowledge that some preconceived notions are invalid, and that they are, no matter how well trained and experienced, still in a learning situation. Members of this team cannot hide behind cliches, titles, or language indigenous to their own profession.

Under the new concept, each member of the team sheds some of his identity as Psychiatrist, Pediatrician, Psychologist, Educator, Opthalmologist and the like, in favor of becoming the Child Developmentalist. Each discipline contributes to the decisions in a cooperative manner that regards the child's problem simultaneously in the light of every other discipline. This new light, instead of separate rays, is merged into one broad and bright beam flashed onto the subject.

The theoretical approach, which cements the relationship of these professional Child Developmentalists, and possibly the most important of their considerations, rests upon the developmental notions of the Swiss biologist Jean Piaget. These theories provide a framework upon which the multiaxial physician-educator team bases its work. According to Piagetian principles, there are developmental aspects of every child which interact and affect each other. These include the development of the neurological and endocrine systems, social interactions and perturbances, and the role of exercise, or physical and logico-mathematical learnings. Thus, physiological, affective, and cognitive development are interfaced and cannot be readily separated. Intervention and the solving of problems require attention from several sources acting as a unit.

While this is a simplified explanation of a Piagetian approach to mental development, it nevertheless lays the groundwork for an attack on inadequate mental development, both cognitive and affective. This attack should have profound implications for the future of education, psychology, and medicine.

First, a simplistic stimulus-response approach to learning, in the writer's view, cannot remedy mental impairments significantly. Atomistic-based programs are extremely self-limiting. Programs utilizing operant conditioning, effective in specific instances, stumble in terms of transfer or generalization. Secondly, remedial attempts which are not interacting fail to deal with the problem in the most effective manner. It appears that since all of the forces are at work simultaneously, the most economical methodology to reduce the effects of developmental lag would be molar in approach. This suggests the integration of the author's educational program (which focuses on the logico-mathematical and social transmission parameters) with Dr. Handford's multiaxial system, which blends all of the disciplines into one coherent attack on mental disabilities. The professionals in such an endeavor are the Child Developmentalists, the designation advocated by Dr. Shaffer.

The multiaxial team currently represents neurology, psychiatry, ophthalmology, psychology, education, and learning and curriculum theory. The team is interested in formulating questions and seeking their solutions. Examples:

Are there experiences which a child may have in a preschool educational setting which will have a marked effect on emotional adjustment?

Are the more-than-expected results of the author's program due to an originally unplanned attack on emotional difficulties? A breakthrough of emotional blocs?

What are the tie-ins between cognitive and affective progress and neurological development? Are there measurable neurological changes concomitant with learning and achievement?

Can neurological and psychiatric tests be developed, comparable to psychological tests of intellectual potential and educational measures of achievement, to measure growth, adjustment, and development?

Would Piagetian-type measures of advancement on a cognitive scale shed light on psychiatric and physiological (CNS) development?

Can electroencephalograms be used to measure changes in brain wave patterns that will correlate with development resulting from the curriculum used in the program?

SPECIFIC PROGRAMS AND/OR APPLICATIONS

Dr. Henry W. Baird III, Chief of Neurology at St. Christopher's Hospital in Philadelphia, Pennsylvania, has helped form a new doctor-educator team. Dr. Baird became convinced that the Piaget-based curriculum, designed as a child development effort, required the services of the medical profession, not in a supportive role but as an integral part of the program. Dr. Baird based his contention upon his own observations of the Piaget-based curriculum now in operation.

Other members of the newly formed team include Dr. Frank Shaffer, medical director of the Child Development Center in Norristown, and Dr. Allen Handford, director of the Children's Unit, Haverford State Hospital. Dr. Handford's psychiatric work in alleviating the effects of mental illness in children has become part of the foundation of the new medical-educational cooperation. Dr. Shaffer, a pediatrician, at an early period saw the possibilities of this new approach and was instrumental in bringing the disciplines together.

SUMMARY AND CONCLUSIONS

The multiaxial physician-educator child development team represents a major change in attempting to solve the learning disability problems which beset children with cognitive and/or emotional handicaps. The approach not only recognizes the intimate connections among the child's affective, physical, and cognitive development, but also brings about a concerted effort by all the disciplines which are involved in the child's welfare.

Since the measurement of the child's learning ability (or disability) serves as the occasion for the initial disability diagnosis (and, indeed, provides the continuing motivation for a child study team to show interest in a child's progress), it is entirely proper that an educational philosophy should underpin the decisions and efforts made on behalf of the child. In the new cooperative approach, the educational program of the author, based on the notions of Jean Piaget, serves to funnel the efforts of the several professions into the same direction. A new breed of professional emerges from the experience: the Child Developmentalist.

The new approach is able to be more effective than traditional team methods because it incorporates the many disciplines of the medical profession, as well as non-medical professionals. Most present approaches fail to recognize the efficacy of medicine and physiology in the solution to a child's learning disability problem. Another advantage of the new approach is the utilization of horizontal cooperation of the various disciplines, in contradistinction to a vertical relationship that has failed to produce the most efficacious results for the child. The new concern is with the child as an integrated person who should be treated by an integrated team. Thus, in place of disciplines acting as entities is a group of Child Developmentalists utilizing a common theory of development (Piaget's) to resolve the many problems facing the children in question.

REFERENCES

Adams, James F. *Problems in Counseling.* New York: MacMillan Company, 1962.

American Association of School Administrators. *Profiles of the Administrative Team.* Washington, D.C., 1971.

Arbuckle, Dugald S. *Pupil Personnel Services in the Modern School.* Boston: Allyn and Bacon, Inc., 1966.

Campbell, Ronald F., Cunningham, Luvern, and McPhee, Roderick. *Organization and Control of American Schools.* Columbus, Ohio: Charles E. Merrill Books, 1965.

Educational Service Bureau, Administrative Leadership Service. *Administration, Organization of Schools.* Arlington, Virginia: The Bureau, 1966.

Fensch, Edwin, and Wilson, Robert. *The Superintendent's Team.* Columbus, Ohio: Charles E. Merrill Books, 1964.

Froehlich, Clifford P. *Guidance Services in Schools,* New York: McGraw-Hill, 1958.

Griffiths, Daniel E. et al. *Organizing Schools for Effective Education.* Danville, Illinois: Interstate Printers and Publishers, 1962.

Jenson, Theodore, and Clark, Daniel. *Education Administration: The Library of Education.* New York: Center for Applied Research and Education, 1964.

Kanezevich, Steven J. *Administration of Public Education.* New York: Harper and Brace, 1962.

———, ed. *Administrative Technology of the School.* Washington, D.C.: American Association of School Administrators, 1969.

Landy, Edward, and Kroll, Arthur M., eds. *Current Issues and Suggestive Active Guidance and American Educators II.* Cambridge, Massachusetts: Harvard Press, 1965.

Levitan, Sar, and Siegel, Irving H. *Dimensions of Manpower Policy: Programs and Research.* Baltimore: Johns Hopkins Press, 1966.

Morphet, Edgar L., and Jesser, David L. *Emerging Designs for Education: Programs, Organizations, Operation and Finance.* Denver: Designing Education for the Future, An Eight State Project, May 1968.

———, eds. *Preparing Educators to Mutual Emerging Needs* (Reports Prepared for the Governor's Conference on Education for the Future). Denver, Colorado, 1969.

National Association of Secondary School Principals. *Looking Ahead, Bulletin #332.* Washington, D.C.: A Department of the National Educators Association, December, 1968.

Tyler, Leona E. *The Work of the Counselor.* New York: Appleton-Century-Crofts, 1953.

Wynn, Richard. *Organization of Public Schools.* Library of Education, New York Center for Applied Research in Education, 1964.

PART II

ADMINISTRATION AND MANAGEMENT OF EDUCATION

23

SYSTEM APPROACHES TO EDUCATION

by Roger Kaufman
Professor of Psychology and Human Behavior
School of Human Behavior
United States International University
San Diego, California

An array of useful educational tools called "system approaches" currently are available to measurably improve educational processes and outcomes. All have been developed to make the educational adventure more successful, holistic, planful, responsive, responsible, logical, orderly, self-correctable, and flexible, rather than wholly intuitive, unordered, undefinable, and doubtful. The field is relatively new, and differences exist between specialists in the area—but this contributes to self-renewal and useful modification of the concepts and tools which are becoming increasingly available and used in a host of educational settings and situations.

Most opposition to system approaches seems to lie in allegations that they are arbitrary, mechanistic, dehumanizing and inflexible. Like with any other tool, all of these charges could be true if it were used incorrectly— but this does not have to be the case. This overview provides a brief understanding of what are the major alternative models, and what are their relationships, and concurrently it attempts to interest the reader to try one or more of these approaches to make educational activities more responsive and responsible.

WHY USE A SYSTEM APPROACH?

Currently there is considerable use of the several forms of system approaches. Use varies from application by a single teacher in an individualized classroom, to governments planning and deciding among alternative programs for improved education. Depending upon one's definition, a system approach or one of its possible components is being used in almost every state of the union and most State Educational Agencies, as well as by the Federal Government. Industry (such as application on the McDonnell-Douglas DC-10) and the military (such as the U.S. Navy and U.S. Army applications) are using this relatively new set of tools, with increasing evidence that it can measurably improve the effectiveness and efficiency of behavior change programs. To name but a few educational applications, California (e.g., Newport-Mesa Unified School District, Commission for Teacher Preparation and Licensing, Los Angeles County Department of Education, San Diego Community Colleges), Arizona (e.g., Mesa), and Florida (e.g., Duval and Sarasota Counties) have been active in attempting to implement a system approach, which starts with a formal assessment of needs and proceeds to delineate measurable requirements; identifies and selects the best methods and means; implements, evaluates, and revises, based upon

formal systematic thinking and doing.

Educational agencies such as these frequently start with a faculty and administrator workshop which discuss what the system approach is, and what it is not, and these agencies explore its utility for them and the learners they serve. After detailed study and questioning, there is usually some period of learning the tools and techniques of needs assessment and system planning, and an application of some of the tools to current conditions. Frequently, the starting point for a system approach is an inappropriate one—a solution such as differentiated staffing, or measurable objectives having been mandated by the legislature or the board before the problems for which they might be responsive have been identified and documented. Thus educational ventures into using a system approach have often been made after the professional staff has discovered that they are down-the-road with a solution for no known problem! After having noted this, the implementation of a system approach has been considered as a way of determining needs before solutions are selected. Still other districts and educational agencies have begun at the beginning, and taken the time to conduct a needs assessment and a system analysis before undertaking programs and projects.

Systematic approaches are being emphasized in response to "accountability" legislation enacted by some states, which emphasizes achievement of results rather than specification of procedures. Concurrently, the Federal Government increasingly is requesting a statement and documentation of needs (as gaps between current results and required results) as a funding requisite. Management by objectives and a planning-programming-budgeting system (PPBS) are being used and required in many states and districts. The Program Evaluation Review Technique (PERT) is now standard procedure for many local districts.

The importance of system approach tools and needs assessment in contemporary education is underscored by the fact that the National Academy of School Executives (NASE) provides regular training programs for its members. Additionally, the American Management Association and other agencies continually are holding workshops and meetings to provide understanding of such tools to educators. Moreover, the concepts and tools are coming to be topics of courses in colleges and universities.

System approaches are useful. When used sensibly, they can help make the educational adventure a creative and responsive undertaking. They can help identify and document learning requirements based upon delineated needs, rather than having objectives based upon historical precedent and raw intuition. We can validate what we are doing and determine how well we are doing, moving from a reaction mode to an action mode. We can become accountable for humanism and responsiveness, and make sure that we are adequately and appropriately serving the learners who come to us for preparation for coping with and shaping both our world and theirs. By being systematic and responsive we can make sure that the whole person can contribute in the world with increased self-confidence, heightened self-concept, and abilities to occupationally and personally survive and contribute to themselves and to others.

Basic to the notions underlying a system approach are the assumptions that (1) hope is not reality, (2) more is learned from error than from ignorance, and (3) we are better off when we decide what should be accomplished *before* we select how we are going to do the job. A system approach is defined here as:

> A process by which needs are identified, problems selected, requirements for problem solution are identified, solutions are chosen from alternatives, methods and means are obtained and implemented, results are evaluated, and required revisions to all or part of the system are made so that the needs are eliminated. (Kaufman, 1972)

Seen in this light, a system approach is a process for identifying as well as for solving problems. A system is defined as:

> The total resultant from the interactions of the parts working independently and working together to achieve required results or outcomes based on documented needs. (Based, in part, upon Kaufman, 1972)

System approaches are useful in achieving planned change—to bring about a positive set of actions which are responsive to needs of learners, educators, and community members, rather than waiting for demands to be made, resulting in reaction.

A system approach increases the likelihood of obtaining responsive results because it insists upon a formal assessment of needs as a first step in the systematic process, rather than going forward from objectives set only by conventional wisdom and historical ritual. A need is defined as:

> The measurable discrepancy (or gap) between current outcomes and desired or required outcomes. (Kaufman, 1972)

All system approach activities start with a solid documentation of needs and resulting problems (needs selected for closure), rather than merely trying to find more efficient ways of doing what we always have done. By thus taking the time and trouble (and pain) of challenging our basic educational assumptions and myths, we better assure that our efforts and expenditures of resources will be more responsive than previously. It distinguishes the differences and relationship between ends and means, while much of education currently (and often tragically) emphasizes means (processes) and assumes or ignores ends (or product).

WHAT ARE SYSTEM APPROACHES?

Taken together, the various system approach models provide an array of tools, techniques, concepts, and models for the systematic improvement of education. They have a number of labels, and we will try to cover most of them here in this brief space. Not all professionals will agree with this presentation, for it will have a number of limitations—it is suggested that the interested reader would do well to read the various original writings and choose the one or ones most appropriate to his

or her application. This section will use a formulation first described in Part III of *Social and Technological Change: Implications for Education* (Kaufman, 1970), where there was a somewhat arbitrary delineation of three types of system approaches: (1) Descriptive Mode, (2) Solution-Implementation Mode, and (3) Design-Process Mode. In a very useful writing, Hoetker et al. referred to these three as "Systems II," "Systems III," and "Systems I" to correspond to the above three categories.

Descriptive Mode

This mode seems to derive most closely from the thinking of many scholars and practitioners in an area of the literature generally called "General System(s) Theory." The most notable of these authors include (but are not limited to) Von Bertalanffy, Banathy, Buckley, Carter, Churchman, Etzioni, Silvern, and Weiner.

Over-generalizing a bit, this position seeks to describe the aspects of any given system in terms of its characteristics, its components, the interrelationship between the components, and the extent to which the system interacts with the external world. It can thus compare two or more "systems" in these terms, providing a description of any system or any group of systems. It is invaluable, for it reminds us that the world is not fragmentary and disassociated, but is comprised of organized and describable "systems." We can further characterize any system in terms of its entropy (unpredictability) and its information (predictability). This mode provides a set of concepts and a set of tools by which we can get a "handle" on our world and describe it for possible future use.

The Solution-Implementation Mode

This model is in the best tradition of our national heritage to get things done more efficiently than ever before. It attempts to provide sets of systematic and responsive tools for selecting among alternatives the best ways to meet objectives in a world of uncertainty. Contributors in this area include (but again are not limited to) Banathy, Heinich, Briggs, Carter, Silberman, Churchman, Cleland, King, Cook, Gagne, Hartley, Lessinger, Ofiesh, Odiorne, Silvern, and Ryan.

This mode contributes to the field by identifying and defining tools and techniques for progressing from measurable objectives to more efficiently achieved outcomes. Generally (but not always) those using this model tend to start with a measurable definition of the outcomes to be achieved, and then seek the most "cost-beneficial" ways and means for achieving the desired objectives. Lessinger, in *Every Kid a Winner*, characterizes this approach as "educational engineering" in that it finds and uses the best ways and means for meeting objectives. In the daily work of education, this approach can be invaluable, providing that you are assured that the objectives are, in fact, valid.

The Design-Process Mode

This model attempts to integrate the other two modes for use by those who cannot or do not want to make assumptions about the validity of existing objectives, and who want to move from the description of two systems (the current system and a desired system) to measurable educational success. Rather than rejecting the two previously identified modes, this model recognizes the critically important contribution these concepts and tools can provide, and attempts to organize them into a more holistic approach.

It consists, basically, of steps presented in Figure 1 (see below). Again, it should be emphasized that (1) these three modes are not mutually exclusive; (2) no single one of the three is either right or wrong (although it is strongly held here that the design-process mode is essential to assure that a holistic approach is realized); and (3) the professionals associated with each of the above are not narrowly defined by that category; in fact, many of them have made contributions in several of these categories, as well as in other, wider professional areas.

Another interesting observation is that in actual practice many of these "system" professionals have produced models and activities which increasingly tend to widen the scope and depth of their work. This is especially noticeable in the increased inclusion of system elements concerned with "needs assessment," a process by which outcome gaps are identified and documented before systematic problem resolution is begun.

The above categories and the formulation which follows are intended to allow the interested reader to sort and order some of the current notions and tools. Following is a listing based upon a previous analysis (Kaufman, 1971) to show current "system approach" tools and their relationship with a Design-Process Mode of System Approach. Let us review some of the current (and quite useful) tools.

Needs Assessment. Generally conceived, this is an outcome gap (or discrepancy analysis) (Kaufman, 1972) where the gaps between current and desired skills, knowledges, and attitudes of the educational partners of learners, teachers, and community members are identified and sorted into categories of agreement and disagreement; the disagreements are reconciled; and priorities are placed among the agreed-upon gaps. Examples in a variety of contexts include studies and work conducted in San Diego (Heinkel, 1973); Mesa, Arizona (Zaharis, 1973); and Sarasota, Florida (English and Pillot, 1973), to name a few.

A number of techniques may be used in a Needs Assessment (including the Delphi Technique). A number of models for this exist, including those of Corrigan, Sweigert, Kaufman, Joyce Krutop, Center for Advanced Study of Educational Administration, University of California at Los Angeles, Research for Better Schools, Inc., Pillot and English (Sarasota, Florida), Eastmond, Alabama State Department of Education, and the Northwest Regional Educational Laboratory.

As Read (1973) points out, the term "system analysis" (in its singular form) seems unique to those who worked, for a while at least, with Operation PEP in California. This technique was developed by Kaufman, Robert, Betty Corrigan, D. L. Goodwin, and others to identify a set of tools (mission, function, task, and methods-means analysis) which were intended to identify the requirements for meeting a need without actually selecting the "how-to-do-its." Thus conceived, it provides a bridge between the Descriptive Mode of a System Approach and the Solution-Implementation Mode.

Measurable Objectives. Unfortunately, more than a few educators think that if they use measurable objectives (such as those described by Mager, Popham, or Smith) they are using a system approach. Not so. Measurability is not the same as validity. However, measurable objectives, especially when written in interval scale terms, provide an invaluable referent for planning, management, and evaluation.

Planning, Programming, Budgeting System. This tool usually is known by its abbreviation PPBS. It is a tool primarily for deciding among alternative methods-means and providing a budget for the related costs for the achievement of specified and agreed-upon measurable objectives. Much has been written about this tool, including the works of Hartley, Corrigan, Katzenbach, Quade, and Rath. This technique, for better or worse, is most often linked to the costing of education.

Systems Analysis. This is an important tool which first gained wide currency in application to complex weapon systems. It is described frequently as being a tool for the selection of the most effective and efficient alternative actions based on alternative resource cost and benefits within a consideration of uncertainty. Note that this is a different tool from "system analysis" described above, since systems analysis does include the actual selection of methods-means, while system analysis is a planning tool where requirements (based upon needs) are delineated along with a determination of possible methods-means, including a feasibility analysis which attempts to determine the probabilities of each alternative's accomplishing the derived objectives.

Methods-Means Selection. This is a tool (Corrigan, 1965) where alternative how-to-do-its are compared with the objectives and then are selected on the basis of the best "fit." It is less mathematical than other tools in this category, and gives tacit recognition to the relatively impoverished state of the art concerning precise ways of matching methods, means, and media in education to the required outcomes.

Games, Modeling and Simulation. These are a variety of ways used to select alternative solution strategies and procedures from among alternatives. Basically, they call for the contained, controlled reproduction of various elements of reality, in order to obtain data and information relative to possible methods and implications of their use.

Network-Based Management Tools. Best known, perhaps, in education, through the works of Cook (1966, 1970, 1973), these comprise the tools where milestones and events are identified and progress is plotted in a

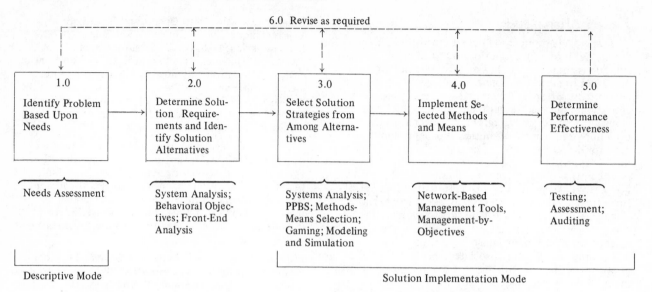

FIGURE 1. A possible integration of the various tools used in System Approaches with a Design Process Mode of A System Approach. Also shown are the other possible modes of system approaches, including the Descriptive Mode and the Solution-Implementation Mode. (Based on Kaufman, 1970, 1971, 1972)

management when what is to be done has been selected, as well as how-to-do-its. Among these tools are Program Evaluation Review Technique (PERT), Critical Path Method, Line of Balance, and Gantt charting (the simplest form, which, unlike the others, does not account for complex interactions between the milestones).

Management by Objectives. Popularized by Odiorne (1965), it is used to assure that objectives which have been identified will be accomplished. It uses delegation of functions, and the reporting back of functions accomplished (and those not accomplished), as the basis for an effective management and control tool.

Testing, Assessment, Auditing. These are all tools for what Scriven might call "summative evaluation," in that they are designed to tell what objectives have and have not been accomplished at the end of a program or activity. Lessinger's concept of the Independent Educational Accomplishment Audit is relatively new to the educational manager, and provides for a public accounting of outcomes.

A POSSIBLE INTEGRATION

All of these tools go together in an interesting possible integration. Figure 1 shows a model of a Design Process Mode of a System Approach—the five functions, plus a sixth function (revise as required) shown as a broken line. Also included in the figure is a suggested manner in which the various system approach tools go together. Additionally noted are the zones which might be considered to define the three suggested modes of system approaches.

In many respects this integrated formulation indicates the usefulness of all of the tools and techniques. It has been suggested (Kaufman, 1971, 1972) that the six steps

of the depicted system approach model, and the associated tools form a "taxonomy of planning" there the first step is called Alpha Planning, the next is Beta Planning, and so forth. Thus conceived, planning, decision-making, and evaluation goes on at each step of this model; the only difference in what is done and how it is done is the assumption of, or the actual data on hand at, the initiation of each of the six steps.

There are a number of system approaches to education, all of which are potentially useful to the educator who measurably wants to improve the current outcomes. The question is not which one is correct, but rather which one is best suited for a specific application.

CURRENT CONTROVERSIES

There are plenty of controversies. One is the suggestion that the differences between a system approach and a systems approach is mere semantic quibbling. It is not. (See, for instance, the previously cited comments of Read.) The system approach intends to design from scratch a system which will identify and meet documented needs. Systems approaches, by and large, tend to start with more assumptions (usually at Gamma Planning or occasionally at Beta Planning) and go forward.

Another controversy is that system(s) approaches (either singular or plural) dehumanize. Frankly, at one time this writer would have dismissed this argument, but he currently sees some possible concern for its validity. The argument goes that system(s) approaches only are interested in measurable outcomes and the efficiency of getting them accomplished, tending to shove children and other humans into cubbyholes—to be treated but not educated. This could happen, especially if one were to arbitrarily choose the solution-implementation mode of a system approach and fail to take into consideration the unique needs and characteristics of learners, implementing educators, and community members. The recent swing to needs assessment procedures should eliminate much of this problem, providing that these assessments are of outcome gaps (needs) rather than assessment of solutions (which many tend to be, as of this writing).

When a needs assessment is a formal part of a system approach, then, there tends to be a humanizing thrust—what could be more humanizing than formally considering the individual and unique characteristics of all of the educational partners in the planning and doing? By using this mode, we will be successful in being accountable for humanism.

Another controversy seems to revolve around the tools used in system approaches. There are those who opt only for mathematical tools and formulations, and those who prefer the "soft" approach to planning and accomplishment. William James referred to this kind of conflict as being between the "tough-minded" and the "tender-minded." The answer to this controversy, like many others, is that both positions are correct—it isn't an "either-or" situation. Naturally, when hard empirical data is available, then mathematical formulations, models, and procedures are preferable. For those many instances where we must operate on a nominal or ordinal-scale set of properties, "softer" methods must be used.

Another controversy is over just plain jargon. Each practitioner, including this one, uses terminology which he or she thinks is necessary to describe the exact tools and procedures which are important. Cook (1973) has spoken to this problem. This controversy promises to resolve itself once the specialists stop trying to push their own models and start to see the vast amount of commonality between formulations.

SUMMARY

This brief overview was designed to illustrate that (1) system approaches offer an efficient and effective set of tools for travelling the road toward humanism and accountability; (2) there are a number of formulations and tools, almost all of which are useful for some applications at some time; and (3) a referent is available for the possible integration of the various tools, models, and procedures. All of the approaches intend to improve the educational enterprise in a systematic manner, and all measurably can contribute to that goal.

REFERENCES

The Alabama State Department of Education. A Study of Educational Needs in Alabama Schools. Montgomery, Alabama, April 1969.

Alkin, M. C., and Bruno, J. E. System Approaches to Educational Planning. Part IV of *Social And Technological Change: Implications for Education.* ERIC/CEA, University of Oregon, Eugene, 1970.

Banathy, B. H. *Instructional Systems.* Palo Alto, Calif,: Fearon Publishers, Inc. 1968.

Barson, J., and Heinich, R. A Systems Approach, *Audiovisual Instruction.* June 1966.

Beals, R. L. Resistance and Adaptation to Technological Change: Some Anthropological Views. *Human Factors.* December 1968.

Bloom, B. S., Hastings, J. T., and Madaus, G. F. *Handbook on Formative and Summative Evaluation of Student Learning.* New York: McGraw-Hill, 1971.

Brickell, H. M. Organizing New York State for Educational Change. New York State Department of Education, Albany, New York, December 1961.

Briggs, L. J. et al. *Instructional Media: A Procedure for the Design of Multi-Media Instruction.* American Institutes for Research AIR-F-63-2/67FR, Pittsburgh, Pa., March 6, 1967.

Buckley, W., ed. *Modern Systems Research for the Behavioral Scientist.* Chicago, Ill.: Aldine Publishing Co., 1968.

Carter, L. F. The Systems Approach to Education—The Mystique and the Reality. System Development Corp., Rept. SP-3291, January 27, 1969.

_____, and Silberman, H. The System Approach, Technology and the School. System Development Corp., SP-2025, 1965.

Churchman, C. W. *The Systems Approach.* New York: Dell, 1969.

Cleland, D. I., and King, W. R. *Systems Analysis and Project Management.* New York: McGraw-Hill, 1968.

_____. *Systems, Organizations, Analysis, Management: A Book of Readings.* New York: McGraw-Hill, 1969.

Conner, J. E., Kaufman, R. A., Lessinger, L. M., and McVity, R. L. *Independent Educational Management Audit: A System Approach.* College/University Press, Washington, D.C., 1973.

Cook, D. L. *PERT: Applications in Education,* OE-1214, Cooperative Research Monogr. No. 17. Washington, D.C.: U.S. Government Printing Office, 1966.

_____. Management Control Theory as the Context for Educational Evaluation (prepublication draft). Educational Program Management Center, College of Education, Ohio State University. Final draft April 1, 1970.

_____. Systems for Education and Training. *AV Communication Review,* Vol. 21, No. 2, Summer 1973.

Corrigan, R. E. Method-Media Selection. OPERATION PEP, Tulare County, California, Department of Education, 1965.

_____, Associates. *A System Approach for Education (SAFE).* R. E. Corrigan Associates: Garden Grove, Calif., 1969.

_____, Corrigan, Betty O., and Kaufman, R. A. The Steps and Tools of the System Synthesis Process in Education. OPERATION PEP. San Mateo County, Calif., Department of Education, December 1967.

Crump, W. A. Management System for Administration of the Georgia Proprietary School Act. State of Georgia, Department of Education, 1973.

Cyphert, F. R., and Gant, W. L. The Delphi Technique: A Case Study. *Phi Delta Kappan,* Vol. 57, No. 5 (January 1971).

Dalkey, N. Use of the Delphi Technique in Educational Planning. Sacramento, Calif.: *Educational Resources Agency Herald,* Vol. 4, No. 2 (November-December 1970).

Dubin, R., and Taveggia, T. C. *The Teaching-Learning Paradox.* Center for the Advanced Study of Educational Administration, University of Oregon, Eugene, 1968.

Eastmond, J. N. *Need Assessment: Winnowing Expressed Concerns for Critical Needs.* Salt Lake City, Utah: World-Wide Education and Research Institute, April 1969.

English, F. W. Change Strategies That Fail. *California School Boards,* May 1969.

_____, and Kaufman, R. *Needs Assessment: Focus for Curriculum,* Washington, D.C., Association for Supervision and Curriculum Development (ASCD), June 1975.

Etzioni, A. *Modern Organizations.* Foundations of Modern Sociology Series. Englewood Cliffs, N.J.: Prentice-Hall, 1964.

Frankl, V. L. *Man's Search for Meaning: An Introduction to Logotherapy.* Boston: Beacon Press, 1962.

Gagne, R. M., ed. *Psychological Principles in System Development.* New York: Holt, Rinehart and Winston, 1962.

Glaser, R. Psychological Bases for Instructional Design. *A V Communication Review,* Winter, 1966.

Harman, W. W. Nature of Our Changing Society: Implications for Schools. Part I of *Social and Technological Change: Implications for Education.* ERIC/CEA, University of Oregon, Eugene, 1970.

Hartley, H. J. Twelve Hurdles to Clear Before You Take on Systems Analysis. *American School Board Journal,* July 1968.

———. Limitations of Systems Analysis. *Phi Delta Kappan,* May 1969.

Heinkel, O. A. Priority Determination for Vocational Education Through a Formal Needs Assessment Process. San Diego, San Diego Community Colleges, Office of Research, 1973.

———. Development of Management and Information System Skills for Vocational Education in California Community Colleges." San Diego, San Diego Community Colleges, Office of Research, 1973.

Hitt, W. D. Two Models of Man. *American Psychologist,* July 1969.

Hoetker, J., Fichtenau, R., and Farr, Helen. *Systems, Systems Approaches and the Teacher.* The National Council of Teachers of English, 1972.

Johnson, D. W. A Look at the Future of California Education. *California School Boards,* September 1968.

Katzenbach, E. L. Planning, Programming, Budgeting Systems: PPBS in Education. The New England School Development Council, March 1968.

Kaufman, R. *Needs Assessment: What It Is—And How to Do It,* University Consortium for Instructional Development and Technology, United States International University, San Diego, 1975.

———, and English, F. W. *Needs Assessment: A Guide for Educational Managers.* American Association of School Administrators (AASA), Arlington, Va. In press.

———. A System Approach to Education: Derivation and Definition. *A V Communication Review,* Winter 1968.

———. A System Approach, a multimedia presentation. Department of Audiovisual Extension, University of Minnesota, Minneapolis, 1970a.

———. System Approaches to Education—Discussion and Attempted Integration. Part III of *Social and Technological Change: Implications for Education,* ERIC/CEA, University of Oregon, Eugene, 1970b.

———. A Possible Integrative Model for the Systematic and Measurable Improvement of Education. *American Psychologist,* Vol. 26, No. 3 (March 1971).

———. *Educational System Planning.* Englewood Cliffs, N.J.: Prentice-Hall, 1972.

———, Clinkenbeard, W., and Wood, R. A Generic Educational Planning Model. The Los Angeles County Supplementary Education Center, Los Angeles, Calif., May 1969.

———, and Corrigan, R. E. The Steps and Tools of System Analysis as Applied to Education. OPERATION PEP. San Mateo County, Calif., Department of Education, Dec. 1967.

———, Corrigan, Betty O., and Goodwin, D. L. Mission Analysis in Education. OPERATION PEP. San Mateo County, Calif., Department of Education, December 1967a.

———. Functional Analysis in Education. OPERATION PEP, San Mateo County, Calif., Department of Education, December 1967b.

———, and Levine, S. L. Task Analysis in Education. OPERATION PEP. San Mateo County, Calif., Department of Education, December 1967.

———, Rand, M. J., English, F., Conte, J. M., and Hawkins, W. An Attempt to Put the Ten Objectives of Education Developed for Pennsylvania by Educational Testing Service Into Operational Definitions. Temple City, Calif., Unified School District, April 1968.

———, Corrigan, R. E., and Johnson, D. W. Toward Educational Responsiveness to Society's Needs—A Tentative Utility Model. *Journal of Socio-Economic Planning Sciences,* Vol. 3 (August 1969).

———, and Harsh, J. R. Determining Educational Needs—An Overview. California State Department of Education, Bureau of Elementary and Secondary Education, PLEDGE Conference, October 1969.

Krutop, Joyce O. Program Development Needs Assessment Form. National City School District, National City, Calif., 1973.

Lessinger, L. M. *Every Kid a Winner.* Chicago: Science Research Associates, 1970.

———. The Powerful Notion of Accountability in Education. Paper presented to Academy on Educational Engineering, Bowman's Lodge, Wemme, Oregon, August 10-14, 1970.

———. Engineering Accountability for Results in Public Education. *Phi Delta Kappan,* Vol. 57, No. 4 (December 1970).

———, Parnell, D., and Kaufman, R. A. *Accountability, Policies, and Procedures.* Croft Educational Services. Vol. I, Learning; Vol. II, Students; Vol. III, Personnel; Vol. IV, Management, New London, Conn., 1971.

Lieberman, M. An Overview of Accountability. *Phi Delta Kappan,* Vol. 52, No. 4 (December 1970).

Mager, R. F. *Setting Instructional Objectives.* Palo Alto, Calif.: Fearon Publishers, Inc., 1961.

———. *Developing Attitudes Toward Learning.* Palo Alto, Calif.: Fearon Publishers, Inc., 1968.

———, and Beach, K. M. Jr. *Developing Vocational Instruction.* Palo Alto, Calif.: Fearon Publishers, Inc., 1967.

Maslow, A. *Toward a Psychology of Being,* 2nd ed. Princeton, N.J.: D. Van Nostrand Company, Inc., 1968.

Mauch, J. A Systems Analysis Approach to Education. *Phi Delta Kappan,* January 1962.

Meals, D. Heuristic Models for Systems Planning. *Phi Delta Kappan,* January 1967.

Mood, A. M. Some Problems Inherent in the Development of a Systems Approach to Instruction. Paper prepared for the Conference on New Dimensions for Research in Educational Media Implied by the "Systems Approach to Instruction," Center for Instructional Communications, Syracuse University, April 2-4, 1964.

Odiorne, G. S. *Management by Objectives.* New York: Pitman Publishing Corp., 1965.

Ofiesh, G. D. *Programmed Instruction: A Guide for Management.* New York: American Management Association, 1965.

———, and Meierhenry, W. C., eds. *Trends in Programmed Instruction.* National Association for Programmed Instruction and National Education Association Dept. of Audiovisual Instruction. Washington, D.C., 1964.

Olson, A. R. Colorado People and Colorado Education—An Assessment of Educational Needs Based on the Population, Economy, and Social Structure of Colorado. Colorado Dept. of Education, Denver, June 1970.

Parker, S. PPBS. *California Teachers Association Journal,* May 1969.

Parnell, Dale. To Achieve Significant Improvements in Education, State Government Must Take the Lead in Systematic Planning and Evaluation. Paper presented to Academy on Educational Engineering, Bowman's Lodge, Wemme, Oregon, August 10, 1970.

Pennsylvania Department of Public Instruction. A Summary Statement of Assessment of Educational Needs in the Commonwealth of Pennsylvania in Response to Section 305 (b) (1) of P. L. 90-247-ESEA Title III. Dept. of Public Instruction, Harrisburg, Pa., 1969.

Piele, P. K., Eidell, T. L., and Smith, S. C., eds. *Social and Technological Change: Implications for Education.* ERIC/CEA.

University of Oregon, Eugene, 1970.

Pillot, G. M., and English, F. W. Annual District Comprehensive Educational Plan. The School Board of Sarasota County, Florida, August 1973.

Popham, W. J. *Educational Objectives.* Los Angeles, Calif.: Vimcet Associates, 1966.

———. Probing the Validity of Arguments Against Behavioral Goals. A presentation made to the American Educational Research Association, Chicago, Feb. 1968.

Quade, E. S. Systems Analysis Techniques for Planning-Programming-Budgeting, in D. I. Cleland and W. R. King's *Systems, Organizations, Analysis, Management: A Book of Readings.* New York: McGraw-Hill, 1969.

Randall, R. S. An Operational Application of the CIPP Model for Evaluation. *Educational Technology,* Vol. 9, No. 7 (July 1969).

Rapoport, A. Foreword to "Modern Systems Research for the Behavioral Scientist," W. Buckley, ed. Chicago: Aldine Publishing Company, 1968.

Raser, J. R. *Simulation and Society: An Exploration of Scientific Gaming.* Boston: Allyn and Bacon, 1969.

Rath, G. J. PPBS is More Than A Budget: It's A Total Planning Process. *Nation's Schools,* Vol. 82 (Nov. 1968).

Read, E. A. Book Review of Educational System Planning. *American Educational Research Journal,* Vol. 10, No. 2, Spring 1973.

Rogers, C. Toward a Modern Approach to Values: The Valuing Process in the Mature Person. *The Journal of Abnormal and Social Psychology,* Vol. 68, No. 2 (1964).

Rogers, E. M. Developing a Strategy for Planned Change. Paper presented at the Symposium on the Application of System Analysis and Management Techniques to Educational Planning in California, OPERATION PEP, Chapman College, Orange, California, June 1967.

Rucker, W. R., Arnspiger, W. C., and Brodbeck, A. J. *Human Values in Education.* Dubuque, Iowa: William C. Brown Book Company, 1969a.

Ryan, T. Antoinette. Systems Techniques for Programs of Counseling and Counselor Education. *Educational Technology,* June 1969.

Scriven, M. The Methodology of Evaluation. *AERA Monograph Series on Curriculum Evaluation,* No. 1. Chicago: Rand-McNally, 1967.

Silvern, L. C. Cybernetics and Education K-12. *Audiovisual Instruction,* March 1968.

———. Introduction to special issue, "Applying Systems Engineering Techniques to Education and Training," *Educational Technology,* June 1969a.

Smith, R. G. The Development of Training Objectives. The George Washington University Human Resources Research Office Bull. 11, June 1964.

Stevens, S. S. Mathematics, Measurement and Psychophysics, in Stevens' *Handbook of Experimental Psychology.* New York: John Wiley & Sons. 1951.

Stowe, R. A. Research and the Systems Approach as Methodologies for Education. *AV Communication Review,* Vol. 21, No. 2, Summer, 1973.

Stufflebeam, D. L. Toward a Science of Educational Evaluation. *Educational Technology,* Vol. 8, No. 14 (July 1968).

Sweigert, R. L., Jr. Assessing Educational Needs to Achieve Relevancy. *Education,* Vol. 91, No. 4 (April-May 1971).

Thoresen, C. E. The Systems Approach and Counselor Education: Basic Features and Implications. *Counselor Education and Supervision,* Vol. 9, No. 1 (Fall, 1969), 3-17.

Von Bertalanffy, L. General System Theory—A Critical Review. In W. Buckley, ed., *Modern Systems Theory for the Behavioral Scientist.* Chicago: Aldine Publishing Company, 1968.

Weaver, W. T. The Delphi Forecasting Method. *Phi Delta Kappan,* Vol. 52, No. 5 (January 1971).

Weiner, N. Cybernetics in History. In W. Buckley, ed., *Modern Systems Research for the Behavioral Scientist.* Chicago: Aldine Publishing Company, 1968.

White House Conference on Children, Report to the President, Washington, D.C., 1970.

Zaharis, J. Differentiated Staffing Project Report. Mesa, Arizona, Mesa Arizona Schools, 1973.

24

PROGRAM PLANNING AND EVALUATION

by Roger Hiemstra, Professor
Department of Adult and Continuing Education
Teachers College
University of Nebraska
Lincoln, Nebraska

The term Program Planning and Evaluation does not have a commonly agreed-upon meaning. The three words —program, planning, and evaluation—are commonly thought of together as part of an educational process for organizing and administering programs; however, an understanding of this process begins with separate definitions:

Program—a single activity, or sequential series of activities, designed to achieve one or more educational objectives determined as necessary or desired in promoting change in people.

Planning—the procedures or steps utilized in designing a program.

Evaluation—an assessment of a program's effectiveness, usually in terms of its achievement of objectives.

The implementation of a program is considered as part of the total process.

Planning and evaluation are widely discussed topics in education, with a variety of procedures being utilized to plan and implement educational activities. Added to this diversity in procedures are large numbers of commercialized approaches to planning. Literature on planning and evaluation, gaming and simulation devices on problem solving, courses and workshops to improve planning skills, and related research reports are readily available. Much of this information and many of these procedures are referenced at the end of this chapter.

This abundance of information is one indication that the design of effective education is a complex process. In addition, the process is dynamic in nature, in that developed plans are frequently subject to change based on new and evolving information. Thus, there is no simple recipe for successful program planning. Perhaps it is this complexity and dynamic quality that have made a sinple definition of program planning and evaluation so elusive.

However, there are procedures and steps commonly employed in the systematic development of educational activities. For example, the design of instruction, the development of an annual conference program, the planning of an inservice training session for teachers, or the development of a workshop for the continuing education of a group of professionals, will be based on a process made up of differentiated but interrelated steps. The focus of this chapter will be to describe this process and its various components.

Finally, any discussion of planning and evaluation will normally be based around the assumption that some type of change—be it change in knowledge, skill, or attitude—is an expected educational program result. However, the focus of this chapter's discussion is the planning and evaluating of primarily short-term programs based on some determined need for change. Consequently, curriculum planning which tends to focus on anticipated or long-range needs does not relate directly to the process to be described. Parts of the process certainly are related to, and can be used for, curriculum planning, but the sequencing of, and emphasis placed on, the various components usually are different.

RELATED LITERATURE

Literature on program planning and evaluation is as diverse as are the approaches or models utilized for planning purposes. Some literature centers on the level at which one designs programs. Verner (1964) has suggested that at least two levels should be considered: the first level deals with fulfilling assigned social roles of the institution organizing the program; the second deals with activities, learning tasks, and needs at the client or program participant level. Knowles (1970) and Theide (1964) support this contention, but add that community or societal goals also need to be considered in the planning process.

Another portion of the literature relates to establishing program objectives. Bloom (1956), Krathwohl, Bloom, and Masia (1964), Mager (1962), Popham and Baker (1970), and Tyler (1950) have been some of the pioneers in encouraging the utilization of "instructional" or "behavioral" objectives in educational programs. Although variations exist regarding what encompasses an educational objective, most educators agree that desired learner behaviors should be specified. Furthermore, the task of designing appropriate learning activities is facilitated by precise behavior specifications.

Somewhat related is the discussion by Delbecq and Van de Ven (1970), Dutton (1970), and Knowles (1970) suggesting that program participants should be involved in the planning process, which includes the specification of objectives. This assumes that involving the participant in the planning process will build personal interest in resulting educational activities, and promote learning more central to actual need. This assumption is supported by McLoughlin (1971); he found that experimental subjects who had been involved in objective-setting and program-planning had more positive attitudes toward the educational experience, and achieved as well as control subjects.

The conceptualization and development of planning models is another topic found frequently in the literature. For example, Beal, Ross, and Powers (1966) approached planning from a sociological view, and designed a community level model that includes such functions as determining groups to be involved in the planning process, obtaining legitimation for the developed plan, and seeking community commitment. Variations on this community-oriented approach can be found in Biddle and Biddle (1965), Lindeman (1959), Sower (1957), and Thelen (1954). More recently, Boone, Dolan, and Shearon (1971) used these various community-level models to develop a conceptual scheme for planning that focuses on the decision-making process. Houle (1972) has developed some thoughts toward using a decision-making process and planning system in redesigning current educational programs.

Another approach to model development for educational planning has stemmed from the systems analysis procedures used by business and industry. Several authors (Carter, 1969; Churchman, 1968; Lehmann, 1968; Silvern, 1969, 1972) have developed educationally-related systems analysis models. The critical path analysis approach (Cook, 1966; Justus, 1967; Kaimann, 1966) and Program-Planning-Budgeting Systems (Hartley, 1968; Stauber, 1968) are two additional systematic planning approaches that have received considerable attention.

The assessment of needs prior to designing educational programs has received attention, too. Individual needs and how to assess or define them (Dobbs, 1966; Johnston, 1963; Knowles, 1970; Knox, 1965; Leagans, 1964; Sheasga, 1961), needs of groups or certain population segments (Dowling, 1969; Dublin, 1972; Hiemstra, 1972a; Long, 1972), and needs at a community or institutional level (Baumel, Hobbs, and Powers, 1964; Habib, 1970; Hiemstra, 1972b; McMahon, 1970) are the more common categories around which this portion of the literature has been organized.

The literature on evaluation is immense. It ranges from textbooks or general informational books on evaluation (Beatty, 1969; Byrn, 1959; Gottman and Clasen, 1972; Suchman, 1967; Thorndike and Hagen, 1969; Tyler, 1969) to specific evaluation materials or topics (Stake, 1970; Wedemeyer, 1969), to critiques or discussions of evaluation problems (Alexander, 1965; Cohen, 1970; Guba, 1969; Scriven, 1972; Tyler, 1967). The information on educational evaluation is so broad and extensive that the above citations provide only a starting-point.

A final body of literature to be noted here centers on a growing awareness of research needs in program planning and evaluation. Caro (1969), Hemphill (1969), Merriman (1970), Mezirow (1971), Verner (1962), and Worthen (1968) are but a few of the authors attempting to apply research techniques and findings systematically in building a comprehensive body of knowledge regarding planning. These efforts should lead to a better understanding of the total process.

NEEDS ASSESSMENT

Need can be defined as a discrepancy between what is known or can be determined about a behavior and what should be (Gottman and Clasen, 1972; Knowles, 1970). The educator's role is to create an environment in which learning activities are utilized to reduce or remove the discrepancy.

Thus, needs assessment becomes a necessary and crucial aspect of the planning and evaluating process. A determined need becomes the basis for one or more objectives. Without needs assessment the planned educational activities could promote behavioral changes with limited or no relationship to existing discrepancies.

Various tools and techniques are available at the individual, group, institutional, and community levels. These include observational techniques, projective techniques, questionnaire approaches, community surveys, and job performance analysis procedures. Space limitations do not permit their description, but McMahon (1970) provides an extensive bibliography regarding needs assessment. In addition, references are included at the end of the chapter relating to each component in the planning and evaluation process.

DEVELOPMENT OF OBJECTIVES

Most educational programs revolve around assessed change requirements of three types: (1) attitude modification, (2) behavioral change, and (3) skill or content mastery. An objective is the description of an educational intent to bring about one or more of these changes. Identification and specification of desired change are prerequisites to the design of appropriate learning activities.

Wording objectives so that they are precise enough to be useful is a frustrating and often poorly done part of educational program planning. However, designing those appropriate learning activities, and measuring whether or not they have met some determined need, are dependent upon clearly stated objectives. Mager (1962) suggests that a useful objective must identify the expected change, define the important conditions under which the change is to occur, and define the related criteria for measuring the change achievement. Some of this chapter's references will provide direction on writing and using objectives.

PLANNING THE ACTIVITIES

Planning appropriate learning activities entails the following: the identification of learning tasks necessary for achieving a desired performance or change, the sequencing of these tasks, and the determination of instructional techniques appropriate for both the tasks and the program participant.

The program planning and evaluation process can, and often does, begin at this component in the model. This occurs, for example, when a program is built around a desired speaker or topic. However, including the earlier described needs assessment and objective setting components can strengthen the resulting programs. Thus, a program can be made more relevant if actual needs are being met; the measurement of a program's success can be facilitated if precise objectives have been identified; and the actual design of learning activities can determine if objectives are realistic or achievable. (Various tools, procedures, and techniques are available to facilitate this component's activities. Note the cited sources at the end of the chapter.)

IMPLEMENTATION OF ACTIVITIES

Operating the learning environment and activities, although not unimportant to the planning process, simply means to carry out the activities planned during the three components of the model described above. This function can include such activities as managing the instructional effort, guiding learning activities, collecting evaluative information, meeting the comfort needs of the program participants, and making appropriate decisions as situations warrant them. Various references at this chapter's conclusion provide information pertaining to this component.

EVALUATION

The importance of evaluation cannot be overstressed; however, the activities required for effective evaluation cannot be discussed adequately in the space allotted to this chapter. The reader should refer to a variety of sources, such as Byrn (1959), Gottman and Clasen (1972), Tyler (1969) and others included at the chapter's conclusion, to obtain some understanding of how effective evaluation can be incorporated into the program planning process.

Evaluation is crucial to successful program planning if educators are to know how effective their programs have been. Consequently, evaluation must be included throughout the planning process. Evaluation is depicted in the model as taking place near the end of the process (summative evaluation), because the analysis of whether or not a program's objectives have been met usually cannot be determined until the learning activities have been completed. However, evaluative information often is obtained both before and during the learning activities (formative evaluation), in order to measure actual change. Thus, information gathered from evaluation efforts becomes useful in improving and supplementing ongoing programs, as well as in planning subsequent programs.

FEEDBACK AND MODIFICATION

This feature of the planning process provides a means for utilizing evaluative findings in strengthening the planning efforts, in making adjustments in methods or techniques used throughout the process, and in providing information for future programs regarding educational needs. Feedback is the utilization of evaluative information to modify functions within other components, and as a means whereby adjustments and decisions can be made by the educator even before formal evaluation procedures are carried out.

For example, the educational planner might find that

certain objectives were not achieved by a majority of participants. In a subsequent program, different or supplemental instructional techniques could be planned for the objectives. Another use might involve discovering that it was impossible to design appropriate instructional activities because of unclear objectives. The planner would return to the objective writing component and re-examine the related objective. As a final example, evaluative information could be used for needs assessment; this would occur when the educational planner discovered that participants would have liked more learning activities on a certain topic. That topic could become the partial need basis for a follow-up or improved program.

CONTROVERSIES

One of the current controversial issues in planning and evaluation involves the function of behavioral objectives. It has been suggested that behavioral objectives restrict the learning activities in a program to a narrow focus, and that an impersonal, mechanistic measuring of objective achievement in effect reduces participants to pawns of the teacher's will (Arnstine, 1964). This argument has some merit, in that the behavioral objective approach can be misused or misunderstood.

Another argument relates to goal-free evaluation of programs. Scriven (1972) has suggested that program goals are often vague or unrealistic; therefore, evaluative confirmation of their achievement means little. This indicates the necessity of well-designed objectives based on the real need to prevent, as Kneller (1972) suggests, a poorly designed program plan.

Another issue involves the question of when a program should be evaluated. Dressel (1971) and Tuckman (1972) have suggested two types of evaluation: formative evaluation, the on-going assessment of a program which aids in its development, and summative evaluation, the assessment of a program's overall effectiveness.

Controversy also exists because of the varied approaches to evaluation, only a few of which will be described here. One approach is the school accreditation model (National Study, 1960), which involves outside experts making judgments about effectiveness through onsite visitations. Another approach is the focus on analyzing the achievement of objectives (Tyler, 1950). The utilization of collected information for decision-making (Stafflebeam, 1968, 1969) is another variation described in the literature. Still another version is the judgment based approach (Stake, 1967), where the worth of a program is determined through a very complex data collection and analysis procedure.

These controversies will not be resolved easily or quickly. Each points to the fact that program planning and evaluation is a complex and time-consuming process. Consequently, to be successful the educational planner must be systematic in the development of a program. At the same time, the development of programs for people means that flexibility must be a necessary feature of the planning process.

REFERENCES

Alexander, F. D. A Critique of Evaluation. *Journal of Cooperative Extension,* 1965, *3,* 205-212.

Arnstine, D. G. The language and values of programmed instruction: Part 2. *The Educational Forum,* 1964, *28,* 337-346.

Baumel, C. R., Hobbs, D. J., and Powers, R. C. *The Community Survey. Sociology 15.* Ames, Iowa: Iowa State University, Cooperative Extension Service, 1964.

Beal, G. M., Ross, C., and Powers, R. C. *Social Action and Interaction in Program Planning.* Iowa State University Press, 1966.

Beatty, W. H., ed. *Improving Educational Assessment and an Inventory of Measures of Affective Behavior.* Washington, D.C.: Association for Supervision and Curriculum Development, 1969.

Biddle, W. W., and Biddle, L. J. *The Community Development Process: The Rediscovery of Local Initiative.* New York: Holt, Rinehart, and Winston, Inc., 1965.

Bloom, B. S., ed. *Taxonomy of Educational Objectives: The Classification of Educational Goals.* Handbook 1, *Cognitive Domain.* New York: David McKay Co., 1956.

Boone, E. J., Dolan, R. J., and Shearon, R. W. *Programming in the Cooperative Extension Service: A Conceptual Scheme.* Miscellaneous Extension Publication 72. Raleigh, North Carolina: North Carolina State University, Agricultural Extension Service, 1971.

Byrn, D., ed. *Evaluation in Extension.* Topeka, Kansas: H. M. Ives & Sons, Inc., 1959.

Caro, F. G. Approaches to Evaluative Research: A Review. *Human Organization,* 1969, *28,* 87-99.

Carter, L. F. The Systems Approach to Education: Mystique and Reality. *Educational Technology,* 1969, *9* (4), 22-31.

Churchman, C. W. *The Systems Approach.* New York: Dell, 1968.

Cohen, D. K. Politics and Research: Evaluation of Social Action Programs in Education. *Review of Educational Research,* 1970, *40,* 213-238.

Cook, D. L. *Program Evaluation and Review Technique: Applications in Education.* U.S. Office of Education Cooperative Research Monograph No. 17, OE-12024. Washington, D.C.: U.S. Government Printing Office, 1966.

Delbecq, A. L., and Van de Ven, A. H. A Group Process Model for Problem Identification and Program Planning. *Journal of Applied Behavioral Science,* 1970, *7,* 466-492.

Dobbs, R. C. Self-Perceived Educational Needs of Adults. *Adult Education,* 1966, *16,* 92-100.

Dowling, W. D. How to Identify Needs of Groups for Continuing Education. *American Journal of Pharmaceutical Education,* 1969, *33,* 721-728.

Dressel, P. E., ed. *The New Colleges: Toward an Appraisal.* Iowa City, Iowa: American College Testing Program and the American Association for Higher Education, 1971.

Dubin, S. S. Obsolescence or Lifelong Education: A Choice for the Professional. *American Psychologist,* 1972, *27,* 486-498.

Dutton, D. Should the Clientele be Involved in Program Planning? *Adult Leadership,* 1970, *19,* 181-182.

Gottman, J. M., and Clasen, R. E. *Evaluation in Education: A Practitioner's Guide.* Itasca, Illinois: F. E. Peacock, 1972.

Guba, E. G. The Failure of Educational Evaluation. *Educational Technology,* A Special Report, 1969, *9* (5), 29-38.

Habib, W. Problems in Determining Training Needs in an Organization. *Training and Development Journal,* 1970, *24* (7), 44-48.

Hartley, H. J. *Educational Planning, Programming, Budgeting: A Systems Approach.* Englewood Cliffs, N.J.: Prentice-Hall, 1968.

Hemphill, J. K. The Relationships Between Research and Evaluation Studies. In R. W. Tyler, ed., *Educational Evaluation:*

New Roles, New Means. 68th Yearbook of the National Society for the Study of Education, Part 2. Chicago: University of Chicago Press, 1969.

Hiemstra, R. P. Continuing Education for the Aged: A Survey of Needs and Interests of Older People. *Adult Education,* 1972, *22,* 100-109. (a)

____. *The Educative Community.* Lincoln, Nebraska: Professional Educators Publications, Inc., 1972. (b)

Houle, C. O. *The Design of Education.* San Francisco: Jossey-Bass, 1972.

Johnston, J. W. C. The Educational Pursuits of American Adults. *Adult Education,* 1963, *13,* 217-221.

Justus, J. E. PERT. *School Management,* 1967, *11* (12), 24-29.

Kaimann, R. A. Educators and PERT. *Journal of Educational Data Processing,* 1966, *3,* 43-57.

Kneller, G. F. Goal-Free Evaluation. *Evaluation Comment,* 1972, *3* (4), 7-8.

Knowles, M. S. *Modern Practice of Adult Education.* New York: Association Press, 1970.

Knox, A. B. Clientele Analysis. *Review of Educational Research,* 1965, *35,* 231-239.

Krathwohl, D. R., Bloom, B. S., and Masia, B. B. *Taxonomy of Educational Objectives: The Classification of Educational Goals.* Handbook II. *Affective Domain.* New York: David McKay Company, Inc., 1964.

Leagans, J. P. A Concept of Needs. *Journal of Cooperative Extension,* 1964, *2,* 89-96.

Lehmann, H. The Systems Approach to Education. *Audiovisual Instruction,* 1968, *13,* 144-148.

Lindeman. E. C. Ten Steps in Community Action. In E. Harper and A. Dunham, eds., *Community Organization in Action.* New York: Association Press, 1959.

Long, R. W. Continuing Education for Physical Therapists in Nebraska: A Survey of Current Practices and Self-Expressed Needs with Recommendations for Program Development. Unpublished doctoral dissertation, University of Nebraska, 1972.

Mager, R. F. *Preparing Instructional Objectives.* Palo Alto, California: Fearon Publishers, 1962.

McLoughlin, D. Participation of the Adult Learner in Program Planning. *Adult Education,* 1971, *22,* 30-35.

McMahon, E. E. *Needs of People and Their Communities and the Adult Educator.* Washington, D.C.: Adult Education Association of the USA, 1970.

Merriman, H. O. From Evaluation Theory into Practice. *Journal of Research and Development in Education,* 1970, *3* (4), 48-58.

Mezirow, J. Toward a Theory of Practice. *Adult Education,* 1971, *21,* 135-147.

National Study of Secondary School Evaluation. *Evaluation Criteria,* 1960 edition. Washington, D.C.: National Study of Secondary School Evaluation, 1960.

Popham, W. J., and Baker, E. L. *Systematic Instruction.* Englewood Cliffs, N.J.: Prentice-Hall, Inc., 1970.

Scriven, M. Pros and Cons about Goal-Free Evaluation. *Evaluation Comment,* 1972, *3* (4), 1-4.

Sheasga, T. A Definition of Needs and Wants. *Adult Education,* 1961, *12,* 52-53.

Silvern, L. C. *Systems Engineering of Education IV: Systems Analysis and Synthesis Applied Quantitatively to Create an Instructional System.* Los Angeles: Educational and Training Consultants Co., 1969.

____. *Systems Engineering of Education V: Quantitative Concepts for Education Systems.* Los Angeles: Educational and Training Consultants Co., 1972.

Sower, C. et al. *Community Involvement: The Webs of Formal and Informal Ties that Make for Action.* Glencoe, Illinois: The Free Press, 1957.

Stake, R. E. The Countenance of Educational Evaluation. *Teach-ers College Record,* 1967, *58,* 523-540.

____. Objectives, Priorities, and Other Judgment Data. *Review of Educational Research,* 1970, *40,* 181-212.

Stauber, R. L. PPBS for Extension? *Journal of Cooperative Extension,* 1968, *6,* 229-235.

Stufflebeam, D. L. Evaluation as Enlightenment for Decision-Making. In W. H. Beatty, *Improving Educational Assessment and an Inventory of Measures of Affective Behavior.* Washington, D.C.: Association for Supervision and Curriculum Development, 1969.

____. Toward a Science of Educational Evaluation. *Educational Technology,* 1968, *8* (14), 5-17.

Suchman, E. A. *Evaluative Research: Principles and Practices in Public Service and Social Action Programs.* New York: Russell Sage Foundation, 1967.

Theide, W. Evaluation and Adult Education. In G. E. Jensen, A. A. Liveright, and W. Hallenbeck, eds., *Adult Education: Outlines of an Emerging Field of University Study.* Washington, D.C.: Adult Education Association of the USA, 1964.

Thelen, H. A. *Dynamics of Groups at Work.* Chicago: The University of Chicago Press, 1954.

Thorndike, R. L., and Hagen, E. *Measurement and Evaluation in Psychology and Education.* New York: John Wiley and Sons, 1969.

Tuckman, B. W. *Conducting Educational Research.* New York: Harcourt, Brace, Jovanovich, 1972.

Tyler, R. W. *Basic Principles of Curriculum and Instruction.* Chicago: University of Chicago Press, 1950.

____, ed. *Educational Evaluation: New Roles, New Means.* 68th Yearbook of the National Society for the Study of Education, Part 2. Chicago: University of Chicago Press, 1969.

____, Gagne, R. M., and Scriven, M. *Perspectives of Curriculum Evaluation.* AERA Monograph Series on Curriculum Evaluation, No. 1. Chicago: Rand McNally & Company, 1967.

Verner, C. *A Conceptual Scheme for the Identification and Classification of Processes for Adult Education.* Chicago: Adult Education Association of the USA, 1962.

____. Definition of Terms. In G. E. Jensen, A. A. Liveright, and W. Hallenbeck, eds., *Adult Education: Outlines of an Emerging Field of University Study.* Washington, D.C.: Adult Education Association of the USA, 1964.

Wedemeyer, C. A. Evaluation of Continuing Education Programs. *American Journal of Pharmaceutical Education,* 1969, *33,* 793-810.

Worthen, B. R. Toward a Taxonomy of Evaluation Designs. *Educational Technology,* 1968, *8* (15), 3-9.

25

PROGRAM-PLANNING-BUDGETING SYSTEMS

by Harry J. Hartley
Dean, School of Education
University of Connecticut
Storrs, Connecticut

PPBS offers a mode of thinking that enables educators to plan programs and allocate funds more effectively than with traditional planning concepts. For purposes of simple definition, one might consider PPBS as a play comprising three distinct and interrelated acts. Act I is *Program Planning,* with its emphasis on preparing explicit goals based on projected organizational needs. Act II is *Program Budgeting,* which includes the assignment of line-item direct costs (such as teachers' salaries, textbooks, and supplies) to clearly defined instructional and supportive programs. Act III is *Program Evaluation,* which includes a wide range of activities to determine the degree to which the stated objectives are in fact being achieved. In the brief span of several years, PPBS has progressed from the stage of conceptual blueprint to operational implementation in educational institutions throughout the country. Approximately 2,000 local schools were phasing in PPBS during 1974. What distinguishes PPBS from other innovations is that its methods are not only newer, but better. The inception of a PPB System offers the basic distinction from traditional planning in its ability to focus upon organizational outputs (such as reading achievement) rather than inputs (such as teachers' salaries), thus providing a clearer means of portraying goals and objectives. Relating costs of programs to desired accomplishments enables educators to respond to increasing demands for accountability.

The theme of this paper is that PPBS is currently assisting educators in allocating scarce resources to instructional programs within the framework of the annual budget cycle. The major objectives in the paragraphs that follow are to:

1. describe the advantages and characteristics of PPBS
2. suggest a strategy for implementing PPBS
3. provide examples of PPBS in practical use
4. identify several possible misuses or abuses of this concept

BUDGET DEFICIENCIES

Present school budgets meet the minimum requirements for legal and fiduciary accounting for funds received and expended. But they do not show that a budget supports well-defined curriculuar programs. Virtually no information can be extracted from the school's financial reports concerning the costs of programs. The conventional concept of budgeting is fallacious and shortsighted. As a result, budget formulation by educators in 1974 is incremental, fragmented, and nonprogrammatic. The budget is prepared for the convenience of accountants, rather than educators or the public. It is not surprising that the schools continue to face a fiscal crisis. Educational administrators simply have not done a commendable job of reporting program expenditures, requesting public funds, planning new programs, establishing priorities, evaluating performance, and describing program accomplishments to a discerning public.

ADVANTAGES OF PPBS

The professional literature contains many definitions and conceptualizations of PPBS, but basically it is a term applied to a set of interrelated organizational activities. PPB Systems are intended to aid educators in

the following ways:

Formulate goals, objectives, and learner skills

Design curricular programs to achieve stated objectives

Analyze more systematically the feasible alternatives

Provide staff with better planning information and resources

Compare costs with accomplishments of programs

Increase teacher involvement in planning and decision-making

Identify direct instructional costs in a program budget

Specify program priorities and educational values

Promote innovative programs, teaching, and evaluation criteria

Increase public understanding of, and support for, the schools (Hartley, 1968)

Schools generally have been provided with ineffectual devices for planning their activities and reporting to an "accountability-conscious" public their program accomplishments. The problem has been compounded by the lack of consensus as to what constitutes desired educational "output." With uncertainty and controversy surrounding the notion of educational productivity, the schools have suffered hardships in designing programs, assessing performance, and developing suitable budgeting procedures.

What was lacking before the advent of PPBS was a district-wide model for participative planning that related desired outcomes and scarce resources. By portraying specific school activities as part of an overall organic system, PPBS serves to integrate the formerly autonomous elements of curriculum development and financial administration. For too long the tail (budget) has been wagging the dog (curriculum).

It is interesting to note that even a best-seller like *Future Shock* contains a layman's praise for PPBS. Toffler (1970) states that a ". . . significant effort to tidy up governmental priorities was initiated by President Johnson with his attempt to apply PPBS throughout the Federal Government. . . . PPBS is a method for tying programs much more closely to organizational goals. . . . The introduction of PPBS and the systems approach is a major governmental achievement (p. 472)."

IMPLEMENTING PPBS IN EDUCATION

PPBS is clearly intended to be a practical tool that can operate in the earthy reality of local schools. The process of diffusing any innovation varies according to the setting and staff. Personal visits to schools in 30 states in the past three years have convinced this author that there is no single best way to "do" PPBS. Rather, the implementation process must be adapted to the unique strengths and needs of each school. My suggestion to educators wishing to pursue PPBS is that they concentrate initially on the following three steps (Hartley, 1972):

1. *Develop a district-wide program structure.* This identifies and categoriezes into programs all organizational activities, both instructional and supportive. The hierarchical arrangement of programs and subprograms identifies the level of specificity for subsequent goals, objectives, and evaluation. It provides the basic framework for all planning and reporting within the district.

> *End Product:* A chart listing programs in descending order of detail.
> *Coordinator:* Superintendent.

2. *Select target curricular area(s) for program analysis.* This enables teachers and administrators to focus attention on a specific program, such as reading, in order to develop a procedural model to guide subsequent analyses of other programs. The format includes program goals, learner skills, instructional objectives, evaluation criteria, alternative methods, predicted effectiveness, program constraints, major accomplishments, future plans, and direct budget costs.

> *End Product:* A concise program memorandum (20 pages) for each subject.
> *Coordinator:* Curriculum administrator and/or principals.

3. *Identify all direct costs in a program budget.* This classifies each program as a "cost center," and is based on cost accounting procedures. The school district's overall budget could be displayed in terms of Function (i.e., Instruction), Object (Teacher's Salary), Program (Social Studies), Location (Jones Elementary School),

or Level (Primary Education). The program budget includes the direct costs (teachers' salaries, benefits, supplies, textbooks, etc.) for each instructional and supportive program.

> *End Product:* A budget containing both programs and function-objects.
> *Coordinator:* Business administrator.

POSSIBLE CONSTRAINTS

Admittedly, this is a pragmatic, opportunistic approach to PPBS. Yet it takes into account the operational constraints confronting local school officials, such as: (a) lack of funds; (b) lack of time (when can teachers be spared to prepare objectives and analyze programs?); (c) understaffing (administrators cannot devote full attention to PPBS); (d) resistance to change (in addition to a small minority who cannot be bothered, some of the more conscientious staff may, for the sake of price, be fearful of failing at something that appears new and uncertain); (e) short attention span (educators seldom stay with one innovation for longer than two years; interest wanes and attention shifts to a new panacea); and (f) day-to-day crises (trying to install PPBS into local schools is a bit like trying to change a flat tire on a moving car; the school must keep moving).

EXAMPLES OF PPBS COMPONENTS

Limitations of space permit only a few PPBS components to be included here. Table 1 contains a fairly

TABLE 1. ILLUSTRATIVE CALENDAR FOR IMPLEMENTING PPBS IN A SCHOOL SYSTEM

Phase 1: Planning and Development
Phase 2: Orientation
Phase 3: Implementation

Task	Beginning Date	Completion Date	Responsibility
Phase 1			
1. Introduction of PPBS concept to administrative staff	September 1972	September 1972	Central Admn.
2. PPBS Task Force Begins work	September 1972	September 1972	Central Admn.
3. Develop program structure	September 1972	November 1972	PPBS Task Frc.
4. Select 2 programs as models for detailed analysis	November 1972	November 1972	PPBS Task Frc.
5. Program profiles developed for 2 model programs	December 1972	February 1973	Prog. Chrmn.
6. Develop budget request forms	December 1972	February 1973	PPBS Task Frc.
7. Develop communication plan	March 1973	May 1973	PPBS Task Frc.
8. Progress report to Board of Education	March 1973	March 1973	PPBS Task Frc.
Phase 2			
1. Orientation workshop for staff	March 1973	May 1973	Task Frc. Consultant
Phase 3			
1. Formation of teacher program committees	June 1973	June 1973	Prog. Chrmn.
2. Program profiles developed for all programs	June 1973	August 1973	Teach. Comm.
3. Key program committees develop program analysis	September 1973	June 1974	Prog. Comms. Prog. Chmn.
4. PPBS budget developed for admission to city admn.	April 1973	January 1974	All Staff

TABLE 2. TYPICAL PROGRAM STRUCTURE FOR A SCHOOL SYSTEM

Regular Instruction		Complementary Instruction		Instructional Services		Administrative Services		Operational Services	
Code		Code		Code		Code		Code	
001	Art K-12	031	Continuing Ed.	040	Guidance	050	Board of Educ.	060	Food Services
002	Business Training 9-12	031	E. S. L.	041	Improvement of Instruction	051	Building Leadership	061	Maintenance
003	Driver Training 9-12	032	Individualized Instruction	042	Learning Resources	052	Central Direction	062	Plant Operation
004	Educ. of Handicapped K-12	033	Remedial Read.	043	Student Welfare Services			063	Professional Technical Services
005	English 9-12	034	Special Educ. Programs	044	Testing			064	Transportation
006	Foreign Lang. 9-12	035	Student Activities	045	Employee Benefits				
007	Head Start	036	Summer School	046	Other Instructional Support				
008	Home Ec. 6-12								
009	Ind. Arts 6-12								
010	Lang. Arts K-8								
011	Math K-12								
012	Music K-12								
013	Other Instructional Activities								
014	Phys. Ed.-Health K-12								
015	Science K-12								
016	Social Studies K-12								
017	Voc. Ed. 9-12								

typical calendar for initial implementation of PPBS in a local school system. Table 2 portrays a program structure for a district. In this case, programs are defined in terms of subject matter rather than buildings or grade level. Table 3 provides a comparison between the old budget format (function-object budget) and the new approach (program budget). Table 4 provides some learner objectives (stated as behavioral objectives) for one of the programs contained in the program budget; in this case, objectives from an 8th grade science program.

POTENTIAL MISUSES OR ABUSES

Any new planning technology has its limitations, but the key to judging the worth of a concept such as PPBS lies in an objective comparison of the potential opportunities and benefits to be gained, against the possible risks and misuses. The evidence, which thus far is limited mostly to testimonials by local practitioners, indicates that PPBS is clearly worth the effort.

What follows is a brief discussion of some potential misuses that planners should avoid. (The list is indicative rather than complete, and does not include the predictable charges made by some who misunderstand PPBS; i.e., PPBS is dehumanizing; decision-making by computer; limited to quantified outputs; anti-curriculum; and too sophisticated for educators.

People problems. The anxiety level of a staff rises very quickly if PPBS is not introduced in a way that indicates sensitivity to the personal needs of teachers. Reassurance as to how PPBS will make life simpler and better should be given regularly.

Excessive paperwork. Most schools already have more than enough forms, paperwork, and bureaucratic procedures. PPBS can compound this problem if not properly supervised.

Use of jargon. Students should never be called outputs, teachers are not inputs, and the curriculum is not a throughput. The new "systems" terminology should be minimized during inservice training sessions.

Cult of testing. Tests are important, but they should not be overemphasized. Testing that is based on poor instruments, disputable assumptions, incorrectly interpreted data, and purposely manipulated data can offset the advantages afforded by PPBS.

Centralizing bias. Care must be taken to see that PPBS does not overcentralize decision-making within a tightly defined chain of command. Actually, it can be used to help decentralize budget and instructional decisions if that is the goal.

Curricular rigidity. Once a program analysis has been performed and documented, there is a danger that the program will become "frozen." Systems renewal can be achieved only by constant review and revision of objectives, scope and sequence, evaluation, and methods.

Paralysis by analysis. With new analytical tools, there is a tendency for some to overformalize, overritualize, and overdocument. The result is that excessive formal analysis itself can prevent school officials from making decisions in a reasonable, intuitive, commonsense manner.

Instant cost reduction. Many boards of education have adopted PPBS because they thought it was a mathemati-

TABLE 3. TWO TYPES OF EXPENDITURE SUMMARIES FOR ONE SCHOOL DISTRICT

Conventional Budget (without PPBS)		Program Budget (with PPBS)	
Auxiliary Agencies	$ 799,124	Adult Education	$ 86,497
Capital Outlay	84,297	Art	272,471
General Control	248,386	Business Education	142,386
Instruction	9,000,133	Building Administration	251,560
Maintenance	415,082	Central Direction	149,500
Operation	779,197	Classic-Foreign Language	504,763
		Data Center	210,500
		English Language Arts	1,860,948
		Food Services	133,706
		Home Economics	134,096
		Industrial Arts	235,778
		Kindergarten	293,873
		Learning Resources	421,312
		Mathematics	854,382
		Music	345,076
		Physical Education-Health	514,952
		Plant Maintenance	415,082
		Plant Operation	779,197
		Pupil Personnel Services	187,990
		Research Development	137,653
		Science	621,342
		Social Studies	733,606
		Special Education	365,254
		Special Projects	900,020
		Student Activities	85,252
		Summer School	134,300
		Supervision of Instruction	198,440
		Transportation	356,353
TOTAL	$17,326,219	TOTAL	$11,326,219

TABLE 4. EXAMPLES OF LEARNER OBJECTIVES FOR AN EIGHTH GRADE SCIENCE PROGRAM

Course Name: Introductory Physical Science

Course Number: 881

Objective Number:

8801 — Given a definition or hypothetical situation, the student will demonstrate knowledge of the basic metric units by identifying the appropriate metric terminology for measurements of length, volume, and mass.

8802 — Given a measure of length, volume or mass in metric units, the student will demonstrate his knowledge of metric conversions by converting the measure to any other appropriate metric unit or identifying a correct conversion from a list.

8803 — Given a list of properties of matter, the student will demonstrate his comprehension of mass and volume as measurable properties by identifying them from a number of distractors.

cal messiah that would automatically reduce costs. In practice, PPBS is neutral on the issue of cost reduction. It will promote efficiency, but even so the overall budget for next year is likely to increase because of personnel costs.

Inadequate time. The major unanticipated costs of phasing in PPBS is staff time. It is difficult to place an accurate dollar value on this item, but it is clear that schools must allocate staff time to PPBS activities (Alioto and Jungherr, 1971). Otherwise, PPBS is done in sporadic spurts of activity, and the result is frustration and uneven progress.

Unrealistic expectations. PPBS cannot be accomplished in one year, nor perhaps even two or three. By its very nature, PPBS is a developmental process that cuts across all activities of the organization. To prevent disappointments over time delays, I suggest that a time-phased schedule of PPBS implementation be developed to show who is to do what, and when, over perhaps a three-year period.

CONCLUSION

The greatest disservice that can be provided a concept such as PPBS is to create a mythology of systems procedures. Such a myth would hold that educational salvation lies in applying to schools any technique that is assumed to have been successful in private industry, defense, or aerospace settings. On the other hand, not to believe in the usefulness of PPBS and the systems approach is to deny the value of reason, common sense, and the scientific method. Success with this innovation, and any other, depends ultimately on the artistry of the user.

Although PPBS is like a well conceived play, it cannot guarantee that each actor's performance will be a success.

REFERENCES

Alioto, Robert F., and Jungherr, J. A. *Operational PPBS for Education.* New York: Harper & Row, 1971.
Hartley, Harry J. *Educational Planning-Programming-Budgeting: A Systems Approach.* Englewood Cliffs, New Jersey: Prentice-Hall, Inc., 1968.
_____. PPBS: Status and Implications. *Educational Leadership,* May 1972, 659.
Toffler, Alvin. *Future Shock.* New York: Bantam Books, Inc., 1970.

ADDITIONAL RESOURCES

Alioto, Robert F., and Jungherr, J. A. *Operational PPBS for Education: A Practical Approach to Effective Decision-Making.* New York: Harper & Row, 1971.
Haggart, Sue A., ed. *Program Budgeting for School District Planning.* Englewood Cliffs, New Jersey: Educational Technology Publications, 1972.
Knezevich, Stephen J. *Program Budgeting.* Berkeley, California; McCutchan Publishing Corporation, 1973.
Novick, David, ed. *Program Budgeting.* Cambridge, Massachusetts: Harvard University Press, 1965.

26

QUANTITATIVE ANALYSIS IN EDUCATIONAL ADMINISTRATION

by James Edward Bruno
Associate Professor
Graduate School of Education
University of California
Los Angeles, California

Quantitative analysis in educational administration refers to those techniques of a mathematical nature which assist managers and administrators of educational institutions in decision-making. Since education departments at most major colleges and universities have developed, or are in the process of developing, programs and courses in quantitative analysis (Bruno, Fox, 1973), skills in this area of decision-making are becoming one of the important bodies of knowledge in educational administrator preparation. This paper presents a taxonomy of the various areas of application of quantitative analysis, discusses some of the important quantitative techniques, and attempts to highlight issues surrounding the effective application of these techniques in education.

It might be useful, at this point, to briefly summarize the historical role of quantitative analysis in decision-making, and to distinguish the traditional and modern modes of decision-making.

Simon (1966) defined the decision-maker as a man at the moment of choice, in an environment that permits freedom to make a selection and provides a set of alternatives from which to choose. He explored the differences between traditional and modern decision-making techniques and developed the taxonomy in Table 1 (see below). According to Simon, the principal difference between the two approaches of decision-making is the increasing emphasis accorded analysis, especially quantitative analysis, in modern decision-making.

EMERGENCE OF QUANTITATIVE ANALYSIS IN THE EDUCATION

In my judgment, well informed legislators and governors and administrators will no longer be content to know in mere dollar terms what constitutes educational need of the schools. The politician of today is unimpressed with continuing requests for more input without some idea of school output.
—Jess Unruh (Hartley, 1968)

Such critical statements from state legislatures as the above, concerning the way schools were managed, became very common in the early 60s. Society began to pay more attention to what the schools produced for their tax dollars than merely what schools spent for their educational programs. The accountability movement in public education was generated during this period, and today it is the single most important influence on the course of education.

As public pressures for greater school district efficiency and accountability became more intense, school administrators began to search for techniques, theories and practices found in the quantitatively-based disciplines of business, policy analysis, and economics to assist them in decision-making. As the transition from input orientation (salaries, facilities, buildings) to output orientation (reading scores, attendance, dropout) become more complete, the dependence upon quantitative analysis as the cornerstone of educational evaluation became more pronounced.

With this change in fiscal orientation came a very important change in the way school administrators viewed their role. The school administrator who rose from the teaching ranks, and believed in the unity of the teacher-administrator professional team philosophy, is today being supplanted by a more management- or decision-oriented individual. It is a moot point whether the school administrator desired this managerial function, whether he was forced by societal demands for accountability to assume it, or whether the development of managerial skills was needed to maintain or legitimize the administrator's status in the school district. It is certain, however, that the exclusion of the administrator from the powerful new teacher bargaining groups has tended to alienate him from the professional team philosophy common to education in the 40s and 50s. Today he is more a manager of the educational enterprise with a managerial class; he had to develop their skills and techniques—notably, he had to develop skills in analysis.

CURRENT INTEREST IN QUANTITATIVE ANALYSIS IN EDUCATION

Quantitative analysis is by no means a new concept in educational administration. As early as 1909, Ayres published his "Index of Efficiency." As Callahan says about Ayres, "He was one of the first educators to picture the schools as a factory and to apply the business and industrial values and practices in a systematic way" (1962, pp. 15-16).

Application of quantitative tools and techniques to educational administration has also been demonstrated on international, federal, and professional levels. International interest is illustrated by two symposia sponsored by the Committee for Scientific and Technical Personnel of the Organization for Economic Cooperation and Development (OECD). The first symposium, held in 1967, dealt mainly with the efficient use of resources at the individual institution and local school system levels (OECD 1969a). The second, held in April 1968, addressed broader issues, such as budgeting, cost-benefit analysis, and cost-effectiveness analysis in educational administration (OECD 1968).

Federal interest has been evidenced by the formation of the Division of Operations Analysis (DOA) in the National Center for Educational Statistics (NCES), and by DOA's subsequent sponsorship in 1967 of a symposium—Operations Analysis in Education. About 1,100 educators, statisticians, mathematicians, economists, representatives of related sciences, and observers from foreign countries attended the symposium. This is believed to be the first nationwide conference devoted exclusively to quantitative analysis in education (Stoller, 1969).

Professional interest in quantitative analysis is indicated by the American Association of School Administrators' (AASA) Commission on Administrative Technology. The commission, created in 1966, was charged with the responsibility of identifying new approaches in management of other fields that can be adapted to school administration. The Commission includes a mix of practitioners (i.e., superintendents) and professors concerned with the preparation of future practitioners. It is concerned and impressed with the possibilities of applying the systems approach to school administration (Knezevich, 1969, p. 131).

The University Council for Educational Administration (UCEA) also demonstrated interest in quantitative analysis when it sponsored, early in 1966, "one of the first multi-institutional seminars devoted to the use of systems analysis in education" (Hartley, 1968, p. 63). The seminar was attended by professors from 20 major universities, who met to study the relevancy of systems procedures for education (Davis and Hendrix, 1966).

Finally, the Division of Administrative Studies of the American Educational Research Association (AERA) entered the field and has, at its annual conventions, sponsored symposia on the application of quantitative analysis to educational administration. The 1970, 1971, and 1972 symposium titles were, respectively, "Application of Quantitative Techniques to School District Decision-Making," "Operations Research-Systems Analysis in School District Planning," and "Educational Operations Research."

At the university and college level, formal interest in educational quantitative analysis can be demonstrated by the emergence of several excellent texts on the subject geared specifically to programs in administrator preparation. These texts include those by Hartley (1968), Banghart (1969), Tanner (1971), Thompson (1971), Van Dusseldorp et al. (1971), and Van Gigh and Hill (1971).

When viewing the domain of problem issues facing educators, and the piecemeal applications of these quantitative techniques to specific problems, certain broad areas of application are apparent. We also notice that tools and techniques applicable in one area are of little substantive use in another. The following section discusses the areas of application of these tools in education in an attempt to establish the appropriateness of these quantitative techniques.

Specific application of tools, and techniques of quantitative analysis, are best summarized in several research studies and books devoted to reviewing the literature on the application of quantitative analysis to problems in education. These special literature review studies include Alkin and Bruno (1970); Bruno and Fox (1972); Hammond (1970); and McNamara (1971, 1972). The diversity of educational planning problems addressed by these techniques demonstrates the wide applicability of these quantitative techniques. For example, linear programming, probably the most widely used of the quantitative techniques of operations research, due to the availability of computer software packages, has been successfully used in allocating funds to local school districts under school finance plans (Bruno, 1969); wage salary evaluation for school district personnel (Bruno, 1970); allocation of funds for vocational and technical education (McNamara, 1970); evaluation of instructional programs (Bruno, 1972); school busing and racial desegregation (Clarke and Surkis, 1968); subsidies for college students (Froomkin, 1969); and resource allocation to education in a developing country (Bowles, 1967).

Mathematical models where one or more of the variables are stochastic or probabalistic in nature are solved by Markov chain analysis and Monte Carlo techniques. These models are specific to the problem situation, so no standard computer software package exists for performing the analysis. However, Markov analysis has been used to project the flow of personnel through a system (Merck, 1965), project the growth of student teacher populations (Zabrowski and Zinter, 1968), and project the needs for higher education (Monstad, 1967).

Monte Carlo techniques have been applied to determining the optimal size of substitute teacher pools (Bruno, 1972), and for the projection of enrollments (Guffin and Schmitt).

AREAS OF APPLICATION OF QUANTITATIVE ANALYSIS IN EDUCATION

It is important to understand the differences between the various tools and techniques of quantitative analysis and the types of educational problems they address. Table 1 shows some traditional and modern approaches. Table 2 illustrates types of problems facing school administrators and the techniques available.

TABLE 1

Types of Decisions	Traditional	Modern

Programmed
   Routine, repetitive decisions
	1. Habit
	2. Clerical routine
	   Standard operating procedures
		Operations research
		Mathematical analysis
		Computer simulation

	3. Organization, structure, common expectation of sub-goals, well defined information channels	Educational Data processing

Nonprogrammed
   One-shot, ill-structured novel policy decision
	1. Judgment, institution
	   Rules of thumb
	   Selection and training
		Heuristic problem solving

TABLE 2. TYPES OF PROBLEMS HANDLED BY QUANTITATIVE ANALYSIS

Tactical Problems	Policy Problems
Objectives, Constraints, and Criteria Predetermined	Objectives, Constraints, and Criteria Subject to Challenge
Concerned with the Question "How?"	Concerned with the Questions "What?" and "Why?"
Typical Tools: Operations Research, Operations Analysis, Cost-Effectiveness Analysis, Cost-Benefit Analysis	Typical Tools: Cost-Effectiveness Analysis, Cost-Benefit Analysis, PPBS, PPBES, Systems Analysis, Policy Analysis
Mathematical Orientation	Social Science and Philosophical Orientation
Technician Plays Major Role	Technician Plays Supportive Role

The polar extremes of the types of tasks are labeled "tactical problems" and "policy problems." Tactical problems include areas such as school bus routing, repair/replace and maintenance decisions regarding equipment, and student scheduling. At the other end of the continuum, under policy problems, are listed wage and salary negotiations, integration policies, and curriculum issues.

Table 2 can also be described by the type of analysis employed. In general, there are two types of analysis. First there is descriptive analysis, which attempts to describe the state of the system and gives no prescription for decision-making. The second type of analysis, called normative analysis, is decision-related, and attempts to evaluate alternative courses of action and delineate criteria for evaluation of the system. Normative analysis can itself be viewed in two parts. First there is input trade-off analysis, where operational control is desired, which asks the question of how well a system is mixing its inputs. Its main goals are efficiency and management. The highest level of analysis, output trade-off analysis, attempts to ask how well a system is mixing outputs. Its main goals are system effectiveness and organizational planning and policy. Essentially, input trade-off normative analysis focuses on the means of a productive process,

while output trade-off normative analysis focuses on the results of a productive process. Table 3 summarizes the three types of analysis and their principal use in school administration.

The three types of analysis can now be placed in a table and compared with administrative functions in a district. Notice in Table 4 how the transitions from line item to performance to program budgeting in American education nicely paralleled societal concerns for control (40s–50s), efficiency (60s) and effectiveness (70s).

TABLE 3. TYPES OF EDUCATIONAL ANALYSIS

Type	Principal Use
Descriptive Analysis	Quantitatively simulate, measure or describe the system Input to normative analysis Asks the question "What?"
Normative Analysis Input Trade-Off Analysis	Management decision-making Operational or tactical planning Strives toward efficiency Input to output trade-off analysis Asks the question "How?"
Output Trade-Off Analysis	Policy or high level goal-oriented decision-making Long range or strategic planning Strives toward effectiveness Asks the question "Why?"

Thus, while descriptive analysis might describe, or ask the question "what," about a reading program in terms of costs/facilities/personnel, input normative analysis asks how these inputs can be mixed to maximize reading scores. Output normative analysis asks questions related to the goals of society and the schools, and are reflected in the reading program and attempts to establish the "why" of a reading program. The techniques in quantitative analysis can also be classified, as in Table 2, with types of problems (tactical, planning, and policy) and types of analysis (descriptive-normative). For further description of specific techniques, the reader is directed to standard textbooks on operations research, multivariate analysis, or statistics.

TABLE 4

	Descriptive Analysis	*Input Trade-Off Analysis*	*Output Trade-Off Analysis*
Principal Purpose	Central	Management	Planning
Unit of Analysis	Function and objects of expenditure	Resources	Programs
Principal Goal	Cost control	Efficiency	Effectiveness
Type of Budget	Traditional line item	Performance budget	Program budget
Applicable Tools and Techniques	Cost accounting	Operations research	Systems analysis PPBS
Economic	Cost analysis	Production theory	Utility
Principal Orientation	Job functions	Departments	Organization
Question	What	How	Why

CONCLUSION

The increasing demand for accountability and school-site decision-making has placed new pressures on school administrators. At the same time, developments in the tools and techniques of quantitative analysis have provided administrators with increased potential of quantitative analysis to school problems.

However, the application of quantitative analysis methods in the schools is by no means a simple and straightforward process. Both practical and theoretical problems must be dealt with. Practical problems include the complexity and confusion associated with quantitative analysis, and the fact that its promise often exceeds its results. Also, quantitative analysis is often biased toward quantifiable data. Finally, this kind of analysis is often expensive, making it more readily available to rich districts than to poor ones.

TABLE 5. QUANTITATIVE TECHNIQUES IN EDUCATIONAL ADMINISTRATION

1. a. Normative Analysis (output trade-off)	Systems Analysis
Challenges organizational goals and effectiveness criteria	PPBS
Answers questions related to organizational effectiveness and policy problems	Utility Theory Policy Analysis Cost Effectiveness
b. Normative Analysis (input trade-offs)	Mathematical Programming Production Functions
Answers questions related to organizational efficiency achieve organizational goal at least cost or some other well-defined criterion of effectiveness	Dynamic Programming Game Theory
2. Descriptive Analysis	Multivariate Analysis Computer Simulation Traditional Statistical Analysis
Answers questions related to description of the system or measurement of change within a system; no criterion of effectiveness stated except for significant/nonsignificant change	Statistical Inference

The theoretical issues center on the question, "Can the schools be viewed as factories?" Production theory is far more developed than educational theory. Educators know very little about what produces educational outcomes (the dynamic of learning remains a mystery). Moreover, much difficulty exists in defining and identifying both the inputs and the outputs of the educational process.

While these practical and theoretical issues exist, the trend towards greater utilization of quantitative analysis by school administrators continues. In 1967, the chairman of the AERA Committee on Educational Organization, Administration, and Finance observed: "There seems to be a growing tendency to assume that administrative procedures, instructional approaches, schools, and fiscal structures must be analyzed as systems or systems components" (Erickson 1967, p. 376). This trend has been projected into the present decade:

> School systems will see the advent of new staff specializations in the next five to ten years. . . The new unit . . . may include computer and data processing experts, systems analysists, and operations researchers. . . . Problems that can be submitted to quantitative analysis will be increasingly solved using OR techniques. . . . Application of the systems approach will place greater emphasis on planning, thoughtful analysis, and increased information requirements. (Culbertson et al., 1969, pp. 185-186)

Unfortunately, the problems associated with limitations of quantitative analysis will continue to be evident in the 1970s.

> There will be improper adaptation of models developed elsewhere to educational situations, an overemphasis on the gathering of quantitative data through crude testing devices, and overemphasis on economic efficiency. It would also seem likely that , because of the complexities involved in comprehensive analysis and lack of adequate data concerning educational outputs, extensive use of formal methods of analysis will be somewhat limited during the next five to ten years. There will be a quantitative increase in the use of the techniques, but formal analysis will be directed at new programs, middle-range programs with similar objectives, programs where information is available or can be obtained at minimum cost, and programs where there is a clear relationship between input and output. However, even within these limitations a number of new trends associated with the use of management technologies may emerge that will affect educational organization and administration. (Culbertson et al., 1969, p. 182)

It appears that as educational administrators become more proficient in the application of quantitative analysis, the scope and effectiveness of these tools and techniques will be dramatically increased. A primary limitation of educational quantitative analysis in the past has been that studies were often conducted by those who were insufficiently trained—including analysts who were not sufficiently acquainted with quantitative analysis. It appears that the bridge between quantitative analysis and educational problems is becoming increasingly stronger. This closer relationship should result in analyses of higher quality that, in turn, should generated increased confidence in the applicability of these tools and techniques.

REFERENCES

Alkin, Marvin C., and Bruno, James E. System Approaches to Educational Planning. Part IV in *Social and Technological Change: Implications for Education,* edited by Philip K. Piele et al. Eugene, Oregon: Center for the Advanced Study of Educational Administration, 1970.

Ayres, Leonard. *Laggards in Our Schools.* New York: Kelley, 1909.

Banghart, Frank W. *Educational System Analysis.* New York: Macmillan, 1969.

Blaug, Mark. Cost-Benefit and Cost-Effectiveness Analysis of Education. In *Budgeting, Program Analysis and Cost-Effectiveness in Educational Planning.* Paris: Organization for Economic Cooperation and Development, 1968.

Boulay, Peter C. Systems Analysis: Tonic or Toxic. *Arizona Teacher, 57, 5* (May 1969).

Bowles, S. S. The Efficient Allocation of Resources in Education. *Quarterly Journal of Economics,* No. 2, 1967.

Brown, Daniel J. The Poverty of Educational Administration. Paper presented at the annual meeting of the American Educational Research Association, Chicago, 1972.

Boulding, Kenneth E. The Schooling Industry as a Possibly Pathological Section of the American Economy. *Review of Educational Research, 40, 1* (winter, 1972).

Bruno, James E. An Alternative to Simplistic Formula Approaches to School Finance, *American Educational Research Journal,* Vol. 6, No. 4, pp. 1-20 (November 1969).

_____. How to Build Salary Schedules Which Reflect School District Priorities and Objectives. Swarthmore, Pa.: A. C. Croft Publishers, 1970.

_____. Integrating Substitute Teachers into School District Instructional Programs. Swarthmore, Pa.: A. C. Croft Publishers.

_____. A Methodology for the Evaluation of Instruction or Performance Contracts which Incorporate School District Utilities and Goals. *American Educational Research Journal,* Vol. 9, No. 2, (Spring 1972) pp. 175-195.

_____, and Fox, James Norman. Quantitative Analysis in Administrative Preparation. Monograph #7, ERIC Clearinghouse, Eugene, Oregon.

Callahan, Raymond E. *Education and the Cult of Efficiency.* Chicago: The University of Chicago Press, 1962.

Clarke, A., and Surkis, J. An Operations Research Approach to Racial Desegregation of School Systems. *Socio-Economic Planning Sciences,* 1968, pp. 259-272.

Coleman, James E. et al. *Equality of Educational Opportunity.* Washington, D.C.: U.S. Government Printing Office, 1966.

Committee for Economic Development. Innovation in Education: New Directions for the American. New York, 1968.

Conner, Forrest E. Foreword to *Administrative Technology and the School Executive,* edited by Stephen J. Knezevich. Washington, D.C.: Commission on Administrative Technology,

American Association of School Administrators, 1969.

Coombs, Philip M., and Hallak, Jacques. *Managing Educational Costs.* New York: Oxford University Press, 1972.

Counts, George S. *The Social Composition of Boards of Education.* Chicago: The University of Chicago, 1927.

Cubberley, Ellwood P. *Public School Administration.* Boston: Houghton-Mifflin, 1916.

Culbertson, Jack A., Farquhar, Robin H., Gaynor, Alan K., and Shibles, Mark R. *Preparing Educational Leaders for the Seventies. Final Report.* Columbus, Ohio: University Council for Educational Administration, 1969.

Davis, Donald E., and Hendrix, Vernon L. *Systems Analysis in Educational Administration.* Minneapolis: University of Minnesota, and University Council for Educational Administration, 1966.

Dror, Yehezkel. Policy Analysis: A New Professional Role In Government Service. Public Administration Review, *27, 3* (September 1967).

_____. Review of Educational Planning-Programming-Budgeting: A Systems Approach by Harry J. Hartley. Santa Monica, California: The Rand Corporation, 1969.

Durstine, Richard M. Technical Trends in Educational Management: Opportunities and Hazards. Papers and Proceedings: Annual Conference of the Comparative and International Education Society, Atlanta, Georgia, March 22-24, 1970. *Comparative Education Review, 14, 3* (October 1970).

Enthoven, Alain. Systems Analysis and the Navy. In *Planning Programming Budgeting: A Systems Approach to Management,* edited by Fremont J. Lyden and Ernest G. Miller. Chicago: Markham Publishing Company, 1968.

Erickson, Donald A. Foreword to *Review of Educational Research, 37, 4* (October 1967).

Farmer, James. *Why Planning, Programming, Budgeting Systems for Higher Education?* Boulder, Colorado: Western Interstate Commission for Higher Education, 1970.

Froomkin, Joseph. Cost/Effectiveness and Cost/Benefit Analyses of Educational Programs. In *Proceedings of the Symposium on Operations Analysis of Education,* a conference sponsored by the National Center for Educational Statistics, Office of Education, U.S. Department of Health, Education, and Welfare, Washington, D.C., November 19-22, 1967. *Socio-Economic Planning Sciences, 2,* 2/3/4 (April 1969).

Guffin, M., and Schmitt, J. A Monte Carlo Model for the Prediction of School Enrollments. Paper presented at the Annual Conference of AERA, Chicago, 1967.

Harmes, H. M. Improvement in Education: Criteria for Change. *Educational Technology, 10,* 11 (November 1970).

Hartley, Harry J. Economic Rationality in Urban School Planning: The Program Budget. *Urban Education, 3,* 1 (1967).

_____. *Educational Planning, Programming, Budgeting: A Systems Approach.* Englewood Cliffs, New Jersey: Prentice-Hall, 1968.

Hinds, Richard H. Educational Program Planning and Related Techniques; Annotated Bibliography. Unpublished Report, Miami, Florida: Dade County Public Schools, 1969.

Hirsch, Werner Z. The Budget as an Instrument for Medium and Long-Range Planning and Programming of Education. In *Budgeting, Program Analysis and Cost-Effectiveness in Educational Planning.* Paris: Organization for Economic Cooperation and Development, 1968.

Hovey, Harold A. *The Planning-Programming-Budgeting Approach to Government Decision-Making.* New York: Frederick A. Praeger, 1968.

James, H. Thomas. The Impending Revolution in School Business Management. Paper presented at the Asosciation of School Business Officials, Houston, Texas, October 22-24, 1968.

_____. The New Cult of Efficiency and Education, Horace Mann Lecture 1968. Pittsburgh: University of Pittsburgh Press, 1969.

Kaufman, Roger. Systems Approaches to Education: Discussion and Integration. Part III in *Social and Technological Change: Implications for Education*, edited by Philip K. Piele et al. Eugene, Oregon: Center for the Advanced Study of Educational Administration, 1970.

———. *Educational System Planning*. Englewood Cliffs, New Jersey: Prentice-Hall, 1972.

Keppel, Francis. Operations Analysis—The Promise and the Pitfalls. In *Proceedings of the Symposium on Operations Analysis of Education*, a conference sponsored by the National Center for Educational Statistics, Office of Education, U.S. Department of Health, Education, and Welfare, Washington, D.C., November 19-22, 1967. *Socio-Economic Planning Sciences, 2*, 2/3/4 (April 1969).

Kiesling, Herbert J. *Multivariate Analysis of Schools and Educational Policy*. Santa Monica, California: the Rand Corporation, 1971.

Knezevich, Stephen J. The Systems Approach to School Administration: Some Perceptions on the State of the Art in 1967. In *Proceedings of the Symposium on Operations Analysis of Education*, a conference sponsored by the National Center for Educational Statistics, Office of Education, U.S. Department of Health, Education, and Welfare, Washington, D.C., November 19-22, 1967. *Socio-Economic Planning Sciences, 2*, 2/3/4 (April 1969).

———, ed. Administrative Technology and the School Executive. Washington D.C.: Commission on Administrative Technology, American Association of School Administrators, 1969.

———. *The American School Superintendent*. Washington, D.C.: American Association of School Administrators, 1972.

Kraft, Richard H. P., and Latta, Raymond F., eds. Special Issue on Systems Techniques in Educational Planning and Management. *Education Technology, 12*, 2 (February 1972).

McNamara, James F. A Mathematical Model for the Efficient Allocation of Vocational Technical Education. Bureau of Educational Research, Pennsylvania Dept. of Education, 1970.

———. Mathematical Programming Models in Educational Planning. *Review of Educational Research, 41*, 5 (December 1971).

———. Mathematics and Educational Administration. *Journal of Educational Administration, 10*, 2 (October 1972).

Minck, J. W. A Markovian Model for Projectory Movements of Personnel Through a System. Lackland Air Force Base, Texas: Air Force Systems Command Personnel Research Laboratory, Aerospace Medical Division, PRL-TR-65-6, 1965.

Mood, Alexander M., and Stoller, David S. USOE is Knee-Deep in Operational Analysis. *Nation's Schools, 80*, 4 (October 1967).

Operation PEP. *Symposium on the Application of System Analysis and Management Techniques to Educational Planning in California*. Chapman College, Orange, California, June 12-13, 1967; Burlingame, California, 1967.

Organization for Economic Cooperation and Development (OECD). *Budgeting, Program Analysis and Cost-Effectiveness in Educational Planning*. Paris, 1968.

———. *Efficiency in Resource Utilization in Education*. Paris, 1969.

———. *Systems Analysis for Educational Planning: Selected Annotated Bibliography*. Paris, 1969.

Peat, Marwick, Mitchell, and Co. *Educational Planning and Evaluation Guide for California School Districts*. Sacramento, California: California State Advisory Commission on School District Budgeting and Accounting, 1972.

Pfeiffer, John. *New Look at Education: Systems Analysis in Our Schools and Colleges*. New York: Odyssey Press, 1968.

Phi Delta Kappa. *Educational Goals and Objectives: Model Program for Community and Professional Involvement*. Bloomington, Illinois, n.d.

Schultze, Charles L. Why Benefit-Cost Analysis; In *Program Budgeting a Benefit-Cost Analysis*, edited by Harley H. Hinrichs

and Graeme M. Taylor. Pacific Palisades, California: Goodyear Publishing Company, Inc., 1969.

Simon, Herbert A. *The Shape of Automation for Men and Management*. New York: Harper and Row, 1966.

Sisson, Roger L. Can We Model the Educational Process? In *Proceedings of the Symposium on the Operations Analysis of Education*, a conference sponsored by the National Center for Educational Statistics, Office of Education, U.S. Department of Health, Education, and Welfare, Washington, D.C., November 19-22, 1967. *Socio-Economic Planning Sciences, 2*, 2/3/4 (April 1969).

———. Operations Analysis: Some Definitions and an Evaluation. Proceedings of American Association of Collegiate Registrars and Admissions Officers, Annual Meeting. *College and University, 45*, 4 (Summer 1970).

Stoller, David S. Foreword to *Proceedings of the Symposium on Operation Analysis of Education*, a conference sponsored by the National Center for Educational Statistics, Office of Education, U.S. Department of Health, Education, and Welfare, Washington, D.C., November 19-22, 1967. *Socio-Economic Planning Sciences, 2*, 2/3/4 (April 1969).

———, and Dorfman, William, conference eds. *Proceedings of the Symposium on Operations Analysis of Education* a conference sponsored by the National Center for Educational Statistics, Office of Education, U.S. Department of Health, Education, and Welfare, Washington, D.C. November 19-22, 1967. *Socio-Economic Planning Sciences, 2*, 2/3/4 (April 1969).

Tanner, C. Kenneth. *Designs for Educational Planning: A Systematic Approach*. Lexington, Massachusetts: Heath Lexington Books, 1971.

Thomas, J. Allen, Efficiency Criteria in Urban School Systems. Paper presented at the annual meeting of the American Educational Research Association, New York, February 1967.

———. *The Productive School: A Systems Analysis Approach to Educational Administration*. New York: Wiley, 1971.

Thompson, Robert B. *A Systems Approach to Instruction*. Hamden, Connecticut: The Shoe String Press, Inc., 1971.

Thonstad, T., Mathematical Models in Educational Planning, A Mathematical Model of the Norwegian Educational System, Paris. OECD, 1967.

Van Dusseldorp, Ralph A., Richardson, Duane E., and Foley, Walter J. *Educational Decision-Making through Operations Research*. Boston: Allyn and Bacon, 1971.

Van Gigh, John P., and Hill, Richard F. *Using Systems Analysis to Implement Cost-Effectiveness and Program Budgeting in Education*. Englewood Cliffs, New Jersey: Educational Technology Publication, 1971.

Weisbrod, Burton A. *External Benefits of Public Education: An Economic Analysis*. Princeton, New Jersey: Industrial Relations Section, Department of Economics, Princeton University, 1964.

Wildavsky, Aaron. Rescuing Policy Analysis from PPBS. (PPBS Reexamined). *Public Administration Review, 29*, 2 (March-April 1969). Reprinted in *Educational Investment in an Urban Society*, edited by Melvin R. Levin and Alan Shank. New York: Teachers College Press, 1970.

Wright, Chester. The Concept of a Program Budget. In *Program Budgeting and Benefit-Cost Analysis*, edited by Harley H. Hinrichs and Graeme M. Taylor. Pacific Palisades, California: Goodyear Publishing Company, Inc., 1969.

Zabrowski, E. K., Zinter, J. R., and Okada, T. Student-Teacher Population Growth Model. Washington, D.C., USOE, OE 10055, 1968.

27

VOUCHER PLANS

by Rita Hegedus
Supervisor of Evaluation
Planning, Research, and Evaluation Division
Delaware Department of Public Instruction
Dover, Delaware

At no time in the history of American education has the worth of the public school system been so highly questioned and criticized as it has been in the last decade. In a debate sparked by the Coleman Report and by the fight for school decentralization in the cities, praise has been virtually nonexistent. Problems concerning the disadvantaged, segregation, busing, teacher strikes, and parochial aid are part of the public school system's plight.

Various solutions have been offered to these problems. Among them are education voucher plans. Education vouchers are an attempt to bring change to the system by restructuring the way schools are financed.

BACKGROUND

The idea of vouchers for education is not new. John Stuart Mill, in his classic work, *On Liberty* (1859), was among the first to propose an educational system that could be classified as a voucher system. He suggested that public education, or education established by the state, be one among many competing experiments. Competitive schools were seriously offered as an alternative in American education in 1955 by the noted conservative economist, Milton Friedman. His listeners were few. During the middle and late 1960s the idea of competition for public schools recurred, and was debated in journals, newspapers, and other public forums. Educational leaders such as Kenneth B. Clark, Theodore R. Sizer, and Christopher Jencks asserted that the public school system was a protected public monopoly facing only minimal competition from private and parochial schools. They believed that like any monopoly, neither change nor confrontation of critical problems would happen from within the system.

In order to break up the monopolistic system of public schools, another means of financing them had to be devised. Under the direction of Christopher Jencks, and supported by an Office of Economic Opportunity (OEO) Grant, in December 1969 the Center for the Study of Public Policy (CSPP) in Cambridge, Massachusetts began exploring alternative ways for financing education. Their answer to the problem was education vouchers. They reasoned that money for schools, while locally controlled, is controlled by the community as a whole. Hence, one way to change control over schools is to take the money from the community as a whole and give it to parents of school-age children in the form of a voucher. Parents could then shop for a public school much the way a potential college student shops for a college.

According to Jencks, and many others, such a system would free public schools from existing constraints by eliminating their "monopolistic privileges." If parents did not like what a school was doing, they could send their children elsewhere. The result would be pressure on schools to improve the quality of their educational programs if they were to keep the children they serve. If they did not, such schools would decline and others would grow.

In order to explain what an educational voucher system is and how it would operate, the CSPP issued a report, *Education Vouchers,* in December 1970. It is the most definitive document available on voucher plans. The report explains what an education voucher system is and how it would operate in a proposed five-year experiment.

EDUCATION VOUCHER SYSTEM DEFINED

According to the report, the first step in operating a voucher system is the establishment of an Educational Voucher Agency (EVA). EVA is designed to be a locally controlled body which will receive Federal, state and local funds for financing the education of all local children. It will not operate any schools of its own; rather, EVA's chief duties would be to issue and redeem vouchers, provide student transportation, and disseminate information on participating voucher schools.

In the spring every family would submit to EVA the names of schools it wanted to send each of its school-age children to in the fall. As long as it had room, a voucher school would be required to admit all students who applied. The local board of education would be responsible for ensuring enough places in publicly managed schools to accommodate every school-age child in the district who did not want to attend a privately managed school.

The voucher school could be an existing public school, a new school opened by the public school board to attract families who would otherwise withdraw their children from the public system, an existing private school, or a new private school opened especially to cater to children with vouchers. In order to cash vouchers, a school would have to:

accept the voucher as full payment of tuition;

accept any applicant as long as it had places;

fill at least half its places by random selection if they had more applicants than places, and the other half as they saw fit, but not discriminate against ethnic minorities;

accept uniform EVA standards regarding suspension and expulsion;

agree to make a wide variety of information about its facilities, teacher, programs, and students available to EVA and the public;

maintain accounts of money received and distributed in a form allowing parents and EVA to determine whether the school was getting its entitled resources, whether a church-operated school was subsidizing church activities, and whether a school operated by a profit-making corporation was siphoning off excessive amounts to the parent corporation; and

meet existing state requirements for private schools.

No participating school would be permitted to discriminate against applicants on the basis of race or religion. Further, revenue could be used only for secular instruction. Except for existing state regulations, there would be no restrictions on staffing, curriculum, and the like.

Having enrolled their children, parents would give their vouchers to the school, which in turn would redeem them at EVA. The redemption value of a middle- or upper-income family's voucher would approximate what the local public schools currently spend on upper-income children, while vouchers for children from low-income families would have a higher value. The monetary incentive for the disadvantaged is regarded as essential in order to overcome their multiple educational handicaps, and to make these students attractive to schools.

THE PROPOSED EDUCATION VOUCHER EXPERIMENT

The Center's 1970 report also contains extensive information on a proposed OEO-sponsored experiment on vouchers. As described in the report, the demonstration was to be confined to a single municipality for a minimum of five to eight years. All children in grades K through six in the designated area were to be eligible. In general, all of the model guidelines on vouchers were to be observed. That is, no voucher school was to be allowed to charge tuition in excess of the vouchers. Pupils attending parochial schools were to receive vouchers redeemable at no more than the cost of secular education. Vouchers for the disadvantaged were to have a higher value than the others. In the case of an overflow in the number of applicants, voucher schools were to be allowed to fill up to 50 percent of their places as they wish, with the restriction that minority groups be represented by the same percentage as the minority group applicants. At least 50 percent of the remaining places were to be filled by lottery.

The demonstration area selected was to have at least ten privately controlled, secular, voucher schools; several parochial voucher schools; and several neighborhood public schools. In order to have a suitable population, at least 12,000 children between the ages of five and eleven were to be within the experimental boundaries. Members of EVA were to be elected or appointed so as to represent minority as well as majority interests. Control groups and extensive evaluation were also to be part of the proposed experiment.

Among the problems to be resolved by the evaluation were whether the education voucher system would

increase the share of the nation's educational resources available to disadvantaged children;

produce at least as much mixing of blacks and whites, rich and poor, clever and dull, as the present system;

ensure advantaged and disadvantaged parents of equal chances of getting their children into the school of their choice;

provide parents (and influential organizations) with information they think necessary to make intelligent choices among schools; and

avoid conflict with both the Fourteenth Amendment prohibition against racial discrimination and the First Amendment provisions regarding church and state.

FEASIBILITY STUDIES

In February 1971 the Office of Economic Opportunity awarded grants to Gary, Indiana, Seattle, Washington, and Alum Rock, California to conduct feasibility studies on the voucher system. All three areas met the basic requirements outlined for a demonstration area. The communities were expected to tell OEO whether or not they could conduct the proposed experiment. The districts had to propose:

how many public schools would be included in the voucher district;

how to establish new schools and stimulate existing ones to participate;

how to enlist the support of parochial schools;

how much autonomy individual principals should have in designing curriculum, hiring staff, and experimentation; and

to what extent parents should participate.

The Gary school system, described as being in a deteriorating black urban area, subcontracted the work to the Institute for Advancement of Urban Education in New York. The study in Alum Rock, which has a large Spanish-speaking population, was subcontracted to the Santa Clara County Office of Education. Seattle, which has substantial minority groups, contacted the Bureau of School Service and Research from the University of Washington to conduct the study.

Additional grants for the feasibility studies were made in the summer of 1971 to Alum Rock and Seattle. Gary, Indiana elected to drop out of consideration and was replaced by Rockland, Maine. Approximately one year later, based on their reports, Alum Rock was selected for the site of the first voucher experiment. Nearly $2 million was granted to the city by OEO for the experiment.

ALUM ROCK

The details of the 1972-1973 voucher experiment in Alum Rock are too numerous to recount in full. Based on its feasibility study, however, it was obvious that a full-scale system could not be implemented, and a compromise version was reached. The plan differed in some significant aspects from the CSPP's model. Only one-third of the schools in the district were involved for a one-year period. Parochial schools could not participate because of California law. In addition, although an Education Voucher Advisory Committee was formed, the Alum Rock Board of Education retained responsibility and control of the voucher schools. Finally, the emphasis in competition was among competing school programs rather than among competing schools. Because of these differences from the CSPP model, OEO labeled the experiment as "transitional."

The results of Alum Rock's first year are generally considered to be favorable. Teachers liked it because there was "less red tape" and they had a "better chance to do what they wanted." In fact, two-thirds of the faculty voted to expand the experiment for the 1973-1974 school term.

Besides greater involvement for the second year, other positive effects were seen in a sharp reduction in absenteeism and truancy and a larger parent turnout at public meetings. A great deal of the success was credited to the efforts and support of William Jefferds, the Alum Rock district superintendent. Some adverse effects were that some schools and teachers were becoming sales-oriented, and many of the parents still remained uninterested.

NEW HAMPSHIRE

A voucher plan of another type is waiting trial in the state of New Hampshire. The proposed $5 million project is based on an "unregulated" model developed by Milton Friedman. Unlike the voucher plan at Alum Rock, New Hampshire would encourage participation of nonpublic schools, and would permit schools to operate under their own selective admissions plans, instead of requiring them to accept all applicants regardless of special qualifications. They would, however, prohibit racial discrimination. It was decided not to include parochial schools in New Hampshire's experiment, in view of the Supreme Court's "severe" antiparochial stand in decisions handed down in June 1973. The experiment is tentatively set for the fall of 1974. During the 1973-1974 school year, groundwork will be laid with parents, teachers, and citizens, school districts will be chosen, and other administrative procedures will be implemented.

DISCUSSION

During 1972-1973 OEO continued to finance other voucher studies. A continuing grant was made to CSPP to study problems teachers encounter with vouchers, and to provide technical assistance to other communities studying voucher plans. These communities include Rochester, New York, New Rochelle, New York, Milwaukee, Wisconsin, and Hartford, Connecticut. The CSPP is also studying areas such as policies for transferring or expelling students; the effect of the lottery; transportation costs; and the accreditation of voucher schools. OEO considers the Alum Rock experiment, although transitional and possibly short-lived, useful because of the data it can offer on the effectiveness of admissions procedures, parent counseling, and financing. The Alum Rock experiment may also offer some indication of the social and political changes, and the effects on student achievement.

The voucher idea has not been without opponents. In general, most organized educational groups, both union and professional, are opposed to vouchers. Since 1970 opposition toward vouchers has solidified and increased in strength and numbers. Arrayed against it are the National Education Association (NEA), the National School Boards Association, the American Association of School Administrators, the American Federation of Teachers, the American Parents Committee, the National Association of School Boards of Education, and the Council of Chief State School Officers. At the NEA July 1970 convention, a resolution was passed stating vouchers "could lead to racial, economic, and social isolation of children, and weaken or destroy the public school system." The resolution further warned that competition would widen the gap between rich and poor schools, since students would desert poor schools to attend better ones, leaving a dumping-ground for students whose parents do not have the sophistication to use the system. The American Civil Liberties Union opposes vouchers on grounds that they would undermine goals of education. the NAACP condemned voucher plans in principle at its July 1970 convention, fearing "the result would be the perpetuation of segregation in schools."

Meetings before U.S. Congressional Committees have given spokesmen for these groups the opportunity to voice their opinions. The disadvantages they see are numerous. Included among them are the beliefs that education vouchers will

> destroy the public schools;
>
> play havoc with the stabilizing factors in our democratic society;
>
> bring religious, economic, social, and political divisiveness;
>
> encourage racism;
>
> become educational hucksterism;
>
> create an unmanageable bureaucracy;
>
> dilute educational opportunities;
>
> make a farce of constitutional separation of church and state;
>
> encourage parents to chose schools based on prejudices; and
>
> contradict tradition of local support and control.

However, the list of advantages is equally as great. According to advocates, vouchers will

> promote general improvement in education through competition;
>
> promote democratic freedom of choice;
>
> increase educational diversity;
>
> give parents some control and responsibility;
>
> promote accountability;
>
> overcome racial and economic limitations of neighborhood schools;

drive bad schools out of business;

improve the education of the disadvantaged;

improve equity among taxpayers; and

increase total expenditures for education.

THE FUTURE

Without actual data, it is difficult to support either point of view on vouchers. There are some obvious limitations to the voucher system. For example, the EVA must vigorously regulate the marketplace if it is not to become another layer on the encrusted bureaucracy. Other problems are still to be considered: How will new school construction be financed? Who is responsible for tax apportionment formulas? Who will supervise the EVAs? What about the relations between EVA and the local school board? Finally, the constitutionality of the education voucher system is quiestionable.

It may be that some form of an education voucher system will offer a viable alternative to the present American system of education. Short of a demonstration, however, all discussion of it remains theoretical. Given the popularly held opinion of the present unsatisfactory state of affairs in education, an experimental operation of vouchers seems worth a try. The idea may be long overdue.

REFERENCES

Bane, M. J. On Tuition Voucher Proposals. *Harvard Educational Review*, 1971, *41*, 79-86.

Business Week. A Market Economy for the Schools. *Business Week*, February 6, 1971, 76-78.

Center for the Study of Public Policy. *Education Vouchers.* Cambridge, Mass., 1970.

Cohodes, A. Voucher System Gets Chance to Show How It Would Work. *Nation's Schools*, 1970, *86*, 20.

Fox, E. J., and Levenson, W. B. In Defense of the Harmful Monopoly: Merits and Limitations of the Voucher Plan. *Phi Delta Kappan*, 1969, *51*, 131-135.

Heller, R. W. Education Vouchers: Problems and Issues. *Educational Leadership*, 1972, *29*, 424-429.

Janssen, P. A. Education Vouchers. *American Education*, 1970, 9-11.

Kornegay, W. Open Market: A New Model for Our Schools? *Phi Delta Kappan*, 1968, *49*, 583-586.

La Noue, G. R. *Educational Vouchers: Concepts and Controversies.* New York: Teachers College, 1972.

Mecklenburger, J., and Hostrop, R. W., eds. *Education Vouchers: From Theory to Alum Rock.* Homewood, Ill.: ETC, 1972.

Overlan, S. F. Do Vouchers Deserve at Least a Sporting Chance? *American School Board Journal*, 1972, *159*, 20-22.

ADDITIONAL RESOURCES

American School Board Journal. Boardmen Can't Think of One Good Thing to Say About Voucher Plans. *American School Board Journal*, 1970, *158*, 33-37.

Clark, K. B. Alternative Public School Systems. *Harvard Educational Review*, 1968, *38*, 100-113.

Clayson, A. S. Vital Questions, Minimal Responses: Education Vouchers. *Phi Delta Kappan*, 1970, *52*, 53-54.

Coleman, J. S. *Equality of Educational Opportunity.* Washington,

D.C., HEW, OE-38001, 1966.

Committee on Education and Labor, U.S. House of Representatives, Washington, D.C., April 2, 1971.

Heller, R. W. Education Vouchers: Problems and Issues. *Educational Leadership*, 1972, *29*, 424-429.

Jencks, C. Speaking Out: The Public Schools are Failing. *Saturday Evening Post*, 1966, *14*, 18.

———. Giving Parents Money for Schooling: Education Vouchers. *Phi Delta Kappan*, 1970, *52*, 49-52.

Kirp, D. L. Vouchers, Reform, and the Elusive Community. *Teachers College Record*, 1972, *74*, 201-207.

Mecklenburger, J. Vouchers at Alum Rock. *Phi Delta Kappan*, 1972, *54*, 23-25.

Overlan, S. F. Do Vouchers Deserve at Least a Sporting Chance? *American School Board Journal*, 1972, *159*, 20-22.

Sizer, T. R. Case for a Free Market. *Saturday Review*, 1969, *52*, 34-42.

Subcommittee on Employment, Manpower and Poverty of the Committee on Labor and Public Welfare, U.S. Senate, Washington, D.C., April 27, 1971.

Swankeo, E. M., and Donovan, B. E. Voucher Demonstration Project: Problems and Promise. *Phi Delta Kappan*, 1970, *52*, 244.

Welsh, J. The New Hampshire Voucher Caper. *Educational Researcher*, 1973, *2*, 16-17.

28

PERFORMANCE CONTRACTING IN PRINCIPLE AND PRACTICE

by Robert A. Feldmesser
Educational Testing Service
Princeton, New Jersey

This article is based on a report (*TM Reports*, No. 20) originally prepated in 1972 for the ERIC Clearinghouse on Tests, Measurement, and Evaluation, Educational Testing Service, Princeton, New Jersey. The report has been revised somewhat to take account of subsequent developments and information. For a more complete and up-to-date study, see Robert A. Feldmesser and Gary J. Echternacht, *Performance Contracting as a Strategy in Education* (Princeton, N.J.: Educational Testing Service, 1975). The ERIC Clearinghouse operates under contract with the U.S. Office of Education, Department of Health, Education, and Welfare. Contractors are encouraged to express freely their judgment in professional and technical matters. Points of view expressed do not necessarily, therefore, represent the opinions or policy of any agency of the United States Government

Stripped to its essentials, a performance contract is a formal agreement between local educational authority (LEA) and some other organization, in which the organization undertakes to provide instruction to students who are in the LEA's jurisdiction and the LEA promises to pay the organization a fee which is to depend upon the measured amount of learning acquired by those students during the contract period. While LEAs have, of course, long entered into contracts for instructional services with individuals and organizations, these have usually been "contracts for best efforts" (Mecklenburger, 1972), in which the LEA engages a teacher, for example, on the presumption that he will do his best to teach a group of students, in return for which the LEA pays him a fixed salary, determined in advance and thus necessarily independent of how much the students may learn. By contrast, a performance contract is a "contract for results" (Stucker and Hall, 1971). The unique provision in such a contract is that the payment for services is set so as to vary with the learning outcomes; the magnitude of the payment must therefore be determined when the instruction is completed rather than before it begins.

Two basic assumptions underlie the proposition that performance contracting can bring about improved instruction: (1) that the primary criterion of success in teaching should be the amount of learning it induces—or, in the language that is often used, how much learning is "produced"; and (2) that, in teaching as in other activities, monetary rewards scaled according to production are an effective device for motivating people to maximize their efforts and hence are a likely way of increasing production. Both these assumptions may be questioned; nevertheless, it is undoubtedly "this no-nonsense insistence on results" (Mecklenburger, 1972) that has attracted so much attention to performance contracting in the brief period since the first such contract in modern times was signed in 1969.

Even in that brief period, a number of features have come to be so commonly associated with performance contracting that, although they are not intrinsic to it, the concept cannot be discussed without reference to them. The most important of these are:

1. The organization offering the instructional services is usually a private profit-making firm, called an "educational technology company" or a "learning systems contractor." The reason for this is that it is generally regarded as more appropriate for a private company to base its actions on considerations of monetary reward than for professional persons to do so. Hence, most contractors either have been divisions or subsidiaries of large private corporations, often those which had previously been selling instructional materials or equipment, or even services, but under fixed-price contracts; or they have been private, relatively small firms established more or less explicitly to take advantage of performance-contracting opportunities. Many of these contractors, however, employ the LEA's teachers as their own instructors (they may even be required to do so), either under conventional contracts or with incentive provisions (see 5 below). In principle, a local teachers' organization may itself enter into a performance contract directly with an LEA, and a few have done that; in such cases, the fee either may be paid to the teachers as additional income or may be paid into a fund to be used for instructional purposes.

2. Along with the performance contract itself, auxiliary contracts are almost always signed with a mangement support group (MSG) and an evaluation agency, and sometimes with a so-called "auditor" as well. The MSG helps the LEA deal with the unfamiliar intrica-

cies of the performance contract, identifies potential bidders and assists in selecting the final contractor, provides liaison between the LEA and the contractor, and aids in the determination of contract costs. The evaluation agency serves as an impartial organization in measuring the learning achievements on which the instructional contractor's payments are based, and perhaps also in ascertaining the other effects of his program. The auditor verifies the work of the evaluation agency, in the manner of a fiscal auditor, and may advise the LEA on proper evaluation procedures; but the distinction between evaluation and auditing is fuzzy, and where the LEA has sufficient confidence in the evaluation agency it may dispense with an auditor. The MSG, and particularly the evaluator and the auditor, are more likely than the instructional contractor to be non-profit companies (and they may sometimes be public agencies), because it is important that their judgments be regarded as disinterested by all parties and by the community at large. Again, however, the LEA could in principle perform any or all of these functions itself.

3. Instruction under a performance contract is often carried out with heavy reliance on "hardware" (tape cassettes or some type of "teaching machine") and on paraprofessional personnel. This is because it is hardly worthwhile for an LEA to enter into a performance contract if all it obtains thereby is a conventional sort of teaching that could be done by its own professional staff. But the performance contract is an administrative arrangement, and no particular instructional strategy is inherent in it. Some LEAs have placed restrictions on the teaching methods that can be used, or have even required that one designated method must be employed, but such provisions are extraneous to the nature of the contract. Indeed, since the performance contract is a contract for results, it implies that the instructional contractor ought to be free to use whatever method he deems effective, and even to change it as he goes along.

4. Most performance contracts have involved the teaching of "disadvantaged"—or, to use the term suggested by Stone (1972), "disequalized"—students. It is for these students, many of whom are members of minority groups, that educational innovations have seemed most urgent, in view of the widespread failure to bring their learning up to "grade level." There have been a number of instances, however, of performance contracts involving students not characterized by any marked disadvantage (e.g., see Mecklenburger and Wilson, 1971).

5. Apparently because it is a natural corollary of the performance-contracting rationale, many instructional contractors use techniques of "contingency management" in their classrooms; that is, they offer rewards to teachers and/or students in accordance with learning outcomes (Frieder, 1971; Homme, 1969). For teachers the rewards may be cash, or stock in the company; for students, they are usually commodities

(for example, small transistor radios), free time to engage in activities of their own choice, admissions to various kinds of entertainments, or tokens redeemable for one or the other. Another form of incentive, aimed at increased learning but not directly tied to it, is the provision of special classrooms (which may be given a distinctive name, such as "rapid learning centers") for the contractor's program, furnished with air-conditioning, carpeting, and other attractive accoutrements, which either the LEA or the contractor may pay for. Because these incentive practices are so common and do reflect the basic principles of performance contracting, some critics (Shanker, 1971) have identified them with performance contracting proper. Actually, contingency management can be used outside a performance contract, and a performance contract does not necessarily imply the use of contingency management; some LEAs have forbidden its use in their contracts. In any case, it should be clear that the incentive principle of the performance contract is applied to the instructional contractor, who may or may not choose to extend it to teachers or students.

6. Most contracts require that, if the instructional company's teaching methods prove successful, the company, the MSG, or both, are to help the LEA's professional staff incorporate them into the routine operations of the school system. This provision, called "turnkeying,"[1] evidently arises out of the reluctance of LEAs—perhaps even their legal disability—to be dependent on a private company over a long period of time. Since such dependence probably would cause serious difficulties (for example in teachers' morale, if nothing else), turnkeying comes closer to being a necessary part of performance contracting than any of the other auxiliary features listed above.

THE PAYMENT SCHEDULE AND PROBLEMS OF MEASUREMENT

The heart of a performance contract is its "payment schedule." In this schedule, the amounts of learning which might occur among students during the contract period are listed, typically in terms of grade-equivalent gains, and attached to each gain is the fee to be paid for each student who achieves it. Sometimes a minimum gain is specified, below which no payment is made. This is called the "guaranteed" or "insured" level, and in a contract running for one year (the duration of most performance contracts so far), it is usually a gain of one year. A base payment—for example, $50—is made for each student who reaches the guaranteed level, and premiums are paid for additional gains; for example, $20 for each month beyond a year (the figures are taken from an actual contract).[2] A maximum total payment is also stated, so that the LEA can be certain that contract costs will not exceed available funds. The same schedule may be used for each subject to be taught under the contract, or different schedules may be applied to different subjects.

If a legal document such as a performance contract is to attach a specific monetary reward to a specific amount of learning, both quantities must be measurable with a high degree of precision and objectivity. This requirement causes no problems as far as the monetary reward is concerned: number of dollars is widely accepted as a precise and objective form of measurement. "Amount of learning" is far harder to measure, and the efforts at measuring it have won by no means universal acceptance.

Measurement efforts have come closest to acceptance in the areas of reading and mathematics. Consequently, nearly all performance contracts have been limited to instruction in either or both of those subjects, and this will probably be a major restriction on the scope of performance contracting for some time to come. It is conceivable that other subjects like vocational training, science, and history could be added (they have been included in a few contracts[3]), but the prospects are remote for precise measurement in important dimensions of pupil growth such as social maturity, self-esteem, or civic responsibility.

Proponents of performance contracting argue that this limitation should not be a deterrent to the use of the device. They point out that disequalized children almost always are seriously deficient in reading and mathematics; that these are vital skills in their own right, and prerequisite to much other learning; and that progress should be made in whatever areas it can be made, rather than holding back until it is possible in all areas (Lessinger, 1970). Critics contend, however, that many commonly used test instruments stress "lower-level" kinds of skills such as a knowledge of vocabulary or recall of facts, rather than "higher-level" skills such as expressive abilities or application of generalizations; and that the excitement aroused by a performance contract, the rewards attached to it, and the resources devoted to it will lead LEAs, teachers, and students alike to depreciate the areas not included in it (Shanker, 1971). These areas will not merely remain as before: they will be "under-taught"; and while reading and mathematics are important, it does not follow that every increment in knowledge of those subjects is worth the sacrifice of everything else.

Even in reading and mathematics, measurement of learning gain is beset with a plethora of problems. The typical procedure is to select one of the nationally standardized tests already on the market and administer one form of it to the students before the instructional program begins; administer an equated alternate form (to avoid "practice" effects) when it has ended; convert the scores for each child into grade equivalents according to the test publisher's norms; and calculate the differences between the pretest and posttest grade equivalents as the basis for payment to the instructional contractor. The following are among the defects in this procedure:

1. No nationally marketed test will closely reflect any one contractor's instructional program. To the extent that it does not, the learning that has occurred will be underestimated.

2. Most of the marketed tests were designed to rank-order students in terms of their relative knowledge at one point in time. Psychometricians are skeptical about the propriety of using them to measure change

over a period of time.

3. The reliability of the difference between two scores for a single individual is apt to be quite low.

4. Conversion of test scores into grade equivalents is a dubious, though common, practice. On many tests, the difference between the norms for two successive grades corresponds to only a small number of additional correct responses; and because of differences in norming populations and procedures, as well as in test content, the knowledge indicated by a grade-equivalent score on one publisher's test is not necessarily the same as the knowledge indicated by the same grade-equivalent score on another publisher's test.

5. The measurement of gain as described ignores the "regression effect"—the probability that a person who scores extremely low on a test at one administration will score higher on it (or an alternate form of it) at the next administration, simply by chance and regardless of how much he may have learned or not learned in the interim. It is true that regression works the other way around, too—a high scorer tends to score lower when he takes the test again— but this is less likely to receive attention, since the instructional contractor is paid premiums for score gains of more than a year but his fee is not reduced for score losses of more than a year. Moreover, the disequalized students at whom performance contracts are usually aimed are much more likely to be initially low scorers than high scorers—a reflection, of course, of the very reason why special efforts are being made to improve their instruction. (In some cases, they score so low that the test norms are not applicable to them.) Thus, the instructional contractor may appear to be producing more learning than he actually is, and to be paid accordingly, merely by a statistical artifact. (For further discussion of these and related problems, see Feldmesser, 1971; Lennon, 1971; Sigel, 1971; Stake, 1971).

6. Because his fee depends on his students' posttest scores, the instructional contractor may orient his program excessively toward the posttest items ("teaching to the test") or may even use his program to coach students on the correct answers ("teaching the test"). The former practice is generally regarded as undesirable; the latter is plainly unethical, since it produces spuriously high scores—that is, students may come to know the correct answers without acquiring the knowledge that the test is presumed to measure. Yet in the very first performance contract, in Texarkana, Texas-Arkansas, test items were deliberately and repeatedly included in the contractor's lessons just prior to administration of the posttest (Bumstead, 1970). Despite the scandal that erupted, it may have happened again in a performance contract in Providence, Rhode Island (Wardrop, 1971). Thus, what is supposed to be the major strength of performance contracting has, as its obverse, a serious weakness: The monetary reward can become an end in itself, and those who pursue it will sometimes re-

sort to illegitimate means that defeat the original purpose of the reward. Examples of this are legion in the marketplace, leading some critics to argue that performance contracting threatens to corrupt the very nature of the educational enterprise.

Various solutions have been offered to these problems. Payment schedules could be based on the mean gain of a class, which would be a more reliable statistic than individual gains; or the unreliability of individual score differences could be reduced by extending the duration of the contract to two or three years. Payment schedules could also be based on standard or percentile scores rather than on grade equivalents, and gains could be expressed as residuals derived from a regression analysis rather than as simple differences. Deductions from the fee could be provided for score losses, in the same magnitude as premiums for score gains. Penalties could be imposed for test items discovered in the instructional program, and/or the identity of the test could be concealed from the contractor.

Some of these solutions have been adopted, but many of them give rise to problems of their own: the fear that may be aroused (perhaps unjustifiably) that a contractor paid according to the mean gain of a class will "lose sight" of the individual pupils in it, or at least not distribute his efforts evenly among them; the legal difficulties of a long-term contract with a private firm; the loss of public understanding that might come with the elimination of grade equivalents or with the use of regression analysis; the unfairness to the contractor of paying him according to a standard whose content is kept hidden from him.

A more sweeping solution that has been suggested is to reduce the reliance on standardized tests, or to do away with them altogether, in favor of "criterion-referenced" tests. This is a complicated topic which cannot be explored at length here (for fuller treatment, see Jackson, 1970). However, for present purposes, a criterion-referenced test may be defined as one on which the items are drawn from a clearly and rigorously circumscribed domain of learning—for example, a specific instructional program—and each item is construed to be a self-evident criterion (hence the name) of whether an element in that domain has been acquired.

If this is so, then gains from one test administration to the next can be measured directly, without resort to the norms of a standardized (or "norm-referenced") test. Contractors in particular seem to favor criterion-referenced testing, since it allows—indeed, requires—the test to be exactly matched to the program content: by the same token, "teaching the test" becomes the proper and necessary course of action. Criterion-referenced tests have formed the basis of a proportion of the total maximum payment in many performance contracts.

But there are grave objections to the use of criterion-referenced tests for this purpose (Feldmesser, 1971; Lennon, 1971). Their statistical properties are poorly understood, and there is little agreement on the standards for identifying suitable items. They are probably even more vulnerable than norm-referenced tests to the criticism that they do not adequately measure the "higher-level" kinds of knowledge. In part because they are new, they are not widely available on the market. As a result, when they have been used the items have often been supplied by the contractors themselves, which leaves open the possibility that the items may be made so easy that they are not a convincing measure of the knowledge that has been acquired; this has occurred (Office of Economic Opportunity, 1972), and it seems to amount to another kind of "cheating" induced by the lure of monetary reward. Even at that, the creation of a test de novo is a time-consuming and expensive process. In the large-scale trial of performance contracting sponsored by the Office of Economic Opportunity in twenty districts in 1970-1971, criterion-referenced tests were supposed to determine 25 percent of the contractors' payments, but the burden of developing the tests proved to be unmanageable, partly because OEO tried (unsuccessfully) to have the items reviewed by the evaluator prior to administration to prevent the abuse just mentioned (Office of Economic Opportunity, 1972). Finally, a criterion-referenced test may have a drawback opposite to that of a norm-referenced test: It may be *too* closely matched to program content. That is, it may show whether a student has mastered a contractor's reading program but not necessarily whether he "knows how to read" in a broader sense.

For the time being, there appears to be no set of wholly satisfactory solutions to all the problems of measuring learning increments for performance-contracting purposes. The partial solutions currently available may, however, be considered sufficient if performance contracting offers hope for significant improvements in the educational system.

PROS AND CONS OF PERFORMANCE CONTRACTING

A number of consequences beneficial to education generally are claimed to flow from performance contracting. For each alleged benefit, however, counterarguments have been put forth, to the effect that the presumed consequences are not actually obtained, that they can be obtained equally well by other and better means, that they are outweighed by other nonbeneficial yet inseparable consequences, or that the consequences themselves are not benefits at all. Three major controversial issues will be reviewed here.

Stimulus to Accountability

One of the virtues most frequently attributed to performance contracting is that it furthers the movement toward educational accountability (Carpenter and Hall, 1971; Lessinger, 1970; Sigel, 1971). In the present context, "accountability" may be defined as the principle that persons charged with producing learning in students should bear the consequences of the amount of learning they produce. (Thus, it is distinguished from the point of view which holds that only *students* should be the beneficiaries—or victims—of the learning they acquire or fail to acquire.) The effect of this principle would be that those most successful in producing learning in their

students would be rewarded, and so would tend to remain in the education profession, while those less successful would be discouraged from remaining. Hence, accountability is viewed by some as a powerful tool both for increasing the learning that takes place in school and—because it would tend to eliminate ineffective producers—for reducing the cost of producing it. Since a performance contract seeks to establish a direct tie between amount of learning and the reward to the producer of learning (in the form of the fee paid to the instructional contractor), it is clearly a move toward this kind of accountability. Even if, as Lennon (1971) has said, it will eventually "be seen as a rather primitive, simplistic approach" to implementation, it nevertheless may help focus attention on the principle and pave the way for more sophisticated mechanisms.

Some of the objections to this claim rest on the difficulties in measurement that have already been discussed. It may be noted that, to the extent that such objections are valid, they cast doubt on the possibility of instituting any sort of accountability whatever.

Other objections are based on the suspicion that performance contractors may not be primarily concerned with increasing student learning at all; they may be motivated instead by the desire "to break into new markets heretofore largely dominated by textbook publishers" (Carpenter and Hall, 1971), or by the hope that the publicity attendant upon their novel ventures will raise the price of their stock. For such purposes, they may even be pricing their contracts lower than their anticipated costs, and without regard to how much knowledge they expect to convey to students; if so, the experience with performance contracting does not further the move toward accountability. A related objection is that performance contracts do not give an accurate picture of instructional costs, because the LEA sometimes bears a portion of these costs (teachers' salaries and fringe benefits, classroom renovation) and because contracts may require the LEA to purchase some services (e.g., teacher-training) that it could probably provide more cheaply itself (Stucker and Hall, 1971; Locke, 1971).

It must also be pointed out that there are criticisms of the concept of accountability itself as it has been defined above. Some observers fear that it may all too easily turn into cost-cutting for its own sake (Sigel, 1971). Others, especially spokesmen for teachers' organizations, have asserted that a professional person can be held accountable only for following "proper professional practices," not for bringing about any specific result which depends on factors outside his control (Shanker, 1971).

Improvements in Administration

Another claim for performance contracting is that it promotes improvements in educational administration. Organizations providing MSG services sometimes have backgrounds in industrial management, and it is felt that they can offer a model of "scientific management" and help train the local administrators in its techniques. Apart from the effects of the MSG's presence, it has also been argued that the performance contract itself sets a precedent for objectively described and clearly understood relationships between an LEA and an instructional corps. The contract is supposed to specify exactly what responsibilities each party has and what will be the price of failure to meet those responsibilities. It has some of the same no-nonsense air about it that the emphasis upon results has. If these characteristics can subsequently be transferred to the relationships between the LEA and its own professional staff, educational administration, so the argument goes, will be placed on a sounder footing.

How much one is impressed with the first of these contentions depends inevitably on what one thinks of the techniques of "scientific management." That aside, the record of the MSGs so far has not been auspicious. A careful and thoughtful study of eight performance contracts found that they were plagued with managerial problems that the MSG evidently did not solve; that teachers continued to be indispensable to the proper design and planning of the contract; and that—scientific management or no—the effectiveness of the contract as a "change agent" demanded that "someone in the LEA's administration with ability, position, and respect adopts the program as his personal project" (Carpenter and Hall, 1971). It has even been suggested that the MSG, instead of being a "mediator" between the LEA and the instructional contractor (Lessinger, 1970), could be a barrier between them, reducing interaction below the level necessary to assure proper guidance and understanding and ultimate acceptance of the results (Stucker and Hall, 1971). It must also be mentioned as an ironic peculiarity that the MSG companies—often the strongest supporters of the accountability principle—themselves operate under contracts that do not hold them accountable in the same strict way that the instructional contractors are (Sigel, 1971).

The second contention—that performance contracts help build sounder relationships for the future between the LEA and its own professional staff—is also weaker than it might appear, at least at the present stage of development. In the first place, each performance-contract venture entails not one but three or four separate contracts (see above), and this has led to "fragmented responsibility and authority among several parties" (Carpenter and Hall, 1971). Secondly, the contract with the instructional firm alone has its complexities. The spirit of performance contracting, as has been explained, requires that the instructional contractor have a good deal of latitude for changing his program when he finds it desirable to do so, but such changes sometimes necessitate changes in the contract that are not easily accomplished. Carpenter and Hall (1971) conclude, from their study of the execution of eight performance contracts, that "the contracts as they were written actually hampered the [program] development effort." The experience of the OEO project has been even more instructive; the agency's first report on it (Office of Economic Opportunity, 1972) says:

> . . . the original terms [of the contracts] specified that a definite number of students would be present for definite periods of instruction. Teacher strikes, absenteeism, bad weather, student drop-outs, and other factors made it impossible for school districts to fulfill those guarantees.

"Adjustments for these factors," it adds, "are presently being negotiated." On the other hand, the report also points out that "the initial contracts allowed too much room for difference in interpretation . . . and . . . the roles of the various . . . participants were not spelled out clearly enough."

Questions about the legality of an LEA's delegation of instructional duties to a private company have already been mentioned. In addition, teachers' organizations have charged that performance contracts may violate the terms of their contracts with LEAs, especially insofar as the firm involved employs low-paid and uncertified paraprofessionals. Even if these charges are inspired by teachers' apprehensiveness about their jobs or the threat of merit pay, they are not for that reason false, they may nevertheless lead to expensive litigation, and they hardly suggest that performance contracts lead to healthy relationships between LEAs and their teaching staffs.[4] The American Federation of Teachers has declared its unequivocal opposition to performance contracting, and the National Education Association has adopted what is at most a lukewarm attitude (Dickinson, 1971). All of these difficulties are probably going to become more rather than less severe, because in many places they have been "left unresolved on the grounds that these were experimental programs. . . . In future years challengers are less likely to hold their fire" (Carpenter and Hall, 1971).

Facilitating Innovation

Performance contracting has, finally, been heralded as a way of bringing badly needed changes into the content and conduct of educational programs. Indeed, to some, this is its major long-run significance. Three kinds of reasons are given for this view:

> The typical public bureaucracy, such as a school system, is encumbered with rules and regulations that make it cautious and slow-moving, but private firms can by-pass many of these obstacles and may also be "more flexible [organizations], able to adapt more rapidly and easily to changes in the state of the art" (Stucker and Hall, 1971).

> A private firm can spread its research and development (R&D) costs over all the school districts in which it operates, so that innovation in any one of them can be less expensive than if the LEA had to bear all the costs itself. This would be of particular advantage to a small school district, in which R&D costs would otherwise be a prohibitively large proportion of its budget. Moreover, the performance contract ensures that, if the innovation is ineffective (fails to increase learning), the fee paid to the contractor will be relatively small; innovation can thus be undertaken at low financial risk.

> Private firms have fresh ideas, resources, and talents, uninhibited by educational traditions. This is especially important for innovations that constitute instructional "*systems,* as opposed to loose collections of components. . . . An outside organization may find it

easier to design a new program 'from the ground up' than could someone already in the system" (Stucker and Hall, 1971).

These theoretical advantages may not be so appealing on closer examination, or they may not be manifested in practice. The regulations that a private firm can ignore may be needed for the protection of students, teachers, or the general public. Moreover, a private firm may have its own bureaucratic requirements, which can be just as constricting. The reduction in a district's R&D expenses may be made up for by the extra costs of contract preparation and monitoring and the fees paid to the MSG, the evaluator, and the auditor—and these costs are no less if the instructional program is a failure (although in most contracts to date, such costs have been covered by a Federal grant, outside the district's ordinary budget).

On the other hand, if the program is a success, there will be the costs of training teachers and administrators to work with it, costs which could have been avoided had they received their training while attempting to install the program themselves. Perhaps most important, it has become apparent that few, if any, instructional contractors do in fact have prepackaged, ready-to-install programs, tradition-free or otherwise. The early efforts at performance contracting, in particular, found the contractors improvising almost from day to day, misjudging student responsiveness, failing to supply equipment and materials on time and in good working order, etc. (Carpenter and Hall, 1971; Office of Economic Opportunity, 1972).

Even when contractors did develop more smoothly operating programs, it should not be assumed that these programs would necessarily be superior to those now in use, or to those that can be developed within the public educational system or by its affiliated (and nonprofit) R&D organizations. There are, after all, numerous instances in which the ideas, resources, and talents of private firms have been put to frivolous or injurious—not to say disastrous—use. Nor is it unambiguously clear that private firms have a better understanding of human learning processes than professional educators do (Block, 1970). What they do know probably comes from the educational research literature, in which case it is "available to any school system free for the taking" (Mecklenburger, 1972). Or, if they *have* put that knowledge into an effective program, it can often be bought on the market in the ordinary way, without the apparatus of a performance contract (Locke, 1971). Some performance-contract projects have, in fact, been used simply as opportunities to acquire an instructional program that could have been acquired under an ordinary fixed-fee contract.

CONCLUSIONS

An LEA's decision to enter upon a performance contract involves considerations of preferred types of risk, instructional and managerial capabilities relative to those of potential contractors, legal and other institutional hazards, costs, and expected effectiveness; some of these considerations are incalculable, intangible, or peculiar to local situations (Stucker and Hall, 1971). If the decision is affirmative, the LEA must be prepared to cope with a compliated set of contractual relationships, tangled problems in the measurement of learning gain, possible protests from teachers, and anxieties over the non-contracted parts of the curriculum. And if the contractor's work proves successful, the LEA may not know to what to attribute the success, and consequently may not know exactly what ought to be turnkeyed: the incentives of the payment schedule, the technological devices, the contingency management or other instructional techniques, the paraprofessionals, the special classroom furnishings, the freedom from bureaucratic impediments, the work of the MSG, or some combination of these.

Yet many a school-board member, superintendent, and principal would gladly endure all these perplexities if he could be assured that performance contracting was, in the end, a reliable way of increasing student learning over what it presently is. No such assurance can be provided. The results of the OEO project were, in a word, dismal. The agency bluntly summed up its evaluator's findings thus: "Was performance contracting more successful than traditional classroom methods in improving the reading and mathematics skills of poor children? The answer . . . is 'No' " (Office of Economic Opportunity, 1972). The eight contracts studied by Carpenter and Hall (1971) displayed the same picture. It is true that these results came out of what were to a large extent ill-planned ventures and hastily installed programs. But later contracts have not materially altered the conclusions. It is an understatement to say that performance contracting does not appear to be the "Educational Millenium" (Sigel, 1971).

NOTES

[1]The term was adopted from the housing-construction industry, where it referred to an arrangement whereby public housing was built by a private contractor, who carried out all the planning, site acquisition, construction, etc., so that the authorizing public agency had only to "turn the key" in the door in order to make the housing available.

[2]Questions have been raised (Office of Economic Opportunity, 1972) about the scale of values implicit in a payment schedule. Are all gains of less than one year truly "worthless"? Is one student's gain of 1.5 years actually equal to three students' gain of one year each? Does a gain of one month for a student in the sixth grade have the same worth as a gain of one month for a student in the fourth grade? It is difficult to know how an LEA, or its community, might go about deciding what are, for it, the right answers to these questions.

[3]The performance contract in Gary, Indiana, was unique in that the contractor was responsible for instruction in all subjects for an entire elementary school, but it is noteworthy that the company was paid on the basis of gains in reading and mathematics only. This contract was also unusual in that it was scheduled to run for four years, though it was actually terminated midway through the third year.

[4]In one instance, the paraprofessionals employed by an instructional contractor staged a brief work stoppage themselves, to demand the dismissal of the contractor's project administrator and improvements in their conditions of work (Shanker, 1972).

REFERENCES

Block, A. H. Viewpoints about Performance Contracting. *National Society for Programmed Instruction Journal,* 1970, *9,* 11-12.

Bumstead, R. Performance Contracting. *Educate,* 1970, *3,* 15-27.

Carpenter, P., and Hall, G. R. *Case Studies in Educational Performance Contracting: Conclusions and Implications,* 1971. Santa Monica, Cal.: Rand Corporation (Part I of Report R-900).

Dickinson, W. E., ed. *Performance Contracting: A Guide for School Board Members and Community Leaders.* Evanston, Ill.: National School Boards Association, 1971.

Feldmesser, R. A. Measurement Problems in Performance Contracting. *National Council on Measurement in Education Measurement News,* 1971, *14,* 6-7.

Frieder, B. Motivation and Performance Contracting. *Journal of Research and Development in Education,* 1971, *5*(1), 49-61.

Homme, L. *How to Use Contingency Contracting in the Classroom.* Champaign, Ill.: Research Press, 1969.

Jackson, R. Developing Criterion-Referenced Tests. Princeton, N.J.: ERIC Clearinghouse on Tests, Measurement, and Evaluation, 1970, TM Report No. 1 (ED 041 052).

Lennon, R. T. To Perform and to Account. *Journal of Research and Development in Education,* 1971, *5*(1), 3-14.

Lessinger, L. M. *Every Kid a Winner: Accountability in Education.* New York, N.Y.: Simon and Schuster, 1970.

Locke, R. W. Accountability, Yes; Performance Contracting, Maybe. *Proceedings of the Conferences on Educational Accountability, Washington, D.C., Hollywood, California, March 1971.* Princeton, N.J.: Educational Testing Service, 1971, pp. E1-E9.

Mecklenburger, J. A., Performance Contracts? One View. *Educational Leadership,* 1972, *29,* 297-300.

_____, and Wilson, J. A. Performance Contracting in Cherry Creek? *Phi Delta Kappan,* 1971, *52,* 51-54.

Office of Economic Opportunity. *An Experiment in Performance Contracting: Summary of Preliminary Results.* Washington, D.C.: Office of Economic Opportunity, Office of Planning, Research, and Evaluation, 1972 (OEO Pamphlet 3400-5).

Shanker, A. Possible Effects on Instructional Programs. *Proceedings of the Conferences on Educational Accountability, Washington, D.C., Hollywood, California, March 1971.* Princeton, N.J.: Educational Testing Service, 1971, pp. F1-F11.

_____. Performance Contract in District 9: A Bronx Cheer for OEO, *New York Times,* January 2, 1972.

Sigel, E., and Sobel, M. *Accountability and the Controversial Role of the Performance Contractors: A Critical Look at the Performance Contracting Phenomenon.* White Plains, N.Y.: Knowledge Industry Publications, 1971.

Stake, R. E. Testing Hazards in Performance Contracting. *Phi Delta Kappan,* 1971, *52,* 583-589.

Stone, C. The Psychology of Whiteness vs. the Politics of Blackness: An Educational Power Struggle. *Educational Researcher,* 1972, *1*(1), 4-6.

Stucker, J. P., and Hall, G. R. *The Performance Contracting Concept in Education,* 1971. Santa Monica, Cal.: Rand Corporation (Report R-699/1-HEW).

Wardrop, J. L. Performance Contracting Game Continues. *Educational Products Information Exchange Report,* 1971, No. 38.

29

STATE EDUCATIONAL ASSESSMENT PROGRAMS

by Joan S. Beers
Pennsylvania Department of Education
Harrisburg, Pennsylvania

Paul B. Campbell
Educational Testing Service
Princeton, New Jersey

Center for Statewide Educational Assessment

and the

ERIC Clearinghouse on Tests, Measurement and Evaluation
Educational Testing Service
Princeton, New Jersey
in collaboration with
Education Commission of the States

This publication was originally prepared for the ERIC Clearinghouse on Tests, Measurement and Evaluation, Educational Testing Service, Princeton, New Jersey, 1972. The Clearinghouse operated under contract with the U.S. Department of Health, Education and Welfare, Office of Education. Contractors are encouraged to express freely their judgment in professional and technical matters. Points of view expressed within do not necessarily, therefore, represent the opinions or policy of any agency of the United States Government.

Considerable expansion of statewide assessment has occurred in the two years since the results of the previous survey were published. In the report of that survey, Dyer and Rosenthal (1971) present a concise statement of the history and development of assessment programs. They also identified some apparent trends which were beginning to emerge. Against this background, the present survey was designed to allow specific analysis of the nature of statewide assessment programs, as planned or as placed in operation.

To provide the information for this analysis, the survey utilizes a uniform set of questions and a common format. The District of Columbia, the Virgin Islands, and Puerto Rico were included with the 50 states, and for the purposes of this survey are reported among the states. The most obvious development is that there are now many more operational assessment programs than existed at the time of the earlier survey. Each of the states has reported assessment activities either as operational, in a developmental process, or in a planning stage.

THREE GROUPS OF STATEWIDE ASSESSMENT PROGRAMS

After a first reading of statewide assessment program descriptions, it is easy to be deceived into thinking that statewide assessment programs are more alike than not.

The similarities are many. State agency personnel are in charge. They select tests or guide and direct their construction, specify target populations, arrange for test administrations, make provisions for scoring, analyze the results (or have them analyzed), and assemble and disseminate reports. Assessment purposes are similar also— to assess development, to measure influences on learning, to assess needs, to measure growth. It takes a second and more careful reading, even a third and a fourth reading, to begin to detect that real differences do exist among programs. These differences, we discovered, center on one question: Who gets to use the results? When the 30 operational programs are divided into those for which data is collected for decision-making by state agency personnel and those for which data is collected for decision-making by teachers and administrators, many other differences fall into place.

The distinction between these two types of programs is sometimes subtle. Many programs are designed to serve both levels of decision-making. Nevertheless, we took the risk of categorizing the 30 operational programs into two groups, based upon program emphases. We screened the program summaries, separating those whose major focus is collecting information for state-level use, from those whose major focus is collecting information for local use. A third group of 24 programs we labeled "emerging" because they are not yet operational. A first cycle of testing, analyzing and reporting has not been completed.

New York state has three assessment programs. The Pupil Evaluation Program is in Group 1 and The System for Pupil and Program Evaluation and Development is in Group 2. Therefore, New York is included twice. The Regents Examination, the third New York state program, is not categorized.

The 17 programs for which the emphasis is on collecting information for state-level decision-making are in the following:

Arizona	Nevada
California	New Jersey
Colorado	New York
Connecticut	North Carolina
District of Columbia	Rhode Island
Florida	South Carolina
Maine	Tennessee
Massachusetts	Texas
Michigan	

The 13 programs for which the emphasis is on collecting information for local-level decision-making are in these states:

Alabama	Mississippi
Arkansas	New Hampshire
Delaware	New York
Hawaii	North Dakota
Idaho	New Mexico
Iowa	Pennsylvania
Kentucky	

The 24 emerging programs are in these states:

Alaska	Georgia
Illinois	Oregon
Indiana	Puerto Rico
Kansas	South Dakota
Louisiana	Utah
Maryland	Virgin Islands
Montana	Vermont
Minnesota	Virginia
Missouri	Washington
Nebraska	West Virginia
Ohio	Wisconsin
Oklahoma	Wyoming

In the matrix on the following page, essential features of each of the three groups of programs are described. Reading across the matrix, differences are highlighted.

COMPARISONS AND CONTRASTS AMONG THE THREE GROUPS OF PROGRAMS

Legislative Mandates

Legislative mandates are the impetus for statewide assessment programs in 16 states. In all other states, assessment was introduced by state education agency personnel. Many programs began in response to ESEA Title I and Title III requirements. Of the 17 operational programs which have as their emphasis the collection of information for state-level decisions, more than half of them began with legislative mandates. In contrast, of the 13 operational programs which have as their emphasis the collection of data for local-level decisions, only the Pennsylvania program has a legislative mandate. Although the focus for most of the emerging programs is the collection of data for state-level use, few states have legislative mandates.

Reporting of Assessment Results

A consequence of legislative mandates is the required reporting of assessment results to legislators. Legislative reports are more likely to accompany programs designed for state-level decision-making and less likely to accompany programs designed for local-level decision-making.

Use of Data for PPBS and/or MIS

The use of assessment results highlights a third contrast between the two groups of operational programs. State agency personnel who direct programs intended primarily for state use are more likely to apply assessment results to Planning, Programming and Budgeting Systems (PPBS) and/or Management Information Systems (MIS) than are state agency personnel who direct programs intended primarily for school district use. Effective use of assessment data is a problem mentioned frequently by many of the interviewees. The ways in which assessment data are used for PPBS or MIS, and the effectiveness of such data for these purposes, might be some areas for further study.

THREE GROUPS OF STATEWIDE ASSESSMENT PROGRAMS

Group 1	Group 2	Group 3
Program emphasis: Collecting information for decision-making at the state level. N = 17	Program emphasis: Collecting information for decision-making at the local level. N = 13	Emerging Programs. N = 24
Assessment is mandated by the state legislature in 9 states (52%).	Assessment is mandated by the state legislature in 1 state.	Assessment is mandated by the state legislature in 6 states (25%).
Assessment results are reported to the state legislature in 13 states (76%).	Assessment results are reported to the state legislature in 3 states (23%).	Reports are not yet compiled but the focus for 20 (89%) of the programs is the collection of data for state-level decision-making.
The collection of data for PPBS and/or a statewide MIS is specified for 7 programs (41%).	The collection of data for PPBS and/or a statewide MIS is specified for 4 programs (30%).	The collection of data for PPBS and/or a statewide MIS is planned for 9 programs (37%).
Assessment data are used to allocate state and federal funds in 8 states (47%).	Assessment data are not used to allocate state and federal funds in any state.	Assessment data will be used to allocate state and federal funds in 10 states (42%).
Participation is required in 10 states (59%).	Participation is voluntary in 12 states (92%).	All but 3 states report that participation will be voluntary.
Samples of students rather than all students in the target populations are tested in 12 states (70%).	All students in the target populations are tested in 12 states (92%).	Seventeen states (71%) plan to draw samples of students for testing.
Cognitive skills only are assessed in 11 states (65%).	Both affective and cognitive skills are assessed in 9 states (69%).	Thirteen states (59%) plan to assess both cognitive and affective skills.
Criterion-referenced tests are administered in 9 states (52%).	Norm-referenced tests only are administered in 9 states (69%).	Of the 17 states which specified whether norm-referenced or criterion-referenced tests will be used, 11 states plan to administer criterion-referenced tests.
Assessment is financed by state funds only in 6 states (35%), federal funds only in 4 states (24%), a combination of state and federal funds in 5 states (29%), and a combination of local, state, and/or federal funds in 2 states (11%).	Assessment is financed by state funds only in 2 states (15%), federal funds only in 3 states (23%), a combination of state and federal funds in 4 states (31%), and a combination of local, state, and/or federal funds in 4 states (31%).	Assessment is financed by state funds only in 5 states (21%), federal funds only in 14 states (58%), a combination of state and federal funds in 3 states (12%), and a combination of loca, state, and/or federal funds in 2 states (8%).
All but one of the interviewees reported that program objectives are being met successfully.	Five of the interviewees reported that program objectives are being met successfully; one reported that objectives are being met to a limited extent; three reported that objectives are not being met successfully; and four did not answer the questions.	It is too early to determine whether or not program objectives are being met successfully for most of the emerging programs.
Interviewees reported the following as major problem areas: Not enough money. Not enough staff. Difficulty with program coordination at the state level. Resistance from teachers to outside testing. Lag in the development of systematic use of the data. Mandatory rather than voluntary participation. Voluntary rather than mandatory participation. Lack of acceptance by teachers who see the program as a threat without providing any direct benefits. Magnitude of the program. Inability to use the data in significant ways.	Interviewees reported the following as major problem areas: Not enough money. Not enough staff. Inability to make adequate use of project results. Difficulty in getting the program data into decision-making hands. Negative attitudes toward testing. Lack of understanding about the usefulness of tests by teachers and students. Difficulty in making meaningful interpretations of results. Difficulty in developing awareness at the local level. Difficulty in inspiring use of data at the local level. Inadequate dissemination. Improper use of results.	Interviewees reported the following as major problem areas: Not enough money. Not enough staff. Lack of coordination at the state level. Lack of agreement on future directions.

Group 1	Group 2	Group 3
Inability to help school systems use the data. Inadequate dissemination. Difficulty in acclimating school personnel to the rationale and purposes of criterion-referenced testing. Opposition from teachers' organizations. Inability to use the program data to make decisions. Lack of understanding at all level of the program and its purposes	Improper interpretation of results.	

Use of Assessment Data for Allocating Funds

In eight states where achievement data is collected primarily for state purposes, the results are used to allocate state and Federal funds to school districts. In 10 other states, the intentions are to use assessment information to distribute funds. When the results of achievement tests are linked to the distribution of money, do teachers and administrators treat the assessment program differently? The question might be worth exploring.

Voluntary Versus Required Participation

There is a definite trend toward voluntary participation and away from required participation on the part of school districts, although most interviewees report that practically all invited schools do, in fact, participate. In 5 of the 10 states in which participation is required, interviewees reported that teacher resistance to statewide testing is a major problem. Whether or not teachers are more likely to resist statewide testing programs when they are required, rather than voluntary, is another possible area for further study. In the group of programs where the emphasis is on collecting information for school district purposes, only in Hawaii is participation required.

Sampling Versus Testing of All Students in Target Populations

The contrast is striking between the two groups of operational programs on the issue surrounding testing all students versus testing samples of students. Samples of students from target populations are tested in the majority of states where assessment data is used for state-level decisions. All students from target populations are tested, except in Iowa, in the states where assessment data is intended for local-level decisions. In most of the states where programs are not yet operational, samples of students from target populations, rather than all students from target populations, will be tested. Target populations are defined, usually, by age and grade levels. Target populations include, usually, specified students in elementary schools, middle schools, and high schools. Rarely is every student at every age or grade level tested.

Measurement of Cognitive and Affective Achievement

What is measured provides another area of contrast between the two groups of operational programs. The measurement of verbal and mathematical achievement only is the focus for the majority of programs in the group where the emphasis is on information for state-level use. In contrast, in the group where the emphasis is on local-level use, attitudes as well as verbal and mathematical skills are assessed in the majority of states. In the group of states with emerging programs, there is a definite trend toward the measurement of attitudes, also. The large number of states which do or plan to assess attitudes and personal development represents a significant change since the 1971 study was conducted. At that time, Dyer and Rosenthal wrote that states were concerned mainly with how well their educational systems were succeeding in imparting basic skills. Few assessment programs measured beyond the three Rs. The inherent complexities in measuring attitudes and personal-social development were once thought to be overwhelming in those states which were pioneers in this area. Interestingly, these difficulties are hardly mentioned by the interviewees in this study. Can it be that we are beginning to reach a stage in measurement where affective skills are no more difficult to assess than cognitive skills?

The affective domains mentioned number at least 12, but there are four which are most prevalent: attitudes toward school, self-concept or self-acceptance, citizenship, and career development or orientation.

Norm-Referenced Versus Criterion-Referenced Testing

On the issue of norm-referenced versus criterion-referenced measurement, contrasts and comparisons among the three groups of programs again are evident. There is a definite trend toward the use of criterion-referenced testing in those states where the results are used for state-level decision-making. This trend continues in those states where assessment is not yet operational. In the majority of states where results are used for local-level decision-making, norm-referenced tests only are administered. The underlying reasons for these findings do not seem obvious. The findings may have occurred by accident rather than design. If the findings did occur by design, the implication is that state-level decision makers consider the results from criterion-referenced testing more suitable for their purposes than the results from norm-referenced testing. As a corollary, the implication is that local-level decisionmakers consider the results from norm-referenced testing more suitable for their purposes than the results from criterion-referenced testing. Since the current push for the development of criterion-referenced testing comes from its use in individually prescribed instruction, a highly localized decision-making situation, this finding is a most curious anomaly. The issue should not be left here, but should be explored further.

Financing Statewide Assessment

Funding is varied among all groups of programs. State funds only is the most frequently mentioned source of money for programs in which the emphasis is on collecting information for state use. A combination of state and Federal funds and the use of local funds in combination with state and/or Federal funds are the most frequently mentioned sources of money for programs in which the emphasis is on collecting information for local use. In this group of programs, local funds are more likely to be appropriated than in any other group of programs. Federal funds only is the most frequently mentioned source of money for emerging programs. One question that might be asked is whether programs which are financed in full or in part by the state are more likely to be accompanied by a greater commitment on the part of the state agency than are programs which are supported solely by Federal funds. A second question that can be asked is: In those states where school districts contribute money for statewide assessment, do school district personnel also play a policy-making role?

Meeting Program Objectives

Are program objectives being achieved satisfactorily? In those states where program emphasis is on state-level decision-making, the interviewees were almost in unanimous agreement that they were meeting objectives. In those states where program emphasis is on local-level decision-making, few interviewees stated that program objectives were being met satisfactorily.

Major Problems

What are the major problems related to assessment programs? This open-ended question brought forth answers that may say as much or more about statewide assessment as all of the other questions combined. Two eternal problems, not enough money and not enough staff, appear in practically all reports. What constitutes enough money is hard to define, but a close look at staff numbers leads one to wonder how assessment can be accomplished at all. Twelve states have but one full-time staff member responsible for the program and not more than 10 states have five or more full-time staff members. If the objectives of the programs are being met satisfactorily, as many interviewees claim they are, other

agencies must be assisting statewide educational assessment personnel. In 20 states, the state university cooperates with the state department to implement the programs. In nine states, school district staff assist with assessment programs. In 30 states some aspect is contracted to outside personnel.

Interviewees in states with emerging programs report few problems. They can look forward to a great number, judging from the many problems reported by interviewees in states with operational programs. In states where the program emphasis is on collecting information for state use only, practically no problems were mentioned. It is in states where assessment results are used for both state-level and local-level decisions that problems are most numerous. Moreover, the difficulties reported from these states are more similar than different from the difficulties encountered by states where assessment results are used primarily for local-level decisions. The dissemination, interpretation, acceptance, understanding, awareness, and utilization of assessment results by teachers and administrators are problems for state department personnel. Lack of money and staff may be contributing factors, but negativism and resistance on the part of teachers and administrators are factors which cannot be treated lightly.

GOALS

The 1971 survey of state assessment programs suggested that there was an increasing concern with the involvement of citizens in goal-setting. This involvement, although not universal, has continued as a major trend in the 1972-1973 survey. Several such projects have been completed.

The usual approach is represented by procedures such as those used in Wyoming, where, with the assistance of the University of Wyoming, a series of discussions were held with the participation of a State Sounding Committee, the State Superintendent of Public Instruction, the State Board of Education, the State Education Agency, students, teachers, administrators, the teacher's association, staff from the National Assessment of Educational Progress, and other educational experts. Goals were prepared during these discussions which were presented to the State Board for anticipated endorsement.

A very scholarly and thoughtful approach is represented by the Georgia Assessment Project. A series of papers on Georgia's future were commissioned from knowledgeable people in many professions. These papers were in turn critiqued by additional experts. From these activities a series of educational goals were derived, which in turn were assigned priority by a representation of Georgia citizens, including students, through use of the Delphi Technique (Weaver, 1971). The goals were then used to derive objectives which provided the basis for instrumentation in the Georgia Assessment Program.

The result of this goal setting activity has produced a list of goals ranging from 1 to 78. They can be classified in three general categories: learner outcome goals, process goals and institutional goals. The learner goals may be further classified among the following subsets:

Basic Skills
Cultural Appreciation
Self-realization
Citizenship and Political Understanding
Human Relations
Economic Understanding
Physical Environment
Mental and Physical Health
Creative, Constructive and Critical Thinking
Career Education and Occupational Competence
Lifelong Learning
Values and Ethics
Home and Family Relations

The general recognition of the societal expectation that school is more than a reading, writing, and arithmetic class is evident from these goals. They constitute the bulk of the goal-setting activity, with the other categories appearing as facilitating learner outcomes.

The process category includes such ideas as the involvement of students and citizens in the planning of curriculum (Kansas) and the designing and implementation of instructional programs (Idaho).

An example of institutional goals can be found in Virginia, where the goals include standards for personnel, instructional materials and programs, planning and management. Another example, from South Carolina, is a goal to promote programs to provide adequate and qualified professional and paraprofessional personnel to staff the state's educational systems.

Although thoughtful and productive approaches have been demonstrated by the goal-setting activities of the states, a major problem appears at the point where goals are translated into program objectives and into data collection procedures. As a typical example, 27 of the 53 states have stated a goal concerned with human relations. However, only three states report that they have been able to conduct an assessment of progress toward such a goal. Several are in the process of developing the necessary instrumentation, but have not yet achieved results which are a satisfactory solution to the measurement problems, although tentative use of these instruments in a few states appears to offer positive benefits in that schools are encouraged to make instructional provision for the achievement of goals in human relations. While there appears to be some stability in group trends, measurement in an affective area such as this is in need of much additional development

The unfortunate side-effect of the limited application of assessment to noncognitive achievement is that many educators, failing to see assessment programs applied in affective areas, doubt the genuineness of the state commitment to these areas.

Finally, consideration of the worthy and carefully developed goals reported by most of the nation leads one to ask, do assessment programs increase our chances of attaining the stated goals? Are program changes occurring because of assessment results? It is too early to specify a positive or negative answer to these questions, because most programs have not been in operation long enough. There is, however, spotty evidence from several states indicating that at least some assessment programs are stimulating change at the district level. For example, several Michigan districts have asked for their assessment results in punched card form so that they can conduct their own intensive analysis. At least one district has designed a pre-post analysis of an intervention program which attempts to improve school attitude. Many Pennsylvania districts have also undertaken program changes as a result of assessment activities. A somewhat different example is Colorado's accreditation plan, which depends on objectives selected through assessment activities for program design. In general, however, state assessment programs have not had enough operational time to demonstrate the nature and extent of their influence on the goal orientation of programs.

RELATED DATA

One expressed purpose for many statewide assessment programs is to measure influences on learning. How program designers define "influences on learning" can be illustrated best by the kinds of related data assessment specialists collect. Related data can be grouped under four categories: pupil characteristics, school characteristics, community characteristics, and process variables. The specifics under each of these categories are:

Pupil Characteristics

age
sex
socioeconomic status
racial/ethnic background
bilingual or not

School Characteristics

dropout rate
attendance rate
percent minority
pupil/teacher ratio
per-pupil expenditure for education
cost of instructional programs
teacher data—salaries, education, course loads
use of paraprofessionals
transportation costs

Community Characteristics

size
geography

Process Variables

classroom practices

No one state collects all of this information. Some states collect a great deal, others collect age and sex only and still others collect none. The question that must be raised is: What, if anything, do states do with this information?

The kinds of facts gathered under Pupil Characteristics and Community Characteristics can provide information about relationships between these variables and pupils' achievement, but the characteristics are impossible to change. The kinds of facts gathered under School Characteristics can be manipulated, to a greater or lesser degree, and may provide some clues as to what schools can do to improve the learning process. The best possibilities for measuring influences on learning probably can be found under Process Variables. However, only one state, Pennsylvania, reports that information about classroom practices is collected.

It is probably safe to say that statewide assessment will not produce any startling revelations about what can be done by teachers to help children learn more effectively. This conclusion is not meant to be as much an indictment of statewide assessment as it is a statement of its limitations. Revelations in teaching practices and methods can come only from intensive analysis within each school building and each classroom. If statewide assessment data can whet the appetites of teachers and administrators for doing the kinds of evaluation only they can do for themselves, statewide assessment will serve its purposes well.

ACCOUNTABILITY REVISITED

The word "accountability" is not mentioned very often in the 53 statewide assessment summaries. But the concept can be detected easily in most of the program writeups. Accountability is the heart and soul of most assessment programs. More importantly, state education agencies in every state in the union are taking the leadership in helping (or coercing) school administrators to answer to the public's cries for better information about what children know and how well schools are doing their job.

Do statewide assessment programs, and the manner in which they are conducted, adequately define the dimensions of accountability? At least one authority does not think so. Stake (1973) defines an accountable school as one that discloses its activities, makes good on staff promises, assigns staff responsibility for each area of public concern, and monitors its teaching and learning.

> Most state accountability proposals call for more uniform standards across the state, greater prespecification of objectives, more careful analysis of learning sequences and better testing of student performance. These plans are doomed. What they bring is more bureaucracy, more subterfuge, and more constraints on student opportunities to learn. The newly enacted school accountability laws will not succeed in improving the quality of education for any group of learners. . . . If state accountability laws are to be in the best interests of the people, they should protect local control of the schools, individuality of teachers, and diversity of learning opportunities. They should not escalate the bureaucracy at the state or local level. They should not allow school ineffectiveness to be more easily ignored by drawing attention to student performance. They should not permit test scores to be overly influential in schoolwide or personal decisions— the irreducible errors of test scores should be recognized. The laws should make it easier for a school to be accountable to the community in providing a variety of high-quality learning opportunities for every learner.

To agree with Stake's vision of what accountability could or should be is uncomfortable. Not only are the ingredients of most statewide assessment plans an antithesis to what Stake is promoting, but the idea that these plans may in fact be harmful or damaging to the educational system is a serious charge.

The supposed dangers resulting from mass testing have been voiced before. Dyer (1966) reminds us how loudly the critics shouted in response to the plan for a National Assessment of Educational Progress. Some of the arguments raised against National Assessment were: (1) the tests would put undue pressure upon students; (2) the findings would lead to unfair comparisons; (3) teachers would teach for the tests, to the neglect of important educational objectives; (4) the program would ultimately force conformity and impose Federal control on the schools.

Dyer reacts by stating that ". . . one would suppose that to assess the educational enterprise by measuring the quality of its product is an egregious form of academic subversion" (1966, p. 69). Dyer sees the need for statewide testing programs for two reasons: continuity in the educational process and stability in educational systems. Statewide testing can help to bring greater continuity into the educational process if it can bring to teachers a continuous flow of information about the developmental needs of students, regardless of where they are or where they have been, and if tests are seen not so much as devices for selection or classification or evaluation, but as instruments for providing continuous feedback indispensable to the teaching-learning process. Statewide testing can help to bring greater stability into the educational process by steering a well-planned educational program toward well-considered educational goals.

The issue should not be one of state-imposed accountability versus locally initiated accountability. State education agencies and state legislatures have their own reasons, and suffer their own pressures, for collecting information about students' educational achievements. School districts' accountability to the state should not be confused with school districts' accountability to their own communities, or with teachers' accountability to their own school systems. The issue should be whether state-imposed accountability systems encourage or discourage school administrators and teachers from developing their own accountability plans.

It can be said that accountability laws are the signs of the public's lack of faith in the effectiveness of schooling. It also can be said that accountability laws are the signs that school officials did not, or could not, respond on their own to accountability demands.

Whether or not statewide assessment programs emphasize local use of results, helping teachers and administrators interpret and use the results is a job most state assessment specialists either try to do or feel they should do. It is also the area where they report the greatest difficulties and frustrations.

Baker (1973) says it well: ". . . the fallacy of accountability is that it can be legislated in a monolith. Perhaps, like most worthwhile things, it should be allowed to have an infancy and mature." Perhaps state education agencies are doing the best they can do and as much as they should do. Perhaps school board members, administrators, and teachers now should do more.

REFERENCES

Baker, E. L. Opening Accountability: A Story in Two Parts. *Evaluation Comment.* February 1973, *4*(1), 7-8.

Dyer, H. S. The Functions of Testing—Old and New. In *Testing Responsibilities and Opportunities of State Education Agencies.* Albany, New York: New York State Education Department, 1966, pp. 63-79.

_____, and Rosenthal, E. An Overview of the Survey Findings. In *State Educational Assessment Programs.* Princeton, N.J.: Educational Testing Service, 1971, pp. ix-xix. (ED 056 102).

Stake, R. E. School Accountability Laws. *Evaluation Comment,* February 1973, *4*(1), 1-3.

Weaver, W. T. The Delphi Forecasting Method. *Phi Delta Kappan,* 1971, *52,* 267-271.

30

STATE TESTING PROGRAMS

by Richard O. Fortna
and
Eleanor V. Horne
Educational Testing Service
Princeton, New Jersey

The purpose of the survey herein described was to obtain information to prepare a profile of state testing programs. Because changes are always being made, many of the facts presented in this report may be outdated in a matter of months. Therefore, the entire survey should be viewed only as a picture of what was reported about 1972-1973 programs and what was planned as of Spring/Summer 1973. Because so many changes were anticipated by so many of the programs we hope to be able to repeat this type of survey periodically to keep the information as current as possible.

In the first section we shall describe the procedures used in carrying out the survey. In the second we shall summarize and discuss the findings of the survey.

THE SURVEY PROCEDURES

The information obtained by this survey was gathered mainly by means of telephone interviews. Initial contact was made by a letter addressed to an individual in each state (usually in the state education agency) who appeared most likely to be able to give us the information we needed. A follow-up telephone call confirmed the appropriateness of our selection of the individual, and set a date and time for an in-depth telephone interview. Prior to the date of the interview, the person identified was provided a copy of the Interview Guide[1] and, when requested, a copy of the state's program description from the 1968 publication, *State Testing Programs: A Survey of Functions, Tests, Materials and Services.*[2]

The telephone interviews were completed between June and the early part of August. Each interviewer completed the guide and tape-recorded the interview. Some states were not willing to describe their assessment programs as testing programs; others were; therefore, in conducting the interviews no attempt was made to restrict the definition of a state testing program, or to go beyond what state personnel were willing to describe as their testing program. Following the interview the state descriptions were sent to the individual interviewed for approval or revision. The approved summaries are presented state-by-state in the main body of this report.

In addition, each interviewee was asked to submit program publications which could be used as reference materials. To ensure availability, these materials have been submitted for inclusion in the ERIC system. These documents have been assigned a "TM" or ERIC clearinghouse accession number. All will eventually be given an ERIC document (ED) number by which they must be ordered. Copies of these documents may be purchased from the ERIC Document Reproduction Service (EDRS), P.O. Drawer O, Bethesda, Maryland 20014. Specific information on how to order these documents may be obtained from any current issue of *Research in Education,* ERIC's monthly abstract journal.

SUMMARY OF FINDINGS

This section summarizes data on 42 testing programs that were operating in 33 states during the 1972-1973 school year. Although there are more than 42 program descriptions in the state-by-state section, we omitted from the analysis those which were planned for future years or which offered only a scoring and reporting service.

The District of Columbia, Puerto Rico, and the Virgin Islands are in this survey and reported with the states; therefore, the total number of states in the survey is 53. States having programs are listed below. Multiple programs are indicated by a number in parentheses after the state name.

Alabama	Illinois	North Carolina
Arizona	Iowa (2)	North Dakota
Arkansas	Kansas	Puerto Rico (2)
California	Massachusetts	Rhode Island
Colorado	Minnesota	South Carolina
Delaware	Mississippi	South Dakota
District of Columbia	Nebraska	Tennessee
Florida (2)	Nevada	Texas
Georgia	New Jersey	Virginia
Hawaii	New Mexico	Virgin Islands
Idaho	New York (7)	West Virginia

The summary which follows is arranged in eight major areas covering all questions asked during the interviews.

We rearranged some sections to make our discussion more meaningful. Question numbers after section titles refer to the Interview Guide.

1. *Purposes of Programs and Use of Data*
   (Questions, 2, 19, 20, 21, 22)
   What are the major purposes of the program? How are the results of the program being used? What efforts are undertaken to assist local interpretation and use of program results? Who provides this help? For whom is this assistance provided?

2. *Management Aspects of Programs*
   (Questions 3, 4, 5)
   Who determines program policy? What agency coordinates the program statewide? How are the activities of the coordinating agency funded?

3. *Population Tested*
   (Questions 6, 7, 8, 9)
   In what grades is the program administered? Is school participation required? What percent of eligible schools were included last year? How many students were tested last year?

4. *Instrumentation*
   (Questions 10, 11, 12, 12a, 13, 14)
   What tests are used in the program? What cognitive and noncognitive areas are assessed? Were any measures tailor-made, or revised for use in the program? Who developed these tailor-made tests? Who selected the tests used in the program?

5. *Data Collection and Processing*
   (Questions 15, 16, 17)
   What months of the school year are the tests administered? Who is responsible for giving the tests? Who is responsible for scoring?

6. *Norms*
   (Question 18)
   What types of norms are used?

7. *Dissemination*
   (Questions 23, 24, 25, 26)
   What kinds of reports are prepared? Who prepares the reports? Who receives a copy of the program reports?

8. *Prospects for the Future*
   (Questions 27, 28)
   What elements of your program are most likely to change in the near future? What are the major problems related to the program?

The tabulations presented in each of the eight sections which follow were prepared from the responses to questions in the Interview Guide. In almost every instance, more than one response could be given in answering a question. For example, only seven state programs listed but one purpose. Eleven programs listed three, ten programs listed four purposes, and so on. (See Response Summary, question number two.) Therefore, one should not expect the tables to total either to the number of programs or the number of states.

1. Purposes of Programs and Use of Data

The data in this section was derived from questions 2, 19, 20, 21, and 22 of the interview guide. Following each question is the number of programs and states responding.

Question 2. What is the major purpose of the program?
(42 programs in 33 states responding)

	Programs	States
1. Instructional evaluation	27	23
2. Identification of individual problems and talents	23	19
3. Guidance	22	20
4. Provide data for the management information system	14	14
5. Placement and grouping	14	13

Question 19. How are the results of the program used?
(42 programs in 33 states responding)

	Programs	States
1. Instruction	28	24
2. Program evaluation	26	22
3. Program planning	26	23
4. Guidance	23	22
5. Comparative analysis across schools	14	13

Note the similarity of purposes and uses. Instructional evaluation was the most frequently mentioned purpose. Instruction, program evaluation, and program planning were cited most frequently as uses. While there are a few exceptions—programs where purposes cited and uses mentioned do not agree—across all programs the uses are generally consistent with purposes cited.

The most frequent combination of purposes was the following: instructional evaluation, guidance, and identification of individual problems and talents (13 programs in 13 states). The most frequent combination of uses was: instruction, comparative analysis across schools, guidance, program planning, and program evaluation (mentioned by six programs in six states).

Question 20. What efforts are undertaken to assist local interpretation and use of program results?
(42 programs in 33 states responding)

	Programs	States
1. Workshops	31	30
2. Consulting	26	25
3. Publications	24	21
4. Audio-visual aids	11	11
5. Nothing	5	2

Question 21. Who provides this help?
(37 programs in 33 states responding)

	Programs	States
1. State Education Agency	30	28
2. Test publisher	10	10
3. College or university	10	8
4. Local education agency	6	6
5. County or district education agency agency	5	5
6. Consultant/contractor	2	2

Question 22. For whom is this assistance provided?
    (37 programs in 33 states responding)

	Programs	States
1. Administrators	32	29
2. Classroom teachers	26	25
3. Guidance counselors	25	25
4. School boards	10	10
5. Community groups	8	8
6. PTA	6	6
7. Students	5	5

Most states provide some sort of assistance to local schools to help them with the interpretation of program results. Responses to the next three questions indicate what is done, who provides the help, and for whom the help is provided.

Seven state programs provide all four kinds of service for local school personnel: workshops, consulting, publications, and audiovisual aids. Five programs provide no help with interpretation. Three of these five are for individuals not enrolled in school—candidates for a high school equivalency diploma or college credits. Two of the programs are for classroom teacher use only.

With the exception of one state program, the state education agency and the college or university are the only two agencies providing services to schools on their own. Any time a test publisher, local education agency, county or district education agency, or consultant/contractor is mentioned it is always cited in combination with a state education agency or the college or university responsible for the program.

It is interesting to note that relatively little assistance in the interpretation and use of the program results is provided for the nonprofessional members of the community.

2. Management Aspects of Programs

Information in this section was obtained from questions 3, 4, and 5.

Question 3. Who determines program policy?
    (42 programs in 33 states responding)

	Programs	States
1. State Board of Education	21	15
2. State Education Agency	16	15
3. Advisory council	10	10
4. Chief State School Officer	9	9

A single agency is mentioned as responsible for program policy in 24 programs in 16 states. In this group, the most frequently mentioned are the state board of education (10 programs in four states), the state education agency (6 programs in five states), and some type of advisory council (four programs in four states). Two other programs in one state claimed that the university was responsible for program policy. In the other two programs, each in a different state, one attributed program policy to the state legislature; the other, the Chief State School Officer. The advisory councils were usually formed by some combination of representatives from school systems—i.e., teachers, guidance counselors, ad-

ministrators; college and university faculty members; and various departments of state education agencies.

Question 4. What agency coordinates the program statewide?
    (42 programs in 33 states responding)

	Programs	States
1. State Education Agency	35	28
2. College or university*	7	5

*One program in one state does make some use of SEA.

Generally, divisions or departments of state education agencies which administer programs represented some combination of the following three: planning, evaluation and research (mentioned by 11 programs in 11 states). Pupil personnel services or guidance departments were involved in nine programs in nine states.

Question 5. How are the program activities of the coordinating agency funded?
    (42 programs in 33 states responding)

	Programs	States
1. State monies	29	23
2. ESEA Title III monies	17	16
3. Other federal monies	9	8
4. School or school district monies	5	4
5. Other	3	2

Sixteen programs in 10 states are funded solely by state monies. The combination of state and Federal funds was noted by 12 programs in 11 states. Federal funds were the sole source of funding in nine programs in nine states.

3. Population Tested

Information in this section was obtained by looking at the responses to questions 6, 7, 8, and 9. Only two tabulations are presented; both deal with grades tested. Responses to the other three questions (school participation, percentage participating and the number of students tested) are summarized in the text.

The "Other" category represents two high school equivalency testing programs and one program offering tests for college credit. Only one state reports testing in kindergarten.

Responses to question 6 were used to determine the number of grades tested.

Question 6. In what grades is the program administered?
    (42 programs in 33 states responding)

Grade	Programs	States
12	11	8
11	15	13
10	7	5
9	15	11
8	16	16
7	7	7
6	12	12
5	8	8
4	13	13
3	9	9
2	3	3
1	6	6
K	1	1

Question 6. How many different grade levels are tested?
(All 33 states with programs included)

Number of Grades	States
1	8
2	9
3	4
4	4
5	2
6	3
7	0
8	0
9	2
10	0
11	0
12 (All but K)	1
13	0

Seventeen states, over half, test in only one or two grades.

In this section questions were also asked about program participation. Sixteen programs in 15 states reported that school participation was required. Participation of schools is voluntary in 26 programs in 21 states. One state reported that student participation was voluntary. In most states conducting voluntary programs, between 70 and 90 percent of all eligible schools participate.

Interviewees were also asked to record the number of students tested during 1972-1973. The range of responses for programs was 5,800 to 1,625,000. By state the range was 5,800 to 2,104,000. The total number of students tested in all programs during that period was over seven million.

4. Instrumentation

This section was based upon responses to questions 10, 11, 12, 12a, 13, and 14. Test use was obtained by responses to question 12a of the Interview Guide.

There is a great deal of similarity between what is tested at the elementary level (kindergarten through grade 8) and the secondary level (grade 9 and beyond). The next tabulation was derived from question 10. It shows how frequently an area is tested at the two levels. States did not report elementary and secondary programs separately. For purposes of analysis, we tallied the two separately. For example, if a state reported that grades 3 and 10 were tested, we tallied this as "one" elementary and "one" secondary program. Therefore, the sum of programs and states in the two categories does not amount to 42 programs and 33 states.

With two exceptions, all programs which test aptitude also test one or more subject areas. There was only

Question 10. Which of the following cognitive areas are being tested?
(41 programs in 32 states responding)

	Programs	States
1. Mathematics	36	30
2. Reading	32	30
3. Language skills	27	22
4. Natural science	25	21
5. Social science	22	18
6. Aptitude	20	20
7. Study skills	9	8

Question 10. Which of the following cognitive areas are being tested?
(41 programs in 32 states responding)

	Elementary		Secondary	
	28	28	30	24
	Programs	States	Programs	States
1. Reading	28	28	21	19
2. Mathematics	27	27	24	21
3. Language skills	18	18	20	17
4. Natural science	14	14	18	15
5. Aptitude	13	13	12	12
6. Social science	11	11	17	15
7. Study skills	7	7	2	2

one program in which achievement tests were not used; an aptitude test was sufficient for achieving the program's purpose.

Some of the subject areas tested form constellations which are fairly consistent across states and programs. Reading, mathematics, and language skills testing is a very common pattern, occurring in 24 programs in 23 states. This core plus one other area forms a recognizable pattern in at least one-third of the states. The core areas plus natural science is used in 15 programs; aptitude plus the core in 14; and social science plus the core in 11.

The information in this tabulation was derived in the same manner as the preceding one. The total number of programs and states does not equal our real total because of the artificial dichotomy we created.

Question 11. Which of the following noncognitive areas are being tested?
(9 programs in 9 states responding)

	Elementary		Secondary	
	6	6	5	5
	Programs	States	Programs	States
1. Attitudes toward school	5	5	2	2
2. Self-concept	4	4	1	1
3. School plans and aspirations	2	2	1	1
4. Interests	1	1	4	4
5. Biographical data	–	–	2	2

Thirty-two programs in 22 states do not test noncognitive areas. Nine programs in nine states do. There is almost an even split between elementary and secondary programs testing noncognitive areas; however, there is little agreement between the rank order of the areas tested at the elementary and secondary level.

A variety of instruments is used in state testing programs. No single test or test series occupies a dominant position. Some of the measures are purchased "as is" from the test publisher; others are revised for use in the programs; and some are developed from scratch specifically for use in a particular program.

Of 41 programs in 32 states, 20 programs in 20 states use only tests purchased "as is" from test publishers. Thirteen programs in seven states use only tests which have been tailor-made, and in eight programs in eight states a combination of purchased, tailored, or revised measures is used.

Question 12a. What tests are used in the program and at what grades?
(28 programs in 28 states responding)

Tests	States	1	2	3	4	5	6	7	8	9	10	11	12
1. Differential Aptitude Tests	7								1	4		2	
2. Comprehensive Test of Basic Skills	6		1	1	1	1		3					1
3. Iowa Tests of Educational Development	6									3	1	4	2
4. Iowa Tests of Basic Skills	5	1	2	1	3	3	3	2	3	1			
5. SRA Achievement Series*	5				2	1	1	1	2				
6. California Achievement Tests	4	1	1	1	2	2	1	1	3	1	1	2	1
7. School and College Ability Tests	4			2		1		2	1		1		2

*Includes one test listed as the SRA Survey.

In determining which tests available from publishers are most frequently used in state testing programs, only instruments prescribed for use were tallied. Tests which may be administered at the discretion of the local education agency were not included because the data did not reveal whether optional tests were administered, the frequency with which the tests were administered, or the grades in which they were used.

Question 14. Who selected the tests used in the program?
(42 programs in 33 states responding)

	Programs	States
1. State Education Agency	27	21
2. Committee of professionals from various fields	14	12
3. Committee of college and university personnel	7	6

The state education agency is most frequently mentioned as having the responsibility for instrument selection. It is reported that in 15 of the 27 programs in nine of the 21 states, the state education agency is solely responsible for test selection.

Question 13. Who developed these tailor-made tests?
(21 programs in 13 states responding)

	Programs	States
1. State Education Agency	13	8
2. Committee of professionals	8	3
3. College or university	5	5
4. Test publisher	5	4
5. Outside contractor	4	4

Responses to question 13 show who developed the tailored or revised measures. In almost one-half of the programs using these tests, a single agency is cited as having sole responsibility for their development. The state education agency is cited in three programs in three states. College and universities, test publishers, and outside contractors are each credited in two programs in two states.

5. Data Collection and Processing

The information in this section was summarized from questions 15, 16, 17, and 18.

Question 15. What months of the school year are the tests administered?
(37 programs in 28 states responding)

	Programs	States
September	15	13
October	20	18
November	8	7
December	4	4
January	7	6
February	5	4
March	4	4
April	13	12
May	10	9
June	6	3
July	2	2
August	4	2

Question 15. What months of the school year are the tests administered?
(42 programs in 33 states responding)

	Programs	States
Fall	31	26
Winter	9	7
Spring	21	19
Summer	7	3

Question 15 elicited multiple responses from most programs. While 16 programs reported testing in only one month, 26 programs reported testing in two or more months.

Five programs in 5 states reported only "fall," "midwinter," or "spring" as the time of testing; therefore, these programs are excluded from the monthly tally. All programs are included in the "season" tally.

The most frequently mentioned period of the school year for testing was fall. Thirty-one programs in 26 states mentioned this as the period of testing. The most frequently mentioned month of testing was October. Spring testing was mentioned by 21 programs in 19 states. The most frequently mentioned month during this period was April. Winter testing was mentioned by only nine programs in seven states. Five programs in two states, all for nonschool populations, report testing during July and August; these programs are for high school equivalency.

Question 16. Who is responsible for giving the tests, inventories, etc., for the program?
(42 programs in 33 states responding)

	Programs	States
1. Classroom teachers	21	17
2. Guidance counselors	15	15
3. School administrative staff	9	9

For 10 programs in nine states the administration of tests could not be categorized, since it was reported that this decision was made at the local level. We can only assume that in these cases the job of test administration was assigned to classroom teachers, guidance counselors, or school administrative staff.

Ten programs in six states indicated that only classroom teachers are used to administer the program tests. Guidance counselors were mentioned as the sole administrators in only four programs in four states.

Five programs in five states report that two agencies score program tests. Usually, one agency scores one test used in the program; the other scores a different test. Where only one agency is listed as the organization providing scoring services, we find that test publishers are mentioned in 11 programs in 11 states, contractors by nine programs in eight states, state education agencies in seven programs in five states, and colleges or universities by six programs in six states.

Question 17. Who is responsible for scoring the tests?
(42 programs in 33 states responding)

	Programs	States
1. Test publisher	15	15
2. Outside contractors	11	10
3. State Education Agency	9	6
4. College or university	7	7
5. Local schools or school districts	3	3
6. Classroom teachers	3	1

6. Norms

Information in this section was derived from question 18. With the exception of three programs in two states, norms of some kind are produced.

Question 18. What types of norms are used?
(41 programs in 33 states responding)

	Programs	States
1. State	33	27
2. National	21	20
3. Local	20	19
4. Regional	7	7
5. County	4	4

Eleven programs in 10 states use only the three-set combination of local, state and national norms. The only type of norm mentioned that was not used in combination with any other was state norms. Seven programs in six states use only state norms.

7. Dissemination

Information in this section was summarized from questions 23, 24, and 25.

Question 23. What kinds of reports are prepared?
(40 programs in 33 states responding)

	Programs	States
1. School summaries	33	31
2. State summaries	30	28
3. Student summaries	28	25
4. School system summaries	24	24
5. Class summaries	20	19
6. County summaries	9	8

The three-set combination of school summaries, state summaries, and student reports is used by 20 programs

in 19 states. Two programs provide a transcript service to candidates so that score reports are available upon request. Two programs indicated they do not prepare reports. In both cases the programs are intended for instructional evaluation, one at the classroom level by the classroom teacher, the other at the school level. No data from these programs are submitted to the state education agency. One state reports that a magnetic computer tape of the program results is made available for research use.

Question 25. Who prepares the reports?
(40 programs in 33 states responding)

	Programs	States
1. State Education Agency	29	24
2. Test publisher	11	11
3. College or university	8	7
4. Outside contractor	4	4

Reports are generally prepared by the state education agency, either alone or in association with test publishers, colleges or universities, or some outside contractor/consultant.

In 17 programs in 13 states the reports are prepared by the state education agency. Three programs in three states report that the local education agency, or the local school, is involved in producing the reports without the help of any other agency.

Question 24. Who receives a copy of the program reports?
(40 programs in 33 states responding)

	Programs	States
1. Schools	31	28
2. School districts	27	25
3. State Education Agency	23	21
4. Students	20	14
5. Principals	17	16
6. State Board of Education	16	16
7. Teachers	15	14
8. Colleges or universities	12	11
9. Newspapers	11	11
10. Governor or Legislature	8	8

Only seven programs in seven states report that parents are given reports of results, and only six programs in six states distribute reports to the general public—most often only upon request. Tying this with the information from question 22, one can conclude that little assistance in the interpretation and use of program results is provided for nonprofessional members of the community, and the results of programs are not often shared with these individuals.

8. Prospects for the Future

The information in this section was summarized from questions 26, 27, and 28.

No problems are reported by 19 programs in 13 states. Responses to question number 27 show the areas most frequently cited as problems in the remaining 23 programs in 20 states.

Sixteen different areas were listed as problems. However, there is little consistency from program to program.

Funding was mentioned as the only problem in 5 programs in 5 states.

Question 27. Are there major problems related to the program?
(23 programs in 20 states responding)

	Programs	States
1. Funding	11	11
2. Use of results	5	5
3. Local education agency acceptance	4	4
4. Lack of staff	3	3
5. Scoring and data processing	3	3

Question 26. Which of the following elements in your program are most likely to change in the near future?
(29 programs in 26 states responding)

	Programs	States
1. Tests	19	19
2. Areas assessed	18	18
3. Funding	10	10
4. Target population	10	10
5. Dissemination	10	10
6. Data processing procedures	9	9
7. Use of data	9	9
8. Goals of testing program	8	8
9. Interpretive materials	7	7

Ten programs in five states mentioned that no changes are expected in the near future. Responses to question number 26 show the areas most frequently cited by the remaining 32 programs in 28 states. Three programs in three states responded that the programs are constantly changing to meet the needs of the state education agency or local schools. These programs did not list any specific changes. Only three of the programs which reported that funding is a problem also report that funding is an element that may be changed.

All tables in this section were derived from the state-by-state Response Summary which we prepared. Obviously, we could not tabulate and discuss all possible combinations within or across categories. We had neither the time nor space to do so.

NOTES

[1] *State Testing Programs Interview Guide* (Princeton, N.J.: Educational Testing Service, 1973).

[2] *State Testing Programs: A Survey of Functions, Tests, Materials and Services* (Princeton, N.J.: Educational Testing Service, 1968). (TM 003 001)

REFERENCES

State Testing Programs Interview Guide. Princeton, N.J.: Educational Testing Service, 1973.

State Testing Programs: A Survey of Functions, Tests, Materials and Services. Princeton, N.J.: Educational Testing Service, 1968. (TM 003 001)

State Educational Assessment Programs: 1973 Revision. Princeton, N.J.: Educational Testing Service, 1973. (TM 003 098)

State Educational Assessment Programs. Princeton, N.J.: Educational Testing Service, 1971. (ED 056 102)

31

ISSUES AND PROCEDURES IN THE DEVELOPMENT OF CRITERION REFERENCED TESTS

by Stephen P. Klein
and
Jacqueline Kosecoff
ERIC Clearinghouse on Tests, Measurement and Evaluation
Educational Testing Service
Princeton, New Jersey 08540

This publication was prepared pursuant to a contract with the National Institute of Education, U.S. Department of Health, Education and Welfare. Contractors undertaking such projects under government sponsorship are encouraged to express freely their judgment in professional and technical matters. Points of view or opinions do not, therefore, represent official National Institute of Education position or policy.

A visitor to our planet Earth, surveying the current state of educational testing, would very likely be confused by what he found. He would observe, for example, the increasing use of tests in all phases and facets of the educational process, including the evaluation of instructional personnel. He would learn, too, about the great technological improvements that have been made in tests and in their administration, scoring, and reporting procedures. All of these factors would tend to support the notion that tests are fulfilling an important and vital role. On the other hand, this same observer might also hear the valid complaints of the growing cadre of test critics. These critics complain that present tests are inappropriate for most educational decision-making and, if a test is not going to be used for decision-making, why bother giving it in the first place?

Perhaps one of the quickest ways of alleviating our visitor's confusion is to point out to him certain changes that have been occurring in education and testing during the past few years. For example, most expert test construction in the past has focused upon a relatively few kinds of assessment instruments, such as those that are used to decide whether a student should be accepted for college. Comparatively little help has been given to the classroom teacher to diagnose individual student needs, or assess the outcomes of particular instructional programs. Now, however, there is growing desire to individualize instruction, to assess validly the outcomes of instructional programs, and to hold teachers and administrators responsible for actual gains in student performance. These trends have increased the demand on test developers for appropriate tools to facilitate the measurement process, because existing measures are useful for some important educational decisions but are not designed to meet all needs. It is evident, therefore, that test critics are complaining not about tests per se, but about the need for certain kinds of quality measures that are not currently available.

It is within this context of increased need for, and reliance on, valid test results that the movement toward so-called "criterion referenced tests" (CRT) has been given new impetus. A criterion referenced measure is essentially "one that is deliberately constructed so as to yield measurements that are directly interpretable in terms of specified performance standards."[1] (Glaser and Nitko, 1971). The pertinent question is whether or not the individual has attained some significant degree of competence on an instructional performance task (Harris, 1972).

Measures with these characteristics are, of course, not new to education. What is new is the range of importance of the decision areas for which they are being employed or emphasized, and the attention they are being given by measurement and curriculum experts alike (Airasian and Madaus, 1972; Baker, E., 1972; Keller, 1972; Davis, 1972, 1973; Hawes, 1973). It would not be surprising, therefore, for us to witness during the next few years a number of major contributions to testing theory and methodology arising from the use of criterion referenced tests. Further, the improvement of such measures is likely to have many ramifications for instructional practice, since with improved tools even more reliance is likely to be placed upon the results obtained. For example, a bill before the United States Congress would require criterion referenced test data in order to make funding decisions affecting thousands of schools and involving several million dollars (Quie, 1973).

It is appropriate at this point in time, therefore, for us to examine how criterion referenced tests are constructed and, more importantly, the basic issues and procedures associated with these steps. It is hoped that such an appraisal will clarify some of the basic methodological and theoretical concerns associated with criterion referenced tests that will be examined during the next few years.

This paper is divided into two parts. In the first section the major issues and steps in the development of CRTs are considered. In the second section representative CRT systems in mathematics, as well as important efforts in other content areas, have been selected for review.

MAJOR ISSUES AND STEPS IN CRT DEVELOPMENT

This section of the paper provides a review of the basic steps in the development of CRTs and the major issues associated with these steps. Although many of the steps and issues have their counterpart in classical test development, the present focus is upon those considerations unique to CRTs, and especially those relating to the development of such measures in mathematics. It should be kept in mind, however, that the method chosen to resolve a particular issue at one stage in the development of a CRT is likely to have ramifications for other stages in the developmental process, as well as in the interpretation of the scores obtained. In addition, the most important but not necessarily self-evident of

these implications are noted, and the primary techniques and procedures that have been used, as well as their most important advantages and limitations, are identified.

Purpose and Defining Characteristics of CRTs

It is a generally accepted principle that somewhat different kinds of measures have to be constructed for different purposes. This principle also appears to carry over into the development of CRTs. For example, to ensure an adequate level of test reliability, a CRT or series of CRTs that will be used in making a decision about an individual's level of performance will need to be longer than one used for group assessment. Similarly, the focus of the CRTs used for managing an individualized learning segment of a small mathematics unit would be narrower than that used to measure end-of-year performance of all students in a classroom. The characteristics of the target audience, such as their ages and ethnic backgrounds, are also likely to influence the test construction process in terms of the appropriateness of various kinds of stimuli and response formats. Further, the anticipated number of students to be tested and the context in which the testing will occur influence test format, production, distribution, administration, scoring, and analysis.

Figure 1 lists some of the basic purposes that have been noted for using CRTs in terms of the decisions to be made and the focus of the testing (Harris, 1973; Skager, 1973). Three major kinds of decisions have been identified. Decisions relating to the organization of an instructional program are classified as planning decisions. Validating the quality and competency of a program is encompassed by certification decisions. Decisions based on additional investigation of the instructional program are included in a research category. With respect to the focus of the testing program, three classifications are considered. First, a CRT can be primarily involved with the individual student. Second, groups of students such as a classroom or ethnic group can be the focus. And third, the instructional program itself might be the primary unit of concern.

Figure 2 illustrates how differences in the target audience would result in different test items for the same objective. From an inspection of these figures and the foregoing discussion, it is apparent that the different uses of CRTs may require different kinds of measures and test models. The fundamental issue underlying these differences is the degree to which the CRT or set of CRTs will provide precise and reliable information about student performance relative to various feasibility constraints associated with gathering this information, such as costs and testing time.

Objectives Chosen

As noted in the preface to this paper, one of the essential features of CRTs is their foundation in clearly defined educational objectives. There are, however, a number of issues associated with how these objectives should be developed and stated. The essence of these issues may be summarized by the question: "What kinds of objectives should form the basis for a CRT system?"

Focus of the Testing Program	Planning	Type of Decision Certification	Research
Student	Diagnosis, Prediction, and Placement	Determination of "mastery," grades, and success of placement	Interactions between the student, the group, and the program
"Group" (Classroom, ethnic, SES cultural, or geographical groups)	Classroom management Curriculum selection	Instructional and administrative accountability	Interactions between group(s) and program, e.g., do students with certain characteristics function better than others in a given situation?
"Program" (A program may be used with one or more groups)	Organization and sequencing of instruction, Curriculum and product development, Needs Assessment	Program Evaluation Analysis of subject matter domain	Comparisons between types of programs, Analysis of program components, Development of measurement methodology

FIGURE 1. Purposes for Criterion Referenced Tests

Almost all developers of CRTs agree that to assess performance within a given area requires the construction of a set of CRTs rather than a single measure. The problem then arises as to which objectives within an area should become the basis for the CRTs and how broadly or narrowly these objectives should be stated—that is, the extent of each objective's coverage. The statement of an objective may be further delineated by defining the conditions under which the measurements are made (e.g., open vs. closed book, with or without the aid of a sheet containing needed formulas, and so forth) and/or the standards of performance to be reached in order for the objective to be achieved (e.g., "80 percent correct," "in less than 2 minutes," and so forth) (Mager, 1962; Popham, 1965). Implicit or explicit assumptions about the relative importance of the objectives and the characteristics of the area to be assessed (such as the logical and/or sequential organization of the objectives in it) also influence decisions as to which objectives should form the basis for a CRT system (Popham, 1972).

The resolution of the issues associated with choosing a set of objectives usually hinges upon the anticipated purpose(s) of the CRT system. Thus, there is a consideration of the degree of precision needed relative to various practical considerations. This balance is illustrated by the IOX Criteria for Objective Selection (Popham, 1972) presented in the Appendix.

Some of the procedures that have been used to develop the objectives bases for CRTs systems are described briefly below:

Expert Judgment. A small group of experts within the

Objective

The student will indicate by marking the appropriate choices on an attitude scale his/her appreciation of the importance of mathematics in everyday life.

	First Graders	*Twelfth Graders*
Format	The student is given a test booklet. Each page is a different color and has a familiar symbol at the top of the page, such as a rabbit. Each page also has the words "Yes" and "No." Directions are provided to the student so that he/she understands to mark the choice that answers the question that is read by the teacher.	The student is given a set of statements and a series of choices ranging from "Strongly Agree" to "Strongly Disagree." The student marks the number of his choice on a machine-scorable answer sheet.
Sample Items	The teacher reads the following kinds of directions and questions: "Now turn to the red page with the rabbit at the top. . . . Now I am going to read you the next question. 'Do you have to know how to work with numbers to tell time?' . . . . Now turn to the yellow page with the duck at the top. . . . 'Do you have to know how to add and subtract numbers to catch a ball?' . . . . Now turn to the page with the table at the top. . . . 'Do you have to know how to work with numbers to buy something at the store?' ". . . . and so forth.	The following kinds of items might appear on a scale to measure the objective: Persons who fill medical prescriptions need to use mathematics frequently in their work. Only a very small part of a carpenter's job requires him to use mathematics. It is more important for a bank teller to make friends easily than it is for him or her to make arithmetic computations accurately. In order to be a good plumber, one would have to be able to do basic arithmetic computations with fractions.
Comments	Note that the child does not have to read the questions; the questions are asked about himself or herself, rather than some other person; and the language level and activities are within the students' repertoire of experiences.	The statements are balanced with respect to being positive or negative regarding the importance of mathematics, so as to reduce any irrelevant tendency to agree or disagree.

FIGURE 2. Comparison of General Item Formats for the Same Objective at Different Grade or Age Levels

area to be assessed meet and, on the basis of their knowledge and experience in the field, jointly decide which objectives are the most important to measure. These objectives are then screened to determine the feasibility of measuring them and, where necessary, to clarify and/or redefine them. This is probably the most common approach.

Consensus Judgment. Various groups, such as community representatives, curriculum experts, teachers, and school administrators, decide which objectives they consider to be the most important. A measurement and/or curriculum expert is then responsible for defining and stating these objectives in a way that would permit them to be assessed (Klein, 1972; Wilson, 1973).

Curriculum Analysis. A team of curriculum experts analyzes a given set of curriculum materials such as testbooks in order to identify, and where necessary infer, the objectives that are the focus of these materials (Baker, R. L., 1972).

Analysis of the Area to be Tested. An in-depth analysis is made of an area such as mathematics in order to identify all contents (such as single-digit numerals) and behaviors (such as multiplication with replacement) that are included in that area (Glaser and Nitko, 1971; Nitko, 1973). The objectives associated with these contents and behaviors are then organized in some systematic fashion, such as in terms of a hierarchy and/or sequence of objectives for the components of the subject area (in mathematics usually referred to as "strands") (Nitko, 1971; Roudabush, 1971; Popham, 1972).

Item Construction and Selection

Once the purpose(s) and the objectives for the CRT system have been delineated, the next step is to construct and/or select test items or tasks to measure the objectives chosen. This is one of the most difficult steps in the total developmental process because of the vast number of test items or tasks that might be constructed for any given objective, even those that are relatively narrowly defined. For example, consider the following objective: "The student can compute the correct product of two single-digit numerals greater than 0 where the maximum value of this product does not exceed 20." The specificity of this objective is quite deceptive, since there are 29 pairs of numerals that meet this requirement and at least 10 different item types that might be used to assess student performance (see Figure 3). Further, each of the resulting 290 combinations of pairs and item types could be modified in a variety of ways that might influence whether the student answered them correctly. Some of these modifications are:

Vary the sequence of numerals (e.g., 5 then 3 versus 3 then 5).

Use different item formats (e.g., multiple choice versus completion).

Change the mode of presentation (e.g., written versus oral).

Change the mode of response (e.g., written versus oral).

The student can compute the correct product of two single-digit numerals greater than 0 where the maximum value of this product does not exceed 20.

a. $\begin{array}{r} 5 \\ \underline{\times 3} \end{array}$

b. $5 \times 3 =$

c. $(5)(3) =$

d. $5 \cdot 3 =$

e. 5 times 3 =

f. The product of 5 and 3 =

g. $5 \times \underline{\hspace{1cm}} = 15$

h. If $x = 5$ and $y = 3$, what is the value of xy?

i. What numeral multiplied by 3 will equal 15?

j. John has 5 apples. Sally has 3 times as many apples as John. How many apples does Sally have?

FIGURE 3. Item Types using the Content of Numerals 3 and 5 for the Objective

It soon becomes evident that even a highly specific objective could have a potential item pool of well over several thousand items (Hively, 1970, 1973; Bormuth, 1970).

The number of items to construct for each objective is influenced by several factors. Some of these factors are the amount of testing time available and the cost of making an interpretation error, such as saying that a student has achieved mastery when he has not. A survey of current measures reveals that the usual practice is to use about three to five items per objective. This practice appears to stem more from feasibility constraints than any sound foundation in psychometric theory or technology.

The particular item construction and selection approach (or combination of approaches) chosen to define a CRT program is a major consideration. One reason for this is that the methods used have a direct bearing on the utility and content validity of the CRTs developed and the interpretation of their scores. For example, if there is a hierarchy of objectives, and if a CRT is to be based on an objective at a given level of generality in this hierarchy, then it is likely that the items used will be sampled from the relevant subobjectives. Unless there is a specified hierarchy or an organization of objectives, such systematic sampling is impossible. When this latter situation occurs, one has much less confidence that the measure(s) developed really assess the whole objective. One reason for this concern is that without a systematic plan for guidance it is very easy to just construct items for those aspects of an objective that are most amenable to measurement, rather than those aspects that might be considered most germane or critical. On the other hand, it also seems likely that responsible test developers working without an overall plan are more likely to focus their attention on the most salient (and perhaps most frequently taught) facets of an objective, than on those aspects that may be just tangential to what a student must really know or be able to do. Thus, the best compromise between systematic sampling (and thereby improved content validity) and potential instructional relevance is to first develop a provisional systematic plan, then assign items to some or all the components of this plan based upon their perceived relative importance. This latter approach is the one most frequently adopted by major test publishers (Wood, 1961).

A related issue in construction and selection of CRT items is the degree to which the items should be sampled with respect to their relative difficulty within an objective. It is a well known and frequently used principle of test construction that slight changes in an item can affect its difficulty. This is most readily accomplished by varying the homogeneity of the alternatives in a multiple choice item, such as in the two examples below:

Eight hundredths equals	Eight hundredths equals
a. 800	a. 800
b. 80	b. .80
c. 8	c. .08
d. .08	d. .008

The extent to which the items within an objective are sampled with respect to difficulty has, of course, a direct bearing on the interpretation of the scores obtained. In other words, if only the most difficult items are used, then the phrase "mastery of the objective" has a very different meaning than if the items were sampled over the full range of difficulties. The fact that the difficulties of items on CRTs (and thus their scores) can be influenced so easily poses real problems to CRT users. To blindly assume that the scores obtained indicate an accurate appraisal of the degree of mastery achieved, merely because a measure is called a "CRT," is an exercise in self-deception.

A third consideration influencing the construction and selection of items is the degree to which an item is dependent upon, or related to, a particular set of curriculum or institutional materials and techniques (Baker, R., 1972; Skager, 1973). For example, if the instruction only gave students practice in solving multiplication problems in the form used in item types a-e in Figure 3, and if the CRT for this unit only used these same item types, then the CRT would be said to be "instructionally dependent," or biased. It is readily apparent that the more instructionally dependent the CRT, the more likely the effects of instruction would be evidenced in the scores obtained with it, and the less generality one could draw from these scores regarding the student's mastery of the objective. On the other hand, instructionally independent tests are more likely to reflect a student's general ability. Thus, an instructionally biased test might be preferred for such purposes as teacher accountability, while an instructionally independent test might be preferred for school accountability and for evaluation studies comparing the effects of different programs.

A fourth issue, and one which has perhaps not received as much attention as it should, is the potential interaction between the objective and how it is measured. It is often assumed, for example, that selected response items (e.g., multiple choice) serve as an effective proxy for constructed response items (e.g., completion or short answer) because the performance of students on the two kinds of items are highly related. Although this may be generally true, it may not be true for certain kinds of objectives; and further, the degree of mastery required to answer a constructed response item is usually greater than it is to answer the selected response item.

The relative scoreability of the latter format, however, has led to its use almost exclusively in published measures, including CRTs. It should be recalled that anything affecting item difficulty on a CRT will influence the total score on it, and thereby the interpretation of that score.

The foregoing considerations have led to a number of different methods of selecting and constructing items for CRTs. The general features of these methods are described below, but it should be remembered that each of these approached begins with, or involves the development of, well-defined statements of the educational objective(s) to be measured.

Panel of Experts. A group of measurement and curriculum "experts" decide which items to use based on their knowledge and experience of the field (Zweig, 1973). When the experts involved are classroom teachers, this approach may lead to highly instructionally dependent measures.

Systematic Sampling. This approach is basically a variation of the classical test construction technique. It involves developing for each objective a matrix of contents and behaviors (or tasks) to be assessed. Items are then systematically sampled within this matrix, and perhaps along a third continuum of item difficulty as well (Wilson, 1973; CTB/McGraw-Hill, 1973).

Systematic Item Generation. This is the most sophisticated of the various approaches, and starts with the assumption that all the relevant contents, behaviors (or tasks), stimulus and response characteristics, and related factors can be defined for a given domain or universe of objectives (Hively, 1970, 1973; Cronbach, 1971; Skager, 1973). Basic item forms, or "shells," are then constructed. Various techniques can then be used to generate the necessary items, including the use of a computer (especially in the field of mathematics) to meet certain prespecified criteria for coverage of the objectives (Kriewall and Hirsch, 1969).

It is evident from these descriptions that as the sophistication of the method improves, generality of the results and the costs of test construction tend to increase. Further, the particular method chosen will be influenced by the nature of the efforts that have been devoted to the generation of the objectives on which the CRTs are based and the purposes for which they will be used. Finally, the degree of sophistication may be limited still further by the clarity of the domain to be assessed, such as mathematics versus "citizenship," and the measurement technology available for constructing measures in that domain (e.g., academic achievement versus personality development).

Improving Item Quality

It is axiomatic that all tests and measures be field-tested prior to basing decisions upon them. Although it appears that this axiom is often ignored, there are a number of methods that have been suggested for analyzing CRT items in order to identify those that are "faulty." It should be noted, however, that an item that is considered "faulty" or "good" using one method of analysis may not be identified as such using another method (Popham and Husek, 1969). This is illustrated in Table 1. It is apparent, therefore, that the final version of a test may be influenced greatly by the method of item analysis chosen for its construction (Cox and Vargus, 1966; Roudabush, 1973).

TABLE 1. RESULTS OF DIFFERENT ITEM ANALYSES

Item No.	Item Difficulty		Possible point biserial r with score on test	Possible sensitivity to instruction
	Pretest	Posttest		
1	0%	100%	0	High
2	50%	50%	1.00	Low

There are two basic concepts underlying the item analysis techniques associated with CRTs, and at least one of these constructs is present in each analysis method. These two constructs are as follows:

1. An item is considered "good" if it is *sensitive* to instruction, that is, if performance on it is related to the degree of instruction obtained. The methods that rely heavily on this construct are usually used when there is little or no variation in student scores at any one testing. There are problems with such methods, however: they assume that the instruction was indeed effective; they tend to produce instructionally dependent measures; and they are biased by maturation and other irrelevant systematic factors that might tend to improve scores over time. Further, the use of a technique emphasizing sensitivity could easily lead to some rather interesting circular reasoning, if one tried to improve the test and an instructional program at the same time.

2. An item is considered "good" if it *discriminates* between those who did well versus those who did poorly on the test as a whole, or on some "outside" criterion such as performance in the next step in a sequence of instruction. This involves all the classical item analysis approaches and as such one must accept all the assumptions, advantages, and disadvantages that are normally associated with these techniques (especially item and test variance).

The kinds of analysis methods and their variations that have been suggested are listed below:

Comparison Group. Give the test to two groups who are known to possess different degrees of skill with respect to the objective(s) measured. One way of doing this is to give the test to those who have, versus those who have not, received instruction dealing with the objective. A second method is to give the test to those whose normal activities require different levels of attainment of the skill measured (e.g., carpenter versus auto mechanic for an objective dealing with computing the size of various geometric objects). The next basic step is to identify those items that discriminate best between the groups in the desired direction (that is, the presumably more able should do better). It is important for the purposes of CRT interpretation that if two separate groups are involved, they have the same general intellectual ability or

other characteristics that might bias the test results.

Single Group, Pre- and Posttest. Give the test to the same group twice, once before instruction and again after instruction. Identify those items that discriminate between the two test sessions. A number of item analysis techniques designed specifically for CRTs have used this approach (Popham, 1970; Ozenne, 1971; Kosecoff and Klein, 1973; Roudabush, 1973).

Single Group, Posttest Only. Give the test to one group of individuals after a fixed period of instruction; that is, all examinees have had the same amount of opportunity to achieve the objective. If the time allotted is somewhat less than that needed for *all* the students to achieve the objective, and the students are somewhat heterogeneous in their ability (as is common in most classrooms), then the typical item analysis procedures, such as computing point biserial correlation coefficients, may be employed to identify faulty items. An internal criterion (total score on test) or an external criterion (success in achieving a more advanced skill) may be used (Glaser, 1963). One weakness in this approach is that items having very high or low difficulties will tend to have low biserial coefficients, even though they may be very sensitive to instruction. An extreme case would be an item that would be failed by everyone prior to instruction but passed by everyone after instruction. A second weakness is that general intellectual ability, as well as the effects of instruction, may influence the results, and there is no way of cleanly separating these influences.

Single Group, Repeated Measures. Each student periodically takes the complete test until he is able to achieve mastery. A record is kept of the number of times the student passes and fails each item. Analysis is then made to determine whether the item generally exhibits the desired pattern of failure than success (with no reversals); i.e., a desired pattern would te FFPP and an undesirable pattern would be PFFP. This approach is only applicable where there are no carry-over effects from test session to test session, or where truly parallel items may be constructed for each test session and then systematically counterbalanced across sessions and examinees. The advantages of this approach are that it permits relevant scaling of an item within an objective and the analysis is made after all students have become "masters." The labor involved in this approach, and the likelihood of finding items that scale well, however, have not contributed to this method's popularity.

One issue that is related to item analysis procedures, and that seems to be neglected with respect to CRTs, is the problem of knowing whether the final set of items provides adequate coverage of the objective. In other words, how many items are really needed to sample sufficiently a given objective? Further, a procedure is needed for determining whether some of the items are redundant. Although these kinds of issues have been examined in part with the more traditional kinds of tests, the unique demands of CRTs will correspondingly require new ways of dealing with this general problem of knowing when one has appropriate and efficient coverage.

Content Validity

A major concern of CRT developers is in establishing the content validity of their instruments. The three most common ways that have been used to do this are as follows:

Systematic Test Development. This approach involves presenting the rationale for the systematic procedure employed in terms of why it should result in a content-valid test (Hively, 1970, 1973).

Expert Judgment. Content experts are given a variety of objectives and the items used to measure them. They are then asked to assign the items to their "appropriate" objective. The degree to which they are able to do this accurately reflects on item-objective consistency, and thereby on content validity; that is, is a given item really measuring the objective for which it has been constructed? (Dahl, 1971).

Item Analysis. It is possible to compute internal consistency indices for a CRT and/or see whether an item on a given objective correlates more highly with other items for this objective than it does with items on other objectives. These approaches are limited by all the dangers of internal consistency validation techniques plus the potential problem of no variance on the measures (that is, the students all receive the same score). The latter problem, however, usually appears to be more theoretical than actual, because students do vary in their performance. This variation may be due to a number of factors, including the students' general intellectual ability, cultural and environmental backgrounds, and the quality of instruction they receive. If enough students are tested, then one will discover sufficient variance in the levels of performance and/or in the time it takes to achieve a given level. Reports of "no variance" usually stem from failure to sample enough students and/or the failure to examine the rate at which students master items and objectives. Thus, although one might conceive of a situation in which no variance might occur in a given classroom, it is hard to imagine how this might arise across a variety of classrooms—unless, of course, the test was totally inappropriate for the full range of examinees for whom it was constructed. The real problem, therefore, is not in finding variance but in identifying just that portion of the variance that is due to the student's degree of mastery of the particular objective on which the CRT is based, rather than variance due to some extraneous influence.

Item and Test Bias

"Item bias" may be defined as a group by item interaction; that is, the profiles of performance of different groups (such as males versus females) across all items in the test are not parallel. "Test bias" is defined as a group by test interaction; that is, groups do not have the same shaped profile of scores across the various tests being considered (Cleary, 1966; Cleary and Hilton, 1968). Little attention has been paid to CRTs with respect to these kinds of biases, although they have become important topics within the general measurement field.

It should be noted, however, that the identification of a test or set of tests as being "biased" with respect to certain groups does not necessarily mean that the measures should be revised. The reason for this is that such "bias" may only mean that the educational and cultural experiences of the groups taking the tests are systematically different, and the basis for these differences and how to deal with them should be examined. It is entirely likely, for example, for a test to appear biased simply because it draws more on the vocabulary from certain texts than it does from others, and the use of the more test-dependent texts is not random in the population of examinees. Wider use of the more dependent texts would, therefore, remove the supposed "bias" in the test; changing the test to be more representative of the texts used would also achieve the same result.

Test Scores

As noted in the preface to this paper, one of the two essential features of a CRT is that an individual's or a group's score on it is interpreted in terms of the level of performance obtained with respect to the achievement of the objective(s) on which the CRT is based. This type of score reporting is contrasted to the norm referenced approach, in which a student's or a group's score is interpreted with respect to the performance of other individuals or groups (Popham and Husek, 1969). The primary advantage of the CRT approach is, therefore, its ability to provide a means for describing what the student (or group) can do, or what it knows or feels, without having to consider the skills, knowledge, or attitudes of others.

There is some question, however, as to whether a CRT can really do this (Klein, 1970; Davis, 1971; Ebel, 1972). For example, if parents are told that their child has mastered a given objective or set of objectives, their first question is, "Is this performance satisfactory?" In other words, they are asking whether the child is progressing satisfactorily, and the only frame of reference one can give in this situation is the rate of progress of other students. The fact that such a normative frame of reference can easily be provided also points out that one can make norm referenced interpretations of CRT scores. The distinctive feature of a CRT score must, therefore, lie in its emphasis on describing the absolute, rather than the relative, level of performance with respect to an objective or skill. Because of this emphasis, different kinds of scores are generally reported for CRTs than for norm referenced measures. Some of the different kinds of scores that can be reported for CRTs that reflect emphasis on objectives are listed below:

The number or percent correct on a given objective or set of items that encompass a few highly related objectives.

"Mastery" of a given objective or set of items where "mastery" is defined in terms of a certain level of performance, such as 90 percent correct.

The time it takes (such as in class hours or calendar days) for an individual to achieve a given performance level (including what has been defined as "mastery") (Harris, 1973).

The time (in minutes or hours) it takes a student to perform a certain task or set of tasks related to an objective (such as correctly computing the product of all single-digit numerals).

The probability that the student is ready to begin the next level of instruction (this may be based on both the number of items correct and the pattern of answers given to these items).

The percentage of students who "pass" each item; that is, the item's difficulty. This kind of score is used exclusively in program evaluation, where each item or task is considered important in itself.

Of all the scores listed above, the ones that have been the focus of most discussion are those that imply that the student has achieved "mastery" (Millman, 1972). The reason for this attention is that while such a score comes closest to the underlying spirit of a CRT, there is rarely a good way of definiting exactly what is meant by "mastery." Arbitrary definitions, such as 85 percent correct, are rampant; but there is rarely any satisfactory criterion for setting such standards of performance. Further, a mastery score often hides the true level of student performance. In other words, if the student failed to achieve mastery, did he miss by a little or miss by a great deal; or, if he made it, did he just squeak by? Finally, the problems inherent in the construction of items for a CRT, and especially those dealing with the defining of the acceptable item types, item selection procedures, and item difficulty, severely limit the interpretation of what is means by "mastery."

Packaging and Other Considerations

How a CRT is finally put together and packaged is again a function of the purpose(s) for which it will be used, relative to the various kinds of constraints imposed on its development and use. When there is a vast number of objectives to be assessed and it is not considered reasonable to develop a separate CRT for each, one or more of the following techniques are used:

Combine objectives that are considered highly related to one another into a single measure.

Select a group of objectives from the total pool of objectives based on a set of appropriate criteria (such as those presented in the Appendix).

Limit the scope of each objective so as to reduce the potential number of items and/or tasks that might be needed to measure it.

All of these techniques do, of course, require the use of experts in the fields of measurement and curriculum in order to make sound compromises from both content and methodological points of view.

The methods of packaging and distributing CRTs are quite varied. One of the potentially most functional techniques involves printing tests on spirit masters, so that each teacher can duplicate the copies needed for a given class without having to purchase large numbers of test booklets. A second innovation that appears to have promise is referencing the objective, and even the test item, to specific instructional materials. In one such case, the test form was printed in such a way that the teacher was told immediately whether the student passed the item, and in the event of a failure a manual then directed teachers to materials for additional instruction.

PRESENT EFFORT IN CRITERION REFERENCED TESTING

This section summarizes the results of a survey conducted to assess current efforts in criterion referenced testing. All information is based on data provided directly by the projects themselves or through associated technical reports, journal articles, and interviews.

Although special emphasis was given to criterion referenced measures in mathematics, related developmental efforts in other content areas were also reviewed. The list of projects reported here is not exhaustive but can be viewed as representative of the general state of the art in criterion referenced testing.

Five defining characteristics of criterion referenced testing programs have been identified. They include program focus, instructional dependence, objective and item generation, test models and packaging, and test scores. Each of these characteristics has already been discussed in the first section of this paper; however, some further explanation regarding the scale used for the instructional dependence category is needed.

California Test Bureau—McGraw-Hill (CTB) Prescriptive Mathematics Inventory (PMI)

Focus. CTB is interested in the construction of CRT programs for classroom management. In particular the PMI was designed to measure 351 objectives representing the mathematics curriculum nominally taught in grades 4 through 8.

Instructional Dependency. Small. Neither the objectives nor the test items reflect any instructional bias.

Objective and Item Generation. Using a "consensus approach," objectives were culled from the text materials most widely used in schools, collated from each source into a single list, classified into broader objectives classifications, and analyzed with respect to content and a hierarchical structure. Items were then developed to measure these objectives. (Note: On the PMI only one item is used to assess each objective.)

Test Model and Packaging. The PMI is divided into four levels, based on the objectives most commonly taught in grades 4 and 5, 5 and 6, 6 and 7, and 7 and 8. The test items sample various levels of difficulty in each of the content categories represented. In responding to the PMI, the student records his answers on unique, item-specific, machine-scoreable answer grids specially designed to eliminate guessing.

In addition to the actual PMI test, CTB/McGraw-Hill offers the following support materials and services:

Complete scoring and reporting services (i.e., that provide information on objectives mastered and not yet mastered)

Practice exercise booklets, an examiner's manual and class information sheet (to identify the class and tests)

An Individual Diagnostic Matrix (reporting the student's score on each objective)

A Class Diagnostic Matrix (reporting average class scores on each objective)

An Individual Study Guide (that references pages in texts where material can be found for objectives which the student did not master)

A Class Grouping Report (that lists students according to their deficiencies in major content areas)

Test Scores. Because one item is used to measure each behavior, the mastery criterion for each objective is that the student correctly solve the associated item (Roudabush, 1971). Test scores are then reported in terms of mastery or non-mastery for each objective.

Four different types of reports are available for reporting test scores: two individual reports for each student, and two reports for the class. The Individual Diagnostic Matrix shows a profile of the student's mastery or nonmastery of the objectives. The Individual Study Guide gives page references for a selected textbook covering those objectives not yet mastered by the student. The Class Diagnostic Matrix summarizes test results for the whole class in terms of the percentage of students mastering each objective. And finally, the Class Grouping Report indicates how students fall into achievement groups within the mathematics curriculum, and provides page references to the textbook being used in the classroom for materials covering objectives that were frequently missed.

Additional information available from:

CTB/McGraw-Hill
Del Monte Research Park
Monterey, California 93940

Comprehensive Achievement Monitoring (CAM)

Focus. CAM is designed as a computer-assisted, multipurpose evaluation system useful at individual, group, district, or state levels.

The CAM model is based on two attributes: (1) a flexible time-series design (testing at frequent intervals), which can be varied to meet the financial limitations and information needs of the user, and (2) a procedure for sampling students and items which both introduces economy into testing and increases the comprehensiveness of behavior samples available from each testing session.

At present, the New York State Department of Education has installed a CAM or modifications of CAM in five school districts. Although programs have mostly involved math, they are currently being extended to science and reading.

Instructional Dependency: Large. CAM is constructed to be most effective when the items relate directly to course objectives.

Objective and Item Generation. Curricula are defined by behavioral objectives which are systematically coded for easy identification, retrieval, and grouping, and by one or more classifications. This process is typically carried out by potential system users (that is, teacher groups).

With respect to objectives specification, a "behavioral analysis" of course content requires that the user (1) prepare a topical course outline, (2) specify the general course objectives derived from the content (in nonbehavioral terms), (3) specify the terminal course objectives (in behavioral terms), and (4) specify enabling objectives (in behavioral terms). Objectives are then organized into classifications, typically utilizing Ammerman and Melching's (1966) classification system for the specificity of instructional objectives by their relationship to terminal student performance.

Items are developed by system users (teachers) directly from objectives, and are then judged (typically by the item writers themselves) for their consistency with the objectives. Considerations of error from guessing, ease of scoring, criterion referenced versus norm referenced test interpretations, and general item writing skills (that is, "the item stem must be worded to require specific response") guide item construction activities.

Test Model and Packaging. The typical set of CAM tests is constructed around the stated objectives of the course or program to be evaluated. Objectives, items, and test forms are typically generated by system users in accordance with instructions provided in a user's manual.

Generally, a pool of items is constructed with approximately four to 10 samples per objective. Through random stratified sampling items are assigned to test forms, creating parallel test forms or monitors. Students receive the test forms in a random order at fixed testing intervals (determined by the user's information needs). Each test form contains a fixed number of items, representing objectives which are taught between test administrations. Test forms are usually short, requiring from 10 to 30 minutes of testing time.

Test Scores. Through sampling of test items and testing at frequent intervals, CAM generates performance data on all course objectives in relation to three phases of time: before instruction, immediately after instruction, and retention over long periods of time.

After each test administration, each student receives a report listing the correct and incorrect responses to every item, as well as total scores on current and previous tests. Group data area also provided, in the form of percent achievement by designated objectives for each test administration. Finally, achievement profiles, which graphically display the level of achievement (in terms of percent correct test scores) for all previous and current tests on selected objectives, are available quarterly.

Additional information available from:

Robert O'Reilly
Chief, Bureau of School & Cultural Research
University of the State of New York
State Education Department
Albany, New York 12224

William Gorth
School of Education
University of Massachusetts
Amherst, Massachusetts 01002

Individualized Criterion Referenced Testing (ICRT)

Focus. ICRT offers criterion referenced testing programs emphasizing individual student achievement and providing two basic kinds of information: first, the specific knowledge and skills which the student has learned, and second, the specific knowledge and skills which are the next instructional steps to be mastered. At present such testing programs are available in reading and mathematics; the following comments will focus primarily on the mathematics system.

Instructional Dependency: Large. The basis for the criterion referenced tests is a set of specified instructional objectives which describe the Continuous Progress Laboratory's Math program.

Objective and Item Generation: Instructional objectives referenced to the Continuous Progress Laboratory's math curriculum are arranged from the most elementary to the most difficult, forming an instructional continuum. From this instructional continuum those objectives common to most curricula, and expected of most students, are selected as testing objectives. These selected objectives, arranged with respect to item difficulty, constitute a testing continuum. The testing continuum is then used as a basis for item and test generation.

Test Models and Packaging: ICRT provides test kits for each grade level, 1–8. Each test kit has sufficient tests for an average class, a teacher's manual, a scoring template and an orientation kit. In addition, each kit (with the exception of level 1) contains multiple copies of the grade level test booklets as well as multiple copies of booklets for up to two levels below the indicated grade level of the kit.

Tests are designed to be self-administered or administered with teacher guidance. All the tests are power tests with no implied time limit. Each test has approximately 16 items (two items per objective). The student records his responses to the test items on computer cards. Directions for test scoring are included in the teacher's guide.

Four kinds of score reports are available: A District Summary, a Building Summary, a Class Summary, and a Student Summary. The Student Summary provides prescriptive instructional resources.

Test Scores: Students' scores on each objective are reported to District, Building, and Class Summaries: students' scores are reported in terms of how many students are at various working levels (a student's approximate working level is determined by the first test booklet in which he or she missed three or more objectives). The Student Summary is intended as a prescriptive instrument, indicating which objectives have been mastered, which require review, and which should be learned next. In addition, prescriptive instructional resources are suggested for objectives which the student needs to review or learn. These prescriptive guides are referenced to the Continuous Progress Laboratory Math Program, the supplementary drill tapes, and three additional curricula selected by the user.

Additional information available from:

Louis Miller, Vice President
Educational Progress Corporation
3000 Sand Hill Road
Menlo Park, California 94025

Charles Carlson
Educational Progress Corporation
4900 South Lewis Avenue
Tulsa, Oklahoma 74105

Instructional Objectives Exchange (IOX)

Focus. A criterion referenced test program has been developed to complement the IOX objectives collections. The decision to develop these objectives-based tests represents an effort to provide readily usable support materials, to assess individual student progress and to facilitate classroom management.

Instructional Dependency: Small. Neither the objectives booklets nor the criterion references tests are based on any particular curriculum or instructional program.

Objective and Item Generation. Within each subject area objectives are defined in terms of relevant topics and skills at three levels of generality. Criteria for sampling the most general categories include importance of the area, economy of production into tests, and practical scoreability. Selection of the type of learner behavior to serve as the specific objective is then guided by considerations of transferability or generalizability within a content area, importance, terminality (that is, the highest step in a hierarchy), transferability outside the area, ease in scoring, and amenability to instruction.

Rooted in Wells Hively's (1970, 1973) item form analysis, expanded objectives (called amplified objectives) are used to define permissible stimulus and response options for item generation. For each objective only one type of test item is used; the associated item format is then carefully defined by an amplified objective.

Test Models and Packaging. IOX provides manuals listing objectives, sets of criterion referenced tests, and a user's guide or test manual. In the area of elementary mathematics, for example, there are five independent sets of criterion referenced measures which cover the nine mathematics strands identified by the California State Department of Education. For each set of tests a parallel set is available to facilitate pre- and posttesting (that is, each set of tests is available in a form A and a form B, which contain parallel tests).

Tests are distributed on one-page, preprinted spirit masters which can be used by teachers to duplicate sufficient copies for their students. The typical test is multiple choice in format, contains five to 10 items, and requires about 30 minutes to complete. The test manual provides a list of objectives in that area, sample test items, complete instructions for test administration, answer keys, and a guide for classifying scores in terms of achievement levels (whether or not the student attained mastery).

Test Scores. Although directions are provided in a user's guide for classifying scores into mastery groups, IOX does not provide forms for reporting scores or suggestions for tabulating test scores.

Additional information available from:

Instructional Objectives Exchange
Box 24095
Los Angeles, California 90024

MINNEMAST Curriculum Project— University of Minnesota

Focus. The MINNEMAST Project represents an experimental effort to develop a coordinated and sequential mathematics and science curriculum for the elementary school. As part of the evaluation of this project, a technology for criterion referenced test construction was developed by Hively and his associates at the University of Minnesota. These tests were primarily intended to assess the MINNEMAST Program itself, rather than individual students' progress.

Instructional Dependency: Small. Test items were generated that reflect the entire range of skills and behaviors associated with a given objective.

Objective and Item Generation. Relevant learner behaviors and skills associated with a given content area were organized (by the MINNEMAST staff) into classes called learning domains. The basic notion underlying this process is that important classes of content and skill would be completely defined in terms of behaviorally stated, structured sets, or domains.

Rules for generating test items for a given learning domain are organized into formal schemes called item forms. There are three major components to an item form: (1) instructions (directions given to students), (2) stimulus characteristics (the skills and behaviors an item can cover, and rules for constructing specific kinds of items), and (3) response characteristics (acceptable way of responding to an item, for example written or oral responses).

Test Models and Packaging. (It should be noted that the MINNEMAST efforts reported here were field test activities, and consequently a final packaging mode was not available). The MINNEMAST curriculum was divided into discrete units. For each unit the teacher was provided with a handbook containing a sequence of lessons, general statements about goals, explanatory background information, and lists of materials needed for lessons.

Test construction was computer-assisted and conducted by the MINNEMAST staff. A system of student-item sampling was utilized to gather information on all test items with a minimum of testing time. To this end computer printout labels were generated for each student, listing his or her name, identifying data such as class and school, and the items assigned to him or her. When all the items specified from an item form had been written, the computer printout labels were attached to them and the items were then collated into tests for the individual students.

Test Scores. The principal data derived from the MINNEMAST testing program were the proportion of correct responses. Whenever possible, however, additional information was reported concerning the kinds of correct and incorrect responses being made.

Although no set format for reporting scores was stipulated, data were usually presented in tables showing complete item-by-item listings of actual responses, as well as frequencies of various categories of responses (for example, frequencies for individual items, item forms or objectives, and groups of objectives). Due to the absence of empirical evidence, desired levels of achievement were not established in advance of testing.

Additional information available from:

Wells Hively
Department of Psychology
University of Minnesota
Minneapolis, Minnesota 55455

National Assessment of Educational Progress (NAEP)

Focus. The purpose of NAEP is the assessment of educational attainments on a national basis.

Instructional Dependency: Small. Neither objectives nor items are referenced to any curriculum test or instructional program.

Objective and Item Generation. NAEP defines its objectives and the associated skills and behaviors (the "domain of reference") through a national consensus regarding the important goals and outcomes of education with respect to a given subject area.

Objectives developed by NAEP's Exercise Development Department are reviewed by external subject matter experts and lay groups. Following the development of objectives, contracts are awarded for item generation. The amount of items developed for a given objective is based on a weighting scheme determined by the subject matter experts. A framework for item writing is provided by a system of exercise prototypes that define four characteristics of an item: (1) administrative mode (can the item be administered individually or to a group), (2) stimulus mode (audio, visual, and so on), (3) response mode (multiple choice of free response), and (4) response category (written, verbal, roll playing, and so on).

Test Models and Packaging. Tests are designed exclusively for measuring student achievement on a national scale.

The number of items for a given objective is determined by a weighting scale based on priorities identified by the subject matter experts. Tests are available at four age levels (9, 13, 17, and adult). Two subject areas are currently being assessed each year, with a five-year reassessment cycle. (Mathematics is scheduled for the 1972-1973 school year.) Two hundred and ten minutes of testing are allotted annually to each subject at each age level.

Test Scores. Scores are generally reported as the percentage of correct responses by items, and for various classes of items. For example, items dealing with solving algebraic equations might be compared with items on mathematical induction. In addition, scores are broken down in terms of typical performance by region, sex, SES, and so on.

Additional information available from:

> National Assessment of Educational Progress
> 822 Lincoln Tower
> 1860 Lincoln Street
> Denver, Colorado 80203

Southwest Regional Laboratory (SWRL)

Focus. SWRL is involved in the development of text-referenced instructional management systems that operate in conjunction with a developed curriculum. At present such a classroom management system in reading is available at the kindergarten level, and a math system is under development. Criterion referenced tests have been incorporated into this system to assess student progress.

Instructional Dependency: Large. The SWRL program is specifically based on a predefined curriculum: ". . . to be minimally useful the (CR) test must be specifically referenced to a prespecified structure of achievement. To be maximally useful the tests must be specifically referenced to defined instructional materials" (Baker, R. L., 1972).

Objective and Item Generation. Hively's (1973) item form approach and related processes are utilized to define classes of behaviors and skills associated with specific content areas. A collection of item forms, sequentially organized, together with a list of constraints on item generation, provide the framework for defining total content areas in behavioral terms (a "universe of content"). Strings of item forms are then organized into tentative sequences, or "instructional specifications," that map out the instructional and evaluation efforts consistent with the item forms.

Test Models and Packaging. With respect to evaluation activities each instructional management system provides:

> A means (vis-a-vis testing) for student placement

> Criterion referenced measures on three to eight instructional outcomes 10 to 15 times during the year. (Note: These tests are constructed for specific information purposes—to assess student progress

on objectives attended to by a specific curriculum.)

> Additional practice materials for the instructional outcomes which have continuity throughout the text

> A midyear and end-of-year evaluation measure

> A Quality Assurance System (a user's manual, providing directions and pacing information)

Test Scores. The Quality Assurance Manual provides forms for reporting the means, standard deviations, and percent of students attaining criterion performance. Regression analyses between criterion scores on final and midyear criterion referenced tests are also reported, based on a large student sample.

Additional information available from:

> Southwest Regional Laboratory for
>   Educational Research and Development
> 4665 Lampson Avenue
> Los Alamitos, California 90720

System for Objectives Based Assessment—Reading (SOBAR)
Center for the Study of Evaluation: UCLA

Focus. SOBAR basically constitutes an item bank integrated into a selection/delivery system intended as a multipurpose evaluation procedure appropriate at the individual, group, or program level. Designed to serve as an exemplary objectives based assessment system, SOBAR includes a set of performance objectives covering the entire spectrum of a content area (in this case that of reading, grades K-12), a classification system for selecting objectives, and a bank of assessment items keyed to specific objectives.

Instructional Dependency: Small. SOBAR is seen as a flexible, multipurpose test generation system that is not dependent on a given instructional program or information need.

Objective and Item Generation. A set of objectives was developed by the SOBAR staff (with the help of reading experts) to cover the complete content area of reading. These objectives were then classified into categories reflecting various skill areas and levels of generality. Upon completion of objective specification, the SOBAR staff constructed items keyed to the objectives. During item writing special attention was given to the independence (nonredundancy) of items, objective item congruence, and the comprehensiveness of items. The system is referenced to performance objectives.

Test Models and Packaging. Among the materials and services provided to users SOBAR includes:

> A comprehensive catalogue of nearly 500 objectives. (These objectives cover grades K-12 and are divided into six major skill categories.)

> A guide and selection chart to aid the user in selecting objectives appropriate to local priorities.

> Computer-generated reports of the outcome of the objective selection process.

Tests for each SOBAR objective. These measures are leveled by grade clusters: K-3, 4-6, 7-9, and 10-12. Depending on the nature of the objective, a test for an individual objective may contain from five to 20 test items.

Test construction is viewed in terms of the user's specific information needs. Items are selected for tests according to the test model appropriate for a given test situation. In addition, tests can be assembled at different levels of objective generality.

Test Scores. At present SOBAR has not begun to field-test methods of score reporting and interpretation.

Additional information available from:

> SOBAR Project
> Center for the Study of Evaluation
> University of California
> 145 Moore Hall
> Los Angeles, California 90024

Zweig and Associates

Focus. Zweig offers a criterion referenced testing program based on behavioral objectives and indexed to prescriptions for teaching alternatives. At present such testing programs, designed for classroom management within the context of individualized instruction, are available in reading and mathematics. The Fountain Valley Teacher Support System in mathematics was reviewed for this paper. Comments are largely based on the Fountain Valley System.

Instructional Dependency: Small. Objectives and items cover the entire spectrum of skills reflected in the nine mathematics strands for California.

Objective and Item Generation. Objectives and items are generated by teacher groups (followed by a review from experts) and reflect skills in each of the nine mathematical strands developed by the California State Department of Education. Strands are measured at each grade level, K-8, for which there is pertinent instruction. Typically, three to five items are constructed for each objective.

Test Models and Packaging. The Fountain Valley System includes:

> 785 objectives organized by strand and grade level
>
> 196 self-scoring, self-administering tests
>
> Continuous Pupil Progress Profiles to record individual student achievement
>
> Class ditto masters to document group performance
>
> Teacher Manuals for each grade level (that include a listing of all objectives at that level)
>
> Manuals of criterion referenced teaching alternatives

All materials are color-coded. Tape cassettes at each level provide directions for test administration. Each test is printed on a sealed form made of treated paper that automatically records student's responses on the reverse side of the test sheet as the student takes the test. In addition, the reverse side indicates correct or incorrect responses by a number code which corresponds to the objective and strand being tested, and provides a score interpretation key to classify scores into "proceed" and "reteach" categories.

At each grade level a Teaching Alternatives Manual documents (by number code) prescriptive activities (for skills falling into the reteach category) listed by number code under each publisher's name and series.

Test Scores. Student scores in each skill for each of the nine strands are recorded on a Continuous Pupil Progress Profile (CPPP). The objectives for each strand are arranged on the CPPP in a hierarchy of difficulty, grouped by grade levels and designated by color and number codes. Objectives measured by each test are then grouped between heavy lines. Student scores are recorded on the CPPP as either "reteach" or "proceed" in accordance with scoring instructions on the answer sheet. These instructions give the number of incorrect answers that determine the classification for each skill.

Additional information available from:

> Richard L. Zweig Associates, Inc.
> 20800 Beach Boulevard
> Huntington Beach, California 92648

Summary and Conclusions

This paper has attempted to outline the basic steps and procedures in the development of criterion referenced tests, as well as the issues and problems associated with these activities. In addition, representative CRT systems have been reviewed. From this analysis it is clear that the developer of a CRT must answer a number of questions in order to clarify the nature and purpose of a CRT:

> For what decision areas and purposes is the CRT most applicable?
>
> What areas and objectives does the CRT cover, and how were these objectives derived and organized?
>
> How broadly or narrowly are the objectives defined?
>
> How were the test items, or tasks chosen to measure the objectives, defined and developed?
>
> How dependent are the items on particular instructional materials or programs? And what is their applicability to different kinds of students?
>
> What methods were used to improve the items on the CRT, and why were they chosen relative to the purpose of the instrument?
>
> How was the validity of the CRT established?
>
> What kinds of scores should be reported for a CRT, and what is the justification for these scores, especially those involving "mastery"?
>
> How was the test finally put together, what compromises had to be made, and how were they resolved?
>
> In what ways will packaging of the CRT facilitate its use?

These questions will hopefully serve three functions. The first is that they will guide CRT developers to the issues that must be addressed in both the construction process and in the manual that accompanies the final instrument. The second purpose these questions may serve is to guide researchers to those problems of major interest within the field of criterion referenced testing. Finally, they will help the purchasers of CRTs to understand better the kinds of variables they must consider, in order to make a wise selection of instruments and an appropriate interpretation of the results obtained with them. Certainly the publication of a set of minimum standards for CRTs by an appropriate professional organization would go a long way toward ensuring that these functions have been carried out successfully.

APPENDIX:
IOX Criteria for Selecting Objectives*

The following criteria should be applied in deciding on the type of learner behavior which will serve as the specific objective, thereafter to guide the test construction:

Transferability Within Domain. The form of learner behavior selected should be the most generalizable of those represented in the content general domain; i.e., a learner mastering the designated behavior requirements would likely be able to transfer that mastery to most, if not all, of the other eligible behavioral requirements in the content-general domain.

In making such a selection it is important to consider the entire range of learner behaviors with which we are concerned, i.e., both test-like events and real world events. For instance, in surveying an individual's mathematical competence we should be attentive not only to the X_1, X_2, and X_3, which we can represent via standard test formats, but to the X_{17}, X_{18}, and X_{19}, which might reflect such skills as the ability to make change in a supermarket or to complete one's annual income tax report.

The test constructor should sketch out as wide a range of alternatives as possible, then select the one testable learner behavior which will most readily transfer to the other learner behaviors delimited by the content-general objective.

Widely Accepted. The objective selected should be the most widely accepted as important by those in the field. Unlike the IOX objective collections, where we present a wide array of alternatives and then encourage educators to choose among them, here we will have to go with the majority preference. Clearly, this criterion is not unrelated to the first criterion cited, but it may be profitable to apply it independently.

Terminality. If there is a degree of possible hierarchy present in the contending types of learner behaviors under consideration, such that some are considered pre-

cursive or enroute to others, the chosen specific objective should represent the most terminal learner behavior.

Transferability Outside the Domain. Another consideration in selecting a specific objective is the degree to which that behavior, once mastered, will be transferable outside the content-general domain, for example to domains which might be learned by students in the future. For instance, certain skills acquired by students in one course (such as the ability to distinguish between fact and opinion) may have reference to many other courses. Such high-transfer skills and intellectual constructs should be given high priority in the selection of specific objectives.

Ease of Scorability. In an effort to produce tests which have considerable practical utility, we must try to select learner behaviors which, other factors being equal, can be easily scored by those educators employing them. Again, this does not limit us to selected response items, for in some instances we shall surely find it necessary to utilize constructed response formats. (This may help distinguish the IOX tests from typical standardized tests.) Nevertheless, scoring practically is an important consideration.

Now how should these five criteria be employed in selecting the specific objectives? Should they be weighted equally, in descending order, or in reverse order (stratified according to number of two syllable words in the descriptive paragraphs)? Sorry, but no handy scheme is available for mechanical translation into decisions. Test constructors must, however, be self-consciously attentive to each of the five points. We may devise a check sheet or other shorthand form to encourage such attention. If the test developer has exhausted all rational alternatives, an arbitrary selection is always possible.

Having chosen the specific objectives, that is, the categories to be used in generating a pool of homogeneous test items which assess a given learner behavior, the next task involves the production of a defensible set of such items.

NOTES

[1] These performance standards are usually behaviorally stated, for example: "The student will be able to perform all fundamental mathematical operations involving single-digit integers."

REFERENCES

Airasian, P., and Madaus, G. Criterion Referenced Testing in the Classroom. *Measurement in Education,* 1972, *3* (4), 1-8.

Baker, E. L. Using Measurement to Improve Instruction. Paper presented at Convention of American Psychological Association, Honolulu, Hawaii, 1972, ED 069 762.

_____. Measurement Considerations in Instruction Product Development. Paper presented at Conference on Problems in Objectives Based Measurement, Center for the Study of Evaluation, University of California, 1972.

Bormuth, J. P. *On the Theory of Achievement Test Items.* Chicago: University of Chicago Press, 1970.

Cleary, T. Test Bias: Validity of the Scholastic Aptitude Test for Negro and White Students in Integrated Colleges. Research Bulletin 66-31. Princeton, New Jersey: Educational

---

*Excerpted with permission of the author, W. J. Popham, from *Selecting Objectives and Generating Test Items for Objectives-Based Tests,* Los Angeles, IOX, 1972.

Testing Service, 1966. ED 018 200.

_____, and Hilton, T. An Investigation of Item Bias. *Educational and Psychological Measurement,* 1968, *28* (1), 61-75.

Cox, R., and Vargus, J. C. A Comparison of Item Selection Techniques for Norm Referenced and Criterion Referenced Tests. Pittsburgh: Center for the Study of Instructional Programs, Learning Research and Development Center, University of Pittsburgh, 1966.

Cronbach, L. J. Test Validation. In L. Thorndike, ed., *Educational Measurement* (2nd ed.). Washington, D.C.: American Council on Education, 1971.

Dahl, T. A. The Measurement of Congruence Between Learning Objectives and Test Items. Unpublished doctoral dissertation, University of California, Los Angeles, 1971.

Davis, F. B. Criterion Referenced Tests. Paper presented at Annual AERA Meeting, New York, 1971. ED 050 154.

_____. Criterion Referenced Measurement. 1971 AERA Conference Summaries, ERIC/TM Report 12, 1972. Princeton, New Jersey: ERIC Clearinghouse on Tests, Measurement, and Evaluation, 1972. ED 060 134.

_____. Criterion Referenced Measurement. 1972 AERA Conference Summaries, ERIC/TM Report 17, 1973. Princeton, New Jersey: ERIC Clearinghouse on Tests, Measurement, and Evaluation, 1973. ED 073 143.

Ebel, R. L. Evaluation and Education Objectives: Behavioral and Otherwise. Paper presented at the Convention of the American Psychological Association, Honolulu, Hawaii, 1972.

Glaser, R. Instructional Technology and the Measurement of Learning Outcomes: Some Questions. *American Psychologist,* 1963, *18,* 519-521.

_____, and Nitko, A. Measurement in Learning and Instruction. In R. L. Thorndike, ed., *Educational Measurement* (2nd ed.). Washington, D.C.: American Council on Education, 1971, pp. 652-670.

Harris, C. Comments on Problems of Objectives Based Measurement. Paper presented at Annual AERA meeting, New Orleans, 1973.

Hively, W. Introduction to Domain Referenced Achievement Testing. Symposium presentation, AERA, Minnesota, 1970.

_____, Maxwell, G., Rabehl, G., Sension, D., and Lundin, S. Domain Referenced Curriculum Evaluation: A Technical Handbook and a Cast Study from the MINNEMAST Project. CSE Monograph Series in Evaluation, Volume 1. Center for the Study of Evaluation, University of California at Los Angeles, 1973.

Keller, C. M. Criterion Referenced Measurement: A Bibliography. Princeton, New Jersey: ERIC Clearinghouse on Tests, Measurement, and Evaluation, 1972. ED 060 041. Bibliography ERIC/TM Report 7, 1972.

Klein, S. P. Evaluating Tests in Terms of the Information They Provide. *Evaluation Comment,* 1970, *2* (2), 1-6. ED 045 699.

_____. An Evaluation of New Mexico's Educational Priorities. Paper presented at Western Psychological Association, Portland, 1972. TM 002 735.

Kosecoff, J. B., and Klein, S. P. Analyzing Tests and Test Items for Sensitivity to Instructional Effects. CSE Working Paper No. 24, Center for the Study of Evaluation, University of California at Los Angeles, 1973.

Kriewall, T. E., and Hirsch, E. The Development and Interpretation of Criterion Referenced Tests. Paper presented at Annual AERA Meeting, Los Angeles, California, 1969. ED 042 815.

Mager, R. F. *Preparing Instructional Objectives.* San Francisco: Fearon Publishers, Inc., 1962.

Millman, J. Passing Scores and Test Lengths for Domain Referenced Measures. Paper presented at Annual AERA Meeting, Chicago, 1972. ED 065 555.

Nitko, A. J. A Model for Criterion Referenced Tests Based on Use. Paper presented at Annual AERA Meeting, New York, 1971. ED 049 318.

_____. Problems in the Development of Criterion Referenced Tests. Paper presented at Annual AERA Meeting, New Orleans, 1973.

Ozenne, D. O. Toward an Evaluative Methodology for Criterion Referenced Measures: Test Sensitivity. CSE Report 72, Center for the Study of Evaluation, University of California, Los Angeles, 1971. ED 061 263.

Popham, W. J. *The Teacher-Empiricist; A Curriculum and Instruction Supplement.* Los Angeles: Lennox-Brown, Inc., 1965.

_____, and Husek, T. R. Implications of Criterion Referenced Measurement. *Journal of Educational Measurement,* 1967, *6* (1), 1-9.

_____. Indices of Adequacy for Criterion Referenced Test Items. Presentation at joint session of NCEM and AERA, Minneapolis, Minnesota, 1970.

_____. Selecting Objectives and Generating Test Items for Objectives Based Tests. Paper presented at Conference on Problems in Objectives Based Measurement, Center for the Study of Evaluation, University of California, Los Angeles, 1972.

Roudabush, G. Some Reliability Problems in a Criterion Referenced Test. Paper presented at Annual AERA Meeting, New York, 1971. ED 050 144.

_____. Item Selection of Criterion Referenced Tests. Paper presented at Annual AERA Meeting, New Orleans, 1973. ED 074 147.

Skager, R. Generating Criterion Referenced Tests from Objectives Based Assessment Systems: Unsolved Problems in Test Development, Assembly, and Interpretation. Paper presented at Annual AERA Meeting, New Orleans, 1973.

Wilson, H. A. A Humanistic Approach to Criterion Referenced Testing. Paper presented at Annual AERA Meeting, New Orleans, 1973.

Zweig, R., and Associates. Personal communication, March 15, 1973.

Selected References on Test Item Construction

Ebel, Robert L. *Essentials of Educational Measurement.* Englewood Cliffs, New Jersey: Prentice-Hall, Inc., 1972.

Gronlund, N. E. *Constructing Achievement Tests.* Englewood Cliffs, New Jersey: Prentice-Hall, 1968.

Wood, Dorothy A. *Test Construction.* Columbus, Ohio: Merrill, 1961.

32

RECORDS CONFIDENTIALITY
by Robert R. Wright
Office of Science Indicators
National Science Foundation

The rapid growth and potential for computer-based record keeping in the schools has raised to public attention the delicate balance between the educational institution's need for information about students and the students' basic rights to privacy and confidentiality, which are to be accorded all citizens. The policies and practices of the collection, maintenance, access, and dissemination of student data in the school setting have been severely criticized in recent years, and several major efforts have been made to establish guidelines for combatting the intentional or inadvertent invasion of student privacy and confidentiality. Then, in 1974, the "Buckley Amendment" (P.L. 93-380, as amended) gave Federal protection to most student records.

SCOPE AND REVIEW OF DEVELOPMENTS

This presentation discusses the nature of student records and their confidentiality. It then describes some of the current guidelines and makes suggestions for their implementation.

A brief historical perspective may explain why in recent years there has developed a need for records confidentiality. The first pupil record was established in 1838 in order to have more reliable attendance information. The compulsory education movement encouraged larger numbers of students to enter the schools, making it necessary to supplement teachers' memories with a permanent format for recording children's achievements. A wider variety of students were entering the schools, requiring variations in school programs and services. Guidance activities, including testing, were initiated to maximize the placement and progress of students, and records became an important professional tool. The acceptance of the elective course approach by secondary schools increased the variety of credentials being presented for graduation, and formal knowledge of these different patterns was necessary. Schools and school systems became much more complex, requiring a statistical information base to support policy-making, planning, and evaluation. There has been the very great increase in college-bound youth, who must provide extensive official information about their high school years in order to apply even to the most open-door of colleges. It has only been since the late 1960s that a widespread concern has developed over possible abuses and privacy invasion inherent in the uses of student records, forcing educators to examine openly their responsibilities to students, to the schools, and to the larger society.

What are the proper uses of pupil records? Most school personnel would strongly agree that records should serve only the educational mission of the school, but considerable disagreement exists on the scope of that mission. "Is not the school an instrument of society?" some would ask, and these would expect that all information on a child be housed in a single place and be available for society's convenience—including court or arrest records, family social service agency involvement, and much other information not usually related to the instructional process. As one participant in a survey (Allen, 1972) of the privacy of student files said, "The schools must give everyone, colleges, employers, the police, the F.B.I., businesses, and others that might have dealings with the students whatever information they request. This would help people know what kind of a person they are dealing with" (p. 94). This attitude implies that the end justifies the means, assumes that the filed data are accurate and that the information recipient will use the information ethically, and overlooks the inequity of the requestor having considerably more

"knowledge" about the student than the student does of himself, since one's school records are often unavailable for student inspection.

Basically, school records should serve two purposes: instruction and management. Since education is change, records are used to record changes in the performance of both students and teachers. Records serve as surrogates for future performance, and therefore are very important to the student. Records are increasingly the basis for reporting to school systems, state and Federal agencies involved in planning, program evaluation, resource allocation, and educational research. But underlying all these uses of student records is the principle that "the interest of the student must supercede all other purposes to which records might be put" (*Code of Student Rights and Responsibilities*, p. 12).

Have abuses of the privacy of student information files occurred? Information gathered for one purpose has been used for other purposes. Inaccurate data are sometimes inserted in a file, without the opportunity for its verification by school staff or by the pupils. Data held for a long time after a student has outgrown a trait (or the behavior is no longer considered serious) can be a lasting handicap to the person. Subjective records tend to be negative, while exemplary behavior or characteristics are not equally recorded. School medical records are often available to teachers. Barone (1971) found that over three-fourths of his responding districts permitted access to the records for nonprofessional staff, and half of these districts permitted external third parties to receive file information from these nonprofessional staff members. Sixty percent of Barone's districts permitted the release of personality test results and disciplinary records by telephone to third parties (p. 19). In the Goslin and Bordier survey (1970), parents had the lowest access of all other groups, even less than nonschool requestors such as juvenile courts without subpoena, health department officials, C.I.A. or F.B.I. agents, and prospective employers.

Releasing information to persons other than for educational purposes, and without the student's or his parents' consent, is what is generally meant by the invasion of records privacy. More important, however, is what the recipient does with the information received; once the information has been released, even with proper consent, there is seldom any way to control subsequent dissemination. The conference on the ethical and legal aspects of school record-keeping sponsored in 1969 by the Russell Sage Foundation concluded that from the widespread lack of formal confidentiality policies, substantial opportunity exists for privacy invasion by the improper use of school records (*Guidelines,* 1970).

There has been a tendency for the keeper of records to bear the total responsibility for privacy abuses. However, we must not forget the all-too-human tendency to be curious about our neighbors and yet hold ourselves apart from others. But whether the reason for keeping records is allegedly benign (as in claims for more efficient decision-making) or as a means of controlling people (as in identifying "predelinquents"), the *user* of the information from personal files must be the proper focus of potential abuse. It would be useful to have studies of the deeper psychological reasons why some records systems have accumulated far more data than needed for educational purposes, why educational systems are expected to be informers to the larger society, how students are distorting their records with an eye toward real or imagined uses and misuses, and what the factors are that account for varying tolerance toward records confidentiality violations among different people.

Searching in the law for guidance on issues of records privacy until recently has not been of much assistance. As Vanderpool (1971) pointed out, little mention is made in state statutes regarding pupil personnel records, but there is a growing protection of privacy being provided by the courts. He found that only nine states had statutes specifying closed pupil personnel files, three states permitted release of data from these files, and the remaining 38 states' statutes were mute on this topic. Steim (1971) reports that most states have no legislative guidelines relating the concept of privileged information to the field of education, and therefore student records are confidential only by an ethical obligation, rather than "privileged", because there is usually no legal power to prevent disclosure (as is necessary for the privileged status of patient/physician communication, for example). In 1974, the Congress initiated a section of the General Education Provisions Act which set out requirements designed to protect the privacy of students and parents (P.L. 93-380, as amended).

The only court decision dealing directly with student personnel records has been in New York State (*Van Allen*, 1961), which concluded that student records are open for inspection by school personnel and a child's parents. This access is based on the in loco parentis delegation of educational authority to the school by parents.

Prominent in the commonly accepted rationale for the need to have better records privacy is the great potential for abuse represented by advanced technologies, particularly computers. Unquestionably, the centralization of data files and the lowering of unit costs have been accompanied by expansion of the file contents and the tendency to merge what were once separate files, rather than simply a lessening of administrative costs. Reubenhausen expressed well the contrast between automated and manual files (*Guidelines*, 1970): "There was a time when among the strongest allies of privacy were the inefficiency of man, the fallibility of his memory, and the healing compassion that accompanied both the passing of time and the warmth of human recollection. These allies are now being put to rout" (pp. 5-6). But what is often overlooked is the easier physical access to non-automated files, with the same personal injury if file contents are inappropriately disseminated. Computerized files are less likely to contain subjective notes and narrative information—the very kind of material least likely to be verifiable and most likely in need of confidential handling.

Unlike adults, children cannot give an informed consent for data collection or dissemination, because they cannot comprehend the possible uses and misuses of data. They often trust the school, and either do not know they can refuse, for example, to be interviewed or have their personalities assessed, or believe they must concur

in a request for information or suffer retribution. As Allen (1972) has said:

> A special relationship of trust and confidence exists between the school and its students. In most matters concerning this relationship the student has no effective appeal to a higher authority, nor can the disclosure of unauthorized information be recalled after the damage has been done. The school and the student do not meet on equal terms, nor do they at arm's length. The school plays a dominant role in a relationship to which the student is an involuntary party." (p. 5)

No voluntary set of principles and recommendations about records confidentiality has had such a widespread input and dissemination as the report of a conference sponsored in 1969 by the Russell Sage Foundation (*Guidelines*, 1970). While this report was generally hailed by civil libertarians and supported by counseling professionals, it was often considered impractical by administrators who saw it as requiring a considerable increase in staff effort. However, as the report itself indicated, there may also be a substantial reduction in workload as ad hoc decisions are replaced by more routine procedures.

The N.E.A. published a subsequent report (*Code*, 1971) which differs from the Russell Sage *Guidelines* only slightly. The studies by Vanderpool (1971), Soto (1971), Allen (1972), and Wheeler (1970) provide additional suggestions for specific policy provisions. All of these outstanding sources have been drawn on heavily for the following description of the development of a policy on school records confidentiality.

SPECIFIC RECOMMENDATIONS

Every school or school system should have a formal, written policy covering the contents and accessibility of school records, with sanctions for violations. A specific individual should be assigned the responsibility of planning and organizing the implementation of the policy, for coordinating the policy across the system's several schools, and for training those personnel who will be involved. The policy should be developed cooperatively by all those affected (parents, teachers, counselors, administrators, and students), because of the considerable variety of laws and legal interpretations, because the Jeffersonian common wisdom should prevail in such a personal area of governmental policy, and because this involvement will strengthen commitment to the policy, which is essential to its success. The policy should be established within the staff resources available, or the necessary additional staff must be budgeted and made available to support the policy, particularly for notifying parents and students regarding the content of files, obtaining parental and/or student consent, and reporting to them on releases made of file information. A strategy should be outlined for adopting the policy, which will undoubtedly mean changing or formalizing records handling procedures.

Important questions regarding the information to be recorded in school files include the following: Why is each item of information necessary? What are the relevant decisions to be made by the school in using that element of information? Is it legitimate to collect and record it? Is the information duplicated elsewhere? What information may not be included? Is parental or student consent required before the information is collected? In what instances may representational consent suffice? Who is to be permitted to place information in a file? Will the information be complete on all students? What is the standing mechanism for insuring accuracy? What are the routine procedures for updating the file? What is the routine method for the challenging of file contents by parents, students, or others? Do students and parents have the right to counsel, to cross-examine witnesses, and to present evidence in challenging the contents of their file?

Planning for the physical organization of the files requires answers to these key questions: Are there to be different files for different purposes, or should there be a single, cumulative file? Should the files be centralized, say, in the system office, or decentralized at each school? What forms will be used to collect information? What forms will be used to record the information? What information from nonschool sources can be included? Shall the files be computerized, on microfilm, or consist only of paper documents? How does the policy apply to computerized files? How will impressionistic and narrative information be recorded objectively in the files? What is the most reliable source of each piece of information to be included? Are the files kept locked? Is there a regular schedule for destroying the information not part of the permanent file, which becomes less relevant and often more likely to result in privacy abuses when released? Are there formal procedures for handling inactive records with the same care as the active records of currently enrolled students?

The most effective means of keeping a file current and accurate is periodic inspection by the student or his parents. Do they know of the existence of school records and their contents? Are the specific uses of these records made known? Are they notified when new material is added? Are confidential materials, such as personal recommendations, protected even from student and parent scrutiny?

The most conspicuous focus of privacy invasion is in the release of information from student files. Is it unambiguous who may receive what information, and for what purpose? Are limits placed on subsequent use by the requestor? Does the policy differentiate between school and nonschool requestors? Is the consent of both parents of a confidential communication necessary before releasing it? Are subpoenas brought to parents' attention? Must requests be in writing? Are certain data identified as not available to requestors? Who is available to interpret the information? Are records released for research without identification? Is a notation made, and is the student or his parent notified of information releases, particularly to nonschool requestors?

Policy and practice often are inconsistent. Is there a formal mechanism to monitor the policy and its implementation? Is there a periodic evaluation by a review board to demonstrate to the schools' constituencies that an adopted policy is working, or, for identified reasons, should be altered?

"If a reasoned response to these policy issues is forthcoming, it should help to prevent an irrational revolt against record-keeping, and to protect the positive functions record-keeping serves for any modern society" (Wheeler, 1970, p. 25).

RECENT DEVELOPMENTS

The Family Educational Rights and Privacy Act (P.L. 93-380, as amended), which became effective in late 1974, provides that schools receiving any monies from the U.S. Office of Education must provide parents of students access to official records directly related to the students, and an opportunity for a hearing to challenge such records on the grounds that they are inaccurate, misleading, or otherwise inappropriate. Schools must obtain the written consent of parents before releasing personally identifiable data about students from records to other than a specified list of exceptions. Parents and students must be notified of these rights. The statute and its accompanying regulations (45 C.F.R., Part 99) govern access to records and the release of such records, and are likely to be adopted by most school systems.

REFERENCES

Allen, W. E. *Student Permanent Record Files: The Right to Privacy Related to the Content and Accessibility of Student Records in Massachusetts Public High Schools.* (Doctoral dissertation, University of Massachusetts) Ann Arbor, Mich.: University Microfilms, 1972, No. 72-19486.

Barone, M. J. *Survey of School Districts to Determine Local Policy Regarding Maintenance, Release and Use of Pupil Personnel Information.* Wilkes-Barre, Pa.: Wilkes College, 1971.

Code of Federal Regulations. Vol. 45, part 99, "Privacy Rights of Parents and Students."

Considerations of Data Security in a Computer Environment. White Plains, N.Y.: International Business Machines Corp., 1968.

Department of Health, Education, and Welfare, Secretary's Advisory Committee on Automated Personnel Data Systems. *Records, Computers and the Rights of Citizens.* Washington: Superintendent of Documents, 1973.

Goslin, D. A., and Bordier, N. Record-Keeping in Elementary and Secondary Schools. In *On Record: Files and Dossiers in American Life,* S. Wheeler, ed. New York: Russell Sage Foundation, 1970.

Guidelines for the Collection, Maintenance, and Dissemination of Pupil Records. New York: Russell Sage Foundation, 1970.

Miller, A. R. *The Assault on Privacy.* Ann Arbor: University of Michigan Press, 1971.

National Education Association, Task Force on Student Involvement. *Code of Student Rights and Responsibilities.* Washington: N.E.A., 1971.

Public Law No. 380, 93rd Congress (August 21, 1974, as amended). "The Family Educational Rights and Privacy Act."

Rosenberg, J. M. *The Death of Privacy.* New York: Random House, 1969.

Soto, J. I. *The Development of Guidelines for the Handling of College Student Records and Information.* (Doctoral dissertation, George Peabody College for Teachers) Ann Arbor, Mich.: University Microfilms, 1971, No. 71-26191.

Steim, B. L. *A Study of Privileged Communications with their*

Relationship to the Collection, Use and Release of Student and Faculty Records. (Doctoral dissertation, University of Utah) Ann Arbor, Mich.: University Microfilms, 1971, No. 71-25659.

Van Allen v. *McCleary,* 211 N.Y.S. 2d 501 (N.Y., 1961).

Vanderpool, F. A. *Confidentiality of Pupil Personnel Records in the Public Schools of the United States.* (Doctoral dissertation, University of Denver) Ann Arbor, Mich.: University Microfilms, 1971, No. 71-8747.

Westin, A. E. *Privacy and Freedom.* New York: Atheneum, 1967.

———, and Baker, M. A. *Databanks in a Free Society.* New York: Quadrangle Books, 1972.

Wheeler, S. *On Record: Files and Dossiers in American Life.* New York: Russell Sage Foundation, 1970.

33

ADMISSION OF FOREIGN STUDENTS

by James S. Frey
Assistant Director of Admissions
Indiana University
Bloomington, Indiana

The enrollment of foreign students in U.S. educational institutions expanded dramatically after World War II. One of the results was the development of a new profession within educational administration, that of the foreign student admissions officer. Although still found primarily at university-level institutions, this position is beginning to emerge at the elementary and secondary levels too. This is particularly true in cities such as New York and Washington, where large numbers of foreign diplomats and consular officials and their families reside, and in those major metropolitan areas which attract large numbers of foreign businessmen and immigrants.

There are several working definitions of the term "foreign student" currently in use in the United States. One of the most inclusive applies the term to all students who are not yet citizens of the United States, without regard to their current visa status or the location of their previous education. This definition includes immigrants who have attended one or more schools in the United States. Another broad definition refers to "international students," and includes all persons who have studied in one or more countries other than the United States. It includes U.S. citizens who study abroad. A more restrictive definition applies the term "foreign student" only to those who have come to the United States for educational purposes, thereby limiting it primarily to persons who hold F (student) or J (exchange visitor) visas. The definition which any given academic institution will use will generally be determined by a mixture of the attitude of the foreign student admissions officer and the foreign student advisor toward administration in general, and in particular toward their institution's role in international educational and cultural

exchange. Generally speaking, persons for whom work with foreign students is a major responsibility usually opt for a broad definition, while those for whom work with foreign students is just one of a number of responsibilities usually choose a more narrow definition.

A fairly large number of closely related administrative functions can be encompassed by the term "admissions." When specifically applied to foreign students, however, four main areas of concern are generally involved: an analysis of the quantity and quality of the student's previous education, as represented by academic records; an evaluation of his English proficiency, as measured by test scores; a review of his financial resources, as explained in a financial statement; and the preparation of the necessary nonimmigrant visa forms needed to enter the United States (or to extend the permission to stay in the U.S., if the student is already here on a nonimmigrant visa). The visa forms are obviously not needed in the case of a permanent resident, and the review of finances may not be as important in his case, but his previous education and his English proficiency usually need the same attention as do those of nonimmigrants.

Although the admissions function is probably as old as formal education itself, the process of admitting students into institutions of higher learning did not begin to evolve into a separate administrative profession until the early part of the twentieth century, when several U.S. college and university administrators received the official designation of "Director of Admissions." Foreign student enrollment is also probably as old as formal education, and the related foreign student admissions function too, but the development of this area of educational administration into a separate administrative profession is even more recent.

Prior to the Second World War, most U.S. colleges and universities absorbed the task of evaluating foreign educational credentials and the process of admitting foreign students somewhere within the admissions/ registration/records complex. These duties were assigned to a clerical employee, or to a subordinate professional employee, or performed by the registrar or director of admissions himself, depending upon the relative importance (or lack thereof) which these particular functions had with respect to the overall administration processes of a given institution. No matter where these duties resided, however, foreign student admissions was almost always a minor assignment, and the person who performed this function was seldom recognized within the institution as one who had developed any special or notable expertise.

In the years following the Second World War, foreign student enrollment in U.S. colleges and universities increased remarkably, from approximately 26,759 in 1949 to 121,300 twenty years later (Moore, 1970). Whereas in previous years a large proportion had come from Canada and Western Europe, now the developing countries of Africa, Asia, and Latin America were the primary sources. As a result of these changes, it became necessary to study many more educational systems, to decipher new types of academic records, and to interpret more complicated grading scales. Because the majority of the educational systems of the world were involved in postwar reorganization or postcolonial redevelopment, it also became necessary to conduct more frequent and more thorough investigations into the educational systems of other countries, particularly for providing accurate and current statistical information and quality clues as to the quantity and quality of the academic achievement which foreign academic credentials represent.

As the admission of foreign students grew in both volume and complexity, there was a tendency at many institutions to coordinate the evaluation and processing of foreign applications, and to delegate this responsibility to professional rather than clerical employees. Consequently a greater degree of centralization developed in this area than in the admission of U.S. students to the various undergraduate, graduate, and professional schools of most U.S. institutions.

A reflection of the gradual transfer of the foreign student admissions assignment to professional employees can be seen in the activities of the American Association of Collegiate Registrars and Admissions Officers (AACRAO). Topics related to the admission of foreign students began to appear with greater frequency on the programs of annual AACRAO conferences, and when the Association was reorganized in 1966 a separate international education section emerged as one of its five major divisions, composed of committees which are primarily concerned with the admission of foreign students. Similar processes were at work within the National Association For Foreign Student Affairs (NAFSA), and in 1965 a separate foreign student admissions section (ADSEC) was established within that association.

Both ADSEC and the international education section of AACRAO are members of the Council on Evaluation of Foreign Student Credentials, together with six other organizations which are concerned with the admission of foreign students, viz., the American Association of Community and Junior Colleges, the Association of American Colleges, the Association of Graduate Schools, the College Entrance Examination Board, the Council of Graduate Schools, and the Institute of International Education. The primary purpose of the Council is the formal approval of placement recommendations to accompany those publications of AACRAO and the U.S. Office of Education which relate to foreign educational systems. The Council is recognized as the primary source of definitive placement recommendations in the field of foreign student admissions.

In 1963, AACRAO, NAFSA, the College Entrance Examination Board (CEEB), and the Institute of International Education (IIE) cosponsored the first in a continuing series of two-day workshops concerned with the details of foreign student admissions. In 1965, ADSEC developed an intensive two-week workshop to study in depth the educational systems of four Asian countries. Nine similar workshops have been held since then in Honolulu, San Juan, Santo Domingo, West Germany, Western Africa, Scandinavia, and the Middle East. Each of these workshops produced a report which contributed significantly to the literature of this field.

In order to coordinate their varied activities relating to the admission of foreign students, AACRAO, CEEB, IIE, and NAFSA formed the National Liaison Committee on Foreign Student Admissions (NLC). They were joined later in this enterprise by the Council of Graduate Schools (CGS). One of the major accomplishments of the NLC was the development of four regional credential evaluation projects, staffed by experienced foreign student admissions officers on a voluntary basis to assist institutions which do not have their own experienced foreign student admissions officers. Evaluations are provided without charge to colleges and universities which have 100 or fewer foreign students. The NLC has also organized a series of regional workshops overseas, which are designed to improve the counseling which is available in other countries to persons who want to study in the United States (Jameson, 1972).

As a result of the activities of the NLC and of its five member organizations within the past ten years, a number of college and university administrators have been identified professionally as foreign student admissions officers. Only 55 of them work full-time at that specific assignment, and only 22 have that specific title, but more than 300 now hold membership in the Admissions Section of NAFSA (NAFSA Directory, 1972). Many of them have professional visibility not only within this field but also within their own institutions, and among other institutions in their region. The two foreign student admissions officers at Indiana University, for example, received 224 requests for assistance from 125 other U.S. institutions located in 33 states during the calendar year 1974.

As has been indicated above, the profession of foreign student admissions has had a brief but active history. All indications point to an even more active and stimulating future. Despite the rising costs of college and university education in the United States, recent conferences (Board of Foreign Scholarships, 1967; Council of Graduate Schools, 1969; Education and World Affairs, 1969; Board of Foreign Scholarships, 1971) have concluded that the number of foreign students coming to this country will probably continue to increase in the future. (Perhaps the primary reason for this anticipated steady increase is the fact that opportunities for secondary-level education are increasing in the developing countries of the world at a rate which is not likely to be matched in this century by postsecondary opportunities, particularly at the graduate level). In addition to an anticipated increase in volume, foreign student admissions will also continue to increase in complexity, as educational systems continue to change in order to meet the demands of increasing enrollments and expanding technology. Major colleges and universities in the U.S. will therefore continue to need professional staff members who are familiar with educational systems and institutions throughout the world, and who can simplify the tasks of other administrators by distinguishing between well- and poorly-prepared foreign applicants, and by recommending for admission only those who are likely to succeed in academic programs in the United States.

Professionally active foreign student admissions officers are being consulted more frequently by more persons in regard to their own institution's international educational activities, including special contracts with foreign educational institutions, the hiring of foreign-educated faculty, and the development of study-abroad opportunities for U.S. students. Similarly, the various educational arms of the U.S. Government, especially the Office of Education, the Agency For International development (AID), and the Bureau of Educational and Cultural Affairs (CU) of the U.S. Department of State, are increasingly consulting with foreign student admissions officers when planning and evaluating their own international educational activities. In addition to the professional development opportunities which such consultations represent for the foreign student admissions officer, there are many others. An intensive, two-week admissions workshop was held in 1975, and several more are in the planning stage. The NLC is planning two additional regional workshops overseas, and the NAFSA Field Service Program is continuing to send selected foreign student admissions officers as consultants to U.S. institutions. There will continue to be opportunities for foreign study and travel through programs such as those which are funded by the American Friends of the Middle East and administered by AACRAO and NAFSA; also, the program funded by AACRAO in connection with its World Education Series, i.e., publications dealing with the educational systems of other countries with an emphasis on the placement of students in postsecondary institutions in the United States.

There will also be continued opportunities for involvement in educational exchange policy deliberations through the special contracts which AID has with AACRAO and NAFSA. And there will be many opportunities for the exchange of information and ideas at the state, regional, and national conferences of AACRAO and NAFSA, and at numerous local and regional foreign student admissions workshops.

As U.S. institutions enter an era of declining domestic enrollment, rising costs, and tight budgets, existing policies and procedures pertaining to the enrollment of foreign students will be reviewed and modified. Three major issues can be identified:

The Enrollment of Undergraduate Foreign Students

Some institutions feel that foreign student enrollment should be limited to the graduate level, with exceptions at the undergraduate level only in those fields of study which are both high in need and short in supply in developing countries, such as veterinary science; on the assumption that undergraduates are younger, tend to stay longer, and consequently are more likely to remain in the U.S. permanently, thus contributing to the brain drain. Others feel that, subject to the availability of funds, each person ought to be given an opportunity to proceed through formal educational programs as far as his ability and motivation will take him, without regard to country of birth, and that each student's academic accomplishments contribute to the welfare of mankind even if his own nation does not benefit directly. Persons responsible for the administration of financial assistance programs, and those who work with groups of students, tend to favor the former policy, while those

who have little or no financial assistance to offer, and who work with individual students, tend to favor the latter.

Because of falling domestic enrollments, it is likely that the latter policy will continue to dominate the foreign admissions field for the foreseeable future. This is particularly true at institutions which have new and relatively nonprestigious graduate programs. Enrollments of foreign students at these institutions, and at undergraduate liberal arts colleges and junior/community colleges, will continue to outnumber those at major universities, although the latter institutions will continue to account for almost all professional foreign student admissions personnel.

The Availability of Financial Assistance

At most U.S. institutions, the costs of tuition, room, and board are increasing at a faster pace than the availability of financial assistance for nonimmigrant students. Consequently, fewer students are being assisted each year, although the total amount of dollars expended is increasing steadily. It is not likely that this situation will change in the foreseeable future. Any new funds which do become available are likely to come from local religious and service groups, and not from federal, state, or local governments or from alumni contributions.

Financial assistance for undergraduate foreign students will be available almost exclusively at junior/community colleges and private liberal arts colleges. Institutions which offer graduate degree programs will continue to limit almost all of their assistance to graduate students, and little of this will be available for the student's first year of study at that institution, no matter where or how well the undergraduate work was completed. Teaching and research assistantships will continue to provide the largest portion of financial assistance available at the graduate level, but the number of these awards will continue to decline until there is a resurgence of federally funded graduate research programs to provide financial assistance to domestic graduate students at a level at or above that which existed in the late 1960s.

The Enrollment of Foreign Students in "Exotic" Ph.D. Programs

There will continue to be controversy concerning the enrollment of foreign students in Ph.D. degree programs which currently have little applicability to developing countries, such as computer science, aeronautics, and atomic physics. However, it is not likely that many universities will deny admission to such programs to qualified foreign applicants, and recipients of these degrees will most probably continue to remain in the United States or emigrate to other developed countries, as is currently the case.

In addition to these concerns, there is a continuing need for additional research on the educational systems of other countries. Since workshop reports and other publications only have an accuracy span of approximately five years, some type of systematized updating of current data is needed, as well as a coordinated effort to fill existing gaps. The latter concerns not only countries which have not yet been studied, but also those fields of study, such as teacher training, which have been covered only peripherally in existing works.

Another area which needs attention in the immediate future is the granting of transfer credit at the undergraduate level for advanced secondary (e.g., the thirteenth year) and postsecondary work. Although there is some agreement in this area, it is not nearly as conclusive and well articulated as it ought to be, particularly given the fact that at this level most foreign students are enrolled at institutions which do not have professionally active foreign student admissions officers. It is therefore necessary that a guide for determining appropriate undergraduate transfer credit be prepared which can be easily used by admissions officers who work with small numbers of foreign applicants each year.

In conclusion, it can be said that the foreign student admissions officer has evolved from a clerical interpretor of academic records and decipherer of grading scales, to an evaluator of academic achievement and potential and a coordinator of the academic placement of persons who study in more than one educational system. This transition occurred in the 1950s, and was codified by the reorganization of AACRAO and NAFSA in the mid-1960s. Current signposts in the field of international educational exchange point to continued professionalization in the future, as does the existence of a large number of varied professional development opportunities. It is probable that there is both a larger number and a greater variety of professional development opportunities in this profession, in proportion to the number of members, than in any other area of educational administration in the United States. A relatively bright and reasonably ambitious inexperienced newcomer can, if he or she wishes, become locally recognized as an expert in one year, regionally recognized in two, and nationally recognized in three. It is therefore a field which can confidently be recommended to persons who are seeking an opportunity in educational administration.

REFERENCES

Board of Foreign Scholarships. *Diversity and Interdependence Through International Education.* New York. Education and World Affairs, 1967.
_____. Educational Exchange in the Seventies. *International Educational and Cultural EXCHANGE.* Washington: U.S. Advisory Commission on International Educational and Cultural Affairs, Fall, 1971, Vol. 7, No. 2.
Council of Graduate Schools. *University, Government, and the Foreign Graduate Student.* New York: College Entrance Examination Board, 1969.
Education and World Affairs. *Internationalizing the U.S. Professional School.* New York. Education and World Affairs, 1969.
Jameson, Sanford C. Counseling Counselors Abroad on U.S. Higher Education. *International Educational and Cultural EXCHANGE.* Washington. U.S. Advisory Commission on International Educational and Cultural Affairs, Fall, 1972, Vol. 8, No. 2.
Moore, Forrest G. International Education in the Seventies: Revolution or Turmoil on the Campus? *International Edu-*
cational and Cultural EXCHANGE. Washington. U.S. Advisory Commission on International Educational and Cultural Affairs, Summer, 1970, Vol. 6, No. 1.
NAFSA Directory. Washington. National Association For Foreign Student Affairs, 1972.

MAJOR ORGANIZATIONS

American Association of Collegiate Registrars and Admissions Officers, One Dupont Circle, N.W., Washington, D.C. 20036
College Entrance Examination Board, 1717 Massachusetts Avenue, N.W., Washington, D.C. 20036
Institute of International Education, 809 United Nations Plaza, New York, N.Y. 10017
National Association For Foreign Student Affairs, 1860 19th Street, N.W., Washington, D.C. 20009

34

COLLEGE GRADING SYSTEMS

by Jonathan R. Warren
Research Psychologist
Educational Testing Service
Berkeley, California

Almost every educational institution in the country, from elementary school through graduate school, has some procedure for recording and reporting the performance of its students. These procedures—the grading systems—have been the subject of chronic controversy and periodic minor adjustment since their inception about a hundred years ago. Yet the vehemence and persistence of the controversy are puzzling. Grades are peripheral to the educational process, yet disputes over the form they should take absorb amounts of faculty time and energy that would seem justified only by major educational issues. And in spite of the long history of the controversy, attention has been given almost exclusively to form; purposes have been almost ignored.

That grades are peripheral to the educational process is apparent in their use primarily by persons who were not involved in the instruction to which the grades refer. In elementary and secondary schools grades function as reports to parents. In secondary schools and colleges they are used by persons at the next higher educational level in admission decisions. Neither reporting to parents nor selection to higher educational programs plays any role in the instruction or learning that produces the grade that is recorded and reported. The common assertion that evaluation of student performance and knowledge of results are important to sound instruction, while true, has no bearing on grades. Evaluation occurs and its results are communicated to students in a variety of ways—through written and oral teacher comments, results of tests and quizzes, observations by the students themselves of the ease or difficulty with which they carry out assigned tasks, and other formal and informal classroom experiences. The end-of-term grade is, then, no more than a gross summary statement of the results of all these evaluative activities, largely for administrative purposes.

Because the current controversy over grading systems is greatest at the college level, as indicated by the volume of literature on grading at each level, the emphasis here will be on college grading systems. On one side of the controversy are a large number of students and a moderate number of faculty members who want to abolish or substantially change the most common grading system, A through F. A 1969 survey of 70,000 students and 30,000 faculty members across the country showed more than half the students and one-third of the faculty members agreeing that grades should be abolished (Carnegie Commission, 1972). The primary objection to grades is that they interfere with learning, that the activities students feel obliged to follow to get good grades are not always the most beneficial activities the students could engage in if learning were their only goal. Many students assert that the time they spend studying to get good grades does not help their learning or understanding, that the competitive aspect of grades discourages students from helping each other, and that grades turn students and teachers into adversaries (Becker, Geer and Hughes, 1968; Education at Berkeley, 1968; Katz and Associates, 1969; Stallings and Leslie, 1970). Yet no evidence other than student perceptions can be cited in support of these common beliefs.

The other side of the grading controversy rests largely on two propositions. One, prominent in the comparison of Pass-Fail with A-F grading systems, holds that grades are sometimes necessary and usually valuable in inducing students to study, that without the distinction among several levels of acceptable performance provided by a multilevel grading system students would not learn as well. The evidence available from Pass-Fail studies tends to support this view (Feldmesser, 1969; Karlins, Kaplan, and Stuart, 1969; Sgan, 1970), but it is vulnerable to alternative interpretations and far from conclusive. The second major argument for maintaining a multilevel grading system, or any grading system at all, is that grades are essential for the effective selection of students to college from high school and to graduate or professional schools from undergraduate colleges (Raimi, 1967).

PURPOSES OF GRADING SYSTEMS

The purposes of grades, as well as the intensity of the controversy, shift with increasing educational level. In the elementary and intermediate years, the primary purpose is to inform parents about the academic performance of their children. Elementary school grades lead to no educational action. Even tracking of students at the elementary level is likely to be based on test scores or other direct measures of performance, rather than on end-of-term grades. While grades have no administrative educational consequences in elementary school, such as modifying the instructional program for students whose grades are low, they do affect pupils' self-definitions, their expectations of themselves, their future educational decisions, and the expectations of their teachers. Educational consequences therefore do occur, but seldom in the service of any planned educational purpose.

As the secondary level grades continue to serve as a report to parents, but they are also used more extensively than in the earlier years in decisions about tracking, placement in special programs (both for particularly capable students and for those who are educationally deficient), admission to college, and the award of scholarships. In college the function of grades as selectors is still more pronounced, while their function as reports to parents is minimal. Grades must be maintained at a specified level to permit continued enrollment and eventual graduation. Although grades are strongly associated with withdrawal from college (Astin, 1972), the relationship is complex and has not been effectively studied. Grades continue to exercise a strong selection function in the award of honors at graduation, in selection to graduate and professional schools, and in the award of graduate fellowships and assistantships. The basis for this heavy influence of grades on continuing educational selection is the belief that the same kinds of performance recognized and rewarded at lower educational levels are those that assure success at higher levels. The low relationships between grades separated by two or more years, however, raise questions about this belief (Humphreys, 1968).

The extent to which college grades are used in selection to employment is not known, but one survey suggests that it may not be great (Bailey, 1972), and evidence that college grades are related to the qualities desired for any particular job is usually missing. The American Telephone and Telegraph Company has shown moderate relationships between college grades and several measures of job performance (Kappel, 1962), but it is an exception. Most studies relating college success and job success typically show a negligible relationship (Berg, 1970; Hoyt, 1966). Yet many faculty members feel an obligation to students and to employers to provide grades for use in employment selection.

At all levels, from elementary school through graduate school, teachers use grades to induce students to perform as the teacher desires (Raimi, 1967). Good grades act as rewards to students and poor grades constitute punishment. Grades therefore give teachers a powerful tool for controlling students, as long as students need grades to move farther up the educational selection process. In view of the limited educational value of grades, this may be the primary reason for the vehemence with which many faculty members resist changes to the grading system.

FORMS OF GRADING SYSTEMS

The most common form of grading system at the secondary level and in colleges and universities is the five-symbol ABCDF system (AACRAO Survey, 1971; Burwen, 1971). The F indicates failure, but its meaning varies with the consequences of failure. In some instances it means only that no progress toward graduation can be credited from that course. In higher education, an F usually has the further consequence of subtracting some number of credits from the total earned by the student in other courses. If the course is one required for graduation or for a particular major field, the student may have to repeat the course.

Ds are more ambiguous than Fs. They usually do not cause a student's total store of credits to be depleted, and they may or may not allow the course to count toward graduation, or require that it be repeated. Their ambiguity gives instructors, academic advisers, and institutions flexibility in interpretation, with the consequences of a D often depending on the student's other grades. If they are good the D is ignored; if bad, the D may take on the characteristics of an F in decisions about the student's further educational activities.

The three passing grades simply represent three levels of acceptable academic performance, with C usually intended to indicate adequate performance, B somewhat better than that, and A quite good. In recent years, though, grade distributions at a number of colleges and universities have shown the C to be taking on the qualities described above for Ds, while the most common grade, indicating acceptable performance, has become the B rather than the C. Ds and Fs are barely distinguishable, and in combination probably account for well under 10 percent of the grades given. Thus without any formal change in the grading system, colleges and universities have moved from a five-level system to what is, in effect, a four-level system, with the lowest level—the combination of Ds and Fs—rarely used, and then probably almost entirely in the freshman year. Further, the operational meaning of the traditional grades has changed without any formal recognition of its happening. Changes in the high school grades reported by entering college students surveyed nationally by the American Council on Education suggest that a similar shift in grading patterns may have occurred in high schools between about 1968 and 1970.

The most popular recent change in grading systems in higher education has been to offer students a limited option to choose one course per term to be graded Pass-Fail, rather than on the A–F system (AACRAO Survey, 1971; Burwen, 1971). The effects of that change have been small, eliminating distinctions among various levels of acceptable performance in fewer than 10 percent of the grades awarded at the institutions offering the option. Failing grades were not affected by the change, but the limited number of Fs actually awarded makes that of questionable importance, except in the attitudes of students toward the grading system.

Changes occurring at a number of institutions, but too recently for their incidence yet to be known, have abolished both Ds and Fs while maintaining three levels of acceptable performance. Stanford and Brown Universities, and a substantial number of California junior colleges, are among the institutions that have adopted this ABCX System (Ladd, 1970; Smith, 1969). The X indicates only that the student did not perform well enough to be given credit for the course, and does not affect his or her grade-point average. Whether it is recorded at all varies with different institutions. At both Brown and Stanford the students are also given a Pass-No Credit option under the same conditions usually applying to the Pass-Fail option—one course per term

not in the student's major field. The University of California at Santa Cruz, where Pass-Fail grading plus instructor comments has been used since 1965, recently shifted from Pass-Fail to Pass-No Credit. The heart of the Santa Cruz system, though, remains the instructor comments.

The descriptive grading system at the University of California at Santa Cruz, used in conjunction with Pass-No Credit, has been used for some time at a small number of colleges such as Bennington and Sarah Lawrence. The student's performance is described in whatever descriptive prose the instructor considers appropriate. The collection of faculty comments then becomes the student's record.

The major objections to the descriptive grading system are the time required of faculty members to write descriptive comments about each student and the difficulty people evaluating transcripts have in making comparisons among students. Both difficulties exist, however, in every grading system; they just escape being ignored when descriptive comments are required. In recording a student's performance, the faculty member has the same amount of information about the student—derived from tests, papers, and observations of classroom performance—whether a single letter is recorded or a descriptive paragraph is written. If nothing more can be said than "Good student"—the kind of written comment that does occur at times in descriptive grading—that is also all that is implied by the corresponding letter grade, probably a B. The deficiency, then, is in the evaluation process that gives the instructor so little information, not in the grading system that records and reports the information. A parallel situation exists in evaluating transcripts. The information conveyed by a letter grade or by a grade-point average is easy to compare superficially, but two Bs, or two grade-point averages of 3.0, are no more comparable in actuality than the descriptive comments that might have been written about the same students.

A modified system of descriptive grading has been proposed in which faculty members would use from 15 to 25 rating scales, each with three to five levels, on which to check the performance of their students (Elbow, 1969). The content of the rating scales would be established collectively by the faculty in advance, to ensure that the most important elements of student performance were included. Each faculty member would be free to use whichever scales were pertinent to his or her courses or to any particular student. Two students in the same class, for example, may require different terms to describe their performance. Dogged persistence may be an important attribute of one student's performance but immaterial to another's. Each faculty member would also have the option of using only a single scale, probably labeled academic performance, which would retain the present multilevel, undifferentiated system.

A grading system that goes beyond descriptive grading in the detail and scope of information provided is one that consists of portfolios of the student's work. Test papers, written work, photographs or slides of work too bulky to be placed in a portfolio, and audio tapes can all be made part of a student's portfolio. The major problems with such a system are in the time required and difficulty encountered in evaluating the portfolio. Whether these problems are too great for the system to be feasible depends on the nature of the decisions to be based on student records. When decisions must be made quickly about large numbers of students, or when the decisionmaker is not clear about the purposes of the selection process he is engaging in, and must therefore rely on a general evaluation of competence by the student's former professors, portfolios are impractical. A distinct advantage the portfolio has over other systems, however, is the placement of decisions about the nature of the desired performance in the hands of the persons making the selections, rather than in the hands of the former faculty members who grade students without knowledge of the purposes for which the grades will later be used. As might be expected, schools and departments in the graphic and performing arts are most likely to use a portfolio system of recording and reporting student performance. At the California Institute of the Arts, where such a system is in use, the student selects from his or her portfolio the items to be sent as a transcript, and different items may be selected for different purposes.

The current innovation in grading systems that seems most likely to have an important and lasting effect is the abandonment of failing grades. The Pass-Fail options that have been popular are too limited to be important, but changing the consequences of poor performance is likely to have important effects on the enrollment patterns and academic attitudes of students. One argument for retaining failing grades is to have a mechanism to deny continued enrollment and expensive educational resources to students who are not using them effectively. But any grading system can be used for that purpose, and the belief that the level of a student's grades indicates how well he is using the resources of the institution needs examining in any case. Continuing deficiencies in the voluminous literature on grading systems are identification of the purposes they are to serve, determining the importance or validity of the several purposes, and assessing the effectiveness with which they serve the desired purposes.

REFERENCES

The AACRAO Survey of Grading Policies in Member Institutions. Washington, D.C.: American Association of Collegiate Registrars and Admissions Officers, 1971.

Astin, A. W. College Dropouts: A National Profile. *ACE Research Reports,* Vol. 7. No. 1. Washington, D.C.: American Council on Education, 1972

Bailey, R. P., ed. *A Report of the Sub-Committee to Survey the Acceptance of Non-Traditional Grading Patterns by Government, Industry, and/or Graduate Institutions—1972.* Athens, Ohio: American Association of Collegiate Registrars and Admissions Officers, 1972.

Becker, H. S., Geer, B., and Hughes, E. C. *Making the Grade: The Academic Side of College Life.* New York: Wiley, 1968.

Berg, I. *Education and Jobs: The Great Training Robbery.* New York: Praeger, 1970.

Burwen, L. S. *National Grading Survey.* Office of Institutional Research, San Francisco State College, San Francisco, California, 1971.

The Carnegie Commission on Higher Education. *Reform on Campus: Changing Students, Changing Academic Programs.* New York: McGraw-Hill, 1972.

Education at Berkeley: Report of the Select Committee on Education. Berkeley: University of California Press, 1968.

Elbow, P. H. More Accurate Evaluation of Student Performance. *The Journal of Higher Education,* 1969, *40,* 219-230.

Feldmesser, R. A. *The Option: Analysis of an Educational Innovation.* Hanover, N.H.: Dartmouth College, 1969.

Hoyt, D. P. College Grades and Adult Accomplishment. *Educational Record,* 1966, *47,* 70-75.

Humphreys, L. G. The Fleeting Nature of the Prediction of College Academic Success. *Journal of Educational Psychology,* 1968, *59,* 375-380.

Kappel, F. R. *From the World of College to the World of Work.* New York: American Telephone and Telegraph Co., 1962.

Karlins, M., Kaplan, M., and Stuart, W. Academic Attitudes and Performance as a Function of Differential Grading Systems: An Evaluation of Princeton's Pass-Fail System. *The Journal of Experimental Education,* 1969, *37,* 38-50.

Katz, J., and Associates. *No Time for Youth: Growth and Constraint in College Students.* San Francisco: Jossey-Bass, 1969.

Ladd, D. R. *Change in Educational Policy: Self-Studies in Selected Colleges and Universities.* New York: McGraw-Hill, 1970.

Raimi, R. A. Examinations and Grades in College. *AAUP Bulletin,* 1967, *53,* 309-317.

Sgan, M. R. Letter Grade Achievement in Pass-Fail Courses. *The Journal of Higher Education,* 1970, *41,* 638-644.

Smith, L. G. Non-Punitive Grading in California Junior Colleges. El Cajon, California: Grossmont College, 1969.

Stallings, W. M. and Leslie, E. K. Student Attitudes Toward Grades and Grading. *Improving College and University Teaching,* 1970, *18,* 66-68.

ADDITIONAL RESOURCES

Elton, L. R. B. The Assessment of Students—A New Approach. *Universities Quarterly,* 1968, *22,* 291-301.

Marshall, M. S. *Teaching Without Grades.* Corvallis, Ore.: Oregon State University Press, 1968.

McKeachie, W. J. Research on Teaching at the College and University Level. In N. L. Gage, ed., *Handbook of Research on Teaching.* Chicago: Rand McNally, 1963, pp. 1118-1172.

Miller, S. *Measure, Number, and Weight: A Polemical Statement of the College Grading Problem.* Knoxville, Tenn.: Learning Research Center, The University of Tennessee, 1967.

Thorndike, R. L. Marks and Marking Systems. In R. L. Ebel, ed., *Encyclopedia of Educational Research.* (4th ed.) Toronto: Macmillan, 1969, pp. 759-766.

Wallace, W. L. *Student Culture: Social Structure and Continuity in a Liberal Arts College.* Chicago: Aldine, 1966.

Warren, J. R. College Grading Practices: An Overview. Report 9. Washington, D.C.: ERIC Clearinghouse on Higher Education, 1971.

35

PASS-FAIL GRADING SYSTEMS

by H. M. Davidovicz
Center for the Study of Higher Education
Hofstra University
Hempstead, New York

Based on: Davidovicz, H. M. Pass-Fail Grading—A Review. *Abstracts and Reviews of Research in Higher Education, No. 17,* Hofstra University (New York), 1972.

While the concept of Pass–Fail courses is rather old, its widespread acceptance is a recent innovation. Burwen (1971) estimated that currently about 67.5 percent of all institutions use some sort of nontraditional grade. Furthermore, the innovation of eliminating all failing grades is beginning to emerge. Several authors have investigated the procedures used in Pass-Fail grading (Beven et al., 1969; Simpson et al., 1970; Quann, 1970; Johnson, 1970; and Burwen, 1971). Usually students take about one Pass-Fail course per semester. In most cases the student has to demonstrate good academic ability before he can utilize this option. Furthermore, the Pass-Fail course cannot be in the student's major area. As is reported by Simpson et al. (1970), a failing grade does not affect the grade point average in about half the schools they surveyed. One procedure, which has not been adopted as widely as the others, is to eliminate dual grading standards by having instructors submit letter grades for all students, and then having the registrar convert these to Pass-Fail grades (Johnson, 1970). This has the fortuitous advantage of facilitating research on the subject of Pass-Fail grading.

In his review of the literature on college and university grading practices, Yuker (1969) concluded that an increasing number of universities were adopting limited Pass-Fail options even though few of them used Pass-Fail grades exclusively. The issue he found to be most serious was that graduate and professional schools preferred traditional grading systems for selection of students and that students with all Pass-Fail grades "tend to be discriminated against."

Beven et al. (1969) reported that those who favor Pass-Fail grading argue that it relieves the pressure on students, and channels them to learning by making it easier to take courses they would not have taken otherwise. Those who argue against it claim that students take advantage of it by not working as hard, and that many administrative problems arise with respect to such things as the dean's list, academic probation, academic suspension, computation of grade point averages (GPA), admission to graduate and professional schools, and admission of transfer students. As will be demonstrated, these are not areas of major concern to those institutions that operate with a limited Pass-Fail option, though they are for those institutions that are totally on Pass-Fail. But those that operate on a total pass-fail system have suggested some solutions.

HYPOTHESES AND PROBLEMS IN THE RESEARCH

Research in the area of Pass-Fail grading has not progressed much in recent years. Weems et al. (1971) found that 85 percent of the institutions with Pass-Fail options had no evaluative data on their programs. The majority of the literature reports opinions and offers little substantiating data. From a research point of view, the Pass-Fail option is a difficult independent variable to manipulate (Stallings et al., 1968). The criterion problem (i.e., which variables can be measured to get at the consequences of selecting a Pass-Fail option) seems to be primary. There seems to be self-selection as to which students elect the Pass-Fail option. This, however, has yet to be substantiated with data. To date, the criteria used to measure the effects of Pass-Fail grading have been either grade point average or grades in Pass-Fail courses. As will be demonstrated, these two measures have yielded some facts that are disappointing to advocates of Pass-Fail grading.

CHARACTERISTICS OF PASS-FAIL STUDENTS

Stallings, Wolff, and Moehr (1969) explored the possibility that students who were high in "fear of failure" elect a Pass-Fail option, regardless of their interest in the subject matter, in order to avoid an undesirable test experience. They studied 83 education majors from the University of Illinois. The sample was divided into those students who took their course work under an A to F grading system and those who were enrolled for Pass-Fail credits. While the authors expected that the Pass-Fail students would have the greatest amount of test anxiety, as measured by the Test Anxiety Questionnaire, they found that there were no differences between groups. They also found that the Pass-Fail sample showed a higher GPA and carried heavier course loads. Since the authors also found no difference between the groups in their reasons for choosing Pass-Fail courses, this would not indicate that people who elect Pass-Fail courses do so in order to avoid evaluation.

Another study designed to get at attitudes associated with advocating Pass-Fail grading was carried out by Priest (1971). He hypothesized that students who favored noncompetitive grading also favored both less competition in testing and noncompetitive peer interactions. He further hypothesized that those students who had not achieved high grades in past competition would dislike competing.

In order to test his hypotheses a questionnaire was administered to a sample of 433 students. The majority of those sampled favored a Pass-Fail grading option. Those who favored Pass-Fail grading aspired to high grades, and expressed a negative attitude towards grading as being competitive. It was found that those who favored Pass-Fail grading also tended to believe that competition for grades does not promote learning, and that there is too much competition for high grades. In addition, these same people reported that they did not enjoy studying, and preferred evaluation of their performance on original projects. In contrast, those who favored traditional grading believed that competition stimulates learning; they wanted to be graded on their work, and went to their instructors for answers to questions. In general, there appeared to be a clear distinction between the types of students who favored Pass-Fail grading and those who did not. But neither attitude was closely related to either aspirations for grades or actual school achievement.

ACHIEVEMENT UNDER PASS-FAIL GRADING

A study carried out at Knox College (Helville and Stamn, 1967), which examined the grades of students enrolled in Pass-Fail courses, found that GPAs increased directly in proportion to the number of Pass-Fail courses the students took, and that the average academic performance within Pass-Fail courses was lowered. McLaughlin et a. (1972) found partial support for this in a study carried out on 300 undergraduate students at Virginia Polytechnic Institute and State University. Their sample of Pass-Fail students received higher GPAs and took heavier course loads than non-Pass-Fail students.

A carefully controlled study, with conflicting results as to increased GPAs, was done by Gold et al. (1971) at the State University College of New York at Cortland. They used samples of freshmen and juniors matched for GPA, Scholastic Aptitude Test scores, and sex. Grades were submitted for all students, although some were converted to Pass-Fail grades. The experimental subjects were permitted to take Pass-Fail courses, while control subjects who wanted to take the same courses on a Pass-Fail basis were denied the opportunity. The authors found that the average GPA for both freshmen and juniors was significantly lower for those students who took Pass-Fail courses. The experimental subjects demonstrated no compensatory improvement in the non-Pass-Fail courses, and even after they returned to a system of traditional grading they continued to get significantly lower grades than the control subjects. Somehow, in this case, taking Pass-Fail courses had an adverse effect on college achievement.

Studies done by Sgan (1970) and Quann (1971) lend further support to the argument that students do not perform well under Pass-Fail grading. Quann reported that students at Washington State University who took Pass-Fail courses or traditional courses did not differ significantly in GPA initially, but after the courses were completed the regularly enrolled students received five times as many As and 50 percent more Bs than Pass-Fail students. Sgan found that at Brandeis University freshmen, sophomores, and juniors received significantly poorer grades under Pass-Fail than they did under letter grading. There were no significant differences between seniors who either took or did not take Pass-Fail courses. Since first-year students did most poorly, Sgan concluded that "There would seem to be some need for special preparation and attention to first-year students if Pass-Fail is opened to them as an option. Merely allowing it may not be a responsible educational effort (p. 643)."

Von Wittich (1972) used 895 Iowa State University students enrolled in elementary foreign language courses in a single blind study (instructors filed A to F grades which were converted to Pass-Fail by the registrar). She found that even students with high GPAs did significantly more poorly in the courses they took as Pass-Fail than in those they took with letter grading. Further, a multiple regression analysis she carried out (to control for extraneous variables) indicated that the difference between Pass-Fail and non-Pass-Fail students was due to the grading system alone.

ATTITUDES IN PASS-FAIL GRADING

It is frequently stated that Pass-Fail grading causes students to report a reduction in the amount of tension they perceive (Hales et al., 1973). Stallings and Leslie (1970) were particularly critical of the effects of regular grading. They concluded that:

> The undergraduate perceives grades as that proverbial sword hanging over his head which forces him to study content he otherwise might not study. The power of "the grade" is strong enough to restrict his studying to material which he anticipates will be on tests. In most cases this material is factual, regardless of the level of the instructor's objectives. If he should happen to stray from factual material and become somewhat imaginative, the student expects his efforts to go unrewarded. . . . Once a grade is received, it is not perceived as feedback. . . . Pressure mounts and can lead to cheating. Cheating is perceived as a side-effect behavior, partly attributive to the pressure to obtain high grades. (p. 67)

They argued that students should be allowed to take Pass-Fail alternatives when they desire to do so, and that if graduate schools complain they should be defied.

Those who have investigated attitudes towards the Pass-Fail system (Sgan, 1969; Karlins et al., 1969; Cromer, 1969; and the Office of Institutional Educational Research at Washington University, 1970) have consistently found that students are overwhelmingly in favor of it. There is a question whether students work as hard for Pass-Fail grades as they do for numerical grades, but the evidence seems to indicate that they do not. Karlins et al. (1969), found that with numerical grades, students completed 80 percent of their readings and attended 85 percent of the lectures, while Pass-Fail students reported that they had done 61 percent of the readings and attended 74 percent of the lectures. While some researchers reported that students explored courses outside of their own major (Sgan, 1969), others said they did not (Johnson, 1970; Weems et al., 1971). This could be a function of varying student characteristics at the different universities. While it is difficult to draw a firm conclusion, on the whole it seems that students do not take Pass-Fail courses to explore other areas, but rather use it to relax in some of their course work (Cromer, 1969; Weems et al., 1971; and Hales et al., 1973).

PROBLEMS ASSOCIATED WITH PASS-FAIL GRADING

While graduate and professional schools prefer applicants with traditionally graded transcripts, a survey done by Goldstein and Tilker (1969) on institutions of higher learning in New York State indicated that graduate schools preferred a four-point or less grading system (i.e., Pass-Fail or a similar system) for their own internal purposes. Professional schools, on the other hand, preferred a five-or-more-point scale (i.e., traditional A to F grading) for grading their students. Warren (1971) claimed that grades fulfill an administrative rather than an educational purpose, but that administrative needs such as awarding financial aid or honors are legitimate educational purposes. He said that graduate and professional schools are the primary beneficiaries of grades for selection, and thus they are the ones most concerned about departures from traditional grading patterns.

Needham (1970), of Simmons College, quoted the Law School Admissions Test Council as saying that "College grades make a contribution to the prediction of law school grades that is not supplied by the Law School Admission Test." In his own research at Simmons College, Needham asked students if they thought the Pass-Fail grades on their transcripts had an adverse effect on their applications to graduate schools, transfer applications, employment applications, etc. The number of students who perceived unfavorable reactions against their transcripts was relatively small, in all cases except transfer students. So it seems that transfer students perceive themselves to be most negatively affected by Pass-Fail grading.

A survey done by the American Association of College Registrars and Admissions Officers (1971) found that 44 percent of the institutions reported that they disregard the Pass-Fail grades of transfer students. Another 18 percent have yet to establish a policy, 21 percent request "further information," and seven percent assign an arbitrary quantitative value to the grades. A total of 26 percent of the graduate schools that responded indicated that admission to their programs is either jeopardized or delayed by the presence of a substantial number of Pass-Fail credits. This indicates that the effects of Pass-Fail grading on transfer students is unclear but that graduate school applicants experience some harmful effects.

The results of a survey done by Rossman (1970) are in accord with these findings. His sample consisted of 45 schools which were frequently attended by Macalaster College graduates. This small sample had 60 percent of the administrators indicating that the reputation of the school would be considered in admission decisions. It was also found that 75 percent of the administrators indicated that achievement test scores would take on great importance for students with many Pass-Fail grades. He reported that students who have 75 percent or more of their grades in traditional formats should not experience any difficulty in admissions. So it would seem that students who do not do well on standardized achievement tests, and students who come from schools that do not have established reputations, suffer most from Pass-Fail grading.

Only a small number of colleges are run completely on a Pass-Fail system, and very few students graduate with more than ten percent of their grades in Pass-Fail form (Hofeller, 1971; Warren, 1971). It would seem that the majority of students who have a high percentage of Pass-Fail grades and apply to graduate schools are admitted, but perhaps not always to their first choice of school. The effect on loss of fellowships and scholarships, however, has not yet been determined (Warren, 1971).

As far as honors are concerned, Phi Beta Kappa (1969) reported that about 60 percent of those schools that responded to their questionnaire kept their usual grades in addition to indicating whether the course was passed or failed, and about 80 percent ranked students in their respective classes by GPA. About 64 percent of the Phi Beta Kappa chapters reported no problems with Pass-Fail grading, another 12 percent indicated problems, and 24 percent were not sure as yet. Thus, Pass-Fail grading was not a major problem for these schools.

SOLUTIONS

One method of dealing with Pass-Fail grading was described by Tragesser et al. (1968). He suggested that College-level examinations which measure achievement in specific course areas might be used when transferring credits is a problem. Each school would develop its own norms. Schools such as the University of California at Santa Cruz and Raymond College, which normally assign Pass-Fail grades, provide letter grades in science courses for premedical students at their own request. Other schools, such as Goddard College and Nasson College, issue "descriptive analysis of course work for transferring students."

Massey et al. (1969) described a method used at Ohio Northern University (where one-third of a student's work goes ungraded and GPAs are based on graded courses) for determining such things as dean's list, eligibility for honor societies, graduation honors, class rank, etc. Instructors fill out separate honors recommendations, which are used only for internal decision-making and are not part of the student's permanent record. A similar method is used at Tarkio College (Aven and Breazier, 1969), where student teaching grades for education majors are Pass-Fail. There, the student's supervisor writes an evaluation which becomes part of the student's academic credentials. Of the school superintendents who receive these written evaluations, 81 percent said that they were sufficient. These students do receive letter grades in other courses.

The Department of Vocational Teacher Education at the University of Massachusetts, whose students spend 50 percent of their time on noncourse experiences, uses a method of written evaluation to record individual student progress when traditional grading is not feasible (Johnson and Lauraesch, 1969). Leiseming et al. (1970) described another alternative. At Westminster College, where a four-point grading system was adopted in 1965, academic progress is assessed by comparing hours earned each semester with a norm of 15.5 hours. No GPA is obtained, but students are ranked via this procedure. It can be seen that for schools on a total Pass-Fail program the most practical solution is to keep a dual record of grades so that traditional transcripts are available on student request. Another possibility is to include descriptive summaries of course work in the student's record. There is no need to resort to either of these procedures if only a limited Pass-Fail option exists.

SUMMARY

This review of the literature on pass-fail grading leads to the following conclusions:

Students do not take Pass-Fail courses in order to avoid evaluation, but once having taken them their performance in both those courses and in traditionally graded courses declines (Sgan, 1970; Gold et a., 1971; Quann, 1971).

Students do not take Pass-Fail courses to explore areas outside of their own major, but rather do so in order to make things easier for themselves in terms of course work (Johnson, 1970; Weems et al., 1971).

Freshmen suffer most academically from taking Pass-Fail grades, and so they should not be permitted the option; or they should receive special guidance when they elect to do so (Quann, 1971).

The elimination of failing grades on transcripts is being practiced more widely than previously (Simpson et al., 1970).

Most schools do not have major problems with Pass-Fail grading because they offer it only as a limited option (Needham, 1970).

While students with a substantial number of credits in Pass-Fail courses can transfer to other colleges, or be admitted to graduate and professional schools, they are less likely to get into the school of their choice. The possible detrimental effect on financial aid for them has not yet been determined (Needham, 1970; Rossman, 1970; AACRAO, 1971).

Double bookkeeping systems or written evaluations can serve to supplement transcripts of students who have a large percentage of Pass-Fail courses (Tragesser et al., 1968; Aven et al., 1969; Johnson et al., 1969; Massey et al., 1969; Johnson, 1970).

When students with many Pass-Fail grades apply to graduate or professional schools, the schools tend to give more weight to scores on achievement tests (Rossman, 1970).

Institutions are still not doing the required research, or using adequate research techniques, in research regarding Pass-Fail grading.

REFERENCES

The American Association of College Registrars and Admissions Officers. *Survey of Grading Policies in Member Institutions.* Washington, D.C.: American Association of Collegiate Registrars and Admissions Officers, 1971.

Beven, J. E., D'Andrea, J. E., Moore, J., Ruller, F. E., and Cate, G. Transcript Adequacy—P's, F's and other letters. *College and University, 44*(4), 1969, 502-503.

Burwen, L. S. *National Grading Survey.* San Francisco, California: Office of Institutional Research, San Francisco State College, 1971.

Cromer, W. An Empirical Investigation of Student Attitudes Toward the Pass-Fail Grading System at Wellesley College. *College Student Personnel Abstracts, 5*(2), 1970, 189.

Gold. R. M., Reilly, A., Silberman, R., and Lehr, R. Academic Achievement Declines Under Pass-Fail Grading. *The Journal of Experimental Education, 39*(3), 1971, 17-21.

Goldstein, K. M., and Tilker, H. A. *A Review of Grading System Practices in the Higher Education Institutions of New York State.* New York, 1969, 81 pp.

Hales, L. W., Bain, P. T., and Rand, L. P. The Pass-Fail Option: The Congruence Between the Rationale for and Student Reasons in Electing. *The Journal of Educational Research, 66*(7), 1973, 296-298.

Helville, G. L., and Stamn, E. *The Pass-Fail System and the Change in the Accounting of Grades on Comprehensive Examinations at Knox College.* Illinois: Galesburg, 1967, 25 pp.

Hofeller, M. A. *Survey of U.S. Graduate School Attitudes Toward Non-Traditional Grading Systems.* New York: Hofstra University, 1971.

Johnson, J. T. Evaluate Program, Not Grading. *College and University Business, 49*(3), 1970, 77-78.

Johnson, R. A., and Lauroesch, W. Pass-Fail System with Options for the Learner. *American Vocational Journal, 44*(6), 1969, 16-18 and 65.

Karlins, M., Kaplan, M., and Stuart, W. Academic Attitudes and Performance as a Function of Differential Grading Systems: An Evaluation of Princeton's Pass-Fail System. *Journal of Experimental Education, 37*(3), 1969, 38-50.

Leiseming, L. B., Elliott, C., Fuller, G. L., King, H. C., Warren, R. J., and Parish, J. B. Evaluating Evaluations—grading practices. *College and University, 45*(4), 1970, 349-359.

Massey, G. H., D'Andrea, J. E., Moore, J., Papaulos, G., and Williams, J. N. Transcript Adequacy—P's and F's and Other Letters. *College and University—44*(4), 1969, 520-527.

McLaughlin, G. W., Montgomery, J. R., and Delhorey, P. D. A Statistical Analysis of a Pass-Fail Grading System. *The Journal of Experimental Education, 41*(1), 1972, 74-77.

Needham, J. G. *Honors-Pass-Fail: A Report.* Boston: Simmons College, 1970.

Office of Institutional Educational Research at Washington University. *Pass-Fail Evaluation: Phase II: Questionnaire Analysis.* Seattle, 1970. 30 pp.

Pass-Fail Study Committee. *Report to the Senate.* Washington, D.C., Phi Beta Kappa, 1969.

Priest, R. F. Why College Students Favor Grading Reforms. *The Journal of College Student Personnel, 12*(2), 1971, 120-125.

Quann, C. J. *The Pass-Fail Option: Analysis of an Experiment in Grading.* Athens, Ohio, 1971, 18 pp.

_____. Survey Shows Variations in Grading Trends. *College and University Business 49*(3), 1970, 77-78.

Rossman, J. E. Graduate School Attitudes to S-U Grades. *Educational Record, 51*(3), 1970, 310-313.

Sgan, M. R. Letter Grade Achievement in Pass-Fail Courses. *The Journal of Higher Education, 41*(8), 1970, 638-644.

_____. The First Year of Pass-Fail at Brandeis University: A Report. *The Journal of Higher Education, 40*(2), 1969, 135-144.

Simpson, C., Quann, C., King, H., Shantz, H., and Moen, C. Pass-Fail—What are the Trends? *College and University Business, 49*(3), 1970, 78-79.

Stallings, W. M., and Leslie, E. K. Student Attitudes Towards Grades and Grading. *Improving College and University Teaching, 18*(1), 1970, 66-68.

_____, Wolff, J. L., and Moehr, M. L. Fear of Failure and the Pass-Fail Grading Option. *The Journal of Experimental Education, 38*(2), 1969, 87-91.

_____, Smack, H. R., and Leslie, E. K. The Pass-Fail Grading

Option. *School and Society, 96*(2305), 1968, 179-180.

Tragesser, E. F., Arbolino, J., Huntly, S., Melville, G. S., Smith, R. E., and Montgomery, I. Are New Developments in Achievement Testing an Adequate Answer to Pass-Fail Grading Systems? *College and University, 43*(4), 1968, 565-567.

Von Wittich, B. The Impact of the Pass-Fail System upon Achievement of College Students. *Journal of Higher Education, 43,* 1972, 499-508.

Warren, J. R. *College Grading Practices: An Overview.* Washington, D.C., 1971, 29 pp.

Weems, J. E., Clements, W. H., Quann, C. J., Smith, K., and Schefelbein, B. E. Pass-Fail: Were the Hypotheses Valid? *College and University, 46,* 1971, 535-556.

Yuker, H. E. Grades and Grading Systems. *Higher Education Research Abstracts No. 6,* Hempstead, New York, 1969.

36

RECRUITMENT AND SELECTION OF EDUCATORS

by Kenneth A. Erickson
and
James L. Shinn
Field Training and Service Bureau
University of Oregon
Eugene, Oregon

The term "recruitment" will be used to describe activities designed to attract the quality and quantity of personnel necessary to fill the teaching and administrative vacancies in a school district. "Selection" will be used to designate activities designed to choose the best candidates from those recruited.

While the number of candidates for positions in education may make recruiting appear to be less necessary, the recruiting and selection process continues to be one of the most important facets of educational administration. The competency of the personnel administrator at one time was measured by whether all vacancies were filled; now his competency is evaluated on the basis of the quality of his choices from the candidates available. The personnel administrator, today, must be accountable for hiring errors which formerly might have been excused by a shortage of qualified candidates.

This chapter outlines two recruitment and selection plans—one designed to provide the best candidates for teaching positions, the other for administrative positions. While the suggestions given are designed for districts large enough to have a full-time personnel administrator, minor modifications would make them applicable to districts in which the building administrator or the superintendent is personally responsible for all recruitment and selection activities.

RECRUITMENT AND SELECTION OF TEACHERS

The first step in developing a recruiting plan is to analyze the needs of the district. Because so many of the best beginning teachers are hired early in the spring and are unavailable later, this needs analysis must be completed before most vacancies are known. Therefore, early assessment should be made of how many new teachers will be needed in a district. Both the few positions known to be vacant and a prediction of expected vacancies must be considered. Predictions can be based on anonymous questionnaires to teachers, in which they are asked to state the probability of their returning; predictions by building administrators and department heads; and district enrollment forecasts. Analysis of this data should predict the probable number of vacancies which will occur in various subjects and grade levels, and with this information it can be estimated how many candidates must be selected.

After this district analysis has been made, building principals should provide the personnel administrator with two types of position guides (or job descriptions). The first should be a detailed position analysis for each position already known to be vacant—detailed to the extent that the recruiting team can look for and employ specific candidates. This position analysis must include any special subject matter or methodology needed for the position, plus any co-curricular activity which the teacher must direct. A second, less detailed position analysis also should be prepared which outlines general teacher qualities needed when anticipated vacancies occur. Both of these descriptions will assist the personnel administrator in designing interview forms, and instruct the recruiter(s) regarding special employment needs.

The next task in completing a recruitment plan is to identify sources of prospective candidates to fill the vacancies. An often overlooked source consists of teachers in the district who have asked for reassignment, or whose reassignment is requested by their supervisors. Consideration of such requests results in more effective placement of teachers, and therefore higher staff morale. Another source consists of employees who are on leaves of absence and have requested assignments.

The major source of candidates for most districts is the new college graduate in education. Traditionally, school districts have asked interested graduating seniors to sign up for personal interviews. However, the larger number of education graduates who may sign up often is too great in relation to the number of vacancies normally available; thus, this plan may prove too costly both for districts and candidates.

A more up-to-date plan (designed by Dr. Forest Gathercoal of Oregon State University) features a group information session to which all candidates interested in a particular district are invited. This session is commonly held on campuses of colleges of education. A sufficient number of district staff members (who have been selected as recruiters) are sent to accommodate all interested candidates. A sign-up system is unnecessary and no candidates are turned away. Several group meetings may be held throughout the day to accommodate class schedules of the students and interested teachers from neighboring districts. At these group meetings the recruiters answer students' questions and discuss the district and its needs. Greater credibility in the sessions can be gained by having teachers from the district available to describe the working conditions of the district and to answer candidates' questions.

Those students interested in pursuing employment are asked to complete a preliminary application and leave it with the district recruiter. This application, together with the candidate's placement file, is examined by the recruiter, and a decision is made the same day as to whether the probability of employment for the candidate justifies a personal interview. If so, the placement office contacts that candidate by phone to schedule a later, in-depth interview. If there is little or no interest in the candidate, the district's personnel office writes and explains that a personal interview would not be profitable. Early use and evaluation of this plan indicates that students and recruiter feel it more desirable than the more traditional program.

Another source of candidates consists of teachers in other school districts. The most effective way to interest these teachers is to build exemplary working conditions, so that local staff members voluntarily encourage their friends, who may be teaching elsewhere, to apply. A well-designed recruitment brochure can be widely distributed to inspire interest from many areas.

TEACHER RECRUITMENT ACTIVITIES

Knowing the projected needs, the personnel officer is able to begin the recruiting effort. He must select any recruiting aides, decide on the geographic extent of the effort, and write correspondence necessary to communicate with candidates.

The skill of the interviewers is one of the most crucial ingredients of a successful recruiting effort. Bolton (1970) suggests the following criteria for selection of the interviewer:

Alertness to cues

Ability to make fine distinctions, perceive accurately

Ability to make immediate and accurate records

Willingness to use criteria established by the organization

Ability to suppress biases

Bolton also emphasizes that in addition to selecting interviewers carefully, attention should be paid to providing them with training and practice.

In choosing members of the selection team, it would be well to keep in mind the following conclusions from Bolton's research (1970):

Training and experience of a decision-maker influences his interpretation of information

Ability to interpret data is not related to sex

More accurate judgments are made by those who do not become emotionally involved or who are socially detached

Use of multiple raters tends to improve prediction

The selection decision is improved by using a single-page summary document, and by providing instructions on how to process information

Intensive recruiting activities will involve a minimum of three months, and requires concentrated effort by a number of district personnel. While some administrators work outside the district, others may interview local candidates. Recruitment activities conducted during college vacations assure that college students soon to graduate in education may seek an interview. Saturday interviews assure that interested employed teachers can be scheduled (necessary if experienced teachers are needed). Districts adopting a complacent attitude because of the abundance of candidates often find that outstanding candidates will be hired by the aggressive districts before these candidates have time to contact the less aggressive "competitors."

Interview questions may be designed in such a way that comparisons can be made between candidates interviewed by different team members. A simple set of questions, or a structure as sophisticated as a subset of the Ryan Characteristics of Teachers (Ryans, 1960), may be formulated by the administrative team. Discussions of interview techniques and report forms can be found in texts on personnel administration, which are included in the Bibliography.

Upon completing the screening process, the personnel office should have applications, placement files, and interview reports for a number of preferred candidates. All candidates who have been eliminated from consideration should be so informed promptly, to allow them time to search for employment elsewhere. Those in the preferred files should be contacted periodically and informed of their status until either they are hired or it is known they will not be needed.

TEACHER SELECTION PROCEDURES

A dilemma in some districts concerns who should make the final teacher selection. Technically, the school board does the hiring. In practice, however, the superintendent may delegate the nominating responsibility to the personnel office. The principal, if he is to become increasingly accountable for his building, should become more involved in selecting teachers. As specific vacancies in a particular school become known, the personnel administrator may refer one or more preferred candidates to the building administrator, from which he makes his recommendation. In some instances, the department chairmen seek involvement in the selection of teachers. In smaller districts, school board members may wish to involve themselves more in the selection process than in larger districts. However, most board members are in no way qualified by training or experience for the selection of teachers.

Even more important than who makes the final decision is how much time is spent on selection procedures by the various administrators. The personnel administrator is challenged to maintain a delicate balance between obtaining the best candidates and keeping time demands on administrators within reason. By carefully considering this balance, most vacancies can be filled with the right persons, and well in advance of the new school year.

If, during the selection process, a candidate is hired who does not meet each requirement of the position, the personnel office should note the deficiencies and report them both to the principal and to the department responsible for staff development. Compensatory inservice training should be designed to increase the teacher's effectiveness. A competent personnel department is responsible not only for recruitment and selection, but for making every effort to see that each teacher in the district has an opportunity to succeed.

RECRUITMENT AND SELECTION OF ADMINISTRATORS

The following section deals specifically with the selection of new school superintendents. However, many of these recommendations apply equally well to the selection of principals and other school administrators.

Because today's administrators face tremendous pressures and heavy responsibilities, it is essential to allocate adequate time and resources to search out and hire the most competent school administrators available. Some school boards seem to feel that a new face from a great distance may be the best candidate. Others may feel that someone working alongside the former administrator would make the smoothest transition, and therefore be a desirable candidate. Neither reasoning is necessarily sound. Indeed, if the top candidate is thought to be available within the local district, it is unfair both to all applicants and their sponsors to go through the motions of an extensive search. However, if any doubts exist concerning the in-district applicant, a wide-open search is advisable. One study has found that the larger the area of search for a new superintendent, the greater the satisfaction of the school board with the new superintendent in subsequent years.

Next, a time schedule should be developed showing dates for the following major recruitment decisions and activities: a general search plan, which includes qualifications desired, need for an advisor, compensation range, screening committee composition, geographical scope of search, type of vacancy announcement, and budget for the search; advertising of the vacancy, receipt of applications, completion of all files, screening of applicants, report to the board; disbanding of screening committee, establishment of interview schedule, visits to home district of board finalists, offer of contract, notification of unsuccessful candidates, and preparation of media announcements. This total process may require a minimum of four months.

There is a widely accepted statement to the effect that a school eventually reflects the nature of its principal. Similarly, a school superintendent has a strong effect on the potential progress or the perennial problems experienced by a school district. Those skills which make one an excellent teacher, counselor, or coach are not identical to those which make an excellent administrator. It is essential to develop criteria according to district needs, against which to measure prospective administrative candidates.

An early determination that must be made is whether the board will handle the selection process by itself or seek the assistance of an advisor. Because a thorough search takes both expertise and time, it is common practice for boards to choose a consultant to assist in securing the new superintendent. Such an advisor, who may be a former superintendent and/or a professor of educational administration, may help the board formulate criteria to be used in the selection process; contact important segments of the district to help assess the special needs and educational goals of the community; help outline contents of the recruitment brochure; advise on the composition and responsibilities of the screening committee; and assist with travel and interview suggestions when finalists are contacted.

VACANCY ANNOUNCEMENT

Since only the most competent applicants are being sought, and since such individuals are normally secure in their present positions, an attractive brochure may be necessary to arouse the interest of highly desirable candidates. An administrative job description is basic to the preparation of this brochure. The announcement should also indicate the reason for the vacancy, the educational philosophy of the school district, the application deadline and planned date of the announcement of the appointment, the salary range, information to be required of the applicant, and the person to whom applications should be sent. A statement of required and desired qualifications, and a description of the school district and the community, should be included.

Vacancy announcements or brochures may be distributed through county or intermediate school superintendents, university placement centers, key professors of educational administration, and state departments of education. The board's consultant will be aware of other helpful contacts for receiving names of outstanding applicants.

SCREENING OF APPLICANTS

Normally, a screening committee is appointed by the school board with assistance from its consultant. Some districts include both an administrative and a teacher representative on a screening committee. Each individual appointed by the school board must be completely trustworthy, should function as an individual and not as the representative of an organization, and be able to treat all information in a professional and confidential manner. Otherwise, it is safer to appoint a screening committee of professionals from outside the district, such as two school superintendents, a representative of the state department of education, a university representative with qualifying experience in public school administration, and one reliable community member (such as a former school board chairman) who is highly respected. In the interest of efficient screening, it is preferable to have a relatively small number of screening committee members, all highly qualified.

When selecting administrators other than superintendents, the screening committee usually consists of local district staff members. Their screening of final candidates becomes a recommendation to the superintendent who must initiate the final employment recommendation to the school board.

The screening committee should have an early meeting with the school board to explore the special attributes board members feel are necessary for the successful candidate. For example, does the board prefer a young candidate with less experience but very high potential or a candidate with considerable experience regardless of age? The screening committee also may meet with organizational representatives who will give their input prior to the screening process.

The school board's consultant coordinates the work of the screening committee as it reduces the number of applicants to the board's requested five or so finalists. This committee should carefully review all confidential papers and application material on each candidate, share information known about various candidates, and make all the telephone calls necessary to narrow the field of those considered to be semifinalists. It is helpful if the screening committee prepares a written one-page summary, based on phone contacts on each finalist recommended to the board.

The screening committee report is submitted to the board in executive session. This report should explain why certain candidates have been recommended, and answer any board questions about other applicants. The screening committee members must understand that the committee is officially disbanded once its report has been presented to the school board.

SCREENING OF FINALISTS

When superintendent candidates have been selected for board interview, one board member, or a selected district staff member, is designated as host to meet each visiting candidate and give him a tour of the district. Each candidate should be accorded the same length of visit—a minimum of one-half day and an evening. The consultant may be asked to suggest questions that might be asked of all candidates.

The local school board should pay all travel and subsistence costs involved in bringing a candidate to the community for an interview. The only exception to this practice may be an advance agreement with each finalist that these expenses will be paid unless the position is offered and turned down by the candidate. This practice may ensure that only serious candidates will accept the board's invitation for an onsite visit and interview.

After the school board reduces the number of finalists to one or two candidates, it should arrange for a visitation by a board representative to the candidates' home communities to interview such persons as school board members, the mayor, city manager, ministers, teachers association officers, a banker, and PTA officers, to learn more about the candidate. While interviewing these community leaders, the reputation of the local candidate must be safeguarded; it is helpful to remind those being interviewed that other excellent individuals are under con-

sideration, so the local candidate will not be embarrassed if unsuccessful. Questions asked the community leaders should include: Is the candidate able to make sound decisions? Are board policies carried out with sincerity? What is the quality of staff morale? Is the administrator ethical in all of his contacts? Does he bring full information in well-prepared form to the board? Are his personal traits appropriate for this type of position? Also, to learn more about the candidate it is important to meet with him and his wife sometime during this visitation.

After the board has agreed on a finalist, he may be brought to the school district again to discuss salary and related matters. The new superintendent may also be interviewed by the press, and simultaneous announcements should be made in the home community and the employing community.

UNSUCCESSFUL APPLICANTS

A major complaint of unsuccessful candidates is that they seldom hear anything as to the status of their application. Once consideration has been narrowed to several finalists, a letter should go to all other applicants thanking them for their interest and telling them they are no longer in contention. Finalists not selected for the position also should receive a personal letter from the board chairman thanking them for their participation, recognizing that they became finalists and indicating that an announcement of the board's final selection will be made within a few days.

SUMMARY

This article has emphasized the continuing importance of the recruitment function for teachers and educational administrators, and has presented ideas useful to the reader in developing selection procedures to fit local needs.

A district must be concerned not only with the development of a selection process, but with the evaluation of that process. This evaluation must not only be well planned, but must be a continuing process. Bolton (1970) states, "The implication of research findings and advice from measurement specialists is that any measure of success of a selection process is likely to be only temporary. This means that the value of the procedure should be checked periodically."

Whatever system the reader develops, concern for the welfare of the unsuccessful candidates should not be overlooked. A well-planned, well-administered selection program will not only provide excellent teachers and leaders for youth, but will add materially to a district's reputation.

REFERENCES

Bolton, Dale L. *The Selection and Evaluation of Teachers.* Final Report, Project No. 9-0572, U.S. Department of Health, Education and Welfare, 1970.

_____. *The Use of Simulation in Educational Administration.* Columbus, Ohio: Charles E. Merrill Publishing Co., 1971.

_____. *Variables Affecting Decision Making in the Selection of Teachers.* Final Report, Project No. 6-1349. U.S. Office of

Education, 1968.

Castetter, W. B. *The Personnel Function in Educational Administration.* New York: The Macmillan Co., 1971.

Ryans, David G. *Characteristics of Teachers, Their Description, Comparison and Appraisal.* Washington, D.C.: American Council of Education, 1960.

McIntyre, Kenneth E. *Selection of Educational Administrators.* Austin, Texas: University Council of Educational Administration, 1966.

37

CAMPUS SIZE: SOME RECENT DEVELOPMENTS

by Donald J. Reichard
Director of Institutional Research
University of North Carolina at Greensboro

In recent years, a number of factors have emerged which heighten interest in the question of how big a single campus of a college or university should be, and the manner in which institutions are dealing with size-related problems. Foremost in importance has been the vast increase in enrollments in higher education during the 1960s, and the accompanying increases in the size of individual institutions.

Concern with possible dysfunctional social-psychological, organizational, and economic aspects of institutional size has also attracted the interest of both academicians and legislators to the question of "ideal" institutional size. At the same time, an increasingly stringent financial situation, affecting public and private institutions of all sizes, has encouraged administrators and higher education researchers to examine the possibility of achieving various economies of scale in internal operations.

Despite the increasing amount of attention being devoted to the topic, a review of the literature and institutional experience in dealing with size-related problems reveals the lack of widely applicable answers to how big a college or university should be, as well as the necessity for each institution to find its own answers to its own problems.

SCOPE

In the period 1960 to 1970, higher education enrollments increased by 212 percent in public institutions and 38 percent in private institutions (Shell, 1973). Along with the increase in overall enrollments came a dramatic increase in the average size of colleges and universities, from 1,828 students in 1960 to 3,146 students in 1969 (Gaff, 1970). Gaff's figures with regard to average institutional size (p. 9) contrast with Carnegie Commission on Higher Education figures showing Fall, 1970 median FTE enrollments of 1,820 in public institutions and 664 in private institutions (see Table 1, below).

Nationally, during the period 1960-1970 the percentage of public and private institutions enrolling less than 1,000 students dropped from 63 percent in 1960 to 47 percent in 1970, while institutions enrolling more than 5,000 represented nine percent of all institutions in 1960 and 16 percent in 1970 (American Council on Education, 1972).

Over a somewhat longer time period, the percentage of all students who were enrolled in higher education institutions with less than 1,000 students dropped from 32 percent in 1937-1938 to eight percent in 1967-1968. On the other hand, the percentage of students attending institutions enrolling 2,500 or more students increased from 49 percent in 1937-1938 to 79 percent in 1967-1968 (Southern Regional Education Board, 1971).

REVIEW OF THE LITERATURE AND DEVELOPMENTS

Apart from the statistics relating the changes in higher education enrollments, institutional size, and patterns of student enrollments in institutions of various sizes, published literature relating to institutional size is largely of a fragmented, single-issue-oriented nature. Individual scholars or researchers have become interested in size-related problems as a result of their academic backgrounds, or interests developed in special areas which often reflect the orientations of the researcher's institution. The literature on institutional size consists mainly of general overviews of the topic, discussions relating to economic aspects of size, and discussions of the relationship between size and institutional quality.

General Overviews

The most extensive effort to review a wide variety of literature relating to size of institutions has been made by the California State Colleges (1970). The publication contains pertinent excerpts from articles and books, as well as several complete documents dealing with size-related questions.

Reichard's (1971) selective review of literature, relating to the economic, organizational, and social-psychological aspects of institutional size, notes findings relative to large multiversities as well as smaller liberal arts colleges. The review of literature with regard to social-psychological aspects of size cites literature relative to organizational and attitudinal correlates of size, the supposed virtues of smaller sized institutions, the effect of size upon the learning environment, and the complex relationship between student protest and institutional size. The review takes an intra-institutional view in examining the cluster college as an alternative organizational adaptation to increased size.

An insightful general discussion of university size by two staff members of the Iowa State Board of Regents reflects a state-wide, interinstitutional orientation in exploring the consequences of alternative policies to be considered relative to institutional growth (Porter and McMurry, 1970). They note the nature of the increasing state interest in higher education and the possibility of achieving economies of scale in several areas of university operations. The authors also consider the feasibility of greater utilization of regional consortia and cluster colleges, and the establishment of enrollment limitations for existing institutions (or the establishment of new institutions) as means of dealing with possible dysfunctions of increased size.

Hodgkinson (1971, pp. 26-33) found that presidents of colleges and universities of varying size reported different perceptions of the extent of changes affecting the student body, faculty, and administration over the period 1958-1968. As size of institution increased, so did the percentage of presidents of institutions in the various size categories who reported increases in the quality of student preparation in high school. The percent of an institution's graduating class planning further education increased as size increased, as did the percentage of students participating in community volunteer programs, the percentage of students who had transferred into the institution, and the ratio of graduate to undergraduate students.

Hodgkinson's data indicate that tenure appeared to be awarded at an earlier average age to faculty in progressively larger institutions. Commitment to research generally increased, while commitment to teaching declined, as size of the institution increased. In keeping

with the relatively greater increase in research, larger institutions reported a larger percentage of their total budget to be based upon Federal support.

Activities of the Carnegie Commission on Higher Education, and the deteriorating financial condition of institutions of higher education, have been particularly influential in adding to the volume of literature with regard to the economic aspects of institutional size. In one of the first publications in the Carnegie series, Dunham (1969) raised the question of the relationship between size and cost, and stressed the need to pay more attention to the influence of size upon students, faculty, and institutional cohesiveness. Subsequent staff reports of the Carnegie Commission on Higher Education (1971, 1972b) have posed recommended enrollment limitations, and have dealt in detail with possible sources of economies of scale in institutions of various types and sizes.

After an extensive analysis of secondary data adapted from U.S. Office of Education sources, the Carnegie Commission on Higher Education (1971) recommended full-time equivalent enrollment ranges for public institutions of 5,000-20,000 in doctoral institutions, 5,000-10,000 in comprehensive colleges, 1,000-2,500 in liberal arts colleges, and 2,000-5,000 for two-year colleges (pp. 82-83). If the recommended enrollment ranges are accepted as having some validity, Table 1, citing Fall,

TABLE 1. NUMBER AND PERCENTAGE OF INSTITUTIONS OF HIGHER EDUCATION IN U.S. BY TYPE OF CONTROL UNDER, WITHIN, OR OVER FTE ENROLLMENT LIMITATIONS SUGGESTED BY CARNEGIE COMMISSION ON HIGHER EDUCATION—FALL, 1970

Type of Institution	Total Number	Percent Underenrolled	Percent Within Suggested Enrollment Range	Percent Overenrolled	Median FTE Enrollment
Doctoral Granting (5,000-20,000)					
Public	101	3.0	74.3	22.7	14,885
Private	63	31.8	61.9	6.3	7,053
Comprehensive Colleges (5,000-10,000)					
Public	316	58.0	29.4	12.6	4,340
Private	147	89.8	10.2	–	2,282
Liberal Arts Colleges (1,000-2,500)					
Public	27	74.1	–	25.9	784
Private	676	67.6	28.8	3.6	804
Two-Year Institutions (2,000-5,000)					
Public	805	61.4	31.0	7.6	1,140
Private	256	96.1	3.9	–	326
All Institutions	2,391	65.0	28.3	6.7	
Public	1,249	56.0	33.5	10.5	1,820[1]
Private	1,042	74.9	22.7	2.4	664[1]

[1]Including specialized institutions not shown.

Adapted from Carnegie Commission on Higher Education. *New Students and New Places.* New York: McGraw-Hill, 1971, pp. 68-69.

1970 FTE enrollments, demonstrates conclusively that problems associated with underenrollment, rather than overenrollment, are much more common in the nation's colleges and universities.

The Commission (1971) found that various types of institutions faced special problems in attempting to achieve economies of scale, with regard to educational costs per student which were defined as educational, and general expense less expenditures for organized research. In doctoral institutions, educational expenditures per full-time student fell sharply as FTE enrollments increased to about 5,000. Per-student costs fell less sharply thereafter until FTE enrollments approached 15,000. Possible economies of scale tended to be offset by an increased ratio of graduate to undergraduate students, increases in the number of faculty members per field, and increases in the number of degree fields as enrollment grew. Among public comprehensive colleges (primarily master's degree-granting institutions), instructional costs per FTE student showed no economies of scale beyond enrollments of 2,000-2,500, due to increased costs associated with expanded program offerings (pp. 69-73).

In "quality" liberal arts colleges, characterized by relatively high per-student expenditures and higher selectivity, educational costs per FTE student dropped sharply up to about 900 FTE, and dropped less sharply until FTE enrollments neared 2,000. As enrollment increased in liberal arts colleges with lower per student expenditures, the Commission (1971) found that economies tended to be offset by a wider range of courses, an increased number of faculty per field, and higher average salaries. Similar factors tended to offset possible economies of scale after enrollment reached about 2,000 FTE in public two-year institutions (pp. 75-78).

A more extensive analysis of data collected by the U.S. Office of Education's Higher Education General Information Survey was made by the Carnegie Commission on Higher Education (1972b). It points out significant economics of scale in expenditures for administration and student services, plant maintenance and operation, and libraries (p. 172). This study revealed a consistent inverse relationship between educational costs and increased enrollments. The study also showed that total per-student expenditures were higher in private two-year institutions with less than 1,000 students than in similar publicly supported institutions. As enrollments in two-year institutions increased, total expenditures remained higher for private than public institutions, although less was spent on instruction and departmental research due to higher administrative expenses (p. 183).

Apart from the Carnegie efforts to identify economies of scale in institutional operations, Maynard (1971) and Jenny and Wynn (1970, 1972) have pursued the question of economies of scale with reference to particular institutional types. Realizing the vast differences in expenditures among institutions with varied resources, Maynard attempts to derive a meaningful relationship between size and cost per student among 123 presumably homogeneous state colleges in 13 states. Maynard notes that a FTE enrollment of around 5,400 students is the point where "maximum economies of scale are realized." His

study is noteworthy primarily as an attempt to subject the operations of higher education institutions to systematic economic analysis.

Jenny and Wynn (1970, 1972) have investigated the possibility of achieving economies of scale among 48 liberal arts colleges which enrolled from 476 to 2,513 students in 1968. Jenny and Wynn (1972) conclude that "individual institutions may have to increase their enrollments so as not to pass all the new fixed costs on to the present number of students enrolled (p. 64)."

Parden (1971) also distinguishes between fixed and variable costs in applying breakeven analyses, all income and expense categories must be classified as fixed or variable with respect to changes in enrollment. The author notes that economies of scale occur only when increased enrollment generates more income than the additional variable costs incurred without adding to fixed costs. Otherwise, there would be no advantage to enrollment growth.

Ruml and Morrison's study (1959) deals clearly with the question of institutional size, and remains as timely today as when it was first written. It demonstrates that any enrollment from 800 to 3,000 can be "ideal" for a given liberal arts college, provided that prior planning indicates how revenues derived from specified enrollments are to be allocated in a manner consistent with institutional purposes.

Bowen and Douglas (1961) confine themselves primarily to analyzing the possibilities of achieving efficiency and curricular diversity through the use of various instructional modes in liberal arts colleges enrolling around 1,200 students. They also note the effects of enrollment growth in achieving decreased instructional costs by demonstrating the increased average section sizes possible when institutions offering identical curricula increase their enrollments from 1,200 to 2,400. The Ruml and Morrison and Bowen and Douglas studies are both extremely important because they demonstrate the necessity of, and benefits possible through, comprehensive, institution-side planning in small colleges.

Size and Institutional Quality

Astin and Lee (1972) use size and selectivity of institutions as the two primary variables in identifying some 494 "invisible" colleges. Private four-year institutions enrolling less than 2,500 students, and having combined mean SAT Verbal and Mathematical scores of less than 1,000, were regarded as "invisible" colleges. Their characteristics were contrasted with those of larger, more selective institutions.

The authors concluded that a substantial enrollment size almost guaranteed a moderate degree of selectivity. Thus the least selective institutions were concentrated among the smallest colleges, and relatively few very large institutions were found in the very low selectivity levels. Approximately 81 percent of private four-year colleges enrolling less than 500 were classified as "invisible," as were 65 percent of institutions enrolling 500-999, and 47 percent of institutions in the 1,000-2,499 enrollment category. In larger enrollment categories, the percentage of institutions enrolling student bodies with total mean

SAT scores of less than 1,000 decreased steadily as enrollment increased (pp. 10-11).

Blau (1973) noted that size exerts a pervasive influence on organizational characteristics in all organizations, and that academic institutions are no exception. Blau notes the dilemma created by the fact that the financial assets of larger institutions allow for higher faculty salaries and the recruitment of faculty oriented to scholarly research, while at the same time "the impersonal atmosphere in multi-universities, independent of other conditions, appears to make them less attractive for the best students as well as the best faculty members and to weaken faculty allegiance to the institution (pp. 253-254)." Twenty-one direct effects of size are classified under the main categories of economic and manpower resources, impersonality, and administrative load. Blau's work is significant in that he examines the effects of size from a formal organizational view, by applying such concepts as differentiation of function, span of control, and bureaucratic and professional authority, to academic institutions.

In his 1973 article, Sutherland considered the optimum size for a traditional, single-campus university offering the main academic disciplines as well as several professional areas of training. Sutherland was less concerned with determining an optimum economic size than with determining an optimum size with regard to academic distinction.

Sutherland builds a theoretical model of an academically distinguished university by noting that such an institution (without professional schools) should have approximately 25 departments, with an average of 25 faculty members in each department and a student-staff ratio of 8:1-10:1. These figures would yield an institution with a minimum enrollment of 5,000-6,250. If six professional schools with about 250 students each were added, minimum "ideal" enrollments would rise to about 7,750. Sutherland hesitantly reaches an ideal maximum size by expanding the number of departments to 30 while maintaining an average of 25 faculty members per department and raising the student-staff ratio to 12:1. These figures yield 9,000 students in general studies, to which another 3,000 professional students are added, giving a totel optimum maximum enrollment of 12,000 (p. 77).

In arriving at an optimum enrollment range for a university of between 7,750 and 12,000 students, Sutherland acknowledged that larger institutions could offer high quality programs. However, he indicated a strong preference for several universities, located in separate regions and enrolling less than 15,000 each, than for a single multiversity enrolling 30,000 to 40,000 students.

Gallant and Prothero (1972) also seriously question the assumption that bigger is necessarily better. Using the biological analogy of "scaling up," they argue against the proposition that continuous growth should be accepted as unavoidable, or should be assumed to be manageable. The authors cite diffusion, absence of community, dead-end overspecialization, administrative complexity, bureaucracy, alienation, and a tendency to engage in status games as outcomes or correlates of dysfunctional growth. Possible economies of scale, the achievement of a critical

mass, and increased flexibility are cited as potentially functional aspects of growth.

Cartter (1966) urged that the concept of optimal size also be applied to departments, as well as the university as a whole (pp. 113-114). In this regard the National Science Board (1969), after an intensive investigation of Cartter's (1966) departmental ratings, tentatively concluded that at least seven faculty members were generally needed to form a critical mass capable of facilitating communication within a department (pp. 98-99). The Board further noted that higher quality departments tended to be large departments, but that the achievement of adequate departmental size did not mean that high quality would follow. Thus, in examining the relationship between departmental size and Roose and Anderson's (1970) ratings of the quality of graduate faculty in the fields of biochemistry, economics, philosophy, physics, and physiology, Gallant and Prothero found significant but conflicting Spearman rank-order correlations between departmental size and "quality" ratings only in biochemistry (-.65) and in economics (+.49) (p. 384).

DEALING WITH SIZE

With some exceptions (University of Virginia, 1972), institutions of higher education have seldom made extensive efforts to determine optimal enrollments. Thus, the fact that only 28 percent of the campuses of higher education institutions in the nation have enrollments which the Carnegie Commission on Higher Education views as economically and/or operationally feasible (Table 1) should stir institutional and state level higher education planners to investigate the various effects of institutional size more thoroughly.

Although only seven percent of the nation's institutions might be regarded as overenrolled by Carnegie Commission criteria, most of the attention in the popular press and in state legislatures has centered upon the problems of the multiversity. On the other hand, the efforts of 65 percent of the nation's institutions to reach economically efficient enrollments, or make ends meet in the face of stable or dwindling enrollments, go largely without notice.

Attempts to solve problems associated with large size have varied among the approximately 70 institutions currently enrolling over 20,000 students. Some institutions, such as the University of Washington (Gallant and Prothero, 1972), have created special faculty councils charged with examining institutional growth and related matters (p. 388). The University of Florida (Southern Regional Education Board, 1972) has attempted to identify optimum enrollment levels for colleges, departments and other subunits. Elsewhere, the vulnerability and incapacity of large institutions during a time of disruption has served as an impetus for reorganizing administrative structures (University of Maryland, 1970).

One of the most significant adaptations to increased size which is gaining increased acceptance (Assembly on University Goals and Governance, 1971) has been the establishment of cluster colleges, in an attempt to create smaller, more personalized learning environments within larger universities (Gaff, 1970; Lichtman, 1971; Dressel, 1971; Southern Regional Education Board, 1971). In a more cautious vein, Sutherland (1973) notes that "the majority of the Oxford and Cambridge colleges are living on the accumulated wealth of several centuries (p. 60)." He therefore appears less optimistic that many American universities will have either the resources or the authority to grant the autonomy necessary if cluster colleges are to become a viable, widely adopted organizational form in American higher education.

State-level decisions to establish upper division colleges in Illinois, Texas, New York, and Florida have in effect placed limitations on the size of existing institutions (Altman, 1970; Southern Regional Education Board, 1971). Also at the state level, decisions to establish new two- or four-year institutions, particularly in metropolitan areas (Carnegie Commission on Higher Education, 1971, 1973a), would relieve growth pressures upon existing institutions.

At the other end of the size continuum, underenrollment appears to be a problem facing the great majority of liberal arts colleges and two-year institutions. Size-related problems faced by the liberal arts college center upon efforts to obtain minimum enrollments which will provide a stable fiscal base. The fate of the small college appears precarious, especially with the failure to pass Federal institutional aid legislation which would have had a particularly favorable effect upon smaller institutions (Carnegie Commission on Higher Education, 1972a).

The decreasing pool of applicants in private institutions, and the increasing tuition differential between private institutions and low-cost public colleges, make it unrealistic to expect that a large percentage of currently underenrolled institutions could increase their enrollments significantly. Smaller institutions may be aided by proposed Carnegie Commission on Higher Education (1973b) recommendations if enacted, which call for raising public tuition charges—thus making private institutions more competitive price-wise. In any event, institutions wishing to stay small, in the hope of retaining or creating a more personalized learning environment, must be aware of the additional cost per student. Some institutions—as suggested by the Carnegie Commission and others—may do well to consider merging with other colleges or universities.

The recent establishment of a large number of publicly supported two-year institutions might explain why so many have not yet attracted the minimum of 2,000 students recommended by the Carnegie Commission. On the other hand, few branch campuses of senior institutions may be expected to reach a minimum enrollment figure of 2,000 students due to the more limited nature of their course offerings. The tendency for each county to want its own public two-year institution regardless of programs offered in surrounding communities, may place unjustifiable demands on state and local tax resources, and make it unlikely that a large percentage of two-year institutions will reach economically efficient enrollment levels.

CURRENT CONTROVERSIES

The debate on the optimum size of a college or university continues to take place, and some consensus is beginning to emerge in various countries throughout the world (Carnegie Commission on Higher Education, 1972a; Walsh, 1972). In the United States, however, no consensus has emerged as to how big a given college or university campus should be. Furthermore, with the present decentralization of decision-making in American higher education, no consensus is likely to emerge. Nor should it, if institutional diversity is to be encouraged and/or preserved.

The debate on institutional size does not center upon the virtues of planned versus unplanned growth, or the virtues of large or small size. Rather it centers upon the determination of functional versus dysfunctional size or growth, the establishment of new institutions versus the expansion of existing institutions, or the advisability of state-level-initiated planning versus institutionally initiated planning.

In a time of declining enrollment growth, and actual enrollment decreases in some colleges and universities, institutions of all sizes are going to have to face the fact that the extra 100, 500, or 1,000 students anticipated for the next year may not materialize. Learning to live with existing size levels will shift the emphasis from determining optimal university size to determining possible economies of scale, or optimum sizes for individual colleges, divisions, departments, and programs.

Other than noting that institutions enrolling less than 1,000 students are going to be high-cost operations, and that institutions generally experience very little reduction in unit costs beyond an enrollment of 15,000, there are few, if any, rules of thumb to indicate how big a college or university should be. Indeed, without the specification of well-defined institutional objectives, necessary financial resources, desired program content, organizational characteristics, and interpersonal relationships, there can be no single optimal size for an individual institution, let alone a group of institutions.

As individual institutions gain clearer pictures of the purposes they serve and the resources available to them, they will come to realize that almost *any* size may be optional, provided adequate prior planning has taken place.

REFERENCES

Altman, Robert A. *The Upper Division College.* San Francisco: Jossey-Bass, 1970.

American Council on Education. *A Fact Book on Higher Education: Third Issue.* Washington, D.C.: American Council on Education, 1972.

Astin, Alexander W., and Lee, Calvin B. T. *The Invisible Colleges: A Profile of Small, Private Colleges with Limited Resources.* New York: McGraw-Hill, 1972.

Assembly on University Goals and Governance. *A First Report.* Cambridge, Massachusetts: The Assembly on University Goals and Governance, 1971.

Blau, Peter M. *The Organization of Academic Work.* New York: John Wiley and Sons, 1973.

Bowen, Howard, and Douglass, Gordon K. *Efficiency in Liberal*

Education: A Study of Comparative Instructional Costs for Different Ways of Organizing Teaching. New York: McGraw-Hill, 1971.

California State Colleges. *How Big? A Review of the Literature on the Problems of Campus Size.* Los Angeles: Division of Institutional Research, Office of the Chancellor, the California State Colleges, 1970.

Carnegie Commission on Higher Education. *New Students and New Places: Policies for the Future Growth and Development of Higher Education.* New York: McGraw-Hill, 1971.

_____. *Institutional Aid: Federal Support to Colleges and Universities.* New York: McGraw-Hill, 1972a.

_____. *The More Effective Use of Resources: An Imperative for Higher Education.* New York: McGraw-Hill, 1972b.

_____. *Reform on Campus: Changing Students, Changing Academic Programs.* New York: McGraw-Hill, 1972c.

_____. *The Campus and the City: Maximizing Assets and Reducing Liabilities.* New York: McGraw-Hill, 1973a.

_____. *Higher Education: Who Pays? Who Benefits? Who Should Pay?* New York: McGraw-Hill, 1973b.

Cartter, Allan M. *An Assessment of Quality in Graduate Education.* Washington, D.C.: American Council on Education, 1966.

Chickering, Arthur W. *Education and Identity.* San Francisco: Jossey-Bass, 1969.

Dressel, Paul L. *The New Colleges: Toward an Appraisal.* Iowa City, Iowa: American College Testing Program, 1971.

Dunham, E. Alden. *Colleges of the Forgotten Americans: A Profile of State Colleges and Regional Universities.* New York: McGraw-Hill, 1969.

Gaff, Jerry G., and Associates. *The Cluster College.* San Francisco: Jossey-Bass, 1970.

Gallant, Jonathan A., and Prothero, John W. Weight Watching at the University: The Consequences of Growth. *Science,* 1972, *175,* 381-388.

Hodgkinson, Harold L. *Institutions in Transition: A Profile of Change in Higher Education.* New York: McGraw-Hill, 1971.

Illinois Board of Higher Education. *Institutional Size and Capacity: Report of Committee L, Master Plan Phase III Committee to the Illinois Board of Higher Education,* 1970.

Jenny, H. H., and Wynn, G. Richard. *The Golden Years: A Study of Income and Expenditure Growth and Distribution of 48 Private Four-Year Liberal Arts Colleges 1960-1968.* Wooster, Ohio: The College of Wooster, 1970.

_____. *The Turning Point: A Study of Income and Expenditure Growth Distribution of 48 Private Four-Year Liberal Arts Colleges 1960-70.* Wooster, Ohio: The College of Wooster, 1972.

Lichtman, Jane. *The Experimental Sub-College.* Washington, D.C.: ERIC Clearinghouse on Higher Education, 1971.

Maynard, James. *Some Microeconomics of Higher Education: Economies of Scale.* Lincoln, Nebraska: University of Nebraska Press, 1971.

National Science Board. *Graduate Education: Parameters for Public Policy.* Washington, D.C.: National Science Foundation, 1969.

Parden, Robert J. The Use of Breakeven Analysis in Developing an Optimum Institutional Size. *Institutional Research and Communication in Higher Education: Proceedings of the 10th Annual Forum on Institutional Research.* Association for Institutional Research, 1970, 209-214.

Porter, Paul V., and McMurray, Robert G. How Big Should A University Be? *Toward an understanding of Higher Education.* Council of State Governments, 1970, 15-22.

Reichard, Donald J. *Campus Size: A Selective Review.* Atlanta: Southern Regional Education Board, 1971.

Roose, Kenneth D., and Anderson, Charles J. *A Rating of Graduate Programs.* Washington, D.C.: American Council on Education, 1970.

Ruml, Beardsley, and Morrison, Donald H. *Memo to a College Trustee.* New York: McGraw-Hill, 1969.

Sanford, Nevitt R. *Where Colleges Fail.* San Francisco: Jossey-Bass, 1967.

Shell, Helene I. Enrollment Trends in Higher Education. *ERIC Higher Education Research Currents. College and University Bulletin,* June, 1973, *25,* 5-8.

Southern Regional Education Board. Cluster and Upper Division Colleges: New Organizational Forms in Higher Education. *Issues in Higher Education,* No. 2, 1971.

_____. Underenrollment a Problem?: Examining the Size of Southern Institutions. *Regional Action,* December 1972, *23,* 4-5.

Sutherland, Gordon. Is There an Optimum Size for a University? *Minerva,* 1973, *11,* 53-78.

University of Maryland. *Academic Organization Study Committee Report to the Chancellor.* College Park, Maryland: November 1970.

University of Virginia. *The University of Virginia in the Decade of the Seventies: A Report of the Findings and Recommendations of the Committee on the Future of the University.* Charlottesville, Virginia: The University of Virginia, April, 1972.

Walsh, John. French University Reorganization: Voila: Thirteen Universities of Paris. *Science,* 1972, *176,* 621-622.

38

THE SCHOOL BUSING ISSUE

by Howard Ozmon
and
Sam Craver
Virginia Commonwealth University
Richmond, Virginia

HISTORICAL BACKGROUND

In the earliest days of the American public school, the problem of transportation for school children was considered the family's responsibility. Wherever possible, children walked to the nearest one-room school, or, in more sparsely populated areas, families would cooperate in providing transportation for their children. As early as 1838, Horace Mann was urging the public to recognize that a school could not be built within walking distance of every child; therefore some type of transportation would have to be provided.

This early consideration of transportation went with another public school dilemma: the proliferation of small, poorly operated, one-room, one-teacher schools. Educators and the concerned public soon realized that combining small schools into larger ones would more efficiently utilize economic resources, as well as provide a better educational environment. Thus, at an early date school consolidation and pupil transportation at public expense developed together—the growth of one spurring the growth of the other. More and more states followed the lead of Massachusetts in passing legislation providing for transportation funds in 1869, and several years later for consolidation. According to Noble (1940), by 1913 the 48 states had all passed some form of school consolidation law, and by 1920 all states had provided laws with regard to the transportation of school pupils at public expense. By the end of the school year 1923–1924, more than 800,000 students were being transported in the United States, and busing had become the chief means of conveying these students. By the school year 1937–1938, more than three million students were being bused.

But there was another aspect to the busing story. Myrdal (1944) reported that in ten southern states in the school year 1935–1936, blacks constituted 28 percent of the public school enrollment, but they received only 3 percent of the total expenditures for transportation. While bus service was generally provided for whites, it was less adequately provided for blacks. Many black families had to pay for private bus service or do without, and a significant number did without. Even if bus service were provided for blacks, they were often bused greater distances over longer periods of time so they could attend an all-black school.

So long as blacks were bused in segregated buses to segregated schools during the decades from the 1920s to the 1950s, there was no public outcry. But when busing began to be used as a serious tool in the desegregation process, there was heated opposition from some sectors of the public. Thus, busing became a controversy which has crucially divided the public in recent years. Even though busing is only a part of the larger desegregation effort, it is nontheless a problem with no simple solutions.

It may be said that the heart of the issue involved in busing is the concept of equality of opportunity, which has historically been a part of the American experiment and implied in the Declaration of Independence. The busing controversy strongly indicates contemporary confusion about equality, a confusion marked by uncertainty, disharmony, and a dismaying lack of clarity. Indeed, it could be said that it exemplifies America's confusion over moral and social values.

LEGAL ASPECTS

Much of the drama of busing has occurred in the courts. Few legal decisions in the twentieth century have so affected American life as the *Brown* case (1954 and 1955). While *Brown* did not deal with busing, it did delineate unconstitutional racial inequalities in the schools. The legal doctrines and precedents established by *Brown* were to have long-range repercussions in American education, and on busing as a traditional adjunct to education.

In the years immediately following 1954, very little progress was made in eliminating school segregation maintained by state laws. Finally, in *Green v. County School Board* (1968), the Court was faced with a number of "freedom of choice" programs which were used to preserve a dual system more than a decade after *Brown*. While the Court realized that a freedom of choice plan could have desirable consequences in some circumstances, the plan's failure to be effective in *Green* required that stronger efforts be made by school boards to end segregation immediately. School authorities were "clearly charged with the affirmative duty to take whatever steps might be necessary to convert to a unitary system in which racial discrimination would be eliminated root and branch." The "root and branch" wording of *Green* left little doubt about the Court's intent; however, eliminating legal (de jure) segregation was one thing, and eliminating nonlegal (de facto) segregation, such as housing patterns, was another. Busing appeared to many people as the easier course in dealing with de facto segregation.

The court battle was extended in the Charlotte-Mecklenburg schools of North Carolina by *Swann* (1972). In *Swann*, the Supreme Court held that if school authorities failed in their obligation to develop desegregated, unitary school systems, then the courts had the power to provide a remedy insuring a unitary system. There was a need to find means to hasten desegregation, and busing was deemed an appropriate measure. The Court concluded that the argument against busing would have validity only when the distance of travel was so great as to risk either the health of the children or to impinge significantly on the educational process.

The legal aspects of the busing controversy came to a head in two very similar cases, the Richmond case and the Detroit case. In *Bradley v. the School Board of the City of Richmond, Virginia* (1972), the District Court brought forth a storm of protest when it ordered the counties of Henrico and Chesterfield (which had been separate districts since 1871) to be merged with the City of Richmond to create a single unitary school system for the purpose of desegregation. Although this case was not one dealing with busing per se, busing was held to be the most feasible way in which to achieve immediately a more equitable distribution. The schools in the City of Richmond were found to be substandard when compared with those in surrounding areas. They were marked by deteriorating architecture, a proliferation of drugs, and violence. Inner-city schools were predominantly black, and even with inner-city busing, more black than white children attended schools in the City of Richmond. The decision meant that many students would be bused, and black students would then constitute a minority of the overall school population.

On June 5, 1972, the United States Circuit Court of Appeals for the Fourth Circuit, in a five-to-one vote, reversed the District Court decision. The majority opinion held that the District Court's decision was an attempt to restructure the internal government of a state, and in attempting this restructuring the District Court was exceeding its authority. It was emphasized that the Supreme Court, in *Swann,* ruled that local school authorities had broad powers, and that judicial authority could intervene only when local authority defaulted, or when there was a constitutional violation. The decision to consolidate Henrico and Chesterfield counties with the City of Richmond was unfounded, since there was no constitutional violation and no default by local authority. Each of the separate units was a unitary system, and once a local authority had achieved a unitary school system it met the requirements of law. In addition, the majority opinion of the Court of Appeals was that the increasingly black population of Richmond was not brought about and perpetuated by the state or by a collusion of the affected counties and the City of Richmond. The Court maintained that it was not known exactly how this state of affairs came into existence, either in Richmond or in other cities across the country.

Interestingly, the Court's reversal was not based on any apparent considerations of busing. The word "busing" was not even used in the text of the majority opinion. Reversal was based on the grounds that the District Court had exceeded its authority in ordering consolidation of three distinct unitary systems. The Court of Appeals did not rule on the legality of crossbusing for the purposes of integration; thus, the legality of busing for the purposes of integration within the boundaries of a unitary school district was not overruled.

The case was then appealed to the United States Supreme Court. Because one of the nine justices, Lewis Powell, a native of Richmond, had been involved in the case prior to his appointment to the Court, he disqualified himself. The Court tied, four-to-four, on the case. In effect the Court did not decide the issue, but allowed the Court of Appeals decision to stand, with the practical result that conditions in Richmond did not change.

Litigation, however, was still active in the Detroit case. In *Bradley v. Milliken* (1972), the District Court ordered a metropolitan remedy through the consolidation of 53 districts, both urban and suburban, into one large district in which increased busing would be used for desegregation. This decision was appealed to the U.S. Circuit Court of Appeals for the Sixth Circuit, which in turn upheld the principle of a metropolitan solution but set aside lower court busing plans. This was done in order to allow the 52 suburban districts involved to air their objections in court. Eventually the case found its way to the U.S. Supreme Court. In a controversial decision, delivered on July 25, 1974, and one which Mr. Justice Marshall called a "giant step backward," the Court remanded the case to the district court to be handled on a "Detroit-only" basis. The rationale of the majority decision, delivered by Mr. Chief Justice Burger, was that the remedy must be determined by the extent of the constitutional violation, and since the violation occurred within the Detroit school system the remedy must also occur within that system. In effect, this decision, along with the Court of Appeals decision in the Richmond case, further established the doctrine that unless it could be shown that constitutional violations involved inter-district segregation, then the remedy must be maintained on a within-district basis only.

In the Denver case (*Keyes v. School District No. 1, Denver, Colorado, 1973*), the U.S. Supreme Court handed down a ruling which so broadened the de jure standpoint that it could cover many instances formerly considered de facto. According to Shannon (1973), the Court found that if seven of Denver's 119 schools were proven to be de jure segregated, then it was necessary to show that each additional school within the district was legally desegregated. The implication was that schools

could no longer remain segregated simply on the excuse of de facto conditions. While the Court did not require de facto segregated schools to be integrated, and while the de jure/de facto question was not resolved, the decision did provide practical considerations whereby lower courts had "discretion to determine, as an issue of fact and not as a question of law, whether or not a local school board presides over a de facto or de jure segregated school district." However, only time will tell if this development will have effect in easing the de jure/de facto dichotomy.

One new development which may have an impact on the legal aspects of the busing issue is a case recently decided by a Superior Court in the state of California. The presiding judge, Max F. Deutz, ruling on a case arising in the city of Inglewood, stated that when a school system whose white population had fallen to 20 percent or less, there was no longer any need to bus students for the purpose of racial balance. Thus white flight was taken into account in the California decision, although it had never been a deciding factor with Federal courts. The city of Inglewood has returned to neighborhood schools, with the judge reversing a busing decision he himself had made five years earlier. Whether or not this decision will have any future impact on other state and Federal court decisions remains to be seen.

THE PUBLIC DEBATE

Although the problem of busing has had many court hearings, it has also received widespread attention in other sectors of public life, including government agencies, academic institutions, private organizations, and committees of ordinary citizens.

Some opponents of busing have championed "freedom of choice" as the most viable way of meeting the requirements of *Brown* and subsequent court decisions. In the South, according to a report issued by the United States Commission on Civil Rights in 1967, freedom of choice was overwhelmingly favored by over 1,700 school districts desegregating voluntarily, (i.e., not under court order). Proponents argued that freedom of choice was democratic and helped preserve the neighborhood school. At that time, some Federal courts agreed with freedom of choice, for in the Fifth Circuit as late as March 1967, 129 districts under court order were also using freedom of choice to desegregate the schools, while only 11 were using geographical zoning.

But there were growing concerns with freedom of choice plans. The Civil Rights Commission found that in many cases freedom of choice plans did little or nothing to effectively desegregate the schools. In some instances more busing was used than would have been the case under a device such as geographical zoning. Investigators reported several instances where separately bused blacks and whites were transported en masse ten to 30 miles to identifiably black or white schools, often passing a school of the opposite race on the way to their destination. The report of the Lambda Corporation (1971) indicated that busing has been used substantially to maintain segregated schools, and that the amount of busing necessary to provide complete desegregation could be as little as one-third to one-fourth for the nation as a whole.

The Civil Rights Commission found that where black children did choose to attend a white school, various pressures were exerted against that choice. The report contains several pages of examples where intimidation and sometimes violence were employed against blacks. Intimidation by violence included shootings, threats on life, and at least one threat of castration. Economic coercion was exerted, including the ejection of sharecroppers from property and livelihood if they chose to send their children to white schools. Threats were made, using black parents' jobs and welfare aid. In the schools themselves, harrassment by white students was a means of coercion and intimidation. This usually manifested itself in racial epithets, assaults, threats on lives, knocking books out of hands, and changing seats away from blacks in class. While the Commission reported that school officials were generally very helpful, with a few going out of their way to cooperate, there were instances where teachers and administrators allowed students to use racial epithets in class, refused to recognize black achievement, and refused to recognize freedom of choice decisions. The Commission concluded that there were serious doubts about freedom of choice as an adequate desegregation device.

Although a few reports, such as the Armor study (1972), indicated that "mandatory" busing was ineffective, there have been a number of reports which indicate that busing has worked to combat de facto segregation and to improve the learning ability of both white and minority students. In Hartford, Connecticut (Satz and Hoffman, 1971), "Project Concern" bused inner-city elementary children into nearby suburban schools, where they "thrived intellectually and emotionally." In September, 1968, Berkeley, California (Melville, 1970) developed a two-way, crosstown busing plan which was highly successful. White (1971) conducted a study of fourth-, fifth-, and sixth-grade students in Midwest City, Oklahoma. His investigation indicated that bused students showed greater achievement on test scores and a higher attendance rate than nonbused students.

Yet, for all the studies showing that busing may not have the ill effects some opponents have predicted, there remained a deep-seated resentment to busing among large segments of the population. This condition is perhaps best represented by the situation in Boston, Massachusetts. In the fall of 1974, the Federal District Court issued a temporary order to bus several thousand students to further desegregate the schools. School boycotts, demonstrations, and violence resulted, particularly in the South Boston area. By the spring of 1975, the Court came forward with a final plan superceding the temporary one, a plan calling for the busing of around 21,000 students to reflect the racial mixture on a city-wide basis. This plan was met with almost immediate resistance. Part of that reaction was voiced by a meeting in Boston of an organization calling itself ROAR (Restore Our Alienated Rights). Ironically, the event was held on the weekend of May 17, 1975, the twenty-first anniversary of the historic *Brown* decision in 1954.

But a closer look at the pro-busing attitude itself may reveal some perplexing weaknesses. Busing may be too simple a solution, a patchwork bandage applied to a large and festering cultural sore. As more and more research is conducted, the general trend of the findings (exemplified by the Coleman Report, 1966, and Jencks, 1972) indicates that socio-economic background and family circumstances may play a greater role in educational achievement than what goes on in school. As the evidence mounts, it seems that busing must be seen in terms other than schooling. Yet, acknowledging these considerations, there are many who still feel that busing may be the only viable solution at this time toward achieving integration in the schools. In these respects busing is only a stopgap measure, for if busing takes a pupil out of his immediate neighborhood to enjoy wider cultural and educative contacts, it will most likely return him to that same neighborhood, and his immediate circumstances are not drastically altered.

Those who are fully committed to busing may find themselves on the horns of a dilemma. Even though they realize that integration goes far beyond busing, they are caught with the problems of time and expediency. Thus they accept busing as a readily available course, realizing that open housing and other paths may take considerably more time. Those who oppose busing on educational and child-welfare grounds may have sincere concerns, too. They point to disruptions in the lives of children who are pulled from a familiar environment and forcibly thrown into a more alien one. They show the unlikelihood of close family allegiance to a school some distance from home, the inconvenience of parents and children participating in extracurricular activities, and the dangers incurred in more lengthy distances of travel. They oppose the extra time involved in bus rides to a different school or the safety of children forced to attend tough inner-city schools where crime and violence are more prevalent.

The social and moral issues involved in busing are by no means simple. The issue of equality of opportunity seems paramount in dealing with the controversy, but there are various interpretations as to what equality of opportunity really means. What we need in education, as in other aspects of life, is not only a verbal commitment to the principles of a democratic society but a sincere effort to promote social justice in every aspect of life.

REFERENCES

Books, Monographs, and Studies by Organizations

Coleman, James S. et al. *Equality of Educational Opportunity.* Washington: Department of Health, Education, and Welfare, Government Printing Office, 1966.

Crain, Robert L. *The Politics of School Desegregation: Comparative Case Studies of Community Structure and Policy Making.* Chicago: Aldine Publishing Company, 1968.

Editorial Board of Harvard Educational Review. *Equal Educational Opportunity.* Cambridge: Harvard University Press, 1969.

Featherstone, E. Glenn, and Culp, Delos P. *Pupil Transportation.* New York: Harper and Row, 1965.

Hill, Roscoe, and Feely, Malcolm, eds. *Affirmative School Integration: Efforts to Overcome De Facto Segregation in Urban*

Schools. Beverly Hills: Sage Publications, 1968.

Jencks, Christopher et al. *Inequality: A Reassessment of the Effect of Family and Schooling in America.* New York: Basic Books, Inc., 1972.

Lambda Corporation and Concord Research Corporation. *School Desegregation With Minimum Busing.* A Report to the Secretary for Planning and Evaluation, U.S. Department of Health, Education, and Welfare, December 10, 1971. Arlington, Virginia: Lambda Corporation, 1971.

Melville, Keith. *School Desegregation Plan, Berkeley, California.* New York: Center for Urban Education, 1970.

Myrdal, Gunnar. *An American Dilemma: The Negro Problem and Modern Democracy.* Two Volumes. New York: Harper Torchbooks, 1962; originally published by Harper and Row, 1944.

Noble, Marcus C. S., Jr. *Pupil Transportation in the United States.* Scranton, Pennsylvania: International Textbook Company, 1940.

Orfield, Gary. *The Reconstruction of Southern Education: The Schools and the 1964 Civil Rights Act.* New York: Wiley-Interscience, 1969.

Satz, Arthur, and Hoffman, Martin. *Project Concern, Hartford, Connecticut.* New York: Center for Urban Education, 1971.

Teele, James, Jackson, Ellen, and Mayo, Clara. *Family Experience in Operation Exodus: The Busing of Negro Children.* Community Mental Health Monograph Number Three. New York: Behavioral Publications, Inc., 1967.

U.S. Commission on Civil Rights. *Southern School Desegregation, 1966-1967.* A Report of the U.S. Commission on Civil Rights, July, 1967. Washington: U.S. Government Printing Office, 1967.

Periodicals

Armor, David J. The Evidence on Busing. *The Public Interest,* No. 28, (Summer, 1972), pp. 90-126.

Beckler, John. Washington Report. *School Management, 15:* 8 (June 1971).

Brazziel, William F. Quality Education for Minorities. *Phi Delta Kappan, 53:* 547-552 (May 1972).

Busing Decision. *School Management, 15:* 8 (June 1971).

Busing: The North Reports. *Saturday Review, 54:* 52 (June 19, 1971).

Buskin, Martin. City-Suburb Busing: What Next for Great Neck? *School Mangement, 13:* 58-65 (April 1969).

Cooper, Charles R. An Educator Looks at Busing. *The National Elementary Principal, 50:* 26-31 (April 1971).

Craig, Benjamin L. Richmond and Detroit: A Tale of Two Cities. *NOLPE School Law Journal, 4:* 12-18 (1974).

Foerster, Leona M. Beyond Busing. *American Teacher, 56:* CE-6 (April 1972).

Forced Busing Vetoed by 90% of Schoolmen. Opinion Poll, *Nation's Schools, 85:* 100 (June 1970).

Goodman, Walter. Busing for Integration is Working Well in Central 7 School Ditrict—Knock Wood. *New York Times Magazine, 121:* 31, 100-106 (April 9, 1972).

Green Light for Busing. *Saturday Review, 54:* 68-69 (May 22, 1971).

Green, Robert L., Smith, Eugenia, and Schweitzer, John H. Busing and the Multiracial Classroom. *Phi Delta Kappan, 53:* 543-546 (May 1972).

Grieder, C. Busing: Wrong Prescription for Discrimination Ills. *Nation's Schools, 85:* 9 (June 1970).

Gross, N. N. Reaching for the Dream: An Experiment in Two-Way Busing. *Children, 17:* 133-136 (July 1970).

Harvey, James C., and Holmes, Charles H. Busing and School Desegregation. *Phi Delta Kappan, 53:* 540-542 (May 1972).

If Not Busing, What? *Time, 99:* 60-61 (April 24, 1972).

Is Busing the Answer? *Instructor, 79:* 123-124 (October 1969).

It Can Work: Busing Inner City Pupils to Suburban Schools. *The Clearing House, 46:* 158-162 (November 1971).

Newsnotes: Busing in Los Angeles. *Phi Delta Kappan, 53:* 600 (May 1972).

Phase Two for Boston. *Time, 105:* 64 (May 26, 1975).

Primack, Robert. Knuckleheads and Neighborhoods. *Phi Delta Kappan, 52:* 363-365 (February 1971).

Research Division of the National Education Association. Busing. Teacher Opinion Poll, *Today's Education, 58:* 7 (March 1969).

Reutter, E. Edmund, Desegregation: Where the Law Stands Today. *Nation's Schools, 87:* 59-70 (March 1971).

Scudder, B. T., and Jurs, S. G. Do Bused Children Affect Achievement of Non-Negro Children? *Integrated Education, 9:* 30-34 (March 1971).

Shannon, Thomas A. The Denver Decision: Death Knell for Defacto Segregation? *Phi Delta Kappan, 55:* 6-9 (September 1973)

Simpson, Robert J., and Gordon, William M. School Desegregation—Is Busing for U.S.? *NOLPE School Law Journal, 3:* 27-36 (Spring, 1973).

Spence, Ralph B. Best Education for All Children Includes Busing. *Phi Delta Kappan, 53:* 539, 573 (May 1972).

Stone, I. F. Moving the Constitution to the Back of the Bus. The New York *Review of Books, 18:* 4, 6, 10-11 (April 20, 1972).

A Study of Transportation of Public School Pupils in Virginia, for the Session 1936-37. Virginia State Board of Education *Bulletin, 20:* 1-21 (March 1938).

Wagoner, David E. The North, Not the South, Is Where School Desegregation Isn't Happening. *The American School Board Journal, 159:* 31-34 (September 1971).

Wayward Busing. *Time, 11:* 49 (June 5, 1972).

The Wayward Busing Issue. *Phi Delta Kappan, 53:* 537-538 (May 1972).

White, Dan A. Does Busing Harm Urban Elementary Pupils? *Phi Delta Kappan, 53:* 192-193 (November 1971).

Encyclopedia Articles

Cooper, Shirley, Dawson, Howard A., and Isenbert, Robert M. Transportation of Students. *Encyclopedia of Educational Research* (Third Edition), pp. 1543-1551. New York: Macmillan Company, 1960.

Culp, Delos P. Transportation and School Busing. *Encyclopedia of Education. 9,* 227-279. New York: The Macmillan Company and the Free Press, 1971.

Cubberly, Edwood P. Consolidation of Schools. *A Cyclopedia of Education, 2,* 185-189. New York: Macmillan Company, 1911; reprinted by Gale Research Company, Book Tower, Detroit, 1968.

Heck, Arch O. Transportation of Pupils. *Encyclopedia of Modern Education,* 840-841. New York: Philosophical Library, 1943.

Isenberg, Robert M. Transportation of Students. *Encyclopedia of Educational Research* (Fourth Edition), pp. 1493-1499. New York: Macmillan Company, 1969.

Unpublished Materials

Citizens for Excellent Public Schools. "Analysis and Interpretation of School Consolidation Survey," Richmond, Virginia, March 31, 1972. (Mimeographed)

Jones, Nathaniel R. "Statement of Nathaniel R. Jones, General Counsel, NAACP Before the House Committee on the Judiciary, Subcommittee No. 5," Washington, D.C., March 16, 1972 (Mimeographed)

Levit, Martin. "The Ideology of Accountability in Schooling," a paper presented at the Conference of Accountability held at Lehigh University, March 9, 1972.

Mitchell, Clarence, "Statement of Clarence Mitchell, Director of Washington Bureau of NAACP, Before House Judiciary Subcommittee No. 5," Washington, D.C., April 13, 1972. (Xeroxed)

Nixon, Richard Milhouse. "Remarks of the President on Nationwide Radio and Television." Press Release from the Office of the White House Press Secretary, March 16, 1972. (Mimeographed)

Wilkins, Roy. "Statement of Roy Wilkins, Executive Director of NAACP, Before House Judiciary Committee," Washington, D.C., March 16, 1972. (Mimeographed)

Newspapers

Antibusing Rally Ends in Boston. *Richmond Times-Dispatch*, May 19, 1975, p. A-2.

Busing Will Help Solve Problems. *Hard Times*, South Carolina Council on Human Relations, Columbia, South Carolina, April 1972, p. 3.

Cox, Charles. Area School Merger Case Aired. *Richmond Times-Dispatch*, April 14, 1972, pp. 1, 4.

———. Two Sociologists Say School Busing is a Fake Issue. *Richmond Times-Dispatch*, April 25, 1972, p. B-3.

Farber, M. A. Lawyer's Group Fears an Overreliance on Educational Studies. *New York Times*, June 11, 1972, p. 47.

Harris, Louis. Attitudes Toward Busing Harden Past Year. *The Progress Index*, Petersburg, Virginia, April 10, 1972.

Herbers, John. Fear of Busing Exceeds Its Use. *New York Times*, May 28, 1972, p. 1, 34

Landers, Jim. Whither Busing? *Richmond Mercury*, May 28, 1975, pp. 5-6.

Court Cases

Bradley v. School Board of the City of Richmond, 338 F. Supp. 67 (1972).

Bradley v. School Board of the City of Richmond, 462 F 2nd, 1058 (1972).

Bradley v. Milliken, 345 F. Supp. 914 (1972).

Brown v. Board of Education, 347 U.S. 483 (1954).

Brown v. Board of Education, 349 U.S. 294 (1955).

Davis v. School District of the City of Pontiac, 131 F. Supp. 734 (1970).

Green v. County School Board of New Kent County, 391 U.S. 430 (1968).

Griggs v. Duke Power Co., 401 U.S. 424 (1971).

Hobson v. Hansen, 269 F. Supp. 401 (1967).

Keyes v. School District No. 1, Denver, Colorado, 313 F. Supp. 61 (1970), 313 F. Supp. 90 (1970).

Keyes v. School District No. 1, Denver, Colorado, 93 S. Ct., 2686; 413 U.S. 189 (1973).

Milliken v. Bradley, 418 U.S. 717 (1974).

Plessey v. Ferguson, 163 U.S. 544 (1896).

Stuart v. School District No. 1 of the Village of Kalamazoo, 30 Mich. 69 (1874).

Swann v. Charlotte-Mecklenburg Board of Education, 402 U.S. 1 (1971).

PART III

TEACHER/FACULTY ISSUES

39

TEACHER CERTIFICATION

by Robert A. Roth
Teacher Preparation and Professional Development
Services
State of Michigan, Department of Education
Lansing, Michigan

Certification is a process of legal santion, authorizing the holder of a credential to perform specific services in the public schools of the state. Its widely accepted purpose is to establish and maintain standards for the preparation and employment of persons who teach or render certain nonteaching services in the schools (Kinney, 1964, p. 3)

The authority for establishing requirements and issuing and revoking certificates is, with a few exceptions, delegated by state legislative action to the state board of education. The certification program is administered by the state department of education under the direction of the chief state school officer (commissioner or state superintendent). Stinnett (1970) reported that in nine states "the legal authority for certification is shared to some extent with other agencies (p. 31)," such as county authorities, cities, and certain colleges.

All states currently require certification for public school teachers, and most require administrators and special services personnel (guidance counselors, etc.) to hold a certificate. Some states require certificates in areas such as nursery schools, junior colleges, and state teachers colleges. Nineteen states require it for nursery school teachers, and eight for junior college personnel. Twenty-nine states require teachers in private, parochial, or independent schools to hold state certification (NEA, 1974).

Standards for certification can be classified into two broad categories, general and educational requirements. General requirements include elements such as age, citizenship, and loyalty oath. Eighteen is the more common minimum age requirement, while 25 states require U.S. citizenship, and 13 states require an oath (NEA, 1974). Educational prerequisites include a baccalaureate degree, which is required by all states in most areas of certification. Vocational education is a common exception to this rule.

Currently, there are over 500 different types of certificates issued in the United States. The predominant practice of endorsing secondary teaching credentials with the subjects one is authorized to teach would increase this number. Stinnett (1970) has reported that 45 states issue endorsements on high school certificates, 11 states issue blanket high school certificates, and five issue both types. Although there is an attempt to reduce the number of types of certificates in order to facilitate interstate reciprocity, the endorsement practice has confused the issue. As Kinney (1964) points out, "The ostensible number of certificates listed for any given state may no longer provide a true index to the com-plexity of the credential structure (p. 29)."

The use of proficiency examinations for certification purposes appears to be increasing. In 1970, 21 states reported some use of examinations (Stinnett, 1970). Tests commonly used are the Modern Foreign Language Association Examination for teachers, the National Teachers Examination (NTE), and the Graduate Record Examination. The examinations are generally used to grant credit equivalents for areas in which formal course work has not been taken, rather than as a substitute for a degree program. They are also frequently used to validate work taken in unaccredited colleges. In only three states (Mississippi, North Carolina, and South Carolina) a passing score on the National Teachers Examination is a prerequisite to certification (NEA, 1974).

Several states have developed procedures which provide more flexibility in the certification process. Sixteen states have established review or appeals committees to process applications of candidates whose records may indicate that they do not have the precise requirements for a credential as specified in state certification regulations (Stinnett, 1970). The candidate, however, may have related experience, equivalent course work, or unusual qualifications which provide him with a comparable degree of expertise, as the specific requirements intend. The appeals committees grant certification to these individuals who qualify.

The relationship between teacher certification and teacher education has been approached in a variety of ways, and has also seen an effort to provide more flexibility and diversity. A few states still use a transcript analysis or course-credit approach to the issuance of certificates. Almost all states, however, use the approved-program approach to accreditation and certification, at least to some extent. This is a process by which a teacher education program is approved (accredited) by the state education agency. The graduates of these colleges are issued the appropriate teaching certificate by the state upon completion of the degree program and recommendation by the preparing institution.

In 1974, 48 states reported use of the approved program approach (NEA, 1974). Most states (40) use a special committee as a visitation team, which evaluates a program using state standards. About 44 states use some type of state standards (Stinnett, 1970). The certification standards in an approved-program approach are usually broadly stated, to allow institutional flexibility and diversity, whereas transcript analysis usually requires a more prescriptive course-list as the certification standard.

The teacher education program approval standards vary from state to state. Only two states rely on regional accreditation or regional standards for evaluation programs. There are six regional accrediting associations which evaluate the overall strength of institutions (Western, Northwest, North Central, Southern, Middle States, and New England Associations of Colleges and Secondary Schools). These regional associations are not specifically interested in teacher education; it is the entire institutional quality that they are concerned with.

The National Council for Accreditation of Teacher Education (NCATE), established in 1952, is a "voluntary accrediting body devoted exclusively to the evaluation and accreditation of teacher education programs. It is recognized by the National Commission on Accrediting as the only national accrediting agency for the field of teacher education (NCATE, 1973-1974, p. 3)." The 1973-1974 list of NCATE-approved colleges and universities contained the names of 522 institutions representing every state except Alaska, Delaware, and Hawaii. There are approximately 1,265 teacher education institutions in the United States (NEA, 1974). Although there are varying reports, it appears that at least 75% of new teachers are from NCATE-accredited institutions. In 1970, 27 states relied somewhat upon NCATE standards for program approval (Stinnett, 1970). NCATE approval "requires that an institution be accredited by the appropriate regional association and approved or accredited by the State Education Agency prior to Council accreditation (NCATE, 1973-1974, p. 5)."

Another set of standards for approval of teacher education programs has been developed by the National Association of State Directors of Teacher Education and Certification (NASDTEC). Over 30 states and the District of Columbia have officially adopted the NASDTEC standards, and a list of colleges approved by each state appears in the 1973-1974 list of approved programs (NASDTEC, 1974).

An area of increasing interest in teacher certification is reciprocity, or an agreement between states to issue certificates to each other's graduates. A growing number of states have entered into such agreements, and this has developed into a significant trend in teacher certification. Thirty-one states have an official policy of accepting out-of-state graduates of NCATE-accredited institutions as being sufficiently qualified for the appropriate certificate (NCATE, 1973-1974). Stinnett (1970), however, reported that 24 states used NCATE approval significantly and 16 used it somewhat in granting certificates to out-of-state applicants.

Twenty-two states are members of the NASDTEC Certification Reciprocity System, with each participating state using the NASDTEC program approval standards. The reciprocity agreement, therefore, is based on the use of a common set of approval standards. Stinnett (1970), however, has reported that a total of 28 states will issue initial certificates to graduates of programs approved by NASDTEC standards.

Another approach to reciprocity has been the development of regional compacts. In 1949, an eight-state certification reciprocity compact was initiated by the states of New England, New York, and New Jersey. In 1957, an 11-state agreement was entered into by the states of New England, New York, New Jersey, Pennsylvania, Delaware, and Maryland. This Northeast Regional Reciprocity Plan applied to graduates of approved elementary teacher education programs only. These agreements were both terminated as of October 1, 1973.

Recently the Interstate Certification Project was initiated with funds provided by ESEA Title V, and administered by the state of New York. This project has not established approval standards; the approach has been to design model-enabling legislation and contracts which are used independently by cooperating states. Al-

though a state may participate in the Interstate Project, it signs contracts only with other states in the Project that it wishes to. Since its inception in 1968, the Project has grown to include 31 states who have passed the enabling legislation and 28 who have signed multilateral contracts with other states. The development of this Interstate Project obviated the eight- and 11-state agreements.

The basic contract of the Project includes only teachers who have graduated from programs approved by the state within which the institution is located. For those states who have signed the contract, there is also a codicil which covers pupil service personnel and administrators (except superintendents). Twelve states have signed this codicil. A second codicil has been developed for vocational education teacher, because they frequently are not required to have four-year college degrees. Nine states have signed this codicil thus far (Hartle, 1974).

An increasingly important area in teacher certification is the establishment of advisory councils or legal commissions on teacher preparation and licensure. "By 1970 all states reported some form of advisory board on teacher education and certification (Frinks, 1971, p. 5)." A particularly interesting development has been the passage of professional standards acts which have led to the creation of teacher standards and practices commissions. In most cases this is an attempt to broaden the base of decision-making and put the control of the profession more into the hands of teachers.

The National Education Association has advocated that each state establish two categories for the regulation of the profession: standards of preparation and standards of practice. Professional standards boards would deal with issues such as certification and accreditation, while professional practices commissions would be concerned with standards of practice such as ethics, competence, and academic freedom. These committees are to serve as juries of peers, and promote self-governance of the teaching profession (Frinks, 1971).

A recent NEA directory indicated that 19 states have now established, through legislative action, either professional practices commissions or standards boards. In two states, Kansas and Oregon, both have been established. In all cases except two, these groups are advisory to the State Board of Education, which gives them considerable influence. In California, the Commission for Teacher Preparation and Licensing is autonomous, having considerable legal power, but the State Board of Education has veto power (NEA, 1973). The Oregon Teacher Standards and Practices Commission establishes rules for certification and accreditation, issues teaching certificates, and approves teacher education programs. Oregon was the first state to grant certification and accreditation authority to a Commission made up predominantly of educators.

The distinction between boards and commissions, as defined by NEA, does not appear to always fit the functions of current committees, but generally they coincide. In six states responsibilities include establishing criteria for certification and preparation, while in three others they only recommend such criteria. Only two states provide the committees with responsibilities in teacher education accreditation. The remaining commissions and boards deal with professional practices issues such as competency, ethical conduct, and the adoption of rules and procedures (NEA, 1973).

It is the author's opinion that the most significant movement today in teacher education and certification is the development of competency-based teacher education and certification programs (the terms competency-based and performance-based are generally used synonymously, although distinctions are sometimes made). Recent surveys have shown that over 35 states are either seriously studying or actively developing some form of competency-based teacher education or certification (Roth 1974), and close to 500 teacher education institutions are operating or developing competency-based programs (Schmieder, 1973).

Although there is no concensus of program elements, competency-based teacher education has been defined by Elam as having the following essential elements:

> Competencies (knowledge, skills, behaviors) to be demonstrated are derived from explicit teacher roles, make possible assessment of behavior, and are made public;

> Criteria to be employed in assessing competencies are based upon specified competencies, state explicit levels of mastery under specified conditions, and are made public in advance;

> Assessment of student's competency uses performance as primary evidence, accounts for knowledge, and strives for objectivity;

> Rate of progress is determined by demonstrated competency;

> The instructional program is intended to facilitate the development of specified competencies.
>
> (Elam, 1971)

Competency-based certification has been approached in a variety of ways, and thus also has not been clearly defined. State plans range from the adoption of specific competencies by the state to development of process standards only. If performance certification were to be defined as a distinct process separate from teacher education, then some type of performance examination would be required. No state has instituted a comprehensive program of this type thus far.

In the approved-program approach, the distinction between certification and teacher education becomes less clear, and this is the procedure being followed by states involved in the competency movement. Within the approved-program approach, however, there also exists a great diversity of methods. New Jersey, Arizona, Utah, and Pennsylvania are currently developing statewide competencies for certain certification areas. In these programs, the state may issue a certificate upon the recommendation of a college that the individual has completed the approved program and achieved the state-adopted competencies.

In Arizona and California, efforts are directed toward the recertification of teachers. California enacted the Stull Bill (Assembly Bill 293, 1971), which requires each school district to develop evaluation based on student progress and teacher competence. Arizona has stipulated that certificates other than the initial one will be issued on the basis of teacher effectiveness, which will be determined by teacher performance and student growth utilizing performance objectives.

Although the major thrust in Utah is the development of competency-based teacher education programs, a set of competencies was adopted in July, 1972 by the State Board of Education for certification (endorsement) in media. A bachelor's degree and a teaching certificate are prerequisites. An examination for proficiency conducted by a recommending institution (approved-program) is then administered. The candidate must demonstrate proficiency in certain major areas: cataloging and classifying, selection of media, utilization of media, media production, and media administration. Examples of competencies are as follows:

> The candidate will identify five professional journals for the media specialist and five others for the teacher.

> The candidate will produce one acceptable example of each of the following methods: thermo transparency, diazo, picture transfer of lift.

> From a group of twenty books provided, the candidate will select, classify, and catalog ten according to *Cataloging and Inventorying Instructional Materials in Utah Schools*. No more than two errors in cataloging and classifying that violate any major principle in those references shall be permitted.

> The candidate will identify and describe three activities a media coordinator might initiate to encourage reluctant students to use the school instructional media center.
>
> (Utah, 1972, pp. 3, 5, 8, 19)

In most states the development of competencies is left to the colleges, but the programs are approved by the state for certification purposes. A recent survey revealed that 11 states have now mandated competency-based programs for the preparation of teachers or administrators (Wilson and Curtis, 1973). These states are Alabama, California, New York, North Carolina, Oregon, Pennsylvania, South Dakota, Tennessee (administrators only), Texas, Vermont, and Washington. Not all of these states have set implementation dates, and Texas has since rescinded its mandate. Another survey indicated that 17 states have some legislative and/or administrative support for a competency procedure (Schmieder, 1973).

A more flexible approach to the competency movement has been taken by several other states. For example, Florida's teacher education institutions have the option of maintaining the more traditional course-list system or of specifying the competencies which its graduates will be expected to demonstrate. In either case, the program is approved by the state of Washington.

Perhaps the most unique and flexible approach is the system developed by the State of Washington. The emphasis is on decentralization of the certification process, and state regulations are process rather than content in nature. Under standards adopted in 1971, teacher preparation programs in Washington are to be developed and implemented by a consortium of agencies including colleges, school organizations, and professional associations. The state standards require that each of these agencies have a role in development of the program. Performance criteria or other content standards are not established at the state level; however, the consortia are to develop competencies which are derived from teacher roles.

There are a number of problem areas in certification which have caused controversy and criticism. A meeting of state leaders in education in 1970 yielded the following concerns:

> The rigidity of state requirements discourages flexibility and creativity in teacher education programs.

> There should be a simplification of standards and a reduction in the number of certificates.

> The diversity of certification requirements in the United States creates serious problems in the mobility of teachers.

> Certification should be concerned with output, not input.

> The profession has little responsibility for certification of teacher competence, and should be given a larger role in its own governance.   (Frinks, 1971)

Another problem is the development and application of competencies. Who should write the criteria, how will they be applied, how specific should they be, and can they apply to all aspects of teaching? Opponents of competency-based certification point out that we know very little about what constitutes good teaching, particularly from an empirical standpoint, and therefore cannot put teacher competencies into state standards until validated. Those supporting the competency approach argue that demonstrated ability is a better indicator of competence than amount of time spent in class; therefore, standards should be based on performance and derived from whatever knowledge we have, including expert opinion. This appears to be the most controversial area in teacher certification today.

A related concern deals with specificity of standards. Advocates of reciprocity desire flexible standards, but with a certain degree of uniformity, to facilitate movement among the states. The competency approach implies specificity of standards, although a few states have used it as a vehicle to introduce more flexible standards. The specificity in these latter programs is not at the state level, but rather within the preparation program.

Although the approved program is generally viewed as a means of providing greater flexibility, there are dissenting viewpoints. Conant's address, "Teacher Certification: The Restricted State-Approved Program Approach," is indicative of the concern. He is basically opposed to regulatory practices in teacher education, and recommends the university faculty as the most plausible place to turn for responsible control of teacher education (Conant, 1964). Also, without proper approval procedures institutions may not strive to improve, and may even neglect certification standards.

On the other hand, the approved-program approach avoids the weakness of checking courses against prescriptive state course requirements. Its strength is in placing greater responsibility upon preparing institutions, providing for differences in philosophy, staff, and facilities (Stinnett, 1969). It is also argued that transcript analysis merely assesses quantity, while program approval determines the quality of a certification program (Frinks, 1971). The approval approach admits that specified courses may not be crucial or relevant, gives incentive to institutions to develop exciting programs, and reduces the chance of rejecting an outstanding teacher for lack of "required" courses (Allen and Wagschal, 1969).

In summary, there are a number of discernible trends in teacher certification today. A general movement is toward the decentralization of the certification process, a broadening of the decision-making base. Evidence of this is found in the competency approach where consortia and local districts are making certification recommendations. Providing further evidence are the trends in development of advisory councils, the increasing use of the approved-program approach, and professional practices acts, as part of the move toward self-governance of the teaching profession.

Also notable is the increasing flexibility of standards to support both the approved-program approach and the strong efforts to develop reciprocity agreements. Finally, the most significant movement in teacher education and certification is the competency-based approach.

REFERENCES

Allen, D. W., and Wagschal, P. A New Look in Credentialing. *The Clearinghouse*, 1969, *44*, 137-140.

Conant, J. B. The Certification of Teachers: The Restricted State Approved Program Approach. Fifth Charles W. Hunt Lecture. Washington, D.C.: American Association of Colleges for Teacher Education, 1964.

Elam, S. Performance-Based Teacher Education: What is the State of the Art? *American Association of Colleges for Teacher Education PBTE Series*, 1971, No. 1.

Frinks, M. L. Planning and Effecting Improvements in the Preparation and Certification of Educators: Emerging State Relationships and Procedures. Report of a special study, April, 1971, Denver, Improving State Leadership In Education.

Hartle, H. Questions and Answers on Interstate Certification. *Journal of Teacher Education*, 1974, *25*, 248-249.

Kinney, L. B. *Certification in Education*. Englewood Cliffs, New Jersey: Prentice-Hall, 1964.

National Association of State Directors of Teacher Education and Certification. *1974 List-Approved Programs*. Trenton: 1974.

National Council for Accreditation of Teacher Education. *Twentieth Annual List*. Washington, D.C.: 1974.

National Education Association. *Teacher Standards and Practices Commissions*, March 15, 1973, Washington, D.C.

_____. *A Manual on Standards Affecting School Personnel in the United States, 1974 Edition*. Washington, D.C. National Education Association, 1974.

Roth, R. A. *Performance-Based Teacher Certification: A Survey of the States, 1974*. Lansing: Michigan State Department of Education, 1974.

Schmieder, A. A. Competency-Based Education: The State of the Scene. *American Association of Colleges for Teacher Education PBTE Series*, 1973, No. 9.

Stinnett, T. M. Teacher Certification. In R. L. Ebel, ed., *Encyclopedia of Educational Research.* Toronto: Macmillan, 1969.
_____. *A Manual on Certification Requirements for School Personnel in the United States.* Washington, D.C.: National Education Association, 1970.
Utah State Board of Education. *Recommended Proficiency Guidelines for Media Endorsements,* July 21, 1972, Salt Lake City.
Wilson, A. P., and Curtis, W. W. The States Mandate Performance-Based Teacher Education. *Phi Delta Kappan,* 1973, *15,* (1), 76.

ADDITIONAL RESOURCES

American Association of Colleges for Teacher Education PBTE Series. AACTE, Washington, D.C.
New Directions In Certification. T. E. Andrews. Association of Teacher Educators, Washington, D.C.
Guidelines and Standards for the Development and Approval of Preparation Leading to the Certification of School Professional Personnel. Superintendent of Public Instruction, State of Washington, Olympia, Washington, July 9, 1971.
What Has Been and Should Be the Role of State Education Agencies in the Development and Implementation of Teacher Education Programs (Both Pre and Inservice)? K. P. Daniel and W. Crenshaw. U.S. Office of Education, Washington, D.C., September 3, 1971.
Requirements for Certification, Thirty-eighth Edition, 1973-74. E. H. Woellner, University of Chicago Press, Chicago, 1973.

GROUPS AND ORGANIZATIONS

American Association of Colleges for Teacher Education. One Dupont Circle, N.W., Washington, D.C. 20036.
Multi-State Consortium on Performance-Based Teacher Education. Theodore Andrews, New York State Education Department, Albany, New York, 12210.
National Association of State Directors of Teacher Education and Certification. Vere A. McHenry, President of Executive Committee. Utah State Department of Education, Salt Lake City, Utah.
National Council for Accreditation of Teacher Education. 1750 Pennsylvania Avenue, N.W. Washington, D.C. 20006.
National Education Association, 1201 Sixteenth Street, N.W., Washington, D.C. 20036.

40

TEACHER MILITANCY

by Dewey H. Stoller
Head, Department of Educational Administration
and Supervision
University of Tennessee
Knoxville, Tennessee

Teacher militancy is not a downtrodden group's reaction to the present and future; rather, it reflects the hope of an increasingly important segment of the total society. Militancy is not just personnel negotiation, but a professional group, with increasing specialization, reacting to receiving the brunt of the criticism by the public for educational problems over which the teachers are not generally responsible.

It should be indicated that probably only a minority of teachers are militant; still, an even smaller minority can be classified as militant professionals. A conclusion that can be reached is that given the growing concentration of the population, small percentages can be numerically large enough to be important. The militant professionals constitute a core leadership group having the support of a majority of teachers. In comparison with their colleagues, they are better educated and more respected, better integrated into their peer groups, and have more support from their peers. Generally, instead of the youngest, least mature teachers, the leaders are usually middle-aged, well-established men.

PRESENT UNREST

The current unrest is predicated upon a number of socio-economic and professional factors. A major source of militancy is the economic problem. Greater competition is developing for available tax dollars. Teachers are developing political skills that will enhance their opportunity to capture scarce dollars. Although teachers' salaries have increased tremendously over time, the teachers' relative salary position has not improved. The merger discussions by the American Federation of Teachers and the National Education Association highlight the militancy issue. Certainly the shift to militant liberalism by the previously conservative and conforming teacher, with emphasis upon non-violent civil disobedience, is a way of protesting unjust social conditions. The increasing size and bureaucratization of the educational system, the changing role of administration, and the lack of community identification have promoted the alienation of teachers from both educational institutions and the communities served. Teachers are younger, brighter, and have greater self-assurance. All of these factors contribute to teacher militancy.

FEDERAL INTERVENTION

As many states are struggling with the difficult problems related to teacher militancy and extending collective bargaining to public employees, two U.S. Congressmen, Mr. William Clay (Dem., Mo.) and Mr. Carl Perkins (Dem., Ky.), have introduced into the 93rd Congress a bill (H.R. 8677) which would require collective bargaining in the public sector on a nationwide basis.

At a time when substantive differences between public and private sector bargaining are beginning to be recognized, H.R. 8677 would attempt to create a body of theory and practice for the public sector based primarily on experience in the private sector. The proposal contains clauses which would extend the right to strike to all public employees, permit the inclusion in a single unit of supervisors and non-supervisors, and force creation of either an agency shop or a union shop among employees of public bodies. Although staff negotiations are not the substance of teacher militancy, it is a measure of the state of the art. There are many measures of teacher militancy. Many of these measures would be difficult to research and relate the data.

EXTENT OF AGREEMENTS

Since 1966-67 when the first survey of written agreements was conducted, the number of school systems with negotiation agreements has increased by 158.5 percent. In the 1966-67 survey, 1,531 school systems reported negotiation agreements; the 1972-73 survey found 3,958 systems with such agreements. The number of teachers covered by collective bargaining agreements has more than doubled. In 1966-67, 648,322 teachers were covered by negotiated agreements, while during 1972-73, 1,482,476 teachers were working under collective bargaining agreements. More than four-fifths of the teachers employed in the nation's largest school systems (25,000 or more pupils) are covered by collective bargaining agreements. The largest percentage of negotiated agreements were found in the Far West, where 93.7 percent of the school systems have negotiated agreements. Only the Southeast and Southwest have less than three-fifths of the school systems with negotiating agreements, and more than 50 percent of teachers in all regions, except the Southeast, are covered by collective bargaining agreements. (*Negotiations Research Digest,* June 1973, p. 14)

The role of the administrator is changing in educational decision-making. The administrators' traditional jurisdictions, which are being undermined by the growing influence of the Federal Government and of local, militant groups, is increasingly being challenged by the classroom teachers. The logical distinction between "policy decision" and "administrative decisions" has never really been an effective division of labor between administrators and school boards. The presumed division between administrative and teaching responsibilities will

be no real barrier against the encroachment of teachers on traditional administrative prerogatives. The shifting role of the administrator can be seen in Table 1 (*Negotiations Research Digest,* January 1973, p. 11).

Over the years, the percentage of school district negotiating teams made up of boards members only, or superintendents only, declined, while mixed teams of school-board members and school administrators increased. The percentage of other school administrators who participate in negotiations has increased steadily since 1966-1967. The percentage of school systems in which the superintendent negotiates with full or limited authority remained fairly constant from 1966-1967 to 1969-1970, but declined slightly thereafter.

Today, the superintendents are most likely to be advisors to the school-board negotiators only, whereas five years ago they were most likely to be advisors to both the school board and teacher negotiators (*Negotiations Research Digest,* January 1973, p. 11).

It can be concluded that the organizational rivalry between the NEA and AFT has intensified the drive toward greater teacher militancy. At all levels, the two organizations and their affiliates at the state and local levels have come under great pressure to achieve more expanded benefits than would be the case if the two organizations were not competing. A representative election generally causes the competing organizations to demonstrate a more militant stance in order to show their effectiveness in achieving teacher goals. Failure to present a strong, militant posture in achieving teacher objectives becomes a threat to organizational survival. Both the national and state organizations have a heavy stake in local elections, particularly in large cities with large teacher populations. Because of this rivalry, both organizations are much more

TABLE 1. PERCENT OF SCHOOL DISTRICTS HAVING NEGOTIATION AGREEMENTS, BY ROLE OF SUPERINTENDENT AND SCHOOL-BOARD MEMBERS IN NEGOTIATION SESSIONS, 1966-67 TO 1971-72

Item	Survey response year					
	1966-67	1967-68	1968-69	1969-70	1970-71	1971-72
1	2	3	4	5	6	7
NEGOTIATORS FOR SCHOOL BOARD						
Board members only	33.2	17.4	14.6	13.3	13.2	14.7
Superintendent only	26.3	17.7	13.4	10.5	9.4	8.2
Other school administrators	3.6	4.3	7.1	9.4	12.7	14.2
Board members and superintendent	21.2	32.9	32.5	31.4	27.8	26.0
Board members and other school administrators	0.9	2.9	5.5	6.7	7.4	8.1
Board members, superintendent, and other school administrators	6.8	12.8	13.9	15.4	14.1	12.6
Superintendent and other school administrators	8.0	12.1	13.0	13.4	12.9	12.1
Outside negotiator	–	–	–	–	2.4	4.0
	100.0	100.1	100.0	100.1	99.9	99.9
ROLE OF SUPERINTENDENT						
Negotiator with full authority	21.7	20.2	20.3	19.4	18.5	16.4
Negotiator with limited authority	16.0	17.7	17.2	16.1	15.5	14.4
Advisor to school-board negotiators only	13.4	19.8	30.3	37.8	42.4	45.6
Advisor to school-board and teacher negotiators	41.1	34.6	25.2	19.6	15.0	13.9
Neutral resource person	6.8	6.4	4.9	4.3	4.5	4.6
Nonparticipant	1.1	1.3	2.0	2.8	4.1	5.1
	100.1	100.0	99.9	100.0	100.0	100.0

closely attuned to teacher objectives. If the merger comes about it should tend to increase teacher militancy in some areas and reduce militancy in other areas.

Some of the teachers' reporting procedures now being negotiated are shown in Table 2; and some of this author's analyses, as they appear in *Negotiations Research Digest* (Feb.-May 1973) follow.

TABLE 2. TEACHERS' REPORTING PROCEDURES

Item	Number	Percent
1	*2*	*3*
TOTAL AGREEMENTS ANALYZED	1,529	100.0
Agreements containing report-in and absence report procedures	475	31.1
Absence report procedure only	352	23.0
Daily report-in procedure only	87	5.7
Daily report-in procedure and absence report procedure	36	2.4

Provisions concerning reporting on the availability for teaching duties are incorporated in 475 (31.1 percent) of 1,529 classroom teacher collective bargaining agreements with 1,000 or more pupils enrolled.

During the two-year period 1968-1969 to 1970-1971, the total number of teacher collective bargaining agreements collected for analysis by NEA Research increased from 978 to 1,529, a gain of 56 percent. The growth in number of agreements containing negotiated health and life insurance coverage provisions exceeded this gain.

Agreements with group health insurance provisions increased from 716 to 1,320 (an increase of 604 agreements, or 84 percent). A corresponding increase in the percent of agreements providing health insurance, from 73.2 percent in 1968-1969 to 86.3 percent in 1970-1971, was recorded.

TABLE 3. NUMBER AND PERCENT OF AGREEMENTS WITH HEALTH AND LIFE INSURANCE PROVISIONS, 1968-69 AND 1970-71

Group insurance	1968-69		1970-71	
	Number of agreements	Percent	Number of agreements	Percent
1	*2*	*3*	*4*	*5*
TOTAL NUMBER OF AGREEMENTS	978	100.0	1,529	100.0
Health Insurance TOTAL	716	73.2	1,320	86.3
Hospitalization, medical-surgical, and major medical	329	33.6	315	20.6
Hospitalization and medical-surgical	212	21.7	589	38.5
Other combinations or not identified	175	17.9	416	27.2
Life insurance	298	30.5	525	34.3

Similarly, the number of agreements with life insurance plans rose from 298 to 525, a gain of 76 percent. However, when viewed in the context of all recorded agreements, the percentage of agreements with life insurance coverage increased from 30.5 registered in 1968-1969 to 34.3 in 1970-1971.

An examination of employer participation in the payment of insurance premiums indicated that more school boards are paying part or all of the insurance premiums, the percentage rising from 66.3 to 80.6. The number of agreements wherein employers are required to pay the full cost of health insurance premiums doubled, from 25.1 percent to 50.1 percent.

The number of agreements containing life insurance provisions under which the employer pays part or all of the premium has increased slightly, from 25.3 to 28.2 percent. Again, those provisions under which the school board agreed to pay the full cost of life insurance have accounted for most of this increase—from 12.4 percent in 1968-1969 to 17.1 percent in 1970-1971.

This analysis is restricted to those agreements (effective in school systems with 1,000 or more pupils enrolled) on file with NEA Research. Since this analysis does not account for state, school district, or nonnegotiated health or life insurance programs not included in agreements, coverage may be even more widespread than indicated here.

Dismissal procedure provisions regarding the termination of classroom teachers are incorporated in 250 (16.4 percent) of 1,529 collective bargaining agreements in school systems with 1,000 or more pupils enrolled. Sixty-two agreements, or every fifth agreement with at least one from each state having a negotiated contract, were selected for further analysis. The selected sample of agreements taken from the 1970-1971 data base are representative, and are indicative of the prevalence of dismissal procedure provisions in negotiated contracts. This analysis is restricted to what appeared in negotiated contracts; specific reference to dismissal procedures where mandated by state law were not analyzed. All data appearing in the tables are not mutually exclusive, and percentages may not add to the totals shown because of rounding.

Negotiated provisions regarding dismissal procedures are usually supplemental to state tenure laws in those states which have tenure laws. Such negotiated procedures serve to provide another avenue through which dismissal or nonrenewal may be processed. State labor boards and courts have upheld this principle.

Provisions concerning inservice training were contained in 35.0 percent of 1,529 comprehensive teacher agreements comprising NEA Research's Survey of 1970-1971 Written Negotiation Agreements. By culling every fifth agreement, with at least one from each state having negotiated agreements, 110 provisions were selected for further analysis. The negotiated contents of these selected provisions were divided into three groups: (a) 12.7 percent contained stipulations concerning salary credit for participation in inservice training programs; (b) 36.4 percent made general statements either agreeing to establish an inservice program or recognizing an existing program which had not been included in the agreement; and (c) 50.9 percent established guidelines for the exist-

**TABLE 4. EMPLOYER PAYMENT OF HEALTH AND LIFE INSURANCE PREMIUMS,
1968-69 AND 1970-71**

	Percent of all[a] agreements with group insurance coverage							
	Employer pays all		*Employer pays part*		*Employer pays none*		*Not indicated*	
Type of group insurance	*1968-69*	*1970-71*	*1968-69*	*1970-71*	*1968-69*	*1970-71*	*1968-69*	*1970-71*
	2	*3*	*4*	*5*	*6*	*7*	*8*	*9*
Health Insurance								
TOTAL	25.1	50.1	41.2	30.5	–	0.5	6.9[a]	5.2[b]
Hospitalization, medical-surgical, and major medical	14.3	14.2	17.9	6.0	–	0.1	1.4	0.4
Hospitalization and medical-surgical	6.4	21.1	13.4	14.1	–	0.2	1.8	3.1
Other combinations or type of coverage or not indicated	4.4	14.8	9.9	10.4	–	0.2	3.6	1.8
Life Insurance	12.4	17.1	12.9	11.1	0.3	2.0	4.9	4.1

[a]Total of all agreements in 1968-69 was 978. Total of all agreements in 1970-71 was 1,529.

[b]Subitems do not add to total shown owing to rounding.

ing inservice training program (Table 6). As the last-mentioned category, which comprised over half of the selected provisions (56), was the most comprehensive insofar as these provisions related to functional programs, a subcategory was established for intensive analysis.

Over one-third of the teacher collective bargaining agreements on file with NEA Research contain provisions granting extra compensation for a variety of duties assigned in addition to the regular teaching load or the annually compensated guidance of student extracurricular activities. Of the 1,529 agreements negotiated during 1970-1971 in districts with 1,000 or more pupils enrolled, 521 agreements contained such provisions.

This analysis is intended to show the variety of activities and duties for which teachers are compensated, and the frequency with which compensation for them is negotiated, not the specific dollar amounts received.

Normal curricular duties, extracurricular activities for which a seasonal or yearly stipend is paid, adult education, night school, and summer school are considered to be part of the regularly conducted teaching load, and are not included in this analysis. These tables only depict some of the items included in teacher negotiations. These are only examples of some of the issues negotiated by militant teacher groups.

Many writers are suggesting that teacher militancy is on the wane. It is questionable whether this is true, because teacher militancy is being accepted by a larger segment of society. In addition, as negotiations become accepted as a way of life by boards of education, the spectacular teacher strikes that captured the headlines have diminished.

Problems involved in the unionization of the public sector cover the complete range of those in the private sector. If there is a major difference, it is that those in the public sector are more complex.

The initial problem is the law. In reality there is an entire series of problems due to the many existing state and local laws. The second problem is the lack of a comprehensive Federal law similar to the Taft-Hartley Act (which applies only to the private sector), to serve as a base upon which local laws can be built. To a degree,

this problem is solved by Executive Order 11491, which provides the framework for collective negotiations in the Federal government. The third problem area is the determination of what items can be negotiated. The list of negotiable items has expanded explosively. Courts have entered into the definition of negotiable items, and the growing number of cases in the courts attests to further increases. Both the National Education Association and the American Federation of Teachers have provided members with detailed descriptions and analysis of welfare conditions to be included in school board contracts, and the list grows daily.

Basic salaries are the most consistent source of conflict between teachers and the board of education. However, many agreements cover recognition clause, scope of the agreement, time, working conditions, benefits, safety, obligations of teachers, grievance and impasse procedures, salary and general wage provisions, use of the bulletin board and mail boxes, seniority, merger or consolidation of districts, transfer and assignment, promotion, removal and dismissal.

In negotiations it is extremely difficult to distinguish between "educational policy" and "salaries and working conditions" where collective negotiation is taking place.

**TABLE 5. NEGOTIATED CONTENT OF DISMISSAL
PROCEDURE PROVISIONS**

Item	*Number*	*Percent*
1	*2*	*3*
Tenure laws and other legislation mentioned or referred to	22	35.5
Reasons for dismissal stated	36	58.1
Prior written notice of dismissal required	45	72.6
Meetings/conferences regarding dismissal required	5	8.1
Suspensions	5	8.1
Hearing required	24	38.7
TOTAL SAMPLE OF PROVISIONS ANALYZED	62	100.0

TABLE 6. INSERVICE TRAINING PROVISIONS, 1970-71

Item	Number	Percent
1	2	3
AGREEMENTS CONTAINING INSERVICE TRAINING PROVISIONS	534	100.0
Inservice training provisions selected for analysis	110	20.6
INSERVICE TRAINING PROVISIONS SELECTED FOR ANALYSIS	110	100.0
Specified only salary credit for inservice training	14	12.7
Contained general statement agreeing to establish or recognizing an existing inservice training program	40	36.4
Contained guidelines for an established program of inservice training	56	50.9
GENERAL CONTENT OF PROVISIONS CONTAINING GUIDELINES FOR AN ESTABLISHED INSERVICE TRAINING PROGRAM	56	100.0
Purpose of inservice training specified	29	51.8
Teacher involvement in developing inservice training program required	24	42.9
Types of inservice training activities offered	39	69.6
Requirements for attending inservice training stated	30	53.6
Time inservice training activities are to be conducted	29	51.8
Incentives for participating in inservice training stated	31	55.4

For instance, it is generally accepted that salary schedule and teacher benefits are "bargainable" if anything is. However, if raising teacher benefits forces a budget reallocation of sums set aside for textbooks, hiring of additional professional personnel, building maintenance, or even new school construction, a decision on school district policy is clearly involved. Negotiations on working conditions in the schools has to some extent substituted centralized decision-making for decentralized decision-making on the management side. School principals have lost significant discretion in this process, and in a number of systems they not only resent this loss, but are becoming militant and are actually undertaking organization as a means of securing a stronger voice in centralized decision-making.

Delegates to the 1973 NEA Convention, in Portland, Oregon, approved plans for merger talks between NEA and the American Federation of Teachers, an AFL-CIO affiliate. But the delegates voted to require that any resulting merger be outside the AFL-CIO. "The NEA and its affiliates will not enter into a merger requiring affiliation with the AFL-CIO or any other labor organization," says new business item 52 as passed by the delegates.

The delegates endorsed a merger proposal to be submitted to the AFT, setting forth three basic concepts

TABLE 7. NEGOTIATED EXTRA-DUTY, OVERTIME, AND PREMIUM PAY PROVISIONS, 1970-71

Paid Extra Duties	Number	Percent*
1	2	3
TOTAL NUMBER OF AGREEMENTS	1,529	
NUMBER OF AGREEMENTS WITH EXTRA COMPENSATION	521	100.0
Duties during the school day	380	72.9
Regular teachers as substitutes	187	35.9
Overload, extra class period	126	24.2
Lunch, hall, recess, bus loading, cafeteria, and other duties	56	10.7
Excessive class size, combined classes	11	2.1
Duties before or after school	469	90.0
Student supervision, athletic and supplemental support services at unspecified events	152	29.2
Chaperones	123	23.6
Curriculum development	42	8.1
Field trips	18	3.4
Faculty meetings, parent-teacher conferences, conferences, etc.	11	2.1
Support services for dramatic and musical	9	1.7
Inservice participation	8	1.5
Debate and speech contest judges	7	1.3
Undefined activity	81	15.5
Undefined Saturday, Sunday, holiday duty	18	3.4
Extended school year	72	13.8

*Since provisions are not mutually exclusive, the percent of agreements containing specific provisions falling within a broad category cannot be determined accurately.

which NEA is not prepared to compromise during merger discussions:

1. No affiliation with the AFL-CIO and no obligations to the institutional positions and objective of the AFL-CIO.

2. Guaranteed minority group participation in the governance and operation of the new organization.

3. Use of the secret ballot to elect the officers and change the governing documents of the new organization.

The proposal also includes a one-year moratorium on all merger discussions at the state and local levels and on organizational rivalry at the local level.

Based upon the consensus that is developing in some areas and the uncertainties remaining in others, it seems to me that these conclusions can be identified in the evolution of teacher militancy:

Teacher militancy is going to increase rapidly and in more subtle forms.

Teacher organization action in the foreseeable future is going to be militant.

The achievement of collective power is going to become a major objective of teacher groups for a considerable period.

The combination of political and economic bargaining strategies and tactics will disturb for some time the pattern of collective bargaining between school administrators and teacher unions and associations.

The civil service concept of personnel policy and arrangements is going to suffer and be severely modified.

The public is going to pay a big price for what public employees gain.

Despite this, nothing is going to stop the introduction and spread of collective bargaining in the public schools.

REFERENCES

Stollar, Dewey. National Education Association. *Negotiations Research Digest.* Washington, D.C., January 1973.
_____. National Educational Association. *Negotiations Research Digest.* Washington, D.C., February 1973.
_____. National Education Association. *Negotiations Research Digest.* Washington, D.C., March 1973.
_____. National Education Association. *Negotiations Research Digest.* Washington, D.C., April 1973.
_____. National Education Association. *Negotiations Research Digest.* Washington, D.C., May 1973.
_____. National Education Association. *Negotiations Research Digest.* Washington, D.C., June 1973.

ADDITIONAL RESOURCES

Carlton, P. W., and Goodwin, H. I. *The Collective Dilemma: Negotiations in Education.* Worthington: Charles A. Jones Publishing Company, 1969.
Chamberlain, N. W., and Kuhn, J. W. *Collective Bargaining.* (2nd ed.) New York: McGraw-Hill, 1965.
Chanin, R. H. *Protecting Teacher Rights.* Washington, D.C.: National Education Association, 1970.
Elam, S. M., Liberman, M., and Moskow, M. H. *Readings on Collective Negotiations in Public Education.* Chicago: Rand McNally & Company, 1967.
Greene, J. E. *School Personnel Administration.* Philadelphia: Chilton Book Company, 1971.
Lieberman, M., and Moskow, M. H. *Collective Negotiations for Teachers.* Chicago: Rand McNally & Company, 1966.
Randle, C. W., and Wortman, M. S., Jr. *Collective Bargaining.* (2nd ed.) Boston: Houghton-Mifflin Company, 1966.
Shannon, T. A. Resolving Management Conflicts Through Associations. *The Administrative Team.* Arlington: National Association of Elementary School Principals, 1972.
Woodworth, R. T., and Peterson, R. B. *Collective Negotiations for Public and Professional Employees.* Glenview: Scott, Foresman and Company, 1969.
Yoder, D., Heneman, H. G., Jr., Turnbull, J. C., and Stone, C. H. *Handbook of Personnel Management and Labor Relations.* New York: McGraw-Hill, 1958.

41

PREGNANT TEACHERS

by Larry L. French
Chief Counsel
Oklahoma State School Boards Association
Oklahoma Association of School Administrators
Seminole, Oklahoma

Pregnancy has been described as a possible "impediment" (French, L. L., The School Administrator's Legal Handbook, Oklahoma University Law Center, 1973), particularly when such "status" occurs while one is employed as a teacher within a public education system. Essentially, the maternal status of a teacher relates directly to the prospect of that teacher's continued employment within the school assigned, depending generally upon local school board policy and perhaps politics as well. An additional aspect that complicates the issue is the marital status of the pregnant teacher. An attempt to rectify the situation (marry prior to delivery) might well remedy the teacher's plight, as recently, in the first Illinois case of its kind, the state court ordered a school board to reinstate with back pay a Kindergarten teacher with thirteen years tenure who was fired because she didn't marry until the eighth month of her pregnancy. The Judge said the 1970 Illinois Constitution gives equal protection to the sexes, and cited two recent rulings holding that pregnant students could not be excluded from classes and that school boards could not require pregnant teachers to take maternity leave.

Now as to the first ruling cited by the Illinois Court, there exists no argument; but as to the second, there does exist a disparity as between crucial decisions, as will be explored hereafter. It is noted that the United States Supreme Court has agreed to rule on whether school districts which require pregnant teachers to take a leave of absence four or five months before delivery are discriminating against these teachers on the basis of sex.

Other issues than the maternity leave question, though, revolve around the pregnant teacher, one being whether or not pregnancy qualifies as "sick leave." Another would be the transferability of a pregnant teacher to perhaps a higher level (or lower level) of instruction because of her "impression" upon impressionable students, the morality factor being of significance as well. Finally, the issue of discrimination as applied to male teachers who desire to obtain paternity leave during that particular critical period of their wives' pregnancy cycle, to wit the birth.

REVIEW OF RECENT CASES AND DEVELOPMENT

It was not that long ago when school boards delved into the then common practice of denying employment and dismissing female teachers solely on the basis of marriage alone. Well into the 1940s, the courts tended to affirm dismissals, especially in situations involving statutory or contractual provisions precluding marriages (Delon, 1973). For the most part, states prohibitions against marriage have disappeared, and in 1971 a Federal District Court ruled that refusal to hire married women violates the Civil Rights Act of 1964 (*Srogis v. United Airlines, Inc.*, 444 F. 2d 1194 (7th Cir. 1971) Cert. Den. 92 Su. Ct. 536 (1971)).

The courts have apparently not yet dealt with a situation involving a school board's refusal to hire pregnant teachers, although there are such policies in existence still today; but the court have ruled that a school board, while they may grant a leave period, cannot terminate a teacher solely upon the basis of pregnancy. Somewhere in between would be the regulation which prohibits a teacher from reporting to work the ensuing semester, following factual determination of the pregnancy. Regardless, the disposition of a pregnant teacher must meet the "constitutional" test as dictated by our courts.

REVIEW OF DEVELOPMENTS

A great many writings and court decisions have essentially ignored the premise of a school board's inherent and/or statutory authority, and responsibility, for the continued efficient and effective operation and maintenance of the public school system by which they were elected to so govern (French, 1973). This edict establishes the other side of the coin to the balancing test, which is determinative of any reasonable test as to the action and/or inaction of a governing body.

The Fourteenth Amendment to the United States Constitution provides in part that "no state shall ... deny to any person within its jurisdiction the equal protection of the laws." This clause has been applied to all state legislation (and regulations of state agencies) where classification of individuals is involved. The Supreme Court has consistently recognized that the equal protection clause

does not deprive the states of all power to classify, but does require that the treatment of different classes in different ways bear some rational relationship to a legitimate state objective. Thus the Constitution forbids not just discrimination but "invidious discrimination."

The determination of whether or not a statute or regulation constitutes an invidious discrimination has become refined in recent years. In economic and regulatory cases the test has been whether there is some "reasonable basis" for the discrimination. This test focuses on the purpose of the classification, and has been applied to give the states much leeway in providing different treatment for different classes. Under this test a regulation will be invalidated only where no "state of facts reasonably can be conceived that would sustain it." It has been said that in economic and regulatory matters the Court has presumed the regulation valid, placed the burden of showing no rational basis on the complaining party, and in fact almost abandoned the review of such equal protection questions.

Where a "suspect classification" or "fundamental right" is involved, a much stricter test has been applied to state regulations. Under the "compelling state interest" test, the state must be able to point to some compelling governmental interest promoted by the regulation or statute in question before it will be upheld. Thus a significant burden of justification is placed on the state.

What constitutes a "suspect classification" or a "fundamental right" is not altogether clear, because the Supreme Court has not enunciated "a rational Standard, or even points of reference, by which to judge what differentiations are permitted and when equality is required." Classifications based on race, national ancestry, alienage, and wealth have been treated as "suspect," with racial classifications receiving the strictest treatment. Personal interests found to be "fundamental" include procreation, education, voting, rights respecting criminal procedure, and the right to travel.

In testing regulations against the equal protection clause, one must look first to the classification to determine whether it is "suspect." If not, the compelling state interest test may still be invoked if there is a "fundamental interest" involved. If neither a "suspect classification" nor a "fundamental interest" is present, then the regulation needs only to have some reasonable basis in order to withstand an equal protection challenge (Hodges, 1973).

Obviously the courts have ruled that such regulations, if affected, must be applied uniformly and without discrimination. For example, one court ruled that if a school board permits maternity leave to a teacher with tenure, then the district must afford such privilege to the teacher without tenure (probationary), as well as to assure full compliance with the Equal Protection Clause of the Fourteenth Amendment to the United States Constitution.

To effectually determine the status of pregnant teachers as to employment rights and remedies, an attempt must be made to define exactly what pregnancy, per se, is. Basically, two extreme arguments exist: (1) pregnancy is an illness, and as such should qualify for sick leave benefits; (2) pregnancy is a disability, and should exist as a failure to perform situations pursuant to the teacher's employment contract. Closely related arguments are those related to the physiological condition, and, further, an incapacitated state of condition.

As to defining pregnancy, it is clear that pregnancy does exist as a "condition" (*State v. Sudol,* 129 A.2d 29, 32, 43 N. J. Super. 481; *State v. Comer,* 132 A.2d 325, 329 45 N. J. Super. 236). An Oregon case has further said that pregnancy is definitely not a disease or an injury (*Carter v. Howard,* 86 P.2d 451, 455, 160 Org. 507). Normally, pregnancy is treated as a separate condition pursuant to normal hospitalization and life insurance policies (*John Hancock Mutual Life Insurance Co. v. Serio,* D.C. Municipal Appellate, 176 A.2d 874, 876). An earlier case indicated that pregnancy was not, per se, a condition of unsound health, disease, or ailment within the meaning of such terms in a policy providing for payment of disability benefits (*Lee v. Metropolitan Life Insurance Co.,* 186 S.E. 376, 382, 180 Sup. Ct. 475).

On the other hand, "sick leave" has been broadly defined as leave of absence from duty granted on account of sickness, injury, or disability, (*Nelson v. Dean,* 168 P.2d 16, 27 Cal. 2d, 873, 168 ALR 467). More specifically, the word sickness has been held to not necessarily include pregnancy (*Mutual Benefit Health & Accident Association v. United Casualty Co.,* CCA Mass. 142 F.2d 390, 394). An extremely old case held that an able-bodied woman who was pregnant was not sick within the meaning of the statute in question. (*Regina v. Huddersfield,* 7 EL, BL 794, 796). More recently, under a professional disability policy providing indemnity for loss of time caused by sickness, pregnancy, and confinement for delivery per se, could not be construed as sickness within the intent and meaning of the policy. (*Sullivan v. National Casualty Co.,* 125 N. Y. Supp. 2d, 850). The only exception therein would be a case where the pregnancy itself was complicated or carried unusual and disabling consequences, and as such could be viewed as a sickness within a professional disability policy. (*Sullivan v. National Casualty Co.,* 128 N. Y. Supp. 2d., 717, 283 Appell. Div. 516). Such case citations would generally make clear that the state of an "uneventful" pregnancy would not so qualify as sick leave.

The transferability of teachers usually depends upon the teacher's contract of employment. Where the statute or the rules of a school board provide for the assignment and/or transfer of teachers to such work or such positions as the board may determine, a teacher, of course, is bound thereby, and may be assigned work in the system at the discretion of the board. (*Alexander v. School District #1,* 84 Org. 172, 164 Pac. 711). It is noted, however, that the rule is well established that a teacher cannot be required to perform service of a kind, other than that provided for in his contract. Assignment of a teacher to perform work substantially different from that which he has agreed to perform constitutes something other than that agreed upon (*School District #21 v. Hudson,* 277 S. W. 18). The impressionable student is obviously not a thing of the past, but community values as to the existence of a "woman with child" within the classroom may not be as strained as it obviously was many years earlier. The difficulty, though, can be ex-

treme in the case of the pregnant teacher without benefit of marriage, which would be a fact not unknown to the students.

SPECIFIC APPLICATIONS

While the entire area of employment policies of school districts relating to pregnancy and childbirth has seen much change recently, it is important to consider the guidelines now adopted by the United States Equal Law Employment Opportunities Commission which relate to pregnancy and childbirth policies:

> Section 1604.10–Employment Policies Relating to Pregnancy and Child Birth.
>
> (a) A written or unwritten employment policy or practice which excludes from employment applicants or employees because of pregnancy is in prima facie violation of Title 7.
>
> (b) Disabilities caused or contributed to by pregnancy, miscarriage, abortion, child birth and recovery therefrom are, for all job related purposes, temporary disabilities, and should be treated as such under any health or temporary disability insurance or sick leave plan available in connection with employment. Written and unwritten employment policies and practices involving matters such as the commencement and duration of leave, the availability of extensions, the accrual of seniority and other benefits and privileges, reinstatement, and payment under any health or temporary disability insurance or sick leave plan, formal or informal, shall be applied to disability due to pregnancy or child birth on the same terms and conditions as they are applied to other temporary disabilities.
>
> (c) When the termination of an employee who is temporarily disabled is caused by an employment policy under which insufficient or no leave is available, such termination violates the act if it has a disparate impact on employees of one sex and is not justified by business necessity.

These guidelines appear to make it clear that a board of education may no longer lawfully require a pregnant employee to cease work after any specific period of being pregnant. Many boards continue to have a policy requiring teachers and other female employees to take a leave of absence after the fifth month of pregnancy. The guidelines heretofore indicated clearly preclude this practice. Thus, if a teacher can successfully perform her duties as a teacher while she is pregnant she must be permitted to do so, or, to put it another way, a teacher may teach up to the day of delivery, provided she can perform efficiently. However, if the teacher's performance is affected by the condition of being pregnant, this may well give a board of education sufficient reason to ask the teacher to take a leave of absence.

The guidelines also seem to make it clear that if an employee is disabled and unable to work because of being pregnant, or because of a miscarriage, abortion, childbirth or recovery therefrom, then such disability must be treated as an illness under any existing sick leave policy in effect. Most school districts now have sick leave policies which do not provide for disability payments because of pregnancy, for the reason that pregnancy has not until now been considered to be an illness. It appears that the EEOC, with the obvious backing of Congress, has now made pregnancy an illness insofar as sick leave policies are concerned. Such continues to be debatable. Also, because of the position of the EEOC it is doubtful whether a teacher who becomes pregnant, and because of such pregnancy is unable to perform her duties as a teacher, has violated or breached her contract of employment. There continues to be some speculation as to whether pregnancy is a result of an accident or an intentional act. Under normal contract law, failure to act is usually construed to be a breach of contract, unless the accident is an act of God, in which case the decisions seem to indicate that both parties are then relieved from further duties pursuant to the contract. These guidelines obviously present some real problems for school districts. One of these problems would be what type of contract should be given to an interim teacher, e.g., the teacher who fills in for the pregnant teacher during her period of disability. It has been recommended that the interim teacher be given a contract which contains specific language to the effect that the contract is not subject to the continuing contract law, if one is applicable under normal circumstances; that the teacher who signs the contract waives any and all rights the teacher might be entitled to receive pursuant to such continuing contract law; and, finally, that the contract have a specific expiration date, either a date certain or the date when the pregnant teacher actually returns to her teaching duties (Kansas Association of School Boards, Jan. 1973).

The basic maternity leave regulation, which generally requires that a teacher be required to take a leave beginning at the fourth or fifth month of pregnancy, and often continuing for several months after delivery, has been challenged in many courts throughout this country. The essence of the issue boils down to two United States Court of Appeal decisions, each having reached opposite conclusions regarding the maternity leave regulation validity pursuant to the Equal Protection Clause of the Fourteenth Amendment of the United States Constitution.

In one (*LeFleur v. Cleveland Board of Education,* 465 F.2d 1184, 6th Cir. 1972), the Sixth Circuit struck down a school board rule requiring an unpaid leave of absence from school duties beginning five months before expected delivery and continuing until the beginning of the first term after the child reaches three months of age. The school board attempted to justify its regulation as providing for continuity of classroom education, relieving the board of burdens of administrative problems, and removing pregnant teachers as a source of pointing, giggling, and snide remarks; but the court found the regulation arbitrary and unreasonable in its overbreadth, and thus denied pregnant teachers equal protection of the laws. The court reasoned that any teacher disability (including the common cold) causes some administrative problems; that the basic rights involved in the employment relationship could not be made to yield to embarrassment; that the medical evidence presented no support for the regulation; and that there was no employer interest at all involved in the three-month postdelivery

leave requirement.

In the other (*Cohen v. Chesterfield County School Board,* 467 F.2d 262, 4th Cir. 1972), the Fourth Circuit reversed its earlier panel opinion in the same case by upholding a school board regulation that required the notice of the fact of pregnancy be given six months in advance of the date of expected birth, and that employment terminate four months prior to that date. The teacher had contended that the decision as to when to start maternity leave was an individual one, otherwise she would be subjected to an impermissible discrimination based upon her sex. The majority of the closely divided court disagreed, holding that the regulation was not an invidious discrimination based on sex, and that the school board had a legitimate interest in fixing reasonable dates for maternity leaves.

One difficulty that does exist, in attempting to analyze the reasonableness of such a regulation, is the term of leave in question. Possibly, for example, a one-month required leave period might be acceptable, such being a shorter period of time, and, even though many considerations would be the same, the justification for such a leave, per se, would become more reasonable. If the period of leave requirement was directly related to the medical difficulties normally encountered by a woman during the course of her pregnancy, such would be difficult to sustain, as it is clear that many women do not experience any difficulty during the course of their pregnancy—and then again, other experience extreme and continuous difficulties. Obviously, this would seem to support the position of the women litigants, in that they prefer to determine the leave timing pursuant to a determination made between themselves and their doctor and essentially precluding the input of the school administration. On the other hand, though, the school administration does have some responsibility to bear with respect to the efficient and effective continued operation of its school system; and (as is true with any personnel matter) administrative tasks are required, a substitute must be found and incorporated, determination must be had as to the substitute's contractual arrangement, and provisions are necessary with respect to notice by the pregnant teacher to the school system of her proposed effective leave and return dates.

In a large school system these various procedures could and would require a great deal of time, as oftentimes in a system of 2500 teachers, anywhere from 100 to 300 will become pregnant during the course of any school year. In essence, an independent staff could be required to handle the problem of pregnant teachers. In a small school system the problem would not be as significant, but still too, administrative tasks would have to be employed to assure smooth transition and continued normal operation of the school (Singer, Anne, Comment, 4 U. Cinn. L.R. 857, 1971).

CONCLUSION

Title VII of the Civil Rights Act of 1964 was an attempt to eliminate discrimination based upon race, color, religion, sex, or national origin. Although the Act was a significant step toward the elimination of discriminatory practices, it did not provide complete protection against discrimination in the employment field. Although there were earlier attempts to revise Title VII, it was not until the Equal Employment Opportunities Act of 1972 was enacted that teachers were given standing to challenge the employment practices of educational institutions. Clearly, discrimination by a school district may now be attacked; however, invalidation of maternity leave policies pursuant to Title VII requires that you have a determination that such policies constitute sex discrimination; this the United States Supreme Court will decide.

On January 21, 1974, the United States Supreme Court decided the maternity leave controversy dealing with both *LaFleur* and *Cohen*. The Court held as follows:

1. The mandatory termination provisions of board maternity rules violate the due process clause of the Fourteenth Amendment;
   a. The arbitrary cutoff dates (which obviously come at different times of the school year for different teachers) have no valid relationship to the State's interest in preserving continuity of instruction, as long as the teacher is required to give substantial advance notice that she is pregnant;
   b. The challenged provisions are violative of due process since they create a conclusive presumption that every teacher who is four or five months pregnant is physically incapable of continuing her duties, whereas any such teacher's ability to continue past a fixed pregnancy period is an individual matter; and the school boards' administrative convenience alone cannot suffice to validate the arbitrary rules.
2. The Cleveland three-month return provision also violates due process, being both arbitrary and irrational. It creates an irrebuttable presumption that the mother (whose good health must be medically certified) is not fit to resume work, and it is not germane to maintaining continuity of instruction as the precise point a child will reach the relevant age will occur at a different time throughout the school year for each teacher.
3. The Chesterfield County return rule, which is free of any unnecessary presumption, comports with due process requirements.

It is important to note, though, that the Court did hold that required advance notice of the state of pregnancy by the teacher is reasonable, and, further, that a school board may institute alternative administrative means in support of the legitimate goals of education. Specifically, boards may demand in each case substantial advanced notice of pregnancy, and, subject to certain restrictions, they may require all pregnant teachers to cease teaching at some firm date during the last few weeks of pregnancy.

As to re-entry, boards may in all cases restrict same to the outset of the school term following delivery, preceded by submission of a medical certificate from the teacher's physician. Finally, then, the Court has held that a school board in determining such regulations, cannot utilize unnecessary presumptions that broadly burden the exercise of protected constitutional liberties.

REFERENCES

Alexander v. School District #1, 84 Org. 172, 164 Pac. 711.
Carter v. Howard, 86 P.2d 451, 455, 160 Org. 507.
Cleveland Board of Education, et al., v. LaFleur.
Cohen v. Chesterfield County School Board, 467 F.2d 262 (4th Cir. 1972).
Cohen v. Chesterfield County School Board, et al., 42 L. W. 4186 (January 21, 1974).
Delon, Floyd G. Women's Rights: An Area of Concern. *Missouri School Boards Association School Lawletter.* Vol. 1, No. 3 (September 1973).
French, L. L. Maternity Leave. *American School Board Journal*, p. 30, Mar. 1973.
_____. The School Administrator's Legal Handbook. OU Law Ctr., 1973.
Hodges, George R. Mandatory Maternity Leaves for Teachers. 51 N. Car. L.R. 768 (1973).
John Hancock Mutual Life Insurance Co. v. Serio, D.C. Municipal Appellate, 176 A.2d 874, 876.
E.E.O.C. Guidelines. *Negotiation News.* Kansas Association of School Boards, January 1973.
Lee v. Metropolitan Life Insurance Co., 186 S.E. 376, 382, 180 Sup. Ct. 475.
LeFleur v. Cleveland Board of Education, 465 F.2d 1184 (6th Cir. 1972).
Mutual Benefit Health & Accident Association v. United Casualty Co., CCA Mass. 142 F.2d 390, 394.
Nelson v. Dean, 168 P.2d 16, 27 Cal. 2d, 873, 168 ALR 467.
Regina v. Huddersfield, 7 EL, BL 794, 796.
School District #21 v. Hudson, 277 S. W. 18.
Singer, Anne. Comment, 40 U. Cinn. L.R. 857, 1971.
Srogis v. United Airlines, Inc., 444 F.2d 1194 (7th Cir. 1971) Cert. Den. 92 Su. Ct. 536 (1971).
State v. Comer, 132 A.2d 325, 329 45 N. J. Super. 236.
State v. Sudol, 129, A.2d 29, 32, 43 N. J. Super. 481.
Sullivan v. National Casualty Co., 125 N. Y. Supp. 2d, 850.
Sullivan v. National Casualty Co., 128 N. Y. Supp. 2d., 717, 283 Appell. Div. 516.

42

LEGAL WORK STATUS OF THE HOMOSEXUAL PUBLIC SCHOOL TEACHER

by M. Chester Nolte
Chairman, Educational Administration
University of Denver
Denver, Colorado 80210

THE PROBLEM

Current court decisions dealing with sexual deviation among public school teachers have now reached a point where a new principle of common law is emerging: a board of education must bear the burden of proof that a duly certificated teacher's homosexuality, absent conviction for same, is sufficient grounds for that teacher's discharge. Coming in a decade of the 1960s as an adjunct of the civil rights movement, the drive of homosexuals for equal protection and due process of law has emphasized the need for boards of education to re-examine the puritanical sanctions they have applied to public school teachers. This article deals with the legal work status of the deviant public school teacher as the courts had enunciated it by the middle of 1975.

BACKGROUND

Sexual deviation is apparently older than recorded history. In Genesis XIX, Lot, not wishing to displease God, fled from Sodom in abhorrence at the evil sexual abuses rampant there. Later, the term "sodomy" was applied to those practices. The Greek poetess, Sappho, described how in the sixth century B.C. a group of women on the Aegean island of Lesbos fell prey to what was later known as "lesbianism," denoting homosexuality among females. The Apostle Paul, in his Letter to the Romans (I:26-27), indicated the wickedness of those who lusted after others of the same sex. Among the Greeks, homosexuality was accepted and even encouraged; some of the most revered Greek statesmen, as well as Romans of later date, were homosexuals. It is likely that the condemnation of homosexuality by the early Christian church was a reaction against the unbridled homosexuality of these earlier notables, whose lives were being emulated in the Middle Ages.

Nevertheless, even within the Church homosexuality was widely practiced, and the homosexual priest was often depicted in Renaissance drama. With the decline of the Church's influence, secular authority adopted prohibitions against homosexual activity. Such laws became more stringent during the Victorian era, and both England and the United States established sanctions against homosexuality as "an infamous crime against Nature."

In the law, up until the 1960s, the legal definition of a homosexual was anyone *apprehended* in a sexual act with another of the same sex. Two complications then arose: (1) some states, urged on by the changing sexual code and by pressures from civil libertarians, passed statutes which permitted homosexual acts between consenting adults, leaving only the *solicitation to commit a homosexual act* as illegal; and (2) some individuals, including those employed in public school teaching, voluntarily admitted their homosexuality and demanded equal rights with heterosexuals. In addition to the actions taken by state legislatures, there were numerous court tests to clarify the status of homosexuals, with particular emphasis on their right to work in public employment.

CASES

Socially regulatory law comes from two sources: the written law, including statutes and constitutions of the various governmental units, and the unwritten law, consisting chiefly of court decisions. By these two means, the social order seeks to uphold and enforce what are considered to be acceptable standards of propriety

among its public servants; to say that these standards are subject to change is to belabor the obvious. All 50 states have enacted laws forbidding or limiting the act of sodomy. Yet, in light of research on human sexual deviation, many college-educated males would be institutionalized if the statutes were to be vigorously enforced. Either the research findings are invalid or the laws are honored more in their breach than in their enforcement. Were we to accept the findings of Dr. Kinsey (1948), the statistical probability that there are homosexuals among duly certificated public school teachers is obvious. The question then arises, "To what extent may the State, in the form of local school boards, constitutionally regulate the personal and private lives of those who teach?" The cases make interesting reading, if for no other reason than that they are so new and so different from the traditional teacher-employment cases of the past.

Sarac. One of the earliest cases involving a homosexual public school teacher occurred in California (*Sarac v. State Board of Education*, 57 Cal. Rptr. 69, 1967). The plaintiff, a certified teacher in California, was convicted in a municipal court on a charge of homosexuality on a public beach, for which the State Board of Education revoked his teaching credential on the statutory grounds of immoral and unprofessional conduct and "evident unfitness for service." Claiming that such an action, without a hearing on the merits, deprived him of due process of law, the plaintiff claimed double jeopardy, since he had been tried and punished under the penal code as well as at the hands of civil authorities. The Supreme Court of California did not agree:

> Homosexual behavior has long been contrary and abhorrent to the social mores and moral standards of the people of California as it has been since antiquity to those of many other peoples. It is clearly, therefore, immoral conduct within the meaning of the Education Code, section 13202. It may also constitute unprofessional conduct within the meaning of that same statute as such conduct is not limited to classroom misconduct or misconduct with children. . . . It certainly constitutes evident unfitness for service in the public school system within the meaning of that statute. . . . In view of appellant's statutory duty as a teacher to 'endeavor to impress upon the minds of the pupils the principles of morality' (Education Code, Sec. 7851) and his necessarily close association with children in the discharge of his professional duties as a teacher, there is to our minds an obvious rational connection between his homosexual conduct on the beach and the consequent action of respondent in revoking his teaching credential on the . . . grounds . . . used. Needless to say, we find no abuse of discretion by respondent (state board) in the penalty it here imposed on appellant, nor *any constitutional questions whatsoever* with respect to such action on its part. (Emphasis added)

This case, and others subsequent to it, have developed the principle of law that teachers, who must be examples of their charges, have no constitutional protection when convicted in a state court on charges of public homosexuality. They do not "possess" continuing rights to public employment constitutionally, and hence may not protest that something of value, such as a license to teach, has been denied them illegally. The only right they seem entitled to is against discriminatory action at the hands of the State, since working for the state has always been considered a privilege rather than a right.

Morrison. It appears, however, that the board must prove the nexus between the teacher's homosexuality and his effectiveness as a teacher in the classroom. This plaintiff, also a duly certified California teacher, engaged in a limited, noncriminal physical relationship of a homosexual nature with another male teacher. Neither sodomy nor oral copulation was involved. The second teacher revealed the circumstances about six years following the event. Plaintiff enjoyed a good record as a teacher, having never been accused or convicted of any criminal activity whatsoever, and his record contained no evidence of any abnormal activity. The State Board of Education revoked his credential, charging "moral turpitude" under the same section of the Education Code outlined in *Sarac, supra.* The teacher brought suit, challenging the Board's action as a violation of his right to continue teaching. His suit was successful. Said the Supreme Court of California in ordering his credential reinstated:

> . . . we are not unmindful of the public interest in the elimination of unfit elementary and secondary school teachers. But petitioner is entitled to a careful and reasoned inquiry into his fitness to teach by the Board of Education before he is deprived of his right to pursue his profession. The power of the State to regulate professions and conditions of government employment must not arbitrarily impair the right of the individual to live his private life apart from his job, as he deems fit. We do not hold, of course, that homosexuals must be permitted to teach in the public schools of California. What is required is that the Board properly find, pursuant to the precepts set forth in this opinion, that an individual is not fit to teach. The Board called no medical, psychological, or psychiatric experts to testify as to whether a man who has had a single, isolated and limited homosexual contact would be likely to repeat such conduct in the future. The Board offered no evidence that a man of his background was any more likely than the average adult male to engage in any untoward conduct with a student. . . . The lack of evidence is particularly significant because the board failed to show that plaintiff's conduct in any manner affected his performance as a teacher. There was not the slightest suggestion that plaintiff had ever attempted, sought or even considered any form of physical or otherwise improper relations with any student. There is no evidence that plaintiff's conduct affected students, or his co-workers. We therefore order his certificate reinstated. (*Morrison v. State Board of Education,* 82 Cal. Rptr. 175, 1969)

The court distinguished between this case and *Sarac,* pointing out that in the latter the homosexual behavior was public rather than private, and that Plaintiff Morrison had not been convicted. The extent to which the passage of six years' time affected the court's reasoning is not clear, but it did allow time for Morrison to establish his competency and obtain a property right to his position (see *Board of Regents v. Roth,* 92 S. Ct. 2701, and *Perry v. Sindermann,* 92 S. Ct. 2694, 1972). The California Supreme Court thus reached its decision prior to the United States Supreme Court's holding that one who teaches for a length of time establishes a "property" right

to that position, and the State must show cause if it is going to deprive that individual of continuing employment by providing him due process of law as outlined in the Fourteenth Amendment.

Some of the earlier cases likewise foreshadowed this conclusion. In 1896, the Supreme Court of Arkansas held that the state's power to revoke a teacher's certificate for lack of good moral character must be exercised in such a way as to take into account the right of the teacher to an opportunity to defend his good name at a hearing (*Lee v. Huff,* 33 S.W. 846, 1896). In 1962, the Florida Supreme Court (*Neal v. Bryant,* 149 So. 2d 529, 1962) held that a local board could not dismiss a teacher without a hearing on a charge of moral turpitude in the practice of homosexuality. The board had illegally proceeded without affording plaintiff his statutory right to an investigating committee to make a preliminary determination of probable cause for dismissal. These two cases were not founded on the constitutional right of due process, but rather upon whether a state statute had been complied with in dealing with an employee of the school district.

Norton. The court in *Morrison* cited with approval from *Norton v. Macy,* 417 F. 2d 1161, 1969, in which a Federal Court of Appeals had held that a Federal employee could not be dismissed for homosexuality alone, if he had committed no act with an ascertainable deleterious effect on the efficiency of the public service. Since the government was unable in *Norton* to show such an effect, the employee was ordered reinstated. (Homosexuals in mystery stories are depicted as individuals notoriously susceptible to blackmail, therefore being considered poor security risks.)

Wentworth. Another Federal court granted summary judgment to an employee of Bell Laboratories on grounds that "an order to deny clearance to an admitted ongoing homosexual (not to mention fornicators, adulterers, and those who offend in other ways the mores of our Judaeo-Christian tradition)" must be accompanied by proof of a nexus or of a rational connection between such (sexual) condition and the ability to safeguard classified information. The government had failed to provide such a nexus (*Wentworth v. Laird,* 346 F. Supp. 1152, 1972).

Richardson. An applicant who was denied employment until he proved himself rehabilitated from former homosexual conduct was further denied employment because he had failed to prove, to the satisfaction of the court, that he had indeed been fully rehabilitated (*Richardson v. Hampton,* 345 F. Supp. 600, 1972).

Moser. Does one who makes a public display of his homosexuality become unfit for service as a teacher because of such display? The California Supreme Court had occasion to decide such a question in 1972. Plaintiff, a certified public school teacher, had his credential revoked by the State Board of Education on evidence that he had masturbated while in public view in a public restroom, and had touched the private parts of another male. The court held that such conduct on the part of the plaintiff was sufficient, in an of itself, to establish obvious unfitness for service to teach, and also held that the state was within its rights in revoking a teacher's credential without a hearing on the merits of unfitness to teach (*Moser v. State Board of Education*, 101 Cal. Rptr. 86, 1972).

Grossman. A New Jersey teacher underwent sex rearrangement and became a female. The evidence established that the children in the teacher's classes would be harmed by the individual's appearance as a female teacher, and he/she was ordered dismissed for reason of just cause due to incapacity. The board was ordered to process an application for a disability pension on behalf of the teacher (*In the Matter of the Tenure Hearing of Paula M. Grossman, also known as Paul M. Grossman*, N.J. Comm. of Educ. Decision, 1972).

Burton. The homosexual teacher cases are predominantly male, but an Oregon case illustrates that there must be no double standard for the sexes (*Peggy Burton v. Cascade School District*, 353 F. Supp. 254, Oregon 1973). The Oregon statutes vest in the board of education the power to dismiss teachers for "immorality" without defining in more detail what that term means legally. In her second year of teaching, plaintiff let it be known that she was a homosexual, although the board admitted that she was one of its best teachers in the classroom. She was granted relief under the Civil Rights Act of 1871 (42 U.S.C. §1983). The statute was unconstitutionally vague, said the court, in that it failed to give fair warning of what conduct was proscribed, and permitted erratic and prejudiced exercise of authority by the state. The statute also created serious constitutional problems because it did not require a nexus between conduct and teaching performance. Said the court in explaining how definitions may change with the times:

> Immorality means different things to different people, and its definition depends upon the idiosyncrasies of the individual school board members. It may be applied so broadly that every teacher in the state could be subject to discipline. The potential for arbitrary and discriminatory enforcement is inherent in such a statute.

But the school board may not draw its lines so far afield that it can sweep anyone into its net. Quoting from an earlier case, the court told why this is so:

> It would certainly be dangerous if the legislature could set a net large enough to catch all offenders, and leave it to the courts to step inside and say who would be rightfully detained and who should be set at large. (*U.S. v. Reese*, 92 S. Ct. 214, 1875)

A statute so broad makes those charged with its enforcement "the arbiters of morality for the entire community." In doing so, it subjects the livelihood of every teacher in the state to the "irrationality and irregularity" of such judgments. The statute is vague, said the court, because it fails to give fair warning of "what conduct is prohibited," and because it permits "erratic and prejudiced" exercise of authority. Attorneys for the sides were directed to get together and work out an appropriate remedy within two weeks' time. Should the attorneys

fail to agree, the court said it would hold a hearing to resolve the issues.

McConnell. Plaintiff was an avowed homosexual pressing for more freedom and equality for homosexual individuals in our society. He had been offered a job as librarian at the University of Minnesota, St. Paul campus. Before the regents had an opportunity to confirm his appointment, he and another man applied for a marriage license, a news item which gained considerable notoriety in the national press. The regents thereupon refused to confirm his appointment on the grounds that his personal conduct was not consistent with the best interests of the university. The librarian then brought an action in Federal District Court claiming a denial of due process of law. At the district court level, the court held that the librarian should be reinstated, because the regents had failed to show how his homosexuality, which was freely admitted, would impair his efficiency as a librarian (*McConnell v. Anderson*, 316 F. Supp. 809, 1970). The circuit court reversed, reasoning essentially that the case involved not mere homosexuality propensities of a prospective employee, or exclusion from employment because of a desire to pursue homosexual conduct clandestinely, but rather a desire to pursue "an activist role" in implementing his unconventional ideas concerning the societal status to be accorded homosexuals, and thereby to foist tacit approval of his socially repugnant concept upon his unwilling employer. The court added, "We know of no constitutional fiat or binding principle of decisional law which requires an employer to accede to such extravagant demands (*McConnell v. Anderson*, 451 F. 2d 193, VIII Circ. 1971, *cert. denied*, 405 U.S. 1046, 1972)."

Acanfora. What of the teacher who failed to inform the board of his propensity toward homosexuality at the time of making application to teach? A school board in Maryland had a policy of not knowingly employing any homosexual teachers. The court held that mere knowledge that a teacher is a homosexual is not sufficient to justify his transfer or dismissal. But it did hold that the teacher had gone beyond his needs in engaging in activities such as TV appearances, radio and news broadcasts, and active participation in the cause of greater civil rights for homosexuals. He had sparked controversy outside the constitutional realm of his protection, although the court was inclined to want to protect his rights even then. What finally resulted in the teacher's legal dismissal was his practice of fraud, in lying on the application blank that he was not a homosexual. While homosexuality, said the court, is not in and of itself grounds for dismissal, lying (i.e., fraud) is (*Acanfora v. Bd. of Educ. of Montgomery Co.*, 491 F. 2d 498, 1974).

Lewis. Potential degenerates may be precluded from the vicinity of the school in order to protect the state's interests, according to a recent case in New York. Defendants stood on a public sidewalk and handed out leaflets to students. They were found guilty of loitering without having a legitimate reason for being on school property without written permission from any one authorized to grant such permission. The court held that

the state has a valid interest and responsibility to protect students and their schools from drug peddlers, degenerates, vandals, and the like. Appellants failed to
offer any proof of arbitrary and discriminatory application of the requirement of prior restraint in the requirement of prior approval by school authorities (*People v.
Lewis,* 332 N.Y.S. 2d 929, 1972).

Purifoy. A statute which provides for suspension and/or
revocation of a teaching credential upon conviction of a
sex offense is not a denial of due process of law, since
the teacher was accorded a hearing in a criminal proceedings, thus meeting the due process guarantee (*Purifoy
v. State Board of Education,* 106 Cal. Rptr. 201, 1973).
Plaintiff was certified for life to teach in the public
schools of California. However, his credential was revoked when, after a jury trial, he was convicted of loitering in and around a public toilet for the purpose of engaging in or soliciting any lewd or lascivious act. He
thereupon sued for the return of his certificate and his
former position on grounds that he had been denied due
process of law and been placed in double jeopardy. The
court could not agree with his contention:

> The Fourteenth Amendment protects the right of an indi-
> vidual to pursue his chosen profession without interference
> by arbitrary state action.... The requirements of due process,
> however, are not inflexible, but rather are dependent upon
> the nature of the governmental function involved and the
> private interest affected.... (Automatic) disbarment is an
> automatic fact based upon the violation of a statute and con-
> viction thereupon, and is not a denial of due process since
> an individual is assumed to know the law.... The statute
> was based upon a compelling state interest in removing school
> teachers from classrooms. The state has the right to so pro-
> tect its interests and those of its citizens enrolled in the
> public schools.

Wishart. Finally, a case arising in Massachusetts illustrates the old adage that where there's smoke there's fire.
Action was brought by a dismissed tenured sixth grade
teacher against the board for injunctive relief and monetary damages. The district court denied relief, and the
teacher appealed. The United States Court of Appeals
for the First Circuit held that the board had sufficient
evidence to warrant the teacher's dismissal, and that its
actions were not arbitrary or damaging.

Charges against the teacher were related to "conduct
unbecoming a teacher," which the teacher claimed were
unconstitutionally vague. The board heard evidence that
the teacher, in public view on his property located in the
small town where he taught, in a lewd and suggestive
manner carried a dress mannequin that he had dressed,
undressed, and caressed, notwithstanding the teacher's
claim that reasons for his dismissal were unrelated to the
educational process or to the working relationship
within the schools themselves. A psychiatrist testified
that his behavior was symptomatic of a personality disorder brought on by severe depression over the death of
his first child, born with a serious neurological deficit.
Since his behavior was in full view of the neighbors, one
of whom informed the school committee, the dismissal
was not arbitrary or capricious on the part of the school

committee (*Wishart v. McDonald,* 500 F, 2d 1110,
1974).

SUMMARY

Mere homosexuality per se in a public school teacher
is insufficient to deny further employment to a duly
certified teacher. States vary considerably in the attention they give to this problem statutorily, and one must
of course become acquainted with the state's position on
this issue. Further than that, there seems to be no property right which attaches to teachers until one has put in
at least three years' employment. Since all cases involving
homosexual teachers must rest entirely upon the particular set of circumstances in each instance, categorical
standardization of this area is particularly difficult, if
not indeed risky.

One does not have a right to work for the government; however, once that employment has been granted,
the teacher may not be discriminated against on account
of his/her homosexuality without proof by the board of
education that such a lifestyle has a deleterious effect on
classroom efficiency. Since this is sometimes difficult to
accomplish, school boards have found that dismissal or
transfer of a teacher on the grounds of "immorality"
may not stand up in court.

This area of the law is still murky, but it seems well
settled that what the teacher does in private, absent
notoriety which may destroy his/her credibility with
students, is still protected under the right to privacy.
The right to do those things in private is lost when the
same acts are done in public and become matters of
general gossip and notoriety.

43

LEGAL CONTROLS ON TEACHER BEHAVIOR

by Floyd G. Delon
Associate Dean
University of Missouri
Columbia, Missouri

This article examines current statutory and case law
representing legal controls on teacher behavior both inside and outside the classroom. Legal writers sometimes
use the term "teacher discipline" to describe the application of these controls. The applications presented here
identify both the types of behavior leading to disciplinary
action and the punishments involved in disciplinary action.

Significant changes in teacher discipline occurred in
the last five years. It follows, then, that most of the pertinent illustrative court decisions are of rather recent
origin. Because the court decisions involving Federal constitutional questions are of general applicability, this ar-

ticle places emphasis on them rather than on court decisions involving the interpretation of specific state statutes.

Since the early history of this country, the public has been far more restrictive in its expectations for the conduct of teachers than for the conduct of the average lay citizen. This attitude is readily apparent in state legislation and court decisions up to the beginning of the last half of this century (Elsbree, 1939; Beale, 1971).

A study of reported causes for teacher dismissal (Anderson, 1939) revealed that in most states teacher dismissal was on "a personal rather than a professional basis (p. 8)." The distribution of causes in the samples reviewed was: incompetency and inefficiency (34), reassignment and transfer (26), insubordination (24), marriage and childbirth (25), neglect of duty (22), abolition of position (21), abandonment of position (18), immorality and rumors of immorality (17), general unpopularity (8), unprofessional conduct (7), anticipated causes (6), and political activity (4).

Bolmeier (1960) observed that teachers were "more restricted than most citizens in the exercise of their freedoms guaranteed by the constitution (p. 206)." This conclusion was based on a review of court decisions on teacher involvement in subversive, political, union, and other controversial out-of-class activities.

On the other hand, Firth (1960), advocating self-discipline by the teaching profession, declared: "Existing legal machinery is apparently inadequate for the removal of incompetent or unethical teachers from our classrooms (p. 24)." In this same vein, Garber (1964) expressed doubt that a teacher could be fired for "unprofessional conduct" because of his public criticism of the school system, unless such criticism can be shown to impair or disrupt discipline or the teaching process. Garber (1968) later concluded that "the right of a school board to control the dress or appearance of the teacher is limited to occasions where the matter it desires to control has an adverse effect on student and/or learning conditions of the school (p. 50)."

A number of articles on teacher immorality were published in the late 1960s. Punke (1965) wrote, "the moral code for teachers is more rigid than for people in many vocations (p. 53)." Through an analysis of court decisions, Koenig (1968) identified the various meanings ascribed to teacher immorality and misconduct. According to Nolte (1967), the board of education "may legally expect a teacher to exhibit exemplary behavior and to comply with the local mores in dress and conduct, especially in public (p. 29)."

Williams (1967), in his doctoral dissertation, analyzed the legal causes for dismissal of public school teachers. He noted that the states' statutory causes for dismissal lacked "unity" and the courts' interpretations displayed "a great deal of ambiguity among the causes (p. 1)." He recommended the adoption of a uniform tenure law by each of the 50 states.

Union activity, which has increased significantly in the last ten years, has become a frequent source of disciplinary action against teachers. Nolte (1969), pointing out the constitutionally guaranteed right of freedom of assembly or association, advised school boards not to penalize teachers for participation in unions. However, in cases of illegal strikes, board action and withholding pay has been upheld (Nolte, 1968). Furthermore, *Instructor* magazine (1968), from a survey of teachers, found that only 16 percent of those responding thought striking teachers should receive their regular salaries.

Two recent books provided detailed listings of cases dealing with teacher dismissal (Punke, 1971; Peterson et al., 1969). Delon (1972) analyzed both statutory and case law pertaining to the broad area of teacher discipline. He found marked changes in teacher discipline associated with new legislation, recent Federal court decisions, and developments in the total social context.

Nolte (1973) examined academic freedom in the public school setting. He concluded: "Although there seems to be an inclination on the part of the courts to broaden the protected area of academic freedom in the classroom, this territory is still ill-defined, and subject to further litigation. . . (p. 47)."

Shannon (1973) discussed new tactics used by plaintiffs, including teachers, in imposing their views and enforcing their rights against school boards. While making no value judgment concerning these tactics, he pointed out that they are "realities" with which public school people must deal (p. 87).

More recently an article appeared in *The Wall Street Journal* (January 28, 1975) entitled, "More Teachers Fight Efforts to Fire Them for Personal Conduct (p. 1)," and another in *Newsweek* (February 24, 1975) under the byline, "Private Lives (p. 87)." These articles discussed such behaviors as unwed pregnancies, posing in the nude, and union activism.

State agencies, namely, state boards of education and local boards of education, derive their authority to discipline teachers from the statutes. The statutes of most states specify ground for disciplinary action as well as resulting penalties. The major category of penalties, certificate revocation, dismissal, and fines and/or imprisonment, serve as the subheadings in this section.

CERTIFICATE REVOCATION

Nearly every state has legislation authorizing the revocation of a teaching certificate for certain stated causes. The listing typically includes such grounds as incompetency, neglect of duty, inefficiency, insubordination, immorality, contract violations, and other good, just or sufficient cause. This penalty is an extreme one which is not often imposed; therefore the body of case law dealing with it is not extensive

Certificate revocation for immorality is perhaps the most frequent source of litigation in this area. A series of recent cases in California illustrate recent developments. While these decisions are not binding on the courts of other states, they may exert some influence under similar circumstances, when the wording of the statutes are nearly identical and when the state has no judicial precedents of its own.

The first of these cases, decided in 1967, was brought by a teacher to compel the state board of education to restore his certificate (*Sarac v. State Board of Education*, 249 Cal. App. 2d 58, 1967). The court upheld the revocation after it was established that the individual did engage in a homosexual act on a public beach. The California courts followed this ruling last year, again holding that homosexual behavior in a public place constitutes unfitness to teach in the public schools (*Moser v. State Board of Education,* 22 Cal. App. 3d 988, 1972).

In 1969, in *Morrison v. State Board of Education,* the California Supreme Court reviewed a revocation action resulting from homosexual incidents in the privacy of the teacher's apartment. The court, in ruling for the teacher, distinguished between "public conduct" and "private conduct" of a teacher, and placed the burden of proof on the licensing agency to establish a relationship between the questioned behavior and fitness to teach. According to the opinion, "the power of the state to regulate professions and conditions of government employment must not arbitrarily impair the right of the individual to live his private life apart from his job as he sees fit (p. 394)." The California court said also that a teacher's credential may not be revoked solely for the conviction of the crime of possession of marijuana (*Comings v. State Board of Education,* 23 Cal. App. 3d 94, 1972). Again, the court indicated that the board must show a connection between the offense and fitness to teach—for example, adverse school relationships, or excessive notoriety impairing these relationships.

In 1973, however, the California Supreme Court affirmed the revocation of an elementary teacher who was active in a "swingers" or "wife-swapping" group (*Pettit v. State Board of Education,* 513 p. 2d 889). The Iowa Supreme Court ruled that adulterous behavior was insufficient reason to justify revoking a certificate on the basis of immorality (*Erb v. Iowa State Board of Public Instruction,* 217 N.W. 2d 339, 1974).

For the past several years, penalties connected with loyalty oaths and organizational memberships have been subject to the careful examination of the courts. In 1970 a three-judge district court ruled that the California loyalty oath is an unconstitutional condition for certification (*MacKay v. Rafferty,* 321 F. Supp. 1177, 1970). The weight of evidence now indicates that membership in a political organization, per se, is not a permissible ground for disqualifying applicants for the profession, or for revoking their certificates or licenses to teach. The state may probably go no farther than to require that the teacher be willing to affirm a general commitment to uphold the Constitution and to perform the duties of his position (Van Alstyne, 1970).

DISMISSAL AND SUSPENSION

The statutory grounds for teacher dismissal parallel those listed for certificate revocation. It is apparent from an examination of the extensive body of cases that there are no standard definitions of the stated grounds, and that the same behavior may be associated with a variety of charges.

The most significant recent developments related to teacher dismissal are the restrictions on a school board's action brought about by the vigorous court enforcement of teacher's constitutional rights. Most relevant to a treatment of legal controls on teacher behavior are the

court decisions involving the substantive rights of the First Amendment, namely, speech, press, assembly, and the right to petition government for the redress of grievances.

Personal Behavior

Constitutional protections do not extend to immoral conduct, either outside or inside the classroom. For example, the Michigan Court of Appeals upheld the school board's action suspending a teacher for giving barbituates to a person they thought to be a former student (*Mullally v. Board of Education,* 164 N.W. 2d 742, 1968); and the California Appellate Court affirmed the discharge of a male teacher discovered intimately embracing one of his female students in a parked car (*Board of Trustees v. Stubblefield,* 16 Cal. App. 3d 820, 1971). An Illinois case is illustrative of discharge for immoral in-class behavior. A band director lost his job because of substantiated complaints that he fondled several of the junior high school girls during his classes (*Lombardo v. Board of Education,* 241 N.E. 2d 495, 1968).

Speech and Expression

What teachers say and write have been frequent bases for dismissal actions. The specific legal controls in this area began to be redefined with the *Pickering* decision (391 U.S. 563, 1968), when the United States Supreme Court ruled that the teacher's right to speak out on issues of public concern should not serve as a basis for his discharge. Subsequently, in a similar case involving a letter to the newspaper, the Alaska Supreme Court ruled that personal verbal attacks affecting the operation of the schools were not protected by the Federal constitution (*Watts v. Seward Board of Education,* 454 P.2d 732, 1965).

In general, the courts' position on speech and expression in the classroom may be only slightly more restrictive on the teacher. A Federal District Court in Nebraska upheld the dismissal of a teacher who criticized her substitute and encouraged her students to oppose the corporal punishment policies of the school (*Ahern v. Board of Education,* 325 F. Supp. 1391, 1971). The court said:

> I am persuaded that the exercising of the constitutional right was not the reason for the discharge. Although a teacher has a right to express opinions and concerns, as does any other citizen on matters of public concern, by virtue of the First and Fourteenth Amendments, ... I doubt that she has the right to express them during class in deliberate violation of a superior's admonition not to do so, when the subject of her opinion and concern is directly related to the student and teacher discipline. (p. 1397)

The courts have also considered the extent to which choice of subject matter is protected by the First Amendment. For example, in *Parducci v. Rutland* the court ordered reinstatement of an English teacher discharged for using a short story by Vonnegut (316 F. Supp. 352, 1970). The courts have consistently held that it is constitutionally impermissible to ban arbitrarily subject matter selected by the teacher.

Assembly and Association

The past decade has witnessed a dramatic change in teacher/school board relationships with the adoption of collective bargaining arrangements. Conflicts have developed resulting in teacher dismissals. These dismissals in many instances have been overturned as violative of teachers' constitutional rights.

In *McLaughlin v. Tilendis,* the courts said that probationary teachers may not be discharged or denied a contract solely because of union membership or activities (398 F. 2d 387, 1968). In the words of the opinion, "public school teachers have the right of free association. . . . Unless there is some alleged legal intent, individual rights to form and join a union is protected by First Amendment (p. 288)." The weight of evidence is that a teacher may not be denied a teaching contract because of his activities in a professional association, regardless of how vigorous they are.

A teacher may not be denied initial employment because the board disapproves of her living on a communal farm. Because the teacher was otherwise qualified, a Federal District Court in Georgia ruled that such action of the board violated the teacher's constitutional right of freedom of association (*Doherty v. Wilson,* 356 F. Supp. 35, 1973).

LOSS OF PAY, FINES AND IMPRISONMENT

The statutes of several states authorize boards of education to deduct teachers' salaries for a number of offenses. These offenses include failure to submit reports, refusal to attend institutes, unauthorized absences, and unlawful strikes. The salary losses can be significant, as evidenced by the penalties in Stamford, Connecticut, where teachers were docked a total of $285,665 for a four-day strike (Educators Negotiating Service, 1972).

Fines and imprisonment are almost without exception assessed by the courts. While the state statutes may call for fines and/or imprisonment for such offenses as failure to display the flag, teaching overthrow of the government by force, and failure to perform certain specified duties, applications of these statutory provisions are extremely rare. Most of the cases in which fines or imprisonment do result involve either unlawful strikes and picketing or assault and battery.

Usually, the school district's most formidable defense against an illegal strike is the court-ordered injunction. Defiance of the injunction can lead to heavy fines against the teacher organization and its officers, who may also receive jail terms. Teachers engaged in illegal picketing, in violation of a restraining order, may suffer similar consequences. For example, three North Dakota Teachers were fined $250 plus court costs and were given 30-day suspended sentences (*State v. Heath,* 177 N.W. 2d 751, 1970).

Few assault and battery cases involving teachers have moved beyond the trial courts. However, one such case illustrates the type of teacher conduct involved. In *City*

of McComb v. Gould, a teacher engaged in supervisory duty at a football game allegedly struck a male student several times in the face after ordering him to leave a given area. The court upheld the teacher's conviction for violating a city ordinance prohibiting fighting, and assessed a ten-dollar fine (244 N.E. 2d 361, 1969).

CURRENT CONTROVERSIES

The controls on teacher behavior remain in a state of change, and the rate of change continues to accelerate. In reviewing disciplinary actions the ever-present task of the courts is to balance the public interest with the individual rights of the teacher. Current and future litigation will require that the courts examine further, and define more precisely, limitation on teachers' personal lives and on their freedom of expression.

An increasing number of states have enacted negotiation laws. The effects of collective bargaining on teacher discipline are uncertain. School districts and teachers may benefit by resolving problems through negotiation rather than litigation. Organizational support and formalized grievance procedures may deter arbitrary action. On the other hand, adoption of the labor-management model may multiply the number of illegal strikes.

Professional practice laws, also a product of the past decade, add a new dimension to the legal controls on teacher behavior. Such laws provide the legal machinery and authorize self-discipline by the teaching profession. Although past performance of teachers in self-policing their ranks casts doubt as to the success of this approach, perhaps official recognition of this responsibility will make a difference. As most teachers and administrators will agree, some new and effective form of regulation is needed.

REFERENCES

Anderson, W. *Trends in Courses of Teacher Dismissal as Shown by American Court Decisions.* Unpublished doctoral dissertation, George Peabody College for Teachers, 1939.

Beale, H. *A History of Freedom of Teaching in American Schools.* New York: C. Scribner's Sons, 1941.

Bolmeier, E. C. Legal Scope of Teacher Freedoms. *Educational Forum,* 1960, *24,* 199-206.

Delon, F. Substantive Legal Aspects of Teacher Discipline. *ERIC/CEM State of the Knowledge Series,* 1972, No. 23, *NOLPE Monograph Series,* No. 2.

Educators Negotiating Service. Educators Negotiating Service Newsletter. Washington D.C., January 1, 1972.

Elsbree, W. *The American Teacher.* New York: American Book Co., 1939.

Firth, G. Teachers Must Discipline Their Professional Colleagues. *Phi Delta Kappan,* 1960, *42,* 24-27.

Garber, L. O. Can You Fire a Teacher for Un-Professional Conduct? *Nation's Schools,* April 1964, *73,* 90 and 114.

———. To Shave or Not to Shave: That is the Requirement. *Nation's Schools,* December 1968, *82,* 50.

Koenig, R. Teacher Immorality and Misconduct. *American School Board Journal,* January 1968, *155,* 15-19.

Nolte C. From Scopes to Epperson and Beyond: Academic Freedom in the Schools. *Nolpe School Law Journal,* Spring 1973, *3,* 37-47.

———. How *Not* to Pay Damages: Don't Penalize Teachers for

Unionism. *American School Board Journal,* April 1969, *156,*
8-10.

_____. Teacher Image, Conduct Important. *American School
Board Journal,* July 1967, *55,* 27-29.

Peterson, L., Rossmiller, R., and Volz, M. Public School Law.
New York: Harper & Row, 1969.

Punke, H. Immorality as Ground for Teacher Dismissal. *NASSP
Bulletin,* 1965, *49,* 53-69.

_____. Cause and Grounds in Teacher Dismissal. *The Teacher
and the Courts.* Danville, Illinois: Interstate Publishers, 1971.

Shannon, T. The New Tactics Used by Plaintiffs in Imposing
Their Views on, or Enforcing Their Rights Against, Public
School Boards—A Commentary. *Journal of Law and Educa-
tion, 2,* 1, 77-87.

TABLE OF CASES

Ahern v. Board of Education, 325 F. Supp. 1391, 1971.
Board of Trustees v. Stubblefield, 16 Cal. App. 3d 820, 1971.
City of McComb v. Gould, 244, N.E. 2d 361, 1969.
Comings v. State Board of Education, 23 Cal. App. 3d 94, 1972.
Doherty v. Wilson, 356 F. Supp. 35, 1973.
Erb v. Iowa State Board of Education, 217 N.W. 2d 339, 1974.
Lombardo v. Board of Education, 241 N.E. 2d 495, 1968.
MacKay v. Rafferty, 321 F. Supp. 1177, 1970.
McLaughlin v. Tilendis, 398 F. 2d 387, 1968.
Moser v. State Board of Education, 22 Cal. App. 3d 988, 1972.
Mullally v. Board of Education, 164 N.W. 2d 752, 1968.
Parducci v. Rutland, 316 F. Supp. 352, 1970.
Pettit v. State Board of Education, 513 P. 2d 889.
Pickering v. Board of Education, 391 U.S. 563, 1968.
Sarac v. State Board of Education, 249 Cal. App. 2d 58, 1967.
State v. Heath, 177 N.W. 2d. 751, 1970.
Watts v. Seward Board of Education, 454 P. 2d 732, 1965.

44

WOMEN IN HIGHER EDUCATION

by Ruth M. Oltman
Dean of the Graduate Program
Hood College
Frederick, Maryland

In the nineteenth century there was much controversy over the value of higher education of women and
the dangers of both coeducation and certain curricula.
Although President Finney of Oberlin, in 1837 the first
college to admit women to a degree program, acknowledged that "with us the results are quite satisfactory
and even, we think, admirable" (McGuigan, 1970, p. 21),
President Tappan expressed his grave concern over admitting women to the University of Michigan in 1870:
"Men will lose as women advance, we shall have a community of defeminated women and demasculated men.
When we attempt to disturb God's order, we produce
monstrosities (McGuigan, 1970, p. 18)."

Today, with over three million women enrolled in
institutions of higher education each year, the question
is no longer whether they should be educated. The concerns, instead, are about the nature of that education,
full access of women to educational programs at all levels,
special needs of women students, and equality of opportunity for professional women educators. Social factors
and educational structures which discourage women
from consideration of a broad range of educational and
vocational options are being examined critically. The
civil rights and new women's movements, demanding
full participation as citizens and equality of treatment in
all aspects of life, have contributed to this examination of
higher education and to methods for dealing with barriers which still exist.

"Denial of full development of individual potential
is, or should be, the concern of educators everywhere
(Cross, 1972, p. 5)." Yet the Newman Task Force (1971)
concluded: "Discrimination against women, in contrast
to that against minorities, is still overt and socially acceptable within the academic community (p. 80)." An
increasing accumulation of data developed on individual
campuses, in specific disciplines, and by educational research groups indicates that "at every level—student body,
administration, faculty, and trustees—women are underrepresented or placed in positions with little power in decision-making (Oltman, 1970, p. 24)." The organizational,
nonlegal, and legal forces to increase opportunities for
women in higher education are growing rapidly and
beginning to have a significant impact on change. The
"male university" is being challenged.

THE WOMAN STUDENT

Enrollments at all levels of education have risen greatly
since 1900, as secondary education has become available at all. At the same time, access to higher education
has been facilitated by possibilities of financial aid,
rising family incomes, and the growth of community
colleges. In 1971, 60 percent of both men and women
20 years of age or over were high school graduates (U.S.
Bureau of Census, 1971). Increasing numbers of students
are attending colleges—3,735 women were enrolled in
degree credit programs in 1973-1974. Forty-three percent of the total bachelor's degrees in June 1972 were
awarded to women (ACE, 1973, 1974).

As women constitute 51 percent of the population,
obviously many are lost in the educational process before entering college. Cross (1972) points out that this
is especially true of bright young women in the lowest
economic quarter, 40 percent of whom never go beyond
high school (only 25 percent of the men do not).

More women than ever before also are going on to
graduate school, as are more men, women earning 40
percent of the master's degrees in 1971—about the same
proportion as in 1930. However, in 1971 women received only 14 percent of all doctorates (proportionately
less than 1920) and only 6 percent of first professional
degrees (though this was 11 percent in 1960). However,
figures released by the National Research Council (1974)
indicate a surprising upturn to 18 percent in 1973.

Attrition of women between the undergraduate and
graduate levels is a matter of concern, particularly in
the professional fields. Why are women only 7 percent
of our doctors, 19 percent of our college faculty (but

PERCENTAGE OF DEGREES EARNED BY WOMEN

Year	All Degrees	Bachelor's	Master's	Doctor's	First Professional
1947-48	35	35	32	12	–
1959-60	34	35	32	10	11
1965-66	38	40	34	12	5
1971-72	42	43	42	16	6

ACE Fact Book–4th, 1973

only 8 percent of full professors), 9 percent of our scientists, 3 percent of our lawyers, and 1 percent of our engineers? The reasons are complex, and are embedded in attitudes of men toward women, of women toward themselves, in social stereotypes, in training for "role" which girls and boys experience from the cradle, in models which are provided, and in rigidity of the educational structure.

During the past five years there has been a sharp decrease in the number of women's colleges, as more and more single-sex colleges have become coeducational. Financial difficulties, geographical isolation, social factors, and need for diversity in curriculum have all contributed to the trend. Coeducation, it is argued, provides a natural association of men and women students which the single-sex college does not, and makes possible broader programs of curriculum and activities. When Hampshire College was organized, it was specifically designed to avoid the stereotypes so often prevalent in coeducational schools. Many women's colleges, however, have made extensive studies of what they have to offer women, and have decided not to change their structure (notably Chatham, Hood, Wellesley, Goucher, Smith, Bryn Mawr, Stephens, Mills, and Mt. Holyoke), but to commit themselves firmly to contemporary women's education. The day of the postsecondary "finishing school" for women (which perseverates stereotypes) is over, but the women's colleges which provide viable role models and relevant training for young women in today's world are flourishing.

Lack of equal opportunity for women in coeducational higher education has been evidenced by sex differentials in admission requirements, in quotas, and in financial aid. Traditional curriculum has been inflexible, and less has been invested in programs (such as physical education) for women than for men. Facilities, counseling and scheduling have been insufficient to meet the needs of the older woman student who wishes to resume her education. Women have learned little about their roles in history, literature, or art, and have been taught almost nothing about their own psychology or the social factors in their development as individuals. They see few "models" among professional women educators. Health and counseling services for women have been inadequate, social regulations have been restrictive, placement offices have permitted differential treatment of women by recruiters on campus. The Women's Education Equity Act was introduced by Representative Patsy Mink (D-Hawaii) in the 92nd Congress, in fact, for the purpose of remedying some of these inequities and of making education for women more relevant to their needs.

Recent trends, however, point to developments which may make basic changes in higher education of women. During recent years women have been applying and admitted in greater numbers than ever before to professional schools such as law and pharmacy. Even medical schools have opened some of their doors, with women students comprising 18 percent of those enrolled in 1972-1973, almost three times the percentage in 1962-1963 (J. Med. Ed. 1975). All evidence shows that they do as well as men during medical training and that dropout rates are low. Astin's study (1969), and a survey made for the American Medical Women's Association (Renshaw and Pennell, 1969), indicate that most women who achieve the Ph.D. or M.D. do use that training professionally. "Once a women decides to invest herself, her time and her energy in pursuit of specialized training, the likelihood of her maintaining a strong career interest and commitment is very high (Astin, 1969, p. 149)."

Women's Studies courses are growing rapidly and several institutions now offer master's degree programs (Robinson, 1973; Howe, 1973). Many of these developed out of continuing education programs for women, which first sensitized higher education to the educational needs of mature women ten years ago (Women's Bureau, 1971). Women's resource centers are being formed on campus. Nontraditional approaches are making higher education more accessible to women through easier transfer of credits, credit by examination and experience, convenient class hours, and individualized counseling (Campbell, 1972). There is every indication that these trends will continue in the future, as broader opportunities open to women and as attitudes change concerning previously accepted stereotypes about the "female mind."

THE PROFESSIONAL WOMAN IN EDUCATION

The issue of equal rights is now of vital concern in the employment of women at all levels of higher education. Statistics tell a consistent story of underemployment, lack of promotion and tenure, and differentials in salaries and fringe benefits.

Nationally, women comprise 19 percent of all faculty, although the figure was 25 percent in 1950 and 28 percent in 1940. The proportion of faculty women is particularly low at prestige institutions, and women are consistently lacking in responsible administrative positions or on Boards of Trustees, particularly in the large public institutions.

Mean salaries of women faculty, no matter what rank, level, or type of institution, are uniformly lower than those of men. While differences in experience and degrees account for some of the differentials, there are

PERCENT OF WOMEN ON FULL-TIME FACULTY IN DEGREE-GRANTING INSTITUTIONS

Faculty rank	1959-60	1965-66	1971-72
All ranks	19.1	18.4	19.0
Professor	9.9	8.7	8.6
Associate professor	17.5	15.1	14.6
Assistant professor	29.3	32.5	39.4

NEA, 1973, p. 2

clear salary dislocations along sex lines, and men receive more pay regardless of their work experience or status. Few women have been appointed department chairmanships or hired for jobs which are stepping-stones to more important academic responsibilities. Many women are not familiar with the processes of academic recruitment and advancement, and generally have been considered outside the "prestige system" of the academic marketplace (Caplow and McGee, 1958). Nepotism rules, originally devised to protect the man who was the main wage earner in a family in the past, in practice discriminate against women. The position of women professionals in academia has been further depressed by the current economy. As colleges and universities cut back budgets and reduce staff, often among the first to go are women who have never been given tenure (*Chronicle of Higher Education*, 1975), who have little status as part-time instructors, or who have expressed complaints over unequal treatment.

SALARIES AND PERCENTAGES OF FACULTY, BY SEX

	Median Salary		Percent of
Group of institutions	Men faculty	Women faculty	faculty who are women
All 4-year institutions	$13,359	$11,026	19.0
Public universities			
Enroll 10,000 or more	14,342	11,519	15.6
Enroll 5,000-9,900	13,112	11,140	19.7
Enroll less than 5,000	12,887	10,960	23.5
Nonpublic universities			
Enroll 5,000 or more	14,944	11,367	13.6
Enroll less than 5,000	13,127	10,787	15.6
Public colleges	12,648	11,421	22.5
Nonpublic colleges			
Enroll 1,000 or more	11,841	10,283	21.6
Enroll 500-999	10,773	9,580	29.1
Enroll less than 500	10,388	8,925	29.6

NEA, 1973, p. 1)

While academic women may now seek equity through a number of legal and nonlegal avenues which did not exist a few years ago (discussed below), improvements have been slow, as academic structures and attitudes take time to change. Roby (1972) pessimistically predicts that "neither educational equality for women nor the hybrid model of social relations is likely to be realized within the present economic structure (p. 138-139)." In any case, "the transition to a fully nondiscriminatory policy will be painful (Pifer, 1972, p. 12)."

WHAT THE LAW REQUIRES

Sex discrimination in higher education was first challenged on January 31, 1970, when the Women's Equity Action League (WEAL) filed a class action complaint directed against all universities and colleges receiving Federal contracts, under Executive Order 11246, charging sex discrimination in employment. Since then WEAL, NOW, and individual women have filed similar complaints against many institutions for failure to comply with the nondiscrimination requirements of their contracts. The Higher Education Division, Office of Civil Rights of HEW, is charged with the responsibility of securing compliance and of delaying issuance of contracts until compliance is assured. Contracts totaling $750,000 have been withheld from six universities alone. Others have experienced a "freeze" on new contracts. This economic tool was intended to develop affirmative action policies and programs on the campus in the same manner that it has been useful in business and industry, but it has not been effectively enforced. In October of 1972 HEW issued official guidelines to assist institutions in developing affirmative action programs. These guidelines clarified Revised Order No. 4, issued by the U.S. Department of Labor in December 1971, which covered the application of Executive Order 11246 (as amended) to institutions of higher education holding contracts, as well as to other types of contractors.

Other laws for which women have effectively lobbied have since been passed which further support action against discrimination. The Comprehensive Health Manpower and Nurse Training Amendments of 1971 both include clauses prohibiting sex discrimination in admission to all types of health training programs, with power to withhold funding if such discrimination occurs. The Equal Employment Opportunity Act of 1972 amended Title VII of the Civil Rights Act of 1964 so that professional employees in education are no longer excluded from coverage. The Women's Education Equity Act (PL 93-380), passed in the summer of 1974, has not at this writing been funded but should be sometime soon. It will provide means for resolving problems of educational inequity through training and counseling programs, research, development of model programs and resource centers, and evaluation of curricula and textbooks. The Equal Pay Act of 1963 was amended by Title IX of the Education Amendments Act of 1972 to include professional, executive, and managerial personnel. The Amendments also broadly prohibit discrimination on the basis of sex in any educational program or activity receiving Federal aid. Regulations for Title IX of the 1972 Amendments were not issued by HEW until June 1975, after lengthy debate and controversy. The ECS (1975) has published two comprehensive compendiums of state and Federal laws affecting women in higher education.

Depending on the nature of the complaint, therefore, the academic woman has several sources through which to seek redress. Problems in processing complaints have arisen related to release of information considered confidential by the institution, harassment or even discharge of a complainant, lack of communication and follow-through on adjustments required, and slowness of processing cases (Abrahamson, 1975). The compliance process unfortunately has created an adversary relationship. Demands for equal pay have come at a time when institutions already are hard pressed to meet financial obligations. Monitoring of hiring policy challenges institutional methods of governance and departmental authority. The enforcement of other laws has been less than effective because of insufficient government funding and personnel, over-reliance on general assurances of compliance, institutional evasion, and jurisdictional limitations. Fields (1975) has described the courts' handling of affirmative action cases, and Goodwin (1975) has shown the devious ways some institutions have found to avoid real compliance.

NONLEGAL APPROACHES

Whatever the law requires, each institution must develop an affirmative action plan to meet its own needs and unique organization. In most cases this has meant the appointment of an affirmative action commission or advisory council to make an analysis of the existing inequities, to recommend nondiscriminating methods of recruitment and hiring of all personnel, to develop means of facilitating upward mobility, to examine benefits and policies and recommend corrections of any which are discriminatory, and to provide an avenue for the hearing and processing of grievances. Usually this commission reports to the chief administrative officer. Such a commission should be given authority to effect and coordinate affirmative action programs, so that it does not become merely a review and recommending body. The first committee in a university system was appointed at the City University of New York (CUNY, 1972), which includes 20 institutions. Many schools have examined their salary distributions and voluntarily have made substantial adjustments.

Women on many campuses have organized themselves as action committees and caucuses to develop data and to press for affirmative action. The first report on a campus study was done at SUNY Buffalo in 1970, and its recommendations laid the groundwork for most of the current issues under consideration (Scott, 1970). Women also have organized committees or caucuses within their professional associations to lobby for more voice in policy, to study the status of women in their professions, to create awareness of problems, to recommend improvements in recruitment, and to solicit support for policies which contribute to the advancement of women (Oltman, 1971). More than 65 such groups have been organized within the past five years (AAUW, 1975). The Report of the Task Force on the Status of Women in Psychology (APA, 1973) describes the considerable accomplishments of one such group over its first two years and the still unresolved problems. A permanent committee has now been appointed by the APA Council.

As awareness has grown, and the need to recruit professional women becomes more urgent, many aids have been developed to assist both women and the universities. AAUW (1973) coordinated the preparation of a position paper on women in higher education, endorsed by 13 national groups and covering education, employment, and participation in decision-making institutional services and practices. It has already been endorsed by nine national groups. The Office of Civil Rights, HEW, published a source book of availability data on minorities and women (OCR, 1973), and the U.S. Office of Education a review of the law (USOE, 1973). Tinsley et al. (1975) has prepared an action handbook to assist professional women. The Association of American College's Project on the Status and Employment of Women has been effective in disseminating needed information. The Intercollegiate Association of Women Students has taken positions on student issues and has cooperated on campuses with women's committees.

"Institutions have the opportunity to make constructive changes without the trauma of legal action," says Sylvia Roberts (1973), President of NOW Legal Defense and Education Fund. "It is my hope that the far-reaching issues raised by women and minorities will be resolved in the most positive fashion at the conference table; if not, they will surely have to be resolved in the courts (p. 213)."

CURRENT ISSUES

In attempting to solve the many problems of equity, related issues arise which must be addressed or defined. It should be recognized that "equity of opportunity" does not mean that higher education should be the same for men and women. Rather, it may necessitate programs to meet the special needs of women, counseling to fit their differing life patterns, curricula designed to fill the gaps in knowledge, recruiting through resources not previously used, and adapting teaching or class schedules.

Affirmative action requires the development of data which have not heretofore been collected in an organized way. This has created additional work for institutional research and personnel staffs at a time of financial cutbacks. Without adequate statistics, however, discrimination cannot be proved and affirmative action goals cannot be developed. Yet statistics may not tell the full story, because of peripheral factors which need to be considered. For example, Astin and Bayer's study (1972) of college faculty examined some of these factors, but found that even "when women are statistically matched with men on the variables that determine rewards they still fall below men in rank and salary (p. 117)."

The provision of opportunities to study or teach on a part-time basis will require adjustments in traditional higher education. While nontraditional and continuing education programs are meeting some of the needs of undergraduate women students, many graduate schools still have strict rules on residence and full-time enrollment which discourage women. "And is there any reason," Sandler (1972) asks, "other than academic tradition, that prevents schools from giving scholarships on a part-time basis? (p. 87)" The status of part-time teachers is under much fire. Many women instructors are in this category, never having faculty status, fringe benefits, opportunity for promotion or tenure, or vote in the faculty council. Women in almost all professional caucuses and committees are pushing for academic recognition of the regular part-time teacher.

"Goals" vs. "quotas" in hiring new faculty have not been well understood in affirmative action planning. "Quotas" imply a percentage which must be hired, without regard for qualifications. This is not the intent of the law. "Goals", however, are flexible, and are targets which should be sought in good faith, in view of the availability of eligible women in the employment pool. This process involves careful study of the resources which at this point are scattered, often confusing, and difficult to interpret in terms of institutional requirements. To date, no funding has been provided by either the government or educational foundations to create a national roster or data bank on women to alleviate this problem, though many academic associations have rosters within their own disciplines. These are being tapped, and national statistics on the numbers of women earning degrees in various fields are being used to establish "goals."

Child care also is needed for both the woman student or faculty woman if she is to participate fully. Should the institution provide this? Who should pay for it? The Carnegie Commission report (1973) suggests: "We believe that colleges and universities should be responsive and cooperative in relation to requests . . . for child care service, and that they have a responsibility to ensure that child care arrangements associated with the campus are of high quality." Many institutions already have developed such programs.

Admissions of women at all levels of education, particularly at the graduate and professional levels, must be examined critically for discrimination on the basis of sex. Quotas and percentages will no longer be acceptable. The professional school which accepts ten percent of all applicants may be discriminating against women if the pool of women applicants is already highly selective, as is too often the case. Acceptance must be solely on the basis of merit; subjective judgments must be eliminated. In particular, the older women students desiring to return for study should be provided opportunities, through flexible arrangements and counseling, to do so without penalty.

"Positive attitudes on the part of faculty members toward the serious pursuit of graduate study and research by women are greatly needed (Carnegie, 1973)." Women must not only see "models" of women who have achieved as faculty or administrators, but also be encouraged to consider a broad range of educational and vocational objective. Such attitudinal changes will take time, but can be hastened by the adoption of positive policies by the institution and by enlightened counseling from educational advisors.

Our institutions of higher education will never be the same after the Executive Orders, even though not fully enforced, and the legislation which has been passed since 1970. As Newman (1971) has said, "colleges and universities have an unparalleled opportunity to affect the status of women. . . . Their role in the transmission of values and the preparation of men and women for careers makes this opportunity a responsibility that these educational institutions must not ignore if they are to be responsive to the needs of society (p. 56)."

REFERENCES

AAUW. *Joint Statement on Women in Higher Education.* Washington: American Association of University Women, 1973.
_____. *Graduate and Professional Education of Women,* 1974.
_____. *List of Professional Women's Caucuses and Organizations,* 1975.

Abrahamson, J. *The Invisible Woman.* San Francisco: Jossey-Bass, Inc., 1975.

ACE. *A Fact Book on Higher Education,* First Issue 1974, Enrollment Data. Fourth Issue, 1973, Earned Degrees. Washington: American Council on Education.

APA. Report of the Task Force on the Status of Women in Psychology. *American Psychologist,* 1973, *28,* 611-616.

Astin, H. S. *The Woman Doctorate in America.* New York: Russell Sage Foundation, 1969.
_____, and Bayer, A. E. Sex Discrimination in Academe. *Educational Record,* 1972, *53,* 101-118.

Bird, C. Women's Colleges and Women's Lib. *Change,* 1972, *5,* 60-65.

Campbell, J. W. Utilizing the Resources of Traditional Institutional Structures, or the Non-Traditional Student in Academe. In Furniss, W. T., and Graham, P., *Women in Higher Education.* Washington: American Council on Education, 1973.

Caplow, T., and McGee, R. J. *The Academic Marketplace.* New York: Basic Books, 1958.

Carnegie Commission on Higher Education. *Women in Higher Education: Their Current Participation, Prospects for the Future and Recommendations for Action,* by M. S. Gordon. Berkeley: Carnegie Commission on Higher Education, 1973.

Cross, K. P. Women Want Equality in Higher Education. *The Research Reporter,* 1972, Vol. 7, No. 4, 5-8 (Center for Research and Development in Higher Education, University of California, Berkeley).

CUNY, *Public Hearings and Testimony, An Edited Summary and Evaluation.* Chancellor's Advisory Committee on the Status of Women at CUNY, September 1972.

DATAGRAM: U.S. Medical Student Enrollment, 1970-71 through 1974-75. *Journal of Medical Education, 50,* March 1975, 303-306.

ECS. *A Handbook of State Laws and Policies Affecting Equal Rights for Women in Education.*
_____. *A Digest of Federal Laws for Women in Education.* Denver, Colorado: Education Commission of the States, 1975.

Faculty Members with Tenure, 1974-75. *Chronicle of Higher Education,* April 21, 1975, p. 8.

Fields, C. How Courts Will Enforce Laws on Sex Bias. *Chronicle of Higher Education,* Feb. 24, 1975, p. 6.

Goodwin, C. Playing Games with Affirmative Action. *Chronicle of Higher Education,* April 28, 1975, p. 24.

Howe, F. Women's Studies and Social Change. In Rossi, A., and Calderwood, A., eds., *Academic Women on the Move.* New York: Russell Sage Foundation, 1973, 393-423.

McGuigan, D. G. *A Dangerous Experiment.* Ann Arbor: University of Michigan, 1970.

NEA. *The Status of Women Faculty and Administrators in Higher Education Institutions,* 1971-72. Research Memo 1973-7. Washington: NEA, April, 1973.

Newman, F. (Chairman). *Report on Higher Education,* Task Force on Higher Education, USOE. Washington: Government Printing Office, 1971.

NRC. *Summary Report 1973, Doctorate Recipients from United States Universities.* Washington: National Academy of Sciences, May 1974.

OCR, HEW. *Availability Data: Minorities and Women.* Washington: Higher Education Division, Office of Civil Rights, HEW, 1973.

_____. *Higher Education Guidelines,* Executive Order 11246. June 1973.

Oltman, R. M. Women in the Professional Caucuses. *American Behavioral Scientist,* 1971, *15,* 281-302.

_____. *Campus 1970: Where Do Women Stand?* Washington: American Association of University Women, 1970.

Pifer, A. A Fuller Role for Women. *The Chronicle of Higher Education,* Vol. 6, No. 13, 1972.

Renshaw, J. E., and Pennell, M. Y. Distribution of Women Physicians, 1969. *The Woman Physician,* 1971, *26,* 187-195.

Roberts, S. Equality of Opportunity in Higher Education: Impact of Contract Compliance and the Equal Rights Amendment. *Liberal Education, 59,* 1973, 202-216.

Robinson, L. H. *Women's Studies: Courses and Programs in Higher Education.* ERIC Higher Education Research Report No. 1. Washington: AAHE, 1973.

Roby, P. Women and American Higher Education. *Annals of the American Academy,* 1972, *404,* 118-139.

Sandler, B. Equity for Women in Higher Education. In Vermilye, D., ed., *The Expanded Campus.* San Francisco: Jossey-Bass, 1972.

Scott, A. The Half-Eaten Apple. *Reporter,* May 14, 1970. Available from NOW Task Force on Higher Education.

Tidball, M. E. Perspective on Academic Women and Affirmative Action. *Educational Record,* 1973, *54,* No. 2, 130-135.

Tinsley, A., Reuben, E., and Crothers, D. *Academic Women; Sex Discrimination and the Law: An Action Handbook.* MLS Publications Center, New York, 1975.

U.S. Bureau of Census. Educational Attainment: March 1971. *Current Population Reports,* Series P-20, No. 229. Washington: U.S. Government Printing Office, December, 1971.

U.S. Office of Education. *Education and Women's Rights: What the Law Now Says,* DHEW Publication No. (OE) 73-01003. Washington: U.S. Government Printing Office, 1973.

Women's Bureau, USDL. *Continuing Education for Women: Current Developments.* Washington: U.S. Government Printing Office, 1974.

ADDITIONAL RESOURCES

ACE. Sex Discrimination and Contract Compliance: Beyond the Legal Requirements. *ACE Special Report.* Washington: American Council on Education, 1972.

Atwood, C. L. *Women in Fellowship Training Programs.* Washington: Association of American Colleges, 1973.

Carroll, M. A. Women in Administration in Higher Education. *Contemporary Education,* 1972, *43,* 214-218.

Furniss, W. T., and Graham, P. A., eds. *Women in Higher Education.* Washington: American Council on Education, 1973.

LaNoue, G. R. The Future Antidiscrimination Enforcement. *Change,* June 1974, *63,* 44-45.

Robinson, L. H. *The Status of Academic Women.* Review 5, ERIC Clearinghouse on Higher Education. Washington: George Washington University, April 1971.

Rossi, A., and Calderwood, A., eds. *Academic Women on the Move.* New York: Russell Sage Foundation, 1973.

Shulman, C. H. *Affirmative Action: Women's Rights on Campus.* Report No. 6, ERIC Clearinghouse on Higher Education. Washington: AAHE, 1972.

Temko, J. Women in Post-Graduate Education. *Women's Rights Law Reporter,* 1973, *1,* No. 4, 10-20.

USCCR. *Statement on Affirmative Action for Equal Employment Opportunities.* Clearinghouse Publication No. 41, Feb. 1973, U.S. Commission on Civil Rights

Women's Bureau. *Trends in Educational Attainment of Women.* Washington: U.S. Dept. of Labor, 1969. *Careers for Women in the '70's.* 1973.

MAJOR PUBLIC DOCUMENTS AFFECTING WOMEN IN HIGHER EDUCATION

Executive Order 11246 as amended by 11375
  Sex Discrimination Guidelines (June 1970)
  Revised Order No. 4 (December 1971)
  Obligations of Contractors and Subcontractors (May 1968)
  HEW Higher Education Guidelines, Executive Order 11246 (October 1972)

Title VII of the Civil Rights Act of 1964 as amended by the Equal Employment Opportunity Act of 1972
  Guidelines on Discrimination Because of Sex (April 1972)
  Guidelines on Employer Selection Procedure (August 1970)

Equal Pay Act of 1963 as amended by the Education Amendments Act of 1972
  (The Equal Pay Act is an amendment to the Fair Labor Standards Act of 1938)
    Equal Pay for Equal Work—Interpretative Bulletin 800 (August 1971)
    Extension of the Equal Pay Act of 1963—Fact Sheet (September 1972)

Title IX of the Education Amendments Act of 1972
  (Higher Education Act)
    Memorandum to Presidents of Institutions of Higher Education Participating in Federal Assistance Programs (August 1972 and December 1974). Guidelines for Administration, 1975.

Title VII (Section 799A) and Title VIII (Section 845) of the Public Health Service Act as amended by the Comprehensive Health Manpower Act and the Nurse Training Amendments Act of 1971.
  HEW form No. 590—Assurance of Compliance (March 1972)

Public Law 93-380, Women's Education Equity Act

See also ECS reference to two compendiums on state and Federal laws.

MAJOR INTEREST GROUPS AND ASSOCIATIONS

American Council on Education, Office of Women in Higher Education, 1 Dupont Circle, Washington, D.C. 20036

American Association of University Professors, Committee W, 1 Dupont Circle, Washington, D.C. 20036

American Association of University Women, Higher Education Office, 2401 Virginia Ave., N.W., Washington, D.C. 20037

Association of American Colleges, Project on the Status and Education of Women, 1818 R Street, N.W., Washington, D.C. 20009

Citizens Advisory Council on the Status of Women, Washington, D.C. 20210

Federation of Organization for Professional Women, 1346 Connecticut Ave., N.W., Washington, D.C. 20036

Intercollegiate Association of Women Students, 2401 Virginia Ave., N.W., Washington, D.C. 20037

Interstate Association of Commissions on the Status of Women, 1249 National Press Building, Washington, D.C. 20004

National Association of Affirmative Action Officers

National Foundation for the Improvement of Education, Resource Center on Sex Roles in Education, Suite 918, 1156 – 15th Street, N.W., Washington, D.C. 20005

National Institute of Education, 1200 – 19th Street, N.W., Washington, D.C. 20036

National Organization for Women, Task Force on Higher Education, 37A Davis Square, Somerville, MA 02144 (c/o M. J. Pollock)

Office of Civil Rights, Higher Education Division, HEW, 330
Independence Avenue, S.W., Washington, D.C. 20201
Project on Equal Education Rights (PEER), 1522 Connecticut
Avenue, N.W., Washington, D.C. 20036
U.S. Equal Employment Opportunity Commission, 1800 G
Street, N.W., Washington, D.C. 20506
Wage and Hour Division, Employment Standards Administra-
tion, U.S. Department of Labor, Washington, D.C. 20210
Women's Bureau, U.S. Department of Labor, Washington,
D.C. 20210
Women's Equity Action League, 538 National Press Building,
Washington, D.C. 20004

45

FACULTY EVALUATION

by Emmett T. Kohler
Director of Institutional Research
Mississippi State University
Mississippi State, Mississippi

Student evaluations have been by far the most prevalent of the feasible procedures available for gathering
systematic evidence about teaching. There have been a
surprisingly great number of scholarly publications related to the dimensions of good teaching and the adequate measurement of these dimensions. Although student evaluation is an admittedly narrow conceptualization of faculty evaluation, it has been required by space
constraints and, more importantly, because of the great
interest in this activity on the part of students, administrators, and certainly teachers. An extensive historical
review is not intended, but one can easily support the
contention that interest existed in teacher evaluation in
the early 1900s. Beginning in the 1960s there was a considerable increase in the desire to evaluate college teaching, although one investigator (Gustad, 1961, 1967)
reported a decline in the systematic use of ratings from
1961 to 1966. However, from 1966 or 1967 to the
present there has been an apparent renewed interest in
the evaluation of college teachers. One of the major activities this increased interest has promulgated has been
the development and use of formal rating scales completed by students about faculty.

It is recognized that course and teacher evaluations
are probably inseparable, and that any evaluation of
teachers that doesn't encompass the traditional activities
of teaching, research, and service will be incomplete. However, the individual teacher functioning in the instructional mode is the focus here.

Reports reflecting an interest in faculty evaluation as
conceived in this paper appear early in the American educational literature. As early as 1922, the School of Education of Oklahoma A&M distributed questionnaires
among the student body for the purpose of gathering
information about the faculty. A guarantee was offered
assuring the confidential use of the information obtained.

About 1925 the University of Washington and the University of Texas began faculty evaluation programs.
Probably the best known series of experiments on student evaluations of faculty were conducted at Purdue
University (Remmer, 1928, 1930; Remmers and Stalnaker, 1928). These studies focused on the improvement
of teaching through the teacher's knowledge of his effect
upon his students.

When contemplating the use of student ratings of
teachers, one must concern himself with the questions
of the validity and reliability of the rating scales used.
An excellent review of student ratings of college teaching can be found in the *Review of Educational Research,*
Volume 61 (Costin, Greenough, and Menges, 1971). This
review can give the interested reader at least partial answers to these questions. In regard to reliability, they
reported that test-retest correlations ranged from .48
to .89, and internal consistency reliabilities were reported to range from .77 to .94. Coefficients of this
magnitude indicate that rating scales tend to possess
sufficient reliability for evaluation of faculty.

The question of validity was not so easily answered.
In order to meaningfully answer the question of validity,
one must know the purpose for which the ratings are
to be used. This is an important question, and one that
has had no firmly agreed-upon answer, for to answer
this question one must define an effective teacher, and
at this point this has meant different things to different
investigators. Nevertheless, Costin et al. (1971) said students were reported to be at least partially capable of
identifying certain aspects of teaching which increased
their knowledge or motivation.

When student ratings were compared to other criteria the results were mixed. Correlations between supervisor or colleague ratings and student ratings of the
same teacher generally have been low but positive. This
has been interpreted as indicating the student's contribution of an independent dimension to the evaluation
process. One might argue that student achievement or
gains in knowledge would provide a more acceptable criterion, but when ratings were correlated with grades the
correlations tended to be low but positive. Interpretation was difficult; however, since the correlations were
low, this negated arguments in support of contamination
of the ratings by implied awarding of good marks. Additionally, it did not seem unreasonable to argue that effective teaching should produce good marks; therefore, the
relationship between ratings and marks should be positive. For a discussion of the use of a gain criterion as
an ultimate criterion measure see Cohen and Brawer
(1969).

What is the relationship between student evaluations
and research and service productivity? There have been
several studies on the relationship between research productivity and student ratings, but virtually none on the
relationship between service activities and student ratings.
The findings related to research productivity and student
ratings have been mixed, and no definite conclusions can
be drawn. Part of the problem here lies in the inability
to provide an adequate definition of either research or
effective teaching.

Most questionnaires have what was formerly called

"face validity." From examination of the content of many evaluation items it would be difficult to support any argument that the positive possession of these traits would be harmful, even though there is slim evidence they would enhance instruction. See Simpson and Seidman (1962) for example items. Also, the questionnaires are valid on their face if the objective is to gather opinions about a teacher at a given point in time. Of course, the usefulness of such opinions will need verification.

Although the literature disclosed a somewhat cloudy picture, it appeared that sufficient justification exists for the use of student ratings as one dimension in the evaluation of teachers. It can by no means be argued that they are the sole dimension or the most important one.

Much instruction occurs in modes other than what is typically thought of as the teacher lecturing to the class. Thesis and dissertation advising, laboratory instruction, development of materials, and many other activities are all part of the teaching/instructional process, and all should be evaluated in the interest of fairness; but even an evaluation of limited scope requires the completion of several activities.

In order to implement any faculty evaluation procedures, administrative support, candidness, and adequate time for planning are required. Several distinct steps come to mind. Eble (1970) has enumerated a list that appears to be complete and adaptable to most institutions. Below are the steps, and each is illustrated with an example from experience.

Eble (1970) offers the following, which are necessary for successful student evaluation:

Gaining the cooperation of the faculty

Defining purposes, objectives, and uses

Arriving at means and procedures

Making crucial policy decisions

Establishing an office for administering the program

Keeping the campus community informed

Financing a continuing program

Maintaining student and faculty interest and involvement

Conducting follow-up activities and studies

Relating evaluation to other efforts to recognize, reward, and improve teaching (p. 29)

GAINING THE COOPERATION OF THE FACULTY

Our experience in faculty evaluation has supported the contention of Eble (1970) that the faculty desires "(1) a reasonable basis for making judgments; (2) fair and responsible assessments; (3) a clear idea of the purposes, objectives, and uses to be made of the instruments and data [p. 29]." There is no doubt the initial effort for faculty evaluation came from the students. In fact, an evaluation was conducted manned entirely by students on our campus in the early 1960s. In this state many problems were caused by uncertainty and poor communi-

cation among the persons involved. As a result, a student/ faculty committee was established by the administration for the purpose of conducting faculty evaluation. The committee has grown to eight or more members, approximately half of whom are students. The Director of Institutional Research is an ex officio member for the purpose of representing the office in charge of administering faculty evaluation. The Faculty Council has one of its members as a voting member of this evaluation committee, and of course the students are full members. In short, all interested groups, with the notable exception of the administration, have representation on the committee. This approach has been beneficial in keeping the lines of communication open and permitting the entire process to be actively and knowledgeably participated in by all concerned.

The Director of Institutional Research and other members of the committee have participated and continue to participate in open forums sponsored by the AAUP and other similar campus groups, for the purpose of informing the campus community of the progress being made toward the development of an equitable faculty evaluation system.

DEFINING PURPOSES, OBJECTIVES, AND USES

This step is undoubtedly of primary importance, and it must begin early. However, in our experience it also has been a continuing process and, unfortunately, one that we have not mastered fully. We have not yet decided in explicit terms what the purposes, objectives, and uses of faculty evaluation are to be One of the early reasons cited by students in support of faculty evaluation was the information collected would improve instruction. It was implied that instruction was less than outstanding. It is interesting to note, however, that surprisingly high averages were obtained on each item presented in the questionnaire.

Full disclosure of the results was not accomplished immediately. In the early stages the results were for the instructor's eyes only. Next, the averages were also made known to the teacher's department head and dean. Then, we moved to publication of results in addition to the above. These have been illustrated only to point out what appear to be changing uses reflecting changing opinions about the purpose of faculty evaluation. Also, we are changing forms for the third time. This is also offered as evidence that consensus was not maintained, if it ever was attained, as to the purpose of faculty evaluation.

ARRIVING AT MEANS AND PROCEDURES

The provedure we followed parallels the thoughts of Eble closely. At first the students surveyed institutions then conducting faculty evaluation. From this survey the first questionnaire was developed. Later, a new survey was conducted because of expressed dissatisfaction on the part of faculty with the earlier form. A new form was developed by a coalition of faculty and students. The tryout of this new proposed form was done on an informal basis, utilizing only faculty who supported the concept of student evaluation of faculty members. A more encompassing tryout is recommended.

To fully utilize the information contained in the extensive literature is recommended; however, those assigned the responsibility for faculty evaluation should do a careful and thorough job of mapping the proposed questionnaire onto the explicitly stated goals of faculty evaluation at their institution. Any form developed through a committee should receive extensive trials, and any feedback should be incorporated into the final form to be used.

MAKING CRUCIAL POLICY DECISIONS

Among the questions that need to be answered are: Who will be evaluated? How often will they be evaluated? Will the results of the evaluation be published? What will the official use be?

There are many, many questions that need to be answered early in the development of a faculty evaluation system. All the answers may not be known at the beginning. For example, our faculty evaluation began as a voluntary activity with the results for the teacher's eyes only. To accomplish this, an elaborate scheme was devised to assure complete privacy of the ratings. Now, however, we publish the results, which can be purchased at the campus store.

Each institution is more or less unique, with its own peculiar problems and their associated solutions. The institution is certainly not a monolithic entity since each division, each school, and, more likely than not, each department has its own set of objectives and procedures. Nevertheless, many of the decisions that must be made related to a faculty evaluation system will be institution-wide. While here is not the place to debate this state of affairs, the lack of congruence between the operating unit's goals, etc., in an institution-wide policy can be troublesome. An example illustrates this point. Early in the faculty evaluation program there was some clamoring to publish openly the results. This proposal was presented to the president. Several months passed before his decision was handed down. During this intervening period a vocal group of students and faculty pushed hard for publication, and eventually the Faculty Council endorsed the idea. Following the Faculty Council's decision, the president agreed to the publication of the faculty evaluation results. At this point one might naively have assumed the matter was settled; not so. The faculty, as it turns out, was not totally happy with the concept of publication, and as a result of this unhappiness the Faculty Council decided to reconsider its position. At the writing of this article the faculty now has scheduled a survey of the faculty to determine their opinion about publication.

On our campus, publication has probably had a mixed effect. It seems that publication can be useful to the student whose program allows selection from among several instructors or electives. However, when the student has no choice the utility of publication is doubtful, since many of the professed goals of faculty evaluation, such as improving instruction, could be achieved under the system whereby only the teacher or the teacher's im-

mediate superior sees the results.

ESTABLISHING AN OFFICE FOR ADMINISTERING THE PROGRAM

Someone must handle the "nuts and bolts" of the evaluation process. Students could do it or a committee could do it, but neither of these groups really has the time or the needed resources, such as secretarial services, space, etc., nor do they have continuity from one year to the next. On our campus the Office of Institutional Research was assigned this task. Within the Office of Institutional Research a half-time graduate assistant has the responsibility for the program. This student is employed for 12 months. The half-time position is augmented at peak times by other office employees. Particularly this is true during the dispersion and collection stages of the evaluation. This approach seems to be adequate for our program.

KEEPING THE CAMPUS COMMUNITY INFORMED

This is certainly an important function. Several avenues for information exchange are open on our campus. The Faculty Evaluation Committee is active and accessible, and they frequently interact with the campus community on the topic of faculty evaluation through open forums conducted by several campus organizations.

FINANCING A CONTINUING PROGRAM

There are certainly costs associated with any faculty evaluation. True cost estimates have been difficult to obtain because much of the work is "donated" by students and faculty alike. Eble (1970) cited the figure of $1.00 per student at Princeton, and in 1967-1968, $2,500 for surveying 180 classes at Michigan State University. No information was given as to the approximate number of evaluation forms processed by this latter endeavor. Jenkins (Miller, 1972) reported computer cost figures for North Carolina State University were $3,585 to $7,315 for the period 1967-1968 to 1970-1971. The announcement introducing *The Student Instructional Report,* a faculty evaluation system published by Educational Testing Service (1972), stated the costs to be "Materials: 10 cents per answer sheet. . . . Scoring: 25 cents per answer sheet for the first 5,000 scored and 20 cents per answer sheet thereafter." This latter document also indicated special rates could be obtained for large volume scoring.

Computerization is required for most large-scale evaluation projects. "Optical scanning" of the form seems to be the most feasible method of preparing the information obtained from the evaluation document for data reduction and analysis by computers. Optical scanning equipment can be expensive, but part of this cost can be defrayed by using the equipment for test scoring, the processing of research questionnaires, and for other programs on campus. Computer processing procedures can be expensive regardless of method of preparation of input, and these dollar costs may vary greatly because of equipment differences and charge policies in effect at the various institutions.

A cost figure of $10,000 has been used on our campus. This is a conservative estimate for our surveying of approximately 1,800 sections, producing 45,000 evaluations. This cost is certainly too much to ask of students, but even if it were not, faculty evaluation is an instructional activity and should be financed by the institution (Kerlinger, 1971). Our present arrangement—and it seems to be workable—is that a special fund for faculty evaluation has been established by the Vice President for Academic Affairs, with the Office of Institutional Research initiating the requests for expenditures.

MAINTAINING STUDENT AND FACULTY INTEREST AND INVOLVEMENT

Publication, at least to this date, has been the primary device for maintaining interest on the part of faculty and students. Several publications are compiled annually. The first is the Instructor's Report. It is a description of the average rating the instructor receives on each item. These averages are aggregated in several ways. In addition, the several averages associated with the instructor's department, school, and university are provided on the Instructor's Report. See Figure 1 for a sample page of this publication.

An Interpretive Guide is also distributed to the campus community. This publication briefly discusses the local research findings related to our questionnaire, and gives the percentile ranking of each average attained. In the past the entire university distribution was taken as the reference group for ranking purposes.

The remaining publication is produced by the Student Association. All the analyses for this document are computed and properly formated by the Office of Institutional Research. This publication lists each course and its teachers. The average rating by teacher within the course and by department is shown for each item. These averages are based on the last evaluation obtained. In

Jones, A. B.		AN Department		Arts and Sciences			
			Item Averages				
Course	Section	1	2	3	15	16	17
AN 1103	1	3.8	4.1	4.3	4.4	4.6	4.6
AN 4413	1	3.8	4.2	4.8	4.6	4.3	3.4
Average by Student Classification							
Instructor							
Freshman		4.0	5.0	5.0	4.0	4.0	5.0
Sophomore		3.9	4.3	4.4	4.5	4.5	4.5
Junior		3.5	3.6	4.2	4.4	4.6	4.5
Senior		3.3	4.2	4.3	4.0	4.3	3.8
Graduate		4.0	5.0	5.0	4.0	4.0	4.0
Special		4.3	4.3	4.7	4.9	4.9	4.9
Average		3.8	4.1	4.4	4.4	4.5	4.4
Department							
Freshman		3.7	4.1	4.2	4.1	4.6	4.1
Sophomore		3.4	4.3	4.3	4.0	4.6	4.0
.		.	.	.	.	.	.
.		.	.	.	.	.	.
.		.	.	.	.	.	.
Average		3.6	4.3	4.3	4.1	4.5	4.1
College							
Freshman		3.6	4.2	4.1	4.7	4.4	4.3
Sophomore		3.6	4.3	4.1	4.7	4.4	4.3
.		.	.	.	.	.	.
.		.	.	.	.	.	.
.		.	.	.	.	.	.
Average		3.6	4.3	4.1	4.7	4.4	4.3
University							
Freshman		3.7	4.2	4.1	4.7	4.5	4.3
Sophomore		3.6	4.3	4.1	4.7	4.4	4.3
.		.	.	.	.	.	.
.		.	.	.	.	.	.
.		.	.	.	.	.	.
Average		3.7	4.3	4.1	4.6	4.4	4.3

FIGURE 1. Instructor's Report

Course & Faculty	Term	Item Averages						
		1	2	3	15	16	17
AN 1103								
Jones, A. B.	FA72	4.2	4.8	4.7	4.2	4.0	4.4
Smith, C. B.	FA72	4.2	4.4	4.3	4.0	4.1	4.7
Average		4.2	4.5	4.5	4.1	4.1	3.9
AN 5213								
Caine, J.	FA72	4.8	3.1	4.6	2.2	5.0	4.3
.	.	.	.	.	.	.	.
.	.	.	.	.	.	.	.
.	.	.	.	.	.	.	.
Average		4.3	3.7	4.7	3.1	4.5	4.2
AN Departmental Averages		4.3	4.2	4.5	3.7	4.2	4.3

FIGURE 2. Student Publication

future publications, in addition to the averages above, a cumulative average based on all previous evaluations, excepting the last, are shown in Figure 2.

In addition to publication, the Faculty Evaluation Committee has a rotating membership which brings in new people and new ideas. These new members are informally recommended by the various schools and colleges to the Committee on Committees before appointment.

CONDUCTING FOLLOW-UP ACTIVITIES AND STUDIES

These are important activities, and they can lend research respectability to the endeavor. These studies should certainly be programmatic. On our campus the studies have tended to be technical measurement activities, or descriptive. Two areas of inquiry that deserve more attention are faculty personality correlates of the evaluation ratings, and student characteristics relating to their perceptions of teaching. Both areas are difficult to research because of the restrictions of anonymity and the possible invasion of privacy problems that are inherent in this type of study.

RELATING EVALUATION TO OTHER EFFORTS TO RECOGNIZE, REWARD, AND IMPROVE TEACHING

We have an active, faculty-originated committee established for the purpose of improving instruction. This Instructional Improvement Committee has been actively involved with the evaluation of faculty. In a cooperative effort the Instructional Improvement Committee, the Office of Institutional Research, the Faculty Evaluation Committee, and other interested faculty have begun investigation of other modes of evaluation. These have concentrated on variations in the visitation process and in the development of devices other than questionnaires for gaining consensus. The emphasis of these activities has not been to punish the "bad" teachers or necessarily to reward the "good" teachers, but rather to develop multimode systems of faculty, course, and student evaluations, with the objective being to enhance the instruc-

tional process.

No reasonable professional would deny the necessity of evaluation, but teachers in higher education have escaped this realistic assessment. Many, if not most, of the issues or controversies surrounding faculty evaluation can be grouped into two general categories. The first is who will evaluate. The second is what will be evaluated. Mayhew (1967, p. 8) specifies four reasonable sources of evidence concerning teacher evaluation. They are (1) the teacher, (2) the student, (3) observation of the teaching process, and (4) demonstration of desired behavior modifications. If these steps are incorporated into the evaluation procedure the evaluation process can be greatly improved, because it expands the number of people actively involved in the evaluation process, thus providing several different points of view, and it will provide a set of criteria for determining the validity of these observations. This absence of good validity criteria has been a great detriment in the research of teacher evaluation. It must be remembered that the goal of faculty evaluation is improvement in the teaching/learning system, but without means to translate these evaluations into actions for the improvement of instruction, the maximum benefits to be derived from evaluation cannot be realized.

REFERENCES

Cohen, A. M., and Brawer, F. B. *Measuring Faculty Performance.* Washington, D.C.: ERIC Clearinghouse for Junior College Information, 1969.

Costin, F., Greenough, W. T., and Menges, R. J. Student Ratings of College Teaching: Reliability, Validity, and Usefulness. *Review of Educational Research,* 1971, *41,* 511-535.

Eble, K. E. *The Recognition and Evaluation of Teaching.* Salt Lake City: Project to Improve College Teaching, 1970.

Gustad, J. W. Policies and Practices in Faculty Evaluation. *Educational Record,* 1961, 208.

_____. Evaluation of Teaching Performance: Issues and Possibilities. In C. B. T. Lee, ed., *Improving College Teaching.* Washington: American Council on Education, 1967.

Kerlinger, F. N. Student Evaluation of University Professors. *School and Society,* 1971, *99,* 353-356.

Mayhew, L. B. A Tissue Committee for Teachers. *Improving College and University Teaching,* 1967, *15,* 5-10.

Miller, R. I. *Evaluating Faculty Performance*. San Francisco: Jossey-Bass, 1972.

Remmers, H. H. The Relationship between Students' Marks and Students' Attitudes toward Instructors. *School and Society*, 1928, *28,* 759-760.

_____. To What Extent do Grades Influence Student Ratings of Instructors? *Journal of Educational Research*, 1930, *21,* 314-316.

_____, and Stalnaker, J. M. Can Students Discriminate Traits Associated with Success in Teaching? *Journal of Applied Psychology*, 1928, *12,* 602-610.

Simpson, R. H., and Seidman, J. M. *Student Evaluation of Teaching and Learning*. Washington, D.C.: The American Association of Colleges for Teacher Education, 1962.

ADDITIONAL RESOURCES

Werdell, P. R. *Course and Teacher Evaluation*. Washington, D.C.: United States National Student Association, 1966.

PART IV

EDUCATION AND TRAINING OF TEACHERS AND ADMINISTRATORS

46

CURRENT ORIENTATIONS IN TEACHER EDUCATION

by Ron Iannone
Associate Professor of Education
College of Human Resources and Education
West Virginia University
Morgantown, West Virginia

In teacher education programs across the country there are five distinct orientations. While any two specific programs may overlap at times, there are definitive assumptions which can be clearly identified for each, placing it in one of five philosophical orientations. More specifically, these orientations exhibit a continuity based upon dimensions such as performance, community, models of teaching, humanism, and realism. Their major assumptions and discontinuities will be delineated in the following discussion.

PERFORMANCE ORIENTATION

In the late sixties and early seventies the teacher education literature has been filled with such terms and concepts as "competency-based," "cost-effectiveness," "cost benefits," "delivery system," "feedback loop," "modules," "hardware," "software," "parity," "input-output," and so forth.

Both the cry for accountability and the Federal government's interest in a systems approach for education have influenced teacher education program designers to start looking at these terms and concepts for application in the teaching-learning process. One basic assumption underlying performance based teacher education is that there are observable outcomes in the teaching-learning process, and these should be the core of the teacher education curriculum. In short, this view is based on B. F. Skinner's theory of Operant Conditioning and behavioral modification, which posits that learning is observable, can be modified by the environment, and can be reinforced by environmental conditions. Moreover, the teacher must accept responsibility for mediating and manipulating the environmental conditions for the learner.

In 1968, criteria based on this orientation were used by the U.S. Office of Education for accepting proposals for Elementary Teacher Education Models. Nine were accepted out of the 80 that were submitted (Engbretson, 1969). A constant theme that runs throughout eight of the nine models is the orientation toward modules (small segments) of learning experiences, with built-in cognitive, and sometimes affective, performance specifications (behavioral objectives) for the training of teachers. The Michigan State University Model (1969) had over 2,700 learning experience modules, highly concentrated in the fields of behavioral sciences.

Explicitly, or implicitly, the performance-oriented

models purported that teachers in training could gain a body of understandings and skills which then could be observed, and that the consequences of teacher behavior on the learning outcomes of pupils could also be observed and evaluated. This was the basic rationale for the University of Georgia's model (Johnson et al., 1968) for teacher education. Three basic elements underlie the Georgia program: first, pupils' behavioral outcomes were designated; second, teachers' behavioral outcomes were determined according to the specified pupil behavioral outcomes; and finally, behavioral specifications were suggested for the teacher education program to facilitate orchestration of the first two elements. Some of the criterion measures proposed to evaluate this orchestration were pupil achievement, parental attitudes, peer ratings, supervisory ratings, and use of videotape.

The University of Georgia model, and other performance oriented teacher education programs, have come under pointed attacks from humanistically oriented teacher educators. Humanistic educators' arguments are usually predicated on a variety of metaphors related to the mechanistic philosophy underlying the performance orientation. Certain humanistic educators argue quite passionately that teaching is an art, and by designating competencies for teaching one loses the humanity, creativity, spontaneity, imagination, and even mysticism that good teachers seem to exhibit in the classroom. Others argue that present attempts at delineating teaching behaviors have been myopic, citing as evidence that most performance oriented teacher education programs have revolved around the cognitive aspects of teaching; because of the complexities related to the learning outcomes of children, the teaching-learning process has been overemphasized regarding the teaching component, to the expense of the learning component. Thus, teacher educators who profess this orientation are presently only superficially treating such areas as the emotional, social, and intellectual growth of children. Another criticism is that when the performance orientation is accepted by teacher training institutions, many teacher educators just change the names of their courses by calling them modules, while the structures and processes of their courses remain the same.

Results of performance oriented teacher educators' facing these criticisms head-on are somewhat uncertain at this time. But one thing is clear: performance orientation has helped many teacher educators in delineating observable aspects of teaching related to "didactics" and "theory of teaching," and for this performance orientation should be praised.

COMMUNITY ORIENTATION

During the upheaval of the sixties the consciousness of communities, and their complexities, both in the inner city and in rural areas, was felt by almost everyone in this nation. Likewise, some teacher education institutions responded by designing teacher education programs to meet the needs of specific communities. The emphasis in many of these community oriented teacher education programs was to shift the center of teacher education programs from the universities to the communities. The community oriented teacher educators argued that there was a great need to expand the vision of teachers to see that their role required active involvement with parents and participation in community life. To do this, teachers would have to synthesize a body of knowledge with concepts in community development, sociology, anthropology, ethnography, and cultural history. Typically, in community oriented teacher education programs members of the community, university people, and public school people attempt to work cooperatively in designing the pre- or inservice training for teachers.

An illustration of such a cooperative effort is taking place in Chicago, where a Cooperative Program in Urban Teacher Education has been implemented (Talmage and Monore, 1970). This program is built upon the development of different centers in individual schools. Some of the characteristics of these centers are: appointment of an advisory committee drawn from the community, the school, and the university; and a working committee comprised of university personnel, the school's community coordinator, and representatives of teachers in training. Suggestions are made for each teacher in training by the advisory committee and implemented by the working committee, which also meets with the teachers in training to discuss their experiences.

Larry Cuban (1969, pp. 253-272) points out the differences between a community oriented, as opposed to a traditionally oriented, teacher education program. His main points are:

> The control of the teacher education program would not be with the university, but centered in school system with cooperation of a university.

> The approach would not be deductive and didactic but would be practical, inductive, and inquiring, with trainees relating theory to teaching.

> The sequence of learning experiences would be treated in formal courses, but would be related to clinical experience through group and individual study and personal investigation.

Many community oriented programs have been implemented, either on a small scale or experimentally. In an attempt to develop more concrete community teacher education programs, the University of Maryland, Indiana University, Multi-Institutional Kanawha County Student Teaching Center in Charleston, West Virginia, and others have devised a concept usually identified as "teacher education centers," or "teacher centers." This concept calls for a new partnership in teacher education between teacher training institutions and community public school systems. Goals usually listed for this concept fall into the following categories: they should be vehicles for general change in the community and their schools; they should offer inservice education; they should include a broad trainee population; they should offer preservice education in the teacher center; they should encourage cooperation; they should serve children; they should have a parity governmental body. These and other related concepts are treated by Lorraine Poliakoff (1972) in the *Journal of Teacher Education.*

Educators such as Jonathan Kozol (1972) and Paulo Freire (1970) see the school and its teachers as a political entity, where both the pupils and their parents are given an opportunity to see more clearly the culture that shapes their behavior and how they may gain control over those things that shape their daily lives. Moreover, Freire discusses the role of the teacher in the community as one of working in a reflective-dialogical fashion, so that teachers, together with pupils and their parents heighten their consciousness with regard to the realities that surround them. Once heightened consciousness is achieved, the dialectic can turn into action programs for the community in which its members may celebrate their individual potentials.

One major problem area underlying many community oriented teacher education programs is the existence of considerable naiveté, revolutionary fervor, and vagueness, combined with a lack of concrete substance to their clamors. Those uncertainties cause many community oriented educators to outstrip the realities of the communities they were hoping to help. In fact, the frustrations, turbulence, contradictions, unwillingness to change, and prejudices of some trial communities were at times almost too difficult for teachers in training to cope with. Definitive and concrete support systems for them were lacking in many experimental community oriented teacher education programs. These same problems, and others of greater magnitude, also seem to prevail within the teacher education center concept; that is, many courses formerly offered at the universities were simply displaced to teacher education centers with very little change in the structure and processes of courses— only the name of the course and place of presentation was altered. New terms and titles such as "clinical professors," "learning centers," "cooperative teachers," "internship," "resident professors," and so forth belie the reality of the same old traditional teacher education programs that simply give fancier names for methods courses and student teaching.

Nevertheless, the attempts by community oriented teacher educators and teacher education center advocates should not be disparaged or demeaned. What should be encouraged is a rigorous attempt on the part of these teacher educators to identify the structures and processes that are needed for community oriented teacher education programs.

MODELS OF TEACHING ORIENTATION

In a historical sense, the basic foundation for this orientation was articulated by such educators as Arno Bellack (1963), Nathaniel Gage (1963), B. O. Smith (1963), Hilda Taba (1964), and others. Some of their work revolved around identifying basic pedagogical movements in the classroom (Bellack), delineating relationships between variables in the classroom (Gage), determining the logical aspects of teaching (Smith), and focusing on questioning-and-answering aspects of teaching relative to cognitive development (Taba). Of course there were many more teaching related concepts developed by these authors, and others, but other aspects are beyond the scope of this discussion.

At present, an integration and synthesis of their ideas

can best be illustrated by briefly examining some of the work accomplished by Bruce Joyce and his associates at Columbia University. Joyce (1968) was the major author of one of the nine proposals which were funded by the USOE Elementary Teacher Education Project. Since then, some teacher educators have felt that the teacher education model developed by Columbia University represented the most imaginative, creative, and scholarly attempt of all plans submitted to this USOE Project. The Columbia Model is not locked into the performance orientation of the other eight models.

The underlying rationale for the Columbia Model was to help future teachers to be interactive teachers, institutional builders, innovators, and scholars. More recently, Joyce co-authored a book with Marsha Weil (1972) entitled *Models of Teaching*. Cogently, they point out that the teacher in training should understand the processes and the philosophical bases for different models of teaching in areas of information processes, and in social, personal, and behavioral orientations. Joyce and Weil indicate that there are 16 submodels of teaching which are derivative from these four broad categories. For instance, the inquiry model of teaching is related to the informational processes area, the nondirecting model of teaching is related to the personal area, the value clarification model of teaching is related to the social area, and so forth for all sixteen models of teaching. The Joyce and Weil basic outline (1972, pp. 96-97) for presentation of these models to teachers in the training is as follows:

Part I: Theoretical Background

Read basic sources. Read an annotated transcript or narrative account of a model. Read related research or related theoretical references. Listen to and discuss the summary lecture on the salient features of the model: objectives, syntax, social system, principles of reaction, and points of conceptual or practical difficulty.

Part II. Application of the Model

Watch and analyze a video-tape or live demonstration. Practice exercises focusing on a component behavior or particular phase of the model. Peer-practice teaching of the model over specified lessons or topics. Implement the model in the classroom over different content areas.

Currently, this model of teaching orientation is being implemented in a one-year master's degree program at Columbia University. Joyce and his associates are hopeful that once teachers in training have assimilated the structure and processes of these models, they can then select one model or combinations of models for their particular purposes in the classroom.

Several remarks seem appropriate at this time regarding the feasibility of using this type of orientation for teacher education programs. One cannot but suspect that a Models of Teaching orientation would be very liable to the pitfalls of mechanistic teaching. This type of orientation could easily become dull, unimaginative, and stifling. One of the major reasons this could happen is related to the complexities of some of these models themselves. The analytical nature of many of the Models of Teaching models is well beyond the level (or needs) of many beginning teachers. For example, Kohlberg's (1966) model for teaching moral development strongly suggests that the teacher in training should be an expert in the principles of cognitive psychology; and the Oliver and Shaver (1966) model for jurisprudential teaching argues that teachers in training should be quite proficient in the techniques and assumptions used in jurisprudence!

On the positive side, this rigorous and sophisticated approach to the training of teachers may be indicative that the teaching profession is to move beyond its present technical level. This orientation may be one of the alternatives to the present intellectual sloppiness that is prevalent in many teacher education programs.

HUMANISM ORIENTATION

Primarily the "self" and "becoming" are the underlying concepts for the Humanism Orientation. Often quoted for support of this position are Carl Rogers, Abraham Maslow, Arthur Combs, William Purkey and some of the existential theorists such as Maxine Greene, Jean-Paul Sartre, and others. To be more human, open, honest, real, and sensitive are usually the goals of avowed humanistic teacher education programs. Proposed humanistic models include the University of Massachusetts (Allen and Cooper, 1969), Syracuse University (Benjamin, 1969), and West Virginia University (Iannone and Carline, 1971). Basic themes in these three models are quite similar. A teacher needs to be a fully developed human being, a person who is warm and understanding and perceptive, a person with a positive self-concept who is able to match the realities of his values with those of the youngsters he is to teach.

The nondirective approach and group oriented techniques seem to be the core of experiences outlined for the training of teachers under these models. Strong emphasis is placed upon helping teachers in training learn how to facilitate conditions in the classroom whereby pupils can become self-directed learners. Thus, the so-called "open classroom," which has received much pro and con attention, coincides neatly with expectations of humanistically oriented teacher educators. Motivated by the romantic critics like Holt, Kozol, Dennison and others, theirs was a child-centered approach to teaching. That is, traditional teaching methods were considered too authoritarian. Humanistic teaching methods ideally should free children to explore and actualize their individual potentials. A marriage between humanistically oriented teacher educators and the open classroom advocates became a reality. Yet a certain amount of criticism was being aimed at this marriage for its lack of intellectual goals and concrete programs for the training of teachers for this type of classroom. Throughout the whole free schools, or alternative schools, phenomenon teachers were being called paragons of sloppy permissiveness. Many humanistically oriented teacher educators and romantic critics were being blamed for producing undesirable conditions both in the public and private sector of education.

To answer some of these criticisms, the humanistically oriented teacher educators look to the British Infant School concept of informal curriculum, and they also look to the psychologist Jean Piaget for both the structure and processes of training teachers for classrooms other than traditional ones.

Consequently, schools like the University of North Dakota, which was brought to fame by Charles Silberman (1970), began to develop a highly structured, humanistically oriented, teacher education program, based upon the concepts of Piaget and practices used in the British Infant Schools. Innovations such as learning centers, integrated curriculum, and self-directed learning packets were tried. Criticisms around and about humanistically oriented teacher education programs are loud and clear. As mentioned previously, some of these criticisms are centered on their vague goals, intellectual sloppiness, ephemeral "training" experiences (such as sensitivity groups), excessive psychological orientation, being too understanding, too compassionate, too analytical, and many more, which are too numerous to list. Many educators also complain that humanistic teacher educators are naive regarding the social, political, economic, and cultural circumstances of student's lives, thinking idealistically that the pain, anguish, and frustrations of living in our country can be wished or loved away.

Even though some of the romantic critics and the humanistic oriented teacher educators may have been overly zealous in their claims, they have made more than a passing contribution. They have made many become aware of the human variable in the teaching-learning process in an age of increasing dominance by impersonal technology. For this we should be thankful.

REALISM ORIENTATION

During the lull of the early seventies, and after the rhetorical sensationalism about "killing," "murdering," and "oppressing" in schools, there seems to be a climate of settling down. Realism appears to be emerging as a counterforce to the clamor of late sixties' radical/romantic critics. A leading force toward realism in education is Harry Broudy (1972), who has been an observer and scholar of teacher education for the last 20 years. He has come to grips with the romantic critics and their views about teaching and learning in today's schools. Convincingly, Broudy points out that despite the excessive claims that have been made, we do not have a scientific theory of teaching. Further, the pedagogical theory available is not very reliable, and in many respects is highly technical in design. The theory that does exist, Broudy argues, should be found in the form of foundation studies in the teacher education curriculum. Concepts from such disciplines as philosophy, history, sociology, and anthropology place the problems in what Broudy defines as the "rational context" of education. These subjects have an interpretive utility which Broudy (1972, p. 57) feels ". . . affects the general strategy of education, of appraising the teaching situation in many dimensions and for making decisions that take account of these dimensions."

It is interpretive rigor that Broudy believes will create a new professionalism among teacher educators. Broudy's solutions to reforming teacher education deal concretely with many of the problems and seeming enigmas which face teacher educators in this decade. More specifically, Broudy suggests that perhaps we could start training people in the secondary schools to perform most normal classroom functions of teachers. Objectives and criteria for success in particular content areas could be made quite explicit, so didactics and necessary pedagogy could easily be handled by programmed instruction. Technicians could be trained to perform most classroom functions with very little difficulty.

In turn, Broudy suggests, there would be in existence a small cadre of professional teachers, graduates of four-year specialized schools, with their teacher program having been of an interpretive nature. These graduates would oversee what he calls the didactics, heuristics, and philetics of schools. Different potentials of students, he writes, in elementary, secondary, and collegiate schools seem to require different mixes of instructional staff and instructional approach. In more detail, Broudy (1972, p. 184) says:

> In the elementary school the strategy of instruction could be:
> 1. Didactics for certain skills in language, writing, and composition.
> 2. Heuristics, or the method of learning by discovery, for a varied assortment of items in history, mathematics, geography, and science.
> 3. Philetics to provide a psychologically healthy relationship between teacher and pupil, between pupil and pupil, as well as to provide conditions favorable to school attendance and learning.

Throughout efforts for realism as a basis for teacher education, Harry Broudy, B. O. Smith (1969), and others are concerned with upgrading the teaching profession by "educating" teachers and not with "training" them in an apprenticeship-like system and deprofessionalizing the role of the teacher. The realism orientation for teacher education contends that as professionals, the role of teachers requires that they extend their knowledge beyond their own specified "subject" areas, and in turn delineate a larger, more coherent pattern of life for their students. Universals that exist in science, history, literary criticism, art, poetry, religion, and mathematics will help the student understand humanity and the patterns of life by which humanity lives. These universals transcend anything vocational, and their truths can be explored for eternity. For example, how could one attempt to understand the complexities of the modern political sphere without having read the views of Mill and Emerson on liberty, justice, and freedom? One can gain a sense of form and a sense of reality by absorbing laboriously the great authors and poets. In short, this orientation stresses a need for teachers to look for a cross-fertilization from all disciplines in their pursuit of the "real."

One final word regarding this orientation and some of the criticism generated by its opponents. It is difficult for an existentialist to accept the belief that children should be led to some set of universal values existing in a real world. It may also be difficult for those who are concerned with minorities to accept this position, when a "foreign" accent or an unfilled stomach is felt by some minorities to be their major problem. Quality education and use of technological skills, as defined by Broudy, may translate to mean more manipulation and control of people. However, these criticisms are trivial in comparison to the clarity that Broudy and the realism orientation has given us in forcing the issues of teacher education.

CONCLUSIONS

In speaking about teaching, Emerson states: "I confess myself utterly at a loss in suggesting particular reforms in our ways of teaching," (Emerson, 1946, p. 269); after all is said and done, this is where we find ourselves in teacher education today. A great deal of lip service has been given to many of the orientations for teacher education discussed above, but many never reach realization beyond the talking or designing level. Very few teacher education institutions have implemented any of the above-mentioned orientations, except perhaps on a small-scale or experimental basis.

Unable to generate the commitment and energy among teacher educators to move beyond their methods courses and student teaching programs, teacher educators like myself hide from this reality by being concerned with the application of ideas such as "operant conditioning," "sensitivity procedures," "open classrooms," "simulation games," "multimedia" gimmicks, "cultural pocket" observations, and "ad hocracy" solutions. A great poet once said, "Out of the quarrel with others we make rhetoric and out of the quarrel with ourselves we make poetry—the most useful of all quarrels is the quarrel with ourselves."

Unless we in teacher education start being honest about our own feelings, insecurities, and struggles, we won't be able to bring any sort of cogency, or "balanced wheel approach," to the orientations presented here. Too often, because of our attitude of inertia, and because of our attitude of resignation, and because of our shortsightedness, we lack the insight, skill, and courage to move beyond pharmacological solutions and the technical skills of teaching. Areas which are unsafe, and areas which force teacher educators into the darkness, frighten us immensely. Once we move into this darkness, then the adolescent's cry for "doing it" will also become a reality for teacher educators. Then, instead of talking and fantasies about the beauty of a specific orientation to teacher education, we too will be "doing it."

REFERENCES

Allen, D. W., and Cooper, J. M. *Model Elementary Teacher Education Program: Final Report.* Washington, D.C.: U.S. Government Printing Office, 1969.

Bellack, A. C. et al. *The Language of the Classroom: Meanings Communicated in High School Teaching.* (U.S. Office of Education Cooperative Research Project 1497) New York: Institute of Psychological Research, Teachers College, Columbia, University, 1963.

Benjamin, W. et al. *Specifications for a Comprehensive Undergraduate and Inservice Teacher Education Program for Elementary Teachers: Final Report.* Washington, D.C.: U.S. Government Printing Office, 1969.

Broudy, H. S. *The Real World of Public Schools.* New York: Harcourt-Brace-Jovanovich, 1972.

Cuban, L. Teacher and Community. *Harvard Educational Review,* 1969, *39* (2), 253-272.

Emerson, R. W. In M. Van Doren, ed., *The Portable Emerson.* New York: Viking, 1946.

Engbretson, W. E. *Analysis and Evaluation of Plans for Comprehensive Elementary Teacher Education Model: Final Report.* Philadelphia: Temple University, 1969.

Freire, P. *Pedagogy of the Oppressed.* New York: Herder & Herder, 1970.

Gage, N. L., ed. *Handbook on Teaching: A Project of the American Educational Research Association.* Chicago: Rand McNally, 1963.

Iannone, R. V., and Carline, J. L. A Humanistic Approach to Teacher Education. *Journal of Teacher Education,* 1971, *22*(4), 429-433.

Johnson, E. C. et al. *Georgia Educational Model Specifications for the Preparation of Elementary Teachers.* U.S. Office of Education, Washington, D.C.: U.S. Government Printing Office, 1968.

Joyce, B. R. *The Teacher-Innovator: A Program to Prepare Teachers.* (ED027284) Sections 1 and 2, U.S. Office of Education, Washington, D.C.: U.S. Government Printing Office, 1968.

_____, and Weil, M. *Models of Teaching.* Englewood Cliffs, N.J.: Prentice-Hall, 1972.

Kohlberg, L. Moral Education in the School. *School Review,* 1966, *74,* 1-30.

Kozol, J. *Free Schools.* Boston: Houghton-Mifflin, 1972.

Michigan State University. *Behavioral Science Elementary Teacher Education Program: Final Report.* (ED027285) Vol. 1, U.S. Office of Education, Washington, D.C.: U.S. Government Printing Office, 1969.

Oliver, D. W., and Shaver, J. P. *Teaching Public Issues in the High School.* Boston: Houghton-Mifflin, 1966.

Poliakoff, L. Teacher Centers: An Outline of Current Information. *Journal of Teacher Education,* 1972, *23*(3), 389-397.

Silberman, C. *Crisis in the Classroom.* New York: Random House, 1970.

Smith, B. O. *Logical Aspects of Teaching.* Urbana: University of Illinois Press, 1963.

_____ et al. *Teachers and the Real World.* Washington, D.C.: American Association of Colleges for Teacher Education (ED027267), 1969.

Taba, H. et al. *Thinking in Elementary School Children.* (U.S. Office of Education Cooperative Research Project 1574) San Francisco: San Francisco State College, 1964.

Talmadge, H., and Monore, G. E. The Teacher as a Teacher Educator: A Self-Regenerating System. *Educational Leadership,* 1970, *27,* 609-613.

47

PREPARATION PROGRAMS IN EDUCATIONAL ADMINISTRATION

by Robin H. Farquhar
Assistant Director
The Ontario Institute for Studies in Education
Toronto, Ontario, Canada

Preparation for educational administration is a process that continues throughout a person's career and is obtained in a variety of ways—through individual study, university programs, on-the-job training, and continuing education opportunities offered by school boards, government agencies, professional associations, private corporations, and institutions of higher learning. The most significant preparation occurs in graduate programs offered by universities' Schools of Education, typically through their Departments of Educational Administration. Such programs are designed to provide preservice training for prospective administrators in schools, school systems, state and federal education agencies, other organizations, and associations concerned with education—and for future professors, researchers, and developers in the field of educational administration. It is with these university-based graduate programs in educational administration that this article is concerned.

A recent study (UCEA, 1973) produced considerable information about the current scope of preparation programs in educational administration. In 1972, 363 universities in the United States were offering such programs. (There are also about 20 in Canada, approximately ten in other countries of the British Commonwealth, and around a dozen scattered throughout additional nations in Africa, Asia, Europe, and South America.) Among the 284 American institutions responding to the UCEA survey, 261 had master's programs, 161 had Specialist or two-year programs, and 118 had doctoral programs (20 with the Ph.D. only, 42 with the Ed.D. only, and 56 with both the Ph.D. and the Ed.D.). The most rapidly expanding of these has been the Specialist, or two-year program, with the number of institutions involved growing from seven to 145 between 1940 and 1970. The slowest growth has been in Ph.D. programs, which increased from 38 to 73 during the same time period. Since 1965, the number of graduate degrees awarded in educational administration has risen by almost 40 percent at the master's level and by over 70 percent at the doctoral level (more than 1,000 doctorates in educational administration were awarded during 1970).

The nature of preparation programs in educational administration has also changed substantially in recent years (Culbertson et al., 1969; Farquhar and Martin, 1972). Whereas they were once viewed as an opportunity for formerly successful administrators to pass along the lore and wisdom accumulated during their careers to groups of neophytes who needed to be told "how to do it," they now reflect the belief that educational administration is a sophisticated applied social science with a body of knowledge comprised of relevant concepts from a variety of academic disciplines. This major shift in perspective is reflected in the content, instructional approaches, and personnel involved in today's programs.

The predominant characteristic of program content is an emphasis on the social sciences—notably anthropology, economics, political science, social psychology, and sociology (Culbertson et al., 1973). Many universities require their students to go "across campus" and take minors in one or more social science areas on the assumption that, through exposure to some of the concepts and modes of inquiry in a discipline, the student will be able to distill knowledge, skills, and attitudes that he can eventually apply within the educational context, as he performs such administrative functions as goal setting, decision-making, and problem-solving. Whether or not such transfers actually occur has never been empirically demonstrated. Other institutions pursue a more direct approach by employing social scientists in Departments of Educational Administration where their role is to teach particularly relevant administrative theory, and to focus their disciplinary insights directly upon the problems encountered in contemporary education. While the latter approach is preferable, it is not always possible because of certain territorial imperatives, organizational rigidities, and academic reward systems within universities. But regardless of the approach used, there are few preparation programs in educational administration that do not include a substantial dose of social science content.

As the social science movement began to pay off, in terms of both more theoretically knowledgeable graduates and more academically respectable programs, the expansion of educational administration as a field of study continued into other areas, two of which are currently noteworthy. One such excursion resulted from a growing concern with the importance of value definition and clarification. This concern has led professors of educational administration to the arts, humanities, and futurism (Farquhar, *Humanities*, 1970). Unlike those in business administration, who embraced the arts and humanities during the fifties and early sixties in the belief that more liberally educated and "cultured" graduates would make better corporation executives, those in educational administration are drawing upon these fields in an effort to help their students come to grips with their basic beliefs and values, those of others, and the potential conflicts between the two. It is felt that classic and contemporary literature, philosophy, film, music, and art can be used effectively to portray crucial moral dilemmas and value conflicts, and that through examining these the prospective administrator will be in a better position to perform such essential functions as purpose definition, conflict resolution, and cross-cultural communication. It is also hoped that his creative capacities will be enhanced by direct contact with the work of artists and futurists. One of the most innovative expressions of this hope is found at the University of Iowa, where the doctoral dissertations of some recent graduates have been presented in the forms of a novel, a motion picture, and a photographic essay.

The other major source of academic content is found in the newer management technologies, for which educational students are often sent to schools of business and public administration. Sophisticated planning and evaluation techniques, program-planning-budgeting systems, operations research, systems analysis, quantitative management methods, man-machine communications, and management information systems—all originated in government, industry, or the military—are now viewed as having relevance to the administration of educational systems. While it is recognized that schools are not factories and teachers aren't soldiers, it is also becoming increasingly apparent that educational administration involves the allocation of scarce resources, and that certain techniques which have proven successful in other managerial contexts can be adapted for use in education (Bruno, 1973). The challenge is to determine and exploit their utility within the uniquely human setting of schools.

In addition to the above sources of academic content, most preparation programs in educational administration also include a substantial component of field experience (Horoschak and Cronin, 1973). It must be remembered that, because educational administration is almost exclusively a field of graduate study, the vast majority of students have had previous training in education and experience as teachers. Thus, the field-related activities in their graduate programs focus specifically on the kinds of realities they will confront as administrators. In the past, such experiences typically took the form of single-subject internships, in which the student was assigned to a particular practicing administrator and spent up to a year following him around as an observer, assistant, and confidant. Today, however, it is becoming common to find administration students involved in a series of rotating internships, wherein they spend a few weeks with responsibilities in each of several education-relevant establishments, such as mayors' and city planners' offices, health and welfare agencies, local police and recreation departments, business organizations, professional associations, and state legislatures. This approach was introduced at Teachers' College, Columbia (Creswell and Goettel, 1970). Such experiences give the interns a variety of opportunities to apply what they have learned on campus within different practical settings.

Other efforts to integrate academic content with the realities of the field are found in some of the instructional approaches employed by professors of educational administration (Wynn, 1972). For many years the case study technique, pioneered in the field of business administration, has been employed in education. More recently, a number of comprehensive, sophisticated sets of simulation materials have been developed for use in educational administration programs. These sets are typically multimedia in character, containing a wealth of written, taped, and filmed information on a community, its schools, and the particular role being simulated. After studying this material, the student "gets into role" and proceeds to deal with a variety of administrative problems presented to him through written items in his in-basket, taped telephone calls and interruptions, and filmed incidents. He then has an opportunity to analyze his problem-solving behavior with the supervising pro-

fessor and relate it to the cognitive knowledge he has gained during his program. A few universities (including Texas and Wisconsin) are now using computer-based simulations (Bessent and Piele, 1973), and several are employing management games, laboratory training exercises, and numerous other clinical approaches. The popularity and productivity of such reality-based instructional methods are rapidly rendering the lecture-and-textbook technique obsolete.

This trend has contributed to a growth in the flexibility and individualization of preparation programs in educational administration. Students are no longer "batch-processed" through their graduate studies. Independent learning is now common, and is arranged in a variety of ways which are much more ambitious than the traditional "Individual Reading and Research" courses found in the bulletins of many universities. New York University, for example, has introduced "Individual Learning Systems for Administrators" (Rose, 1973), in which students plan a major portion of their programs around a variety of experiences in the university and the field which are directly relevant to their interests, but are not tied to courses being offered on campus—although the students may choose to attend particular segments of regular courses as a part of their programs if they wish. Another example is the program at the University of Massachusetts (Flight, 1973), in which a number of modules (of varying length and credit value) are made available to students on demand; groups of students and faculty are able to continually generate new modules in line with the individual needs and aspirations of those concerned.

The impression should not be left, however, that administrative preparation has become a random mixture of personal preferences. On the contrary, there is more concern with integration and rationalization than ever before. The emphasis on accountability, the emergence in some states of performance-based certification for administrators, and the demand that professors of education practice what they preach about behavioral objectives, have combined to force upon preparation programs a strong concern with relevance, purpose, and competency orientation. Program designers are paying increasing attention to the specific knowledge, skills, and attitudes that their graduates will require when they enter their chosen fields of practice. This is reflected in the content of programs, wherein the criteria for electing various components are being carefully examined, and an intensive effort to develop competency-based modules is underway—notably at the University of Utah (McCleary, 1972). It is reflected in the structure of programs, wherein clearly rationalized distinctions are being made between those experiences designed to prepare professional practitioners of educational administration, and those for training academic scholars in educational administration (a distinction that is evident between the two new doctoral programs at the Ontario Institute for Studies in Education); in addition, carefully developed options are being made available to students who wish to supplement their core experiences with specializations in particular sub-areas of educational administration. And it is reflected in admission criteria for programs, wherein the predominant concern with previous academic records is gradually being replaced by a focus on the applicants' evidence of leadership performance and potential—although progress in this direction remains slow, as will be indicated later in this article.

Related to this last point is the fact that considerable expansion is occurring in the talent pools from which candidates are sought for preparation in educational administration (Stout, 1973). While current teachers and beginning administrators still constitute the majority of applicants, an effort is underway to recruit individuals who have demonstrated leadership ability in organizations other than schools. This endeavor is best reflected in the National Program for Educational Leadership, a five-university project funded by the U.S. Office of Education which is designed exclusively to recruit into school administration established leaders in such fields as law, social work, the ministry, business, industry, and government service. It does not lead to a university degree; its curricular and instructional approaches are highly individualized, and include internships, clinical services, and observations, as well as access to courses, seminars, counselling, and independent study on participating campuses (Cunningham and Muth, 1972). Another current emphasis in recruitment for preparation programs is found in special attempts to attract more women, black, Chicano, and American Indian candidates than in the past.

The nature and functions of staff personnel in administration programs are also undergoing change. The emphasis on content and experiences outside of Education has resulted in fewer professors who are graduates with long school experience, and more young scholars with training in the cognate disciplines being employed by university Departments of Educational Administration. In the past, professorial areas of expertise were typically defined in terms of educational levels (e.g., secondary administration) or task areas (e.g., personnel administration). More recently, specializations have been described according to academic subdisciplines (e.g., politics of education) or bodies of theory (e.g., organizational behavior). Currently, some professors of educational administration are beginning to view themselves primarily as researchers (generating new knowledge), synthesizers (collating existing knowledge), teachers (transmitting knowledge to students), or developers (applying knowledge to the resolution of problems in the field). This trend in staffing is reflective of a growing emphasis on knowledge utilization in educational administration. It also illustrates the emergence of functionally-oriented program budgeting in universities generally.

It is clear from the foregoing that preparatory programs are in a state of flux. Educational administration is relatively young as a field of study, and the number of leaders involved in its development is comparatively small. This has facilitated considerable communication and cooperation among the individuals and organizations contributing to its advancement. Interuniversity relationships have been enhanced particularly by the National Conference of Professors of Educational Administration, an association of academics in North America who meet annually for one week to hear presentations on new developments, to cooperatively generate new program ideas, to discuss shared interests and concerns, and to plan publications on contemporary topics in the field; and by the University Council for Educational Administration (Farquhar, *Planning & Changing*, 1970), a group of almost 60 leading universities in the U.S. and Canada that have met qualitative criteria for admission to the Council, and cooperate to improve the study of educational administration through joint projects to generate and disseminate new program content, conceptualize and implement new preparation strategies, develop and test new instructional programs; and publish a newsletter, two journals, and a variety of position papers, books, and reports. Cooperative relationships between universities and practitioners are influencing program improvement through such mechanisms as advisory groups of local administrators for universities, regional university-based school development councils, activities planned jointly by professors and statewide professional associations, and national projects in which organizations of practitioners (such as the American Association of School Administrators and the National School Public Relations Association) work with groups of universities to develop new program plans for the professional development of their members. On the international level, the recent establishment of the Commonwealth Council for Educational Administration has stimulated a number of cooperative activities to serve the mutual interests of scholars and practitioners of educational administration throughout the Commonwealth of Nations (Thomas, 1971).

The progress through cooperation that characterizes the current state of preparation programs in educational administration has not left the field devoid of problems or controversies. The most crucial need currently confronting university personnel in the field is for the systematic evaluation of their preparatory programs. There are at present three typical ways of assessing a program's quality: (1) measures of the completion rate by students, which are subject to all problems of self-fulfilling prophecies; (2) observations of graduates' career progression, which are dependent on numerous personal and situational factors other than professional preparation; and (3) surveys of alumni opinions about the value of their programs, which represent a classic example of sampling bias. The lack of systematic, valid program evaluation results from some weaknesses that lie at the heart of administrative preparation; program designers are not agreed on the performance indicators of "good" educational administration; thus their instructional objectives are not explicated in clear behavioral terms; therefore, their criteria for determining the nature of their programs are vague, and consequently they have no specific standards against which to judge their effectiveness. The inevitable result of these lackings is that efforts to improve preparation programs in educational administration—like those in many other professional fields—tend to be incremental, irrational, and nonconsensual.

A related problem area concerns the selection of candidates for admission to the programs (McIntyre, 1966). Because of the lack of agreement on what good educational administration is, it is difficult to identify the characteristics of those who are most likely to practice it. Without an understanding of what these characteristics are, it is impossible to develop tests to determine the extent to which they are possessed. And lacking such tests, there are no valid ways of selecting students for admission to preparation programs, or of predicting the success of their eventual administrative performance. Moreover, there is a disquieting hunch held by many that the most significant characteristics of leadership potential are qualities upon which training can have little or no impact anyway —traits such as vision, commitment, courage, creativity, integrity, and tolerance. Since few of these can be reliably measured, they have little influence on criteria for student admissions. Accordingly, selection decisions are typically based on such traditional kinds of evidence as previous academic records, letters of reference from friends, and (infrequently) opinions formed during short interviews—all of which, as McIntyre (1966) has noted, are invalid and nonproductive. Consequently, many students are admitted to preparation programs in educational administration who probably shouldn't be there.

This leads to a third problem currently confronting program designers—that of "birth control." As indicated at the beginning of this article, the supply of personnel trained in educational administration has increased substantially in recent years. Yet, the demand for their services is decreasing (UCEA, 1973). Most states now have a considerable oversupply of individuals holding certificates in school administration, an imbalance which is being exacerbated by declining enrollments, especially at the elementary level. At the same time, there is now an overabundance of persons trained for the professoriate in educational administration, and this problem too is worsening because of the staff cutbacks increasingly being required by the dismal financial state of most universities. Thus, the need for graduates of preparation programs in educational administration is lessening drastically; yet their production continues unabated. The critical unresolved issue in this matter is whose responsibility it is to exercise the necessary control: Should universities lower their intake of students in order to lessen their output of graduates? Should state agencies adopt quotas or more stringent requirements for their issuance of certificates in school administration? Or should the market be left to control itself, on the assumption that employers will only hire according to their needs and that prospective students of educational administration, recognizing this, should be permitted to take their chances by enrolling in preparation programs if they wish? Opinion is sharply divided on this issue, with the result that despite much lamentation little is being done about it at present.

Critical as these problems are, they are not unknown. Efforts are underway to grapple with them, particularly under the auspices of UCEA. The brief history of educational administration as a field of study would seem to justify a favorable prognosis for their resolution. Within the past 20 years obvious progress has been made in dealing with such erstwhile problems as the lack of substantive quality in preparatory programs, the irrelevance of preparation to the realities of contemporary education, and the inattention to values in training for such a value-laden activity as administration. There is reason to suspect that today's problems will be met with equal success, and that progress through cooperation will continue to characterize preparation programs in educational administration.

REFERENCES

Bessent, Wailand, and Piele, Philip K. *The Use of Computers in Administrator Preparation.* Eugene: ERIC Clearinghouse on Educational Management, 1973.

Bruno, James E. *The Preparation of School Administrators in Qualitative Analysis.* Eugene: ERIC Clearinghouse on Educational Management, 1973.

Culbertson, Jack et al. *Preparing Educational Leaders for the Seventies.* Columbia: UCEA, 1969.

_____, eds. *Social Science Content for Preparing Educational Leaders.* Columbus: Merrill, 1973.

Cunningham, Luvern L., and Muth, Rod. NPEL—The National Program for Educational Leadership. *UCEA Newsletter,* 1972, *12,* 9-12.

Cresswell, Anthony M., and Goettel, Robert J. Rotating Internships and Situational Analysis. *UCEA Newsletter,* 1970, *11,* 7-9.

Farquhar, Robin H. Improving the Preparation of Educational Leaders. *Planning & Changing,* 1970, *1,* 58-70.

_____. *The Humanities in Preparing Educational Administrators.* Eugene: ERIC Clearinghouse on Educational Administration, 1970.

_____, and Martin, W. Michael. New Developments in the Preparation of Educational Leaders. *Phi Delta Kappan,* 1972, *54,* 26-30.

Flight, David. UMass Program Seeks Maximum Flexibility, Individualization, and Involvement. *UCEA Newsletter,* 1972, *13,* 10-12.

Horoschak, Peter P., and Cronin, Joseph M. *Innovative Strategies in Field Experiences for Preparing Administrators.* Eugene: ERIC Clearinghouse on Educational Management, 1973.

McCleary, Lloyd. The Development of a Competency-Based Individualized Program. *UCEA Newsletter,* 1972, *14,* 2-4.

McIntyre, Kenneth E. *Selection of Educational Administrators.* Columbus: UCEA, 1966.

Rose, Gale W. ILSA—An Individualized Learning System for Administrators. *UCEA Newsletter,* 1971, *12,* 17-20.

Stout, Robert T. *New Approaches to the Recruitment and Selection of Educational Administrators.* Eugene: ERIC Clearinghouse on Educational Management, 1973.

Thomas, A. Ross. The Commonwealth Council for Educational Administration: A New Centre for Educational Leadership. *The Journal of Educational Administration,* 1971, *9,* 128-134.

University Council for Educational Administration. *The Preparation and Certification of Educational Administrators: A UCEA Commission Report.* Columbua: UCEA, 1973.

Wynn, Richard. *Unconventional Methods and Materials for Preparing Educational Administrators.* Eugene: ERIC Clearinghouse on Educational Management, 1972.

ADDITIONAL RESOURCES

Baron, George, Cooper, Dan H., and Walker, William G., eds. *Educational Administration: International Perspectives.* Chicago: Rand McNally, 1969.

Culbertson, Jack A., and Hencley, Stephen P., eds. *Preparing Administrators: New Perspectives.* Columbus: UCEA, 1962.

Farquhar, Robin H. Current Issues and Trends in the Preparation of School Teachers and Administrators. *Improving School Effectiveness.* Princeton: ETS, 1973.

_____, and Piele, Philip K. *Preparing Educational Leaders: A Review of Recent Literature.* Eugene: ERIC Clearinghouse on

Educational Management, 1972.

Leu, Donald J., and Rudman, Herbert C., eds. *Preparation Programs for School Administrators: Common and Specialized Learnings.* East Lansing: Michigan State University, 1963.

Thomas, A. Ross, Farquhar, Robin H., and Taylor, William, eds. *Educational Administration in Australia and Abroad: Issues and Challenges.* Brisbane: University of Queensland Press, 1974.

MAJOR RELEVANT ORGANIZATIONS

American Association of School Administrators
1201 Sixteenth Street, N.W.
Washington, D.C. 20036

Center for the Advanced Study of Educational Administration
University of Oregon
Eugene, Oregon 97403

Commonwealth Council for Educational Administration
University of New England
Armidale, N.S.W. 2351
AUSTRALIA

ERIC Clearinghouse on Educational Management
University of Oregon
Eugene, Oregon 97403

National Conference of Professors of Educational Administration
c/o Wayne K. Hoy, Secretary-Treasurer
School of Education
Rutgers University
New Brunswick, New Jersey 08903

University Council for Educational Administration
29 West Woodruff Avenue
Columbus, Ohio 43210

48

TRAINING-IN-COMMON FOR EDUCATIONAL, PUBLIC AND BUSINESS ADMINISTRATION

by Erwin Miklos
Professor of Educational Administration
The University of Alberta
Edmonton, Alberta, Canada

Surveys of the literature and of existing practices confirm that the most useful approach to defining training-in-common is to include all formal arrangements for bringing prospective administrators for two or more different types of organizations together for some common learning experiences during at least part of their preparation programs. These formal arrangements might range all the way from a series of seminars to a completely integrated program of common experiences. A more restrictive definition would include only those programs in which there is an undifferentiated approach to preparing administrators for governmental, business, and educational organizations. Although this definition might be useful in outlining possible alternatives when designing programs, it proves to be far too limited for describing the current reality in administrator preparation.

The generic study of administration—administration qua administration—and training-in-common are recurring discussion topics in various specialized administrative fields. A considerable amount of attention was given to the concept within educational administration during the middle and late fifties; however, the interest did not persist. In recent years, the proposals for integrated or common programs appear to have come more frequently from those associated with public and business administration. The concept has sufficient continuing appeal to result in various training innovations: common seminars are organized, existing programs are changed to give them broadened scope, and some totally new types of programs are developed. Proposals for highly integrated programs have proven to be difficult to implement; in North America there are still fewer than five centers which attempt to offer in-common preparation for administrators.

PROPOSALS FOR TRAINING-IN-COMMON

The literature on this subject suggests that the proponents of common training for administrators accept at least two basic assumptions. A first assumption is that there are similarities of sufficient significance among administrative processes in different types of organizations to warrant a generalized approach to the preparation of researchers, students of administration, and practitioners. A related second assumption is that some body of content, a core, which will serve the needs of administrators in all fieds can and should be developed. Scholars who emphasize the unique characteristics of different types of organizations, and who deny the possibility of developing a useful general theory of administration, are not likely to be found among the proponents of common preparation programs.

Using these two basic assumptions—either explicitly or implicitly—as points of departure, the proponents of training-in-common may stress any one of a number of desirable ends which could be achieved through appropriately designed programs. These outcomes include upgraded preparation programs, more rapid progress toward developing a science of administration, and preparation which is in accord with emerging organizational realities.

The general upgrading of preparation programs presumably would result from having fields which are at different stages of development associate with each other. Hinderaker (1963) proposes that the differences in stages of development are the result of the particular histories of the specialties, of their location within the university, and of their different associations with basic disciplines. He suggests that business administration has the most to offer to, and educational administration the most to gain from, the general study of administration.

Critics of specialized programs suggest that fragmentation of the field has seriously impaired the development of the discipline of administrative studies. Litchfield (1956) has expressed disappointment in the state of the field, and indicates that we "make general theory more difficult of attainment by developing separate schools in these fields in our universities (p. 7)." Both Thompson (1956) and Snyder (1969) affirm that administrative studies have reached the stage at which scholars from various disciplines could and should collaborate systematically to accelerate the development of the discipline.

Another argument for training-in-common is that this is more realistic preparation for administrators, since they will be working in a complex network of interorganizational relationships (Waldo, 1968). Specialized preparation programs may tend to hinder the development of necessary communication among organizations; Snyder (1969) proposes that the basis for the communication must be laid during the preparation program. Closely related to this argument is the suggestion that organizations in different institutional areas are becoming more similar. Crozier (1968) expresses the opinion that "the role of the administrator in the public sector now seems much nearer to that of managers in the private sector (p. 8)" as a result of changing environmental and organizational characteristics. Culbertson (1969) also notes signs of the erosion of differences between public and private sectors, and suggests that a convergence of administrative activities and concerns is taking place.

Giving recognition in preparation programs to organizational interrelationships, and to the convergence of organizational characteristics, might also result in broadened career opportunities for administrators. Preparation which does not emphasize narrow specialization would make it easier for administrators to move from one type of organization to another.

These and other rationales for greater commonality in preparation programs lead to various strategies and proposals. At the lowest degree of integration is the single joint course, or seminar, which offers a beginning on a common core of experiences for administrator trainees in education, business, and public areas. A second possible strategy involves redefining the content of management studies in order to emphasize that which is common in the management of different types of organizations. Yoon (1968) proposes that management schools should "incorporate into their curricula courses oriented toward administrative problems and environments of nonbusiness enterprises (p. 286)." There are signs of a movement toward combining schools of business and public administration; the extent to which management schools will play a leadership role in such developments remains to be seen.

Writers who have a particular interest in the development of an administrative science tend to propose the establishment of centers which would work toward achieving that specific objective. One example of such a proposal, put forward by Culberson (1965), takes the form of a Graduate College of Public Policy and Administration. The staff of the college would be an interdisciplinary group, consisting of scholars from basic disciplines as well as from specialized areas of administration. A similar proposal has come from Caldwell (1968) who suggests that "the establishment of centers, institutes, or schools to facilitate multidisciplinary focus upon administrative phenomena (p. 217)" would be the best ap-

proach to designing an appropriate organization. Proposals such as these are reminiscent of the Administrative Science Center, which was initiated at the University of Pittsburgh in the mid-fifties.

The graduate school of administration concept is the one which combines all strategies and holds out the promise of achieving the broadest range of possible outcomes. Such a school would be designed to develop the generalized aspects of the study of administration, while at the same time allowing for the specialized needs of administrators in particular fields. Hinderaker (1963) was among the first to propose a graduate school of administration, "even though the few attempts which have been made to combine business and public administration have not, for varying reasons, been notably successful (p. 9)." More recently, the concept has been supported by Gordon (1967) and Caldwell (1968), among others.

TRAINING-IN-COMMON PRACTICES

A recent survey of practices (Miklos, 1972) resulted in the identification of schools or centers which have adopted various forms of the strategies that have been outlined above. The only strategy for which no current example was identified is the center for the study of administration. No new centers of this type appear to have been established since the Administrative Science Center at the University of Pittsburgh ceased to operate.

Several long-established schools of management now indicate that their programs have relevance for areas other than business administration. Among these schools are Carnegie-Mellon University, Yale University, and MIT's Alfred P. Sloan School of Management. The Carnegie-Mellon catalogue of 1971 mentions that it seeks to prepare students for general management in business and government. Yale (1971) describes an approach in which "teaching and research in Administrative Sciences are directed toward the development and application of behavioral/social sciences to the study of goal-seeking organizations (p. 1)." Similarly, the MIT program in 1971 was described as being designed to prepare people "to function effectively as managers in private and public organizations (p. 5)." Presumably, the general characteristics and flexibility of these programs permit designing individual programs appropriate for careers in different organizations.

A number of other schools have attempted to provide for common and differentiated preparation through core programs. The Graduate School of Business and Public Administration at Cornell University offers programs which lead to degrees in public, business, and health services administration. A major portion of formal study during the first year of two-year programs consists of courses common to the three areas; in the second year, studies tend to focus on the specialized field. The Faculty of Administrative Sciences at York University in Toronto offers a similar program, which has a common core for students of business and public administration.

One of the few programs which links education and business administration was developed at Stanford University. The Joint Program in Educational Administration is intended to serve the needs of both the generalist administrator who wishes to develop some competence in financial analysis, as well as the prospective specialist in this field (Kirst, 1970). To a large extent existing courses were used to build a three-year program in which candidates qualify for both the doctorate in education and the Master of Educational Administration degree, which is awarded jointly by the Graduate School of Business and the School of Education. This program appears to be a highly promising strategy for using resources from two areas in a manner which provides for both general and specific administrative components in a preparation program.

The survey by Miklos (1972) identified three different types of integrated approaches to administrator preparation: general administrative studies at the undergraduate level, a special purpose common program, and a generic approach to the training of administrators and the study of administration.

The program which leads to the Bachelor of Administration degree at the Regina Campus of the University of Saskatchewan is based on the assumption that administration is a universal phenomenon in all types of organizations (Bolstad, 1968). The developers of this program have rejected the narrowness of the traditional school of business administration, in favor of a program which attempts to prepare people for careers in business, education, health, government, and other types of organizations. Program components include the foundations for administrative studies, breadth in applied areas, and specialization in an area closely related to practice. Because institutional specialization and broader conceptions of administration are intentionally left to graduate schools, the content of the program tends to focus on technical-administrative tasks and skills.

Sangamon State University has developed a Master of Arts (Administration) program which is designed to serve part-time students employed in governmental, business, and educational organizations, as well as full-time students. About one-half of the courses required for the degree are drawn from a common core and the remainder from the major area of concentration—business, public, or school administration. Courses in the common core deal generally with human and decision-making aspects of administration; heavy emphasis is placed on the application of behavioral science concepts and management skills development.

The prototype for training-in-common may well be the program of the Graduate School of Administration at the Irvine Campus of the University of California. This program has been in operation since 1966, and is based on the concept proposed by Hinderaker (1963) and developed by those involved in the academic planning for the new campus. Snyder (1969) has summarized the assumptions, rationale, and initial features of the program; more recent development of the program has proceeded from that base. Specialization in one of the three institutional levels—education, business, or public—is possible at both the Master of Sciences (M.S.) and Doctor of Philosophy in Administration degree levels.

Although candidates are recruited from a variety of academic and professional areas, a background in specific areas is assumed or must be acquired. This background includes mathematics, statistics, economics, psychology or sociology, and political science. The Master of Science degree normally requires two full years of study, while the Ph.D. degree requires at least three, and probably four, years of full-time study after an undergraduate degree.

Course requirements and other activities at the M.S. level are intended to contribute to development of general knowledge, conceptual and empirical knowledge of organizations, specific knowledge about administration in a particular area, skill in management techniques, and a professional orientation. The basic requirements for the Ph.D. include extensive preparation in the core disciplines, expertise in areas of technical competence, and demonstrated competence in research. Individualized programs within the general framework permit preparation for roles ranging from corporate managers and federal executives to researchers and policy analysts.

A comparison of existing practices leads to the conclusion that there appears to be substantial agreement on what might be considered as common to all administrator preparation programs. The two broad areas of quantitative skills and human managerial skills appear to form the core of in-common administrative study. Much greater variation is evident in the extent to which content from specific institutional areas is included; presumably, the goals of particular programs, and the circumstances in which they are developed, determine this variation.

PROBLEMS AND ISSUES

Developments in training-in-common are spurred on by convincing proposals grounded in the rationales which were outlined above. The examples of the implementation of in-common preparation programs are evidence that the concept is accepted, and receives support, in various institutions. However, the relatively limited extent to which training-in-common has been implemented is evidence that there are some very real problems and unresolved issues which tend to retard development. The problems and issues have not received much attention in the literature, but some speculation about them is possible.

Perhaps the basic issue surrounding generic preparation programs concerns the content and scope of administrative studies. The concept of an administrative science holds much appeal for some scholars; however, the substance of the discipline has proven to be elusive. Although there have been attempts to carry out comparative studies of administration, to develop generalizations, and to theorize about administration in general, there is still no systematic body of thought on administration qua administration. The absence of this content forces the specialized areas to focus on improving themselves, and contributes further to the slow rate of progress in developing the science of administration.

Closely related to this problem is the continuing uncertainty about the relative importance of common and unique elements in the study of organizations generally, and of administration specifically. In spite of the rationales which have been presented, there are those who argue that the common features of organizations tend to be trivial, and not of high relevance to the work of administrators. It is proposed that what administrators really need to know is specific to each type of organization. Even though what is common to all might be recognized, it should not form the basis for administrator preparation programs. The debate is not enhanced by the absence of empirical research on these questions. Until there is more adequate research and an evaluation of programs, the uncertainties surrounding the generalizability of knowledge about organizations and administration will continue to impede developments.

Training-in-common is also retarded by various institutional and organizational barriers. Traditional disciplinary boundaries are highly resistant to change. Even strong proponents of generic approaches tend to weaken when the identities of their disciplines are threatened or their location within the university becomes uncertain. The proponents have also tended to be vocal within specialized fields, rather than across boundaries. Unless there is discussion which involves scholars and program planners from various fields, progress is likely to proceed slowly. There are numerous other specific institutionalized sources of resistance to change. The background preparation of professors, professional identifications, available instructional materials, and costs involved in program reorganization are among the factors which make change difficult if not unlikely. Outside of the training institutions, career patterns for administrators across institutional boundaries have not been established; consequently, there is little demand for preparation programs which might facilitate such movement.

These problems point to the areas which require further attention from scholars and researchers if the implementation of training-in-common is to be accelerated. Specifically, there is need for:

More emphasis on the cross-institutional study of organizations and administration

Greater communication about preparation programs across existing administrative disciplinary boundaries

More research about various aspects of administrator preparation

Evaluation research which focuses on programs attempting some form of training-in-common

The future of generic studies of administration and training-in-common will depend, in part, on progress in carrying out this needed research and analysis.

REFERENCES

Bolstad, W. G. A New Approach to Administrative Studies at the Undergraduate Level. Paper presented at the Annual Conference of the Canadian Schools of Business in Calgary, Alberta, 1968.

Caldwell, L. K. Methodology in the Theory of Public Administration. In *Theory and Practice of Public Administration: Scope, Objectives and Method*, edited by J. C. Charlesworth. Philadelphia: The American Academy of Political and Social Science, 1968, 205-222.

Carnegie-Mellon University. *Graduate School of Administration: Masters and Doctoral Programs 1972-73*. Pittsburgh: Carnegie-Mellon University, 1971.

Cornell University Announcements. *Graduate School of Business and Public Administration, 1971-72*. Ithaca: Cornell University, 1971.

Crozier, M. The Present Convergence of Public Administration and Large Private Enterprises, and Its Consequences, *International Social Science Journal*, 1968, *20*, 7-16.

Culbertson, J. A. Trends and Issues in the Development of a Science of Administration. In *Perspectives on Educational Administration and the Behavioral Sciences* by W. W. Charters, Jr. et al. Eugene: University of Oregon, 1965, 3-22.

———. Preparation of Special and General Educational Administrators. In *Common and Specialized Learning Competencies and Experiences for Special Education Administrators*, Proceedings of the National Conference, edited by C. Meisgeier and R. Sloat. Austin: The University of Texas, 1969, 72-83.

Gordon, P. J. Administrative Strategy for a Graduate School of Administration. *Academy of Management Journal*, 1967, *10*, 351-364.

Hinderaker, I. The Study of Administration: Interdisciplinary Dimensions. *The Western Political Quarterly*, 1963, *16*, 5-12.

Kirst, M. W. Stanford Joint Program in Educational Administration. *UCEA Newsletter*, 1970, *11* (also mimeographed).

Litchfield, E. H. Notes on the General Theory of Administration. *Administrative Science Quarterly*, 1956, *1*, 3-29.

Massachusetts Institute of Technology. *The Master's Program and The Doctoral Program, Alfred P. Sloan School of Management*. Cambridge: Massachusetts Institute of Technology, 1971.

Miklos, E. *Training-in-Common for Educational, Public and Business Administrators*. Columbus, Ohio: The University Council for Educational Administration, 1972.

Sangamon State University. Proposal for a New Unit of Instruction: Master of Arts Degree in Administration. Mimeographed. Springfield, Illinois: Sangamon State University, 1971.

Snyder, R. C. The Preparation of Educational Administrators: Some Problems Reconsidered in the Context of the Establishment of a New Graduate School of Administration. In *Educational Administration: International Perspectives*, edited by G. Baron, D. H. Cooper, and W. G. Walker. Chicago: Rand McNally and Company, 1969, 269-299.

Stanford University. The Joint Program in Educational Administration: Graduate School of Business—School of Education. Mimeographed. Stanford, California: Stanford University, 1970.

Thompson, J. D. On Building an Administrative Science. *Administrative Science Quarterly*, 1956, *7*, 102-111.

University of California. *Graduate School of Administration*. Irvine, California: University of California, 1970; Description of core courses in M.S. program, and M.S. program. Graduate School of Administration. Mimeographed, Fall, 1971.

University of Saskatchewan. *Administration Calendar 1971-72*. Regina: University of Saskatchewan, Regina Campus, 1971.

Waldo, D. Scope of the Theory of Public Administration. In *Theory and Practice of Public Administration: Scope, Objectives and Method*, edited by J. C. Charlesworth. Philadelphia: The American Academy of Political and Social Science, 1968, 1-26.

Yale University. *Administrative Sciences*. New Haven, Connecticut: Department of Administrative Sciences, Yale University, 1971.

Yoon, B. M. Management Discipline in a School of Administration: Reappraisal in the Public Service Perspective. *Academy of Management Journal*, 1968, *11*, 279-289.

York University. *Faculty of Administrative Sciences, Calendar 1971-72*. Downsview, Ontario: York University, 1971.

ADDITIONAL RESOURCES

Boulding, K. E. Evidence for an Administrative Science: A Review of the *Administrative Science Quarterly*, Volumes 1 and 2, *Administrative Science Quarterly*, 1958, *3*, 1-22.

Campbell, R. F. What Peculiarities in Educational Administration Make it a Special Case? In *Administrative Theory in Education*, edited by A. W. Halpin. Chicago: Midwest Administration Center, University of Chicago, 1958, 166-185.

Hilling, H. C. Public Administration: Study, Practice, Profession. *Public Administration Review*, 1966, *26*, 320-328.

Leu, D. J., and Rudman, H. C., eds. *Preparation Programs for School Administrators: Common and Specialized Learnings*. East Lansing: Michigan State University, 1963.

McNulty, N. G. *Training Managers: The International Guide*. New York: Harper and Row, 1969.

Ridley, F. F. Public Administration or Administrative Science. *Political Studies*, 1968, *16*, 441-445.

49

INSERVICE EDUCATION

by Kenneth A. Erickson
and
Robert L. Rose
Field Training and Service Bureau
College of Education
University of Oregon

"Inservice education" according to Carter Good (*Dictionary of Education*, 1973), means the efforts of administrators and supervisors to promote professional growth and involvement of educational personnel. Harris and Bessent (1969) indicate that inservice education is the collection of limited tasks which have a direct impact on the quality of instruction offered. The emphasis is on instruction rather than supervision of instruction. Some specific tasks which likely have this kind of impact on the quality of instruction are: (1) discussing and eventually solving indigenous problems; (2) presenting new ideas and methods of teaching; (3) keeping up-to-date on subject matter; (4) orienting new teachers and reorienting old teachers to new philosophies (Kilpatrick, 1967). Inservice education then, implies that every individual is both able to and wishes to improve his work, and will be receptive to intelligent efforts which provide opportunity for professional growth.

Similarly, the American Association of School Administrators sees inservice training of superintendents and principals as the strengthening of leadership potential at strategic times, so that school programs can be improved for students presently enrolled. "Bringing about changes in people is the focal point in the organization and operation of an inservice program." (Inservice Education..., AASA, 1963, p. 191).

PROBLEMS OF INSERVICE EDUCATION

Inservice education per se is no panacea. As with all other cultural tools, it can be effective or ineffective in achieving its goals, depending on a variety of factors. Several studies have reported staff reaction to typical inservice programs. For example, a survey of 165 teachers and 155 administrators made by O'Hanlon and Witters (1967) revealed the following:

Seventy-seven of the 165 teachers believed they had received no inservice experience of value.

Approximately 40 percent of the 155 administrators were unable to describe an effective inservice activity in the last three years.

Both experienced and new teachers thought the effectiveness of the programs would be improved if teachers played a larger role.

Both experienced and new teachers wanted help and generally wanted similar help.

A number of controversies and concerns which hamper effective inservice programs include:

Credit. It is difficult to design inservice programs which offer college credit because inservice usually is offered away from campus and does not meet a predetermined number of hours. Educators are accustomed to receiving a certain number of hours of credit for additional college training, which they can apply to a pay scale in their district. Thus, they tend to expect credit for most inservice activities, and may avoid committing themselves to programs which do not offer credit. If continuous education is to be part of the growth of professional educators, new ways should be found to relate these activities to the granting of credit.

Certification. Today there is much concern about competency-based certification in all areas of education, especially in certifying teachers and administrators. If competency means the ability to function adequately in the position, inservice training is a logical and flexible vehicle for the completion of certification requirements.

Board posture. School boards traditionally have not allocated any sizable amounts of money for inservice training. This is unfortunate, since public schools are a labor intensive industry. If a school board fails to appropriate maintenance and improvement dollars for the continuing education of its staff, it guarantees rapid obsolescence of the school's most important and expensive asset—its educators.

Boards of education must give stronger support to efficient inservice training. Training individuals while on the job demands both time and ample funds. Finding such resources is the responsibility of the employing organization. Local boards must realize that inservice activity will be beneficial to educators, and therefore to the children served.

Consultant mystique. There is a pervasive mystique that

suggests that a local consultant may be less effective than one who comes from a great distance. Many capable consultants who work outside their own state are seldom requested to work in their own area or region. Efforts should be made to identify and use local talent.

Overloading. If teachers and administrators are expected to participate in training programs at the end of a busy day or week, they'll inevitably suffer from work overload and not benefit fully from the training offered. It is necessary that school districts look upon inservice training as important for improving education programs for children, and therefore worthy of adequate allocations of time.

Inappropriate activities. Inservice education suffers if it consists primarily of speeches from program leaders and long periods of sitting and listening for participants. Learning experiences must be selected which require active involvement of participants. In planning such activities, genuine consideration of staff wishes should be sought. The planning of inservice programs only by the superintendent, school board, or principal may produce irrelevant programs with minimal teacher acceptability.

Results of training. One of the major stumbling blocks to the continuation of inservice education is the demand for immediate results. The *AASA Yearbook* on Inservice Education for School Administration (1963, p. 192) says in this regard that change is "imperceptible at the time of its making, yet it becomes part of total growth...." Results are evident not necessarily at the time of inservice activities, but as inservice participants put what they've learned to work in actual situations.

Evaluations. Rarely are careful evaluations of programs undertaken—either while the program is in progress or at its termination. This is essential if it is to be determined how well the participants' needs are being met.

Attitudes. One of the quickest ways to create uninterest in an activity is to announce that it will be part of an inservice program. This image has not been wholly undeserved, as many irrelevant programs have been forced upon professional educators under the guise of inservice training. Only by carrying out meaningful and dynamic inservice programs will this negative image be erased.

WHY INSERVICE EDUCATION?

If typical inservice education programs have been inadequate, and their reputation is precarious today, what justifies their continuance? As society changes there is a compelling need for our monolithic education structure to change. Yet the schools cannot change in ways that really matter unless educators themselves change. As a result, inservice, or continuing, education is the key to our schools being able to meet new challenges today.

Other reasons (summarized from Harris and Bessent, 1969) that suggest why inservice education is important include:

Preservice preparation of professional staff members rarely is completely comprehensive.

Social and educational change makes current professional practices, tools, and knowledge obsolete and/or ineffective in a very short period of time.

New understanding of the learning process makes the sharing of new and more effective pedagogical techniques mandatory. Effective changes in instructional practices require changes in people.

Morale can be uplifted and maintained by way of inservice education.

The decreasing amount of turnover of both teachers and administrators reduces the infusion of new ideas normally received as new personnel join a staff. Through inservice programs, new and vital ideas can be generated.

There are all kinds of precedents in other areas of American life which suggest that inservice training in education suffers from cultural lag. For example, medical centers throughout the United States offer postgraduate training programs for practicing doctors which range from several days to a month. The American Academy of General Practice requires postgraduate training each year if a doctor is to retain his membership in that organization. Most people would object to placing their health in the hands of a doctor who had not been back to school for 10 to 20 years. Yet, generally speaking, school systems are little concerned about placing the mental welfare of the nation's children in the hands of educators who do not regularly add to their efficiency through some form of continuing education.

PLANNING INSERVICE PROGRAMS

A number of factors should not be overlooked in the planning and development of inservice programs:

Involvement of participants in planning. There is a close relationship between involvement in an enterprise and the commitment to its goal. Yet teachers and other inservice participants all too often are never involved in choosing, planning, and executing their own inservice education activities. Those who plan continuing education programs should regularly communicate with those who will be the participants.

Staffing. To cut down unnecessary expenses, greater use should be made of qualified professional staff members within the state and/or the school system. There also is potential for follow-up that is not available when a person "blows in, blows off, and blows out." Only in cases where needed services are not available in the district or in the general area should consultants from a distance be utilized.

Finances. Offering financial assistance to staff members generally helps encourage their participation in inservice programs. School systems themselves must increasingly assume financial responsibility for inservice education.

Involvement of participants in the program. Brian Cane (1969) found in his study on inservice training that the learning methods which appeal most to teachers were those involving active participation. For example, three-quarters of the teachers would like to observe and discuss demonstrations of lessons or teaching activities of another teacher.

Inservice programs can and should place a great deal more emphasis on doing rather than listening. Teachers may participate in meaningful exercises, after which general principles can be deduced from the experience. Then practical applications of these principles can be made in the everyday work of the teachers or administrator. Role-playing activities and small group discussions also increase the participation, interest, and morale of educators. Demonstrations also can be given with children and/or teachers in realistic situations.

Presentation techniques. Activities such as small group discussion, role-playing, case studies, panels, discussion, and lecturettes, in addition to video and audio equipment, can be used to more efficiently and creatively present many kinds of subject matter. The selection of the medium or activity should be guided by the content and purpose of the particular program.

Inservice planning through professional associations. Professional associations should cooperate with either local districts or institutions of higher education in developing inservice programs. The professional associations should encourage their members to update training and improve the skills necessary to deal with changing demands on public schools today. Particularly those associations organized at the state level are in a position to react more quickly to changing training needs than are either local districts or training institutions. For example, the Oregon Association of School Executives (superintendents) has contracted with the Field Training and Service Bureau of the College of Education at the University of Oregon for several years to put on three different inservice education programs (fall, winter, and spring) in various parts of the state. Funds for this program came from membership fees paid by individual members, who may participate in the seminars at no additional cost.

Inservice programs from business and industry. Outstanding examples of continuing education programs, many of which may be adaptable to the needs of the public schools, have been designed by major industries. Appropriate portions of such programs should be evaluated for possible incorporation into educational inservice programs.

Evaluation. All continuing education programs should be evaluated through some formal questionnaire, during or at the end of the program session, and also several months after the session, to determine the practical value of the inservice training.

VARIETIES OF INSERVICE EDUCATION

A Research Summary of the National Educational Association (1966) has given the following types of inservice education:

Classes and courses

Institutes (a series of lectures designed to give as much information as possible in a short time, usually two or three days)

Conferences (gives participants an opportunity to question others and discuss ideas presented)

Workshops (usually a moderate-sized group, where each person has a problem to solve that is closely related to his field). A skilled consultant works with each group.

Staff meetings (may perform a useful inservice function, but generally used to acquaint teachers with administrative procedures and policies)

Committee work (five to seven members work on a problem that would be impossible for the whole school staff to tackle)

Professional reading (with the aid of professional library, study groups, book reviews, etc.)

Individual conferences (dependent on feeling of mutual understanding and support existing between teacher and supervisor)

Visits and demonstrations (opportunity to observe actual teaching techniques)

Work experience (usually in lines related to teaching fields)

Teacher exchanges

Cultural experiences (travel, lectures, concerts, plays, operas)

These above major types fall into two kinds of inservice programs. The short-term, one-shot program involves workshops or seminars concentrating on a particular topic for a short time (one day to several days). This kind of program is most appropriate when the purpose is to develop an awareness of new concepts, provide information which may be used by the participants in their job assignment, or serve a large number of individuals in a short length of time.

A second major kind of inservice involves long-range, concentrated effort, often within some organization like a school district. Such an effort may be planned over a long time (from several weeks to a year or more). The goal is to cause a change in behavior of individuals within the organization or in its environment. Sending an individual away to a workshop whose goal is to cause change within an organization may be relatively ineffective. In such cases an individual often returns highly motivated and enthusiastic about his experience, only to find it very difficult all by himself to effect a change in the working environment.

During the past five years the College of Education at the University of Oregon has provided both short-term and long-range inservice activities for administrators and teachers. The University's Field Training and Service Bureau, in conjunction with state professional associations and local school districts, has presented workshops and seminars of one-to-three-days' duration on a variety of topics in demand by the participating school personnel. The greatest success has been evident when a combination of activities have been included in one program—for example, some lecture, small group discussions, some role-playing, and problem-solving activities of a participatory nature. Fundamental to any success, however, has been a serious effort to identify participant needs in advance.

ADMINISTRATIVE INSERVICE PROGRAMS

Traditionally, most inservice education opportunities have been planned for teachers. Until recently, little has been done for inservice training of school administrators. The current need for administrator inservice programs has been amplified by critical problems for which traditional formal training has not prepared the school administrator. The challenges facing today's school administrator that were little known in the early 1960s include teacher militancy, student militancy, program budgeting, professional negotiations, teacher strikes, court orders regarding integration, minority studies, performance contracting, differentiated staffing, and accountability. Notable among recent efforts to meet the inservice needs of public school administrators has been the National Academy for School Executives—begun in January of 1969 by the American Association of School Administrators. Since then, the Academy has presented some 30 seminars annually, throughout the country. These have attracted more than 1,000 participants each year. In 1972, the National Association of Secondary School Principals, supported by a grant from the Danforth Foundation, established the National Institute for Secondary School Administrators. NISSA was modeled after the Academy program developed by AASA.

UNIVERSITIES AND INSERVICE EDUCATION

Relatively few universities have accepted their responsibility to develop programs of inservice training. The University of Oregon, through the Field Training and Service Bureau, College of Education, has designated one full-time staff person to develop inservice educational opportunities for school employes in Oregon. During the past three years, the Field Training and Service Bureau has made new inservice opportunities available to Oregon educators. A number of these programs vary from traditional inservice activities provided by institutions of higher education. The programs include:

The Externship in Educational Administration. The Externship is a year-long experience for practicing administrators. It involves statewide and regional meetings scheduled monthly during the school year. Participating Externs identify topics of concern to them and the Bureau develops the agenda and staffs the monthly program to cover these topics. Participants receive University credit toward their administrative certification. The program is currently in its fifth year of existence and has been judged very valuable by participants for two

major reasons:

Qualified and capable consultants deal with the current problems facing participants.

There is the opportunity for Externs to share with consultants and peers their operational problems carrying out specific administrative assignments.

Teacher Evaluation Workshop. Workshops have been set up for single districts or groups of districts to train principals in teacher evaluation techniques. Two unique factors have contributed highly to the workshops' success and acceptance:

Each workshop has been staffed by a college instructor and a competent practicing school administrator. This combination helps to establish credibility with the workshop participants.

Workshops have been scheduled throughout the school year so that instruction related to specific evaluation skills is provided at the times most needed by participants.

Communication and Organizational Development Programs. Two workshops designed to improve an administrative team's function have been carried out under the direction of the Field Training and Service Bureau. Both of these workshops use organizational development tools developed in the private sector and adapted to the public school administrative team.

Oregon School Study Council Visitations. On a quarterly basis, the Field Training and Service Bureau, acting in behalf of the Oregon School Study Council, plans conferences, tours, and visitations of exemplary school plants and programs for members of the Study Council and guests.

The Field Training and Service Bureau. This arm of the College of Education has had contractual arrangements with the Oregon Association of School Executives (superintendents), and an informal arrangement with the Oregon Association of Secondary School Administrators (secondary principals), to provide inservice opportunities for members of their respective organizations.

The relationship with the superintendents' association involves presenting a series of quarterly seminars throughout the state for OASA members. Topics for these seminars are chosen by an OASE committee, and the Bureau is responsible for selecting staff and developing agenda.

In cooperation with the secondary principals group, the Bureau has established a summer institute for members of their association. This involves one week of training dealing with topics chosen by the OASSA inservice committee.

Other schools and colleges are beginning to recognize the need for providing follow-up inservice to teachers or administrators on the job. Because of the resources available to institutions of higher education, colleges and universities are in a position to contribute to the continuous training needs of their graduates. Thus a direct tie can be made between the problems of the professional educator and the activities of college staff conducting inservice training. This two-way communication is beneficial and essential to both parties.

SUMMARY

Inservice education is most effective when it is simple and flexible; when planning is jointly shared by those who receive the service; then the program meets the needs of the local community being served; when the leadership personnel are capable of inspiring, refreshing, and strengthening the learners; when enough funds are available to implement potentially successful programs; and when the inservice program stands up well under the rigid test of usefulness. The ultimate test of usefulness is the extent to which it has brought about better schools—richer and more varied opportunities for children to learn and grow, stronger and better prepared teachers, more flexible school facilities, and improvement at every point along the way toward achievement of the educational program that is presently wanted and needed (AASA Yearbook, 1963).

REFERENCES

Cane, Brian. Inservice Training: A Study of Teachers' Views and Preferences. National Foundation for Educational Research in England and Wales, Slough, England. 1969.

Good, Carter V. *Dictionary of Education.* 1973.

Harris, Ben, and Bessent, W. *Inservice Education: A Guide to Better Practice.* Englewood Cliffs, New Jersey: Prentice Hall, Inc., 1969, p. 15.

Inservice Education for School Administration. American Association of School Administrators, Washington, D.C. 1963, p. 191.

Inservice Education for School Administrators. *American Association of School Administrators Yearbook.* 1963, pp. 191, 192, 197.

Inservice Education of Teachers. *National Education Association Research Summary.* 1966.

Kilpatrick, Gordon. *Inservice Education With Recommendations Concerning Its Implementation in American Junior Colleges,* El Camino College, California. 1967.

O'Hanlon, James, and Witters, Lee. Breakthrough. *Inservice Education For All Schools,* Nebraska State Department of Education. 1967.

50

INSERVICE EDUCATION OF VOCATIONAL AND TECHNICAL EDUCATORS: A RESULTS-ORIENTED APPROACH

by William Gary Ward
Assistant Professor of Vocational/Technical Education and Director of the Kansas Vocational/Technical Curriculum Materials Center
Kansas State College of Pittsburg
Pittsburg, Kansas

The inservice education of vocational and technical educators is conceptualized as the formalized activities conducted to change educators to meet the expectations held for them by the planners of such activities (Gibson, 1967; Thompson, 1967; Thelen, 1971). This approach includes Lefforge's (1971), who saw in-service as "an instrument for change," and Edmonds' (1966), who considered it a "vehicle for change"; yet, it is more usable because it specifies a measurable result (Dayton, 1970). That dependent measure is the degree of change by the educators toward the role-expectations held by the planners. The conceptualization is more realistic than Florida State Department of Education's, which stated, "in-service is to cause some, more or less, permanent changes in what a teacher knows, how he feels, or how he acts, that will have a positive effect on his pupils (Florida, 1971)." Their approach means the measuring of the effect of in-service by the changes in the educators' pupils. Effects on students may be the end purpose, but we are lacking in sound techniques to accurately measure a group which is once removed from the in-service. Research of this nature rarely shows any measurable difference.

The conceptualization includes the two elements identified by 35 vocational educators who had the responsibility for inservice education in ten states. The elements were the teacher (1) as a change agent in the ongoing process of social change, and (2) as an integrating agent in terms of values and philosophical concepts (Scarborough, 1966).

The conceptualization is not as naive as Jackson's (1971) statement, "in-service is a strategy for improving education." As Tyler (1971) has so candidly written, "since 1917 the majority of in-service training is done to assist educators in meeting certification requirements." In regard to teachers, this action, Tyler (1971) wrote,

had a deleterious effect both on the institutions and on the teacher enrolled. Instead of planning for summer courses that were new and exciting to the professor who offered them, colleges and universities sought to identify and offer old courses that teachers had not taken previously. The teachers came not with the purpose of getting new insight, understanding, and competence, but rather with the purpose of getting certificates renewed by patching up their backgrounds.

He noted that in the 1960s (we may add well into the 1970s), in-service revolved around implementation of national policies like disadvantaged, career education, and accountability. By the time educators were indoctrinated with an ideal, it was time to switch; one replacing another until educators became suspicious of adopting anything presented from the hierarchy. This built-in antiquity has generated an entire field of problems. It is little wonder that local in-service has become a negotiating issue between teacher organizations and school boards. Is it too improbable to forecast that it may become a negotiating issue between state boards and state-level teacher organizations?

The conceptualization appears defensible. It is a more accurate reflection of the reality of in-service than other reviewed definitions, and states that in-service is conducted to change the educator from what he is to what the planner wants him to be. That sets up the evaluative criteria: specify in the planning stages what changes are desired; then, in the evaluation stages, those changes can be measured. The validity of the measures will vary, but there are very few items which are unmeasurable. Yet, one must accept and deal with measures of varying confidence levels. This is a results-oriented approach, and requires justification.

RATIONALE FOR RESULTS ORIENTATION

The higher bureaucratic job positions which control the federal and state monies for in-service are staffed by at least three distinct groups. One is the gold-plated migrant workers who set out to cause vested change. Their changes are based on gaining personal prestige or instituting the policies of every changing political base. That statement is self-legitimizing via observation. This can be carried closer to home by specifying college and university professors, state department officials, and members of boards who establish certification requirements. Personal motivation may displace the purpose of vocational and technical education. Sincere vocational educators are the second group who control in-service. The statements calling for a results orientation will aid their attempts at improvement. Specificity in results, which is demanded during the planning stages, could cause a rejuvenation of faith with in-service. It allows a separation of short-term political ideologies from the improvement of educators' competencies. It also forces the third group, who have inservice responsibilities as extra additional duties, to do something. These individuals are either deadwood, who are either being carried by the organization or hold more prestigious jobs. To the latter type, inservice responsibilities are merely a way to have a portion of their salary paid by federal or state funds. Their main job demands their time and in-service is left to a low-potential subordinate or a secretary. A results-oriented approach, if mandated by funding agencies, would force a change in this problem.

This orientation does not have to come from a funding agency mandate. There are many competitive federal grants for in-service. A review of the *Federal Catalogue of Domestic Assistance,* updated yearly and available from the Superintendent of Documents, will yield more possibilities than most people have time to write. With the tenet of our times, a proposal which specifies measurable results, even when political persuasion is involved, is more acceptable than less quantifiable ideas. The competitiveness might cause applicants to move to a results orientation.

EDUCATORS' COMPETENCIES

It is this writer's finding that the concept of competency, the measurable areas of results, can be divided into at least five areas. The efficiency and effectiveness with which one performs a job, any job, is founded in (1) knowledge, (2) skill, (3) values, (4) organizational climate, and (5) experience. These are closer to a valid reflection of those items which effect competency than are the three aspects identified by Borg (1968)—curriculum content, professional knowledge, and classroom skills. The five components are clearer than the four forms of in-service Bush (1971) pursues. He classified these as expository exhortations, demonstration teaching, supervised trials, and analysis of performance.

The five components of competency require some defining. Each allows the purposes of any particular inservice activity to be classified, which leads to measurement. The first, knowledge, is defined as cognitive understanding. With teachers, there are at least two types: the technical knowledge of their teaching field, and knowledge of the science of learning and the art of teaching. Administrators need at least two types: knowledge of how to accomplish objectives via people; and knowledge of the bounding rules, regulations, and laws which establish the parameters of operation. With service support personnel (technicians, such as secretaries, accountants, maintenance people, and operators or monitors of machines, who are required to support the inner workings of any organization), there are also two types: knowledge in their technical field, and knowledge of the overall purpose of education and their organization.

Too often we neglect that latter item. We write off their high turnover in low-level jobs to other factors, and refer to them as nonprofessionals in official communiques. The organization will work only as well as these individuals fulfill their role expectations. There is also the other extreme with service support. Finance personnel and head secretaries make many educational decisions with only a folklore knowledge of education. Knowledge about education would assist both extremes in better accomplishing their jobs. The technician could feel more a part of the organization, and the high-input, low-educational-knowledge person might begin to realize that other factors, aside from financial rules and regulations, are considered in educational decision-making. We are tremendously out of balance with the service support group.

The second component of competency, skill, is defined as the vehicle through which knowledge is applied to one's work. Here again, we could take each of the groups and delimit the major skill areas. Given the specific position and particular job functions of an individual, it would be possible to list many of the exact skills and knowledges each needs.

The third component, values, requires explanation. We are familiar with the folklore statement, "he has the ability, but because of his attitude he just won't do it!" The difference this writer has with that statement is the word attitude. Attitudes have a poor reputation for measurement. Yet, by conceptualizing attitudes as parts of a larger value domain, a more accurate measurement is possible. Baier (1969) defined a value as a feeling "for or against an event or phenomenon, based on a belief that it benefits or penalizes some individual, group, or institution." It allows values to be measured via behavior. A review of Super's (1957, 1970) activities with work values documents that values can be measured. Sciara (1972) documented that teachers' values toward in-service are the strategic factor in whether or not in-service is effective. The major point is that competence requires certain work values; and we rarely do anything but complain about this area. Some of the in-service in the 1970s attempted to instill new values, like career education. Specificity in the planning stages which lists desired behavioral outcomes could be, as justified earlier, beneficial.

The fourth component, organizational climate, is defined as those organizational constraints which effect the ability of role-incumbents to fulfill their job expectations. Some organizations, because of the placement of people in the hierarchy, or because of rules and regulations, will not allow one to perform well. Management by Objectives workshops are examples of in-service to correct problems in this area. University courses in management for administrators' certificates are also examples.

The last component is experience. It welds all other components together, and is defined as participation in events. It speaks to the feedback from the application of knowledge, via skills, to events. This invariably leads to modification of techniques and changes in knowledge. The worth of experience is possibly the least measurable of all the components! Yet, the changes in behavior can be monitored.

These five components, and perhaps others, allow a classification system for competency which sets up areas of measurement and allows specificity in desired results. The application of this system to recent inservice programs allows a critique of its worth and a trial application of a results orientation. This writer selected randomly 14 in-service articles from over 80 reviewed for this article. The purpose of each was classifiable into one or more of the areas of competency. The authors were: Thurber (1971), Syhlman (1971), Dietz (1971), Davis and Trout (1971), MacAuthor (1970), Ritter (1972), Miller (1969), Miller and Valentine (1968), Reed and Wright (1968), Matthews (1968), Reynolds (1967), Hull (1967), Parsons (1971), and Shibata and Roberson (1969). All were classifiable, but only one, Parsons' (1971), was results-oriented. How the others justified the expenditures is unknown to this writer. Additional reports which would allow the reader an opportunity for classification are Doherty (1967), O'Hanlon and Witters (1967), Bessent (1967), Dagne (1968), and Crockett

et al. (1968).

MEASUREMENT OF RESULTS

Given the nonrandomness of the participants of most inservice programs, "textbook researchers" might immediately disdain accepting the results orientation. However, many practitioners in behavioral research should embrace the approach. In reality it bends the textbook experimental design and one may desire to call this approach a para- or quasi-experimental design. However, given the reality of the situation, a results orientation must be developed. See Dayton (1970), Van Dalen (1966), Kerlinger (1973), and Popham (1973) for research designs.

For measurement techniques see Parsons (1971), Ward (1973), Shibata and Roberson (1969), and Johnsen (1969). Video tape, along with the concept of microteaching, offers a measurement method. See Cooper and Allen (1971) for its history of development, Allen (1967) for a description, and Borg (1968) for its rationale. An implementation manual has been developed by Crandall and Shibata (1969). Also check Doty and Cotrell (1971); Acheson (1964), Aubertine (1964), Blanke (1967), Bruner (1964), Bush and Allen (1964), Cotrell and Doty (1971), Cruickshank (1967), Dixon (1967), Golhar (1969), McNemar (1972), Olivero (1964), Winer (1962), King (1970), and Bosley and Wigress (1967). The self-analysis aspect of video tape is a way of measurement. It also appears that a videotape self-analysis may not be superior to student or peer critique of teaching competency. For recording instruments see Rosenshine (1970).

Television in its various forms can also be used as a delivery system, but its cost tends to be prohibitive (Lehmann, 1971). King (1970) found it similar in effects to a live teacher. Wyoming University (1970) used cable television to reach rural areas. Television as a delivery and recording device has potential yet it is expensive. Video tape does offer a unique way for teachers to critique themselves and, coupled with Rosenshine's (1971) list of instrumentation, allows an avenue for self-instruction (Fischer, 1971).

SUMMARY

This writer has stressed the need, may we call it a demand, for a results orientation. Given, on one side, the past lack of adjustment of educators' time, attitude, and pay, and on the other a drive for autonomous educator negotiating groups, there are few alternatives (NEA, 1966; Bush, 1971; Meade, 1971; Sorohan and Colbert, 1966; Rubin, 1971). It is not that major a forecast to state that soon educators will be selecting the in-service they desire. The past lack of rigor has discouraged many (Bush, 1971). Alternatives to this educator's approach are presented by Massachusetts (1970), Monahan and Miller (1970), and Knoll and Stephens (1968). On the supporting side are Brantner (1964); Pyatte (1972); Brown (1968); Roberson (1969); Ohio (1970); and Bauman et al. (1970). The very near future has been programmed —educators, the practitioners, will decide what training they require (Boulding, 1964; Ayres, 1969; Clark, 1973; Drucker, 1968; and Toffler, 1970).

REFERENCES

Acheson, K. A. *The Effects of Feedback from Television Recordings and Three Types of Supervisory Treatment on Selected Teacher Behavior.* Unpublished doctoral dissertation, Stanford University, 1964.

Allen, Dwight W. *Micro-Teaching, A Description.* ERIC (Microfiche ED 019 224), 1967.

Aubertine, H. E. *An Experiment in the Set Induction Process and Its Application in Teaching.* Unpublished doctoral dissertation, Stanford University, 1964.

Ayres, Robert U. *Technological Forecasting and Long-Range Planning.* New York: McGraw-Hill Book Company, 1969.

Baier, Kurt, and Rescher, Nicholas. *Values and the Future.* New York: The Free Press, 1969.

Bauman, Daniel et al. *A Guide to the Instruments Developed for Evaluation of In-Service Institutes.* ERIC (Microfiche ED 011 591), 1967.

Bessent, E. W. et al. *Designs for In-Service Education.* Austin: Texas University. ERIC (Microfiche ED 011 591), 1967.

Blanke, V. E. *Reporting on MOREL.* Michigan-Ohio Regional Education Laboratories, 1967.

Borg, Walter R. *The Minicourse: Rationale and Uses in the In-Service Education of Teachers.* Berkeley: Far West Lab for Educational Research and Development. ERIC (Microfiche ED 018 978), 1967.

Bosley, Howard E., and Wigress, Harold E. *Television and Related Media in Teacher Education, Some Exemplary Practices.* Baltimore: Multi-State Teacher Education Project. ERIC (Microfiche ED 018 978), 1967.

Boulding, Kenneth E. *The Meaning of the 20th Century: The Great Transition.* New York: Harper and Row, 1964.

Brantner, S. T. *Trade and Technical Teachers' Opinions on In-Service Education.* University Park: Penn State University, ERIC (Microfiche ED 016 044), 1964.

Brown, William J., Jr. *The Effect of In-Service Education and Resource Unit Components on Teacher and Student Learning.* Raleigh, N.C.: Research Coordinating Unit. ERIC (Microfiche ED 042 885), 1968.

Bruner, J. S. Some Theorems in Instructions. *Theories of Learning and Instruction,* E. R. Hilgard, ed. Chicago: National Society for the Study of Education, 1964, pp. 316-317.

Bush, Robert N. Curriculum-Proof Teachers. *Improving In-Service Education,* Louis Rubin, ed. Boston: Allyn and Bacon, Inc., 1971, pp. 37-70.

_____, and Allen, D. W. Micro-Teaching: Controlled Practices in the Training of Teachers. Paper presented at the Santa Barbara Conference on Teacher Education of the Ford Foundation, April 30, 1964.

Clarke, Arthur C. *Profiles of the Future: An Inquiry into the Limits of the Possible.* New York: Harper and Row, 1973.

Cooper, James M. et al. *Microteaching: Selected Papers.* Washington, D.C.: National Center for Educational Communications. ERIC (Microfiche ED 055 960), 1971, pp. 8-23.

Cotrell, C. J., and Doty C. R. *Assessment of Micro-Teaching and Video Recording in Vocational and Technical Teacher Education: Phases I-III.* Columbus: Center for Vocational and Technical Education, Ohio State University, 1971.

Crandall, Curtis R., and Shibata, Kenneth E. *A Guide to Implementing the Video In-Service Program.* Milford, Nebraska: Nebraska Educational Service Unit 6. ERIC (Microfiche ED 054 055), 1969.

Crockett, Walter H. et al. *Teachers as Students: Report on the Experienced Teacher Fellowship Program.* Milford, Nebraska:

Nebraska Educational Service Unit 6. ERIC (Microfiche ED 054 055), 1969.

Cruickshool, D. R. *The Longacre School: A Simulated Laboratory for the Study of Teaching.* Knoxville: University of Tennessee, 1967.

Dagne, Frank A. *In-Service Education for Teachers.* Niles, Illinois: East Maine School District Number 63. ERIC (Microfiche 031 456), 1968.

Davis, J. Clark, and Trout, Len L. *Improving Preparation of Professional Personnel for Vocational Education in Metropolitan Areas.* Reno: Nevada University. ERIC (Microfiche ED 055 241 and 062 523), 1971.

Dayton, C. Mitchell. *The Design of Educational Experiments.* New York: McGraw-Hill, 1970.

Dietz, Thomas S. *An Institute Program Designed to Train Vocational Education and Academic Teachers for the Development of Performance Objectives.* Washington, D.C.: Office of Educational Bureau of Research. ERIC (Microfiche ED 055 037), 1971.

Dixon, W. J. *Biomedical Computer Program.* Los Angeles: University of California Press, 1967.

Doherty, Victor W. The Carnegie Professional Growth Program, An Experiment in the In-Service Education of Teachers. *Journal of Teacher Education.* Vol. 18 (Fall, 1967), pp. 261-268. ERIC (Microfiche ED 020 162).

Doty, Charles R., and Cotrell, Calvin J. *Feedback Techniques in In-Service Methods Courses.* Columbus: Center for Vocational and Technical Education, Ohio State University. ERIC (Microfiche ED 057 206), 1971.

Drucker, Peter F. *The Age of Discontinuity.* New York: Harper and Row, 1968.

Edmonds, Fred. *In-Service Teacher Education: Crucial Process in Educational Change.* Lexington: University of Kentucky, College of Education. ERIC (Microfiche ED 031 424), 1966.

Fischer, Louis. In-Service Education. In *Improving In-Service Education,* Louis Rubin, ed. Boston: Allyn and Bacon, Inc., 1971, pp. 227-243.

Florida State Department of Education. *Individualized In-Service Teacher Education: A Performance-Based Module.* Tallahassee: Florida State Department of Education. ERIC (Microfiche ED 055 049), 1967.

Gibson, Dorothy. *In-Service Education—Perspectives for Educators.* ERIC (Microfiche ED 015 161), 1967.

Golhar, M. B. *Questionnaire Analysis, Weighted Scoring and/or T-Tests.* Columbus: Ohio State University, 1969.

Hull, William L. et al. *Training Institute to Upgrade Teachers of Vocational Agriculture in Distributive Education and Supervised Training in Off-Farm Agricultural Occupations,* Final Report. Stillwater: Oklahoma State University. ERIC (Microfiche ED 016 846), 1967.

Jackson, Philip W. Old Dogs and New Tricks. In *Improving In-Service Education,* Louis Rubin, ed. Boston: Allyn and Bacon, Inc., 1971, pp. 19-36.

Johnsen, Mel. *Model Program for Teacher In-Service Training: Emphasizing the Affective Dimension.* Arlington Heights, Ill.: Elk Grove Training and Development Center. ERIC (Microfiche ED 034 747), 1969.

Kerlinger, Fred N. *Foundations of Behavioral Research.* New York: Holt, Rinehart and Winston, Inc., 1973.

King, Franklin J. *Feasibility of Incorporating Telecture in Presenting a Teacher Methods Course to Vocational Teachers.* Unpublished doctoral dissertation, University of Missouri, 1970.

Knoll, Peter F., Jr., and Stephens, John F. In-Service Training for Vocational Teachers in Utah. Salt Lake City: Research Coordinating Unit, 1300 University Club Building. ERIC (Microfiche ED 021 128), 1968.

Lefforge, Orland S. *In-Service Training as an Instrument for Change.* Gainesville: University of Florida. ERIC (Microfiche ED 055 577), 1971.

Lehmann, Phyllis E. *Teacher Training Takes to the Road. Mobile Van, Computers Add Convenience and Quality to Continuing Education.* University Park, Pennsylvania State University. ERIC (Microfiche ED 054 063), 1971

MacAuthor, Earl W. *Improving Vocational Education in Post-High School Institutes.* Delhi, New York: State University of New York Agricultural and Technical College. ERIC (Microfiche ED 038 541), 1970.

Massachusetts University School of Education. *In-Service Training Design Simulation.* Amherst: Massachusetts University School of Education. ERIC (Microfiche ED 051 091), 1970.

Mathews, Mildred. *Leadership Development Institute for Vocational and Technical Personnel in the Western States: Final Report.* Corvallis: Oregon State University. ERIC (Microfiche ED 042 037), 1968.

Meade, Edward J., Jr. No Health In Us. In *Improving In-Service Education,* Louis Rubin, ed. Boston: Allyn and Bacon, Inc., 1971, pp. 211-226.

McNemar, Q. *Psychological Statistics.* New York: John Wiley and Sons, Inc., 1962.

Miller, A. J., and Valentine, I. E. *National Program Development Institutes in Technical Education.* Columbus: Center for Vocational and Technical Education, Ohio State University. ERIC (Microfiche ED 021 069), 1968.

Monahan, William G., and Miller, Howard E. *Planning and Developing In-Service Education.* Iowa City: Iowa University Center for Research in School Administration. ERIC (Microfiche ED 045 611), 1970.

NEA. *In Service Education of Teachers; Research Summary 1966.* Washington, D.C.: National Education Association. ERIC (Microfiche ED 048 684), 1970.

O'Hanlon, James O., and Witters, Lee A. Breakthrough. *In-Service Education for All Schools.* Lincoln: Nebraska State Department of Education. ERIC (Microfiche ED 015 147), 1967.

Ohio State Department of Education. *Evaluation Report of the Workshop for Vocational and Special Education Teachers,* Cincinnati Public Schools, 1969-1970. Columbus: Ohio State Department of Education. ERIC (Microfiche ED 048 684), 1970.

Olivero, J. L. *Video Recording as a Substitute for Live Observations in Teacher Education.* Unpublished doctoral dissertation. Stanford University, 1964.

Parsons, Theodore W. *Guided Self-Analysis Professional Development Systems. Education Series: Overview.* ERIC (Microfiche ED 052 151), 1971.

Popham, W. James. *Educational Statistics.* New York: Harper and Row, 1973.

Pyatte, Jeff A. *The Effectiveness of Performance Based Training Modules on Planning and Presenting.* Pensacola: University of West Florida. ERIC (Microfiche ED 062 299), 1972.

Reed, Jack C., and Wright, Lucille B. *In-Service Education of Office Occupations Teacher-Coordinators.* Cedar Falls: University of Northern Iowa. ERIC (Microfiche ED 021 137), 1968.

Reynolds, Robert R. *In-Service Training in Computer Assisted Instruction for Vocational Teachers: Final Report.* Providence, Rhode Island: Providence College. ERIC (Microfiche ED 023 918), 1967.

Ritter, Ken. *A One Year Follow-Up Evaluation of a Training Program for Vocational and Technical Education Administrators.* Stillwater: Oklahoma State University, 1972.

Roberson, E. Wayne. *Effects of Teacher In-Service on Instruction and Learning.* Tucson: EPIC Evaluation Center. ERIC (Microfiche ED 037 383), 1969.

Rosenshine, Barak. Evaluation of Instruction. *Review of Educational Research,* Vol. 40, No. 2 (April 1970), pp. 279-300.

Rubin, Louis J., ed. *Improving In-Service Education.* Boston: Allyn and Bacon, Inc., 1971.

Scarborough, C. Cayce. *Regional Seminar for State Leaders in Vocational Education.* Raleigh, North Carolina: Center for Occupational Education. ERIC (Microfiche ED 015 264), 1966.

Sciara, Frank J. et al. *Report on the Triple I Project, An Individualized In-Service Teacher Education Program.* Muncie: Ball State University. ERIC (Microfiche ED 059 162), 1972.

Shibata, Kenneth, and Roberson, E. Wayne. *V.I.P. Video In-Service Program; Teacher Guide for Self-Appraisal.* Washington, D.C.: Office of Education, ERIC (Microfiche ED 029 824), 1969.

Sorohan, Lawrence J., and Colbert, W. P. A Proposed Approach to Individualized Professional Growth. *Remaking the World of the Career Teacher.* Washington, D.C.: National Commission on Teacher Education and Professional Standards. ERIC (Microfiche ED 031 419), 1966, pp. 161-164.

Super, Donald E. *The Psychology of Careers.* New York: Harper and Brothers, 1967.

_____. *Work Value Inventory.* Boston: Houghton-Mifflin Company, 1970.

Syhlman, Bill D. *The Professional Internship Exchange Program for Vocational Education, 1970-71.* Olympic, Washington: State Coordinating Council for Occupational Education. ERIC (Microfiche ED 054 377), 1971.

Thelen, Herbert A. A Cultural Approach to In-Service Teacher Training. In *Improving In-Service Education,* Louis Rubin, ed. Boston: Allyn and Bacon, Inc., 1971, pp. 71-104.

Thompson, James D. *Organizations in Action.* New York: McGraw-Hill Book Company, 1967.

Thurber, John C. *Individualized In-Service Teacher Education (Project In-Step) Evaluation Report, Phase III.* Boynton Beach, Florida: Palm Beach County Board of Public Instruction. ERIC (Microfiche ED 059 161), 1971.

Toffler, Alvin. *Future Shock.* New York: Random House, 1970.

Tyler, Ralph W. In-Service Education of Teachers. In *Improving In-Service Education,* Louis Rubin, ed. Boston: Allyn and Bacon, Inc., 1971, pp. 5-17.

Van Dalen, Deobold B. *Understanding Educational Research: An Introduction.* New York: McGraw-Hill Book Company, 1966.

Ward, William G. *Conducting Evaluation Within a State: Information for State Leaders.* Clearinghouse on Vocational and Technical Education, The Ohio State University, Information Series No. 73. ERIC (Microfiche VT 020 268), 1973.

Winer, B. J. *Statistical Principles in Experimental Design.* New York: McGraw-Hill Book Company, 1962.

Wyoming University College of Education. *In Service Programs for Wyoming Education Via Video-VERB.* Laramie: Wyoming University College of Education. ERIC (Microfiche ED 051 115), 1970.

51

MINICOURSES: A MICROTEACHING APPROACH TO TEACHER TRAINING

by Beatrice A. Ward
Associate Laboratory Director
and
Fred S. Rosenau
Far West Laboratory for Educational Research
and Development
San Francisco, California

The Minicourses developed by the Far West Laboratory for Educational Research and Development, San Francisco, are self-contained, self-instructional training packages that enable preservice and inservice teaching personnel to learn specific classroom skills without leaving the buildings in which they work. Seven Minicourses are already available nationally, through The Macmillan Company, each having been rigorously field tested during development. They include:

Minicourse 1—Effective Questioning: Elementary Level
Skills to increase pupil involvement in class discussions (pausing, redirection, prompting, etc.) and to reduce "teacher talk" and other "bad habits."

Minicourse 2—Developing Children's Oral Language
Strategies to help young children speak and think with more precision and flexibility (extend phrases to sentences, model new language patterns, use positional language in context, etc.).

Minicourse 5—Individualizing Instruction in Mathematics
Skills to use in tutoring—diagnosis, demonstration, evaluation, and practice. Compatible with new math curricula and with individualized programs.

Minicourse 8—Organizing Independent Learning: Primary Level
Skills to prepare young children (K-3) to work independently, so the teacher can be freed to work uninterruptedly with small groups or individual children; also to teach pupils to solve problems and wait for delayed teacher response.

Minicourse 9—Higher Cognitive Questioning: Intermediate and Advanced
Skills that parallel Bloom's taxonomy—asking higher order questions (especially analysis, synthesis, and evaluation) and evaluating the quality of pupil responses.

Minicourse 15—Organizing Independent Learning: Intermediate Level
Skills to establish an instructional program in which pupils assume increasing responsibility for planning and evaluating their learning experiences. Provides strategies for assessing pupils' levels of independence, establishing performance contracts based upon clear statements of objectives and work plans, and introducing independent learning in the classroom.

Minicourse 18—Teaching Reading as Decoding
Skills to determine where pupils are in the decoding process, to present decoding skills to pupils, to respond to pupil errors, evaluate lessons, and guide toward independence in decoding.

The Minicourse model has evolved from the microteaching studies conducted at the Stanford Center for Research and Development in Teaching (Borg et al., 1970). The Laboratory shaped that technological research so that it became the foundation of these new teacher-training packages that rely on individual videotape feedback.

By using school audiovisual equipment and Minicourse instructional materials, a teacher can learn or sharpen skills required for more effective pupil learning. The trainee working with a Minicourse spends about three hours a week for approximately five weeks, during regular school hours, planning his microteaching lesson, videotaping himself in a special small room near the classroom, and evaluating on video tape his own performance.

Each Minicourse presents specific, observable, precisely defined teaching skills. Model performances are shown on color film. Continual practice sessions provide immediate videotape (or audiotape) feedback. The learning sequence is study, observe, practice, and refine; that is, read about a cluster of skills, view illustrations and models on film, plan and conduct microteach lessons to apply the skills, evaluate use of skills, replan and conduct another lesson, and evaluate the skills in the "reteach" lesson.

To elaborate, first the trainee reads in his teacher handbook a section that explains one to three specific teaching skills (e.g., how to evoke higher cognitive responses from pupils). Then he observes, on film, examples that describe and illustrate the skills. Next he sees on film a model lesson that provides a clear performance model, showing each skill being used in an instructional context and guiding the trainee to recognize and discriminate the behavior as it occurs. Prompt feedback is provided in the same films.

Next the trainee practices the skills in a microteaching situation (no more than ten minutes) with a handful of pupils from his own classroom. This practice session is recorded on video tape for later feedback and evaluation, using special forms provided in the handbook. Finally, with another small group of pupils, the trainee refines his use of the skill(s) in a "reteach" lesson, again using the video tape available for his use during training. After the reteach lesson, the trainee once more evaluates his performance on video (or audio) tape. Each Minicourse includes four to six sequences of this type.

A single, complete Minicourse training package will contain four or more color films, a coordinator handbook, a teacher handbook for each participant, follow-up activities, evaluation forms, and research documentation. Every Minicourse released by the Laboratory has successfully completed a full R&D development cycle that includes at least three cycles of field testing and revision (Hemphill and Rosenau, 1972). As a result, the Laboratory has amassed a significant body of formative and evaluative data demonstrating that both preservice and inservice trainees readily learn the skills and retain them permanently in their teaching repertoire (Borg et al., 1970).

Minicourses, though a rather new development in teacher training, are already widely used by preservice trainers, by inservice supervisors, and by Teacher Corps centers (Ward et al., 1972). Because each Minicourse is priced at $1,000 or more, the packages are best suited to training institutions and to school districts that can efficiently shape their programs to enable groups of teachers to move through the instructional sequences under the guidance of an experienced coordinator. With repeated cycles of six to ten trainees using a single videotape system (camera, monitor, recorder, and microphone) in one microteaching room, the cost-per-trainee can be kept quite modest (Hutchins et al., 1971).

The role of the coordinator is fully defined in the coordinator handbook for each Minicourse. He keeps the teachers on a designated schedule for individual and group use of films and videotape (or audiotape) equipment, and sees that the materials move along to another site as soon as the first group of trainees has completed one sequence. However, neither the coordinator nor any administrator evaluates the trainee's video tapes unless invited to do so; in this way, trainees learn in a totally nonthreatening atmosphere. In actual practice, teachers tend to share their own videotaped performances in small-group critiquing sessions. The coordinator also helps the teachers learn to operate the videotape equipment, if they happen to be neophytes in its operation, and protects them from unwanted visitors while they are microteaching—another way of reassuring trainees that the experience will be comfortable and nonthreatening. A suitable coordinator may be chosen from the ranks of administrators in school districts, or from AV specialists or teacher supervisors at training institutions. Often the coordinator is able to arrange inservice (or preservice) credit from cooperating higher-education institutions.

Performance data are collected by the Laboratory for each Minicourse during development. This applied research demonstrates to what extent each Minicourse makes specific changes in teaching behavior. For example, in the case of Minicourse 1, mean scores for the main field test showed that the length of pupil responses in words was increased from 5.63 to 11.78 for pupils whose teachers completed the training. Further, teachers reduced the number of times they repeated pupil answers from 30.68 to 4.36, and (most important of all) the percentage of teacher talk declined from 51.64 to 27.75.

The Minicourse development group had anticipated a need for a refresher course, but this precaution proved to be unfounded. For the main field test sample, when the time for restimulation arrived (4 months later) the teachers proved to have retained the skills at the level attained after completing the course, or, in some cases,

to have internalized the skills and to have been able to demonstrate them at an even higher level (Borg et al., 1970). A follow-up study indicated posttraining use of the skills also was maintained by the teachers three years later (Borg, 1972).

Other field test results have proved equally encouraging. For example, the data on Minicourse 5 have been summarized in a technical report reprinted in Hemphill and Rosenau (1972). Other field test reports are on file at the Laboratory, and/or are summarized in teacher handbooks or coordinator handbooks for the individual courses.

The major current controversy regarding the Minicourse method of teacher training revolves around the question as to whether the special skills learned in these packages actually make a difference in pupil outcomes. Under the aegis of the National Institute of Education (NIE), the teacher education division of the Laboratory has launched a three-year research program to examine to what extent teacher behaviors do affect pupil outcomes. Heretofore, the Laboratory staff has assumed, on the basis of the published research of others, that if teachers exhibit in their classrooms certain behaviors (e.g., asking higher cognitive questions, individualizing instruction, tutoring in math, etc.), their pupils will learn more than they would have in the classrooms of teachers who did not possess and use these clusters of skills. Now data are being collected in several careful studies which will determine the accuracy of these earlier assumptions.

Meanwhile, Minicourse development and field testing are being held in abeyance, since all available resources have been targeted for applied research on pupil outcomes. Several Minicourses have been shelved following some phases of testing; others may one day inch toward completion under other auspices. Researchers are encouraged by the Laboratory to use any of the fully developed and available packages to carry out their own research studies on topics of local interest or concern. Work with Teacher Corps sites (Ward et al., 1972) is only one example of this type of synergistic activity. Laboratory staff can help with the planning and design of such studies, though only on a consultancy basis.

Another under-researched domain is the question of how best to install and utilize Minicourses in school districts and training institutions. The Laboratory has been unable to obtain funds to carry out monitoring studies or to evaluate longitudinal use of these training packages. There is a pressing need for a case-study evaluation of sites where multiple Minicourses are available and are being continually used. What is the optimum mode of utilization? How many courses can an individual trainee profitably work through? Is there a desirable sequence when more than one Minicourse is administered? What techniques have proved most useful in reducing the number of substitute teachers required to "cover" the classrooms of elementary-school teachers who must leave their pupils briefly to microteach? These—and other—questions could well be investigated by teacher trainers or university-based researchers outside the Laboratory, with or without NIE support.

REFERENCES

Borg, Walter R. et al. *The Minicourse: A Microteaching Approach to Teacher Education.* Beverly Hills, California: Macmillan Educational Services, 1970.

_____. The Minicourse as a Vehicle for Changing Teacher Behavior: A Three-Year Follow-Up. *Journal of Educational Psychology,* 1972, *63,* 572-579.

Hemphill, John K., Rosenau, Fred S. *Educational Development: A New Discipline for Self-Renewal.* Eugene, Oregon: Center for the Advanced Study of Educational Administration, 1972.

Hutchins, C. L. et al. *Minicourses Work.* Washington, D.C.: Superintendent of Documents, 1971.

Ward, Beatrice A. et al. *The Minicourse in Teacher Education.* Washington, D.C.: Teacher Corps, U.S. Office of Education, 1972.

PART V

STUDENTS AND PARENTS

52

STUDENT RIGHTS AND INVOLVEMENT

by Ronald Armstrong
Assistant Professor, Sociology
University of South Florida
St. Petersburg, Florida

Student Rights refers to the specific freedoms and responsibilities granted to public school students by the Constitution of the United States of America. It refers also to the freedoms and responsibilities of public school officials as their actions impinge upon the constitutionally granted rights of students.

Student Involvement refers to the participation of students in decision-making processes relating to the total educational process, including the specific fields of facilities planning, curriculum and instruction, student government, student discipline, and student activities.

STUDENT RIGHTS

In spite of the fact that the Constitution of the United States was written and adopted two centuries ago, much controversy still rages over its interpretation, the extent of its protection to individuals, and specific behaviors either pre- or proscribed. Amendments to the constitution have specifically extended the protection of that document to former slaves, women, and 18-, 19-, and 20-year-olds in the Fourteenth, Nineteenth, and Twenty-Sixth Amendments, respectively. Additionally, several states have extended full majority rights to 18-year-olds. The full ramifications of adults as regular high school students have yet to unfold. However, recent court tests have supported constitutional freedoms for students of all ages. In *Tinker v. Des Moines,* the majority of the United States Supreme Court held that

> First Amendment Rights, applied in the light of the special characteristics of the school environment, are available to teachers and students. It can hardly be argued that either students or teachers shed their constitutional rights to freedom of speech or expression at the schoolhouse gate. (Gaddy, 1971, 14)

Relevant court decisions will be considered in the following broad areas: freedom of expression, freedom of dress and appearance, freedom from discrimination, freedom from unreasonable regulations, and the right to due process.

Freedom of Expression

According to the ACLU (1968), student expression of opinions about national, local, or other nonschool political policies is, in a technical sense, not the concern of the school. When schools have become involved in political expression, court tests have supported expression in the wearing of buttons, armbands, or other symbols.

Schools may make regulations governing the distribution of symbols and discussion of opinion, providing that regulations are reasonable, consistent, and uniform. In *Blackwell v. Issaguena County Board of Education,* the court held that the banning of buttons was reasonable, for the regulation prohibited all symbols, not merely objectionable ones. Rules banning specific symbols, such as antiwar buttons, have not been upheld by the courts, unless they can be shown to constitute a reasonable anticipation of disruption of the legitimate and orderly process of education.

With respect to written expression, relevant court decisions generally conclude that the restrictions school officials can place on the issuance and distribution of student publications are those in effect in the adult community. Officials may prohibit publication and/or distribution of printed matter, whether sponsored by the school or not, only when the publication or distribution would endanger the health or safety of students, clearly and imminently threaten to disrupt the educational process, or constitute libel (ACLU, 1968). The school newspaper should not be considered an official image of the school, and censorship should not be invoked unless material is of a libelous nature. Indeed, if a single publication is incapable of fully representing the opinions of students, school officials should encourage multiple and competing periodicals. Student groups representing differing viewpoints have equal rights to school resources.

The legal principle to follow in situations of written, symbolic, or verbal expression is considered of the question of disruption. According to the disruption principle, school authorities are not permitted to infringe on the freedoms of students unless behavior substantially and materially interferes with the discipline and good order of the school (Griffiths, 1968).

Freedom of Dress and Appearance

Court litigation on this topic covers three areas: clothing, beards and mustaches, and length and style of hair. In two clothing cases, courts ruled that clothes should not be a condition of attendance. In the first, a high school girl argued that the prescribed gym suits were immodest, as were some of the prescribed physical exercises. The court held that purchase and wearing of the gym suit was not a necessary requirement but that the girl must satisfy the curriculum requirement, namely attend the class (Mitchell, 1962). In the other case, the Nassau County (New York) Supreme Court ruled that females could not be prohibited from wearing slacks to school. School Board Regulation of clothing was acceptable only to the extent necessary to protect the safety of the wearer, or to control disturbance or distraction interfering with the education of other students (Scott, 1969). Examples of dress regulations which are justifiable include prohibitions on bell- or flair-bottomed slacks which interfere with movement or constitute a safety hazard, clothing that is sexually provocative and distracting to others, jewelry or accessories that make distracting noise, and clothing so voluminous that it might get stepped on, caught in machinery, or otherwise constitute a safety hazard. Articles of clothing that scratch or damage furniture or floors, such as cleats, rivets, or buckles, can be reasonable proscribed.

Clothing and its appearance must meet what this writer calls the Unisex Principle. Each provision of a dress regulation must apply to males and females alike. Slacks cannot be prohibited for females and simultaneously permitted for males. Earrings, bracelets and necklaces, if permitted for females, cannot be summarily proscribed for males.

As regards beards and mustaches, the California Court of Appeals (Akin, 1968) held that school regulations demanding a clean-shaven appearance would stand. School officials had testified that wearing of beards in the past had resulted in disruptions. Though the court has apparently settled this issue, it will surface again. Beards and mustaches have traditionally been regarded as symbols of adulthood and maturity, not as political expression. As long as laws do not grant majority rights to certain individuals, school officials may regulate for those individuals the activities normally covered by majority rights. When individuals are granted the legal status of adults, schools may not prohibit the symbols of that status. Beards and mustaches, as symbols of adulthood, cannot be prohibited for 18 year-old students where states may have granted them legal majority rights.

Court decisions concerning length and style of hair are equivocal. Some cases have ruled that school officials can dictate length and style of hair, especially for boys; others have held the opposite. This is an area where the Unisex Principle may operate, and where the disruption principle certainly operates. The disruption principle, as applied to hair, states that school officials may regulate length and style of hair when it involves a health or sanitary risk to the wearer or others, or will interfere with his or others' performance of school work, or will create disciplinary problems of a kind reasonably thought to be of concern to public officials (Richards, 1969).

In Griffin (1969), the Court stated that until one's appearance carries with it the substantial risk of harm to others, that appearance should be dictated by one's own taste or lack thereof. That is, authorities may not set standards of taste, but may guarantee the safety of others and of the process of education.

It should be noted here that standards of safety vary with the activity. The standards of safety for the chemistry lab are different from those of the football field, and both are different from the English classroom. Regulations on length of hair can be made if they clearly relate to typical safety standards for each activity.

Freedom from Discrimination

The courts have generally been consistent on the question of racial discrimination since the 1954 *Brown v. Board of Education of Topeka*. The ACLU (1968) says that no student should be granted preference or denied privilege on the basis of race, religion, color, or national origin. This has since been applied to relative affluence and area of residence of parents. Tokenism, i.e., having a few minority students in a school, does not meet the requirements of the courts.

The courts have also consistently struck down any local or state action designed to circumvent the intent of the *Brown* decision. Public funding of private schools, prohibiting certain modes of transport, repealing compulsory attendance laws, gerrymandering school districts, and various tracking systems that result in either de facto or de jure segregation and discrimination have been prohibited.

In another area, schools have in the past often discriminated against married students, mothers and mothers-to-be. Again the courts are clear on the rights and obligations of students and schools. School policy that bars any student from participation in extracurricular school activities on the grounds of marriage or parenthood is reasonable and may stand. In marriage and parenthood, individuals assume certain responsibilities which are important to society, and the schools should take care to prevent placing competing demands and obligations on the student. The outright prohibition of married students, parents, or parents-to-be from the regular scholastic program is not reasonable, and must be revised to provide for reasonable educational opportunities for all. In a case involving a pregnant student, the court stated that she could be prevented from going to the regular school classes, provided she were given the opportunity to continue her regular education through home study or other special programs.

The disruption principle can be invoked in the cases of unwed mothers. If the board of education is firmaly convinced that a girl's presence will taint the education of other students, she can be excluded. But the fact that a girl has a child out-of-wedlock is not prima facie evidence of moral turpitude (Perry, 1969). Presumably, any student convicted of a criminal offense may be excluded from regular public education opportunities. However, skin color, marriage, and pregnancy are not criminal offenses.

Freedom from Unreasonable Regulations

In the past, many school boards or officials have reserved the right to "make any rules and regulations promoting the best interests of the school." Students have also met with disciplinary action under the auspices of this broad authority, or for violating unwritten school regulations or general school policy. The courts have usually ruled in favor of students where regulations have been vague, broad, or standardless. Any regulation governing the school as a whole should be clearly and explicitly formulated, published, and made available to all members of the school community. Any behaviors that are either demanded or forbidden must be completely specified.

Several cases have been adjudicated concerning disciplinary action by schools against students for behavior alleged to be "against the best interests of the school," but which occurred off-campus and out-of-school. Again, courts have usually held for the student, ruling that school authorities have limited jurisdiction over a student's free time away from campus. Two such cases involved suspension without a hearing, one for participation in a civil rights demonstration on a Saturday, the other for possession of narcotics and associated paraphernalia. The courts ruled that these activities did not present a material threat to the health and safety of the other students, and suspension was unjustified. The courts did, however, draw the distinction between possession and use of narcotics, conceding that the use of heroin by students off school premises might endanger the health, safety, or morals of other students (Howard, 1969). Further, the courts directed the schools to remove from the students' records any reference to legal action by civil authorities. Students should not be placed in jeopardy at school for out-of-school activities, and it is a violation of the student's rights for the school to punish such activity, enter it on school records, or report it to employers or other agencies, unless authorized by the student.

The Right to Due Process

The rulings of courts indicate that students are generally granted civil and constitutional rights, including the right to due process under the law. *In re Gault* (1967) discusses the specific provisions of the due process right, and concludes that children have the right to counsel, the right to notice of charges, the right to confrontation with the accuser, the right of cross-examination, the right to a transcript of the proceedings and the right to appellate review. The right to be represented by an attorney does not apply to hearings which are administrative in nature (Cosme, 1967).

One final issue under the topic of the due process concerns the right of law officers to pursue violators on school grounds, and the procedures for searching student lockers, desks, and personal effects. Schools are not sanctuaries for law violators, and officers may pursue and apprehend violators on school premises. It is assumed that the police will conduct their activities in an orderly fashion, taking care not to disrupt the orderly operation of the school. Police should contact the principal or some designated faculty member and notify him of their intentions. Any search, apprehension, or interrogation procedures should be conducted in the presence of school officials, as much to guarantee the neutrality of the school as to preserve the rights of students and officers. Courts have ruled that lockers and desks are not the private property of the student, and may be legally searched upon the consent of school officials and presentation of a proper search warrant. Since ownership of lockers is thought to reside in the school, students do not have to consent to a search, but it is advisable that students be informed of their rights prior to, and be present during, the search.

STUDENT INVOLVEMENT

There are three basic reasons why students should be involved in educational decision-making. The most frequently cited reason is the effect such participation has on student unrest. Student involvement is a technique suggested to channel student interests and efforts into responsible activities, and to prevent the disruption of the educational process.

A second reason is the potential utility of student decision-making as a teaching method. Schools must not only train students to cope with problems of the future, but also to be contributing, participating, members of a democratic society. Given that experience is a very effective teaching technique, there is probably no better way to learn participatory democracy than through sharing in actual decision-making activities in the relatively sheltered school environment.

The third reason supporting student participation is that students, as a legitimate interest group, ought to have their interests represented in decisions affecting them. Nothing in the discussion of student rights can be construed to mean that school officials may prevent student involvement. The extent of proper student involvement varies from area to area, and the following discussion contains suggestions, all of which have been successful, for ways to involve students in planning, implementing, and strengthening school programs.

Increased Communication

Communication appears to be the strongest "preventive medicine" administrators can use to reduce student unrest, and especially to eliminate administrator misperception of student desires. Informal contacts with students are especially helpful. Periodic dinner or luncheon meetings, or even eating with students in the school cafeteria, is an excellent practice, as is attending sports events, dances, or other social events. More formalized channels include open office hours, regular gripe sessions, suggestion boxes, a student ombudsman, retreats, and sensitivity training groups. Administrators should read student newspapers and publications, even the underground variety, as they often provide a reliable source of student opinion. Clues of hostility and dissatisfaction may be gotten from these media and acted upon before disruption occurs.

Increased communication, while desirable, is not a panacea. Administrators must act sincerely on some student recommendations, because communication is a means to effect educational reform, not the substance of reform itself. Bailey (1970) and Gudridge (1969), remind us that the culture we live in contributes to student unrest and to demands for greater participation. School officials, who are powerless to change these outside causes, should accept some conflict as inevitable, and develop skills in conflict management, including arbitration and mediation skills and compromise techniques, while maintaining an unbiased stance to all parties.

Committee Memberships

A few school districts report that students serve as nonvoting members of the Board of Education. Student representatives may be elected by the student body or selected by student government subject to final approval by the board. They usually participate in all deliberations except personnel items and executive sessions. Student representatives provide advice in the areas of direct pupil concern, studying board materials and then reporting to their own constituents.

A more common procedure for student participation is through membership on advisory committees at the local school level. There are almost as many committees, either standing or ad hoc, as there are issues, and students can make important contributions to library, curriculum, building and grounds, community relations, student-faculty, discipline, staffing, and student activities committees.

Instruction Methods

Increased student participation in the educational process should be reflected in the classroom, where students spend the greater part of their school time. Historically, the classroom has been dominated by the teacher. He sets the goals, methods, and subject matter of a course. He usually lectures—an excellent means for imparting information, but one which inhibits the participation of students.

One alternative is participatory education. This method relies on the use of small groups, often without the instructor's presence. Groups are structured to insure maximum involvement of all students, and to guide each student in assuming responsibility for his own learning and development. Not only does the student assimilate the facts of the subject matter, but he learns from group interaction, problem-solving, analysis, and evaluation. Students learn to work together, communicate, and support each other in their efforts.

Another means of involvement in the classroom is student evaluation of teachers. Teacher evaluations, widely used in higher education, may prove to be a valuable technique for student participation on the secondary level.

Curriculum Planning

The biggest student complaint in secondary schools is the lack of relevant courses in the curriculum. Relevance has been enhanced by the following: expanded offering of courses; greater individual choice of courses; fewer required courses; minicourses that last only a few weeks, so students can elect more courses in a term; independent or individualized programs, assuming the student has a voice in the subject matter; and courses taught wholly or in part by students themselves.

Currently, the usual avenue of student involvement in curricular matters is through suggestions for course content. Combs (1970), reporting on the results of a survey sent to 500 California high schools, notes that 27 percent of the responding schools had inaugurated new courses from students' suggestions. These new courses occurred in nearly all areas, but were concentrated in Ethnic Studies, Computer Technology, and Vocational Education. Combs suggests permanent involvement for students, with full membership rights, on a curriculum advisory committee composed of administration, faculty, students, and parents. He also suggests a "Special Interest" period each day so students could study what they want. In one California School, the faculty submitted 200 topics that they could, and would, teach to interested students in this program. In other areas, 20 Buffalo

students were paid out of regular curriculum development funds to serve on the summer curriculum committee, which produced revisions in Language Arts, Vocational Education, and Black History programs. In one Maryland school (House, 1970), the regular curriculum was suspended for two weeks and a student-recommended curriculum was followed, including field trips to Washington, work with underprivileged children, and independent study.

Student Organizations

There are two separate issues in the area of student organizations: (1) the participation of students in student organizations, and (2) the participation of student organizations as representative bodies in the decision-making process of the school.

If student organizations, and especially student governments, are to be a training ground for democratic participation, they should guarantee the participation and representation of all students. Administration-imposed restrictions or qualifications on student council membership, such as minimum grade point average or exemplary behavior, deprive a considerable number of students of representation. Elimination of these conditions would provide a more representative student council. Activities and organizations, except those of an honorary academic nature, should be open to students of all types of backgrounds, and students should be allowed to join at any time in the year. Activities fees should be kept low or subsidized to encourage the economically disadvantaged to become involved, and grade requirements should be dropped. School districts ought to provide transportation to and from events whenever possible, and activities buses should be made available in the late afternoon so students without private transportation can remain for after-school activities. If time is made available during the school day for extracurricular activities, then students who have jobs or other responsibilities after school can participate.

Just as some students may be underrepresented in student government, the student council may be underrepresented in the policy- and decision-making activities of the school. The student council should not be a rubber stamp congress or a mechanism to siphon off student energies into some meaningless exercise. The student government, if truly representative of students, can serve as an ideal instrument of institutionalized communication, conveying the needs and opinions of students to the board of education and the school administration.

SUMMARY

Students have generally the same constitutional rights as have adults. They are limited in their activities only to the extent those activities present a danger to others or materially threaten to disrupt the educational process. Students can, and probably ought to, involve themselves in every aspect of education. Lack of imagination by either students or school officials is the only limitation on student participation.

REFERENCES

American Association of School Administrators and National
  Education Association. Framework for Student Involvement.
  Educational Research Service Circular, 1970, 6.

American Civil Liberties Union. *Academic Freedom in the Secondary Schools*. New York: 1968.

Akin v. Board of Education of Riverside Unified School District,
  68 Cal. Rptr. 557 (1968).

Armstrong, Ronald. *Student Involvement*. Eugene: ERIC Clearinghouse on Educational Management, University of Oregon,
  1972.

Bailey, Stephen K. *Disruption in Urban Public Secondary Schools.
  Final Report*. Syracuse, New York: Syracuse University Research Corporation, 1970.

Brown v. Board of Education of Topeka, 347 U.S. 483, 74 S. Ct.
  686, 98 L. Ed. 873 (Kansas, 1954).

Calkins, Carl J., Kukenbill, Ronald W., and Mateer, William J.
  Children's Rights: An Introductory Sociological Overview.
  Peabody Journal of Education, 1973, *50*, 89-109.

Chesler, Mark A. Shared Power and Student Decision-Making.
  Educational Leadership, 1970, *28*, 9-14.

Combs, Stanley L. A Summary of a Survey on Student Involvement in Curriculum. *Journal of Secondary Education*, 1970,
  45, 243-249.

Cosme v. Board of Education, 50 Misc. 2d 344, 270 N.Y.S. 2d
  231 (1966); aff'd mem., 27 App. Div. 2d 905, 281 N.Y.S. 2d
  970 (1967).

DeCecco, John, Richards, Arlene, Summers, Frank, Harrison,
  Josephine, Brussel, Edward, and Mandel, James. *Civic Edu-
  cation for the Seventies: An Alternative to Repression and
  Revolution: Volume I*. New York: Center for Research and
  Education in American Liberties, Columbia University, 1970.

Ferguson, Donald G. *Student Involvement. A Working Paper*.
  Paper presented at the annual meeting of the American
  Association of School Administrators, Atlantic City, Feb-
  ruary 1971.

Gaddy, Dale. *Rights and Freedoms of Public School Students:
  Directions from the 1960s*. Topeka, Kansas: National Organization on Legal Problems of Education, 1971.

Griffin v. Tatum, 300 F. Supp. 60 (Alabama, 1969).

Griffiths, William E. Student Constitutional Rights. The Role of
  the Principal. *The Bulletin of the National Association of
  Secondary School Principals*, 1968, *52*, 30-37.

Gudridge, Beatrice M. *High School Student Unrest. Education
  U.S.A. Special Report: How to Anticipate Protest, Channel
  Activism, and Protect Student Rights*. Washington, D.C.: Na-
  tional School Public Relations Association, 1969.

Hollister, C. A. Why the Courts Will Allow School Officials to
  Treat Students Unfairly—Up to a Point. *The American School
  Board Journal*, 1973, *160*, 37-39.

House, James E. Can the Student Participate in His Own Destiny?
  Educational Leadership, 1970, *27*, 442-445.

How Student Involvement Pays Off. *School Management*, 1970,
  14, 29-32.

How to Involve Students in Decision-Making. *School Management*, 1969, *13*, 12, 17.

Howard v. Clark, 299 N.Y.S. 2d 65 (1969).

In re Gault, 387 U.S. 1 (Arizona, 1967).

Johnson, T. Page. The Constitution, the Courts, and Long Hair.
  *The Bulletin of the National Association of Secondary School
  Principals*, 1973, *57*, 24-33.

Lovetere, John P. Student Involvement on School Committees.
  *The Bulletin of the National Association of Secondary School
  Principals*, 1973, *57*, 132-137.

Marquis, Romeo. Curriculum Development: Can Students be
  Involved? *The Bulletin of the National Association of Secondary School Principals*, 1973, *57*, 127-131.

McGrew, Jean B. Student Participation in Decision-Making. *The*

*Bulletin of the National Association of Secondary School
  Principals*, 1970, *54*, 124-133.

Mitchell v. McCall, 273 Alabama 604, 143 So. 2d 629 (1962).

New Jersey State Federation of District Boards of Education.
  *Student Activism—and Involvement in the Educational Pro-
  gram. Federation Ad Hoc Committee Report, January, 1970*.
  Trenton: 1970.

Nolte, M. Chester. Sometimes, Four-Letter Words are OK for Use
  in Classrooms. *The American School Board Journal*, 1973,
  160, 28-31.

North Carolina State Board of Education. *Student Involvement:
  A Bridge to Total Education. Revised Edition*. Raleigh: Task
  Force on Student Involvement, Department of Public In-
  struction, 1971.

Pearson, George. How Free Should Student Publications Be?
  *The Bulletin of the National Association of Secondary School
  Principals*, 1971, *55*, 50-58.

Perry v. Grenada Municipal Separate School District, 300 F. Supp.
  748 (Mississippi, 1969).

Petrillo, F. Interpretation of Pupil Authority in School Government. *School Activities*, 1966, *37*, 13-15.

Richards v. Thurston, 304 F. Supp. 449 (Massachusetts, 1969).

Ritchie, Ritchard M. Due Process and the Principal. *Phi Delta
  Kappan*, 1973, *54*, 697-698.

Scott v. Board of Education, 305 N.Y.S. 2d 601 (1969).

Smith, H. Stuart, Jr. An Analysis of Court-Ordered Desegregation.
  *The Bulletin of the National Association of Secondary School
  Principals*, 1973, *57*, 34-42.

Squires, Raymond. Do Students Have Civil Rights? *The PTA
  Magazine*, 1968, *63*, 2-4.

Student Involvement: Channeling Activism into Accomplishment. *Nation's Schools*, 1969, *84*, 39-50.

Triezenberg, George. Student Communication Rights. *The Bulletin of the National Association of Secondary School Principals*, 1973, *57*, 13-23.

The Underground Press. *NASSP Spotlight on Junior and Senior
  High Schools*, 1969, *87*, 1-2.

Vernon, Sarah A. *The Task Force for Student Involvement*.
  Denver and Raleigh: Improving State Leadership in Education;
  and Department of Public Instruction, North Carolina State
  Board of Education, 1970.

Weldy, Gilbert R. Building Democrat Values Through Student
  Participation. *The Bulletin of the National Association of Secondary School Principals*, 1970, *54*, 72-79.

Winston, Sheldon. Expulsions and Due Process. *Phi Delta
  Kappan*, 1973, *54*, 699.

53

TRAINING EVALUATION AND STUDENT ACHIEVEMENT MEASUREMENT

by Brian A. Bergman
Administrator of Personnel Research
and Communications
Standard Pressed Steel Company
Jenkintown, Pennsylvania
and
Arthur I. Siegel
Director
Applied Psychological Services, Inc.
Wayne, Pennsylvania

This research was carried out under the provisions of Air Force Contract F41609-71-C-0025.

Methods and procedures for evaluating training courses and student achievement have been slowly evolving, and assuming increased stature within any training program developmental paradigm which aims to be at all complete. This increased emphasis on training evaluation and student measurement is due, in part, to the increased realization that there can be no training system without quality control. Training in this sense is viewed as a process (analogous to a chemical or manufacturing process) in which raw material (students) is converted from one form to another (skilled craftsmen). Within such a construct, there must be a quality control stage; training evaluation and student measurement represent the quality control stage in the training process.

TRAINING EVALUATION AND STUDENT ACHIEVEMENT MEASUREMENT

Training evaluation and student achievement measurement in some ways involve similar constructs, and in some ways they involve different constructs. Moreover, several different meanings have been attached to the term "training evaluation."

There are at least three major and quite different reasons for measuring student achievement. The most time-honored of these is for determining whether the student has mastered the prescribed subject matter, and hence can be promoted, graduated, certified, licensed, or in some other way acknowledged. This type of student measurement takes place for purposes of evaluating the student; and it is completely distinct from evaluating the training provided to the student, or from other reasons for student measurement.

A second reason for student measurement is to determine his subject matter areas of strength and weakness, for reinforcement and feedback purposes and for diagnosis and subsequent remedial action. Many automated, or programmed, instructional tests and devices provide for this type of measurement, as do most good tutors. This student measurement is an instructional technique, and it is completely distinct from evaluating either the student or the training.

Finally, the student measurement is employed for the purpose of drawing inferences about the effectiveness of instruction provided to the student. Other things being equal, it can be inferred that the more the students have achieved, the better the quality of the instruction. Student achievement in this case is indeed a method of training evaluation. Only one, then, of the three uses of student measurement overlaps the topic of training evaluation. In the other two uses, student measurement is a distinct topic of interest without any necessary reference to training evaluation.

The term training evaluation also has multiple meanings and has been applied in a number of different contexts. At a minimum, one should distinguish comparative or relative training evaluations from more absolute evaluations of training. The first case involves the determination of which is best among a number of methods or programs for presenting the training content. The second case involves determination of how good the training is.

CURRENT TRENDS AND NEW DEVELOPMENTS

Due to the broad scope of the training evaluation and student achievement measurement field, we will be very selective in our presentation of current trends and new developments. Only those trends and developments which are either innovative or controversial are presented. Since this selection is judgmental, many areas of interest considered important by other investigators may not be discussed. This article will include: testing methods, learning styles and moderator variables, cross-cultural evaluation, programmed instruction, computer-assisted instruction and testing, and cost-benefit analysis.

Testing Methods

Hierarchical and Sequential Testing. Hierarchical and sequential tests involve a sequence of branching in which the student only gets items at his own level. This procedure decreases testing time, increases reliability, and increases student motivation, because he is not forced to take (and guess at) the more difficult items. The concept was introduced in early intelligence tests and has recently received new emphasis. An example of the application is the work of Cleary, Linn, and Rock (1968a, 1968b) who wished to use programmed tests to decrease testing time while leaving reliability and validity the same. In the procedure described by Cleary, Linn, and Rock, each student receives a different set of items along a scale. Sequentially programmed tests have a routing section which branches the subject to the appropriate items, and a measurement section containing items of suitable difficulty. The routing section can be used alone, although these investigators used a combination. The sequential method uses fewer items for those easy to classify, and more items for those at the borderline of categories. Computer-based testing could facilitate this procedure because of speed, flexibility, convenience, and immediacy of feedback. This method is especially suited to persons at the extremes of the distribution, because they can be quickly routed and thus save time.

Criterion- and Norm-Referenced Testing. Glaser (1963) and his colleagues (Glaser and Cox, 1968; Glaser and Klaus, 1962; Glaser and Nitko, 1971), as well as Popham and Husek (1969), Carver (1970), Holtzman (1971), Siegel and Bergman (1972), Berman and Siegel (1972), Siegel, Schultz, and Lanterman (1964), and Siegel and Fischl (1965), have all written on the topic of criterion-referenced testing versus norm-referenced testing. The characteristics of criterion-referenced tests are that they (a) indicate the degree of competence attained by an individual with regard to specified absolute standards of performance; (b) minimize individual differences; and (c) consider variability irrelevant.

Generally, from these statements it can be seen that criterion-referenced tests tell how the student is performing with regard to a specified standard of behavior. Individual differences are considered irrelevant, since the student is graded against a single standard rather than against all the others taking the test. Assigning grades of competency to students on the basis of relative performance, when it is not really known whether any of the students have attained a specified behavioral objective, makes very little sense. One can, though, derive individual differences from criterion-referenced tests by specifying the degree of competency reached by each student.

Glaser (1963) and Glaser and Cox (1968) discuss the use of norm-referenced achievement tests and criterion-referenced tests in differentiating among individuals and treatment groups. When evaluating individuals, one needs to use an achievement test containing items with different difficulty levels. For evaluating treatments or experimental conditions, though, one needs perfect post-treatment answers and incorrect pretreatment answers, so that the dependent measure is maximally sensitive to training change. In this latter case, criterion-referenced tests are most appropriate.

Gain Scores and Final Examination Grades. Carver (1966, 1969, 1970) presents a rather conclusive argument against the use of gain or difference scores in evaluation research. The problem in the before-and-after measurement of gain scores is that when small significant increases are registered, there may actually be a tremendously large increase in knowledge. This paradoxical result comes from the inequality of measurement at different points along the scale. Carver hypothesizes that a curvilinear relationship exists between test scores and knowledge, with knowledge increasing faster than test scores. One can rarely find a significant positive correlation between initial test scores and gain scores (often there is an inverse correlation). This is contrary to expectation, since it is expected that the more intelligent student will learn more and that the more interested student will be motivated to study more. One

can partially explain this finding on the basis that students who already know a lot do not have much left to learn. Another related problem is the ceiling effect, which occurs when the initially bright student already has most of the items on the pretest correct and does not have much room for improvement. Carver indicates that final examination grades constitute a dependent variable measure that is superior to gain scores, but with certain restrictions: the ratio of final knowledge to initial knowledge must be considerably greater than one; the correlation between initial knowledge and final knowledge must remain high; and the variance of final knowledge must be greater than the variance of initial knowledge.

Confidence Testing. Confidence testing involves a method which provides for weighting the selected alternatives of a multiple choice test item, so as to allow the examinee to reflect his belief in the correctness of his response. The basic concept behind confidence testing is that there is additional information available from the students' degree of belief (confidence) probabilities. The method, accordingly, allows the student to maximize his expected score if he truly reflects the degree of his belief, or the probability that a specific alternative is correct.

Confidence testing evolved because of the feeling among student measurement experts that knowledge, as measured by achievement tests, has more dimensions than those indicated by the typical multiple choice and true-false test. Some students can respond to a multiple choice test item with 100 percent certainty of the correct choice. Other students may be able to eliminate several alternatives as being incorrect, and have to make a decision between one or the other of the two remaining alternatives. Still other students may approach the same test item and not be able to eliminate any of the alternatives. The question then arises, does the student who can eliminate all of the incorrect alternatives have more knowledge than the one who could eliminate all but two? And by the same token, does the student who is uncertain of his response (and so indicates through his statement of his confidence in his answer) have more knowledge than the one who selects the same incorrect response, but feels certain that his response was correct? Confidence testing advocates would respond in the affirmative to these questions (Shuford, Albert, and Massengill, 1966; Shuford, 1967).

LEARNING STYLES AND MODERATOR VARIABLES

Scope of the Problem

The sensitivity and predictive power of student measurement and training evaluation techniques can often be increased through the use of moderator variables. This is because certain attributes of select groups tend to make the testing evaluation methods more or less appropriate for the groups. Some of the factors which can be used as moderators are achievement level, personal and environmental variables, social background factors, cognitive style, and affective reactions.

Cognitive styles are modes of thought, perception, and memory; they are also information-processing habits. Some of the various types of cognitive styles that have been identified are field dependence-independence; attention span (or span of awareness); breadth of categorizing (e.g., lumpers and splitters); conceptual styles (e.g., modes of categorization); complexity versus simplicity in word perception; reflective-impulsive; leveling versus sharpening; susceptibility to cognitive interference; and ability to accept unrealistic experiences.

Rundquist (1969) contends that item analysis, factor analysis, and moderator variables have not helped to increase efficiency because these various methods fail to take into account the fact that different antecedents can produce the same behavior across individuals (e.g., visual recall via eidetic imagery, or by short term memory). According to Rundquist, one must learn the mediating processes used by individuals in learning to do a job, and then construct tests for the antecedent behaviors. These new tests would be better measures of an ability than more global tests, and they could avoid confounding effects. The new test or measure may be slanted more toward one antecedent than another, thus increasing the validity coefficient.

Cohen (1970) feels that one must be careful when using cognitive styles as moderators and instructional aids, since they can change over time. For example, much of Piaget's work has shown that the child's problem-solving style and conceptual mode of thinking will qualitatively change from infancy to adulthood. Cohen concludes that a valid decision about an individual's cognitive style at one time may prove to be invalid at another time.

Tucker (1966) recently presented a rather unique application of factor analysis to the measurement of student learning. Using the Ekhart-Young theorem (a Fundamental matrix decomposition theorem of factor analysis), Tucker found that individuals learn in qualitatively different ways over trials, such that individuals can be grouped or clustered according to the way they perform or learn. Tucker would not use a single, homogeneous learning curve to describe what is in fact a heterogeneous phenomenon.

Motivation and Types of Intelligence

There has been a plethora of recent research emphasizing the effects of differential motivation and differential thinking styles (erroneously termed "intelligence") on student achievement. These concepts certainly should be held in mind by anyone concerned with student achievement, from either the measurement or the instructional point of view.

Rimland (1969) suggests that there are two types of intelligence, practical and abstract. Rimland hypothesizes that practical intelligence is needed for job performance, and that abstract intelligence is needed for academic work. Such thinking would imply that most trade schools should rely heavily on job performance testing to measure student achievement. Rimland says that the traditional g, or the ability to abstractly manipulate symbols and events in the head, is the ability required of test-takers. Others are better at "extracerebral events," or the ability to sustain attention on and perform simple tasks which simulate the job (e.g., perceptual speed). Rimland posits that these two types of intelligence are mutually exclusive. In his research, he found that intelligence test scores correlated much higher with school grades than did performance test scores, but that performance test scores correlated much higher with job performance than did intelligence test scores. He concludes that different types of training and separate types of measurement are needed for students with different types of intelligence.

Rotter (1966) conceives the effect of reinforcement on behavior as dependent on whether the person perceives a causal relationship between his own behavior and the reward. If not, the result is attributed to luck or to the control of others. *Internal control* exists when the student thinks reinforcement is contingent upon his own behavior, while *external control* is when the student thinks reinforcement is controlled by others or by chance events.

Atkinson (1966) presents a somewhat more rigorous theory of motivation involving achievement motivation, incentive, and goal expectancy. Atkinson's theory is depicted by the formula:

Motivation = f(motive $\times$ expectancy $\times$ incentive)

With motivation to approach a goal (nAch) held constant at 1.00, and with expectancy and incentive equal to .5, then the probability of goal approach is .25 (the highest possible). Atkinson defines incentive as the goal attractiveness, and motive as the ability to strive for satisfaction or to accomplish. "The strength of motivation to approach a goal decreases as probability of success increases from .50 to a near certainty (p_s = .90), and it also decreases as p_s decreases from .50 to certainty of failure (p_s = .10) (p. 17)."

From this formulation, it is easily seen that the young, deprived black child will rarely encounter a probability of success of .5 or greater. Because he perceives a certainty of failure, he then lacks the motivation to approach a goal; therefore, he does not perform as well in student measurement situations as the nondeprived white child who perceives a higher probability of success.

Katz (1967) more or less integrates the two earlier theories into a coherent two-stage theory of development which possesses implications for student measurement. During the first stage (up to two years of age) of development, the child's verbal efforts are normally reinforced by parental approval. Selective approval on the part of the parents can develop strong habits of striving for proficiency in the child. During the second stage, the parental standards and values of achievement are internalized by the child. "The child's own implicit verbal responses acquire, through repeated association with the overt responses of the parents, the same power to guide and reinforce the child's own achievement behaviors. . . . Internalization doesn't take place until strong, externally reinforced achieving habits have developed (p. 5)." Lower class children (including most blacks) are most dependent upon others for social reinforcement in academic situations. Lacking internalization, they will avoid achievement situations and concentrate on other situations regarded as more promising. "Lower class Negro children tend to be externally oriented in situations that demand performance. That is, they are likely to be highly dependent on the immediate environment for the setting of standards and the dispensing of rewards (p. 8)."

Hess and Shipman (1965) present a very interesting and alternative developmental formulation. They feel that cognitive growth is ". . . fostered in family control systems which offer and permit a wide range of alternatives of action and thought, and that such growth is constricted by systems of control which offer predetermined solutions and few alternatives for consideration and choice (p. 870)." In the deprived family context, the parent-child control system ". . . restricts the number and kind of alternatives for action and thought that are opened to the child; such constriction precludes a tendency for the child to reflect, to consider and choose among alternatives for speech and action. It develops modes for dealing with stimuli and with problems which are impulsive rather than reflective, which deal with the immediate rather than the future, and which are disconnected rather than sequential (pp. 870-871)."

CROSS-CULTURAL EVALUATION

Brislin (1970) presents a rather acid critique of most military cross-cultural training programs. The aim of cross-cultural programs, according to Brislin, is to allow the military to function behaviorally and effectively in a foreign environment. Most programs, though, do not have data on effectiveness, and the evaluative methods used are inadequate. When evaluations were conducted, they were too dependent on verbal and written reports of the trainees. Most data needs to be collected on the actual overseas behavior of trainees; therefore, responses to attitudinal questionnaires need to be verified by other means. Evaluation needs to be conducted by researchers not associated with the program. Also, the attitudes of foreign nationals should be sampled. Techniques should be available to assess transfer of training to the actual foreign situation with more replication and followup training.

Fiedler, Mitchell, and Triandis (1970), and Worchel and Mitchell (1970), have recently described an exciting new technique known as the Cultural Assimilator, which is based upon the critical incident technique. In this technique, critical incidents are obtained in which the norms or behaviors across cultures are quite different. Questions are asked about the incident with multiple-choice answers and immediate feedback. A target sample from the host culture selects the correct multiple-choice responses.

PROGRAMMED INSTRUCTION

Mager (1970a, 1970b) maintained that it is impossible for the instructor to apply all the principles of learning in the classroom. This is not because he does not want to, but because the learning environment is prohibitive. "We still put large groups of students in front of a single instructor and insist that they all learn at the same rate (p. 4)." This procedure may be convenient and inexpensive, but it is inefficient. Programmed learning devices and machines are held to possess the potential for solving these problems, since they usually present instruction in small steps; reinforce the student along the way; help the student proceed at his own pace; and feed back responses into the device to modify instruction to fit the particular needs of the student.

Lindvall and Cox (1969) present a Structured Curriculum Model (SCM) for developing a programmed instructional course. They state that one must define specific objectives and organize them according to difficulty or prerequisites. This organization provides a structural sequence which is a frame for determining the student's present status and for his future planning. In the SCM, the curriculum materials must be matched to the objectives, and one must keep in mind that students can master the same objectives with different kinds of material. In addition, the student must be given a diagnostic evaluation to place him in the proper location along the learning continuum. The placement test should "select items which test representative objectives along the continuum (p. 170)." Pretests are also suggested prior to each instructional unit, because the student may be able to cope with some of the objectives in the unit and not others. Evaluation in this model is by way of "curriculum embedded tests" and "post-unit" tests. Curriculum embedded tests measure one objective of a unit; they are content-references, they are short, and they enable the teachers to make decisions regarding student advancement. Post-unit tests help the teacher to decide whether the pupil should progress to the next unit or be given remedial work.

COMPUTER-ASSISTED INSTRUCTION (CAI) AND TESTING

Computer-assisted instruction represents one of the most recent innovations in training methodology. One of the main problems of CAI is its cost when compared with other similar methods which might give equivalent results (e.g., TV). Another, more serious objection to CAI is that it does not allow the student enough opportunity or freedom to chart his own progress (Hammel, 1969).

Seidel (1969) discusses the purposes of project IMPACT, which is to provide the Army with an appropriate and efficient CAI system adaptable to the individual trainee. Programs are to be branched and adapted to the entry characteristics of the trainee and his performance throughout instruction. Some of the important decision factors involved are: entry characteristics; education and background; responses of trainee; response latency; pattern and history of errors; relation of individual and group norms to responses; and subject matter.

Ferguson (1970) described how computer-assisted criterion-referenced measurement was applied to an experimental school in individually prescribed instruction (IPI). Addition and subtraction skills were taught in a sequence in which each stage built onto, and was required for, the next stage. After each answer the computer made a decision, on the basis of percentage correct and number of problems of this type attempted, whether to go to the next level or continue presenting problems of the same type. Each item was randomly selected from a population of similar items.

COST-BENEFIT ANALYSIS

Alkin (1970) has written an extensive treatise on cost-benefit analysis. Some of his comments and suggestions are reviewed in the ensuing paragraphs.

Generally, cost-benefit analysis is the analysis of the costs and benefits of various alternative courses of action. The decision maker selects the method giving the largest yield at a given cost, or the most benefit for the least cost. Input and output must be measured in dollar terms. Cost-benefit studies are usually large-scale. For instance, the cost of college education can be compared with the resultant increase in productivity yielded by the college education.

The manipulable characteristics are the conditions whose variations maximize or minimize student output. The manipulatable characteristics which affect student output are (a) student inputs measuring the achievement starting point of the student; (b) financial inputs, or funds allocated; (c) external system, which is the giver of inputs and the receiver of outputs (e.g., society); and (d) instruction, supplies, tests, and similar items.

With regard to the outcomes of cost-benefit analysis, the analyst's interest is in how the student has changed in short- and long-term ways (e.g., how well he deals with other schoolwork and his society). Although there are financial inputs, there are no financial outcomes except those derived from behavior changes. There are also nonstudent outcomes, which comprise items such as teacher salaries and number of personnel used in the program.

Alkin sees three major problems in evaluating the cost effectiveness of manipulatable variables. They include difficulty in getting accurate cost data; difficulty "in dealing with cost effectiveness in the light of system interrelationships (p. 235)"; and problems in generalizing to specific individual cases.

APPLICATIONS

A specific example which employs many of the concepts discussed in previous sections of this paper is shown by the work of Siegel, Bergman, and Miller (1973) in two parallel programs in diverse Air Force specialties (AF Contract F41609-72-C-0014). One purpose of this program was to describe, on an introductory basis, methods for providing a unifying core within the Instructional System Development (ISD) technique as employed within the Air Force technical training context. A second purpose was to demonstrate the adaptability and utility of several advanced measurement and evaluation techniques to Air Force student measurement.

Multidimensional scaling (factor analytic) and cluster analytic techniques were employed to order job analytic data for two Air Force technical specialties—electronics and administrative specialist. For both specialties the results from both techniques were similar. Accordingly, it was held that either the multidimensional scaling or the clustering technique will provide the required definitional nexus within the ISD system.

A number of advanced measurement methods and techniques were developed on the basis of the job factors extracted from the job analytic data for each specialty. Forty-one electronics students and 31 administrative students were administered the respective advanced measurement techniques. The students also completed a questionnaire regarding their attitudes toward some of the advanced measurement techniques. In addition, ten instructors from each school were interviewed in order to assess their opinion of the new measurement methods.

The scores derived from the advanced measurement techniques were analyzed in regard to validity, reliability, uniqueness, and cost-effectiveness. Within each specialty, several of the advanced measurement techniques were indicated to possess psychometric, cost-benefit, and related properties which support a contention favoring their adoption. For the electronics specialty, these included sequential testing, figural systems, confidence testing, and scoring on the basis of theory of signal detection (d'). For the administrative specialist, the supported advanced measurement techniques included technical words (job-related vocabulary), absurdity recognition, partial knowledge scoring (a variation of confidence testing), and d' scoring. At least for the two job specialties considered here, the following conclusions appear warranted:

The multidimensional scaling and the cluster analytic techniques appear to possess merit as methods for ordering job analytic data and for providing coherency within ISD application.

Extension of student achievement paper and pencil testing beyond the multiple choice format is warranted.

REFLECTIONS ON THE CURRENT STATE OF THE ART

Training evaluation and student achievement measurement research has been, in the past, characterized by the use of rational (i.e., "armchair") rather than empirical evaluation methods. Similarly, research in these areas has been frequently subjective when objectivity was needed. Finally, research has too often been limited by monetary considerations. The monetary criticism is probably the most important, since many of the other criticisms can be reduced to it. What investigators fail to realize is that cost cutting actually wastes money, because the results of inadequate evaluations are at best uninterpretable and at worst misleading and invalid. Agencies, contractors, and others performing evaluation studies might be well advised to conserve their money, or to perform one or two sound evaluation studies rather than five or six poor ones.

REFERENCES

Alkin, M. Evaluating the Cost-Effectiveness of Instructional Programs. In M. Wittrock and D. Wiley, eds., *The Evaluation of Instruction.* New York: Holt, Rinehart & Winston, 1970, pp. 221-238.

Atkinson, J. Motivational Determinants of Risk-taking Behavior. In J. Atkinson and N. Feather, eds., *A Theory of Achievement Motivation.* New York: Wiley, 1966, pp. 11-30.

Bergman, B., and Siegel, A. I. *Training Evaluation and Student Achievement Measurement: A Review of Literature.* AFHRL-TR-72-3. Lowry AFB, Colo: Technical Training Division, Air Force Human Resources Laboratory, January 1972.

Brislin, R. *The Content and Evaluation of Cross-Cultural Training Programs.* Report No. P-671. Arlington, Virginia: Institute for Defense Analysis, 1970.

Carver, R. The Curvilinear Relationship Between Knowledge and Test Performance: Final Examination as the Best Indicant of Learning. In K. Wientge and P. Du Bois, eds., *Criteria in Learning Research.* Technical Report No. 9. St. Louis, Missouri: Washington University, 1966.

_____. A Model for Using the Final Examination as a Measure of the Amount Learned in Classroom Learning. *Journal of Educational Measurement,* 1969, *6,* 59-68.

_____. Special Problems in Measuring Change with Psychometric Devices. *Evaluative Research: Strategies and Methods.* Pittsburgh, Pa.: American Institutes for Research, 1970, pp. 48-66.

Cleary, T., Linn, R., and Rock, D. Reproduction of Total Test Scores Through the Use of Sequentially Programmed Tests. *Journal of Educational Measurement,* 1968, *5,* 183-187. (a)

_____. An Exploratory Study of Programmed Tests. *Educational and Psychological Measurement,* 1968, *28,* 345-360. (b)

Cohen, L. Comments on Professor Messick's Paper. In M. Wittrock and D. Wiley, eds., *The Evaluation of Instruction.* New York: Holt, Rinehart & Winston, 1970, pp. 204-210.

Ferguson, R. *Computer-Assisted Criterion-Referenced Measurement.* Pittsburgh: Learning Research and Development Center, University of Pittsburgh, 1970.

Fiedler, F., Mitchell, T., and Triándis, H. *The Culture Assimilator: An Approach to Cross-Cultural Training.* Seattle: Washington University, 1970.

Glaser, R. Instructional Technology and the Measurement of Learning Outcomes: Some Questions. *American Psychologist,* 1963. *18,* 519-521.

_____, and Cox, R. *Criterion-References Testing for the Measurement of Educational Outcomes.* Pittsburgh: Learning Research and Development Center, University of Pittsburgh, 1968.

_____, and Klaus, D. Proficiency Measurement: Assessing Human Performance. In R. Gagne, ed., *Psychological Principles in System Development.* New York: Holt, Rinehart & Winston, 1962, pp. 419-472.

_____, and Nitko A. *Measurement in Learning and Instruction.* Pittsburgh: Learning Research and Development Center, University of Pittsburgh, 1971.

Hammel, D. *Flexible Teaching Methods for CAI Systems.* Austin, Texas: Texas University Electronics Research Center, 1969.

Hess, R., and Shipman, V. Early Experience and the Socialization of Cognitive Modes in Children. *Child Development,* 1965, *36,* 869-886.

Holtzman, W. The Changing World of Mental Measurement and Its Social Significance. *American Psychologist,* 1971, *26,* 546-553.

Katz, I. Some Motivational Determinants of Racial Differences in Intellectual Achievement. *International Journal of Psychology,* 1967, *2*(1), 1-12.

Lindvall, C., and Cox, R. The Role of Evaluation in Programs for Individualized Instruction. In R. Tyler, ed., *Educational Evaluation: New Roles, New Means.* Chicago Press, 1969, 156-188.

Mager, R. *Teaching: Today and Tomorrow.* Collected papers prepared under work unit TEXTRUCK. Methods of instruction in technical training. HumRRO Professional Paper No. 34-70, 1970-11. (a)

_____. *Preliminary Studies in Automated Teaching.* Collected papers prepared under work unit TEXTRUCK. Methods of instruction in technical training. HumRRO Professional Paper No. 34-70, 1970-12. (b)

Piaget, J. The Origins of Intelligence in Children. New York: International University Press, 1952.

_____. The Psychology of Intelligence. London: Routledge and Paul, 1950.

Popham, W., and Husek, J. Implication of Criterion-Referenced Measurement. *Journal of Educational Measurement,* 1969, *6, 1-9.*

Rimland, B. *The Search for Measures of Practical Intelligence: Research Project 100,000.* Paper presented at the American Psychological Association Meeting, Washington, D.C., 3 September 1969.

Rotter, J. Generalized Expectancies for Internal vs. External Control of Reinforcement. *Psychological Monographs,* 1966, *80*(1) (Whole No. 609).

Rundquist, E. The Prediction Ceiling. *Personnel Psychology,* 1969, *22,* 109-116.

Seidel, R. *Discussion of a Unique Approach to CAI: Project Impact. Innovations for Training.* HumRRO Professional Paper No. 6-69, 1969, 10-24.

Siegel, Schultz, D., and Lanterman, R. *The Development and Application of Absolute Scales of Electronic Performance.* Wayne, Pa. Applied Psychological Services, 1964.

Siegel, A., and Fischl, M. *Absolute Scales of Electronic Job Performance: Empirical Validity of an Absolute Scaling Technique.* Wayne, Pa.: Applied Psychological Services, 1965.

_____, Bergman, B., Federman, P., and Sellman, W. *Some Techniques for the Evaluation of Technical Training Courses and Students.* (AFHRL-TR-72-15) Lowry AFB, Colo.: Technical Training Division, Air Force Human Resources Laboratory, February 1972.

_____, Berbman, B., and Miller G. Adaptation of Advanced Measurement and Evaluation Techniques for Utilization in Air Force Technical Training Systems. AFHRL-TR-73-18. Lowry AFB, Colo.: Technical Training Division, Air Force Human Resources Laboratory, November 1973.

Shuford, E. *Confidence Testing: A New Tool for Measurement.* Lexington, Mass.: Shuford-Massengill Corp., 1967.

_____, Albert, A., and Massengill H. Admissible Probability Measurement Procedures. *Psychometrika,* 1966, *31,* 125-145.

Tucker, L. Learning Theory and Multivariate Experiment: Illustration by Determination of Generalized Learning Curves. In R. Cattell, ed., *Handbook of Multivariate Experimental Psychology.* Chicago: Rand McNally, 1966.

Worchel, S., and Mitchell, T. *An Evaluation of the Effectiveness of the Culture Assimilator in Thailand and Greece.* Report No. TR-70-13. Seattle, Washington: Washington University, Department of Psychology, 1970.

ADDITIONAL RESOURCES

Cronbach, L. Course Improvement Through Evaluation, *Teachers College Record,* 1963, *64,* 672-683.

Gagne, R., ed. *Psychological Principles in System Development.* New York: Holt, Rinehart & Winston, 1962.

Tyler, R., ed. *Educational Evaluation: New Roles, New Means.* Chicago: University of Chicago Press, 1969.

Wittrock, M., and Wiley, D., eds. *The Evaluation of Instruction.* New York: Holt, Rinehart & Winston, 1970.

54

COLLEGE STUDENT MORALE

by Lora H. Robinson
Special Assistant to the President
Grand Valley State Colleges
Allendale, Michigan

This paper has been previously published as an ERIC/Higher Education Research Current at, and published by, the American Association for Higher Education, Washington, D.C. (May 1, 1972).

College campuses have not been nearly as calm as many people think. A study by Bayer and Astin (1971) showed that almost 20 percent of higher educational institutions (an estimated 462) experienced at least one severe protest in 1970-1971. This figure is only slightly lower than the estimate for 1968-1969, a year viewed as one of extreme disruption. Consequently, it is timely to be concerned about the sources of student disaffection and alienation today.

This study covers several potential sources of impact within the college environment—students, faculty, administration, and student role expectations. Students' interaction with these people within their environment, and their own social role expectations, determine the nature of their student experiences and determine the type of student-college relationship that evolves. Data on actual student experiences within these four realms of impact are presented to provide a basis for assessing the character of the student-college relationship both in terms of its quality and content.

The research findings reported were obtained by the author in a study of 372 college students at two liberal arts colleges (Robinson, 1972). The "Student Experiences Questionnaire" was administered to a representative sample of all class levels at both schools. The instrument was designed to elicit students' estimates of the frequency of occurrence of a number of college experiences.

STUDENT-ADMINISTRATION RELATIONS

Students frequently criticize administrative policies and procedures. In the research literature there are a number of studies pertaining to administrative policies that reveal student feelings and attitudes about how adequately they have been integrated into the academic system. In this realm, Chase and Warren (1969), Goodman (1967), *Graduate Students' Opinions* . . . (1968), Stordahl (1969), and Taylor in Oxtoby (1967) provide examples of either the areas or the intensity of student criticism. For example, Chase and Warren found an increase in students' desire for more responsible participation in university affairs after a period of submersion in campus life.

The fact that students feel disassociated from administrators is suggested by Taylor's report. He found stu-

dents thought of the administration as the higher echelon, where decisions are made in absentia. Furthermore, students complained that they were not consulted about decisions affecting their future lives, that an atmosphere of "we" and "they" permeated the halls, and that administrative procedures resulted in depersonalization and alienation.

In *Graduate Students' Opinions . . .*, students were asked to list five satisfactory and five unsatisfactory aspects of their undergraduate experience. They criticized the administration for inadequately communicating and interpreting policy decisions, as well as for not providing visible and accessible channels through which student opinions or complaints could reach administrative ears. This study, along with Taylor's, depicts a few students' notions of defects in student-administration relations.

Part of the author's questionnaire results relate to student experiences that *indirectly* reflect administrative policies. For these questions, students were asked to judge their experiences with nonacademic personnel (defined as administrators, secretaries, clerks, counselors, health service personnel, campus police, attendants, janitors, etc.). The figure below summarizes student responses to five different experiences that correspond to aspects of the student-administrator relationship. The percentage of students who encountered a specific experience "once or twice," "occasionally," "commonly," or "never" is presented. *In dealings with nonacademic personnel, students have:*

	Never	Once	Occasionally	Commonly
found that information was easy to get	7%	22%	36%	35%
not been notified about changes which concerned them	37%	37%	16%	10%
encountered lack of interest in suggestions or complaints	28%	31%	28%	13%
been frustrated by the complexity with which things are done	17%	27%	27%	28%
had a voice in determining or influencing policies or procedures	49%	27%	21%	4%

These percentages indicate that even at small schools procedures do not remain simple. Over half of the sample had been upset by the complexity of some aspect of college operations. The data also suggest that while administrative personnel listen to complaints, students actually have little concrete involvement in policy-making. Finally, students seem to be well informed both in terms of the accessibility and dissemination of information.

In the area of administrative procedures, students also are affected by their *direct* contact with nonacademic personnel. Indeed the quality of these contacts are believed to play a significant role in students' education. Kauffman (1968) and Price (1968) urge the recognition of the importance of student-staff relations. For example, Kauffman suggests colleges and universities recognize that all their administrative personnel play a role in education, since they are the ones the students most frequently deal with. One wonders how much of the student unrest could be attributed to authoritarian policy, rude clerks, hostile and unfriendly secretaries, and testy tellers. . . . No matter how unimportant a staff position may seem to the administration and faculty, it must be recognized that the students have to deal with many of these people constantly.

The figures below summarize the kind of treatment students report experiencing from college staff. *In dealing with nonacademic personnel students have:*

	Never	Once	Occasionally	Commonly
gotten the run-around	30%	38%	22%	10%
been treated unfairly	53%	34%	10%	3%
felt that they sincerely tried to be helpful	1%	18%	34%	47%
been treated courteously	3%	6%	25%	67%
felt that they were interested in their welfare	9%	22%	41%	28%

STUDENT-FACULTY RELATIONS

Probably the one need most often expressed about student-faculty contact is the student's desire for sympathetic relationships. Foley and Foley (1969), Hunt (1963), Trotter (1967), Wedemeyer (1951), Shamos (1969), and Townsend (1956), among others, document this.

Responses to two questions indicate how frequently students encounter the desired sympathetic relationship with instructors. *Students report having an instructor who:*

	Never	Once	Occasionally	Commonly
became interested in them as a person	11%	37%	37%	22%
made it easy for them to talk to him (her)	2%	20%	37%	40%

Although communications between faculty and students flow fairly easily, establishing closer relationships seems much rarer.

Sympathetic understanding is not the only quality students value in teachers. Traits appearing often in evaluations of effective teachers include: cooperativeness, democratic attitude, patience, wide interests, personal appearance, pleasing manners, fairness and impartiality, sense of humor, good disposition, consistent behavior, flexibility, and expression of recognition and praise for efforts (Nelson, 1955).

Hussain and Leestamper (1968) asked samples of student, faculty, and alumni to rank criteria for effective teaching in order of importance. All samples ranked *being well prepared for class* first; however there was a great deal of disparity in priorities among groups. Students ranked *motivating students to do their best* 13th (faculty, third); faculty ranked *being able to show prac-*

tical application of subject matter 21st (students, ninth); students ranked *being fair and reasonable to students in evaluation procedures* second (faculty, eighth). It is not surprising that students consider fairness as a high-priority item: it is directly related to their success and status in their student role. Other studies that indicate students desire fairness, impartiality, and trustworthiness from their instructors include those by Bousfield (in Nelson, 1955), Goodman (1962), Erickson (1969), Reid (in Ellis, 1954), and Trotter (1967).

The content of four questions related directly to these teacher attributes. Responses indicate how frequently students were likely to encounter teachers with undesirable traits. *Students report having an instructor who:*

	Never	Once	Occasionally	Commonly
showed more respect for one or two students than for the rest of us in the class	30%	42%	21%	7%
was not entirely fair in his dealings	40%	51%	7%	2%
made us feel that some later or hidden penalty might come from displeasing him	37%	42%	18%	2%
handed out grades in a capricious or arbitrary way	38%	46%	13%	3%

These percentages indicate that many students will experience these unfavorable teacher traits at least once in their student career. In the student-teacher relationship currently the "power" is held by the teacher. It seems possible that the recent call for external exams and nongraded courses may have been motivated by the past abuse of this power.

How a course is conducted is also an area of interest to students; yet, information on the actual experiences of students is rare. In this study students were asked a number of questions about their actual class experiences *Students report having an instructor who:*

	Never	Once	Occasionally	Commonly
assigned coursework which seemed pretty irrelevant and meaningless	17%	38%	32%	13%
had such vague course objectives that we had to guess what he wanted us to know	20%	55%	21%	4%
treated class members as though he viewed us as capable and responsible	1%	11%	36%	51%
was genuinely interested in students' ideas, comments and suggestions about how the class might be run	6%	30%	37%	26%

Contradictions appear in students' responses to these questions. Fifty-one percent reported that frequently they were treated as responsible people. Yet this did not extend to ideas about running the class, reported "common" by only 26 percent. Although most students will probably encounter vague course objectives, the occurrence of meaningless coursework is even more frequent, and is by far the most commonly encountered negative course experience.

STUDENT-STUDENT RELATIONS

Although an effective student-teacher relationship may be of much consequence, the student-student relationship holds even more promise for the undergraduate. A number of educators believe students' peers have a greater impact on them than any other group in college (Freedman, 1960; Riesman and Jencks, 1962; and Newcomb, 1962). Given the potential effect of peer influence, it is surprising that there is so little attention paid to the student-student relationship by the higher education community. The prevailing attitude is that "they will take care of themselves."

This study explored the student-student relationship in some detail. Ten questions covered many aspects of student interactions. The percentages below show what kind of student relationships can be found on campus. *With peers, students:*

	Never	*Once*	*Occasionally*	*Commonly*
found that upperclassmen were active in helping them to adjust to campus life	5%	28%	39%	28%
met others whom they just couldn't respect	7%	30%	45%	18%
pitched in to help get the job done	11%	28%	38%	23%
been unacquainted with most of the other members in class	10%	29%	37%	24%
shared many attitudes and opinions	1%	12%	36%	51%
found little help and sympathy for their problems	32%	41%	20%	7%
felt they could "be themselves"	3%	6%	25%	66%
found others critical but fair	8%	26%	43%	23%
watched a class develop hostility toward a student who turned out more work than anyone else	52%	31%	13%	4%
discovered that the competition in class hindered the development of friendships	64%	24%	9%	3%

A few of the item response patterns deserve comment. There is little known about the actual effects of academic competition on students. The questionnaire results reveal a clear denial that competition affects student friendships; however, the competition climate at the sample schools may not be as keen as elsewhere, since

most also denied that class members became hostile toward an aggressive competitor. On the whole, campus relationships appear to be good: students are cooperative, helpful, fair, and sympathetic. Despite the fact that some students did not merit respect, and some remained strangers, those with whom contacts were shared allowed them to feel comfortable and communicate ideas freely.

THE STUDENT ROLE

So far student reactions have been assessed in relation to significant personages in the academic environment. There are many other aspects of the student educational experience that are not tied to particular people. While every aspect of an institution's climate might be blamed or credited to someone, there are aspects that are simply a function of general feelings, not assigned to any particular source, yet are important to a student's educational experience.

For example, Trotter (1967) noted students expressed the feeling that they were under the "power" of the academic system, that information was not readily available to them, and that there was not much they could do about either. The longer the student remained in school, the better informed he felt; yet there was still a feeling of "powerlessness" and of only being able to "submit." Other students have expressed similar feelings.

> Despite all of the efforts so far, the U. is just one big Computer in the minds of most students. It's too big to be friendly; any concern for the individual's welfare must be achieved at the Departmental or Residence Hall level. However, the U. should still try to do away with its mechanical air. (*Reflections by College Students . . .,* 1968)

How accurately do these individual perceptions reflect student experiences at large? The responses of the student sample to several general questions concerning their student role provides some perspective on this question. *As students, we have:*

	Never	*Once*	*Occasionally*	*Commonly*
not felt part of campus life	29%	36%	23%	12%
had a chance to do things we really like	4%	20%	37%	39%
been stimulated to do our best	8%	27%	48%	17%
wondered whether the work we have to do is preparing us adequately for the future	5%	17%	33%	45%
felt like an individual, not just a number	2%	9%	32%	57%
seen time pass quickly when studying	5%	14%	37%	44%
been afraid of failing	24%	34%	19%	23%
noted changes which are a sign of growth and progress	4%	10%	44%	42%
felt pride in being at this school	12%	24%	36%	28%
wished we were elsewhere doing other things	10%	28%	37%	25%

There are indications that students on the two campuses studied had experiences supportive of student role actualization. Most reported engaging in desirable activities, being stimulated, making progress, and being immersed in studies. Even with the implied positive value of these experiences, a significant group of students have doubts about the value of their activities, and a large number are concerned as to whether they will "succeed" or not. And there are indications of students' integration into the campus community—most feel they are a part of campus life, that they have an individual identity, and have pride in their school—still a significant portion wished they were elsewhere doing other things.

Viewed from this perspective, some of the responses seem contradictory; however, there is one possible interpretation that would account for this. Students seem to view the college experience as necessary and even challenging, as well as being satisfying and rewarding in many respects; still, at the same time, they see the student role as only a temporary one that ends abruptly when they leave college. To most students there seems to be little correlation between the demands made upon them in college and future "life" demands after graduation.

SUMMARY AND CONCLUSION

The data presented in this study provide information on a wide variety of student experiences. Taken together, the results offer a view of the quality and nature of the student-college relationship at two liberal arts colleges. Analyzed in more detail, specific items reveal the frequency with which both positive and negative experiences are encountered on campus. Frequently encountered positive experiences include:

accessible information;

notification of pertinent changes;

fair, sincere, courteous and interested treatment from administrative personnel;

communicative, respectful, fair and noncapricious treatment from faculty members;

supportive, communicative, sympathetic, comfortable and fair treatment from peers;

friendly, nonhostile behavior under competition;

chances to do things really liked;

growth and progress;

engrossment in studies; and

feelings of individual worth.

Frequently encountered negative experiences include:

no voice in policies or procedures;

administrative run-around;

vague course objectives; and

worries about the relevance of college to their future work.

On balance, at the two colleges that form the basis of this study, students encounter more positive than negative experiences. And the source of the most frequent positive and least frequent negative experiences are students' peers.

Hopefully, these results will provide some illumination into the nature of college students' experiences, and serve as an example of a method for exploring other college climates. Such exploration is likely to help educators determine the quality and nature of their own campus environment and locate places for remedial action. In this way an assessment can ultimately be used to facilitate an institution's enterprise.

REFERENCES

Bayer, Alan E., and Alexander W. Astin. "Campus Unrest, 1970-71: Was it Really all that Quiet?," *Educational Record 52*, (1971), pp. 301-313.

Chase, Clinton I., and Warren, Suzanne. *Freshmen View the College Scene: Opinions Before and After the Initial Semester.* Bloomington, Indiana: Indiana University, Bureau of Educational Studies and Testing, 1969. 20 pp. ED 029 592.

Ellis, Elmer, ed. *Toward Better Teaching in College.* Columbia, Missouri: University of Missouri Press, 1954.

Erickson, Stanford C. Earning and Learning by the Hour. In *The Quest for Relevance: Effective College Teaching* 4. Washington, D.C.: American Association for Higher Education, 1969, pp. 3-45. ED 027 858.

Foley, James A., and Foley, Robert K. *The College Scene.* New York: Cowles Book Company, 1969.

Freedman, Mervin B. *The Impact of College.* New Dimensions in Higher Education, No. 4. Washington, D.C.: U.S. Department of Health, Education and Welfare, Office of Education, 1960.

Goodman, Paul. *The Community of Scholars.* New York: Random House, 1962.

_____. A Usual Case—Nothing Fancy. In *College Decision,* ed. by Richard M. Lyon and Rhee Lynon. Belmont, California: Brooks/Cole Publishing Company, 1967. pp. 20-25.

Graduate Students' Opinions of the Undergraduate Experience. *Journal of the National Association of Women Deans and Counselors, 31* (1968): pp. 88-90.

Hunt, Everett L. *The Revolt of the College Intellectual.* New York: Human Relations Aids, 1963.

Hussain, K. M., and Leestamper, Robert. *Survey on Criteria of Teaching Effectiveness at New Mexico State University.* Las Cruces, New Mexico: New Mexico State University, 1968. 53 pp. ED 023 365.

Kauffman, Joseph F. *Report of the Committee on the Student in Higher Education.* New Haven, Connecticut: The Hazen Foundation, 1968. 72 pp. ED 028 735.

Nelson, A. Gordon. Better Teacher-Student Relations, *Phi Delta Kappan, 36* (1955): pp. 295-302.

Oxtoby, R., ed. *Staff-Student Relations.* Report of a conference organized by the United Kingdom Council of World University Service. London: World University Service, 1967.

Newcomb, Theodore M., Student Peer-Group Influence and Intellectual Outcomes of College Experience. In *Personality Factors on College Campus: Review of a Symposium,* ed. by Robert L. Sutherland and Wayne H. Holtzman et al. Austin, Texas: Hogg Foundation for Mental Health, 1962. pp. 69-91.

Price, William, The Role of the Student. In *Leadership and Responsibility on the Changing Campus: Who's in Charge Here?* Papers presented at the eighth annual meeting of the American Association of State Colleges and Universities. Washington, D.C.: American Association of State Colleges and Universities, 1968. 12 pp. ED 029 605.

Reflections by College Students on Their Environments, A Survey Report. Amherst, Massachusetts: University of Massachusetts,

Office of Institutional Studies, 1968.

Riesman, David, and Jencks, Christopher. The Viability of the American College. In *The American College: A Psychological and Social Interpretation of the Higher Learning,* ed. by Nevitt Sanford. New York: John Wiley and Sons, Inc., 1962. pp. 74-192.

Robinson, Lora H. The Assessment of College Student Morale. Unpublished doctoral dissertation. Los Angeles: University of California, 1972.

Shamos, Morris H. The Art of Teaching Science. In *The Quest for Relevance: Effective College Teaching 2.* Washington, D.C.: American Association for Higher Education, 1969. pp. 3-25. ED 027 856.

Stordahl, Kalmer E. *Student Satisfaction With Northern Michigan University.* Marquette, Michigan: Northern Michigan University, Office of Institutional Research, 1969. 19 pp. ED 045 020.

Townsend, Agatha. *College Freshmen Speak Out.* New York: Harper and Brothers, 1956.

Trotter, Marilyn L. Characteristics of University Teacher-Student Relationships. Unpublished master's thesis. Kansas State University, 1967.

Wedemeyer, Charles A. Use of the Morale-Type Survey on the College Level. *Junior College Journal 21* (1951): pp. 434-443.

55

STUDENT DISSENT: ALWAYS WAS AND ALWAYS WILL BE

by Kenneth G. Goode
Assistant Vice Chancellor
University of California
Berkeley, California

In July 1973, Willis A. Shotwell, full-time disciplinarian at the University of California, Berkeley, the cradle of the Free Speech Movement, was returned to his previous assignment of giving preprofessional counseling to students. The administrators at Berkeley had "held a mirror to the nostrils of expiring rebelliousness and detected no life there." Said Shotwell, "the draft is gone, the war is more or less over, and the threat of interruption of life has ended. The passionate, impromptu politics of the 60s has long since closed down, and may have to await renewal until Jane Fonda's and Tom Hayden's new baby comes of age (Time, 1973)."

Observers of the student protest movement would not agree that "the passionate, impromptu politics of the 60s have long since closed down." Student dissent always was and always will be, and this was best stated by Sir Eric Ashby, who said that one of the university's intellectual purposes is to carry it "from the uncriticized acceptance of orthodoxy to creative dissent over the values and standards of society (1973)."

STUDENT DISSENT ALWAYS WAS

Since medieval times when universities and colleges were first established, students have thrown garbage, threatened professors, shot at presidents, protested infringement of their right of privacy, rioted, demanded a voice in institutional governance, protested against wars, demanded an end to *in loco parentis,* and otherwise revolted. However, the one thing that is different about student unrest today in the United States is that it is qualitatively and quantitatively different. Never before has it been so apparent and its manifestations so widespread, especially in our colleges and universities. Student activism before 1960 had no major impact on national policy. Now it has (Altback and Peterson, 1967).

The first signs of organized student interest in social and political issues on a national scale began to appear in the early 1960s. It was catalyzed when black students sat down at lunch counters in the South to challenge the legacy of slavery and Jim Crow, and it has continued through the Montgomery Bus Boycott, Freedom Rides, Free Speech Movement, Filthy Speech Movement, Anti-War Movement, Third World Cultural Revolution, Anti-House Un-American Activities Movement, United Farm Workers Movement, Free Political Prisoners Movement, Anti-Death Penalty Movement, and Anti-Draft Movement. These demonstrations constitute the most dramatic manifestations to date of what has come to be called "the student protest movement (Mayhew, 1967)."

WHO REVOLTS AND WHY

If it can be understood why these movements and others of the 1950s and 1960s occurred, then a great deal of the basis of student dissent will be understood. But comprehending the mood of the student dissenters who participated in these movements means coming to grips with much that many people, including many administrators in higher education, would rather ignore, or simply write off with some such sweeping term as "communist-inspired" or "beatnik" or "misguided." These same people concentrate their attack on the participants' dress, cleanliness, and length of hair. Out of the accumulated residue of such reactions comes an impression to student dissenters as some sort of rabble scraped from the bottom of the social heap of America (Mayhew, 1973, p. 247).

Interestingly enough, the rabble turns out to be the sons and daughters of America's middle class, who grew up believing that they lived in a great democratic nation which was dedicated to providing its citizens with equal education opportunities, equal job opportunities, the highest standard of living in the world, and all other ingredients of America's middle class. Somehow this post-depression, post-World War II generation, who had everything their middle-class parents could give them, found the gift hollow and rejected it. And in their rejection they began to fashion a movement which has raised many issues and touched on a number of the nation's most exposed nerve ends, i.e., racism, poverty, unemployment, militarism, corruption, etc.

Although it is estimated that only one or two percent of the student dissenters participate in demonstrations, a large segment, if not the majority, of today's college students from all points of the political spectrum share the activists' discontent with institutions of higher education and also their disillusionment with society. Behind their superficial differences in rhetoric, rightwing, middle-of-the-road and leftwing students are in astonishing agreement about higher education. They agree that campus discipline is unjust and politically motivated; they agree that universities and colleges systematically indoctrinate their students with abhorrent political ideas; they agree that higher education in the United States has become a tool of the military-industrial-union "Establishment" (Keniston and Lerner, 1970).

They question the values and priorities of higher education, such as inadequate channels of communication, a lack of responsiveness by administrators, the impersonality of university life, limitations on their freedom of expression, and their inability to participate in decisions that affect their lives. They charge that universities and colleges are hypocritical, in that they fail to practice what they preach, especially in the areas of faculty commitment to teach, labor relations with nonacademic employees, fairness on disciplinary hearings, and institutional concerns for community problems (American Bar Association, 1969). They see universities and colleges are reflections of the larger society, mirroring its institutional racism, its support for the recolonization of the Third World, its repression of new lifestyles and the maintenance of the status quo.

Because of this, student dissenters see an attack on institutions of higher learning as an effective act of resistance to a corrupt society, as opposed to a symbolic gesture of protest (Wallerstein and Starr, 1971). As a result, what has emerged is a clearer critique of American democracy, a more articulate enunciation of some of its contradictions, and a demand for reform. The belief in the constitutional guarantees of life, liberty, and the pursuit of happiness is blurred by the stench of Southern justice, the debris of the inner-city riots, the Kent State, Jackson State, and Southern University deaths, the burning flesh of old women and children in Southeast Asia. The myth of the great American middle class, which projected the image of an endless, prosperous suburb, is now contradicted by the fact that more than 30 million Americans still live in poverty (Horn, 1971).

VIOLENT VS. NONVIOLENT DISSENT

Arson, willful destruction of property, assault and battery, occupation of buildings, interruption of classes, disruption of meetings, barring entrances to buildings, holding administrators captive, violations of injunctions, and other willful and unlawful conduct have all been a part of student dissent. Highly politicized student groups, sometimes aided by nonstudents, have been able to halt the normal operations of institutions of higher education and thwart the normal disciplinary proceedings of universities and colleges. And on a few campuses there is reason to believe that a determined group of revolution-

aries seek to destroy the university or college they attend if they cannot transform it to the image they desire. Therefore I cannot share the calm of the historian Will Durant, who cautioned educators against being unduly alarmed over dissent on college campuses and the turbulence that was marking the 1960s, which he referred to as "foolishness" and just the "measles of intellectual growth (Mayhew, 1967, pp. 252, 216-217)."

However, contrary to the widespread impression created by the mass media (and reinforced by some politicians) that disruptive and violent disorders are typical of campus unrest, the overwhelming majority of campus protests in recent years have been peaceful, orderly, and clearly within the bounds of dissent protected by the First Amendment of the Constitution. A study of campus protest in 1968-1969 showed that more than three-quarters of America's 2500 colleges and universities either had no protests at all or had peaceful protests. Violent protests involving property damage or personal injury occurred on fewer than seven percent of all campuses. During academic year 1968-1969, the American Council on Education found that incidents of student dissent occurred on two-thirds of all campuses, but only about nine percent reported violence. And in May 1970, after Cambodia, Kent State, and Jackson State, only four percent of 1800 college presidents reported violent protest on their campuses. Furthermore, the absolute number of protests on American campuses did not increase dramatically between 1964 and 1970, as some observers of student dissent led the public to believe. From a 1964-1965 study of 849 colleges and universities it is estimated that there were about 370 student protests per 100 colleges and universities. A roughly comparable study conducted in 1969-1970 showed only a small rise to 386 protests per 100 colleges and universities. The evidence, then, is clear—violent and disorderly protests are the exception, not the rule, at institutions of higher education in the United States. The vast majority of students, while becoming more frustrated, more opposed to the military-industrial-labor union complex, less confident in basis American institutions, and more confident that social change will come about only as a result of radical pressure from outside the system, will remain committed to peaceful dissent. Unfortunately, however, political rhetoric and selective reporting by the mass media will continue to conceal the complexity of the situation on the campuses (Keniston and Lerner, p. 28).

DISINTEGRATION OF THE MOVEMENT

Today the student movement is facing a crisis. What once was a loosely knit but unified movement following a widely accepted leadership, with broad but uniform goals, is now a hodge-podge of groups, projects, and styles with no uniform sense of direction and, more often than not, with hostile differences. Evidence of a schism emerged as far back as 1964, when New Left student leaders at the Atlantic City Convention of the Democratic Party denounced trade unionists, mainstream civil rights leaders, and other party liberals for having refused to completely remove the Mississippi delegation and seat the delegates of the Mississippi Freedom Democratic Party. Such denunciation caused alienation, and thereby destroyed the possibility of the New Left's ever becoming a viable mass movement with the support of a national political organization (League for Industrial Democracy, 1970, pp. 1-3).

The most destructive internal rift, however, resulted from a clash between those two groups whose coming together had created the modern student protest movement—black and white students. As the cultural revolution gained momentum, a separatist position was adopted by many black student activists. This trend could have been curtailed by interaction with white student activists who were devoted to racial equality and integration, but the opportunity for such interaction was lost as white student activists, instead of pressing for integration, supported the blacks' non-negotiable demands for their own dormitories, courses, houses, etc. This trend toward separatism was further exacerbated by the peace movement, the ecology movement and the womens' rights movement, all of which instilled a deep resentment in many black student leaders who felt that there was no longer any hope for building a broad-based integrated movement for carrying out major social reform. Hence they turned to "black concerns." As a result, integrated student organizations that grew out of the struggle, such as SNCC and CORE, began to fade away (League for Industrial Democracy, 1970, p. 3).

The breadth of this breach never became clear to many white students until it had become virtually unbridgeable. The responsibility for the breach lay with white students who, in their self-righteousness, believed that until the war was ended, the physical environment saved, and sex discrimination ended, the blacks—along with the poor and the mentally ill—had to wait. Needless to say, this approach had little appeal to black student activists who were nurtured by lectures on patience (League for Industrial Democracy, 1970, pp. 3-4).

Fragmentation was also occurring among white student leaders. The most serious was the split that took place at the 1969 convention of the Students for a Democratic Society, when one faction, unable to agree on tactics and philosophy, expelled another, and this culminated in the creation of two, three, and then many SDS-type organizations.

As the New Left moved from verbal intimidation to disruption to terrorism, in an effort to impose its will on institutions of higher education, other students began to seriously reappraise the philosophy and tactics of change, and to move toward a more peaceful and democratic approach to change. It was clear that many students had become dissatisfied with the dogmatism, self-righteousness, and violence of the New Left. They displayed their abhorrence with the philosophy and tactics of the New Left by establishing such student organizations as the New Politics, Democratic Radicals, Campus Americans for Democratic Action, and the Moderate Left. Other evidence of this dissatisfaction can be seen in the growing interest in student government, where "moderate left radicals" have continued to unseat New Left officeholders; the rebirth of fraternities and sororities; the es-

tablishment of alternative models of careers; and the overall willingness to work within the system in order to effectuate change (League for Industrial Democracy, 1970, p. 6).

THE FUTURE

The student protest movement of the 1950s and 1960s, although violent at times, created a greater sense of reality about our democratic society, and although institutions of higher education, local and state governments, and the Congress have responded to the disruptive disturbances and to the underlying causes of student unrest in a variety of ways, to clearly understand the student protest movement means to come to grips with the powerful forces which motivate students to challenge a system that so effectively reinforces itself and so convincingly challenges the students' own self-confidence.

The great majority of the students in the movement will choose to remain in the colleges and universities and maintain some loose connection with "the system." However, they will also more and more aggressively and directly challenge the basic premises and missions of our institutions of higher education. There is little hope of immediate, radical change; nevertheless, the student movement to reform the colleges and universities, as a part of the movement to reform society, will continue to gain constant and more compelling strength, fragmentation notwithstanding.

REFERENCES

Altbach, Philip G., and Peterson, Patti. Before Berkeley: Historical Perspectives on American Student Activism. *Annals,* Vol. 395, May 1971, pp. 1-14; Richard Glacks, The Liberated Generation: And Exploration of the Roots of Student Protest. *Journal of Social Issues,* Vol. 23, July 1967, pp. 52-75.

Ashby, Eric. The Structure of Higher Education: A World View. New York: International Council for Educational Development, 1973.

Astin, A. E., and Astin, A. W. Violence and Disruption on the U.S. Campus, 1968-1969. *Educational Record,* Fall 1969, Table 1.

Campus Tensions: Analysis and Recommendations. Washington, D.C.: American Council on Education, 1970.

Campus Tensions: Analysis and Recommendations. Winston-Salem: Mary Reynolds Babcock Foundation, 1970.

Cerese, Sarah, and Koon, Jeffrey. College Seniors View Campus Unrest and National Issues—Spring 1970. Berkeley: Center for Research and Development in Higher Education, 1970.

Constructive Changes to Ease Campus Tensions. Washington, D.C., National Association of State Universities and Land Grant Colleges, 1970.

Holmes, Grace W., ed. Law and Discipline on Campus. Ann Arbor: Institute of Continuing Legal Education, 1971.

_____. Student Protest and the Law. Ann Arbor: Institute of Continuing Education, 1969.

Horn, Francis H. Challenges and Perspective in Higher Education. Carbondale, Ill.: Southern Illinois University Press, 1971.

Joint Statement on Rights and Freedoms of Students. Washington, D.C.: Association of American Colleges, 1967.

Keniston, Kenneth, and Lerner, Michael. The Unholy Alliance Against the Campus. *The New York Times Magazine,* November 8, 1970.

Kroepsch, Robert H., and Buck, Dorothy, eds. Governing the

Restless Campus. Boulder, Colorado: Western Interstate Commission for Higher Education, 1970.

Mayhew, Lewis B., ed. Higher Education in the Revolutionary Decades. New York: McCutchen Publishing Co., 1967.

Peterson, R. E. The Scope of Organized Student Protest in 1964-65: An Extrapolation. Princeton: Educational Testing Service, 1966.

Report of the American Bar Association Commission on Campus Government and Student Dissent. Chicago: American Bar Association, 1969.

Report of the Commission on Campus Unrest. Washington, D.C.: United States Government Printing Office, 1970.

Singletary, Otis A. Freedom and Order on Campus. Washington, D.C.: American Council on Education, 1968.

The State of the Student Movement—1970. New York: League for Industrial Democracy, 1970.

Student Protest. The Annuals of the American Academy of Social and Political Science, May 1971.

Wallerstein, Immanuel, and Starr, Paul, eds. *The University Crisis Reader*. Two Volumes. New York: Random House, Inc., 1971.

56

STUDENT-INITIATED CHANGES IN THE ACADEMIC CURRICULUM

by Janet Dinsmore Shoenfeld
ERIC Clearinghouse On Higher Education
The George Washington University
Washington, D.C.

This paper has been previously published as an ERIC/Higher Education Research Current or ERIC/Higher Education Research Report prepared by The George Washington University and published by the American Association for Higher Education, Washington, D.C.

The literature on student unrest at colleges and universities cites dissatisfaction with the learning experience as a major, and sometimes *the* major, cause of student rebellion. Student charges that many college courses are irrelevant to social realities and needs, and that the traditional structure of the academic curriculum results in a fragmented and superficial educational experience, are familiar to all concerned with higher education. Not only has the substance of particular courses and academic programs come under attack, but also the methods of packaging them, such as the A-to-F grading system, the use of lectures rather than independent study, and inflexible course and degree requirements.

N. N. Betts, Jr., observed in 1970:

> There is a good bit of evidence to suggest that student concerns will be more and more with academic policy, with the nature of the curriculum, the quality of teaching, the depersonalization of education.

The findings of the survey reported here certainly add to this evidence. Studies have indicated that in the past only a few colleges and universities provided effective means for students to design or shape accredited academic programs, most relegating student-initiated efforts to extracurricular activities. Now, however, it is clear that institutions of all types, sizes, and geographic locations are not merely bowing to student pressures for participation in educational reform, but are actively encouraging student suggestions for change.

METHODOLOGY

This survey of 234 diverse institutions of higher education was undertaken in December 1969, a time when the movement toward student-initiated educational reform was well under way. About 70 percent of the sample surveyed were institutions cited by students attending a recent U.S. National Student Association conference as having at least one student-initiated course. The remaining 30 percent, however, were chosen at random. Both groups responded at approximately the same rate.

A letter accompanied by a brief five-item questionnaire was sent to the staff member in charge of academic affairs asking for information on courses, programs, or activities that had been established or modified at the direct request of students. Learning experiences that were not awarded credit were not to be included. In addition, the survey form asked whether the institution, in response to specific student pressure (in contrast to general student activism) had adopted new grading practices, dropped courses, or altered degree requirements. The respondents were further asked to describe how students were instrumental in effecting these changes. Of the 234 institutions surveyed, 132 responded, a response rate of 56.4 percent. This report presents and discusses the findings.

ORGANIZATION

The report is divided into two major sections: *Types* of Curricular Reform and *Processes* of Curricular Reform. The sequence of discussion in Part I generally reflects the frequency of responses concerning the topic under consideration. It begins, for example, with the most commonly reported student-initiated change—the establishment of Black Studies courses and programs. Findings concerning Ethnic Studies programs are discussed separately, since these programs usually refer not to black experience but to the role and history of other minorities in the U.S.

Courses established in response to student desires for "relevance" are the third group under discussion. These courses relate directly to current social and/or political issues. Although the subjects of these courses sometimes overlap with those of Black or Ethnic Studies courses (when the topic is "racism," for example), the category is distinct enough to warrant separate treatment. The findings reported include both individual course innovations and the creation of entire departments.

The next topic deals with student-initiated courses that fit comfortably within the established curriculum, and includes examples of new courses in the arts, the freshman-year program, and courses concerning the role of higher education and the university.

Changes in degree requirements and course load are considered next. Although the tendency was in the direction of reducing requirements, institutional methods of doing this varied. Grading reform, principally the introduction of the pass/fail system, is the last item under "Types of Curricular Change." Again, while a large number of institutions introduced pass/fail, there was great variation in the extent of and constraints on its use.

Part II deals with the processes or methods of curricular change, and considers *how* students effected innovations. Eight approaches are identified, ranging from service on academic committees concerned with specific courses or practices, to the formulation of comprehensive plans calling for, and outline the reconstruction of, entire academic programs and structures.

I. TYPES OF CURRICULAR REFORM

Black Studies

The most common student-initiated change reported was the establishment of Black Studies courses or programs. Fifty-nine institutions, ranging from small, private, rural colleges to large, public, urban universities, reported the inclusion of Black Studies courses in their curricula, often following recommendations from black student groups. Black students, in fact, frequently shared responsibility with faculty for developing new courses, locating faculty, and recruiting new students.

A majority of institutions, such as the universities of Alabama, Colorado State, and Arizona, Cornell College (Iowa), and Kansas State College of Pittsburgh, chose to include new Black Studies courses within existing departments. Thus, on many campuses, Afro-American literature was added to the English Department, The Negro in the United States (or some version thereof) to the History Department, such courses as Economic Development of the Black Community and Economics of Poverty and Discrimination to the Economics Department, and Swahili to the Department of Foreign Languages. The scope of traditional fields was stretched to encompass topics such as: The Black Community as Internal Colony (at Indiana University), Black Nationalism (at Chatham College), Black Philosophy (at Swarthmore), The Mind of Black America (at the University of Arizona), and Black Experience (at the University of West Virginia). Most institutions, however, chose to offer courses that fell clearly into the established disciplinary categories of literature, history, sociology, and the arts.

About 20 of the responding colleges and universities, including such differing institutions as Fordham, the universities of Akron, Montana, Houston, and California at Santa Barbara, initiated full-fledged degree programs in Black or Afro-American Studies. Like Temple University and the University of Ohio, Fordham established an Afro-American Institute at the urging of black students. In the first semester, Fall 1969, courses were offered in

history, social thought, economic structure of the community, social institutions from antiquity, psychology, comparative social and cultural systems, and Swahili.

The University of Houston's program was more elaborate. It offered: Afro-American Culture, People of Africa, Black Identity, Community Organization and Development, American Minority Peoples, Social Movements, Economics of Slavery, Human Resources and Poverty, Afro-American Literature, History of East, Central and West Africa, Elementary and Intermediate Swahili, Topics in Political Dynamics, Africa in World Affairs, Government, Politics and Geography in Africa, Educating the Disadvantaged, and Independent Study.

Independent and field studies and the requirements of community service were common features of newly established Black Studies courses and departments. A student-engendered course, Study of Poverty and Ghetto Life, at the University of California, Berkeley, required students to live in homes in the Oakland poverty area while investigating the organization of the black ghetto, the roles of existing institutions, the culture, and possible planning solutions. Berkeley students taking The Politics of Race Relations conducted field research on the structural, ideological, and social psychological dynamics of the political process surrounding a Poor People's" demonstration in Washington, D.C. The proposed community service component of the Black Studies program at University of California, Santa Barbara, was typical in its inclusion of urban programs, workshops, cultural offerings, social activities, and programs dealing with relations between black students and their parents.

Extensive turmoil, attracting national attention, surrounded the establishment and role of the Black Studies Department at San Francisco State College in 1969. A listing of course titles indicates the department's special flavor: Black History, Black Psychology, Black Involvement in Scientific Development, Black Arts and Humanities, Literature of Blackness, Black Writers Workshop, Black Intellectuals, Black Fiction, Black Poetry, The Painting of Blackness, The Sculpture of Blackness, Black Radio, Television and Film, Black Journalism, Black Oratory, Black Philosophy, Black Classics, Black Politics, Sociology of Blackness, Economics of the Black Community, Geography of Blackness, Social Organization of Blackness, Field Work in Black Organization, Social Structure of Black Organization, Field Work in Black Community, Development of Black Leadership, Demography of Blackness, Black Counseling, and Black Nationalism and the International Community.

Third College at the University of California, San Diego, was in the process of development at the time of the survey. Oriented toward ethnic and urban studies, the College is designed to include black and Mexican-American studies programs. Students were engaged in planning the curriculum and developing the philosophy to guide future academic plans for the college. "In anticipation of Third College there are certain courses in ethnic studies which are currently available. These were (established) in direct response to stated requests of our students and their awakened interest in ethnic and cultural matters."

Ethnic Studies

Seventeen mostly Western and Southwestern institutions (eight of them in California) reported the establishment of ethnic studies courses or programs at the urging, or with the participation, of students. The heavy involvement of students in the development of such programs as Indian Studies at the University of Montana, and American Ethnic Studies at Sonoma State College (California), was emphasized by respondents. The Dean of the Faculty at Sonoma State wrote: "All of the initial cadre of ethnic studies faculty were interviewed and approved by the students who worked toward the development of the program. We hired no faculty member who was not approved by the students."

In contrast to the common academic practice of randomly adding more courses to various departments, most of the responding institutions initiated comprehensive degree-earning programs. Some examples are the new College of Ethnic Studies at Western Washington State College and three degree programs in Mexican-American Studies at the University of Arizona. The Arizona program concentrates on preparing students for teaching in the field, "rather than merely contributing to broader cultural understanding"—evidence of genuine commitment to this new area of study.

While preparing the proposal for a program in American Ethnic Studies, the Educational Policies Council of Sonoma State College's Academic Senate, in which students hold 15 voting memberships out of 62, sent out two questionnaires to assess community and student reactions to this new field of study. The response was "most favorable." The number of students who expressed interest and approval far exceeded the number of students in each ethnic group enrolled at the college—an indication to the Council that they need not be concerned that ethnic studies courses would become segregated courses. The response from the community indicated that the public school system and other public service organizations were ready to employ graduates of an ethnic studies program, and suggested a wide range of possible positions graduates might be called upon to fill. Because of high public interest in the provision of ethnic studies in the college's service area, Sonoma State developed courses, institutes, and workshops in its extension and continuing education programs.

As in Black Studies programs, community service is a typical aspect of ethnic studies. A student-initiated course at the University of California, Berkeley, entitled Education of Deaf Mexican Children, calls for students to teach and work with youngsters at the School of Deaf Children in Tijuana, Mexico. While tutoring at the school, students live with local families.

The proposed Center for Chicano Studies at the University of California, Santa Barbara, would offer community workshops, cultural events, nonresearch publications, etc. A course in "Brown Power" is offered in the extension program of the University of California, San Diego, in addition to courses in the regular academic program on Spanish-American-Mexican history and culture. American Indians and Mexican-Americans were not the only focus of ethnic studies programs. Puerto Rican Studies were offered at Fordham, and Asian-American Studies were offered at several California institutions. The Asian-American Studies program at San Francisco State was the most extensive reported. It offers courses such as: Practical English Skills for Asian-Americans; Third-World Community Workshop; Sociocultural and Political History; Asian-American Communities and the Urban Crisis; The Asian-American: A Psychological Profile; Asian Perspectives on Western Literature Traditions; Asian-American Workshop in Creative Writing; Asian-American Studies: Curriculum, Research and Evaluation; Conversational Cantonese; The Chinese in America; The Chinese-American Community; Mental Health Problems in the Chinese-American Community; The Japanese-American: A Social and Psychological Profile; The Japanese-American in the United States; Japanese-American Community Workshop; Selected Topics in Japanese-American Studies; Introductory Tagalog; Introductory Ancient Philipino History; Introductory Modern Philipino History; Philipino Arts; and the Philipino Community Workshop.

The respondent from the University of Hawaii wrote:

> In the spring of 1969, student radicals of the Black Student Union and the Third-World Liberation Front demanded a program in ethnic studies. After several meetings in which the University administration tried to facilitate the development of the proposal, the students insisted that the initiative should be theirs. However, during the intervening summer the student leaders lost interest in the program and the idea died. Upon prodding of certain students by the administration, we have revived the idea and a student-faculty committee has been appointed and a coordinator is about to be hired to develop plans for a program which will study the life of minority ethnic groups within the American culture, particularly in Hawaii.

Montclair State College attributed to student initiative a college requirement that students take at least one of a specified group of courses that aim to increase student awareness and understanding of the problems and culture of minority groups and their contribution to the nation's heritage and future.

Many respondents noted that students were not only instrumental in developing academic programs in black and ethnic studies, but that their suggestions also resulted in the establishment of programs to recruit minority students. Frequently, admissions officers used minority students already enrolled in the institution as members of recruiting teams, and as staff in their offices.

Social and Political Problems

As might be expected, and as the proliferation of black and ethnic studies indicates, student-initiated courses are overwhelmingly concerned with contemporary social and political issues in the U.S. Many of the new courses deal with urban problems, and encourage or require service in a city community. Typical examples of these problem-centered courses are Xavier University's (New Orleans) The University and the City and Community Health Seminar; Oberlin College's Urban Political Analysis and Seminar in Teaching the Disadvantaged; Kalamazoo College's Racism and Culture; and Indiana University's Poverty Seminar and Rise and Fall of Urban Decay— The Ghetto.

At several institutions, students succeeded in raising the status of community service from an extracurricular activity to a college requirement. At Iowa Wesleyan, for instance, students are required to spend at least seven weeks engaged in service to a community. Central State University in Wilberforce, Ohio, has designed a university-wide "Community Participation Program," in which students are awarded three hours of credit for six hours of active community work per week.

The creation of formal urban studies institutes or centers was rarely mentioned by respondents as a direct outgrowth of student requests, despite the fact that many of the institutions had established such programs or centers. Two cited exceptions were the Division of Urban Education in Indiana University's School of Education and a concentration in urban affairs instituted at Colgate University. In contrast to black and ethnic studies, students appear to have been responsible more for specific courses dealing with urban conditions, rather than for comprehensive programs.

"Relevance" is provided at Southern Illinois University by a student-suggested course entitled Issues of Today. Empowered to choose both topic and teacher, students selected "Election '68" as the first topic for the Winter 1969 quarter. The course covered: the American party system, who votes and why, the Democrats, Republicans, Vietnam, the economy, civil rights, the poor, the American city, fringe and mainstream political participants, myth and reality of public opinion, what the politicians said or failed to say, and the 1968 Congressional elections. Black militancy was the next "Issue of Today," and students studied material on the history of slavery, abolitionist thought and activity, early militant spokesmen and activists, twentieth-century militants and movements, foreign philosophies and militant influences, related organizations and degrees of militancy, freedom movement activities, and contemporary militant newspapers, magazines, music, movies, dress, and manners.

Indiana University's "J" Series in the College of Arts and Sciences offers further examples of socially relevant new courses: Politics and the New Left, Evolution of the Use of Drugs, Role of the Mafia in Contemporary America, Rock and Folk Lyrics and the Counterculture, The Penal Code System, Attitudinal Racism, and Contemporary Political Problems—which covers political aspects of environmental management, radical black politics and related Third-World movements, the Marxian revolutionary idea, the white "problem" in the American city, ancient Hebrew and modern black prophets, and crisis in European integration.

At Colgate University, students were responsible for the establishment of courses in civil disobedience and problems of war and peace, as well as one on environmental issues. At the Chicago branch of the University of Illinois, courses in Institutional Racism in Social Welfare and Social Action were added to the curriculum in response to student suggestions.

Student pressure on colleges and universities to provide socially relevant learning experiences resulted not only in the establishment of individual courses, but also of entire programs and departments. Sonoma State College's Dean of the Faculty wrote of a newly established masters program in political science:

> The Political Science MA clearly originated with a group of graduating seniors in political science. It differs from conventional MA degrees because it involves an internship program and has an emphasis on learning the techniques of securing change within the present system.

The request for approval of the new degree stated:

> Many contemporary students are deeply disturbed by inconsistencies they find in the American Society. Of special concern to them is the gap between the high ideals of justice, equality and freedom set forth in the Deceleration of Independence, the Constitution of 1787, and the Bill of Rights, and the actual performance of the society where they find inequality, injustice, and poverty. Some students wish to destroy the hypocrisy they see about them through total revolution. Others seek to escape the dilemma through self-immolation. On the other hand, there are students who wish to operate within the system to bring about social reform; to bridge the gap between ideals and practice. For this latter group of students this program is designed.

The emphasis on active involvement with concrete political issues through internships, and the view that academic learning should have practical objectives, are characteristic of student-initiated courses.

This problem-centered approach is demonstrated in the new Department of Applied Behavioral Sciences at the University of California, Davis. Students played a significant role in its establishment, and a student committee designed its undergraduate major. The program's focus is similar to that of the Sonoma State Political Science MA.

> APPLIED BEHAVIORAL SCIENCES prepares students for creative work with people in helping them improve their social and their physical environments. The study of human social behavior together with the study of processes and strategies of social change are emphasized. Knowledge of the behavioral and environmental sciences is integrated with the development of skills necessary to apply this knowledge to the solving of complex social problems.
>
> The curriculum is intended primarily for students whose career goals are oriented toward public and community service. Community development, education, environmental design, and inter-group relations are examples of fields offering opportunities for employment of graduates in a wide variety of settings.

The curriculum includes such courses as: Scientific Bias and Social Myths, Directed Group Study, Special Study for Undergraduates, Orientation to Community Resources, Housing, Community Development, The Disadvantaged, The Continuing Learner, Man, Work and Technology, Research Methods and Applied Behavioral Science, Tutoring in Applied Behavioral Sciences, Community Tutoring, and Special Study for Advanced Undergraduates.

While students suggested material and helped develop programs of study at some campuses, they actually ran courses at others. Two examples of student-run courses dealing with socially relevant topics are Rosary College's

(Illinois) course on racism and Loyola University's (Louisiana) course on drugs. The Loyola course was dropped after one semester because the Dean of Students decided it would be possible to reach more students with information about drugs by inviting guest lecturers to the campus. Another example is Boston University's The Radical Critique of the American Political Economy, which has the following course description:

> The Radical Critique of the American Political Economy is an innovative course which attempts to subject the major political, social and economic institutions of the United States to a systematic and radical inquiry. The course has an explicitly radical perspective, although within that perspective many points of view contend. The major topics covered by the course include racism, the oppression of women, imperialism, labor and the working class, and a brief overview of Marxist economic and social theory. The structure of the course combines outside lecturers and student-led discussion groups weekly, and the course is governed by the student section leaders.

Some students not only want a voice in choosing curricular content, but seek reform in the overall decision-making process as well. This is indicated by the description of the administration of The Radical Critique:

> The course is administered by the Radical Course Collective; i.e., the section leaders and co-leaders. It should be noted that most sections have both male and female leaders, one or the other acting as a co-leader and both members of the Collective. All decisions as to content of the course, schedule, speakers, readings, etc., are made democratically by the Collective, in consultation with members of the Faculty Liaison Committee.

Here the administrative structure is similar to that of free universities, which students have established to provide learning experiences that are generally unavailable at most institutions of higher education. The chairman of a faculty Academic Policy Committee made the following assessment of the course:

> Generally it was agreed that the student faculty and the student audience demonstrated enthusiasm, a curiosity rarely found among college courses. Lecture sessions are followed by extremely vigorous spontaneous discussions between the floor and the speaker. Some discussion sections have been found to be well attended and filled with talk and the exchange of ideas. Some committee members found that contrary to their expectations no monolithic ideological view was to be found in lecture or discussion. There is a very generous sense of inquiry to be found among the students in the course, and, to a lesser degree, among the faculty.

However, he went on to say that "the course could be materially improved by adequate and concerned faculty supervision."

Another new accredited course organized, conducted, and evaluated by students is Experiments in Learning at Our Lady of the Lake College (Texas). It is described as a "seminar on interdisciplinary topics of contemporary relevance."

Courses run by Swarthmore College students include: Radical Education, Black Philosophy, Technology and the Environment, Human Ecology, Theories of Psycho-

therapy, and The Film in America. In addition, students at Swarthmore initiated and participated in the planning and administration of a course entitled Technology and Freedom, a general survey course of issues in the evolution of technology and social organization and their relationship to individual liberty and privacy.

In a student-initiated Action Studies Program ("a 'free university' which nevertheless is integrated within the University of Iowa"), graduate students share teaching duties with some faculty members. This program was established in response to student demands for

> courses more relevant to current social problems, action-oriented courses in which learning would not be divorced from doing, and a program sufficiently flexible and experimental that courses could be given on topics that departments would not ordinarily consider. Students could suggest courses, have a say in class decorum (no classes are strictly lecture), and even determine much of the material to be read and discussed.
>
> In addition to sponsoring courses, the program was broadened to include conferences, speakers, and panels, generally of a controversial nature.

Fourteen courses were offered at the beginning of the program in Spring 1968: History of Vietnam, Teaching in Urban Ghetto, Critique of Business Life, The New Industrial State and the Question of Peace, Applied Behavior Analysis, The Media and McLuhan, The Nature of Sex, Literature and Theology, Literature and Revolution, Mythology and American Folk Literature, Contemporary Afro-American Literature and Thought, Underground Newspaper Workshop, Practical Creativity for Poets, Writers and Other People, and Poverty Action. As a direct result of the actions of some of the participants in the Poverty Action course, city records on housing that failed to meet standards of the local code were made available to the public. A tutorial program for socially deprived, low-income children was also begun.

The Program's general policy was not to repeat courses; however, some have become a part of the regular University curriculum. Although academic credit is not automatically awarded, in the Action Studies Program (even when the subject is The Organization of a Coffee House) credit is sought and often granted through individual departments if the course conforms to certain rigorous academic requirements.

New Courses in General

Although the majority of new courses deal with social and political issues previously considered outside formal academic concern, there are many new student-initiated courses that have been easily accommodated within the traditional college curriculum. Some examples are: Latin American Economics, Political Systems of Sub-Saharan Africa, The Creative Imagination in Contrasted Civilizations, and Aesthetics of Environmental Art, offered at Oberlin College; Karate, History of Religion—Old and New Testaments, and Calculus for Non-Science Majors, offered at Mt. Hood Community College (Oregon); New Directions in Theatre, Mathematics and Everything Else, Human Sexuality, Stylistic Techniques in Creative Writing and Introduction to Clinical and Community Psychology, offered at Indiana University; Major Writers of the European Tradition, offered at Wilson College; Behavioral Science Survey, at Maryville College (Missouri); Broadcast Journalism, at Xavier University; Seminar on Ecclesiology, at Union Theological Seminary; and Contemporary Vietnam, at the University of Hawaii.

Students at some institutions (e.g., Cornell College and Albright College) sought an end to compulsory attendance at weekly convocations and artist-lecture series; however, at other universities more cultural programs and courses in the arts were created. At the University of Montana, the visiting lecture and concert programs were broadened extensively, primarily because of the financial contributions of students. Five courses in dance have been added to the curriculum at Wilson College (Pennsylvania), and student-initiated courses on film-making have been popular additions to many academic curricula. Emory University is one example.

The freshman-year course regimen came under attack on some campuses. Noting "a relative lack of intellectual stimulation" during the freshman year at Carleton College, a student curriculum committee report recommended various reforms that were subsequently adopted. The changes included a freshman-year humanities course, freshman seminars, and modification of the grading system to extend a pass/fail option to most freshman courses. Students also participated in developing a freshman seminar program at Southwestern College in Memphis.

As the demands for "relevance" and opportunities for community service show, there is great interest among students in the practical applications of knowledge. At student request, the College of Education at the University of Illinois, Chicago Circle, established a requirement that all students taking Social Foundations of Education must spend three hours each week in a school. The experience enables students to test and evaluate concepts presented through lectures and readings, their own feelings about the teaching profession, and their preconceptions about education, schools, and learning. Class discussion about this field experience have become an integral part of the course.

The role of the university and the nature of teaching and learning form another category of student concern. Students at the University of California, Santa Barbara, were the major sponsors of a program on the Structure and Purpose of the University. Classes were offered on the University and Society, History of the University and Society, Nature of the University, and The University and Politics. University of Texas students received credit for a pass/fail course entitled Self and Campus Society. University of Utah students studied The University of Utah as an Educational Institution. Marymount College (New York) students were awarded credit for participation in an Innovation Workshop, covering: Changing Educational Objectives of Colleges and Universities, Critique of Undergraduate Teaching, Course Innovations for Fall 1970, and Evaluation of the Course Innovations (to take place a year later).

At SUNY Buffalo, students took courses in Education, Cooperation and Society; Experiments in Education

Change; Experimental College: Self-Study and Comparative Analysis; Students and Their Institutions; Planning a New University; and Justice in the University. At the University of California, Berkeley, a student-initiated course, Social and Behavioral Factors in College Commitment, combines a concern for minority problems with an interest in the university experience. The course description reads:

A critical evaluation of social and behavioral problems of academic achievement among minority students with major emphasis being placed on the Negro, Mexican-American, and American Indian and other low-income students. The team approach is used to provide the theoretical and empirical framework for discussion and application of basic principles.

Student interest in a broad interdisciplinary course of study, as opposed to specialization within one field, was evident at a number of institutions. Rhode Island College students who were enthusiastic about a freshman and sophomore, 12-hour, required humanities sequence in general studies, developed a minor program in the humanities. Students taking the humanities sequence determine the specific topics and texts to be studied in each course, along with the faculty member who is to teach it. The major themes selected are considered from a variety of standpoints—literary, artistic, historical, philosophical, and scientific. Courses themselves are given as seminars, and pass/fail evaluation is made on the basis of reading and participation in the discussions. High priority is placed on "vocal combat."

A new degree program, a Bachelor's in General Studies, was established at the University of Michigan in May 1969. It represents a restructuring of the bachelor of science degree away from discipline orientation and toward student orientation.

(The program) would assign to the student responsibility for planning an appropriate academic program. Thus, the student will, if he elects the B.S. in General Studies, enjoy the advantages of greater freedom and flexibility; and he will incur the risk that his decisions will occasionally be contrary to his best interests.

At the University of Hawaii, student involvement on the Undergraduate Instruction Committee contributed to the adoption of another "nonmajor major," a B.A. in Liberal Studies.

Students strongly supported the establishment of a department of religion at the University of North Carolina, Greensboro. Not only were they actively involved in a committee making the original request, but also in deciding what kind of department was desired.

Among the institutions that reported current involvement in the process of planning or self-study were Miami University of Ohio, Denison University and the University of Scranton. Schools that had recently undergone self-examination with the active participation of students, and adopted sweeping curricular reforms, will be discussed in Part II, Methods of Curricular Change.

Changes in Requirements

The second, fourth, and fifth questions in the questionnaire asked respondents to list courses or accredited activities (such as ROTC) that had been modified or withdrawn as a result of student pressure. The results indicated that ROTC became optional and/or lost accreditation at the Universities of Arizona, Michigan, Montana, Scranton, Pittsburgh, Howard, and Colgate. Tuskegee Institute, in deference to student wishes, reduced its ROTC requirement to one year. Other institutions, such as Moorhead State College, reported that their ROTC programs were under study.

Twenty-three schools, including such institutions as Maryville College of the Sacred Heart, the University of Pennsylvania, SUNY Buffalo, Wilson College, and Union Theological Seminary, specifically reported reducing their degree requirements. Additional schools, such as Lawrence University, eliminated certain course requirements in the process of general curricular overhaul. No institution reported an increase in credit requirements for graduation, but there was little similarity in the kinds of courses that did become optional. They included courses in English composition, physical education, philosophy, theology, physical chemistry, general studies, and languages. Comprehensive examinations as a requirement for graduation were dropped or modified at Hamilton College, Southwestern at Memphis, and Howard University, and were under review elsewhere. Regulations governing class attendance and residency for graduate students also became less stringent at a number of schools.

Among the institutions that modified fixed-distribution requirements were SUNY Buffalo, Hamilton College, and Emory College of Emory University. In a major revision of undergraduate degree requirements in 1969-1970, SUNY Buffalo reduced student workloads to four courses per semester and replaced the former distribution requirements with a simplified system that left students with "an extraordinary amount of latitude." Undergraduates gained the opportunity to design individual fields of concentration, subject to the approval of faculty members in the field and the Dean of the Division of Undergraduate Studies.

The University of South Carolina reported that the faculty completely revised undergraduate requirements in response to a student analysis of the curriculum. Hamilton College replaced its policy requiring freshmen and sophomores to take courses in six prescribed areas by creating a board of faculty advisors to "assist freshmen and sophomores in the development of programs of study that will best serve their educational interests and needs." Emory reduced its uniform requirements from 86 to 51 quarter hours and dropped all specified course requirements. Instead, the college required that students take 15 hours each, in any combination of courses, in the humanities, social sciences, natural sciences and mathematics. Six hours of physical education were also required. The changes came about "very largely in response to student and younger faculty opinion that the requirements were too particularly specified and too numerous, and represented a false assumption that the College had the right or obligation to make so many decisions regarding student academic programs."

A proposal for reduction of the course load at the University of Pennsylvania by the Student Committee on Undergraduate Education states the generally accepted rationale behind such changes in degree requirements.

> Because of the nature of the student's academic schedule, the SCUE suggests that there are valid considerations in favor of a reduction in the undergraduate course load. The current requirement of five courses per semester severely hampers the individual's ability to pursue any single discipline beyond a superficial level. If the student has selected his courses judiciously *and* if he is fortunate, two or more of his courses will complement one another in such a way that he can effectively use his time to integrate concepts suggested by the separate courses. If, however, he is not so fortunate, and this is a frequent occurrence, the student does not have a substantial opportunity to study a field in even moderate depth or to attempt a more subtle evaluation of the ideas he works with. One cannot carry five courses and deal effectively with them all.

After presenting the details of the proposed credit reduction, the paper goes on to say:

> There are several advantages which are by-products of such changes. The student who plans to teach will have an opportunity to take additional education courses during four credit semesters. Departments will be able to reduce the number of man-hours they devote to courses whose main purpose is to fulfill distribution requirements. The implications of this are obvious. Class size will tend to decrease; while this proposal is not designed to remedy overcrowding, it will improve the situation. In addition, the quality of individual classes should increase since student enrollment is more likely to indicate student interest than institutional pressure. While these are benefits of the system, they are not the vital ones. It is important that we understand the intent of the primary proposal. Course load reduction should grant the student additional latitude, not deny it. If the student feels that he can better serve his ends by taking five or more courses, then he should be permitted to do so. It is for this reason, also, that we have suggested that the qualified student be permitted to take an unlimited number of Pass-Fail courses.

When asked about course modifications as a consequence of student demands, several institutions cited a greater use of independent studies. The results, however, showed no other common types of student-initiated changes in continuing courses. For example, at West Virginia University, a sociology course on race relations became one on black experience; Wilson College modified all its American civilization courses; Bemidji State College consolidated its biology sections; Chatham College revised an arts course; Maryville College of the Sacred Heart modified its honors program; and SUNY Buffalo's School of Nursing revised its curriculum to put more emphasis on community public health and health topics related to sex.

Grading Reforms

Pass/fail or credit/no credit grading was introduced at the request or with the support of students at 53 institutions, but there was tremendous variation in the extent of and regulations covering its use. Most schools, including such institutions as Manhattanville College, Maryville College of the Sacred Heart, Oklahoma State University,

Eastern Kentucky University, the University of Arizona, and the University of Alabama, restricted the pass/fail option to juniors and seniors having a B average, or to honors students. They further stipulated that the option could be chosen only for one course per semester, thus allowing undergraduates to take a maximum of four courses on a pass/fail basis. Usually, only courses that were "purely elective" (outside major, minor, or other campus requirements for graduation) were permitted, and then only if the instructor teaching the course agreed to offer it on a pass/fail basis. In addition, students were generally required to obtain permission to take the course from the department chairman or the academic dean.

At the other end of the spectrum are a few institutions, such as the University of California at Santa Cruz, that employ a pass/fail grading system throughout its undergraduate and graduate programs; and Florida Presbyterian College, with only three symbols on its grading scale: High Pass, Pass, and Fail.

Pass/fail policies of the remaining responding institutions fall somewhere in between. Swarthmore records only pass/fail grades for freshmen. The State University of New York at Buffalo permits students to select a satisfactory/unsatisfactory system of evaluation for any course during the first 4 weeks of a semester, or choose to receive written evaluations at any point during the semester. Buffalo students can also choose letter grades if they so desire. The University of Michigan offers language courses on a pass/fail basis. University of Missouri undergraduates are allowed to take six pass/fail courses; University of North Carolina undergraduates may take eight. Harvard and University of Pennsylvania law schools adopted pass/fail grading throughout their curricula.

Descriptions of the pass/fail option stress that there is no reduction in course work in such classes: "It is not the same as auditing," states Rosemont College. Courses taken under the pass/fail option are not included in computations of a student's grade point average, but credits earned under the option count toward graduation requirements. "Pass" is generally considered the equivalent of A, B, C, or D, although C is the lowest grade for which credit is awarded at some schools (e.g., the University of Missouri at Kansas City).

The purpose of offering a pass/fail option is the same at most schools. It enables students to explore subject areas outside their majors without fear of damaging their academic records. They can thereby enrich their educational experience free of the pressure of grades. Like most of the other student-initiated changes, it encourages students to assume responsibility for their own education.

Respondents at four institutions (the Universities of Pennsylvania, Missouri at Kansas City, Indiana, and North Carolina at Greensboro) include studies of the pass/fail option based on surveys at their schools. Both Missouri and Indiana reported low usage of the option. A total of 62 students in the University of Missouri's College of Arts and Sciences elected a course on the credit/no credit option the first semester it was available, Spring 1969. The number represents 1.5 percent of the total enrollment, which, however, includes ineligible freshmen. At Indiana University, approximately ten percent of the eligible juniors and seniors in the College of Arts and Sciences elected the pass/fail option in Fall 1967, and 20 percent in Fall 1968. The majority of students at both institutions were seniors, who tended to select courses within their major field. Despite the small numbers of students taking advantage of the option (a factor noted by other respondents), there was overwhelming support by the student bodies of all four institutions for continuation or expansion of the grading option.

II. PROCESSES OF CURRICULAR REFORM

Although the methods used by college students to effect changes in the academic curriculum vary from institution to institution, depending upon the college environment, it is possible to identify eight overlapping approaches from the responses. They are discussed here in order of their comprehensiveness or ambitiousness, from the least to the most.

Committee Membership

By far the most common means used by students to influence the selection of course and program offerings is membership on committees. And while student representation on curriculum or departmental committees is not generally equal to that of faculty members, there appear to be few committees completely closed to them. (Students do predominate in committees responsible for generating proposals concerning the establishment of black and ethnic studies, and they are usually heavily involved in developing such programs.)

The fact that many curricular innovations were initiated by committees, including faculty and administrators as well as students, led a good number of respondents to state that it was difficult to isolate the exact origin of course changes. This was particularly true of small campuses at which faculty, administrators, and students were closely in touch with, and responsive to, one another's needs. Nevertheless, respondents attempted to list only courses, programs, or grading changes that were clearly the result of student wishes. Usually, while students were responsible for the initial suggestion of a new course, the implementation was up to the faculty and administration. The response from the School of Physical Education at the University of Illinois, Chicago Circle, was fairly typical:

> [An] examination of the undergraduate curriculum is being conducted via the committee process. Students have been invited to attend all committee meetings. . . . This action is the result of student oriented movement which began during the 1968-69 academic year. At that time this office invited both students and faculty to attend a series of three open forum discussions. From this type of symposia setting there emerged a healthy stream of student-faculty communication. Curricular problems were discussed and the concept of increased student participation in the development of curriculum was initiated.

A Brigham Young University respondent wrote:

While students have been deeply involved in reviewing grading procedures, credit by examination, and the development of programs in environmental control, they could not accurately be described as either "initiating" or being "instrumental" in effecting them. Students and faculty work so closely that giving credit to either at BYU is unfair.

A respondent from SUNY Buffalo wrote:

> A student-faculty committee, with an equal number participating from each group, proposed major revisions of grading to the Faculty Senate in the fall of 1968. On one of the recommendations, the joint committee split. Student members of the Committee took their position to the floor of the Faculty Senate, and their proposal was adopted. As a result, the State University of New York at Buffalo has a three-fold grading system. . . . These alterations went into effect in 1969-70.

Student Government

A somewhat more traditional, but not the most common, current approach whereby students were instrumental in initiating change was through formal recommendations of the student government. At Eastern Kentucky University, for example, the Student Council formally requested the Council on Academic Affairs to consider the merits of a pass/fail system. The plan described was then worked out by a subcommittee of the Council on Academic Affairs, approved by that body, the Faculty Senate, and the Board of Regents.

Course and Teacher Evaluation

Student courses and teacher evaluations have been widely responsible for course and degree modifications. Frequently, the evaluation projects are not only initiated, organized, and run by students; they are also financed entirely by student fees. The respondent from SUNY Buffalo commented:

> Through the mechanism of SCATE—Student Course and Teacher Evaluation—and through student participation on a significant number of committees within departments, a variety of alterations have occurred within existing curricula. The changes are too extensive to list in detail. However, the teaching style adopted in experimental courses, such as the freshman seminars or the college courses, the rapid growth of independent study, and student insistence upon inclusion of neglected elements in certain curricula . . . testify to the vital role undergraduates have played.

A more extensive survey of student opinion was that conducted by the University of Iowa. Concerned with the College of Liberal Arts, it covered the advisory system, pass/fail courses, the need for a teacher and course evaluation program, the honors program, requirements, cheating, graduate teaching assistants, lectures versus independent study, course load, and the importance of the instructor. Presumably, the findings were used to generate changes in these areas.

Free Universities

The incorporation of "free university" courses into the regular, accredited college curriculum has been another method of introducing student-designed material. At the University of Alabama, credit was secured for two courses initially offered by the New Alabama Experimental College. One deals with poverty and religion and the other involves a tutorial project in the black community. The courses were left on a completely experimental basis, just as in the College, and students were allowed to structure them as they wished. Dartmouth University is another institution that has incorporated into its regular curriculum formerly experimental college courses, Black American History, Film Criticism, and The Relationship Between Religion and Science.

The evaluation of previously extracurricular community service activities to accredited status is a similar method by which student-initiated curricular innovations have crept in through the back door. At Michigan State University, for instance, 180 student ombudsmen receive credit for their work. One of their activities has been to establish a "crisis center."

Interim Term

The introduction of a January term, or "Four-One-Four" plan, is a fifth method by which institutions have accommodated student demands for "relevant" study. The Four-One-Four calendar plan, which has gained wide popularity, provides an interim semester of one month—usually January—during which students can concentrate on a single course or project. Students are urged to develop during this period interest in and knowledge of subjects outside their major fields. The provision of a pass/fail grading option is frequently a further encouragement for students to engage in studies for which they might not have an extensive background.

Students have not only been instrumental in speeding the adoption of interim terms on many campuses, but have suggested and designed many of the courses offered during the term. Students at St. Olaf College (Minnesota), for example, have suggested such January term courses as The Negro: A Minority Group in American Society; The Radical Argument in Politics; and Musical Acoustics. Macalester College offered over 200 courses in its 1970 January interim term. They ranged from Art Criticism to Botanical Technique; Biological and Geologic field study of the Tucson Region; Current Economic Issues and Public Policy; European Economic Institutions; Principles and Practice of Life Insurance; The English System of Education; Child and Adolescent Life Styles; Encounter Group Experience; Study at The Institute for the Study of Non-Violence; Women and American Society; The Art of Muckraking; The Homosexual in Literature; French Canada; The Geography of Peace and War; Neighborhoods and Perception of Territoriality—a St. Paul Field Project; Introduction to Crystal Optics; Sir Winston Churchill; The Lost Cause in America, Past and Present; or Power to the People; Research in Washington, D.C.; Number Theory for Neophytes with Computer Applications; Making a Harpsichord; Utiliarian Ethics; Survey of Aquatic History; Neuromuscular Relaxation; Spontaneous and Forced Exercise of Small Animals (rats); Avalanche—The

Physics of Snow and Ice; The Impact of 20th Century Physics on Modern Thought and Society; Astronomical Instrumentation and Telescope Making; Law and the Ghetto; Violence and Politics; The College and University as a System of Political Behavior; The Mental Hospital; Personality in Gambling and Game Playing; European Psychological Laboratories; Biblical Eschatology and Contemporary Man; The Christian-Marxist Dialogue (abroad); Russian Culture and Conversation (Tolstoy Farm at Valley Cottage, New York); Madness; Here comes the Judge: Anthropology of Court Rituals; City Problems: Views of the Activists; A Comparison of the Interpretations of Spanish History in the Writings of José Ortega, Miguel de Unomuno, and Américo Castro; Radio and Television in Sweden (abroad); and Norway: A Welfare State? (abroad). Students themselves directed four courses: Introduction to Cobol Programming, Theories and Applications of Counseling for College Students, The Era of the Silent Cinema, and Institutional Analysis. In addition, faculty advisors were provided to supervise individual projects both on and off campus.

The respondent from Florida Presbyterian College pointed out that the January term gives students the opportunity to recommend and take the kind of courses that elsewhere they could take only from a free university. At Florida Presbyterian, for example, a group of 15 students spent January 1970 in the San Francisco Bay area studying humanistic psychology, and visiting such places as the Esalen Institute and the Haight-Ashbury Clinic. The interim terms at New Mexico State University and St. Edwards University (Texas) are similar.

As the partial listing of Macalester College's interim term courses indicates, the January term can frequently be spent in study abroad. Florida Presbyterian's syllabus lists courses to be taken in Britain and Jamaica.

The University of Hawaii chose a theme, "Hawaii and Its Future," for its first two-week interim session in January 1970. The session was devoted to a critical analysis of four general areas of Hawaiian life—culture and life styles, education, economics, and the environment— and was intended to produce concrete proposals which would then be channeled into the State Legislature. It was hoped there would be broad participation of both the campus and the public communities. In addition, special courses were offered for credit and special activities sponsored by 22 departments.

Special Facilities

A sixth method is more ambitious, because it requires an ongoing commitment on the part of the college or university to curricular innovation. It involves the establishment of special institutional channels or structures for initiating student-desired courses. One example is the University of Utah's joint student-faculty committee called the "Experimental Curriculum Board." Established in the 1968-1969 academic year, the Board is authorized to receive and approve, for two quarters of credit, courses that are initiated by either students or faculty and taught outside the regular curriculum. Two courses that have resulted from its creation are Workshop for Student Government Officers and The Great Basin

as an Ecological System.

A related practice is the designation of one experimental course per year. Southern Illinois University's "Issues of Today," and Florida Presbyterian College's "Junior Seminar" are examples of course time set aside for study of a student-suggested topic. The topics generally vary from year to year, depending upon student interest.

The University of Michigan's "Course Mart," developed in the fall of 1968 by a planning committee that included two administrators, two faculty members, and six students, represents another effort to inject flexibility into the curriculum. The Course Mart is described as a "stock market in courses," whereby students may suggest courses they wish to be taught and instructors may submit proposals for courses they wish to teach. Faculty members who don't want to teach courses themselves may sponsor courses to be taught by qualified graduate students. Credits are arranged for each course individually, and can be applied toward distribution requirements in the humanities and natural and social sciences on approval of a curriculum committee. All courses offered through the Course Mart are graded on a pass/fail basis.

SUNY Buffalo has a similar "Bulletin Board" arrangement, whereby students and faculty can propose new courses available for credit following approval of the curriculum committee. By the second semester of 1969-1970, 24 such courses (some extending over two semesters) had been offered. About 60 percent of the courses were proposed by students and the remainder by faculty. The subjects ranged from contemporary political and social issues to education, music, literature, biology, film, and higher mathematics.

The University of Hawaii's "Clearinghouse for Innovation" was created at the urging of "one persistent student." To stimulate change in the curriculum, this body maintains files of new programs at the University and other campuses, and holds weekly discussion meetings concerning new courses and programs. A student and faculty member serve as co-chairmen and anyone may attend the meetings.

The Center for Participant Education, at the University of California, Berkeley, is a well established formal vehicle for student-designed courses. The courses it generates fit into existing departmental categories: i.e., the Department of Dramatic Arts absorbed Studies in Avant Garde Theater and Its Antecedents; the Department of Social Analysis added Existentialism and Freedom; the Nature Studies Department added The American Wilderness as Myth, Hope and Experience; Literature absorbed Mysticism: Theory and Practice and Writing Seminar Workshop; and Mathematics added Modern Algebra and Number Systems.

Alternative Curricula through Independent Study

The seventh method involves the expansion of the concept of independent study to a completely separate curriculum within the college or university. Paul Tamminen's paper, "Powerlessness Corrupts" (1969), discusses this approach.

[One] approach is developing a total alternative plan but seeking its implementation on a limited scale– e.g., in an "inner college" or "residential college" in which only a small part of the total student body participates, but does so on a full-time basis. This approach is gaining increasing consideration, as it offers the advantages of (1) allowing an "experimental" approach to larger change; and (2) requiring a smaller group of willing student and faculty to initiate it. These advantages are particularly important at large universities, where the problem of sheer size presents acute obstacles to reformers, leading many to advocate the formation of "cluster colleges" as a necessary prerequisite for other changes.

This expanded use of independent study is often combined with "learning contracts"–agreements between a student and faculty member concerning course content and methods of study and evaluation–and plainly permits students a much wider range of course choice than the traditional college curriculum. At New College (Florida), a student, with the aid of two faculty members, can write a contract defining his academic program for three months at a time. Contracts can involve seminar work, classroom study, tutorials, independent projects, or study at another college. If the student fails to fulfill the contract, the faculty sponsor can declare the contract void, or, in cases of default, recommend dismissal of the student.

The Inner College Experiment (ICE) was the creation of a group of about 30 Macalester College students who met for many sessions during the 1968-1969 academic year to discuss education at Macalester and develop the proposal for the ICE. It calls for a group of about 35 students to participate in a program of independent study that lasts throughout the fall term. The interim session is devoted to evaluation and analysis of the results; and the spring term to involvement in the regular curriculum in such a way as to build upon the independent study experience. In the fall, each student selected for the ICE prepares a written statement of his educational objectives during the year, and plans a program of study around one or several topics. The students follows an honor procedure in grading, in that he or she indicates to the registrar at the end of the fall term and interim session whether elective course credit should be awarded. The rationale is that

> With the removal of external motivations, there will be plenty of opportunity for the development of self-discipline and internal motivation. The community that the Inner College will attempt to build is designed for the maximum educational growth that cooperative learning, independent study, and interdisciplinary study lend to the educational experience.

The University of South Carolina's program of "Independent Study and Contemporary University" is another example of an attempt to build a new kind of academic community within the university structure. Like the Inner College, the formulation and implementation of the program fall essentially under the rubric of independent study; but also, like the Inner College, the program attempts to transcend purely independent study by placing strong emphasis on the development of close relationships among participating students and the coordinat-

ing faculty. In short, both programs represent efforts to build new educational communities. The Independent Study-Contemporary University program allows selected undergraduates to develop individual or group programs of study for one semester and receive up to 15 hours of credit for their work. Participants can submit finished work in any form they wish–a paper, novel, movie, seminar series, etc.–as long as the product can be evaluated by the faculty advisor. In a review of the program, which concludes with a recommendation for its continuation and expansion, a faculty committee commented that the program afforded students the chance "to formulate and follow through their own ideas with a maximum of freedom. After a year's experience, the program has proven that it is not a haven for would-be dropouts, disrupters, or misfits but an enriching academic opportunity for a broad spectrum of students."

New Curricula

The last and most comprehensive method is development of a master plan for the total reconstruction of the curriculum. The success of this approach at Brown University attracted national attention in 1969, when the University agreed to abandon completely its existing curriculum and adopt, with few changes, an alternate curricular structure proposed by two students in a voluminous document reviewing the system of American higher education in general and Brown University in particular.

Unlike Brown, which serves as an inspiration to many student reformers, most efforts to restructure the total academic curriculum of an institution are not spurred solely or even mostly by students. The great majority of wholesale curricular overhauls are the product of committees, including administrators, faculty members, trustees, and alumni representatives, as well as students. However, the revisions the committees propose are uniform in giving students greater freedom to design their own education and greater responsibility for meeting self-imposed objectives.

Lawrence University's Select Committee on Planning, which was composed of 14 faculty and administrators, three trustees, and three students, was charged with examining the University in detail and making recommendations. Its report, issued in September 1969, covers the institution's tradition of liberal education; the curriculum and a host of special programs; athletics; the faculty and all regulations pertaining to it; and government of the University, its structure and facilities. Among the many changes that were recommended and subsequently adopted were the elimination of almost all uniform course requirements and the stipulation that departmental requirements may not exceed 50 percent of a student's total course load. In addition, students were to be allowed to design their own courses, to be graded on a satisfactory/unsatisfactory basis.

Indiana University's Educational Policies Committee, consisting of faculty and students, was appointed to examine the College of Arts and Sciences as a whole, and report on both the internal organization and operation of the College, and its functions within and relation to other components of the University. Underlying its wide-ranging recommendations, which involve complete re-organization of the College, is the notion that the University has an obligation—heretofore unmet because of unnecessarily rigid requirements and a general lack of educational goals or mission—to provide a setting for intellectual growth and excitement.

Hiram College's new curriculum

> is based upon the premise that by giving students more free-dom and more responsibility, along with the opportunity for more individual faculty guidance, a college can create an atmosphere in which both academic inquiry and personal growth will flourish.

Hiram's committee was particularly concerned with re-casting the freshman year program, because of its im-portance in the development of student attitudes toward education and because of its traditional weakness. Dis-tribution requirements were replaced by new courses focusing on issues and cutting across disciplinary lines, and the number of required courses was halved.

Students had a prominent role in the Union Commis-sion that conducted a major examination of Union Theological Seminary during the 1968-1969 academic year. The Commission was created as the result of a "free university" meeting called to discuss the state of the institution following the crisis at Columbia Univer-sity, and the preface of its report refers to this beginning:

> In this time of campus upheaval, many educational institu-tions are struggling to free themselves from traditional and often inflexible patterns in order to discover new forms and roles for the next decade.

The report and its recommendations, which were ap-proved by the student body, the faculty, the board of directors, the alumni council, the staff, and the nonteach-ing administration, discussed the nature and purpose of theological education (which includes all the proposals for curricular reform), governance, and an interpretation of the course of the Commission.

The Colorado College Plan was formulated under the auspices of the college planning office directed by Dr. Glenn E. Brooks, a faculty assistant to the president, and was put into effect September 1970.

> It is a comprehensive plan which integrates academic, leisure, and residential programs of the College. The Plan is designed to assure substantially more active student involvement in education; to give faculty and students more productive con-trol of their time; and to make more effective use of campus and off-campus environments.
>
> Distinctive features include: (1) a concentrated course sys-tem in which students normally will take—and faculty will teach—only one or two courses at a time, or will work in in-terdisciplinary courses; (2) course size will average 14, and strict upper limits will be placed on all course enrollments; (3) courses will vary in length from three to ten-and-one-half weeks, and courses of differing length will run simultane-ously in a modular schedule; (4) within courses, students and faculty will have no set class schedule, but rather will be free to determine their own meeting times; (5) each course will have a specially reserved courseroom or laboratory for meet-ings, study and research; (6) some academic work will be carried on in residence halls; (7) new emphasis will be placed

on field studies and independent research; (8) extensive leisure activities, ranging from conventional lectures and con-certs to a new program of support for individual student projects, will complement the concentrated course work; (9) half-week breaks once a month will be used for symposia and other special activities.

Student initiative was responsible for sweeping changes in the academic programs of Eastern Connecticut State College and the University of Pennsylvania. At Eastern Connecticut, student pressure resulted in the reduction of required background credit hours from 65 to 36, elimination of a language requirement for all students, a cut in the physical education requirement, and reduc-tion of credits needed for graduation from 125 to 120. Periodic reports of the Student Committee on Undergrad-uated Education (SCUE), at the University of Pennsyl-vania, have stimulated discussion and reform in many areas of the University. Their 1966 report on undergraduate life at the University was based on a survey of the student body, committee studies, and a series of teach-ins. It covers the atmosphere at the University, facilities, the College and College-for-Women dichotomy, student-faculty contact, advising systems, entrance to the major, field of concentration program, size of classes, problems of course orientation, teaching and teachers, graduate students as teachers and graders, methods of testing, grading and the pass/fail system, the seminar system and senior colloquia, independent study and auditing, student evaluation of teachers and courses, and the roll of the student in tenure decisions and policymaking.

SCUE summarizes its mission as follows:

> If every student is urged to define his own goals and values, instead of having them dictated to him, we believe that a more committed, responsible, and thoughtful student will be the result. It will have become difficult for a student to be apathetic, [and] unfeasible to take no interest in the ed-ucational process. Education will have become a way of life.

CONCLUSION

Although the number of students actively involved in academic reform is very small in comparison to the total number of students enrolled in institutions of higher education, they have had a significant impact nationwide both on the content and the structure of college curricula. Their impact on the content of the academic program is evident in the proliferation of problem-centered courses dealing with urgent social and political issues of the day. Their effect on the structure of the curriculum is clear in the growth of interdisciplinary, independent, and field studies which call for new, more flexible, and essentially more demanding relationships among students, instruc-tors, and institutions.

The movement of student-generated educational change is uniformly in the direction of greater freedom and greater personal responsibility. Behind demands for more pass/fail grading options, for elimination of cer-tain course and attendance requirements, and for con-cern with practical rather than theoretical matters, lies a feeling that higher education has become too much involved with trivia and too little with individual development and social change. The consistency of the types of reform sought by students, as reported in responses to this survey, indicate a widespread desire for personal involvement with the processes and purposes of American academic learning.

REFERENCES

Bess, James L., Curriculum Hypocrisies: Studies of Student-Initiated Courses. *Universities Quarterly,* Spring, 1970.

Brick, Michael, and McGrath, Earl J. *Innovation in Liberal Arts Colleges.* New York: Teachers College Press, 1969.

Constructive Changes to Ease Campus Tensions. Washington: National Association of State Universities and Land-Grant Colleges, January 1970.

Danish, Paul. *Champaign Report, A Conference on Educational Reform—A Student View.* Washington: U.S. National Student Association, 1966.

Draper, Hal. *Berkeley: The New Student Revolt.* New York: Grove Press, 1965.

Dressel, Paul L. *College and University Curriculum.* Berkeley: McCutchan Publishing Co., 1968.

_____, and DeLisle, Frances H. *Undergraduate Curriculum Trends.* Washington: American Council on Education, 1969. ED 028 695.

Duncan, Karen. *Community Action Curriculum Compendium.* Washington: U.S. National Student Association, 1968.

Eberly, Donald J. Service Experience and Educational Growth. *Educational Records, 49* (Spring 1968), pp. 197-205.

Free Universities and Experimental Colleges. Washington: U.S. National Student Association, 1971.

Furniss, W. Todd. Racial Minorities and Curriculum Change. *Educational Record, 50* (Fall 1969).

Grieder, Jerome B. *Freedom to Learn: A New Curriculum for Brown and Pembroke.* Providence, R.I.: Brown University, 1969. ED 032 727.

Hamlin, Will, and Porter, Lawrence. *Dimensions of Change in Higher Education.* Workshop Conferences to Foster Innovation in Higher Education (First Magnolia Manor, Mass., May 19-23, 1966).

Harvey, James. *Reforming the Undergraduate Curriculum: Problems and Proposals.* Washington: ERIC Clearinghouse on Higher Education, 1971. ED 048 518.

Hefferlin, Lon, J.B. *Dynamics of Academic Reform.* San Francisco: Jossey-Bass, 1969.

Heiss, Ann. Today's Graduate Student—Tomorrow's Faculty Member. *The Research Reporter, 4* (1969).

Hodgkinson, Harold L. Students and an Intellectual Community. *Educational Record, 49,* pp. 398-406.

Jerome, Judson. *Culture out of Anarchy: The Reconstruction of American Higher Learning.* New York: Herder & Herder, 1970.

Johnson, B. Lamar. *Islands of Innovation Expanding.* Beverly Hills: Glencoe Press, 1969.

Klawitter, Robert. Degrading Education: A Proposal for Abolishing the Grading System. Washington: U.S. National Student Association Center for Educational Reform, 1968.

Lichtman, Jane. *The Experimental Subcollege.* Washington: ERIC Clearinghouse on Higher Education, 1971. ED 051 437.

Martin, Warren Bryan. *Alternative to Irrelevance: Strategy for Reform in Higher Education.* New York: Abingdon Press, 1968.

Mayhew, Lewis B. *Contemporary College Students and the Curriculum.* SREB Research Monograph Number 14, Atlanta, Ga., 1969. ED 028 731.

Meehan, Mary. *Student Programs to Supplement the Curriculum.* Washington: U.S. National Student Association, 1966.

New College Student Handbook, 1969-1970. Sarasota, Fla.: New College. ED 040 656.

The Other Revolution: Student Culture in the Classroom. Higher Education Executive Associates (n.d.).

Robinson, Lora, and Shoenfeld, Janet. *Student Participation in Academic Governance.* Washington: ERIC Clearinghouse on Higher Education, 1970. ED 035 786.

Sanford, Nevitt. *Education for Individual Development.* New Dimensions in Higher Education 31. Durham: Duke University, April 1967. ED 013 353.

Schwab, Joseph J. *College Curriculum and Student Protest.* Chicago: University of Chicago Press, 1969.

Shoben, Edward Joseph, Jr. On Student-Initiated Courses: Some Reflections. In *In Search of Leaders,* ed. G. Kerry Smith. Washington: American Association for Higher Education, 1967.

Student Initiative for Curricular Change. *Improving College and University Teaching,* Summer 1969, pp. 64-65.

Student Participation in Campus Affairs. University of Illinois at Urbana-Champaign, *Campus Report, 3* (January 1970).

Students. *Improving College and University Teaching, 18,* Summer 1969.

Tamminen, Paul G. *A Guide to Resources for Undergraduate Academic Reform.* Washington: American Council on Education, June 1970.

_____. *Powerlessness Corrupts. A Report on the U.S. National Student Association National Congress with Commentary and a Few Suggestions.* Washington: American Council on Education, Commission on Academic Affairs, September 1969.

Taylor, Harold. *How to Change Colleges: Notes on Radical Reform.* New York: Holt, Rinehart & Winston, 1971.

_____. *Students Without Teachers. The Crisis in the University.* New York: McGraw-Hill, 1969.

Tussman, Joseph. *Experiment at Berkeley.* Oxford: Oxford University Press, 1969.

Urofsky, Melvin I. An Ideal Curriculum Designed by Students. *The Journal of Higher Education, 39* (1968), pp. 515-517.

Werdell, Philip. *Course and Teacher Evaluation.* Washington: U.S. National Student Association, 1966.

57

NONRESIDENT STUDENTS IN PUBLIC COLLEGES: MOBILITY, TUITION AND LEGAL ISSUES

by Robert F. Carbone
Professor of Higher Education
University of Maryland
College Park, Maryland

Each year nearly half a million American students attend a public college or university in a state other than the one in which they are legal residents. These nonresident students (or out-of-state students, as they are sometimes called) are at the center of a cluster of educational, fiscal and legal issues that continue to plague college administrators and trustees. The primary issue, briefly stated, is: How easy should it be for nonresident students to earn resident status, and thus qualify for the lower tuition rates traditionally enjoyed by resident students?

SCOPE OF THE PROBLEM

All publicly supported institutions of higher education in the United States employ a differential tuition system to collect student charges. This means that the children of in-state taxpayers who attend one of the public institutions their parents help support pay less than students whose parents live out-of-state. This phenomenon is universal in this country—even local community colleges charge "out-of-district" fees to students who live in the same state but in another community. Since no other country in the world has a similar arrangement, the differential tuition system must be seen as one of the distinguishing characteristics of American public higher education.

In the past, when college tuition was relatively low, few educators and legislators paid much attention to nonresident students. Each year institutional budgets showed an item of anticipated income from out-of-state students, and the procedures for student classification and fee collection were handled routinely. However, when inflationary pressures forced tuition upward,and when institutional budgets began to get tight, the matter took on new importance. All of this coincided with a wave of radical student activity on many campuses, much of which was blamed on "outside agitators"—in other words, nonresident students.

Students, encouraged by their newfound voice on campus, began to question the regulations for classifying nonresidents. A sharp increase in nonresident rates—differentials of $1000 were not uncommon—prompted some students to appeal original classifications and even carry their cases to the courts. New student lifestyles helped many of them substantiate claims that they were no longer dependent on parents in distant states. It was, however, the 1972 elections that most clearly defined the student-vs.-institution conflict in this area.

The Twenty-Sixth Amendment to the Constitution extended voting rights in Federal elections to all citizens above the age of 18. Subsequently most states followed this example, by either lowering the age of majority or authorizing voter registrars to list as official voters persons at age 18, 19, or 20—the legislation varied from state to state. All of these actions, obviously taken without much thought about consequences in areas other than the election process, gave students yet another tool to use in residency matters. If a student, originally from out-of-state, could now vote in the community where he or she goes to college, was it legal for the college to still collect higher nonresident tuition from that student?

Despite these mounting pressures, many colleges were not overly concerned. Their regulations said that a student who was originally classified as a nonresident must stay in that status as long as he or she was in attendance. This "irrebutable presumption of nonresidents," as the lawyers called it, proved to be thin ice. In June 1973, the United States Supreme Court, ruling on a suit brought by two University of Connecticut students, said that freezing students in that status violated the Fourteenth Amendment of the Constitution.

The impact of that decision was clear: nonresident students in all public colleges and universities could qualify for lower in-state tuition rates if they met the obligations of citizenship (paying taxes, obtaining a driver's license, registering to vote, etc.) and were physically present in the state for some given durational period (normally one year, but in some cases as little as six months). If large numbers of nonresident students take advantage of this opportunity, the resulting loss of income for all public colleges and universities could be as much as $150 million a year, and the future of the low tuition system will be threatened (Carbone, 1973).

RULES AND REGULATIONS

When a student migrates to another state to enter college, he or she immediately comes under the jurisdiction of a set of regulations that define tuition status. Often detailed and complicated, these regulations determine whether the student will pay several thousand dollars more for a college education than do fellow students who are residents of that state.

The residency rules are created by a variety of groups—state legislatures governing boards, state-wide coordinating agencies, or administrative committees. As a result, there is a great variance in the rules. They differ from state to state, from institution to institution within a state, and sometimes from campus to campus within a college or university system. A comprehensive review of all state and institutional regulations (Carbone, 1970) illustrated the diversity. For example, most states require a one-year durational period to qualify for resident status, while others require six months. In some states students can claim residence in their own right at age 18, but other states set the age at 19, 20, or 21. Some states allow women to earn resident status through marriage to an in-state male, and other states say marriage does not influence this status, but few permit nonresident men to become residents by virtue of marriage to resident females. In some states, special circumstances will result in reclassification as a resident. Examples of this include waivers for children of faculty, fee remissions for graduate teaching assistants, being under military orders in the state, and exceptions covering disadvantaged students, children of clergymen, diplomats and their dependents, and part-time students. The variety is at best confusing, at worst unfair. The title of two articles illustrate the point: "Are Nonresident Students Receiving Fair Treatment?" (Carbone, 1970) and "States Urged to Examine Residency Requirements" (Carbone, 1970).

After considerable study of residency regulations, some guiding principles become evident. Regulations should be reasonable and equitably applied; they should be flexible, and include some appeal mechanism; and they must not forever freeze students into the nonresident category, but provide some reasonable means that will permit the student to overcome initial classification.

STUDENT MIGRATION

Statistics on the number of students who migrate across state lines to attend college are reported every decade by the U.S. Office of Education. The most recent data (Wade, 1968) reported a total migration of

1,221,909 to both public and private colleges in 1968. Of this number, 490,185 attended public institutions. A more recent sampling (Fenske, Scott, and Carmody, 1972) suggests that the proliferation of local community colleges and the use of admission quotas tended to reduce interstate migration of students. In another article based on this research (Fenske and Scott, 1973), an interesting profile of migrating students is reported. The authors find them to be better than average on admissions tests; possessing education expectations beyond a bachelor's degree; from a rural or suburban community; of moderate to high family income; not planning to work part-time while in college; and little concerned with low cost as a factor in selecting a college, but more interested in the national reputation, or the special curriculum, of the college they did select. In contrast, resident students presented a quite different profile. These authors conclude that if these student profiles ". . . become even more clearly differentiated, then American higher education may become sharply stratified purely on socio-economic bases, a trend that has always been counter to democratic ideals (p. 31)."

Without doubt, economic factors have become a major impediment to student migration in this nation. Because of the differential tuition system, institutions were able to control the influx of out-of-state students by sharply increasing the nonresident fees. In earlier years, when the differential was small, this factor had little influence on student migration, but since the mid-sixties the ever-increasing cost of nonresident tuition has become the single most important element in determining how many students will seek admission to a college in another state (Carbone, 1973).

Data provided by the Office of Institutional Research of the National Association of State Universities and Land-Grant Colleges reveals that the differential between resident and nonresident tuition in the major public institutions has increased faster than the total growth rate for either resident or nonresident tuition during an eight-year period. From 1965-1966 to 1972-1973, resident tuition increased 66 percent and nonresident tuition increased 78 percent. However, the differential between resident and nonresident tuition increased 90 percent during that same period (Carbone 1973).

Dollars are not the only important factors at work in the migration situation. Two other barriers to student migration continue to be utilized. Quotas on the number of nonresident students a campus may enroll are a common practice in public institutions. Higher admission standards for nonresidents is a somewhat less widely used technique. These barriers were described as follows:

Admissions quotas—In a number of institutions, policies generated by the state legislature, governing board, or administrative officers limit the number of nonresident students who may matriculate. The limitations are either in the form of percentage quotas (e.g., a specified proportion of the freshman class, of all undergraduates, or of the total campus enrollment) or finite numbers (e.g., 1,000 new freshmen plus 500 transfer students). About a third of all public colleges and universities in the nation employ some form of quota system to control nonresident admissions.

Differential admission standards—In order to be admitted

to some colleges or universities, nonresident students must meet admission standards that are higher than those applied to resident students. Through the use of this technique, the institution protects itself against admitting students whose academic backgrounds prevented them from entering public institutions in their home states. Admissions officers are thus provided a handy tool for sorting out preferred candidates for admission on campuses where the number of applications exceeds the number of nonresidents the institutions desire to admit. Also, the technique provides the institution with a way of maintaining (or perhaps improving) its academic quality. Reports from institutions indicate that the use of higher admissions standards for nonresidents is not widespread. It is estimated that only about one in ten colleges or universities has formally established such standards. (Carbone, 1973, p. 13)

These barriers to migration had had an uneven effect on public colleges and universities. The major state universities, institutions that traditionally attracted sizeable numbers of nonresident students, have continued to do so. It is the smaller state colleges and regional universities that experienced marked reductions in out-of-state enrollments. Most of these institutions—former teachers' colleges that expanded to become general undergraduate institutions—have traditionally attracted few nonresidents. However, those located near state borders, and those with unique curricula, have appealed to students from other states. Now that nonresident enrollments have dropped, many of them face serious financial problems because of unfilled dormitory rooms and lower faculty workloads that do not justify projected budget requests. Worse yet, the lack of students from other sections of the country, especially those with diverse ethnic and economic backgrounds, deprives students in these colleges of the educational values inherent in a cosmopolitan student mix. Now, more than ever, they are becoming "Colleges For The Forgotten Americans," as they were characterized by the Carnegie Commission on Higher Education (Dunham, 1969).

LEGAL ISSUES

There is a long history of litigation resulting from the inability of students and colleges to agree on tuition classification. In his review of cases Van Dyne (1973) categorizes them under three general rubrics: Can a public university require new arrivals to the state to wait a certain length of time before applying for in-state rates? Can a state set up a rule that prevents a student who was originally classified as a nonresident from ever becoming a resident for tuition purposes? Can a university which has set up a "waiting period" for acquiring residence require that it be met while a person is not in school? (p. 33).

The body of legal opinion cited by Van Dyne tends to give clear answers to these questions. Colleges and universities have the legal right to set waiting, or durational, periods which a student must satisfy before being classified as an in-state student. A 1969 case (*Kirk v. Board of Regents of University of California*, p. 37) affirmed the right of the University to set a durational period. More recently, in a Minnesota case (*Starns and Mack v. Malkerson*, p. 38) the United States Supreme

Court ruled that the one-year durational period required in that state was not unreasonable, and that it did not violate the "equal protection" clause of the Constitution.

If a student is originally classified as a nonresident, it is unconstitutional to forever freeze the student in that status. This was the opinion of the Idaho Supreme Court in 1960 (*Newman v. Graham,* p. 35) and of the U.S. Supreme Court in a more recent ruling on this issue (*Kline and Catapana v. Vladis,* p. 41). This later case also spoke to the issue of whether or not a student must drop out of school in order to satisfy the durational period. The court clearly mandated that students can work off the established waiting period (one year in the University of Connecticut, where these students had attended) while they were enrolled. The opinion handed down in the Connecticut case also reinforced earlier opinions that it was defensible for a university to assess differential tuition, and to expect students to meet reasonable tests of residency, before qualifying for the lower in-state tuition rates (Law Week, 1973).

A more wide-ranging discussion of the legal and social issues involved in residency was offered by Hendrickson and Jones (1973). They related student residency in divorce actions, welfare matters, and voting rights, and predicted that changes in society will ". . . continue to pressure the states and federal governments to eliminate the residency-nonresidency distinction, and the courts will also be consistently resorted to for redress (p. 460)."

VOTING RIGHTS

The extension of voting rights to younger citizens prior to the 1972 elections dramatically changed the student residency picture. A survey aimed at assessing the impact of this landmark change in national policy produced a "doomsday estimate" of its fiscal implications. It assumed the most extreme set of circumstances: What if all nonresident students attending all public colleges and universities registered to vote, and were thus eligible for in-state tuition rates? The total tuition loss to all institutional budgets would be more than $250 million a year (Carbone, 1972). Fortunately (for the institutions, at least), relatively few nonresident students attempted to parlay their voting rights into reclassification. Universities contacted in an informal survey, following the 1972 elections, indicated that there was only a modest increase in the number of students seeking reclassification

The new voting laws, however, coupled with the Supreme Court decision in the Connecticut case, have provided students (and the parents who support them) with an opportunity to elude the higher nonresident fees for at least a major portion of their college careers. At the same time, these events have made it mandatory for colleges and universities to reexamine their residency criteria to make certain that the rules are reasonable and evenly applied. In "How To Spot A Nonresident Student" (Carbone, 1973), this writer provided some guidelines and suggestions that took cognizance of the new conditions.

CONCLUSION

As things stand now, colleges and universities will maintain the differential tuition system, and they will continue to require nonresident students to meet a reasonable durational period. However, many nonresident students will remain nonresidents for only one year. After that, those students who can demonstrate they have assumed the obligations of citizenship in their communities will be able to make a good case for reclassification. The resulting loss of tuition income will hurt (but not cripple) institutional budgets. Unfortunately, the immediate reaction of governing boards and state legislatures will be to increase tuition for all students to cover the loss. This will mean that the traditional concept of low tuition in our public colleges will give higher educators a golden opportunity to devise new and creative methods of dealing with tuition issues. Hopefully they will find a way to keep tuition low and also keep their doors open to nonresident students. If that way can be found, higher education and society in general will benefit.

REFERENCES

Carbone, R. F. Are Nonresident Students Receiving Fair Treatment? *College Board Review,* 1970, *76,* 22-24.
_____. *Resident or Nonresident? Tuition Classification in Higher Education.* Denver: Education Commission of the States, 1970.
_____. States Urged to Examine Residency Requirements. *Compact,* 1970, Vol. 4, No. 2, 39-40.
_____. Quotas and Dollars. *Compact,* 1971, Vol. 5, No. 5, 23-25.
_____. *Voting Rights and the Nonresident Student.* Washington: National Association of State Universities and Land-Grant Colleges, 1972, mimeo.
_____. Future of the Low Tuition System. *The Educational Record,* 1973, Vol. 54, No. 4, 265-270.
_____. How to Spot a Nonresident Student. *College Board Review,* 1973, *86,* 17-18.
_____. *Students and State Borders: Fiscal/Legal Issues Affecting Nonresident Students.* Iowa City: American College Testing Program, 1973.
Dunham, E. A. *Colleges for the Forgotten Americans.* New York: McGraw-Hill, 1969.
Fenske, R. H., Scott, C. S., and Carmody, J. F. *College Student Migration.* Iowa City: American College Testing Program, 1972.
_____, and Scott, C. S. Migration to College. In Carbone, *Students and State Borders.* Iowa City: American College Testing Program, 1973.
Henrickson, R. M., and Jones, M. E. Nonresident Tuition: Student Rights v. State Fiscal Integrity. *Journal of Law and Education,* 1973, Vol. 2, No. 3, 443-460.
The United States Law Week. Washington, D.C., June 12, 1973, 41 LW 4796-4804.
Van Dyne, L. The Courts Speak. In Carbone, *Students and State Borders.* Iowa City: American College Testing Program, 1973.
Wade, G. H. *Residence and Migration of College Students.* Washington: Office of Education, Department of Health, Education and Welfare, 1968.

COURT CASES

Kirk v. Board of Regents of University of California, 78 Cal. Rptr. 260 (1969).
Vlandis v. Kline, 93 S. Ct. 2230 (1973).

Newman v. Graham et al., 82 Ida 90, 349 Pac (2nd) 716 (1960).
Starns v. Malkerson, 91 S. Ct., 1231 (1971).

58

COMMUTER STUDENTS IN URBAN COLLEGES

by Thomas F. Harrington
Professor
Northeastern University
Boston, Massachusetts

Two-thirds of all the full-time students today commute to college. The development of junior colleges and branches of the state college and university systems will also contribute to a continuing rise in the proportion of commuters. Hardwick and Kazlo (1974) project a 90 percent commuting rate by 1985. The commuter, unlike the resident student, generally spends only about 15 to 20 hours a week at the college. A prevailing but changing characterization of the commuter is Peterson's (1965) description:

> . . . coming from a working- or lower-class home. He looks upon his formal education as a ladder of mobility toward improved social status. His parents—relatively impoverished economically, educationally, and culturally—share this instrumental view of education and have nourished his strong yet narrow commitment to some occupational career. . . . His higher education consists largely of a body of information and/or skills to be mastered. His preference is to ingest passively, rather than to explore or examine critically. . . . He is apolitical and culturally plebian.

Only belatedly is attention being given to the development of these students not living on campus. Now a body of knowledge is accumulating to show what factors influence students' decisions to commute or reside on campus, and to select a local urban community college as opposed to a residential four-year institution. More important is the evidence indicating that the educational, social, and psychological development of commuters is different from that of residential students (Harrington, 1974, and Trivett, 1974). Freedman (1969) wrote, "The future of American higher education is increasingly the large, urban, commuter campus. . . . The urban campus reflects the conflicts of urban society. . . . The traditional campus community also belongs to another age (p. 85)."

DEVELOPMENT, LIFESTYLE, AND PERSONAL QUALITIES

Separation from home—whether to enter the military service, to work in another locality, or to go away to college—is a normal developmental experience for the young adult; but the young commuter's experience is different. Making a less explicit transition from life in high school to life in college, commuters find it difficult to realize the change, to understand the new behaviors expected of them, or to meet the college faculty's expectation for self-direction. Commonly they are slow to alter ineffective study patterns that they relied on in high school (see Stark, 1965), and to accept the freedom that goes with college status. Moreover, they must still relate daily with their siblings and parents, and they have to cope with difficult study conditions at home. During any transition from social, religious, and political views held by the family and neighborhood to newer values that they learn in college, they may receive little empathy or tolerance. Furthermore, in the nature of commuter schools the students often have no strong relationships with college peer groups who can offer them emotional support in working through the crisis of achieving independence from home. Political and social attitudes that depart from the families' outlooks are often great producers of stress and unhappiness in the lives of commuting students, since they may have to suppress their thinking at home or else defend their "radical" views.

Schuchman (1974) identified four critical tasks with which commuters need to cope: learning to deal with authority, management of impulses, maintenance of self-esteem and establishing a suitable identity. Mass techniques for dealing with students and faculty fail to provide the means to constructively deal with conflicts which can increase frustration and anger. Students who experience activities unfamiliar to their parents must take greater responsibility for establishing their controls, frequently without the support of peers. Especially during the first year or two, young adults will experience in the intellectual, academic, and in social and sexual identification, feelings of inadequacy, which can be serious threats to self-esteem. In addition, the learning process will provide opportunities to develop one's own identity, provided the person is psychologically free to do so and separated from the family sufficiently to allow a conscious choice.

The commuting student may have very scant experience of any environment outside his city. Coulton (1955) observed that nine-tenths of Brooklyn College's students had never lived outside New York City and half of them had never traveled beyond the city's immediate environs. Dated as this report is, and incredible though some may find it, this author believes it will still apply to many students in our urban colleges in 1976.

Commuters also experience a social deprivation. Continuing to identify chiefly with people they knew during high school, they commonly have relatively few college friends and acquaintances. Both students and teachers often retreat to their own peer groups immediately after classes, and thereby abort the valuable student-teacher interaction that contributes to mental health, social development, and growth of knowledge.

Differences between the lives of urban commuting students and resident collegians are numerous. For instance, at Wayne State University, where the proportion of resident students is negligible, Ward and Kurz (1969) found that only 20 percent of all students graduated in four years. Most undergraduates worked while they attended school: 55 percent of the full-time and 80 percent of the part-time students. Of those who worked, ten percent worked 1 to nine hours, 19 percent ten to 19 hours, 22 percent 20 to 29 hours, eight percent 30 to 39 hours, and 41 percent 40 hours or more. The parents of 44 percent of the students made no financial contribution; many students made some financial contribution at home. Late afternoon and evening students in particular complained of the loss of energy and mental acuity at the end of the day. Commuters arranged their class schedules to minimize their on-campus time. Afternoon labs, field trips, desired courses, even required courses frequently were avoided to make a tight schedule to accommodate car pools and work demands. Withdrawal from classes was common because of unexpected changes in working hours.

> The commuting student, it appears, does not share with his campus counterpart the long idyllic days of meditation and concentration, broken only by a few hours in class. Instead his day often consists of a frantic daily rush frustrated by slow buses and filled parking lots.

Dating is another part of life where the styles of resident students and commuters differ. It is not necessary to specify or document the differences, nor possible to succeed in doing so. One sees them and sees them changing, even across the generation gap. Some of the most significant have to do with living arrangements and dating, e.g., the family home is compared to the college dormitory; these differences alone are enough to make the two worlds very unlike. And it may be that "dating" is in some places a term almost out of use, a concept of the past.

Literature concerning the personal qualities of commuting students, as compared with resident students, has not been ample. Among the more recent is the 1971 publication of Arthur Chickering and Ellen Kuper (1971). Working from a series of longitudinal studies conducted by the American Council on Education (ACE), and using their findings from the Project on Student Development in Small Colleges, these investigators presented several generalizations on the comparative development of residents and commuters as a result of attending college. The commuters' transitions were slower, and they had greater constraints associated with internal conflicts, parental pressures, and peer relationships formed before entering college. In intellectual development the college experiences of commuters and residents were similar. In out-of-class experiences and interpersonal relationships, however, substantial differences existed and persisted; nonintellectual changes proceeded more slowly for the commuters.

Dormitory students exhibited a greater range of competencies than commuters at the time of entering college; this gap between the groups increased during the freshman year. The ACE studies also revealed that students who lived in private housing, such as apartments or rooms, reported college experiences and activities very similar to the commuters from home. The former, while definitely exhibiting a wide range of differences, had a more restricted group with which to cope and interact— one or two roommates, in comparison to residents, who

had to adjust to a broader range of persons. These off-campus students, as commuters, also had less time for extra-curricular activities and, while they had less traveling to do than the commuter from home, the saved time was used in cooking and housekeeping chores.

When Graff and Cooley (1970) compared commuters to resident students, they found that the commuters had poorer mental health and curricular adjustment, and showed less maturity in goals and aspirations. It was their conclusion that commuters were less satisfied with their chosen curricula, perceived less relevance in their course work, and showed less responsibility in satisfying academic requirements. Interestingly, commuters also manifested a lack of self-confidence, feelings of failure and insecurity, and excessive anxiety when confronted with petty annoyances. But with regard to their achievement, study skills, planning use of time, and interpersonal relations with peers, no differences between resident and commuter students were found. Stark (1965), however, found commuting students often slower to alter ineffective study patterns carried over from high school, and suggested establishment of special remedial programs. In a study of commuting students from the St. Louis area, George (1971) found them to have a greater manifest personality need for autonomy and dominance than resident students, while resident students manifested a greater need for change and aggression than commuters.

Dodgens (1971) similarly found differences in the development of psychosociological characteristics between residents and nonresidents. The characteristics studied were those considered important for social living and interaction: dominance, capacity for status, sociability, self-acceptance, and responsibility. Their findings supported the hypotheses that psychosociological growth continues during the first two years of college, faster for the resident student and faster for the female student than for the male.

Black college students in three different educational settings, a large urban university, a medium-sized urban college, and a small urban center, were found to have varying degrees of alienation toward their institutions. Students from the urban center, (commuters, in contrast to the college and university students) the majority of whom lived on campus, were the least alienated from their educational setting. In contrast to white commuters, Babbitt, Burbach, and Thompson (1975) hypothesized "that the familiar surroundings of the inner city and the continuation of family life may act as supportive elements among urban blacks in building a more positive orientation to institutions of higher education."

First-generation commuting students—those whose parents never attended college—experience special psychological tensions, associated with the dream of upward mobility plus the need to maintain, simultaneously, the roles of student, worker, and son or daughter still residing in the parents' home. In contrast, second-generation collegians tend to enroll more frequently in residential colleges (Jencks and Riesman, 1968). Commuting students may place undue value on working their way through college, an attitude that Demos (1967) finds based more upon myth than on fact: "It is desirable to work your way through college—in fact, the more work, the better."

Some commuting students may not have been raised in an urban environment. When they first arrive in the city as young adults they may feel confronted with normlessness, isolation, powerlessness, and a multiplicity of entirely new experiences. Dressell (1970) wrote:

> The environment of an urban university may be effectively restricted to the facilities provided for instruction and to the social and psychological characteristics of the formal educational process provided in classes, offices, libraries, and laboratories. The environment of a residence institution comprehends residence halls, food services, recreational facilities, and the social and cultural opportunities of a large city. The resident institution is not, however, despite tradition and mythology, inevitably a better learning environment than the former. Indeed, the more diverse and rich and environment, the greater the possibility of interference and conflict between it and the central goals of learning. Confusion, incoherence, and disillusionment may result as the student expends vast energy coping with a multiplicity of uncoordinated and unrelated aspects of his environment without perceiving any undergirding or unifying goals.

REASONS FOR ATTENDING AN URBAN COLLEGE

Many students choose urban colleges (if "choose" is the word) because urban colleges and commuter living are what they can afford. In a large-scale study of the plans of high school seniors in New York (University of the State of New York, 1970), it was found that students were forced to make adjustments, the most significant of which were related to cost: to enroll in public institutions instead of private institutions; to enter a two-year college instead of a four-year school; to commute instead of living on campus; to work part-time instead of not working at all.

Attending an urban college while living at home may reduce a college student's subsistence costs by one-third; moreover, students living in high-density populated areas have a better chance at part-time employment to help them finance their education. Kerr (1967) remarked that one-quarter of all college students were self-supporting and three-quarters were partly self-supporting. Pearson (1968) added that more than one-quarter of all families in the United States lack the financial resources to meet *any* of the expenses of college attendance, even at a low-cost community college or university. Skaggs (1970) noted that at community colleges with open-admissions policies most students in occupational programs, and four out of ten men in academic programs, go to school part-time, compared to fewer than one in ten men in four-year collegiate institutions. For example, at the Community College of Denver 75 percent of the student body work full- or part-time and carry a course load of no more than nine credits.

The open admissions policies of many urban colleges encourage matriculation by students who cannot meet requirements concerning prescribed courses and grade averages in secondary school, or who achieved minimum test scores in scholastic aptitude. These deficiencies are often correlated with socio-economic status—with being

poor. In a chronology of the five-year history of the most celebrated case of open admissions, City University of New York, Bard (1975) reports on the two views of it as being a "tentative" success and the failure rate of fifty percent.

The decision to attend an urban college includes, if it is not explicitly preceded by, the decision to attend college. Some people choose not to go to college. We expect parental influence and family outlook to influence the decision; these may have social and ethnic aspects; and all may be correlated in some degree with high or low socio-economic status. Whatever, the expectations of a college education do differ between blacks and whites (Gibbs, 1973) and Mexican- and Anglo-Americans (Garza and Nelson, 1973).

The fact of access to a college undoubtedly enters into the decision to attend college. Hollinshead wrote in 1952:

> Colleges play a major role in the determination of college-going. They do this by the way they develop a clientele and engage in recruiting. They influence college-going by their purposes and their activities. They stimulate college-going by being widely scattered and by having both high and low academic standards. They encourage a larger clientele by low costs. (p. 55)

Experience long ago showed that when a college was present in a community the percentage of youth who attended college from the local area increased (Cowen, 1946).

THE ENVIRONMENTAL CLIMATE

A commuting college has been described by Riesman and Jencks (1965, p. 173) as a social organization that resembles a factory to which students come each day for a limited number of hours. The need for a specialized orientation program to reflect the lifestyle of a commuter campus was reported on by McCoy (1973). Urban colleges must consciously plan to create their desired environments. Vocationally oriented, upwardly mobile youth from the working class and lower middle class, desirous of accumulating course credits for a degree and credentials, reject the stereotyped collegiate culture—perhaps especially those who aspire to enter graduate school or a profession. Mass higher education also tends to work against the development and maintenance of informal student subcultures with a serious interest in ideas.

The environment to be created must have a place for students at opposite extremes of maturity. Although we have scant data concerning the different personality need characteristics of commuter students who choose to attend two-year or four-year metropolitan colleges and universities, Minkevich, George, and Marshall (1970) found that high school students selecting to commute to two-year colleges, compared to those selecting metropolitan four-year colleges and universities, tended to be more dependent upon others, more frequently let others make decisions, sought suggestions from others, did what was expected, conformed to custom, and avoided the unconventional; in contrast, students selecting the four-year schools were more inclined to form strong attachments, to share things with friends, to form new relationships, to do things with a friend rather than by oneself, to participate in groups, and to remain loyal to friends. In a longitudinal study, Fry (1974) found that a university environment had a differential impact on the psychosocial development of youths coming from urban and rural communities. The rural youths developed greater identity achievement than did students from urban backgrounds. At the other extreme from such young commuters are those who for one or another reason are pursuing learning as a possibly lifelong process, young and old: professionals pursuing inservice education; the disadvantaged adult who did not complete high school, now a new careerist receiving vocational training as a paraprofessional; the divorcee pursuing the education that an early marriage and children interrupted; widows and housewives bored by bridge and volunteer work; blue- and white-collar workers dissatisfied with their stagnated careers and slow advancement, working toward promotions through education; nurses, having trained in their applied art and now desirous of supervisory positions, working on their degrees, etc.

It becomes obvious that the more one develops an educational and training system for a heterogeneous group of people moving along at different paces, the more important it is that colleges grow to understand their students' backgrounds to build and maintain meaningful programs.

REFERENCES

Bard, Bernard. College for All: Dream or Disaster? *Phi Delta Kappan,* 1975, *56*(6), 390-395.

Babbitt, Charles E., Burbach, Harold J., and Thompson, Myron A., III. Organizational Alienation among Black College Students: A Comparison of Three Educational Settings. *Journal of College Student Personnel,* 1975, *16*(1), 53-56.

Chickering, Arthur W., and Kuper, Ellen. *Them That Has, Gets.* Washington: Office of Research, American Council on Education, 1971.

Coulton, Thomas. *A City College in Action.* New York: Harper and Brothers, 1955.

Cowen, Philip A. *A Study of the Factors Related to College Attendance in New York State.* Albany: New York State Education Department, 1946.

Demos, George D. Problems of Integrating the Commuter College Student to the College Campus. *Journal of the American College Health Association,* 1967, *15,* 291-294.

Dodgens, Charles. Developing Competence. In Arthur W. Chickering, *Education and Identity,* 2nd ed. San Francisco: Jossey-Bass, 1971.

Dressel, Paul L. Evaluation of the Environment, the Process, and the Results of Higher Education. In Asa Knowles, ed., *Handbook of College and University Administration.* New York: McGraw-Hill Book Company, 1970.

Freedman, M. B. San Francisco State: Urban Campus Prototype. In G. Kerry Smith, ed., *Agony and Promise.* San Francisco: Jossey-Bass, 1969.

Fry, P. S. (Dua). Developmental Changes in Identity Status of University Students from Rural and Urban Backgrounds. *Journal of College Student Personnel,* 1974, *15*(3), 183-190.

Garza, Raymond T., and Nelson, Darwin B. A Comparison of Mexican- and Anglo-American Perceptions of the University Environment. *Journal of College Student Personnel,* 1973, *14*(5), 399-401.

George, Rickey L. Resident or Commuter: A Study of Personality Differences. *Journal of College Student Personnel,* 1971, *12,* 216-219.

Gibbs, Jewell Taylor. Black Students/White University: Different Expectations. *The Personnel and Guidance Journal,* 1973, *51*(7), 463-469.

Graff, Robert W., and Cooley, Gary R. Adjustment of Commuter and Resident Students. *Journal of College Student Personnel,* 1970, *11,* 54-57.

Hardwick, Mark W., and Kazlo, Martha P. Designing and Implementing A Commuter Services Program: A Model For Change. *Commuter Research Report No. 3-73.* College Park, Maryland: Office of Commuter Student Affairs, June 1974.

Harrington, Thomas F. *Student Personnel Work in Urban Colleges.* New York: Intext Educational Publishers, 1974.

Hollinshead, Byron S. *Who Should Go to College.* New York: Columbia University Press, 1952.

Jencks, Christopher, and Riesman, David, *The Academic Revolution.* New York: Doubleday and Company, 1968.

Kerr, Clark. Broadcast interview, *Face the Nation.* CBS Radio Network, February 5, 1967.

McCoy, Robert D. Commuter College Orientation: The Walkthrough. *Journal of College Student Personnel,* 1973, *14*(6), 551.

Minkevitch, George, George, Rickey L., and Marshall, Jon C. Students Commuting to Two-Year and Four-Year Colleges: Some Personality Differences. Paper presented at the Annual Convention of the American Personnel and Guidance Association, Atlantic City, New Jersey, April 1971.

Pearson, Richard. Can Colleges Reclaim the Non Student? Maybe— With Hard Cash. *College Board Review,* 1967-1968 (Winter), 14-19.

Peterson, R. E. On a Typology of College Student. *Educational Testing Service Research Bulletin.* Educational Testing Service, Princeton, New Jersey, 1965.

Riesman, David, and Jencks, Christopher. The Viability of the American College. In Nevitt Sanford, ed., *The American College.* New York: John Wiley and Sons, 1965, 74-192.

Schuchman, Herman. Special Tasks of Commuter Students. *The Personnel and Guidance Journal,* 1974, *52*(7), 465-470.

Skaggs, Kenneth C. Finishing School for Workers. In Rose Weiner, *Manpower,* 1970, *2,* 3-7.

Stark, Matthew. Commuter and Residence Hall Students Compared. *Personnel and Guidance Journal,* 1965, *44,* 277-281.

Trivett, David A. The Commuting Student. *ERIC Higher Education Research Currents,* American Association for Higher Education, June 1974.

University of the State of New York, The State Education Department. *A Longitudinal Study of the Barriers Affecting the Pursuit of Higher Education by New York State High School Seniors, Phase II,* July 1970.

Ward, Richard, and Kurz, Theodore. *The Commuting Student— A Study of Facilities at Wayne State University.* Final Report of the Commuter Centers Project; Study Made Possible by Educational Facilities Laboratories. Detroit, January 1969.

59

THE OMBUDSMAN IN AMERICAN HIGHER EDUCATION

by David G. Speck
Director of Student Activities
The George Washington University
Washington, D.C.

A new position—the ombudsman—has come into the organizational structure of over 50 American colleges and universities since 1966 (Rowland, 1970), and many more institutions are considering such a position or a similar one. During its brief history, the ombudsman seems to have made significant strides toward restoring the human factor to a complex and impersonal system of higher education, and in assisting in the resolution of grievances which are commonplace on many campuses.

The word "ombudsman" is borrowed from Sweden, where it means agent or attorney. The position, which has distinct legal overtones, existed there for almost a century; but when the new constitution of 1809 established a democratic monarchy, it specifically provided for the appointment of a *Justitie-ombudsman* ("Procurator for Civil Affairs") by the Parliament to

> . . . supervise the observance of laws and statutes as applied, in matters not coming under the Military Procurator, by the courts and by public officials and employees . . . institute proceedings before the competent courts against those who, in the execution of their official duties, have through partiality, favouritism, or other cause committed any unlawful act or neglected to perform their official duties properly. (Sawer, 1964)

Since that time, the duties of the ombudsman have been modified and the prosecutor's role minimized. His main functions are to receive complaints of maladministration from citizens, investigate fully such complaints, report to the official and department responsible for righting the wrong, and carry out a continuous inspection of random departments and authorities at work. He does not have the power to overrule an official decision, and usually does not question the use of discretionary power if it is within the law. Several countries—including Finland, Denmark, Norway, New Zealand, Japan, Yugoslavia, and the Soviet Union—have instituted positions patterned after the Swedish model (Sawer, 1964). Although many people (including U.S. Representative Henry S. Reuss) have suggested that such a governmental function would be beneficial in the United States, and legislation has been proposed in the Congress, it is on the campuses that a form of the ombudsman position is being implemented.

The greatly increased size of higher education institutions, and the complexity of their administrative structures, have resulted in a steady decline in personal contact among the major academic constituents—students, faculty, and administrators. Students, especially, have perceived a lack of concern for their individuality, and have been loudest in voicing resentment and in expressing grievances.

The creation of the position of ombudsman is an attempt to decrease some of the frustrations caused by burgeoning size and/or impersonal bureaucracies. Not all of the individuals filling such positions are called "Ombudsmen." Often the title reflects the particular needs of the school; so one might be called "Counselor at Large," "Director of Innovations in Student Life," or "Consultant in Student Affairs" (Bloland and Nowak, 1968).

Specific titles or previous occupations are irrelevant, except to the extent that the person serving as the ombudsman is recognized and respected by the university community as competent. Although the job description for the ombudsman may vary from school to school, the underlying theme is an awareness of the individual and the problems of the bureaucracy.

RESPONSIBILITIES

At the University of Washington, the Ombudsman outlined six general areas of responsibility:

> To serve as a source for information and assistance that is available to all University community members concerning both academic and nonacademic rules, regulations, and procedures of the University.

> To receive complaints from students and members of the faculty and staff about alleged inequities.

> To bring any complaint to the attention of the appropriate University agency if it has not already been heard by the agency.

> To investigate complaints already heard, if the individual concerned still feels aggrieved and seeks to resolve the difficulty between the individual and the University agency involved.

> To recommend redress to the President when the Ombudsman believes that an individual has been improperly treated, and when the Ombudsman has been unable to resolve the matter himself.

> To recommend to the President and to appropriate authorities such changes in rules, regulations, and procedures as he deems necessary or desirable (Aagaard, 1969).

At St. Cloud State College ("Working Draft . . .," 1970), a proposal for a campus ombudsman presented six general premises in developing the position:

> His two main functions are to receive and attempt to resolve individual student grievances pertaining to the College, and to recommend procedural changes aimed at keeping student grievances at a minimum.

> He has no authority to take disciplinary action, reverse decisions, or circumvent existing rules and regulations. He will supplement, not replace, other means of redress for student grievances.

> He has access to all college offices and files, except medical or psychological records.

He will make periodic, general, and widely publicized reports.

He will be responsible for establishing and maintaining confidential records.

He will have a private office conveniently located for students.

In a proposal ("Proposal for . . .," 1969), for the creation of an ombudsman at Cornell University, the five general functions for the position were noted: investigation, recommendation, information, encouragement of and participation in special services during emergencies, and encouragement of the establishment of counterparts to the ombudsman's office. This report also outlined some "don'ts" in the responsibilities of the office:

he can, of course, exercise no powers that are beyond the legal authority of the University, although he may make recommendations concerning the authority of the University or of its constituent parts;

he does not himself make University policy or replace established legislative or judicial procedures, although he may investigate any and all of these, raise questions about them, and make such recommendations as he feels proper for their improvement and efficient functioning;

while he may have access to personal and personnel records, he must respect their confidentiality unless he has written permission from the affected parties for releasing the information;

while he has wide latitude in making public his findings and recommendations, he must preserve the requests of the complainants that their anonymity be preserved.

From these and other descriptions of the functions of the ombudsman, a general description can be developed that outlines the role the ombudsman will perform, although the specific functions vary according to need from school to school and from situation to situation.

Investigation. At the request of an individual or group in the school community, the ombudsman will investigate instances of discrimination, misuse of power, or unreasonable penalty.

Recommendation. The ombudsman may recommend modifications of policies, procedures, or regulations that have caused a grievance or have the potential to do so, but he will not *make* modifications.

Information. The ombudsman will serve as a general information source for all members of the school community.

Encouragement. The ombudsman will encourage members of the university community to respond to complaints and grievances, to be aware of patterns of problems, and to develop an atmosphere in which his services will no longer be required.

Several ombudsmen have suggested, and most seem to agree (Cook, 1970; Norman, 1968; Rowland, 1969; Rust, 1968), that a specific appointment of two or three years is desirable. A one-year reappointment system, or tenure system, is undesirable because it has the tendency to stress performance as the criterion for continued appointment. It is important to note that there is no such concept (and probably never will be) of a professional ombudsman in higher education. The ombudsman generally plans to return to his original field of interest after a specific term of appointment as ombudsman. However, it is necessary for the ombudsman to have a time period of more than one year, to develop the position within his own framework and to be free of the political pressures of regular reappointment.

San Diego State's ombudsman (Norman, 1968) supplemented some of the specific concerns of ombudsmen with a checklist of provisions which must be considered in developing the position:

Length of term, method of appointment, and termination.

Clear statement of accessibility to officials, records, committee meetings and minutes, and organs of communication.

Clarification of his role: Is he the faculty's, administration's, or the students' man? To whom, if anyone, does he report? Is he responsible or answerable to any official or body?

What types of problems can he accept? Is secrecy assured?

What help is available for informational and referral functions?

What official status does he have in regular campus structures?

What ultimate power does he have to advance stalemated but justified appeals?

What aspects of the job are left to the discretion of the appointee? Office management? Method of operation? Records kept?

Who pays his salary, and what strings does that imply?

What guarantees are provided for his invulnerability?

Obviously, all of the above questions should be qualified with a consideration of the particular needs of the school.

Howard Rowland (1969) went further in delineating aspects of both the institution and the job that are important to the effectiveness of a college or university ombudsman:

The institution with a campus ombudsman should have a relatively stable organizational structure, supported and trusted by most of the people within it most of the time.

The office of ombudsman should be equivalent in

salary and prestige to high-level academic and administrative positions.

The campus ombudsman should be a long-term faculty member at the institution, experienced in teaching and advising, and highly respected by students, colleagues, and administrators. Regardless of his academic discipline, he should have some rudimentary knowledge of law and be thoroughly acquainted with the civil ombudsman concept.

He should be carefully selected by a committee representing students, faculty, and administration. The actual appointment should be made or confirmed by the governing board of the institution upon the recommendation of its chief administrative officer.

He should be appointed for a two-year term, renewable by mutual agreement of the ombudsman and the selection committee.

The ombudsman should make widely publicized, periodic general reports to all members of the institution. He also may make confidential reports with recommendations to the chief administrative officer, who should determine the extent of their circulation.

While serving as ombudsman, he should not be required to teach or perform other faculty duties.

He should have a private office, apart from the main administration building and easily accessible to students, with a secretary but not a staff.

The ombudsman should be receptive to individual student grievances, both academic and nonacademic, concerning the institution. He should decide which complaints are within his jurisdiction and competence and which of those merit his investigation.

He should use reasoned persuasion to bring about redress of genuine student grievances as expeditiously and equitably as possible.

Where a pattern of student grievances develops, he should work for a change in regulations, procedures, or personnel to prevent recurrance.

He should not conduct investigations on his own initiative, but rather in response to student complaints.

The ombudsman should have access to all campus offices and files except medical, psychological, and classified government records.

He should keep confidential records on each case he considers.

When rebuffed during an investigation, he should have the authority to appeal to the chief administrative officer for intervention.

He should not have authority to take disciplinary action, reverse decisions, or circumvent regulations. His power should lie in his prestige, persuasiveness, and persistence in stating his views to persons involved in a grievance, and, if necessary, to their organizational superiors.

He should supplement, not supercede, other means of redress for student grievances.

Decisions about continuing the office should be based on systematic sampling of students who have consulted the ombudsman.

Although the position of ombudsman is new in American higher education, and has had relatively limited acceptance, the ombudsmen themselves and those who have utilized their services contend that it has produced definite benefits. In 1968, the ombudsman at San Jose State College (White) drew some tentative conclusions on the value of the ombudsman after having served in that position for one year: the ombudsman can restore a sense of accessibility to the student; furnish alternative channels to at least some of the confrontations taking place; help form administrative decisions; offer some hope that real concerns are not lost in the shuffle of events; assure students that he is not there to defend the status-quo; help bring about equality for all in the college community; and help overcome the administration's tendency to deal with complaints by reinforcing current procedures, rather than meeting the problems causing the grievances.

Dr. Nelson Norman (1968), at San Diego State, estimated that approximately two-thirds to three-fourths of the students seeing him received the help they desired; one-fifth presented situations "which would require restructuring the whole institution or persuading the governor to change his mind, and five to ten percent were not successful due to my mishandling or other circumstances."

As part of his doctoral dissertation, Dr. Ray Rowland surveyed students who had consulted the campus ombudsman at Michigan State University during the Fall semester, 1968. He reported (1969):

> Nearly half of the 218 students surveyed had taken their problems to two or more persons in authority before consulting the ombudsman. Two-thirds indicated that the problems they brought to the ombudsman were completely or partially solved, while one-third considered their problems "not solved at all." Two-thirds of the respondents thought the campus ombudsman helped relieve student frustration and hostility. None wanted to see the functions of the ombudsman discontinued, although one-third recommended changes. Nearly all indicated that they would return to the ombudsman if they had similar problems and would recommend him to other students. Only 13 of 207 respondents claimed to have experienced "unpleasant treatment" by anyone concerned with their complaints after they consulted the ombudsman.

Earle Clifford, formerly Dean of Student Affairs at Rutgers University, criticized the ombudsman concept when he argued (1968) that establishment of the ombudsman merely compounds the problems of institutional bureaucracy, and that permissive institutions and overdemanding youth are the causes of organizational weaknesses—not the organizational structure itself. He contends that the ombudsman is "educational gimmickry" in its focus on the effects rather than the causes of an institution's problems, and that an effective student personnel staff can adequately assume the duties of an ombudsman and avoid one more step for students in the resolution of problems. However, although a dynamic and respected dean of students can do much to affect the mood of a campus, student personnel workers are often unable to deal effectively with controversy over academic matters. Administrators, regardless of faculty status, are usually not viewed as academians by faculty members, who generally resist attempts by nonacademic personnel to control their performance. Both administrators and faculty have, in fact, occasionally resented the presence of an ombudsman. As Monroe Rowland stated (1970), "the very fact that the ombudsman is hired because of problems in the system, and to change the system, is a threat."

In addition, while it would be convenient to use an already existing administrative position, the administrator functioning as an ombudsman should have more authority than that of the dean of students. He should have access to anyone or any section within the institution, and the only administrator with that type of power now is the president. Unfortunately, most college and university presidents do not have time for the duties of an ombudsman, so schools that have developed the position have delegated certain presidential powers to the ombudsman. At Michigan State University, for example, Ombudsman Dr. James D. Rust functions—like the dean of students—as a traffic cop, directing students through the bureaucracy. Unlike the dean of students, however, Dr. Rust has the organizational authority to follow up a referral—by crossing departmental lines if necessary—to ensure that the student's questions or problems have been dealt with adequately.

Herein lies one of the most critical concepts of the ombudsman. Any office with the necessary knowledge at hand can be set up as an information and referral center. Students can be instructed to come to this office if they have problems and questions, and referrals will be made to the specialized office which, theoretically, is prepared to meet the situation. However, as long as this referral office remains a part of the bureaucracy its power is limited, for there are usually other offices with similar administrative authority. The ombudsman, on the other hand, has no organizational affiliation to a specific office except to that of the president or chief executive officer. Having access to all offices and all officials, he is able to see that decisions are not made without the benefit of careful consideration and that there are means to rectify problems.

It should be noted, however, that the decline of serious, overt unrest on the campuses, coupled with a multitude of positive steps by many colleges and universities, has lessened the demand for ombudsman-type functions. Such actions as more student involvement in decision-making, improved communication, representative governance structures, better relationships among students, faculty, and administrators, and the development of existing structures (i.e., judicial systems) for the resolution or adjudication of grievances, have affected the popularization of the ombudsman, and caused many institutions to review carefully the possible impact of such a position.

However, while the ombudsman may always be a controversial position, often misunderstood (more often mispronounced) and sometimes resented, it generally has great potential usefulness. Nelson Norman (1969) summed it up well when he wrote,

> . . . a motto for the position might be: "Maximum Service and Significant Change Rapidly." Another college or university, with all conditions different, still would find the office serviceable. There can be no single pattern: the assignment is capable of widest changes. "Ombudsman" is the greatest word in projective psychology since "Rorschach": everyone can make of it what he wants.

REFERENCES

Anderson, Stanley V. Canadian Ombudsman Proposals. Berkeley, California: Study presented to the Institute of Governmental Studies, University of California, Berkeley, November 1966.

Ascher, C. S. Grievance Man or Ombudsmania. *Public Administration Review, 27,* June 1967, pp. 174-178.

Bloland, Paul, and Nowak, Daniel. The Ombudsman: An Informal Survey of the Implementation of the Ombudsman Concept. Student Personnel Report Number 4. Los Angeles: University of Southern California, Office of the Dean of Students, October 1968.

Brann, James W. The Campus Ombudsman: College Students' Defender. *The Chronicle of Higher Education, 3,* November 11, 1968.

Buccieri, Claudia. Campus Troubleshooter Resetting his Sights. *College and University Business, 45,* December 1968, pp. 51-53.

_____. Ombudsman: New Troubleshooter on Campus. *College and University Business, 44,* March 1968, pp. 52-55.

Caffrey, John, ed. *The Future Academic Community: Continuity and Change.* Washington: American Council on Education, 1969.

Clifford, Earle W. Second Thoughts on the Ombudsman in Higher Education. Detroit: Paper presented at the University of Detroit Conference on Ombudsman in American Higher Education, October 25, 1968. Reprinted in the *NASPA Journal, 7,* April 1970.

Constructive Changes to Ease Campus Tensions. Washington: Office of Institution Research, National Association of State Universities and Land-Grant Colleges, January 1970.

deSmith, S. A. Anglo-Saxon Ombudsman. *Political Quarterly, 33,* January 1962, pp. 9-19.

Downs, Anthony. *Inside Bureaucracy.* Boston: Little, Brown and Company, 1967.

Egan, J. Ombudsman: Danish Official to Protect the Private Citizen From Government. *Holiday, 40,* November 1966, p. 28.

Gellhorn, Walter. *Ombudsman and Others.* Cambridge: Harvard University Press, 1966.

_____. Ombudsman or Ombudsmania. *Student Lawyer Journal, 14,* April 1969, pp. 14-17.

_____. *When Americans Complain.* Cambridge: Harvard University Press, 1966.

_____. Colleges and Universities with Campus Ombudsman or Ombudsman-Like Operations. Portion of a paper presented at the Higher Education Executive Associates Conference on the Ombudsman, Chicago, March 1, 1970.

_____. A Study of the Campus Ombudsman in American Higher Education with Emphasis on Michigan State University. Abstract of doctoral thesis, 1969.

Rowland, Monroe. Quotes. *NASPA Journal, 7,* April 1970, p. 245.

Rust, James D. A report on the Ombudsman at Michigan State

University. 1968. Mimeographed.

_____. A Campus Ombudsman Looks at His Job. July 23, 1969. Mimeographed.

Sandler, Ake et al. An Ombudsman for the University. *The Journal of College Student Personnel, 9,* March 1968, pp. 112-115.

Sawer, Geoffrey. *Ombudsman.* Melbourne: Melbourne University Press, 1964.

Schlossberg, Nancy. The Ombudsman in Current Status and Theory. Paper presented at the Consultation on the Ombudsman in American Higher Education, Detroit, Ocrober 24, 1968.

_____. An Ombudsman for Students. *NASPA Journal, 5,* July 1967.

Sellin, Thorsten, ed. The Ombudsman or Citizen's Defender: A Modern Institution. *The Annals of the American Academy of Political and Social Science, 377,* May 1968.

Speck, David G. *A Collection of Literature on the Ombudsman in Higher Education.* Material prepared for the George Washington University, Washington, D.C., November 15, 1969.

_____. A Proposal for the Creation of an Ombudsman at the George Washington University. A report made to the Vice President for Student Affairs at the George Washington University, Washington, D.C., December 19, 1968.

Sweden's Remedy for Police Brutality: Ombudsman. *Harper's Magazine, 229,* November 1968, p. 132.

Wainwright, L. For the Ombudsman, a Hearty Skoal. *Life, 61,* December 16, 1966, p. 126.

We Can, Indeed, Fight City Hall: The Office and Concept of Ombudsman. *American Bar Association Journal, 53,* March 1967, pp. 231-236.

Werner, R. W. Educational Tyranny and the Ombudsman: Protecting Pupils and Teachers. *School and Society, 95,* October 28, 1967, pp. 391-392.

ADDITIONAL REFERENCES

Hamilton, Randy S. Can You Fight City Hall and Win? *Public Management, 49,* October 1967, pp. 268-275.

Little Man's Champion: The Ombudsman. *Newsweek, 68,* December 12, 1966, p. 28.

Montgomery, Paul L. Cornell's New Faces Turn to Student Unrest. *The New York Times,* October 13, 1969, p. M41.

Mundinger, Donald. The University Ombudsman: His Place on the Campus. *Journal of Higher Education, 38,* December 1967.

Norman, Nelson F. The Ombudsman: A New Bird on Campus. San Diego: San Diego State College, 1968.

The Ombudsman. *Newsweek, 74,* December 15, 1969, pp. 100-104.

The Ombudsman. New York: Report of the 32nd American Assembly, October 26-29, 1967.

Ombudsman, Anyone? *National Review, 13,* August 28, 1962, p. 127.

The Ombudsman in Higher Education. *NASPA Journal, 7,* April 1970.

The Ombudsman in Higher Education: Advocate or Subversive Bureaucrat. Burlingame, California: Papers from a conference on the ombudsman in American higher education, May 4-6, 1969.

Osborn, R. J. Citizen Versus Administration in the USSR. *Soviet Studies, 17,* October 1967, pp. 226-237.

Peterson, Richard. *The Scope of Organized Student Protest in 1967-68.* Princeton, N.J.: Educational Testing Service, 1968.

Rabinovich, Abraham, The Jerusalem Ombudsman. *Hadassah Magazine, 51,* March 1970, p. 10.

Reuss, Henry S. An American Ombudsman. *Public Management, 49,* October 1967, pp. 265-267.

_____. Ombudsman for America: Scandinavian-Style Grievance

Man to Investigate Complaints about the Work of Bureaucrats. *The New York Times Magazine, 113,* September 13, 1964, p. 30.

Rowat, Donald C., ed. *The Ombudsman: Citizen's Defender.* London: George Allen & Unwin, Ltd., 1968.

_____. Ombudsman for North America. *Public Administration Review, 24,* December 1964, pp. 230-233.

Rowland, Howard Ray. The Campus Ombudsman: An Emerging Role. *Educational Record, 50,* Fall, 1969, pp. 442-448.

White, J. Benton. The Ombudsman in Practice. Report by J. Benton White, Ombudsman, San Jose State College, 1968.

Working Draft of a proposal for a Campus Ombudsman. St. Cloud, Minnesota: St. Cloud State College, February 1970.

60

PARENT EDUCATION

by Frank W. Freshour
Associate Professor
University of South Florida
Tampa, Florida

Most of the programs in parent education have been in kindergarten, first grade, and second grade in the area of reading, although there is a trend toward preschool parental involvement in compensatory education. Reading and early childhood are two of the areas which have been receiving the greatest emphasis in the field of education. Children do not succeed in school because they cannot read, and early childhood educators maintain that many children are doomed to failure before they reach first grade.

Thus it logically follows that the efforts of many educators would come to be directed to the area of reading readiness activities which actively involve parents. It might be wise to examine the recent literature and developments in parent education from several different viewpoints. For example, what are some of the home factors which have an influence on the success of a child in school? What differences are there between middle-class situations and the disadvantaged? (For lack of better terminology, the term "disadvantaged" is used, and is defined in a broad sense to include family situations in which the income falls below the level of $4,800 per year.) What different kinds of studies have been carried out, and with what success? What different kinds of parent education programs look promising? Can educators muster the cooperation of the public schools and the parents, and also gain the financial support of the government? Can education afford to carry out parent education programs of such proportions as to make a worthwhile impact on the success of children in school? Quite possibly, the present confused state of our society might make a more appropriate question read, whether we can afford not to carry on parent education.

THE LITERATURE

Studies have suggested a variety of home factors which have a bearing on the success of a child in school. The effect of the amount of independence of a child was found to be an important factor by Stewart (1950) and Winterbottom (1958). Freeberg and Payne (1967) found parental pressure and parental assistance to succeed, particularly in the area of verbal skills, to be important factors. Gordon (1969) found the degree to which a child matches the maternal expectations to be a strong influence on child performance. His work was carried out with disadvantaged mothers and their preschool children. Mothers were trained to go into the homes. Their main objective was child stimulation. He found that mothers can be trained to be effective with their children. Milner (1951) found that rich verbal environments and parent-child interaction were positive factors, while Fodor (1966) points out the value of reading to preschool children. Cazden (1965) found that exposure to models of good speech was effective in language acquisition.

Some studies have examined the differences between middle-class and disadvantaged home situations. Miller (1969), for example, found home prereading experiences to be related to reading readiness but not to first grade reading achievement. She provided typical middle-class experiences, among them alphabet learning, library usage, discussions, and field trips. Miller (1967) also found that middle-class mothers were more person-oriented in their control system, while lower-class mothers were more status-oriented. Willmon (1967) dealt with parent participation in a Head Start Program. She found significant differences in reading readiness in favor of those children whose parents were active participants. Five hundred forty-one children were involved in her study. McConnell et al. (1969) collected data from training offered in language development and sensory perception. Their study covered two years of compensatory education in a day-care center. They found significant differences in intelligence and in readiness in favor of the experimental group upon first grade entrance. In the Murfreesboro (Tennessee) Early Training Project, Gray and Klaus (1965) dealt with 60 disadvantaged Negro children and their parents. Their objectives were achievement motivation, language stimulation, and the ability to order and classify objects. In the Perry Preschool (Ypsilanti, Michigan) Project, Weikart (1967) found a significant difference in IQ scores of blacks over a two-year period. Home visits were a part of the program. From his work with black parents, Freshour (1970) suggests that some of the problems that future research will need to deal with are inappropriate tests, irregular parent attendance, and overly theoretical presentations (as opposed to practical applications). He suggests that longitudinal studies of several years are needed, as opposed to short-term studies. Involvement of the school principal and teachers might help improve parent participation. Freshour makes a final suggestion that researchers work at least part of the time with parents and children together.

Two studies are reported which produced favorable results in reading over a period of several years in Denver. Brzeinski and Driscoll (1971) and McManus (1964) carried out these parent education programs with middle-class parents over television. Parents had study guides to use, and were to spend 30 minutes a week with their children. Alphabet and phonics cards were among the materials used. MacLaren (1965) offered a parent information program to parents of first-grade, middle-class students. He found significant differences in favor of his experimental group. Ryan (1965), on the other hand, found little difference in second-grade children whose parents were involved in a home reading program. The experimental group did read more extensively and visited the library more often.

SOME PROBLEMS

Some ideas for future directions in parent education programs seem to be appropriate at this point. Based on the successes and failures of some of the previously mentioned review of literature, it would appear that parental involvement in preschool and first grade is an important and promising field in education. Educators need to look more closely at the importance of attitudes and values of both parents and their children. Parents are for the most part unaware of the part that self-concept plays in the success of children at school. In turn, lack of success in school shows a positive correlation with delinquency, a growing concern of our country today.

A particularly perplexing problem is that the parents and children that the schools need to reach most are the most difficult to reach. Success with the disadvantaged has been very limited, despite the large sums of money and time which have been invested. Often only one parent lives in the home; usually it is the mother, and usually she is employed and has very little time for her children, even if she is interested in helping them.

Sesame Street, the well-known television program which received large sums of federal money in an attempt to reach the disadvantaged preschooler, has not succeeded in its main goal. It seems that Sesame Street is having more effect on middle-class children, quite possibly because middle-class parents take the time to watch and discuss the program with their children. Parents of the disadvantaged most likely do not have the time for, or do not realize the value of, watching and discussing the program. The Electric Company, another television program along the same lines, is aimed more toward the school and teacher, rather than the home. Perhaps future efforts might be aimed at helping parents of the disadvantaged to work with their children by providing guidelines for parent-child activities in conjunction with television programs such as these.

Another problem with the disadvantaged has been in finding and/or developing appropriate tests to measure anything other than skills. Carrying out studies over a period of several years is becoming more and more difficult, for various reasons: our society is becoming more and more transient; children are being bused to one school this year and to a different school next year; often the children are bused so far from home that it is impossible for the parents to visit the school or attend workshops.

EXEMPLARY PROGRAMS

Successful programs in general tend to show some commonalities. Most of them tend to be with the middle class, quite probably because these families have more time and money, are more easily reached, and are academically oriented, in that they see success in school as being all-important to occupational possibilities for their children. Studies show success in school to be related to parental occupation, parental assistance with school activities, the number of books in the home, the breadth and depth of parent-child conversation, and the breadth and depth of experiences that parents provide for their children. Early success is related to reading to a child and providing a good model for the child. Setting aside a time after supper in which the television is turned off and everyone in the family reads is certainly a good example. Parent education programs in which parents are asked to carry out particular activities have been more successful than programs which were more lecture- and information-giving in nature.

Gordon (1969) has carried out one of the few successful programs with the disadvantaged over a period of several years. He trained mothers to go into the community and work with other mothers and their preschool children. He succeeded in training the mothers and was able to enhance the development of the children. His program has served as a model for parent-and-child-center programs throughout the country. The Chattanooga Parent and Child Center has made use of his program. The Jacksonville, Florida, Parent and Child Center has made use of this model, and representatives from as far away as Barton, Vermont, Cleveland, Ohio, Minneapolis, Minnesota, and Atlanta, Georgia have come to study the model that Gordon has developed at the University of Florida at Gainesville.

Follow Through programs, which have used his Florida Follow Through Model, include such cities as Philadelphia, Richmond, Jacksonville, Tampa, and Houston. These and other cities have sent representatives to Gainesville for training. Gordon also has available a list of booklets for purchase; among the items available are such booklets as The Stimulation Series Booklet and a Piaget-oriented activities booklet. The work of Gordon offers promise for helping parents of disadvantaged children to work with their children from the infant stage through the early years of school. Here is an attempt to help those children who are "doomed to failure before they start school."

The studies in Denver by Brzeinski and Driscoll (1971), and by McManus (1964), are examples of large-scale longitudinal programs which have been carried on with middle-class children and their parents. As was stated earlier, their programs made use of television presentations to parents. Guidebooks were given to the parents in conjunction with the television programs. Approval of the program by parents was high, and the children showed significant progress in their reading abilities.

More recently, the Calgary Catholic School District in Alberta, Canada, has launched a parent education program and has compiled "A Collection of Articles on Beginning Reading," which it has used in its program.

In England, which has a more centralized educational setup than the United States, they have invested large sums of money into the nursery school concept of providing a variety of pressure-free experiences for children who otherwise would not have much more in the way of preschool experiences than the busy city streets. For those children who show they are ready to read, a more structured opportunity is available, but this is not the aim of the program. The Minister of Education oversees this vast program, and she has indicated that parental involvement and approval are good.

There are various other parental involvement programs scattered throughout the United States, and it seems appropriate to mention some of them. The Baltimore City Schools sponsored The Baltimore Early Admission Project, in which they did not hold traditional classes but based group activities on the concerns of parents. In Los Angeles, teacher-led classes were held for parents in The Child Observation Project. After the classes, the parents worked with their children in play activities. This was a preschool program. This same project also had a program which covered kindergarten through sixth grade and was coordinated with the schoolwork of the children. Oakland Public Schools held a preschool project in which parents were employed as aides, and efforts were made to develop the language and personalities of the children. The Ypsilanti Schools conducted three different programs which were set up to help parents work with their children in the home. One program was for retarded children and two were for disadvantaged children. The Detroit Great Cities Project used school-community workers and assistants in an effort to go into homes to help parents work with their children. Prince George's County, Maryland, had a similar program, Operation Moving Ahead. Parent Helpers worked in the homes of the disadvantaged to help parents prepare their children for school (Gordon, 1970).

ATTACKING THE PROBLEMS

Although there is still some controversy in the area of parent education, most of the issues have been compromised to the satisfaction of most educators. One problem has been whether parents should try to teach their children in a formal or technical manner, similar to that of a teacher, or to function in more of a supportive, informal role. Most educators agree that a parent can be trained to teach a child in a manner similar to that of a teacher, but most question the wisdom of such training because of the emotional problems which are likely to result and the ensuing family friction which is likely to follow. The parent-child relationship is likely to suffer when the parent tries to become a teacher. Games, discussions, trips, and other informal activities are considered to be more beneficial than actual teaching.

Another problem which seems to have lessened is that of teachers' not wanting parents in the schools, for fear of interference with their teaching. However, as more and more parents participate in school activities the barriers begin to fall. Teachers are beginning to realize that, given direction, parents can be an asset. Many of the problems come from lack of understanding about what the goals and methods of the teachers are. As parents and teachers begin to realize the fears and problems that each have, a coordinated effort brings about a better learning situation for all concerned.

One final issue which bears mentioning is that of early reading. It, too, has been resolved to the satisfaction of most reading specialists. Children can learn to read before entering school, but most children are better off in an informal environment of readiness activities. Too often overly ambitious parents pressure their children into early reading. If the child pushes to learn to read, let him, but parental pressure often results in emotional problems and a dislike of reading.

In closing, one final suggestion for future efforts of the schools, in the area of parent involvement: why not hold high school classes in parent education that are required of all students? It seems to make sense to try to prepare our teenagers for one of the most important and difficult tasks that they are likely to face, that of being a parent.

REFERENCES

Brzeinski, J., and Driscoll, H. Early Start in Reading—Help or Hindrance? *Parents and Reading.* Newark, Delaware: IRA, 57-75, 1971.

Cazden, C. B. Environmental Assistance to the Child's Acquisition of Grammar. Dissertation, Harvard University, 1965.

Fodor, M. E. The Effect of the Systematic Reading of Stories on the Language Development of Culturally Deprived Children. Dissertation, Cornell University. Ann Arbor, Mich.: University Microfilms, 1966, No. 66-10,261.

Freeberg, N. E., and Payne, D. T. Parental Influence on Cognitive Development in Early Childhood: A Review. *Child Development,* 1967, *38,* 65-87.

Freshour, F. W. The Effects of a Parent Education Program on Reading Readiness and Achievement of Disadvantaged First Grade Negro Children. Unpublished doctoral dissertation. University of Florida, 1970.

Gordon, I. J. Early Child Stimulation Through Parent Education. Final Report, June 30, 1969, Institute for the Development of Human Resources, University of Florida, Project No. PHS-R-306, PHS-R-306(01), Dept. of Health, Education and Welfare.

_____. *Parent Involvement in Compensatory Education.* Champaign-Urbana, I..: University of Illinois Press, 1970.

Gray, S. W., and Klaus, R. A. An Experimental Preschool Program for Culturally Deprived Children. *Child Development,* 1965, *36,* 887-898.

MacLaren, F. W. The Effect of a Parent Information Program upon Reading Achievement in First Grade. Dissertation, University of Oklahoma. Ann Arbor, Mich.: University Microfilms, 1965. No. 65-12,958.

McConnell, F., Horton, J. K., and Smith, B. R. Language Development and Cultural Disadvantagement. *Exceptional Children,* 1969, *35,* 597-606.

McManus, A. The Denver Prereading Project Conducted by WENH-TV. *The Reading Teacher,* 1964, *18,* 22-26.

Miller, W. H. Relationship Between Mother's Style of Communication and Her Control System to the Child's Reading Readiness and Subsequent Reading Achievement in First Grade. Dissertation, University of Arizona. Ann Arbor, Mich.: University Microfilms, 1967. No. 67-12,179.

_____. Home Prereading Experiences and First-Grade Reading Achievement. *The Reading Teacher,* 1969, *22,* 641-645.

Milner, E. A Study of the Relationship Between Reading Readiness in Grade One School Children and Patterns of Parent-Child Interaction. *Child Development,* 1951, *22,* 95-112.

Ryan, E. M. A Comparative Study of the Reading Achievement of Second Grade Pupils in Programs Characterized by a Contrasting Degree of Parent Participation. Dissertation, Indiana University. Ann Arbor, Mich.: University Microfilms, 1964. No. 65-2392.

Stewart, R. S. Personality Maladjustment and Reading Achievement. *American Journal of Orthopsychiatry,* 1950, *20,* 410-417.

Weikart, D. P. A Home-Teaching Program. *Journal of Special Education,* 1967, *1,* 183.

Willmon, B. J. The Influence of Parent Participation and Involvement on the Achievement of Pupils Attending the Leon County Head Start Program as Measured by a Reading Readiness Test. Dissertation, Florida State University. Ann Arbor, Mich.: University Microfilms, 1967. No. 67-14464.

Winterbottom, M. The Relation of Need for Achievement in Learning Experiences in Independence and Mastery. In J. Atkins, ed., *Motives in Fantasy, Action and Society.* Princeton, New Jersey: Van Nostrand, 1958.

ADDITIONAL RESOURCES

Gordon, Ira J. College of Education, University of Florida, Gainesville, Florida.

The International Reading Association Committee on Parents and Reading, 6 Tyre Avenue, Newark, Delaware 19711.

PART VI

SPECIAL INTEREST GROUPS

61

EDUCATION FOR CHILDREN OF MIGRANT FARMWORKERS

by Gloria Mattera
Director, Geneseo Migrant Center
Professor of Education
State University College of Arts and Science
Geneseo, New York

While their parents migrate to harvest the crops of a nation that prides itself on the quality of its educational system, the children of migrant farmworkers reap a harvest of so substandard an education that approximately 90 percent of them do not finish high school (*On The Season*, n.d.). Even though economic factors play an important role in this high dropout rate, a basic problem is that the migrant child, as he travels from school to school and state to state, does not enjoy the continuity of learning so essential to intellectual development and scholastic success.

Before Federal funding, local school interest in the migrant child was nil—he was always the one "from someplace else." While some states—notably, Colorado since 1953 and New York since 1956—have made attempts to utilize their own funds to improve the situation, it was not until the 1966 Migrant Amendment to the Title I Elementary and Secondary Education Act (ESEA) that national concern brought special programming for this "national" child. At last, efforts were commencing that would, hopefully, enable the migrant child to move from learning center to learning center in his "open" classroom, the nation, so that educational continuity could be realized.

GEOGRAPHIC SCOPE

The Title I ESEA Migrant Amendment allocates funds directly to 49 states (all except Hawaii). Many stateside programs, in an effort to provide follow-up, send the children's transfer records to such "home bases" as Canada, Puerto Rico, and Mexico. Thus, the geographic scope of the program encompasses much more than the 49 states.

FUNDING SOURCES

In addition to approximately $92 million from the Title I ESEA Migrant Amendment, funds for migrant children are also provided by:

The Economic Opportunity Act as amended; section 222. This $2.5 million, administered by the Indian and Migrant Programs Division (IMPD) of the Office of Child Development, supports 18 child-care and Headstart programs (*Impact of Federal Programs . . .*, 1973).

The Economic Opportunity Act as amended; Title III B. Administered by the Department of Labor, $4.2

million is for High School Equivalency and College Assistance Programs and $1.5 million for day care (*Impact of Federal Programs . . .*, 1973).

CULTURAL GROUPS SERVED

While approximately 90 percent (*Children at the Crossroad*, 1970) of the workers are Spanish-speaking, other cultural groups are represented in the migrant stream. Thus, a classroom in Edinburg, Texas may have Mexican-American children only, whereas a classroom in Geneseo, New York may have as many as five cultures represented—Algonquin Indian, Black, Caucasian, Mexican-American, and Puerto Rican!

These three aspects of program scope—geographic, funding sources, and cultural groups served—help illustrate the uniqueness of the migrant program.

REVIEW OF RECENT LITERATURE AND DEVELOPMENTS

Many publications are available that describe particular state programs. Three national reports, however, make recommendations designed to improve the migrant program in general. Among these recommendations are:

"That the chief State school officers encourage and permit intrastate, interstate and regional cooperation and communication by the state migrant coordinators and local school officials to develop compacts and programs that will provide educational continuity for migrant children (*America's Educationally Neglected...*, 1973, p. 34)."

That HEW develop an effective monitoring and evaluation system (*Impact of Federal Programs...*, 1973).

That the USOE give a high priority to staff development and take the initiative in getting the states to set a like priority (*A Policy Statement...*, 1973).

While these recommendations are in various stages of implementation, new programs continue to develop as needs are identified. Currently, there is an emerging nationwide thrust to reach the very young migrant child who is not in a school setting, and also the older student who may have to or has dropped out.

SPECIFIC PROGRAMS

The variety in number and types of migrant programs precludes adequate examination of them all. Instead, general program types will be presented and, where desirable, specific examples cited. Unless indicated otherwise, the programs described are funded by the Title I ESEA Migrant Amendment.

Generally, these programs focus on specific age groups: day-care/preschool, elementary, older students, parents, staff. Resources for these groups, such as the Migrant Student Record Transfer System, mobile units, migrant centers, etc., will be described separately.

Day Care/Preschool Programs

While legislation has sorely neglected migrant children during the critical 0-3 years, imaginative multiply-funded models in some states have been successful in reaching some children in this age group.

California's Pilot Program in Group Infant Care combines funds from the Social Security Act, Title IV-A, Human Resources and the ESEA Migrant Amendment, to provide Child Development Centers in four migrant camps. Parents leave their children there the entire working day, assured of full and competent attention to their physical, social, emotional, and educational needs.

Oregon's Migrant and Indian Coalition for Coordinated Child Care has a corporation which secures funds from such sources as H.E.W.'s Indian and Migrant Programs Division (IMPD), ESEA Migrant Amendment, and Title IV-A. It provides resources, training, planning, and co-ordination for local communities desiring quality day care.

New York's Migrant Day Care Interagency Committee enables the Department of Agriculture and Markets, which has the legislative mandate for migrant day care centers, to coordinate with other funding sources to meet the needs of young migrant children throughout their stay in New York. Represented on the Committee are Social Services, Migrant Health, Bureau of Migrant Education, and IMPD.

Thus, at least some migrant children 0-3 receive appropriate services, but in too few states. Until this critical need is met, babies will be taken to the fields or be cared for by older siblings while their parents work.

In states that now mandate educational services for children ages 3-5, the Migrant Amendment has had some success in reaching down at least to 3-year-old migrant children. However, since the Migrant Amendment does not count for funding purposes children under 5, these states are forced to utilize funds generated by the children who are counted; namely those 5-17. The inevitable result is that the 0-5 years are an educational wasteland for migrant children.

Elementary Programs

While Migrant Amendment funds may be used for children aged 3 to 21, the lion's share has gone to school-age children 5 to 17 for the reason stated above. The ultimate goal—that of a child's being able to move from school to school and state without serious interruption of educational services—has been a most difficult one to reach because the Migrant Program is not controlled nationally (as is Headstart). Educational continuity has been left to the individual states, each with its own laws and regulations regarding curriculum, credits, etc.

Nevertheless, migrant educators have taken some significant steps—many of them focused on individualization of instruction—toward bridging this continuity gap. Some are:

Experience-Based Approach. One of the most immediate problems confronting migrant educators is the lack of relevant commercial instructional materials. It has been partially solved by utilizing the child's experiences to serve as a basis for reading, writing, and other academic skills.

A strong component, initiated in Florida's Markham School in Broward County, and since spread among programs nationwide, has been "peer-produced" books, written and illustrated by the children (and often taped for nonreaders to enjoy). The children's feelings of accomplishment and success thus experienced have often been an important first in the school setting.

Criterion-Referenced Materials. The long overdue emergence of commercial criterion-referenced materials may be the key to sequential learning for migrant children. Reading and math programs are in use in several state migrant programs.

Michigan Criterion Mathematics Assessment and the Texas Reading Assessment programs, developed for migrant children, are being considered for national implementation by the state migrant coordinators.

Tutorial Program. A third effective way of reaching individual migrant children has been through tutorial programs. These range from peer-tutoring in Arizona and Texas to New Mexico's "Home Livelihood Program" in which teachers work with families at home. The Florida and New York programs pay trained tutors to work with migrant children in the schools.

Older Students

The economic necessity of having young people help support the family has been a major cause of the 90 percent dropout rate. Whereas in previous years many of these children were never motivated in school, those now emerging from the migrant program are making more visible the need for creative and work-experience programming for older youth. Among the current approaches are:

Career Development. New Jersey was the first state to make extensive use of mobile vocational education units. North Carolina provides counseling and prevocational training for young male adults, and Missouri has two exemplary high school programs focused on preparation for the world of work.

Initiated in Broward County, Florida's "Learn and Earn" is now a state-mandated program. Occupational exploration and training on special vocational mobile units, as well as experiences in local businesses, combine to keep students in school.

In-Camp and Weekend Programs. One manner of serving young people who must work has been to take programs to the migrant camps. Examples may be found in Virginia, New York, North Carolina, Florida, and Idaho.

Weekend programs provide an alternative to camp life by involving workers in community activities and field trips to areas of interest, and making available community resources. A university in New York opens its recreational (pool, bicycles, tennis and squash courts, TV, pool tables, etc.) and cafeteria facilities for anywhere from 50 to 150 migrants every Sunday.

High School Equivalency. This program, funded by OEO, is a type of "external degree" program. It places migrant dropouts on college campuses, provides a weekly stipend, and works individually with them until they secure a high school diploma.

Opportunities for older youth to go to school and also earn wages must have high priority. The expenditure of $92 million for elementary students will be hard to justify if 90 percent of them continue to drop out of school as soon as they are old enough the help support the family.

Parents

A fact recognized by migrant educators is the need for parental involvement in programs and programs for the parents themselves. Accordingly, some common approaches have been: (1) having parents serve on advisory committees that help plan, implement and evaluate programs, as in California and North Dakota; (2) training parents and hiring them as aides, as in Washington; and (3) providing special programs on nonworkdays or during evenings that meet their literacy, child-rearing, or other needs, as in New York and Arizona.

Staff Development

Materials and methods have little effect if the staff has no empathy with the children. In an effort to overcome this weakness, several approaches to staff development are being implemented.

Generally national, regional, statewide, and local conferences are held annually. Agendas focus on the needs of migrant children and suggested methods and materials.

University-based programs and courses vary, from Oregon's unique Master's Degree program, in which participants live for seven weeks in a migrant camp, to Washington's student teaching undergraduate program. Individual university courses are available, such as those offered in California, New York, and Arizona, in which participants implement their course work suggestions in methodology and materials with migrant children.

In some cases paraprofessionals receive special training, as in the Associate Arts Degree for Paraprofessionals sponsored by the Center for the Study of Indian and Migrant Education at Toppenish, Washington.

California's Mini-Corps prepares college students of Mexican descent to work in summer migrant programs as teacher assistants. A two-week training program precedes work with the children and a week of evaluation follows it.

MIGRANT STUDENT RECORD TRANSFER SYSTEM

The above programs related to age groups are supported by a variety of resources. As has been stated, the Title I ESEA Migrant Amendment allocates monies directly to the states, leaving no discretionary funds at the national level. Therefore, any national thrust must be agreed upon by all the states. Such was the case with the Migrant Student Record Transfer System. The states agreed, in 1969, to set aside funds for the development and implementation of the MSRTS.

Presently, this computerized system operates in 48 states through 140 terminals tied to the central data bank in Little Rock, Arkansas. Education, health and family background information for each child, recorded on a newly revised form, is transmitted quickly upon request to schools receiving the migrant children so that continuity of services may be maintained.

It is too early to adequately assess the effectiveness of the system in improving the education of migrant children. Its potential, however, to achieve this goal as well as that of transmitting information about young children in Child Development Centers and adults in vocational programs, certainly warrants a continuing period of experimentation.

NATIONAL OFFICES

The Migrant Programs Branch of the U.S. Office of Education does not administer the $92 million in Migrant Amendment funds. It has a small staff that provides such leadership as establishing national goals and making recommendations to the state migrant coordinators for program improvement. (See Appendix A for List of National Goals.)

Two national offices that do administer funds (a total of approximately $8.2 million) are in a better position to control and coordinate programs. These are the Indian and Migrant Programs Branch of the Office of Child Development, and the Department of Labor, which now has the Office of Economic Opportunity (OEO) High School Equivalency, College Assistance, and Day Care Programs. Their meager funds, however, preclude providing the needed impact of services.

MIGRANT CENTERS

The need for information, materials, and methodology specifically for teachers of migrant children has led several states to establish "Migrant Centers." While these centers presently form a loose network of services nationwide, the Migrant Programs Branch plans to link them, to avoid duplication of materials production and research, and to better share products of their individual expertise. (See Appendix B for a list of the Centers.)

There are two national clearinghouses for information on migrants. ERIC/CRESS (Clearinghouse for Rural Education and Small Schools), funded by N.I.E., is located on the New Mexico State University campus as Las Cruces. The Juarez-Lincoln Center, funded by OEO through the Colorado Migrant Council and Antioch College, is in Austin, Texas.

RECRUITMENT AND SOCIAL EDUCATOR PROGRAMS

Recruitment of children by the school districts has been a major problem. Accordingly, several states, led by New Jersey, have initiated recruitment programs wherein a state team recruits for the schools. A corollary to recruitment is the provision of needy services to migrant families. New Jersey's recruitment team works with settled-out families during the winter months.

Florida renders a similar service through its unique Social Educator program, wherein 34 social educators assist families, make out transfer record forms, recruit children, etc. 70 percent of the social educator's time is spent with the preschool mobile units program and 30 percent with the Learn and Earn program.

BILINGUAL/BICULTURAL PROGRAMS

The many cultures represented in the migrant stream necessitate meeting language and cultural needs. Persuading states to allow children to speak and learn in their own language has been no easy task. While ESL (English as a Second Language) is the initial step taken in many programs, the growing awareness of the strengths of the cultures is resulting in some implementation of bilingual/bicultural programs. For example, New Jersey's Pilot V program produces matching Spanish and English TV programs especially for migrant children.

The hiring of bilingual teachers and staff, as well as the publications of bilingual notices, pamphlets, etc., have encouraged greater involvement of families in school programs. A Palm Beach County school utilizes FM radios in the homes of Spanish-speaking families to communicate about school programs, as well as programs of interest to the parents themselves.

MOBILE UNITS

Mobile units have filled several needs. Most, like Florida's Learn and Earn and preschool units, provide additional appropriately equipped space for school, camps, and day care centers. Oregon's Migralab, in addition, provides inservice for teachers in the schools it serves. Michigan's two mobile units take G.E.D. and reading and writing to the camps, while Colorado's diagnostic unit provides hearing aids, glasses, etc., and other health and educational services. The Texas Migrant Council, funded by IMPD, provides continuous day care services to migrant crews by traveling with them while they are "on the season."

INTERSTATE/INTERAGENCY COOPERATION

Interstate cooperation is critical to fulfillment of migrant program goals. Despite the problems of overcoming state regulations, there has been success in co-sponsoring conferences and workshops, and sharing information, staff, and materials. Texas, for example, sends personnel to 18 states that receive its children, to provide the assistance of an educator familiar with the Texas program.

IMPD is currently implementing an Eastern Stream Project which is attempting to provide continuity of child development services for children in the eastern seaboard, Florida to New York.

Interagency involvement improves not only the quality of a program, but also community attitude towards migrants. Thus, services from a variety of agencies are utilized by resourceful programs such as New Mexico's, which incorporates services from as many as 22 agencies, including even the Karate Club!

CURRENT CONTROVERSIES

No major disagreement exists among migrant educators themselves. Nor would it be correct to say that there is controversy between the educators and legislators. Since, however, legislation was passed before the migrant education problem had been adequately explored, progress has been hampered by the inevitable time lag before legislation can catch up with the migrant programs' emerging needs. For example:

Whereas experience has shown that migrant children continue to need special services after their families "settle out" of the migrant stream, the original 1966 ESEA Migrant Amendment permitted the establishment of programs for "true" migrant children, allowing settled-out children in only to fill empty slots. No programs could be initiated for settled-out children.

Legislative Change: In 1974 Migrant Amendment funds were increased and the migrant child definition expanded to include settled-out children (and children of fishermen), thus more adequately compensating for the deprivations of migrancy.

Whereas it is self-evident that the amount of money allocated to each state should depend upon the number of migrant children, the original Migrant Amendment based the allocation on a formula depending upon the number of adult migrant workers.

Legislative Change: The basis for allocation of migrant amendment funds was changed in 1974 to the number of migrant children as determined by the Migrant Student Record Transfer System.

Whereas interstate programs like Head Start have shown effectiveness of control and coordination of funds and programs by a national office, the Title I Migrant Amendment—which has the greatest amount of funds for migrant children and can therefore make the greatest impact—is powerless, because the states receive the money directly.

Needed Legislative Change: An amount of money (approximately one percent of the Migrant Amendment funds) should be specified by a statute and set aside specifically for the Migrant Program at the Federal level to institute, spur, or promote activities that would be of benefit to migrant children nationwide.

Whereas it is evident that the entire migrant family—from baby to adult—is in need of coordinated and comprehensive services, the present laws produce devastating gaps (such as in the area of day care) or overlaps (common in most migrant service areas), and are not consistent as to who may be served. (For example, some laws define "migrant" strictly, whereas others include "seasonal" workers.)

Needed Legislative Change: Provide coordination at the national level and institute one definition of the population to be served.

Whereas young migrant children are in need of educational services, the present Migrant Amendment counts them for program purposes only, thus effectively depriving them of participation, since they do not generate funds.

Needed Legislative Change: The Migrant Amendment should be changed to include, as eligible for generating monies, children aged 0-17 instead of the current ages 5 to 17.

Whereas millions of dollars are being spent to educate migrant children, a recent study revealed that approximately 90 percent of them still drop out of school.

Needed Legislative Change: Legislation is needed in the areas of labor, health and related services that guarantee year-round employment at a wage that could provide healthful working and living conditions, and also free migrant children from having to help support their families. Until this occurs, migrant programs must focus on creative programming that will keep the youngsters in school and also attract the dropouts.

The Senate Subcommittee on Migratory Labor, which was a boon and a blessing to migrant children, has been eliminated. Current efforts by educators and concerned agencies to initiate legislative changes may partially compensate for this loss. Without an effective national voice, however, migrants will, as in the past, be overlooked because they are the ones "from someplace else."

CONCLUSION

While Federal funds have moved mountains for them, migrant children will continue to be educationally underprivileged until, as Robert Coles (1975) sensibly suggests, they cease to be migrants. This will not occur, however, unless harvests are totally mechanized or picked by local help—a rare prospect indeed.

In the meantime, educators must continue to compensate as much as possible for the regrettable lack of continuity in migrant education. And they can rejoice in the knowledge that not only migrant children, but eventually all children, will reap the harvest of their ingenuity and devotion.

REFERENCES

Arizona State Department of Education. *Arizona Evaluation for Migrant Children Educational Programs, Fiscal Year 1971.*
Phoenix: State Department of Education, 1971.

Arkansas State Department of Education. *Love and Understanding of the Migrant Child.* Jonesboro: State Department of Education, 1969.

_____. *Program for Effective Learning.* Little Rock: State Department of Education, 1969.

Association for Childhood Education International. *Migrant Children: Their Education.* Washington: A.C.E.I., 1971.

Brunstein, J. J. *The Somerton Story-Part II.* Phoenix: Arizona Department of Education, 1970.

California State Department of Education. *Mini-Corpsmen.* Sacramento: State Department of Education, 1968.

_____. *California Plan for the Education of Migrant Children.* Sacramento: Santa Clara County Superintendent of Schools, 1970.

Center for the Study of Migrant and Indian Education. *An Assessment of Needs Related to the Education of Indian Children in the State of Washington.* Toppenish: Central Washington State College, 1971.

_____. *An Overview of the History and Purpose of an Educational Service Center for Teachers of Migrant and Indian Children in the State of Washington.* Toppinish: Center for the Study of Migrant and Indian Education, n.d.

Coles, R. *Uprooted Children.* New York: Harper & Row, 1970.

Colorado Department of Education. *Colorado Migrant Education Program: Summary and Evaluation Report, September 1, 1970-August 31, 1971.* Denver: Colorado Department of Education, 1972.

Comptroller General of the United States. *Report to the Congress—Impact of Federal Programs to Improve the Living Conditions of Migrant and Other Seasonal Farmworkers.* Washington: U.S. General Accounting Office, 1973.

End, W. J. *FM Radio for Migrant Children in Palm Beach County, Florida.* Belle Glade: School Board of Palm Beach County, 1966.

ERIC/CRESS. *Migrant Education, A Selected Bibliography, Supplement 1.* Las Cruces: ERIC/CRESS, 1970.

_____. *Migrant Education, A Selected Bibliography, Supplement 2.* Las Cruces: ERIC/CRESS, 1971.

_____. *Migrant Education, A Selected Bibliography, Supplement 3.* Las Cruces: ERIC/CRESS, 1973.

Florida Department of Education. *The Ones from Someplace Else.* Tallahassee: Department of Education, n.d.

_____. *The Florida Migratory Child Compensatory Program ... Facts and Figures.* Tallahassee: Department of Education, n.d.

_____. *The Florida Migratory Child Compensatory Program— Annual Evaluation Report, Fiscal Year 1971-72.* Tallahassee: Department of Education, 1972.

Florida Migratory Child Compensatory Program. *Aqua Arriba— Up the Stream.* Tallahassee: Florida Department of Education, 1973.

Guernsey, T. *Rise and Shine.* Portland: Portland Oregonian, n.d.

Idaho State Department of Education. *State Annual Evaluation Report, Fiscal Year 1969.* Boise: State Department of Education, 1969.

Juarez-Lincoln Center. *Migrant Programs in Florida.* Austin: Juarez-Lincoln Center, 1973.

_____. *Migrant Programs in Texas.* Austin: Juarez-Lincoln Center, 1973.

Markham Elementary School. *The Markham Story.* Pompano Beach: Markham Elementary School, n.d.

Mattera, Gloria, and Steel, Eric M. *Exemplary Programs for Migrant Children.* Las Cruces: ERIC/CRESS, 1974.

Migrant and Indian Coalition for Coordinated Child Care, Inc. *MIC Newsletter.* Hood River, Oregon: MIC, 1973.

Minkler, E. D. *To Teach a Migrant Child.* Salem: Oregon Board of Education, 1969.

Missouri State Department of Education. *Migrant Education in Missouri.* Jefferson City: Missouri State Department of Education, 1972.

National Advisory Council on the Education of Disadvantaged Children. *Annual Report to the President and the Congress: America's Educationally Neglected.* Washington: N.A.C.E.D.C., 1973.

National Committee on the Education of Migrant Children. *Wednesday's Children.* New York: N.C.E.M.C., 1971.

_____. *A Policy Statement on Staff Development.* New York: N.C.E.M.C., 1973.

Nebraska State Department of Education. *Orphans of Wealth.* Lincoln: Nebraska State Department of Education, 1971.

New Mexico Department of Education. *Project Information, Title I ESEA, Albuquerque Public Schools.* Santa Fe: Department of Education, 1969.

New York State Bureau of Migrant Education. *An Aid to Comprehensive Planning for Migrant Programs.* Geneseo, N.Y.: N.Y.S. Migrant Center, 1972.

New York State Education Department. *Measuring the Difference: Report of the Fiscal 1972 Program for the Education of Children of Migratory Agricultural Workers.* Albany, N.Y.: State Education Department, 1972.

North Carolina Department of Public Instruction. *Serving Migrant Families.* Raleigh: Department of Public Instruction, 1970.

_____. *Migrant Education Administrative Handbook.* Raleigh: Department of Public Instruction, 1971.

_____. *1973 Migrant Education State Evaluation Report.* Raleigh: Department of Public Instruction, 1973.

_____. *On the Season.* Raleigh: Department of Public Instruction, n.d.

North Dakota Department of Public Instruction. *Summer Educational Program for the Children of Migrant Agricultural Workers.* Bismarck: Department of Public Instruction, 1973.

Office of Economic Opportunity. *HEP—One Way Up for Migrants.* Washington: Office of Economic Opportunity, n.d.

Pennsylvania State Department of Education. *The Opened Door— An Experiment in Education for Migrant Children.* Dallas, Pa.: State Department of Education, 1970.

Smith, V. *Texas Migrant Council.* Washington: Office of Child Development, 1973.

Southwest Educational Development Laboratory. *Educational Services for Migrants.* Austin: Southwest Educational Development Lab., n.d.

Stockburger, C. *Statement of Child Labor.* New York: National Committee on the Education of Migrant Children, 1973.

Sutton, E. *Knowing and Teaching the Migrant Child.* Washington: National Education Association, 1960.

_____. *Working More Effectively with Migrant Children in Our Schools.* Geneseo, N.Y.: New York State Migrant Center, 1969.

Texas Education Agency. *A Guide for Programs for the Education of Migrant Children.* Austin: Texas Education Agency, 1968.

_____. *Texas Child Migrant Program—Migrant and Preschool Programs.* Austin: Texas Education Agency, 1972.

Texas Migrant Educational Development Center. *Handbook for a Parent-School-Community Involvement Program.* Austin: Southwest Educational Development Corporation, 1969.

U.S. Department of Health, Education, and Welfare. *Children at the Crossroad.* Washington, D.C.: U.S. Government Printing Office, 1970.

_____. *Questions and Answers—Migrant Children Under ESEA Title I.* Washington: Department of Health, Education, and Welfare, 1971.

U.S. Government Printing Office. *Computer Harvests Migrant Records.* Washington: U.S. Government Printing Office, 1971.

U.S. Office of Education. *Directory of Consultants on Migrant Education.* Washington: U.S. Office of Education, 1965.

Virginia Beach City Public Schools. *A Curriculum Guide for Migrant Education.* Virginia Beach: Virginia Beach City Public Schools, 1970.

Wyoming State Department of Education. *A Handbook for Teachers of Migrant Children in Wyoming.* Laramie: State Department of Education, 1968.

ADDITIONAL RESOURCES

Data Bank, Migrant Student Record Transfer System, Arch Ford Education Building, Little Rock, Arkansas 72201

ERIC Clearinghouse on Rural Education and Small Schools, Box 3AP, New Mexico State University, Las Cruces, New Mexico 88003

Indian and Migrant Programs Division, Office of Child Development, P.O. Box 1182, Washington, D.C. 20013

Juarez-Lincoln Center, National Migrant Information Clearinghouse, 3001 South Congress Avenue, Austin, Texas 78704

Migrant Centers (Appendix B)

Migrant Programs Branch, U.S. Office of Education, 7th and D Streets, S.W., Washington, D.C. 20202

National Association Migrant Education (NAME), Elsberry Building, 224 South Main Street, Belle Glade, Florida 33430

National Committee on the Education of Migrant Children, 145 East 32nd Street, New York, New York 10016

State Directors of Migrant Education (for listing, contact Migrant Programs Branch, USOE)

Major Interest Groups

American Friends Service Committee, 160 North 15th Street, Philadelphia, Pennsylvania 19102

East Coast Migrant Project, 1325 Massachusetts Avenue, N.W., Washington, D.C. 20005

Migrant Legal Action Program, 1820 Massachusetts Avenue, N.W., Washington, D.C. 20036

National Association Migrant Education (NAME), Elsberry Building, 224 South Main Street, Belle Glade, Florida 33430

National Committee on the Education of Migrant Children, 145 East 32nd Street, New York, New York 10016

National Sharecropper Fund, Inc., 1346 Connecticut Avenue, N.W., Washington, D.C. 20036

Rural Education Association, 515 Education Center, U.N.I., Cedar Falls, Iowa 50613

APPENDIX A
NATIONAL GOALS OF MIGRANT EDUCATION

Instructional Services

Provide the opportunity for each migrant child to improve communications skills necessary for varying situations.

Provide the migrant with preschool and kindergarten experiences, geared to his psychological and physiological development, that will prepare him to function successfully.

Provide specially designed programs in the academic disciplines (Language Arts, Math, Social Studies, and other academic endeavors) that will increase the migrant child's capabilities to function at a level concomitant with his potential.

Provide specially designed activities which will increase the migrant child's social growth, positive self-concept, and group interaction skills.

Provide programs that will improve the academic skill, prevocational orientation, and vocational skill training for older migrant children.

Implement programs, utilizing every available Federal, state, and local resource through coordinated funding, in order to improve mutual understanding and appreciation of cultural differences among children.

Supportive Services

Develop in each program a component of intrastate and interstate communications for exchange of student records, methods, concepts, and materials to assure that sequence and continuity will be an inherent part of the migrant child's total educational program.

Develop communications involving the school, the community and its agencies, and the target group to insure coordination of all available resources for the benefit of migrant children.

Provide for the migrant child's physical and mental well-being by including dental, medical, nutritional, and psychological services.

Provide a program of home-school coordination which establishes relationships between the project staff and the clientele served, in order to improve the effectiveness of migrant programs and the process of parental reinforcement of student effort.

Increase staff awareness of their personal biases and possible prejudices, and upgrade their skills for teaching migrant children by conducting inservice and preservice workshops.

APPENDIX B
MIGRANT CENTERS

Arizona
Arizona Migrant Child Education
    Laboratory (AMCEL)
College of Education, Arizona State
    University
Tempe, Arizona 85281

Provides inservice for teachers and aides, consultant services, comparative oral language study, Oral Language Assessment Inventory; disseminates informational packet of migrant publications; conducts Summer Institute for Teachers of Migrant Children.

Florida
Broward County Migrant Education Center
650 North Andrews Avenue
Fort Lauderdale, Florida 33311

Conducts programs for children and adults, and inservice for administrators, aides, teachers, staff; provides consultant services, media utilization, materials dissemination; conducts mini-projects and Earn and Learn and Tutorial Programs.

Idaho
Migrant Education Resource Center
312-3rd Street South
Nampa, Idaho 83651

Conducts inservice for teachers and aides; serves as liaison between parents and schools; disseminates information; makes available multimedia materials; operates State Migrant Student Transfer Record System; produces teaching materials.

Michigan
Migrant Education Center
Central Michigan University
Mt. Pleasant, Michigan 48858

Conducts studies, preservice (Major in Elementary Education for Teaching Spanish-Speaking Bilingual Children) and inservice for teachers and aides; produces and disseminates special materials; develops curriculum and evaluates state migrant programs.

North
Carolina
Migrant Education Center
P.O. Box 948
Grifton, North Carolina 28530

Operates migrant media center, State Migrant Student Transfer Record System, two automotive tune-up units; provides consultant services and training sessions for LEAs; produces and disseminates handbooks and other publications.

New York
New York State Migrant Center
State University College
Geneseo, New York 14454

Conducts studies, inservice for teachers and aides, programs for children and adults; serves as dissemination and information center on migrant matters, and instructional materials resource center; produces handbooks and other publications; provides consultants.

Oregon
Migrant Education Service Center
3000 Market St. S.W., Suite 316
Salem, Oregon 97304

Provides teaching resources, consultants; develops individual skill analysis programs; designs and conducts state academic and acculturation inservice; conducts statewide monitoring and evaluation; coordinates statewide migrant preschool program and two trailers.

Texas
Migrant Educational Development Center
800 Brazos Street
Austin, Texas 78701

Produces bilingual-bicultural instructional materials; develops curriculum; provides parental involvement; conducts programs for preschool and high school youths; produces and disseminates publications; conducts studies.

Washington   Center for the Study of Migrant and
              Indian Education
            P.O. Box 329
            Toppenish, Washington 98948

            Provides inservice workshops for professionals, preprofessionals and paraprofessionals; develops curriculum programs and instructional materials; prepares and disseminates publications, information and evaluations.

62

SUMMER COMPENSATORY EDUCATION

by Bruce G. Rogers

by Bruce G. Rogers
Assistant Professor
Education Measurement and Statistics
University of Maryland
College Park, Maryland

Summer compensatory education refers to those educational programs conducted during the summer months with the expressed purpose of providing remedial instruction to students identified as being below grade level. While reading and mathematics are the most common areas of emphasis, almost every school subject has been represented to some extent. Because of the high expense of the programs, most have been funded by the Federal government (about 16,000 districts received Title I ESEA funds last year, while additional districts were funded from other legislative acts, e.g., migrant student programs), and for all these programs an evaluation report was required. This article will address itself to the effectiveness of summer compensatory education programs by analyzing the many documents available to the public.

REVIEW OF THE LITERATURE

Summer school is basically a twentieth-century development, begun to accommodate pupils with diverse backgrounds and needs. Originally it provided opportunities for repeating previously failed subjects, remediation in basic skills, recreation, accelerating progress, etc., but not until mid-century did a widespread interest in compensatory education develop. Since many disadvantaged pupils could not afford to attend a tuition-supported facility, some cities allocated tax funds in order to eliminate tuition charges. When Chicago adopted this policy in 1954,

an increase in attendance was noted (Gordon and Doxey, 1966, p. 93). Because of the individualization necessary, almost all of the recent compensatory programs owe their existence to Federal funding, primarily through the Summer Compensatory Education Program component of Title I of the Elementary and Secondary Education Act of 1965. This act had as its goal "to provide financial assistance . . . to local educational agencies serving areas with concentrations of children from low-income families to expand and improve their educational programs . . . (to meet) the special educational needs of educationally deprived children (USOE, 1969, pp. 1, 2)."

To ensure the accountability of those who received funds, an evaluation program was required to be submitted before a project could be approved, and a report had to be filed annually with the USOE. However, since the annual reports have not been released to the U.S. Superintendent of Documents for reprinting, they are unavailable to the general public through the repositories of documents in each state. A number of reports have been submitted by their authors to the ERIC system and to research journals, and it is from these public sources that the references in this article will be drawn.

It is tempting to write a prescriptive article describing how a compensatory summer educational program should be operated, and no doubt readers would anticipate the result to be of great value. But such a prescription should be based upon research findings, and at present an adequate base does not exist. On the other hand, the experience of those who have conducted well-planned evaluations should not be disregarded by those who will be contemplating future projects. Accordingly, this article will attempt to summarize the state of the art in research and illustrate by reference to typical programs.

Austin, Rogers, and Walbesser (1972) reviewed the existing literature on the effectiveness of summer compensatory education, and concluded that there was evidence of modest cognitive achievement gains from programs emphasizing elementary mathematics, reading, and language communication. Student attitudes were also found to improve during the summer, but no data were found to demonstrate that either cognitive or attitudinal change persisted over time. They recommended that future programs state their objectives in behavioral terms, and establish an evaluation program around those objectives.

EXPECTED SUMMER GAINS WITHOUT INSTRUCTION

In order to assess the effectiveness of summer programs, it would be useful to compare the achievement, at the beginning and end of summer, of pupils who receive no intervening instruction. Unfortunately, however, there have been few such studies, and the results are somewhat less than unequivocal.

A common method of comparing achievement between pupils is the use of grade equivalents, where, for example, the value 4.7 represents the average (or median) performance of pupils tested in the seventh month of the fourth grade. For this method, it is usually assumed that equal growth occurs during each of the nine school months and that the equivalent of one more month of growth occurs during the summer vacation (Ahmann and Glock, 1971, p. 266). The Iowa Tests of Basic Skills, for example, are normed on this assumption (Beggs and Hieronymus, 1968, p. 91).

Some writers assume that no growth, on the average, occurs over the summer months, while others assume that there is an average decline in performance. The difficulty of validating these claims is illustrated by the conflicting research reports. Soar and Soar (1969) found achievement gains of three to five months between the fifth and sixth grades. Practical limitations required that the tests be given about a month before the ending of school and about a month after its opening. How much of the achievement occurred during school time and how much occurred during the summer months? While this question could not be answered with absolute assurance, Soar and Soar did feel confident in interpreting their data as showing that definite summer achievement gains are shown by many pupils.

Fitzsimmons (1969) found no differences in the reading and language skills of intermediate grade pupils between July and September. But Mosteller and Moynihan (1972) refer to "evidence suggesting—but only suggesting—that . . . learning during the summer . . . almost ceases for the lower-class child, while it continues apace for his middle-class schoolmates (p. 48)."

Certainly further research is needed to establish expected summer gains or losses under various conditions and with various populations, if project directors are to base their curricula on the needs of the recipients.

COMPARISONS OF SUMMER GROWTH WITH AND WITHOUT INSTRUCTION

In an experimental study to ascertain whether instruction during the summer enhances achievement, Weinberg (1971) requested teachers to select 96 white boys from fourth, fifth, and sixth grades on the basis of having serious reading disabilities. Three groups were formed, with pupils matched on age, grade, IQ, reading level, and socio-economic background, and then assigned to a reading program, a recreation program, and an untreated control group. Each reading class consisted of eight students, who met for one hour a day for six weeks. The teachers were allowed to choose any materials they wished. Although pupils in all three groups made gains during the program, there were no significant differences between groups at the end of the program or one year later. Unfortunately, the study did not incorporate a controlled instructional system (since the teachers could choose their own materials), a defect which may have prevented the obtaining of significant results.

The effect of instruction upon disadvantaged tenth- and eleventh-grade pupils (who were participating in an Upward Bound summer session) was investigated by Gwaltney (1971). Sixty pupils were randomly divided between an experimental and a control group, and the former group received a seven-week reading improvement course. Immediate and delayed posttests were administered to both groups, but no significant differences were found on either test. In attempting to explain this result,

the author suggested that perhaps the course content was not sufficiently flexible to meet individual needs, and that some pupils were in the program even though they did not desire to participate.

PREVIOUS REVIEWS OF THE FIELD

The experimental literature is not particularly encouraging with respect to the value of summer compensatory education. While this may be due to methodological defects, that cannot be proven until better studies are designed. On the other hand, the results of these studies are not inconsistent with the judgments of most reviews of compensatory education.

During the spring of 1965, Project Head Start was launched with great expectations. Approximately 70 percent of the pupils participated in summer programs, while the rest participated in full-year programs. Three years later, a follow-up evaluation project was commissioned which compared 2,000 randomly drawn Head Start participants with 2,000 matched controls in grades 1 through 3. According to one of the consultants to the evaluation, no positive effects of the Summer Head Start programs could be detected in any of the three grades (White, 1970, p. 174).

A 1972 report on the effectiveness of compensatory education, published by the Office of Program Planning and Evaluation, of the U.S. Office of Education, likewise concluded that most pupils in full-year Head Start Programs did not show evidence of cognitive gains (Menges et al., 1972, p. 9).

After reanalyzing the famed Coleman Report data, Mosteller and Moynihan (1972) reached the following conclusion with respect to compensatory education in general: "The large Negro-white differences in verbal skills before formal schooling even begins is one of the strongest pieces of evidence for the importance of family and community background characteristics, and the failure of six years of schooling to narrow the gap raises hard questions about the ability of schools alone ever doing so (p. 39)."

The available evidence suggests, unfortunately, that compensatory education, in its usual applications, has had relatively unsuccessful results (Beilin, 1972, p. 165; Jencks et al., 1972, p. 255).

SPECIFIC PROGRAMS

Since the experimental literature appears to be inadequate to determine the worth of summer compensatory education, we must now attempt to draw inferences from one-shot case studies. Methodologically, such designs are in low repute (Campbell and Stanley, 1963, pp. 6-12) when compared with experimental designs, but they can be of value in the generation of testable hypotheses.

Illustrative of large-scale programs are those conducted in New York City (Erickson et al., 1971). In one program the basic skills expected of a child entering kindergarten or first grade were categorized into four areas: learning school routine, reading readiness, social behavior, and physical development. Detailed objectives were then written; for example, "speaks freely to peers," "knows the concept of up and down," "uses feet alternately on stairs," "washes hands after using toilet," etc. Six hundred and twenty children in ten scholls participated, and class size was limited to 20 pupils.

Since it was not feasible to conduct an in-depth evaluation for each child, a random sample of five pupils was chosen from each classroom and the teacher evaluated the progress of those five pupils with respect to the detailed outline of 47 objectives. Over three-fourths of the pupils were reported to have shown some improvement in at least three of the four general areas.

Kindergarten pupils who needed extra help were selected as participants in the Kindergarten Star Program. Each week they and their parents were visited for up to an hour in their own homes by paid nonprofessionals, who helped the parents provide reading readiness training. Although the parents reported favorable attitudes toward the program, no improvement was found in language ability.

In the Homework Helper Program, teenagers were recruited to individually tutor pupils in grades 4 through 9. During the summer months 500 pupils received two hours per day of tutoring from 220 tutors. Taken as a whole, the data suggested that the group met the objective of an average .2 grade-level gain in reading skills.

In interpreting the results of these projects, the reader must be cautious, bearing in mind that no comparison data were gathered to infer if the gains under instruction surpassed gains that would have occurred without instruction. Descriptions of other programs follow in the next section.

CURRENT CONTROVERSIES

Cognitive vs. Noncognitive Goals

What are the appropriate goals for summer compensatory education? While the Federal law states that the purpose of the program is to meet "the special educational needs of educationally deprived children (USOE, 1969, pp. 1, 2)," it is not precise on how those needs are to be met. Many have maintained that cognitive skills should receive first priority, and have constructed programs to include reading, mathematics, general science, etc. Others have contended that the purpose of the legislation is to improve the future economic and social standing of the pupils when they became adults, and that there may be more effective ways to bring about this goal than with a direct concentration on cognitive skills (Cohen, 1970, pp. 217-220). Gadjo and Hayden (1972) found that most teachers in a migrant summer program felt that the affective domain was more important than the cognitive.

For another summer migrant program (Eiszler and Kirk, 1973), both cognitive and affective objectives were developed, with exercises, following the model of the National Assessment of Educational Progress. But the results appeared paradoxical: The bilinguals showed more cognitive improvement than the monolinguals, yet they declined in positive attitude, while the monolinguals showed no affective change. The authors suggested that perhaps cognitive change was not sufficiently rewarded in the classroom, thus leading to disenchantment.

Inasmuch as the relative importance of cognitive vs. non-cognitive goals has been extensively discussed in the literature, most program directors are aware of the significance of both. In the opinion of this reviewer, while the term "compensatory education" logically implies cognitive aims, a positive attitude on the part of the student should usually aid in the attainment of those goals.

Behavioral vs. Nonbehavioral Objectives

When the expectations of a program are not translated into behavioral objectives, the result is likely to be an unstructured program, and when evaluated by objective measures the results are likely to be less than satisfactory. Illustrative of this point was a summer prekindergarten (Robinson, 1970) whose objectives were to facilitate perceptual development and language skills. The selection of instructional activities was left up to each individual teacher. When pre- and posttest data were entered into a contingency table by quartiles, it was seen that about one-third of the pupils had improved their performance, while the majority remained at the same level.

For the next summer program (Robinson, 1971), 16 behavioral objectives were identified, e.g., to identify each letter in his first name, to demonstrate an understanding of digits to five, to state the name and purpose of major body parts, etc. The curriculum was then structured to meet these objectives. At the conclusion of the program, 14 of the objectives had each been achieved by 70 percent or more of the pupils.

Well-structured, teacher-directed language programs, i.e., those in which the teacher's activities are designed to ensure that each child has full opportunity to acquire the desired skills, have been much more successful in improving both IQ and achievement test scores than the loosely structured, child-centered general enrichment approaches. Unfortunately, however, only a small proportion of the programs have had this strong instructional emphasis. (Bereiter, 1972, pp. 5, 6; McLaughlin et al., 1971, pp. 1, 2).

In this reviewer's opinion, it seems clear from the evidence that objectives should be specifically stated and used as the basis for constructing the curriculum for all summer compensatory education projects.

Evaluation Design and Types of Evaluation Data

From a study of the effectiveness of summer compensatory education programs, Austin, Rogers and Walbesser (1972) concluded that "few objective measures have been used to measure the possible range of student accomplishment. Even when objective measures were used, the unavailability of a control group jeopardizes the interpretation of the results (p. 179)." They recommended that "a goal of future evaluations should be to compare, under controlled conditions, summer growth gains and retention for students under compensatory education with those of students not so benefited (p. 179-180)."

Probably not all project directors share this viewpoint. In a four-week program, with the goal of motivating and inspiring high school students to seek a college education, discussions and lectures were conducted on astronomy, social protest, Hispanic history, etc. (Chappel and Baur, 1971). Out of 21 pupils who attended the program after the tenth grade, 12 entered college following high school graduation. The authors said that they decided not to collect objective data, owing to the expense. "Because the program is small, allowing personal knowledge of *all* the students . . . we feel confident when we say the program is a success (p. 16)."

A review of summer compensatory education reports, and Title I reports in general, reveals a lack of controls, randomization, and unconfounded treatment effects, making it difficult to extract valid information from many of the documents. A multitude of conclusions are made in the reports without supporting data, and thus there is little evidence on a national level of a positive impact on children (McLaughlin et al., 1971, p. 7; Wargo et al., 1970, p. 7).

Promptness of Funding and Materials

One of the problems related to the effectiveness of the summer programs concerns the late allocation of funds. Many project directors have claimed that funds have been made available so close to the onset of the project that it was not possible to operate the program as scheduled, or to implement the planned evaluation procedure. In the previously mentioned program in New York City (Erickson et al., 1971), half the teachers never received the planned instructional materials, and another 45 percent received them late. Since most summer programs only run from four to six weeks, it follows that a few days' or weeks' delay can have serious consequences in the planning for both instruction and evaluation.

CONCLUSION

Has summer compensatory education been a success? Should it be continued? To deny the need for it would be folly, but to continue to fund programs that do not have well-structured curricula would be futile. The literature appears to suggest that successful programs in the past have been characterized by a clear statement of behavioral objectives, a structured program designed to achieve those objectives, and a well-planned evaluation procedure to determine the extent to which the objectives have been realized. Planners of future programs will want to seriously consider these aspects as they prepare for successful and effective instructional experiences.

REFERENCES

The author wishes to thank Julian Stanley, Johns Hopkins University, and William Sedlacek and Henry Walbesser, University of Maryland, for their criticisms of earlier drafts of this article.

Ahmann, J. S., and Glock, M. D. *Evaluating Pupil Growth.* (4th ed.) Boston: Allyn & Bacon, 1971.

Austin, G. R., Rogers, B. G., and Walbesser, H. H. The Effective-ness of Summer Compensatory Education: A Review of the Research. *Review of Educational Research, 42*(2), 171-181.

Beggs, D. L., and Hieronymus, A. N. Uniformity of Growth in the Basic Skills Throughout the School Year and During the Summer. *Journal of Educational Measurement,* 1968, *5*(2), 91-97.

Beilin, H. The Status and Future of Preschool Compensatory Education. In Julian Stanley, ed., *Preschool Programs for the Disadvantaged.* Baltimore: Johns Hopkins University, 1972, pp. 165-181.

Bereiter, C. An Academic Preschool for Disadvantaged Children: Conclusions from Evaluation Studies. In Julian Stanldy, ed., *Preschool Programs for the Disadvantaged.* Baltimore: Johns Hopkins University, 1972, pp. 1-21.

Campbell, D. T., and Stanley, J. C. *Experimental and Quasi-Experimental Designs for Research.* Chicago: Rand McNally, 1963.

Chappel, W. R., and Baur, J. F. A Physics Oriented College Motivation Program for Minority Students. Boulder: University of Colorado, 1971. ERIC: ED 058977

Cohen, D. K. Politics and Research: Evaluation of Social Action Programs in Education. *Review of Educational Research,* 1970, *40*(2), 213-238.

Eiszler, C. F., and Kirk, B. Achievement and Attitude Change in Michigan Migrant Education Summer Classrooms, 1972. Mt. Pleasant: Central Michigan University, 1973. ERIC: ED 072876

Erickson, E. et al. Final Report of the Evaluation of the 1971 District Title I Summer Program. Brooklyn: New York City Board of Education, 1971. ERIC: ED 066520

Fitzsimmons, M. E. *An Analytical Study of the Retention of Selected Skills by Intermediate Grade Pupils After the Summer Recess.* Doctoral dissertation, Fordham University. Ann Arbor, Michigan: University Microfilms, 1969. No. 70-11,461.

Gadjo, H. W., and Hayden, L. 1972 Sodus New York Migrant Summer Program. Sodus, New York: Sodus Central School, 1972, ERIC: ED 071833

Gordon, E., and Doxey, A. W. *Compensatory Education for the Disadvantaged.* New York: College Entrance Examination Board, 1966.

Gwaltney, W. R. An Evaluation of a Summer Reading Improvement Course for Disadvantaged High School Students. *Journal of Reading Behavior,* 1971, *3*(4), 14-21.

Jencks, C. et al. *Inequality. A Reassessment of the Effect of Family and Schooling in America.* New York: Basic Books, 1972.

McLaughlin, M. et al. The Effects of Title I, ESEA: An Exploratory Study. Cambridge, Mass.: Harvard University, 1971. ERIC: ED 073216

Menges, C. et al., The Effectiveness of Compensatory Education: Summary and Review of the Evidence. Washington, D.C.: Office of Program Planning and Evaluation (DHEW/OE), 1972. ERIC: ED 062475

Mosteller, F., and Moynihan, D., eds. *On Equality of Educational Opportunity.* New York: Vintage Books (Random House), 1972.

Robinson, B. Final Report: 1970 Summer Pre-Kindergarten. Columbus, Ohio: Columbus Public Schools, 1970. ERIC: ED 061350

_____. 1970-71 Pre-Kindergarten and 1971 Summer Pre-Kindergarten Final Report. Columbus, Ohio: Columbus Public Schools, 1971. ERIC: ED 061351

Soar, R. S., and Soar, R. M. Pupil Subject Matter Growth During Summer Vacation. *Educational Leadership,* 1969, *2*(4), 577-587.

United States Office of Education. *History of Title I ESEA.* Washington, D.C.: USOE (DHEW), 1969.

Wargo, M. J. et al. ESEA Title I: A Reanalysis and Synthesis of Evaluation Data from Fiscal Year 1965 Through 1970. Palo Alto, Calif.: American Institutes for Research, 1972.

ERIC: ED 059415

Weinberg, W. A. et al. An Evaluation of a Summer Remedial
Reading Program—A Preliminary Report on the Development
of Reading. *American Journal of Diseases of Children,* 1971,
122, 494-498.

White, S. H. The National Impact Study of Head Start. In Jerome
Helmuth, ed., *Disadvantaged Child.* Vol. 3. New York:
Brunner/Mazel, 1970, pp. 163-184.

63

HEAD START

by James S. Payne
Department of Special Education
University of Virginia
Charlottesville, Virginia
and
Cecil D. Mercer
Department of Special Education
University of Florida
Gainesville, Florida

Operation Head Start has charged the citizenry of
the United States with the task of disrupting the cycle
of poverty via democratic processes. Its purpose involves
the development of human resources at all ages through
local community action. In conjunction with the educational facets of Head Start, some common features of
programs include parental participation, medical and
dental services, career development programs for staff,
and the use of community volunteers. Thus Head Start
represents much more than just another Federally sponsored program, for it not only reflects the spirit of the
democratic process but challenges its efficacy. Brazziel
(1967) noted the scope of the Head Start venture when
he referred to it as "the country's biggest peace-time
mobilization of human resources and effort (p. 244)."

HEAD START IN PERSPECTIVE

Halcyon Period

Head Start has emerged through three rather distinct
periods. The initial period (1965-1967) was characterized by generous funding and massive support. Prior to
Head Start movement, studies reported by Kirk (1958),
Hunt (1961), Skeels (1966), and Kugel (1967) generated
an optimistic tone among professionals concerning the
potential effect that early experiences could have on the
development of human resources. Likewise, the general
public viewed operation Head Start as a means for eliminating the debilitating effects of poverty on U.S. communities. This "war on poverty" was given further
impetus when heart-warming case studies flooded in
from Head Start centers all over the country. Typical
examples include:

Five-year-old boy whose life was saved because a Head
Start medical examination detected a serious heart
disease.

Eastern Ohio dentist closed his door to Head Start
staff seeking his paid services and three days later
volunteered to be the Dental Director.

Head Start center was burned to the ground, and today a new one stands in its place, built entirely by
volunteer community efforts (Richmond, 1967, pp.
6-7).

Many of the youngsters responded to the question,
'What does a policeman do?' with such answers as
'arrest you,' 'puts daddy in jail,' or 'shoots people.'
For most, this answer was changed to 'helps you' or
'is your friend.'

One (teacher) was bitten by a small, frightened boy
who wanted to leave after being deposited by an older
sister on the first day. Later, however, on a field trip,
he confided, 'You know, I might like you by the time
this is over' (Richard, 1966, p. 23).

Another volunteer was a 78-year-old retired librarian
who came daily to the centers in groups of children
or, as she said, 'I sometimes just hold a child in my
lap for a while. I can do this, for I have plenty of time.'

One 15-year-old boy who was a potential school dropout worked as an aide and never missed a session
(Levens, 1966, p. 482).

. . . to the girls who used to ask for candy and pop-
corn when we went to town, but now asks for a picture
book and crayons (Broman, 1966, p. 483).

These were truly the halcyon days of the Head Start
movement. By 1967 Head Start centers had served over
one million children.

Critical Period (1967-1969)

Evaluations of Head Start programs during the halcyon
period consisted mostly of descriptive reports which were
characterized by subjective impressions and case studies.
However, in 1967 articles began to appear which questioned the lasting effects of Head Start. The skepticism
gathered momentum, due to the impact of two events
which dominated the literature concerning Head Start
during the 1968-1969 period. The first event was the release of the Westinghouse Report, and the second event
concerned the transfer of Head Start from the Office of
Economic Opportunity to the Department of Health,
Education, and Welfare. The Westinghouse Report was
the first large-scale evaluation of Head Start (Cicirelli,
Evans, and Schiller, 1969). As reported by Payne, Mercer, Payne, and Davison (1973), the main points of the
study were:

1. Summer Head Start programs did not produce early
cognitive and affective gains that continued in the
first grade and beyond.

2. Full-year programs produced marginal cognitive gains which continued through the first three grades, but no affective gains were made.

3. Programs worked best in Negro centers, in some urban areas, and in the Southeast region of the nation.

4. Project children were below national norms on the Illinois Test of Psycholinguistic Abilities (I.T.P.A.) and the Stanford Achievement Tests, although Metropolitan Readiness Test scores approached national norms.

5. Parents liked the program and took active part in it. (pp. 93-94).

Although the authors of the Westinghouse Report acknowledged the limitations of the study, the news media began to release articles indicating that Head Start had failed. The release of the study seemed to prompt a nationwide sigh of disappointment. The Westinghouse Report, coupled with the heated debates that occurred concerning the transfer of Head Start from OEO to HEW, jeopardized the survival of the Head Start movement. To illustrate this controversy, Eveline Omwake (1969a), Presiding President of the National Association for the Education of Young Children, boldly purported that:

> At the close of 1968, after three years of a grand effort, we have to face the reality that the once promising Head Start project had already begun to go downhill . . . negative effects are by now clearly observable. . . . One can speculate that with the anticipated budget cuts, with the continued push to involve nonprofessionals in place of professionals and to appoint sketchily trained paraprofessionals to positions of authority, Head Start programs may contain little else than the children enrolled, angry, frustrated, tired adults, broken crayons, incomplete puzzles, torn books, and diluted paints left over from the halcyon days of early Head Start. . . . They [federal agencies] muffed it when they began to exploit the children's programs to bolster the economy. (pp. 130-131)

Omwake's comments triggered a response from Richard Orton (1969a), Associate Director of Project Head Start. It appeared in the March issue of *Young Children*. Orton defended Head Start with some salient facts, and the two articles (Omwake, 1969b; Orton, 1969b) reappeared back-to-back in the March, 1969, issue of *Voice for Children*.

Consolidation and Refinement Period (1969-1973)

The current state of the art finds Head Start being administered directly from the Office of Child Development within HEW. Head Start employees are no longer preoccupied with discussing the virtues and vices of the Westinghouse Report or the administrative transfer to HEW. Fortunately, they are more concerned with delivering high-quality services. It was learned from the halcyon days that the breaking of the poverty cycle through early intervention is no easy task. Although the importance of early intervention is widely accepted, it was discovered that effective preschool programs cannot be achieved in haphazard fashion. It has been realized that

faith in the mission of Head Start is essential, but that faith alone is not sufficient for the implementation of quality programs. Finally, our early experiences with Head Start programs indicated that effective programs included specific objectives and well-formulated intervention strategies (Bissell, 1972).

Even though the Westinghouse Report has long since passed, it was a valuable lesson, and provided impetus for introspection and self-criticism. Early childhood specialists throughout the nation were challenged to deliver a viable program that would unquestionably facilitate the development of children. In essence, early childhood specialists went back to their drawing boards and returned with a refined "game plan."

To begin with, the experts realized that it was senseless to evaluate the impact of Head Start programs on a national scale, since all programs were operated in highly dissimilar ways. For example, large differences appeared in "curriculum, techniques and methods for handling children, equipment, materials and supplies available, facilities used, professional staff training, salaries, age of children, recruitment and screening process of children, community variables, and racial balance (Payne et al., 1973, p. 61)."

The efforts of early childhood specialists culminated in a proliferation of well-defined programs. The implementation of these models in Head Start centers enables Head Start directors to articulate the specific components of their respective programs, thus allowing, for the first time, an understanding of similarities and differences among Head Start programs. Also, for the first time the availability of these models provided Head Start centers with some definitive alternatives concerning intervention strategies. Some of the more popularized models being employed and evaluated today are:

The behavior analysis model was developed by Don Bushell of the University of Kansas. It stresses the teaching of academic content via systematic reinforcement procedures which encompass the use of tokens and individualized programmed instruction.

The cognitive model was developed by David Weikart of the High School Educational Research Foundation. It was derived on the basis of Piagetian theory, and emphasizes home training sessions with mothers and decision-making roles for teachers. Although teachers plan detailed lessons and activities, they are given continuous assistance from classroom supervisors.

The Tucson early education model was designed by Marie Hughes, and is currently sponsored by the University of Arizona. The model emphasizes the development of language competence, intellectual skills, motivation, and social skills. The environmental setting for obtaining these skills is characterized by the freedom to choose activities, a fostering of cooperation among children, and systematic positive reinforcement from teachers.

The academically-oriented preschool model is advocated by Wesley Becker and Siegfried Engelmann, of the University of Oregon. It promotes academic learning in reading, arithmetic, and language. Teaching sessions are highly structured, and are characterized by drills and positive reinforcement. Small study groups are set up by teachers in order to facilitate the presentation of patterned learning materials (usually DISTAR).[1] Teachers focus on eliciting constant verbal responses from children.

A pragmatic action-oriented model was inspired by the English Infant Schools and is currently sponsored by the Education Development Center in Newton, Massachusetts. Its main objective is to tailor classroom environments that are responsive to individual needs and styles of children and teachers. The model has advisory-consultant systems, which encourage teachers to experiment with a variety of ways to effect children's development in such areas as self-respect, respect for others, imagination, curiosity, openness to change, ability to challenge ideas, and persistence.

The Florida parent-educator model was developed by Ira Gordon of the University of Florida. The model stresses home instruction as well as classroom instruction, by involving parent-educators. A parent-educator is identified as a mother from the community who works as a teacher's aide in the classroom and with parents in their homes. The program is based on the theories of Piaget and is cognitively oriented. The curriculum is flexible, in order to accommodate the needs of particular individuals and classes.

The responsive model was designed by Glen Nimnicht, of the Far West Laboratory for Educational Research and Development. Within a responsive environment, which features the use of self-pacing and self-rewarding materials, the program focuses on helping children develop a positive self-image and intellectual ability. In addition, the materials stress the development of sensory discrimination, language ability, and problem-solving ability, while providing immediate feedback and enjoyment from learning.

The Bank Street College model was developed by the Bank Street College of Education in New York City, and represents a "whole child" approach. The ultimate objective of this approach is to enable each child to become intensely involved and self-directed in his learning. Bank street teachers help children build positive images of themselves as learners by functioning as trustworthy adults, being responsive to the needs of individual children, and sensitizing children to sights, sounds, and ideas.

Although the final data analysis concerning the effectiveness of the various models has not been released, it is important to realize that these models do present Head Start centers with some well-formulated and briefly tested alternatives. These resources alone indicate that operation Head Start has generated a proliferation of identifiable programs for educating young children.

Planned Variation and Follow Through are two longitudinal research programs initiated on a national level which have recently released a sparse amount of data concerning the effectiveness of various Head Start models. These studies are designed to assess the cumulative impact on participating children of systematic programs which begin during the preschool period and extend into the early elementary grades. It is anticipated that a complete interpretation of the data generated by these studies will be available in the near future. Until the complete report is released, it is noteworthy to examine the early findings of these two major research efforts. Bissell (1972) found:

Participants in Head Start and Follow Through programs achieved greater gains in both academic achievement and cognitive development during the school year than did children not in the programs.

Children in well-implemented Head Start programs were consistently ahead of nonparticipants in such areas as academic achievement, cognitive growth, and attitude growth. Likewise, children in Follow Through programs consistently out-performed nonparticipants.

The differences among Planned Variation approaches suggested a specificity of effects as related to specific program objectives. Programs having specific objectives with well-formulated strategies were superior to other, less structured programs.

In the wake of these tentative results reported by Bissell (1972), it is feasible to forecast that the efficacy of Head Start will soon be more firmly grounded on the basis of objective evaluations. Until final research reports are available, it appears that the Office of Child Development has chosen to operate the programs on the basis of current findings. By establishing guidelines for program performance standards, HEW has encouraged the development of specific objectives and well-formulated intervention strategies in the Head Start centers.

Increased support and confidence, at both the national and local level, are implicit in Head Start's newest program thrust, i.e., to ensure at least two percent enrollment of handicapped children in the program (Jordon, 1973). Finally, it is hoped that through refinement and expanding resources Head Start will acquire the necessary skills for achieving its appointed mission— to disrupt the poverty cycle and minimize the debilitating effects of handicaps on young children.

NOTES

[1]DISTAR (Direct Instructional System for Teaching Arithmetic and Reading) refers to a commercial packaged program distributed by Science Research Associates, Inc., 259 East Erie St., Chicago, Illinois 60611.

REFERENCES

Bissell, J. S. *Planned Variation in Head Start and Follow Through.* Washington, D.C.: Department of Health, Education, and Welfare, 1972.

Brazziel, W. Two Years of Head Start. *Phi Delta Kappan,* 1967, *48,* 344-348.

Broman, B. L. Parents' Reactions to Head Start Program. *Childhood Education,* 1966, *42,* 483-487.

Cicirelli, V. G. *The Impact of Head Start: An Evaluation of the Effects of Head Start on Children's Cognitive and Affective*

Development. Vol. 1. Springfield, Va.: Clearinghouse, 1969.

Hunt, J. M. *Intelligence and Experience.* New York: Ronald Press, 1961.

Jordon, J. B. O.C.D. Urges Special Education's Support for New Head Start Services to Handicapped Children. *Exceptional Children,* 1973, *40,* 45-48.

Kirk, S. A. *Early Education of the Mental Retarded: An Experimental Study.* Urbana, Ill.: University of Illinois Press, 1958.

Kugel, R. B. Familial Mental Retardation—Fact or Fancy? In J. Hellmuth, ed., *Disadvantaged Child.* New York: Brunner-Mazel, 1967.

Levens, D. A Look at Project Head Start. *Childhood Education,* 1966, *42,* 481-483.

Omwake, E. B. From the President. *Young Children,* 1969, *24,* 130-131. (a)

——. The Federal Agencies Muffed It. *Voice for Children,* 1969, 4-8. (b)

Orton, R. E. Comments on the President's January Message. *Young Children,* 1969, *24,* 246-248. (a)

——. A Serious Charge that Needs Full Airing. *Voice for Children,* 1969, 5-8. (b)

Payne, J. S., Mercer, C. D., Payne, R. A., and Davison, R. G. *Head Start: A Tragicomedy with Epilogue.* New York: Behavioral Publications, 1973.

Richard, F. Giving Them a Head Start. *Education Digest,* 1966, *31,* 21-24.

Richmond, J. B. Beliefs in Action. *Childhood Education,* 1967, *44,* 4-7.

Skeels, H. M. Adult Status of Children with Contrasting Early Life Experiences. *Monograph of the Society for Research in Child Development,* 1966, *31*(3), 1-65.

ADDITIONAL SOURCES

Implementation of Planned Variation in Head Start: Preliminary Evaluations of Planned Variation in Head Start According to Follow Through Approaches (1969-1970). Interim Report: First Year of Evaluation, Part II. Menlo Park, Calif.: Stanford Research Institute, 1971.

Implementation of Head Start Planned Variation Testing and Data Collection Effort: Final Report. Menlo Park, Calif.: Stanford Research Institute, 1972.

Payne, J. S., Mercer, D. C., Payne, R. A., and Davison, R. G. *Head Start: A Tragicomedy with Epilogue.* New York: Behavioral Publications, 1973.

Shipman, V. C., Barone, J., Beaton, A., Emmerich, W., and Ward, W. *Disadvantaged Children and Their First School Experiences: ETS-Head Start Longitudinal Study: Structure and Development of Cognitive Competencies and Styles Prior to School Entry.* Princeton, N.J.: Educational Testing Service, 1971.

Shipman, V. C. *Disadvantaged Children and Their First School Experiences: ETS-Head Start Longitudinal Study: Demographic Indexes of Socioeconomic Status and Maternal Behaviors and Attitudes.* Princeton, N.J.: Educational Testing Service, 1972.

——————

64

THE MENTALLY RETARDED

by Paul Heintz
Associate Professor of Educational Psychology
New York University
School of Education
Department of Educational Psychology
Washington Square
New York, New York

Mental retardation is a concept which has been used over the years to refer to individuals who exhibit both significantly subaverage intellectual functioning *and* impaired adaptive behavior in such areas as maturation, learning, and social adjustment. Since mental retardation is a concept (like intelligence, motivation, anxiety, and similar terms in psychology and education), or a construct, when used in formal theoretical schemes, definitions of mental retardation will depend largely on the theoretical positions held by the individuals defining the concept. More importantly to the child who may be affected by local classification policies, the educator's and psychologist's conception of mental regardation will influence such factors as prevalence figures, identification procedures, labeling practices, educational placement, curricula, and instructional strategies, among others.

DEFINITIONS

Gelof's (1963) analysis of 23 formal systems for classifying mental retardation, based on different levels of behavior and functioning, emphasized the differences that can and do exist among various professional organizations and/or authorities in the field. Despite a number of critical differences in constructs and rationale among the classifiers, however, intellectual subnormality and problems in social adaptation were central to most conceptualizations of mental retardation.

Contemporary educational programs for the mentally retarded continue to be influenced by a combination of the various definitions which appeared before and after approximately 1960. Prior to the 1960s, definitions of mental retardation frequently described the condition in terms of adult behavior, yet stressed the appearance of retardation during childhood, its constitutional nature, and its incurability (Robinson and Robinson, 1965). Other early definitions have, in varying degrees, connected mental retardation with such factors as disease, defect, injury, central nervous system pathology, incomplete cerebral development, insanity, criminality, and mental illness (Clausen, 1967; Doll, 1962). These early definitions continue to exert considerable influence on general and special educators as they formulate programs and services for the mentally retarded.

Recognizing the confusion generated by the variety of definitions of mental retardation in use, the American Association on Mental Deficiency (AAMD) developed a definition which has received wide acceptance since the 1960s by most of the workers in the field of mental retardation, who represent a variety of disciplines. The AAMD definition, which involves three criteria that must be met concurrently by the individual, is as follows: "Mental retardation refers to significantly subaverage general intellectual functioning existing concurrently with deficits in adaptive behavior and manifested during the developmental period (Grossman, 1973; Heber, 1959, 1961)." Although subaverage intellectual functioning, as measured by an individual intelligence test, initially was operationally defined as being greater than one standard deviation (SD) below the population mean for the age group involved, the AAMD adopted the criterion of greater than two SDs below the population mean in 1973. The four word descriptions of degree of mental retardation, together with ranges in SD values and IQ scores for tests with an SD of 15, are: (1) mild, −2.01 to −3.0, 55-59; (2) moderate, −3.01 to 4.00, 40-54; (3) severe, −4.01-5.0, 25-39; and (4) profound, <5.00, <25.

The developmental period, although not precisely defined, is regarded as being approximately the first 18 years. The inclusion of this long developmental period suggests that the condition of mental retardation conceivably could occur relatively late in a pupil's school career. Most mildly retarded children are, however, identified by the time they reach the age of 8 or 9.

The AAMD's criterion of impaired adaptive behavior may be manifested in the broad areas of maturation, learning, and social adjustment. The vast majority of moderately, severely, and profoundly mentally retarded children show disabilities in such maturation areas as mobility, communication, and self-care skills; while few, if any, children later identified as mildly retarded exhibit noticeable slowness in these areas. "Learning" refers to the ability of the individual to acquire knowledge as a result of experience, and is particularly important during the school years, when all children are expected to acquire academic skills. It has been speculated that most pupils classified as mildly retarded during their school years would not meet the AAMD's criteria for mental retardation if compulsory schooling were not part of their experience. Finally, "social adjustment" is the degree to which the individual is able to maintain himself independently and to conform to personal, social, and vocational standards appropriate for his age group.

The current AAMD definition specifies that subaverage intellectual functioning must be accompanied by impairment in adaptive behavior. It also clearly states that mental retardation is a term descriptive of the *current* intellectual functioning and adaptive behavior of the individual. A pupil may therefore meet the criteria of mental retardation at one time and not at another. These latter notions concerning mental retardation, while being crucial to the development of appropriate educational classification, placement, and programming policies, have yet to replace the earlier criterial attributes of constitutional origin and cerebral impairment held by some psychologists and educators providing direct services to the child who may meet the AAMD criteria at a given time.

It should be emphasized that these earlier attributes, and others, may be quite legitimate in developing a theory of mental retardation; but they too frequently lead to stereotyped treatment of the retarded child if they are permitted to directly or indirectly influence educational services.

The President's Panel of Mental Retardation (1963) estimated that three percent of the population of the United States is mentally retarded. Based on this national incidence figure, the number of individuals who meet the criteria of mental retardation at some time during their lifetime approximates 6 million. Prevalence figures of mental retardation reported for individual localities in the past have been dependent on two major factors: (1) socio-economic level of the community, and (2) degree of subaverage intellectual functioning and/or impaired adaptive behavior used to define mental retardation (Kirk, 1972).

Within the IQ range of 50 ± 5 to 75 ± 5 ("educable" mentally retarded), Kirk (1972) estimated that 50, 25, and ten pupils per 1,000 school-age children could be expected in low, middle, and high socio-economic communities, respectively. Approximately four of each 1,000 pupils obtain IQs between 30 ± 5 and 50 ± 5 ("trainable" mentally retarded), with this prevalence rate remaining constant for communities representing all socio-economic levels.

Program development for the mentally retarded since 1940 has far outstripped provisions for all other types of exceptional pupils. As a result of this rapid growth period, close to one-third of the nearly three million children receiving special education services in local public systems during 1971-1972 were enrolled in special classes for the educable and trainable mentally retarded child (Dunn, 1973). It was estimated that from approximately one-third to one-half of all special education teachers were working with the mentally retarded by the end of the 1960s. While California reported a recent drop from previous years in the number of pupils in special classes for the mildly retarded, the increment from 1970-1971 to 1971-1972 in this area for the United States as a whole was 144,500, against an average annual increase of almost 40,000 over the 1952-1966 period (Dunn, 1973). Thus, even though there have been recent calls for a drastic reduction in the number of pupils classified as mildly retarded and assigned to self-contained special classes (Dunn, 1968, 1973; Kirk, 1972), the data available suggest that actual cut-backs may not be occurring as rapidly as some special educators would like them to happen.

EDUCATIONAL CONSIDERATIONS

Terminology

There are few, if any, areas in the education of the mildly retarded that presently are free from controversy or wide disagreements regarding practices. Basic to most of the issues, however, is the question of whether the vast majority of pupils in the schools who come from lower-income (and usually minority) backgrounds, and who meet the AAMD criteria of mental retardation at some time during their school years, should be classified as mentally retarded for educational purposes. There is increasing agreement that the answer to this question is no, but the supporting arguments provided for this response vary widely.

Dunn (1973), in addressing himself to this issue, urged that the term "mentally retarded" be restricted to the lowest one percent of each ethnic or racial subgroup, who are so low in general intellectual ability that they are unable to care for themselves. He also proposed that the term no longer be used for educational classification purposes. In its place he suggested the use of the term "general learning disabilities" (GLD), which he defined as follows:

> Pupils with general learning disabilities are those who require special education because they score no higher than the second percentile for their ethnic or racial subgroup on both verbal and performance types of individual intelligence test batteries administered in their most facile language (Dunn, 1973, p. 69).

Dunn further proposed that terms "moderate GLD" (IQ 35 ± 5 to 60 ± 5) and "severe GLD" (IQ 20 ± 5 to 35 ± 5) be substituted for the labels of "trainable" and "custodial," respectively, now used by educators.

As for the child traditionally labeled "educable mentally retarded," Dunn urged the use of "mild general learning disabilities," which includes the following criteria' (1) lower age limit of 6 years; (2) an IQ score which is between the one-half and second percentile for the child's ethnic subgroup and obtained on an individual test in the pupil's most facile language: Anglo children, IQ = 70; American Indian Children, IQ = 65; and inner-city black children, IQ = 55 (Dunn, cited in MacMillan, 1971a); and (3) general school achievement which does not exceed the level predicted from an IQ score obtained on a nationally standardized intelligence test given in the language used for instruction in school.

Basing his arguments primarily on educational grounds, Dunn (1968) has argued against labeling the estimated 60 to 80 percent of socio-culturally deprived and minority group children whose IQ is below 70, who experience difficulty with school learning and are routinely assigned to special classes for the educable retarded. His proposal for the use of separate regional and/or ethnic norms for low-income children in defining the pupil with mild general learning disabilities, however, is also tenable, when examined in the light of theoretical schemes accepted by many as being valid to explain intelligence and its measurement. A commonly held view of intelligence specifies that it is the ability to profit from experience. In order for the measurement and subsequent comparison of individuals on intellectual ability to be valid (as opposed to current intellectual functioning), the individuals must have had prior similar experiences or opportunities to learn. Since the vast majority of pupils placed in special classes for the mildly retarded over the years have been from lower socio-economic backgrounds, and also frequently held membership in a minority group, there can be little doubt that their opportunities for intellectual and educational development differ in many respects from that of the majority, middle-class pupil. It

is also commonly held that intelligence is more or less normally distributed, and within large, well-defined subgroups of the population having a similar range of experiences, there will always be approximately two percent who fall at the lowest end of the distribution. While this is a "psychometric definition," the lower-ability population within these subgroups usually exhibits psychologically and educationally significant impairment in behavior (unless the environment is considered to be uniformly superior). Thus, Dunn's suggestion for using different IQ cut-off points to define various populations of low-functioning pupils is consistent with the long-held, but rarely-acted-on, belief that intelligence is affected by opportunities to develop this capacity; and a pupil's intellectual ability therefore should not be estimated without consideration of this factor. As in the past, when the term "educable mentally retarded" was in use, there is of course no point to classifying any child as having "mild general learning disabilities" for educational purposes unless this will lead to education and treatment with clearly demonstrable benefits.

Dunn's definition of GLD focuses on racial, regional, and nationality differences on IQ test scores, while failing to note that the overlap among various subgroups in IQ test scores is substantial. For example, while the mean IQ of Anglo persons is approximately one standard deviation above that of inner-city black persons as a group, 15 percent to 20 percent of the latter group in this country have IQ scores above the group mean for Anglo individuals; and, because of total population differences, there are more Anglo persons who score below the mean of inner-city black persons than there are inner-city black individuals who score below this mean (Cleary et al., 1975). Dunn's definition attempts to compensate for the fact that the proportion of low-income minority pupils whose IQ score falls within the lower half of the nation's population is larger than that of majority pupils.

A further limitation of Dunn's suggestions for defining pupils with GLD for educational pruposes is that it is based on traditional theories of intelligence which define it as "an innate capacity" (or capacities) of the person. There are of course no tests of innate capacity, although certain limited inferences about future performances can be made from measures of current performance, and these are independent of race or socio-economic status (Cleary, Humphreys, Kendrick, and Wesman, 1975).

There probably always will be a need for some type of shorthand term in education in order to direct the attention of educators to the underdeveloped and/or undeveloped abilities of certain pupils. The term must be beneficial to the child, and based on an adequate understanding of the range of appropriate uses, limitations, and interpretations (in psychology and education) of the concepts and constructs, or tests and measurements, on which educational decisions are made. A failure to proceed in this manner increases the danger of blindly engaging in the invalid but common assessment and placement practices in special and regular education described by Mann (1971). Theoretical orientations or biases which are inconsistent with providing the mildly retarded with maximum opportunities for growth, development, and even eventual average functioning in cognitive ability, language learning, affective development, and socialization, should not be permitted to influence any aspect of special educational programming in the schools. Since most of the information available on intelligence and its origin, development, permanence, and related concepts are of a tentative nature, each pupil should be required to empirically demonstrate his upper limit of functioning within programs designed to promote developmental abilities. The educational and psychological effects of such an approach probably will be related to such overlapping factors as the child's degree and extent of previous stimulation, age, and previous opportunities for growth.

Reynolds and Balow (1972), in an especially perceptive article, have pointed out that special education is particularly vulnerable to criticism for its common practice of using simplistic categories for human beings because of the exclusive use of negatively loaded terminology in doing so. It is crucial, however, that pupils whose intellectual functioning is between 50 ± 5 and 70 ± 5 upon school entry be singled out and guaranteed early, individualized instruction, and, if a category is required, these pupils should be classified as children with *unactualized developmental abilities* until at least the age of 8. After the age of 8, the term *unactualized general learning abilities* would seem preferable to others proposed, or now in use, for pupils up to the age of 18 who continue to function at a level that is greater than 2 SDs below the average in intellectual abilities and adaptive behavior.

A great deal has been written about the variety of devastating and long-lasting consequences of labeling a child mentally retarded independent of other factors (MacMillan, Jones, and Aloia, 1974), particularly children who exhibit minimal levels of retardation. These deleterious effects, which are commonly accepted as fact among special educators, include lowered feelings of worth and aspirations among children labeled, and inappropriate treatment by others, which leads to lowered opportunities to develop up to one's potential. MacMillan's review and analysis of the literature on the effects of labeling reveals that the studies conducted to date have either failed to find clear-cut evidence to support the negative effects of labeling children as mentally retarded, or confounded labeling with such a variety of other variables as to make their findings uninterpretable. The most convincing argument against labeling pupils as mentally retarded would be that they themselves object strongly to being so labeled.

Using the different IQ cut-offs for various subgroups within the schools described earlier, coupled with the belief that the label mentally retarded has deleterious effects, may lead to the practice of simply delabeling and ignoring pupils who are in need of special assistance in learning. Differences in IQ test performance of even one standard deviation (IQ of less than 84-85) generally do have such important consequences that they cannot be ignored (Cleary et al., 1975). Delabeling children as mentally retarded is probably the first crucial step in a long series of steps required to provide them with educational opportunities which will prove to be superior to those currently provided.

Administrative Arrangements

The most commonly used administrative plan for educating mentally retarded pupils in the United States has been the special class-unit, housed in the regular school building. Although the primary motive for originally creating separate, special classes was to benefit nonretarded pupils and their teachers, the placement of mentally retarded children in separate classes during the schools' period of most rapid growth (1940-1963) was based on the belief that retarded pupils deviate from other children to such a degree that they require a modification of school practices in order to develop to their maximum capacity (Kirk, 1962). There has been a continuing concern among special educators for the effectiveness of special classes from the very beginnings of their existence; Bennett (1932) stated that "It is not surprising, in a field of education that has had such a rapid growth, that there is considerable variance as to procedures and objectives, and that many assumptions have been made that are unverified by accurate data (p. 1.)" Thirty years later, after reviewing the special class efficacy studies, Johnson (1962) concluded that mentally retarded pupils enrolled in special classes achieved significantly less than comparable children who remained in regular classes, despite smaller class size, higher costs, and specially trained teachers in the special classes. He also concluded that advantages in personal and social development which appear to be associated with special-class enrollment are probably slight and not particularly meaningful. Johnson attributed the disappointing findings of the special class efficacy studies primarily to the negative attitudes of teachers, which emphasized the inability of retarded pupils.

Dunn's (1968) criticism of special classes is more severe: he urges that alternative educational placements be found for at least the vast majority of socio-culturally deprived children labeled as "educable mentally retarded." According to Dunn, the current practices followed in determining eligibility for special class placement has in large measure led to "digging the educational graves of many racially and/or economically disadvantaged children by using a WISC or Binet IQ score to justify the label 'mentally retarded.' This term then becomes a destructive, self-fulfilling prophecy (p. 9)." Kirk (1972) also cautioned about the possible drawbacks of placing children in special classes who come from lower socio-cultural backgrounds, in view of the fact that many special class teachers' expectations may not be sufficiently high. Data gathered by Heintz (1974), however, indicated that the possible negative consequences of pupils interacting with teachers having low expectations in special classes may be applicable to any pupil labeled as retarded, regardless of the child's socio-economic status. He found that more than one-half of a sample of experienced special class teachers believed that retarded pupils are not able to achieve at a level expected on the basis of their mental age.

All of the major special class efficacy studies carried out since the early 1930s have had serious weaknesses in their design (Blackman and Heintz, 1966; Kirk, 1964).

Despite these methodological flaws, most special educators have accepted their findings as being reasonably accurate in showing that, as far as academic achievement is concerned, educable mentally retarded pupils in regular classes were performing at least as well as, and often significantly better than, those in special classes. It should be noted that the recent recommendations that a moratorium be declared concerning the placement of most mildly retarded pupils in special classes stem from a general dissatisfaction with the results obtained from these classes, rather than a knowledge that particular alternative instructional arrangements will indeed lead to maximum growth and development among this part of the school population.

Despite the lack of clear-cut findings on the efficacy of regular versus special classes, most special educators favor placing mildly handicapped pupils, including mildly retarded pupils, in the mainstream of education, with special educators serving as consultants, instructional specialists, and itinerant or resource teachers (Dunn, 1968; Lilly, 1971). The resource-room model, which is now perhaps the preferred plan when possible, is any arrangement in which pupils attend the regular class, in which they are based for pupil accounting purposes (e.g., homeroom), for part of the day, and in addition receive special instruction or training in a separate instructional setting on a part-time basis. The major advantages of the resource-room model are that the pupil's primary educational involvement is associated with a regular grade, or home room, while attempts to meet the child's special learning needs are being continued. This plan also permits pupils to remain with their friends and peers, and to receive help without being categorized and labeled as handicapped. The plan is also less expensive, and serves more children than the self-contained special class (Hammill, 1972).

Although the resource-room plan appears to be free of some of the practices objected to by recent critics of the special class unit, its success will depend on a variety of other factors within the schools. These include the attitudes of administrators, teachers, and pupils toward pupils who exhibit obvious difficulty in learning, as well as the ability of the integrated pupil to perform within the range of acceptable behavior as defined by their peer groups. Goldberg and Blackman (1965) suggest that true integration of pupils labeled mildly retarded is an administrative and pedagogical "state of mind," in addition to being a physical arrangement. Thus, it is possible for pupils to be physically integrated into regular classrooms, yet isolated socially and psychologically, with the negative consequences, if any, to the "integrated" pupil unknown at this time.

Further concern for the social and psychological environment of integrated arrangements arises from the empirical data which indicate that, as a group, mentally retarded pupils have not been well received by either teachers or their fellow pupils. Johnson (1950) found mentally retarded children in the regular grades to be isolated and rejected by their normal peers, while Goldstein, Moss, and Jordan (1965) generally confirmed these findings and suggest that the amount of isolation and re-

jection may be related to the degree of emphasis and level of academic achievement in any given regular class setting.

Initial findings on teachers' reactions to the integration of mildly retarded pupils into the regular class program blend into previous negative findings in this area, and raise questions concerning the appropriateness of this approach in schools which use the conventional grade organizational pattern (Shotel, Iano, and McGettigan, 1972). These investigators reported a decline in the number of elementary school teachers who expressed agreement with the practice of integrating retarded children as part of a resource-room plan, after being involved in such a program for a year. The teachers in the study reported that the retarded pupils were among the lowest achievers, did not participate in general class activities, and were frequently teased by their classmates. Whether similar findings would be obtained with older mildly retarded pupils, who have had more time to develop social skills, is yet to be determined.

The initial empirical data obtained on the effects of integrating mildly retarded pupils into the regular classes, taken together with Goldberg and Blackman's (1965) theoretical analysis of the potential social and psychological consequences of various integration patterns, should not lead to further idle discussions of whether these pupils should be integrated. Rather, local educators should decide which pupils, at what time in their school career, and exhibiting what levels of academic and social competence, should be integrated with what teachers and pupils, and under what types of instructional/organizational patterns. Although there are exceptions, most educators feel that the self-contained special class is probably the most suitable administrative arrangement for educating the more severely and profoundly retarded children (Smith and Arkans, 1974).

Psychoeducational Modifications

Special educators over the years appear to have given lip-service to the notion that what takes place within the administrative arrangement, once it is established, is the most crucial factor in determining what and how well pupils learn. The major efforts and resources of special education personnel have been directed toward administrative and organizational aspects, and have largely ignored the development of curricular and instructional approaches for mentally retarded pupils (Meyer, 1968). It is not surprising, therefore, that until recently the only "special" instructional modifications made for retarded pupils have been based on just a few, rather simplistic principles which emphasize the use of concrete educational materials and experiences which are presented at a gradual rate. Although their development have generally been fragmented, the curriculum and instructional approaches currently in use in special education, and described in greater detail elsewhere (Heintz and Blackman, in press), tend to parallel those in regular education. The major sources for formulating curriculum objectives in regular education and in special education include subject matter as a data source, society as a data source, and the learner as a data source.

Past research findings strongly suggest that mentally retarded learners, in contrast to intellectually average pupils, are not naturally set to learn academic skills. The mentally retarded have demonstrated relatively lower ability in a variety of concept utilization skills, short-term memory, information processing, and incidental learning, among others. As a result of these characteristics (generally observed among mentally retarded learners, but in varying degrees in individual pupils), academic material should be presented in a highly organized state, in which key concepts underlying the structure of specific subject matter and subareas are emphasized at all levels (Bruner, 1960; Phenix, 1964), and in a sequence empirically established as being efficiently organized for learning (Gagne, 1970; Coleman, 1970), in order to maximize success. A higher-than-average expectation of failure, a greater tendency to decrease effort following failure experiences, and a greater dependency on external, rather than internal, reinforcements may also influence the retarded child's school performance. In examining these influences, MacMillan (1971) emphasizes the critical need to include modifications during instructional activities which are appropriate for the motivational patterns frequently found among mildly retarded children. Interestingly, he points out that when faced with mastering a cognitive task, mentally retarded pupils often are more interested in behaving in ways that will increase the amount and frequency of time periods in which they are able to interact with approving persons, and are less motivated to solve a task or provide correct answers, than are most intellectually average pupils.

The daily needs and activities of individuals living in contemporary society have served as a second major source of curriculum content in special education, from the very beginning of special classes. More recent efforts in developing a social learning curriculum (SLC) (Goldstein, 1969, 1970) also have as their major goal social occupational competence. The SLC represents a departure from most traditional curriculum building efforts, in that its content is based on empirically derived needs and problems encountered by mentally retarded persons in their attempt to adjust in an increasingly complex society.

The major goals of the SLC are to teach mentally retarded pupils to think critically and to act independently, in order to enhance their chances of making adequate social-occupational adjustments. Goldstein suggests the exclusive use of an inductive teaching approach to instruction, organized so that the pupil is systematically guided through problem-solving steps involving a series of increasingly complex, teacher-initiated questions requiring responses of labels, details, inferences, predictions and generalizations. A unique feature of this approach is that the teacher does not provide the pupils with the correct response, hopefully resulting in a reduction of dependency behavior encouraged by some special class practices in the past.

Since the 1960s, the deviant characteristics of the mentally retarded learner have served as an additional major source of curricular for the special education program. Kirk (1962) had long emphasized that a common characteristic of any exceptional child was his discrep-

ancies in growth within himself in such areas as motor, language, speech, academic, and social development. As a result of the popularity of a learning disability approach among educators of retarded pupils, instructional objectives in academic and social areas in many programs have taken a position of secondary importance, behind that of training perceptual, linguistic, and motor abilities (Bateman, 1967; Kirk and McCarthy, 1971). Mann (1971), however, has raised questions about the validity of a number of the central principles and procedures underlying a learning disability approach, as well as the sophistication of the testing instruments identified with this curriculum model.

OTHER ISSUES

From the beginnings of history, man has generally expressed skepticism, if not open ridicule, regarding the possibility of modifying the intelligence of persons. This reaction is quite consistent with the traditional conceptions of intelligence which define it as a "capacity" of the person. Recent formulations of intelligence, which anchor the concept to measurement operations and the functional relationships among current tests (Cleary, Humphreys, Kendrick, and Wesman, 1975), require a reexamination of commonly held beliefs regarding the "educability of intelligence." Intelligence has been described as "the entire repertoire of acquired skills, knowledge, learning sets, and generalization tendencies considered intellectual in nature that are available at any one period in time (Cleary et al., 1975)."

There have been preliminary discussions and efforts to assess and, directly or indirectly, remedy childrens' weaknesses within the general framework of cognitive models or theories of intellectual structure (Meeker, 1969). A number of studies have also focused, in part, on research questions dealing with the degree of IQ changes among retarded children as a result of exposure to special programs. Goldstein, Moss, and Jordan (1965), in their special class efficacy study, reported substantial gains in IQ among young mildly retarded pupils, with a gain of 12 points not uncommon. Gains among a group of young psychologically deprived children whose initial IQs were between 50 and 85 were approximately one standard deviation or more (15 to 21 points) after exposure to a diagnostically based curriculum (Hodges, McCandless, and Spicker, 1971).

The most dramatic study to evaluate the results of early (and largely direct) training and/or stimulation of intellectual skills among preschoolers was that of Heber, Garber, Harrington, Hoffman, and Falender (1972), who selected 50 recent mothers with IQs of less than 75 and assigned them at random to experimental and control groups. One-half of the infants of those mothers received an intensive stimulation program beginning shortly after birth and lasting some five years throughout the preschool period. During the child's first four months an "infant teacher" spent the entire day in the home interacting with the child, while the mother was provided with training outside of the home. At approximately four months of age, most experimental infants were taken to a learning center for eight hours each day, where intensive one-to-one and small-group training continued in such areas as receptive language, reading readiness, and mathematical-problem-solving skills.

At the end of approximately 5 years of intensive training, the experimental children obtained an average IQ score of 128, while the mean scores of the control- and a contrast-group were 94 and 85, respectively. Thus, the experimental group surpassed the control group by more than 2 standard deviations, and the contrast group by almost 3 standard deviation units.

The Heber et al. study has been criticized by Page (1972) on the grounds that the stimulation program contained materials which were similar to those in infant intelligence tests. Page suggested that the study merely demonstrated that it is possible to train subjects on items that are similar to those used in intelligence tests. Scrutiny of the toys, books, and games selected for the preschool child in most middle-class homes, as well as the language models available, indicates that these materials and models would also have to be described as being very similar, and in some cases identical, to intelligence test items. Thus, the preschool program used by Heber and Dever may be viewed as having replicated the environment and experiences of those middle-class children for whom materials, activities, and skills are selected because of their high "educability value."

The validity of Heber's findings cannot be determined until the experimental pupils enter school and their ability to succeed in the academic and social areas is evaluated. However, until these follow-up data become available, it appears reasonable for special educators to begin to formulate curriculum objectives that are more consistent with current conceptualizations of intelligence that do not necessarily lock children into the category of mental retardation because of their initial low performance on intelligence tests or school tasks. Guarded optimism over the future of many of these children with unactualized developmental or learning abilities appears to be warranted, on the basis of the following views, expressed by a group of distinguished psychologists with particular expertise in the area of intelligence and its assessment:

Intelligence is not a fixed trait in a population. There are good data which show that the intellectual level of Americans, as well as the levels of other Western nations (use of tests is essential to test the hypothesis), has risen even during the relatively short history of the use of intelligence tests. The variables responsible for such increases are not known with sufficient detail that a course of action can be described, but the increases are real. It is also a very reasonable hypothesis that the level of a particular subgroup could be raised. The amount and specific kinds of effort required, however, are unknown. The following recommendation is justified: It is undesirable to underestimate the amount of effort required or to view narrowly the kind required. An effective compensatory program may take years and involve the family, the neighborhood, the peer group, and the schools. (Cleary et al., 1975, p. 23)

REFERENCES

Bateman, B. Implications of a Learning Disability Approach for Teaching Educable Retardates. *Mental Retardation,* 1967, 5, 23-25.

Bennett, A. *A Comparative Study of Subnormal Children in the Elementary Grades.* New York: Bureau of Publications, Teachers College, Columbia University, 1932.

Blackman, L. S. The Dimensions of a Science of Special Education. *Mental Retardation,* 1967, 4, 7-11.

_____, and Heintz, P. The Mentally Retarded. *Review of Educational Research,* 1966, 36, 5-36.

Bruner, J. S. *The Process of Education.* New York: Vintage, 1960.

Clausen, J. Mental Deficiency–Development of a Concept. *American Journal of Mental Deficiency,* 1967, 71, 727-745.

Cleary, T. A., Humphreys, L. G., Kendrick, S. A., Wesman, A. Educational Uses of Tests with Disadvantaged Students. *American Psychologist,* 1975, 30, 15-41.

Coleman, E. B. Collecting a Data Base of a Reading Technology. *Journal of Educational Psychology,* 1970, 61(4), Part 2.

Doll, E. E. A Historical Survey of Research and Management of Mental Retardation in the United States. In E. P. Trapp and P. Himelstein, eds., *Readings on the Exceptional Child.* New York: Appleton, 1962.

Dunn, L. M. Special Education for the Mildly Retarded–Is Much of It Justifiable? *Exceptional Children,* 1968, 35, 5-22.

_____, ed. *Exceptional Children in the Schools: Special Education in Transition.* New York: Holt, Rinehart & Winston, 1973.

Gagne, R. M. *The Conditions of Learning.* New York: Holt, Rinehart & Winston, 1970.

Gelof, M. Comparisons of Systems of Classification Relating Degree of Retardation to Measured Intelligence. *American Journal of Mental Deficiency,* 1963, 68, 297-317.

Goldberg, I. I., and Blackman, L. S. The Special Class: Parasitic, Endophytic, or Symbiotic Cell in the Body Pedagogic? *Mental Retardation,* 1965, 3, 30-31.

Goldstein, H. et al. *A Proposal for a Research and Development Center in Curriculum for the Mentally Retarded.* New York: Yeshiva University, 1970.

_____. Construction of a Social Learning Curriculum. *Focus on Exceptional Children,* 1969, 1, 1-10.

_____, Moss, J., and Jordon, L. S. *The Efficacy of Special Class Training on the Development of Mentally Retarded Children.* Urbana, Illinois: University of Illinois, 1965.

Grossman, H. J., ed. *A Manual of Terminology and Classification in Mental Retardation: 1973 Revision.* Washington, D.C.: American Association on Mental Deficiency, 1973.

Hammill, D. The Resource-Room Model in Special Education. *The Journal of Special Education,* 1972, 6, 349-354.

Heber, R. A Manual of Terminology and Classification in Mental Retardation. *American Journal of Mental Deficiency Monograph Supplement,* 1959, 64, entire issue.

_____. Modifications in the Manual on Terminology and Classification in Mental Retardation. *American Journal of Mental Deficiency,* 1961, 65, 499-500.

_____, Garber, H., Harrington, S., Hoffman, C., and Falender, C. *Rehabilitation of Families at Risk for Mental Retardation: Progress Report.* Madison, Wisconsin: Rehabilitation Research and Training Center in Mental Retardation, University of Wisconsin, 1972.

Heintz, P. Teacher Expectancy for Academic Achievement of Mentally Retarded Pupils. *Mental Retardation,* 1974, 12, 24-27.

_____, and Blackman, L. S. Psychoeducational Considerations with the Mentally Retarded. In I. Bialer and M. Sternlicht, eds. *The Psychology of Mental Retardation: Issues and Approaches.* Chicago: Aldine, in press.

Hodges, W. L., McCandless, D., and Spicker, H. *Diagnostic Teaching for Preschool Children.* Arlington, Virginia: Council for Exceptional Children, 1971.

Johnson, G. O. A Study of the Social Position of the Mentally Handicapped Children in the Regular Grades. *American Journal of Mental Deficiency,* 1950, 55, 60-89.

330 SPECIAL INTEREST GROUPS

Kirk, S. A. *Educating Exceptional Children.* Boston: Houghton-
Mifflin, 1962.

_____. *Educating Exceptional Children.* New York: Houghton-
Mifflin, 1972.

_____. Research in Education. In H. A. Stevens and R. Heber,
eds. *Mental Retardation.* Chicago, Illinois: University of
Chicago Press, 1964.

_____, and McCarthy, J. J. Learning Disabilities. *The Encyclo-
pedia of Education,* 1971, *5,* 441-446.

Lilly, M. S. A Training Based Model for Special Education. *Exceptional Children,* 1971, *37,* 745-749.

MacMillan, D. L. Special Education for the Mildly Retarded:
Servant or Savant? *Focus on Exceptional Children,* 1971a,
2(9), 1-11.

_____. The Problem of Motivation in the Education of the
Mentally Retarded. *Exceptional Children,* 1971b, *37,*
579-586.

_____, Jones, R. L., and Aloia, G. F. The Mentally Retarded
Label: A Theoretical Analysis and Review of Research.
American Journal of Mental Deficiency, 1974, *79,* 241-261.

Mann, L. Psychometric Phrenology and the New Faculty Psychology: The Case Against Ability Assessment and Training.
The Journal of Special Education, 1966, *33,* 77-81.

Meeker, M. N. *The Structure of Intellect: Its Interpretations
and Uses.* Columbus, Ohio: Charles E. Merrill, 1969.

Page, E. B. Miracle in Milwaukee: Raising the IQ. *Educational
Researcher,* 1972, *1,* 8-16.

Phenix, P. *Realms of Meaning.* New York: McGraw-Hill, 1964.

President's Panel of Mental Retardation. *Report to the President.
A Proposed Program for National Action to Combat Mental
Retardation.* Washington, D.C. Government Printing Office,
1963.

Reynolds, M. G., and Balow, B. Categories and Variables in
Special Education. *Exceptional Children,* 1972, *38,* 357-366.

Robinson, H. B., and Robinson, N. M. *The Mentally Retarded
Child: A Psychological Approach.* New York: McGraw-Hill,
1965.

Shotel, J. R., Iano, R. P., and McGettigan, J. F. Teacher Attitudes Associated with the Integration of Handicapped Children. *Exceptional Children,* 1972, *38,* 677-683.

Smith, J. O., and Arkans, J. R. More Than Ever: A Case for the
Special Class. *Exceptional Children,* 1974, *40,* 497-502.

Suppes, P. et al. *Computer Assisted Instruction.* New York:
Academic Press, 1968.

ADDITIONAL RESOURCES

Major Organizations Involved in Mental Retardation

American Association on Mental Deficiency (AAMD)
5201 Connecticut Avenue, N.W.
Washington, D.C. 20012

National Association for Retarded Children (NARC)
2709 Avenue E East
Arlington, Texas 76011

    Membership includes parents and other persons interested in
mental retardation, as well as professional workers in the
field.

Council for Exceptional Children (CEC)
Jefferson Plaza Suite 900
1411 S. Jefferson Davis Highway
Arlington, Virginia 22202

    CEC has divisions with major interest in various areas of ex-
ceptionality, including a division of mental retardation.

Journals in Mental Retardation

American Journal of Mental Deficiency
Education and Training of the Mentally Retarded
Exceptional Children
Journal of Special Education
Mental Retardation
Teaching Exceptional Children

65

COMMUNICATION DISORDERS
by Rolland J. Van Hattum
Professor and Chairman
Communication Disorders
State University College
Buffalo, New York

Communication disorders have been labeled by various
terms, such as speech problems, speech defects, speech
disorders, hearing loss, and deafness. Regardless of the
major heading utilized, two basic divisions of communication disorders are those involving expression and those
involving reception.

Disorders of Expression. Disorders of expression have
been subdivided into articulation, voice, rhythm, and
language. The specialist responsible for remedying these
disorders is called a Speech Pathologist in most settings
and a Speech Clinician in the schools, as well as occasionally being referred to as Speech Correctionist or
Speech Therapist. Children in the schools generally continue to use the designation of "Speech Teacher" in addressing the specialist. In fulfilling responsibilities to
the communicatively handicapped, the specialist diagnoses, prognosticates, prescribes for, and provides
therapy for communication disorders, primarily in the
expressive disorders.

Disorders of Reception. Receptive deficits of the communication process primarily consist of deficiencies in
auditory function. Hearing loss or hearing impairment
are the terms most often used to represent these problems.
However, in a broadening concept of auditory dysfunctions, difficulties in other aspects of auditory processing,
such as in auditory discrimination, auditory sequencing,
and auditory closure, have been receiving increasing attention. Diagnosis and prescription of remedial measures
are provided by a specialist referred to as an Audiologist.
The Speech Pathologist usually provides a number of
remedial measures, such as speech therapy, speech reading, and auditory training. It is not unusual that one individual is certified as both a Speech Pathologist and
Audiologist. A third specialist is the Teacher of the Hearing Impaired (Teacher of the Deaf), who provides classroom programming for those individuals with hearing

disorders severe enough to warrant special class placement. A specialist called Teacher of the Language Impaired is becoming increasingly evident, and assists those children whose difficulty with the language system interferes with their ability to profit from the educational experience without special assistance. These children are sometimes included in the group labeled "learning disabled." In fact, many learning disabled children have a linguistic deficit as their basic handicapping condition.

SCOPE OF THE PROBLEM

About nine percent of the population have communication disorders severe enough to interfere with educational, emotional, and/or eventual economic adjustment. Communication can be labeled disordered when it interferes with message transference; specifically when its expressive component is characterized by verbal behavior which is difficult or impossible for the listener to understand, or which detracts from the individual by being inappropriate to the individual's age, sex, or appearance; or when its receptive component interferes with the individual's ability to receive messages without distortion, confusion, or obliteration. Of the nine percent, approximately 3.5 percent are expressive problems of articulation, voice, and rhythm, 5 percent expressive or receptive problems related to the linguistic system, and .5 percent receptive problems in hearing impairment (Dunn, 1973). It is estimated that 30,000 Speech Pathologists and Audiologists are currently functioning in the United States. Two hundred fifty colleges and universities offer programs preparing persons to enter this field. It is further estimated that 75,000 to 80,000 specialists would be needed to adequately meet the needs of the communicatively handicapped. The majority of communication disorders are found in school-aged children, and the majority of services are provided there.

Emergence of Language

The most significant occurrence in the profession in the approximately 50 years since its inception has been the emergence of language as the major focus. This has resulted in a restructuring of classifications, alterations in training programs, and changing priorities in clinical programs. These developments are understandable. Language is the primary conveyer of information. In the delivery of a message from a sender to a receiver, language is the system or code which is utilized. In language, sequences of letters are used for the non-oral code, and strings of sounds are used for the oral code, to form words which represent people, places, things, and abstract concepts, and also provide a connective fabric of words to support those words which provide the major meaning. Oral language uses speech as its primary method of delivery. Speech consists of the production of speech sounds (articulation) to produce words which are produced with adequate voice quality and rhythm. The words and the method by which they are arranged (syntax) comprise the grammar of the language. Two other elements of language are the semantic aspect, or the relationship between the word and the object, and the prag-

matic aspect, or the relationship between the man and his words.

Language contributes significantly to many facets of human behavior. Its relationship to learning is not difficult to describe. Learning is a process whereby the symbol system of a culture is learned in order to profit from the past and present knowledge of that culture. Without the mastery of the symbol system, information cannot be gathered, organized, retained, and retrieved for problem-solving—the basis of education. Thus, the ability to communicate adequately is basic to the educational process.

Not only does each individual use the communication system to communicate, but it is basic to his internal verbal functioning. Man uses language to talk to himself, to think, and, in addition to the educational implication of this, he uses language to commune with himself and to describe to himself the world he sees. Thus, language plays a vital role in human adjustment. Verbal language is a distinctively human trait. In many respects, man *is* his language.

EXPRESSIVE COMMUNICATION DISORDERS

With the pervasiveness of language, it is no wonder that the former classification system, which placed language as one division of communication disorders, along with articulation, voice, and rhythm, is considered outmoded. More recent classification tends to retain the headings of articulation, voice, and rhythm under disorders of expression, but as subheadings under language in describing communication disorders. Grammatical disorders then become a fourth heading. Each disorder may exist in isolation or may be found in some combination accompanying conditions such as cleft palate, cerebral palsy, hearing impairment, brain dysfunction, intellectual deficit, or behavioral disorders.

Articulation Disorders

Articulation problems are found in approximately two to three of every 100 individuals, and can be described as the inability to produce vowel or consonant sounds correctly. Types of articulation problems are omissions, or the absence of a sound where one should occur; distortion, or producing the sound defectively; and substitution, in which another sound is produced in the place of the correct and appropriate sound. Articulation errors are common in young children until about 5 years of age. Maturity of articulation should be complete in all children by 7½ years of age. The presence of an articulation error in a young child does not necessarily denote a communication disorder. Speech Pathologists are able to determine whether the errors that exist in young children are a normal part of the maturational process or are disorders in need of remedial attention. Common causes of articulatory defects are organic factors, such as faulty dentition; psychological factors, such as manipulative behavior; and intellectual factors, such as mental retardation.

Voice Disorders

Voice disorders are present in fewer than one in 200 persons. It is difficult to accurately quantify the prevalence, since it appears that society is willing to accept a wider range of communication behavior in voice production than in other aspects. Typical voice problems include inadequate volume, too loud or too soft; inappropriate pitch, too high or too low; and quality disorders, either phonatory (hoarse, harsh, breathy) or resonatory (nasality). Voice disorders are principally caused by organic or structural problems, such as paralysis of the velum, or cleft palate; vocal abuse, such as the result of excessive and continued volume, or from alcohol or tobacco; functional factors, such as imitation of poor models; of psychological factors, such as shyness or more severe problems such as hysterical symptoms.

Rhythm Disorders

Rhythm problems are also estimated to be present in slightly fewer than one in 100 persons. There are a number of classification systems which attempt to take into account the likely normalcy of early nonfluencies in young children, and the increasing complexity of the problem if it persists as the child matures. These classification systems tend to provide labels for this early stage, in addition to later transitional stages and the final stage of confirmed stuttering. In general, young children before the age of 7½ who are not aware of their fluency imperfections, or who do not exhibit a form of struggle behavior in their communication attempts, are not considered to be stutterers. Generally, three basic causative agents have been viewed as possible etiologies for stuttering. These are organic, psychological, or developmental factors.

Language Disorders

About five of every 100 persons are considered to have communication disorders in other aspects of language. Classification of these differences is difficult, since the authorities tend not to agree on the development of language or a description of language. Some authorities support a learning theory model, such as Skinner (1957), who explains the acquisition of language on the basis of stimulus, response, and reinforcement. Other linguists, such as Lennenberg (1964), view language on the basis of an inherent ability toward which the individual is disposed, such as in walking. Depending on the theoretical model followed, the deficits are described in different ways. Most authorities agree that grammatical problems are the most significant of language handicaps, but redefined terminology and new terminology have created a confusing picture of language and its disorders, even to the specialists. Their impact, however, is indisputable, and the dramatic increase of special classes for these children attests to this.

RECEPTIVE COMMUNICATION DISORDERS

Hearing Impairment

The primary receptive disorder is hearing impairment. Approximately five persons in 1,000 are thought to have hearing losses of varying severity. About one in 1,000 can be classified as deaf. The function of the Audiologist is to administer a wide variety of tests to determine the extent of the hearing impairment, to aid in determining the type and cause of the problem, and to recommend rehabilitative measures, such as amplification (a hearing aid), speech and language therapy, speech (lip) reading and auditory training, preferential seating in the classroom, or assignment to a special class for the hearing impaired. In such special classrooms, Teachers of the Hearing Impaired provide classroom programming with primary emphasis on the development of adequate communicative behavior, particularly language, to enable the hearing handicapped to participate in the educational program.

PROFESSIONAL FUNCTION

Because of the early beginnings of the profession by both educational and medical personnel; because of the varying natures of the problems previously described; and because of the variety of employment environments in which they function; Speech Pathologists and Audiologists have had difficulty in determining whether to adopt an educational or a medical model. The early medical and educational personnel, who initiated the profession, utilized different methods, equipment, materials, techniques, and procedures. Vestiges of these differences remain within the profession.

In spite of these differences, Speech Pathologists tend to possess similar qualifications regardless of where they are employed. Academic knowledge and clinical skills are not significantly different, whether the specialist functions in the schools or in another clinical setting, such as a hospital clinic. However, the age levels and types of problems of cases treated understandably vary, based on the location of the services.

Speech Clinicians and Audiologists in Schools

In school environments, the Speech Clinician screens classrooms for communication disorders, diagnoses, prescribes for, and remedies these disorders, usually in several schools. Most often, three or four schools are assigned and the case load, or number of children scheduled, averages 75 children. Children are usually seen in small groups of four to six children, or seen individually, in both instances for therapy periods of approximately 30 minutes' duration. The typical Speech Clinician in a school system might visit one school building on Monday and Wednesday mornings and another in the afternoons, and follow a similar procedure on Tuesdays and Thursdays. Fridays may be devoted to staff meetings, diagnosis of new referrals, consultation with teachers, administrators or parents, report writing, preparing letters of referral, demonstration of prevention techniques in a classroom, or consulting with a special class teacher regarding developmental programming in speech and language. Some clinicians use intensive methods of scheduling, wherein they provide services to the same school or schools every day for a period of time, and then change to another school or schools. Other variations are also employed. A school or unit for the physically handicapped may include several speech clinicians on its staff. When Audiologists are employed in the schools, they may conduct screening programs and/or may diagnose children referred by School Nurse-Teachers who conduct screening programs. Audiologists usually play the major role in hearing conservation programs.

Speech Pathologists and Audiologists in Other Clinical Settings

Speech Pathologists function in several types of clinical service centers. As part of rehabilitative teams in medical rehabilitation centers, they assist patients with physical handicaps resulting from illness or injury. Vocational rehabilitation centers utilize the Speech Pathologist to assist the physically handicapped toward improved employment opportunity. Speech and Hearing Centers, often Red Feather or United Way agencies, are concerned with children and adults with communication defects. Veteran's Hospitals, too, provide services. In all of these settings the services range from providing the mother of a cleft palate child with information, in an attempt to prevent the development of aberrant communication behavior; to the specialist, who works with patients who have had their larynges removed and must be taught new means of communication; to persons who have suffered head wounds or strokes and are unable to communicate adequately.

Most colleges and universities operate speech and hearing clinics to provide students opportunity for practice experiences. Faculty members may provide demonstration therapy in such settings, supervise student clinicians, teach cognitive courses, and/or engage in research.

Additionally, Speech Pathologists and Audiologists are increasingly found in Health Departments, functioning as members of maternal and child care teams; associated as consultants of clinicians in early intervention programs, such as Head Start or Early Push; providing services in nursing homes or other facilities for the aging; providing services in all branches of the armed services; or, increasingly, providing professional services in private practice. Speech Scientists and Hearing Scientists also play vital roles in the further exploration and understanding of the nature of communication and its disorders, and more effective methods of remediation. Many businesses and industries concerned with aspects of communication employ such specialists in laboratory settings. Specialists within the profession continue to play an active role in the study of noise as a public health problem.

PROFESSIONAL PROBLEMS

A number of problems confront the speech and hearing profession, some internal and some external. No clear professional unity, and accompanying identity of role, has been established. Thus, Speech Pathologists and Audiologists often do not agree on their relative roles or their areas of cooperation. One area of specialty may feel that the other does not really comprehend the importance of an issue confronting it. This is currently demonstrated in the issue of whether Audiologists should dispense hearing aids, and, if they do, whether they should ethically be allowed to do so for profit. Even the Audiological profession is almost equally divided on these issues.

Lack of identity has resulted in insufficient impact on national and state legislation related to the communicatively handicapped. In some of the legislation, the specialist is not allowed his rightful responsibility for independent function, but must work under the prescription of a physician. This is particularly important where third-party payments are concerned.

Another crucial area, alluded to earlier, is that of learning disabilities. Even though many of these problems are rooted in symbolic deficits, the profession has only recently offered its expertise. In the meantime, specialists from other fields, such as mental retardation and psychology, have challenged for this area of responsibility.

PROFESSIONAL CHANGE

Speech Pathologists are accepting increasing responsibility with the educable and trainable retarded. Results with the trainable to this time have been marginal at best. But new methods are under study, and the expressions of interest in this neglected area are encouraging. More success is reported with the educable retarded. Whereas this group was considered homogeneous and static in intellectual behavior, results of some programs of language remediation suggest that certain segments of this population may be mentally retarded as a result of language deficits, rather than possessing these deficits as a result of intellectual restriction. This has significant implication for future educational programming for these individuals.

Services to Minority Group Children

Both preschool programs and elementary grade programs which provide black children assistance in learning standard English have yielded impressive gains in academic achievment (Bereiter and Engelmann, 1966). However, the controversy continues as to whether these children should be required to develop competence in standard English in order to succeed in schools. Those who do respond in the affirmative cannot agree on when and how this should be accomplished. The decisions in this area, which affect the lives of millions of children, badly need early resolution. This is not likely to occur, since there is little evidence of growing agreement over the basic issues. A related issue is the communicative behavior of Spanish-speaking children. The issues of bilingual education has considerable meaning for the communication expert, and for our society.

Early Services and New Delivery Systems

Other changes involve greater emphasis on early prevention and early intervention for children with communication disorders. Also, new service delivery systems are being utilized in schools and clinics, such as taped systems and Communication Aides. Such programs have proven successful, and not only provide assistance to children, but relieve the clinician so that other expanding areas of responsibility can be fulfilled (Van Hattum et al., 1974).

Rather than being a well-defined, tradition-bound profession, the youthful members of the profession are currently producing a constant state of change. While problems of identity, unity, responsibility, and direction exist, the activity of the professionals in many areas, as they search for a resolution, offers opportunity for dynamic and expanding professional growth.

Many sources describe aspects of the profession in greater detail. Among these, the following texts are recommended for additional information:

For an overview of the disorders of communication:
Travis, L. E. *Handbook of Speech Pathology.* New York: Appleton-Century-Crofts, 1972.

For descriptions of disorders and remedial measures:
Dickson, S. *Communication Disorders: Remedial Principles and Procedures.* Chicago: Scott-Foresman, 1974.

For descriptions of school programs:
Van Hattum, R. *Clinical Speech in the Schools.* Springfield, Illinois: Charles C. Thomas, 1969.

For language disorders in children:
Berry, M. *Language Disorders of Children.* New York: Appleton-Century-Crofts, 1969.

For hearing remediation:
Sanders, D. *Aural Rehabilitation.* Englewood Cliffs, New Jersey: Prentice-Hall, 1971.

For audiology:
Newby, H. *Audiology.* New York: Meredith Publishing Company, 1964.

The national organization which consists solely of these specialists is the American Speech and Hearing Association, 9030 Old Georgetown Road, Washington, D.C. 20014. The association has a certification program for Speech Pathologists and Audiologists. It also certifies training programs and professional services.

The Division for Children with Communication Disorders, of the Council for Exceptional Children, also includes many of these specialists, but primary focus is on these services as they are provided in schools, and the entire council also includes other areas of exceptionality. One of its primary goals is to foster communication among special services for the handicapped in the schools.

REFERENCES

Bereiter, C., and Engelmann, S. *Teaching Disadvantaged Children in the Preschool.* Englewood Cliffs, New Jersey: Prentice-Hall, 1966.

Dunn, L. M. *Exceptional Children Education.* New York: Holt, Rinehart and Winston, Inc., 1973.

Lennenberg, E. H. *The Capacity for Language Acquisition.* Englewood Cliffs, New Jersey: Prentice-Hall, 1964.

Skinner, B. F. *Verbal Behavior.* New York: Appleton-Century-Crofts, 1957.

Van Hattum, R., Page, J., Duguay, M., Baskervill, R. D., Conway, L., and Davis, T. A Taped, Aide-Presented Program for Articulation Remediation. *Language, Speech and Hearing Services in Schools,* Vol. 9, No. 2, 1974.

66

THE PROFESSIONAL EDUCATION OF MILITARY OFFICERS

by Lt. Col. Harold Markowitz, Jr.
and
Lt. Col. Edward E. Jernigan
Air University, USAF
Maxwell AFB, Alabama

Views or opinions expressed or implied in this paper are not to be construed as carrying official sanction of the Air University or The Department of the Air Force.

The purpose of this article is to describe professional education in the American military services. Extensive programs designed to build the professional competence of officers are offered by each branch of the service, as well as by the Department of Defense. As a working definition, professional military education is any curriculum designed to enhance the competence of officers through broad knowledge and behaviors that are not job-specific, usually as a part of a coherent program (Air University, 1975; US Army, 1971).

This paper will avoid presenting aspects of these educational programs that are common to higher education in general, and focus on the remarkably utilitarian programs and the complex interrelationships of military institutions. To further limit the article, the authors have not attempted an historical review of military education, since this has been done adequately by Shelburne and Groves (1965, 1969; and Reeves, 1914). Finally, we have permitted ourselves a minimum of space-consuming digressions on the role of professional education in the unique sociology of military groups; through it must be said that to analyze professional education as purely an exercise in skill-acquisition is to miss much of the point, whatever the profession.

On the role of professional education in the sociology of the military, the standard reference is Janowitz (1960). And for a political scientist's view, one turns to Huntington (1964).

DEFINITIONS

The terms "professional" and "education" do not carry unusual definitions as they are employed in the services, but the precision with which these terms are used requires comment. The attributes of the military "profession," though clouded by catchword abuse, go beyond the mere possession of skill or office (Lang, 1969). Expertise, responsibility, and corporateness are the characteristics which lead Huntington (1964) to state unequivocally, "the modern officer corps is a professional body and the modern military officer a professional man (p. 7)." Lang (1969) accepts criteria of objective performance and self-enforcement of standards (Goode, 1957) as the marks of this and other professions.

The military usually distinguishes education from training. Training is a matter of skill acquisition, while education involves the acquisition of knowledge and behavior patterns that are not job-specific (Lang, 1969; US Army, 1971; Shelburne and Groves, 1965, 1969; Masland and Radway, 1957). Learning to fly an airplane or to operate a computer requires training, though theory and principles may be involved. Building a sensitivity to the relevant aspects of a leadership or management problem requires education, though specific cases and incidents may be the vehicles by which these are taught. Professional military education attempts to focus on that which is judged to be needed by all officers, and the acquisition of the specialized knowledge needed for a specific job occurs elsewhere. It is speculated that the behavioral movement has eroded the precision of this distinction in the services' educational literature, though the concept is widespread.

A THREE TIER SYSTEM

One may envision the professional military education programs as composed of a system having a base and three succeeding levels, though variations between the services preclude more precise generalization.

Precommissioning Education: The Professional Base

At the base is the precommissioning education, which qualifies a cadet for his commission. With minor variations in program, there are three main sources of precommissioning education: the Reserve Officer Training Corps program, taken concurrently with a civilian college curriculum; a cadet program (sometimes requiring a bachelor's degree as a prerequisite), taken subsequent to schooling and prior to officer service; and the services' academies.

The first two of these programs are designed to augment the cadets' education by providing supplemental education and training in military subjects (Air University, 1975; US Army, 1971). The assumption is made that the attitudes, skills, and background knowledge necessary for officership have not been acquired through other educational means. Though the curricula of the services vary considerably, they generally consist of about 600 hours of instruction, in subjects ranging from the specificity of marksmanship to the generality of military management, administered in periods varying from three months to four years. In every case, the curriculum is derived from actual or presumed service mission requirements (Shelburne, Groves, and Brokaw, 1969; Masland and Radway, 1957). In times of national emergency criteria of entrance are generally lowered, to increase the population base from which officers may be chosen. Higher education is universally accepted as an index of the quality of the officer corps, and is highly valued as the appropriate base for further professional development.

The Air Force Academy, located near Colorado Springs, Colorado, has a maximum strength of 4,417 cadets. This maximum, established by Congress in 1964, is the same for all military academies but the Coast Guard Academy. The teaching faculty is entirely composed of military officers (U.S. Air Force Academy, 1975). The four-year curriculum requires 187 semester-hours for graduation, 22.5 of which are earned in mandatory summer programs of physical education, military training, and orientation conducted at a variety of Air Force bases. A core of basic education courses totaling 140.5 semester hours is required of all cadets, including 14.5 hours of physical education, 27 hours of leadership and military training, 99 hours of academic subjects (sciences, mathematics, English, social sciences, and a foreign language), and 46.5 hours in an academic major field. Cadets may major in any of 14 scientific and engineering fields, or seven social sciences. The core subjects dominate the first year ("Fourth Class") and progressively give way to the academic major, which dominates the final year ("First Class') (U.S. Air Force Academy, 1975).

Admission to the Army, Navy, and Air Force Academies is based upon a three-step process: nomination, examination, and appointment. Nominations are made by U.S. senators and representatives, the President, the Vice President, the services, military schools, ROTC programs, outlying U.S. areas, and the District of Columbia. The sons of Congressional Medal of Honor winners are also eligible for appointment.

The U.S. Military Academy, at West Point, New York, serves as the Army's undergraduate program. Student body size and admission procedures are as described above. This academy is the nation's oldest, having been established in 1802.

The curriculum consists of a minimum of 48 one-semester courses, including at least six elective courses. This academic work is supplemented by intensive summer training in military skills. Essentially an engineering program that also requires courses in the liberal arts, the U.S. Military Academy curriculum requires courses in mathematics, sciences ,engineering (general, civil, nuclear, electrical, or weapons systems), English, social sciences and a foreign language, as well as extensive physical training. Cadets may concentrate their electives in a single area, if they choose, but there is no choise of academic majors, as in the Air Force program (Meyerson, 1971; U.S. Military Academy, 1975).

The U.S. Naval Academy is at Annapolis, Maryland. Again, student body size and admission procedures are aligned with the other academies. The teaching faculty is unique among the academies, being composed of roughly equal numbers of military officers and civilians (Hurd, 1971).

The curriculum consists of 140 semester hours and leads to a Bachelor of Science degree. Cadets undergo naval instruction and take training cruises during the summers. Each cadet completes 40 courses, of which 34 are in the core curriculum (sciences, engineering, social sciences, naval science, English, and a foreign language). A minor subject is required, the six electives being used for this purpose. An independent study program allows outstanding scholars to devote their fourth year ("First Class") to a research thesis (Hurd, 1971; U.S. Naval Academy, 1975).

The U.S. Coast Guard Academy, located near New London, Connecticut, is the smallest of the American military academies. It has a student enrollment of 1,100 cadets. Also, unlike the other academies in its selection criteria, Coast Guard Academy appointments are based on standardized test scores, academic accomplishment, and evidence of a well-rounded background (U.S. Coast Guard Academy, 1975).

During the first two years of the four-year curriculum, the cadet follows a standard program of studies. This core program stresses mathematics, engineering, and science. Diversified scientific studies and social science courses form the core program during the last two years of the curriculum. Electives taken during the last two years are on the basis of individual interest. As in the case of the Naval Academy, selected scholars may pursue an independent research program during their fourth year. Each summer includes a six-week cruise. A Bachelor of Science degree is granted to all graduates.

There is, of course, no agreed-upon "best" foundation for the career of a professional military officer. But out of the descriptions above emerges a broad consensus that one should possess depth in the sciences and in an engineering field appropriate to the needs of his service; that he should be exposed to the broadening influence of the social sciences and humanities; that he communicate effectively in English and passibly in another language; that he should be physically fit; and that he demonstrate the qualities of self-discipline and acceptance of authority that are required to successfully complete a rigorous and comparatively inflexible academic program. And in each curriculum there is a recurrent theme—that the desired context within which the cadet's preprofessional studies occur should be practical knowledge of, and actual experience in, the professional environment the cadet will enter after graduation.

Professional Military Education: Career Development

Lang (1969) stated the sociological and historical context within which the modern military functions:

The armed forces, like all organizations, are responsive in varying degrees to changing internal and external requirements. Developments in the technology of warfare . . . and changes in the level of skill, force adaptations in the structure of military organization. The broad outline of historical change is unambiguous. Armed forces whose mainstay was once a postfeudal aristocracy . . . have everywhere been professionalized. (p. 39)

As mentioned previously, each service has a multitiered system for the professional military education of its officers. The Army and Marine Corps professional schools are sequential; that is, an officer must study at the first level before he is eligible for the second, and so on. In contrast, the Air Force and Navy take a less structured approach, in which their officers may be chosen to attend a second- or third-level school without a prerequisite of professional schooling. For those officers not selected to attend professional schools, correspondence or group study programs ("nonresident seminars") are available. The correspondence or nonresident programs parallel, as closely as possible, the educational content of the resident programs.

The skills and techniques taught at each of the three levels of professional military education are those appropriate to the students' rank and responsibilities. As a consequence of this explicit keying of education to career requirements, a military officer's professional education is necessarily incremental over a career, rather than predominately at the beginning, as is the case in most other professions. The rationale for this is that the officer corps is a "specialized profession (Janowitz, 1973, p. 1)." In this context, the periodic return to school has the distinct advantage of promoting currency in scientific, technological, environmental, strategic, and tactical changes in his chosen field. Contrasting this approach with customary civilian methods, Janowitz (1960) wrote that unlike "the concentrated single dosage" in the education of a physician or a lawyer, "an officer, as he moves up the hierarchy, is sent to various schools at prescribed intervals, to acquire new skills and new perspectives (p. 126)."

The early years of commissioned service, like similar periods in other professions, determine in large measure the direction and level of performance of a career. "Much time is devoted to training activities. Most of it is spent in the field with troops, at sea in ships of the fleet, or with operating air and support units. Generally this experience is developed within a defined area of specialization, such as one of the branches in the Army, Naval aviation or submarine-warfare in the Navy, or with fighters or bombers in the Air Force (Masland and Radway, p. 275)." Assignment to military schools constitutes an integral part of these early years in an officer's career.

First Professional Level

While serving in diverse line and staff positions, officers in the Army, Air Force, Navy, and Marines may attend the first level of professional military education. The term "first professional level," as used here, refers to those schools whose student body consists of relatively junior officers (with from three to eight years in their service), and whose curricula incorporate professional education, as distinguished from job-specific training. There are 18 such schools in the Army (the "advanced" schools, organized by branch within the Army), the Marine Corps' advanced program at Quantico, Virginia, the Navy's General Line School at Monterey, California, and the Air Force's Squadron Officer School at Montgomery, Alabama.

The first-level schools vary considerably in duration, ranging from the Air Force's 11-week Squadron Officer School to the Army's 39-week Field Artillery and Signal Schools. With the exception of the Air Force school, only a portion of each first-level curriculum could be considered "professional" education, since much of the material studied is job-specific. These courses are designed to prepare their students for subsequent duties at the intermediate level in the military hierarchy, e.g., command of a small unit or staff work at an intermediate headquarters.

The mixture of specialist training and more general education is illustrated by the "mission statement" of the Army's advanced courses, which cites the need to prepare the officer students for command and staff duties at battalion level. While studying a specialty, emphasis is placed on the exercise of command, where applicable, or else focusing on a knowledge of functions and responsibilities and the "development of managerial and specialist skills (US Army, 1971, pp. 2-3)." The courses provide perspective through orientation and instruction in, among other things, the general functions of a staff.

As previously noted, the Air Force has elected to divorce its first-level professional education from its specialist schooling. The original concept of the school was that it would be an eight-week course offered by the Air Command and Staff School (later College), for the benefit of officers recalled to active duty during the Korean War. Thus, since its inception in 1950 the Squadron Officer School has clearly maintained the professional orientation of its parent staff college. The mission statement of the school does not involve training in any job-related skills, but instead focuses on the preparation of junior officers for command and staff tasks, as well as to "strengthen those professional values necessary for a full career of dedication and service . . . and to provide . . . a foundation for further professional development (Air University, 1971, pp. 1-4)."

The substance of first-level professional military education may be pictured as the intentional cultivation of a broad outlook. Though junior officer specialists are needed, the perspective of a manager is cultivated in these early years.

Second Professional Level

All of the military services conduct command and staff courses for selected mid-career officers. This is the first level at which there is a joint school—the Armed Forces Staff College. Joint schools are operated under the supervision of the Joint Chiefs of Staff, rather than of an individual service, and provide professional military education for those who are to serve in middle- and high-level positions dealing with more than one specific service of DOD agency. Both faculty and student body in joint schools come from all services, and the curriculum emphasizes subjects of interest to all (Armed Forces Staff College, 1973). The total number of students from all services at the five schools is approximately 2,100 per year. The National War College and the Industrial College of the Armed Forces are joint military colleges that conduct professional education at the highest level (U.S. Air Force, 1974).

The Armed Forces Staff College is located at Norfolk, Virginia, and is indeed a unique college in the intermediate school structure. It is the only United States intermediate-level joint military college, and conducts two five-month courses each year, whereas all other intermediate level courses are approximately ten months in duration. Its mission is to conduct a course of study in joint and combined organization, planning, and operations, and in related aspects of national and international security, in order to prepare selected military officers for duty in all echelons of joint and combined commands (U.S. Air Force, 1974). Even though Armed Forces Staff College students are not exposed to as much of their service viewpoints on staff techniques as those who attend their own service's college, they are given the same credit for completion of intermediate professional military education.

The oldest and best-known course at this level is Army's Command and General Staff College. Its primary mission is to prepare selected Army officers for duty, in peace or war, as commanders of large units and as general staff officers (Kloke, 1970; Just, 1970). Some time between their ninth and 15th year of service, about one-half of all eligible Army officers are selected to attend this second professional level of education. Since this will be the final general military educational experience for the vast number of these officers, the college focuses its attention on bringing all students to a high level of staff competence and to a common understanding of the principles of military leadership and command of forces in the field (Armed Forces Staff College, 1973; Just, 1970).

The Marine Corps Command and Staff College is similar to the Army's in objectives. It provides professional education for majors and lieutenant colonels to prepare them for command at the regimental or group levels, and for duties with joint- and high-level service organizations (Kloke, 1970). It is the highest-level professional education school in the Marine Corps; however, a few Marine officers are selected to attend the senior service schools of the other services.

The Navy's Command and General Staff course is also ten months in length, and is also devoted to "emphasis upon the operational functions of command including operational planning—and upon the organization, functions, and procedures of operational staffs (Armed Forces Staff College, 1973, p. A-6)."

The Navy intermediate level school "differs somewhat from the Army and Marine Staff colleges in devoting considerable time to military history and Navy and global strategy, probably because it is colocated with the Naval War College (at Newport, R.I.) and shares some of the latter's lecturers (Armed Forces Staff College, 1973, p. A-7)."

The Air Command and Staff College is located adjacent to the Air War College at Maxwell AFB, Alabama. The college offers a 39-week course annually for approximately 600 students. The mission is to improve the professional ability of selected officers for command and staff assignment normal to their rank, and to contribute to the development of sound Air Force doctrine and effective command and staff practices. The college's environment is oriented toward the free expression of ideas and independent, analytical, and creative thinking (U.S. Air Force, 1969).

In its unpublished March 1973 study, the Armed Forces Staff College characterized the intermediate-level school graduate as being marked by professional competence.

> Carefully selected to begin with, they have been through a rigorous course of study focused squarely on the kinds of problems that will be theirs over the next few years. Perhaps their minds have not been stretched enough in view of the pace of technological advance and the changing politico-military environment, nor have they been sufficiently encouraged in innovative and creative thinking, but these are difficult objectives for a single year's schooling. . . ."
> (Armed Forces Staff College, 1973, p. A-8)

However, the more promising of the graduates will have further opportunity to cope with such problems at the next level of general military education—the senior service schools.

Third Professional Level

At the apex of the pyramid of military education stand five coequal institutions: two "joint" (more than one service) colleges—the National War College and the Industrial College of the Armed Forces—and the Army, Navy, and Air War Colleges. The approximately 40-week course of each institution has a goal of preparing "selected officers to man the highest level command and staff positions within their own services and with national and international forces and headquarters (Armed Forces Staff College, 1973, p. A-8)." All five colleges have students from each service, as well as from civilian agencies with defense-related responsibilities (e.g., Department of State and the CIA). Annual enrollments approximate 1,000 students.

All five colleges examine the military and international environment, the strategic threats to the nation, allied and U.S. capabilities to meet those threats, and optimal strategies and programs to use those capabilities. The differences in curricula among the services' colleges are principally traceable to the importance each service attaches to assuring that its graduates are steeped in its own perspective and doctrine. For example, the Air Force places particular emphasis on aerospace power and making the student "capable of performing as an effective advocate of aerospace power (U.S. Air Force, 1974, p. 17)." Similarly, one of the Army's objectives is "to stress Army doctrine, higher tactics, and operations

against an appropriate background of National strategy in the joint and international environment (Kloke, 1970, p. 21)." The Industrial College of the Armed Forces has a somewhat different mission and curricular emphasis from the others, in that it focuses on the "economic and industrial aspects of national security and in the management of resources under all conditions (U.S. Air Force, 1974, p. 19)." The mission of the National War College is to "conduct a study of those agencies of government and those military, economic, scientific, political, psychological, and social factors of power potential in order to enhance the preparation of selected personnel of the Armed Forces and State Department for the exercise of joint and combined high-level policy, command and staff functions, and for the planning of national strategy (Kloke, 1970, p. 25; Masland and Radway, 1957)."

Current thinking about the education of military officers takes into account the national and international environment within which today's leaders must operate. Huntington (1963) indicated that a general must be a generalist as well; it is not enough to be knowledgeable in a single field. Partridge (1969) corroborates this, saying that education for "generalist" officers is:

> an education which is broader, more diversified and more 'liberal' in the sense of being less concerned in its earlier stages with practical training in a narrowly vocational way; one that provides for more advanced and vigorous theoretical or academic study . . . (p. 6).

This has been a rapid tour of the professional education of the military officers. We looked first at the educational base from which academy officers are commissioned, then examined the educational pyramid that is identified with a professional military career.

UNRESOLVED QUESTIONS

There is no universal agreement on just which problems facing professional military education are the paramount ones. Indeed, equally qualified authorities may debate whether a particular problem is a problem at all. The unresolved questions that follow were selected wholly on the basis of their prominence in the literature and their recurrence in the discussions of informed individuals.

The Granting of Degrees

For over 40 years the military has granted academic degrees—at the academies, at the Naval Postgraduate School, at the Air Force Institute of Technology, and, most recently, at the Army Command and General Staff College. As Shelburne, Groves, and Brokaw (1969) have pointed out, it is "a moot point . . . whether military schools should grant degrees (p. 849)." Excepting the academies, proponents of both sides of the issue may be found in both the military and the civilian academic community. The central argument in favor of the issue is that the services offer college-level academic programs that are not offered elsewhere. The arguments against this are either that the programs are not of college caliber or that the academic content is indeed available elsewhere. The degrees granted are authorized by Congress, but the schools that grant them are accredited by civilian agencies (American Council on Education, 1964). Should the military grant degrees? It is possibly a "moot point" overtaken by events.

Military Scholarship

Many of the subjects that concern the student of professional military education are also of vital concern to the nation. The choice of an appropriate international strategy, the function of the services in the American domestic scene, the ethical and moral aspects of weaponry, the impact of (and alternatives to) defense spending—all of these are central concerns, and in none of these is military scholarship noteworthy, much less preeminent (Fleming, 1969; Feld, 1964). As a general recently lamented, "these important fields have been preempted by civilians, and the officers simply do the pick-and-shovel work." Proponents of the scholar-soldier concept envision broad benefits in the application of military expertise to significant issues, as well as greater control by the military over its own destiny. Opponents within the services hold that officers are not, and should not be, recruited primarily for their scholarly characteristics, and outside critics see little advantage in increasing the power of the military. Should military scholars advise the nation's policy-makers? Probably we must wait for another Mahan to don the epaulet.

The All-Volunteer Force

The moral and institutional strength of the armed forces in the volunteer era will depend upon their response to the challenges posed by social ferment, reordering of national priorities, cultural changes in the American society, continued antimilitarism, and pragmatic determination of national interests abroad. One effect of ending the draft has been to eliminate large numbers of highly capable men who would seek officer status in preference to being drafted as enlisted men. Thus smaller in total strength, and perhaps less selective in its officer input, the armed forces must seek greater efficiency in using manpower to maintain combat efficiency. Further, as Shelbourne and Groves (1965) have noted, a continuously expanding economy provides more career opportunities in the civilian community, which increases the difficulty of recruiting qualified personnel for military careers. Clearly, since the military draft was discontinued, the services have been faced with demanding tasks of maintaining viability as a fighting force while evolving solutions to simultaneous social and manpower problems. To accomplish these tasks would seemingly require high levels of professional competence—a goal that becomes more difficult as austere manning makes extended schooling increasingly a luxury. Sorenson (1971) is quite correct in stating, "all the services must earn the attention and respect of all Americans. They must reestablish themselves as purposeful, reliable, educated, and efficient managers of people as well as weapons (p. 50)." These are the challenges to

which the professional military education system must contribute solutions, though faced with the possibility of reduced quality and quantity of input into the officer ranks.

REFERENCES

Air University. *Air University Catalog.* Montgomery, Ala.: U.S. Air Force, 1975.

_____. *History of the Squadron Officer School, 1946-1971.* Maxwell AFB, Ala.: U.S. Air Force, 1971.

American Council on Education. *The Integrity of the Academic Degree: Statements of Policy by The National Commission on Accrediting and The American Council on Education.* Washington: American Council on Education, 1964.

Armed Forces Staff College. Study on Military Training and Education for Officers. Unpublished study, March 1973.

Feld, M. D. Military Self-Image in a Technological Environment. In M. Janowitz, ed., *The New Military.* New York: Norton, 1969.

Fleming, T. J. *West Point.* New York: William Morrow, 1969.

Goode, W. J. Community Within a Community: The Professions. *American Sociological Review,* Vol. 22, April, 1957, pp. 194-200.

Huntington, S. P. Power, Expertise, and the Military Profession. *Daedalus,* Fall 1963, pp. 785-807.

_____. *The Soldier and the State.* New York: Vintage, 1964.

Hurd, R. C. Military Academies: US Naval Academy. In L. C. Deighton, ed., *Encyclopedia of Education.* New York: Macmillan, 1971, Vol. 6, pp. 376-379.

Janowitz, M. *The Professional Soldier.* New York: Free Press, 1960.

_____. The US Forces and the Zero Draft (Adelphi Papers No. 94). London: International Institute for Strategic Studies, 1973.

Just, W. *Military Men.* New York: Alfred A. Knopf, 1970.

Kloke, J. Stepping Stones to the Stars. *Army Digest,* June 1970, pp. 21-25.

Lang, K. Technology and Career Management in the Military Establishment. In M. Janowitz, ed., *The New Military.* New York: Norton, 1969.

Masland, J. W., and Radway, L. I. *Soldiers and Scholars.* Princeton: Princeton University Press, 1957.

Meyerson, D. W. Military Academies: US Military Academy. In L. C. Deighton, ed., *Encyclopedia of Education.* New York: Macmillan, 1971, Vol. 6, pp. 373-376.

Miller, J. W., and Sullivan, E. J., eds. *A Guide to the Evaluation of Educational Experiences in the Armed Forces.* Washington: American Council on Education, Office on Educational Credit, 1974.

Partridge, P. H. *Educating for the Profession of Arms: Comments on Current Thinking and Practice in Britain and the United States.* Canberra: Australian National University Press, 1969.

Patte, C. Who Goes to Senior Service Schools? *Army,* April 1975, pp. 41-48.

Reeves, I. L. *Military Education in the United States.* Burlington: Free Press, 1914.

Shelburne, J. C., and Groves, K. J. *Education in the Armed Forces.* New York: Center for Applied Research in Education, 1965.

_____, and Brokaw, L. D. Military Education. In R. L. Ebel, ed., *Encyclopedia of Educational Research* (4th ed.). New York: Macmillan, 1969, pp. 839-866.

Sorensen, N. G. Implications of a Volunteer Force. *Air University Review,* Vol. 22 (3, March-April 1971), pp. 47-52.

United States Air Force. United States Air Force Officer Professional Military Education System, Air Force Manual 53-1. Washington: US Air Force, January 1975.

United States Air Force Academy. *Air Force Academy 1975-1976 Catalog* (Annual catalog number 20). USAF Academy, Colo.: May 1975.

United States Army. Military Education and Training, Army Manual 351-1. Washington: US Army, August 1971.

United States Coast Guard Academy. *Bulletin of Information, United States Coast Guard Academy, 1975-1976.* New London, Conn.: US Coast Guard Academy, 1975.

United States Military Academy. *United States Military Academy Catalog, 1975-1976.* West Point, N.Y.: US Military Academy, 1975.

United States Naval Academy. *Annapolis: The United States Naval Academy Catalog, 1975-76.* Annapolis, Md.: US Naval Academy, 1975.

67

WOMEN'S STUDIES: COURSES AND PROGRAMS FOR HIGHER EDUCATION

by Lora H. Robinson
Special Assistant to President
Grand Valley State Colleges
Allendale, Michigan

This paper has been previously published as an ERIC/Higher Education Research Current or ERIC/Higher Education Research Report prepared by the George Washington University and published by the American Association for Higher Education, Washington, D.C. (1973).

This publication was prepared pursuant to a contract with the National Institute of Education, U.S. Department of Health, Education and Welfare. Contractors undertaking such projects under government sponsorship are encouraged to express freely their judgment in professional and technical matters. Points of view or opinions do not, therefore, necessarily represent official NIE positions or policy.

OVERVIEW

Women's studies emerged as a field of interest because traditional disciplines either devoted too little attention to women or presented biased and stereotypical notions of women. There are several indices of the impact of women's studies on higher education. They include the number of articles and reports that urge the creation of women's studies courses and programs; the inclusion of women's studies courses and programs in campus affirmative action plans; the number of conferences and workshops on women's studies; the increase in journal space devoted to women's studies; the proliferation of women's studies courses; and the growth of women's studies programs.

Persons starting women's studies programs faced a number of problems. However, their main one centered on finding a means to promote women's studies on campus while, at the same time, not becoming isolated as a women's field or creating an institutional place for women. Programs have tried to solve this dilemma in a number of ways, ranging from refusing to seek official university sanction to the creation of programs with multiple links within the campus community. This variety in program approach led to difficulties in identifying campuses with established women's studies programs. To incorporate as many as possible, campuses were included where activities in women's studies involved more than the offering of women's studies courses. This could mean the existence of a women's studies major or an organizational unit responsible for women's studies. Using this definition, 32 campus women's studies programs were identified.

The main feature of programs is women's studies courses, offered either within a single discipline or with a multidisciplinary[1] approach. The multidisciplinary course is a requirement of the two BA and three MA programs in women's studies.

Teachers report that women's studies courses have attracted large enrollments and changed the attitudes and behavior of students. It is common for students to take two or three more women's studies courses after their first exposure. In fact, on campuses where degrees in women's studies are not offered, students are using alternate routes to specialize in women's studies by designing individualized majors and minors.

Several features of program operation demonstrate an attempt to foster multiple links to the rest of the campus and to the community at large. First, programs utilize minimized hierarchical structures, along with large advisory bodies to insure the participation of a variety of persons, including students, staff, and community women. In addition to their participation in decision-making, students, community women, and faculty also teach courses. Often faculty participate on either a joint-appointment or released-time basis. Second, programs sponsor or promote a number of other activities that clearly are intended to build connections within the institution and to the community beyond. Lecture series, career counseling, and program publications are three examples of activities designed to broaden program impact.

The future of women's studies and women's studies programs is uncertain. However, there are three conditions that may ensure their continuation. There is a need for empirical data on women; for theories to adequately conceptualize both new and old knowledge about women; and to create a balance in the presentation of the sexes in existing bodies of knowledge. As long as these three conditions persist, current programs will probably be continued and new ones will be established.

BACKGROUND OF WOMEN'S STUDIES

Women's studies is primarily a by-product of the Women's Liberation Movement. Groups of women began to examine their status in society, and found many institutions, including colleges and universities, seriously wanting in their treatment of women. One of the ways colleges were found lacking was in the manner intellectual knowledge is taught, studied, and researched.

Feminists who criticize the current status of intellectual knowledge question particularly the status and treatment of women. Their perception is that knowledge, texts, research, and courses have two common failings. Frequently coverage of women is not commensurate with their numbers and actual contributions. Or at times materials on women are stereotypic and/or biased against women.

Lack of attention to women, feminists assert, results from a viewpoint that takes male supremacy for granted; consequently, books and courses focus heavily on men's actions, organizations, theories, perceptions, ideas, and concepts. To support their case, feminists marshal evidence that half the human race is either omitted with forethought, omitted unintentionally, given footnote status only, treated as an appendage or exception, or presumed to be included when the content really deals with men only: ". . . one soon realizes that when the author talks about 'man,' he means male (Freeman, 1971, p. 474)."

Textbook studies have been used to support the notion of women's invisibility and appendage status.

> . . . in one study of the 27 leading textbooks used in college level American history courses, women were virtually absent: no book devoted more than 2% of its pages to women; one had only 5/100 of 1% of its pages devoted to women. In many books Harriet Beecher Stowe and Eleanor Roosevelt are not even mentioned. (Sandler, 1971, p. 6)

> Major books have been written on such relevant topics as the occupational structure, in which whole sections are devoted to "minority groups," but only a footnote to women (one third of the labor force). (Freeman, 1971, p. 474)

Textbooks are not the only medium where the absence of references to women is commonplace. Women's studies advocates have been asking why women writers are not included in literature course syllabi, why noteworthy women aren't covered in history courses, why we don't learn about the special treatment of women under the law, and so on. So the absence of women has been questioned across most of the scholarly disciplines.

A related criticism focuses not on women's omission or minor treatment, but the fact that a male norm has been adopted to which women are the exception. The study of achievement motivation is one frequently cited example where women were considered an exception to the norm, i.e., their behavior did not fit the theoretical model. Yet the model was neither modified to fit both sexes, nor has been fully developed to account for women alone.

> Some years ago, for example, the subject of achievement motivation was considered closed by psychologists. They had done their studies, and written up their conclusions. It didn't seem to matter, at the time, that their results in no way explained atypical patterns shown by women on their tests. It was considered not just sufficient but conclusive to have successfully dealt with male achievement motivation. Matina Horner, a psychologist and Radcliffe's new president, has reopened the subject, is doing extensive and imaginative research on achievement motivation in women, and her work is profoundly disturbing. (Benson, 1972, p. 285)

That this issue is still current is illustrated by a recent copy of *Behavior Today,* in which Aletha Stein is cited as questioning traditional notions of achievement. She suggests that they are loaded against women.

> Since achievement is usually correlated with traditionally masculine personality characteristics—competitiveness and independence—women's lack of these characteristics has led to the conclusion that they are not motivated to achieve. . . . Stein suggested that women often translate achievement motivation into the context of feminine interests and activities culturally and socially prescribed as "feminine domains." ("To Be or Not to Be," 1973, p. 1)

Those observing biases in the treatment of the sexes feel that there is a great need to achieve a more balanced view. However, since women's status now is usually inferior or subordinate to men, they feel remedial efforts should focus primarily on women.

Feminists try to upgrade the status of women in modern knowledge in a number of ways. One common approach is to reorient the material on a familiar topic in college courses. Benson (1972) provides an example of the feminist perspective applied to the study of novelist Jane Austen:

> Jane Austen is usually taught as a "lady novelist," a novelist of manners, even of an economic phenomenon in that she records the rise of a new class in her society. In a different kind of course, we also look at how Austen portrays the female experience in her novels, we look at her heroines' consciousness of themselves as women in an environment she perceived as less open to women than to men. (p. 284)

Another approach is to develop new tools of analysis, especially for the study of women within a particular field. Lerner (1969) is a good example of an attempt to arrive at a new framework for the analysis of women in American history. Similar efforts are underway in other disciplines.

A third approach commonly employed is the reexamination of major theoretical works. A work frequently cited in this category is Freud's theory of sexuality. Recently, Gilman (1971) analyzes the feminist view of Freud's work. He states:

> . . . as I read on through the feminist critique . . . and, more decisive than that, went back to Freud's own writings, the evidence of his radical bias against women and the existence of that bias in the very texture of psychoanalysis came to seem indisputable. . . . The astonishing thing, which had only rarely been pointed out until the feminists began waving their arms at it, is that Freud's entire theory of sexuality is built from a masculine model. In psychoanalysis, maleness is the norm and femaleness an incomplete or, even worse, deficient aspect of it. (pp. 10-11)

In addition to the approaches cited above, feminists hold that ideas and philosophy should be intellectually compatible with actions. This link between attitudes and actions has led to the rejection of the traditional notion of a separation between the academic and the political and social world. This rationale is reflected in contemporary definitions of women's studies:

The major goal of women's studies courses and programs to-day is the fostering of intellectual and personal autonomy in women. (Sicherman, 1972, p. 85)

... women's studies reexamines the traditional disciplines—psychology, literature, history, economics, and so on. (Benson, 1972, pp. 283-284)

Women's Studies is a political and academic endeavor, and the two are inseparable. The courses should seek to awaken women to the realities of American society as well as to the reasons for their secondary status. (Salper, 1971a, p. 5)

... the purpose of the Women's Studies Program is to examine all aspects of the lives of women and men in contemporary society, in order to develop a comprehensive understanding of the nature and potential of women and men, and to encourage the fuller development and utilization of their talents. ("Women's Studies Program," 1972, p. 1)

And this is what women's studies really amounts to: analysis of the role of women (past and present) for the purpose of contemporary and future change. ("Women's Studies at Towson," 1972, p. 2)

Female Studies is the intellectual examination of the absence of women from history; the fresh look in a non-Freudian way at the social psychology of women; the study of women in literature and the images of women in the Arts; [and] the economic and legal history of the family. . . . (Tobias, 1970c, p. 1)

The definitions above indicate a deliberate linking of an intellectual outlook to women's lives.

In summary, the field of women's studies can be defined by three types of activities. First, women's studies means learning more about women, and bringing this knowledge to the classroom or publishing it in scholarly journals. Second, work is being done to develop new ways of analyzing, approaching, and arranging both new and old bodies of knowledge from a feminist perspective. The development of a feminist theoretical orientation, however, is still in the preliminary stages. Third, women's studies proponents are sharing their work with men and women students in the hope of fostering changes in their attitudes and behaviors.

Women's Studies Gains Visibility in Higher Education

For years some academics have written about or considered women's thoughts and experiences in their work. For example, Lloyd Miller, Professor of the History of Art at Towson State College,

... was convinced many years ago . . . of the importance of the contributions of women in the arts, indeed of their leadership in originality and influence, and has been gathering materials and doing research in this area. (Coulter and Hedges, 1972, p. 5)

Similarly, Annette Baxter, Professor of History at Barnard, chose "women" as the topic for an American History colloquium in 1966, before the Women's Liberation Movement had brought the need for women's studies into national prominence. Now there are a number of indications that there is support for women's studies in higher education. First, there are a number of journal articles that urge that women's studies courses and programs be created on

campus (Alexander, 1970; Cohen, 1971; Husbands, 1971; Newman, 1971; Oltman, 1972; Sandler, 1972; Tobias, 1970c; Trecker, 1971; and Trow, 1972).

Second, committees charged with investigating the status of women on campus have felt there was a need for women's studies on their campus. As a result, their reports often include the recommendation that women's studies courses and/or programs be started on campus. This was true of the Steering Committee of the Association of Faculty Women at the University of Wisconsin (Madison and Extension). Their proposal to the administration contains an outline of a proposed women's studies program as one of its fourteen sections ("An Affirmative Action Program . . .," 1972, pp. 33-36).

Third, different types of meetings in the past two or three years have reflected increased interest in women's studies. A number of conferences, institutes, and workshops on women's studies have been organized in different parts of the country.[2] In addition, a number of professional associations, such as the American Historical Association, the National Council on Family Relations, The American Sociological Association, the American Psychological Association, and the Modern Language Association, have devoted significant portions of time to the subject at annual meetings.

Fourth, more journal space has been devoted to topics in women's studies. This is evident in scholarly journals in the traditional disciplines that have increased markedly the number of pages devoted to women. Also, five new journals have been started that focus specifically on the topic: *Women's Studies; Feminist Studies; Journal of the International Institute of Women's Studies; Women's Studies Abstracts;* and a *Women's Studies Newsletter.*[3]

Fifth, there has been a proliferation of women's studies courses on campuses across the country. Even though the estimates of the numbers of courses vary widely, there is no doubt of their phenomenal increase. The fall 1972 issue of the *Women's Studies Newsletter* announced a recent counting of upwards of 1,000 courses in women's studies (Howe, 1972b). This number is remarkable, when one considers that there were essentially none prior to 1969.

Courses evolved naturally from the awakening of interest in women's studies. On campus, informal groups of women, both students and faculty, shared their experiences and talked about women's status. Reading lists, reprints of articles and papers, and position papers circulated freely. Subsequently, similar activities began to appear in slightly more formal places such as "free universities," experimental colleges, and other locations where study could be introduced quickly and with few constraints.

Concurrently, those mechanisms that facilitated the introduction of women's studies courses on campus were quickly utilized. Courses appeared in noncredit programs, continuing education programs, and extension programs. Some instructors changed the content of an existing course; others added major portions dealing with women. In some cases, courses were offered under a form that allowed the topic focus to vary, such as independent study or readings or the "pro-seminar." And in many cases, courses were shepherded through channels to become regular parts of the college curriculum.

The mushrooming of courses in the short space of three years simply reflects the acknowledgement of the real need for women's studies as urged by the Women's Liberation Movement and others. As Howe (1972a) points out, the net results have far outstripped what any organized effort to foster women's studies could have done.

Sixth, and finally, women's studies programs have been established at a number of colleges and universities. Like courses in women's studies, programs have rapidly increased in number. In 1970, there were two programs, San Diego (California State University) and Cornell University; in December 1971, case studies of several women's studies programs covering 20 educational institutions appeared in *Female Studies III* (Howe and Ahlum, 1971). By the fall of 1972, Howe (1972b) announced that the Clearinghouse on Women's Studies had information on 46 programs.

The emergence of women's studies courses was the real beginning of women's studies programs. There was no case where a program preceded courses in women's studies. In an oversimplified way, the introduction of women's studies courses led to interest in their coordination and promulgation. A mechanism was needed to recruit faculty to teach women's studies, to develop new women's studies courses, or a formal sequence of courses in the curriculum, and to generally promote women's studies throughout the institution.

Women's studies programs have had to struggle for acceptance and support in the educational community. Groups attempting to start programs have faced many hurdles, including, in some instances, open hostility. Freeman (1971) points out that despite the precedent of area and cultural studies:

> . . . both black studies and women's studies programs have been treated with controversy and scepticism [sic] as illegitimate ways of structuring knowledge; which leads one to the feeling that perhaps it is the illegitimacy of the groups proposing them—rather than the programs—which generates the hostility. (p. 475)

In the same vein, Benson (1972) notes that the definition of "legitimacy" is itself political, and is used as "a strategy to keep the in-people in, and the out-people out (p. 283)." However, despite the problems, within Astin and Parelman's (1973) sample of programs, there was consensus among respondents that, in their case, approval came relatively quickly and easily.

On the basis of the evidence outlined above, one might conclude that women's studies as a feature in higher education has gained a substantial foothold and deserves a closer look. The purpose of this paper is to create an understanding of women's studies programs in higher education through a description of their development and basic features. First, some of the problems faced by those attempting to institute programs is reviewed. This is followed by a short section on the identification of existing programs. The programs reviewed for this paper are listed in the following section. Finally, several brief case studies illustrate the variety of ways programs begin.

The remainder of the paper is devoted to basic program features—women's studies courses, and program organization and activities. Programs have created multiple links to the rest of the institution and the community through their organizational structure, personnel utilization, and extracurricular activities. Examples from each of these areas are cited to illustrate the network effect created by women's studies programs.

DEVELOPMENT OF WOMEN'S STUDIES PROGRAMS

A number of complex issues have faced those creating women's studies programs. Most of the problems center on determining whether there should be a separate niche for women's studies programs and, if so, what kind of a niche it should be. The basic conflict revolves around the fact that there are almost as many compelling reasons for not establishing identifiable programs, and especially departments, as there are for it.

One of the most fundamental disagreements arises from varying views of women's studies. There are women's studies advocates who recognize the need for fuller coverage of women in the academic disciplines, but claim that women do not have a separate history, society, or culture. They view women's studies, therefore, as most properly only a special interest topic within the traditional disciplines, and are against moves to separate out the study of women.

On the other hand, others in women's studies feel that there is enough uniqueness to women's experiences to justify the separate study of women. Freeman (1971) points out "that women, as a group, have a different relationship to society than men, as a group, and thus have a different set of experiences and a different perspective (p. 475)." It is this perspective that proponents feel needs to be researched, written about, and added to the intellectual realm. Further, they see no reason to expect men-in-general or male-dominated departments to take on the task of researching and incorporating this new knowledge. Consequently, many express the need for an institutional base for building a cohesive body of feminists who will tackle the work, and who have the control needed for self-determination.

Even those who argue for the separation of women's studies recognize the problems that can beset a department or program that strikes out on its own. Freeman (1971) notes that once before there was a women's movement organized to meet the needs of women. The departments of women's studies created to meet these demands were called home economics. The result was a denigration of academic content, the segregation of knowledge into female fields, and an institutional place to put women.

While there is some concern about the efficacy of establishing women's studies programs and departments, persons expressing reticence are definitely in the minority in the literature on women's studies. The creation of so many programs in such a short space of time, plus the number of places where additional programs are on the drawing board, seem to indicate that many persons believe arguments for a program are more compelling than any arguments against.

Proponents of the programs, however, are aware of

the dangers in establishing separate academic units. So those sponsoring programs are very concerned about designing a format that will both meet women's needs and, if possible, at the same time not result in isolation. Their goal has been to create an organization for legitimacy and advocacy that simultaneously is inextricably entwined with the regular, day-to-day functioning of the institution. The result has been the creation of programs whose organizational structure and activities result in a network of multiple links to the rest of the college.

Some programs have taken a roundabout way of avoiding the problems, beset by units academically sanctioned. In these cases, e.g., Portland State University, the programs have been organized and sustained by groups of students, faculty, and community persons with an interest in women's studies. These ad hoc programs rely heavily on the volunteer efforts of those involved. Although the utilization of volunteer workers creates its own difficulties, those in the program feel that their independence gives them needed latitude in formulating the direction of the program. The emergence of these strong ad hoc activities in women's studies, that do not fit the traditional academic mold, can be labeled programs only under a broader conception of the term than usually used.

Identifying Programs on Campus

During the preliminary stages of this study, it became apparent that there would be difficulties in identifying those campuses with bona fide women's studies programs. There are so many activities related to women and women's studies happening on campuses across the country that sometimes it is hard to determine when these activities have achieved program status. For the purposes of this paper, institutions were not included that simply offered courses in women's studies, or where ideas for programs or majors and minors in women's studies were at an incipient stage. However, the criteria were not rigid; basically, programs were included if they indicated the commitment of significant institutional or human resources (including volunteer work), the existence of an organizational structure, or some indication of the "legitimization" of women's studies on campus, such as the availability of a major or minor in women's studies. In addition, only programs linked in some way to recognized institutions of higher education were included.

These broad guidelines were utilized to identify campuses with women's studies programs. Campuses with programs were asked to describe them and to share any written materials about it. The list of campuses where women's studies programs have been identified, as of December 1972, appears below.

Women's Studies Programs

Alverno College (Wisconsin)
Barnard College (New York)
Berkeley (University of California)
Buffalo (State University of New York)
Cambridge-Goddard Graduate School for Social Change (Massachusetts)
Cornell University (New York)
Douglass College of Rutgers University (New Jersey)
Five-College Women's Studies Committee (Amherst, Hampshire,

Mount Holyoke, and Smith Colleges, and the University of Massachusetts)
Fresno (California State University)
George Washington University (District of Columbia)
Goddard College (Vermont)
Governors State University (Illinois)
Laney Community College (California)
Long Beach (California State University)
Mundelein College (Illinois)
Northeastern Illinois University
Old Westbury (State University of New York)
University of Pennsylvania
University of Pittsburgh
Portland State University
Richmond College (City University of New York)
Rockland Center of the Rogger Williams College "University Without Walls" (New York)
Sacramento (California State University)
San Diego (California State University)
San Francisco (California State University)
San Jose (California State University)
Sarah Lawrence College (New York)
Sonoma State College (California)
University of South Carolina
University of South Florida
Towson State College (Maryland)
University of Washington

On the whole, programs are an East Coast phenomenon. Seventeen of the 32 programs are in eastern seaboard states. Four are in the midwest and 11 are in the far west. Howe (1972a) notes that the geographic dispersion of programs parallels closely the spread of the Women's Liberation Movement, lending further credence to the notion of a link between the Movement and academia.

At this point, there is very little published information available on existing programs. *Female Studies III* (Howe and Ahlum, 1971) contains brief individual case studies for 16 of the above programs. One research study of 18 women's studies programs has been completed but has not been published yet (Astin and Parelman, 1973). Two other surveys on women's studies in general have some material relevant to programs in particular. The first survey (Foxley, 1972) sent questionnaires to 500 colleges and universities. As of now only a brief summary of the data collected is available. The second survey does not review existing programs; instead individuals interested in women's studies were asked to discuss arguments for and against programs, to analyze types of program structures, and to relate personal experiences with women's studies programs, courses, research, and the development of women's studies in their discipline (*A Descriptive Analysis . . .,* 1972).

There is also a lack of information from the programs themselves. Few programs have prepared lengthy descriptions of their history and development. Materials about specific programs are scarce, and many times have been developed for purposes other than presenting an historical picture. Therefore, information about programs must be gleaned from bits and pieces of information found in widely scattered sources. The information available right now suffers from both a lack of comparable data across programs and a lack of extensive descriptive materials for each. In light of the current status of knowledge about programs, generalizations about them can only be tentative at this time.

Part of the reason very little is known about programs is, of course, their very newness. The first fully recognized women's studies program on campus was established in the fall of 1970 at San Diego (California State University). Many programs have existed for a year or less; as such, women's studies programs are still in the introductory stage.

So far only general comments have been made about the background of women's studies programs. For better understanding, it would be valuable to present details about the development of all 32 programs, but there is neither sufficient data available nor adequate space for such coverage here. However, a brief synopsis of the development of a few programs will be given. The ones discussed were chosen to illustrate the diversity among programs.

Examples of Program Development

Five-College Committee on Women's Studies

Women in the Northampton area of Massachusetts saw a need for interinstitutional sharing of information on women's studies. After several meetings, they proposed the Five-College Committee on Women's Studies to be comprised of representatives from each of the five institutions: Amherst, Hampshire, Mount Holyoke, and Smith Colleges, and the University of Massachusetts. Their proposal outlines the general goals and specific activities to be undertaken by the Committee. It also spells out the reasons for convening the Committee:

> The committee has been formed because people teaching courses on women [felt] a need to get together and talk on a regular basis; to exchange information about speakers, faculty members, bibliographic and other materials for teaching and research; and to collect and make available information for people who would like to become more familiar with the history and present status of women. To facilitate information-sharing and efficient use of resources, we felt that at least one readily identifiable person should be available at each institution and should maintain contacts with counterparts at other institutions. ("Description and Proposed Activities," 1971, p. 2)

Since its formation, the Committee has continued to carry out many of its general goals and proposed activities. Most recently, the Committee sponsored a faculty seminar on "Women and the Curriculum," in which members explored the use of the generic term "man" and values implicit in its use; attitudes toward women in the disciplines that limit the understanding of human experience; and ideas for improving the liberal arts experience for men and women students.

University of Pennsylvania

A unified group of women have worked hard and long for a women's studies department at Pennsylvania. The working group, comprised of students and faculty at the University, is called the Penn Women's Studies Planners. In April 1972, they submitted a proposal for a Department of Women's Studies to the president. The proposal is quite comprehensive, covering: Purposes and Goals; Women's Studies within the University Structure; Academic Personnel for 1972-73; Governance of the Department of Women's Studies; Administration of the Department; Curriculum; Research and Graduate Concerns; Development for the Department; Library Facilities and Materials; and Outside Funding ("Proposal for a Department . . .," 1972). At that time, the president requested a more thorough report on the development of women's studies. During the summer of 1972, the group designed and implemented a project to obtain the information needed. A questionnaire was developed and sent to 1,000 persons who had demonstrated some interest in women's studies. The questionnaire attempts to determine experiences in women's studies and reactions to developments in women's studies. Sample items include:

> What do you think are the major arguments for or against programs focusing on the study of women?

> In what ways has your commitment to women's studies changed your professional or personal lifestyle?

> Can you give us a brief summary of the state of knowledge in the subspecialty on women in your discipline?

> Have students assisted you in your research?

> If you have taught a course in women's studies, did you notice any difference in response by women students to this course as compared to more traditional courses you have taught? (*A Descriptive Analysis . . .*, 1972, Appendix B)

The 100-page report of the responses to the questionnaire is now ready for use by those designing a more detailed plan for a women's studies department. Until the approval of a formal department or a program, 12 courses in women's studies have been introduced into the College of Thematic Studies for the spring of 1973.

Cornell University

As a result of issues raised at a 1969 Cornell Conference on Women, a number of persons became particularly interested in the curriculum. They developed the first multidisciplinary college course on women, entitled "Evolution of the Female Personality: History and Prospects." The student response to the course was so great that plans began for a program. A one-day conference was held to explore the future of female studies at Cornell and other campuses in the area. Needed areas of research were identified, and an ad hoc Female Studies Committee sought funds to sponsor research and develop new courses. Funds were received from various sources within the University to operate an experimental Female Studies Program starting in September 1970. Sustained interest on campus led to the formal approval of Cornell's Women's Studies Program in May 1972. The program was accepted by a majority of the faculty of the College of Arts and

Sciences, and as such is a fully-accredited academic program. In general, the Faculty Board and Director, who are responsible for the program, continue efforts to expand the teaching about women, research on women, and promotion of public service activities for and about women.

San Diego (California State University) and Others

Quite a few women's studies programs have gained official recognition and approval on their campus through the "committee route," as did the Cornell program above. The first program to receive official sanction on a campus was San Diego (California State University). The struggle to establish a women's studies program there is one of the best documented (See Salper, 1971a and 1971b). A mixed pressure group of staff, students, faculty, and several community women worked for months to establish the nation's first autonomous program. The fall of 1969 was spent organizing an informal spring program in women's studies. It consisted of five already existing courses, with the contents changed to "emphasize the role, status, identity and potential of women ("Fall Women's Studies Program," 1970, p. 1)." Next, a group of 20 women, working as a committee, drafted a proposal for a Center for Women, one component of which would focus on women's studies. The Center for Women never became a reality on campus; however, a women's studies program, including allotted teaching staff, was started and is still in existence.

Fresno (California State University)

Fresno had a few courses in women's studies in the Experimental College and the English department before an administrator and a faculty member developed a proposal for a multidisciplinary program. The program was approved at Fresno without opposition in 1971 and began operation in the fall of 1972. Other campuses where the committee route was utilized successfully include: Buffalo (State University of New York); George Washington University; University of Pittsburgh; Richmond College (City University of New York); and the University of Washington. The proportion of programs that rely almost entirely on ad hoc groups and organizations for sustenance has diminished significantly, as an ever-increasing number of programs are receiving institutional approval and support.

WOMEN'S STUDIES COURSES

Women's studies courses are the foundation of women's studies programs. Course offerings in the area have drawn large numbers of students, and feminists report the desire on the part of students for second and third courses after an initial course in women's studies. Burgeoning interest created an overnight need for complete listings of the courses offered within and across institutions. For example, one of the first goals of the Five-College Women's Studies Committee was to oversee the routine preparation of a list of the women's studies courses being offered at colleges in the Northampton area.

The task of creating pamphlets or leaflets of course offerings to be distributed to those interested in women's studies set the stage for programs on many campuses. This chapter will review the types of women's studies courses offered, examples of program offerings, types of women's studies degrees, and student response to women's studies courses.

Single and Multidisciplinary Courses

Quite a few types of courses have appeared on course listings of women's studies. There is as yet no consensus as to which courses properly belong to the field. For example, those compiling lists of courses have included ones which serve women's needs, such as self-defense; ones which are about traditional women's interests, such as child care; ones in which women are an integral part of the topic, such as sex roles and family; and ones which are about women only, such as feminism and the Women's Liberation Movement. The main intent of those compiling the lists seems to be to include all courses that are for or about women.

There are few visible attempts to specify courses that should be listed as women's studies. The Five-College Committee on Women's Studies did develop six categories of women's studies courses. They include:

Those dealing primarily or exclusively with women and taught under the auspices of a particular department by a person trained in a specific discipline.

Interdisciplinary approaches to the subject of women, usually taught collectively by a number of people representing various fields of study.

Courses which deal with sex roles or male-female reactions in general, such as Sociology 391, "Sex and Sex Roles in Changing Society."

Courses on the Women's Movement.

Discipline or field courses . . . which [have] a unit on [women].

Discipline courses which ordinarily are assumed to deal primarily with women, such as "Marriage and the Family." ("Description and Proposed Activities," 1971, p. 1)

These categories indicate an attempt to create a comprehensive list of women's studies courses. However, courses in these categories may or may not actually be in the field of women's studies, as defined in this paper and by others in the field. For example, courses in home economics and sociology, which would be included using these categories, have been cited by some feminists as perpetuating stereotypic notions of women.

The crucial factor is not the title or the type of course, but the actual course approach. The distinguishing feature of a women's studies course, whether covering old or new material, is whether or not the course takes a feminist perspective. Marilyn Salzman-Webb points out the distinction between content coverage and approach when analyzing the field of women's studies:

This is to say I don't particularly feel any body of knowledge is more or less relevant to feminist curricula, but it is how we look at that knowledge, what questions we ask of it, and how it is useful for an understanding of our own struggle that makes it relevant or not. (Siporin, 1972, p. 69)

Therefore, courses in home economics and other disciplines may or may not adopt a feminist perspective. (For a description of a feminist course taught in a department of home economics, see Tobias and Kusnetz, 1972.) Further, as long as women's studies course lists are compiled primarily from course titles, this distinction will continue to be blurred. Some typical course titles which have appeared on women's studies lists include:

Women and Communism: The Chinese Experience – Cornell University

The Educated Woman in Literature – Douglass College of Rutgers University

Judeo-Christian Tradition and Historical Perceptions of the Role of Women – Smith College

Image of Women in Western Civilization – University of South Florida

Women and Social Welfare – Fresno (California State University)

La Raza Women's Seminar – San Francisco (California State University)

Psychology of Women – San Jose (California State University)

The Sportswoman in American Society – Towson State College

Language of Sexism – University of Washington

Women and the Movies – Wesleyan University

The substantial number of women's studies courses offered in regular college and University departments has provided a solid foundation for program offerings. From their inception, the majority of women's studies courses have been in the humanities ("Women in Literature since 1900"; "Feminism in Modern French Literature"; "The Idea of Women in Philosophy"; and "Linguistic Behavior of Male and Female") and social sciences ("Position of Women in the Middle Ages"; "Sociology of Women"; "Role of Women in Modern Economic Life"; "Psychology of Women"; and "Cross-Cultural Perspectives of Women"), fields where the most women teachers are found traditionally. In the 1970-1971 academic year, Astin and Parelman (1973) found that 75 percent of the women's studies courses offered could be classified in either the humanities or social sciences. With time, a number of courses have emerged in the arts, sciences, and professions.

The single disciplinary course offering reflects one view of women's studies as a subspecialty or special interest area within an existing discipline. The fact that women's studies teachers have been trained in their own professional field, to which an interest in women has been added, reinforces this perception. Programs depend on faculty in the regular departments to develop and add

women's studies courses to their offerings, and actively promote an interest in women's studies throughout the institution. Since few programs have been allocated faculty slots of their own (partly due to the current financial stringencies in higher education), freeing up one of a faculty member's courses for women's studies has been the most feasible method of increasing course offerings.

In addition to the single disciplinary course, programs promote a wider perspective through multidisciplinary courses. This type was especially characteristic of the first women's studies courses that were comprehensive, introductory, or issue oriented. Issues such as abortion, divorce laws, sexual attitudes, sex roles, child care, and child rearing required examination from more than one perspective. An example of such a course is "Contemporary Women in the United States" (University of South Florida):

Economic, political and social considerations of woman's role in modern society. Changing life-styles and family patterns. Generational differences among today's women. Effects of the media in shaping attitudes, self-concept, and expectations of men and women in our society. ("Women's Studies Program: Curriculum Proposal," 1972, p. 6)

Multidisciplinary courses continue to remain a staple in women's studies programs.

In some cases, multiple perspectives are provided by one instructor. Tobias (1972) describes her experience of teaching a women's studies course in which she touched six different disciplines: sociology, literature, economics, law, history, and psychology:

I found myself often in the course of a single sentence touching on a number of disciplines. More than that, I was teaching the tools of the several fields—statistics, literary exegesis, macroeconomics. I am no genius. It is merely that one masters what one needs to make sense of the material, and in three years I have mastered large parts of quite a number of fields. (p. 261)

Other times, a multiple perspective is introduced through the use of team or group teaching. For example, 27 women faculty members from 20 departments and 24 disciplines took part in the University of Wisconsin's first women's studies course. Participation took the form of a guest lecture. There are also numerous instances where groups of teachers were present at and responsible for the entire course (e.g., see Cless, 1971). Under this condition, those responsible for the course work together to plan course content, requirements, and conduct.

Since multidisciplinary courses are a standard feature of women's studies programs, there has been some concern about its effectiveness as a technique. Teachers note that it is very hard to create a good multidisciplinary course because of overlapping content and difficulties in integrating materials. Work is being planned at Towson State College that would evaluate introductory, multidisciplinary core courses in women's studies for their effectiveness:

We would wish to determine how effectively the disciplines have been integrated in the presentation of the subject matter in each course and whether there has been any real advantage in bringing several disciplines together. We would hope that insights can be achieved through well integrated interdisciplinary work that would not otherwise be possible, but our evaluation would necessarily have to determine if this indeed is happening, and if so, how and to what extent. (Coulter and Hedges, 1972, p. 7)

Since multidisciplinary courses are such an important feature of women's studies programs (they are even required in the degree programs), research work like Towson's will make a significant contribution to the field of women's studies.

Examples of Program Offerings

At times it is difficult to tell the credit from the noncredit courses. Usually the program lists cover all institutional offerings in women's studies of which some may be extension or reduced credit courses. Similarly, such a comprehensive list blurs the distinction between courses that are actually departmental, but cross-listed with women's studies, and those that are offered by the program only. On the whole, it seems safe to assume that most of the courses have been prompted by the program, but few operate from program funds entirely.

San Jose (California State University)

For the fall 1972, the San Jose schedule of classes lists 18 courses under the women's studies umbrella. All have departmental numbers; for example, English 196A—"The Heroine of the American Novel" and Speech-Communication 196A—"The Rhetoric of Feminism." Seven were developed by the women's studies program and approved as departmental offerings.

Cornell University

During the fall 1972 term, the Cornell program offered four women's studies courses. Women's Studies 282—"The Social Psychology of Women"—was cross-listed for credit under sociology and psychology. "Studies in Fiction: Heroes and Heroines" was listed also under English; "Women and Communism: The Chinese Experience" under government. Only "Feminist Art" had no other departmental classification indicated.

Buffalo (State University of New York)

The Women's Studies College at Buffalo is in its sixth semester and second year of existence. Each semester between 20 and 30 courses are offered, enrolling up to 500 students. Three types of courses are offered in the program: those which combine study of the position of women with field work; those which develop a theoretical analysis of women's oppression; and those which teach skills which are critical for women ("Women's Studies College," 1972, p. 15).

Some of the courses are designed for the College, while others are cross-listed with separate departments. Courses include: "Philosophy of Human Nature: A Feminist Perspective on Philosophy"; "Marxism and Women's Liberation"; "Women's Automotive Course";

"The Political Economy of Women's Liberation"; "Theories of Feminism"; and "Women, Careers, and Advising." In all, 28 courses are mentioned in the spring 1973 catalog.

University of Washington

Most programs offer both strictly disciplinary and multidisciplinary courses. To illustrate this, both course titles and descriptions are included from a Washington program listing. The abbreviation GIS refers to those courses which are offered under General and Interdisciplinary Studies, a department in the Undergraduate Studies of the College of Arts and Sciences. Thus, all the courses are departmental offerings.

GIS 256. *Introduction to Women Studies:* An interdisciplinary course introducing women studies through lectures, readings, and discussions, drawing from the following fields: art history, economics, history, law, literature, psychology.

GIS 353. *Women in Cross-Cultural Perspective:* An anthropological study of socio-cultural roles of women in selected societies, including the United States: an analysis of women's strategies, resources, and limitations, with emphasis upon the physiological parameters, development of personality, position in kinship, economic and political organizations, religion, expressive culture, and social change.

GIS 355. *Women and the Law:* A general introduction to the legal process with focus on the present status of women and the law: the legal status of single vs. married women, and the legal disabilities that both suffer under present laws; the rationale for protective legislation, and the present status of such legislation in light of Title VII of the Civil Rights Act of 1964 and the proposed Equal Rights Amendment. The course will also examine the civil rights legislation and the Equal Rights Amendment generally, and will explore the potential of their impact on present sex discrimination practices. A significant portion of the course will be devoted to a study of the current litigation on such topics as abortion, education, child care, tax laws, Social Security benefits, etc.

GIS 430. *Problems and Topics in Women Studies:* Independent study in some area of women studies, supervised by a faculty member with appropriate academic interests.

English 431. *English Literature since 1930.*

English 499 H.B. *Problems of Women in 19th Century English Literature.*

Sociology 482. *Issues in Analytic Sociology—Sex Roles in Contemporary Society:* Male, female sex roles according to both sociological and psychological perspectives, with particular reference to role theory and stratification theory. Emphasis on power in relationships. ("Women Studies: College of Arts . . .," 1972, pp. 1-2)

The seven courses comprise the program's first-quarter offerings for 1972.

Degree Programs

Richmond College (City University of New York) and the University of Washington offer bachelor's degrees in women's studies. At Richmond, women's studies is a major within the social science division. At Washington, students earn a Bachelor of Arts in General Studies. In both programs, multidisciplinary courses or field work are integral features of the course of study. For example, at the University of Washington, requirements for a women's studies major include:

One core course in Women Studies which presents an overall view of the field.

35 credits in a single department offering courses relevant to Women Studies.

At least four upper-division Women Studies courses designated as such on the curriculum list.

A senior thesis on some aspect of Women Studies.

In addition to the requirements for a major, all students must fulfill the University and College of Arts and Sciences requirements for total credits and distribution. ("Women Studies Major," 1972, p. 1)

The course that fulfills the first requirement, "Introduction to Women Studies," is multidisciplinary in nature; it introduces the study of women using the fields of art history, economics, history, law, literature, and psychology.

There are also three graduate programs in women's studies. Sarah Lawrence College offers an individualized master's program in women's history. Candidates are expected to take three year-long, 10-credit courses of graduate work and submit a thesis. In addition to history courses, and women-in-history courses, candidates are expected to do individual work in fields of study such as literature, anthropology, economics, and psychology related to some aspect of women's history.

The Cambridge-Goddard Graduate School for Social Change, a program of Goddard College, offers a master's degree in women's studies. The School is an experimental program in graduate education designed for people interested in combining research and social action. Student-faculty collectives are formed around mutual interests. The group is responsible for developing their own study plan and degree requirements. Once a plan or set of activities is formulated, it becomes the group's work for the academic year. Five possible topics were offered for the 1972-1973 academic year in the Feminist Studies Program: family, socialization, sexuality, work, and forms of female expression.

The George Washington University recently approved a graduate degree in women's studies. Students in the field of women's studies earn a Master of Arts in Special Studies, awarded by the University's Graduate School of Arts and Sciences. Requirements of the program include two core courses in women's studies that are multidisciplinary. The first course will be conducted by five women professors, plus three guest lecturers in the spring of 1973. The rest of the students' courses will be selected from other University offerings with the consultation of an academic advisor.

Even if the program does not offer a degree, at many institutions students can specialize in women's studies. On many campuses across the country students can earn their BA degree through self-designed majors with special emphasis in areas of their own choice. For example, at the University of Minnesota there are four ways a student can earn a BA with special emphasis in women's studies: (1) Through the Experimental College, in which each student designs his or her own undergraduate education; (2) through the University College, in which a student may design his or her own major, drawing from all the colleges; (3) interdepartmentally within the College of Liberal Arts, by selecting from programs in the College; (4) and through a special Bachelor of Electives Studies program, in which 100 students participate each year.

At Berkeley (University of California), the Center for the Continuing Education for Women is drawing up sample majors in women's studies, to be used by students taking advantage of the individualized major. If these model plans receive formal approval, students wishing to concentrate in women's studies may adopt them, thereby eliminating the need to be cleared on a case-by-case basis. At San Francisco (California State University), a similar arrangement has been made under the Inter-disciplinary Studies in Social Sciences degree program. The major that crosses disciplinary boundaries in the social and behavioral sciences consists of 12 units of required courses and at least 24 units of electives centered around a theme. Several clusters of electives are suggested for those students who wish a major with a focus on women. In situations such as these, it is understandable why there might be less concern about establishing a recognized major or degree in women's studies. However, proposals for majors and minors in women's studies are currently being considered at many institutions.

Student Response

Women's studies courses have been attracting large numbers of students. In the spring of 1970, when a team of teachers introduced The Evolution of Female Personality at Cornell University, the course attracted 204 undergraduates and about 150 auditors (Tobias, 1970b). This phenomenon is not unique. Similar occurrences are reported at other institutions starting women's studies courses.

The student composition has run from all female to all male (Showalter and Ohmann, 1971). In 1971, White et al., estimated that one in ten students was male. A national survey done by Astin and Parelman (1973) and one done by Foxley (1972) also found the enrollment rate of male students to be about ten percent. Although classes have not been closed to males, in a few instances class procedures have been designed to minimize traditional sex role behavior. One common device is the creation of sex-segregated discussion groups.

One institution, the University of Washington, asked students why they were taking women's studies courses.

The students gave many reasons for taking their particular Women Studies course(s). Basic to all replies, however, was a concern for knowledge in an area all felt was generally ignored at the University. Again and again both men and women students indicated "personal growth," and "self-knowledge" as reasons for their initial interest. Also, many indicated that they enrolled because the role of women must be changed and education was the basis for social reform. ("Report of the ad hoc Committee . . .," 1971, p. 8)

Some students view women's studies courses as a way to learn about the Women's Liberation Movement and not be identified as a "women's libber." Others are attracted by the possibility of work with nontraditional source materials and innovative teaching techniques. It is clear that some of the attraction of women's studies will wear off with time. It is impossible to predict how much and at what rate.

Secondhand reports of students' responses to women's studies courses would indicate that they are enthusiastic. Most of the reporting has been done by the course instructors or organizers. Lerner reports:

Several of the students expressed the conviction, in their evaluations, that their ideas of what to do with their lives had undergone change, as a result of the seminar. They were more open to different options of life patterns, different ways of making use of the many opportunities open to them, different educational goals. Two of them were reinforced in their desire to go on to graduate study; one or two thought, for the first time, they might like to become historians. The sampling was, of course, small, but the experience of the seminar would indicate that to a group of female students the opportunity for frank discussion of these troublesome questions can be of great vocational and intellectual significance. (Howe, 1970, p. 87)

Other reported student reactions to women's studies courses have included: increased valuation of own intellect; increased awareness of the male orientation of other courses; increased awareness of professorial comments that embody mythical views of women and their roles; more positive feelings toward personal potential; significant reorientation of attitudes and views; depression; anger; a feeling that the course had personal meaning; and increased awareness of male chauvinism in aspects of day-to-day life.

A number of writers have commented on the depth of emotion that women's studies courses seem capable of evoking.

At the end of a literature course, one girl came up to Buffalo's Ann Scott and Declared: "I want you to know that you've ruined my life. Everything I read now fills me with rage." ("Studying the Sisterhood," 1972, p. 91)

Another problem encountered is deep depression on the part of women students who see little hope after lengthy documentation of sex discrimination. Teachers are struggling to combat potential despair and depression, and to provide support for students who find their attitudes and values challenged, or find the course structure threatening.

Another interesting area of student response that has been chronicled by teachers of women's studies is men students' reactions. The experience of being in the minority led to new insights on the part of some men. Strong observes:

For the first time in these men's university experiences they were not only in a minority, but a frighteningly small minority, which made a second element in the class more difficult to handle. Not only were they a minority, but they were in a situation in which they did not possess a naturally assumed authority because of their sex. In history and political science, disciplines which usually explore such traditionally male activities as war, politics, and power, it is somehow assumed by both men and women that these are subjects which men "innately" understand better than women. Thus women, because they are usually in a minority and outside their "natural" sphere, tend to participate less. In a feminism class, however, things are quite the opposite, and a number of women made it clear that women, by their very nature, possessed special insights into the problems of women and that men could never understand the quality of woman's subordination, either historically or contemporarily, because they were the oppressors. By their very womanhood, women possessed a bond with Elizabeth Cady Stanton which men were incapable of understanding, for only the oppressed could understand the oppressed. (Showalter and Ohmann, 1971, p. 43)

Other teachers report men students' behavior ranged from subtle to blatant in their attempt to regain power and status within the classroom. Some actions are clearly intended to be disruptive. Others reveal their inability to relate to the instructors on a professional level and to take the subject matter seriously. Tobias (1972) reports that only male students complain that the course is offering "no solutions" and is "beating a dead horse," which might be "a denial of the complexity of the issue and its relation to *their* lives" (p. 262). Benson (1972) describes an instance where the male students did not, or could not, treat the women instructors as professionals.

From the first day, our male students behaved towards us as they never would have toward our male counterparts. They called us by our first names immediately. They wanted us to keep the class from laughing or groaning at males who asked stupid, facetious, or deliberately provocative questions. (They apparently weren't as concerned about the egos of the women students.) They gave us unsolicited advice on everything from our lecture styles to our hair styles and clothes. What we women teachers objected to was not that relations between students and teachers could be much more informal than they are now. We were concerned that men students could not relate to women teachers as professionals. They thought, like many of their male mentors, that because we were women, they could relate to us immediately in a very personal way more or less as mothers and sweethearts. On one level, this is merely offensive. On another, it's a way for men to deny that what we are saying is valid and relevant to them. (pp. 285-286)

On the other hand, there have been some reports of real behavioral changes by men as the result of their encounter with women's studies courses. One male student observed that some men had become less emotionally inhibited, had reduced their strivings for dominance, and generally became more human ("Studying the Sisterhood," 1972, p. 91).

Summary

The women's studies course is by far the most important element of women's studies programs. Historically, programs were built on women's studies offerings. Most of the initial courses were in the humanities and social sciences. Programs have continued to encourage courses in these and other disciplines. In addition to courses in the traditional disciplines, programs commonly feature multidisciplinary courses. Sample program listings and degree requirements feature some kind of multidisciplinary work. Reports indicate that students find women's studies stimulating and interesting. At present, programs continue to build in response to student enthusiasm. The following section will review organizational structures and program activities as mechanisms of support for women's studies.

PROGRAM OPERATION

While women's studies courses are the backbone of women's studies programs, another basic program feature centers on the mechanism of operation. Most characteristic is the attempt to maintain and foster links to both the campus and the community. This chapter will cover three areas in which programs utilize the multiple-link approach to program operation: organizational structure, faculty and staff utilization, and specific program activities. Examples which illustrate program approaches will be cited under each of these areas.

Organizational Structure

Women's studies programs are characterized by either nonhierarchical or minimized hierarchical structures. Such structures many times have built-in mechanisms for receiving input from various campus constituencies in addition to a large governing board or committee. Program planners frequently note that these structures were adopted in the hopes that wide participation would be ensured.

One type of nonhierarchical structure that has been utilized is the collective. Collectives are those programs that do not designate one person as the head. Programs conducted essentially on a collective basis include: Buffalo (State University of New York); Cambridge-Goddard Graduate School for Social Change; Goddard College; Portland State University; Richmond (City University of New York); and Sacramento (California State University).

At Sacramento, the guiding body of the program is an elected women's studies board. It consists of three elected faculty with one vote, three students with three votes, and two staff with one vote. This board develops policies, controls funds, allocates positions, and, when necessary, the faculty members assume departmental chair duties.

Right now, it is unclear whether the collectives are successful. The longest operating one is beginning its sixth semester. So, for over a year now, the Buffalo Women's Studies College has carried on its work through committees composed of students taking women's studies courses and teachers. Even this seems too short a time in which to make an evaluation. The fact that the energy and time required to make group decisions is substantial is probably one reason that some collectives are currently reassessing their governing structure. So some collectives may evolve into forms with increased delegation of responsibilities and functions.

A somewhat modified collective structure is popular among women's studies programs. It consists primarily of a committee or board with one or two persons designated as program head. An example of this structure may be found at Towson State College. The women's studies program there is run by a Women's Studies Committee composed of eight faculty members, two of whom are designated program coordinators. San Francisco (California State University) has essentially the same structure. The program there is run by a 12-member Advisory Committee on Women's Studies, chaired by one person. At Fresno (California State University) the academic vice president appointed a 13-member advisory committee to direct the Women's Studies Program. One faculty member was designated coordinator of the group that has five other faculty members and seven students. Other examples of this structure type include: Barnard College; Mundelein College; Northeastern Illinois University; University of Pittsburgh; San Diego (California State University); and the University of Washington.

The program at Cornell University is a good example of one that operates with input from diverse sources. Decision-making for the program rests with the Faculty Board, which is composed of faculty holding the rank of assistant professor or above. Mechanisms exist so that elected representatives from other constituencies, such as graduate students, will be added as the program evolves. The director of the program is a member of the Faculty Board, and coordinates the program on a half-time basis. In addition there is the Advisory Group, composed of fifty graduate students, undergraduates, lecturers, postdoctoral associates, instructors, and academic staff members. They serve on 12 subcommittees that are the source of ideas, womenpower for projects, and a sounding board for plans of the Faculty Board. An adjunct to the Advisory Group consists of faculty members who are called Friends of Women's Studies. Cornell exemplifies the network type of program structure that relies on a fairly representative body for decision-making and ties to an even wider body (or bodies) for ideas and input.

Personnel Utilization

One of the prime ways for programs to maintain a link to the rest of the academic community has been to utilize faculty from various departments and colleges to teach women's studies courses. Programs report great interest in women's studies among campus faculty members, and a willingness to participate in program activities.

On occasion, joint appointments are a feature of the program. If this is the case, faculty are shared between women's studies and a regular department on the basis of their appointment, rather than through the use of release time. For example, at the University of Pittsburgh the program plan called for new faculty ". . . incumbents to be appointed in established departments, who will form an interdisciplinary program with a portion of their time allocated to the program ("FAS Votes . . .," 1971, p. 1)." Appointments were made by a joint decision of the particular departments and a women's studies search committee, appointed by the provost in consultation with the dean of the Faculty of Arts and Sciences.

Sometimes, persons serving as the designated coordinators, directors, or program heads also are part-time. In this case, their time is divided between women's studies and regular departmental or administrative duties. More commonly, faculty members have been released from a class or other duties to devote time to the development or operation of the program.

Students and community women have also been involved in all aspects of women's studies programs. For example, at San Diego (California State University) lecturers are women who have their BAs and formerly were teaching assistants in the program. ("Proposal to Establish Women's Studies as an Official Minor . . .," 1972, p. 3). At Sacramento (California State University), women with "grass-roots" community movement experience serve on the program's faculty ("Request for Approval of a Minor in Women's Studies . . .," 1972, p. 10). And at Cornell University any person interested in teaching a women's studies course can submit an application that includes a course proposal and an outline. These are reviewed by a board, which then offers one-term appointments as lecturer to those with good course ideas and academic qualifications. In addition to participation in program teaching, many governing boards have students and staff members.

Extracurricular Program Activities

Many activities reflect attempts to maintain and build links between the program and the rest of the institution or the community at large. A number of proposals for programs indicate that building these links were considered a high priority goal. Plans for the proposed women's studies center at Northeastern Illinois University reflect this concern. Suggested center activities include:

Providing resource materials on women and men to all interested community people, students, and faculty.

Encouraging research for our own use and periodic publication.

Encouraging and helping plan seminars and conferences relating to issues of equality, career planning, and alternative social structures.

Helping students and community people to implement their career plans, as well as providing support for individuals who desire to broaden their career options.

Providing some form of child-care assistance to parents who wish to take courses.

Disseminating information and providing counseling on birth control, legal rights, and health care.

Maintaining a speaker's bureau. ("Women's Studies Program," 1972, p. 2)

Further, both the University of Wisconsin (Milwaukee) and Mundelein College's proposals for women's programs have large sections devoted to public service or outreach activities. They urge publicity for the program and college to surrounding area women; vocational guidance and placement services; development of community projects through which students could obtain degree credit for field work; provision of information services to the community; and the establishment of a state Women's Studies Information Clearinghouse ("Proposal for a Women's Studies Program . . .," 1972, pp. 3-4, and "The Report Investigating . . .," 1971, p. 1).

Actual program activities also reflect attempts to establish connections between the program and the campus or the program and the community. For example, contracts between programs and the campus faculty have been fostered by women's studies surveys. A brief questionnaire was directed to all Cornell faculty asking them if any sections of their courses focused on women; if such courses could be publicized; whether any research projects pertinent to women's studies were anticipated or underway in their department; and if they would serve as an advisor to the program from time to time. Responses indicated that 56 projects related to women's studies were being planned or executed by Cornell faculty and students, and 75 faculty members consented to being advisors.

Alverno College, as a women's college, felt it inappropriate to start a separate women's studies program within the institution. Personnel at the College feel that all of its programs, classes, and activities should be relevant to and serve women's needs. As a result, self-study efforts are currently underway to reevaluate the College program. As part of the self-study, a survey was done to assess the usage of a feminist orientation in class. A questionnaire asked each faculty member to cite approaches or changes in course content, methodology, etc., that reflected an awareness of women students' needs. The results were reported in five categories: content; concepts to be incorporated in class; methodology of teaching; extracurricular activities; and career opportunities ("Summary of Departmental Presentations . . .," 1971).

Although women's studies programs are concerned with the development of women's studies courses that receive academic credit within the institution, their educational focus is much broader. They also participate actively in extension, continuing education, and community-based educational efforts. At Cornell University the women's studies program served as a resource for several projects undertaken by the Cooperative Extension divisions of the University, including the preparation of the "Women in Employment" sections of a training program for Cornell's first-line supervisors. Similar efforts are reported at the University of Washington, where work is done with the Division of Continuing Studies that offers noncredit courses to the general public.

Women's studies programs have also been instrumental in establishing popular courses for women in the basic skills or self-help area. These courses are usually offered on a noncredit or reduced credit basis, and instruct students how to do things in areas traditionally relegated to men. Self-defense, automobile mechanics, industrial arts, and legel self-help are among the types of courses offered.

Academic counseling is routinely provided by women's studies programs. In addition, some programs are concerned to some extent with career counseling. This is considered an important function of the Barnard Women's Center. "Educating women means more than giving them academic courses. Programs to help them plan careers, before and after the B.A., are an integral part of the Center (Stimpson, 1971, p. 8)."

Women's studies programs have sponsored or promoted a wide variety of other activities. These include: conferences; institutes; workshops; symposia; seminars; lecture and film series; day care centers; consciousness-raising groups; area family planning services; musical and theater groups; and several publications. Along with bringing speakers and artists to campus, a number of programs have provided speakers to interested organizations. Cornell University reports providing speakers to at least 30 Cornell campus groups, to local organizations such as Girl Scouts, Business and Professional Women's Clubs, and Ithaca Women's Clubs, and to nearby colleges such as Bucknell University, Keuka College, and Eisenhower College.

In each case, the number and variety of program activities seem to depend on local interest and resources, as well as individual talents and energies. Still, they all serve as examples of the many ways programs promote themselves on campus and within the wider community.

UP-DATE

The following section has been provided by the Clearinghouse on Women's Studies, Old Westbury, New York. It has been extracted from the publication *Female Studies VII: Going Strong, New Courses/New Programs* (1974). This information has been written by Deborah Silverton Rosenfelt, Editor, The Feminist Press.

The growth of women's studies in the past two years has been phenomenal. In 1971, there were about 600 courses and about 20 programs. There are now well over 2,000 courses and over 80 programs. Geographically they range in the United States from Orono, Maine to Honolulu, Hawaii, and there is a small but growing number of courses in the United Kingdom and Canada. I have examined descriptions of some 30 programs and syllabi for over 200 courses.

Courses

The criteria for the selection of courses were initially these: (1) Would the syllabus provide significant assistance, in organization, bibliography, project suggestions, etc., to women developing their own courses in the area? (2) Would it extend, rather than repeat, material already

available, especially in the first three volumes of *Female Studies*? (3) Would its origin help indicate the geographic and institutional diversity of women's studies? (4) Was it innovative in perspective, materials, methods, structure, etc.?

The second criterion means that this volume must be read in conjunction with others for an accurate sense of the scope of women's studies. In applying it I regretfully eliminated some excellent syllabi, particularly for broad departmental courses in History of Women and Sociology of Women, both well represented in other volumes. (History, like literature, is probably overrepresented here anyway; but it is in these two disciplines that the most diverse and innovative courses seem to appear.)

Another criterion evolved as I worked: Does the syllabus suggest the diversity of women—in terms of class, race, culture, nationality? Most of the courses generally available in the past have focused on women in America, particularly white, middle-class women. Most still do, though the introductory, interdisciplinary syllabus almost inevitably includes a section on cross-cultural studies, a section on working women, and/or a section on Third World women. It seemed to me, though, that there was a special need for materials on Third World women and women in non-Western societies, so I included most available course descriptions in this area: Women in Contemporary Society; Cross-Cultural Studies: Women in Revolutionary Societies (the only course antedating 1972); La Chicana in the United States; Women in African History; American, Indian, African Women; Race, Sex, and Ethnic Groups in America; Black Matriarch; Status of Women in Various Political-Economic Systems; and, its innocuous name notwithstanding, Images of Women in Literature. Rayna Reiter's thorough bibliography, Anthropological Perspectives on Women, includes references to women throughout the world.

In some instances I could not meet my criteria so well as I had wished. There are, for example, no courses from other than traditional academic institutions (though these range from the two-year community college to the graduate school), and there are no how-to courses: self-defense, auto mechanics, and so on. In each case, these omissions were the result not of choice, but of the absence of material. These courses exist, and we have listings for some; but either they do not lend themselves to the fine art of syllbaus-making, or, the most likely explanation in the first instance, their originators have chosen to work outside the communications network of academia.

Two other omissions require an explanation. I included no courses in foreign language and literature, because a forthcoming volume, edited by Sidonie Cassirer for the MLA Commission on the Status of Women, will be devoted exclusively to that topic. And there are no courses at the high school level, because *High School Feminist Studies,* a collection of high school materials, bibliography, and syllabi, edited by Carol Ahlum and Jacqueline Fralley, will soon be available from The Feminist Press.

In spite of these omissions, the courses included here, taken altogether, are representative of the ongoing development of women's studies in academic institutions throughout the United States—not to mention Canada and the United Kingdom. But they are not always proportionally representative. For example, I had one syllabus each in Classics, Film, Law, Music, and Journalism; I included all of them. I had two in Theology and two in Social Work; I included all four. Lise Vogel sent not only a syllabus on Women, Art, and Feminism, but a thoughtful essay and lengthy bibliography; knowing the scarcity of such materials, I included all of it.

In order to provide a more accurate picture of the overall status of women's studies on the campuses than the courses here would suggest on their own, I have analyzed the offerings for one academic year, 1972-1973, listed by institution, in *Guide to Female Studies, II* and *III* (The Feminist Press: October 1972 and Summer, 1973). All the college courses listed in *Guide III,* and the 1972-1973 courses in *Guide II,* are included in the following breakdown. The sample is not exhaustive, but it is large enough to be representative—765 courses in all. Complete information on courses offered since the inception of women's studies are available in the directory *Who's Who and Where in Women's Studies,* The Feminist Press, Spring, 1974.

As when *Female Studies III* was published, the largest categories are still history, sociology, and especially literature, along with a consistently large group of interdisciplinary courses. But education and psychology are increasingly well-represented, and political science, anthropology, and law are making gains. A hopeful development is the increase in courses in the area of health sciences, home economics, etc., which focus on issues ranging from human sexuality and the pragmatics of contraception and abortion, to child care and alternate lifestyles. These trends, on the whole, were reflected in the syllabi from which I actually made my selections. (Some of these are included in the data base; others are new courses offered during the 1973-1974 academic year.) I had 41 syllabi to choose from in literature, 33 in history, 25 in sociology, 18 in psychology, 11 in education. Again, then, these were the largest categories, and, except for history and sociology, in the same order as in the larger sample.

Such statistics, of course, tell us little about the content, method, or atmosphere of the courses themselves. Nor is this the place for a detailed analysis of these concerns. But I do want to make several observations which seem especially important. First, if anyone still has fears about the academic validity of women's studies, those fears may once and for all be laid to rest. The proliferation of specialized or advanced courses, particularly in literature and history, but in other fields as well, itself bears witness to that validity; obviously the broad interdisciplinary course, or the broad disciplinary one, is no longer enough to encompass the work to be done and the materials to be studied. Instructors and students feel the need to focus on more concentrated areas, to ask more specific questions: Was Shakespeare a chauvinist, does it matter, and if so, to whom? Can sex be used as the basis for concerted political action? To what extent is there/

should there be a female/feminist art? How much power do black women really have, and how is it exercised? Specialization may take the form of a thematic focus, exemplified by, but certainly not limited to, the increasing number of courses examining feminism per se: Feminism as a Contemporary Social Movement, Rhetoric of Feminism, Feminist Politics, Feminist Thought Workshop. Or it may involve concentration on women of a particular class, race, or era: Black Matriarchy; La Chicana; Women as Intellectual in Modern European History. A promising variant on the latter approach encourages students to research local but often neglected materials on women in their institution's geographic area: Boston Women in the Progressive Era, for example, or the project assignment for the Nineteenth-Century Woman Movement.

The trend toward specialization exists, of course, side by side with the interdisciplinary perspective characteristic of women's studies since their inception. The coexistence of these two approaches provides the field generally with both scope and depth. Obviously, though, the range varies with the institution. Instructors who wish to offer more specialized courses at schools lacking introductory ones often feel frustrated at having to spend course time on basics. Not surprisingly, the broadest spectrum of courses, from the general and introductory to the more specialized and/or advanced, is to be found at institutions with well-developed programs. That fact explains the inclusion here of more than one course from several such schools: SUNY Buffalo; SUNY College at Old Westbury; the University of Michigan; the University of Pittsburgh; and San Jose State University.

Women's studies courses, moreover, are characterized by a thoughtful structuring of topics, by lengthy yet selective reading lists—not infrequently including unpublished papers and manuscripts; and by a careful articulation of the questions to be raised, often with a sophisticated conceptual frame for both students and instructors. Many of them call for original research; virtually all require papers and/or projects. Few are simply lecture courses; time and again, the emphasis is on student participation, student times for reports, panels, project presentations, and often for discussion or work in small groups. This emphasis no doubt reflects the connection of women's studies with the women's movement at large—its dislike of authoritarian techniques, but more, its sense that each woman is, at least potentially, an intelligent, productive, responsible being, capable of genuine contributions to the work of the group.

And at least part of the work in many of these classes is group-oriented. Individual competition for grades is de-emphasized, replaced by a stress on the cooperative production of useful materials, or some form of cooperative participation in both learning and teaching. Many syllabi suggest that projects be done in groups. In other classes—such as the introductory course at Sonoma State—the course is taught collectively, in the latter instance entirely by students who have taken the class in preceding semesters. The essay by Joan Borod, Susan Dorsky, Carol Hull and Ellen Keller, of Case Western Reserve University, discusses the use of a collective methodology in class evaluation—an issue that will be of increasing concern in the future of women's studies. Again, the stress on cooperation rather than competition suggests the link between women's studies and feminist belief.

Obviously, many courses are more traditional in method. But one generalization I would risk: the quality of student performance in women's studies classes is unusually high. Perhaps that is because the work done in them is real work for a real audience, and not just another academic exercise. I have seen original research papers, excellent annotated bibliographies, almost professional curricular units for teaching women's studies in the public schools, imaginative and careful creative work, social histories based on interviews with members of the student's own family, and additional research on the period. These courses, then, are exploring new methodologies, raising and answering new questions, and making available a wealth of new materials. Across the country, students and teachers in these classes have a sense of involvement in a collective endeavor—to discover women's history, their past; to understand their condition in the present; to play an active role in shaping the future.

The belief that the subjective experience matters, that lives will be changed, that social and political institutions will be challenged, is reflected in these descriptions in several ways. Some instructors make this assumption explicit in their statements—the one from the introductory Adult Education course at the University of Wales, for example, or Education of Women in Historical Perspective, from Cornell. Most frequently, it emerges in the assignment for a journal: a "general recording . . . of your reactions to what you see-hear-feel going on about you in relation to women" (Images of Women in Music); or "a cumulative record of your cognitive and affective learnings" (Perspectives on Human Sexuality). These assignments are not substitutions for hard study and serious thought; rather, they stress the seriousness of the academic endeavor by allowing the student to integrate what is learned in the classroom with what is lived outside. And some courses require projects that will formulate and even implement strategies for social change. Students are asked to design curricular units in women's studies, to initiate consciousness-raising groups, to create nonsexist worship services, to write nonsexist children's books or devise methods for persuading publishers to eliminate stereotypical sex roles from their publications, and to investigate cases of sex discrimination at their own institutions. These classes, then, do not stop with the personal; though, unlike traditional college classes, they may stop *for* it.

In summary, the typical women's studies course is likely to provide for at least one, and often all, of the following: self-actualization and consciousness-raising; the feminist reinterpretation of "received doctrine" and familiar materials, or the discovery or creation of new or neglected materials; and the formulation of strategies for social change. They foster an understanding of both self and world, and the capacity to act on that understanding in a context larger than the classroom. And, judging from conversations and correspondence with teachers and students across the country, there is a final quality that many of them have in common: a sense of excitement, of discovery, of commitment, and of the importance of the work in which the class is engaged. These courses seem to matter to those who are teaching and taking them, to matter profoundly; that alone may make them almost unique in academia.

Programs

Female Studies VII includes a list of women's studies programs as of November 1973: 83 in all, at community colleges, four-year colleges, and universities. Several others—at least five—are in the planning stages. This flowering of programs is as impressive as the proliferation of courses—in one respect moreso, for while it is relatively easy to institute a new course, it is quite a different matter to organize and win acceptance for a program. A program is inherently a political unit; and it requires an outlay of institutional support—office space, services, funding, and released time for teaching and coordination. The spread of programs, then, is a testament to the commitment, hard work, and strategic skill of the scores of women and men who organized them.

Two years ago (as noted in *Female Studies III*) the geographic distribution of programs followed in the path of the women's movement along the East and West Coasts. The great majority are still concentrated in East and West: 21 in the Northeast (14 in New York, all but one of the rest in Massachusetts); ten in the mideast; and 34 in the far West (21 in California alone). But the Midwest now offers 14 programs, the South at least three. An examination of recent materials from some of those included in *Female Studies III* (Buffalo, Cornell, Pittsburgh, Cambridge-Goddard, the Five Colleges in Massachusetts, Sacramento, and the University of Washington) revealed generally an expanded array of course offerings, an increased number of core faculty, and such structural evolutions as the establishment of the Women's Studies College at Buffalo and an officially recognized minor at Sacramento.

At 11 institutions a student may now graduate with a major in women's studies. Since few programs exist as separate departments, most of the BAs are either individually structured by the student (as are the MAs at George Washington, Cambridge-Goddard, and San Jose), or are offered in conjunction with a BA from an existing School or Department of which the women's studies program is a part. The programs at the College of Old Westbury and the University of Hawaii represent the latter type. Eight programs offer minors or concentrations, five MAs, and one, a community college in Southern California, an Associate of Arts. Most programs do not offer degrees. At some this is a conscious choice, designed to avoid energy-draining entanglements with bureaucratic red tape, and to stave off hardening of the arteries in terms of requirements. At others, like the programs at California State University, Hambolt, and the University of South Florida included here, that option is held in reserve for the future.

In spite of this diversity, however, I decided early on to emphasize courses, rather than programs, in this collection. The programs in *Female Studies II* and *III* provide material that is more analytic of the purposes and goals of women's studies, and more informative about the political struggles involved in their establishment, than most of the statements (often little more than brochures) from newer programs. These earlier programs were consciously pioneering new territory. Most of the women who initiated them came out from the antiwar movement or the women's movement, or both. They brought with them their political perspective and their activist commitment. Most believed that women's studies programs should be far more than a body of courses; they should contribute to the work of the women's movement in other ways as well, at least by improving the status of women on campus, and providing needed services to campus and community women in the form of consciousness-raising groups, day care, and counseling.

They were concerned primarily with three overarching issues: the program's governance, its structural relationships to the institution, and its responsibility and responsiveness to the larger community. Generally, they argued that the governance of programs should reflect feminist ideology: collective or democratic decision-making rather than hierarchy; and maximal student participation, and sometimes student control, in formulating goals and policy, in developing the curriculum, even in sacrosanct matters like the hiring of personnel. Women in the community should be involved, they felt, not only as the recipients of benevolently provided services, but as shapers of policy—or, more often, as teachers, whether or not they possessed traditional academic credentials. To implement these beliefs the programs would require considerable autonomy within the institution. The question of separatism was hotly debated: should women fight for an independent program, with its own faculty and course offerings, or could they evolve a structure that would provide the necessary autonomy while infusing courses and faculty throughout the institution? (See Robinson, 1973.) Often, as they attempted to implement their beliefs, the organizers found themselves locked in a fierce struggle with the administration. Their program rationales, emerging out of this context of debate and struggle, were often persuasive manifestoes; their histories, detailed analyses of their endeavors.

Many programs are still engaged in tactical struggles for support from their institutions. And the issues that occupied early program planners are far from dead—as recent women's studies conferences on the East and West Coasts demonstrated. But my impression is that most of the new programs have dealt with or avoided them in pragmatic ways. In governance, most have preserved the ideal of collectivism in modified form—a board or council or committee with representatives from various segments of the campus community—but have opted against leaderlessness, electing or appointing one or two women as coordinators. Important decisions are usually made by the board; the coordinator's functions are primarily administrative. The typical structure is triangular, with power distributed along the base and middle levels, rather than concentrated at the peak.

In the relation of programs to their institutions, neither rigid separatism nor complete assimilation is the pattern. To avoid the isolation of women's studies in small pockets of feminism, apart from the rest of campus life, most programs encourage the spread of courses and faculty throughout the various departments. But to ensure at least a measure of autonomy in hiring, allocating funds, and shaping goals and policy, most have evolved independent core structures of some sort that can also offer courses unavailable elsewhere on campus.

Several of the programs included here casually mention the existence of Women's Resource Centers on or near campus. My impression is that the responsibility for such services is increasingly assumed by segments of the campus community other than the women's studies program per se—not infrequently, the Women's Caucus or Union. These centers, and other services, do frequently benefit community women. But on the whole, while programs or women's groups on campus may reach out to the community through courses and services (the main function of Continuing Education for Women), the lines of communication and influence do not so frequently run the other way.

More recent materials from programs tend to be less detailed, less analytic, and less passionate than their predecessors. Perhaps that is an indication of the increasing acceptance of women's studies programs as legitimate presences on campus. It certainly suggests a relaxation of the pressing need of the pioneers to communicate with other women about their struggles for recognition. But it may also indicate a certain falling-off from their deliberate insurgency.

Many of the newer programs emerged not from the coordinated efforts of a coalition of women implementing a developed body of political beliefs, but from the coalescence of individual courses initiated independently by faculty women or men whose main interest was, at least at first, a scholarly one. Frequently their feminist perspective evolved from teaching and research rather than prior movement ties. The more recent program descriptions emphasize traditional academic concerns: faculty credentials, requirements for a major or minor, and course listings. Often these listings are impressive in their length and variety, and increasingly in their coherence.

One promising development in women's studies is inter-institutional cooperation. The Five College Consortium in Western Massachusetts—ranging from the small liberal arts college of Hampshire to the University of Massachusetts, with its 24,000 student body—paved the way for a program that has thrived since its beginning three years ago. Students may cross-register for classes between institutions, accessible through an extensive bus service. Cooperation has enabled diverse course offerings, team teaching by instructors from the different schools, and faculty exchanges. A similar effort is now underway in Mid-state New York through the Hudson Valley Association of Colleges and Universities, with members ranging from Vassar College to the Culinary Institute. A Women's Studies Steering Committee, composed of representatives from each college in the Association, pooled their resources to compile a cooperative course listing, a collection of syllabi, and information on library materials, speakers, and jobs. Students at these schools may also cross-register for courses. These two examples do not really constitute a trend, but they do offer a potentially powerful model for other programs in the future.

The next obvious step for women's studies in higher education is to begin a systematic evaluation of their impact. One measure of their effect will be the extent to which they can assist public school teachers to bring nonsexist materials and teaching techniques into their own classrooms. For it is in the elementary and secondary school classrooms that education for social change must begin. Efforts in this direction are well under way in school districts in Berkeley, Kalamazoo, Ann Arbor, Princeton, etc. The growing number of courses on sexism and education in Schools of Education throughout the country, and such projects as the one on Inservice Education and Curriculum Development at SUNY/Old Westbury, suggest the role that higher education can play in facilitating such efforts. The effect of women's studies on other institutions—legal, economic, political, religious, social—and especially on deeply held cultural attitudes, will be harder to assess. But it will be greatest if women's studies programs can fulfill their unique potential as agents for change. They can bring together numbers of women and men with a wide range of knowledge, skills, and experience to discuss goals and directions; to evolve ideology and strategy; to work toward changing the patriarchal attitudes and institutions that we teach and learn about in our courses. It is the energies of such women and men, working patiently to implement their vision of a more humane and equitable society, that account for the unquestionable vitality and strength of the women's movement.

WOMEN'S STUDIES AND THE FUTURE

At this point it seems imperative to entertain some conjecture about the future of women's studies and women's studies programs. Few programs are adequately funded, and grants to programs are rare occurrences. A few programs report special donations or bequests, but primarily programs have subsisted on institutional support and the volunteer efforts of individuals. This is not surprising, since research, teaching, course planning, and curriculum revision are some of the activities traditionally sanctioned by colleges and universities. However, those program activities that might be viewed as of special interest to and for women will continue to compete with other programs for funds.

Despite these problems, there are three major reasons that will justify the continued existence of women's studies and women's studies programs. First, there is the demonstrated need for building a systematic body of knowledge about women. This state of affairs is one of the primary reasons for the enthusiasm for women's studies among students and teachers. Both find it stimulating to be engaged in research and study in an area where original work is needed. Teachers such as Wendy Martin report that their students are excited over the prospects of doing research in a new field:

> Many students were radicalized by having to write a portrait of a nineteenth-century feminist; singly and together, they searched the shelves of the Queen's College Library, their

local libraries, and finally the New York Public Library and discovered that there was very little information available on many of the most important feminists. When they were able to locate materials such as letters, diaries, autobiographies and tracts, they discovered that in addition to being improperly catalogued, these materials were left to crumble in an obscure corner. . . . Surprisingly, the men students were most outraged by this sexist influence on the distribution of knowledge, probably because this was the first time they confronted it on a very practical and immediate level. (Showalter and Ohmann, 1971, p. 11)

And the number of new journals in the field alone signifies the increased interest in women's studies among faculty members and scholars.

Second, there is a need to build theories from data on women and sex differences. Researchers have found, and are finding, that women's experiences and perceptions do differ from men's. Sex differences have always been an important, mediating variable in research in the social sciences. Women's studies reemphasizes the need to research and learn about these differences and their implications. The Women's Studies Committee at Towson expresses this view: "Men and women are, in fact, socialized in very different ways. Contemporary concern with this process dictates the necessity for scholarly study ("Women's Studies at Towson State . . .," 1972, p. 1)."

Right now the collection of empirical data on women and the development of theories adequate to conceptualize this data is the first order of business for women's studies. Institutions of higher education are the proper place in our society to conduct this work. Faculty of the Women's Studies Program of the University of South Florida point out the social benefits to be derived from scholarly work in women's studies:

> Crucial social issues, about which many generalizations exist, are giving rise to policies which have no adequate and critical scholarship to support them. For example, the relationship among women's role priorities, effective birth control programs, and urbanization; alternatives to the nuclear family as a basic unit of social organization; the role of society as an agent of early socialization (day care), and the interest of society in matters of abortion and population planning. ("Women's Studies Program: Curriculum Proposal," 1972, p. 2)

Thus, the amount of work to be done in terms of gathering data and developing theories, by itself, could easily justify the existence of women's studies programs in institutions of higher education.

Third, women's studies programs will be started and maintained as long as women's interests need special advocacy on campus. If bodies of knowledge remain unbalanced in their coverage of humanity, women will continue to utilize programs to promote a more positive and adequate presentation of women. As such, women's studies programs provide a legitimate place for women to bring these concerns and to organize their efforts.

In the long range, the future of women's studies programs will depend on how well women's studies develops as a field of interest. There is the possibility that knowledge about women will be integrated into the disciplines that exist today. However, most feminists feel that this is not likely to happen for some time. In the meantime, women's studies courses and programs are providing a place for feminists to promote the study of women.

NOTES

[1]The term multidisciplinary is adopted here in line with Tobias (1972). She prefers the word multidisciplinary because it sounds comprehensive, whereas interdisciplinary sounds "homeless" (p. 260).

[2]For a publication from one of these conferences, see *Notes: Midwest Conference on Women's Studies,* 1971; Siporin, 1972; Tobias, 1970f; or *Women and Education: A Feminist Perspective,* 1971. Additional conferences on women's studies have been held at the University of Pennsylvania, Santa Cruz (University of California) and Tufts University.

[3]*Women's Studies:* Gordon and Breach Science Publishers Inc., 440 Park Avenue South, New York, 10016; *Feminist Studies:* 606 West 116th Street, New York, 10027; *Journal of the International Institute of Women Studies:* International Institute of Women Studies, 1615 Myrtle Street, N.W., Washington, D.C. 20012; *Women's Studies Abstracts:* Box 1, Rush, New York 14543; *Women's Studies Newsletter:* The Feminist Press, Box 334, Old Westbury, New York 11568.

REFERENCES

Ahlum, Carol, and Howe, Florence, eds. *The Guide to Current Female Studies II.* Old Westbury, New York: The Feminist Press, 1972.

Alexander, Anne. Who's Come a Long Way, Baby; *The Johns Hopkins Magazine, 21* (April 1970): 10-15.

An Affirmatice Action Program to Redress Past Inequities and to Establish a Policy of Equal Treatment and Equal Opportunity at the University of Wisconsin for all Women. Report of the Steering Committee of the Association of Faculty Women. Madison, Wisconsin: University of Wisconsin (Madison and Extension), May 1972. ED 067 982

Astin, Helen, and Parelman, Allison. Women's Studies in American Colleges and Universities. *International Social Science Journal, 25* (Summer 1973): 389-400.

Benson, Ruth Crego. Women's Studies: Theory and Practice. *AAUP Bulletin, 58* (September 1972): 283-286.

Bowman, Barbara, Freedman, Ann, Norton, Eleanor H., and Ross, Susan D. *Women and the Law: A Collection of Reading Lists.* Pittsburgh: KNOW, Inc., 1971.

Cambridge-Goddard Graduate School for Social Change: A Program of Goddard College. School bulletin. Cambridge, Massachusetts: Cambridge-Goddard Graduate School for Social Change, 1972.

The Center for Women's Studies at California State University, Long Beach. Pamphlet. Long Beach: California State University, 1972.

Cheskis, Nancy. Female Studies at 24 Schools Here. *Chicago Sun-Times,* October 10, 1971.

Chmaj, Betty E. *American Women and American Studies.* Pittsburgh: KNOW, Inc., 1971.

Cless, Elizabeth L. *Evaluation of the National Endowment for the Humanities Sponsored Course: "The Idea of Woman."* Claremont, California: The Claremont Colleges' Office for Continuing Education, 1971. ED 063 888

Cohen, Audrey C. Women and Higher Education: Recommendations for Change. *Phi Delta Kappan, 53* (November 1971): 164-167. ED 051 769

Coulter, Sara, and Hedges, Elaine. Core Curriculum for Women's Studies. Grant Proposal. Baltimore: Towson State College, 1972.

Counterpoint: Womens' Studies. *The Harvard Independent,* October 15-21, 1970.

Description and Proposed Activities. Report of the Five-College Committee on Women's Studies. Amherst, Massachusetts: Amherst, Hampshire, Mount Holyoke and Smith Colleges, and the University of Massachusetts, March 1971.

A Descriptive Analysis of the Results of a National Survey. Philadelphia: New Morning Press, 1972. HE 003 760 (RIE May 73). Available from Penn Women's Studies Planners, 3601 Locust Walk, Philadelphia, Pennsylvania 19174.

Drake, Kirsten, Marks, Dorothy, and Wexford, Mary. *Women's Work and Women's Studies: 1971.* Pittsburgh: KNOW, Inc., 1972.

Fall Women's Studies Program. Press release. San Diego: California State University, July 1970.

FAS Votes: O.K.'s Women's Studies Program. *University Times,* November 4, 1971.

Farians, Elizabeth. *Institute for the Study Redefinition and Resocialization of Women: A Program for Colleges and Universities.* Cincinnati: NOW's Ecumenical Task Force on Women and Religion, 1971. ED 065 079.

Foxley, Cecelia H. Summary Report of Women's Studies Survey. Mimeographed. Iowa City: University of Iowa, December 1972.

Freeman, Jo. Women's Liberation and its Impact on the Campus. *Liberal Education, 57* (December 1971): 468-478.

Gilman, Richard. The FemLib Case against Sigmund Freud. *The New York Times Magazine,* January 31, 1971.

Ginsburg, Ruth B. Treatment of Women by the Law: Awakening Consciousness in the Law Schools. *Valparaiso University Law Review, 5* (1971): 480-488.

Hoffman, Nancy, Secor, Cynthia, and Tinsley, Adrian, eds. *Female Studies VI: Closer to the Ground—Women's Classes, Criticism, Programs.* Old Westbury, New York: The Feminist Press, 1972.

Howe, Florence, ed. *Female Studies: No. 2.* Pittsburgh: KNOW, Inc., 1970. ED 065 075

_____. Identity and Expression: A Writing Course for Women. *College English, 32* (May 1971): 863-871.

_____. Neither Bridge nor Barrier: A Place to Work for Change. Speech given April 1972a at Radcliffe College. Mimeographed.

_____. On the Campus. *Women's Studies Newsletter,* no. 1 (1972b): 2.

_____. Women Studies and Social Change. In *Academic Women on the Move,* edited by Alice S. Rossi and Ann Calderwood. New York: Russell Sage Foundation, 1973.

_____, and Ahlum, Carol, eds. *Female Studies III.* Pittsburgh: KNOW, Inc., 1971. ED 065 076

Husbands, Sandra Acker. Women's Place in Higher Education? *School Review, 80* (February 1972): 261-274.

Isenberg, Barbara. Boosting 'Liberation:' Women's Studies Rise in College Popularity. *The Wall Street Journal,* June 9, 1971.

Kazickas, Jurate. College Courses on "Her Story." *The Herald Traveler,* September 11, 1970.

Kerber, Linda. Courses in Women's History and Related Fields. Periodic bulletins. Available from Linda Kerber, Department of History, University of Iowa, Iowa City, Iowa 52240.

Lerner, Gerda. The Feminists: A Second Look. *Columbia Forum, 13* (Fall 1970): 24-30.

_____. New Approaches to the Study of Women in American History. *Journal of Social History, 3* (Fall 1969): 53-62.

Louchheim, Katie. Men and Women Studying Women. *The Washington Post,* May 30, 1971.

Marks, Marsha. Paper for Colloquium on "Teaching of Woman's History." Presented to the Southern Historical Association, November 1971, Houston, Texas. Mimeographed. ED 063 909

Miller, Lindsay. Newest Course on Campus: Women's Studies. *New York Post,* May 22-27, 1972. ED 065 108

Mirow, Deena. Interest Here Grows in Women's Studies. *The Plain Dealer* (Cleveland), February 6, 1972.

New College Trend: Women Studies. *New York Times,* January 7, 1971.

Newest Campus Crusade: Equal Rights for Women. *U.S. News & World Report, 71* (December 13, 1971): 79-82.

Newman, Frank. *Report on Higher Education.* Washington, D.C.: Office of Education, Department of Health, Education and Welfare, 1971. ED 049 718. Available from Superintendent of Documents, U.S. Government Printing Office, Washington, D.C. 20402, HE 5.250:50065.

Notes: Midwest Conference on Women's Studies. Milwaukee, Wisconsin: Alverno College Research Center on Women, 1971. ED 063 911

Oltman, Ruth M. Focus on Women in Academe, 1980. *Improving College and University Teaching, 20* (Winter 1972): 73-75.

Proposal for a Department of Women's Studies at the University of Pennsylvania. Report of the Penn Women's Studies Planners. Philadelphia: University of Pennsylvania, April 1972.

Proposal for a Women's Studies Program at the University of Wisconsin–Milwaukee. Mimeographed. Milwaukee: University of Wisconsin, March 1972.

Proposal for an Interdisciplinary Women's Studies Program. Mimeographed. Fresno: California State University, December 1971.

Proposal to Establish Women's Studies as an Official Minor for Undergraduate Students. Mimeographed. San Diego: California State University, November 1972.

The Report Investigating the Feasibility of the Women's Studies Program. Report of the Women's Studies Committee. Chicago: Mundelein College, 1971.

Report of the ad hoc Committee on Women Studies, College of Arts and Sciences. Mimeographed. Seattle: University of Washington, June 1971. HE 003 657 (RIE April 73).

Request for Approval of a Minor in Women's Studies at California State University, Sacramento. Mimeographed. Sacramento: California State University, 1972.

Robinson, Lora H. The Emergence of Women's Courses in Higher Education. *Research Currents.* Washington, D.C.: American Association for Higher Education, September 1972, ED 066 139

Rosenfeldt, Deborah, ed. *Female Studies VII: Going Strong, New Courses/New Programs.* Old Westbury, New York: The Feminist Press, 1973.

Salper, Roberta. The Theory and Practice of Women's Studies. *Edcentric, 3* (December 1971a): 4-8.

_____. Women's Studies. *Ramparts, 10* (December 1971b): 56-60.

Sandler, Bernice. A Feminist Approach to the Women's College. Speech before the Southern Association of Colleges for Women, November 1971, Miami, Florida. Mimeographed.

_____. What Women Really Want on the Campuses. *The Chronicle of Higher Education,* April 24, 1972. ED 061 870

Sanford, Nevitt. The Activists' Corner. *Journal of Social Issues, 26* (Spring 1970): 183-189.

Sarah Lawrence College: Master of Arts in Women's History. Pamphlet, Bronxville, New York: Sarah Lawrence College, 1972.

Schnorrenberg, Barbara. Paper for Colloquium on "Teaching of Woman's History." Presented to the Southern Historical Association, November 1971, Houston, Texas. Mimeographed. ED 063 908.

Schramm, Sarah Slavin, ed. *Female Studies VIII: Do It Yourself: Women's Studies.* Pittsburgh: KNOW, Inc., 1975.

Scully, Malcolm. Women in Higher Education: Challenging the Status Quo. *The Chronicle of Higher Education,* February 9, 1970.

Semas, Philip W. 55 Campuses Now Offering Courses in Women's Studies. *The Chronicle of Higher Education,* November 30, 1970.

_____. Women's Studies. *Improving College and University Teaching, 20* (Winter 1972): 46-47.

Showalter, Elaine, and Ohmann, Carol, eds. *Female Studies IV:*

Teaching about Women. Pittsburgh: KNOW, Inc., 1971, ED 065 077

Sicherman, Barbara. The Invisible Woman: The Case for Women's Studies. In *Women in Higher Education,* pp. 75-98. Washington, D.C.: The American Council on Education, 1972.

Sims, Jane. Colleges Expanding Women's Studies. *The Washington Post,* July 26, 1971.

Siporin, Rae L., ed. *Female Studies V.* Pittsburgh: KNOW, Inc., 1972.

Somerville, Rose M. Women's Studies. *Today's Education, 60* (November 1971): 35-37.

Sopher, Valerie. Women's Studies Courses Proliferate. *The Daily Californian,* February 2, 1971.

Stimpson, Catharine R. What Matter Mind: A Theory about the Practice of Women's Studies. Mimeographed. New York: Barnard College, August 1972. ED 068 078

_____ et al. *The Women's Center.* New York: Barnard College, Fall 1971. ED 063 913

The Study of Woman. *Time, 99* (July 6, 1970): 54.

Studying the Sisterhood. *Time, 99* (March 20, 1972): 90-91.

Summary of Departmental Presentations on Education of Women. Mimeographed. Milwaukee: Alverno College Research Center on Women, Fall 1971. ED 063 892

To Be or Not to Be. *Behavior Today, 4* (January 8, 1973): 1.

Tobias, Sheila. Educating Women for Leadership. *Wesleyan University Alumnus, 55* (Fall 1970a): 6-7, 10.

_____. Female Studies–An Immodest Proposal. Mimeographed. New York: Cornell University, July 1970b. Included in Appendices for ED 056 631.

_____. Female Studies: Its Origins, Its Organization, and Its Prospects. Paper for the Modern Language Association's Annual Convention, December 1970c, New York. Mimeographed. Included in Appendices for ED 056 631.

_____, ed. *Female Studies: No. 1: A Collection of College Syllabi and Reading Lists.* Pittsburgh: KNOW, Inc., 1970d. ED 065 074

_____. New Feminism on a University Campus: from Job Equality to Female Studies. Speech for *Symposium on Feminism,* September 23-24, 1970e, University of Pittsburgh. Mimeographed. ED 065 073

_____. Report of Female Studies Conference. *Cornell Chronicle,* May 21, 1970f. ED 063 910

_____. Teaching Female Studies: Looking Back over Three Years. *Liberal Education, 58* (May 1972): 258-264.

_____, and Kusnetz, Ella. For College Students: A Study of Women, Their Roles and Stereotypes. *Journal of Home Economics, 64* (April 1972): 17-21.

Trecker, Janice Law. Woman's Place is in the Curriculum. *Saturday Review, 54* (October 16, 1971): 83-86, 92.

Trow, Jo Anne J. Higher Education for Women. *Improving College and University Teaching, 20* (Winter 1972): 19-20.

Tucker, Frank H. The Study of Women in History. *Improving College and University Teaching, 20* (Winter 1972): 16-17.

Van Matre, Lynn. Women's Study Courses: Meeting a Need. *Chicago Tribune,* December 27, 1970.

Wallach, Aleta. Genesis of a 'Woman and the Law' Course: The Dawn of Consciousness at UCLA Law School. *Journal of Legal Education, 24* (1972): 309-353.

White, Merry I., Reid, Patricia, and Fox, Barbara J. Women Studies Gain Toehold on Campuses. *The Christian Science Monitor,* November 23, 1971.

Wohler, Milly. Women's Studies set for Year at PSU. *The Oregonian,* September 20, 1971.

Women and Education: A Feminist Perspective. Symposium sponsored by the University of Pittsburgh and the Modern Language Association's Commission on the Status of Women. Pittsburgh: University of Pittsburgh, November 5-7, 1971. ED 060 789

Women in the Curriculum. Mimeographed. Washington, D.C.:

Association of American Colleges' Project on the Status and Education of Women, November 1972.

Women Studies: College of Arts and Sciences Courses Offered 1972-73. Mimeographed. Seattle: University of Washington, September 1972.

Women Studies Major. Mimeographed. Seattle: University of Washington, November 1972.

Women Studies: Richmond College. Mimeographed. Staten Island: Richmond College (City University of New York), September 1971.

Women's Lib Courses Set at Two Colleges. *Association of Urban Universities Newsletter, 23* (Winter/Spring 1971): 6.

Women's Program of Douglass College. Pamphlet. New Brunswick: Rutgers University (The State University of New Jersey), 1972.

Women's Studies. *Newsweek, 76* (October 26, 1970): 61.

Women's Studies at California State University at San Francisco. Mimeographed. San Francisco: California State University, June 1972.

Women's Studies at Cornell University. Mimeographed. Ithaca, New York: Cornell University, November 1972.

Women's Studies at Towson State College. Mimeographed. Baltimore: Towson State College, 1972.

Women's Studies College. Course catalog. Buffalo: State University of New York, 1972.

Women's Studies Get FSC Approval for Fall. Press release. Fresno: California State University, May 1972.

A Women's Studies Institute for the University of South Carolina. Mimeographed. Columbia, South Carolina: University of South Carolina, May 1972.

[Women's Studies Program.] Mimeographed. Chicago: Northeastern Illinois University, 1972.

Women's Studies Program: Curriculum Proposal. Mimeographed. Tampa: University of South Florida, June 1972.

The Women's Studies Program of Laney College. Mimeographed. Oakland, California: Laney Community College, 1972.

[The Women's Studies Program of the University of Pittsburgh.] Pittsburgh: University of Pittsburgh, 1972. HE 003 846 (RIE June 73).

PART VII

TEACHING AND LEARNING STRATEGIES

68

CLASS SIZE: IS IT AN EFFECTIVE OR RELEVANT VARIABLE?

by Dwight Lindbloom
Principal
Bloomington Public Schools
Bloomington, Minnesota

A WIDESPREAD CONCERN

During this entire century, "class size" has been studied, researched, and even negotiated. Causes for this interest in class size have been two-fold: 1) the tremendous financial investment and one-time teacher shortages, calling for larger classes; and 2) perceived student gains and changed teacher behavior supporting a smaller teacher/pupil ratio. The evidence supports smaller classes in their effect on educational processes. However, with hundreds of studies completed the world over, no clear direction exists as to the "magic" number of student/ class or teacher for the several criteria used to measure success. With new and emerging instructional and staffing models gaining broader acceptance, the concept of class size itself becomes vague and lacks definition and meaning.

Beginning with studies by Rice in 1903, there have been well over 300 cataloged studies to date on the subject of class size (Furno and Collins, 1967). Early studies were precipitated largely by rising enrollments and shortages of teachers. Later studies reflected a concern for tax dollars, teachers' working conditions, and student learning.

Controversy has arisen both in the United States and abroad over the issue of class size. Now and in the future the controversy will culminate at the negotiating table, where teachers face school boards and taxpayers. Differences in opinion relate to the discrepancies between the goals of these two groups, and among the conflicting results of the research.

WHAT ARE THE COSTS?

Since personnel costs represent about 80 percent of a district's budget, it is obvious that taxpayers, boards of education, and administrators often view larger classes as a means to relieve the financial crisis facing many of our school districts today. If a district of 20,000 students, an average class size of 30 students, and a mean salary of $10,000 were to reduce class size to 25 students, the additional cost to the district for teachers' salaries alone would be well over one million dollars. Collins (1964), in a special report to congress, showed a variation in the national need for additional classrooms from about 66,000 to 272,000, depending solely on choice of class size. If the average cost of a classroom is $50,000, the difference in total cost of facilities depending upon class-size preference only would be over ten billion dollars. According to a survey of 618,910 elementary classes

from school systems of 3,000 students or more, by regrouping all pupils in classes of more than 25 there would be an increase of 118,629 classrooms, and an equal number of teachers (National Education Association, 1965). This alone represents an increase of 17 percent. In larger districts, having enrollments of 100,000 or more, the increase would be far greater—26 percent increase in both classrooms and teachers. The staggering cost of personnel and buildings is quite evident, and definite drastic economic advantages can be accrued by initiating and implementing policy to provide for larger class sizes.

WHAT ARE THE BENEFITS?

On the other hand, teachers and other professional people, as well as parents vitally interested in the education of their children, view small classes as a means through which greater learning will take place. Large classes are viewed by teachers and other educational leaders as a major problem and issue at all levels. In one of the NEA Research Division's opinion surveys in 1968, nearly three-fourths (72 percent) of the public school teachers throughout the country classified large class size as a problem—34 percent indicated it was a major problem (*NEA Research Bulletin,* 1969). Among teachers in urban classrooms, the proportion increases to over three-fourths.

Opinions regarding the importance of class size have not changed over the past decade. In 1961 the Research Division found that about two-thirds of the teachers and principals in elementary schools believed that classes of 24 pupils or less would allow for more effective teaching than would larger classes (*NEA Research Bulletin,* 1961). In 1972, the same Teacher Opinion Poll indicated that the attitudes toward the importance of smaller classes have not changed (*NEA Research Bulletin,* 1973). Nor has class size decreased to any great extent: the 1972 Survey indicates that nearly three-fourths (72 percent) of the elementary teachers in the country had 25 or more pupils in class. The general public is also convinced that smaller classes made a "great deal of difference." According to the Fifth Annual Gallup Poll of Public Attitudes Toward Education (Gallup, 1973), not only did professional educators believe that small classes made a great deal of difference in regard to achievement and progress of students (85 percent), but public school parents supported this view (83 percent) as well as individuals with no children in school (75 percent).

Although it is quite clear that an increase in class size will drastically reduce expenditures in any district, the case for smaller classes is not quite so definitive. The literature abounds with claims (and confusion) of the merits of small classes contributing to positive educational processes within the classroom, and increased pupil learning as an educational product. Among the specific advantages proported for small classes are greater pupil achievement, fewer behavioral and disciplinary problems, use of a greater variety of methods and materials in teaching, an increased teacher knowledge of the pupil, improved teacher morale, improved interpersonal relations in the classroom, more individualization of instruction, and a decrease in non-teaching duties. The most comprehensive and current review of research and literature on class size and its relationship to teacher behavior and student learning was done by Lindbloom (1970), *Class Size as it Affects Instructional Procedures and Educational Outcomes.* He shows that prior to 1950, the criterion variable used in studies for the assessment of class size factors was pupil achievement, including promotion. In recent years the focus has shifted toward an interest in the criterion variables of the "teaching process" and "desirable classroom conditions." Lindbloom reviewed the research relating to class size using the following two criteria with their individual operational definitions:

1. *Educational Processes.* The means of instruction employed to reach desired ends, including teaching methods and procedures and the classroom environment provided—non-achievement variables. Generally the measurement of the characteristic of educational process is accomplished through the use of classroom observation and inventory.

2. *Pupil Achievement.* An end toward which educational processes are directed. Achievement is generally measured through the use of standardized tests, grades, and promotion data. More recently, attitude inventories have also been used.

In reviewing the research conducted and reported within the past 75 years, this writer sees a sound case for smaller classes when the former criterion is used. No such case exists, however, when pupil achievement is used as a criterion.

Blake (1954), in an unpublished doctoral dissertation, identified 267 written documents concerning class size, of which 85 were based on some type of original research effort. Of these 85 studies, the results reported were as follows:

Smaller classes reported to be advantageous	35
Larger classes reported to be advantageous	18
No difference detected by the researcher	32

Blake applied six criteria of scientific adequacy or acceptability to the 85 studies, and eliminated all but 22 as unsatisfactory pieces of research. Of the 22 studies, 16 favored small classes, three favored large classes, and three were inconclusive. Classified by various criteria, a breakdown of the 22 studies follows:

Criterion	Small Classes Superior	Large Classes Superior	Inconclusive Results
Pupil Achievement	5	3	3
Teacher Opinion	8	0	0
Teacher Knowledge of Individual Students	1	0	0
Class Activities and Teacher Practices	2	0	0
	16	3	3

These data indicate that on the basis of these four criteria; small classes were favored by more than a five-to-

one ratio over large classes. However, the findings based on pupil achievement were far from conclusive.

Blake's results reflect the writer's conclusion after and extensive review of the research: When instructional procedures and educational processes are used as criteria, there is a high degree of support for smaller classes. When pupil achievement is used, no such support exists and results are either mixed or inconclusive.

Studies by Lundberg (1947), Baker (1936), Newell (1943), Richman (Ross and McKenna, 1955), Whitsitt (1955), Otto (1966), and Cannon (1966) generally conclude that smaller classes promote improved attendance, pupil behavior, teacher morale, teacher knowledge of pupils, invention (creativity), introduction and diffusion of newer teaching methods, greater use of individualization and small groups, more meaningful interaction among students, more student leadership, and use of a greater variety of activities.

Although teacher behavior does change when class size is reduced, the change is more pronounced when it is planned and teachers are notified to prepare accordingly (Whitsitt, 1955; Ross and McKenna, 1955). Haberman and Larson (1968), after making 906 observations in small and large classrooms, state, "If small classes are to make a difference in classroom behavior of teachers, it may be that they need to be instructed on how to teach a small class in different ways."

Using a new instrument, *Indicators of Quality,* developed by the Institute of Administrative Research (IAR), Teachers College, Columbia University, Coble (1968) and Olson (1970) both concluded that smaller classes are favorable to larger classes.

This instrument is composed of 51 polarized signs to measure the extent to which elements of individualization, interpersonal regard, creativity, and group activity are observed to be present in the classroom. Olson (Education Summary, 1971) concluded, after a study had involved 18,258 classrooms at all grade levels, that "On both elementary and secondary levels, any way one tries to slice it, smaller classes produced higher scores than large ones (p. 1)."

The results of existing studies are rather conclusive: Small classes are superior to large classes in terms of educational process and methodology. As indicated above, the research on class size and pupil achievement was conducted over a very short period of time, and reveals inconclusive results. Two other studies are interesting exceptions. Barlow (1969), in a two-and-one-half year study, and a five-year study in the Baltimore City Public Schools by Farno and Collins (1967), concluded that increased achievement appears to be a function of class size. These two studies, carefully conducted and longitudinal in nature, suggest that in the areas of reading and arithmetic achievement, small classes are favorable to large classes.

PROBLEMS IN RESEARCH

Lindbloom (1970), in his review of research on class size, focuses on the problems and difficulties in attempting to compare results among several studies. This difficulty stems from inconsistency in precisely defining the variable, and from lack of the use of standard procedures among the many researchers. To summarize briefly, some of these problems are:

Many variables (e.g., teacher quality) which affect results were not always controlled.

The purpose or goals of the class or group being studied were not defined.

Differences occurred in the quantitative definition of class size. Some researchers used 30 as "large," while others used this number to define "small."

Some studies were short-term (i.e., six weeks) while others were long-term (i.e., five years).

Different measures of central tendency (mean vs. medium) were used.

The definition of "class" and "teacher" varied considerably. Some studies used actual class size; others used total student/teacher ratio, while others used student/all professional educators ratio.

Almost exclusively, the research, literature, and general concern have dealt with the class-size question in the traditional sense of "class" and "teacher." Until recently this question has been, "How many students should each teacher have in a class for the most effective teaching and learning to take place?" Traditionally the definitions of "class" and "teacher" were based upon an instructional staff composed entirely of certified *classroom* teachers and a group of students in a self-contained classroom, meeting for one hour every day. The Research Division of the National Education Association (1965), for instance, refers to "class" as "the number of pupils for whom (one) teacher is responsible in a self-contained classroom (p. 7)." Ross and McKenna, in *Class Size: The Multi-Million Dollar Question,* defines class in much the same way—a group of students meeting regularly with "one particular teacher (p. 3)." Considering the problems of measurement mentioned above, the general definitions of "teacher" and "class" have remained fairly constant until recently. As these terms are less clearly defined, the question of class size per se becomes irrelevant and "inoperative" (sic). Many schools are moving away from the self-contained classroom, and traditional staffing patterns are breaking down, causing the concept and definition of these two terms to begin to break down also.

"CLASS"—A CHANGING CONCEPT

The past decade has been one of innovation, particularly in our public schools. Team teaching, differentiated staffing, and flexible modular scheduling, together with the use of teacher aides and paraprofessionals, use of specialists, alternative and community schools, and a host of other new instructional models, have caused the concepts of teacher and class to become fluid and stretched so that their meanings become at the least vague and nearly useless in many cases.

Differentiated staffing, which often causes concern and apprehension among the professional ranks and their organizations, presents a model which changes the definition of "teacher." No longer is a "teacher-a-teacher-a-teacher," but the professionals accept roles and tasks which are determined by their strengths and interest and the professional nature of the task. In addition to staff teachers, the teaching team consists of leadership staff, interns, student teachers, paraprofessionals, and teacher aides. Often this is accomplished by providing additional resources to add teacher aides and paraprofessionals to the existing staff. In other cases the total staffing collar is set, and these resources are differentiated depending on program demands and total staffing needs.

In Bloomington, Minnesota, all seven secondary schools are staffed on a 20:1 ratio. The principal and teaching staff are able to determine staffing needs based on program. The Oak Grove Junior High staff presents an interesting example of how the use of an extensive differentiated staff has implemented a very open variable program—but also has changed the meaning of "teacher." With an enrollment of 1,600 students, 80 staff "equivalencies" are allocated to Oak Grove's program. Instead of utilizing 80 certified professional teachers (i.e., classroom teachers, counselors, principals, and librarians), the Oak Grove staff has chosen to use the same staffing monies in the following manner:

Equivalencies		Full-Time Staff
62	=	62 teachers
14 (14 X 3)	=	42 certified interns
1 (1 X 3)	=	3 paraprofessionals
3 (3 X 4+)	=	13 teacher aides
80 equivalencies		130 full time staff

In addition there is enough money left in the allocated funds to provide about $20,000 in leadership pay for Area Leaders and Team Leaders among the instructional staff. With the initiation of the Staff Development Center[1] at Oak Grove Junior High, about 25 full-time pre-service "teachers" have joined the teaching teams. Adding to these teams the support of about 175-200 part-time community volunteers, the total "teaching" staff numbers well over 300 members, of which over 150 are full-time—a tremendous difference from 80 teachers!

Even the casual reader will ask, "But how many of these 150+ or 300+ are teachers?," or "How many of the noncertified staff are teaching, and is this illegal, unethical, or, even worse, bad for kids?" The class-size controversy is complicated precisely because we are beginning to ask these questions, but more broadly phrased: "What is a teacher and what is his/her role?" The writer and his staff believe that the only two tasks reserved exclusively for the permanent, full-time certified professional teacher are *diagnosis* and *prescription.* All other functions and tasks now done by teachers can be accomplished by well-trained noncertified personnel—at less cost and probably greater effectiveness as well! The differentiated staff allows for more professionalism, and offers a greater variety of activities and more extensive program for students; but at the same time it redefines and leaves as meaningless the traditional concept of "teacher."

With the initiation and development of individualized instruction and education, reflected through continuous progress, nongradedness, flexible modular schedules and the large-group/small-group and independent study modules; as well as community schools; the traditional classroom no longer exists. At Oak Grove, for example, within a modular variable flexible schedule and continuous progress curriculum, blocks of 175 students are scheduled into an instructional area for a block of time. The three to four instructional teams within the area determine, on a daily basis, the group size, location, and staff for these students. Each week team leaders negotiate with each other in scheduling the students. In this way, class size and composition and staffing vary considerably over a short period of time. This "scheduled time" represents about 60 percent of most students' time. The remainder of the students' time is spent on independent study in one or more of the 30-plus labs and resource centers in the building.

In many schools, including Oak Grove, the classroom has moved into the entire community. Use of learning centers, storefronts, business and industry, libraries, museums, and community "teachers" have further complicated and confused the notion of "class." It is quite evident that within this fluid instructional environment, class size as traditionally viewed has no meaning.

A NEW LOOK AT LEARNING NEEDS

Much progress has been made through research on class size. From it, educators do have valid inputs into decision-making regarding sizes of classes. In the future, however, the focus of research efforts must be geared to decisions that will be made in the future. With staffing patterns, instructional groups, and learning facilities becoming more variable and defined more broadly, we must learn to state instructional goals and objectives in terms of student-measurable outcomes. To achieve the multiple objectives of providing growth in the social, emotional, physical, attitudinal, and cognitive areas, one must determine methodology, size of learning group, instructional personnel, and facilities. The learning objective may demand an independent study or a small group discussion. It may call for a group of 500 viewing TV monitors, or a lab course for six at a local hospital. A local banker, university professor, a parent, or a fellow student may be part of the instructional team.

With rapid changes caused by new technology, financial costs, and instructional innovation, decision-makers must have data readily available to help determine a new design for education, now and in the future. Research to this end is not only helpful but imperative!

NOTES

[1]The Center attempts to integrate preservice and inservice education, as well as placing greater responsibility on the professional practitioner for determining the training program for those entering the profession and all members of the teaching team.

REFERENCES

Baker, H. L. Class Size Does Make a Difference. *Nation's Schools*, 1936, *17*, 27-28.

Barlow, I. H. A Longitudinal Evaluation of Reading Achievement in Small Classes. *Elementary English*, 1969, *46*, 184-187.

Blake, H. E. Class Size: A Summary of Selected Studies in Elementary and Secondary Public Schools. Unpublished doctoral dissertation, Teachers College, Columbia University, 1954.

Cannon, G. W. Kindergarten Class Size—A Study. *Childhood Education*, 1966, *43*, 9-11.

Coble, H. M. Some New Insights on Class Size and Differences in Teacher/Pupil Performance in the Various Subjects. *APSS Know How*, 1968, *43*, 16-19.

Collens, G. *National Inventory of School Facilities and Personnel*. Washington, D.C.: U.S. Department of Health, Education, and Welfare. Government Printing Office, 1964.

Education Summary, April 30, 1971, *24*, 1-2.

Furno, O. F., and Collens, G. J. *Class Size and Pupil Learning*. Baltimore: Baltimore City Public Schools, 1967.

Gallup, G. H. Fifth Annual Gallup Poll of Public Attitudes Toward Education. *Phi Delta Kappan*, 1973, *55*, 41.

Haberman, M., and Larson, G. L. Would Cutting Class Size Change Instruction? *National Elementary Principal*, 1968, *47*, 18-19.

Lindbloom, D. H. *Class Size as it Affects Instructional Procedures and Educational Outcomes*. Minneapolis: Educational Research and Development Council of the Twin Cities Metropolitan Area, Inc., 1970.

Lundberg, L. D. Effects of Smaller Classes. *Nation's Schools*, 1947, *39*, 20-22.

National Education Association. Class Size: Attitude and Action. *NEA Research Bulletin*, 1969, *47*, 115-116.

_____. Class Size in Kindergarten and Elementary Schools. Washington, D.C.: NEA Research Division, 1965.

_____. Teacher Opinion Poll. *Today's Education*, 1973, *62*, 11.

_____. Teachers and Principals Agree on Best Class Size. *NEA Research Bulletin*, 1961, *39*, 107.

Newell, C. A. *Class and Adaptability*. New York: New York Bureau of Publication, Teachers College, Columbia University, 1943.

Olson, M. N. Identifying Predictors of Institutional Quality: An Examination of Eleven Internal Classroom Variables in Relation to a School System Criterion Measure. Unpublished doctoral dissertation, Teachers College, Columbia University, 1970.

Otto R. W. Creativity in Teaching. *Childhood Education*, 1966, *43*, 40-43.

Ross, D., and McKenna, B. *Class Size, the Multi-Million Dollar Question*. New York: Institute of Administrative Research, Teachers College, Columbia University, 1955.

Whitsitt, R. C. Comparing the Individualities of Large Secondary School Classes with Small Secondary School Classes Through the Use of a Structured Observation Schedule. Unpublished doctoral dissertation, Teachers College, Columbia University, 1955.

69

SMALL GROUP METHODS OF INSTRUCTION

by Joseph A. Olmstead
Senior Staff Scientist
Human Resources Research Organization
Fort Benning, Georgia

Small-group methods of instruction are specific teaching techniques through which group processes are used to stimulate learning. The term "small group" refers to a collectivity of not more than 20 individuals. This is an arbitrary definition; however, experience strongly supports the view that instructional effectiveness is reduced when groups consist of more than 20 students, while any number less than 20 can be readily managed in most learning situations. Furthermore, this topic refers to methods that are specifically designed to use the social-psychological forces inherent in small groups for learning purposes. Accordingly, mere reduction of class size to less than 20 individuals, or the use of discussion in so-called "class-centered instruction," does not constitute use of a small-group method.

Small-group instruction is burgeoning in such widely disparate contexts as secondary education, colleges, industry, and the armed forces. There are probably many reasons for this popularity, not the least of which is a remarkable tendency for fads to play a major role in the choice of educational methods. However, the principal reason appears to be that the use of small groups, and of certain instructional methods suitable only for small groups, is one means for overcoming some of the well-known objections to mass educational programs.

RATIONALE FOR SMALL-GROUP METHODS

The rationale for small-group methods incorporates a number of assumptions about the nature of learning, the factors that influence it, and ways in which it can be induced. Underlying all of these is the fundamental premise that much of learning involves a social transaction; that is, it requires an exchange between people. On the face of it, this premise is not much different from those underlying conventional instruction. However, in conventional education, "learning" usually refers to the process by which students acquire information or skills from someone—an instructor—who is already in possession of them. In contrast, small-group methods start from a view of learning as a transaction between a learner and other learners, all of whom constitute a group. Under this concept, neither the learners nor the body of knowledge are fixed, and both undergo modification during the transaction.

On the other hand, many of the concepts derived from learning theory apply equally in small-group instruction. Perhaps the most useful are the concepts of "reinforcement" and "feedback." With regard to reinforce-

ment, one learns in groups as elsewhere—by responding to a stimulus. However, in the learning group, the stimulus is the behavior of other members, who are the agents of positive and negative reinforcement.

The major difference appears, however, in determination of which responses are "correct." In conventional instruction, the correctness of the response to be learned tends to be predetermined by instructors or doctrine. This definition of correctness is held constant during the entire learning experience. On the other hand, in small-group instruction, group members function both as learners and as environment, and standards of appropriateness of stimulus and response are worked out through the give-and-take of an evolving discussion.

Closely related is the concept of "feedback." This concept is concerned with the powerful learning effects of prompt reporting to the learner about the effects of his exploratory responses. In all forms of learning, knowledge of results is deemed essential. However, in small-group instruction, feedback is supplied by other group members, or by discussion leaders, depending upon conditions and the method used.

Central to the rationale of small-group methods is the use of social-psychological forces to enhance and optimize the conditions under which learning occurs. The rationale rests upon the premise that learning is partly a function of attitudes and education, or that training is a matter of overcoming resistance to change.

Conditions necessary to overcome attitudes that are resistant to change include a learning climate that provides emotional support to students; opportunity for them to practice an analytical attitude through controlled observation; opportunity to experience varied and realistic learning situations; opportunity for experimentation with new concepts; and opportunity for the student to obtain feedback concerning others' reactions to his newly developed ideas.

These conditions can be provided best within the context of a small group which possesses a common goal for learning, a reasonable degree of cohesiveness, norms conducive to learning, and patterns of effective communication—in short, a learning culture. Small-group methods are designed to systematically use these group forces to influence and increase learning.

COMMON METHODS

Among the more common small-group methods are the following:

Conference Method, which consists of a series of discussion sessions, each with a specific goal, in which the conference leader guides students in exploration of topics or problems relevant to the overall purpose of the instructional program.

Leaderless Discussion, which is a discussion session in which an instructor does not participate and no formal leader is designated. "Topic discussions" and "buzz" sessions are forms of leaderless discussion.

Case Method, which consists of discussions of actual situations, which are analyzed with the objectives of discovering underlying principles and applying the principles to diagnose and solve the problems, in order to develop a problem-solving orientation among students. Variations of the case method include the Harvard Method, the Incident Process Method, and the Abbreviated Case, both printed and dramatized.

Role-Playing, which provides a situation in which students assume roles of actual participants and enact the situation toward some resolution. Other students systematically observe behavior of the actors and, following the scene, report and discuss their observations.

Committee Problem-Solving, which involves the study of real or hypothetical problems by small groups of students who work together toward a final group product.

The Case Method and Role-Playing may be used with large classes; however, much of the effectiveness is lost as size of group increases, and greatest learning is achieved when group forces are free to operate. For this reason, these methods are considered to be small-group instructional techniques.

RESEARCH

Despite their widespread use, systematic research on the effectiveness of small-group methods has not been extensive. Attempts to study the question began as early as 1925 (Thie) and have continued intermittently since that time. However, no comprehensive programs intended to obtain definitive answers have yet been undertaken. By far, the greatest number of studies have compared lectures with some form of "group discussion" in terms of immediate recall of content, measured by achievement tests administered at completion of the course. Content about which students were tested included psychology (Eglash, 1954; Engel and Maes, 1971; Gibb and Gibb, 1952; Johnson and Smith, 1953; Leton, 1961), social relations (Wispe, 1951), sociology (Zeleny, 1927; Zeleny, 1940), communicable disease theory (Kerrick, Clark, and Rice, 1967), political science (Heinkel, 1968), and military leadership and human relations (DiVesta, 1954). In all of these studies, the findings were conclusive. As measured by end-of-course tests, both lecture and group methods were equally effective in teaching information and concepts. This finding is further confirmed for both leadership (DiVesta, 1954; Mayo and DuBois, 1963) and supervisory training (Mosel and Tsacnaris, 1954). The evidence is clear that some small-group methods can be effective for teaching information and concepts (Maier, 1971). On the other hand, they appear to have little advantage over lecture for this purpose.

The findings are somewhat different for the *retention* of information and concepts. Whereas lecture and group methods are equally effective, as evaluated by tests administered at completion of course, information learned through group methods is better retained, as measured by tests administered up to six months after course com-

pletion (Bane, 1925; Gerber, 1972; Thompson and Tom, 1957; Stovall, 1956).

Although the results are mixed, some evidence suggests that group methods may not be equally effective for all students. For example, with some college courses, it has been found that poorer students learn information and concepts better under more directive methods of instruction, while more able students profit better from discussion (Wispe, 1951; Watson, 1953). On the other hand, in leadership training DiVesta (1954) found that students who started the course at the upper levels of leadership scores were not much affected by either lecture or discussion.

There is little doubt that small-group methods are effective for improving problem-solving skills of individuals. For example, in experimental studies (Thorndike, 1938), classroom instruction (Bloom, 1953; Johnson and Smith, 1953; Paploizos and Stiefel, 1971), and leadership training situations (Mayo and DuBois, 1963), discussion and analysis in small groups have resulted in gains in quality of problem solutions. What is more, there is strong support for the idea that such discussion is conducive to a higher level of problem-solving than is a lecture (Bloom, 1953).

Although improvement in problem-solving can be obtained even with brief, leaderless "buzz" sessions (Vinacke, 1957), higher-quality solutions result when discussions are led by a permissive leader (Maier and Solem, 1952). Solutions of even better quality are obtained when a leader uses what Maier and Maier (1957) call "developmental discussion," which appears to be a variation of the directed conference method.

An important consideration in the design of instructional systems is student motivation. One important factor in such motivation is the extent to which students possess positive attitudes toward the course. In general, more students who participate under small-group conditions rate their courses higher than those who participate under lecture conditions (Anderson and Kell, 1954; Asch, 1951; DeVries, Muse, and Wells, 1971; Edwards, 1971; Gibb and Gibb, 1952; Johnson and Smith, 1953; Zeleny, 1940). This finding, however, is not true for all students nor for all situations.

One finding that turns up consistently in studies that compare lecture with group methods is that, where anxiety exists about course grades, lecture is preferred (McKeachie, 1954). This is not to say that such students dislike group discussion, but merely that they like lectures more (Guetzkow, Kelley, and McKeachie, 1954). It should be emphasized that preference for lectures was not found when grades were not determined by examinations (Johnson and Smith, 1953; McKeachie, 1954).

For many instructors, one of the principal goals is to channel the attitudes of students in directions advocated by the course content (McKeachie, 1954). Results of research concerning the effects of small-group methods upon attitudes seem reasonably conclusive. For academic courses, it has been consistently found that group discussion is more effective than lecture for changing content-specific attitudes in directions desired by instructors (Gibb and Gibb, 1952; Heinkel, 1968; Leton, 1961; Zeleny, 1940).

Results are also conclusive where instruction was of a more practical nature such as supervisory training (Foster and Danielian, 1966). Thus, in leadership training, small-group methods have been demonstrated consistently to be effective in changing attitudes (Barthol and Zeigler, 1956; Carron, 1964; Hazeltine and Berra, 1953; Katzell, 1948; Lawshe, Bolda, and Brune, 1959; Mosel and Tsacnaris, 1954; Spector, 1958). What is more, the changes appear to be lasting. Hazeltine and Berra (1953) rechecked their students one year after training and found the same changed attitudes as noted upon completion of the course. Carron (1964) found changed attitudes still expressed by his students 17 months after completion of training. This conclusion does not hold for all methods. For example, Vinacke (1957) found that buzz sessions, while effective in developing problem-solving skills, have little influence upon attitudes. The chief characteristic of buzz sessions is their brevity. Accordingly, the finding that they exert little effect upon attitudes would not be unexpected.

For certain objectives, small-group techniques should be the methods of choice; for other purposes, they are valuable options which can provide an educational system with needed flexibility.

POTENTIAL USES

In general, it is feasible to use small-group methods:

To increase depth of understanding and grasp of course content.

To enhance motivation and generate greater involvement of students with the course.

To develop positive attitudes toward later use of material presented in the course.

To develop problem-solving skills specific to the content of the course.

To provide practice in the application of concepts and information to practical problems.

To generate ideas among students concerning ways of applying knowledge acquired in the course.

To develop commitment of students to recommended ways of handling problems.

To emphasize an important issue or drive home a major point of instruction.

When content experts are scarce or not available as instructors.

CAUTIONS FOR USE

Despite these benefits, small-group methods are not always used in the best possible ways. One reason may be that their flexibility and relative ease of administration can lead to the belief that the methods are foolproof. Of course, this is not the case. Like all instructional methods, the success of small-group techniques depends largely upon the care with which they are designed and used. For this reason, it is important to state

several important cautions with regard to the most effective use of the methods.

First, it is essential that methods be selected and used with the instructional objective clearly in mind. The time, effort, and thought expended in accurate definition of objectives, in selection of methods appropriate to the objectives, and in use of the methods properly will usually be well repaid in the quality of learning that is achieved.

Second, although small-group methods are effective for certain purposes when used alone, they are most successful when students are also equipped with background information concerning the topics or problems under study. The foundation for all small-group methods is discussion, and instructive discussion cannot be accomplished unless students have some informational base from which to talk. This base might derive from experience, from reading, or from formal presentations of information. Therefore, unless most students possess relevant experience, small-group methods are usually more effective when used in conjunction with either printed material or some formal presentations, such as lectures or films. In most instances, informational material should precede the use of small-group methods. The only exception is the use of brief, leaderless discussion or role-playing to introduce a problem or emphasize an issue.

Finally, groups in which members work together over periods of time are, in general, likely to be more efficient and effective vehicles for learning. Therefore, where small-group methods are used repeatedly throughout the duration of a course, it is usually advisable to assign students permanently to groups and allow them to remain together whenever group sessions are considered desirable. An exception is the case where a stated objective is the stimulation of students through exposure to a wide range of ideas and viewpoints. With such an objective, periodic realigning of groups may be advisable.

It is axiomatic that no instructional method is better than the person who uses it. This statement is especially true with respect to small-group methods of instruction. However, the requirements for effective use of the methods are somewhat different from those used for other instructional techniques. For example, it is not always essential that discussion leaders or instructors be content experts, although they should have some preparation in the content, and expertise would certainly contribute to the quality of learning. Since responsibility for most of the learning rests with the students, and since guides for discussion leaders can be prepared by experts, complete mastery of content is not an essential requirement for instructors. On the other hand, solid grounding in the rationale and uses of small-group methods is necessary for their maximum effectiveness.

REFERENCES

Anderson, R. P., and Kell, B. L. Student Attitudes about Participation in Classroom Groups. *Journal of Educational Research,* 1954, *48,* 255-267.

Asch, N. J. Nondirective Teaching in Psychology: An Experimental Study. *Psychological Monographs,* 1951, *65,* No. 321.

Bane, C. L. The Lecture Versus the Class Discussion Method of College Teaching. *School and Society,* 1925, *21,* 300-302.

Barthol, R. P., and Zeigler, M. Evaluation of a Supervisory Training Program with "How Supervise?" *Journal of Applied Psychology*, 1956, *40*, 403-405.

Bloom, B. S. Thought Processes in Lectures and Discussions. *Journal of General Education*, 1953, *7*, 160-169.

Carron, T. J. Human Relations Training and Attitude Change: A Vector Analysis. *Personnel Psychology*, 1964, *17*, 403-415.

DeVries, D. L., Muse, D., and Wells, E. H. *The Effects on Students of Working in Cooperative Groups: An Exploratory Study*. Baltimore: Johns Hopkins University Center for Social Organization of Schools, 1971, Report No. 120.

DiVesta, F. J. Instructor-Centered and Student-Centered Approaches in Teaching a Human Relations Course. *Journal of Applied Psychology*, 1954, *38*, 329-335.

Edwards, K. J. *Students' Evaluations of a Business Simulation Game as a Learning Experience*. Baltimore: Johns Hopkins University Center for Social Organization of Schools, 1971, Report No. 121.

Eglash, A. A Group-Discussion Method of Teaching Psychology. *Journal of Educational Psychology*, 1954, *45*, 257-267.

Engel, A., and Maes, W. R. Teaching Personality Theory: A Games Approach. *Counselor Education and Supervision*, 1971, *11*, 24-28.

Foster, R. J., and Danielian, J. *An Analysis of Human Relations Training and Its Implications for Overseas Performance*. Alexandria, Va.: Human Resources Research Organization, 1966, Technical Report 66-15.

Gerber, L. A. "Coping" not "craziness": Psychology's Contribution to Teaching Psychopathology in Medical Students. *JSAS Catalog of Selected Documents in Psychology*, 1971, *1*, 13-14.

Gibb, L. M., and Gibb, J. R. The Effects of the Use of "Participative Action" Groups in a Course in General Psychology. *American Psychologist*, 1952, *7*, 247 (abstract).

Guetzkow, H., Kelley, E. L., and McKeachie, W. J. An Experimental Comparison of Recitation, Discussion, and Tutorial Methods in College Teaching. *Journal of Educational Psychology*, 1954, *45*, 193-207.

Hazeltine, B. P., and Berra, R. L. Supervisory Development—The Research Approach. *Personnel*, 1953, *30*, 60-67.

Heinkel, O. A. *Evaluation of Simulation as a Teaching Device*. Curriculum and Research Office Report No. R-68-19. San Diego: San Diego Community Colleges, 1968.

Johnson, D. M., and Smith, H. C. Democratic Leadership in the Classroom. *Psychological Monographs: General and Applied*, No. 361, *67*, 1953.

Katzell, R. A. Testing a Training Program in Human Relations. *Personnel Psychology*, 1948, *1*, 319-329.

Kerrick, J. S., Clark, V. A., and Rice, D. T. Lecture versus Participation in the Health Training of Peace Corps Volunteers. *Journal of Educational Psychology*, 1967, *58*, 259-265.

Lawshe, C. H., Bolda, R. A., and Brune, R. L. Studies in Management Training Evaluation: II. The Effects of Exposure to Role Playing. *Journal of Applied Psychology*, 1959, *43*, 287-293.

Leton, D. A. An Evaluation of Course Methods in Teaching Child Development. *Journal of Educational Research*, 1961, *55*, 118-122.

Maier, N. R. F. Innovation in Education. *American Psychologist*, 1971, *26*, 722-725.

———, and Salem, A. R. The Contribution of a Discussion Leader to the Quality of Group Thinking: The Effective Use of Minority Opinions. *Human Relations*, 1952, *5*, 277-288.

———, and Maier, R. A. An Experimental Test of the Effects of "Developmental" versus "Free" Discussions on the Quality of Group Decisions. *Journal of Applied Psychology*, 1957, *41*, 320-323.

Mayo, G. D., and DuBois, P. H. Measurement of Gain in Leadership Training. *Educational and Psychological Measurement*, 1963, *23*, 23-31.

McKeachie, W. J. Student-Centered versus Instructor-Centered Instruction. *Journal of Educational Psychology*, 1954, *45*, 143-150.

Mosel, J. N., and Tsacnaris, H. J. Evaluating the Supervisory Training Program. *Journal of Personnel Administration and Industrial Relations*, 1954, *1*, 23-31.

Paploizos, A., and Stiefel, R. Effectiveness of Participative Teaching Methods. *Alberta Journal of Educational Research*, 1971, *17*, 179-190.

Spector, A. J. Changes in Human Relations Attitudes. *Journal of Applied Psychology*, 1958, *42*, 154-157.

Stovall, T. F. Lecture ve. Discussion. *Social Education*, 1956, *20*, 10-12.

Thie, T. M. Testing the Efficiency of the Group Method. *English Journal*, 1925, *14*, 134-137.

Thompson, O., and Tom, F. Comparison of the Effectiveness of a Pupil-Centered versus a Teacher-Centered Pattern for Teaching Vocational Agriculture. *Journal of Educational Research*, 1957, *50*, 667-678.

Thorndike, R. L. Effect of Discussion. *Journal of Social Psychology*, 1938, *9*, 343-362.

Vinacke, W. E. Some Variables in Buzz Sessions. *Journal of Social Psychology*, 1957, *45*, 25-33.

Watson, G. An Evaluation of Small-Group Work in a Large Class. *Journal of Educational Psychology*, 1953, *44*, 385-408.

Wispe, L. G. Evaluating Section Teaching Methods in the Introductory Course. *Journal of Educational Research*, 1951, *45*, 161-168.

Zeleny, L. D. Teaching Sociology by Discussion Group Method. *Sociology and Sociological Research*, 1927, Nov.-Dec., 161-168.

———. Experimental Appraisal of a Group Learning Plan. *Journal of Educational Research*, 1940, *34*, 37-42.

ADDITIONAL RESOURCES

Auer, J. J., and Ewbank, H. L. *Handbook for Discussion Leaders*. New York: Harper and Brothers, 1954.

Beckhard, R. *How to Plan and Conduct Workshops and Conferences*. New York: Association Press, 1956.

Busch, H. M. *Conference Methods in Industry*. New York: Harper and Brothers, 1949.

Cantor, N. F. *The Teaching-Learning Process*. New York: Holt (Dryden Press), 1953.

Golden, O. H. *Training Techniques: A Bibliographic Review*. Chicago: Industrial Relations Center, University of Chicago, 1955.

Miles, M. B. *Learning to Work in Groups*. New York: Teachers College, Columbia University, 1959.

Olmstead, J. A. *Theory and State of the Art of Small-Group Methods of Instruction*. Technical Report 70-3, Alexandria, Va.: Human Resources Research Organization, 1970.

———. *Handbook of Small-Group Methods of Instruction*. Alexandria, Va.: Human Resources Research Organization, 1971.

Thelen, H. A. *The Dynamics of Groups at Work*. Chicago: University of Chicago Press, 1954.

70

MICROTEACHING

by Bruce M. Shore
Associate Professor
Centre for Learning & Development and
Department of Educational Psychology and Sociology
McGill University
Montreal, Quebec, Canada

Portions of this paper have appeared in two previous publications by the author: "Some Applications of Microteaching in Higher Education," *Learning and Development,* 1972, *3* (6), 1-2 (published by the Centre for Learning and Development, McGill University, Montreal); and "Microteaching: It's Not Just Another Gimmick," *Education Canada,* 1972, *12* (1), 16-20 (published by the Canadian Education Association, Toronto).

Microteaching is real teaching reduced in time, number of students, and range of activities. It was developed in 1963 at Stanford University, and was used initially for the training of secondary school teachers. It is equally applicable to elementary teacher education. Five aims guided the plans for the training of teaching skills: (a) providing a realistic teaching situation, (b) assuring minimum risks for both teachers and pupils, (c) exhibiting theoretical soundness (for example, numerous and distributed practice sessions, prompt feedback of results, immediate opportunity to make corrections), (d) providing a wide range of experiences, and (e) being economical in time and resources (Allen and Clark, 1967).

VERSATILITY AND ADAPTABILITY OF MICROTEACHING

Microteaching can be used to teach a wide range of teaching behavior, including responding to silence and nonverbal cues, maintaining participation, asking different kinds and levels of questions, using good examples, and using visual aids (Allen and Ryan, 1969). It is also very well suited to inservice training, to the training of counseling skills such as in interviewing, and as a research setting in studies of learning and teaching.

The main features of a typical microteaching sequence are as follows: A specific teaching skill is identified, such as asking questions that go beyond facts and stated content. The teacher creates a short lesson of about five to 20 minutes in his area of specialization, with a very specific purpose, and teaches it to about five pupils, either real students or his fellow trainees. For example, if he is a history teacher, his microlesson might be about alternative causes of certain events. He could ask questions about hypothetical implications of each. His lesson would be observed by the instructor, who might also make a videotape recording, keeping a careful note of his use of higher-order questioning. The trainee and instructor immediately get together and review the lesson, viewing the videotape, if one was made. A change to reteach the lesson, followed by another meeting, is usually

suggested, and, with the student's very first microlesson, the feedback should focus on his strong points.

Microteaching is very widely used in teacher training. Cooper and Sadker (1972) report data first published in 1968 indicating that it is employed in about half of teacher training institutions. Within any one college, however, use was more likely to be "a small amount" rather than "a good deal." The pattern of diffusion of this innovation, however, does not appear to have been studied in detail. Cooper and Sadker lament the large numbers of institutions which have not adopted microteaching and other innovations, but perhaps their pessimism is premature. It actually seems quite remarkable that such an innovative practice has achieved widespread acceptance in only a decade. Higher education, in general, does not have a reputation for quick and widespread acceptance of validated innovations.

GUIDELINES FOR USING MICROTEACHING BASED ON RESEARCH

Microteaching is such a validated innovation. Allen and Ryan (1969) summarize several years of research in the development of microteaching procedures. Current research has continued the trend of studies seeking optimal strategies for using microteaching in various situations. There is considerable freedom in how the microteaching format can be adapted to individual circumstances (see Van Mondfrans, Hiscox, Fortune, and Johnson, 1973), and it is not expected that all teaching procedures can be taught this way.

The first question faced in using microteaching is deciding which skill to emphasize. If the trainee is a new teacher who has never taught, any of the basic skills, such as eliciting the participation of pupils, could be stressed. With experienced teachers, the skills are more likely to have been chosen by the participants in some way, and to have a "refresher course" image or be directed to very specific skills, such as interpreting nonverbal pupil behavior. This is quite difficult for someone who has no teaching experience.

How long should the microlesson be? Allen and Ryan (1969) found no differences between four- and seven-minute lessons. They suggest resisting the desire for longer lessons. This is a teacher-centered, not a pupil-centered, technique: the teacher's behavior is of interest. Four minutes are enough for the instructor and the trainee to achieve their goals. Of course, whether the pupils learned what they were supposed to is a crucial test of the effectiveness of the teaching. Microteaching is a way to train specific teaching skills; there is always more to good teaching than these skills themselves, but the microlesson is not enough of a complete lesson to make such broad judgments. This has to wait until the trainee has a real class to teach. The aim is to teach the trainee skills which will transfer to real situations when he meets them.

An ethical problem is introduced in getting pupils to "practice on," since their learning is not the foremost purpose during the actual microlesson. There are answers to this challenge. First, the larger goal of microteaching is to better train teachers, with lasting effects in real teaching. Second, pupils can be paid volunteers, quite different from the captive audiences presented to the neophyte trainee during a more usual first-teaching internship. Microteaching was intended to precede and supplement such internships, not to replace them. All persons serving as students—real pupils, paid volunteers, psychology students, or fellow trainees—are informed of their training role. Third, microteaching is done in the presence of a supervisor, with the exception of trainees working only with each other.

Do the effects of microteaching carry through to the classroom? Apparently so, if the pupils with whom the microteaching is done are similar to those with whom the trainee will actually work (Johnson, 1971). Different pupils or the trainees' colleagues would be second choices when there are shortages of either time, money, or representative students. Studies have also shown no differences between microteaching and two other training frameworks, a programmed videotape and lecture-discussion using still pictures from the videotape, in nonverbal teacher skills designed to encourage classroom interaction (e.g., eye contacts, nodding, moving toward pupils) (Pancrazio and Johnson, 1971). These techniques did share the important feature of very limited purposes, very clearly defined. The proponents of microteaching would be quite satisfied with these results, as microteaching has added to the repertoire of procedures for training. More effective teaching is undoubtedly the most important outcome sought from microteaching during teacher training. There are others. One study has been cited in which teachers trained with microteaching did indeed demonstrate greater teaching skill than colleagues who were not exposed to microteaching, but they also expressed less favorable attitudes to teaching (McPherson, 1971). These broader effects are beginning to receive research attention, but it is always difficult to design studies in which a control group that does not get the "special" treatment of the experimental group is indeed equivalent in every other way.

The importance of supervision in microteaching cannot be overstressed, and it is a major subject of current research. Microteaching is controlled practice of very specific teaching behavior. The choice of material and method would not be, without reference to the supervisor or instructor.

All the reports of the use of microteaching stress the first feedback and discussion following the microlesson. The second microlesson might not always be necessary, and the videotaping is not a crucial part of the process. Video tape does provide an explicit record of a lesson, allows the collection of examples (with permission of the people filmed), and is particularly useful if students work on their own and the instructor views the video tapes at a more convenient time.

AN EXAMPLE OF MICROTEACHING IN USE

Microteaching is a very flexible process, which can readily be adapted to suit an individual instructor's needs. Professor Jan Lobelle, of McGill University's Department of Education in Second languages, has divided classes of about 30 students into four work groups. Each

student in turn is given a "mini-language lesson" to prepare. This would be one unit of course content, generally a grammar problem. The students are instructed to cover two separate phases in their lessons: (a) to present the material or problem, and (b) to elicit a variety of responses which indicate that the student audience is learning.

This preparatory stage in microteaching is generally standard, but beyond this point there are many ways of devising the format of the videotape sessions (if used) and evaluative feedback. Professor Lobelle deviates from the standard format in several significant ways:

The students are collectively responsible for the initial evaluation sessions, which they conduct themselves with the instructor absent for the entire period.

Each student first submits the plan of his "mini-lesson" to seven of his peers for evaluation and discussion. Following this, the lesson is presented "live" and videotaped. The student's performance is evaluated by his peers, using a checklist of language teaching behavior as a guideline. There is no video playback at this time.

Because the instructor is not present for the micro-lesson and taping, each student submits to the instructor a short report on his lesson, including the comments of his peers.

When all of the lessons have been given, the instructor shows selected parts of the video tapes to the entire group, in order to compare performance in specific areas. Comments are made by both the instructor and the student.

This course could have been set up in a variety of ways, depending on the objectives, time, and facilities. In this case, the instructor has chosen to emphasize the development of student responsibility and evaluation skills.

ADVANTAGES OF MICROTEACHING IN TEACHER TRAINING

Allen and Ryan (1969) saw five main advantages, especially if microteaching is a routine part of the training of teachers. First, faculty have to get together to agree on common purposes in its use. Second, it becomes feasible to closely follow trainee performance. Third, the program is individualized, and not bound by any particular "course" structure. Fourth, evidence of suitability for teaching is obtained. Fifth, it is a useful research tool.

Craig (1969) added two others. First, it simplifies the complex teaching process in the trainees' first contact with the tasks involved. Teaching is viewed as including specific skills which can be learned individually, rather than relying on a less useful global point of view (Gage, 1968). This does not imply that complete fragmentation is possible, merely that some is desirable. One result is that, with microteaching, students are able to actually study teaching in simplified situations. It is an opportunity to learn to teach and also to learn about teaching (Johnson, 1967).

Craig's second point is that microteaching is very efficient in terms of staff time and use of real pupils, their classrooms, and training facilities. Kallenbach and Gall (1969) have reported that microteaching can achieve results comparable to those attained by conventional methods in as little as one-fifth the time, and with fewer administrative problems. Finally, most reports mention that trainees' apprehension concerning their first classroom experience is greatly lessened.

Three other advantages are the result of instructors' general experience with microteaching. First, it is flexible and adaptable to local needs. Second, it is very easily initiated. Third, it can be employed fairly independently and unobtrusively by an individual instructor.

CONTROVERSIES CONCERNING MICROTEACHING

The first controversy concerning microteaching is over the use of videotaping. Not much can be said about it other than videotaping is usually used with microteaching, but it does not have to be. Video tape can have two major uses in microteaching: first, as a procedure for identifying which skills need enhancing and convincing a teacher this is so; second, it is a powerful feedback instrument during instruction. Simply using video tape to show a teacher his performance, without the accompanying preparation of a detailed instructional and practice sequence, is not microteaching.

Borg and his associates (1969, 1970) have been particularly concerned about possible detrimental effects of some supervisors. They developed the Minicourse, based on microteaching principles. The Minicourse differs from microteaching in four principal ways: (a) it is primarily an inservice, not preservice, model; (b) it is a self-contained package that can be used wherever videotaping is available; (c) trainees are self-evaluated by a structured critique, not by a supervisor; and (d) films or tapes of model lessons serve as the basis for evaluation.

Studies attempting to compare microteaching and Minicourses have not yielded clear comparisons. One reason is obviously that microteaching is not a single event. It is a process of instructional design, of which the Minicourse is actually an example. This is equally true of other spin-offs, such as microcounselling (Ivey et al., 1968) and microplanning (Waimon, Bell, and Ramseyer, 1972). Borg is correct that microteaching is not self-contained, and that it relies heavily on supervisory feedback. There are surely times when these are not disadvantages—for example, in some voluntary inservice training, and undisputedly in preservice training.

Gillion (1969) cautioned that users of microteaching might get the impression that the "micro" situation is the same as the real classroom. However realistic, it is not the same. Emphasis has to be explicitly on the teaching skills acquired, not on the conditions under which they were learned. Student teaching itself is the introduction to the real classroom.

Like any versatile technique, microteaching can be used to achieve undesirable goals. Skills might be taught which perpetuate obsolete practices of instruction and classroom organization. The individuals involved continue to have the responsibility for concentrating on relevant teacher behavior. It is similarly important to avoid concentrating too much on skills whose contribution to student learning is not wide, such as lecturing.

OTHER APPLICATIONS OF MICROTEACHING IN HIGHER EDUCATION

In addition to its wide use in teacher education, microteaching is used in at least three other ways in higher education:

First, elements of microteaching can be used in the training of other professionals: for example, in theology, learning to deliver a sermon; in engineering, presenting a professional paper; and in social work, meeting a client for the first time. In microcounselling, interviewing skills receive particular attention.

Second, inservice microteaching experiences in leading small groups, diagnostic testing, remedial instruction, or using the blackboard and other audiovisual aids effectively, can be offered to faculty and graduate assistants.

Finally, microteaching is a useful research tool. Learning and teaching involve very complex events. Microteaching is one technique which facilitates their study in simplified situations. It is easily used by any instructor who might be asking questions such as which of several explanations is best understood by students, or in what order certain topics should be taught. It is possible to try out various alternatives, with little risk or expense, and so eliminate some of the guesswork that so often confronts the teacher.

CONCLUSION—LEARNING HOW TO TEACH AND LEARNING ABOUT TEACHING

Microteaching provides opportunities for student teachers and researchers to learn the science of teaching as well as the practice. From what has been said above, there are at least five reasons for this dual advantage.

First, the analytical approach to appropriate teaching skills allows careful monitoring of programs and assessment in terms of mastery criteria. It becomes possible to say with some certainty what the student has learned in this portion of his preparation for teaching.

Second, microteaching (with its variations) is supported by a specific and growing research literature.

Third, by providing simplified teaching settings, microteaching can provide a low-threat environment for experimenting with new ideas. It can allow for some discovery learning in teacher preparation. This is a good example of the idea of learning how to learn, of giving students at all levels techniques with which they can learn on their own. Microteaching, in this sense, is a good example of practicing what we preach in teacher education.

Fourth, microteaching is not dependent on any particular facilities or equipment. The usefulness of recording facilities has been acknowledged, but the technique can be as effectively applied in the middle of a field trip without even portable equipment. The most important ingredients are the people involved.

Finally, microteaching focuses on teaching behavior. This is the heart of the question of studying teaching, and learning how to do it well.

REFERENCES

Allen, D. W., and Clark, R. J., Jr. Microteaching: Its Rationale. *The High School Journal*, 1967, *51*, 75-79.

———, and Ryan D. *Microteaching*. Reading, Mass.: Addison-Wesley, 1969.

Borg, W. R., Kallenbach, W., Morris, M., and Friebel, Allen. Videotape Feedback and Microteaching in a Teacher Training Model. *The Journal of Experimental Education*, 1969, *37*, 9-16.

———, Langer, P., and Kelly, M. L. The Minicourse: A New Tool for the Education of Teachers. *Education*, 1970, *90*, 232-238.

Cooper, J. M., and Sadker, D. Current Trends in Teacher Education Curriculum. *The Journal of Teacher Education*, 1972, *23* (3), 312-317.

Craig, D. G. Microteaching—To Improve Teacher Education. *The Agricultural Education Magazine*, 1969, *41*, 170 and 173.

Gage, N. L. Analytical Approach to Research on Instructional Methods. *Journal of Experimental Education*, 1968, *37*, 119-125. Also in *Phi Delta Kappan*, 1968, *49*, 601-606.

Gilliom, M. E. Microteaching in the Methods Course: Bridging the Confrontation Gap. *Social Education*, 1969, *33*, 165-167, 183.

Ivey, A. E., Normington, C. J., Miller, C. D., Morrill, W. H., and Haase, R. F. Microteaching and Attending Behavior: An Approach to Prepracticum Counselor Training. *Journal of Counseling Psychology Monograph Supplement*, 1968, *15* (5, Pt. 2), 1-12.

Johnson, W. D. Microteaching: A Medium in Which to Study Teaching. *The High School Journal*, 1967, *51*, 86-92.

———. The Effectiveness of Three Microteaching Environments in Preparing Undergraduates for Student Teaching. Paper Presented at the Annual Meeting of the American Educational Research Association, New York, February 1971.

Kallenbach, W. W., and Gall, M. D. Microteaching versus Conventional Methods in Training Elementary Intern Teachers. *The Journal of Educational Research*, 1969, *63*, 136-141.

McPherson, J. J. Recent Developments in Research on the Use of Audio-Visual Media in Teacher Education in the United States. *Educational Media International*, 1971, *1* (2), 3-10.

Pancrazio, S. B., and Johnson, W. D. Comparisons of Three Teacher Training Approaches in Non-Verbal Behaviors which Encourage Classroom Interaction. Paper presented at the Annual Meeting of the American Educational Research Association, New York, February 1971.

Van Mondfrans, A. P., Hiscox, S. B., Fortune, J. C., and Johnson, W. Microteaching: An Examination of the Model and its Variations. Paper presented at the Annual Meeting of the American Educational Research Association, New Orleans, February-March 1973.

Waimon, M. D., Bell, D. D., and Ramseyer, G. C. The Effects of Competency-Based Training on the Performance of Prospective Teachers. *The Journal of Teacher Education*, 1972, *23* (2), 237-245.

ADDITIONAL RESOURCES

Cooper, J. M. (Stanford U., Palo Alto). Developing Specific Teaching Skills Through Microteaching. *The High School Journal*, 1967, *51*, 80-85.

Gregory, T. B. *Encounters with Teaching: A Microteaching Manual*. Englewood Cliffs, N.J.: Prentice-Hall, 1972.

Where the Experts Are

The annual meeting program of Division C, American Educational Research Association, regularly includes sessions on microteaching. The central office address is 1126 Sixteenth Street, N.W., Washington, D.C. 20036; telephone (202)223-9485.

The orignator of microteaching, Dwight W. Allen, is now at the School of Education at the University of Massachusetts, Amherst, Mass. 01002.

71

TEAM TEACHING: COOPERATIVE ORGANIZATIONAL CONCEPT

by Harvey N. Sterns
Associate Dean
School of Education
Lockhaven State College
Lock Haven, Pennsylvania

Team teaching is a cooperative organizational concept for educational personnel which involves the association of two or more team members, who may be of different professional status, in assuming the joint responsibility for planning, preparing, presenting, and evaluating all or part of the instructional program for a group of students on a regular, sustained basis.

Team teaching has been referred to as a grouping plan for teachers, cooperative teaching, team planning, group teaching, team organization, and collaborative teaching. Team teaching has been closely associated with the related organizational concepts of staff utilization and staff differentiation for teachers, and grouping and organizational plans for students, such as nongraded school organization and flexible modular scheduling.

Team teaching is related to, and derived from, earlier grouping and organizational plans for teachers and students, such as the Lancaster Monitorial system, the Dalton Plan, the Winnetka Plan, and, especially, the Cooperative Group Plan of the 1930s. Team teaching has been identified with the reform movements of individualization of instruction, open education, the utilization of paraprofessionals, and the recognition of varying roles and responsibilities for teachers.

In practice, teaching teams have infinite variations, often dependent on the number and qualifications of the personnel involved. There are, however, certain characteristics which are common to the elementary, secondary, and teacher education teams which will be discussed here. Teams may be collegial or hierarchical in structure, and interdisciplinary or unidisciplinary in composition. Student groups or learning teams may vary in size from 25 to 200, while teaching teams may be composed of two to eight or more members.

SCOPE

First mentioned in the *Education Index* in 1957-1959 (Volume 2), the practice of cooperative team teaching has been well documented since the now classic Franklin School Project in 1957 (Anderson et al., 1971), especially at the elementary and secondary levels, and has recently been identified as a noticeable trend in teacher education programs.

At the elementary level, the most recent National Education Association Research Division (1972) data indicate that 43 percent of the elementary schools in systems enrolling 300 or more students were using team teaching in 1971. In large school systems, with 25,000 or more students, team teaching was practiced by 90 percent of the elementary schools. This trend had been identified ten years earlier in 1962, when a national survey indicated that nearly 15 percent of the elementary schools were practicing team teaching, and that this figure was expected to increase to 30 percent by 1966 (NEA, 1962).

At the secondary education level, the same 1972 report indicates that 35 percent of the secondary schools in systems enrolling 300 or more students were using team teaching. In large school systems, with more than 25,000 students, team teaching was being used by 82 percent of the secondary schools. Earlier National Education Association Research Division reports indicated that team teaching was being practiced by five percent of the secondary schools in 1956, 12 percent in 1961, and 31 percent planned use in 1966 (NEA, 1967). Cawelti (1967) found that 41 percent of the high schools in his study reported the use of team teaching. He also found that team teaching was innovative (used by fewer than one-fourth of high schools) in eight states, and used by more than one-half of high schools in 11 states.

At the teacher education level, team teaching was apparently first identified as a trend by Languis and others (1969), with their report on the Ohio Middle Elementary Teaching Team program. In 1969, six of the nine comprehensive models for elementary teacher education contained provisions for team teaching experiences, and all nine provided for some form of staff utilization or staff differentiation (Burdin and Lanzillotti, 1969). In 1970 the trend was further apparent, when 37 percent of the 106 American Association of Colleges for Teacher Education Distinguished Achievement Awards participants, including the award recipient, reported some form of team teaching, staff utilization or staff differentiation (AACTE, 1970). Since 1970, the National Teacher Corps program in undergraduate and graduate teacher education in 38 states has required at least one semester of team teaching for all interns. It is apparent that the practice of cooperative team teaching has been well established in the elementary and secondary schools as an accepted organizational concept.

In teacher education programs, a growing trend toward the use of cooperative team teaching methods in student teaching has been identified, which should be considered innovative until we have more definitive data on the scope of such practices nationally.

REVIEW OF PERTINENT LITERATURE

The extent of the availability of research material on the subject of team teaching may be ascertained somewhat from the fact that during a 12-month period (July 1972 to June 1973) the Educational Resources Information Center offered 17 studies under the subject heading of team teaching in their *Research in Education* publication. These reports deal with the topics of differentiated staffing, male influence, team talk analysis, nongraded school organization, paraprofessionals, planning teams, open education and disadvantaged children; the subject areas of reading and physics; and the levels of kindergarten-early childhood education, elementary education, secondary education and adult basic education (Educational Resources Information Centers, 1972, 1973). This review will center on the major findings concerning student achievement and adjustment in team teaching organizations at the elementary, secondary, and teacher education levels.

Sterns and Cooper (1973), in reporting on an elementary cooperative team teaching experiment, found no significant differences in achievement in reading and language for teamed students, but found significant differences in sociograph rejections received favoring the modified self-contained control groups. They concluded that the problems of unadjusted students may be increased in a dual-teacher, team teaching organization. This finding supported an earlier research report by Bennett (1962), who reported a sharp decrease in group integration for some teamed students.

Thomas and Cresimbeni (1967) cite an elementary team teaching experiment at Dedham, Massachusetts, involving 45 teachers and 1,200 intermediate-grade students, which indicated a 50 to 74 percent increase in achievement and growth, in all subjects, beyond the normal rate for teamed students.

Lambert et al. (1970) cite five studies at the elementary level and report no marked differences in achievement. Lambert (1964) found no significant differences in personal or social adjustment between team and control groups. Lambert et al. (1970) commented on the serious lack of controlled studies, and concluded that "the literature does not provide evidence that achievement is superior with either organizational approach, team or self-contained, on the elementary level (p. 503)." Similar conclusions were reached by Nystrand and Bertolaet, 1967, and Heathers, 1965.

Meehan (1973), in reviewing five research studies at the secondary level conducted during 1965-1970, reports that three of the five found no significant gains in achievement for the teamed students. He does report, however, that teamed students apparently displayed better attitudes toward teachers, greater subject matter interest, an improved sense of personal freedom, and greater self-reliance, which were characterized as positive results in the affective domain. In one study, a saving of 25 minutes a week was reported for teachers and students in a modular scheduling experiment. The study by Schlaadt (1969), in teaching health to high school students, concluded that "Students of superior mental ability taught health by the team-teaching method showed a statistically significant gain over students of superior mental ability taught by the traditional method (p. 162)."

Lambert et al. (1970) cite seven studies at the secondary level, two of which reported significant differences in achievement. Vars (1970), commenting on the evaluation of team teaching generally, wrote: "At the moment the most that can be said about the results of team teaching is that teachers, students, and their parents are generally favorable, and student achievement usually equals or slightly exceeds that expected under more conventional arrangements (p. 322)."

There have been few reported studies on team teaching-teacher education programs to date. One brief report on the 1973 American Association of Colleges for Teacher Education Distinguished Awards program from Western Washington State College indicates that: "Evaluation results, validated by an independent auditor, show significant increases in the rates of cognitive development in elementary students and criterion level performances for most college students in the program (p. 10)."

Comments on the Bowling Green State University Center System (1972) include the reaction that the public schools are able to lower the teacher-pupil ratio and individualize instruction through team teaching. It has also been reported that the cooperating teachers involved are pleased with the increased planning time provided by team teaching, and that parents enthusiastically support the program. Other teacher education programs, involving Wisconsin State University and the public schools of LaCrosse, Wisconsin, have reported that teachers and students are supportive of the team teaching aspect of their programs (Sterns, 1972).

Altman (1973), in reviewing the research on the micro-team teaching program at the University of Wisconsin-LaCrosse, concludes "the micro-team practice teachers . . . showed up as well, and in some instances higher than the interns, indicating a more effective practice teaching experience (p. 88)."

It is apparent from a review of the literature on team teaching that the quantity of studies, if not the quality, has increased noticeably since Anderson (1960) decried the lack of fundamental discussion on the subject. The need for carefully controlled studies continues.

It cannot be concluded from the literature that being involved in team teaching has either increased or lessened student achievement, and the results are about the same for student adjustment. The possible loss of group integration for unadjusted students, the affective domain influence on students, and the effectiveness of student teaching in a cooperative team teaching organization should be considered for further testing in future studies.

SPECIFIC PROGRAMS AND APPLICATIONS

In West Virginia, where the practice of team teaching was found to be innovative by Cawelti (1967) at the high school level, the elementary schools in the Kanawha County Schools began a nongraded-continuous progress program in 1960-1961, which has grown to include some 90 schools and involves cooperative teaching concepts. Since 1968, all elementary buildings have been constructed specifically to facilitate flexible student grouping and team teaching. The Kanawha County Schools Continuous Progress (1971) plan began with two teacher teams housed in pods, and has grown into the open education concept that includes the use of teacher aides, specialists, and student teachers. Specific schools which have been constructed for team teaching include the Grandview, Ruthlawn, Boreman, and Piedmont.

The Piedmont School, which opened in 1970, features a nongraded-team teaching structure, with six learning teams of 85 students instructed by six teaching teams composed of a lead teacher, two generalist teachers, one paid paraprofessional, one student teacher, and one or more volunteer aides. The lead teachers are responsible for two teaching-learning teams. Specialist teachers in mathematics-science, art, music, physical education, reading and instructional media, and special education are additional personnel considered as members of all six teams. The entire second floor of this innovative two-level building features open instructional space with no interior walls.

The Temple City, California plan of differentiated staffing has received wide attention and imitation of its hierarchical structure based on differentiated teacher roles, responsibilities, and compensation. While not specifically a team teaching organization, the Temple City plan contains the necessary elements for conducting cooperative teaching. The plan, influenced by Dwight Allen, provides four levels of responsibility and three support levels: (1) the master teacher, who has a research and teaching responsibility; (2) the senior teacher, who in a team teaching situation would serve as team leader; (3) the staff teacher, who is responsible for individualized instruction, large- and small-group instruction, and tutoring; and (4) the associate teacher, who is a team-teaching partner and assistant in large group instruction. The three levels of support personnel are academic assistants, educational technicians, and clerks. Salaries range from $5,000 to $25,000. The plan was implemented at the secondary level, but has developed into a K-12 model of differentiated staffing with the addition of senior teachers of instruction and technology at the K-to-6 level, and the retention of the master teacher as a subject matter specialist K-12 (Rand and English, 1972).

A relatively new concept which is developing, relating to student teaching in a team teaching organization, involves the teaching center concept, which is based on a closer relationship between the public schools and teacher education institutions. Such programs are operating at the Wisconsin State University Center, Bowling

Green State University Center System, the Kanawha County Student Teacher Center, and the University of Toledo Teaching Center.

Team teaching concepts are being utilized on several levels in the teacher education programs in elementary education, secondary education, and the Teacher Corps programs at the University of Toledo. The elementary undergraduate program is characterized by interdisciplinary team instruction. The Teacher Corps student teaching team is composed of a team leader, two or three cooperating teachers, and five or six interns. The elementary and secondary education teaching center teams consist of a cooperating teacher, a university supervisor, participant teachers, and three levels of student teachers: career decision aides, field students, and student teachers (Silula, 1973).

Perhaps the most recent development in teacher education-team teaching programs is taking place this school year at Indiana University, where four alternative programs in Secondary social studies are being offered. In addition to the regular program, the student has a choice of three plans which involve team teaching concepts and include interdisciplinary instructional teams, public school teachers and supervisors, and graduate students—who cooperatively select students, plan programs, develop materials, and evaluate participants and program. Student teachers select their cooperating teachers for their student teaching from their instructional team teachers (Marker, 1973).

CURRENT CONTROVERSIES

Johnson and Burns (1970) maintain that team teaching is a highly controversial practice because of the many uncertainties regarding just what team teaching is, and suggest that the association of team teaching with other controversial issues, such as ability grouping of students, subject matter emphasis, large-group instruction, and the hierarchal team structure aspect, may be some of the reasons for concern. They conclude that "a great deal more clarification and research is needed before team teaching can be conclusively defined as a desirable elementary school practice (p. 501)."

Silberman (1970) contends that, while team teaching was originally designed to create options for teachers to move from assistant teacher to regular teacher, and possibly gain team leader status, as the differentiated staff concept implies, "This has not happened to any noticeable extent . . . . As often as not, in fact, team teaching is simply a new label for old fashioned departmentalization (p. 162)."

Olds (1970) maintains that the changing role of teachers in a team teaching organization may be the most controversial issue of all, and that: "Perhaps the most drastic change of functions in the traditional classroom is the placing of the teacher in a cooperative relationship with another adult (p. 229)."

The issue of the lack of understanding about team teaching may be inherent in the flexibility of team teaching, in that each team may vary according to the local situation and personnel involved. There may be no satisfactory answer to this issue, except to point out that as

Dean and Witherspoon (1962) stated: "The heart of the concept of team teaching lies not in details of structure and organization but more in the essential spirit of cooperative planning, constant collaboration, close unity, unrestrained communication, and sincere sharing (p. 4)" that is characteristic of team teaching organizations.

The issue of ability grouping is not necessarily germane to team teaching as such. Team teaching plans may include ability grouping, of course, but the better plans provide for various student grouping patterns based on interest and social considerations as well as achievement and potential. The large group instruction aspect is, of course, a basic ingredient of many team teaching plans, such as the Trump Plan. It should be apparent, however, that this suggested plan calls for 40 percent large-group instruction, 30 percent small-group discussion, and 30 percent independent study (Trump, 1960).

Subject matter emphasis is often associated with departmentalized organization. The proponents of team teaching point out that team teaching is a response to the increased need for specialists, and that the cooperative aspects of team teaching tend to minimize the potential danger of subject matter emphasis by specialists because each team member often teaches most subject areas, in addition to an area of specialization. Team teaching is credited as combining the best features of the departmentalized and self-contained organizations (Anderson, 1960).

The hierarchal structure of team teaching organizations, based on the staff differentiation concept, has resulted in a differentiation of compensation according to role responsibility. The salary differential has been most often applied to those individuals charged with team leadership responsibilities. This practice is possibly related to a revival of the merit pay controversy, and is in opposition to the single salary concept. The proponents of team teaching respond that the differentiated roles and responsibilities in highly developed team teaching organizations are compensated for in terms of differentiated salary, and that this feature is long overdue in providing for the differences in teachers.

As to the charge that team teaching was designed to create options for teachers, Shaplin (1964) indicates that the basis for team teaching was threefold: (1) to provide position and rank classifications to make teaching more attractive and satisfactory to teachers; (2) to use teacher aides to relieve teachers; and (3) to use large-group instruction to utilize the special abilities of teachers, and to save teacher time and effort. If teachers have not been able to move upward through the hierarchy of the team teaching structure, which is open to question, it may be a limitation but it doesn't seem to have been a part of the original design as far as the literature is concerned.

There is no doubt that the teacher's role is in the process of changing from a center-stage director of learning activities to a manager-facilitator of instruction. This change is perhaps most apparent in the area of team teaching, where team members are involved interpersonally with team leaders, subject matter specialists, experienced and inexperienced team teachers, student teachers, paraprofessionals, clerical aides, administrators, parents, students, and support personnel such as counselors and school nurses.

Responsibilities within the team may vary according to ability, preparation, and experience. Special leadership skills are required for team leaders. Indeed, this position is viewed as an emerging instructional leadership position, which aids administration by reducing the span of control and requires effective working relationships with teachers, parents, aides, children, and administrators. The team leader must have the ability to coordinate the team's efforts, plan and organize effective learning experiences for children, and assess the quality of the team's effort—often with a large group of students (Hicks, 1970).

Spauling (1970), in defining the role of the teacher for the seventies, has commented:

> There obviously will be a redistribution of functions which are now all performed by the teacher in a self-contained classroom. There will be team approaches to planning and teaching. There will be much more peer-teaching, that is, students planning their own studies and helping each other learn. Specialist administrators will be facilitators, members of the teaching team, providing the resources needed for teaching and learning, rather than inspectors and supervisors, who act as policemen and wardens. (p. 7)

Lauwerys (1971), in discussing the type of teachers needed for the year 2000, writes: "All teachers must learn how to participate actively in group teaching and how to function happily in continuous progress, nongraded schools (p. 6)."

Few teachers, however, have had either preparation or experience with cooperative team teaching methods. They need preparation in small-group dynamics and large-group instructional techniques. One promising solution to this problem is a cooperative effort between teacher education institutions and public school systems using team teaching (Alexander and others, 1971).

Perhaps the changing role of the teacher in cooperative team teaching organizations is the most important issue to be raised here. It is clear that teacher education institutions will have a tremendous responsibility in providing the needed personnel for the many team teaching plans in operation and being planned. The future of this movement may well depend on the degree of cooperative planning, development, and evaluation demonstrated by the public school and higher education personnel involved in formulating the necessary preparation programs for the teachers of tomorrow.

REFERENCES

Alexander, W. M. et al. *The High School: Today and Tomorrow.* New York: Holt, Rinehart and Winston, Inc., 1971.

Altman, B. E., and Williams, E. E. *Monday Morning.* Winona, Minnesota: St. Mary's College Press, 1973.

American Association of Colleges for Teacher Education. *Excellence in Teacher Education, 1970.* Washington, D.C.: The Association, 1970.

_____. *Excellence in Teacher Education, 1973.* Washington, D.C.: The Association, 1973.

Anderson, R. H. *Team Teaching.* CAPCI Bibliography. ASCD-NEA Research Division, November, 1960.

_____. Some Types of Cooperative Teaching in Current Use.

The National Elementary Principal, 1965, *44,* 22-26.

_____ et al. Team Teaching in an Elementary School. *Change and Innovation in Elementary and Secondary Organization,* Second Edition. Edited by M. Hillson and R. T. Hyman. New York: Holt, Rinehart and Winston, Inc., 1971, 111-121.

BGSU Operates Center System for Student Teacher Program. *OSBA Journal,* 1972, *20.*

Bennett, H. K. *Analysis of a Team Teaching and of a Self-Contained Homeroom Experiment in Grades 5 and 6.* Report given at Atlantic City AERA, February 1962. (Mimeographed.)

Burdin, J. L., and Lanzillotti, Kaliopee, eds. *A Reader's Guide to the Comprehensive Models for Preparing Elementary Teachers.* Washington, D.C.: ERIC and AACTE, 1969.

Cawelti, G. Innovative Practices in High Schools: Who Does What—and Why—and How. *Nation's Schools,* 1967, *79,* 56-88.

Dean, S. E., and Witherspoon, C. F. Team Teaching in the Elementary School. *Education Briefs,* No. 38. Washington, D.C.: U.S. Office of Education, 1962.

Educational Resources Information Center. *Research in Education.* Washington, D.C.: U.S. Government Printing Office, 1972, 1973.

Heathers, G. Research on Implementing and Evaluating Cooperative Teaching. *The National Elementary Principal,* 1965, *44,* 27-33.

Hicks, W. V. et al. *The New Elementary School Curriculum.* New York: Van Nostrand Reinhold Co., 1970.

Johnston, A. M., and Burns, P. C., eds. *Research in Elementary School Curriculum.* Boston: Allyn and Bacon, Inc., 1970.

Kanawha County Schools. *Continuous Progress Manual.* Charleston, West Virginia, 1971.

_____. *Kanawha County Student Teaching Center.* Charleston, West Virginia, n.d.

Lambert, P. et al. *Classroom Interaction, Pupil Achievement, and Adjustment in Team Teaching as Compared with the Self-Contained Classroom.* Cooperative Research Project No. 1391, Madison, Wisconsin, 1964.

_____. A Comparison of Pupil Achievement in Team and Self-Contained Organizations. *Research in Elementary School Curriculum.* Edited by A. M. Johnston and P. C. Burns. Boston: Allyn and Bacon, Inc., 1970, 502-511.

Languis, M. L. et al. Teaming: Innovation in Teacher Education. *Educational Leadership,* May 1969, *26,* 806-810.

Lauwerys, J. Crisis and Change in Teacher Education. *Teacher Education,* 1971. Washington, D.C.: International Council on Education for Teaching, 1971, 3-8.

Marker, G. W. Increasing the Options in Social Studies. *Phi Delta Kappan,* March 1973, *54,* 480-482.

Meehan, M. L. What About Team Teaching? *Educational Leadership,* May 1973, *8,* 717-720.

National Education Association—Project on the Instructional Program of the Public Schools. *The Principals Look at the Schools,* 1962, 18.

National Education Association—Research Division. Team Teaching. *NEA Research Bulletin,* December 1967, *45,* 114-115.

_____. *Team Teaching in Public School Systems,* 1971, September 1972.

Nystrand, R. O., and Bertolaet, F. Strategies for Allocating Human and Material Resources. *Review of Educational Research,* October 1967, *37,* 448-468.

Rand, M. J., and English F. W. Differentiated Staffing: Trying on Seven League Boots. *Differentiated Staffing.* Edited by J. A. Cooper. Philadelphia: W. B. Saunders Co., 1972, 103-119.

Schlaadt, R. G. An Analysis of the Effectiveness of Team Teaching Compared to Traditional Teaching of Health to High School Sophomore Students. *Change and Innovation in Elementary and Secondary Organization,* Second Edition. Edited by M. Hillson and R. T. Hyman. New York: Holt, Rinehart and Winston, Inc., 1971, 149-153.

Shaplin, J. T. Antecedents of Team Teaching. *Team Teaching.* Edited by J. T. Shaplin and H. F. Olds, Jr. New York: Harper & Row, 1964, 24–56.

Sikula, J. P., ed. *Educational Comment, 1973: Teacher Education for an Urban Setting.* The University of Toledo, 1973.

Silberman, C. E. *Crisis in the Classroom.* New York: Random House, Inc., 1970.

Spaulding, S. New Developments in Education for the Seventies. *Teacher Education, 1970.* Washington, D.C.: International Council on Education for Teaching, 1970, 1-8.

Sterns, H. N. Team Teaching in Teacher Education Programs. *The Journal of Teacher Education,* fall, 1972, *23,* 318-322.

_____, and Cooper, D. H. Team Teaching: Student Adjustment and Achievement. *The Journal of Educational Research,* March 1973, *66,* 323-327.

Thomas, G. I., and Crescimbeni, J. *Individualizing Instruction in the Elementary School.* New York: Random House, 1967.

Trump, J. L. *New Directions to Quality Education.* Washington, D.C.: National Association of Secondary-School Principals, 1960.

Vars, G. F. Teaching in Teams. *Principles and Practice of Teaching.* Edited by J. F. Ohles. New York: Random House, 1970, 312-323.

ADDITIONAL RESOURCES

Bair, M., and Woodward, R. G. *Team Teaching in Action.* Boston: Houghton-Mifflin Co., 1964.

Beggs, D. W. III, ed. *Team Teaching: Bold New Venture.* Indianapolis: Unified College Press, Inc., 1964.

Clinchy, E. *Schools for Team Teaching.* New York: Educational Facilities Laboratories, Inc., 1961.

Fund for the Advancement of Education. *Decade of Experiment.* New York: The Fund, 1961.

Gross, C. E. *Pupils, Patterns and Possibilities.* Annual Report. Pittsburgh, Pa.: Board of Public Education, 1961.

Heller, M. P. *Team Teaching.* Educational Research Council of Greater Cleveland, 1963.

Mitchell, R., ed. *Claremont Teaching Team Program.* Annual Report. Claremont, California: Claremont Graduate School, 1962-1963.

Norwalk Schools. *The Norwalk Plan.* A two-year study supported by the Fund for the Advancement of Education. Norwalk, Connecticut, September, 1960.

Polos, N. C. *The Dynamics of Team Teaching.* Dubuque, Iowa: William C. Brown Co., 1965.

Smith, J. B. *The Dundee Design.* The History of the Planning for a Team-Teaching Program. Greenwich, Connecticut, October 1962.

72

CORE CURRICULUM

by Gordon F. Vars
Professor of Education
Kent State University
Kent, Ohio

A core curriculum is a form of block-time program in which learning experiences are organized around problems of significance to students, with conventional subject matter brought in only as needed to deal with these problems.

Sometimes the term "core curriculum" is applied to any type of interdisciplinary program, but it is more properly restricted to block-time programs with a distinctive curricular emphasis. That is, instead of mere correlation or fusion of subject matter from several courses, core represents a direct attack on the major personal and social problems confronting manking. Examination of these problems is given higher priority than mastery of any specified subject matter.

As in other block-time programs, a core class may be taught by one teacher or by a team, it may occupy from one-fourth to one-half a student's schedule, and it usually replaces English, social studies, and homeroom. The balance of the school program consists of other subjects, both required and elective, and student activities. Any or all of these may be correlated with the activities of the core class.

STATUS

Core curriculum is recognized by many curriculum experts as one of the few genuinely different approaches to education that have appeared within this century. Although its roots have been traced far back into educational theory, it was a distinct feature of the secondary education programs that evolved during the progressive education era. In its emphasis on student needs, rational inquiry, and democratic processes, core parallels the elementary school innovations of this period, such as the "activity movement," the "project method," or the "experience curriculum" (Vars, 1972).

Programs so unconventional have never been widespread. They constituted approximately 12 percent of the junior high block-time programs identified through surveys carried out in the late 1950s and mid-1960s (Wright, 1958, p. 15; Lounsbury, p. 92). At the high school level they appear to be even less prevalent. The stress on academic learning that followed Russia's space challenge temporarily diverted attention from the core idea, but current efforts to "humanize" and "personalize" education may be viewed as a revival of the core philosophy. Indeed, many of the current radical reformers appear to be re-inventing the core curriculum under such labels as the "humanistic curriculum," "open education," "career education," and the like.

Core is the name given to some block-time programs, such as those in the junior high schools of St. Paul, Minnesota, Omaha, Nebraska, or Prince George's County, Maryland. Yet the leaders of these systems would be the first to admit that core is more the ideal toward which they teachers aspire, rather than a reality practiced in all classrooms. Secondary teachers in particular find it difficult to free themselves from the subject matter emphasis that permeated most of their training, even when they have official encouragement to develop student-centered programs.

It seems even less likely that many of the team-taught, block-time classes approach core curriculum at present. Interdisciplinary teams often are designed to maintain the integrity of each subject while bringing about a modicum of correlation. This is clearly anthetical to core, in which allegiance to subject matter is replaced by commitment to helping students examine problems of both personal and social relevance. Yet some interdisciplinary team programs may, in time, evolve into core programs, as teachers progress from correlation to fusion to genuine core. This happened in the number of cases in the early days of the core movement (Aikin, 1942, pp. 83-85).

Even within conventional courses, creative teachers occasionally involve students in cooperatively planned units that bear many of the earmarks of core. Some interdisciplinary minicourses also may provide a framework for the core approach, provided that the learning experiences are developed through teacher-student planning, not rigidly prescribed in advance. Consider the possibilities in minicourses such as these, offered at Meadowbrook Junior High School, Newton Centre, Massachusetts: "The World Today," "Coping—Who Am I?," "Dialogue in Black and White," or "Love—Hate." Thus we may find elements of core philosophy in many schools that lack a formally organized core curriculum.

RATIONALE

This philosophy recently was elaborated by a task force of the National Association for Core Curriculum (1973). Ten basic assumptions and beliefs were identified, with specific implications for both the core program and the core teacher. For example, here is assumption number I (p. 2):

I. Interests, Concerns, and Needs Expressed by Pupils Provide a Valid Basis for Curriculum Content and are Central to the Learning Process

THEREFORE . . .

Core makes extensive use of problems of personal and social concern or topics of current interest which have been identified by pupils; rather than content predetermined by teachers.

IMPLICATIONS:

A. The core program provides:
1. Opportunities for pupils to express ideas and concerns.
2. Opportunities for pupils to select, or share in selecting, some of the problems and topics to be studied individually or in groups.
3. For several topics or subtopics to be studied at the same time by different small groups or individuals within a class.

B. The core teacher:
1. Encourages pupils to express their ideas and concerns about problems and topics they want to study through the use of such techniques as: surveys, discussions, small group consensus sessions, etc.
2. Helps pupils to develop criteria for selecting topics for study and to apply the criteria during the selection process.
3. Organizes the class so that individuals and small groups may be working on different topics at the same time.
4. Relates the near-at-hand and easy-to-understand—local issues, school problems, student council, class problems and incidents—to issues of broader concern.
5. Keeps continuous records of observations of pupils, which serve as leads to interests, concerns, and needs.

Space does not permit reproduction of all the specific implications, but here are the other major assumptions and their corollaries.

II. Learning Involves changes in Behavior Which are Brought about Through Experience.

THEREFORE . . .

A. Core draws on many disciplines and a wide range of informational sources, materials, and activities relevant to the vital problems and topics of personal and social concern.
B. Core provides experiences in sharing information, respecting the rights and contributions of others, and taking responsibility.

III. A Democratic Society Values the Worth and Dignity of the Individual.

THEREFORE . . .

A. Core seeks the optimum development of each individual and his special aptitudes.
B. Core requires that the teacher treat each pupil with humaneness and respect. In turn, the student becomes aware of his own humanity and of his relationships and responsibilities to other human beings.

IV. A Democratic Society Requires Citizens Who are Skilled in the Decision-making Process.

THEREFORE . . .

A. Core emphasizes the development of problem-solving techniques and procedures.
B. Core requires that students become actively involved in all class activities.

V. Higher Priority must be given to the Development of Learning Skills and the Clarification of Values, Than to the Acquisition of Specific Information in Subject-Matter Areas.

THEREFORE . . .

A. Core includes as its main goals those qualities, competencies, and characteristics needed to become effective and responsible citizens.
B. Core seeks to develop the self-directed learner who will think of education as a continuous life-long process.

VI. Learning Experiences are Enhanced When the Learner is Encouraged and Helped to Draw Upon All Appropriate Sources of Information.

THEREFORE . . .

Core helps the student to correlate and integrate his learning.

VII. The Extent and Nature of Classroom Activity Should Determine the Allocation of Time.

THEREFORE . . .

Core is scheduled in extended blocks of time.

VIII. The Teacher's Primary Roles Should Be those of An Advisor, A Facilitator, A Friend, and A Fellow Learner.

THEREFORE . . .

The core teacher functions as an advisor, friend, facilitator, organizer, co-planner and fellow learner who assists youth in discovering and clarifying what is important for them to learn.

IX. Teaching and Many Aspects of Guidance are Complementary Functions of the Teacher.

THEREFORE . . .

Individual and group guidance are integral elements of core teaching.

X. To Bring About Continuous Improvement in Learning, All Concerned Parties Should be Involved in Evaluation.

THEREFORE . . .

Core benefits from continuous evaluation by teachers, pupils, administrators, parents, and visiting teams.

STRENGTHS AND LIMITATIONS

As a variant of the block-time program, core exhibits all the advantages inherent in the block-time approach to interdisciplinary instruction described elsewhere. In addition, student motivation in core is enhanced by the focus on relevant problems. Through student-teacher planning and small group work, the learning experiences are brought even closer to the lives of a particular group of students. In addition, students learn important problem-solving and decision-making strategies through actual practice.

The guidance advantages of block-time are further enhanced in core, since these classes study directly some of the issues and problems ordinarily examined through group guidance. Small group work enables students to share their concerns; often just knowing that other students are experiencing the same problems is reassuring for young people. Moreover, individual conferences between teacher and student grow naturally out of such core units as "Growing Up," "Understanding My Sexuality," "Teen-Age Problems," "Planning My Career," or "Finding Values by Which to Live." Thus guidance in a core class comes through curriculum, methods, and personal counseling by a teacher who knows the student well.

Probably the major reason why the core curriculum is not more widespread is the shortage of qualified teachers. In addition to having a broad academic background, a core teacher must be committed to the philosophy stated above. That is, he must see his role as primarily guiding students in their own self-directed inquiry, rather than merely purveying subject matter. Few colleges offer professional programs specifically for core teachers. Prospective students are reluctant to prepare for a kind of program that is not widespread, yet school administrators say they cannot initiate or expand core programs without trained teachers—the proverbial vicious cycle. Although colleges could do much more than they are at present, it is apparent that schools wishing to develop core programs must rely heavily on inservice education of available staff.

Research on the core curriculum is hampered by the difficulty of measuring such intangibles as a student's self-concept, critical thinking ability, personal and social adjustment, or "democratic" attitudes (Wright, 1963, p. 11). Jennings' study (1969) also underlined the difficulty of finding enough genuine core classes even in a large school system to compare with the more conventional block-time programs. Too often, studies do not distinguish between types of block-time programs, and many comparisons were made before research techniques were developed to detect subtle differences in such factors as teacher-student interaction. Yet one thing is evident from the more than 55 studies of block-time programs completed to date: students in these interdisciplinary programs acquire the knowledge and skills measured by conventional achievement tests as well as, or better than, those in separate-subject programs (Vars, 1974).

The National Association for Core Curriculum is now at work on evaluation instruments for assessing the degree to which school programs, teacher performance, and administrative practices reflect the philosophy set forth in the task force statement cited above.

CURRICULUM ORGANIZATION

A core curriculum may be classified as either *structured* or *unstructured,* depending upon the limits of planning set in advance by the staff.

In a *structured core* program, the staff decides in advance which broad problem areas or centers of experience the students will explore. These categories of human experience range from those which are primarily of immediate and direct personal concern to adolescents, such as "Personality Development" or "Sex," to broader social problems like "Pollution," "Population," or "Human Rights." Within these areas, students and teachers cooperatively plan learning units focused on the specific problems and concerns of members of a particular class.

Over the years, curriculum experts have proposed several sets of problem areas, or centers of experience, for structuring a core program. Writing for the 1976 yearbook of the National Society for the Study of Education, William Van Til (1975) revised and updated the list he developed originally in 1946. The centers of experience below are derived from his examination of the needs of students, values, social realities, and organized knowledge.

Centers of Experience Recommended by William Van Til

War, Peace, International Relations
Overpopulation, Pollution, and Energy
Economic Options and Problems
Governmental Processes
Consumer Problems
Intercultural Relations
World Views
Recreation and Leisure
The Arts and Aesthetics
Self-Understanding and Personal Development
Family, Peer Group, and School
Health
Community Living
Vocations
Communication
Alternative Futures

Centers of experience ordinarily are elaborated in a set of resource units describing the ramifications of the problem area, possible learning activities for students, pertinent instructional materials, etc. A teacher and his students select from these the learning experiences they consider most promising. Selection is facilitated in schools that have access to computer-based resource units, which list learning activities and materials specifically fitted to the characteristics and objectives of each individual student (Harnack 1965).

In an *unstructured core* program, teacher and students are free to examine any problem they consider worthwhile. For example, here are topics and problems identified by one eighth-grade class when asked to list what they considered worth studying. The student committee that organized the list put some topics under several headings, illustrating the way that many problems interrelate. Trivial items are minimized when students perceive that the teacher is sincere, and that they will be expected to make a serious study of the topics chosen.

SUGGESTED TOPICS FOR STUDY—8TH GRADE, KENT STATE UNIVERSITY SCHOOL

1. School and campus
   dress codes
   religion
   grading systems
   campus unrest
   K.S.U. killings
   race problems
2. Drugs
3. Population
   birth control
   abortion
4. Environment
   pollution
   conservation
   poverty (slums)
5. Fashions
6. Crime
   shoplifting
   rape; sex crimes
   hijacking
   drugs
   riots
   police brutality
   prison conditions
7. Civil rights
   women's lib
   race problems

8. Exploration
   deep sea diving
   space travel
9. Transportation
   cars (new developments)
   planes
   space travel
10. People
    generation gap
    race problems
11. Young people's demands
    ratings on movies
    voting age
12. War
    atom bomb
    Southeast Asia
13. Health
    smoking
    venereal disease
    drugs
    mercy death
14. Beliefs
    the occult (E.S.P.,
    witchcraft)
    respect for country
15. Economy
    prices
    inflation
    depression

Often either the staff or the teacher and students together establish criteria to guide the selection. These serve to eliminate topics that the students have studied before, that interest only a few students, or for which there are insufficient learning resources. Units developed in unstructured core classes may cut across several of the centers of experience proposed for structured core. For example, a class may begin studying boy-girl relations, become concerned with the problem of venereal disease, and end up spearheading a drive for wholesome recreation for young people in the community.

The teaching methods used by core teachers are not unique, although there is apt to be more teacher-student planning and small group work than in conventional courses. Teachers sometimes find it difficult to enter fully into cooperative planning, since it means relinquishing some of their authority. There is a temptation to "go through the motions" of teacher-student planning, while in reality manipulating students to arrive at the decision the teacher wants. On the other hand, teachers may give students too little guidance, allowing them to become bogged down and discouraged with the whole process. Teachers can avoid either extreme if they are sincerely committed to student involvement and willing to work into the teacher-student planning process gradually (Parrish and Waskin, 1967; Zapf, 1959).

A gradual approach also may be needed if students are not used to small group work. Students working in committees *are* noisier than a conventional class, but things will not get out of hand if the process has been carefully planned and the students are working on problems they consider worthwhile (Hock, 1958). Teachers need not relinquish their authority to maintain discipline when they share with students some of the decisions on curriculum and instruction.

As in other block-time programs, skill development in core grows out of, and is motivated by, deficiencies uncovered in the course of a problem-centered unit. Students use literature of all types, art, music, and any other expression of man's accumulated experience as resources for studying problems. In addition, core classes may take time to discuss current affairs, and to enjoy reading and creative writing experiences unrelated to the unit under study. Since core classes usually serve as homerooms, there are the usual school government duties, class recreational activities, and so on.

SOME ADMONITIONS

As with any major curriculum innovation, the development of a core curriculum should not be undertaken lightly. Since core is a variant of block-time, the first step is to consider three questions similar to those discussed in the article on block-time programs, namely: What subjects should be combined or replaced; Should the core curriculum be structured or unstructured? Should each core class be taught by one teacher or by a team? Next, school personnel might well reflect on the following admonitions, which are based on many years' experience with block-time and core programs (adapted from Vars, 1969, pp. 185-187).

Do not be satisfied with half-way measures. Educators may want to start with a subject-area block or unified studies program, or with a conventional interdisciplinary team teaching program, but they must realize that these are merely first steps toward the kind of problem-centered core program required to meet present world conditions. Interdisciplinary and combined-subjects approaches are cursed with the same emphasis on mastery of subject matter per se that makes conventional programs so repellent to students.

Administrators must exert their leadership. Today's educational leader must accept his role as a dynamic change agent, using all the tools of modern administrative theory and research to persuade the staff, students, parents, and the community at large to move in the desired direction. Studies like Brickell's (1961) indicate that teachers who appear at first unwilling to change usually find that they like the new way of doing things after they have tried it awhile. The current educational climate encourages innovations that are student-centered, "humanized," or "personalized." Educational leaders may never have a more propitious time to institute a core program.

Core teachers are made, not born, and most of them are made on the job. Schools unwilling to invest heavily in inservice development programs should avoid core or any other curriculum innovation.

Stay on the growing edge of the profession, but examine proposed innovations carefully. Core teachers must do their best to keep informed of major developments in the supporting disciplines and in professional education. Innovations that appear to offer advantages should be carefully tried out and evaluated. It is no credit to the profession, for example, that the "multiple-core" model proposed by C. Benjamin Cox (1970) has yet to see a major trial in the schools. On the other hand, a current innovation such as the minicourse should not be adopted without careful examination, since to go overboard in this direction may result in a splintering of the curriculum that is exactly counter to the goals of core.

Core teachers should welcome modern individualized approaches to the teaching of skills, yet "prepackaging" an entire program may fractionate the curriculum, eliminate teacher-student planning, and reduce the interaction among students and teachers that is so vital a part of the learning process in core.

Since the interaction between teacher and students is critical in a core class, core teachers should be the first to profit from research and experimentation along this line (Soar, 1972). Some of the simulation games, such as "Ghetto" or "Pollution," seem especially well suited to the problem-solving emphasis in the core curriculum, and value clarification procedures are extremely useful. (Raths, 1966).

After more than 50 years on the educational scene, the core curriculum still has much to offer. How well it fulfills its promise depends upon the wisdom with which it is applied by members of the educational profession.

REFERENCES

Aikin, W. M. *The Story of the Eight-Year Study.* New York: Harper and Brothers, 1942.

Brickell, H. M. *Organizing New York State for Educational Change.* Albany: New York State Education Department, 1961.

Cox, C. B. Involving the Learner in the Multiple-Core. *Ideas Educational,* 1970, *9,* 21-32.

Harnack, R. S. Computer Based Resource Units. *Educational Leadership,* 1965, *23,* 239-245.

Hock, L. E. *Using Committees in the Classroom.* New York: Holt, Rinehart, and Winston, 1958.

Jennings, W. B. Development of the Self-Concept in the Core Program. Unpublished doctoral dissertation, University of Minnesota, 1968. *Dissertation Abstracts,* 1969, *29,* 2439A.

Lounsbury, J. H., and Douglass, H. R. Recent Trends in Junior High School Practices, 1954-1964. *Bulletin of the National Association of Secondary-School Principals,* 1965, *49,* 87-98.

National Association for Core Curriculum. *Core Today: Rationale and Implications.* Kent, Ohio: The Association, 1973.

Parrish, L., and Waskin, Y. *Teacher-Pupil Planning for Better Classroom Learning.* New York: Pitman Publishing Corp., 1967.

Raths, L. E., Harmin, M., and Simon, S. B. *Values and Teaching.* Columbus, Ohio: Charles E. Merrill, 1966.

Soar, R. S. Teacher-Pupil Interaction. *A New Look at Progressive Education.* 1972 Yearbook. Washington: Association for Supervision and Curriculum Development, 1972, 166-204.

Van Til, William, ed. *Secondary Education in the United States.* Chicago: University of Chicago Press (in press).

Vars, G. F. Administrative Leadership—Key to Core Program Development. *Bulletin of the National Association of Secondary-School Principals,* 1962, *46,* 91-103.

_____, ed. *Common Learnings: Core and Interdisciplinary Team Approaches.* Scranton: International Textbook Company, 1969.

_____. Curriculum in Secondary Schools and Colleges. *A New Look at Progressive Education.* 1972 Yearbook. Washington: Association for Supervision and Curriculum Development, 1972, 233-255.

_____. A Bibliography of Research on the Effectiveness of Block-Time Programs. Kent, Ohio: National Association for Core Curriculum, 1974.

Wright, G. S. *Block-Time Classes and the Core Program in the Junior High School.* U.S. Office of Education, Bulletin 1958, No. 6. Washington: Government Printing Office, 1958.

_____. *The Core Program: Unpublished Research, 1956-1962.* U.S. Office of Education, Circular No. 713. Washington: Government Printing Office, 1963.

Zapf, R. M. *Democratic Processes in the Secondary Classroom.* Englewood Cliffs, New Jersey: Prentice-Hall, 1959.

ADDITIONAL RESOURCES

Books

Faunce, R. C., and Bossing, N. L. *Developing the Core Curriculum,* 2d ed. Englewood Cliffs, New Jersey: Prentice-Hall, 1958.

Van Til, W., Vars, G. F., and Lounsbury, J. H. *Modern Education for the Junior High School Years,* 2d ed. Indianapolis: Bobbs-Merrill, 1967. Chapters 8, 10, 11, 12.

Organizations

National Association for Core Curriculum
404F Education Building
Kent State University
Kent, Ohio 44242

Resources: *The Core Teacher* (quarterly newsletter), resource units, bibliographies, films, filmstrips, audiotapes, videotapes.

National Association for Humanities Education
Post Office Box 628
Kirksville, Missouri 63501

Resources: *The Humanities Journal, NAHE Newsletter.*

73

BLOCK-TIME PROGRAMS

by Gordon F. Vars
Professor of Education
Kent State University
Kent, Ohio

A block-time program is one in which two or more subjects that are ordinarily taught separately are combined, or replaced and scheduled for a block of time longer than the usual single-subject class.

A block-time class may be instructed by either one teacher or a team, and it may bear a variety of labels. The names of the included subjects may be hyphenated, as in "English-social studies," or initials may be used, such as "ESSG" (English-Social Studies-Guidance) or "CLASS" (Combined Language Arts and Social Studies). Occasionally special labels may be applied, such as "Unified Program," "Combined Studies," "American Studies," "Humanities," or "Core." Sometimes any type of interdisciplinary program is referred to as "core curriculum," but this term is more properly restricted to a particular type of block-time program, as described later.

Nearly every conceivable combination of subjects has been used in block-time programs. Unified arts programs, embracing art, industrial arts, and home economics, may be found in some middle schools or junior highs. In vocational education, courses like bookkeeping, typing, shorthand, and office practice may be combined and taught in a simulated business-office setting. However, most block-time programs are built around required subjects, usually English and social studies, sometimes with the addition of science, mathematics, art, or music. Some schools have two block-time classes, English-social studies and math-science.

A block-time program may occupy from one-fourth to more than one-half of a student's day. The balance of the program usually consists of more or less conventional subjects and student activities. The block-time class is likely to absorb some of the functions of the homeroom, where students obtain advice on school-related matters and where student government functions, class social affairs, and other activities are carried out. In a sense, block-time represents an extension of the self-contained elementary classroom into the secondary grades, where complete departmentalization is the most common pattern.

STATUS

Although only a few block-time programs may properly be labeled core, they are a phase of the core curriculum movement that was sparked by the progressive education experiments of the 1930s and 40s (Vars, 1972). The percent of junior high schools having one-teacher block-time programs rose from 15.8 percent in 1949 to 40.0 percent in 1960, according to U.S. Office of Education surveys (Wright and Greer, p. 20). Smaller samplings taken by Gruhn and Douglass (1971) showed 46 percent in 1965 and 39 percent in 1969. Percentages have always varied widely from state to state, with figures as high as 87 percent in California in 1957 and 75 percent in Oregon in 1965.

Some schools abandoned block-time during the post-sputnik stampede for academic excellence, but at the same time there was an upsurge of interest in team teaching. For example, Gruhn and Douglass (1971) found that 48 percent of the junior high schools in their 1969 survey had team teaching, of which 31 percent embraced two subjects and 16 percent more than two.

Interdisciplinary team teaching also is a prominent feature of the evolving middle school, both in the recommendations of experts and in actual practice. For example, when Gatewood (1971) compared educational practices at the same grade levels in junior high schools and middle schools in Michigan, block-time and core were most often found in junior highs, and interdisciplinary teams in middle schools (p. 9).

Under the title "humanities," interdisciplinary team teaching also is gaining a foothold in the senior high school, long a stronghold of subject specialization. For example, Cawelti (1967) found humanities programs in 17.7 percent of the 7,237 accredited high schools he surveyed in 1967.

Not to be overlooked are the many modified self-contained classes found in middle schools, especially in grades 5 and 6 (Middle Schools, p. 3). Combining these with the interdisciplinary teams and one-teacher block-time programs, it appears that some form of block-time may be found in a majority of junior high and middle schools. In high schools and senior highs the figure is probably less than 25 percent.

RATIONALE

Block-time programs are instituted to accomplish three major purposes: (1) to enhance the guidance role of the classroom teacher; (2) to promote the integration of subject matter from several disciplines; and (3) to facilitate instructional procedures that require more time than the usual class period.

Guidance

If one teacher handles instruction in a block-time class, the guidance advantages are the result of his having fewer students for longer periods of time. A teacher who has been assigned two two-and-a-half-hour blocks may meet a maximum of 60 students per day, whereas under conventional scheduling he may have 150 or more. Block-time teachers therefore get to know their students better as individuals; they can identify special needs or special talents. And, having longer time period and great scope of subject matter to manipulate, they can more easily make adjustments to meet these individual differences.

Conversely, a student in a block-time program meets fewer teachers every day. He may find security in being well acquainted with at least his block-time teacher, making it more likely that he will seek him out for advice and counsel. In other words, the block-time teacher may assume somewhat the "mother hen" role of the elementary teacher in a self-contained classroom. This is especially important while students are undergoing the stresses and strains of adolescence. It is also valuable as they move into an unfamiliar situation, as in the transition from elementary to middle school or from middle school to high school. The popularity of block-time programs in the early grades of junior high schools and middle schools may be explained, at least in part, by the desire to ease students' transition from a self-contained to a more or less departmentalized program.

In block-time programs taught by a team, the guidance advantages stem less from the continuity of relationship with one teacher than from the variety of staff members that share the instruction of a group of students. In a four-teacher interdisciplinary team, for example, each staff member interacts regularly with 120 or more students, but he shares his insights and experiences with other members of the team. Thus the collective wisdom of four professionals can be brought to bear on the special problems and needs of individual students. The relationship between a particular student and a teacher will be less intense than in a single-teacher block-time program, but the student will have a choice of four different personalities with whom to relate. Some teams capitalize on this possibility by inviting each student to select a member of the team to be his advisor, and scheduling regular times for both group guidance and individual counseling with these "home base" groups.

In either of these arrangements, the guidance carried on by the block-time teachers must be carefully coordinated and supervised by guidance specialists. In team situations this is often formalized by assigning a counselor to each interdisciplinary team, at least on a part-time basis. In any case, guidance specialists need to meet often with block-time teachers to learn what they are doing and how individual students are responding to the educational program. Counselors also can help teachers interpret school records and improve their skills as teacher-counselors.

Curriculum Integration

Combining or replacing two or more subjects in the block of time opens the door to various degrees of correlation or fusion of content. All teachers are familiar with the student who promptly forgets everything he learned in English class as he sits down to write a science report! This is especially unlikely in a single-teacher block-time program, where the same teacher is responsible for the two or more subjects being correlated. The greater the number of subjects in the block-time program, the more the opportunities to apply skills functionally, and with a consistency that is lacking in the usual separate-subject schedule.

Moreover, gaps and duplications between subjects can be corrected when they are taught as part of the same program. Consider the efficiency of dealing with all aspects of a problem such as drug abuse in a block-time program, rather than parceling it out to health, science, and social studies. The time gained by reducing overlap can be used to deal with topics of current importance to

young people that may not fit within traditional subjects, such as boy-girl relations, a school controversy over appropriate lunchroom behavior, or a popular fad such as the recent upsurge in interest in the occult. Various approaches to integration of content are elaborated below.

Instructional Flexibility

The extended period of time makes it easier to use techniques such as teacher-student planning, small group work, creative writing, field trips, and role-playing, all of which may be cramped when confined to a single 40-to-50-minute period. Time allotments can be fitted to the learning activity, rather than vice versa, and activities within the block can be extended or shortened as student interest waxes and wanes. Field trips and community action projects can be scheduled without disrupting so many other classes. Block-time is not the only way to give teachers flexible use of extended periods of time, but it is one of the gains from block-time scheduling.

IMPLEMENTATION DIFFICULTIES

Difficulties in implementing block-time programs are of two types, philosophical and practical. Staff members may reject efforts to modify conventional approaches to teaching the subjects, or they may lack some of the leadership, counseling, and instructional skills needed. The list below should help school personnel anticipate and avoid the most common problems (adapted from Vars, 1969, pp. 12-13).

Guidance

Teachers may lack interest in or preparation for the role of teacher-counselor.

Teachers may be tempted to go beyond their depth in counseling with students.

Teachers may experience role conflict in trying to combine instruction and counseling.

Students also need access to highly trained and impartial guidance specialists. This need may be overlooked in schools that place undue reliance on teacher-counseling.

Curriculum

Combining subject areas may blur the distinctive nature of the disciplines.

The preferred sequence in one subject may be distorted in an attempt to correlate or fuse it with another.

Instruction

If the teacher or team is ineffective, the students will have poor teaching in several subjects instead of in one.

The longer periods of time together may aggravate a personality clash between student and teacher, or among the members of a teaching team.

The extended period may prove tiresome and boring to students if the teachers do not use a variety of activities.

The teachers may stress one subject and neglect the others.

Administration

Continuous inservice education of block-time teachers is necessary to realize the full benefits of the program.

The block-time program, especially if it differs greatly from the conventional, must continually be interpreted to students, parents, other teachers, and the public.

The longer time block may complicate the process of scheduling.

It may be difficult to schedule the common planning time that is so essential for block-time teachers.

Resources

Instructional materials are seldom designed to capitalize on correlation or fusion of subjects.

Teacher Preparation

Teachers fully qualified in two or more teaching fields, as required for the single-teacher block-time program, are relatively scarce.

Few colleges or universities prepare teachers for any type of block-time or interdisciplinary teaching.

It should be noted that inadequately prepared teachers hamper any program, and that many of the criticisms of block-time are essentially criticisms of bad teaching. Lack of financial support lies behind some of the difficulties listed, but this, too, is not peculiar to block-time. A survey of research on block-time programs shows that the real key to the success of this or any other educational innovation lies in the hands of the school leadership, who should be able to muster community support, provide the necessary inservice education, and solve many of the administrative problems inherent in any curriculum innovation (Vars, 1962).

Research studies comparing block-time programs with conventional separate-subject arrangements now total more than 60 (Vars, 1974). In general, they show that block-time students learn the usual subject matter and skills as well as, or better than, those in other programs. Moreover, once the program is firmly established, teachers, pupils, and parents usually favor it. The guidance and interdisciplinary instruction advantages of block-time have proved very difficult to measure.

TYPES OF PROGRAMS

When we look behind the label and the schedule, we may identify four distinct types of block-time programs, classified according to curriculum organization. The vast majority are *subject-area block* programs, in which each subject retains its identity, although areas may be correlated (Wright, p. 10; and Lounsbury, 1965, p. 92). For example, an English-social studies teacher might draw some of his spelling words from the current social studies topic, or encourage students to write themes, poems, or other works relating to that subject. Literature may also be correlated, such as having students read Hunt's *No Promises in the Wind* to help them understand what life was like during the Depression.

Most of the interdisciplinary team programs so prevalent in middle schools are of this type. For example, the sixth-grade interdisciplinary team in the Richmond Heights, Ohio, Middle School correlates learning experiences around the following topics: Racing, Exploration, Man, Conflict, Ecology, and Leisure Time. the team consists of four teachers: English, Social Studies, Science, and Mathematics. If we look more closely at such a team dealing with pollution, we might even find the science teacher dealing with the technical aspects; the social studies teacher helping students examine the political, economic, and social effects; the English teacher engaging students in writing about their feelings concerning the problem; and the mathematics teacher helping them deal with the statistical data.

In a *unified studies* program, the subject matter of two or more areas is fused or merged, usually around the basic sequence or structure of the social studies or science course included. The example, the combined studies program in the Evanston (Illinois) Township High School fuses English and social studies in grades 9 through 12. The courses are organized around broad units, such as "The Nature of Man," "Man's Search for the Ideal Society," and "Processes of Change: Alternatives and Results." Novels such as *Walkabout*, by James Vance Marshall, or *Sounder*, by William H. Armstrong, serve as main vehicles of instruction at certain points, not merely as enrichment of the social studies.

Although much of the language arts and mathematics content is taught through social studies or science units, additional time within the unified studies class usually is set aside for English or math content not related to the unit. Regardless of the degree of fusion, in both unified studies and the subject area block, the primary concern is with teaching subject matter.

A *core* program, on the other hand, is distinctly different. Here the top priority is given to helping students deal with problems and issues they find meaningful. Subject matter from any area may be employed to deal with these problems, but there is no prior commitment to "cover" certain content. Core may be classified as "structured" or "unstructured" according to the limits of planning set in advance by the staff.

In *structured core* the students explore broad "problem areas" or "centers of experience" identified by the staff as most likely to be of significance to students. By definition, a problem area includes both the personal problems, interests, and needs of students, and also the broad social problems confronting society as a whole. Within these areas, students and teachers cooperatively plan learning activities especially pertinent to that class at that time.

In *unstructured core*, students and teachers are free

to study any problem or issue they consider worthwhile. However, selection may be limited by the availability of instructional materials and by the degree of interest shown by the students. Criteria such as these may be established by the staff or developed by the group in the early stages of teacher-student planning.

These four types of block-time programs may be viewed as lying along a continuum, each succeeding type departing further from commitment to conventional subject-matter teaching. All four types may be found in adjoining classrooms of the same school; indeed, the same block-time teacher or team may shift in approach from time to time throughout the year, even in schools that are presumably working toward the core ideal.

Teachers from areas outside the block may aid in planning the interdisciplinary learnings, and may on occasion serve as consultants or "guest lecturers" in the block-time class. Art and music teachers are frequently called upon in this way, especially in core or humanities programs. Courses outside the block may be correlated with the major units under study in the block-time class. Indeed, an entire school may focus its efforts on a broad theme, such as "A Nation of Immigrants," or "World Understanding."

Learning experiences within a block-time class are not limited to major units of study and related skill development. Time also may be set aside for recreational reading, creative writing, current events, student government business, "homeroom-type" activities, and other matters of concern to a particular group.

SOME CRUCIAL QUESTIONS

Before establishing a block-time program, educators must answer three crucial and interrelated questions:

1. What Subjects Should be Combined or Replaced?

In most schools, the block-time program provides a major part of the common learnings, or general education considered essential for all students. Usually the basic curriculum structure of a block-time class is derived from one of the so-called "content" subjects, such as social studies or science. "Skills" subjects like English or mathematics are then blended in, with time set aside within the block for additional work on skill development. Research has demonstrated that the content and skills ordinarily taught in English classes can be learned just as well in a block-time class (Vars, 1956).

The place of mathematics in block-time is less secure, especially in programs that go beyond occasional correlation. The social applications of mathematics can be taught in conjunction with other subjects, but the sequential development of mathematical skills and concepts requires considerable specialized attention. As a result, mathematics may be taught both inside and outside the block-time program, a separate course in mathematics being offered in addition to whatever mathematics is taught in connection with block-time units of study.

Similar considerations may apply to science. This is especially true of the science programs that are build around a carefully sequenced series of laboratory experiences through which students discover basic science concepts. Whereas such a program could be loosely correlated with other subjects through interdisciplinary teaming, it would not fit into a core program. It is evident that the decision on what subjects to include depends on the type of curriculum to be implemented.

2. Should the Block-Time Curriculum Emphasize Correlation, Fusion, or Core?

As may be seen from this article and the one on Core Curriculum, each of these approaches has its merits. A correlated program makes the least demands upon teachers and creates fewer questions in the minds of students and parents. However, it differs so little from conventional programs as to offer very little advantage. Core, on the other hand, requires considerable investment in curriculum planning and teacher development, as well as continuous interpretation to the school's various publics. Yet it is only through some such radical restructuring of the curriculum that education can approach the social relevance and humaneness demanded by modern times. Many educators recommend beginning at whatever level of integration is presently acceptable to the staff, and then moving as far and as fast as possible toward the core ideal.

3. Should the Block-Time Class be Taught by One Teacher or by a Team?

This decision, too, depends upon the degree of integration of curriculum desired. Examination of student problems, as in a core program, seems to require the close rapport between teacher and students that is best established under the one-teacher plan. Correlating subjects, on the other hand, may work best when teachers from several disciplines pool their various perspectives through team planning. As team members learn from one another and become familiar with interdisciplinary approaches to instruction, they may develop both the competency and the desire to teach a block-time class on their own.

Schools may wish to combine both approaches, using the one-teacher model in the lower grades, where the group guidance function of the teacher is most crucial, and then shifting to a team approach with older students who are ready for more formal approaches to instruction.

Considering the individual differences among both teachers and students, both approaches might well function side by side. Students who appear to need a more intense, personal relationship with an adult might be placed with a teacher who functions best in this pattern, whereas students who need the stimulation of a more complex team operation would have that option. Each approach has its own set of rewards and demands, so it would probably be best to allow both teachers and students some choice in the matter.

Whatever the pattern of curriculum organization, a block-time program provides a time-tested vehicle for achieving some of the major goals of education.

REFERENCES

Cawelti, G. Innovative Practices in High Schools. *Nation's Schools*, 1967, *79, 56-88.*

Gatewood, T. E. and Walker, G. H., Jr. *A Comparative Study of Middle Schools and Junior High Schools in the State of Michigan.* Mount Pleasant: Central Michigan University, 1971.

Gruhn, W. T., and Douglass, H. R. Unpublished study of block-time and core programs, 1965.

_____. *The Modern Junior High School,* 3d ed. New York: Ronald Press, 1971.

Lounsbury, J. H., and Douglass, H. R. Recent Trends in Junior High School Practices, 1954-1964. *Bulletin of the National Association of Secondary-School Principals,* 1965, *49,* 87-98.

Middle Schools. *Educational Research and Service Circular,* No. 3. Washington: National Education Association, May 1965.

Vars, G. F. Language Arts in the Core Curriculum. *Progressive Education,* 1956, *34,* 54-58.

_____. Administrative Leadership—Key to Core Program Development. *Bulletin of the National Association of Secondary-School Principals,* 1962, *46,* 91-103.

_____, ed. *Common Learnings: Core and Interdisciplinary Team Approaches.* Scranton: International Textbook Company, 1969.

_____. Curriculum in Secondary Schools and Colleges. *A New Look at Progressive Education.* 1972 Yearbook. Washington: Association for Supervision and Curriculum Development, 1972, 233-255.

_____. A Bibliography of Research on the Effectiveness of Block-Time Programs. Kent, Ohio: National Association for Core Curriculum, 1974.

Wright, G. S. *Block-Time Classes and the Core Program in the Junior High School.* U.S. Office of Education Bulletin 1958, No. 6. Washington: Government Printing Office, 1958.

_____, and Greer, E. S. *The Junior High School: A Survey of Grades 7-8-9 in Junior and Junior-Senior High Schools, 1959-60.* U.S. Office of Education Bulletin 1963, No. 32. Washington: Government Printing Office, 1963.

ADDITIONAL RESOURCES

Books

Adler, R. R., ed. *Humanities Programs Today.* New York: Citation Press, 1970.

Pumerantz, P., and Galano, R. W. *Establishing Interdisciplinary Programs in the Middle School.* West Nyack, New York: Parker Publishing Company, 1973.

Organizations

National Association for Core Curriculum
404F Education Building
Kent State University
Kent, Ohio 44242

Resources: *The Core Teacher* (quarterly newsletter), resource units, bibliographies, films, filmstrips, videotapes, audiotapes.

National Association for Humanities Education
Post Office Box 628
Kirksville, Missouri 63501

Resources: *The Humanities Journal, NAHE Newsletter,* units, reprints, bibliographies.

74

THE INQUIRY METHOD

by William C. Merwin
Associate Professor of Education
University of North Florida
Jacksonville, Florida

The inquiry method is a process, as well as an attitude toward learning and teaching, which employs a variety of intellectual operations to analyze and evaluate alternative solutions to problems under investigation. A student who engages in inquiry learning formulates testable hypotheses for problems under consideration, and searches for valid and reliable data from which solutions, conclusions, or generalizations are established.

While the inception of the inquiry method can be traced to Socrates, with the exception of John Dewey's problem-solving method, it received little attention in either the literature or practice until the decade of the 1960s. More recently, variant forms of inquiry learning-teaching are practiced in thousands of elementary, secondary, and college-level classrooms throughout the United States. Although the inquiry method is employed more extensively in the social sciences, it has become a popular approach in language arts, science, mathematics, art, music and physical education.

DEFINITION

The literature in education reflects a great deal of confusion related to the term "inquiry method." For example, terms such as discovery, reflective thinking, and problem-solving are often used synonymously with inquiry. Some refer to thinking, while others relate to ways of teaching. All of these terms, however, do have at least one common element—they refer to a way in which people engage in or facilitate learning. Learning theorists and teachers alike tend to agree that the most effective teaching methods incorporate practices which are based upon sound principles of learning. The inquiry teaching method is predicated on how inquiry as a way of learning is thought to occur.

Much of the current interest in inquiry teaching, as expressed by Bruner, Suchman, Fenton, and Massialas, can be traced to the work of John Dewey. More than 40 years ago, Dewey (1933) defined a process referred to as "reflective thinking." This process, consisting of five phases (suggestion, intellectualization, hypothesis, reasoning, and action) (pp. 106-116), was to be employed as a classroom teaching method as well as an instructional goal. Dewey did not try to establish a fixed series of consecutive steps involved in thinking. Rather than learn a formula for thinking, he proffered that a learner should develop the "intellectual tact and sensitiveness" to solve problems by inquiring constantly in the classroom. In essence, Dewey argued that school experiences should help students learn how to inquire, or "learn by doing."

A contemporary interpretation of Dewey's reflective thinking idea has been offered by J. Richard Suchman (1961), who has conducted extensive experiments on inquiry training. Suchman points out that many interpretations of "learning by doing" have been a gross oversimplification of what Dewey actually had in mind. Suchman suggests that a much closer approximation of Dewey's intent is summed up by the phrase "discovering by experimenting and thinking." This is the way Suchman presents his case for inquiry training.

> Concepts are . . . most meaningful, are retained the longest, and are most available for future thinking, when the learner actively gathers and processes data from which concepts emerge. This is true (a) because the experience of data gathering (exploration, manipulation, experimentation, etc.) is intrinsically rewarding; (b) because discovery strengthens the child's faith in the regularity of the universe, which enables him to pursue causal relationships under highly frustrating conditions; (c) because discovery builds self-confidence, which encourages the child to make creative intuitive leaps; and (d) because practice in the use of the logical inductive processes involved in discovery strengthens and extends these cognitive skills. (p. 149)

Much of the literature and research regarding the inquiry method is related to the development of inquiry skills and an examination of the conditions which promote and generate discovery and problem-solving. Bruner (1963) suggests that if students are to learn the techniques of discovery they must be given many opportunities in problem-solving. The more practice in problem-solving, the more students gain control of the techniques of inquiry.

Sagl (1966) attempts to clarify the relationship among problem-solving, inquiry, and discovery. She sees problem-solving as a process in which learners inquire into possible solutions to their problems and gather data which they organize to facilitate generalizing. In this concept of problem-solving, learners are guided to discover relationships among data by engaging in problem-solving experiences that facilitate this discovery. Thus, inquiry is a process in which the students study a problem, hypothesize, and formulate theories that get at the why and how.

Fenton (1967) suggests that a mode of inquiry consists of a number of cognitive skills combined in a logical order. Following the model developed by Dewey, he identifies six essential steps in this process: (a) recognizing a problem from data; (b) formulating hypotheses; (c) recognizing the implications of the hypotheses; (d) gathering data; (e) analyzing, evaluating, and interpreting data; (f) evaluating the hypotheses in light of the data (p. 144).

Other authors define the inquiry method in much the same manner as the foregoing. Whether it is labeled reflective thinking, discovery, problem-solving or inquiry, it is essentially the same thing: they are descriptive of a process by which people engage in learning by finding out for themselves. It is the application of purpose to data to develop useful knowledge. According to Beyer (1971), the purpose may be to solve a problem, answer a question, satisfy a curiosity or simply to apply a concept. The data

may be found in many forms: it may be remembered and/or observed experience, either the learner's or that of others, in the form of statistical information shown on maps, graphs, charts, a picture, an artifact, or some bit of written material, such as a textbook, a newspaper article, a poem, or an original document. The kind of knowledge developed is useful knowledge; knowledge that solves the problem, answers the question, satisfies the curiosity, demonstrates or validates the concept, or gives meaning to experience.

IMPLEMENTATION

Many techniques of inquiry teaching are similar to those used in expository teaching, but are arranged in different sequence, managed somewhat differently, and employed to attain different objectives. For example, the use of inquiry techniques is most desirable when the objective is to teach for more than recall of factual information; that is, when it is to develop conceptualized knowledge, to clarify values, or to refine an intellectual skill. There are probably scores of teaching techniques that are applicable to the inquiry process of learning, in which the intellectual operations experienced by the students would be similar. Beyer (1971) states that any inquiry-oriented teaching strategy must provide an opportunity for the learner to identify and clarify a purpose for inquiry; formulate a hypothesis; test the hypothesis; draw conclusions; apply the conclusions in new situation to new data; and develop meaningful generalizations (pp. 21-25).

A teacher who wishes to plan a learning experience that will utilize and foster inquiry should thus include activities in his plan that will enable the learner to engage in each of these operations.

Thus, teaching through inquiry is a process of formulating and testing ideas, and implies an open classroom climate that encourages wide student participation and expression of divergent points of view. According to Massialas (1969), the roles of the teachers who practice the inquiry method fall into six categories. He argues that these are actual, not ideal roles, and that all teachers, regardless of their subject area, can perform them. Briefly, the roles are as follows:

1. *The Teacher as planner.* In this role the teacher collects, organizes, and sequences materials for classroom use.

2. *The Teacher as introducer.* It is important to introduce a new learning experience with material that will serve as a springboard for inquiry and discussion. This introductory material (an anecdote, math problem, quotation, case study, etc.) should create a provocative situation, in which the students are prompted to develop concepts and relationships for themselves. Several other inquiry specialists argue that the students should introduce the provocative issues rather than the teacher.

3. *The Teacher as questioner and sustainer of inquiry.*

The teacher's attitude is that of a fellow learner who has no final or absolute answers. Textbooks and other traditional sources of authority are to be carefully scrutinized and questioned. No knowledge claim is ever better than the data on which it stands. The teacher usually redirects questions addressed to him. In this context, the teacher plays the role of the devil's advocate, constantly probing and redirecting student responses, making them prove the defensibility of their positions. The teacher needs to be a master of the art of questioning.

4. *The Teacher as manager.* The teacher recognizes students, makes announcements, and maintains order. His major function, however, is to provide concepts, techniques, and data sources to engage students in planning and executing inquiries of their own.

5. *The Teacher as rewarder.* The teacher encourages students to play their hunches, and rewards or praises them when they do. He rewards the free exchange and test of ideas that lead to higher levels of motivation and more student participation.

6. *The Teacher as value investigator.* When dealing with value laden issues, the teacher places emphasis on the process of inquiry. The teacher operates on the premise that values are not taught but are identified and analyzed in the open market of ideas. He usually refrains from taking a definite personal stand on an issue early in the discussion. (p. 41)

CLAIMS AND CRITICISM

The past decade has witnessed a dramatic emphasis on cognitive skill development in practically all curriculum areas. The inquiry method has enjoyed a position of prominence in most national, state, and local curriculum revision movements. For example, Sanders and Tanck (1970) critically assessed 26 national curriculum projects in the social studies, and reported that 25 advocated the use of discovery or inquiry teaching strategies. As the use of the inquiry method increased, educators launched informal debates relative to the pros and cons of the approach. Current literature in education abounds with references to the advantages and disadvantages; proponents report phenomenal success related to multitudinous aspects of the educational enterprise; opponents counter that those strong claims are exaggerated.

The following statements represent typical claims echoed by some of its leading advocates. Cox and Massialas (1966) contend that students learn just as many facts, and actually display more interest, enthusiasm, and sense of relevance, using inquiry, when compared with expository instructional approaches. Similarly, Oliver and Shaver (1965) claim there is no loss of knowledge when inquiry techniques are employed. Bruner (1961) holds that discovery (inquiry) increases the intellectual potency, transfer, memory, motivation, and organizational ability of the learner. Fenton (1967) argues that critical thinking and skills of scientific investigation are enhanced by the inquiry approach. Strain

(1970) claims that inquiry is operative and natural to the environment of disadvantaged children, and would therefore be an appropriate teaching strategy.

Critics of the inquiry approach have pointed out that there is little proof that it actually produces all that its advocates claim. In a review of available research on the inquiry-discovery approach, Wittrock (1966) put it this way: "Many strong claims for learning by discovery are made in educational psychology. But almost none of these claims has been empirically substantiated or even clearly tested in an experiment (p. 33)."

Ausubel (1961), in defending expository teaching methods, argues that when greater learning and subsequent transfer occur using discovery, it is because a greater effort has been expended by both teacher and learner. He further contends that inquiry is too time-consuming, and is generally suited only for the creative, intuitive learner.

After a careful examination of the materials and methods that comprise many of the new curriculum projects and packages, Rogers (1970) reveals that the kinds of questions raised, the problems studied, and the discoveries or generalizations arrived at are rarely the children's. In essence, where the inquiry method has failed it has been organized in such a way as to preclude the purposes of the inquiry approach. Brubaker (1970) reports that the inquiry approach, like other, more expository methods, is also used to reinforce and change values in the direction considered "right" by those who wish to influence schools. La Forse (1970) claims that because of the peculiarly American necessity for premature closure and hard feedback, teachers and students cannot tolerate the ambiguity often associated with inquiry learning. Similarly, Fraser (1970) found that both teachers and students experience dissatisfaction with inquiry because of the difficult role changes demanded by the inquiry model.

RESEARCH

Does the inquiry method really make a difference in educational development? The pursuit of an answer to this inquiry into inquiry is as complex as in any social science where the investigator is concerned with students and teachers as both individuals and members of groups. In an effort to disentangle this complex interaction, many sophisticated experimental designs and statistical techniques have been developed. However, the randomization and laboratory-like control essential in the experimental design are seldom possible in an authentic classroom environment. Such limitations have frustrated experimental researchers, and subsequently tend to thwart exaggerated claims. With these problems and known limitations taken into consideration, a review of research literature reported during the past decade was launched with specific focus on the use of inquiry for teaching the social studies. Over 60 research studies, representing elementary, secondary, and college-level investigations, were selected for their potential contribution to the solution of such problems as: Can the inquiry method generate the kinds of cognitive and affective learning outcomes necessary for citizenship in a complex world; Is inquiry effective with diverse student audiences? Will all teachers be capable of employing inquiry?

The research surveyed in response to the first question included more than 40 experimental studies. Eight, each using a different type of inquiry device, reported no significant difference in subject achievement between groups taught by traditional methods and those taught by inquiry; three found subject achievement significantly higher in the inquiry groups; and six others reporting conclusions favorable to the inquiry method were difficult to assess, because instrumentation and statistical methods have been deleted.

Most of the studies measuring the knowledge acquisition potential of inquiry reported other associated learning outcomes, such as cognitive skills and abilities, or affective development; six reported no significant differences between treatment and control groups on measures of critical thinking ability; five reported results favoring inquiry as a teaching method to generate higher cognitive operations, inquiry skills, and critical thinking.

All 11 reports citing affective outcomes of the inquiry process reported positive results. Upon cursory inspection, it would appear that the inquiry method produced distinctive advantages in the affective domain. However, closer scrutiny of these reported findings disclose a paucity of information necessary for objective evaluation. Most of the studies reported clinical observations, and completely omitted any reference to the validity of the instruments employed.

Thus, research findings appeared to indicate that under certain conditions inquiry is at least as effective as the more traditional teaching methods and, within particular circumstances, more efficacious in both cognitive and affective development. However, several unanswered questions persist which tend to threaten the generalizability of the findings to other populations. Did control groups, treated with traditional, noninquiry approaches, employ equally competent instructors, who utilized multimedia devices to produce otherwise equal instruction input, when compared with the instructional input of the inquiry groups? A more prudent conclusion (with subject matter of this nature, inquiry experiences of this type, in this amount produced this pattern of experiences in pupils at this level of development) would further delimit the generalization.

Despite the fact that the reported research pointed up generally favorable learning outcomes for the inquiry method, to be effectively employed in a particular situation, the method must be analyzed in juxtaposition with existing conditions. Is it adaptable to all teachers and all student audiences?

In relation to the question concerning the reactions of heterogeneous student audiences, the reported research is far from conclusive. Although it has been demonstrated that age (grade level) is not a delimiting factor, there is need for far more extensive research regarding mental ability, psychological disposition, and socioeconomic status as learner variables.

Closely related to varied student audiences are the individual differences found among teachers' styles. Studies related to teacher style, as measured by student performance, found that students have more success on divergent questions, critical thinking tests, and attitude scales if their teachers perceive student interaction with peers and teachers as a valuable learning activity. Whether all teachers are willing or able to employ inquiry effectively is dependent upon numerous other factors, few of which have been measured by the research.

The research related to the method of inquiry is neither conclusive nor convincing enough to warrant its universal adoption. To label the inquiry method of this past decade as either a panacea or a total failure would be overgeneralizing from the research findings. However, one cannot ignore the successful learning outcomes of the inquiry method as recorded in several of the reports. For many students and teachers, the inquiry approach provides an exciting and rewarding dimension in learning; for others, it is fraught with intolerable frustration and subsequent failure. In conclusion, like any successful teaching technique, the inquiry method may help students learn to think and solve problems provided it is used in appropriate situations by a competent teacher who proceeds with enthusiasm and confidence.

REFERENCES

Ausubel, David. Reception versus Discovery Learning. *Educational Theory*, 1961, *2*, 20-24.

Beyer, Barry K. *Inquiry in the Social Studies Classroom: A Strategy for Teaching*. Columbus, Ohio: Charles E. Merrill Publishing Company, 1971.

Bruner, Jerome S. The Act of Discovery. *Harvard Educational Review*, 1961, *31*, 21-32.

_____. Structures in Learning. *Today's Education*, 1963, *52*, 26-27.

Brubaker, Dale L. Indoctrination, Inquiry, and the Social Studies. *The Social Studies*, 1970, *61*, 120-124.

Cox, C. Benjamin, and Massialas, Byron. *Inquiry in the Social Studies*. New York: McGraw-Hill Book Company, 1966.

Dewey, John. *How We Think*. Boston: D. C. Heath, 1933.

Fenton, Edwin. *The New Social Studies*. New York: Holt, Rinehart and Winston, Inc., 1967.

Fraser, Graeme S., and Switzer, Thomas Jr. Inquiries in Sociology: Responses by Teachers and Students. *Social Education*, 1970, *34*, 922-926.

La Forse, Martin. Why Inquiry Fails in the Classroom. *Social Education*, 1970, *34*, 65-68.

Massialas, Byron. Inquiry. *Today's Education*, 1969, *58*, 40-45.

Rogers, Vincent R. A Macrocosmic Approach to Inquiry. *Social Education*, 1970, *34*, 74-77.

Sagl, Helen. Problem Solving: Inquiry, Discovery? *Childhood Education*, 1966, *43*, 137-141.

Sanders, Norris, and Tanck, Marlin. A Critical Appraisal of Twenty-Six National Social Studies Projects. *Social Education*, 1970, *34*, 383-447.

Shaver, James, and Oliver, Donald. The Analysis of Public Controversy: A Social Studies Curriculum Project Report. *The Counsellor*, 1965, *24*, 10-14.

Strain, Lucille B. Inquiry and Social Studies for Disadvantaged Learners. *The Social Studies*, 1970, *61*, 147-148.

Suchman, Richard J. Inquiry Training: Builds Skills for Autonomous Discovery. *Merrill-Palmer Quarterly*, 1961, *7*, 147-171.

Wittrock, M. C. The Learning by Discovery Hypothesis. In Lee S. Schulman and Evan R. Keisler, eds., *Learning by Discovery*. Chicago: Rand McNally, 1966.

ADDITIONAL RESOURCES

Allen, Rodney F., Fleckenstein, John V., and Lyon, Peter M. *Inquiry in the Social Studies.* Washington, D.C.: National Council for the Social Studies, 1968.

Beyer, Barry K. *Inquiry in the Social Studies Classroom.* Columbus, Ohio: Charles E. Merrill Publishing Company, 1971.

Bruner, Jerome S. *Toward a Theory of Instruction.* Harvard University Press, 1966.

Crabtree, Charlotte. Inquiry Approaches: How New and How Valuable? *Social Education,* 1966, *30,* 523-526.

Hudgins, Bryce B. *Problem Solving in the Classroom.* New York: Macmillan, 1966.

Massialas, Byron, and Zevin, Jack. *Creative Encounters in the Classroom: Teaching and Learning through Discovery.* New York: John Wiley and Sons, 1967.

Sanders, Norris M. *Classroom Questions: What Kinds?* New York: Harper and Row, 1966.

Shulman, Lee S., and Keislar, Evan R., eds. *Learning By Discovery: A Critical Appraisal.* Chicago: Rand McNally, 1966.

75

SIMULATION AND GAMING FOR LEARNING

by Paul A. Twelker
Professor of Educational Research
Instructional Development Division
United States International University in Oregon
Corvallis, Oregon
and
Kent Layden
Assistant Professor of Instructional Technology
International Institute of Instructional Technology
United States International University
San Diego, California

Educational simulation/gaming combines two basically simple ideas: simulation and gaming. Simulations are simplified reality—the essence of physical or social systems of interaction. Simulations attempt to replicate essential aspects of reality so that reality may be better understood and/or controlled. Reality is replicated to the degree that the simulation designer selects essential elements from reality.

Games are competitive interactions among participants to achieve prespecified goals. These interactions may feature cooperation within groups, but competition either among individuals or groups distinguishes gaming. Games are usually played for entertainment, and clearly identify winners and losers. Participant success is dependent upon skill or chance or some combination of the two. Games make no attempt to replicate real-world behavior—rules of behavior for the game need apply to the game only

From these two ideas—simulation to represent ele-

ments of reality and gaming to stimulate interaction—have been developed a variety of powerful learning contexts, commonly known as educational stimulation/games. These may be distinguished by the particular combinations of simulation and gaming that they employ to facilitate different learning outcomes.

Although the following may not represent mutually exclusive categories, they do serve to differentiate among the variety of simulation/game applications being presented to educators for use.

Non-simulation games are competitive learning contexts in which participant success is determined by the degree of subject matter comprehension—of information, concepts, generalizations, and/or theories—demonstrated during game play.

Planning exercises are nonsimulation games which focus on process rather than content by engaging the participant in the examination of selected social problems requiring solution. Committees cooperate in discussion, and each proposes solutions which are in competition for adoption by the entire group after evaluation criteria have been established and applied.

Interpersonal simulation games are learning contexts in which the participant responds within the simulation game as if he were in the actual system of interaction being simulated. Interaction is structured by rules and physical circumstances. Resultant interaction ranges from the highly restricted participant behavior of a computer simulation game, through the less inhibited behavior with a so-called "board game," to the flexible, open-ended behavior of role-playing simulation games, which allow participant behavior more closely proximate to that in the actual system of interaction being simulated. Whatever the format, interpersonal simulation games combine the competitive aspects of gaming with the reality replication of simulation, to allow the participant a personal glimpse of how it "feels" to be in the dynamics of real-system interpersonal interaction.[1]

Large system simulation games are learning contexts for the examination of the dynamics of complex systems of interaction. Focus may range from looking at the variables affecting the urban community to a thoroughgoing analysis of the nation-state system of the international community. But in all cases the participant engages himself in the simulated systems—as planner, decision-maker, or merely observer—in order to better comprehend the variables affecting the dynamics of aggregate human behavior within the context of the actual complex system being simulated.

STATE OF THE ART

Diversity of technique and application have characterized the field of simulation and gaming from inception. This could be expected, given the roots of simulation and game design development. At present the field reflects debts to mathematics, operations research, systems science, and role theory from both psychology and sociology. Yet this very diversity is at once a strength and weakness: with interdisciplinary perspective has come an increasing understanding of system dynamics as "translated" through a semantic haze fraught with communication problems. One promising step toward theoretical resolution of this semantic haze is represented in the work of Duke (1972).

End user diversity is as great as that of the conceptual underpinnings of the field. From the elementary classroom teacher in Middle America, constructing a simple exercise to actively engage seven-year-olds in the learning process, to the researcher examining the interaction of variables in complex large system simulations—as epitomized by the visibility of the World Dynamics project of Forrester and his colleagues, and others (cf. McLeod, 1972)—simulation and gaming's time has come.

But to what extent use grows may only be inferred. Little data are available to enable us to make a statement about the current use of simulation/gaming techniques for learning. Most authors simply state that the use of these techniques "is common," or that the use "has increased" over the last decade. Klietch (1970) reports that in 1969 about 35 percent of surveyed schools in Minnesota used such techniques, while in 1970 use in the same schools had increased to 40 percent, with at least 10 percent of these games teacher or student-teacher devised. Recently, Chapman and Davis (1973) found that 72 different games were being used by 114 teachers in eight different locations. By and large, the greatest application of simulation/gaming techniques in secondary schools is in the social studies, including content from anthropology, economics, geography, history, political science, psychology, and sociology (cf. Charles and Stadsklev, 1973).

However, if growth in the simulation/gaming marketplace is demonstrative of the acceleration of classroom application, Zuckerman and Horn's (1973) *The Guide to Simulation Games for Education and Training* provides insight. In the 1970 edition, 404 simulations and games available to the public were reviewed. With the 1973 edition, that figure climbed to 613. Neither figure, of course, represents the total population of materials available or "in the works" at the time, due to publication lag-time and on-going development. The number of games that are accessible may be four or five times greater than the number listed in *The Guide*. Clearly, the available choices to the educational consumer are widening. This, too, poses problems.

Introducing simulation/gaming techniques into schools remains difficult. Heyman (1972) hypothesizes that the basic problem is that the educational philosophy implicit in the use of these techniques conflicts with the educational philosophy held by most teachers and administrators. Simulation/gaming techniques restructure the learning situation by altering the roles of students and teachers. Add to this the technical problems associated with inadequate game and game manual design, and commercial producers' inability to train teachers in the proper use of their materials (assuming, of course, that they even know) before or after they are sold, and it becomes a question not of why are there problems, but why have they been so few?

Yet the question of how much use merely begs the question of use for what? The field is hard pressed to present research evidence concerning the "hows," "whys," and "for whats" of game use. Although scores of research projects have been conducted (cf. Marshall and Mulder, 1972) little practical information has come, and virtually none with generalizable significance. Fletcher (1972) summarizes the research situation in this way:

> Most of the claims for the learning value of playing simulation games are extravagant, and for many such games there is no logical mechanism that would enable players to learn what the designers claim they would learn. The quality of the research investigations of these claims for the learning value of simulation games has been poor. The variables have been measured by different instruments in every study. The simulation devices have been used usually with a single play of the game, and usually there has not been careful attention to the actual behavior of the person in the game. Classroom research, in particular, still remains single-shot studies with different measures of different sets of variables that have very little comparability or mutual consistency. There is still no guarantee that findings on one game are at all generalizable to others. (p. 243)

Greenblat (1973), in a review of research studies conducted prior to September 1971, states that:

> . . . it appears that there is a considerable amount of anecdotal material about affective involvement of students at the time of the participation, and some evidence that student interest in simulation is very high. There is, at the moment, little hard data to show that such participation leads to greater interest in the subject matter, the course, or learning in general. (pp. 76-77)

Greenblat concludes that there is a lack of sufficient data to prove that games meet their pedagogical promise, but that this paucity of validation research evidence precludes the use of games in classrooms no more than do other such unvalidated mediums regularly employed.

But research questions, we feel, are beginning to take a turn toward evaluation measures which may yield sound evidence of the learning values of simulation/gaming techniques. Evaluation of simulations and games should provide users with suitable information to make both reliable purchase decisions and provide adaptive strategies for use with specific audiences. Properly conducted evaluations should obtain data about an exercise in a variety of operational settings, so that revisions may be made and so that the impact of an exercise on specific audiences may be reported. Unfortunately, most of what passes for evaluation studies at present fails to provide the needed information to improve user choice. What is needed now is the development of widely accepted and approved criteria for the certification of educational simulations and games. Third-party evaluation reports to consumers would seem a logical next step.

However adequate evaluation of a product may become, such information still may only slowly improve getting the product to users. The state of the art with respect to the distribution of simulation/gaming techniques is frankly embryonic. Very few large, commercial, textbook-oriented publishers are willing to take an interest in publishing games unless they are formatted as, or with, books. The market is seen as too small for large sales, so primary distribution has sifted down to a handful of jobbers, a half-dozen or so publishers, and small distributors of simulation/gaming products exclusively, and a host of "cottage" operations that come and go quicker than they can be catalogued. It has been suggested by Irving B. Naiburg, Jr., of Appleton-Century-Crofts, that developers publish privately and circulate their products on an informal basis, so that two things can happen: debugging may improve the product, and marketability may be determined and made available to prospective publishers (cf. *Simulation/Gaming/News,* 1973). Clearly, there is a need for a group to function as a product clearinghouse to help developers get into contact with consumers and each other.

An important footnote to this whole question was raised by Crow and Noel (1965), but has yet to be seriously considered, though we feel it is an important and useful distinction:

> Establishing the "validity" of simulations, or any other behavioral science method, is difficult. We believe that much more rapid progress could be made by a seemingly simple change in viewing the problem: we should shift attention from the validity of the method itself to the validity of using the information produced by the method. We suggest that validity be measured by asking: *How useful to the purpose for which it is to be gathered is the information produced by this method, as compared to some alternative method?* We believe that this approach to validity brings it more closely in accord with modern concepts of scientific method, and guides research more directly to application.

SELECTED SPECIFIC APPLICATIONS

Classroom Education at All Levels

Commercially available games and simulations exist in practically every discipline and content area, including adult and professional education. Some teachers have designed entire courses around a simulation game, or a series of games. Such saturation efforts often meet with mixed success, as students tire of the prolonged exposure to one dominant learning strategy. We would emphasize that simulation and gaming be viewed as one, and we think powerful, strategy for altering a passive instructional environment to a dynamic learning environment, emphasizing active student participation. We feel a particularly hopeful means to this end might be perhaps the least-used simulation/gaming strategy, but one that has powerful potential—student-designed games. When learners themselves design simulation games, our experience, if not research, suggest greater cognitive learning and sustained positive effect than when teacher-designed games are used. Teachers may well understand this from the old aphorism that "You never learn it so well until you have to teach it." And what happens? The teacher-learner "sees" new associations and insights in content and process, previously opaque but now self-appropriated. We think that is significant learning.

Urban Gaming and Simulation

Urban gaming and simulation techniques have been used for training, research, planning, and policy formation. Since about 1960, this area has undergone steady growth and sophistication, but with some growing pains.

It has been estimated that several hundred urban gaming and simulation techniques are in existence (cf. Feldt, 1972), ranging from simplistic, Monopoly-style board games to very complex, computerized games. To begin with, urban gaming techniques were manually operated (e.g., Community Land Use Game [CLUG], Region I and Region II), but as the number of variables included in the model increased, and as the number and complexity of calculations increased, the computer was used to eliminate the burdonsome accounting and to provide players a tool to facilitate decision-making. Some computer games have become so complex that some have suggested, half in jest, that it would be cheaper and less complicated to rent a real city than to conduct the more complicated of the computer-based models (cf. Becker, 1972, p. 17).[2]

Religious Education

Many people in the church are using simulation games for a variety of purposes. These uses include the training of laymen for church courts; teaching learners about various social problems and issues, such as feeding the world's population and racial unrest; teaching learners about various Biblical events and stories; and teaching church boards to make better decisions in planning, programming, and budgeting (cf. Wilcoxson and Washburn, 1972; Graham, 1972). It is interesting to note that many of the games being used by these groups are commercially available products not specifically designed for religious education purposes, but which have been adapted to meet specific needs and circumstances.

Television-Mediated Simulation

Simulation/gaming techniques need not be limited to the classroom, secular or otherwise. In 1967, a five-program simulation of the Korean Crises of 1950 was broadcast to home audiences over WGBX-TV, a special-service UHF channel in Boston (Lee, 1968). Studio participants represented statesmen of six major nations involved in the dispute, while the home audience took the role of the political elite of one of the teams, who advised the statesmen through telephone calls and letters. This experiment established the feasibility of reshaping television into a participatory experience for family groups, as well as for individuals and informal groups. However, further studies in this area have demonstrated some of the operational difficulties associated with decentralized game play. Edwards et al. (1972) report one such experiment using the CITY model over educational television in the Baltimore area. Further exploration of mass-audience utilization of simulation/gaming techniques seems likely, as products are further refined and as the match with technological developments (such as video cassettes for home use) moves "formal" education increasingly out of the classroom. One prominent development that breaks precedent-setting ground along these lines is the regional educational television network via satellite to the Rocky Mountain states, funded by the United States Office of Education.

Situational Response Testing

In designing the form of a test, an individual has a number of options open to him, ranging from the elicitation of facts to the observation of real-life behavior (cf. Frederiksen, 1962, pp. 323-346). Between these two extremes lies the elicitation of life-like behavior, but in the context of a simulated setting. Some of the most significant work on situational response testing has been conducted under the auspices of the American Board of Orthopedic Surgery, which began to study competence in orthopedics for the purpose of improving its certification procedures. From this effort has come a series of simulation problems in patient management that require sequential analysis and decision-making skills, defined as essential components to competence in orthopedic surgery (cf. Levine and McGuire, 1968, 1970). The results on the reliability and validity of the various measures have led to the investigation of the use of simulation for assessment purposes by other professional groups (cf. Lamont and Henen, 1972; Starkweather, 1967).

CURRENT CONTROVERSIES

The Conflicting Educational Philosophy Controversy

A major controversy has been alluded to above: The use of simulation/ gaming techniques implies the acceptance, on the part of the teacher, of an educational philosophy that is in conflict with the philosophy held by many teachers and school administrators. These techniques restructure the learning environment from an information-processing mode to an experiential learning mode. Livingston et al. (1973) describes each of these modes:

Information-Processing	*Experiential Learning*
1. Reception of information from a symbolic medium (e.g., text).	1. Acting in a particular instance and observing the consequences of that action.
2. Understanding the general principle.	2. Understanding the effects of the action in this particular case.
3. Inferring a particular application from the general principle (particularizing).	3. Understanding the general principle under which this particular instance falls.
4. Acting, using the general principle as understood to apply to a particular instance.	4. Application through action in a new circumstance within the range of generalization.

The controversy is fueled by an insistence that one or the other learning modes is preferable (or right), often to the exclusion of other modes. We sometimes hear from opponents of simulation/gaming techniques words to the effect that "there is no controversy: everyone knows that they aren't worth anything." Gamers should face this issue head-on, and produce the evidence that particular games *do* result in consistent learning gains, both cognitive and affective. A systematic series of well-conducted evaluations could, we feel, if not end, at least diminish, this controversy.

The Debriefing Controversy

To do or not to do often becomes the question. Many games are run without debriefings; apparently some users subscribe to the view that a good game doesn't need a debriefing; or the debriefing is dropped, since considerable means to lead students into the higher reaches of analysis, synthesis, and evaluation require extremely skilled practitioners to mitigate against the potential of the anticlimatic following-game play. Other game debriefings take on the didactic characteristic of lectures rather than that of guided discussion, where students do most of the talking. The controversy centers not so much on whether or not debriefings should be conducted, but how and by what means. Should game designers take the responsibility to outline debriefing sessions, complete with sequential questions? Or should consumers take the responsibility of developing validated debriefing sessions with the same degree of painstaking care characteristic of the better games that have been developed? Answering these questions must await the generation of appropriate learning heuristics, including debriefings.

The Simplistic Game-Complex Game Continuum

For some, the best games are single-concept games that can be prepared for in a few minutes, conducted in a typical class period, and debriefed quickly. The proponents of such simple games argue that they can insert such games easily in their curriculum, with maximum benefit and little disruption of desirable activities (after all, teachers only have a limited amount of time with students). For others, the best games are complex, long-running (and often tedious) games, though sometimes computerized to ease the burden of bookkeeping. Complex games have been used, however, as the backbone of the curricula rather than as adjuncts to the curricula. The consumer is caught in the middle, since he is asked to make purchasing decisions, frequently without preview, among a great variety of materials of varying complexity, together with all that implies for curriculum sequencing and learner outcomes. Most likely, there will come a day when the consumer will have the opportunity to make knowledgeable decisions about a hierarchy of games across the simplistic-complex gap. We believe that eventually a typology of game types—matrixed against anticipated learner outcomes, which clearly identifies the time-benefit tradeoffs of each type—will emerge to assist the educator in making more rational decisions for the learning environment. Until that day, the controversy wages on.

The Advocacy for Value-Free Simulations Controversy

Simulation and gaming techniques strongly reflect their social and behavioral science roots. Consequently, the field has not escaped the rift between those in the social sciences, who maintain that objectivism is preferable and desirable, and those who would criticize the value-free stance as naive. They argue that the applications ought to reflect the implicit and explicit value assumptions of practitioners across the theoretical-to-applied spectrum. Simulation/gaming techniques have expanded predominantly from the social sciences into wide-scale educational usage. The controversy has been compounded with the plethora of educational philosophies in the public schools. Most users remain oblivious of the issue, and designers, as transmitted through the commercial process have steadfastly ducked taking positions until recently.

McClellan (personal communication, 1973) stressed, in a probing analysis, that designers bear the responsibility for making their biases perfectly clear, and that users ought take stands on social policy questions raised in simulation/gaming environments. Cipinko (1973) reviewed recent professional periodicals in the simulation/gaming field and asked if concern with values is totally lacking. We feel this issue will draw increasing attention.

NOTES

[1] Our categories include simulation/gaming activities most frequently employed in the classroom setting, but they are far from inclusive. Other types of interpersonal simulation games which are beginning to find wider usage include media-based training exercises, communication skills exercises, and a wide range of exercises and activities for human relations training. For a more complete introduction to simulation/gaming techniques, refer to Twelker and Layden, 1972.

[2] For a review of the state of the art in urban gaming, refer to the report published by Environmetrics, Inc. (1971).

REFERENCES

Becker, H. A. General Introduction. In H. Becker and H. Goudappel, eds., *Developments in Simulation and Gaming.* Gasgracht 10 at Meppel, The Netherlands: Boom Publishers-Book Division, 1972, p. 17.

Cipinko, Stuart. Concern with S/G Values: Totally Lacking? *Simulation/Gaming/News,* 1973, *1*(9), 10.

Chapman, Katherine, and Davis, James E. *The Use of Simulation/Games in the Social Studies Classroom: A Report.* Boulder, Colorado: Social Science Education Consortium, Inc. and ERIC Clearinghouse for Social Studies/Social Science Education, 1973.

Charles, C., and Stadsklev, R., eds. *Learning with Games: An Analysis of Social Studies Educational Games and Simulations.* Boulder, Colorado: Social Science Education Consortium, Inc., 1973.

Crow, Wayman J., and Noel, Robert C. *The Valid Use of Simulation Results.* La Jolla, California: Western Behavioral Sciences Institute, 1965, p. 25.

Duke, Richard D. The Language of Gaming. In S. Kidder and A. Nafziger, eds., *Proceedings of the National Gaming Council's Eleventh Annual Symposium.* Baltimore, Maryland: The Johns Hopkins University, Center for Social Organization of Schools, 1972.

Edwards, Keith J., Meares, Portia, and Henry, Louise. An Evaluation of a Simulation Combining Television and Computer for High School Government Classes. In S. Kidder and A. Nafziger, eds., *Proceedings of the National Gaming Council's Eleventh Annual Symposium.* Baltimore, Maryland: The Johns Hopkins University, Center for Social Organization of Schools, 1972.

Environmetrics, Inc. *The State-of-the-Art in Urban Gaming Models.* Washington, D.C.: Office of the Secretary for the Environment and Urban Systems, Department of Transportation, 1971.

Feldt, Allan G. Developments in the Field of (Simulation and) Gaming in the United States. In H. Becker and H. Goudappel, eds., *Developments in Simulation and Gaming.* Gasgracht 10 at Meppel, The Netherlands: Boom Publishers-Book Division, 1972, 111-124.

Fletcher, Jerry L. The Direct Simulation of Effective Learning Environments: Enhancing Communication Among Diverse People. In S. Kidder and A. Nafziger, eds., *Proceedings of the National Gaming Council's Eleventh Annual Symposium.* Baltimore, Maryland: The Johns Hopkins University, Center for Social Organization of Schools, 1972.

Frederiksen, Norman. Proficiency Tests for Training Evaluation. In R. Glaser, ed., *Training Research and Education.* Pittsburgh: University of Pittsburgh Press, 1962.

Graham, Randolph. Game Prepares Laymen for Church Courts. *Simulation/Gaming/News,* 1972, *1*(2), 11.

Greenblat, Cathy S. Teaching with Simulation Games: A Review of Claims and Evidence. *Teaching Sociology,* 1972, *1*, 62-83.

Heyman, Mark. Introducing Simulation Games into Schools: Why Is It Difficult? In S. Kidder and A. Nafziger, eds., *Proceedings of the National Gaming Council's Eleventh Annual Symposium.* Baltimore, Maryland: The Johns Hopkins University, Center for Social Organization of Schools, 1972.

Klietch, Ronald. Learning Games and Instructional Simulations in Minnesota Secondary Schools: 1970 Highlights. (Report No. 2) Saint Paul: Macalester College, Instructional Simulation Center, 1970.

Lamont, C. T., and Hennen, B. K. E. The Use of Simulated Patients in a Certification Examination in Family Medicine. *Journal of Medical Education,* 1972, *47,* 789-795.

Lee, Richard H. The Most Dangerous Game: An Experiment in Viewer-Response Television. *Audio-visual Instruction,* 1968, *13,* 473-476.

Levine, Harold G., and McGuire, Christine. Role-playing as an Evaluation Technique. *Journal of Educational Measurement,* 1968, *5,* 1-8.

_____. The Use of Role-Playing to Evaluate Affective Skills in Medicine. *Journal of Medical Education,* 1970, *45,* 700-705.

Livingston, Samuel A., Fennessey, Gail M., Coleman, James S., Edwards, Keith J., and Kidder, Steven J. *The Hopkins Games Program: Final Report on Seven Years of Research.* Baltimore, Maryland: Center for Social Organization of Schools, The Johns Hopkins University, 1973.

Marshall, Mel, and Mulder, Jim. *Simulation Research 1972: A Partial Inventory.* Logan, Utah: Utah State University, 1972.

McLeod, John. McLeod Surveys World Simulation. *Simulation/Gaming/News,* 1972, *1,* 8.

Simulation/Gaming/News. Editorial: It's Cooperation Time for S/Gers. *Simulation/Gaming/News,* 1973, *1*(9), 2.

Starkweather, J. A. et al. Psychiatric Interview Simulation by Computer. *Methods of Information in Medicine,* 1967, *6,* 15-23.

Twelker, Paul A., and Layden, Kent. *Educational Simulation/Gaming.* Stanford, California: ERIC Clearinghouse on Media and Technology, 1972.

Wilcoxson, Georgeann, and Washburn, John. Toward a Theology of Simulation/Gaming. *Simulation/Gaming/News,* 1972, *1*(2), 1.

Zuckerman, David, and Horn, Robert, eds. *The Guide to Simulations/Games for Education and Training, 2nd Edition.* Lexington, Massachusetts: Information Resources, Inc. (P.O. Box 417), 1973.

ADDITIONAL RESOURCES

Adair, Charles H., and Foster, John T. *A Guide for Simulation Design: Theoretical and Practical Procedures for the Development of Instructional Simulation.* Tallahassee, Florida: Instructional Simulation Design, Inc. (P.O. Box 3330, Leon Station, Tallahassee, Florida 32303), 1972. The design process from A to Z in eight chapters and an appendix: Models and Theories; Pedagogical Models; Simulation Media; Assembling the Prototype; Developing your Simulation Evaluation Strategy; Observation; Field Testing; Evaluating and Improving your Simulation; and The Complete Simulation Obstacle Course.

Gordon, Alice Kaplan, *Games for Growth*. Palo Alto, California: Science Research Associates, Inc., 1970. This easy-to-read book explores the history of simulation/gaming and its current uses. It includes specific descriptions of some available games, suggestions for classroom use, guidelines on game design and adaptation, and a discussion of game evaluation.

Raser, John R., *Simulation and Society: An Exploration of Scientific Gaming*. Boston, Massachusetts: Allyn and Bacon, 1969. Somewhat technical in places, yet remains a lucid and readable discussion of modeling and simulation theory. It is primarily aimed at the social scientist who may not be familiar with simulation. The educator will find some sections useful, particularly the chapter on games for teaching.

Simulation and Games: An International Journal of Theory, Design, and Research (Johns Hopkins University, Sage Publications, 275 South Beverly Drive, Beverly Hills, California 90212 ($18 per year, quarterly, professional discounts available). This journal provides a forum for theoretical and empirical papers related to simulations (man, man-machine, and machine) of social processes. It publishes theoretical papers concerned with the use of simulation for research and instruction, empirical studies, and technical papers about new gaming techniques. Book reviews, listings of newly available simulations, and short simulation reviews are included.

Simulation/Gaming/News, Box 3039, University Station, Moscow, Idaho 83843 ($4 for five issues: every other month except in the summer). This tabloid-style, informal publication provides readers with practical, "applicable" information in addition to more theoretical considerations. It treats the application of simulation and gaming in most areas of experience and at different educational levels.

Stoll, Clarice, and Inbar, Michael. *Simulation and Gaming in Social Science*. New York: Free Press, 1972. This book is written for a general audience as an introduction to various simulation techniques (teaching or research, computer or non-computer). It includes six "textbook chapters" written by Inbar and Stoll, and 12 chapters by contributors. Included is a discussion of the history of simulation, and descriptions of several simulations.

Stoll, Clarice, and Livingstone, Samuel A. *Simulation/Gaming: An Introduction for Social Studies Teachers*. New York: Free Press, 1973. A short, practical handbook written for the classroom teacher, K-12. It includes excellent discussions of how to design a simulation game, written in unsophisticated language, and how to use games and incorporate them with other materials into the classroom. It also has a section devoted to conclusions of research to date.

Taylor, John L., and Walford, Rex. *Simulation in the Classroom*. Baltimore, Maryland: Penguin Books (7110 Ambassador Road), 1972. Past and present developments in simulation gaming are covered in one of the best available introductions to the area. A basic primer.

MAJOR ORGANIZATIONS

International Simulation and Gaming Association

Prof. Dr. H. A. Becker
University of Utrecht
Department of Sociology
P.O. Box 13015
Utrecht, The Netherlands

Prof. Dr. R. D. Duke
School of Natural Resources
University of Michigan
109 E. Madison
Ann Arbor, Michigan 48104, U.S.A.

An international organization whose aim is to advance an optimal application of simulation/gaming techniques throughout the world by the facilitation of communication between specialists, policymakers, students, and other persons, and the training of specialists in the field.

National Gaming Council

Peter House
Environmental Studies Division
Environmental Protection Agency
Washington, D.C. 20460

An informal group of people that have to date resisted organization, except to meet once a year.

Simulation and Gaming Association

Michael J. Raymond, Executive Director
4833 Greentree Road
Lebanon, Ohio 45036

Organization dedicated to the classroom teacher interested in exchanging ideas about the use of simulations and educational games.

76

INDIVIDUALIZED LEARNING

by Robert A. Weisgerber
Principal Research Scientist
American Institutes for Research
Palo Alto, California

The fundamental premise of education is that the young shall be afforded the opportunity to develop the knowledge, skills and attitudes which will enable them to lead a satisfying and productive adult life, both personally and socially. Flanagan (1973) has cited a number of findings from a large-scale national survey (Project TALENT) as evidence of the schools' past failure in providing performance standards and appropriate learning activities which develop the full potential in each individual.

Educators have long sought ways to improve the educational process and make it more meaningful to the participants. Among the innovative approaches of yesteryear were the Frederic Buck (California), Dalton (Massachusetts), and Winnetka (Illinois) schools. In recent years, two main thrusts of improvement in educational practice have been the utilization of newer media for effective communication and the general upgrading of teacher training. While potentially beneficial, these "improvements" have often been illusory and their effects unknown. This is principally because they have been aimed at the improvement of what the teacher does rather than what the learner does. Gagné's (1965) important work in differentiating hierarchical levels of learning was instrumental in shifting instructional emphasis from the instructor to the learner, and Glaser's (1966) views on the psychological bases for instructional design were a bridge between theory and practice.

Until the late sixties, individual differences among students tended to be overlooked by many teachers, or were overemphasized, becoming a rationale for the "earning" of grades, including failing grades. This is a practice which Bloom (1968) and many others find less desirable than learning for mastery. Today, educators are discovering ways of capitalizing on individual differences, to maximize the effectiveness of their instruction and to make learning more relevant and more interesting for each student.

A number of educational developments led to the emergence of the process we now know as individualized learning. Among the major contributing developments were programmed instruction; computer-managed and computer-assisted instruction; behavioral objectives and the specification of learner goals; diagnostic and criterion-referenced testing; flexible scheduling and staffing, including the use of tutors and paraprofessionals; and school-based learning centers, equipped with media and materials suitable for individual use. Most recently the trend toward teacher accountability has further strengthened the individualization movement. When most or all of these factors are carefully planned and implemented, the process is often termed a "systems approach," or an application of "educational technology," or "instructional design."

In sum, individualization as a teaching/learning process has been long thought of as an ideal way of fulfilling the fundamental premise of education; but only in the last decade has individualization been demonstrated to be viable within the mainstream of educational practice.

DEFINITION

Individualized learning represents a pervasive change in educational practice, a change which attempts to make instruction responsive to learners' needs and values. Indeed, the definition of individualized learning offered by Weisgerber (1973b) emphasizes the learner's point of view. That is, learning is individualized when the learner feels that the instructional system is responsive to his own needs, and that he has some choice in the determination of:

Time:	rate of instructional presentation, duration of study sessions, frequency of study sessions.
Subject Matter:	choice of topics, sequence of topics, depth of study in topic.
Mastery:	selection of goals or objectives, criteria for evaluation, readiness for testing.
Learning Methods:	media or materials to be used, extent of interaction with classmates, types of learning activities, instructional setting, teacher role.

It is important to realize, however, that the functional definition given above is *not* meant to be descriptive of the entire individualization movement. Individualized instruction and independent study, for example, may have somewhat different connotations (Weisgerber, 1973a). Some of the widely cited variants of individualized learning are personalized instruction, diagnostic and prescriptive education, audio-tutorial methods, individually guided education, and ungraded, continuous progress education. In addition, many forms of individualization are being practiced in the schools and colleges which are not labeled in any way, but which nonetheless involve the "tailoring" of activities and instructional materials, as is generally associated with individualized programs.

SCOPE AND STATUS OF INDIVIDUALIZATION

It is a most difficult and elusive task to attempt any classification or categorization of the varieties of individualization currently identifiable in the schools and colleges. Gibbons (1971) has pointed out that individualized programs can be active, responsive, or permissive in nature, and can exist even in the context of grouping to achieve homogeneity. Certainly, variations in the *degree* of individualization exist along a number of dimensions, including proportion of student body involved; proportion of school day allocated; amount of teacher/administrative intervention or direction; amount of rigidity and linearity within the learning materials or study units; purpose and nature of assessment; and the amount of constraints placed upon the learner when his interests, goals, pace, activities and "learning style" are divergent from his classmates'.

If one defines individualization operationally, that is, based upon its intent rather than its degree of development, then it would seem that the majority of the schools in the country employ it to some extent. Even if one takes a more conservative view, the increasing frequency of published reports and the volume of individualization-oriented instructional materials presently coming into the marketplace makes it appear that the number of students involved is many hundreds of thousands. Clearly, it is no longer a novelty in the schools.

SPECIFIC PROGRAMS AND/OR APPLICATIONS

A number of important, programatic individualization efforts have been described elsewhere (National School Public Relations Association, 1971; Weisgerber, 1972; Duane, 1973, EPIE, 1974). Only a few major approaches will be mentioned here.

A Technological System

In the late sixties various research and development organizations began systematically applying educational technology to individualization at the elementary and secondary school levels. This has had a profound and enduring impact on the nature of the movement.

One of these organizations was the American Institutes for Research, Palo Alto, California, which, by 1970, has developed Project PLAN* (Program for Learning in Accordance with Needs). Perhaps the most comprehensive of the R&D efforts, the developmental phase of PLAN* involved some 14 school districts across the country, included the four major subject matters of language arts, science, social studies and mathematics, and spanned grades 1-12. PLAN* is presently being marketed by Westinghouse Learning Corporation, and the number of students enrolled for the 1974-1975 school year approximates 100,000. A four-volume set of the objectives for PLAN* has been published separately (Flanagan, Mager, and Shanner, 1971). Project PLAN* has been described fully elsewhere (Flanagan, Shanner, Brudner, and Marker, 1975; Flanagan, 1972; Weisgerber and Rahmlow, 1971).

A major premise of PLAN* is that the learner should have responsibility for his own educational development within a structured system that:

uses testing to help the student identify appropriate long-term goals (career fields), as well as to assess his progress on near-term goals (objectives).

allows for his choice of alternate Teaching/Learning Units (TLUs) to achieve particular modular objectives.

encourages interpersonal communication without sacrificing the benefits of private study.

involves the learner in the selection and use of inexpensive multimedia as he acquires information and demonstrates skills.

involves the teacher as a resource person and classroom manager.

utilizes the computer (on an optional basis) to store and process data on student performance, and to play a role in the formulation of programs of study.

A Prescriptive Approach

One of the most widely adopted programs is known as IPI (Individually Prescribed Instruction). It was developed at the Learning Research and Development Center, Pittsburgh, and is disseminated by Research for Better Schools, Philadelphia. IPI mathematics and language arts have been available at the elementary school level for a number of years, while science has been introduced rather recently. IPI has been described fully by Cox and Lindvall (1971), Bolvin (1972), Scanlon (1973), and Glaser and Rosner (1975).

For IPI and its sister project, PEP (Primary Education Project), the approach emphasizes the matching of learning levels and steps to individual differences. This is accomplished by:

detailed diagnosis of the initial state of the learner's mastery of prerequisite behaviors, his aptitude, and his perceptual ability.

the specification of the learner's appropriate starting-point within a sequence of self-instructional materials.

the monitoring of his progress, i.e., the assessment of requisite behaviors prior to his moving into successive instructional materials.

the adjustment of the instructional sequence for each learner in accordance with his demonstrated performance.

Nongradedness

A more modest approach, which has had widespread adoption and is often partially individualized, is nongradedness. Pioneered as early as 1925, it was described and advocated by Goodlad and Anderson (1963), and in 1966 was promoted widely by the Institute for the Development of Educational Ideas (I/D/E/A), with the support of the Kettering Foundation. The concept has been fully described by Rollins (1968), and compared to individualized instruction by McLoughlin (1972). The differentiated staffing, multilevel grouping, and "quest" learning that are often associated with nongradedness became articulated in a League of Cooperating Schools in California, which then became models for implementation in a number of other schools around the country. A key feature of this movement has been the development of "UNIPAC" instructional modules and their dissemination from a "bank" numbering more than 5,000 (Feild and Swensen, 1972). At the Nova School, in Fort Lauderdale, Florida, the instructional module was termed a LAP (Learning Activity Package). It, too, has been widely copied and thoroughly described (Smith, 1972; Cardarelli, 1972). Kapfer and Ovard (1971) have also described the development and use of modular, individualized packages in detail.

Most recently, the I/D/E/A version of individualization has been complemented by another closely allied approach conceived and developed at the Wisconsin Research and Development Center for Cognitive Learning, called Individually Guided Education, or simply IGE (Holzman, 1972; Klausmeier, 1975). It stresses individualization within multi-unit grouping, and emphasizes the motivational aspects of learning.

Higher Education

Bechtol (1972) has reported the development of college-level learning packages modeled after the UNIPAC modules. Termed ComPacs, they have been used for competency-based teacher education at Southwest Minnesota State College. In Utah, where individualization at the higher education level is widespread, Weber State College has begun to use WILKITS (Weber Individualized Learning Kits) for teacher education (Burke, 1972).

For about a decade, the "audio-tutorial system" has been in use to individualize biology instruction at Purdue University. Developed by Postlethwait and his colleagues (Postlethwait, Novak, and Murray, 1972), the approach has spread through the colleges and universities and has been applied in many other subject areas. In essence, the system involves an audiovisual, self-instructional laboratory, augmented by teacher/student seminars and even by large-group lectures. In this sense, then, it is a partially individualized approach, similar in process to many nongraded programs where some homogeneous grouping occurs.

One of the most prevalent of all college-level approaches to individualization is that developed by Fred S. Keller in the mid-sixties. Popularly known as PSI, or Personalized System of Instruction, this approach is distinguishable by its central role for proctors, emphasis on written teacher/student exchanges, and the use of group lectures for motivational rather than informational purposes (Cook, 1974).

IMPACT OF INDIVIDUALIZED LEARNING

Individualized learning is a relatively recent phenomenon in the long history of education, notwithstanding the pioneering ventures referred to previously, which were generally ahead of their time. Consequently, its long-term impact in preparing learners for adulthood has not yet been fully felt. Its near-term impact, however, is already apparent, and in no uncertain way has left its mark upon the mainstream of the educational process. See, for example, the variety of evaluation indices cited by Flanagan, Shanner, Brudner, and Marker (1975) in a range of schools.

Most important, educators at all levels are now more sensitive to the fact that learners in their classes have unique capabilities and needs, who would not be benefited by a fixed-pace presentation of information that is the same for all. Nor would they be benefited by testing that all too often merely proves differences that were evident to begin with, showing little about mastery of the subject matter. In terms of meeting learner needs, the principles of individualized learning have direct import for particular disciplines, such as the special education of the handicapped (Weisgerber, 1974).

Educators no longer blithely make the assumption that extremely low teacher/student ratios and high operating budgets are prerequisite before individualization can be undertaken. Individualization has been demonstrably successful where student/teacher ratios exceed 30:1, and where school districts operate on "lean" budgets.

It has become increasingly clear to educators that many students are able to share a greater part of the decision-making involved in their own education than had previously been thought possible. While this kind of involvement has been no surprise at the college level, it has also been convincingly demonstrated at all other levels, including first grade. It is also clear that students can share in the conduct of instruction, for peer-tutoring plays an important role in most individualized programs.

Through the enabling "how" of individualization, the educational enterprise has begun to revalue the "what" of the curriculum and "why" of accountability. In addition to necessary skills in basic subjects, individualization makes possible an increasing emphasis on the development of self-concept, self-determination and career exploration (Dunn, 1972).

Individualization has stimulated highly innovative approaches to instructional development, media resources management, and functional facilities design. Among the more dramatic innovations is the concept of the Open University in Britain (Hawkridge, 1972), where television and print media are utilized in lieu of a traditional campus, thus making higher education available to thousands of qualified persons who may be holding jobs far from campuses, or who for some other reason cannot attend regular classes. Various American colleges are following this lead, and now encourage individual study for external credit units.

As the locus of responsibility for the acquisition of knowledge, skills, and attitudes shifts from the teacher to the student, so does the responsibility for acquiring the materials essential for learning. A major trend in schools and colleges is the provision of a learning center— a kind of focal point for nontraditional learning that goes far beyond the "repository" status of many audiovisual service centers and libraries—representing a dynamic alternative to the classroom itself (Peterson, 1973). Indeed, the learning center is increasingly being thought of as a community resource which adults can use in furtherance of their own lifetime learning.

CURRENT CONTROVERSIES AND CONSIDERATIONS

In spite of the great promise and benefits that seem evident in systematically developed individualized programs, there are factors or cautions which the prudent educator should anticipate and take into account.

All too often *insufficient planning* handicaps new programs. Specifically, the success of fledgling programs is jeopardized where the administration is passive or noncommittal, where provision has not been made for thorough teacher retraining, where parents have not been involved in meaningful ways, where insufficient or ill-designed instructional materials are employed, and where diagnostic and criterion tests are absent, or are not clearly tied to behavioral objectives and long-range goals. Even though exceptions can be cited in which individual teachers have been able to "go individualized" on their own, the available evidence strongly suggests that program success is directly related to the amount of systematic planning and administrative support that is given to new programs before they begin and during the first several years. For example, the Duluth Public Schools' use of "contracts" to individualize education flourished within a receptive environment fostered by the administration (Esbensen, 1968).

Overexpectations are another risk associated with newly initiated individualized programs. Initially, a "honeymoon period" of enthusiasm, novelty, and experimentation is likely to lead to overoptimism about program results. When ample time is not allowed for the innovative program to shake down before making judgments of a summative nature, there may well be a psychological letdown, especially if academic gains are only equal to, or are slightly less than, in the preceding year. That is not to say that individualized programs should be expected to compare unfavorably with traditional programs, but rather that during transitional periods optimal performance is unlikely for the key participants (learners, teachers, administrators) unless there has been considerable advance preparation. A variety of texts (Weisgerber, 1971a, 1971b; Dell, 1972; Dunn and Dunn, 1972; Davis, Alexander, and Yelon, 1974; and Gagne and Briggs, 1974) may be helpful in providing this essential preparation.

The *requirements for extra time and effort* are usually high when individualized programs are introduced. Not only does the dedicated teacher frequently find herself spending additional time in preparing for class, but she also will spend more time talking with students, meeting with colleagues to discuss individual cases, and explaining the new approach to interested parents. Experience has shown that this extra time commitment is ameliorated in succeeding years, but even during the difficult first year most teachers feel that it is a wise investment of their time.

Much debate has centered on the *role of computers* in individualized instruction. The chief alternatives are computer-assisted instruction (CAI), which directly interfaces the student on-line with the computer and involves branching instructional programs; and computer-managed instruction (CMI), which is generally used off-line for planning students' programs of studies, for monitoring progress, and for summarizing class and individual status. CAI has been fairly widely used for initial reading and math drill and practice at the public school level, an approach developed by Suppes at Stanford University, and for a variety of courses in higher education through PLATO, an approach developed by Bitzer at the University of Illinois.

Computer-managed instruction (CMI) has been successfully employed in the aforementioned Project PLAN*, developed at the American Institutes for Research, and is presently available from Westinghouse Learning Corporation. The Comprehensive Achievement Monitoring (CAM) system, jointly developed by the University of Massachusetts and the New York State Education Department, utilizes the computer for prescriptive, achievement, and maintenance management. The Automated Instructional Management System (AIMS), at the New York Institute of Technology, has applied CMI to college-level courses for a number of years.

The educational community must keep cost benefits in mind; thus, future widespread adoption of CAI or CMI is still uncertain. Nevertheless, experimentation will undoubtedly continue.

Fundamental to improvement in the efficiency of individualized learning is the concept that what is recommended as a course of action for some learners is not the best for others—indeed it may be counterproductive. Research on the relationships between particular learner aptitudes and particular instructional treatments, referred to as *Aptitude-Treatment-Interaction*, or simply A-T-I, has been undertaken by Cronbach and Snow (1969), Salomon (1972), Koran (1972), and others, with mixed results. The field of individualized learning has only been able to make limited use of this concept to date, but with more definitive findings greater precision and efficiency should be possible in the selection of appropriate learning experiences. Eventually, it may well be that A-T-I research will, as Glaser (1972) suggests, lead to the identification of "new aptitudes" and to the release of individual talents in an environment of academic freedom.

REFERENCES

Bechtol, W. M. The ComPac: An Instructional Package for Competency-Based Teacher Education. *Educational Technology,* 1972, *12*(9), 37-41.

Bloom, B. S. Learning for Mastery. *Evaluation Comment* (Center for the Study of Evaluation of Instructional Programs, University of California at Los Angeles), May 1968, *1*(2).

Bolvin, J. O. Materials for Individualized Instruction: An Interpretation of Goals. *Educational Technology,* 1972, *12*(9), 23-27.

Burke, C. D. The Structure and Substance of the WILKIT Instructional Module. *Educational Technology,* 1972, *12*(9), 41-46.

Cardarelli, S. M. The LAP—A Feasible Vehicle of Individualization. *Educational Technology,* 1972, *12*(3), 23-29.

Cook, D. A. *Personalized System of Instruction: Potential and Problems.* EPIE Report #61. New York: Educational Products Information Exchange Institute, April 1974.

Cox, R. C., and Lindvall, C. M. Evaluation in a Structured Curriculum Model for Individualized Instruction. In R. A. Weisgerber, ed., *Developmental Efforts in Individualized Learning.* Itasca, Illinois: F. E. Peacock Publishers, Inc., 1971.

Cronbach, L. J., and Snow, R. E. *Individual Differences in Learning Ability as a Function of Instructional Variables.* Final report, U.S.O.E. contract no. OEC 4-6-061269-121, Stanford University School of Education, California, 1969.

Davis, R. H. Alexander, L. T., and Yelon, S. L. *Learning System Design: An Approach to the Improvement of Instruction.* New York: McGraw-Hill Book Company, 1974.

Dell, H. D. *Individualizing Instruction: Materials and Classroom Procedures.* Chicago: Science Research Associates, Inc., 1972.

Duane, J. E., ed. *Individualized Instruction: Programs and Materials.* Englewood Cliffs, New Jersey: Educational Technology Publications, 1973.

Dunn, J. A. *Individualization of Education in Career Education.* Palo Alto, California: American Institutes for Research, 1972.

Dunn, R., and Dunn, K. *Practical Approaches to Individualizing Instruction: Contracts and Other Effective Teaching Strategies.* West Nyack, N.Y.: Parker Publishing Company, Inc., 1972.

EPIE. *Evaluating Instructional Systems: PLAN*, IGE, PIP.* EPIE Report #58. New York: Educational Products Information Exchange Institute, 1974.

Esbensen, T. *Working with Individualized Instruction: The Duluth Experience.* Palo Alto, California: Fearon Publishers, 1968.

Feild, W. B., and Swenson, G. The UNIPAC: A Form and Process for Individualizing. *Educational Technology,* 1972, *12*(9), 11-13.

Flanagan, J. C. The PLAN System as an Application of Educational Technology. *Educational Technology,* 1972, *12*(9), 17-21.

_____. Education: How and for What. *American Psychologist,* 1973, *28*(7), 551-556.

_____, Mager, R. F., and Shanner, W. M. *Behavioral Objectives: A Guide to Individualizing Learning.* (Language Arts, Science, Social Studies, Mathematics.) Palo Alto, California: Westinghouse Learning Press, 1971.

_____, Shanner, W. M., Brudner, H. J., and Marker, R. W. An Individualized Instructional System: PLAN*. In Harriet Talmadge, ed., *Systems of Individualized Education.* Berkeley, California: McCutchan Publishing Company, 1975.

Gagné, R. M. *The Conditions of Learning.* New York: Holt, Rinehart and Winston, Inc., 1965.

_____, and Briggs, L. J. *Principles of Instructional Design.* New York: Holt, Rinehart and Winston, Inc., 1974.

Gibbons, M. *Individualized Instruction: A Descriptive Analysis.* New York: Teachers College Press, Columbia University, 1971.

Glaser, R. Individuals and Learning: The New Aptitudes. *Educational Researcher,* June 1971, *1*(6), 5-13.

_____. Psychological Bases for Instructional Design. *AV Communication Review,* 1966, *14*, 433-449.

_____, and Rosner, J. Adaptive Environments for Learning: Curriculum Aspects. In Harriet Talmadge, ed., *Systems of Individualized Education.* Berkeley, California: McCutchan

Publishing Company, 1975.

Goodlad, J. I., and Anderson, R. H. *Nongraded Elementary School*. New York: Harcourt, Brace & World, Inc., 1963.

Hawkridge, D. G. Applications of Educational Technology at the Open University. *AV Communication Review*, 1972, *20*, 5-15.

Holzman, S. *IGE: Individually Guided Education and the Multi-Unit School*. Arlington, Virginia: National School Public Relations Association, 1972.

Kapfer, P. G., and Ovard, G. F. *Preparing and Using Individualized Learning Packages for Ungraded, Continuous Progress Education*. Englewood Cliffs, New Jersey: Educational Technology Publications, 1971.

Klausmeier, H. J. IGE: An Alternative Form of Schooling. In Harriet Talmadge, ed., *Systems of Individualized Education*. Berkeley, California: McCutchan Publishing Companh, 1975.

Koran, M. L. Varying Instructional Methods to Fit Trainee Characteristics. *AV Communication Review*, 1972, *20*, 135-146.

McLoughlin, W. P. Individualization of Instruction vs Nongrading. *Phi Delta Kappan*, 1972, *53*(6), 378-381.

National School Public Relations Association. *Individualization in Schools: The Challenge and the Options*. Washington, D.C.: Author, 1971.

Peterson, G. T. Conceptualizing the Learning Center. *Audiovisual Instruction*, 1973, *18*(3), 67-72.

Postlethwait, S. N., Novak, J., and Murray, H. T., Jr. *The Audio-Tutorial Approach to Learning*, 3rd ed. Minneapolis: Burgess Publishing Company, 1972.

Rollins, S. P. *Developing Nongraded Schools*. Itasca, Illinois: F. E. Peacock Publishers, Inc., 1968.

Salomon, G. Can We Affect Cognitive Skills Through Visual Media? An Hypothesis and Initial Findings. *AV Communication Review*, 1972, *20*, 401-422.

Scanlon, R. G. Individually Prescribed Instruction: A System of Individualized Instruction. In J. G. Duane, ed., *Individualized Instruction: Programs and Materials*. Englewood Cliffs, New Jersey: Educational Technology Publications, 1973.

Smith, J. E., Jr. The Learning Activity Package. *Educational Technology*, 1972, *12*(9), 15-17.

Weisgerber, R. A., ed. *Developmental Efforts in Individualized Learning*. Itasca, Illinois: F. E. Peacock Publishers, Inc., 1971. (a)

――――, ed. *Perspectives in Individualized Learning*. Itasca, Illinois: F. E. Peacock Publishers, Inc., 1971. (b)

――――. *Trends, Issues and Activities in Individualized Learning*. Stanford, California: ERIC Clearinghouse on Media and Technology, 1972.

――――. Individualized Instruction, Individualized Learning, and Independent Study. In J. W. Brown, ed., *Educational Media Yearbook 1973*. New York: R. R. Bowker Company, 1973. (a)

――――. Individualized Learning Through Technology. *Audiovisual Instruction*, 1973, *18*(3), 54-55. (b)

――――. Individualizing for the Handicapped Child in the Regular Classroom. *Educational Technology*, 1974, *11*, 33-35.

――――, and Rahmlow, H. F. Strategies for Learning in PLAN. In R. A. Weisgerber, ed., *Developmental Efforts in Individualized Learning*. Itasca, Illinois: F. E. Peacock Publishers, Inc., 1971.

ADDITIONAL RESOURCES

Glaser, R. *Studies of Instructional Technology Relating to Computer-Assisted Instruction*. Final report, Learning Research and Development Center, Pittsburgh University, Pa., 1972. ED 071 422

Coombs, A. M., Jr. et al. *Variable Modular Scheduling. Effective Use of School Time, Plant, and Personnel. New Directions in Education*. Beverly Hills, Calif.: Benziger, Bruce & Glencoe, Inc., 1971. ED 071 200

Frazier, A. *Open Schools for Children*. Washington, D.C.: Association for Supervision and Curriculum Development, 1972. ED 069 035

Stevens, J. L. *Differentiated Staffing, Nongraded–Continuous Progress, Open Concept Schools. A Comprehensive Bibliography*. Houston University, Texas: Bureau of Educational Research and Services, 1972. ED 066 811

Gagne, R. M., and Elfner, E. A. *Plan of Operation for an Individualized System of Elementary Education*. Report no. R-4. Tallahassee: Florida State University, 1971. ED 066 784

Pask, G., and Scott, B. C. E. Learning Strategies and Individual Competence. *International Journal of Man-Machine Studies*, 1972, *4*(3), 217-253. EJ 072 333

Wood, F. H. Individual Differences Count. *NAASP Bulletin*, 1973, *57*(369), 23-31. EJ 070 027

Heathers, G. Overview of Innovations in Organization for Learning. *Interchange*, 1972, *3*(2-3), 47-68. EJ 067 910

Eisendrath, C. R., and Cottle, T. J. Individualizing the College Curriculum. *Urban Education*, 1972, *7*(3), 281-291. EJ 066 111

77

INDIVIDUALLY GUIDED EDUCATION

by Richard A. Rossmiller
Director, Wisconsin Research & Development Center
for Cognitive Learning
Madison, Wisconsin

Individually Guided Education (IGE) is a system of education designed to produce higher educational achievement by accommodating individual differences among students in rate of learning, learning style, and other characteristics. Individually Guided Education currently includes seven major components: (1) an organization for instruction—the multiunit school; (2) a model for instructional programming; (3) instructional materials; (4) measurement tools and evaluation procedures; (5) a program of home-school communications; (6) facilitative environments; and (7) research and development to continuously improve the system.

Eleven years ago Individually Guided Education was little more than an idea in the minds of researchers at the Wisconsin Research and Development Center for Cognitive Learning. Today it is a new way of teaching and learning for teachers and children in approximately 2,000 of the nation's elementary schools organized as multiunit schools; and thousands of others are using one or more of the Center's products. The first schools organized in accordance with the IGE system were formed in 1967-1968, and as recently as 1970-1971 as many as 164 IGE schools were in operation. The rapid spread of IGE to school districts throughout the nation during the past few years is virtually unprecedented for an innovation as complicated and comprehensive as IGE.

Why has Individually Guided Education proven so popular? Although many reasons are cited by elementary school teachers and principals, two seem to stand out. First, IGE is a comprehensive system that provides a workable alternative to the age-graded, self-contained classroom—the traditional form of organization that typically requires children to adapt to the system, rather than adapting the system to meet the needs of individual children. Second, IGE incorporates into a single system some of the most promising educational innovations of recent years—team teaching, differentiated staffing, multi-age grouping, peer instruction, open classrooms, continuous progress learning, programmed instruction, computer-assisted instruction, and many others. The developers of IGE make no claim that it is a panacea for all educational ills. Rather, they view it as an alternative system of education, which has proven to be more effective than the traditional age-graded system in meeting educational goals in a variety of communities.

HISTORY OF IGE

The development of Individually Guided Education began in 1965 at the Wisconsin R&D Center, under the direction of Professor Herbert J. Klausmeier. Members of the Center staff worked closely with elementary schools in Madison, Janesville, Milwaukee, and Racine, Wisconsin, during the 1965-1966 school year, starting with 13 nongraded instructional units, which replaced age-graded classes. These units, which later became known as instructional and research (I&R) units, marked the beginning of the organizational/administrative component of IGE—the multiunit school. In 1967-1968, seven elementary schools were for the first time completely organized into instructional and research units, and the term "multiunit school" was coined to designate these schools. The development of the IGE system was given further impetus during the 1968-1969 school year, when the Wisconsin Department of Public Instruction selected the multiunit school for statewide demonstration and installation. During this initial period of development, it became apparent that merely changing the organizational structure of a school from age-graded classes to I&R units was not sufficient to achieve the desired results. Thus, the seven components which constitute what is now known as the IGE system gradually evolved from these early research and development efforts.

Another important step in the development of IGE occurred in 1969, when the Wisconsin R&D Center and /I/D/E/A/ (Institute for Development of Educational Activities), of the Kettering Foundation signed an agreement dealing with the development of inservice materials. /I/D/E/A/ was authorized to use the prototypic materials developed by the Center, and also incorporated into the materials insights gained from its own study of educational change, which had begun in the spring of 1966.

The spread of IGE was given further impetus when the U.S. Department of Health, Education, and Welfare selected the multiunit school for nationwide installation during the 1971-1972 school year, and authorized the U.S. Office of Education to provide funds which enabled the Wisconsin R&D Center to carry out extensive implementation activities. Support provided by the

Office of Education during the period 1971-1973, and by the National Institute of Education during the period 1973-1975, has enabled the Wisconsin R&D Center to continue working with state education agencies, teacher education institutions, and local school districts in 23 states to extend and refine the implementation of IGE concepts in multiunit schools. Since January, 1972, /I/D/E/A/ and the Wisconsin R&D Center have carried out independent implementation efforts, using different strategies and materials which are designed to accomplish similar purposes.

THE COMPONENTS OF IGE

As noted above, Individually Guided Education is a system of education consisting of seven independent, but conceptually interrelated, components. A brief description of each component should facilitate understanding of the IGE system.

The Multiunit School

The multiunit school is the organizational/administrative component of IGE. It provides a new organizational pattern for instruction and a changed administrative pattern at the building and central office levels. Figure 1 illustrates these interlocking elements. Differentiated staffing, group planning and decision-making, open communication, and accountability characterize the multiunit school.

At the classroom level, the nongraded instructional and research unit replaces the age-graded, self-contained classroom. Research is included in the title to emphasize the fact that the staff must continuously engage in practical research in order to devise and evaluate an instructional program appropriate for each child in the unit. In the typical multiunit school each I&R unit includes a unit leader, or lead teacher, three or four other teachers, one instructional aide, one clerical aide, one intern or student teacher, and 100 to 150 students. The children in a unit typically have a two- to three-year age span.

The second element in the multiunit organization is the Instructional Improvement Committee (IIC). The IIC is building-wide in scope and is comprised of the principal and the unit leaders. The principal organizes and chairs the IIC, and sees to it that its decisions are implemented. The committee takes primary initiative for stating the educational objectives and outlining the educational program for the school building, coordinates I&R unit activities, and arranges for the use of facilities, time, and material. The IIC deals primarily with developing and coordinating instructional functions. Although the principal's leadership responsibility is not diminished under the IGE system, he does share instructional decisions with the IIC.

A third key element of the multiunit school organization is the Systemwide Program Committee (SPC). The SPC is chaired by the superintendent or a designee, and includes central office staff members and representative principals, unit leaders, teachers, and parents. The SPC establishes operational guidelines and coordinates system-wide activities, such as planning for inservice educa-

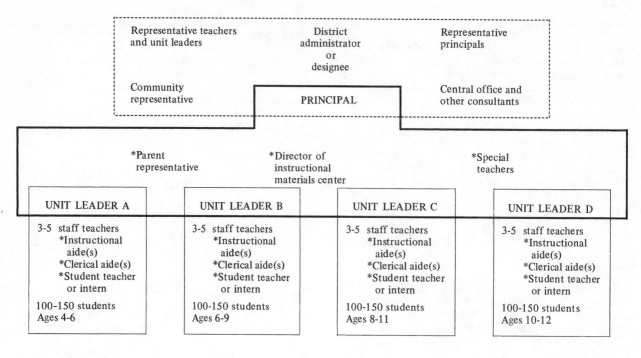

Figure 1. Multiunit organization of an IGE School of 400–600 students.
Adapted from: Herbert J. Klausmeier, Richard G. Morrow, and James E.
Walter, *Individually Guided Education in the Multiunit School.* Madison:
Wisconsin Research and Development Center for Cognitive Learning, 1968.

tion, providing instructional materials, and disseminating information to the community.

Unlike some differentiated staffing programs, in which new roles and titles are proliferated, the multiunit school organization establishes only one new position—the unit leader, or lead teacher. The unit leader is not a supervisor, but a career teacher who plans and coordinates unit activities. The unit leader is responsible for demonstrating new materials and for keeping abreast of research and development. As a member of the IIC, the unit leader helps plan and develop the instructional program of the building, and serves in a liaison capacity between the unit staff and the principal. As unit coordinator, the unit leader is responsible for planning and implementing the unit's educational program. However, each teacher in the unit shares fully in decision-making, and assumes responsibility for the programs of specific children. Unit meetings are held at least two hours a week (during school time), giving teachers an opportunity to pool their knowledge and expertise. They cooperatively plan, carry out, and evaluate an instructional program for each child.

Instructional Programming Model

A model of instructional programming for the individual student is at the heart of IGE. Ideally, each child's program will be based on how and at what pace he learns best, and where he stands on mastering specific skills or concepts. Attempting to achieve this ideal involves a series of steps, which are outlined in Figure 2. The R&D Center is developing curriculum materials which incorporate the instructional programming model, and assists school personnel in applying the model to other curricula. For purposes of illustration, the six steps in the model will be discussed as they might be used in the Word Attack element of the *Wisconsin Design for Reading Skill Development* (WDRSD), the Center's Individually guided reading program.

Step 1 involves the setting by the IIC of school-wide educational objectives in reading. The terminal objective for reading might be: 90 percent of the children attain independence in Word Attack by age 10, 95 percent by age 11, and 99 percent by age 12.

Step 2 calls for identification by the I&R unit staff on a subset of specific instructional objectives appropriate for a given group of children.

Step 3 involves the assessment of each child's level of skill development. For each behaviorally stated objective of the Word Attack element, a short criterion-referenced test has been developed and validated for use in assessing mastery or nonmastery of the skill described. This testing, supplemented with observation, indicates which of the skills each child has already mastered and which he has not.

Step 4 involves setting instructional objectives for each child in the unit. The behavioral objectives related to the skills a child has not yet mastered become his instructional objectives.

Step 5 calls for unit teachers to plan an instructional program for each child in the unit. Each teacher assumes responsibility for the instruction of certain children, who may be grouped together because they need to master the same skills. While children will be involved in several different instructional patterns in the various curriculum areas, each will receive some instruction in small groups,

with other children working on the same skills. The Word Attack element of WDRSD has a teacher's resource file, which keys published materials and suggested activities to each of the 45 skills.

Step 6 of the model involves assessing students to determine their attainment of objectives. Once the student reaches the specified mastery level, he moves on to the next sequence of the program (Step 7). If he has not mastered the skills, the unit staff takes another look at his progress and designs another program for the same or another objective.

Measurement Tools and Evaluation Procedures

A third component of the IGE system is a model for developing measurement tools and evaluation procedures. This includes pre-assessment of children's readiness, assessment of progress and final achievement with criterion-referenced tests, feedback to the teacher and the child, and evaluation of the IGE system and its components. The assessment data are used not only to plan each child's instruction, but also to evaluate whether or not the school is meeting the objectives of its educational program. Such analyses permit judgments about the effectiveness of a school's program to be based directly upon performance related to specified objectives.

Curriculum Materials

Curriculum materials, including statements of instructional objectives, criterion-referenced tests, and observation schedules, are the fourth component of the IGE system. Curriculum materials currently being developed at the Wisconsin R&D Center are described briefly below.

The *Wisconsin Design for Reading Skill Development* (WDRSD) describes essential reading skills and related behaviors, and provides criterion-referenced tests for assessing children's mastery of these skills. The program is organized into six skill areas: Word Attack, Study Skills, Comprehension, Self-directed Reading, Interpretive Reading, and Creative Reading. The program offers a unique management system, which simplifies grouping children for instruction. It also provides suggestions for teacher-directed learning activities and references to commercially published materials.

The *Prereading Skills Program* is designed to prevent reading failures by identifying and overcoming deficits in prereading skills at the preschool and kindergarten levels. Diagnostic tests have been developed for three visual skills (letter order, letter orientation, and word detail) and two auditory skills (sound matching and sound blending). Instructional packages to help children learn these skills include games, songs, and other activities. Information assessment procedures and teacher materials are also included.

Developing Mathematical Processes (DMP)—a comprehensive instructional and management program—integrates arithmetic, geometry, and probability and statistics to learning with IGE practices. Based on an empirical analysis of how children learn mathematics, DMP represents the first attempt to incorporate an activity approach in a carefully sequenced, complete program of

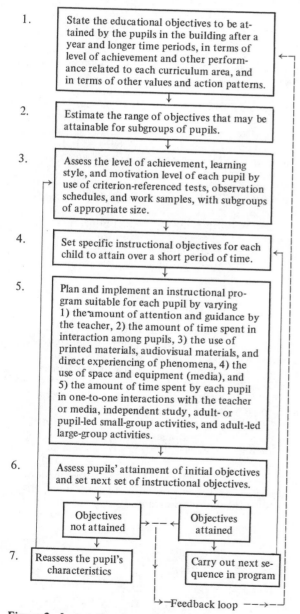

1. State the educational objectives to be attained by the pupils in the building after a year and longer time periods, in terms of level of achievement and other performance related to each curriculum area, and in terms of other values and action patterns.

2. Estimate the range of objectives that may be attainable for subgroups of pupils.

3. Assess the level of achievement, learning style, and motivation level of each pupil by use of criterion-referenced tests, observation schedules, and work samples, with subgroups of appropriate size.

4. Set specific instructional objectives for each child to attain over a short period of time.

5. Plan and implement an instructional program suitable for each pupil by varying 1) the amount of attention and guidance by the teacher, 2) the amount of time spent in interaction among pupils, 3) the use of printed materials, audiovisual materials, and direct experiencing of phenomena, 4) the use of space and equipment (media), and 5) the amount of time spent by each pupil in one-to-one interactions with the teacher or media, independent study, adult- or pupil-led small-group activities, and adult-led large-group activities.

6. Assess pupils' attainment of initial objectives and set next set of instructional objectives.

Objectives not attained → Objectives attained

7. Reassess the pupil's characteristics → Carry out next sequence in program

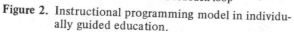

Feedback loop

Figure 2. Instructional programming model in individually guided education.

mathematics instruction for grades K-6. Pilot studies show that children enjoy the activity approach and learn well, and that teachers do not require lengthy inservice education to use the program. Geometry is integrated with the study of arithmetic by taking a measurement approach, where children themselves generate the numbers they work with. Because they are constantly generating numerical data, children also study elementary probability and statistics as they organize and analyze these data.

Individually Guided Motivation is a program designed to increase children's interest in learning, and their self-direction. Multimedia inservice materials describe and illustrate how principles of goal-setting, modeling, feedback, reinforcement, and reasoning may be incorporated into the instructional program. There are four motivational-instructional procedures described in sound motion pictures and associated print materials: Setting Goals with Individual Children, Promoting Independent Reading, Tutoring of Younger Students by Older Students, and Small Group Conferences to Encourage Self-directed Behavior.

In addition to these R&D Center programs, some materials developed at other educational r&d centers and laboratories, as well as certain commercial materials, can be adapted for use in the IGE system. Some schools are successfully using both IGE and Individually Prescribed Instruction (IPI), for example. IPI is an instructional system which allows an individual student to move through a curriculum at his own rate. Available from Research for Better Schools, Inc., a Federally funded, nonprofit educational laboratory in Philadelphia, IPI differs from IGE in several ways. First, IPI can be used in a variety of organizational settings, including the self-contained classroom. Also, as its name implies, IPI is generally more prescriptive than IGE. Each child's progress is monitored daily, and individual lesson plans prescribe instruction. In addition, the student tends to work independently on his own prescription, whereas in IGE the emphasis is on small-group instruction with regrouping every 1-3 weeks. However, both IGE and IPI are built on a cycle of finding out where each child is, what he needs to learn next, selecting the way for him to obtain these objectives, and making certain he has met them. Because they include instructional objectives, corresponding diagnostic tests, and instructional materials and proçedures, IPI programs in math, reading, spelling, science, and social education are compatible with the IGE instructional programming model. Therefore, some IGE schools have adopted IPI materials to meet the need for individualized curriculum materials. Some IPI schools, on the other hand, have implemented the IGE system because the multiunit organization provides for increased teacher participation in decision-making and facilitates small-group instruction.

Home-School Communication

The fifth component of the IGE system is a program of home-school-community relations, that reinforces the school's efforts by generating the interest and encouragement of parents and other adults whose attitudes influ-

ence pupil motivation and learning. Research and development work in this area was initiated by the Center during 1972-1973, and the first materials were field-tested during the 1974-1975 school year.

Facilitative Environments

Facilitative environments in school buildings, school systems, state education agencies, and teacher education institutions are required in order to implement Individually Guided Education in multiunit schools, and to maintain and strengthen them so that each school becomes increasingly self-renewing. A network comprised of the state education agency, local school districts, and teacher education institutions, can cooperatively provide the necessary facilitative environments. (A major project to develop IGE instructional materials for use in the preservice and inservice education of teachers is currently being financed by the Sears Roebuck Foundation.) Other groups, such as teacher associations and parent organizations, also are expected to share in policy development and implementation in the IGE system. The exact role of each agency must necessarily be worked out within each state, and will vary from one state to another.

A national association of persons interested in IGE has been organized by educators from states which have made a major commitment towards establishing Individually Guided Education and multiunit schools. Thirty-one states (and Canada) were represented at the second annual meeting of the association in November 1974. The Association for Individually Guided Education provides a means of facilitating communication and cooperation between state education agencies, local school districts, and teacher education institutions involved in the IGE movement.

Research and Development

The seventh component of the IGE system is continuing research and development, to generate knowledge and produce validated instructional materials and procedures. IGE is a dynamic system, designed to change and improve through continuous research and development. The Wisconsin R&D Center is engaged in several research and development activities to further refine and extend IGE concepts. Included are studies to facilitate application of the instructional programming model; research on modes and styles of learning; development of computer applications, to assist in gathering and assessing the data needed to guide the instructional programming of pupils; cost/effectiveness of multiunit schools; models for extending the multiunit organization to the middle and senior high school levels; and refinement of organizational roles and relationships in multiunit schools.

REFERENCES

Bechtol, William M. *Individualizing Instruction and Keeping Your Sanity.* Chicago, Illinois: Follett Publishing Company, 1973.

Dickson, George, and Saxe, Richard W. et al. *Partners for Educational Reform and Renewal.* Berkeley, California: McCutchan

Publishing Corporation, 1973.

Education U.S.A. Special Report. *Individually Guided Education and the Multiunit School.* Arlington, Virginia: National School Public Relations Association, 1972.

_____. *Individualization in Schools: The Challenge and the Options.* Arlington, Virginia: National School Public Relations Association, 1971.

IGE Newsletter. Madison, Wisconsin: Wisconsin Research and Development Center for Cognitive Learning, 1973.

Hull, Ronald E. Selecting an Approach to Individualized Instruction. *Phi Delta Kappan,* November 1973, pp. 169-173.

Klausmeier, H. J. The Multiunit Elementary School and Individually Guided Education. *Phi Delta Kappan,* November 1971, 181-184.

_____, and Pellegrin, R. J. The Multiunit School: A Differentiated Staffing Approach. In D. S. Bushnell and D. Rapaport, eds., *Planned Change in Education.* New York: Harcourt, 1971, pp. 107-126.

_____, Quilling, M. R., and Sorenson, J. S. *The Development and Evaluation of the Multiunit Elementary School, 1966-1970.* Madison, Wisconsin: Wisconsin Research and Development Center for Cognitive Learning, Technical Report #158, 1971.

_____ et al. *Individually Guided Motivation and the Multiunit Elementary School: Guidelines for Implementation.* Madison, Wisconsin: Wisconsin Research and Development Center for Cognitive Learning, 1971.

_____, Sorenson, J. S., and Quilling, M. R. Instructional Programming for the Individual Pupil in the Multiunit Elementary School. *The Elementary School Journal,* 1971, *72*(2), 88-101.

_____. *Individually Guided Education: An Alternative System of Elementary Schooling.* New Haven, Connecticut: Center for the Study of Education, Yale University, 1972. (Harlan E. Anderson Lecture.)

Morton, Richard, and Morton, Jane. *Innovation Without Renovation in the Elementary School.* New York: Citation Press, 1975.

Schmuck, Richard A. et al. *Consultation for Innovative Schools.* Eugene, Oregon: Center for Educational Policy and Management, University of Oregon, 1975.

The Schools and Individualized Instruction: Six Perspectives. Philadelphia: Research for Better Schools, 1973.

Major Interest Groups

Wisconsin Research and Development Center for Cognitive Learning
University of Wisconsin-Madison
1025 West Johnson Street
Madison, Wisconsin 53706

Institute for Development of Educational Activities
5335 Far Hills Avenue
Suite 300
Dayton, Ohio 45429

Chairperson Leslie Bernal
Association for Individually Guided Education
Merrimack Education Center
101 Mill Road
Chelmsford, Massachusetts 01824

University of Wisconsin/Sears Roebuck Foundation Project
1025 West Johnson Street
Madison, Wisconsin 53706

78

PEER INSTRUCTION IN MEDICAL EDUCATION

by Abigail B. Sher, Ph.D.
Associate Professor
Office of Medical Education Research & Development
Michigan State University
East Lansing, Michigan

Abigail B. Sher is currently on leave to the Technion, Haifa, Israel.

The profession of medicine, however similar it is to other professions, differs from them in the breadth of attributes which a physician must possess to be a qualified and respected practicing professional. Likewise, the problems facing medical educators are unique, in that these persons have responsibility for designing educational environments which foster simultaneously each and all of these aspects. Innovations in medical education are being demanded both from within the profession and from the outside. Although peer-instruction learning formats have been tried only a few times in medical schools, this chapter addresses itself to the development of peer-instruction learning formats in medical schools as a maximal learning environment for achieving the complex professionalization of physicians.

What, then, are the particular aspects of the multifaceted professional role of a physician? First, he is a purveyor of medical care; people come to him seeking compassion and a cure for illness. He is viewed as a skilled expert and an authority regarding medical knowledge and technique. Yet medical knowledge, like other fields of science, is comprised of very tentative knowledge, facts, and understandings, which change often and rapidly. The transient nature of this knowledge requires the physician to be a continuing self-learner. Once out of medical school and postgraduate training settings, the physician has the responsibility to create his own settings and stimuli for further learning. In addition, there are many skills of interpersonal interaction required of the practicing physician. He must elicit information from individual patients, as well as advise each patient as to an understandable course of treatment and health maintenance. Beyond this, a physician is required to listen to, learn from, and teach his peers. Interaction skills are also necessary for the leadership and responsibility physicians share with other members of health-care teams. Physicians, like many other professionals, are required to be quick decision-makers, analytic problem-solvers, and efficient and effective delegators of tasks as well.

Because medical students come into undergraduate medical programs having been selected on some characteristics which are incongruent with those seen as desirable upon graduation, the task for the medical educator seems especially difficult. Medical school admissions are by nature competitive; yet, physicians are expected to be cooperative. Biological and physical science requirements are stressed in most admissions procedures, and yet, the tasks of medicine are based in both the biological and the *social* sciences. Even the breadth of the basic science requirement itself seems counterproductive, in that these survey courses are less oriented to an examination of the nature of scientific inquiry than they should be, if one of the desirable traits discussed earlier was an understanding of the changing nature of knowledge. In addition, skills in oral and written communications are rarely required.

WIDENING HORIZONS: A VARIETY OF EDUCATIONAL FORMATS

Changing the examination system to one which is ungraded and/or comprehensive has been a first attempt for many medical schools to contain, if not eliminate, the competitiveness of their students (Johnson and Abrahamson, 1968). However, this solution has proved inadequate for some schools. In the past year, both Harvard and Yale have reverted to an older system of grades after the achievement of their students on The National Board Examination fell below previous standards (Goldhaber, 1973). Sacrificing academic achievement for the more affective goals appears to be an unworkable alternative.

A second approach to enhancing student self-responsibility has been an introduction of student-run activities, such as student-run health clinics or community-based health visits (Mulvihill, 1968; Record and McKegney, 1969). These projects have the disadvantage of being extracurricular, and are viewed by students as something separate from medical education proper. Whatever solutions can be found for these complex problems, these must be seen by the students as an integral part of the medical curriculum.

Small-group teaching formats represent another approach which has been tried in medical schools. Balancing large group lectures with small-group experiences was introduced to provide settings for discussion, for breaking down reliance on lecturing authorities, and to bring about more communication and cooperation between students. In recent years, attention has been directed toward research on the maximal composition of student groups (Fleisher, 1968; Fleisher and Levin, 1970). Such manipulations increased productivity and learning. However, small groups comprise, in most cases, a minor part of the total time spent in medical school. The few schools (McMaster University, and Michigan State University College of Human Medicine) which have introduced programs using predominantly small-group formats have done so at the cost of tremendous faculty time and resources. The presence of faculty members to ensure exposure to the breadth of knowledge usually covered in the early years is expensive, at a time when the already high cost of large-group medical education is being challenged.

The alternative often suggested is a self-instructional program (Griesen and Kahn, 1971; Kahn, Conklin, and Glover, 1973). The efficiency, as well as the low cost, of such a program, after the initial investment, are hailed as the most salable aspects of these programs. While self-instructional programs can provide students with self-paced and individually-branched learning experiences, they do not provide opportunities to practice those interpersonal interaction skills—cooperation, communication, and leadership—which are vital for the practicing physician.

There are only two series of research papers on peer instruction (Coppola and Gonnella, 1968, 1972; King and Zimmerman, 1963a, 1963b; Zimmerman and King, 1963) reported in the medical education literature. In both, achievement in these groups was as high as achievement in faculty-led groups. The advantages discussed by the authors included an increased student-responsibility for his own education and an increased excitement about learning in general.

The combination of a small-group format with one of peer instruction seems to offer a unique solution to some of the issues raised earlier in connection with the broad task facing the medical educator. It has the advantages of small-group formats, in that students are required to cooperate and communicate with each other. Moreover, in this format students are required to take on some of the roles traditionally delegated to teachers: they must plan educational experiences, evaluate their progress and their programs, and simultaneously learn from and teach their peers. Even more important, they must take responsibility for their own education as well as that of others.

PEER INSTRUCTION: AN EXPERIMENT

During the past year, this author had the opportunity to follow two groups of first-year medical students—one which included four faculty members and one without faculty (Sher and Adams, 1973). The circumstances leading to the participation of a small group in a peer-instructed mode during this term were fortuitous and unplanned. Therefore, the observations that followed were not of an experimental nature, but rather the result of an exploration of a natural state.

Both groups were participating in a six-hour-per-week course entitled Focal Problems, in which paper medical cases were intended to serve as vehicles for teaching the basic science mechanisms underlying the solution of clinical problems. The peer-instructed group was videotaped from their first session until the middle of the term. During the remainder of the term, both groups were alternately video- and audiotaped.

The tapes of both groups, along with achievement data, were analyzed, concentrating on three areas: the content covered, the interactions between members of each group, and the achievement at the end of the term. The analyses showed that during one term, both groups covered essentially the same basic science and medically-oriented content material; both groups made use of the resource lists for the medical problems; and both groups performed equally well on the evaluations provided by the school as indications of satisfactory attainment of the course objectives.

Several students in the peer-instructed group assumed some of the roles of the faculty in the other group. Specifically, some students in the peer-instruction group presented themselves as "discussion leaders," "managers," and "summarizers," in approximately the same frequency as the faculty in the other group. Whereas students in the peer-instructed group had to take responsibility for planning and evaluating their own progress, students in the faculty-led group were freed of this responsibility, and delegated such issues solely to the faculty. Freedom from such responsibility allowed more students in the faculty-led group to take on the role of "questioners" and/or passive recipients of information presented by the faculty.

In addition, the learning process in the peer-instructed group appeared to be more efficient than that in the faculty-led group. Although students in the peer-instructed group appeared to waste much time discussing organizational matters, they did assess their strengths and weaknesses at the beginning of each problem, and focus their discussions on those topics for which they felt the greatest need of further explication. This represented a sorting process which is seldom achieved in a group led by faculty. It is not surprising that a faculty member highly trained in a given discipline should want to share his particular area of expertise. The question of whether this knowledge is that which students need during the class period in which that faculty member is scheduled to attend is seldom left to the students' discretion.

The availability of video and audio tapes of the sessions of the peer-instructed group allowed for a detailed documentation of its process and problems. Organizational problems occupied many of the early sessions. Despite these, the group was able to handle the subject matter using a variety of educational formats, experiences, and resource persons. At the beginning, a conflict never to be resolved was acknowledged, and this was a nagging sense that somehow whatever goals the group set for itself were in conflict with the expectations of the school, or with, as one student said, "what we're supposed to be learning."

It took the group only a few sessions to resolve its concerns about the channels of resources open to it, the manner in which conflicts in content were to be deliberated, the need for focusing discussions, and the issues of leadership and responsibility within the group. However, concerns about group dynamics and interaction could not be dealt with without a framework of goals within which the group was functioning. Until the last day, questions were being raised about the adequacy and sequencing of the course objectives, and paper cases as a framework for learning. In a kind of desperation, the group hoped that the midterm examination would sort things out. It did not, and the question remained as to how were they to integrate basic science mechanisms and their relationship to clinical problem-solving. The presence of a clinical preceptor in the faculty-led group achieved this for his group.

By most standards, the peer-instructed group performed more than adequately, and yet it is not surprising that members of this group found themselves frustrated by a lack of time, and by the immensity of the task facing them.

DISCUSSION: ISSUES FOR THE FUTURE

To medical educators, it is clear that some of the unintended learning which took place in the peer-instructed group was exciting, and should be fostered. Specifically, when one of the obstacles to quality medical care is a lack of communication and exchange of information between medical personnel at all levels, the students in the peer-instruction format participated in an experience in which each of them was at the same time a planner, a teacher, an evaluator, a student, and, perhaps most important, an equal, with responsibility for his own education as well as that of others. Moreover, it is of no small importance to claim that peer-instruction appears to be less costly of faculty time than faculty-led instruction. This is not to say that a peer-instruction format frees the faculty of its instructional responsibilities. The problems encountered by the peer-instructed group point to a different and new role for the medical school faculty. Like the self-instructional formats discussed earlier, peer-instruction formats require that the faculty spend time on the specification of relevant, comprehensive, and comprehensible goals for the graduating student. However, unlike the objectives in self-instructional programs, some of these are not specifiable in behavioral terms (Steinberg, 1972).

It is for the medical educator to find creative solutions. He must build programs which include in their formats those elements of the unmeasurable value goals which he expects students to learn. Peer instruction in small-group formats is one alternative. Those goals which are specifiable in behavioral terms—intellectual abilities and skills—present a different challenge. Their integration into these new teaching formats presents problems of sequencing, among others. An examination of theories of learning, as well as demonstrated programs of skill training, can suggest productive directions for viable changes in the process of medical education.

REFERENCES

Coppola, E. D., and Gonnella, J. S. A Non-Directive Approach to Clinical Instruction in Medical School. *Journal of the American Medical Association*, August 12, 1968, *205*, 75-79.

———. Learning in Medical Schools: An Approach to Student Responsibility. *Surgery*, 1972, *71*, 645-649.

Fleisher, D. S. Composition of Small Learning Groups in Medical Education. *Journal of Medical Education*, 1968, *43*, 349-355.

———, and Levin, J. L. A Second Study in Composition of Small Learning Groups in Medical Education. *Journal of Medical Education*, 1970, *45*, 929-938.

Goldhaber, S. Z. Medical Education: Harvard Reverts to Tradition. *Science*, 1973, *181*, 1027-1032.

Griesen, J. V. Independent Study versus Group Instruction in Medical Education: A Study of Non-Cognitive Factors Relating to Curricular Preferences and Academic Achievement. Unpublished doctoral dissertation, Ohio State University, Columbus, Ohio, 1971.

Johnson, P. C., and Abrahamson, S. The Effects of Grades and Examinations on Self-Directed Learning. *Journal of Medical Education*, 1968, *43*, 360-366.

Kahn, R. J., Conklin, J. L., and Glover, R. A. A Self-Instructional Program in Microscopic Anatomy. *Journal of Medical Education*, 1973, *48*, 859-863.

King, T. C., and Zimmerman, J. M. Application of Group Dynamics to Medical Education: The Student-Centered Group. *Journal of Medical Education,* 1963, *38,* 871-878. (a)
———. Motivation and Learning in Medical School: The Ground Rules. *Journal of Medical Education,* 1963, *38,* 865-870. (b)
Mulvihill, J. J. A Student-Operated Series of Films. *Journal of Medical Education,* 1968, *43,* 1202-1205.
Record, N. B., and McKegney, F. P. The Community Health Visitor Program: A Student-Organized Experiment. *Journal of Medical Education,* 1969, *44,* 193-201.
Sher, A. B., and Adams, K. W. Peer Instruction: A Case Study. Office Paper No. 1973-4, Office of Medical Education Research and Development, Michigan State University, East Lansing, Michigan, 1973.
Steinberg, I. S. Behavioral Definition of Educational Objectives: A Critique. In Thomas, L. G., ed. *NSSE 71st Yearbook: Philosophical Redirection of Educational Research.* Chicago: University of Chicago Press, 1972.
Zimmerman, J. M., and King, T. C. Motivation and Learning in Medical School. III Evaluation of Student-Centered Groups. *Surgery,* 1963, *54,* 152-157.

ADDITIONAL RESOURCES

E. D. Coppola, M.D., Chairman
Department of Surgery
College of Human Medicine
Michigan State University
East Lansing, Michigan

D. S. Fleisher, M.D.
Professor of Pediatrics
Pacific Medical College
San Francisco, California

J. S. Gonnella, M.D.
Associate Dean for Curriculum
Jefferson Medical College
Philadelphia, Pennsylvania

B. L. Hulbert, Ph.D.
Professor of Medical Education
Pacific Medical College
San Francisco, California

T. C. King, M.D.
Professor of Surgery and Provost
University of Utah
Salt Lake City, Utah

V. Neufeld, M.D.
Coordinator for Educational Development Programs
McMaster University School of Medicine
Hamilton, Ontario, Canada

A. B. Sher, Ph.D.
Professor of Medical Education
Office of Medical Education Research and Development
Michigan State University
East Lansing, Michigan

J. M. Zimmerman, M.D.
Professor of Surgery
Johns Hopkins School of Medicine
Baltimore, Maryland

79

TEXTBOOK SELECTION

by David M. Whorton
Assistant Professor of Educational Administration
Flagstaff, Arizona

Textbook selection is the process of determining which texts will be used in the schools. This process includes state-wide textbook adoption procedures as well as procedures used by school districts and individual teachers. Since textbooks are still the dominant source of instructional material in schools, the selection process is extremely important, and has a tremendous effect on the instructional program.

SCOPE

This article will examine some of the procedures and problems in selecting textbooks for use in the schools. This complex and often controversial process is sometimes neglected or done in a casual manner by educators or committees of laymen. A systematic approach, which allows the expression of conflicting points of view, is needed to best serve the need for instructional materials in the schools.

The textbook, in spite of many objections and attempts at change, is still the primary instructional device in today's schools. Most schools have a procedure for selecting textbooks, but there is a need to examine these procedures to be sure that the best material is selected.

Figures from the American Textbook Publishers Institute, and *School Management*'s Cost of Education Index, show a textbook cost-per-student increase from $2.90 in 1957-1959 to $4.30 in 1965-1966 to $9.88 in 1972-1973 (School Management, 1973). Although this was below the rate of increase for education spending in general, it does illustrate the great expense involved in textbook purchases. The increased cost of textbooks has created problems for many school districts. Therefore, not only must the process of textbook selection include assurances that the best material to meet the needs of children are being purchased, but also that such purchases are accomplished at the lowest practical cost.

REVIEW OF RECENT DEVELOPMENTS

The problem of selecting textbooks has been a persistent one for many years. In recent years the problem has been made more complex by development of a publishing industry capable of producing a great range of hardcover and paperback textbooks.

Elwood Cubberley (1927) wrote, "Partly because of the peculiar teaching needs we have had to meet, partly because of the absence here of any European type of standardization and uniformity of instruction and instructional tools, and partly because of the resulting open competition in the preparation and production of textbooks, the business of preparing textbooks for use in the schools has become a great American business of a type unknown in any other land (p. 4)."

With such a powerful industry developed to produce textbooks, there is the feeling expressed by some that it may well control the curriculum of schools by the materials it supplies. Redding (1963), while associated with the American Textbook Publishers Institute, attempted to counter that feeling when he wrote, "Where the schools go, there must go the publishers (p. 16)." The implication is that publishers do not dictate curriculum, they only supply the demand established by the schools through the selection procedures. Redding continues, "From the publisher's viewpoint, it is imperative that the schools study their books needs carefully and announce their requirements with certainty. . . . For the schools so to do, it is essential that educators acquire at least a working knowledge of publishing procedures and potentials (p. 30)."

The possibility exists that the textbook industry dominates curriculum, if indeed it does, only because educators have allowed it to do so. Rice (1960) supports this point by saying, "Primarily by default education has entrusted to the textbook publisher the responsibility for the development and improvement of vast areas of our curriculum content (p. 55)."

Regardless of whether publishers have or have not dictated curriculum, the need exists for a closer relationship between the person selecting textbooks and the publisher. Shugrue (1972) reports that "During 1972-1973 the Association of Departments of English will convene chairmen of college English departments, specialists in other fields, and representatives of the publishing industry for four regional seminars on the development of interdisciplinary studies (p. 189)." Cooperation of this nature is an important aspect of textbook selection, and should be encouraged.

Cooperation in selection of textbooks also extends to educators themselves. A good example of such cooperation is the International Textbook Institute located in Braunschweig, Federal Republic of Germany. Pillsbury (1966) described the activities of the Institute:

The International Textbook sponsors and undertakes qualitative analysis of textbooks through international collaborations by scholars and educators for the purpose of recommending improvements in scholarship, factual reliability, points of view relative to peaceful co-existence and international understanding, and other details of textbooks. (p. 49)

As important as cooperation between educators and publishers is, it is perhaps even more important that selection be done by the individual teacher. Brown (1969) remarks, "Increasingly the choice of a textbook is left to the classroom teacher rather than to the school board, superindent, or supervisors (p. 18)."

A factor which limits a teacher's opportunity to select from the wide range of textbooks available is the procedure of state textbook adoption. Teachers, limited by state adoption procedures to five or so editors of a text, have little opportunity to select with a great deal of detail any text (Brown, 1972). Reuter (1962) goes so far as to say that, "where the state type of selection exists, that it be repealed and that each local district select its textbooks (p. 18)." The topic of state adoption will

be examined in greater detail later in this article.

A statement from *School Management* (1964) summarizes the proceeding discussion well. "He who controls textbook selection in his district, really controls the curriculum (p. 74)." Most articles reviewed agreed with Satlow (1966), that "Principles of democratic control would require that the *teachers* who use the textbook in the classroom should share in the selection of these books (p. 188)."

SPECIFIC PROGRAMS

Selection procedures have been explored by many writers. Maxwell (1921) and Clement (1942) offer rather complete systems for selecting textbooks. Much of what they suggest is quite appropriate for current textbook selection programs.

The Department of Public Instruction for the State of Iowa (1969) provides some important guidelines for textbook selection, prefaced with the caution that "curriculum development determines textbook selection; textbooks should not determine the curriculum (p. 2)." The Department indicates that the quality of textbook selection can be improved when administrators involve the whole staff; the staff makes a continuing study of textbooks; and selection is based on the school system's course of study, local children's needs and interests, materials currently in use, teachers' academic backgrounds, and community attitudes.

Sternig (1966) offers the following procedure for textbook selection:

1. State the purpose of the instructional program that needs the material you select. Do these purposes meet the needs of the community?

2. Involve the text user in the selection process.

3. Involve the producers of the texts.

4. Determine if the aims of the publisher are in harmony with your aims.

5. Do they provide a variety of resources for all levels of learning?

6. Can you interpret the materials to the community?

7. Is there an evaluation of texts currently in use?

These general procedures can be supplemented by more specific selection guides in subject areas. Alexander (1960), Brodbelt (1972), Brown (1965), Caliguri (1971), Chastain (1971), National Council of Teachers of Mathematics (1965), Tortora (1968), and Townsend-Zeller (1969) provide examples of guides and techniques for textbook selection in specific subject areas.

Specialized guides are also available for selection and analysis of textbooks on the basis of treatment of minorities. The reference and other source listings at the end of this article contain articles in which these guides are presented.

CURRENT CONTROVERSIES

There are several major controversies dealing with textbook selection. Perhaps the most important controversy is whether there should be textbooks in the schools at all. The most highly developed argument against the use of textbooks is presented by Beechhold (1971). After citing several modern writers to support his position, Beechhold concludes his chapter entitled "Teaching Without Textbooks" with "What the student will discover is that most textbooks are not worth exploring (p. 18)."

Beechhold, as indicated, is not alone in his contention that textbooks are not useful in the classroom. Glasser (1969) says, "Teachers are also handicapped by the almost universal use of textbooks and their belief that they should rely heavily upon them. A better procedure would be to eliminate texts altogether and have each school district select books from the large variety of relevant, low-priced paperbacks now widely available (pp. 49-50)."

Phillips (1965) offers a different approach. "Do not give a textbook to each student. A supply of texts slightly larger than class size could be placed in each classroom (e.g., 30 students, 40 books). A variety of books, instead of one text, could be purchased, making use of the best three or four in each field (p. 529)."

Another major controversy involved in selecting textbooks is censorship. Nelson and Roberts (1963), probably the best source regarding controversies over textbook censorship, indicate that "While today's textbook battles are among the most widespread and serious ever to hit this country, they are not without deep roots in history (p. 22)."

As an example of a long-standing textbook dispute over censorship, the inclusion of evolutionary theory can be cited. Lesinbee (1965) reports that "An anti-evolution sentiment was initiated during the 1960-61 academic year by the so-called Blue Version of the Biological Sciences Curriculum Study (BSCS) (p. 35)" in Arizona. In the summer of 1973 censorship was still a topic for debate in Arizona, although not specifically aimed at "evolution." The State Board of Education considered adopting a policy on textbook selection which stated, in part, that textbook content "shall not include selections or works which contribute to civil disorder, social strife or flagrant disregard of the law."

It should be recognized that state boards of education, local boards, and perhaps others have a responsibility to censor what books do go into the classroom. Raywid (1963) points out that "It is clearly the right of citizens to protest where schools are failing to accomplish the right things, or where they are succeeding in accomplishing the wrong things . . . but while some criticism has been warranted and helpful, not all has been (p. 1)." Raywid then proceeds to analyze these critics, "the ax-grinders." Right-wing groups have been extremely active in their opposition to points in textbooks, generally in the social studies area. Campbell, Cunningham, McPhee, and Nystrand (1970) point out the extent to which such groups will go to censor textbooks when it was suggested by a member of the Indiana State Textbook Commission that Robin Hood be banned, on the premise that his philosophy of taking from the rich and giving to the poor was the pure Communist line.

Textbook selection procedures should be structured so that those persons objecting to certain material have a legitimate procedure for voicing their concerns. Their concerns should be listened to and taken into consideration by those selecting texts. In this procedure the following caution of Nelson and Roberts (1963) should be heeded.

> Whatever their differences in dress or the nature of their worries, would be textbook censors share the same convictions: that their views are the correct ones, that the child will be subverted if he hears an opposing philosophy. Always, the censors ignore the fact that no textbook can ever be perfect, and that textbooks will always reflect the changing knowledge and the changing interpretations of successive generations. Society, as a result, must decide whether it wants its textbooks to be shaped by pressure groups or by scholars seeking to supply the most accurate information available. Too often, society has yielded to the pressure groups (p. 24)

In recent years, controversies surrounding treatment of minority groups in textbooks have had implications for selection procedures. For example, Carpenter and Rank (1968) conclude that books in relation to Negro History often mention race in a highly selective way, and that crude stereotyping often occurs. The National Education Association (1967) specifies the following criteria for the selection of textbooks in order to reduce problems related to minorities and their stereotyping.

> Does the author develop the role of minority groups in a scholarly, factual way?

> Does the text meet the basic philosophy of our democratic society—particularly as it related to civil rights?

> Does the text demonstrate consideration for human relationships and respect the dignity of all?

> Does the text depict and illustrate adequately the multi-ethnic character of the United States?

> Are stereotypes—racial, ethnic, and religious—avoided?

> Is the approach to the subject matter realistic? Are materials about minorities chosen for their relevance? Are they woven into the fabric of the book, or included as inserted afterthoughts?

> Is the text nonsectarian?

> Does the text include the unique contributions of various minority groups, or does it just present general, categorical descriptions of these groups?

State adoption procedures, as mentioned previously, are a point of controversy. *School Management* (1966) concluded, after a survey of textbook purchasing practices of 1,500 districts, that "State adoption practices seriously hamper the efforts of local districts to provide the most modern textbooks for their students. The survey showed cyclical adoptions to be the single most important reason that textbooks are not adopted more often—and more quickly (p. 138)."

In 1971, 22 states had state textbook adoption committees for elementary textbooks, and 19 states had committees for secondary textbooks. Of those states that have a textbook adoption committee, 21 use a multiple adoption system (Whorton and Miles (1971). Burnett (1950) indicated that the schools are joining in the battle against state control of textbooks. With slightly less than half of the states still controlling adoption procedures, there is still the need for change before local districts have freedom of choice when selecting textbooks.

State adoption procedures allow single states to control textbook content for other states, by virtue of power through total volume. Black (1967) points out, in a chapter entitled "Texas: King Censor," how Texas has, through statewide adoption, caused publishers to create a series of texts for this state only. Smaller states are certainly not able to follow this example. Winn (1967) and Taylor (1969) offer good descriptions of how textbooks are selected in California and Virginia respectively. The method used in Virginia is typical of states using a state textbook adoption committee.

In the selection of textbooks, cost is certainly an important factor. There is a controversy as to whether textbooks should be paid for by pupils or whether the district and/or state should provide free textbooks. Public school students purchase their own textbooks at the elementary level in two states, and at the secondary level in six states (Whorton and Miles, 1971).

An interesting controversy arose in Arizona, when the Arizona Education Association Delegate Assembly defeated a resolution to support legislation favoring free textbooks for secondary school children, while the Arizona State School Board Association *adopted* a resolution favoring such legislation. Part of the A.E.A. argument leading to defeat of the resolution was that purchasing their own books will teach students responsibility (Miles and Whorton, 1971).

SUMMARY AND CONCLUSION

The selection of textbooks will always be a controversial issue. Systematic selection procedures, which include recourse for those who wish to appeal decisions regarding textbooks, should be implemented in each state and school district.

The skyrocketing cost of textbooks, and the controversies they evoke, should cause educators to take a second look at the use of textbooks in today's schools. In some areas it may be, as some critics suggest, that textbooks are no longer needed.

Finally, the extent to which teachers allow the textbook to dictate curricula should be examined by those making selections. If teachers do indeed still teach from the textbook, then textbook selection procedures are of great importance to the schools.

REFERENCES

Alexander, Albert. The Grey Flannel Cover on the American History Textbooks. *Social Education,* 1960, *24,* 21-23.

Beechhold, Henry. *The Creative Classroom.* New York: Charles Scribner's Sons, 1971.

Black, Hillel. *The American Schoolbook.* New York: William Morrow, 1967.

Brodbelt, Samuel. Using Mathematical Criteria for Selecting Social Studies Textbooks. *Clearing House,* 1972, *46,* 487-492.

Brown, R. A., and Brown, Marion. Selecting Social Studies Textbooks: The Challenge of Choice. *Social Education,* 1969, *33,* 314ff.

Brown, R. G. The Great Textbook Rip-Off. *Clearing House,* 1972, *47,* 111-114.

Brown, W. R. Science Textbook Selection and the Dale-Chall Formula. *School Science and Math,* 1965, *65,* 164-167.

Burnett, L. W. Schools are Gaining in the Battle Against State Control of Textbooks. *Nation's Schools,* 1950, *45,* No. 5, 49-50.

Caliguiri, J. P. Teacher Bias in the Selection of Social Studies Textbooks. *Journal of Negro Education,* 1971, *40,* 322.

Campbell, R. F., Cunningham, L. L., McPhee, R. F., and Nystrand, R. O. *The Organization and Control of American Schools,* 2nd ed. Columbus, Ohio: Merrill Publishing Co., 1970.

Carpenter, L. P., and Rank, Dinah. *The Treatment of Minorities: A Survey of Textbooks Used in Missouri High Schools.* Jefferson City, Missouri: Missouri Commission on Human Rights, 1968.

Chastain, Kenneth. Selecting a Basic Text: A Subjective Evaluation. *Hispania,* 1971, *54,* 483.

Clement, J. A. *Manual for Analyzing and Selecting Textbooks.* Champaign, Ill.: Garrard Press, 1942.

_____. *Score Sheet for Analysis and Appraisal of Textbooks.* Champaign, Ill.: Garrard Press, 1942.

Cubberley, E. P. *The School Textbook Problem.* Boston: Houghton-Mifflin, 1927.

Department of Public Instruction, Iowa. *Guidelines for the Evaluation and Selection of Textbooks and Other Instructional Materials.* Des Moines: State of Iowa, Dept. of Public Instruction, 1969 (ERIC ED 070 088).

Glasser, William. *Schools Without Failure.* New York: Harper and Row, 1969.

Lisonbee, Lorenzo. Thwarting the Anti-Evolution Movement in Arizona. *Science Teacher,* 1965, *32,* No. 2, 35-37.

Maxwell, C. R. *The Selection of Textbooks.* Boston: Houghton-Mifflin, 1921.

Miles, F. M., and Whorton, D. M. The Textbook Question. *Arizona Administrator,* 1971, *9,* 8.

National Council of Teachers of Mathematics. Aids for Evaluation of Mathematics Textbooks. *Arithmetic Teacher,* 1965, *12,* 388-394.

National Education Association. The Treatment of Minorities in Textbooks. *Fourth National NEA/PR&R Conference on Civil and Human Rights in Education.* Washington: National Education Association, 1967 (ERIC ED 064 183).

Nelson, Jack, and Roberts, Gene, Jr. *The Censors and the Schools.* Boston: Little, Brown, 1963.

Phillips, H. F. A Different Approach to Textbooks. *Clearing House,* 1965, *39,* 529.

Pillsbury, Kent. International Cooperation in Textbook Evaluation: The Braunschweig Institute. *Comparative Education Review,* 1966, *10,* 48-52.

Raywid, M. A. *The Ax-Grinders.* New York: Macmillan, 1963.

Redding, M. F. *Revolution in the Textbook Publishing Industry.* Washington: National Education Association, Occasional Paper No. 9, 1963.

Reuter, G. S., Jr. *Reforms Needed in the Selection of Textbooks.* Chicago: American Federation of Teachers, 1962.

Rice, A. H. A New Outlook for Textbooks. *Nation's Schools,* 1960, *65,* No. 3, 55-56.

Satlow, I. D. Teachers Share Textbook Selection. *Journal of Business Education,* 1966, *41,* 188-190.

School Management. Textbook Selection: Whose Job? 1964, *8,* No. 4, 74-78ff.

_____. Is your District Using the Right Text Books? 1964, *8,* No. 10, 79-86.

_____. A Survey of Textbook Purchasing Practices. 1966, *10,* No. 3, 138ff.

_____. Instructional Materials and Equipment. 1973, *17,* No. 8, p. 12.

Shugrue, M. F. Restoring a Tarnished Partnership. *College Composition and Communication,* 1972, *23,* 189-191.

Sternig, John. How to Select New Textbooks. *Nation's Schools,* 1966, *77,* No. 3, 114ff.

Taylor, M. G. Travelogue of a Textbook. *Virginia Journal of Education,* 1969, *62,* No. 8, 22ff.

Tortora, Phyllis. Selection and Use of Text and Reference Books. *Forecast for Home Economics,* 1968, *14,* No. 2, 42-43.

Townsend-Zellner, Norman, and Carr, E. R. *A New Look at the High School Economics Texts.* Fullerton: California State College, Center for Economic Education, 1969 (ERIC ED 065 366).

Whorton, D. M., and Miles, F. M. *Free Public Education?* Unpublished paper, Northern Arizona University, 1971.

Winn, I. J. Rafferty and the Sterile Textbook Adoption Struggle. *Phi Delta Kappan,* 1967, *49,* No. 1, 37-41.

ADDITIONAL RESOURCES

Carpenter, Charles. *History of American Schoolbooks.* Philadelphia: Univ. of Pennsylvania Press, 1963.

Cronback, R. J. *Text Materials in Modern Education.* Urbana: Univ. of Illinois Press, 1955.

Department of Public Instruction, Pennsylvania. *The Treatment of Minorities: Guidelines for Textbook Selection.* Harrisburg: Pennsylvania State Dept. of Public Instruction, 1967 (ERIC ED 024 727).

Finkelstein, Barbara, Golden, Loretta, and Grambs, J. D. A Bibliography of Research and Commentary on Textbooks and Related Works. *Social Education,* 1969, 33, No. 3, 331-336.

Fiske, Marjorie. *Book Selection and Censorship.* Berkeley: Univ. of California Press, 1959.

Hilton, Ernest. Textbooks. In R. L. Ebel, ed., *Encyclopedia of Educational Research,* 4th ed. New York: Macmillan, 1969, 1470-1478.

Latimer, B. I. et al. *Starting Out Right: How to Choose Books About Black People for Young Children.* Madison, Wis.: Madison Equal Opportunities Commission, 1972.

McCormick, John, and MacInnes, Mairi. *Versions of Censorship.* Chicago: Aldine Publishing Co., 1962.

Michigan Education Association. *Racial Bias in Instructional Materials: Negotiating for Better Schools Guidelines.* East Lansing: Michigan Education Association, 1970 (ERIC ED 048 285).

Michigan State Department of Education. *A Report on the Treatment of Minorities in American History Textbooks.* Lansing, 1968 (ERIC ED 032 369).

80

NUTRITION AND LEARNING IN PRESCHOOL CHILDREN

by Susan B. Thomas
College of Education
Florida State University
Tallahassee, Florida

In a typical preschool class, some children are alert, curious, and eager to learn, while others appear apathetic and listless. Children may have short or long spans of attention. In part, these variations may be attributable to differences in the children's nutrition.

Adequate nutrition is basic to optimal physical growth and development. Recent research has indicated that nutrition also influences mental development. Much of the research on the effects of malnutrition has been done with animals in experimental laboratory-type situations. Other research studies have involved children from countries in Africa, Asia, and Central and Latin America. Very few malnutrition studies have been done in the United States, although the lack of research in this area does not imply that there is no problem. One impetus for research in this country has been the Head Start program, with its concomitant emphasis on sound nutrition as a basis for efficient and effective learning. Although malnutrition, especially moderate malnutrition, may not affect a child's innate level of intelligence, it may well affect his ability to use his full range of intellectual potential.

MALNUTRITION: WHAT IS IT?

Read (1969) defines malnutrition as a state in which an individual lacks one or more nutrients to such an extent that specific symptoms and conditions appear: anemia, goiter, rickets, vitamin deficiencies, or retardation in physical development. In school, undernourished or hungry children frequently exhibit behavioral alterations, including apathy, lethargy, inability to pay attention, and perhaps overconcern about food to such a degree that responses to classroom stimuli do not occur. A child in such a condition no longer meets the expectations of his family or teachers. He begins to live in a world of his own, and may seek recognition or try to gain attention in ways that disrupt learning experiences. Parents and teachers may react to his social behavior and withdraw some of the stimulation necessary for adequate mental development.

Sulzer suggests that children with poor nutrition also have problems involving concentration, alertness, and learning. Children with low energy levels, Often brought about by poor nutrition, respond to learning situations with apathy or high excitability, neither of which is conducive to learning.

Bakan (1971) suggests that malnutrition interacts with other factors, such as poverty and illness, in the child's environment. These combined factors often perpetuate the cycle of illness, educational failure, and poverty. Compensatory programs such as Head Start and Follow-Through need to consider many interesting factors, rather than nutrition alone. One research finding, which provides evidence of the need for adequate nutrition as well as attention to other environmental factors, is the demonstration of delayed neurointegrative development in children who have grown poorly because of malnutrition and other interacting factors. Inadequacies of intersensory development can contribute to a child's failure to establish an ordinary normal background of experiences in his preschool years. That is, a child must be able to coordinate visual and motor skills, for example, to perform certain tasks. Poor nutrition can interfere with his development when he is too weak or tired to perform these tasks, and thus he might not be able to benefit fully from occurrences in his environment. Early experiences (e.g., Caldwell, 1969; Hunt, 1961) are thought to facilitate intellectual development.

Birch (1968) points out that a child's nutritional inadequacy affects both his neurological maturation and his learning competency. These children suffer from lost learning-time, due to apathy and sluggishness, nutritional deficit during critical learning periods in the preschool years, and adverse motivation and personality changes. In intervening to provide the best learning conditions for a child, educators should recognize the importance of a child's health to his learning efficiency.

Cravioto, DeLicardie, and Birch (1966) suggest that malnutrition can act in two ways: directly, by interference with the central nervous system; and indirectly, through interaction with social and environmental factors, including loss of learning-time due to apathy and sluggishness. Personality and motivational changes may also occur as a result of child-adult interaction. Often an adult will reject an apathetic or sluggish child because of his behavior, thus compounding the biological problem of malnutrition with the social and psychological factors of rejection and lessened social interaction.

Research indicates that severe malnutrition with hospitalization has a long-term, persistent effect on measured intelligence, and on the learning of such basic academic skills as reading and writing (Cravioto and DeLicardie, 1970). Children who suffer from severe malnutrition early in life are handicapped educationally as well as socially. Because of the increased risk of becoming a poor reader, a poor writer, and subsequently a failure in school, the child functions at a sub-optimal level. Children who survive bouts of severe malnutrition are therefore more likely to be victims of their poor socio-economic environment, and less than normally effective in their social adaptations. In addition, children who function marginally grow into adults who function marginally. They marry and raise families in the same tradition, thus perpetuating the cycle of poverty, malnutrition, retarded learning, and intellectual development.

Although severe malnutrition in the United States is rare, moderate malnutrition (cases not severe enough to be hospitalized) is suggested as a contributing factor to the higher morbidity and mortality rates found among low-income groups (Birch, 1968). Although severe malnutrition has been found to be a causative factor in retarded intellectual development, the exact outcomes of moderate malnutrition have yet to be determined. It has been suggested that psychological, social, and cultural factors act synergistically with malnutrition to produce retarded intellectual development as well as learning disabilities. Just what effect each factor has must be determined. However, it is known that malnutrition *does* play a role.

TYPES OF MALNUTRITION

Research on malnutrition will often deal with a specific kind of malnourishment. Two kinds commonly studied include marasmus (or nutritional marasmus), and kwashiorkor. The term "marasmus" applies to young infants who have experienced protein-calorie malnutrition, with general body wasting. It entails the severe inadequacy of all nutrients, usually from the earliest months of life, and produces infants whose physical development is grossly impaired. It is a long-term condition, beginning early, and is thought to be irreversible. The term "kwashiorkor" indicates an affliction among older infants and young children who have been maintained on low-protein, but modest-calorie-intake diets, with accompanying edema and other problems. It is basically the insufficiency of protein, and typically occurs toward the end of the first year or during the second year of life. It often occurs after the birth of a younger sibling, when the sibling is being nursed rather than the older child.

Marasmus appears to be a more severe form of malnutrition, since it occurs in the very young child, whose brain is developing at a rapid rate. Research has indicated that kwashiorkor is not necessarily associated with permanent intellectual damage, at least not if the child was older than 12 months when the condition began (Pollitt, 1970).

CONTRIBUTING FACTORS

How do the outcomes of malnutrition vary as a function of age of onset, severity, duration, and type of malnutrition? This is one of the questions being studied by researchers. Age of onset of malnutrition is an important factor, since by the time a child is one year old the brain is about 70 percent of the size of that of an adult; by the age of four brain growth is almost complete. Results of animal experiments lend support to the hypothesis that the greatest effect of malnutrition on ultimate size and performance of the mature individual is produced during the period of maximum growth. There is a great possibility that children severely malnourished during the first six months of life may retain a permanent mental deficiency. It is therefore important that nutrition programs in compensatory programs include nutrition education for the parents, and perhaps supplemental feeding programs for children too young to be enrolled in the educational component of the program.

Research by Chase and Martin (1970) has indicated that both the time when malnutrition begins and the duration of malnutrition are critical issues. They evaluated the psychomotor development of 19 children some three and one-half years after they had been hospitalized for "generalized malnutrition" during the first year of life. These children were compared with 19 controls who were adequately nourished all their lives. The psychomotor development of children hospitalized before four months of age did not differ significantly from the controls in the study. However, those malnourished children hospitalized after four months of age, who presumably suffered longer from malnutrition, performed at a significantly lower level than either the control children or the malnourished children hospitalized prior to four months of age. These significant performance decrements were found in five areas: gross motor development, fine motor development, adaptive behavior, personal-social development, and, above all, language development.

Naeye (1970) suggests that the age at which malnutrition occurs is important, since the brain is more sensitive to nutritional deficiency at the time of the most rapid cell division. He found that diet therapy started before the age of four months was more effective than treatment begun between four and 12 months. In a review of the literature, Birch and Grotberg (1971) suggest that the effects of inadequate nutrition on growth and development depend to a large extent on the severity, timing (pre- and postnatal), the duration of the nutritional deprivation. Botha-Antoun et al. (1968) suggest that the greatest effects of undernutrition on mental and physical development may be produced at periods of maximal growth, and probably will not be reversed with later, adequate nutrition. They studied children who had been malnourished between three and 18 months, focusing on the later effects of malnutrition on intellectual performance and psychomotor activities. They found that the average IQ was lower for the malnourished children, and that the age of walking and talking were later. In a study of Guatemalan children, Cravioto, DeLicardie, and Birch (1966) found that intellectual development in malnourished young children was related to the age of the child at the time of affliction, and to the duration of the malnutrition. Performance on psychological tests was related to nutritional factors, and not to differences in personal hygiene, housing, cash income, or other social and economic variables.

Klein (1969) suggests that the central nervous system may be particularly susceptible to the effects of malnutrition during the last trimester of pregnancy and the first six months of life. The effects of malnutrition seem to vary inversely with the age of onset and directly with its duration and severity.

To summarize, research studies point up the importance of several factors concerning malnutrition. The earlier the child is malnourished (even beginning during the last trimester of pregnancy), the more severe the effects usually are. Severity of the malnutrition also dictates the child's intellectual development, since early, severe forms of malnutrition generally bring about more retardation, both physical and mental. Duration is an important consideration in the study of malnutrition, since the longer a child is malnourished, especially if the malnourishment begins at an early age, the more

severe, and sometimes irreversible, are the effects. Type of malnutrition is also a consideration, since marasmus, which strikes younger infants, generally causes more damage than kwashiorkor, which strikes older infants.

WHAT ARE THE EFFECTS OF MALNUTRITION?

A study of the effects of malnutrition raises questions like these: Is the retardation permanent or reversible? What areas or abilities are affected? What are the contributions of environmental and socio-cultural factors?

Frisch (1970) suggests that the difference in reversibility of the effects of malnutrition seems to be related to the age at which the child is affected. It appears that the greatest risk of irreversible brain damage occurs in children who suffer deprivation before birth or shortly thereafter. Winick (1969) suggests that a low-protein diet stunts the brain as it stunts the rest of the body, and that damage done to the brain of a human infant may be irreversible if malnutrition occurs before six months of age. Eichenwald and Fry (1969) suggest that inadequate protein nutrition or synthesis, or both, during brain development results in changes in function; and that, if the degree of deprivation were sufficiently severe and prolonged, the change in function might be permanent.

Latham (1969) cites a study in which malnourished children who received nutritionally adequate diets gained an average of 18 points on IQ tests, while the well-nourished children who were used as a control group showed no gain. He suggested that because of dietary deficiencies the malnourished children had not reached their full potential, and that correction of deficiencies resulted in a rise in IQ, whereas the well-nourished control group children showed no changes over the same time period. Lederberg (1968) suggests that stunted physical growth due to malnutrition in childhood is beyond the reach of an adequate diet in later life, and that mounting research evidence indicates that the same may be true for mental development.

Cravioto and Gaona (1967) used Mexican elementary school children from a rural village in an effort to discover the relationships between early malnutrition and auditory-visual integration. The tallest 25 percent and the shortest 25 percent of the children between the ages or 7 and 12 were tested for their ability to integrate auditory and visual stimuli. Short height was considered an indicator of early malnutrition. The 296 children were individually asked to identify visual dot patterns corresponding to rhythmic auditory patterns. Ability improved with age, with rapid improvement occurring between the ages of 9 and 11. At each age level, the average performance of the taller group was better than that of the shorter group. It was suggested that early malnutrition, which produces integration difficulties, may affect the child's ability to read, since reading requires the ability to make these transformations.

Osofsky (1969) reports a study in which malnourished infants were followed up 11 years later. He suggests that malnutrition affects intellectual development, and is apparently irreversible in the age group studied. Eleven years later the children had difficulty in visual-motor ability and pattern perception, and in many ways resembled brain-damaged children.

Rajalakshmi (1968) points out that nutritional remediation alone is not sufficient to overcome the effects of malnutrition and mental retardation in children whose social and cultural environments are totally lacking in emotional and psychological stimulation. Encouraging parent participation through the compensatory programs could help overcome some of the environmental factors which often accompany poor nutrition. For example, the Home Start program, which emphasizes the role of the mother in the education of the child, provides guidance to parents in teaching and intellectually stimulating their children. Adding nutrition education would provide a two-pronged attack on the problem.

Rendon et al. (1969) reports a study with 18 malnourished, hospitalized children and 18 controls, which revealed that the malnourished children evidenced noticeable deficiencies in anthropometric measurements, development, and functioning levels. Deficiencies in all areas of infant mental development, and especially in the development of language and social-personal attitude, persisted even after nutritional recovery was satisfactory. Rendon suggests that the deficiencies of the malnourished group cannot be attributed solely to reduced protein and calorie intake, because of multiple interrelated factors such as lack of environmental stimulation, extreme poverty, poor parent education, and parent intelligence. Sandstead et al. (1971) suggest that other compounding factors include a marginal family income, a lack of parental understanding of nutrition, and a lack of parental supervision, particularly at mealtime. Scrimshaw (1968) suggests that psychological and social deprivation is also common among malnourished children, and can exert a direct influence on intellectual performance. He suggests that malnutrition can interact with heredity, infection, and social and environmental factors to bring about physical and mental impairment.

It thus appears that if malnutrition occurs during early infancy, the damage is probably irreversible. It also appears that virtually all areas of human functioning are affected by malnutrition and the accompanying social and environmental variables.

CONSIDERATIONS IN NUTRITION RESEARCH

Klein and Yarbrough (n.d.) suggest caution in generalizing findings of any particular nutrition study to an extremely different population. Confounding variables in studying the effects of malnutrition include social class and child-rearing practices, hospitalization, and medical factors such as intra-uterine infection and perinatal anoxia.

It thus appears that there are many difficulties in evaluating the effects of nutrition on cognitive development, since mental and social development are multidetermined traits. Malnutrition is one of many adverse environmental effects impinging on the child; others include mother's health and nutritional status, birth injury, pre- and postnatal infections, and complex social and psychological deprivations.

In setting up a study, the researcher must find an adequate control group so he can make meaningful com-

parisons. In selecting a population, the younger the child the better. The effects of malnutrition seem to vary inversely with the age of onset of malnutrition and directly with its duration and severity (Klein, 1969). Children should probably be studied from birth on, since they may suffer from other injuries, especially in an impoverished environment.

Selection of tests should be on theoretical grounds which reflect both the researcher's framework for conceptualizing the effects of malnutrition, and his theoretical point of view on cognitive development.

Very often sensory-motor scales are used to assess mental development in infancy. However, in selecting this type of test, the researcher is making the assumption that the child's level of sensory-motor development is a valid and reliable index of infant intelligence—an assumption which is generally unfounded.

Traditional IQ tests tell little about the relationship between malnutrition and mental development, since most IQ tests are global measures, giving little information about problem-solving, response style, linguistic competence, perception, and memory. Ginsburg (1972) has an excellent discussion of this topic in his book *The Myth of the Deprived Child.*

Studies of malnutrition have typically been conducted in underdeveloped countries. Generally, these countries are culturally and linguistically different from the country in which the test was developed and normed. It thus appears that most existing measures of intellectual development are inappropriate for use in underdeveloped countries, unless they have been constructed for a particular country's population.

Social and cultural factors may confound research on the effects of malnutrition. Socio-economic status differences are important considerations, since it has been shown that lower-class mothers systematically treat children differently than middle-class mothers do. Differences in intellectual development associated with dissimilar styles of child-rearing can be detected early in infancy (Pollitt, 1969).

In designing research in the area of the effects of malnutrition on mental development, one must remember to consider the entire individual, including his complex inner functionings and his societal relationships, in trying to determine the role malnutrition plays in his life. Klein (1969) suggests there are six factors to be considered in designing studies: 1) an adequate control group; 2) supplemental feeding, so that both the experimental and control groups will be adequately nourished at the time of the study; 3) careful institution of the feeding program, so that social variables are not confounded; 4) very young children, preferably newborns, as the population; 5) appropriate tests, theoretically relevant and culturally appropriate; and 6) measurement of family characteristics.

There appear to be two types of study designs in the literature: retrospective and perspective studies. Retrospective studies define children who have been malnourished, as compared to those who were not. They are able to use large numbers of subjects in a relatively short period of time, and contain a peer definition of the nutritional state during the critical period being examined. Controls must also be selected on the basis of nutritional history, and may in themselves have been inadequately nourished. Perspective studies have fewer children, but the children are evaluated nutritionally by the researchers. This evaluation offers better nutritional information and selection of controls at the time the study population is defined.

RECOMMENDATIONS FOR FUTURE RESEARCH

Birch and Grotberg (1971) suggest that an adequate state of nutrition is necessary for good attention and for appropriate and sensitive responsiveness to the environment. It appears from the research that women who were malnourished as children are more likely to have disturbed pregnancies and children of low birth-weight, and increased risk of neuro-integrative abnormality. However, in cases where environmental, cultural, and social factors contribute much to the malnourished state, the emphasis in the programs should be an effort to improve the overall conditions of disadvantaged children.

Foster 1972) suggests that food programs are important aspects of the day-care programs. Concern about inadequate nutrition in the day-care centers came about in part because of research indicating the relationship of intellectual development and infectious diseases to adequate nutrition. Breakfast, lunch, and nutritious snacks will help raise a child's resistance to disease, and may also bring about motivational changes by increasing a child's responsiveness to stimuli. A food service program of a day-care center can also provide a laboratory for learning about food, nutrition, and socialization.

Project Head Start has helped provide information about nutrition, and nutritious food, to thousands of children and their parents across the country. However, North (1968) suggests that these various feeding and education programs now need to be evaluated.

Some of the problems associated with preschool malnutrition include the mother's lack of proper foods for optimal growth and development; the high cost of protein-rich foods necessary for optimal early development; lack of transportation of food; and improper food processing or preservation. Some of the problems can be overcome through educational programs such as those associated with day-care programs. However, broader Federal programs will probably be necessary to overcome the food cost and transportation problems. Future research should also include more longitudinal studies exploring the effects of malnutrition and mental development, taking into consideration the many factors discussed above.

SUMMARY

Research indicates that good nutrition is of major importance to the physical development of the brain, and it enables a child to benefit optimally from the environmental stimulation necessary for cognitive development. Most evidence suggests that malnutrition during the earliest months causes, or contributes to, retarded mental and physical development. If malnutrition occurs after the first year, subsequent adequate nutrition can often bring the child closer to his capabilities. Factors important in the study of malnutrition include age of onset, severity, duration, and type of malnutrition. Also of concern are whether the effects of malnutrition are reversible or permanent, just what areas or abilities are affected, and the contribution of the culture and the environment.

Future research and concern should include more carefully controlled studies attempting to relate malnutrition and mental development. In addition, nutrition education programs in day-care centers should be established to reach disadvantaged populations.

REFERENCES

Bakan, Rita. *Malnutrition and Learning.* Michigan State University: Center for Urban Affairs Report #RR5, 1971. (ED 051 321)

Birch, H. G. Health and the Education of Socially Disadvantaged Children. *Developmental Medicine and Child Neurology,* 1968, *10,* 580-599. Also presented at the Conference on Bio-Social Factors in the Development and Learning of Disadvantaged Children, Syracuse, N.Y., 1967. (ED 013 283)

_____, and Grotberg, E., eds. *Designs and Proposal for Early Childhood Research: A New Look: Malnutrition, Learning and Intelligence.* Office of Economic Opportunity, Office of Planning, Research, and Evaluation, 1971. (ED 053 811)

Botha-Antoun, E., Babayan, S., and Harfouche, J. K. Intellectual Development Related to Nutritional Status. *The Journal of Tropical Pediatrics,* 1968, *14*(3), 113-115.

Caldwell, B. M. The Rationale for Early Intervention. In S. Cohen, ed., *Child Development: A Study of Growth Processes.* Itasca, Ill.: F. E. Peacock Publishers, Inc., 1971, pp. 298-308.

Chase, H. P., and Martin, H. P. Undernutrition and Child Development. *New England Journal of Medicine,* 1970, *282*(17), 933-939.

Cravioto, J., and DeLicardie, E. R. Mental Performance in School Age Children: Findings After Recovery from Early Severe Malnutrition. *American Journal of Diseases of Childhood,* 1970, *120,* 404-410.

_____, DeLicardie, E., and Birch, H. G. Nutrition, Growth and Neurointegrative Development: An Experimental and Ecologic Study. *Pediatrics,* 1966, *38* (Suppl. #2, Pt. II), 319-372.

_____, and Gaona, C. Early Malnutrition and Auditory-Visual Integration in School-Age Children. *Journal of Special Education,* 1967, *2*(1), 75-82.

Eichenwald, H., and Fry, P. C. Nutrition and Learning. *Science,* 1969, *163,* 644-648.

Foster, F. P. Nutrition and Educational Experience: Interrelated Variables in Children's Learning. *Young Children,* 1972, *27*(5), 284-288.

Frisch, R. E. Present Status of the Supposition that Malnutrition Causes Permanent Mental Retardation. *American Journal of Clinical Nutrition,* 1970, *23*(2), 189-195.

Ginsburg, H. *The Myth of the Deprived Child: Poor Children's Intellect and Education.* Englewood Cliffs, N.J.: Prentice-Hall, Inc., 1972.

Hunt, J. McV. *Intelligence and Experience.* New York: Ronald Press, 1961.

Klein, R. E. Some Considerations in the Measurement of the Effects of Food Supplements on Intellectual Development and Social Adequacy. Paper presented to the International Conference on Amino Acid Fortification of Protein Foods, Massachusetts Institute of Technology, September 1969.

_____, and Yarbrough, C. Some Considerations in the Interpretation of Psychological Data as they Relate to the Effects of Malnutrition. Guatemala, C.A.: Institute of Nutrition of

Central American and Panama (INCAP), Division of Human Development, undated.

Latham, M.C. International Nutrition and Later Learning. In *Nutrition and Intellectual Growth in Children.* Washington, D.C.: Association for Childhood Education International, 1969.

Lederberg, J. Evidence Links Poor Diet to Forever Stunted Minds. *Washington Post,* January 27, 1968, A14.

Naeye, R. L. Undernutrition, Growth, and Development. *New England Journal of Medicine,* 1970, *282*(17), 975-976.

North, A. F. *Nutrition of Poor Children.* Project Head Start, Office of Economic Opportunity, Washington, D.C., 1968. (PS 001 802)

Osofsky, H. Antenatal Malnutrition: Its Relationship to Subsequent Infant and Child Development. *American Journal of Obstetrics and Gynecology,* 1969, *105*(7), 1150-1159.

Pollitt, E. Behavioral Correlates of Severe Malnutrition in Man: Methodological Considerations and Selective Review. In W. M. Moore, H. D. Riley, and M. S. Read, eds., *Nutrition, Growth and Development of Native American Children.* Washington, D.C.: U.S. Government Printing Office, 1970.

_____. Ecology, Malnutrition and Mental Development. *Psychosomatic Medicine,* 1969, *31*(3), 193-200.

Rajalakshmi, R. The Psychological Status of Underprivileged Children Reared at Home and in an Orphanage in South India. *Indian Journal of Mental Retardation,* 1968, *1*(2), 53.

Read, M. S. Malnutrition and Learning. *American Education,* 1969, *5*(10), 11-14.

Rendon, R. et al. The Effect of Malnutrition on the Physical and Mental Development of Children. In G. Farrell, ed., *Congenital Mental Retardation.* Austin, Texas: University of Texas Press, 1969, pp. 262-288.

Sandstead, H. H., Freeman, H. B., and Zanderzwaag, R. Nutritional Deficiencies in Disadvantaged Preschool Children: Their Relationship to Mental Development. *American Journal of Diseases of Children,* 1971, *121*(6), 455-463.

Scrimshaw, N. S. Infant Malnutrition and Adult Learning. *Saturday Review,* 1968, *51*(11), 64-66, 84.

Winick, M. Malnutrition and Brain Development. *Journal of Pediatrics,* 1969, *74*(5), 667-679.

81

SYSTEMS FOR THE OBSERVATION OF CLASSROOM BEHAVIOR IN EARLY CHILDHOOD EDUCATION

by Alan R. Coller
Associate in Education
ERIC Clearinghouse on Early Childhood Education
Urbana, Illinois

This paper was produced pursuant to a contract with the Office of Child Development, partially supported by a contract with the Office of Education, U.S. Department of Health, Education and Welfare. Contractors undertaking such projects under Government sponsorship are encouraged to express freely their professional judgment. Points of view of opinions stated do not, therefore, necessarily represent official Government position or policy.

A search through the literature to locate instruments used to systematically observe early childhood classroom behavior has been a reminder that educational researchers did not always consider the study of classroom observation systems a top priority. Few observationally based studies are reported for the late forties and fifties. The next decade began a new era in the use of observational techniques in early childhood classrooms. In addition, the early researchers (with some notable exceptions) were primarily concerned with an examination of child behavior. Researchers today are concerned with teacher behavior and with student-teacher interactional behavior.

Thus it is the purpose of this paper to describe those instruments not reported in the collection listed above. We have also excluded from this report those instruments which the research for Better Schools, Inc., a regional laboratory, now intends to include in a forthcoming collection.

Section I is intended to provide an introduction to observational procedures, and especially to observations in selected situations. Devices and techniques used for the collection of observational data are described and discussed. Section II describes 12 classroom observation instruments not previously described elsewhere.

SECTION I. AN INTRODUCTION TO OBSERVATIONAL PROCEDURES

Direct Observational Procedures

A fundamental characteristic of all direct observational procedures is their emphasis upon overt behavior, including expressive or coping behaviors that can be seen, heard, or otherwise perceived by the human or mechanical recorder. Covert behaviors, or a child's or teacher's perceptions, attitudes, feelings, or intents for their interactions are not directly observable, and must therefore be inferred from overt behaviors, or assessed by other means. The fact that direct observational techniques relate to the recorder's perception of emergent behaviors, and not to his impressions of past behavior, serves to distinguish such procedures from behavioral trace procedures.

Direct observational procedures may be concerned with behaviors as they occur either under naturalistic or controlled situations. Naturalistic observations are concerned mainly with viewing the child in his everyday environment, where behavior can unfold naturally and is not influenced or caused by the observer or his cohorts. Two naturalistic observational techniques are observations in unstructured environments and observations in selected situations. The technique known as "observations in contrived situations" is a controlled-observation technique. In controlled observations the environment is subtly modified by the observer in such a way that behavior of interest to the observer may be elicited from S; Weick (1968) called this approach "tempered naturalness."

Our concern in this paper is to examine systems useful for the observation of behaviors which take place in early childhood classrooms. An analysis of techniques belonging to the observations in selected situations approach, as portrayed in Figure 1, seems to suit this purpose best.

Observations in unstructured environments are concerned with situations in which the subject moves freely about in his everyday environment (e.g., his neighborhood), unrestricted by the observer. Such behavior is usually assessed by any number of different types of "trailing" techniques, usually referred to as *specimen description* techniques (Wright, 1960). These techniques involve following the subject and recording, usually in a detailed sequential narration, his predominant modes of response to various situations he encounters. The specimen description technique can also be used in the classroom situation.

Observations in contrived situations refers to techniques designed to assess behaviors in specially designed situations that are intended to elicit responses of interest. Weick (1968) indicated that there are several reasons why an investigator might decide to modify a natural setting, but basically it is because he cannot afford to just wait for something relevant to happen. Techniques used for observations in contrived situations also provide more control, and the results may be generalizable to other conditions which are similar. An example of an *observation in contrived situations* technique is the instrument *Reaction to Entry of Teachers,* developed by the staff of the National Institute of Mental Health (c) (undated) and described in the next section. In general, the true purpose of the modified situation is hidden from the subject, and he is not (or should not be) aware that he is being observed.

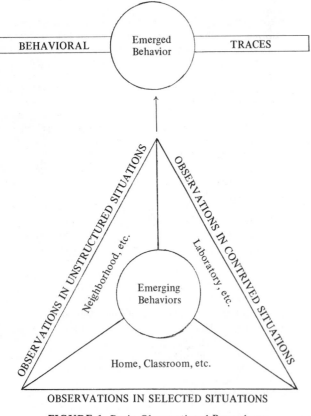

FIGURE 1. Basic Observational Procedures

Observations in selected situations refer to a class of techniques that are designed to assess behavior in given situations (e.g., in the classroom, on the playground, at home, etc.). These procedures are employed because many interesting behaviors occur more frequently under certain conditions than under others. Also, researchers and educators are vitally concerned with classroom behavior. Almost every type of device and technique available has been used to gather observational data in the classroom.

Collecting Observations in Selected Situations

Weick (1968) considers two processes basic to the observational process: *recording* and *encoding.* Recording means that "a considerable portion of observational research consists of making extensive records of events which at some later time are subject to analysis (p. 361)." Encoding is "the simplification of records through ratings, categories, or frequency counts (p. 361)." Weick's distinction, however, does not do justice to the observational processes which use encoding techniques as recording procedures. Another way of looking at these processes is possible: Webb et al. (1966), for example, speak of "accretion," a process whereby materials are "deposited" and later examined by behavioral trace measures. This is an arresting distinction, and is one of which we should be more aware. We may note in this respect that the initial collection or accretion of observational data employs direct observational procedures; the analysis of the already-collected data employs behavioral trace procedures. In any event, we shall use the term "accretion" to refer to any process whereby behavioral data are gathered for future analysis.

Data Accretion Devices

Classroom behaviors can be witnessed live by an observer, or recorded mechanically by a technician, using a videotape recorder, for example. Behaviors observed "live" may be encoded on the scene or otherwise described to be processed later. Regardless of approach, the end result is the accretion of data that are to be analyzed statistically at some future time. There are ten basic accretion devices by which observational data may be "deposited" physically: cinematic, audient, photographic, typographic, miscellaneous mechanical devices, self-as-instrument, diagrammatic, notational, marking, and written. These accretion devices can be combined to form a more extensive set of devices (see Table 1).

Cinematic procedures, in the form of motion picture films, have gained in popularity as an accretion device (e.g., Haggard and Isaacs, 1966; Haworth, 1956; Openshaw and Cyphant, 1966). The *cinematic/audient* combination, which may be in the form of a film with sound or video tape with sound, is even more popular (e.g., Brown, 1968; Kounin, Freisen, and Norton, 1966; Soar, 1970). Miller (1969, 1970) employed a soundless videotape method but combined it with a marking procedure (*cinematic/marking*) to categorize further the events as they occurred.

Audient procedures of all types have been employed

TABLE 1. MATRIX OF ACCRETION DATA DEVICES CURRENTLY USED FOR "DEPOSITING" CLASSROOM OBSERVATIONAL DATA

Cinematic	Audient	Photographic	Typographic	Misc. Mechanical Devices	Self-as-Instrument	Diagrammatic	Notational	Marking	Written	
✓	✓							✓		Cinematic
	✓		✓					✓		Audient
		✓							✓	Photographic
			✓							Typographic
				✓						Misc. Mechanical Devices
					✓			✓	✓	Self-as-Instrument
						✓			✓	Diagrammatic
							✓			Notational
								✓	✓	Marking
									✓	Written

(e.g., Loomis and Meyer, 1959, and Ober et al., 1968). Loomis and Meyer (1959) had two observers watch subjects and describe on tape everything that occurred. The observer's voice was analyzed as well as content. Sher and Horner (1967) used two tracks—one to record what the subject said and the other to keep a record of what the subject was doing. These data were later transcribed for analysis (*audient → typographic*). Caldwell (undated) uses the *audient → marking* procedure, whereby a narrative description of behaviors is tape-recorded and then coded. The *audient → written* approach was used by Schoggen (1964). He used a "Stenomask" into which he narratively described what was going on in the classroom. He obtained a degree of freedom in that he could move about and talk without disturbing anyone. He later wrote down his impressions.

Withall (1956) used time-lapse photography, a *photographic data* accretion device. Gump (1967) obtained a specimen description of a classroom, but supplemented his data by use of photographs (*photographic/written*).

Chapple (1949) invented the "interaction chronograph," which was similar in many respects to a typewriter; the keys differed, and were, in fact, codes for behavior. The *typographic* device is used often to transcribe audiently obtained observational data.

There are a number of different miscellaneous type data accretion devices. Wilensky (1965), for example, used a wristwatch to count the length of time of various periods in a nursery school. Hargreaves and Starkweather (1963) used a voice spectrometer to examine emotive quality. Crawford and Nicora (1964) used an ultrasonic device to examine classroom movement.

Self-as-instrument devices refer to any procedure in which the observer himself is behaving as if he were the recording device. The observer becomes both a cinematic and audient device, and tends to rely upon memory for recording visual and auditory events. Later the observer attempts to recall what it was that transpired. Lofland (1971) and Schwartz and Schwartz (1955) discuss the participant observer approach, which involves the observer living with the type of persons he is concerned with describing. Combs and Soper (1963) describe the self-as-instrument device, and have developed scales (which O, an observer, rates) after he has gathered his inferences about S (*self-as-instrument → marking*).

Coller (1970) used the *diagrammatic* device (which, by definition, also employs notations) to display pictorially a day in the life of a classroom. Coller (1970) also used the *diagrammatic/written* device to describe more fully what the diagrams and the notations on it represented. Wrightstone (1944) used a *notational* system to describe how students at their seats in a classroom were reacting in respect to the lesson.

Marking, of course, is an obvious encoding procedure (a diagrammatic and/or notational system may also be an encoding procedure), and may be employed as a supplementary process for many of the devices mentioned. The observational instruments developed by Medley and Smith (1969) and Wilensky (1966) are typical marking procedures. The Educational Testing Service (1966) and Prescott (1967) developed instruments which employed both marking and narrative description (*marking/written*).

The *written* devices are well known (e.g., specimen description, diary description, anecdotal records, etc.). The work of Kounin (1970) and of Barker and Wright (1955) are good examples of this method.

Implementation of Data Accretion Devices

How to implement a chosen accretion device in the classroom is a problem for the developer of an observational instrument. Wright (1963) and Gordon and Jester (in press) have considered this issue. For example, Wright attempted to schematize six basic methods used in observational child study: diary description, specimen description, time sampling, event sampling, trait ratings, and field unit analysis. These methods may be distinguished from one another on the basis of "continuum coverages," "material coverage," "recording technique," and "analysis procedure." Gordon and Jester added to the number of basic methods by dividing the time sampling category into "time/signs" and "time/categories," and by adding "level of cognitive interaction."

Table 2 presents an alternative to these approaches. Basically, the matrix displayed in Table 2 is described by two dimensions: a set of data systems and a set of sampling units.

Fundamental Data Systems

There are three fundamental data systems: field, sign, and category. *Field data system* refers to that situation in which the observer is not pre-set by instruction to look for and assess specific behaviors. Instead, the observer is to respond to field forces and describe, within predetermined limits, all that occurs. *Sign data system* refers to the approach during which *O* lists "beforehand a number of specific acts or incidents of behavior which may or may not occur during a period of observation (Medley and Mitzel, 1963, pp. 298-299)." *O*, however, is preset by the sign system to look only for certain behaviors. We distinguish between two types of sign systems: the discrete and the hierarchical. *Sign/discrete* systems refer to those observational schedules whose categorical boundaries do not approach the equal-appearing interval type of scale. The categories in the sign/discrete system often are orthogonal to one another and cannot be construed as belonging to the same continuum. The *sign/hierarchical* systems also tend to have discrete categories, but a clear representation of a hierarchy or taxonomy is present in the items. (Note that a debate still exists as to whether or not the evaluative dimension of the cognitive taxonomy [Bloom et al., 19] is actually the highest level of cognition.) *Category data system* refers to the attempt to limit the observation to one general aspect of classroom behavior. The procedure, as described by Medley and Mitzel (1963), is to "construct a definite set of categories into one, and only one, of which every unit observed can be classified (p. 298)." The matrix shown in Table 2 indicates that there are three types of category systems: discrete, hierarchical,

TABLE 2. METHODS FOR IMPLEMENTING DATA ACCRETION DEVICES

	Sampling Units		
Data Systems	*Time/Events*	*Events*	*Situational/Events*
Field Systems	Commentary	Anecdotal Records (critical incidents)	Specimen Description
			Diary Description (comprehensive)
		Diary Description (topical)	Field Unit Analysis
		Commentary	Participant Observation
			Narrative Summaries
Sign/Discrete Systems	Time Sampling	Behavioral Checklists	Behavioral Checklists
		Anecdotal Records (formatted)	Event Sampling
Sign/Hierarchical Systems	Time/Domain Sampling	Point-time Sampling	X
Category/Discrete Systems	Point-fixed time Sampling	Point-time Sampling	Event Sampling
	Time Sampling		Point-time Sampling
Category/Hierarchical Systems	X	Point-time Sampling	Event/Domain Sampling
			Point-time Sampling
Category/Interval Rating Systems	Point-fixed time Sampling		
	Intrasessions Ratings	Point-time Sampling	Intersession Ratings
		Intersession Ratings	Postsession Ratings (Trait ratings)

and interval rating. As in the case of sign systems, discrete category systems refer to those observational schedules whose categorical boundaries do not approach the equal-appearing interval type of scale. Likewise, the categorical boundaries of the hierarchical type of category system tend to be discrete, but a clear representation of a hierarchy or taxonomy is present. The interval rating type of category system provides the observer with scales that tend to approach the equal-appearing interval type; there is a distinct continuum. In general, a category system differs from a sign system in that the category system is supposed to be exhaustive of behaviors of the type to be observed. Both the category and sign systems differ from field systems, primarily because the *O* is pre-set by the sign and category systems to look at very specific behaviors.

Sampling Unit Dimension

The sampling unit dimension is divided into three factors: *time/events, events,* and *situational/events.* The use of events in all three factors is to acknowledge that, regardless of what sampling plan is employed by *O,* the basic unit of analysis is a behavioral action—an event. When *O* samples behavior using the *time/event* factor, he typically employs a fixed time for obtaining an observation; only those behaviors occurring during a fixed time unit are treated as data. If the sampling unit is the *events* factor, *O* will describe, check, code, and/or rate only when a critical, topical or specified event occurs. Observations terminate for the target person or class when the event occurs. The *situational/events* factor refers to a sampling plan during which time is the variable, and the observation terminates only after some specified situation ends—the class, or snack period, for example. We may disregard here the fact that the time/events sampling units may be repeated during a defined situation. Event sampling, a procedure described by Wright (1960) as one which "singles out naturally segregated behavioral events of one or another class and records these events as they arise and unfold (p. 75)," is typically employed as a situational/events measure. Many of the other procedures found in the cells of the matrix of Table 2 are described by Wright (1960). Selected procedures not necessarily discussed by Wright will be examined here.

Wright (1960) defined *trait ratings* as a process that "selects dimensions of behavior and bases judgments about them on observations during extended sequences of behavior (p. 75)." *Postsession ratings* would approach this definition. Other rating schemes, termed *intrasession ratings,* are used during a session, sometimes in a time sampling format. *Intersession ratings* are used from one session to another until all items are observed and rated.

Goodlad, Klein and associates (1970) developed an anecdotal record type of procedure in which they supplied *O* with a list of topics they were to observe intentionally. Such a procedure tends to create a *closed* system and provides different types of data. The anecdotal record/critical incidents and formatted anecdotal record tend to point up these differences.

One final significant addition is the *point-time sampling* procedure. In this procedure the *O* examines the behavior of the target person only long enough to be sure what the behavior is, and then checks off the behavior in the appropriate category. This procedure can be used in a time sampling plan, as long as the fixed unit of time is ample enough for *O* to gather all the information needed. Such a procedure might be called a *point-fixed time sampling* procedure.

SECTION II. INSTRUMENT DESCRIPTION

A Description of Selected Examples of Observations in Selected Situations

1. Classroom Behavior Scale
2. Daily Ratings
3. Discrete Classroom Behavior Schedule
4. Evaluation Scale of Four- and Five-Year-Old Children
5. Intensity of Involvement Scale
6. Nursery School Behavior Record: Juice and Cracker Period
7. Observer Ratings of Children
8. Overview Snapshot Observational Technique
9. Reaction of Entry of Teachers
10. School and Classroom Observation Categories
11. Teachers' Attending Behaviors
12. Weekly Ratings

1. Classroom Behavior Scale

H. N. Sloane, Jr., J. L. Ralph, D. C. Cannon, and W. J. DeRisi

Type of Instrument. This instrument uses both the category/discrete and category/interval rating system combined with a timed sampling plan. Here, then, is a combined use of time sampling and intersession rating methods.

Usage. The instrument was used in a correctional institution for boys. The boys were of junior high school age. The instrument was also used in an "adjustment" class, consisting of students from the first four elementary grades.

Variables Measured. The scale assesses desirable or undesirable student behaviors, the teacher's reactions to those behaviors, and the degree to which the teacher individualizes student contacts. Time spent on academic matters, versus classroom management, is also recorded.

Instrument Description. The scale was developed from a behavior analysis point of view. In each class five (5) children are selected for observation. A rating period lasts 30 seconds: the first ten seconds are used for observing (the target child, teacher, class) and the remaining 20 seconds for scoring. Nine rating periods (or four and one-half minutes) are used for each target while before the observer/rater turns his attention to another of the preselected children. The coding sheet contains a scoring matrix for each student. The horizontal dimensions contain nine columns for the 30-second rating intervals. The vertical dimension displays six categories of student and teacher behavior or interactions: (1) student behavior, (2) nonverbal interaction with the target child, (3) verbal interaction with the target child, (4) nonverbal other, (5) verbal other, and (6) interaction character. The latter category is complex, and contains codes to indicate the type of interaction in respect to group size and academic relationship. In all, 28 different scores or score qualifications can be coded.

Sample Items. *Undesirable Behavior:* To be coded "U," the S must be emitting the following behavior within the 10-second rating period: (a) verbalizing aloud in any manner, when prohibited, (b) making nonverbal noise, (c) unacceptable location, (d) disruptive motor behavior, (e) slow or improper getting or returning of material, (f) failing to begin task upon teacher's signal, (g) not listening or looking at teacher presentation, (h) unauthorized seat leaving, (i) speaking to teacher without raising hand, etc.

Psychometric Description. *Inter-judge Reliability.* Three different studies employing the Classroom Behavior Scale were, in part, useful for supplying inter-judge reliability data. Data are presented in terms of percent agreement for each of the six categories separately.

Agreement for most categories is high. *Validity.* Studies showing change in certain categories for experimental groups were reported.

Comments. None.

Availability. Howard N. Sloane, Jr., The Bureau of Educational Research, 308 MBH, The University of Utah, Salt Lake City, Utah 84112

References. Sloane, H. N., Jr., Ralph, John, Cannon, D. C., and DeRisi, W. J. *The Classroom Behavior Scale.* (Unpublished observational scale, 1969.)

2. Daily Ratings

National Institute of Mental Health

Type of Instrument. This instrument is primarily of the category/interval rating variety and uses the situations/event sampling plan. Basically, the postsession rating method is used. One part of the instrument uses the category/discrete system with the event sampling method.

Usage. Used with preschool children.

Variables Measured. This instrument focuses upon the child, and examines (1) play involvement, (2) nomadic play, (3) peer involvement, (4) separation reaction (upon leaving home), (5) acts of aggressiveness, (6) peer conflicts and (7) excited instances.

Instrument Description. Observations with this instrument may take place at the child's home, in a car going to the center, and indoors and outdoors at the center. The length of observation is variable, and depends upon the length of a particular classroom period or the time it takes to drive from the child's home to the center. For three dimensions O is required to rate S's behavior on continuums. Some scales have 11 points, others 3. For the

aggressiveness dimension, O is to indicate, first, any instance of aggression, and second, the response (on a 4-point scale) of the other child to the aggression. In addition, the nursery school day was divided into 15 different time periods for this schedule, and O was to check any period in which S showed excitement.

Sample Items. *Peer Involvement—Inside free play.* (3) will frequently seek out the other children in the playroom in order to play with them, or talk to them, or boss them, or tease them, or take something from them; (2) some time was spent interacting with some of the other children; (1) very seldom, if ever, had anything to do with another child.

Psychometric Description. No data available.

Comments. Some items on this schedule are not pertinent to other settings.

Availability. Charles F. Halverson, Jr., National Institute of Mental Health, Bethesda, Maryland.

References. National Institute of Mental Health. *Daily Ratings.* (Unpublished observational rating scale, undated) (a)

(This instrument is still in the developmental stages and is therefore subject to change.)

3. Discrete Classroom Behaviors Schedule

Joseph A. Cobb

Type of Instrument. The procedures used here combine the category/discrete system with the timed sampling plan. The commentary method is used to supplement the data.

Usage. Not indicated, but appears useful for observing the young child.

Variables Measured. Basically, a behavioral modification approach. The observed behaviors deal with academically appropriate and inappropriate actions on the part of the child. The categories are: attending, appropriate talking with teacher, appropriate talk with peer, volunteers, imitation, complies, self-stimulation, physical negative, destructiveness, inappropriate locale, noisy, play, inappropriate talk with teacher, inappropriate talk with peer, and noncompliance.

Instrument Description. Every six seconds the observer codes a child's behavior by placing a circle around the appropriate category on the coding sheet. The occurrence of a response to the child's actions is also recorded. Once the behaviors of all children in the classroom are recorded, a new coding sheet is used for a new set of observations. Space on the coding sheet is provided to indicate the academic activity taking place during the coding session, as well as for other types of context description.

Sample Items. *"Appropriate talking with teacher.* This category can be checked when the pupil talks with the teacher about academic material, whether in private as in independent work situations, or answers questions in other situations (p. 2)." "*Noisy*. This category is to be used when the person talks loudly, yells, bangs books, scrapes chairs, or makes any sounds that are likely to be actually or potentially disruptive to others (p. 3)."

Psychometric Description. No data available.

Comments. There is some indication by Cobb that Patterson, Ray, and Shaw (1968) previously defined many of the behaviors described in the manual. However, no bibliographic data were supplied.

Availability. J. A. Cobb, Oregon Research Institute, Eugene, Oregon.

References. Cobb, J. A. *Definitions of Discrete Classroom Behaviors.* Eugene, Oregon: Social Learning Project, Oregon Research Institute, January 1970.

4. Evaluation Scale of Four- and Five-year-old Children

A. L. Butler, M. Church, and M. Swayze.

Type of Instrument. It appears that this instrument uses the category/interval rating system combined with the events sampling plan.

Usage. Twenty-five teachers used the scale in their kindergarten classrooms.

Variables Measured. Four basic areas are assessed with this instrument: self-concept, child in relation to other people, child in relation to his physical environment, and child in relation to the world of ideas.

Instrument Description. No information was available as to how O was to proceed with the observations. There is some indication that the instrument may be used at the very beginning and near the end of the school term. Each of the four major categories contains at least six scales. The second and fourth position of the five scales are described, and S's behavior (the child's) is rated on each of the dimensions.

Sample Items. Involvement in task (self-concept). (2) Flits from one activity to another. Samples but does not become deeply involved. (4) Plans and persists in activity for the sake of the activity.

Psychometric Description. None reported.

Comments. The procedures used here approach those of retrospective trace reports.

Availability. See below.

References. Butler, A. L. An Evaluation Scale for Four- and Five-Year-Old Children. *Bulletin of the School of Education* (Indiana University), 1965, *41* (Whole No. 2).

5. Intensity of Involvement Scale

B. McCandless and W. L. Hodges

Type of Instrument. The procedures used here employ the category/interval rating system with a timed-sampling

plan. The method used is a fixed-time point-time sampling approach.

Usage. This instrument has been used almost entirely with preschool-aged children but the authors feel that it may be equally adaptable for older children.

Variables Measured. The scale is concerned with measuring *task-involvement*, or the degree to which the child is attending to a designated task. Recorded also are indications of *interfering behaviors:* behaviors that distract others. *Activities* are also recorded.

Instrument Description. The observer is asked to make five rounds of the children present in the classroom. Each observation lasts five seconds, and the O is asked to be in a position to observe S's face for all of that time. Immediately after the observation, the O rates the child's involvement by use of one of six categories: (1) unoccupied, (2) onlooking, (3) minimal-minimal, (4) minimal, (5) attention moderate, (6) complete.

Sample Items. 4. Minimal (M): The *S* works in desultory fashion, but has attention flickering on task at hand. He is working, but *O* infers that attention on the task is partial at most. Some unoccupied and on-looking may occur. In stories, he occasionally glances at the story teller, but is not obviously attending to any other activity; he may perhaps be fingering objects or making asides to another child, but is at least partially "with it." Two to four seconds of the five-second observation period are clearly task-involved.

Psychometric Description. *Inter-judge agreement.* Agreements up to 96 percent have been reported.

Comments. None

Availability. Boyd McCandless, Emory University, Atlanta, Georgia 30322

References. McCandless, B. R. *Intensity of Involvement Scale.* (Unpublished observation scale, Emory University, 1968)

6. Nursery School Behavior Record: Juice and Cracker Period

National Institute of Mental Health.

Type of Instrument. This instrument uses two different procedures: (1) a sign system combined with a situational/events sampling plan—event sampling method; and (2) a category/interval rating system interfaced with the situational/events sampling plan—postsession ratings.

Usage. Used with preschool-aged children.

Variables Measured. "Gulping," defined as the amount of food (or liquid) consumed over the number of times the food (or liquid) came to lips, is one dimension measured. Also examined is rate of talk and interest in a story.

Instrument Description. This schedule is designed for a combined snack and story period. The O counts the frequency with which food and/or drink is brought to the S's lips. After the child is finished, he determines how much food and/or liquid was consumed. These two figures are employed to determine a gulping index. During this session O also tallies each statement or attempt at verbalization that is followed by a pause. The child's interest in a story is rated on a five-point scale.

Sample Items. *Attention to story.* (1) Almost completely uninterested in story; (2) slightly interested, or generally no interest, but with a short period of high interest; . . . (5) almost undivided and rapt attention to story.

Psychometric Description. No data available.

Comments. This schedule applicable only under conditions where a snack period and story period are combined.

Availability. Charles F. Halverson, Jr., National Institute of Mental Health, Bethesda, Maryland.

References. National Institute of Mental Health. *Nursery School Behavior Record: Juice and Cracker Period.* Bethesda, Maryland: National Institute of Mental Health, Child Research Branch, 1970 (a).

(This instrument is still in the developmental stages, and is therefore subject to change.)

7. Observer Ratings of Children

W. Emmerich & G. Wilder

Type of Instrument. This instrument uses intersession ratings employing an events sampling plan first and then the postsession rating method.

Usage. Black and white Head Start children, N > 500, were observed during the Fall and Spring semesters. The data were examined both to validate the instrument and to make comparisons between subgroups and programs over time.

Variables Measured. W. Emmerich (1971) describes the instrument as a measure of "personal-social constructs."

Instrument Description. Two judges are required to make "simultaneous paired observations" and to record their perceptions, first on a set of 127 unipolar scales and then on a set of 21 bipolar scales. The unipolar scales assess relatively specific categories of behavior, including social motives, coping mechanisms, and activities of interest (e.g., gross motor behavior). The bipolar scales assess "broad personality dimensions." Each unipolar scale calls for an estimate of a behavior's frequency of occurrence during a specified period of observation, based upon the following four-point scale: (0) totally absent; (1) occurred once; (2) occurred more than once, but not continuously; (3) continuous during the observation period. The inferences called for when rating the bipolar scales are based upon the ratings the observers make on the set of unipolar scales.

Sample Items. (54): Engages in fantasy activity and (73): Deliberately aggressive against property (unipolar scales). (1): Withdrawn-involved and (16): Aimless-purposeful (bipolar scales).

Psychometric Description. *Inter-judge Reliability:* Pearson product-movement correlations were computed on all scales for rater pairs who observed at least 20 children simultaneously. For the 21 bipolar scales as a set, the median of the medians across pairs, sites, and periods was .63. For the 127 unipolar scales as a set, this overall median was .74. Emmerich (1971) notes that there was considerable difference from rater pair to rater pair and over sites.

Comments. The use of ratings from the unipolar scales as the basis for references (self-as-instrument) for the bipolar scales is an interesting procedure that should be investigated further.

Availability. W. Emmerich, Educational Testing Service, Princeton, N.J.

References. Emmerich, W. *Structure and Development of Personal-Social Behaviors in Preschool Settings.* ETS-Head Start Longitudinal Study. Princeton, N.J.: Educational Testing Service, 1971.

_____, and Wilder, G. Classroom Observation Rating Scale (Personality). In Educational Testing Service, *Disadvantaged Children and Their First School Experiences: From Theory to Operations.* Princeton, N.J.: Educational Testing Service, 1969. (OEO Grant H-8256) (ERIC ED 043 397)

8. Overview Snapshot Observational Technique (OSOT)

A. R. Coller

Type of Instrument. This instrument, used to gather data for additional encoding at a later date employs the sign system, the category/discrete system and the category/interval rating systems with a point-time sampling method. A diagrammatic accretion device is employed to gather the data.

Usage. The OSOT has been used to describe pictorially "a day in the life" of a multiaged-group kindergarten class and a "traditional" kindergarten class.

Variables Measured. Besides providing a graphic display of transactions within a classroom context, five dimensions are evaluated by OSOT. These dimensions include: (1) the S's location in the classroom, (2) S's interactions with others, (3) S's encounters with instructional material, (4) S's attention to others, and/or his involvement with instructional materials, and (5) the strenuousness or intensity of his motor activity. Sociometric type choice and various other types of social interactions can also be coded from the basic data.

Instrument Description. OSOT procedures are not fixed, but are intended to be adopted for the particular local purpose. Typically, the OSOT procedure is to focus upon the first child on a list, observe for about ten seconds (or as long as necessary to gather the pertinent data), record the data for about ten seconds, and then focus upon the second child listed. However, if any of these children are interacting, or close to others in the class, the observer reverts to "cluster" observations and records data for all those in the cluster. When this is done, the O focuses on the next child on the list whose behavior has not been recorded and the process continues. The O records notational symbols upon a diagram representing the classroom, with furniture and other important aspects of the classroom displayed and labeled. The O locates the notational symbol on the diagram representing the actual location of the child; other notations are used to represent the social interactions, sex, attention to others, involvement with materials, and level of motor activity. Initials and abbreviations are used to identify S's and type of instructional materials

Sample Items. *Motor Activity Level.* (0) No overt movement; (1) moderate movement, no locomotion; (2) moderate movement, locomotion; (3) intensive movement no locomotion; and (4) intensive movement, locomotion.

Psychometric Description. No data available.

Comments. Initial tryouts with the OSOT indicated that some revision was necessary. A revised version of OSOT will become available in the near future.

Availability. Alan R. Coller, Institute for Development of Human Resources, 520 Weil Hall, University of Florida, Gainesville, Florida 32601

References. Coller, A. R. *Overhead Snapshot Observation Technique (OSOT): Administration Manual.* Urbana, Illinois: Center for Instructional Research and Curriculum Evaluation (CIRCE), University of Illinois, 1970.

9. Reaction to Entry of Teachers

National Institute of Mental Health

Type of Instrument. This instrument employs the post-session rating method.

Usage. Used with preschool children.

Variables Measured. Two scales measure the child's reactions as the teacher (1) entered the doorway (initial encounter), and (2) attempted to move close to the child.

Instrument Description. The two seven-point scales (with each point defined) are rated by O, after observing the child's behavior after the teacher either enters the room or attempts to come close to the child.

Sample Items. *Initial encounter.* (1) child makes no negative responses and makes more than one positive response; (2) child makes no negative responses and makes one positive response; . . . (5) child's reaction is slightly negative; . . . (7) child gives no positive responses and he freezes or runs to mother.

Psychometric Description. No data available.

Comments. When teacher behaviors are "staged," this observational procedure approaches that of observations in contrived situations. This instrument is still in the developmental stages, and is therefore subject to change.

Availability. Charles F. Halverson, Jr., National Institute of Mental Health, Bethesda, Maryland.

References. National Institute of Mental Health. *Reaction to Entry of Teachers.* (Unpublished observational rating scale, undated) (c)

10. School and Classroom Observation Categories

J. I. Goodlad, M. F. Klein, and Associates

Type of Instrument. This instrument employs a sign system with an events sampling plan. The method is best described as a formatted anecdotal record.

Usage. Used to assess about 158 classrooms in 67 schools, grades K-3.

Variables Measured. Basically, a data collection procedure which employs anecdotal records to collect behavior. This instrument provided O with categories for observation. For example, milieu, instructional activities, subject matter, materials and equipment, involvement, interaction, inquiry, independence, curriculum balance, curricular adaptation, etc.

Instrument Description. The technique of anecdotal records was used here, with the categories for observation spelled out in advance for O.

Sample Item. *Curriculum Balance.* The interest in this category is the range of organized human experience with which the class seems to deal. Are subjects and activities concentrated in a few fields, or spread across the major divisions of knowledge? Are emphases identifiable?

Psychometric Description. None reported.

Comments. None.

Availability. See below.

References. Goodlad, J. I., Klein, M. F., and Associates. *Behind the Classroom Door.* Worthington, Ohio: Charles A. Jones Publishing Company, 1970.

11. Teachers' Attending Behaviors

M. Cooper and C. Thomson

Type of Instrument. Two different schedules are combined here. Both use a sign system interfaced with a situational/events sampling plan: the event sampling method.

Usage. Used to assess the attending behaviors of preschool teachers undergoing different treatments in an attempt to modify attending behaviors.

Variables Measured. Teacher behavior in terms of their *attention and/or inattention* to child responses, either appropriate or disruptive.

Instrument Description. It appears as if two observers are necessary. One observer determines if the teacher was attending to appropriate child responses or to disruptive child responses. A second observer, who, like the first observer, records behavior in ten-second intervals, determines occurrences of the teacher's (1) attending to appropriate child responses, and (2) lack of attention to child responses which *could* have been attended to.

Sample Items. Attention to disruptive responses was defined as giving attention to a child when he (1) physically disturbs another, (2) verbally disturbs another, (3) abuses materials, and (4) does not follow directions.

Psychometric Description. *Inter-judge agreement.* Agreements in a study employing the instrument were as low as 73 percent and as high as 95 percent. *Validity.* The instrument apparently is sensitive to treatment effects designed to change the teacher's rate of attending to appropriate and disruptive child responses.

Comments. Another behavioral modification approach.

Availability. The University of Kansas Head Start Evaluation and Research Center, University of Kansas, Lawrence, Kansas.

References. Cooper, M., and Thomson, C. *The Observation of Reinforcement Behavior of Teachers in Head Start Classrooms and the Modification of a Teacher's Attending Behavior.* Lawrence, Kansas: The University of Kansas Head Start Evaluation and Research Center, 1967.

12. Weekly Ratings

National Institute of Mental Health

Type of Instrument. This instrument employs the post-session rating method.

Usage. Used with preschool children.

Variables Measured. This instrument focuses upon the behavior of the child and contains scales for the following dimensions: (1) chronic fear; (2) fear when using equipment; (3) frenetic-impulsive; (4) impatience; (5) positive peer interaction; (6) negative peer interaction; (7) originality; (8) nurturance, female teacher; (9) nurturance, male teacher; (10) indication of intervention; (11) interest in obtaining help; and (12) seeking help.

Instrument Description. The O is asked to rate each target child on the 12 dimensions listed above. An 11-point continuum is employed, with the eleventh, sixth, and first points being defined.

Sample Items. (2) *Fear when using equipment.* Child's general orientation toward approaching physical activity or playground equipment: (11) Confident, daring, bold, adventurous (e.g., likes to swing, climb high, jump from the tree stump); (6) neither characteristically bold nor cautious; (1) timid, over-cautious, needing adult help. Avoids activities, shows fear of heights or loss of balance.

Psychometric Description. No data available.

Comments. Some items on this scale are not generalizable to other settings.

Availability. Charles F. Halverson, Jr., National Institute of Mental Health, Bethesda, Maryland.

References. National Institute of Mental Health. *Weekly Ratings.* (Unpublished observational rating scale, undated) (b)

(This instrument is still in the developmental stages, and is therefore subject to change.)

REFERENCES

Adams, R. S. The Classroom Context. In W. J. Campbell, ed., *Scholars in Context: The Effects of Environments on Learning.* Sydney, Australia: John Wiley & Sons, Australasia Pty Ltd, 1970.

Barker, R. B., and Wright, H. F. *Midwest and Its Children.* Evanston, Ill.: Row, Peterson and Co., 1955.

Becker, W. C., Thomas, D. R., and Carnine, D. *Reducing Behavior Problems: An Operant Conditioning Guide for Teachers.* Urbana, Ill.: ERIC Clearinghouse on Early Childhood Education, University of Illinois, 1969.

Biddle, B. J. Methods and Concepts in Classroom Research. *Review of Educational Research,* 1967, *37,* 337-357.

_____, and Elleva, W. J., eds., *Contemporary Research on Teacher Effectiveness.* New York: Holt, Rinehart & Winston, 1964.

Boyd, R. D., and deVault, M. V. The Observation and Recording of Behavior. *Review of Educational Research,* 1966, *36,* 529-551.

Brown, B. B. *The Experimental Mind in Education.* New York: Harper & Row, 1968.

Butler, A. L. An Evaluation Scale for Four- and Five-Year-Old Children. *Bulletin of the School of Education* (Indiana University), 1965, *41* (Whole No. 2).

Caldwell, B. M., Honig, A. S., and Wynn, R. L. Coding Manual for APPROACH: A Procedure for Patterning Responses of Adults and Children. Unpublished manuscript, undated.

Chapple, E. D. The Interaction Chronograph: Its Evolution and Present Application. *Personnel,* 1949, *23,* 295-307.

Cobb, J. A. Definitions of Discrete Classroom Behaviors. Social Learning Project, Oregon Research Institute, Eugene, Oregon, 1970.

Coller, A. R. Overhead Snapshot Observation Technique (OSOT): Administration Manual. Unpublished manuscript, Urbana, Illinois: Center for Instructional Research and Curriculum Evaluation (CIRCE), University of Illinois, 1970.

_____. *The Assessment of "Self-Concept" in Early Childhood Education.* Urbana, Illinois: ERIC Clearinghouse on Early Childhood Education, University of Illinois, 1971.

Combs, A. W., and Soper, D. W. *The Relationship of Child Perceptions to Achievement and Behavior in the Early School Years.* Gainesville: University of Florida, 1963. (USOE, Cooperative research project No. 814)

Cooper, M., and Thomson, C. The Observation of Reinforcement Behavior of Teachers in Head Start Classrooms and the Modification of a Teacher's Attending Behavior. Lawrence, Kansas: The University of Kansas Head Start Evaluation and Research Center, 1967.

Crawford, M. L. J., and Nicora, B. D. Measurement of Human Group Activity. *Psychological Reports,* 1964, *15,* 227-231.

Dawe, H. C. The Child's Experiences in Communication. In N. S. Light, ed., *Early Childhood Education: Forty-sixth Yearbook, National Society for the Study of Education,* Part II. Chicago: The University of Chicago Press, 1947, pp. 193-208.

Dopyera, J. D., and Lay, M. Assessing the Program Environments of Head Start and Other Pre-School Children. Addendum to Final Report for Office of Economic Opportunity. Syracuse University Head Start Evaluation and Research Project, Syracuse, N.Y., 1969. (OEO Research Contract #4120)

Educational Testing Service. *Classroom Observation Form.* Office of Economic Opportunity, Head Start, 1966.

Emmerich, W. *Structure and Development of Personal-Social Behaviors in Preschool Settings.* ETS-Head Start Longitudinal Study. Princeton, N.J.: Educational Testing Service, 1971.

_____, and Wilder, G. Classroom Observation Rating Scale (Personality). In Educational Testing Service, *Disadvantaged Children and Their First School Experiences: From Theory to Operations.* Princeton, N.J.: Educational Testing Service, 1969 (OEO Grant H-8256) (ERIC ED 043 397)

Goodlad, J. I., Klein, M. F., and Associates. *Behind the Classroom Door.* Worthington, Ohio: Charles A. Jones Publishing Company, 1970.

Gordon, I. J. *Studying the Child in School.* New York: John Wiley & Sons, Inc., 1966.

_____, and Jester, R. E. Techniques of Observing Teaching in Early Childhood and Outcomes of Particular Procedures. In M. W. Travers, ed., *Handbook of Research on Teaching (Rev. Ed.).* (In press)

Gump, P. V. *The Classroom Behavior Setting: Its Nature and Relation to Student Behavior. Final Report.* Lawrence, Kansas: Midwest Psychological Field Station, University of Kansas, 1967. (USOE Cooperative research project #OE-4-10-107)

Haggard, E. A., and Isaacs, K. S. Micromomentary Facial Expressions as Indicators of Ego Mechanisms in Psychotherapy. In L. A. Gottschalk and A. H. Auerbach, eds., *Methods of Research in Psychotherapy.* New York: Appleton-Century, 1966, pp. 154-165.

Hanley, E. M. Review of Research Involving Applied Behavior in the Classroom. *Review of Educational Research,* 1970, *40,* 597-626.

Hare, A. P. *Handbook of Small Group Research.* New York: Free Press of Glencoe, 1962.

Hargreaves, W. A., and Starkweather, J. A. Recognition of Speaker Identity. *Language and Speech,* 1963, *6,* 63-67.

Hartup, W. W. Peer Interaction and Social Organization. In P. H. Mussen, ed., *Carmichael's Manual of Child Psychology (Third edition),* Volume 2. New York: John Wiley & Sons, Inc., 1970.

Haworth, M. R. An Exploratory Study to Determine the Effectiveness of a Filmed Puppet Show as a Group Projective Technique for Use with Children. Unpublished doctoral dissertation, Pennsylvania State University, 1956.

Johnson, O. G., and Bommarito, J. W. *Tests and Measurements in Child Development: A Handbook.* San Francisco: Jossey-Boss Inc., 1971.

Kounin, J. S., Freesen, W. V., and Norton, A. E. Managing Emotionally Disturbed Children in Regular Classrooms. *Journal of Educational Psychology,* 1966, *57,* 1-13.

Lofland, J. *Analyzing Social Settings.* Belmont, California: Wadsworth Publishing Company, Inc., 1971.

Loomis, E. A., and Meyer, L. R. Observation and Recording—A Simultaneous Process. *American Journal of Orthopsychiatry,* 1959, *29,* 574-582.

McCandless, B. R. *Intensity of Involvement Scale.* Unpublished observation scale, Emory University, 1968.

Medley, D. M., and Mitzel, H. E. Measuring Classroom Behavior by Systematic Observation. In N. L. Gage, ed., *Handbook of Research on Teaching.* Chicago: Rand McNally, 1963.

Miller, L. Experimental Variation of Headstart Curricula: A Comparison of Current Approaches. Annual report. University of Louisville, Louisville, Kentucky, 1969. (OEO research project #CG 8199)

_____. Experimental Variation of Headstart Curricula: A Comparison of Current Approaches. Progress report #5. University of Louisville, Louisville, Kentucky, 1970. (OEO research project #CG 8199)

Murray, C. K., ed., Systematic Observation. *Journal of Research and Development in Education,* 1970, *4* (Whole No. 1).

National Institute of Mental Health. *Nursery School Behavior Record: Quiet Room, Games, and Bells.* Bethesda, Maryland: National Institute of Mental Health, Child Research Branch, 1970(b).

_____. *Daily Ratings.* Unpublished observational rating scale, undated(a).

_____. *Weekly Ratings.* Unpublished observational rating scale, undated(b).

_____. *Reaction to Entry of Teachers.* Unpublished observational rating scale, undated(c).

Ober, R. L. Theory into Practice Through Systematic Observation. *Florida Educational Research and Development Council, Research Bulletin IV,* No. 1, 1968.

_____ et al. The Development of a Reciprocal Category System for Assessing Teacher-Student Classroom Verbal Interaction. Paper presented at the annual meeting of the American Education Research Association, Chicago, 1968.

Openshaw, M. K., and Cyphert, F. R. The Development of a Taxonomy for the Classification of Teacher Classroom Behavior. Columbus, Ohio: The Ohio State University Research Foundation, 1966. (USOE Cooperative research project No. 2288)

Prescott, D. A. *The Child in the Educative Process.* New York: McGraw-Hill, 1957.

Schoggen, P. H. Mechanical Aids for Making Specimen Records of Behavior. *Child Development,* 1964, *35,* 985-988.

Schwartz, M. S., and Schwartz, C. G. Problems in Participant Observation. *American Journal of Sociology,* 1955, *60,* 343-353.

Sears, P. S., and Dowley, E. M. Research on Teaching in the Nursery School. In N. L. Gage, ed., *Handbook of Research on Teaching.* Chicago: Rand McNally & Company, 1963.

Sher, A. B., and Horner, V. M. A Technique for Gathering Children's Language Samples from Naturalistic Settings. Paper presented at the annual meeting of the Society for Research in Child Development, New York City, 1967.

Simon, A., and Boyer, E. G., eds. Mirrors for Behavior: An Anthology of Classroom Observation Instruments. *Classroom Interaction Newsletter,* 1968, *3,* (Whole No. 2).

Sloan, H. N., Jr., Ralph, J. L., Cannon, D. C., and DeRise, W. J. *The Classroom Behavior Scale,* Unpublished observational scale, 1969.

Soar, R. Follow Through Model Implementation. Gainesville, Florida: IDHR, College of Education, University of Florida, 1970. (Interim report on project #OEG-0-8-5224 N-4618 (100), U.S. Office of Education.)

Stake, R. E. The Decision: Does Classroom Observation Belong in an Evaluation Plan? In *AERA Monograph Series on Curriculum Evaluation, No. 6. Classroom Observation.* Chicago: Rand McNally, 1970.

Webb, E. J., Campbell, D. T., Schwartz, R. D., and Sechrest, L. *Unobtrusive Measures: Nonreactive Research in the Social Sciences.* Chicago: Rand McNally & Company, 1966.

Weick, K. E. Systematic Observational Method. In G. Lindzey and E. Aronson, eds., *The Handbook of Social Psychology, Vol. 2* (2nd ed.). Reading, Mass.: Addison-Wesley Publishing Company, 1968.

Wilensky, H. Preschool Observations: Description of Instruments and Findings. Unpublished manuscript, Institute for Developmental Studies, New York Medical College, 1965.

_____. Observational Techniques in Preschool Classrooms. Unpublished manuscript, Institue for Developmental Studies, New York University, 1966.

Withall, J. An Objective Measurement of a Teacher's Classroom Interactions. *Journal of Educational Psychology,* 1956, *47,* 203-212.

Wright, H. F. Observational Child Study. In P. H. Mussen, ed., *Handbook of Research Methods in Child Development.* New York: John Wiley & Sons, 1960.

82

GROUP DYNAMICS

by William McLeod Rivera
Consultant, Education Division
Organization for Economic Cooperation & Development
Paris, France

In any human group of any size there are interrelationships between people—some of which are conscious and overt, others which may be conscious but not revealed, and still others which are unconscious. In general, any attempt to analyze a group on the basis of only the overt, conscious aspects of relationships is tantamount to describing only the tip of an iceberg. Advances in the field of human psychology have inevitably led to scrutiny of the unconscious aspects of relationships of human beings within groups. This scrutiny first came to the fore under the rubric of "group dynamics."

Group dynamics is a socio-psychological term first used by Kurt Lewin.[1] It refers to the aims and methods used by T-groups, sensitivity training, encounter groups, and other group experiences which focus on individuals' feelings and needs, on interpersonal communication, and on learning from the processes occurring within a group. The aim of the group dynamics is to stimulate changes in participants, usually through increased awareness of self and others, improved communication skills, and greater openness towards others. The methods and techniques used in group dynamics vary from program to program, and depend considerably on the style and approach of individual leaders, or facilitators.

Originally the most potent vehicle in the group dynamics movement was the "training group," or T-group, format developed by the National Training Laboratories (NTL), established in 1947 at Bethel, Maine. In a T-group, the participants diagnose and experiment with their own behavior and with their interpersonal relationships within the group. Despite slight variations in group training methods, most people refer to these methods interchangeably as T-groups, sensitivity training, encounter groups, or human relations training.

Although it is difficult to distinguish among different group process methods, encounters generally aim to bring people face to face with the object of analyzing and resolving conflictive tendencies in individual behavior. Sensitivity training utilizes the group process to improve individual's responses to stimulae which awaken sensation or other responses, such as irritability and helplessness. According to one exponent (Blumberg, 1971), group dynamics provides "a learning environment centered upon personal, interpersonal, group, or organizational problems in which the participants can learn and change through an inductive process based on experience."

A MAJOR INTERNATIONAL SOCIAL MOVEMENT

Group dynamics bears the earmarks of a major international social movement. In Mexico, in December 1972, the United Nations Educational, Scientific, and Cultural Organization (Unesco), in conjunction with the Latin American Institute for Educative Communication (ILCE), organized an international round-table on the applications of group techniques to education. Thick reports on the development of applied group dynamics were presented by several countries, including Argentina, France, India, Japan, and the United States. This world interest in group dynamics, and its techniques for promoting value and attitude changes, dates from the end of the 1950s and the early 1960s, when group dynamics techniques became increasingly applied to educational settings.

The spreading application of the encounter format has profound implications for education, organizational development, and mental-health services. In the United States, numerous programs have been developed, including: NTL personal growth encounters and T-groups, gestalt therapy, psychodrama, psychoanalytical encounter groups, transactional analysis, reality therapy, Esalen groups, Rogerian marathon groups, and Bell & Howell PEER tape training. "Today's American," according to Lieberman, Yalom, and Miles (1973), "is likely to face the question of membership in an encounter group."

Early work in group dynamics occurred primarily in business and management services. Detailed discussion of applications and research in this area have been put forward by various authors, among them Bradford, Gibb, and Benne (1964), Burton (1969), and Golembiewski and Blumberg (1970). Much of Lewin's early work at his Research Center in Group Dynamics at the Massachusetts Institute of Technology focused on "action research" to promote among management personnel reduction of conflict in working relationships. Since Lewin's pioneering efforts, "organizational development" through group process techniques has become an integral part of much management training in business and other entrepreneurial enterprises.

More recently, group dynamics—and especially the encounter format—has become a highly significant approach to the problems of mental health and therapy. The work of such well-known figures as Carl Rogers, William Glasser, Eric Berne, and Albert Ellis has developed primarily through the group process approach. Each of these therapists has designed specific techniques for relieving psychic stress among individuals and promoting critical changes in their attitudinal and value orientations. The aims of their programs, in general, are to replace feelings of helplessness, depression, and alienation with those of affiliation, self-awareness, and a realization of self-autonomy.

GROUP DYNAMICS IN EDUCATION

Much attention has been given to the application of knowledge about group dynamics to education. The growing concern to make education more responsive to the social-psychological needs and interests of learners, thereby fostering their academic learning, has promoted widespread efforts to integrate group dynamics into the classroom. In the *Handbook of Research on Teaching* (1963), Withall and Lewis review group processes relevant to education in their chapter on "Social Interaction in the Classroom." Bany and Johnson (1964), in their *Classroom Group Behavior*, also review findings from group dynamics research for its applications to the class setting. Articles in the *Encyclopedia of Educational Research* (Ebel, ed., 1969), for example, have appeared concerning group processes, teacher roles, and teaching methods. In most classroom situations, the objective of group dynamics is to develop cooperation among its members, to encourage identification of group goals, and to promote recognition of group problems. For the teacher, the group dynamics approach helps with the understanding of pupils, acceptance of their points of view, and facilitation of verbal and nonverbal communication.

Numerous innovations within the area of group dynamics in education have been developed since the 1960s. Over and above the influence of T-groups and sensitivity training on classroom methods, new methods have been adopted, such as role-playing, team learning, and simulation gaming. A review of these and other techniques has been made by Crist (1972) in her survey of *Group Dynamics and the Teacher-Student Relationship: A Review of Recent Innovations*.

The changing concept of the teacher's role is that of a guide or helper, rather than lecturer or dispenser of information. Hence, students become active participants into the educational effort, rather than passive receivers of facts and knowledge. This changing concept has large implications for education, today and in the future. It means essentially that more emphasis becomes placed on cooperative, rather than the traditional competitive, training that students normally receive in the schools. To date, numerous efforts have been undertaken in the direction of cooperative training. Such approaches are exemplified by the Philadelphia Affective Education Program (Borton, 1970), the Ford-Esalen Project, based at the Esalen Institute and the University of California at Santa Barbara (Brown, 1971), the Human Development Program, based in San Diego (Bessell, 1968; Palomares, 1970), and the Reality Therapy of William Glasser (1969).

The application of T-group methods has been used in educational settings in the United States on school-wide, city-wide, and curriculum-approach projects. O'Donnell and Maxwell (1971) have reported on the application of "reality therapy" in an elementary school. Again, the approach is that of focusing on the feelings of the individual child about himself and about school. The theory is that through interaction with a responsible and sensitive teacher, who recognizes and accepts each child as a person, the child learns to reflect on his behavior and its consequences and to make responsible choices. In Cleveland, Ohio, a city-wide human relations program has been described by Enterline (1970). An open-ended project, "Project Insight," was one in which teachers used any teaching technique that contributed to the program's purpose, i.e., to develop students' awareness of themselves and to promote a climate for facilitating students' talking about themselves and their relationships with other persons. The basic questions with which the program was concerned included: Who am I? Who or what makes me what I am? What is my worth? Am I important to so-

ciety? How do I communicate with others? The project operated for three years at the time of the report in over 60 elementary and secondary schools throughout the city. Human Development Programs have been carried out in California and Australia. The Bessell-Palomares reports found from subjective reports of teachers that its methods led to fewer disciplinary problems, increased personal involvement, greater self-confidence, verbal expressiveness, motivation, improved comprehension, and promoted social interactions.

A study of group process approaches tends to indicate that both students and teachers react favorably to them. As a result of participating in such group approaches, students generally feel that they develop improved awareness of themselves and others, learn to communicate better and more openly, and develop closer interpersonal relationships with other students, as well as with teachers. Certainly, the group approach represents an important step in the improvement of teacher-student relationships and the advancement of affective-cognitive learning.

GROUP DYNAMICS IN ORGANIZATIONS

An enterprise is usually viewed as an instrument for the transformation of the services of persons and things into a completed product. In order to promote the efficient running of an enterprise, it is essential that the different groups involved (divided into unit, division, department, etc.) work in coordination, and with reasonably decent interrelationships. Group dynamics, through the efforts of Kurt Lewin, Elton Mayo, and numerous others, have become an important part of promoting teamwork through group analysis and interaction. The use of group methods in the improvement of management and worker efficiency is now a well-known practice in the United States and elsewhere.

Group dynamics in industry, often referred to as organizational development, is *à la mode*, as Aubry and Saint-Arnaud recognized back in 1963. Its techniques, while contributing primarily to the values of teamwork and motivation, promote exchanges of information and interpersonal understanding that enterprises today recognize to be essential to the fluid operation of organizations. One facet of group dynamics worth noting is the development of achievement-motivation programs.

Harvard and Wesleyan psychologists McClelland and Winter (1971) have essayed with success in various countries (Italy, India, Japan, Mexico, and the United States) the use of achievement-motivation programs utilizing group dynamics. In their book *Motivating Economic Achievement: Accelerating Economic Development through Psychological Training*, they recount their efforts to promote achievement motivation among entrepreneurs and professional people. They claim that achievement need is a powerful motive that can be catalyzed, stimulated, and even "acquired." During a three-year project in India, undertaken with the financial assistance of the U.S. Agency for International Development (AID), and the collaboration of the Indian Small Industries Extension Training Institute (SIET), in Hyderabad, McClelland and Winter gained evidence to show that the effects of motivation training, combined with group process techniques, were not only immediate but long-run. After a two-year period it was ascertained that course participants remained more active, attempted and started more new business ventures, and mobilized increased amounts of capital and labor. The course participants also tended to have relatively larger increases (as compared with a control group) in gross income over the period studied, 1964-1966.

Systematic thinking about group dynamics, as initiated by Gestalt psychologist Lewin, issued from his quest to discover how people can be stimulated "to behave better" as members in and outside a group. Current advocates of organizational development techniques believe that the individual is definitely a changeable being, and that his potential for change depends on the proper situation and catalytic inputs. Personality structures, they say, are temporary, at least in some individuals, and the right environment and stimulus can alter these structures. Hence, in acquiring new perceptions of himself and of the environment, the individual learns new interrelational habits, which sometimes stimulate major and abrupt changes in his personality and attitudinal structures.

GROUP DYNAMICS AND THERAPY

The notion of major and abrupt changes in individuals' values and attitudes, i.e., critical changes, is the aim of most T-groups, sensitivity training, encounter groups, psychodramas, and other group processes. Various techniques, as noted above, have been developed to foster, in particular, adult critical change. Such changes are considered therapeutic, in that they generally release tension and neurotic tendencies among participants. Some participants describe their critical change experiences in religious terms; others see changes in the way they view themselves and others. And still others find through group experiences that changes come about which help them to resolve certain personal or occupational dilemmas.

Leaders of encounter groups differ considerably in their approaches to the problems of others. Some are primarily analytical and interpretive; others function as managers of group forces; still others offer instructional, often nonverbal exercises. Some believe passionately in the importance of love, and others, just as passionately, in the importance of hatred. The idea of primary rage, as with Janov's "primal scream" therapy, may seem alien to the general drift of encounter purposes, but it apparently serves to release inner turmoil and disturbance among certain individuals. Although these various approaches to changing the individual are often effective, recent studies (Lieberman, Yalom and Miles, 1973) point up the "casualty rate" among encounter participants, and raise the question of the permanency of the changes immediately experienced by participants after a therapeutic group experience.

A CRITIQUE OF LAB EDUCATION

It is obvious that the orientation of the leader of a group, or the general objective of a particular group,

forms the standard by which the individuals in the group will be judged. To understand the human process, it is necessary to see clearly that human development is not a process involving one mode of being. It is one thing in a one-to-one relationship to make no claim to absolute truth, and to provide only an individual judgment of an individual's behavior or beliefs. It is quite another to offer the judgment in public, especially within the framework of a group, where the judgment thereby becomes a group judgment. It requires great strength of purpose, and intellectual and emotional clarity, to maintain a position against an onslaught of opposition, especially from those who claim to have one's best interests at heart. An enactive, or kinetic, type of person may readily become self-doubtful before a symbolic-oriented group, or vice-versa.

As is well known from psychological research (Rosenthal, 1966; Friedman, 1967), the most important variable in an educational experience is the variable of what the experimenter expects to happen. Expectations for behavior have a strong influence on what kind of behavior is expressed. Edgar Lee Masters, a great American poet, realized this, and wrote about the importance of expectation for behavior in a superb poem entitled "Aner Clute" (1914), which reads in part:

> Suppose a boy steals an apple
> From a tray at the grocery store,
> And they all begin to call him a thief,
> The editor, minister, judge, and all the people—
> "A thief," "a thief," "a thief," wherever he goes,
> And he can't get work, and he can't get bread
> Without stealing it, why the boy will steal.
> It's the way the people regard the theft of the apple
> That makes the boy what he is.

Encounter and sensitivity training, though often highly effective, tends to become 1) an instrument for adaptive, adjustive resocialization and social integration; 2) an educational tool which promotes personal reconstruction, but not with a view to social reconstruction; and 3) a value-medium which operates to discourage the intellectual, symbolic mode and to disapprove independence regarding task-orientation. In other words, it often attacks the nonconformist as deviant.

Generally speaking, much depends on the leader of a group and his or her particular values and attitudes. The importance of expectations in influencing individuals cannot be denied. Although group dynamics doubtless merits its current and widespread popularity, vigilance and a critical approach to the subject are also needed. The teacher, the organizational developer, and the therapeutic facilitator must be clear not only as to the internal changes sought, but also their consequences for society as a whole. It is all well and good to praise cooperation over competition, for instance, but quite another when cooperation signifies merely adaptive, functional orientations.

SUMMARY

Group dynamics is a major international social movement which is growing in size and influence. The proliferation of this approach and its various techniques within education establishments, organizations, and therapeutic groups is so great that the term "encounter" has become practically a household word. Interest in this approach is not only widespread but valid in many respects, though further critical analysis of its significance and consequences is required.

While a significant tool for education and organizational teamwork, some questions remain as to the use of group dynamics for therapeutical purposes. Before "today's American" decides upon joining an encounter group, he might well ask himself beforehand what kind of changes he wants to see come about in himself, and what sort of changes are likely to be stimulated by the particular group he proposes to join. And finally, he might ask what those changes mean for the local, national, and international society in which he belongs.

Group dynamics, nevertheless, as its exponents claim, is a useful means of promoting openness and communication. As such, it is an approach to interrelationships that promises to improve the mental awareness and flexibility of the individual. In the final analysis, it is an alternative approach to authoritarian teaching and dictatorial management, as well as a valuable means of avoiding costly and long-term analysis of people in times of stress.

NOTES

[1]The term "group dynamics" first appeared in *The Harvard Educational Review* in 1939.

REFERENCES

Aubry, J-M., and Saint-Arnaud, Y. *Dynamique des Groupes.* Paris: Editions Universitaires, 1963.

Bany, M. A., and Johnson, L. V. *Classroom Group Behavior.* New York: Macmillan, 1964.

Bessell, H. The Content is the Medium: The Confidence is the Message. In *Psychology Today, 1*(8), 1968, pp. 32-35, 61.

Blumberg, A. *Sensitivity Training: Processes, Problems and Applications.* Syracuse, N.Y.: Syracuse University, Publications in Continuing Education: Notes and Essays on Education of Adults, No. 68, 1971.

Borton, T. *Reach, Touch and Teach.* New York: McGraw-Hill, 1970.

Bradford, L. P., Gibb, J. R., and Benne, K. D., eds. *T-Group Theory and Laboratory Method.* N.Y.: John Wiley, 1964.

Brown, G. I. *Human Teaching for Human Learning.* New York: Viking Press, 1971.

Crist, J. *Group Dynamics and the Teacher-Student Relationship: A Review of Recent Innovations.* Stanford, Calif.: Stanford University, Stanford Center for Research and Development in Teaching, 1972.

Enterline, J. Project Insight. In *Grade Teacher, 88*(3), 1970, pp. 32-34.

Friedman, N. *The Social Nature of Psychological Research: The Psychological Experiment as a Social Interaction.* New York: Basic Books, 1967.

Glasser, W. *Schools without Failure.* New York: Harper & Row, 1969.

Golembiewski, R. T., and Blumberg, A, eds. *Sensitivity Training and the Laboratory Approach.* Itasca, Ill.: F. E. Peacock, 1970.

Lewin, K. *Resolving Social Conflicts: Selected Papers on Group Dynamics.* New York: Harper Bros., 1948.

Lieberman, M. A., Yalom, I. D., and Miles, M. B. Encounter: The Leader makes the Difference. In *Psychology Today, 6*(10), March 1973, pp. 69-76.

McClelland, D. C., and Winter, D. G. *Motivating Economic Achievement: Accelerating Economic Development through Psychological Training,* New York: The Free Press, 1971.

O'Donnell, D. J., and Maxwell, K. Reality Therapy Works Here. In *Instructor, 80*(7), 1971, pp. 70-73.

Palomares, U. H. Communication Begins with Attitude. In *The National Elementary Principal, 37*(2), 1970, pp. 81-82.

Rosenthal, R. *Experimenter Effects in Behavioral Research.* New York: Appleton-Century-Crofts, 1966.

UNESCO: *Table Ronde sur les Applications des Techniques de Groupe à l'Education.* Paris: UNESCO document EDS/ 2232/0109, 1972.

83

TREATMENT APPROACHES TO SCHOOL PHOBIA

by Eugene W. Kelly, Jr.
Assistant Professor, School of Education
Old Dominion University
Norfolk, Virginia

School phobia is characterized by an extreme reluctance or outright refusal to go to school, as a result of severe anxiety and a dread of some aspect of the school situation. It is accompanied by somatic symptoms that are used as a device to remain at home, and that often disappear once the child is assured that he does not have to attend school (Waldfogel, Coolidge, and Hahn, 1957).

School phobia is distinguished from other forms of school refusal. Johnson, Falstein, Szurek, and Svendsen (1941) noted in their early studies on school phobia that the condition is "fairly sharply differentiated from the more frequent and common delinquent variety of school truancy," and is recognizable by the intense terror associated with being at school, absence maintained over weeks or months, and a neurotic clinging to mother and refusal to leave home (also Millar, 1961). These symptoms are rarely found in the truant (Goldenberg and Goldenberg, 1970). The truant, for example, not only avoids school, but also is usually away from home during his absences. School phobia is also differentiated from the case in which a child is withdrawn from school by the parents for their own purposes (Kahn, 1968; Kahn and Nursten, 1962).

Behavioral symptoms that accompany school phobia include a wide range of somatic complaints (Leventhal, Wineberger, Stander, and Stearns, 1967), such as nausea, vomiting, and other abdominal complaints (Coolidge, Tessman, Waldfogel, and Willer, 1962), and acute panic reactions at school (Talbot, 1957). It is found more frequently in younger children (Davidson, 1961; Leton, 1962), but usually is more serious when it occurs in adolescents (Coolidge, Willer, Tessman, and Waldfogel, 1960). Smith (1970) found that it has a higher incidence in the youngest child in the family. Early data suggested that it occurs most often in average to bright children (Jackson, 1964; Rodriguez, Rodriguez, and Eisenberg, 1959), but more recent research indicates that intelligence is probably distributed among school phobics as it is distributed in the general population (Hampe, Miller, Barrett, and Noble, 1973). If the condition is not resolved during school years, it may result in a form of work phobia in which the adult clings to a familiar setting, such as home, and avoids work and the somatic discomfort it produces (Pittman, Langsley, and DeYoung, 1968; Radin, 1972).

Although the exact frequency of school phobia is not known, it appears to be increasing (Jarvis, 1964; Kahn et al., 1962). Kennedy (1965) gives a figure of 17 cases per 1,000 school children each school year. The impression of many authors that it is more prevalent among girls than boys is not supported by figures indicating about equal occurrence for both sexes (Waldfogel et al., 1967).

TREATMENT APPROACHES

A review of the literature reveals that a variety of theoretical explanations, based on clinical experience, diagnostic testing, and systematic behavioral observation, are given for school phobia. As might be expected, there are also a variety of treatment procedures. Although there is considerable overlapping among these explanations and treatment approaches, it is possible to group them into three broad categories: learning theory or behavioral approaches, psychoanalytic approaches, and nonanalytic psychodynamic approaches.

BEHAVIORAL APPROACHES

Behavioral approaches to the understanding and treatment of school phobia are particularly prominent in recent literature (Hersen, 1971). Behaviorists offer a parsimonious explanation of school phobia on the basis of stimulus-response conditioning and learned maladaptive ways of behaving. These explanations utilize the theoretical models of both classical conditioning (learning via the pairing of stimulus and response) and operant conditioning (learning via the subsequent reinforcement of responses). In behavioral terms, then, school phobia is a conditioned fear and avoidance response which is frequently reinforced by the circumstances that prevail when the child stays at home. Garvey and Hegrenes (1966) offer a specific example of this kind of learning: the child fears loss of his mother as a result of her comments about leaving, and this fear becomes verbally conditioned to ideas about going to school, where he would "lose" his mother. When his fear of school becomes intense, he refuses to go, and staying at home is reinforced because it reduces fear and usually provides other rewards, such as toys and affection.

In the learning theory approach to school phobia, behavioral events, rather than underlying dynamics, are examined in order to establish an appropriate treatment. Stress is placed upon the application of broad learning principles, such as reinforcement via approximations, counterconditioning, desensitization, and interference. The application of behavioral approaches are, however, not instituted arbitrarily, or prior to the determination of the factors that are contributing to the phobia. In each case, an understanding of the relative contribution of the circumstances of conditioned fear (classical conditioning model) and the contingencies of reinforcement (operant conditioning model) will facilitate effective treatment (Lazarus, Davison, and Polefka, 1965).

EXAMPLES OF BEHAVIORAL TREATMENT

Lazarus et al. (1965) describe the successful treatment of a nine-year-old male school phobic with the careful and deliberate use of both classical and operant conditioning methods at crucial phases throughout a four-and-one-half-month period. A long-term shaping process was used, in which the child was gradually reintroduced to school, an example of desensitization in vivo. As the boy's school attendance was gradually reestablished, a system of rewards was established to reinforce him in his new behavior. A follow-up ten months subsequent to the termination of treatment showed that his school attendance was normal.

Successful treatment of school phobia frequently requires close cooperation among school personnel, professional therapists, and the child's parents (Edlund, 1971; Kennedy, 1965; D. L. Miller, 1972). Hersen (1970) reports the successful treatment of a 12½-year-old white male school phobic through the use of a three-part behavior modification program that included cooperation of the boy's parents and school counselor with the therapist. Following the directions of the therapist, the parents kindly but firmly insisted that the boy attend school, and ignored any complaints related to school or discussion of avoiding school. During brief and intermittent contact with the boy during school time, the counselor expressed understanding of his feelings, but otherwise avoided any extended discussion with him. During individual interviews with the boy, the therapist verbally reinforced any evidence of school-approach or independent behavior.

Edlund (1971) describes a school-home behavioral training program in which both school personnel and parents carried out a specific, day-by-day program to eliminate the school avoidance and accompanying crying behavior of a seven-year-old girl. The program was explained to the child by both her teacher and parents. The teacher constructed a daily checklist, which included a frame for each assignment period, and when the child completed an assignment without crying the teacher praised her, and gave her a check on the chart. The chart was taken home each day after school. The parents gave praise for the checks, transferred the checks to a special home chart, and gave activity rewards for the accumulation of specific numbers of checks. Crying behavior ceased completely after four days, and did not recur. The child attended summer school after the regular session with no recurrence of avoidance or crying behavior.

Tahmisian and McReynolds (1971) have highlighted

the important role that parents can play in a behavioral treatment program for a school-phobic child. They report that the parents of a 13-year-old school-phobic girl were trained to use instrumental, behavior-shaping procedures in which the girl was gradually carried through a 15-step school-approach hierarchy, with appropriate rewards for success and no rewards for school-avoidance behavior. Three weeks after the initiation of the treatment the girl was attending school regularly, and a four-week follow-up showed that she had maintained her progress. Total time expended by the therapist was two hours: 90 minutes for instruction and training of the parents and 30 minutes in three follow-up calls.

Kennedy (1965) describes a comprehensive treatment procedure, which emphasizes the need for close cooperation among school, home, and clinic. The first step in this procedure is the correct diagnosis of the type of school phobia which is amenable to his rapid treatment approach. He offers ten behaviorally-oriented criteria by which two types of school phobia (Coolidge, Hahn, and Peck, 1957) can be distinguished. Type 1, which is a neurotic-type, is diagnosed when seven of the following 10 symptoms are present: (1) present illness is first episode; (2) Monday onset, subsequent to an illness the previous Thursday or Friday; (3) an acute onset; (4) subject in lower grades; (5) expressed concern about death; (6) mother's physical health in question; (7) good communication between parents; (8) mother and father well adjusted in most areas; (9) father competitive with mother in household management; (10) parents achieve understanding of dynamics easily. When seven or more of these symptoms are not present, type 2 school phobia, a more resistant form, is diagnosed. The procedural components for treating type 1 school phobia are: (a) good professional public relations, to ensure ready cooperation in identification and treatment of the phobia; (b) avoidance of emphasis on somatic complaints; (c) forced school attendance; (d) structured interviews with parents, to enable them to carry out the therapeutic program in the face of considerable resistance from the child; (e) brief interviews with child, to encourage him to carry on in the face of fear; and (f) follow-up for further support of the parents. Kennedy's report of a success rate of 50 out of 50 for type 1 school phobia suggests that this approach deserves careful consideration by school personnel and therapists.

A frequently used behavioral procedure in the treatment of school phobia is systematic desensitization, either of the imaginal or in vivo type. In the former, a hierarchy of behaviors gradually approaching the target behavior (i.e., full school attendance) is established, and the subject is helped to imagine these behaviors while he is in a relaxed state. He is thereby gradually desensitized with regard to his fear of school. In vivo desensitization is a procedure in which the subject is gradually reintroduced to the school itself (e.g., in terms of time, distance, or separation from parents).

Lazarus (1960) reported the successful treatment of a nine-and-one-half-year-old school-phobic girl with the use of imaginal desensitization, using a seven-item hierarchy centering on gradually increasing periods of separation between the child and her mother. After five sessions

over ten consecutive days, the child willingly went to school, and a 15-month follow-up showed that she had maintained an "eminently satisfactory level of adjustment." Lazarus and Abromovitz (1962) report the use of "emotive imagery," a variant of systematic desensitization, with an eight-year-old enuretic and school-phobic girl. In this procedure, the child's task was to play an imaginary role in which she helped her hero image, "Noddy," gradually overcome his fear of school. School-phobic tendencies were extinguished in four sessions, and enuresis disappeared within two months.

Patterson (1965) reports the use of several behavioral techniques, including desensitization and positive reinforcement, with a seven-year-old boy in the context of semi-play sessions. A doll, with whom the boy identified, was used as the center of stories in which the hero gradually overcame his fear of school. In this manner the boy's fear of approaching school was gradually resolved. M&Ms and verbal praise were used for reinforcement. Interviews were held with the parents to instruct them on how to encourage and reinforce at home the boy's independent and school approach behavior. The boy was gradually reintroduced to school and was going full-time by the eleventh session.

P. M. Miller (1972) reports the case of a ten-year-old multiphobic boy who was successfully treated using systematic desensitization both imaginally and in vivo. Imaginal desensitization was successful in getting the boy to agree to gradually return to the classroom, a thought previously unacceptable to him. At this point in vivo desensitization, via self-induced muscle relaxation, was used to help him gradually increase the length of time he spent near and in the school. Full school attendance was attained by the fifth week after initial re-entry and was maintained for the remaining three and one-half months of school.

Kelly (1971) describes the case of an eight-year-old black female who was treated with in vivo desensitization which relied heavily on the cooperation of the child's parents, teacher, and the school principal and his secretary. On the basis of Kennedy's (1965) diagnostic criteria, it was determined that the girl was amenable to rapid treatment, but, because of her severe panic behavior while on the way to and in school, she should be gradually reintroduced to school. The school counselor helped all the above-mentioned adults understand the elements contributing to the phobia, and elicited their cooperation in keeping the child (and themselves) calm as she gradually returned to school and they praised her for her successes. At first the child returned to school for a half an hour after the other children were dismissed, and the teacher worked with her during this time. Gradually she was brought to school at progressively earlier times. Eighteen days after the treatment was begun, she was attending school all day without crying. On the 64th day she briefly reverted to her panicky behavior. She was calmed and returned to school normally every day thereafter for the remaining two and one-half months.

Desensitizing a school-phobic child in vivo obviously requires the cooperation and/or understanding of school personnel and parents. For example, in a case reported by Garvey et al. (1966), the cooperation and approval of school authorities was obtained to reduce gradually a ten-year-old school-phobic boy's fear of entering and remaining in school. A hierarchy of approach behaviors was established, which included the patient's sitting with the therapist in an automobile in front of school (step 1), leaving automobile and approaching curb (step 2), going to door of school (step 6), entering classroom (step 8), being present in classroom with teacher (step 10), and being present in classroom with full class (step 12). A step was not taken until it could be accomplished in a relatively relaxed manner. For each success the child was given praise by the therapist. The child's phobia was resolved, and a two-year follow-up revealed no remission. Brown, Copeland, and Hall (1974) describe a program in which a gradual return to school, combined with systematic reinforcement, was successfully carried out by an elementary school principal. An 11-year-old school-phobic boy was able to earn football game tickets for himself and his mother by returning first to the school library, then the hall or classroom, and finally the classroom only.

Ayllon, Smith, and Rogers (1970) give a detailed report of the behavioral procedures used to treat an eight-year-old Negro girl from a low-income area. The procedures included desensitization in vivo (increasing amounts of time spent in school each day, starting with short periods near the end of the school day) to initiate school attendance, and, in order to maintain it, the withdrawal of rewards for staying at home; and the establishment of home-based rewards for attendance and punishment for refusal to attend. A nine-month follow-up, subsequent to the child's return to school, showed that she was attending school regularly and performing well academically and socially.

In a study reported by Lowenstein (1973), systematic desensitization was complemented with the use of a treatment approach called "negative practice." In negative practice the subject visualizes and discusses the feared object, in this case school, until fatigue and boredom are developed and the feared object is no longer considered with so much aversion. Lowenstein found that systematic desensitization treatment for five weeks, followed by negative practice treatment for five weeks, resulted in significant improvement in academic performance and reduction of personal distress for six school phobics, ages 9-14 years. A six-month follow-up showed that the improvements were maintained.

Implosive therapy is a form of behavioral treatment based on classical conditioning principles related to the extinction of anxiety responses. In this technique the therapist induces high anxiety in the patient with the use of vivid images of the feared situation or object. Repeated experiences of this image-produced anxiety, in the absence of the actual feared object and real-life aversive consequences, gradually bring about an extinction of the phobia. Smith and Sharpe (1970) report that with the use of this technique in six therapy sessions they enabled a 13-year-old school-phobic boy to return to school and establish a successful pattern of academic and social behavior.

PSYCHOANALYTIC APPROACHES

Until recently, when behavioral approaches began to predominate, the bulk of the literature on school phobia contained psychoanalytically oriented explanations of school phobia and treatment approaches. The psychoanalytic explanations generally stress the overdependency fostered in the child by a mother who herself is often mildly neurotic, and whose own dependency needs frequently are unresolved (Berg, Nichols, and Pritchard, 1969; Klein, 1945). This dependency creates repressed hostility in both the child and mother (Coolidge et al., 1957; Coolidge et al., 1962; Davidson, 1961; Johnson et al., 1941; Talbot, 1957; Waldfogel et al., 1957), and in the child especially a fear of separation (Johnson, 1957; Olsen and Coleman, 1967; Talbot, 1957). The dependency, fear, and hostility inhibit the ego development of the child, and the fear is displaced onto the school as the child anxiously clings to his mother in unresolved dependency (Berg and McGuire, 1971; Broadwin, 1932; Coolidge et al., 1957; Johnson et al., 1941; Millar, 1961; Suttenfield, 1954; Talbot, 1957; Waldfogel et al., 1957). The child attempts to control his anxiety by avoiding the fearful school situation.

In addition to their fear of school, many school-phobic children manifest a more generalized fear of separation from their mother or either of their parents. According to some authorities, school phobia is a specific manifestation of separation anxiety (Johnson, 1957; D. L. Miller, 1972; Olsen et al., 1967; Talbot, 1957). Adams, McDonald, and Huey (1970), and D. L. Miller (1972), have suggested that separation anxiety develops with resistance in the whole individuation and sex-typing process. Other evidence suggests that separation anxiety originated in the parents, who subtly communicate it to their child (Eisenberg, 1958). While separation anxiety may be prominent in younger children, the phobia of older children appears generally to be specific to school (Smith, 1970), and is characterized by withdrawal and depression (Agras, 1959).

Psychoanalytically oriented therapists stress the need of psychotherapy in depth, insight, and the building up of ego-strength and family equilibrium. Therapy is sometimes indicated for the whole family in order to restore balance in family interactions (Davidson, 1961; Messer, 1964), and for the mother in particular in order to resolve her dependency needs and other conflicts (Johnson et al., 1941; Waldfogel et al., 1957). Extensive therapy is suggested to resolve the underlying neurosis (Klein, 1945), but initial action is directed primarily toward symptom relief and a quick return to school.

Coolidge et al. (1957) distinguish between two types of school phobia. The first, termed "neurotic," is in the context of a fairly sound personality and is more amenable to short-term, outpatient therapy. The second, "characterological," is part of a more pervasive and complex personality disorder. For the latter type of school phobia, hospitalization may be beneficial or necessary. Residential treatment should provide an opportunity for the child not only to resolve his fear and dependency needs, but also to make some academic progress in class or group learning experiences (Berg, 1970; Weiss and Burke, 1967; Weiss and Cain, 1964).

Good results are generally reported by psychoanalytically oriented therapists (Coolidge, Brodie, and Feeny, 1964; Johnson et al., 1941; Suttenfield, 1954; Waldfogel, Tessman, and Hahn, 1959; Weiss et al., 1967).

DYNAMIC AND OTHER APPROACHES

Leventhal and Sills (1964) and Radin (1968) suggest that underlying the manifestations of school phobia is a cycle of fear and power. According to this theory, faulty attitudes on the part of the parents cause a school-phobic child to overvalue himself and his achievements, and there is a blurring of the child's ego and ego-ideal. When he goes to school, his unrealistic self-image is threatened by realistic evaluation there; he experiences severe anxiety and runs home to preserve his self-image of power or omnipotence. At home he is frequently succored and indulged by a permissive mother, thereby reinforcing his school avoidance behavior.

In order to resolve the phobia, it is necessary to interrupt this cycle by reducing the child's fears, correcting parental attitudes, and replacing fear with pleasure as a motive (Radin, 1968). According to Leventhal et al. (1967), the power issue must be resolved through a carefully planned strategy in which the child is consistently "outmaneuvered" and persistently pressured, with increasing insistence, to return to and remain in school. A successful application of this approach is described by Weinberger, Leventhal, and Beckman (1973). A school psychologist, with the cooperation of a consulting clinical psychologist and a school guidance counselor, directed a program in which the parents of a 15-year-old school-phobic girl were given sufficient understanding, direction, and support to firmly insist on and enforce their daughter's return to school. A key to the success of the program was the parents' firmness in requiring school attendance, not accepting baseless excuses, and personally seeing that the girl got to school.

Bolman (1967, 1970) has recommended a systems theory approach to the understanding and treatment of the entire school refusal syndrome. In this approach, school refusal is defined and delimited on several different levels, ranging from common truancy to the more serious psychological and behavioral disturbances of school phobia proper. The mode of treatment appropriate to each case of school phobia is based on the form of school refusal diagnosed. For example, a school refusal with a basically organismic cause, such as minimal brain damage, may be treated with medication, while the use of medication in case of classical school phobia, rooted in intrafamilial conflicts, may be harmful. Bolman makes a good point, rarely mentioned by other authors, that a factor contributing to some cases of school phobia may be the fortress-type school that is fearful of the surrounding community. Such a school is constantly on guard, ready to strike back against a community perceived as hostile. It is not difficult to understand how some children would find such a school forbidding, even terrifying. Where such a school exists, community action may be necessary to open up and change the spirit of the school.

Somewhat analogous to the institutional hostility of the fortress school is the animosity that school phobia appears to provoke in some school personnel (Jarvis, 1964). The school-phobic child's extreme resistance to adults' demands that he attend school may provoke in them a deep anger, and a desire to punish the child and get him to school quickly at any cost. Such an approach not only needlessly increases the anguish of the child, but it is also doomed to failure.

Marine (1968) has offered a fourfold categorization of school phobia for diagnostic and treatment purposes. In the first category, simple separation anxiety, the child tries to avoid school by clinging to his mother and tearfully begging to go home. Kind but firm measures for school attendance by the teacher and parents are usually enough to obtain normal attendance. The second category, mild school refusal, is comparable to Kennedy's type 1 school phobia, and is usually treatable through the cooperative efforts of the teacher, school nurse, guidance counselor, and family pediatrician. Category three, chronic school refusal, is comparable to Kennedy's type 2, and usually requires the attention of a psychologist or mental health team. The fourth category is a severe form of childhood psychosis, and requires extensive psychiatric treatment and perhaps hospitalization. In a study of 200 school phobics treated either by school system personnel or at a child guidance clinic, Marine (1973) found that children in her first category indeed responded well to anticipatory guidance, while crisis intervention by appropriate school personnel and mental health workers achieved good results with children in category two.

The use of drugs or medication in the treatment of school phobia has been described by Nice (1968) and Rabiner and Klein (1969). In the former case, sodium pentothal was used to alleviate the patient's fear, thereby enabling him to discuss his condition more calmly with the therapist. Rabiner et al. (1969) reported successful use of imipramine to inhibit the panic attacks of separation anxiety. Lazarus et al. (1965) have suggested that in some cases a placebo may be sufficient to inhibit the development of somatic complaints that accompany school phobia. However, Gittelman-Klein and Klein (1973) found that in the treatment of 35 six-to-14-year-old school phobics, a multidiscipline therapeutic approach with the use of imipramine treatment was significantly superior to similar treatment with the use of a placebo. They noted that side effects of the drugs were not significant. Saraf et al. (1974) reported in another study that 83 percent of a group of 65 school-phobic and hyperkinetic children (ages 6–14) who received imipramine treatment experienced minor side effects, as compared with minor side effects in 70 percent of a group of 37 children who received a placebo. A little less than five percent of the children on imipramine had significant side effects, but none serious enough to require drug withdrawal. However, the authors suggest that physicians use caution in the use of high dosages, since these may interact adversely with individual idiosyncracies.

SUMMARY AND RECOMMENDATIONS

School phobia, if neglected or treated improperly, is a condition with serious psychological and academic consequences. A key to rapid and successful treatment is early detection, intervention and prevention. Teachers and principals, as well as special school personnel such as counselors and school nurses, should be aware of the prominent signs of school phobia: extreme resistance to attending school, various somatic complaints that result from attempts to force school attendance, and a clinging to the home environment. In the case of very mind school phobia or simple separation anxiety (crying, hanging back from school, holding onto mother), a sensitive and informed teacher or principal, who acts with kindness and firmness, may play an important part in helping the child (and his parents) overcome this crisis and attain normal school attendance.

Behavioral techniques have been shown to be quite successful in the treatment of many cases of school phobia. Particularly useful is the process of desensitization, both imaginal and in vivo, in which a child's fear is progressively reduced by gradually reintroducing him to school. At each step the child is kept in a state of relative calm, so that his fear gradually dissipates as he approaches normal school attendance. Also important to the behavioral treatment of school phobia is the appropriate and systematic reinforcement of each of the child's successful steps toward independent and school-attending behavior. Rewards for his new behavior should come both in his home and at school. Even some mild punishment, when used in conjunction with positive reinforcement and desensitization, may be useful. Parents and school personnel should exhibit understanding of the child's fear, but avoid extended conversations with the child about his school fears. Somatic complaints and symptoms (e.g., stomachache) which have been diagnosed by a physician as nonorganic in origin should be handled in a matter-of-fact manner, and generally not allowed to impede the reestablishment of school attendance.

Most authorities agree that it is essential to get the school-phobic child back to school as soon as possible, even if only for a short while each day. Some authors suggest that it is useful to exert considerable pressure to force a child to return to school, but most appear to recommend a more gradual return which stresses appropriate timing, desensitizing of fears, and specific procedures to support and direct the parents as well as the school-phobic child (Lassers, Nordan, and Bladholm, 1973). The evidence indicates that early, simple forms of school phobia will yield to a kind but firm insistence on return to school, while more chronic or severe forms will require a gradual return.

Lazarus and Salzman (1972) suggest that behavioral explanations of phobia may be incomplete, in that they overlook unconscious conflicts present in the genesis and maintenance of the phobia. Indeed, there is extensive clinical evidence that the school-phobic child is excessively dependent on an overly protective mother and/or father, and this overdependency creates a repressed hostility and fear in both the child and his parents (most usually the mother). It is frequently beneficial, therefore, for the parents to be helped to gain some insight into the dependency conflicts and helped to encourage and support more independent behavior by the child. Kelly (1973) has suggested that fear in an older school-phobic child may be based on his anxiety to establish his own strong ego-identity, rather than on a dependency struggle based on anxiety about separation from parents. Getting these adolescent school phobics back to school quickly, and providing them opportunities for success and insight, will give them direct evidence about their worthiness as individuals, thereby fostering their self-acceptance as well as obtaining their compliance to school attendance rules.

In those cases where the phobia is long-standing, resistant to symptom-specific treatment, and complicated by other neurotic tendencies in the child and/or family, a more extensive clinical diagnosis with resulting intensive treatment may be necessary. Medication and the therapeutic use of drugs may be indicated. However, institutionalization and drug therapy should be regarded as drastic measures for severely disturbed children, and should not be used by parents or school personnel as a method to handle difficult or troublesome children.

The school, and indeed certain aspects of the culture itself (Goldenberg et al., 1970), may contribute to the development of school phobia. Schools that are rigid, hostile, or antagonistic toward the community may aggravate a child's personal struggle with his fear of school. Racial and ethnic factors, and the growing role of the woman in careers outside the home, may disturb the relationship between a child and his school and between the school and the community. These environmental and cultural factors, when relevant to the treatment of a particular case of school phobia, need to be considered in addition to the classic psychodynamic factors.

The literature on school phobia is rich with research and clinical and theoretical information for the understanding and treatment of the condition. This survey suggests that well-informed parents and school personnel are in a position to deal effectively with early and simple forms of school phobia. Many of the methods of treatment that are available have been outlined. More severe forms of school phobia will need specialized treatment. In any case, the consequences of neglecting or mistreating the condition, especially in a society where school attendance and independent behavior are crucial to an effective and satisfying way of life, are so serious that school personnel and school-related therapists should be prepared to intervene and initiate effective preventive or remediative measures.

REFERENCES

Adams, P. O., McDonald, N. J., and Huey, W. P. School Phobia and Bisexual Conflict: A Report of 21 Cases. *The American Journal of Psychiatry,* 1966, *123,* 541-547.

Agras, S. The Relationship of School Phobia to Childhood Depression. *The American Journal of Psychiatry,* 1959, *116,* 533-536.

Ayllon, T., Smith, D., and Rogers, M. Behavioral Management of School Phobia. *Journal of Behavioral Therapy and Experimental Psychiatry,* 1970, *1,* 125-138.

Berg, I., and McGuire, R. Are School Phobic Adolescents Overdependent? *British Journal of Psychiatry,* 1971, *119,* 167-168.

_____, Nichols, K., and Pritchard, C. School Phobia—Its Classification and Relationship to Dependency. *Journal of Child Psychology and Psychiatry and Allied Disciplines,* 1969, *10,* 123-141.

Bolman, W. M. A Behavioral Systems Analysis of the School Refusal Syndrome. *American Journal of Orthopsychiatry,* 1967, *37,* 348-349.

_____. Systems Theory, Psychiatry, and School Phobia. *The American Journal of Psychiatry,* 1970, *127,* 25-32.

Broadwin, I. A Contribution to the Study of Truancy. *American Journal of Orthopsychiatry,* 1932, *2,* 253-259.

Brown, R. E., Copeland, R. E., and Hall, R. V. School Phobia: Effects of Behavior Modification Treatment Applied by an Elementary School Principal. *Child Study Journal,* 1974, *4,* 125-133.

Coolidge, J. C., Brodie, B. D., and Feeny, B. A Ten-Year Follow-Up Study of Sixty-Six School Phobic Children. *American Journal of Orthopsychiatry,* 1964, *34,* 675-684.

_____, Hahn, P. B., and Peck, A. L. School Phobia: Neurotic Crisis or Way of Life. *American Journal of Orthopsychiatry,* 1957, *27,* 296-306.

_____, Tessman, E., Waldfogel, S., and Willer, M. L. Patterns of Aggression in School Phobia. *Psychoanalytic Studies of the Child,* 1962, *17,* 319-333.

_____, Willer, M. L., Tessman, E., and Waldfogel, S. School Phobia in Adolescence: A Manifestation of Severe Character Disturbance. *American Journal of Orthopsychiatry,* 1960, *30,* 599-607.

Davidson, S. School Phobia as a Manifestation of Family Disturbance: Its Structure and Treatment. *Journal of Child Psychology and Psychiatry and Allied Disciplines,* 1961, *1,* 270-287.

Edlund, C. V. A Reinforcement Approach to the Elimination of a Child's School Phobia. *Mental Hygiene,* 1971, *55,* 433-436.

Eisenberg, L. School Phobia: A Study in the Communication of Anxiety. *American Journal of Psychiatry,* 1958, *114,* 712-718.

Garvey, W. P., and Hegrenes, J. R. Desensitization Techniques in the Treatment of School Phobia. *American Journal of Orthopsychiatry,* 1966, *36,* 147-152.

Gittelman-Klein, R., and Klein, D. F. School Phobia: Diagnostic Considerations in the Light of Imipramine Effects. *Journal of Nervous and Mental Disease,* 1973, *156,* 199-215.

Goldenberg, H., and Goldenberg, I. School Phobia: Childhood Neurosis or Learned Maladaptive Behavior? *Exceptional Children,* 1970, *37,* 220-226.

Hampe, E., Miller, L., Barrett, C., and Noble, H. Intelligence and School Phobia. *Journal of School Psychology,* 1973, *11,* 66-70.

Hersen, M. Behavior Modification Approach to a School-Phobia Case. *Journal of Clinical Psychology,* 1970, *26,* 128-132.

_____. The Behavioral Treatment of School Phobia. *Journal of Nervous and Mental Disease,* 1971, *153,* 99-107.

Jackson, L. Anxiety in Adolescents in Relation to School Refusal. *Journal of Child Psychology and Psychiatry and Allied Disciplines,* 1964, *5,* 59-73.

Jarvis, V. Countertransference in the Management of School Phobia. *Psychoanalytic Quarterly,* 1964, *33,* 411-419.

Johnson, A. M. Discussion on School Phobia. *American Journal of Orthopsychiatry,* 1957, *27,* 307-309.

_____, Falstein, E. J., Szurek, S. A., and Svendsen, M. School Phobia. *American Journal of Orthopsychiatry,* 1941, *11,* 702-711.

Kahn, J. H. School Phobia. *Acta Paedopsychiatria,* 1968, *35,* 4-10 (*Psychological Abstracts,* 1968, *42,* 1758).

_____, and Nursten, J. P. School Refusal: A Comprehensive View of School Phobia and Other Failures of School Attendance.

American Journal of Orthopsychiatry, 1962, *32,* 707-718.

Kelly, E. W. Jr. Extinguishing School Phobia: A Cast Study. Unpublished manuscript, Old Dominion University, 1971.

_____. School Phobia: A Review of Theory and Treatment. *Psychology in the Schools,* 1973, *10,* 35-42.

Kennedy, W. A. School Phobia: Rapid Treatment of Fifty Cases. *Journal of Abnormal Psychology,* 1965, *70,* 285-289.

Klein, E. The Reluctance to Go to School. *Psychoanalytic Study of the Child,* 1945, *1,* 263-279.

Lassers, E., Nordan, R., and Bladholm, S. Steps in the Return to School of Children with School Phobia. *American Journal of Psychiatry,* 1973, *130,* 265-268.

Lazarus, A. A. The Elimination of Children's Phobias by Deconditioning. In H. Eysenck, ed., *Behavior Therapy and the Neuroses.* New York: Pergamon Press, 1960.

_____, and Abramovitz, A. The Use of Emotive Imagery in the Treatment of Children's Phobias. *Journal of Mental Science,* 1962, *108,* 191-195.

_____, Davison, G. C., and Polefka, D. A. Classical and Operant Factors in the Treatment of School Phobia. *Journal of Abnormal Psychology,* 1965, *70,* 225-229.

_____, and Salzman, L. Phobias: Broad-Spectrum Behavioral Views. *Seminars in Psychiatry,* 1972, *42,* 85-92.

Leton, D. A. Assessment of School Phobia. *Mental Hygiene,* 1962, *46,* 256-264.

Leventhal, T., and Sills, M. Self-Image in School Phobia. *American Journal of Orthopsychiatry,* 1964, *34,* 685-694.

Lowenstein, L. F. The Treatment of Moderate School Phobia by Negative Practice and Desensitization Procedures. *Association of Educational Psychologists' Journal and Newsletter,* 1973. *3,* 46-49.

Marine, E. School Refusal—Who Should Intervene? (Diagnostic and treatment categories.) *Journal of School Psychology,* 1968-1969, *7*(1), 63-70.

_____. School Refusal: Who Should Intervene and How? *Psychiatric Communications,* 1973, *14,* 43-51.

Messer, A. A. Family Treatment of a School Phobic Child. *Archives of General Psychiatry,* 1964, *11,* 548-555.

Millar, T. P. The Child who Refuses to Attend School. *American Journal of Psychiatry,* 1961, *118,* 398-404.

Miller, D. L. School Phobia: Diagnosis, Emotional Genesis, and Management. *New York State Journal of Medicine,* 1972, *72,* 1160-1165.

Miller, P. M. The Use of Imagery and Muscle Relaxation in the Counterconditioning of a Phobic Child: A Case Study. *Journal of Nervous and Mental Disease,* 1972, *154,* 457-460.

Nice, R. W. The Use of Sodium Pentothal in the Treatment of a School Phobic. *Journal of Learning Disabilities,* 1968, *1,* 249-255.

Olsen, I. A., and Coleman, H. A. Treatment of School Phobia as a Case of Separation Anxiety. *Psychology in the Schools,* 1967, *4,* 151-154.

Patterson, G. R. A Learning Theory Approach to the Treatment of the School Phobic Child. In L. P. Ullmann and L. Krasner, eds., *Case Studies in Behavior Modification.* New York: Holt, Rinehart and Winston, 1965.

Pittman, F. S., Langsley, D. G., and DeYoung, C. D. Work and School Phobias: A Family Approach to Treatment. *American Journal of Psychiatry,* 1968, *124,* 1535-1541.

Rabiner, C. J., and Klein, D. F. Imipramine Treatment of School Phobia. *Comprehensive Psychiatry,* 1969, *10,* 387-390 (*Psychological Abstracts,* 1970, *44,* 14824.)

Radin, S. Job Phobia: School Phobia Revisited. *Comprehensive Psychiatry,* 1972, *13,* 251-257.

Radin, S. S. Psychotherapeutic Considerations in School Phobia. *Adolescence,* 1968, *3,* 181-193.

Rodriguez, A., Rodriguez, M., and Eisenberg, L. The Outcome of School Phobia: A Follow-Up Study of 41 Cases. *American Journal of Psychiatry,* 1959, *116,* 540-544.

Saraf, K. R., Klein, D. F., Gittelman-Klein, R., and Groff, S. Imipramine Side Effects in Children. *Psychopharmacologia,* 1974, *37,* 265-274.

Smith, S. L. School Refusal with Anxiety: A Review of Sixty-Three Cases. *Canadian Psychiatric Association Journal,* 1970, *15,* 257-264.

Smith, R. E., and Sharpe, T. M. Treatment of a School Phobia with Implosive Therapy. *Journal of Consulting and Clinical Psychology,* 1970, *35,* 239-243.

Suttenfield, V. School Phobia—A Study of Five Cases. *American Journal of Orthopsychiatry,* 1954, *24,* 368-380.

Tahmisian, J. A., and McReynolds, W. T. Use of Parents as Behavioral Engineers in the Treatment of a School-Phobic Girl. *Journal of Counseling Psychology,* 1971, *18,* 225-228.

Talbot, M. Panic in School Phobia. *American Journal of Orthopsychiatry,* 1957, *27,* 286-295.

Waldfogel, S., Coolidge, J. C., and Hahn, P. B. The Development, Meaning and Mangement of School Phobia. *American Journal of Orthopsychiatry,* 1957, *27,* 754-776.

_____, Tessman, E., and Hahn, P. B. A Program for Early Intervention in School Phobia. *American Journal of Orthopsychiatry,* 1959, *29,* 324-332.

Weinberger, G., Leventhal, T., and Beckman, G. The Management of a Chronic School Phobic Through the Use of Consultation with School Personnel. *Psychology in the Schools,* 1973, *10,* 83-88.

Weiss, M., and Burke, A. G. A Five- to Ten-Year Follow-Up of Hospitalized School Phobic Children and Adolescents. *American Journal of Orthopsychiatry,* 1967, *37,* 294-295.

_____, and Cain, B. The Residential Treatment of Children and Adolescents with School Phobia. *American Journal of Orthopsychiatry,* 1964, *34,* 103-114.

84

CONTINGENCY MANAGEMENT TECHNIQUES IN EDUCATION

by J. S. Birnbrauer
Associate Professor of Psychology
University of Western Australia
Nedland, W. A.

"Contingency management" derives from the writings of B. F. Skinner (1953; 1968; 1969), whose major thesis has been that control of behavior, and hence "understanding" behavior, will be obtained by systematic study of the relationships between antecedent events and behavior; behavior and its immediate effects upon the environment or consequent stimuli; and among the three components—antecedent stimuli, response, and consequent stimuli. These relationships—contingencies—when modified by happenstance or design, result in alterations of behavior.

The purpose of education is to alter behavior: (a) to change its form, e.g., from hastily giving any answer to selecting the best one; (b) to change its frequency, e.g., from reading one page to several pages in the same period of time; and (c) to change the antecedent stimuli which

evoke behavior, e.g., from saying "five" only after "one, two, three, four" to also saying "five" when "V," "5" and an array of five objects is presented. Teaching consists of arranging antecedent and consequent events so that the desired changes in behavior will occur. Contingency management, therefore, refers to planned, systematic manipulation of antecedent and consequent stimuli so as to accomplish the changes in behaviors that, analysis reveals, are the constituents of the educational objectives that have been set.

In the context of education, essentially two approaches may be defined: behavior analysis and precision teaching. Behavior analysts (more commonly called operant conditioners and behavior modifiers) place more emphasis upon applying techniques that are based on behavioral principles and experimental research. Their research methods most often consist of experimental analyses of the behavior of a single subject at a time, following the principles described by Sidman (1960). Behavior analysts emphasize, firstly, reliability of data, in the sense that two independent observers agree that the behavior did, in fact, occur or did not occur; and secondly, that procedures and results be replicated in each study. In other words, steps are taken to ensure that a real effect was obtained (Johnny's reading rate *did* increase), and that the increase was due to the procedures introduced in the classroom at the time, and not to other factors. See the *Journal of Applied Behavior Analysis* (1968ff.), Baer, Wolf, and Risley (1968), Birnbrauer (1971a), Birnbrauer, Burchard, and Burchard (1970), and Leitenberg (1973).

Precision teaching is the creation of Ogden Lindsley, of the University of Kansas Medical Center. This approach is more pragmatic. "Precision Teaching is not a *way* of teaching. Precision Teaching is not another method of teaching. Precision Teaching is not a refined behaviorist approach to teaching. Precision Teaching is one way to *plan, use,* and *analyze* any teaching style, technique, method, or theoretical position—old or new (Kunzelmann, 1970, p. 12.)" Despite Kunzelmann's protest to the contrary, precision teaching and behavioral analysis share much in common. Both groups agree that objectives be stated in terms of the behavior desired and the circumstances in which it is to occur; that behavior be directly and continuously counted, and that the methods of analysis and evaluation are the most important contributions contingency management has to make to education. The research to date suggests little that is new to educators. It says, instead, to be more consistent, more attentive to what pupils are saying and doing, and more willing to look at and *change* the conditions they, teachers and educators, have provided—in short, to teach with more precision.

Programs and research in contingency management can be found at all levels of education: in day-care centers for infants (Doke and Risley, 1972; LeLaurin and Risley, 1972); in universities (e.g., Ferster, 1968; Keller, 1971); in nursery schools (e.g., Harris, Wolf, and Baer, 1964); in TMR and EMR classes (e.g., Baker, Stanish, and Fraser, 1972; Ross and Ross, 1972); in institutional and community residences for delinquents (e.g., Burchard and Barrera, 1972; Fixsen, Phillips, and Wolf,

1972); in hospital and home-based programs for psychotic children and adolescents (e.g., Lovaas, Koegel, Simmons, and Long, 1973; Kaufman and O'Leary, 1972); in sheltered workshops (e.g., Gold, 1973; Schroeder, 1972); in wards for the severely and profoundly retarded (e.g., Azrin and Armstrong, 1973); in after-school programs for culturally deprived youngsters (e.g., Wolf, Giles, and Hall, 1968); in "regular" elementary and secondary school classes (e.g., Glynn, Thomas, and Shee, 1973; McAllister, Stachowiak, Baer, and Conderman, 1969); in homes (e.g., Hall et al., 1972; Patterson, 1971); and in campgrounds and movie theaters (Clark, Burgess, and Hendee, 1972; Burgess, Clark, and Hendee, 1971). The gifted are notably absent from the list; understandably, attention has been focused upon those individuals and groups who have not responded to conventional methods of education, or who, it may be predicted, will not.

Four areas of investigation will be described—Programmed Instruction at the University Level; Response-Consequences Available to Teachers; Token Systems; and Antecedent Stimulus Control. This selection covers the most important points for teachers, while also exposing current issues and problems.

PROGRAMMED INSTRUCTION AT THE UNIVERSITY LEVEL

Programmed Texts

Based on the behaviorist rationale that (a) learning proceeds optimally when immediate feedback (reinforcement) is provided frequently; (b) learning must begin with the behavioral repertoires available to students when they enter a learning situation; and (c) teachers must carefully specify goals in terms of the behavior desired, Holland (1960) conducted studies of programmed instruction which culminated in the text *The Analysis of Behavior* (Holland and Skinner, 1961). The book was designed so that students could acquire basic psychology by merely working through it, and it set the pattern for many texts to follow. Information was presented in fill-in-the-blank sentences, the answers to which the students checked immediately. New information was introduced in small steps, while old information was rehearsed in various contexts. Since then several variants have appeared, but all, to a degree, include the three basic features listed above. For examples that have as their aim the teaching of contingency management, see Becker, Engelmann, and Thomas (1971), Homme (1970), and Patterson and Gullion (1968).

The frontier of programmed instruction has become computer-assisted instruction (Holtzman, 1970). It appears, however, that computer-aided instruction and contingency management are developing as distinct fields of investigation, which is unfortunate for all concerned, for at the moment computers need to be told what to do, cannot determine the final objectives, and sit passively waiting for students to come to them.

Programmed Courses

The Keller Plan. From programmed texts, the natural next step was "personalized," "self-paced," or "programmed" courses of instruction. As described by Keller (1966; 1968; 1971), in a personalized course a student studies a portion of the course contents (such as a chapter or smaller unit) on his own, takes a quiz when ready, and immediately reviews the test with a "proctor." Proctors are volunteers who completed the course in the preceding term with grades of A. If the student's performance indicates mastery of the material, he is congratulated and permitted to study the next unit. He also may become eligible to attend lectures, discussions, or laboratories for which the study unit was a prerequisite. (Lecture and discussion attendance has been so poor in many instances that they have been discontinued.) If performance is less than mastery, the student takes the quiz again with no penalties imposed. With this system, all students may receive As if they apply themselves to studying and taking tests. (Traditional educators are troubled by this feature, and suspect the courses are too easy. The method, of course, was designed to make learning "easy." If "A" means a student met all of the requirements of the course, and every student did just that, then instructors and administrators ought to be pleased. As a matter of fact, students, especially those who ordinarily aspire to grades of C, report studying more in personalized courses.)

The Ferster Plan. Ferster (1968); Ferster and Perrot, 1968) developed an alternative to teach introductory psychology students to talk about psychology—to use psychological concepts correctly in speaking, and to describe findings of psychological research. In addition to the different goal, his method does not employ proctors. Instead, each student in the course must both tell an attentive listener about the material studied, and serve as a listener. Otherwise, the plans are identical in essentials. For more information, see Lloyd and Knutzen (1968), and Malott and Svinicki (1969), and contact the Center for Personalized Instruction (address below).

Some Findings

With either the Keller or Ferster plan, users have found that many students do not organize their time wisely, and consequently "cram" toward the end of term, drop out, or take the grade they have earned at the time. So limits often are imposed on self-pacing for administrative reasons. Keller (1971), however, objects to any restrictions, arguing instead that the plan makes it unnecessary for everyone to begin and terminate learning in conformity with university calendars.

Comparisons with conventional (lecture/discussion) sections of the same course on final examination performance and student ratings have shown the Keller or Ferster sections to be superior (McMichael and Corey, 1969; Sheppard and MacDermot, 1970; Alba and Pennypacker, 1972; Born, Glidhill, and Davis, 1972), but also see Whitehurst (1972) for more information on student attitudes.

Farmer, Lachter, Blaustein and Cole (1972) compared

impersonal feedback and varying percentages of proctoring. The results were that proctoring produced better performance on final examinations than no proctoring, and that the principal advantage of proctoring above some minimum seems to be to facilitate student progress through the study units. Their findings suggest a way of reducing the number of proctors.

Comments

(1) Although personalized courses have surpassed conventional courses statistically, the differences are numerically small, and would be educationally insignificant if it were not for the suggestion that the effects upon "average" and "poor" students are marked (Born et al., 1972). (2) Comparisons with conventional methods, which no one defends, leave much room for further improvement, particularly in teaching that something more than facts and definitions that is expected of a university education. Although both plans should be applicable, implementation awaits behavioral definitions of "something more." (3) To the writer's knowledge, personalized methods have not been employed in lower schools; yet, they appear to be ideally suited for open classrooms, and are consistent with suggestions that students be involved more often in teaching each other. (4) The most important point to recognize is that these plans, as proposed by Keller and Ferster, represent radical educational changes—students are free to study or not, lectures have been abandoned as the core of courses, and examinations are an integral part of *instruction,* and not used as a free evaluation service for employers and graduate schools.

RESPONSE CONSEQUENCES AVAILABLE TO TEACHERS

Most studies of contingency management have consisted of demonstrations of the effects of controlling response consequences on classroom deportment, study habits, and acquisition of knowledge. Investigators have asked: (a) What events and actions will serve as positive reinforcers, i.e., tangible, social, or symbolic events which, when made contingent on behavior, increase the probability of that behavior? (b) How can these events be administered systematically and yet practically? (c) How should teachers repond to instances of inappropriate behavior?

In conducting these studies, contingency managers, as a rule, have had to make other changes in the classes, e.g., in the nature of the lessons; have frequently incorporated instructions, and publicized to the class more clearly defined rules; and, together with the cooperating teachers, worked out definitions of appropriate and inappropriate behavior. Thus, it is not accurate to say that only response consequences have been manipulated. Also, it is impossible to think about (a) and (b) without in the next breath considering (c).

Differential Attention (Approval and Withholding of Attention, Approval and Reprimands, Approval and Time-Out from Positive Reinforcement)

The classic study of the effects of controlling teacher attention was conducted by Allen, Hart, Buell, Harris, and Wolf (1964). The import of the numerous studies conducted since then (e.g., Harris, Wolf, and Baer, 1964); Hall and Broden, 1967; Hall, Lund, and Jackson, 1968; Madsen, Becker, and Thomas, 1968; Broden, Bruce, Mitchell, Carter, and Hall, 1970; Kazdin, 1973) is that if teachers attend frequently to instances of desired behavior, and consistently ignore (withdraw attention from) instances of inappropriate behavior, desired behavior increases and inappropriate behavior decreases.

Broden et al. (1970) illustrate nicely how these studies have been conducted, and provide interesting additional information. Broden and her colleagues were interested in the effects of differential teacher attention on the disruptive behavior of a second-grader, "Jack," in a poverty area school, and also upon the behavior of the boy who sat at the adjacent desk, "Jim." The study, which took place for 30 minutes per day for 60 school days, was divided into five phases. Throughout, observers recorded the boys' on-task behavior and positive teacher attention. The phases of the study were: I—teacher carried on as usual; II—teacher ignored Jack's disruptive behavior and praised his study behavior, while carrying on as usual with Jim; III—the reverse of II: Jim received praise for studying and no attention for not studying; IV—the same as I; and V—both Jack and Jim were attended to positively when they studied and ignored at other times. The results were quite clear: the boy who was the "target" of differential praise and inattention studied much more (80 percent in II compared with 33 percent in I), and so did his neighbor, although his neighbor did not improve as much. In phase IV, the studying of both boys decreased, and finally, in Phase V, both boys studied about 75 percent of the period. Thus, the pupils' attention to assignments, and by implication their disruptiveness, varied perfectly with the way in which the teacher dispensed attention. Why the neighboring child should have been influenced is puzzling, especially since, in a similar study, Kazdin (1973) included controls which rule out the explanations that readily come to mind.

Completely ignoring behavior often is difficult for teachers and others, and should be effective only when teacher attention is a potent reinforcer. Consequently, alternatives to ignoring are needed. Some studies have shown that combining positive teacher attention with instructions which interrupt and redirect the child when misbehavior occurs also is effective (McAllister, Stachowiak, Baer, and Conderman, 1969). Others have combined positive attention with short periods of isolation, on the assumption that isolation will represent "time out from positive reinforcement" (Burchard and Barrera, 1972; Wahler, 1969). For example, Wasik, Senn, Welch, and Cooper (1969) warned the child and gave a redirective instruction whenever aggressive or resistive behavior was displayed. If the child did not comply within 15 seconds, the child was taken to a quiet room for 5 minutes. After the prescribed time, social reinforcement and activities resumed as if nothing had happened.

The important aspect of any of these combinations seems to be that they be applied consistently—every time the behavior occurs; that positive reinforcement of appropriate alternative behavior be frequent; and, of course, that the events actually are positive reinforcers for the children in question.

Attention, it must be emphasized, is not necessarily a positive reinforcer (Herbert et al., 1973), and reinforcement of one dimension of behavior will not necessarily have effects on other aspects. Ferritor, Buckholdt, Hamblin, and Smith (1972) have shown with a third grade sample that reinforcement of studying did not effect improved accuracy of problems completed, and reinforcement of accuracy did not reduce disruptive behavior. When reinforcement of accuracy *and* attention to assignment was arranged, both objectives were achieved.

Tangible Reinforcement

Several alternative procedures to teacher attention alone have been suggested by investigators. Laboratory studies have shown that if praise precedes other positive reinforcers, and these other reinforcers cannot be obtained until praise is obtained first, then the effectiveness of praise will be increased (Lauten and Birnbrauer, in press; Warren and Cairns, 1972). The trouble in using attention as a positive reinforcer often appears to be that praise is given away indiscriminantly and hence loses its value (Paris and Cairns, 1972).

Applied studies have had success in effecting better work habits and cooperation with procedures which employ activities and events which teachers have at hand as positive reinforcers. These procedures have been derived, for the most part, from a rule expressed by Premack (1965). Premack's principle says that behavior which occurs often will serve as a positive reinforcer for behavior which occurs less often in the situation. Translated to the classroom, the rule says that if pupils were regularly to choose games, when given the choice of reading, discussing politics, and playing games, then the opportunity to play games will serve to strengthen taking part in political discussion and reading. The rule has been used for years, e.g., "empty the garbage and *then* you can go out."

Studies have employed free activity periods or special recesses (Osborne, 1969; Salzberg, Wheeler, Devar, and Hopkins, 1971; Wasik, 1970), additional time in favored activities such as gym classes (Schmidt and Ulrich, 1969), and activities which parents administered after school (Edlund, 1971). In Edlund's study, teachers reported how many "privileges" the pupils had earned and the children and parents worked out what the privileges would be.

Barrish, Saunders, and Wolf (1969) tested an interesting variation called the "good-behavior game." The class was divided into two teams. Misbehavior of a team member resulted in a chalk-mark on the board, and the team that had the fewest marks (or both teams if they were both below a prescribed level) received "victory tags," stars, the opportunity to line up first for lunch, and a 30-minute free period. Their fourth graders were significantly more cooperative while the "good-behavior game" was being played. The cost to the school was nil. Another interesting method for use with poverty area preschool children has been described by Jacobson, Bushell, and Risley (1969).

The challenges to the teacher wishing to employ this approach are, firstly, to control access to the preferred activities at times other than those agreed upon; secondly, to devise a scheme for immediately signifying to the pupils that they are earning or losing by their behavior; and thirdly, to state and adhere to very clearly specified rules. Wilson and Hopkins (1973) circumvented these problems in junior high school home economics classes by arranging that the radio which the girls enjoyed be regulated automatically by the noise level in the room. The girls learned rapidly to keep the noise level below that necessary to turn off the radio.

This seems a good time to reiterate that contingency management is distinguished not by the techniques that might be recommended to solve a particular educational problem, but instead by its methods for selecting, applying, and evaluating techniques.

TOKEN SYSTEMS

Numerous studies of token reinforcement systems have been conducted in correctional settings, group homes and institutions, and schools (cf., reviews by Kazdin and Bootzin, 1972; O'Leary and Drabman, 1971; and recent studies by Baker, Stanish, and Fraser, 1972; Burchard and Barrera, 1972; Ingham and Andrews, 1973; Kaufman and O'Leary, 1972; Santogrossi, O'Leary, Romanczyk, and Kaufman, 1973; Walker and Buckley, 1972).

A fully developed token system is a model of a free enterprise economic system applied to a class or school. The only places in which the analogy may break down are: (a) there is not even a pretense of competition; students earn solely on the basis of their own productivity relative to their own base rates, and not at the expense of any other student; and (b) the teacher prescribes, or places limits upon, the assignments that may be undertaken. The rationale of token reinforcement is that students have different hierarchies of reinforcement and do not want the same things every day. A token enables teachers to dispense a common item to all students immediately and frequently, while it represents different things to different students. In technical terms, tokens are "generalized positive conditioned reinforcers" (Skinner, 1953). Thus, for the student who will not work for attention, "victory tags," or a free period there is always something else available.

In the classroom, pupils earn tokens—points, checks (ticks), poker chips, or any tangible item that a teacher finds convenient—by completing items of work correctly, completing assignments, and engaging in behavior appropriate to the educational exercises at the time. The tokens are exchanged later for items from a school store (snacks, trinkets, school supplies, cosmetics, articles of clothing, etc.), for a special outing; for rental of athletic equipment, musical instruments, etc.; and for money. At first, with younger, disturbed, and retarded children, exchange may need to be immediate—to teach the relationship between tokens and "back-up reinforcers"—and then the time may be gradually extended. Zimmerman, Zimmerman, and Russell (1969) describe very clearly the procedures they followed when introducing tokens to a group of profoundly retarded persons.

Comments

Although research leaves no doubt that token systems can produce remarkable changes in class deportment and productivity, several problems should be noted.

First, token systems cannot be regarded as substitutes for well-planned presentations of academic material, although they may facilitate acquisition of arithmetic skills (Hewett, Taylor, and Artuso, 1969; Dalton, Rubino, and Hislop, 1973). Typically, programmed materials have been selected; obviously what the children learn of an academic nature depends upon the quality of these programs. Therefore, in the writer's opinion, token programs usually have not reported impressive academic progress.

Second, students may perform beautifully in the token classroom, but not necessarily perform any differently than before in classes run with conventional methods. This problem of transfer or generalization is discussed in the final section. Related is the finding that performance often deteriorates when a token system is discontinued (Birnbrauer, Wolf, Kidder, and Tague, 1965; O'Leary, Becker, Evans, and Saudargas, 1969).

Third, token systems require careful planning and total commitment. As conceived originally, token systems were like personalized courses, in that the students were free to study or not, and to complete their assignments or not, with the teachers having to rely on the skillful use of positive reinforcement, i.e., their attention and the tokens, to motivate the pupils. Accomplishing these ends requires adjustments in the ratio of work to tokens, the ratio of tokens to back-up reinforcers, and the nature and quantity of work assigned. Managing a token system thus requires teachers who are sensitive to student behavior, skillful in other aspects of contingency management, and willing to keep accurate records of student performance. But, unfortunately investigators and schools were not prepared for the kind of freedom a true token system requires. Hence, from the outset, token classes incorporated punitive tactics, such as seclusion and token loss, for resistive and other misbehavior, and in many instances the token system became a mere veneer for a basically punitive system. Unlike personalized courses in universities, token systems, although exemplifying an equally radical alternative, did not change schools but adapted to them. Other contingency management work is liable to the same criticism (Winett and Winkler, 1972; O'Leary, 1972). In order to develop token system classes as conceived originally, they would have to be housed in schools that operated on a token system. Such schools would have to be freed of any obligation to enforce compulsory attendance laws, an idea that merits serious consideration.

Fourth, token systems are expensive, in comparison to expenditures for classes of comparable size. But they probably would be much less expensive if costs were compared with the costs to society of educational failures, destruction of school property, and so on.

A Note About Punishment

Educators, psychologists, and others believe that contingency managers are advocates of punishment, and that research in contingency management justifies the use of punitive procedures. Neither is correct. To be sure, attitudes about punishment have changed, in that few contingency managers share Skinner's view that punishment is *never* indicated. At the same time, contingency managers are almost invariably critical of the ways in which punishment generally is applied.

The prevailing position is that application of response consequences that will suppress behavior seems necessary in some situations to stop dangerous-self-injurious responses (e.g., Lovaas and Simmons, 1969; Tate and Baroff, 1966) and assaultive actions (e.g., Birnbrauer, 1968), and can be effective *provided* several variables are controlled. Azrin and Holz (1966, pp. 426–427) listed 14 rules for effective use of punishment. Among these are: (a) frequency of punishment should be high, ideally every time the behavior occurs; (b) it should be immediate, intense, and brief, and signal a period of no positive reinforcement; and (c) alternative behavior should be available that will produce more positive reinforcement than the punished response. As can be appreciated readily, (a) and (b) are, in practice, difficult to arrange, and (c) generally meets with considerable opposition.

Rather than justify usage of punitive procedures, contingency management theory and research suggests the opposite. We would be far better off to concentrate upon preventive programs and the development of positive incentives for learning and to abandon it completely as it exists in education today. There will always be a need for punishment, if contingency management principles are correct, for the simple reason that positive reinforcement requires not only giving but also *withholding* positive reinforcers. Thus, punishment will be necessary on occasion to momentarily stop unauthorized procurement of positive reinforcement. When punishment is viewed in that manner, however, application becomes quite different. It is part of an instructional package for the individual; it is neither a deterrent to others nor revenge; the form of punishment is not chosen because it "fits the crime"; the infliction of pain and fear may not be at all necessary; and it is pointless, and harmful, when equally valuable positive reinforcers cannot be gained by alternative behaviors.

As an illustration, the most common form of punishment described in research reports is response contingent presentations of brief periods during which positive reinforcement is unavailable, i.e., when "time out from positive reinforcement" (TO) is enforced. In several studies, TO was applied in the form of removal of the person to another room. Since the rationale was to reduce opportunities for positive reinforcement, mostly social in nature, the rooms were well-illuminated and not cramped. Since the means of teaching alternative behavior was positive reinforcement, the periods of time usually were brief—on the order of five to 15 minutes—and, importantly, classroom conditions were changed so that the pupil would receive positive reinforcement there. To return to the point of this comment, it is a misinterpretation indeed to seclude students (and apply any other punishment) while all other conditions in class continue as usual, and to do so without measuring its effectiveness (cf., Burchard and Barrera, 1972; White, Nielsen, and Johnson, 1972).

ANTECEDENT STIMULUS CONTROL

Contingency management has been criticized, with justification, because of its emphasis upon response consequents at the expense of antecedent stimuli. Yet it must be noted that the procedures employed by contingency managers, with very few exceptions, involve changes in setting and antecedent variables, as well as consequent variables. Typically, instructions, demonstrations, physical guidance, and arrangement of stimuli are used so that the child virtually cannot help but make the correct response. The consensus is that the pupil must be motivated to attend and behave through differential consequences, and guided to attend to particular events and to behave in particular ways through manipulation of antecedents. For a very interesting and well-designed series of studies in which teacher modelling of correct behavior is combined with a token reinforcement system, see S. Ross (1969 a, b), D. Ross (1970), and Ross and Ross (1972).

A large and very important body of literature that shows how children who do not respond to demonstrations and instructions can be taught to do so should be noted. Baer and Sherman (1964) found, in a laboratory study, that some preschool children imitated a puppet's incidental behavior so long as the puppet reinforced imitations of responses that the puppet demonstrated and prompted verbally. They labeled the phenomenon "generalized imitation." This simple finding led Lovaas and his colleagues (Lovaas et al., 1966; Lovaas et al., 1967), Risley and Wolf (1967), and Baer, Peterson, and Sherman (1967) to develop procedures to teach psychotic children and profound retardates to imitate. Those papers describe the procedures in nice detail. Since then, the procedures have been applied also to following instructions (Martin, 1972).

For an appreciation of the issues currently being debated and their applicability, see also Baer, Guess, and Sherman (1972), Bandura and Barab (1971), Garcia, Guess, and Byrnes (1973), Peterson, Merwin, Moyer, and Whitehurst (1971), and Steinman and Boyce (1971). In addition to the practical implications, their literature illustrates how applied research, basic research, and theory development can proceed concurrently, with each influencing the other in the cumulative fashion that applied science should follow.

CURRENT TRENDS AND ISSUES

Contingency management is in a period of self-appraisal and transition, for enough time has elapsed to look back over cases, successes, and failures, and at longer-term gains. For example, Lovaas, Koegel, Simmons, and Long (1973) have summarized their five years of work with psychotic children in a provocative and sobering article. Their data make problems vivid and suggest some solutions.

As the present review indicates, investigators have focused upon response consequences. While no one in the field doubts their importance to learning, the limits of reinforcement and the programs tested to date have become apparent. Rarely does one hear now that behavior analysis is applied easily with a minimum of training.

One limitation is the obvious one that how well students learn to read, compute, solve problems, make plans, etc., depends upon the lessons or programs they study. Contingency management has been shown to improve greatly the willingness of pupils to study. Thus, the writer anticipates a renewed interest in analysis of task requirements, the contents of programs, and the goals of instruction. Perhaps Grimm, Bijou, and Parsons (1973) will be recognized in the future as having initiated that trend. The remarkable capacity of computers to present material, and to store and analyze results, removes some of the tedium from this work.

A second limitation is that improved behavior, in a classroom for example, does not generalize or transfer to other situations, and is not maintained after the contingency management programs have been discontinued. Although these outcomes are predictable from behavioral theory, the problems of transfer and maintenance have received considerable attention of late. Among the tacks being pursued are: (a) to gradually modify the program to conditions more like those found in conventional classes (e.g., Birnbrauer, 1971 b; Walker and Buckley, 1972); (b) to teach teachers, parents and staff to carry out maintenance programs (Azrin and Armstrong, 1973; Foxx and Azrin, 1972; Lovaas et al., 1973; Walker and Buckley, 1972) (in fact, the necessity for including a maintenance program in the total scheme appears to be accepted generally); (c) to shift from teacher-administered evaluation of student performance to self-evaluative systems, the idea being to develop one aspect of self-control (Glynn, 1970; Glynn, Thomas, and Shee, 1973; Kaufman and O'Leary, 1972; Felixbrod and O'Leary, 1973; Santogrossi et al., 1973); and (d) to teach students to modify teacher and peer behavior (Graubard, Rosenberg, and Miller, 1971; Seymour and Stokes, 1973).

Interest in generalization inevitably means that investigators will record more behavior, in more situations, for longer periods of time. Such research promises to produce exciting findings.

Another trend follows from the fact that investigators who have developed program "packages," based on experimentally analyzed components, recognize that information alone is not sufficient. Thus, larger-scale comparative studies have been initiated to answer the questions: How effective? With what groups? At what expense?

Behavior analysts also have become more willing to analyze hypotheses and principles from sources other than behavioral psychology, and to collaborate with investigators from other disciplines. The best example is the realization by Kagel and Winkler (1972) of the relevance of economic theory to token systems, and the implications of token systems for experimental tests of economic principles.

If contingency management continues to be perceived as a method of planning and evaluating educational changes, and as a means of accumulating information about the variables that must be considered, and how they may be controlled, then its contributions to education have no limits. If investigators, on the other hand, cease responding to results, then contingency management will be remembered as a fad of the 1960s. That an appraisal is taking place, and changes in direction are noticeable, suggest the former, rather than the latter, outcome.

REFERENCES

Alba, E., and Pennypacker, H. S. A Multiple Change Score Comparison of Traditional and Behavioral College Teaching Procedures. *Journal of Applied Behavior Analysis*, 1972, *5*, 121-124.

Allen, K. E., Hart, B., Buell, J., Harris, F., and Wolf, M. M. Effects of Social Reinforcement on Isolate Behavior of a Nursery School Child. *Child Development*, 1964, *35*, 511-518.

Azrin, N. H., and Armstrong, P. M. The "Mini-Meal"—A Method of Teaching Eating Skills to the Profoundly Retarded. *Mental Retardation*, 1973, *11*, 9-13.

_____, and Holz, W. C. Punishment. In W. K. Honig, ed., *Operant Behavior: Areas of Research and Application*. New York: Appleton-Century-Crofts, 1966, pp. 380-447.

Baer, D. M., Guess, D., and Sherman, J. A. Adventures in Simplistic Grammar. In R. L. Schiefelbusch, ed., *Language of the Mentally Retarded*. Baltimore: University Park Press, 1972, pp. 93-105.

_____, Peterson, R. F., and Sherman, J. A. The Development of Imitation by Reinforcing Behavioral Similarity to a Model. *Journal of the Experimental Analysis of Behavior*, 1967, *10*, 405-416.

_____, and Sherman, J. A. Reinforcement Control of Generalized Imitation in Young Children. *Journal of Experimental Child Psychology*, 1964, *1*, 37-49.

_____, Wolf, M. M., and Risley, T. R. Some Current Dimensions of Applied Behavior Analysis. *Journal of Applied Behavior Analysis*, 1968, *1*, 91-97.

Baker, J. G., Stanish, B., and Fraser, B. Comparative Effects of a Token Economy in Nursery School. *Mental Retardation*, August 1972, *10*, 16-19.

Bandura, A., and Barab, P. G. Conditions Governing Nonreinforced Imitation. *Developmental Psychology*, 1971, *5*, 244-255.

Barrish, H. H., Saunders, M., and Wolf, M. M. Good Behavior Game: Effects of Individual Contingencies for Group Consequences on Disruptive Behavior in a Classroom. *Journal of Applied Behavior Analysis*, 1969, *2*, 119-124.

Becker, W. C., Engelmann, S., and Thomas, D. R. *Teaching: A Course in Applied Psychology*. Chicago: Scientific Research Associates, 1971.

Birnbrauer, J. S. Generalization of Punishment Effects—A Case Study. *Journal of Applied Behavior Analysis*, 1968, *1*, 201-211.

_____. Contingency Management Research. *Educational Technology*, 1971, *11*, 71-77.

_____. Preparing "Uncontrollable" Retarded Children for Group Instruction. In W. C. Becker, ed., *An Empirical Basis for Change in Education*. Chicago: Science Research Associates, 1971, pp. 213-218. (b)

_____, Burchard, J. D., and Burchard, S. N. Wanted: Behavior Analysts. In R. H. Bradfield, ed., *Behavior Modification*. San Rafael, California: Dimensions Publishing Co., 1970, pp. 19-76.

_____, Wolf, M. M., Kidder, J. D., and Tague, C. Classroom Behavior of Retarded Pupils with Token Reinforcement. *Journal of Experimental Child Psychology*, 1965, *2*, 219-235.

Born, D. G., Gledhill, S. M., and Davis, M. L. Examination Performance in Lecture-Discussion and Personalized Instruction Courses. *Journal of Applied Behavior Analysis*, 1972, *5*, 33-43.

Broden, M., Bruce, C., Mitchell, M. A., Carter, V., and Hall, R. V. Effects of Teacher Attention on Attending Behavior of Two Boys at Adjacent Desks. *Journal of Applied Behavior Analysis*, 1970, *3*, 199-203.

Burchard, J. D., and Barrera, F. An Analysis of Timeout and Response Cost in a Programmed Environment. *Journal of Applied Behavior Analysis*, 1972, *5*, 271-282.

Burgess, R. L., Clark, R. M., and Hendee, J. C. An Experimental Analysis of Anti-Litter Procedures. *Journal of Applied Behavior Analysis*, 1971, *4*, 71-75.

Clark, R. N., Burgess, R. L., and Hendee, J. C. The Development of Anti-Litter Behavior in a Forest Campground. *Journal of Applied Behavior Analysis*, 1972, *5*, 1-5.

Dalton, A. J., Rubino, C. A., and Hislop, M. W. Some Effects of Token Rewards on School Achievement of Children with Down's Syndrome. *Journal of Applied Behavior Analysis*, 1973, *6*, 251-259.

Doke, L. A., and Risley, T. R. The Organization of Day-Care Environments: Required vs. Optional Activities. *Journal of Applied Behavior Analysis*, 1972, *5*, 405-420.

Edlund, C. V. Changing Classroom Behavior of Retarded Children: Using Reinforcers in the Home Environment and Parents and Teachers as Trainers. *Mental Retardation*, 1971, *9*, 33-36.

Farmer, J., Lachter, G. D., Blaustein, J. J., and Cole, B. K. The Role of Proctoring in Personalized Instruction. *Journal of Applied Behavior Analysis*, 1972, *5*, 401-404.

Felixbrod, J. J., and O'Leary, K. D. Effects of Reinforcement on Children's Academic Behavior as a Function of Self-Determined and Externally Imposed Contingencies. *Journal of Applied Behavior Analysis*, 1973, *6*, 241-250.

Ferritor, D. E., Buckholdt, D., Hamblin, R. L., and Smith, L. The Noneffects of Contingent Reinforcement for Attending Behavior on Work Accomplished. *Journal of Applied Behavior Analysis*, 1972, *5*, 7-17.

Ferster, C. B. Individualized Instruction in a Large Introductory Psychology Course. *Psychological Record*, 1968, *18*, 521-532.

_____, and Perrott, M. C. *Behavior Principles*. New York: Appleton-Century-Crofts, 1968.

Fixsen, D. L., Phillips, E. L., and Wolf, M. M. Achievement Place: The Reliability of Self-Reporting and Peer-Reporting and Their Effects on Behavior. *Journal of Applied Behavior Analysis*, 1972, *5*, 19-30.

Foxx, R. M., and Azrin, N. H. Restitution: A Method of Eliminating Aggressive-Disruptive Behavior of Mentally Retarded and Brain Damaged Patients. *Behaviour Research and Therapy*, 1972, *10*, 15-27.

Garcia, E., Guess, D., and Byrnes, J. Development of Syntax in a Retarded Girl Using Procedures of Imitation, Reinforcement, and Modelling. *Journal of Applied Behavior Analysis*, 1973, *6*, 299-310.

Glynn, E. L. Classroom Applications of Self-Determined Reinforcement. *Journal of Applied Behavior Analysis,* 1970, *3,* 123-132.

Gold, M. W. Research on the Vocational Habilitation of the Retarded: The Present, the Future. In N. R. Ellis, ed., *International Review of Research in Mental Retardation,* Vol. 6. New York: McGraw-Hill, 1973, pp. 97-147.

Graubard, P. S. Rosenberg, H., and Miller, M. B. Student Applications of Behavior Modification to Teachers and Environments or Ecological Approaches to Social Deviancy. In E. A. Ramp and B. L. Hopkins, eds., *A New Direction for Education: Behavior Analysis,* Vol. 1. Lawrence, Kansas: The University of Kansas Support and Development Center for Follow Through, 1971, pp. 80-101.

Grimm, J. A., Bijou, S. W., and Parsons, J. A Problem-Solving Model for Teaching Remedial Arithmetic to Handicapped Young Children. *Journal of Abnormal Child Psychology* (in press).

Hall, R. V., and Broden, M. Behavior Changes in Brain-Injured Children Through Social Reinforcement. *Journal of Experimental Child Pshchology,* 1967, *5,* 463-479.

_____, Lund, D., and Jackson, D. Effects of Teacher Attention on Study Behavior. *Journal of Applied Behavior Analysis,* 1968, *1,* 1-12.

_____, Axelrod, S., Tyler, L., Grief, E., Jones, F. C., and Robertson, R. Modification of Behavior Problems in the Home with a Parent as Observer and Experimenter. *Journal of Applied Behavior Analysis,* 1972, *5,* 53-64.

Harris, F. R., Wolf, M. M., and Baer, D. M. Effects of Adult Social Reinforcement on Child Behavior. *Young Children,* 1964, *20,* 8-17.

Herbert, E. W., Pinkston, E. M., Hayden, M. L., Sajwaj, T. E., Pinkston, S., Cordua, G., and Jackson,C. Adverse Effects of Differential Parental Attention. *Journal of Applied Behavior Analysis,* 1973, *6,* 15-30.

Hewett, F. M., Taylor, F. D., and Artuso, A. A. The Santa Monica Project: Evaluation of an Engineered Classroom Design with Emotionally Disturbed Children. *Exceptional Children,* 1969, *35,* 523-529.

Holland, J. G. Teaching Machines: An Application of Principles from the Laboratory. *Journal of the Experimental Analysis of Behavior,* 1960, *3,* 275-287.

_____, and Skinner, B. F. *The Analysis of Behavior.* New York: McGraw-Hill, 1961.

Holtzman, W. H., ed. *Computer–Assisted Instruction, Testing, and Guidance.* New York: Harper & Row, 1970.

Homme, L. *How to Use Contingency Contracting in the Classroom.* Champaign, Illinois: Research Press, 1970.

Ingham, R. J., and Andrews, G. An Analysis of a Token Economy in Stuttering Therapy. *Journal of Applied Behavior Analysis,* 1973, *6,* 219-229.

Jacobson, J. M., Bushell, D. Jr., and Risley, T. Switching Requirements in a Head Start Classroom. *Journal of Applied Behavior Analysis,* 1969, *2,* 43-47.

Kagel, J. H., and Winkler, R. C. Behavioral Economics: Areas of Co-operative Research Between Economics and Applied Behavioral Analysis. *Journal of Applied Behavior Analysis,* 1972, *5,* 335-342.

Kaufman, K. F., and O'Leary, K. D. Reward, Cost, and Self-Evaluation Procedures for Disruptive Adolescents in a Psychiatric Hospital School. *Journal of Applied Behavior Analysis,* 1972, *5,* 293-310.

Kazdin, A. E. The Effect of Vicarious Reinforcement on Attentive Behavior in the Classroom. *Journal of Applied Behavior Analysis,* 1973, *6,* 71-78.

_____, and Bootzin, R. R. The Token Economy: An Evaluative Review. *Journal of Applied Behavior Analysis,* 1972, *5,* 343-372.

Keller, F. S. A Personal Course in Psychology. In R. Ulrich, T. Stachnik, and J. Mabry, eds., *Control of Human Behavior.*

Glenview, Illinois: Scott-Foresman and Co., 1966.

_____. Good-Bye Teacher . . . *Journal of Applied Behavior Analysis,* 1968, *1,* 79-89.

_____. A Programmed System of Instruction. In W. C. Becker, ed., *An Empirical Basis for Change in Education.* Chicago: Science Research Associates, 1971, pp. 506-522.

Kunzelmann, H. P., ed. *Precision Teaching.* Seattle: Special Child Publications, 1970.

Lauten, M. H., and Birnbrauer, J. S. The Efficacy of "Right" as a Function of its Relationship with Reinforcement. *Journal of Experimental Child Psychology,* in press.

Leitenberg, H. The Use of Single-Case Methodology in Psychotherapy Research. *Journal of Abnormal Psychology,* 1973, *82,* 87-101.

LeLaurin, K., and Risley, T. R. The Organization of Day-Care Environments: "Zone" vs. "Man-to-Man" Staff Assignments. *Journal of Applied Behavior Analysis,* 1972, *5,* 225-232.

Lloyd, K. E., and Knutzen, N. J. A Self-Paced Programmed Undergraduate Course in the Experimental Analysis of Behavior. *Journal of Applied Behavior Analysis,* 1969, *2,* 125-133.

Lovaas, O. I., Berberich, J. P., Perloff, B. F., and Schaeffer, B. Acquisition of Imitative Speech by Schizophrenic Children. *Science,* 1966, *151,* 705-707.

_____, Freitas, L., Nelson, K., and Whalen, C. The Establishment of Imitation and Its Use for the Development of Complex Behavior in Schizophrenic Children. *Behaviour Research and Therapy,* 1967, *5,* 171-181.

_____, Koegel, R., Simmons, J. Q., and Long, J. S. Some Generalization and Follow-Up Measures on Autistic Children in Behavior Therapy. *Journal of Applied Behavior Analysis,* 1973, *6,* 131-165.

_____, and Simmons, J. Q. Manipulation of Self-Destruction in Three Retarded Children. *Journal of Applied Behavior Analysis,* 1969, *2,* 143-157.

Madsen, C. H., Becker, W. C., and Thomas, D. R. Rules, Praise, and Ignoring: Elements of Elementary Classroom Control. *Journal of Applied Behavior Analysis,* 1968, *1,* 139-150.

Malott, R. W., and Svinicki, J. G. Contingency Management in an Introductory Psychology Course for One Thousand Students. *Psychological Record,* 1969, *19,* 545-556.

Martin, J. A. The Effect of Incongruent Instructions and Consequences on Imitation in Retarded Children. *Journal of Applied Behavior Analysis,* 1972, *5,* 467-475.

McAllister, L. W., Stachowiak, J. G., Baer, D. M., and Conderman, L. The Application of Operant Conditioning Techniques in a Secondary School Classroom. *Journal of Applied Behavior Analysis,* 1969, *2,* 277-285.

McMichael, J. S., and Corey, J. R. Contingency Management in an Introductory Psychology Course Produced Better Learning. *Journal of Applied Behavior Analysis,* 1969, *2,* 79-83.

O'Leary, K. D. Behavior Modification in the Classroom: A Rejoinder to Winett and Winkler. *Journal of Applied Behavior Analysis,* 1972, *5,* 505-510.

_____, Becker, W. C., Evans, M. B., and Saudargas, R. A. A Token Reinforcement Program in a Public School: A Replication and Systematic Analysis. *Journal of Applied Behavior Analysis,* 1969, *2,* 3-13.

_____, and Drabman, R. Token Reinforcement Programs in the Classroom: A Review. *Psychological Bulletin,* 1971, *75,* 379-398.

Osborne, J. G. Free-Time as a Reinforcer in the Management of Classroom Behavior. *Journal of Applied Behavior Analysis,* 1969, *2,* 113-118.

Paris, S. G., and Cairns, R. B. An Experimental and Ethological Analysis of Social Reinforcement with Retarded Children. *Child Development,* 1972, *43,* 717-729.

Patterson, G. R. *Families.* Champaign, Illinois: Research Press, 1971.

_____, and Gullion, M. E. *Living with Children.* Champaign, Illinois: Research Press, 1968.

Peterson, R. F., Merwin, M. R., Moyer, T. J., and Whitehurst, G. J. Generalized Imitation: The Effects of Experimenter Absence, Differential Reinforcement and Stimulus Complexity. *Journal of Experimental Child Psychology,* 1971, *12,* 114-128.

Premack, D. Reinforcement Theory. In D. Levine, ed., *Nebraska Symposium on Motivation.* Lincoln: University of Nebraska Press, 1965, pp. 123-180.

Risley, T. R., and Wolf, M. M. Establishing Functional Speech in Echolalic Children. *Behaviour Research and Therapy,* 1967, *5,* 73-88.

Ross, D. M. Incidental Learning of Number Concepts in Small Group Games. *American Journal of Mental Deficiency,* 1970, *74,* 718-725.

_____, and Ross, S. A. The Efficacy of Listening Training for Educable Mentally Retarded Children. *American Journal of Mental Deficiency,* 1972, *77,* 137-142.

Ross, S. A. Effects of Intentional Training in Social Behavior on Retarded Children. *American Journal of Mental Deficiency,* 1969, *73,* 912-919. (a)

_____. Effects of an Intensive Motor Skills Training Program on Young Educable Mentally Retarded Children. *American Journal of Mental Deficiency,* 1969, *73,* 920-926. (b)

Salzberg, B. H., Wheeler, A. J., Devar, L. T., and Hopkins, B. L. The Effect of Intermittent Feedback and Intermittent Contingent Access to Play on Printing of Kindergarten Children. *Journal of Applied Behavior Analysis,* 1971, *4,* 163-171.

Santogrossi, D. A., O'Leary, K. D., Romanczyk, R. G., and Kaufman, K. F. Self-Evaluation by Adolescents in a Psychiatric Hospital School Token Program. *Journal of Applied Behavior Analysis,* 1973, *6,* 277-287.

Schmidt, G. W., and Ulrich, R. E. Effects of Group Contingent Events upon Classroom Noise. *Journal of Applied Behavior Analysis,* 1969, *2,* 171-179.

Schroeder, S. R. Parametric Effects of Reinforcement Frequency, Amount of Reinforcement, and Required Response Force on Sheltered Workshop Behavior. *Journal of Applied Behavior Analysis,* 1972, *5,* 431-442.

Seymour, F. W., and Stokes, T. F. Self-Management in Training Delinquent Girls to Increase Work and Elicit Staff Praise. Paper read at the Australian Psychological Society Convention, Sydney, August 1973.

Sheppard, W. C., and MacDermot, H. G. Design and Evaluation of a Programmed Course in Introductory Psychology. *Journal of Applied Behavior Analysis,* 1970, *3,* 5-11.

Sidman, M. *Tactics of Scientific Research.* New York: Basic Books, 1960.

Skinner, B. F. *Science and Human Behavior.* New York: Macmillan, 1953.

_____. *The Technology of Teaching.* New York: Appleton-Century-Crofts, 1968.

_____. *Contingencies of Reinforcement: A Theoretical Analysis.* New York: Appleton-Century-Crofts, 1969.

Steinman, W. M., and Boyce, K. D. Generalized Imitation as a Function of Discrimination Difficulty and Choice. *Journal of Experimental Child Psychology,* 1971, *11,* 251-265.

Tate, B. G., and Baroff, G. S. Aversive Control of Self-Injurious Behavior in a Psychotic Boy. *Behaviour Research and Therapy,* 1966, *4,* 281-287.

Wahler, R. G. Oppositional Children: A Quest for Parental Reinforcement Control. *Journal of Applied Behavior Analysis,* 1969, *2,* 159-170.

Walker, H. M., and Buckley, N. K. Programming Generalization and Maintenance of Treatment Effects Across Time and Across Settings. *Journal of Applied Behavior Analysis,* 1972, *5,* 209-224.

Warren, V., and Cairns, R. B. Social Reinforcement Satiation: An Outcome of Frequency or Ambiguity? *Journal of Experimental Child Psychology,* 1972, *13,* 249-260.

Wasik, B. H. The Application of Premack's Generalization on Reinforcement to the Management of Classroom Behavior. *Journal of Experimental Child Psychology,* 1970, *10,* 33-43.

_____, Senn, K., Welch, R. H., and Cooper, B. R. Behavior Modification with Culturally Deprived School Children: Two Case Studies. *Journal of Applied Behavior Analysis,* 1969, *2,* 181-194.

White, G. D., Nielsen, G., and Johnson, S. M. Timeout Duration and the Suppression of Deviant Behavior in Children. *Journal of Applied Behavior Analysis,* 1972, *5,* 111-120.

Whitehurst, G. Academic Responses and Attitudes Engendered by a Programmed Course in Child Development. *Journal of Applied Behavior Analysis,* 1972, *5,* 283-291.

Wilson, C. W., and Hopkins, B. L. The Effects of Contingent Music on the Intensity of Noise in Junior High Home Economic Classes. *Journal of Applied Behavior Analysis,* 1973, *6,* 269-275.

Winett, R. A., and Winkler, R. C. Current Behavior Modification in the Classroom: Be Still, Be Quiet, Be Docile. *Journal of Applied Behavior Analysis,* 1972, *5,* 499-504.

Wolf, M. M., Giles, D. K., and Hall, R. V. Experiments with Token Reinforcement in a Remedial Classroom. *Behaviour Research and Therapy,* 1968, *6,* 51-64.

Zimmerman, E. H., Zimmerman, J., and Russell, D. Differential Effects of Token Reinforcement on Instruction-Following Behavior in Retarded Students Instructed as a Group. *Journal of Applied Behavior Analysis,* 1969, *2,* 101-118.

Suggested Collections

Becker, W. C., ed. *An Empirical Basis for Change in Education.* Chicago: Science Research Associates, 1971.

O'Leary, K. D., and O'Leary, S. G., eds. *Classroom Management.* New York: Pergamon Press, 1972.

Ulrich, R., Stachnik, T., and Mabry, J., eds. *Control of Human Behavior,* Vol. 2. Glenview, Illinois: Scott, Foresman & Co., 1970.

Organizations and Journals

Association for the Advancement of Behavior Therapy
415 East 52nd Street
New York, N.Y. 10022

Center for Personalized Instruction
Georgetown University
29 Loyola Hall
Washington, D.C. 20007

Society for the Experimental Analysis of Behavior
Department of Psychology
Indiana University
Bloomington, Indiana 47401

Behavior Therapy

Psychological Clinic
Rutgers University
New Brunswick, New Jersey 08903

Journal of Applied Behavior Analysis

Johnny Cake Child Study Center
Mansfield, Arkansas 72944

85

PRINCIPLES OF CURRICULUM DEVELOPMENT: AN ARENA OF STRUGGLES

by Louise L. Tyler
Professor
University of California
Los Angeles, California
and
Harry Handler
Associate Superintendent, Instruction
Los Angeles Unified School District
Los Angeles, California

In his Preface to *Experience and Education,* John Dewey (1938) states that it would not be a sign of health if an important social interest such as education were not an arena of struggles, practical and theoretical. Education consequently can be considered healthy, because it can be characterized as an arena of struggles. Curriculum as one aspect of education is no exception—it too is an arena of struggles.

It is well known that a discussion of curriculum, in the present *zeitgeist,* rarely omits reference to the cultural (social, economic, and political) forces which exert strong influence on the operation of the school. And although currently recognized that the schools can no longer operate in a manner which is culturally innocent, rarely are the educators (whether theoreticians or practitioners), who are involved in curriculum development, perceived as having an active role in the political or economic arena. It is generally accepted that the modern-day educator needs to be well versed in economic and political theory, as well as education. But the education profession has been reluctant to acknowledge the extent to which the operation of schools is influenced by cultural factors, particularly economic and political, and even more reluctant to become involved in these kinds of activities in any substantial way. Undoubtedly there will be much writing in this area in the future, but there is already some foreshadowing in current writing and work.

Although the definition of curriculum has been placed in a context of culture by some few writers, in general curriculum definitions could be thought of as culturally neutral. However, if questioned rigorously, there is probably no definition which can be characterized as culturally neutral, inasmuch as neutrality is also influenced by values of our culture. A cultural slant is given to a definition by Macdonald, Wolfson, and Zaret (1973), who say: "In our view, curriculum is the cultural environment which has been purposefully selected as a set of possibilities for facilitating educative transactions (p. 22)." A definition with less cultural slant is that of Mauritz Johnson's, who stipulates that "curriculum is a structured series of intended learning outcomes (p. 131)."

Goodlad's definition is rather similar, as he says, "A *curriculum,* then, as defined here, is a set of intended learnings (p. 11)." According to Doll (1970), "The commonly accepted definition of the curriculum has changed from *content of courses of study and lists of subjects and courses to all the experiences which are offered to learners under the auspices or direction of the school* (p. 21)." However, whatever definition of curriculum is specified, whether culturally neutral or not, broad or narrow, it does not seem to affect in any significant way the questions or issues dealt with by the curriculum writers. For example, even though Mauritz Johnson (1967) defines curriculum as a structured series of intended learning outcomes, he finds it necessary to include a discussion of instruction and evaluation.

This paper will not posit a definitive curriculum definition. It will, however, focus upon curriculum as a field of inquiry involving questions, problems, and issues of the teaching-learning process. These questions, problems, and issues are theoretical and practical in nature, and involve struggles between theoretical positions and between practical positions, as well as the complex matter of going from theory to practice.

While there are many questions which can be formulated, seven are of great importance. First, who does or should make the decisions about goals, about instructional materials, about evaluation? Second, what are or should be the goals (objectives) of the educational process? Third, what is the nature of the teaching-learning process? How can valid instructional materials be developed? is the fourth question. Fifth, what kind of evaluation studies can be made which provide important information for decision-making? Sixth, how can a staff be continuously refreshed and educated? And seventh, is curriculum development an ends-means (linear) process? For each of these questions there are, of course, many subordinate questions which can be formulated. What is so characteristic of the field of curriculum is the familiar either-or formulation of answers to these questions. Dewey's opening sentences in *Experience and Education* can still be meaningfully stated today (1938): "Mankind likes to think in terms of extreme opposites. It is given to formulating its beliefs in terms of either-ors, between which it recognized no intermediate possibilities (p. 1)." Some of the "either-ors" which presently are encountered are briefly indicated.

In relation to the question as to what the objectives should be, there is the theoretical position that cognitive objectives are the essential goals of the schools. The opposition to this position is that affective objectives are central. In practice, most classroom procedures and activities are concerned with cognitive objectives.

In regard to the teaching-learning process, there are those who take the theoretical position that reinforcement is important and that positive reinforcements from others are to be preferred to negative reinforcements. An opposing theoretical position is that positive or negative reinforcements or rewards, i.e., approval or disapproval, must come from the learner himself; that is, from his ego. In practice, there is little warm, positive response of teachers and learners to themselves.

Currently, evaluation, which can be said to underlie

the matter of accountability, is a center of controversy. There are those who take the position that evaluation is an ends-means process, i.e., formulation of objectives and then selection of measuring instruments related to the objectives. An opposing position is that evaluation is goal-free, or can begin by making measurements and judgments about teaching-learning situations regardless of what the stated objectives have been. In practice, most evaluation involves testing unrelated to the school's objectives, and no revision of the curriculum in light of learner's responses. A last illustration of opposing positions in curriculum is that related to the question of whether curriculum development is linear. One position is that objectives must be clearly specified and learning experiences selected, organized, and evaluated. Another position is that the curriculum planner begins with significant learning experiences and evaluates outcomes along with intended learnings. In practice most instruction is determined by the text which has been adopted.

What has been hinted at in this introduction is that in the arena of struggles in curriculum, there are either-or positions which are being taken. In the following section there will be elaboration of three of the either-ors of the seven outlined curricular questions.

EITHER-ORS

1. Who does or who should make decisions about goals, instructional materials, and evaluation?

We shall discuss only who is and who should be involved in the making of decisions about goals. This question necessitates some clarification of two terms, decision-making and goals. For the purpose of some discussion a decision will be defined as a conscious choice based upon alternatives in regard to questions of goals. Goals are frequently confused with objectives, or the terms are used interchangeably.

California has gone so far as to provide definitions within the State Code, namely, "A goal is a statement of broad discussion or intent which is general and timeless and not concerned with a particular achievement within a specified time period (1972)." "An objective is a devised accomplishment which can be verified within a given time and under specifiable conditions which, if attained, advances the system toward a corresponding goal (1972)."

Goodlad has introduced the important distinction of levels of decision-making, according to the actors and, to a lesser degree, the nature of the decisions (1966). These levels are societal, institutional and instructional. Societal-level decisions are made by some controlling agency, such as a group of legislators or school board. Institutional-level decisions are made by a faculty of a particular school. Instructional-level decisions are made by a teacher or group of teachers responsible for a particular group of students. Tyler (1970) has added a fourth level, the personal, at which level individual students make their own decisions.

A study done by Griffin (1970) showed satisfactory agreement regarding decisions which were made at the societal and instructional level, but not at the institutional

level. This study of Griffin's did not deal with the matter of who should make the decisions, although there has been some discussion by writers that falls into the following pattern.

Position A	Position B
Individual closest to the data should make the decision.	Individual who is most affected by decision should make it.
(Teachers, therefore, should make decisions about objectives for a particular group of learners.)	(Individual learners should set their own goals or objectives.)

Another position would be:

Position A	Position B
Individual most capable should make the decision about objectives.	Individual most responsible should make decisions about objectives.
(Therefore, teacher should make decisions.)	(Therefore, parent should make decisions.)

2. What are or should be the objectives of the educational process?

Here the opposition is between the selection of cognitive or affective objectives in the instructional program. From many writers in curriculum, the emphasis is to develop rationality, critical thinking, or what has been termed the cognitive skills. In practice, however, the cognitive objectives have been of a low-level order, i.e., knowledge and comprehension. Values, appreciations, self-esteem (affective objectives) are highly lauded by some writers, and are considered as more basic than cognitive objectives. However, in practice, little attention other than lip-service has been given to affective objectives.

3. What is the nature of the teaching-learning process?

(Because of the complexity of this question, only one aspect will be singled out for discussion: the "reward" issue.) A prevalent opposition that can be stated is that reward or punishment is something done to a learner by the teacher, versus reward or punishment as something which the individual himself generates. In a very significant article by Havighurst, entitled "Minority Subcultures and the Law of Effect," (1970) a theory of the evolution of reward-punishment is postulated. In this conceptualization, Havighurst's theory involves components of age ranges in relation to the nature of the reward-punishment, to the giver of the reward-punishment, and to the area in which the behavior occurs. For example, during the ages of 5–10, the praise or approval is from outside persons. The givers of the reward-punishment are teachers and other adults in a teaching role, as well as himself, and the action area is in social skills and special motor skills.

In Havighurst's evolutionary conceptualization of the human reward-punishment system, it would appear that from age 10 to 15 years on, the wider community is a

Question	(Either)		(Or)
1. Who does or should make decisions about goals?	Legislators, or Educators, or Parents, or Students, or Community		
2. What are or should be goals (objectives)?	Cognitive objectives	or	Affective objectives
3. What is nature of teaching-learning process (reward)?	Positive and negative rewards administered by others	or	Positive and negative rewards administered by self
4. How can valid instructional materials be developed?	Objectives— effectiveness of materials is empirically verified	or	Materials— developed by subject matter experts. No learner verification.
5. What is nature of evaluation studies?	Evaluation is linear; objectives and instruments developed in terms of objectives	or	Goal-free evaluation
6. How can a staff be refreshed and reeducated?	Personnel development provided external to the institution	or	Personnel development provided within the institution
7. What is nature of curriculum development?	Ends-Means	or	Disregard of ends in planning

FIGURE 1. Illustrative Either-Ors.

giver of reward-punishments (p. 316). However, in the balance of the article he elaborates some additional considerations. These considerations clarify some of the complexities of the reward and punishment system of schooling. In our concerns as educators, the two most significant propositions that Havinghurst proposes are that "an effective reward system in a complex changing society must be based on a strong ego," and "a strongly developed ego gives a sense of personal control and personal responsibility for important events in one's life (p. 319)." However, in our judgment there are few individuals who live without support and encouragement from some significant others.

ASSUMPTIONS WHICH PROVIDE DIRECTION

In the previous section we discussed some of the either-ors of several of the questions, and diagrammed the controversies and presented them in Figure 1. Now we are giving some assumptions which provide direction for finding solutions to the either-or controversies. Prior to discussion of the assumptions, however, it will probably be useful to discuss the kind of person who is to emerge from schooling.

The kind of person who is to emerge from schooling is one who has an attitude toward himself and others, which is characterized by terms such as hopeful, self-controlled, purposeful, competent, faithful, loving, caring, and wise. Secondly, the person should manifest ego strength, and thirdly, be rational. Fourth, the person should understand himself and others. Lastly, the individual should manifest imagining, feeling, playing, fancying, and other qualities of mind. Following are some assumptions which have influenced our thinking. There are seven assumptions, which are pervasive in the processes, which we suggest are useful in formulating solutions to the current either-or controversies in curriculum development.

First Assumption. Education (Curriculum Development) is an art based upon science. Art, in this sense, means working with nature, and by working with it, facilitate the results which occur. To state it as expressed in the Syntopicon, the teacher, like the midwife, merely assists in a natural process which might be more painful and might possibly fail without such help. Dewey's contribution to this idea is that in concrete operation, education is an art (1929, p. 13). It is an art in the sense that it makes integrations of scientific material into its practices.

A few brief comments about the science aspect of this assumption. Science can be viewed as the intellectual manipulation of carefully verified observations which result in knowledge about particular phenomena. As John Dewey expounded, science is a protection from men of unusual power which results in slavish imitation and devotion to them and their ideas. Furthermore, in the subjects best developed from a scientific point of view, uniformity of procedure is not a consequence.

Second Assumption. Application of theory (whether psychological, sociological or the like) to a practical situation is a complex intellectual task. Because of the complexity of going from theory to practice, as well as the simplistic attempts which have been made, disbelief in theory continuously is expressed. Educational practice is highly complex. In classroom instruction, it involves psychological and sociological factors of teachers and students interacting with each other, as well as with content and media of instruction. To attempt to apply in a simple way, some theoretical finding (such as need achievement theory) to a particular group of students in an inner city school is disastrous. Fenstermacher (1967) has outlined an intellectual procedure which makes clear the complexity of going from theory to practice, but which also facilitates our utilization of theory. One conclusion from his work is that the difficulty may not be in theory but in how the practice has been formulated (pp. 86-83).

Third Assumption. Curriculum is a field of inquiry. This assumption implies that questions concerning curriculum are subject to investigation. Goodlad (1968), drawing upon the work of Conant, Dewey, and Schwab, makes four points which are of significance for us. The first is that there must be an interplay between theoretical-deductive and empirical-inductive modes of thought. Second, our inquiries must begin and end in the stuff of educational practice. Third, fluid inquiry reshapes a field, and fourth, invention provides an opportunity to blend theoretical-deductive and empirical-inductive inquiry into educational practice, which provides for fluid inquiry (p. 11).

Fourth Assumption. Effecting educational change is complex, and involves more influences than the teacher using materials for influencing pupil outcomes. Possibly the utilization of a paradigm, shown in Figure 2, as presented by Goodlad (1972), may provide much insight into our knowledge about improving schooling and learning.

Fifth Assumption. Curriculum and evaluation processes are not linear. Educators continue to search for an orderly approach to curriculum development. This orderly approach, as conceptualized, has been characterized by terms such as ends-means or linear. This approach, when briefly summarized, is as follows: first, select our objectives; second, select an activity appropriate to the objectives; third, evaluate the attainment of the objectives. In our judgment, this approach may present a useful way of viewing some aspects of curriculum development, but it is not what occurs or should occur. Rather, curriculum development does not and cannot proceed in a linear manner. Rather, curriculum development proceeds along many dimensions systematically and simultaneously. This is equally true of evaluation.

Sixth Assumption. Human behavior is interrelated and complex, and cannot usefully be analytically separated

into cognitive, affective, and psychomotor domains. For the last 25 years objectives have been classified into domains, and communication between educators has increased considerably. Unfortunately, the publications utilized by many in the field have fostered a conception of objectives as overt, and mainly cognitive. It is now advisable to think of goals and objectives and the three domains (cognitive, affective, and psychomotor) as interrelated facets of curriculum development. It is not possible to discuss one without considering the other. In fact, it is inadvisable to approach the task in a linear manner, since the result is a fragmented, uncoordinated mess. To repeat an earlier statement, a comprehensive approach to curriculum development must proceed along many dimensions systematically and simultaneously.

Seventh Assumption. Adults can make a significant contribution to curriculum development. Until recently the contribution of parents and other adults has been limited to collecting milk money, straightening out the cloakroom, and holding money-raising drives for school equipment, but this is no longer satisfactory to adults, nor does it draw upon the wide range of skills and abilities which they possess and which can facilitate student learning. We therefore strongly hold that adults become involved in a meaningful manner in curriculum development.

ILLUSTRATION OF APPLICATION OF ASSUMPTIONS

It is difficult to provide detailed illustration of the application of these assumptions. Two illustrations are readily available, which are characterized by some of our assumptions. The first illustration is that of the SWRL Kindergarten Reading Program. Baker and Schutz, in Instructional Product Development (1971), have described the character of effective instructional product development. According to Baker and Schutz, there are the following five systems: an instructional system; a training system; an installation system; an accountability system; and a modification system. While these five systems have distinct functions, they share in eleven com-

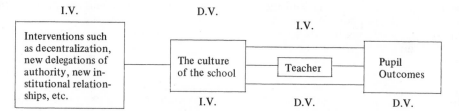

FIGURE 2. A paradigm for studying ends-means relationships and for improving schooling and learning with the teacher extracted from the school as a whole but influenced by it. This figure portrays the well-known paradigm, D. V. standing for dependent variables. This figure depicts the school as a variable dependent on conditions which are subject to adjustments of various kinds. But the school is also a set of conditions (independent variables) which cannot screen out the impact on the student of the total school culture. From Goodlad, John I. Staff Development: The League Model. *Theory into Practice,* 1972, *11*(4), p. 209.

mon characteristics, namely: outcomes, instruction, quality verification, monitoring, personnel, data, interfaces, procurement, information, continuity, and costs (xviii-xx). Baker and Schutz also state that for each of the five systems the requirements, specifications, and procedures of the eleven characteristics must be made explicit; and that the characteristics and systems are interdependent.

A second illustration is that presented by Goodlad (1972). He presents a paradigm for studying ends-mean relationships, and for improving schooling and learning, which extracts the teacher from the school as a whole but is influenced by it. This is, of course, a comprehensive conceptualization of schooling. This paradigm is presented in Figure 2.

These two illustrations are characterized at various points, particularly by assumptions pertaining to curriculum as a field of inquiry, as nonlinear and complex.

CONCLUSION

Throughout the preceding discussion there have been very few references to the person most affected by curriculum development activities, namely, the student. The objective is not that the student succeed in spite of the curriculum, but that the curriculum is a vital factor in student development. Schooling should encompass educational as well as instructional experiences. We wish to facilitate, as stated earlier, an individual who will emerge from the schooling experience as a hopeful, self-controlled, purposeful, competent, loving, caring, and wise person. He should have ego strength, be rational, understand himself and others, and have imaginative, warm qualities of mind. Schools are to facilitate the total development of the individual; curriculum developers can enhance the probability that this will in fact occur.

REFERENCES

Baker, R., and Schutz, R., eds. *Instructional Product Development.* New York: Van Nostrand Reinhold Co., 1971.

California State Legislature, Joint Committee on Educational Goals and Evaluation, and California State Department of Education. Vol. 1, *Guidelines for Total Community Participation in Forming and Strengthening the Future of Public Elementary and Secondary Education in California,* 1972.

Dewey, J. *Experience and Education.* New York: The Macmillan Co., 1938.

_____. *The Sources of a Science of Education.* New York: Liveright, 1929.

Doll, R. C. *Curriculum Improvement: Decision-Making and Process.* Boston: Allyn and Bacon, Inc., 1970.

Fenstermacher, G. Need Achievement Theory and Educational Practice: A Transformation. *Studies in Philosophy and Education,* 1967. (Proceedings of Twenty-Third Annual Meeting of the Philosophy of Education Society.)

Goodlad, J. I., with Richter, Maurice W. Jr. *The Development of a Conceptual System for Dealing with Problems of Curriculum and Instruction.* (The Cooperative Research Program of the Office of Education-U.S. HEW, Contract No. SAE-8024, Project No. 454) Report processed and forwarded by UCLA and /I/D/E/A/, 1966.

_____. Thought, Invention and Research in the Advancement of Education. *The Educational Forum,* 1968, *33,* 7-18.

_____. Staff Development: The League Model. *Theory into Prac-*

tice, 1972, *11*(4), 207-214.

Griffin, G. Curricular Decision-Making in Selected School Systems. Doctoral dissertation, University of California, Los Angeles, 1970.

Havighurst, R. J. Minority Subcultures and the Law of Effect. *American Psychologist,* 1970, *25*(4), 313-322.

Johnson, M. Jr. Definitions and Models in Curriculum Theory. *Educational Theory, 17,* No. 2, 127-140.

Macdonald, J., Wolfson, B., Zaret, E. Reschooling Society: A Conceptual Model. Association for Supervision and Curriculum Development, Washington, D.C., 1973.

Tyler, L. L. New Focus on the Library: Implications for Learning. Annual Conference of the Department of Curriculum, The University of British Columbia, February 12-13, 1970.

86

SYSTEMATIC INSTRUCTIONAL DEVELOPMENT

by Floyd Urbach
Associate Chairman for Instruction
Division of Education
Indiana University
South Bend, Indiana
and
Paul A. Twelker
Professor of Educational Research
Instructional Development Division
United States International University
Corvallis, Oregon

Systematic instructional development may be defined as the facilitation and improvement of the quality of human learning and teaching, achieved through the creative and orderly organization and evaluation of resources, the learning environment, media, and methods. Simply stated, it is a way of being systematic about how every aspect of an instructional problem is examined and interrelated. Judgments are made on the effects of one set of decisions as compared to other sets of decisions. Special attention is paid to the optimal use of resources capable of contributing to the problem solution. The end result of the application of instructional development techniques is a product—sometimes called an instructional system—that is capable of producing a desired result with specified types of learners under specified conditions. Implicit in systematic instructional development is the use of precisely stated objectives, empirically derived information (gained from the students and teachers in trial runs) that allows for the evaluation of the results of the system, and feedback loops that allow for revision based on the evaluative data. A systematic approach to instructional development usually involves:

Needs assessment (to determine what the problem really is)

Solution selection (to meet the needs)

Development of instructional objectives (if an *instructional* solution is indeed needed)

Analysis of tasks and content needed to meet the objectives

Selection of instructional strategies

Sequencing of instructional events

Selection of media

Developing or locating the necessary resources

Tryout/evaluation of the effectiveness of the resources

Revision of resources until they are effective

Recycling continuously through the whole process

(Association for Educational Communication and Technology, 1972, p. 38)

What has prompted the development of this complex but well-related set of techniques? No challenge is greater in education than that of using educational resources wisely (Green, 1972). Teachers, administrators, students, parents, politicians, and taxpayers have come to realize they must not only be concerned with buildings, materials, and equipment, but also, more importantly, with what actually happens to people in the process of learning. There is a growing awareness that the investment being made financially and in terms of people's time, including that of teachers, administrators and students, can result in greater dividends if the investment can be creatively and humanely managed.

> A way must be found to develop, within the educational system as a whole, and in each component, a climate conducive to personal growth, a climate in which innovation is not frightening, in which the creative capacities of administrators, teachers, and students are nourished and expressed rather than stifled. A way must be found to develop a climate in the *system* in which the focus is not upon *teaching*, but on the facilitation of self-directed *learning*. Only thus can we develop the creative individual who is open to all of his experience; aware of it and accepting it, and continually in the process of changing. And only in this way, I believe, can we bring about the creative, educational organization, which will also be continually in the process of changing. (Rogers, 1969)

Systematic instructional development represents a specialized way of thinking about students, teachers, and the total educational setting as related to the process of change. Central to bring "systematic" about processes of change is the use of a specific model that is used to guide the individual developer (or, more frequently, a team of developers). Instructional development models are generalized problem-solving strategies which help the developers organize information by guiding the developers to ask questions in a logical sequence. In this way, no critical component of the problem is overlooked. Different models reflect different ways of looking at people, learning, curricular content, and educational settings.

Although the different models seem quite dissimilar, there exist some general similarities. Essentially, systematic instructional development involves actions that fall into four major categories (see Figure 1): actions that help *define* the problem and organize a means to solve the problem; actions that help analyze and *develop* solutions to the problem; actions that serve to *evaluate* the solutions; and *revisions* that lead to refinement and are interrelated by feedback built into the model. The provision for feedback allows the instructional system to be refined and its effect enhanced.

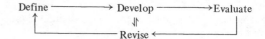

FIGURE 1. A Basic Instructional Development Model

In Figure 2 four major instructional development categories are presented. Note that for simplicity, the feedback loops have not been included. Feedback relationships are obviously possible and desirable between any of the functions.

STATE OF THE ART

No matter what shape or form the model of systematic instructional development, and there are scores of models, the four major categories outlined in Figure 2 must be dealt with in one way or another. Some systematic approaches fit only particular kinds of problems, some will produce only certain kinds of "build-in" solutions, and some do not fit educational settings at all. Model developers seem prone to "do their own thing," which contributes greatly to a confusion of words, jargon, and catch-phrases. Despite the technical jargon, the generalization can be made that the intent of each model is to guide developers by providing a logical flow of information which can be used to define the instructional problem, to develop an instructional solution, to evaluate the instructional solution, and to make thoughtful revisions based on evaluation data collected during tryouts of the instructional solution.

Experience to date has revealed that institutional adoption of systematic instructional development as a planning philosophy, as compared with some optimistic predictions, is moving more slowly and costing more money (in terms of the initial, preclassroom costs), and is supplementing rather than replacing older, less systematic planning approaches. Much of the inertia comes from such standard problems as a lack of a supportive administrative climate for implementing instructional development; the genuine lack of human and material resources to implement educational change on a massive scale; and the lack of effective follow-throughs (cf., Diamond, 1971). By far, the most critical contemporary issue seems to be cost (Stowe, 1971). Since instructional development is an expensive "hand-craft," large amounts of time are required to amortize the benefits that can accrue. The dilemma seems to be heightened by an institutional unwillingness to consider instructional costs in terms sensitive not only to traditional cost-per-student credit hour criteria, but also to "profits" in terms of

I: Definition and Management

1. Define Problems
   —assessment
   —priorities

2. Survey Resources
   —inside
   —outside

3. Establish Controls
   —personnel
   —finances

II: Analysis and Development

4. State Objectives
   —objective analysis
   —evaluation design

5. Analyze Strategies
   —type of learning
   —formats

6. Develop Materials
   —student
   —staff training

III: Tryout and Evaluation

7. Tryout Materials
   —components
   —total system

8. Evaluate Results
   —objective
     achievement
   —system efficiency

9. Decide Next Steps
   —revision
   —implementation

IV: Advertising and Distribution

10. Marketing System

    —advertise to
      target audience
    —procurement
      procedures

11. Dissemination System
    System

    —materials/products

    —people/procedures

12. Management System

    —fiscal procedures

    —legal requirements

FIGURE 2. A Generalized Model of Instructional Development

student-teacher time/energy savings, which can potentially be reinvested in more personal or more creative educational pursuits.

A number of significant efforts are being made to encourage institutional consideration and the adoption of systematic approaches to instructional development. The Carnegie Commission on Higher Education (1972) report emphasizes the need for "the design and utilization of effective instructional programs suitable for use or adaptation by more than one institution." Emphasis is also placed on the use of specialists, "to help faculty members define the objectives of courses of instruction, to plot the learning strategies to be employed, and to evaluate results."

Further support at higher education levels comes from a stimulating report, *The Case for Change* (Cox and Davis, 1972). Although written specifically for the biological sciences, the arguments generalize well to many educational areas.

Many in institutions of higher learning are prepared to scrutinize almost everything—the natural environment, government and industry, all manner of other institutions foreign and domestic—but they are loathe to scrutinize themselves and the institutions they inhabit . . . . It will be necessary to establish priorities that recognize the relative importance of teaching, research, and other activities according to their roles in meeting these objectives. It will require that each department periodically ask itself "Where are we going, what are we trying to accomplish, how will we know when we've done it, and how do these relate to the education of undergraduate students? . . . We are suggesting the same approach to this problem, and with the same standard of scientific logic that is expected in biological research. To do less, in fact, is to submit to the charge of "mindlessness" in higher education.

Another way to communicate the concept of systematic

instructional development is to use the term "curriculum management" (Prentice, 1973). In this approach, "the challenge is to adapt the tools and techniques of management to the special needs and requirements of the curriculum worker. . . ." A useful visual model is presented, illustrating the author's viewpoint of the relationship of the "curriculum component" as a part of the "development process."

A series of articles going into some depth on decision-making techniques of instructional development is presented in the Spring 1973 issue of *AV Communication Review*. Special emphasis is given to different kinds of analyses, including cost evaluation, management, learner analysis, task analysis, validation, and content analysis.

Several programs are concerned not only with individual learning settings, but also with applications aimed at developing "open learning systems" to be used in widespread geographical areas. The SUN Project (State University of Nebraska, 1973) is using an 18-step design/development process "based on extensive curricular and instructional research, which designs, develops, field tests, redesigns, and redevelops all lesson modules into a validated open learning course of superior quality." The design scheme is considered by its developers to be universally applicable at all grade levels. It has been applied in pre- and postsecondary settings and in several international school systems. Systematic development procedures have also been used to guide several emerging instructional systems incorporating cable television, and open circuit television, as well as consortia developmental efforts leading to cooperative exchanges of validated instructional systems.

Trends are developing in three additional areas: (1) a greater concern by developers for the characteristics of the learning system employed in instructional settings (Silber, 1972); (2) the kinds of useful prerequisite training of "change makers (Bhola et al., 1973); and (3) the dissemination and adaptation of already existing instructional systems (Carnegie Commission on Higher Education, 1972). In summary, systematic development procedures have come a long way in the past five years. "Tolerated by most, despised by some, and abused by all . . . systematic approaches are at the cutting edge of the design of learning and instructional systems (Silvern, 1972)."

SPECIFIC APPLICATIONS

Recent survey activities conducted by a variety of organizations, such as the Technological Applications Project (cf. Urbach, 1973); Project ALERT (cf. Henrie, 1972); and the State University of New York (cf. Houston, 1973) reveal thousands of applications of instructional development procedures to all kinds of educational problems, and in all kinds of educational settings. To provide some insight into the range, magnitude, and sophistication of applications of systematic instructional development, a few samples will be described.

Instructional Development Institutes

Instructional Development Institutes (IDI) is a unique instructional system, which was not only developed by the application of systematic instructional development procedures, but is also a system used to train teachers, administrators, and supervisors in the techniques of instructional development. Based on the nine-function instructional development model, this forty-hour institute begins with a review of the critical need to apply systematic procedures, and ends by having teams outline the initial design stages of a problem selected by the trainees. Developed, field tested, and validated over a four-year period, this instructional system has been applied in over 200 institute settings.

Project LIFE

Project LIFE was initially designed for disadvantaged and handicapped children. This sophisticated reading program encompasses a number of related instructional systems. Systematic development has been a keystone.

> The role of Systems Development, as based upon assessed instructional needs, is to design, produce, and developmentally test programmed educational materials. Instructional needs are determined by carefully considering requests from field test centers, trends in curriculum design, and recommendations from consultants in the fields of language and intellectual development. A series of planning sessions are held to determine those filmstrips that will best meet the above needs and also maintain the necessary continuity for a sequentially designed program. Instructional Material Specialists write appropriate educational purposes and behavioral objectives, and design the materials within the constraints of the objectives. These materials go through a series of reviews and revisions before they are produced for developmental testing. After the material is thoroughly tested in this evaluative stage, it is then released to the research department for distribution to the field test centers and to the commercial distributor. (Pfau, 1972)

Project COULD

Project COULD (Career Orientation Utilizing Language Development) has utilized the language arts areas of reading, writing, listening, and speaking as the vehicles to promote vocational awareness and exploration. The first of six pilot instructional systems, developed as part of a forestry career education series extending from grades 3–6, and entitled *Logging*, features field trips, 16mm films, audiotape interviews, overhead transparencies, filmstrips, pamphlets, resource persons and simple competitive games. The content of *Logging* includes 46 learning activities related to 12 logging jobs, logging vocabulary, environmental factors, and economic influence.

Audio-Tutorial Modules

Representative of a large number of audio-tutorial modules is an instructional system on general biology developed by Mary E. Lynch. Developers of audio-tutorial instructional systems typically use a preconceived development model, in which the developmental activities revolve around testing instructional components until they yield the desired level of achievement with the desired population of students. The *General Biology* system is designed to enable students to work independently within a laboratory, and to participate in seminar-discussion activities. Audio tapes direct the student in the use of a variety of materials, including a laboratory manual, slides, film loops, sound films, and television. Students are expected to attend, each week, two lectures, one small group discussion period, and one three-hour audio-tutorial laboratory period. As is the case with other audio-tutorial applications, special carrels are desirable.

Wayne State University

Theodore B. Fleming, Jr., at Wayne State University, has developed an *American Government* system that provides for needs of accelerated students, as well as for those who need assistance in achieving minimum competence levels. The *American Government* System offers concurrently three tracks in this basically self-paced, one-quarter course:

> Track One is required of all students, and incorporates large and small group meetings, supplemented by study guides, audio devices, sound film, and television tapes.

> Track Two allows students the opportunity to pursue specialized, individual, in-depth study of segments of American government. Extra credit is given for participation in this track.

> Track Three is basically a tutorial assistance program for students who score below a predetermined level on exams.

Far West Laboratory for Educational Research and Development

The Far West Laboratory has designed an instructional system for teachers and administrators in elementary schools that describes six new, relatively well-developed programs suitable for science education (Hutchins, 1971). The *Elementary Science Information Unit* addresses the need of teachers and administrators to have information that will serve to decrease the work load of the school personnel responsible for reviewing these developments for possible adoption. Systematic developmental procedures were used to ensure that information is presented clearly and effectively.

From these examples, it is clear that the application of systematic instructional development is not limited to a narrow range of educational problems that involve only students, but rather encompasses a broad range of problems including the communication of information.

CURRENT CONTROVERSIES

Does instructional development dehumanize education or humanize education? Some advocates paint bright pictures of the potential of systematic development for freeing teachers to be more human and creative, by ensuring that teachers know what it is that they are attempting to do; by maximizing the use of available resources; and by creating a supportive atmosphere to carry teachers through the inevitable conflicts and tensions that accompany creative change efforts.

Opponents of advocacy maintain that the systematic procedures too often result in an instructional lockstep which stifles creativity, particularly when a team approach is used. The results are all too often compromises which satisfy no one. There is great concern that the products of systematic instructional development procedures tend to be narrow, sequentially programmed units of instruction, focusing primarily on written responses as evidence of accomplishment and largely ignoring the more exciting, stimulating aspects of interpersonal learning.

As advocates of systematic instructional development procedures, our position is that traditional development has too long been vested in passive acceptance of curriculum materials. Locally produced or adapted materials, when generated by individuals or teams who follow systematic guidelines to development, can produce instructional systems with greater flexibility in use and with application to more students. Although we are aware of excellent learning materials developed by creative individuals, all too often their materials are of value to students only when taught by the developer. Systematic instructional development is particularly valuable when used on sets of learning/instructional problems which involve several subpopulations of students and many teachers (and perhaps many schools), and where the intent is to produce well-integrated instructional systems with wide application. Systematic team development does take time and money, but so do individual efforts, where the costs are simply not as visible and the failures are more easily overlooked.

When does instructional development apply? Should every instructional problem be subjected to an instructional development approach? Some would say that whenever a teacher wishes to develop any unit of instruc-

tion, however small, the systems approach to instructional development should be used. Others point to the costly and time-consuming process of instructional development, and reserve the process for larger projects that have fiscal resources necessary to sustain a sophisticated systematic developmental process.

In the immediate past, most publicized applications of the systems approach have been limited to projects conducted by regional educational laboratories, university and independent research-development agencies, or special curriculum projects well supported by grants. Increasingly, local school systems have budgeted for local development in terms of released time and provisions for the production of instructional materials. A number of school systems of modest size and budgets have now carried on such efforts for several years. Philosophically it would follow that an individual developer, working within whatever resource limits, would find the intellectual process of following systematic procedures helpful. Systematic approaches help to ensure that each aspect of the selected problem is thoroughly thought through, and that the most reasonable design solutions are arrived at. In particular, the concepts related to the basic nine functions, if used as a simple reminder for what should be done, would do much to help many individual developers create a more useful product for their students.

Where should the instructional development approach be applied? Current thought seems to favor the position that major instructional development efforts cannot operate in isolation from the total institutional setting. Educators at all levels must develop their answers to the following kinds of questions:

What of the teacher who wishes to apply the process but cannot gain institutional support (psychological or fiscal)?

What of the emerging educational movements that are noninstitutionally based?

Is systematic instructional development a tool only for elite groups of developers who are fortunate enough to acquire the necessary funds to apply what has been termed a "generic problem-solving model"?

Is instructional development linear, cyclical, or integrative? To some, instructional development is a linear approach, where one begins with specifying what is to be learned, continues with specifying how it is to be learned, and ends with assessing whether it has been learned. For others, this linear approach is too simplistic, and does not reflect the way people actually operate. These proponents consider instructional development as a cyclical system, where adjustments are made by systematically reconsidering each design function. The process is repeated until the system is improved to the point that it can accomplish stated goals with a high degree of replicability. Finally, for others, instructional development is integrative, in that all aspects of the process are worked on simultaneously. The assumption is that each step interacts with the other.

In practice, great variability arises from the background of each developer and personal preferences in problem-solving. In our view the critical criterion for systematic development is the conscientious revision of instructional systems by use of data derived from tryouts. It is desirable, although not essential, that members of a development team subscribe to a common philosophy as to how they prefer to operate in their setting.

SUMMARY

Systematic instructional development may be defined as the facilitation and improvement of the quality of human learning and teaching, achieved through the creative and orderly organization and evaluation of resources, the learning environment, media, and methods. It is a way of being systematic about how every aspect of an instructional problem is examined and interrelated. Judgments made on the effects of one set of decisions are compared to other sets of decisions, while special attention is paid to the optimal use of resources capable of contributing to the problem's solution. The end result of the application of instructional development techniques is a product—usually called an *instructional system*—that is capable of producing a desired result with specified types of learners under specified conditions.

REFERENCES

Association for Educational Communications and Technology. The Field of Educational Technology: A Statement of Definition. *Audiovisual*, 1972, *17*, 38.

Bhola, H. S., Jwa/Deh, A., and Knowlton, J., Training the Change Makers in Education. *Audiovisual Instruction*, 1973, *18*, 22-24.

Carnegie Commission on Higher Education. *The Fourth Revolution: Instructional Technology in Education*. New York: McGraw-Hill Book Company, 1972.

Cox, D., and Davis, L. V. *The Context of Biological Education: The Case for Change*. Washington, D.C.: Commission on Undergraduate Education in the Biological Sciences, American Institute for Biological Sciences, 1972.

Diamond, R. M. Instructional Development—Fact, or Fiction. *Audiovisual Instruction*, 1971, *16*, 6-7.

Green E. Millions for Lemons. *The Sunday Oregonian*, August 6, 1972.

Henrie, S., ed. *ALERT Sourcebook of Elementary Curricula, Programs and Projects*. San Francisco: Far West Laboratory for Educational Research and Development (1855 Folsom Street), 1972.

Houston, W. R., ed. *Performance Education: Resources for Performance-Based Education*. Albany, New York: The State University of New York, The State Education Department, Division of Teacher Education and Certification, 1973.

Hutchins, C. L. *Educational Development Case Study: An Elementary Science Information Unit*. Berkeley: Far West Laboratory for Educational Research and Development, 1971.

Pfau, G. S. Project LIFE: Programming Rationale and Process. *National Society for Programmed Instruction* (NSPI), 1972.

Prentice, M. Management: Curse, Cure-all, or Workable Concept? *Journal of the Association for Supervision and Curriculum Development*, 1973, *30*, 310-312.

Rogers, C. R. *Freedom to Learn*. Columbus, Ohio: Charles E. Merrill, 1969.

Silber, K. H. The Learning System. *Audiovisual Instruction*, 1972, *17*, 10-27.

Silvern, L. C. *Systems Engineering Applied to Training*. Houston: Gulf Publishing Co., 1972.

State University of Nebraska. *SUN Background and Future Plans*. Unpublished monograph. Lincoln, Nebraska: SUN Project, State University of Nebraska, 1973.

Stowe, R. A. The Critical Issue in Instructional Development. *Audiovisual Instruction*, 1971, *16*, 8-10.

Twelker, P. A., Urbach, F., and Buck, J. *The Systematic Development of Instruction: An Overview and Basic Guide to the Literature*. Stanford, California: ERIC Clearinghouse on Media and Technology, 1972.

Urbach, F. *Technological Applications Project Progress Report, June 1973*. Corvallis, Oregon: Instructional Development Division, United States International University, 1973.

ADDITIONAL RESOURCES

Baker, Robert L., and Shutz, Richard E., eds. *Instructional Product Development*. New York: Van Nostrand Reinhold Co., 1971. Wide scope, with sufficient depth to make this a must on the novice's bookshelf.

Cavert, C. Edward. *Procedural Guidelines for the Design of Mediated Instruction*. Washington, D.C.: Association for Educational Communications and Technology, 1973; and Cavert, C. Edward, *An Approach to the Design of Mediated Instruction*. Washington, D.C.: Association for Educational Communications and Technology, 1973. Excellent guidebooks on designing mediated instruction through application of an 18-step model.

Cram, David. *Designing Effective Instruction*. Palo Alto, California: General Programmed Teaching, A Division of Commerce Clearninghouse, Inc., 1970. A practical, programmed treatment of important aspects of instructional development.

Gerlach, Vernon S., and Ely, Donald P. *Teaching and Media: A Systematic Approach*. Englewood Cliffs: Prentice-Hall, Inc., 1970. A combination guide and handbook on selecting and utilizing material to achieve classroom teaching/learning objectives.

Johnson, Rita B., and Johnson, Stuart R. *Assuring Learning with Self-Instructional Packages, or Up the Up Staircase*. Chapel Hill, North Carolina: Self Instructional Packages, Inc. (P.O. Box 2009), 1971. A basic reference for the novice.

Popham, W. James, and Baker, Eva L., *Establishing Instructional Goals*. Englewood Cliffs: Prentice-Hall, Inc., 1970; Popham, W. James, and Baker, Eva L., *Planning an Instructional Sequence*. Englewood Cliffs: Prentice-Hall, Inc., 1970; and Popham, W. James, and Baker, Eva L., *Systematic Instruction*. Englewood Cliffs: Prentice-Hall, Inc., 1970. Useful set of three self-instructional programs covering many aspects of instructional development.

Larson, L. C. *Instructional Technology Graduate Degree Programs in U.S. Colleges and Universities, 1969-71*. Washington, D.C.: Association for Educational Communications and Technology, 1971. Exhaustive listing of institutions offering graduate programs in instructional technology.

Rippey, Robert M., ed. *Studies in Transactional Evaluation*. Berkeley, Calif.: McCutchan Publishing Corp. (2526 Grove St.), 1973. Esoteric, perhaps, but on the cutting edge of evaluation techniques intimately concerned with formative evaluation in instructional development.

Journals

Audiovisual Instruction
Association for Educational Communications and Technology
1201 Sixteenth Street, N. W.
Washington, D.C. 20036

One of the very best publications for the instructional development novice. Volume 16 (December 1971) devoted to instructional development. (Annual subscription $12)

Curriculum Theory Network
Publication Sales
The Ontario Institute for Studies in Education
Department of Curriculum
252 Bloor St. West
Toronto 181, Ontario.

Informal, international forum for both curriculum researchers and practitioners. (Annual subscription $14)

Educational Product Report (Formerly EPIE Forum)
Educational Products Information Exchange
386 Park Avenue So.
New York, New York 10016

Disseminates dependable information about specifications, critical characteristics, and actual school performance of instructional materials, equipment, and systems for preschool through junior college grades. (Annual subscription $35)

Educational Technology
Educational Technology Publications
140 Sylvan Avenue
Englewood Cliffs, New Jersey 07632

Comprehensive, informative, and practical magazine for "managers of change in education." (Annual subscription $18)

Journal of Educational Technology Systems
Baywood Publishing Company
1 Northwest Avenue
Farmingdale, New York 11735.

Systems oriented journal dealing with the interface of instructor-student-curriculum-hardward-software. (Annual subscription $20)

Major Interest Groups, Associations, and Organizations

National Society for Programmed Instruction (NSPI)
P.O. Box 137, Cardinal Station
Washington, D.C. 20017

Members usually include persons concerned with the preparation and use of programmed learning materials for schools, industry, the military, government, and health sciences.

Association for Educational Communications and Technology
1201 Sixteenth Street, N.W.
Washington, D.C. 20036

Members are mainly audiovisual and instructional materials specialists, educational technologists, instructional development specialists, audiovisual and television production personnel, and teacher educators. Two affiliate organizations are especially active in instructional development:

(1) Community College Association for Instruction and Technology. Facilitates the exchange of data, reports, and information pertinent to media and related instructional problems. One of the key groups in the nation encouraging systematic instructional development.
(2) Division of Instructional Development. Dedicated to the study, evaluation, definition, and dissemination both of the process and theory and practical aspects of instructional development. DID is concerned with fostering cooperation and coordination among institutions, agencies, foundations, and organizations concerned with instructional development.

Sources to Contact

Mr. Joe Orndorff
Office of Community Services of the Dayton/Miami
  Valley Consortium
32 N. Maine, Suite 1301
Dayton, Ohio 45402

Dr. Charles Schuller, Consortium Director
University Consortium for Instructional Development
  and Technology
Department of Instructional Technology
University of Southern California
Los Angeles, California 90007

Dr. Glen Pfau, Director
Project LIFE
National Education Association
1201 16th Street, N.W.
Washington, D.C.

Mr. Donald E. Day, Project Coordinator
Coos County Intermediate Education District
2405 Colorado Street
North Bend, Oregon 97459

Ms. Mary E. Lynch
Department of Biology
Manhattan College
Bronx, New York 10471

Mr. Theodore B. Fleming, Jr.
Wayne State University
Detroit, Michigan 48202

Far West Laboratory for Educational Research
  and Development
1 Garden Circle
Hotel Claremont
Berkeley, California

87

CURRICULUM DEVELOPMENT IN HIGH SCHOOLS

by Galen Saylor
Professor of Secondary Education
University of Nebraska
Lincoln, Nebraska

Curriculum development in high schools is the process of planning an educational program for the schooling of adolescents and young adults. The process encompasses these four major aspects: (1) defining the functions and correlative goals of the high school; (2) designing an educational program that will enable students to attain these goals, including the selection of a program of course offerings, extrainstructional activities and out-of-school learning opportunities, the services to be provided students, and seeking to establish the nature of the social and intellectual climate of the school; (3) planning instructional processes and procedures; and (4) formulating methods for determining the outcomes of instruction and the extent to which the goals have been attained.

DEFINING FUNCTIONS

Historically, society has assigned the secondary schools four basic functions:

Transmission of the culture: mastery of learning skills; acquisition of knowledge essential for group life; mastery of one or more major fields of study, to the extent necessary for specialization; and ability to use the methods of rational and intellectual thought.

Socialization of the young: knowledge of and acceptance of the ethos and moral structure of the society; inculcation of the values, mores, traditions, and beliefs of the social group; acquisition of modes of behavior that exemplify the common patterns of living and group conduct; and ability and desire to live the life of the group.

Preparation for adulthood: career selection and preparation at the introductory level; capabilities to fulfill parenthood and citizenship responsibilities; and competency to contribute to the improvement of the life of the social group.

Development of the individual: achievement of self-fulfillment; development of talents and capabilities; competency in self-directiveness and self-discipline; and attainment of personal well-being.

These functions are not discrete elements in schooling; they are intertwined and interrelated aspects of human development. Throughout the history of this country, however, the emphasis given these purposes in secondary schools has shifted relatively, although a continuing, basic program of studies has been evident.

FORMULATING GOALS

Goals give direction to the program of the high school, as it seeks to fulfill the functions assigned it by society. The purposes of a school are usually stated in a hierarchical order. First are the broad, general goals designed to spell out the functions; second are subgoals—more specific and detailed statements of outcomes desired in each category of general goals. Subgoals constitute the basis for planning the curriculum of the school. The final step in goal definition is the formulation of objectives that guide the instructional process.

Until late in the nineteenth century, the general goals of the secondary school were devoted quite largely to the transmission of the culture, the acquisition of knowledge, and preparation for further education. In its 1893 report on the program of the high school, the renowned Committee of Ten (1893) insisted that "their main function is to prepare for the duties of life" (p. 51) the intellectual elite of the nation. The Committee's concept of preparation for life was to pursue a highly academic program of studies, confined to the five basic fields of English, social sciences, science, mathematics, and foreign languages.

Twenty-five years later the Commission on the Reorganization of Secondary Education (1918) defined the "main objectives of education" as "1. Health. 2. Command of fundamental process. 3. Worthy home-membership. 4. Vocation. 5. Citizenship. 6. Worthy use of leisure. 7. Ethical character (pp. 10-11)." It declared that "education in a democracy, both within and without the school, should develop in each individual the knowledge, interests, ideals, habits, and powers whereby he will find his place and use that place to shape both himself and society toward ever nobler ends (p. 9)."

Thus, by 1918 the goals of the secondary school had broadened greatly, to encompass all four of the functions stated above. The secondary schools of this country have endeavored ever since that era to develop a program of education within these seven "Cardinal Principles of Secondary Education." That the ideal has not been fully achieved yet, almost three-quarters of a century later, is recognized by educators and citizens alike; the primary responsibility of the high schools in the future is to implement more fully the concepts of democratic education that have long been accepted as the birthright of every child.

One of the most promising developments in curriculum planning for secondary schools in recent years is the efforts of a number of states, and a large number of local school systems, to involve citizens generally in a study of the aims of education, and in the subsequent formulation of a set of goals for the schools, including the establishment of priorities in curriculum development for implementation of those goals. Examples are statewide programs in California, Florida, Nebraska, Oregon, Colorado, West Virginia, and Pennsylvania.

DESIGNING AN EDUCATIONAL PROGRAM

Curriculum developments in secondary schools in recent years may be classified roughly in these categories: program of studies, course content and organization, individualization of instruction, alternative programs, and extraclassroom activities. Several organizational developments have important curriculum connotations, and will be noted briefly.

Programs of Studies

Secondary schools throughout the country offer a plethora of courses—the U.S. Office of Education, in its most recent survey (Wright, 1965), received reports of 1,100 different titles—but many of them are quire similar in content and goals. The USOE reduced their final list for tabulation to 291 distinct courses, compared to 274 titles included in the previous survey in 1949, and 206 in a similar study in 1934.

The large number of titles reported by the schools represents the subdivision of the basic fields of study into various segments of content. In recent years this procedure constitutes an effort to develop courses that are more specialized in nature for advanced students, provide more meaningful and relevant courses for particular groups of students, and/or add new courses that deal with subjects and topics that school staffs believe serve better the needs of students in today's world.

These developments in the course program of the secondary schools have been stimulated, supported, and often, carried forward by a number of highly influential national curriculum development commissions, professional organizations, learned societies, and civic, social, and political agencies.

Curriculum study and planning commissions at the national level have been established under the auspices of, and supported by, the National Science Foundation and The United States Office of Education. Examples of such planning commissions are the Physical Science Study Committee, Biological Sciences Curriculum Study, Chemical Education Material Study, School Mathematics Study Group, Project Social Studies, The English Program, and the American Industries Project. Some other Federal agencies, such as the National Foundation for the Arts and Humanities, and the President's Council on Youth Fitness, have also spurred curriculum developments in their areas of concern. The National Defense Education Act of 1958, and the Vocational Education Act of 1963, and their respective amendments, have also given impetus to curriculum developments in the areas of science, mathematics, foreign languages, and vocational and career education.

Examples of national professional organizations and learned societies that have prompted significant curriculum developments in their respective areas of interest are the Modern Language Association, the National Council of Teachers of English, the American Association for Health, Physical Education, and Recreation, the Mathematics Association of America, National Council for the Social Studies, and the Joint Council for Economic Education.

Considerable influence on the nature of the high school program in recent years has been wielded by prominent educators who spoke and wrote effectively about needed changes in the program. The most influential of these advocates was James B. Conant, whose book, *The American High School Today* (1959), has served as a guide to program planning in many of the nation's high schools.

All these efforts in curriculum planning have resulted in some important changes in both course programs and nature and organization of content. The fields of science, mathematics, and foreign languages have expanded considerably. Smaller high schools, with only a course or two in science or mathematics, or no offering in the languages, now offer introductory courses in the usual subjects; and at least two years of one, and possibly two, languages. It is in the larger high schools, however, that programs in these fields have been greatly extended.

In addition to introductory level courses in physics, chemistry, and biology, many offer an advanced course or seminar in one or more of these subjects. In addition, new courses in life science, anthropology, earth science, and environmental science are now available in a number of high schools. The most important developments, however, have been in the content of courses and its organization for instructional purposes. The national curriculum commissions in the sciences have devoted much of their efforts to this aspect of curriculum planning. Emphasis is placed on the structure of a discipline and the general

principles that characterize the theory and research of the field.

In mathematics similar developments have taken place. High schools have added a considerable array of advanced courses, such as calculus, analytical geometry, probability and statistics, and a seminar or class in topics in mathematics. Content of all courses has often been drastically revised in terms of modern mathematical processes, particularly those used in computerization of data and analysis.

Offerings in foreign languages expanded greatly in the late 1950s and 1960s. Many small schools that had dropped the subject added at least one, and sometimes two, languages to the program, and in larger schools the offerings in the principal tongues—German, French, and Spanish—were extended to a four-year program. Often these schools introduced other languages, such as Russian, Hebrew, and Chinese. Instructional methods changed greatly with the emphasis on audiolingual procedures and the introduction of language laboratories.

In the field of English, two important developments in secondary schools are the introduction of formal courses and programs in developmental and remedial reading, and of specialized courses that cover only a segment of the traditional general literature and composition courses. Often these consist of short-term unit courses, designated as minicourses or half-semester courses. Thus students are free to select more courses in their English program, and ones that have more appeal. In the composition program, greater attention is given to linguistics, transformational grammar, and literary styles that convey meaning more effectively. Offerings in literature include opportunities to read and study the writings of black authors and other interpreters of the culture of minority groups, the works of non-Western writers, and books and articles that treat present-day social problems in the idiomatic language of the street. Journalism has emerged as an area for serious study by selected students, and the program often serves as a precareer exploratory opportunity.

In the field of social studies, likewise, both course offerings and content have changed quite markedly in recent years. As in English, new courses have been introduced that deal with smaller segments of specialized topics of a subject field, in contrast to the traditional, broad survey courses in history, geography, modern problems, and the like. These may be the new type of minicourses, or short term courses, or regular semester programs. The intent, again, is to enable students to select from a much broader list of offerings, permitting specialization or opportunities to pursue interests. Regular type courses have often been added in economics, psychology, sociology, and geography. Staffs have endeavored to revise course content in the entire program, to give greater attention to the basic principles of the subject, and to deal with the important social issues and problems facing the nation.

Turning to program offerings beyond the five basic academic fields, the area of physical education, health, and safety has expanded in recent years, particularly with the addition of driver education to the program, and a more extensive program in health education. Many schools provide instruction in sex education and drug abuse, either as separate offerings or as part of other health courses.

In the arts, curriculum development has not been as extensive or as broad as in the areas previously discussed. Music has long been an important part of the program of the secondary school, with even the smaller schools sponsoring a "marching" band. The improvement of the program has come principally in upgrading the work of the advanced courses and musical groups. Theory, composition, and trends are studied by these select groups, and the performances of ensembles and groups are often quite superior in quality.

In art, much of the same developments have taken place as in music. Programs have been expanded in most high schools, principally by offering advanced courses in the field and by broadening the program to include opportunities to work in a number of media. Opportunities for individual work are often extensive. The quality of the art produced by gifted students in many schools is outstanding.

A few large city school systems, such as New York, Philadelphia, Newark, Detroit, and Los Angeles, either have established special high schools for the arts and music, or developed specialized programs in selected high schools of the city.

The area of vocational education has been extended greatly in recent years. The Vocational Education Act of 1963, and subsequent amendments, provide large amounts of Federal support for approved programs in the secondary schools. The earlier acts limited subsidies to agriculture, home economics, trades and industry, and distributive education. Now the schools have almost complete freedom to offer any program of vocational preparation that conforms to general Federal and state regulations. Work experience, or types of apprentice training, are aspects of most programs. The U.S. Office of Education launched in the early 1970s a coordinated program designated as career education. It emphasizes not only prevocational and vocational courses, but greatly improved programs of guidance and counseling designed to assist youth in making decisions about careers.

Summarizing curriculum development in terms of total program of offerings, it is noted that secondary schools generally, during the past decade or two, have been endeavoring to provide (1) a great variety of courses and programs, especially of a more specialized and advanced nature; (2) the revision of the content of courses, in an effort to make the program more meaningful and relevant for students, and to prepare them better to continue specialization in a chosen field of study or work; or to deal more effectively with the major social, economic, political, and personal problems and issues confronting youth and young adults; and (3) a greater degree of flexibility and freedom of choice for students in pursuing their programs of study in high school.

INSTRUCTION

Planning instructional modes and procedures is an essential aspect of curriculum development. In recent years significant trends in the teaching process may be sum-

marized as follows:

Use of Technology

Although teachers have used various kinds of audio and visual aids for as long as we have had formal programs of schooling, the variety and sophistication of the aids used has increased greatly in recent years. Motion pictures, still projections, recordings, television, teaching machines, computers, radio, models, electronically equipped laboratories and classrooms, and dial access systems are now commonplace among achools. However, the extent and effective use of such equipment and resources varies greatly among teachers. The electronic equipment enables a school to provide extensive opportunities for students to work individually, and to adapt instruction to personal needs and interests.

Inquiry and Discovery Modes

Most of the national curriculum planning commissions, especially those in science, mathematics, and the social sciences, recommended the use of teaching procedures that encouraged or required students to engage in problem-solving, investigation, simple research, and generalization as aspects of the learning experiences. Courses in health, homemaking, family life, agriculture, industrial arts, psychology, and consumer education also make extensive use of problem-solving methods of instruction. Games and simulation situations also provide flexibility and student participation.

Individualization

Although the individualization of instruction has been a popular slogan for many decades, and especially since the great influx of youth into secondary schools during the 1920s and 1930s, it has only been in the 1960s and the 1970s that high schools have developed effective methods and procedures for providing a significant degree of individualization. The principal method used for many years has been the sectioning of students in the basic academic subjects by achievement or ability levels. But instruction still continued in a class situation.

Some of the newer procedures include independent study projects, contract plans, individual progress by the use of learning packets, instruction in small groups, quest programs, seminars, nongraded schools, individually guided instruction, learning community plans, case study methods, computer-assisted instruction, supervised correspondence courses, use of instructional modules, open laboratories for individual use, the informal or open classroom plan, advanced placement or college-level courses, and dual school enrollment plans, such as central vocational and technical centers.

The alternative school movement is a significant attempt to provide a high degree of individualization of schooling. Not only do these schools offer a program often differing greatly from that available in the regular public or nonpublic high schools, but they have stimulated them to modify courses, programs, and requirements, or offer some new types of opportunities for specific groups of students.

Learning Resource Centers

As an aspect of individualization, many high schools today have established sub-libraries, usually designated as resource centers. In such facilities, various kinds of materials devoted to a single field of study, such as science, social studies, English, or mathematics, are brought together for student use. Such resources include books, films, slides, models, reference works, magazines, specimens, recordings, and a whole array of audiovisual aids to instruction.

EVALUATION

Ascertaining the extent to which students have attained the goals defined by the school is the culminating aspect of curriculum planning. Even to this day, school staffs have failed seriously in appraising their programs in terms of the broad, general goals enunciated by the school. Formal appraisal is usually limited to the administration of tests, success of graduates in college, accreditation by state departments of education and voluntary regional association, and occasionally, in some systems, a survey by an outside agency. Informally, the sentiments of the students themselves, parents, and other citizens may contribute some gross judgments about the merits of a school's program.

Seldom do any of these kinds of evaluation determine to an appreciable extent the attainment of goals of an affective nature, such as attitudes, values, character traits, behavior, human relationships, self-image, and appreciations; nor even of the higher levels of cognitive development, such as analysis, synthesis, generalization, and rationality.

Some progress is being made currently in the improvement of the evaluative process, but secondary schools have not yet taken steps to carry on definitive assessments of their total programs.

THE FUTURE

Schools, especially secondary schools, change slowly in terms of the total, overall program of education for youth. Most innovations in recent years have been directed to the improvement of an existing program, rather than the development of new kinds of educational opportunities. Doubtless this is a proper course of action for such an important social institution.

It is likely that schools will extend and expand their efforts to individualize programs at the secondary level. Much more flexibility in all aspects of the school's administration and program, and many more alternative programs, will be evident in the years ahead. The school will establish and administer programs of various kinds that will be offered outside the school building itself. Youth and young adults will be able to pursue their schooling in a variety of settings and places, and to engage in a variety of programs that best serve their educational needs. And education, whether under the direction of a secondary school, postsecondary-level institutions, colleges and universities, private business firms and offices, or government agencies, will continue for a lifetime.

REFERENCES

Alternatives in Public Education: Movement or Fad. Special Issue. *NASSP Bulletin,* 1973, *57,* No. 374.

Firth, G. R., and Kimpston, R. D. *The Curricular Continuum in Perspective.* Itasca,Ill.: F. E. Peacock, Publishers, 1973.

Saylor, J. G., and Alexander, W. M. *Planning Curriculum for Schools.* New York: Holt, Rinehart and Winston, Inc., 1974.

Tanner, D. *Secondary Curriculum: Theory and Development.* New York: The Macmillan Company, 1971.

Unruh, G. G., and Alexander, W. M. *Innovations in Secondary Education,* 2nd ed. New York: Holt, Rinehart and Winston, Inc., 1974.

ADDITIONAL RESOURCES

Commission on the Reorganization of Secondary Education. *Cardinal Principles of Secondary Education.* U.S. Office of Education, Bulletin 1918, No. 35. Washington, D.C.: Government Printing Office, 1918.

Committee on Secondary School Studies (Committee of Ten). *Report of the Committee on Secondary School Studies Appointed at the Meeting of the National Education Association,* July 9, 1892. Washington D.C.: Government Printing Office, 1893.

Conant, J. B. *The American High School Today.* New York: McGraw-Hill Book Company, 1959.

Wright, G. S. *Subject Offerings and Enrollments in Public Secondary Schools.* U.S. Office of Education, OE-24015-61. Washington, D.C.: Government Printing Office, 1965.

88

PROGRAMMED INSTRUCTION

by Sivasailam Thiagarajan
Assistant Director for Instructional Development
Center for Innovation in Teaching the Handicapped
2805 East Tenth Street
Bloomington, Indiana 47401

Programmed instruction (PI) may be defined in terms of either the product or the process. Early product-oriented definitions identified a program as an instructional sequence. In this sequence the learner was presented with small units of content, kept actively involved in making frequent responses, reinforced with the immediate knowledge of the correct response, and led to the mastery of the instructional objectives through successively closer approximations. This definition is no longer in vogue, because it is too constraining with its references to a particular medium (print), a particular method of programming (linear), and a particular model (operant conditioning). More recent, product-oriented approaches use a "black box" definition, which identifies a program as any instructional material which enables any learner from a defined target population to attain reliably a prespecified set of objectives. In the more popular, process-oriented approach, programming instruction is defined as the process of analyzing an instructional task, deriving behavioral objectives, designing prototype materials, and modifying the materials repeatedly on the basis of expert opinion and student feedback until reliable results are demonstrable.

There is a consensus that PI is dead, the coup de grace having been delivered by the National Society for Programmed Instruction when it changed its name to the National Society for Performance and Instruction in 1973. The causes for its death at such an early age are not hard to find: early adherents of the programming movement made false promises, which were not backed up by the evidence. Fly-by-night companies mass-produced unreliable teaching machines and unvalidated programmed texts. The second-generation programs were poor imitations of earlier ones, without any changes to accommodate differences in instructional objectives or target populations.

In a broader sense, though, PI died of an overabundance of success. The effective elements of the programming process became absorbed into the mainstream of educational practice. Many successful innovations in the field today are either direct offshoots of PI or associated intimately with it. Behavioral objectives got their current impetus from Mager's (1962) best-seller originally entitled *Preparing Objectives for Programed Instruction.* The individualized instruction movement is an outgrowth of management of programmed materials. Educational technology, which is taking over the old audiovisual media field, is another recent derivative of the PI movement. Current interest in formative evaluation—evaluation for the improvement of instruction—is a logical outcome of earlier work on the tryout and modification of programmed materials. Criterion-referenced testing, a new movement in test construction, sprang from the work of Glaser (1963) in relation to the testing of the outcomes of programmed instruction.

RECENT DEVELOPMENTS

The Programming Process

The stages in the basic programming process include instructional analysis, specification of instructional objectives, construction of criterion-referenced tests to measure the attainment of these objectives, design of the initial version of the program, developmental testing (tryout and modification), and validation testing (final evaluation and demonstration of effectiveness).

Within each stage of the programming process there have been a number of recent refinements. In instructional analysis, industrial-type task analysis has been supplemented by concept analysis (Markle and Tiemann, 1971), which is more suited for academic subject-matter areas, and goal analysis (Mager, 1972), which enables the programmer to identify behavioral indicators for affective goals. Specification of behavioral objectives has withstood numerous attacks, and emerged stronger with tech-

niques for stating higher-level cognitive and affective objectives. Criterion-referenced tests have become a legitimate part of test-construction theory, and work is in progress for the identification of suitable statistics to replace traditional notions of reliability and validity. New techniques for the design of instruction have been specified, based mostly on different types of learning. Gagne's (1965) basic hierarchy has been modified by Merrill (1971), which in turn has been modified by Markle and Tiemann (1973) to permit prescription of appropriate instructional strategies.

The work of Horn and his associates (1972) has resulted in related developments in information mapping. In this technique, a standardized information presentation format, called a map, is prescribed for each of seven types of instructional content. Use of these maps results in the production of materials which are highly efficient for both initial learning and subsequent reference.

Another important set of recent developments is the clarification of interrelationships among the stages of the programming process. Harless (1971) and others have indicated how behavioral objectives are derived from the earlier analysis; Mager (1973) has provided techniques for translating objectives into test items; Brethower and others (1964) have shown how these test items may be arranged into an outline for the design of the program; Rummler (1965) has suggested the design of a "lean" program, with a minimum number of frames to maximize feedback during developmental testing; and Markle (1967) has shown how developmental testing and validation testing are related to each other.

Both the beginning and the end of the programming process have recently been expanded with the addition of front-end analysis (Harless, 1971) and contingency contracting (Homme, 1970). Front-end analysis identifies the problem in terms of performance deficiency, and classifies it as motivational, human-engineering, or instructional. Instruction is seen as only one of the many different alternatives available for the solution. In many cases it could be an inappropriate one. A similar approach to performance problem-solving has been presented by Mager and Pipe (1970) in their recent book. The works of Homme (1970) and others have provided the useful technique of contingency contracting for the implementation of programmed (or any other) instruction.

Machines and Media

In its early days, PI was inextricably tangled up with teaching machines. It took the public and programmers some time to realize that it was not the machine but the program that did the teaching. Because the production of software did not keep pace with hardware, many machines had to be discontinued. In addition, as Gotkin and McSweeney (1967) point out, these machines were both unreliable and invalid. Although machines took more time than programmed texts, there were no comparable gains in achievement. Further, neither the machine nor the programmer understood each other: The machine imposed unnecessary constraints upon the programmer and the programmer treated the machine with a total lack of imagination. There was very little creative use of media; the machines were just page-turners.

Today teaching machines are used merely as bonus gifts for buyers of encyclopedias, or as convenient strawmen by critics of educational technology. The principles of programming are being applied to the production of such mediated materials as films, filmstrips, and audio tapes. An excellent example of this trend is the extremely popular children's show, *Sesame Street.* Tosti and Ball's (1970) technique for the selection of appropriate media has benefited instructional developers both within and outside the PI movement.

Topics and Types

Recent trends are noticeable in the types of topics and programs. In the early days, many people, including programmers, agreed that PI was suitable only for factual content and such topics as vocabulary, basic arithmetic, and spelling. A random look through an abstract indicates that current programs deal with such topics as values, empathy, emotional discrimination, interpersonal perception, and self-actualization.

Not so long ago PI was divided into three types. In *linear* programs, all students worked through a fixed set of frames. The student read a frame, made a response, compared it with the correct response, went to the next frame, and repeated the process. In the *branching* programs, the student read a lengthier frame, and chose an alternative to a multiple-choice question. If his choice was correct, he went to the next main-track frame. If not, he went to a remedial frame to receive appropriate instruction, depending upon the type of error revealed by his choice. He was then sent to the original frame to try again. Eventually he worked his unique path through the program. In the *adjunct* program, the student read a conventional textbook chapter, responded to a set of questions based on the content, and restudied those parts suggested by the questions he missed. Although much was written about the logical superiority of each type, empirical results failed to show any consistent advantage. Most of the present-day programmed texts are basically linear, incorporating, whenever appropriate, multiple-choice questions and lengthy passages (panels) for reading. Computer-assisted instruction has taken over the basic branching format. The student is sent through alternative paths depending upon not only his current response, but also a number of such variables as learning style, cumulative errors, and response latency. The basic paradigm of adjunct programming has reappeared as *mastery learning* (Bloom, Hastings, and Mandaus, 1971) strategy.

Human Element in PI

Among the most notable developments in PI in recent years has been the shift from the concept of self-instruction to that of self-contained instruction. The absence of a teacher or other learners is no longer considered to be an essential requirement for PI. Interaction between the learner and a "teacher" or his peers has been successfully programmed to expand the reaches of PI. Groups have been found to be useful reinforcers. A number of complex objectives and interpersonal skills lend themselves admirably to group work. In the attainment of complex decision-making skills by sophisticated learners. Krishnamurty (1969) has used *groupprograms,* in which a small group jointly responds to the frames.

Another recent interactional format, which shares a number of elements with PI, is the personalized system of instruction (PSI) developed by Keller (1968) and others. In this system a course is divided into a number of units, each with predefined, specific objectives. The learner masters each unit, usually by going through printed materials at his own pace. Upon completing the unit, he demonstrates his mastery on a criterion-referenced test, either to the teacher or to a peer proctor. The learner is permitted to proceed to the next one only after achieving perfect mastery of each unit. According to an informal survey, in 1972 about 190 PSI courses were being offered, mostly at the undergraduate level and mostly in introductory, survey-type courses.

Oral responses, which are essential in basic reading, cannot be monitored by even the most complex teaching machine, although even a second-grader can be trained to do it. This fact has given rise to a number of systematic tutoring methods based on PI. These include parent-assisted learning (Niedermeyer, 1969) and structured tutoring (Harrison, 1972). The most comprehensively validated one is the programmed tutoring approach of Ellson (Ellson, Barber, Harris, and Kampwerth, 1965). A unique aspect of programmed tutoring is the separation of the learning content from the tutoring operations. What the child is taught is determined by a series of content programs divided into lessons and frames. How he is taught is determined by an operational program which specifies every move the tutor makes as a function of the child's response. The use of programmed tutoring has spread very rapidly during the past few years, with more than 1,500 paraprofessionals tutoring more than 15,000 children. Tutoring kits are available to accompany all major basal reader series. The technique has also been applied to oral language and basic arithmetic.

SPECIFIC APPLICATIONS

Because many pseudoprograms carry the PI label, while many real ones do not, it is not feasible to tabulate the extent of use of PI materials. However, the trend is toward more programs being used in industry than in academic circles, and more in informal than in formal learning situations. Even in formal education, individualized instruction projects are rapidly becoming major consumers of PI, especially in such areas as beginning reading and arithmetic. Most of the successful uses of PI are reported in the education of handicapped children. The need for individualization is greater here, and the principles of conventional programming (e.g., small steps and redundancy) are clearly applicable. Two specific examples from the education of the deaf are discussed in detail below.

Project LIFE

Language and reading are major problem areas in the curriculum for the deaf, and Project LIFE (Language Improvement to Facilitate Education) (Pfau, 1972) has developed more than 800 programmed filmstrips to increase the language learning rate of deaf children. The materials are profusely and charmingly illustrated, and are presented through a multiple-choice teaching machine. The bulk of the materials comprise the programmed language/reading section, which systematically interweaves language structure and vocabulary in an order of increasing difficulty. The project has also developed series of filmstrip programs on various perceptual and thinking skills which are prerequisite to reading. In the preparation of all these materials, the programming process has been conscientiously applied. An impressive amount of developmental testing has been undertaken locally; validation testing has followed it in approximately 100 different locations.

Electronic Assembly Programmed Learning System for the Deaf

Also designed for deaf learners, but different in many respects from Project LIFE, is the *Electronics Assembly Programmed Learning System for the Deaf* (Persselin, 1972). This program is designed to train high school students in assembling electronic terminal chassis and printed circuit boards. The topic itself was chosen on the basis of systematic front-end analysis because of the available jobs, long-range future, and equal opportunities for men and women. Task analysis involved expert electronic technicians. The design took into consideration reading problems of the deaf by using visual materials in filmstrips and diagrams. Many parts of the program were developmentally tested, and revised as many as ten times. The final validation took place under actual field conditions in four schools for the deaf. Indicative of the effectiveness of the material are the data which show that although there was a great difference in completion times, there was a very insignificant difference in the final performance scores.

The program incorporates a number of unconventional features. It simulates actual working conditions as much as possible, using a workbench equipped with tools, electronic parts, and a filmstrip projector. There are seven programmed units, each coordinated to a filmstrip, an assembly drawing, a final test, and a checklist for the instructor. While working through the program the student is required to give both written and performance responses. At appropriate places he shows some product to the instructor, or has him watch him at work. The instructor's role is patterned after that of a quality control inspector.

RESEARCH AND CONTROVERSIES

Until about the middle sixties, the basic question in PI research was "Which is better: *X* or *Y*?" Diverse variables were pitted against each other: linear vs. branching vs. adjunct type; constructed vs. multiple-choice responses; overt vs. covert responding; prompting vs. confirmation of responses; confirmation vs. no confirmation; large vs. small step size; high vs. low error rates; logical vs. random sequence; and individual vs. group-paced presentation. The variables were vaguely defined, studies were disconnected, and researches were carried out hurriedly, with short, programmed segments. Not surprisingly, the results turned out to be nonsignificant and contradictory. In recent years the basic question has become, "Under what conditions and for what type of learners is *X* more effective than *Y* for attaining a given type of instructional objectives?" A classic example of this type of integrative research was undertaken by Holland (1965) in the area of covert and overt responses. Using the elegant notion of the *blackout ratio*, which indicated the percentage of words in a program which can be obliterated without influencing the error rate, he was able to establish that *overt* responding facilitates learning if, and only if, the responses were relevant to the objective of the program. Kemp and Holland (1966) later reanalyzed data from 12 earlier contradictory comparisons of covert vs. overt responding and reconciled seemingly disparate results.

It is barely two decades since the publication of Skinner's (1954) *The Science of Learning and the Art of Teaching,* which to many marks the modern beginnings of the PI movement. Within this period, the term *programmed instruction* has undergone many changes in its connotation; even today, it means different things to different people. To serious programmers, it always meant, and will continue to mean, the process of systematic development of validated instructional materials. The term programmed instruction may continue to decline in popularity, but its process and principles will increasingly permeate the mainstream of educational endeavor.

REFERENCES

Bloom, B. S., Hastings, J. T., and Mandaus, G. F. *Handbook of Formative and Summative Evaluation of Student Learning.* New York: McGraw-Hill, 1971.

Brethower, D. M., Markle, D. G., Rummler, G. A., Schrader, A. W., and Smith, D. E. P. *Programmed Learning: A Practicum.* Ann Arbor, Mich.: Ann Arbor Publishers, 1964.

Ellson, D. G., Barber, L., Engle, T. L., and Kampwerth, L. Programed Tutoring: A Teaching Aid and a Research Tool. *Reading Research Quarterly.* Newark, Del.: International Reading Association, 1964, *1*(1).

Gagne, R. M. *The Conditions of Learning.* Chicago: Holt, Rinehart and Winston, Inc., 1965.

Glasser, R. M. Instructional Technology and the Measurement of Learning Outcomes. *American Psychologist,* 1963, *18,* 519-521.

Gotkin, L. G., and McSweeny, J. F. Learning from Teaching Machines. In P. C. Lange, ed., *Programed Instruction.* Sixty-sixth yearbook of the National Society for the Study of Education, Part II. Chicago, Ill.: Distributed by the University of Chicago Press, 1967.

Harless, J. H. *An Ounce of Analysis.* Falls Church, Va.: Harless Educational Technologists, 1971.

Harrison, G. V. Tutoring: A Remedy Reconsidered. *Improving Human Performance: A Research Quarterly,* 1972, *1*(4), 1-7.

Holland, J. G. Response Contingencies in Teaching-Machine Programs. *Journal of Programed Instruction,* 1965, *3*(1), 1-8.

Homme, L., Csanyi, A. P., Gonzales, M. A., and Rechs, J. R. *How to use Contingency Contracting in the Classroom.* Champaign, Ill.: Research Press Co., 1970.

Horn, R. E., Nicol, E. H., Razar, M., and Kleinman, J. C. *A Reference Collection of Rules and Guidelines for Writing Information Mapped Materials.* Cambridge, Mass.: Information Resources, Inc., 1971.

Keller, F. S. Good-Bye Teacher. . . *Journal of Applied Behavior Analysis,* 1968, *1*(1), 78-89.

Kemp, F. D. and Holland, J. G. Blackout Radio and Overt Responses in Programmed Instruction: Resolution of Disparate Results. *Journal of Educational Psychology,* 1966, *57,* 109-114.

Krishnamurty, G. B. Programmed Learning in Health Programs. In C. K. Basu, ed., *Programmed Instruction in Industries, Defense, Health and Education.* New Delhi, India: Indian Association for Programmed Instruction, 1969.

Mager, R. F. *Preparing Objectives for Programmed Instruction.* San Francisco: Fearon Publishers, 1962.

———. *Goal Analysis.* Belmont, Calif.: Fearon Publishers, 1972.

———. *Measuring Instructional Intent.* Belmont, Calif.: Fearon Publishers, 1973.

——— and Pipe, P. *Analyzing Performance Problems.* Belmont, Calif.: Fearon Publishers, 1970.

Markle, S. M. Empirical Testing of Programs. In P. C. Lange, ed., *Programed Instruction.* Sixty-sixth yearbook of the National Society for the Study of Education. Chicago, Ill.: Distributed by the University of Chicago Press, 1967.

——— and Tiemann, P. W. Conceptual Learning and Instructional Design. *The Journal of Educational Technology,* 1970, *1*(1).

——— and Tiemann, P. W. A Useful Classification Model for Behavior Analysis. Paper presented at the Eleventh Annual Convention of the National Society for Programed Instruction, San Francisco, 1973.

Niedermeyer, F. C. *Parent-Assisted Learning.* Inglewood, Calif.: Southwest Regional Laboratory for Educational Research and Development, 1969.

Persselin, L. E. Breaking the World Barrier: A Model System of Programmed Learning for Vocational Education. *Improving Human Performance,* 1972, *1*(3), 37-59.

Pfau, G. S. Project LIFE: Programming Rationale and Process. *Improving Human Performance,* 1972, *1*(3), 8-17.

Rummler, G. A. The Economics of Lean Programming. In *Selected N.S.P.I. Talks.* Ann Arbor, Mich.: The Center for Programmed Learning for Business, 1965.

Skinner, B. F. The Science of Learning and the Art of Teaching. *Harvard Educational Review,* 1954, *24,* 86-97.

Tosti, D. T. and Ball, J. R. A Behavioral Approach to Instructional Design and Media Selection. *AV Communication Review,* 1969, *17,* 5-25.

ADDITIONAL RESOURCES

National Society for Performance and Instruction
P.O. Box 137, Cardinal Station
Catholic University
Washington, D.C. 20017

An organization of people working in instructional development through the application of the programming process. The society publishes a monthly newsletter and a research quarterly, *Improving Human Performance.*

Association for Educational Communications and Technology
1201 Sixteenth Street, N.W.
Washington, D.C. 20036

An organization with broader interests. One of the special interest groups of the association is the Division of Instructional Development, which is concerned with "the application of technology to the systematic development of instruc-

tion and the engineering of solutions to instructional problems." AECT publishes a monthly journal, *Audiovisual Instruction* and a research quarterly, *AV Communication Review.*

———

89

RESEARCH AND PRACTICE IN INSTRUCTIONAL MEDIA

by Richard E. Clark, Ed.D.
Chairman, Area of Instructional Technology
School of Education
Syracuse University
Syracuse, New York

One of the most costly experiments in American education is in trouble. Millions have been spent on instructional services such as television, films, and computers since the 1950s, and recent evaluation studies indicate that they generally have not met their promise.

Instructional media, introduced with a passion in the 1950s, were expected to increase the availability, quality, and amount of learning taking place in American classrooms. It is significant that the discussion of how all this can be accomplished proceeds without our knowing much about just how or what people learn from media.

Recent reports by the Carnegie Commission on Higher Education and the Sloan Commission on Cable Communications, for example, provide a comprehensive overview of present and future plans for extending communications technology.[1]

These reports, however, neglect, or delegate the responsibility of, examining the basic processes that permit learning from media to occur. Researchers have been studying educational media for decades, yet recent reviews of the results conclude that "as of today virtually nothing is known about the teaching effectiveness of instructional media."

My purpose here is not to criticize the growth of educational technology, but rather to review the developments in communications and educational psychology that have influenced present educational media strategies, and to show how recent breakthroughs in learning theory and media research offer a new direction in the design and use of instructional media.

NO REAL CHANGE

A recent S.R.I. policy study for the Office of Education concludes that the use of educational media has probably not changed instruction in any essential way, except to make it considerably more expensive.[2] We might agree with one critic who suggested that visible educational media failures have been compared with the invisible virtues of other vehicles of instruction. However, funds for media use are rapidly disappearing.

Films and television, very profitable entertainment-based technologies, have been made available to even the most remote schools by generous Federal and foundation grants, though these funds are tapering off as it becomes evident that they are beyond the technical and financial means of many schools, particularly in a period of diminishing public support for schools. Current Federal and foundation interest is in supporting the development of "software" or instructional materials. Now that we have embraced the new technologies, the question becomes, "what do we do with them?"[3]

Until recently, research in education and communications has made the answer to that question even more elusive than it has to be. Experimental design traditionally focused on the "average" student. Many studies, for instance, compare the learning that results from film with that resulting from television, the relative effectiveness of computer instruction over programmed texts, and so forth. The results of this research is usually that no significant difference in learning results from the use of different technologies.

When an occasional study appears to show an advantage for a given technique, the results are difficult to replicate in other studies or in the classroom. There is little to show for the two decades of concentrated research along these lines. An obsessional quest for the technological key to education has left us with virtually nothing of real usefulness to teacher or student.

The search for a media technique, or treatment which "on the average" results in improved learning, attitude, information-seeking, or problem-solving, results (even if successful) in useful information only about the typical or average student. There has been little realistic concern, however, for those who fall significantly below or above the average. Indeed, anyone who does not fit the average student model is treated as an error in experimental design.

One of the most important consequences of the search for the most successful educational environment, or media technique, is the unwise repudiation of approaches that appear to have failed some students. The traditional classroom, for example, as opposed to the currently fashionable "open" classroom, may be the most productive environment for certain types of students to learn certain subjects in.

Such techniques as the televised lecture, rigid sequencing of materials, and didactic scripting—all out of fashion now—may even be necessary for some students in some contexts. A significant percentage of students actually have their learning inhibited or depressed when one approach is used to the exclusion of all others. Some way must be found to fashion educational environments and instructional media to exploit the special learning capacities of individual students.

Individualizing instruction has been a concern of some American educators since the turn of the century. E. L. Thorndike, in a 1911 book titled *Individuality*, reported that teachers, parents, and students of the era were reacting violently to "the uniformity of method which had clutched and mechanized the schools."[4] Early approaches to the issue were focused on remedial education. Individualization implied special classes or tutorials to bring competence in reading, mathematics, etc., up to a standardized norm. It was assumed that once a student attained the norm, he could thereafter compete with his peers. More recently, individualized instruction has meant using modern technology to give students access to instruction on demand, and some control over the choice and sequence of subject matter.

Although both types of individualized instruction have been extremely valuable interim approaches, the former perpetuates the tyranny of elitism and competition, and the latter handicaps those students who happen not to perform well with that particular style of instruction.

I would like to propose another approach, one that relies on the following assumption: Individualized instruction should imply the matching of knowledge about students' abilities and aptitudes with teaching materials designed or selected to improve their performance and competence.

The essence of this approach is the tailoring of modes of instruction to the aptitudes of individual learners. It assumes that the student's abilities and a given media technique interact to produce learning. For example, studies show that in general the language laboratory and textbook methods of teaching foreign languages work about equally well. When we consider the verbal aptitude of individual students, however, we find that students of high verbal ability learn more from textbooks, and students of low verbal ability perform better with language laboratory training. Yet schools have invested millions of dollars in language laboratories without respect to their differential utility. No wonder the administrators of Federal programs such as the National Defense Education Act feel that research in foreign language instruction has been too inconclusive to merit further support.

Another study investigated the ability of primary students to learn to multiply fractions. Two methods of instruction were compared, the traditional textbook and teacher lecture versus automated devices and flannel boards. Average and above-average students fared equally well with both methods. The below-average students, however, learned much more from the traditional method of textbook and teacher lecture. This finding is particularly interesting, given the widespread assumption that it is below-average students who profit most from teaching machines or elaborate media presentations.

Other studies have indicated that, in a variety of learning tasks, students of lower soeio-economic status (SES) perform better with programmed instruction materials than with traditional classroom teaching. The finding for high-SES students is the opposite—they tend to do better with the traditional approach. When two types of film, a conventionally organized and an "unstructured" version, were tested to determine which resulted in greater factual learning, no differences resulted when the students were considered en bloc. When students were ranked according to their ability to remember parts of a film, however, it was found that the students with below-average memories remembered more factual material from the traditionally structured version of the film. The students with average or above-average memories performed equally well with both types of film. When producing "creative" ideas about the film was required, however, the low-memory students performed best with the unstructured film, and the other students again performed equally well with both versions. In another study, when filmed and "live" instruction were compared for students ranked according to their self-assurance, it was found that the more self-assured students learned most from film.[5]

THE INDIVIDUAL APPROACH

These and similar studies suggest that the most fruitful approach to designing educational experiences lies in a consideration of the interaction between a mode of instruction and the relevant individual differences of students. Used intelligently, this interaction model can help us understand why one student learns more and another student less from a given mode of instruction. To illustrate, the researchers who investigated the foreign language learning problem described above reasoned that students with high verbal ability had already acquired the verbal skills that the other students had to acquire through diligent language laboratory work with voice recording equipment. Similarly, it might be hypothesized that low-SES students find programmed instruction less intimidating and more rewarding than a middle- or high-SES teacher.

In the situations described in these studies and others like them, any effort to find the best instructional technique would have been fruitless, because in every case the best technique for some of the students proved not to be the best technique for a significant number of other students.[6]

This research is not conclusive, of course, and is presented primarily as an illustration of the approach I am suggesting. We must overcome at least three barriers before we can offer practical guidance to the teacher or the designer of instructional materials: 1) media must be categorized in terms of human use rather than mechanical means; 2) aptitudes and abilities must be defined more precisely; and 3) ways of matching instructional media to the capacities of individual students must be devised.

With regard to the first point, at present we categorize instructional media in ways that have little to do with the way students learn from them. We differentiate, for example, between the film and television, when most of the research has shown that no instructional advantages can be attributed to the one over the other. There are obvious esthetic, mechanical, and cost differences between the two media, but in general these factors do not affect learning.

A concerted, systematic effort to identify the learning-relevant aspects of instructional media is vital. One useful result of such an effort might be a taxonomy of media attributes that can realistically be matched with the relevant characteristics of individual students and the demands of various learning tasks. Previous attempts at media taxonomies have resulted in elaborate listings of the machines and technology of instruction. We might reasonably ask what the technical characteristics of mechanical media have to do with the intellectual capaci-

ties of human students. The search for a useful way to categorize instructional media should begin with a knowledge of people, rather than a mastery of machines. If we proceed in this fashion, we may discover that new mechanical devices need inventing.

With respect to the second barrier, learning psychologists have recently expended considerable effort on the problem of uncovering and defining aptitudes. There is a general dissatisfaction with traditional measures of intellectual ability, even though many of them quite accurately predict a student's performance in American schools. The traditional intelligence tests tend to assume a great similarity among testees, an assumption that (a) is unrealistic and (b) gives insufficient weight to the individual student's unique qualities and capabilities. Learning psychologists are now trying to define and describe the components of the process by which something is learned. Once the psychologist has identified the intellectual process involved in a particular kind of learning, he can devise ways of measuring the extent to which the process, or its components, are available to individual students. Examples of newly defined aptitudes and their components are visual and auditory perception, information coding and extracting, cognitive or intellectual style differences, memory and mental elaboration processes, and personality characteristics, such as impulsiveness, anxiety, self-esteem, dogmatism, responsibility, and motivation.

Once we have overcome the first two barriers we will be in a position to tackle the third. Once we can categorize media in human terms and relate them to the whole panoply of student aptitudes, we should be able to offer the teacher some useful advice on the selection of media to teach a given skill to a given student.

Let us see how such an approach can work. A researcher concerned with art appreciation reasoned that a student must be able to notice particular aspects of a painting before arriving at a personally satisfying interpretation of an artist's work. Some students, it appeared, found it difficult to separate out elements from the whole work. It was suggested that the intellectual process involved in noticing parts of a painting might be analogous to the action of a zoom lens on a motion picture camera. A measure of the ability to "notice parts" was designed. After students had been tested for this ability, they were shown extracts from motion pictures illustrating the zoom technique. Predictably, the students who previously had had difficulty noticing parts of paintings did significantly better after seeing the film. They also were able to suggest many more interpretations of paintings they were shown. The two most dramatic results, however, were less predictable. The same students whose perception of parts of paintings had improved after seeing the film were also able to notice more discrete aspects of many other perceptual experiences. That is, their newly acquired skill carried over to other areas; an increased aptitude for "noticing parts" was an unexpected outcome of their exposure to a particular instructional medium.

Equally dramatic was the finding that those students who initially scored high in the ability to notice parts seemed to report fewer parts after seeing the film. Presumably, they had used another kind of intellectual process in selecting out parts of visual materials, and the zoom technique interfered with the individually preferred means by which they achieved the same end.

THE FIRST CONCERN

For the designer and administrator of instructional media, the present state of knowledge is inadequate. The examples presented above are intended to illustrate the usefulness and feasibility of the interaction approach to research. For the time being, however, those who are faced with the day-to-day decisions that shape the media presentations students will experience would do well to focus their attention on the psychological characteristics of the intended audience. The differentiated traits of individual students, relevant to the kind of learning expected, must be the designer's first concern. Put another way, the planning of instructional material should begin with a thorough examination of the psychological, intellectual, and sociological processes that will be engaged, modified, or provided for the learners. Alternative strategies for designing and presenting instructional media should be the end result of such planning, and students should be assigned to one or more of the alternative designs on the basis of their individual aptitudes for the learning in question.

Our goal should be to maximize learning from every student. What may be needed is a team of instructional media designers who combine talents in production, art, and the psychology of learning.

NOTES

[1]The Carnegie Commission on Higher Education, *The Fourth Revolution: Instructional Technology in Higher Education.* New York: McGraw-Hill, 1972; The Sloan Commission on Cable Communications, *On the Cable: The Television of Abundance.* New York: McGraw-Hill, 1971.

[2]Kincaid, H. et al., *Technology in Public Elementary and Secondary Education: An Overview of a Policy Research Effort.* Stanford Research Institute, Menlo Park, California. SRI Project URU-2158.

[3]See, for example, a discussion of the problem by W. H. Allen, "Instructional Media Research: Past, Present, and Future," *A V Communication Review, 19*(1), Spring 1971.

[4]Cited by Robert Glazer in "Individuals and Learning: The New Aptitudes," *Educational Researcher, 1*(6), June 1972, p. 5. This article is a readable review of the search for "new" aptitudes.

[5]Many of the examples of research findings cited in this paper were taken from a prepublication draft of a special issue of *A V Communication Review,* edited by the author, which will be published by the Association for Educational Communications and Technology in the Fall of 1975.

[6]R. Snow and G. Salomon, "Aptitudes and Instructional Media," *A V Communication Review, 16*(4), 1967, pp. 343 ff. A more complete and up-to-date discussion of the approach and existing research may be found in a forthcoming book by L. J. Cronbach and R. E. Snow, of Stanford University. The manuscript is tentatively titled "Aptitudes and Instruction," and should be available late in 1975.

90

MOVABLE-MOBILE LEARNING FACILITIES

by John E. Uxer
Executive Director
Region XIX Education Service Center
El Paso, Texas

The term "learning facilities" refers to the building or structure used for the purpose of conducting school programs. Learning facilities may be permanently anchored to the ground or they may be constructed in such a way that they may be moved.

However, it is a fundamental precept that a concise, universally accepted definition be displayed if a given topic is to be discussed in a meaningful way. In this context, it may be stated that mobile learning facilities include all facilities used for instructional purposes which are not permanently anchored to the ground. Although such a definition is useful in a global discussion, it is much too broad to discuss definitively. Therefore, for purpose of this presentation (and for all practical purposes), mobile learning facilities are categorized as 1) facilities used for instruction which are movable, or 2) facilities used for instruction which are mobile. Mobile facilities may be self-propelled or nonself-propelled; self-contained or nonself-contained.

Obviously, the degree of mobility of a facility inversely relates to the order listed above, while the degree of utilization compares positively with that order. The purpose of this article is to review, for the administrator, the most common uses and current status of usage of mobile learning facilities.

MOVABLE

Any facility used for instructional purposes and not permanently anchored to the ground may be considered, to varying degrees, as being mobile. The following discussion will further describe the essential elements of each of the various categories of mobile facilities.

Movable Facilities

In one sense, practically all school facilities being constructed today could be classed as movable. This is true because most interior walls are nonload-bearing, and thus can be moved or reconfigured to accommodate changing utilization requirements. Although there is merit in this definition, a more prominent concept of movable facility is one which can be moved from one location to another. The term "portable" seems to be the one most frequently used to describe such facilities. Other terms in common usage include transportable, movable, relocatable, temporary, instant classrooms, and convertible schools (Educational Facilities Laboratories, 1964).

The literature is rather barren concerning the beginning and initial surge in the use of nonpermanent facilities. It is generally conceded that the impact of the "baby boom" following World War II caught the nation's schools short-handed and short of buildings. An understandably simple solution appeared to be to stopgap the shortage of facilities with the use of portables.

Although the utilization of portables satisfied some of the elements of floor space shortage, several studies show that their development has been disappointing from almost any measure of design standards. A California study (California State Department of Education, 1969) indicated that most school officials who have the responsibility for construction of school buildings candidly acknowledge that portable buildings do not approach either the quality or functionality required to warrant their use. Aesthetic qualities were less than expected and savings in costs have not compensated for the lack of benefits. The authors of the California study (1969) concluded that "costs are generally higher than the district can justify, when it is apparent that this same money can purchase a custom-designed school with similar space, furnishings, and equipment (p. 3)."

School authorities seldom deliberately plan to use portables as conventional facilities. Rather, one or more of three conditions cause them to resort to portables: unstable enrollments, insufficient time, and the need to reduce costs. Although any one of these conditions could constitute a legitimate reason for using portables rather than permanent structures, the astute administrator will submit each to a thorough examination before arriving at a final decision.

Unstable Enrollments

Shifting populations, resulting in unstable enrollments, continue to challenge school officials. Birth control procedures have ended the "baby boom," but the rural to urban migration, the subsequent urban to suburban move, and the relocation programs sponsored by the Federal government have combined to actually accelerate population mobility. Positive, aggressive planning by school administrators, including close liaison and coordination with city, state, and Federal officials, will assist in determining whether permanent or portable facilities would best meet the need of their communities.

Time Constraints

Such liaison and coordination also can often provide early warning, and preclude last-minute, hastily made building plans. In the event, of course, insufficient time is available to hold a bond election and follow through with a building program, portables may be the only recourse.

Costs

Perhaps the fundamental reason for utilizing portables, either purchased or leased, is the common belief that portables are a more economical solution to space prob-

lems than are permanent facilities. This belief is highly questionable! If costs such as acquisition price, moving and operating expenses, additional restrooms, and other supportive services are considered, it is probable that portables may indeed be more expensive.

Although the California study (1969) reflected rather negatively on the use of portables, other experiences have been quite different. The increasing availability of portable classroom facilities in diverse configurations has attracted much attention. A writer in *American School and University* (1968) expressed this adequacy when he indicated that portable buildings can pass the code for permanent construction and then can be left as permanent buildings, if desired. Such buildings are of a very substantial type, and should give long service with a minimum of maintenance, plus having the advantage of being able to relocate them.

Community involvement, in which resultant problems were focused on schools, caused one school official (O'Grince, 1970) to remark:

> We have only begun to take advantage of this type of construction. Cafeterias and libraries, now crowded . . ., can be moved into a facility of this type. With community activity increasing in all the schools, here is a chance to develop a community hall next to the permanent school, adding immeasurably to the community service concept. (p. 20)

The pros and cons of the use of portables have been debated widely during recent years. Dr. Francis McKeag, Assistant to the General Superintendent of Schools, Chicago, Illinois (Communication Seminars, 1968), referred to the need for semipermanent school buildings that would remain ten to 15 years in a given community. These structures would follow the requirements of the local building code for permanency, but would be constructed in modules of eight-feet length—assembled in any configuration desired—and expeditiously movable when required. McKeag recommended that, for school districts with changing community characteristics where populations are shifting outwardly, it would be advantageous "to build at least one-third or possibly one-half of . . . [the educational facilities] as demountable structure[s] (p. 28)."

McKeag explained that typically, when young families move into new communities and raise their children, there is a tendency for the children to leave the area once their schooling is completed. Consequently, few youngsters remain permanently in the attendance area, and demountable portions of school plants may be disassembled and relocated in high-attendance locales.

Nationally, many school districts have taken advantage of portable or demountable school facilities; the flexibility and economy of these facilities have contributed substantially to the continuing trend of their utilization. Also, when its needs have been met a district can rent or sell its portables to another district.

Mobile Facilities

When considered collectively, mobile educational facilities offer flexibility or programming, expediency, and economy. Mobile facilities differ from portables, discussed in the previous section, in that mobile facilities are designed to be moved frequently. Mobile educational facilities will be discussed as they may fall into one of the following categories.

Mobile, self-contained, nonself-propelled facilities. Mounted in towed trailer- or van-like vehicles, these facilities normally contain all the equipment and furniture necessary to conduct the specific tasks for which they were designed. The units may or may not include a power plant. In the event that a power plant is not included, such units must be capable of using an exterior source.

Mobile, self-contained, self-propelled facilities. This classification includes the majority of the mobile units in use at present. The units essentially feature a separate classroom mounted on a temporary or nonfixed foundation. The units contain heating and cooling units, lights, and possibly plumbing, but must depend upon an exterior source of power and other utilities. Equipment contained in these facilities may be as varied as in any regular classroom.

Within each category of mobile facility, a number of functions may be served. The most common mobile facilities, classified by function, are briefly discussed below.

Regular classroom functions. Regular classes of almost any program may be contained in any category of mobile unit; however, in a vast majority of instances portable self-contained facilities are used.

Simulation. Simulator units contain special equipment which allows instruction to be presented utilizing simulated conditions requiring skill and judgment. For instance, a driver education simulation unit contains all the essential equipment elements found in a car, such as driver seat, steering wheel, brake, clutch, gauges, and others.

Special-purpose functions. Mobile facilities serve a number of special-purpose functions. Although these could be served generally by permanent facilities, the lack of full-time demand negates their establishment. Special-function services include a wide range of applications, such as (1) inservice training for specialized personnel; (2) academic and vocational skills development; (3) diagnostic, appraisal, and therapy functions; and (4) specialized uses in industrial, social service, and educational operations.

Contemporary Uses of Mobile Educational Facilities

The author, along with Charles W. Benson, conducted a rather comprehensive examination of the scope of usage of mobile facilities for inclusion in the ERIC files in 1971. The results of this research, and information gathered subsequently, are included in this discussion.

Migrant Education

Self-propelled laboratories for services to migrant children have been instituted in Oregon, Michigan, and Florida. These units house library resources which are tailored to relate to varying cultural differences among migrant children. Resource materials reflecting different language orientations are manifest in books, films, and filmstrips to serve the interest differential associated with all children—migrant or otherwise.

In Oregon (*Instructor*, 1969), a mobile unit was purchased to serve the needs of migrant children in Willamette Valley. The unit is attended by a head teacher, who remains aboard the facility when it is stationed at a school. A second teacher departs from the unit and works within the regular school classroom in lieu of a regular teacher, who enters the mobile unit with selected migrant children. The head teacher utilizes the mobile unit's special resources to train the regular classroom teacher and to supplement the curricular services available to the migrant children, while the teacher assigned to operate in the regular school strengthens the instructional process as a result of her special training and preparation in advance of the scheduled visit. This *modus operandi* offers direct instructional services of a supplemental nature to children possessing specific educational needs; the setup concurrently allows enriched staff development to occur via a unique inservice training approach.

In 1969, Dr. E. John Kleinhart conducted a study of migrant children in Florida. In his report, Kleinhart reported that some 80 early learning vehicles were providing daily educational programs for 2,000 preschool-age migrant children (Howse, 1971).

Reading Services

Mobile reading laboratories called "Readimobiles" were used in Georgia, Florida, Alabama, South Carolina, and Mississippi to provide a strategy in the teaching of reading to isolated, economically disadvantaged children.

Howse (1971) stated that the basic goals of the Readimobile Project are:

1. To provide readiness experience for children that make them more receptive to formal school programs, and to benefit more fully from formal instruction.

2. To establish communication with isolated groups so that they can gradually become aware of other programs (health, education, legal, etc.).

3. To expose children to other cultures, so that they can become aware of the dimensions of the world and their own place in it.

4. To help children develop awareness of their surroundings and a feeling of their identity through group discussions on films and books.

5. To help children realize their creativity through art music, drama, games, and crafts.

6. To condition children and parents to the needs of a changing society where education means survival. (p. 40)

Adult Education

In many metropolitan areas across the country, a major problem confronting educators is the inadequately educated general populace. Progress of students, it has been repeated numerous times, is inhibited by home-life patterns which are uncontrollable by the educator. Students have natural tendencies to revert to behaviors exhibited in their homes, even though desirable modifications to their educational lifestyles are underway at school.

For years, authorities have attempted to ameliorate the recognized roots of these problems by combating parental educational deficiencies through adult education. Reaching educationally disadvantaged parents and others has historically proved to be a veritable nemesis. Experiences reflect that even if agencies are successful in recruiting adults into the schools for formalized instruction, maintaining their presence constitutes an even greater problem.

An innovative approach for reaching adult education audiences was accomplished in Florida through the use of a specially equipped mobile facility. The latest electronic instructional equipment and materials were installed to assist Puerto Rican target populations to improve their command of the English language, to advance their education, and to improve their economic status (American School and University, 1969).

Teacher Inservice Training

The provision of adequate inservice training of educators has long plagued administration. Personnel who truly contribute to the improvement of the teaching competency of others have typically been in short supply. Although large metropolitan school districts suffer less in this respect, due to the generally increased size of their staffs and concomitant resourcefulness, these districts do experience problems in respect to the optimal distribution of such staff competency to target audiences, or to other educators requiring and/or desiring inservice training.

Mobile educational facilities are operational in several areas of the country for the express purpose of teacher inservice training. An operation of this nature was described by Carter (1968) thus:

Johnston County's mobile unit has been turned into a completely different idea from the "filmobile." Their mobile unit is an inservice teacher-training center. This unit, like the other, has an electric power system, and is air-conditioned. Here the similarities end.

The teacher-training mobile is equipped with: 16mm projector, dry mounting equipment, tape recorder, overhead projector, filmstrip slide projector, record player, and transparency-making equipment.

Whenever the director of the Johnston County Audiovisual Program has made arrangements with a school principal for training the school's faculty in the operation of equipment and the preparation of materials, the mobile unit is driven to the school.

. . . Sometimes the teachers are relieved of duty by a teacher's aide (usually for an hour), while the teacher visits the training mobile and is taught to operate the various pieces of equipment. (p. 47)

Use of a similar mobile unit has been instituted in Rhode Island, with somewhat broader application of the facility than at North Carolina. An elaborate inservice training program for teachers and ancillary personnel is systematized to reach individuals requiring such skills. The Pawtucket School District mobile teacher inservice unit is equipped, according to Cote (1968), to instruct in the utilization of educational technology, and additionally has repair capabilities for servicing virtually any type of audiovisual equipment the district possesses.

There are other configurations of mobile teacher inservice programs that are not limited to only a school district or county area, but serve an expansive geographical region. Colleges have sponsored programs featuring training for educators for which college credit was awarded, and there have been instances where state departments of education have financially sponsored entries of these mobile resource units into their respective states. Since the origin of the units in 1958, they have reached virtually thousands of educators and have delivered demonstrations of instructional activities previously unavailable.

Media and Audiovisual Services

Although most educationally oriented mobile units feature some provision for the use of educational media, several education agencies have designed and instituted special units to train teachers in this regard. School districts in Louisiana have deployed several mobile units which operate in conjunction with the district's respective media centers.

Schools in Maryland are cited by Bryant (1971) as using audiovisual units to train both teachers and students. Teachers are afforded opportunities to participate in three 50-minute sessions, and to follow through with advanced skill development by selecting and completing two minicourses in various audiovisual instructional areas. These courses are chosen by the teacher participant from a total of 14 available. Beyond inservice training capabilities, these units offer advantages as mobile resource centers of audiovisual materials (Pfeil, 1970).

Graduate Training

According to Bryant (1971), in a relatively new scheme, mobile units are being used by several colleges and universities in providing graduate course offerings. In Illinois, a mobile unit is equipped and in service to offer graduate training in special education. The unit, which is stationed at various universities in the state, and accommodates classes for teachers and trainees who enroll in summer courses, enables teachers to take highly specialized course-work without leaving their area of residence or employment. Rural areas as well as urban population centers are reached.

One of the most comprehensive uses of mobile facilitieis in graduate education is in Pennsylvania. An updated mobile unit is scheduled throughout the state by Pennsylvania State University, and offers graduate courses to teaching personnel unable to attend a university. Highly specialized, the unit contains a central computer with 12 terminals to provide individualized instruction to teachers. Featuring flexibility, the facility provides teachers with an opportunity to schedule courses at their personal convenience, and to complete course requirements at an individual pace.

Vocational Education and Counseling

Attesting that mobile units are operational in diversified educational undertakings, New Jersey has effected a mobile unit in the provision of Vocational education for high school students throughout the State.

In Utah, mobile units are functioning in vocational guidance. The MACE (Mobile Assisted Career Exploration) operates in a specially constructed trailer (12 feet by 44 feet) which is partitioned into two general service areas: one for small group sessions or one-to-one counseling activities, and the second for career exploration under the supervision of a vocational guidance career instructor. The unit is scheduled to visit small, rural schools in southern Utah twice yearly, and allows ninth-grade students an opportunity to receive 14 hours with a professional counselor and/or occupational instructor. Fully equipped, the mobile facility houses brochures, pamphlets, and monographs describing diversified job information, as well as procedures a student should follow in responsibly selecting an occupation (Bryant, 1971). Two additional mobile training facilities operated by the Utah State Department of Education provide office occupations and electronics education to predominately rural school students.

Driver Education

From their conceptual beginning in the form of the Link Aircraft Trainers in the 1940s, driver education mobile simulator units have been gaining broad acceptance by numerous educational agencies responsible for driver training.

A quiet, complex unit when fully equipped, the driver education simulator has almost revolutionized driver instruction. Los Angeles, for example, is using mobile driving simulators in its high schools. These simulators are heated, air-conditioned, twelve-place units which can be moved from school to school (Stack, Seaton, and Loft, 1964). Although these units lack flexibility for accommodating training activities in other orientations, they do offer observable advantages in serving their precise purpose.

Few adequate long-term evaluations of driver education are available to date, although numerous such studies are being conducted. Early evidence, however, indicates that economy factors associated with simulation are favorable. One advantage lies with reductions in capital expenditures for permanent classroom facilities in each secondary school. Another advantage is the increased student-teacher ratios without apparent loss of the instructor's ability to monitor and assist the student in his learning. Mobile units for driver education have been purchased by several agencies; however, lease or rental options are popular.

Ford and Uxer (1970) report that, in Texas, one certified teacher, five aides, a simulator, and four driver education cars provide a state-approved program of instruction to 192 students in six weeks on a consistent basis. Without the simulator and aides, it would require one teacher a complete year to teach 192 students.

Other Uses

Throughout the literature appear numerous citations of specialized uses of mobile service and educational units. A noninclusive listing of these is presented, to substantiate the apparent sincerity connected with the intensifying trend of mobile facility utilization in special service and educational domains. Mobile units have been used as bookmobiles, fire rescue vehicles, mobile medical units, sales display coaches, patrol wagons, specialized military vehicles, parcel delivery vehicles, speech and hearing units, innovative teaching techniques units, roving diffusion laboratories, helpmobile teacher training units, audiobus student learning units, mobile classrooms, mobile schools (individualized instruction by computer), special diagnostic units, dental examination clinics, complete dental clinics, space science laboratories, library reading rooms, guidance units, diagnostic hearing and speech therapy units, industrial arts units, ambulances, rural health clinics, X-ray clinics, veterinary clinics, special-purpose vehicles, library classroom units, psychological counseling units, field trip units, vision testing clinics, school medical clinics, learning resource centers, rolling study centers, and educational media units (Howse, 1971).

REFERENCES

American School and University. Portable Units Hold the Line on Facility Needs. Author, 1968, 40.

_____. Wheels: How They Push the Progress of Education. Author, 1969, 41.

Bryant, B. A Study of Portable and Mobile Educational Units. Unpublished research paper, The University of Texas at El Paso, 1971.

California State Department of Education, Bureau of School Planning. Portable School Buildings. Sacramento: State Department of Education, 1969.

Carter, C. Audio-Visuals on the Move. *Educational Screen and Audio-Visual Guide*, Chicago, 1968, 47.

Communication Seminars, Incorporated. An In-Person Interview. *Education Equipment and Materials.* Chicago: Author, 1968, Number 1.

Cote, H. F. A Mobile Media Center. Washington, D.C.: *Audiovisual Instruction*, 1968, *13*.

Educational Facilities Laboratories. Relocatable School Facilities: A Report. New York: Author, 1964.

Ford, L. H., and Uxer, J. E. Education Service Centers Streamline Driver Education. *Texas Outlook*, 1970, *54*.

Howse, J. Preschool Instruction Mobile Facilities; Description and Analysis. Southeastern Educational Corporation, Atlanta, School Practices Report Number 3, 1971.

Instructor. Putting the Migrant Program on Wheels. Author, 1969, *47*.

O'Grince, S. H. Baltimore Expands its Portables. *American School and University,* 1970, *42.*

Pfeil, M. P. Off the Shelf and Into the Classroom: Mobile Educational Technology Unit. *American Education,* 1970, *6.*

Stack, H., Seaton, D., and Loft, B. *Administration and Supervision of Safety Education.* New York: Macmillan, 1964.

Strasser, M., Aaron, J., Bohn, R., and Eales, J. *Fundamentals of Safety Education.* New York: Macmillan, 1964.

ADDITIONAL RESOURCES

Baas, A. M. Relocatable Classrooms. Educational Facilities Review, Series Number 10. Washington, D.C.: National Center for Educational Research and Development, 1973.

Hewitt, B. Readimobile. *Instructor,* 1968, *7.*

Howes, C. B. Chicago's Mobile Classrooms. *American School Board Journal,* 1962, *144.*

Lazar, I. Organizing Child Development Programs. *Appalachia,* 1970, *3.*

Murfreesboro City Schools, Tennessee. *Classroom on Wheels.* Washington, D.C.: Office of Education, 1972.

Pearson, G. Schoolrooms on the Go. *American Education,* 1969, *5.*

Potter, T. C. The Mobile Learning Laboratory: Educational Research and Development on the Move. *Audio-Visual Instruction,* 1968, *13.*

Ontario Department of Education, School Planning and Building Research Section. *Relocatable Learning Facilities.* Toronto: Department of Education, 1970.

Singleton, C. Moveable Teaching Environments for Appalachia. *American School and University,* 1967, *39.*

Tanzman, J. How to Get Rolling with Your Media Centers. *School Management,* 1969, *13.*

91

AEROSPACE EDUCATION

by Frederick B. Tuttle
Director of Educational Programs
Office of Public Affairs
National Aeronautics and Space Administration
Washington, D.C.

Aerospace Education is a term used to denote the efforts by educators to bring to pupils of the elementary and secondary schools an understanding of the nature and the results of mankind's activities beyond the surface of the Earth in atmosphere and space. The term is often used interchangeably with Space Education, Space Age Education, Space Science Education, and Aerospace/Aviation Education.

The Aerospace Education movement began in the late 1950s, about the time that Sputnik was launched. It was an outgrowth of the Aviation Education movement which was so successfully propagated during and after World War II by the Aviation Education Division of the Civil Aeronautics Administration (now the Federal Aviation Administration), and later in the 1950s by the U.S. Air Force's Auxiliary, the Civil Air Patrol.

From a societal point of view, the rationale for introducing aerospace into education is that aviation and space have, on the one hand, opened vast new occupational fields, and, on the other, provided mankind with new understandings of the nature of man, Earth, and the cosmos. From a curricular point of view, the rationale is that aerospace motivates pupil learning.

Aerospace Education takes several forms: (1) teacher education programs for pre- and inservice teachers; (2) efforts by teachers to bring understandings of aviation and space into the teaching of each subject at each grade level; (3) elective courses in secondary schools; (4) nonclassroom and nonschool youth programs; and (5) programs for adults, such as courses, conferences, and meetings.

(1)

Probably the best-known aspect of aerospace education is the effort to introduce pre- and inservice teachers to aerospace. This teacher education activity is frequently carried on through what are familiarly called aerospace courses and workshops, conducted by colleges and universities and local school districts. These aerospace workshops and courses are often colorful and exciting programs, which also provide teachers with practical ideas for incorporating into their classroom teaching what they learn about aerospace.

The college and university aerospace workshops range from those which have a strong orientation toward space, such as the Florida Technological University's (conducted as the NASA Kennedy Space Center), which have been space-oriented, to those workshops which are aviation-oriented, such as the Middle Tennessee State University's and the State of Oklahoma's at its several state college campuses. The Kent State-Baldwin Wallace Workshop, conducted at NASA's Lewis Research Center, and the workshops of the University of Nebraska are representative of the relatively few which devote equal attention to aviation and space.

NASA also assists a number of short courses or workshops that are sponsored by local school authorities. They may involve one or more communities, and generally are conducted during the school year in the afterschool hours. In these school-year workshop programs, the workshop instructional staffers frequently visit the classrooms of the teachers enrolled to work with them and their pupils. These programs range in size from the 25-30 enrollees of Oakland's Chabot Science Center to the 60 or 70 of the Shawnee Mission, Kansas' program.

The typical aerospace education course or workshop usually comprises three elements: lectures, field trips, and activities. By activities is meant teachers practicing ways and means for relating the subject of aerospace to their classroom teaching. Between 150-200 of these courses and workshops are held each year, enrolling an average of 25-30 teachers, with some enrolling 100 or more.

Another means by which aerospace has been introduced into teacher education is through the standard academic and professional courses of the college or university curriculum. The instructor may weave aerospace into his course through units, frequent references to recent developments, selected readings, film viewings, and laboratory and classroom activities.

On a less formal basis, the teacher education aspect of aerospace is carried on through the general and concurrent sessions of local, state, regional, and national conferences of professional education associations.

(2)

The most prevalent aspect of aerospace education is the effort by classroom teachers to integrate aerospace-related understandings into their day-to-day teaching of the standard subjects. Industrial education, science, and social studies courses provide the greatest number of opportunities for teachers to include aerospace. To assist teachers in this effort, a number of curriculum supplement-type publications, units, teacher guides, and outlines have been produced by aerospace industry corporations, airlines, and government and quasi-government organizations.

Large numbers of teachers have had considerable experience weaving aerospace into the subjects they teach. This number is accelerating as the result of the inclusion of aerospace-related units, chapters, and paragraphs in elementary and secondary school standard textbooks. The USOE Elementary and Secondary Education Act, Title III projects included a number of significant aerospace education projects, such as that in the Lincoln, Nebraska, Public Schools; the McPhee Laboratory School in Lincoln has one of the best aerospace education libraries in the nation. The Houston, Texas, Independent School District developed through its Title III program a strong elementary school science curriculum, which included challenging aerospace-related activities. In California, the Newport-Mesa Unified School District, through its Title III project, published a number of booklets, and also outfitted a van to go from school to school to assist teachers. In the Kentucky and Alabama Schools, recent statewide ETV programs on Skylab have stimulated widespread classroom activity and interest.

(3)

The high school elective courses in aerospace have recently been growing in numbers. These, including the courses of the Civil Air Patrol and the Air Force Junior ROTC, number over 1,500. Their course content generally includes a modified aviation ground school, a flight experience in a light aircraft, the principles of rocketry, the nature and accomplishments of manned and unmanned space flight, and the social implications of aviation and space.

Elective courses which are devoted solely to space are fewer in number. They may be categorized as those primarily concerned with astronomy; those dealing with the science and mathematics of rocketry and orbits; and those providing an overview of the space program. As with most elective courses, the orientation of the course depends on the background and interests of the teacher. At the Ben Davis High School, of the Wayne Township Schools outside of Indianapolis, the aerospace elective program has two or more courses, and is oriented toward aviation careers. At Richmond, Washington,

the course was meteorology-oriented. In connection with the Explorer programs at the NASA Lewis Research Center, Cleveland, there were two courses, one devoted to rocketry, the other to aeronautics.

Possibly the best source of information as to the elective aerospace courses in America's secondary schools is the Sanderson Times Mirror's annual *Aviation/Aerospace Education High School Planning Guide.*

(4)

Representative of nonclassroom-related aerospace education activities are contests for highly talented youth, such as the NASA/NSTA Skylab Student Project, the NASA/NSTA Viking Student Project, and the Aerospace competitions sponsored by NASA in Science Services' Science and Engineering Fairs.

There are also projects for the disadvantaged, some of which are sponsored by schools through Title I organizations under the Elementary-Secondary Education Act, and others by local police departments or recreation departments. Those sponsored may be of three to five days' duration, including film showings, talks followed by questions and answers, and activity sessions, which often culminate with participants firing rockets which they constructed.

Of the organized nonschool youth groups, the Scouts have an Aviation Merit Badge and a Space Exploration Merit Badge; the Cub Scouts every two or three years have a Space Month; and the Explorers have posts which devote a large share of their time to the study of aerospace. The 4-H Clubs, as part of their informal education activities, have programs with supporting kits for informal aerospace education activities. Although there are relatively few aerospace model building clubs organized solely for youth, numbers of youth are members of adult model rocketry and model aviation clubs: approximately 80 percent of the membership of model rocketry clubs are under 20 years of age, and 20 percent of the members of the model aviation clubs are under age 20. The Civil Air Patrol has over 400 cadet squadrons and over 900 composite squadrons (adults and cadets). These squadrons carry on a substantial education program in aerospace fundamentals.

(5)

Among adults, Aerospace Education activities include the formally organized courses of state and local education departments, and nongovernment organizations such as YMCAs and YWCAs. An active and exemplary program to provide aerospace courses for adults is that of the Florida State Department of Education, which with NASA's assistance developed a course syllabus and training program for its instructors. These courses, growing in popularity, are generally designed for the layman, often the senior citizen, who possesses little knowledge of aerospace but wishes to broaden his background.

Other adult groups interested in aerospace comprise the adult leadership of such youth and children's organizations as 4-H Clubs and Cub Scouts; for these leaders the programs consist of intensive short courses or workshops. The meetings devoted to aerospace of service clubs, civic groups, church organizations, and PTAs represent a third area of adult interest. Approximately 400 of these are held each year.

A unique feature of the aerospace education activities is the considerable community interest and support they generate; industry associations, aerospace manufacturers, and local, state, and Federal government agencies all lend a hand. They provide or request assistance, such as organizing conferences, courses, and workshops, supplying speakers, helping with field trips, making available films and publications, and occasionally providing funds. The professional organization for aerospace education is the National Aerospace Education Association, a small but dedicated and active group of educators and others interested in space education. This organization, among its many functions, serves as a clearinghouse for information about aerospace education. Its address is Middle Tennessee State University, Murfreesboro, Tenn. 37130.

REFERENCES

Bernardo, J. V. NASA's Services to Teachers. *Current Science* (Teachers Edition), Vol. 55, No. 2, Section 1, September 17, 1965.
Education. Vol. 92, No. 4, April-May 1972. A number devoted largely to aerospace education.
Journal of Aerospace Education. A monthly. First number published February 1974 by the National Aeronautic Association, Suite 610, Shoreham Building, 806 15th Street, N.W., Washington, D.C. 20005
Sanderson Times Mirror. *Aviation/Aerospace Education High School Planning Guide.* An annual report compiled by C. E. Neal. Sanderson Times Mirror, 8065 East 40th Ave., Denver, Colo. 80207.
NASA Report to Educators. A quarterly newsletter. Teachers wishing copies of this newsletter and other NASA publications may write Educational Publications/FE, National Aeronautics and Space Administration, Washington, D.C. 20546.
Strickler, M. K., ed. *An Introduction to Aerospace Education.* Chicago: New Horizons Publishers, Inc., 1968.
Tuttle, F. B., ed. *Science Education in the Space Age, Proceedings of a National Conference.* Washington, D.C.: U.S. Government Printing Office, November 1964.

92

CAREER GUIDANCE: AN OVERVIEW OF ALTERNATIVE APPROACHES

by Robert E. Campbell
and
Louise Vetter
The Center for Vocational Education
The Ohio State University
Columbus, Ohio

This publication was originally published by the ERIC Clearinghouse on Vocational and Technical Education as Information Series No. 45. The material in this publication was prepared pursuant to a contract with the Office of Education, U.S. Department of Health, Education and Welfare. Contractors undertaking such projects under government sponsorship are encouraged to express freely their judgment in professional and technical matters. Points of view or opinions do not, therefore, necessarily represent official Office of Education position or policy.

Traditional counseling (one-to-one and/or group) has been quite successful with the college-bound student population. However, despite the dedicated efforts of many guidance professionals, traditional approaches for assisting youth in planning for the world of work have been deficient in student impact. Alternative approaches for career development and planning are needed which incorporate a broader spectrum of variables such as new techniques and methods, systematic program management, consideration for special populations, innovative models for training career development personnel, and program evaluation. Clearly, new roles and the optimal use of existing roles is required.

Over the past few years, a number of authorities both within and external to the field of vocational guidance have examined the state of the field from different perspectives. Herr (1968) summarized a series of national conferences. Shertzer and Stone (1966) discussed problems from the standpoint of the practicing counselor. Campbell (1968b) did a national survey of guidance programs which studied the points of view of school counselors, administrators, students and parents. Ginzberg (1970) presented the perspective of a national professional service. Rosen (1969), Super (1969), Gribbons and Lohnes (1969), Crites (1969), and Campbell (1968a) examined the career development viewpoint. Hansen (1970) summarized career guidance practices in school and community. Ehrle (1969) synthesized a general overview.

Almost all of the above conclude that vocational guidance is in urgent need of modernization to maximize student impact. Some professional leaders recommend program reorganization; others argue for a closer alliance between counselor education and practice; while still others suggest a considerable reduction of the time lag in the program adoption of research findings to practice. There are also pleas for more "social relevance" in vocational guidance programs; more public support; evaluation systems to judge the effectiveness of systems; student behavioral objectives for career development program planning; and more effective impact on target populations such as the disadvantaged, noncollege-bound youth, and women returning to the labor force.

Wilensky (1966) points out that an orderly career pattern is restricted to a small minority of the labor force. Recent longitudinal career pattern studies confirm his findings and point to the large amount of occupational floundering experienced by a large percentage of the labor force (Gribbons and Lohnes, 1969, and Super, 1967). Many of the "flounderers" are from such special groups as the disadvantaged, women, older workers, and minority ethnic groups.

A number of studies (The Advisory Council on Vocational Education Report, 1968; Campbell, 1968b; Riccio and Waltz, 1967; Rosen, 1969; and Ryan, 1969) have pointed out that 1) counselors do not have enough specialized training for serving the noncollege-bound; and 2) more thought should be given to alternative approaches to career guidance.

The purpose of this article is to present a brief overview of alternative approaches to career guidance programs. No discussion of traditional face-to-face or group counseling procedures is included. A reading list of major sources for further reading is given in Appendix A. The bibliography included is deliberately selective; it includes only those materials used directly in the preparation of this report. Program developers, teacher educators, administrators, counselor educators, and researchers who are interested in further research development and diffusion of innovative approaches to career guidance should find the material particularly pertinent.

ALTERNATIVE APPROACHES

In order to achieve the objective for which this report was written, this section will be divided into two areas. First, exemplary alternative career guidance approaches will be considered. The second section will include recommendations for extrapolations of current exemplary approaches and explorations of possible future systems external to the "establishment."

To avoid misinterpretation, "alternative approaches" will be defined as follows: alternative career guidance approaches are different from the traditional guidance model in that they will deliver on student outcomes; they incorporate all available resources (including the present state of knowledge); they provide for self-evaluation, self-renewal; and are future-oriented.

Exemplary Alternative Approaches

Four types of alternative approaches will be discussed. They are occupational exploration, the developmental (K-14) approach, systems approaches, and computer-assisted approaches. Examples of specific ongoing programs of each type will be included, although discussion of each program will be limited. The reader is urged to consult the original sources cited for more information about each program.

To facilitate discussion, the following is organized around four topics, but the actual division of guidance practices is not quite that clear-cut. For example, developmental approaches may or may not use a systems approach; occupational exploration approaches may or may not utilize computers; systems approaches may incorporate occupational exploration, developmental approaches, and computers, etc.

Occupational Exploration. Budke (1971) defines occupational exploration as "organized educational efforts directed at exposing students to a wide spectrum of career occupations through discussion, films, resource persons, and field trips, as well as exploration of their interests and abilities through participation in manipulative skills and simulations in a laboratory or work setting."

From an extensive review and synthesis of information on occupational exploration programs, Budke (1971) offers the following conclusions:

Little research on specific occupational exploration is available; however, considerable material in the area

of vocational development (with indirect application to world-of-work activities) was found.

Greatest emphasis appeared to be on the development of world-of-work programs and activities at the elementary school level.

At present, programs in the junior high school are most numerous and highly developed.

There is a definite trend toward comprehensive programs or master plans for education. These programs include association with the world of work in the elementary school, orientation to the world of work in the middle school, exploration of the world of work in grades nine and ten, and in-depth exploration of career clusters and skill development in the eleventh and twelfth grades.

Hansen (1970) includes an extensive discussion of programs in her monograph on career guidance practices in school and community. An annotated bibliography on facilitating career development (Bailey, 1970) also contains numerous references.

A sample of programs now underway would include the Detroit Developmental Career Guidance Project (Leonard, 1968); the Atlanta, Georgia Occupational Information Materials Project (Cook, 1968); the Rochester, New York Project BEACON (Stiller, 1968); the Appalachia Educational Laboratory SAVIS—Self-Administering Vocational Information System (Andros, 1967); and the Oregon SUTOE—Seof Understanding Through Occupational Exploration—Program (Oregon Board of Education, 1969).

Media used in occupational exploration are varied, ranging from projected materials, such as films and slides, through games which provide simulations and problem-solving, curricula which provide work experiences, and decision-making exercises on computers.

The University of Pittsburgh Communication in Guidance Project (Martin, 1967) involves the use of slides, filmstrips, video tapes, and movies. Examples of the games approach include the Life Career Game (Boocock, 1967) and Vocational Simulation Kits (Krumboltz, 1968). The Industrial Arts Curriculum Project (1969) provides exploratory experiences for boys of junior high age. Although no girls have been included in the field testing to date, it would seem reasonable to provide such experiences for girls. Super (1970) edited a book on computer-assisted counseling which includes discussions of several exploration systems.

Developmental (K-14) Approach. Hansen (1967) lists the following knowledges and skills needed by a student in a developmental curriculum:

Knowledge of the nature of career development itself—a process which is psychological, tentative, continuous and changing.

Knowledge about the structure and trends of the labor force—obsolescent jobs, demand fields, new occupations, cybernation, and automation.

Skill in the process of decision-making—understanding of the possible, the probable, the desirable, the risks, and the strength of return of certain options.

Skill in synthesizing self-appraisal data and career information into a meaningful concept of self-developing exploratory hypotheses, testing them out, and evaluating them in relation to one's abilities, values, and goals.

A developmental program in vocational education, presented by Bottoms and O'Kelley (1971), indicates that the guidance program should be designed to help students personalize the meaning of their vocational experiences at each educational level, and to assist them at key decision-making points. The counselor is visualized as a resources consultant to teachers in integrating career-oriented experiences into the curriculum and in advising teachers on how to help students interpret the meaning these experiences may have for them. Placement and follow-up would also be necessary components of a developmental system.

Marland (1971), U.S. Commissioner of Education, indicated that he believes all education should be defined as career education. If such a change in focus is adopted by the educational system, it will be crucial to provide superior career guidance.

The program which is under development in Georgia is described by Bottoms and O'Kelley (1971). Ohio and Oregon are two other states which are in the process of developing a K-12 program for career orientation.

Computer Assisted Guidance. Loughary (1970) details five types of computer-assisted guidance programs. They are:

1. Information storage and retrieval systems
2. Library systems
3. Super-support systems (e.g., national work placement)
4. Counseling systems
5. Personal utility systems.

The first three systems are basically information-providing devices. The final two, not much beyond the conceptual stage at this point, could possibly provide many of the routine functions which the counselor provides today.

Tiedeman estimated that there have been approximately 14 different experimental computer-based vocational guidance systems. Most of these are identified in the USOE publication, *Computer-Based Vocational Guidance Systems,* 1969. Examples of these include ECES (Educational and Career Exploration System, Minor, F. J., Meyers, R. A., and Super, D. E., 1969); ISVD (Information System for Vocational Decisions, Tiedeman, D. V. et al., 1970); CVIS (Computer-assisted Vocational Information System, Harris, J., 1967); and SIGI designed to serve Junior College Students (System of Interactive Guidance and Information, Katz, M. R., 1970).

According to Harris et al. (1971), the presently available computer-assisted educational and vocational guidance systems can be divided into the following four types:

1. Indirect inquiry systems;
2. Direct inquiry systems without system monitoring;
3. Direct inquiry with system monitoring; and
4. Direct inquiry with system and personal monitoring.

The basic purpose of all present computer-based guidance systems is to permit inquiry concerning facts bearing on a particular type of institution or realm of activity, such as colleges, vocational-technical schools, financial aids, and occupations. The data file examined in a computer-based system is ordinarily somewhat independent of the system or program necessary to make the data available to the user. In distinguishing among types of computer-based systems, the emphasis is then placed on the scripts and programs which enable the user to tap the data files.

The computer as a tool for career guidance offers a great deal if used wisely. As Harris has pointed out, based upon her rich experience with computers, the guidance staff has to carefully monitor the total guidance program to achieve an optimum blend of man and machine. There can be a danger of relying too heavily on the counselor or the computer for specific tasks; the critical balance involves the appropriate complementary selection of each.

Several additional problems have delayed the wide-scale adoption of computers. One of these is cost. Most schools cannot afford the expensive outlay, but it is very likely that in time solutions such as cost-sharing, and less expensive hardware will emerge. The other problem involves training counselors to accept and use computers. Little effort has been expended thus far to familiarize counselors with them. Wide-scale adoption cannot occur without major educational thrusts.

The recently created commission on computer-assisted guidance systems sponsored by the National Vocational Guidance Association published their first report (Harris et al., 1971). The report is intended to provide practical guidelines for those considering the adoption of computer-based vocational guidance systems, and as such poses a series of "down-to-earth" questions to aid the decision. Many of the questions relate to thinking through the potential usefulness of computers to the present guidance program. In addition to guidelines, the report contains an extensive bibliography.

Systems Approaches. The systems approach can be defined as the selection of elements, relationships, and procedures to achieve a specific purpose (Hare, 1967). Noneducational examples include roadmaps (to reach a specific destination), office procedures (to communicate information), and personnel and equipment combinations to achieve a defense mission or to assemble a product for a corporation.

The primary advantage of using "systems" is in increasing the probability that a given goal will be achieved. The entire approach is target-oriented. Systems models show relationships and flow, from start to finish, and facilitate the management and monitoring of a program. Problems and impediments to achieving the goal can be spotted, modifications installed, resources shifted, and deadlines adjusted. The systems approach identifies alternative methods for achieving a goal, creates a searching attitude, ensures "backup" plans if the primary plan breaks down, and has procedures for determining the success of the program built into the system. Through trial installation, monitoring, and feedback, a program is continuously assessed to determine the degree to which it is achieving its initial goal.

Although the systems approach has been with us for a long time, application of the approach to career guidance has been only within the past several years. Pioneer operational models have been developed by Campbell et al., 1971; Dunn, 1970; Flanagan, 1971; Herr, 1972; and Hosford and Ryan, 1970.

The Campbell et al. systems model for career guidance grew out of a national survey of vocational guidance conducted in 1968, which concluded "if guidance programs are to be effective they must be systematically designed to achieve stated but limited objectives selected from a much larger set of possible objectives."

The model, based on a systems approach, a) emphasizes student behavioral objectives, b) gives alternative methods for accomplishing these objectives, c) provides program evaluation strategies, d) incorporates guidelines for program change adjustments, and e) can be operationally demonstrated in pilot locations and subsequently replicated in other locations. The model consists of 10 procedural phases, each phase reflecting an aspect of the systems approach (such as defining student behavioral objectives, generating vocational guidance methods, and implementing and evaluating the program).

The model was developed over a two-year period in cooperation with a comprehensive senior high school. The project team included staff of The Center, consultants, an advisory committee, and representatives from the public school system in which the model was being developed. The project team embraced a wide range of expertise, e.g., guidance counselors, school administrators, job placement specialists, and students.

Although described in a high school context, the model has been designed for flexible use at many levels, such as the state guidance system, the local school system, and/or the county or area school system. The basic model is not restricted to vocational guidance, and has utility for other aspects of the educational system. All ten phases do not have to be adopted as a total package; each phase is independent, and can be adopted in accordance with individual needs.

Since the model has not been field tested, the model described in the report is viewed as an interim version. A revised model will be published following extensive field testing during the next two years.

The ten phases are outlined below:

Phase I—Context Evaluation
Phase II—Assigning Program Goal Priorities
Phase III—The Translation of Goals to Student Behavioral Objectives
Phase IV—Input Evaluation: Method Selection
Phase V—Input Evaluation: Selection of Techniques
Phase VI—Diffusion: Trial Implementation
Phase VII—Process Evaluation
Phase VIII—Product Evaluation

Phase IX—Adoption
Phase X—Recycling

According to Hosford and Ryan (1970), the critical component for the systems approach (in counseling programs or in any program) is the definition of the product or outcome of the system in behavioral (performance) terms. They list the following functions for a model for developing a counseling and guidance program:

1. Study real-life environment
2. Define problem situation
3. Establish parameters of program
4. Design counseling/guidance program prototype
5. Simulate to test program prototype
6. Pilot-test model
7. Introduce system
8. Operate system
9. Evaluate system
10. Eliminate system.

Dunn and Flanagan have developed a very comprehensive individualized guidance system as a component of Project PLAN. The guidance component, entitled a Comprehensive Career Guidance System (CCGS), employed a systematic approach to develop and evaluate guidance-oriented objectives and related instructional and counseling experiences for youth. The ultimate aim is a comprehensive data bank of behavioral objectives, each keyed to a variety of appropriate instructional, counseling, and evaluational materials and procedures available for student, parent, counselor, and teacher use. With such a bank, guidance personnel should be better able to individualize guidance services and, hopefully, help education in general adjust to the separate needs of each student. It is predicted that during the 1970s, as public and private schools move more and more in the direction of individualized education, greater emphasis will have to be placed upon individualizing youth development and career (i.e., life) planning assistance.

The systematic approach used in the development and evaluation of objectives-based programs in the CCGS involved five types of activities:

Identification of youth development needs; *translation* of these into behavioral objectives which state desired youth outcomes.

Classification of objectives by commonalities and priorities which serve as guidelines for the design of guidance and counseling programs.

Specification of all possible alternative strategies which could be used in individualized instructional and counseling programs and bring about student attainment of previously specified objectives; *selection* of strategies which seem most appropriate for groups of related objectives and groups of youth who have similar learning characteristics.

Design, scheduling, and *implementation* of selected strategies by organizing instructional and counseling materials and procedures into individualized learning units.

Evaluation of the efficiency and effectiveness of

such units in helping students achieve the desired terminal outcomes specified in each unit's behavioral objectives; *corrective feedback* to make modifications in products and procedures developed and used in previous activities.

In regard to the first two activities just outlined, one method for grouping youth needs and objectives is by areas of a person's life (i.e., total career). Preliminary investigation led to the identification of the following six content areas of youth needs:

Vocational. Behaviors related to exploring and making decisions concerning both opportunities in the world of work and personal characteristics related to such opportunities.

Educational. Behaviors required for exploring, making decisions concerning, and pursuing the amount and kind of education and training one wants during school and throughout the rest of life.

Personal-Social. Intrapersonal competencies needed to function effectively as an independent person *and* interpersonal behaviors needed in small group situations, including two-person relationships. Behaviors applicable to various settings including home and classroom.

Academic-Learning. Behaviors involved in handling varied learning tasks more effectively and efficiently. Learning how to learn in varied settings, not just in the formal classroom.

Citizenship. Behaviors differentiated from those in the social behavior area because they are appropriate to secondary (e.g., government) rather than primary (e.g., family) social groups and systems.

Leisure. Behaviors connected with the exploration and utilization of leisure, cultural, and recreational pursuits.

Considerations

Several cautions should be suggested at this point: (1) it would be unwise to impose a rigid national model for career development and planning. Many institutions prefer "doing their own thing," and as evaluations are completed more options will be available. (2) Technology is best used as a tool, not as an excuse for instituting a program. If computers, overhead projectors, etc., will help to implement a well-planned program, use them. If not, don't. According to Walz (1970), "The future of guidance may very well depend upon the capacity of counselors individually and collectively to utilize technology in such ways that minimize the negative consequences and maximize the positive outcomes (p. 182)." (3) Guidance personnel education (both preservice and inservice) is critical. If guidance personnel are not aware of new advances and are not prepared to cope with them, the programs will never get off the ground.

Recommendations

Recommendations will be discussed under two major topics, extrapolations of current options available and future options.

Extrapolations. The major concern about alternative approaches for career guidance is that present methods often do not meet the needs of the students. How much better will the alternative approaches discussed earlier be? At this point, a definitive answer is not available. Many of the experimental systems developed are not yet beyond the field-testing stage. When a program has been implemented, evaluation of it as an operational possibility will need to be completed. When systems have been evaluated and found efficacious, there is still the problem of implementing the system in the schools. Many persons (administrators, school boards, parents, and counselors themselves) have to be convinced that such a program would make their school a better one. Given that such acceptance is obtained, the problems of cost, particularly for the systems which rely heavily on technology, remain.

Another problem with acceptance of alternative systems is the very real fears of human exploitation which arise whenever the introduction of technology into schools is discussed. Dworkin (1970), Tiedeman and Schmidt (1970), Oettinger (1969), Brickman and Lehrer (1969), and Lifton (1970) all speak to the problem. No real conclusions are reached, except that everyone needs to be concerned about the possibilities for dehumanization, and that the danger is much less when people are informed. The glamour of the machines must not be allowed to substitute for concern for the individual's own growth and development.

A third area of concern is the need for training professionals for implementing the innovative approaches. Changes must be considered, in terms of the kinds of educational programs provided and also in the kinds of workers needed. Perhaps a series of specialties should be developed; perhaps more thought should be given to the use of paraprofessionals; perhaps career planning should become part of the curriculum that the classroom teacher presents. Another possibility would be better integration of the career planning function among the schools and industry and community service organizations.

To emphasize the foregoing, three major recommendations are suggested:

1. Meeting student needs with programs which have passed the test of use and evaluation.
2. Protecting against the very real possibility of exploitation.
3. Training professionals for implementing the alternative approaches.

Alternative Futures. Traditionally there has been a time lag of as much as 50 years in the adoption of educational innovations. If this is the case, is it meaningful to talk about what the future holds for alternative delivery systems for career development and planning? It can be, with the stipulation that what is being discussed be forecasts for possible futures (a number of alternatives) rather than predictions of a specific future.

An extensive array of literature exists in the area of forecasting futures. Perhaps the best survey of possible futures for our country is presented in Harman (1970). Two possible ways he sees the country moving toward are to the "second-phase industrial" society and to the "person-centered" society.

In the "second-phase" industrial society, emphasis would be placed on the role of education in accomplishing social goals and alleviating social problems (poverty, racial discrimination, environmental deterioration, etc.). "Behavior-shaping" approaches, involving detailed specification of desired behaviors to be imparted by contingency-management techniques, will be important. Continuing education, in the form of vocational retraining, will also have an important place.

Educational goals that would be emphasized in a "person-centered" society include teaching students to become effective thinkers and learners, and developing their inquiry and problem-solving skills, social skills, and emotional awareness and self-identity. Education would be designed to foster feelings of safety and trust, to promote freedom to explore and inquire, and to provide a responsive environment and directed challenges. There would be reduced emphasis on absorbing specialized information and developing specific vocational skills.

In speaking directly to the question of the future of guidance, Cooley (1969) states: "The probable nature of the future school must be considered along with the probable nature of future guidance functions as we plan computer systems for the schools of tomorrow (pp. 61-62)." He sees the school moving in the direction of individualization of instruction within the next ten years, and states that computers can provide the necessary feedback for managing individually planned instruction, as well as the necessary feedforward information needed in the guidance process. (Feedforward information is that information which the student needs to set goals and develop plans to achieve those goals.)

Another possible future for the schools is indicated by Marland (1971), who states that "all education is career education, or should be." He sees the universal goal of American education as being that every young person completing grade 12 be ready to enter higher education or to enter useful and rewarding employment. The question, according to Marland, is this:

> Shall we persevere in the traditional practices that are obviously *not* properly equipping fully half or more of our young people, or shall we immediately undertake the reformation of our entire secondary education, in order to position it properly for maximum contribution to our individual and national life? (p. 6)

Daley, President-Elect of the American School Counselor association, put it this way:

> Maybe we need to go back and look at what we've done and how effective we've been. If we have anything to account for at all, maybe we need to revamp everything we're doing in counseling, and come up with a completely new model altogether.

The Counseling and Personnel Services Information Center has prepared a bibliography, Counseling in the Future (1970) which is part of a special issue of the CAPS *Capsule* which is entitled, "A Look to the Future."

Almost everyone is agreed that changes need to be made. The question is, what changes, and then, when? Harman (1970) states, and we agree, that choices are not necessarily what the society or its leaders may declare them to be. Choices are inferred from where the society puts its resources. Where will be put ours?

SUMMARY

The purpose of this paper was to look at alternative approaches for career guidance, after documenting the unsatisfactory status quo. The material in this report, supplemented with the sources listed in the bibliography, should aid program developers, teacher educators, and researchers who are interested in further research, development, and diffusion of career guidance systems.

REFERENCES

American Personnel and Guidance Association. Technology in Guidance. *Personnel and Guidance Journal,* Vol. 49, No. 3, November 1970.

Andros, G. C. *Self-Administering Vocational Information System. Development of the Self-Component.* Charleston, West Virginia: Appalachia Educational Laboratory, 1967.

Bailey, L. J., ed. *Facilitating Career Development: An Annotated Bibliography. Final Report.* Springfield, Illinois: Division of Vocational and Technical Education, Illinois State Board of Vocational Education and Rehabilitation; Carbondale, Illinois: Southern Illinois University, July 1970. (ED 042 217)

Boocock, S. S. The Life Career Game. *Personnel and Guidance Journal,* Vol. 46 (1967), pp. 328-334.

_____, and Schild, E. O., eds. *Simulation Games in Learning.* Beverly Hills, California: Sage Publications, 1968.

Bottoms, G., and O'Kelley, G. L. Vocational Education as a Developmental Process. *American Vocational Journal,* Vol. 46, No. 3 (1971), pp. 21-24.

Brickman, W. W., and Lehrer, S., eds. *Automation, Education and Human Values.* New York: Apollo Editions, Thomas Y. Crowell Company, 1969.

Budke, W. E. *Review and Synthesis of Information on Occupational Exploration. Information Series 34.* Columbus, Ohio: The Center for Vocational and Technical Education. The Ohio State University, 1971. (For ED number see future issue of *Research in Education.*)

Campbell, R. E. Career Guidance Practices Transcending the Present. *Vocational Guidance Quarterly,* 1974, *22*(4), 292-300.

_____, Dworkin, E. P., Jackson, D. P., Hoeltzel, K. E., Parsons, G. E., and Lacey, D. W. *The Systems Approach: An Emerging Behavioral Model for Career Guidance.* An interim report of a procedural monograph. Columbus, Ohio: The Center for Vocational and Technical Education, The Ohio State University, April, 1971.

_____, Walz, G. R., Miller, J. V., and Kriger, S. F. *Career Guidance: A Handbook of Methods.* Columbus, Ohio: Charles E. Merrill, 1973.

_____. *The Choice of Vocational Education as an Educational Opportunity: A Bibliography.* The American Personnel and Guidance Interdivision (National Vocational Guidance Association and American School Counselors Association) Commission on Guidance and Vocational Education, February 1968a.

_____. *Vocational Guidance in Secondary Education: Results of a National Survey. Research 36.* Columbus, Ohio: The Center for Vocational and Technical Education. The Ohio State University, December 1968b. (ED 026 534)

Cook, H. E. *Occupational Information Materials. Progress Report No. 4.* Atlanta, Georgia: Atlanta Public Schools, February 1969.

Cooley, W. W. Computer Systems for Guidance. *Computer-Based Vocational Guidance Systems.* Edited by James J. Gallagher. Washington, D.C.: Division of Vocational and Technical Education. Office of Education, 1969. (ED 034 408)

Counseling and Personnel Service. A Bibliography on Counseling in the Future. *CAPS Capsule,* Vol. 4, No. 1 (1970), pp. 13-14.

Crites, J. O. *Vocational Psychology.* New York: McGraw-Hill, 1969.

Daley, T. A Look to the Future. Interview in *CAPS Capsule,* Vol. 4 (1970), pp. 1-12.

Dunn, J. A. The Guidance Program in Project PLAN. *Personnel and Guidance Journal,* Vol. 49 (1970), pp. 232-233.

_____. *The 1970 PLAN Guidance Program.* Palo Alto, California: American Institutes for Research, 1971.

Dworkin, E. P. Input: Beware of False Gods. *Personnel and Guidance Journal,* Vol. 49 (1970), pp. 242-244.

Ehrle, R. A. *Vocational Guidance: A Look at the State of the Art.* College Park, Maryland: University of Maryland, 1969.

Flanagan, J. C. The PLAN System for Individualizing Education. *Measurement in Education,* Vol. 2, No. 2 (January 1971).

Ginzberg, E. *Career Guidance.* New York: McGraw-Hill, Inc., 1971.

Gribbons, W. D., and Lohnes, P. *Career Development from Age 13 to Age 25. Final Report.* Washington, D.C.: Bureau of Research, Office of Education, 1969. (ED 040 477)

Hansen, Lorraine S. *Career Guidance Practices in School and Community.* Ann Arbor, Michigan: ERIC Clearinghouse on Counseling and Personnel Services, 1970 (ED 037 595)

Hansen, L. S. "Theory into Practice: A Practitioner Looks at Career Guidance in the School Curriculum." *Vocational Guidance Quarterly,* Vol. 16 (1967), pp. 97-103.

Harman, W. W. Nature of Our Changing Society: Implications for Schools. *Social and Technological Change.* Edited by P. K. Piele and T. L. Eidell. Eugene, Oregon: University of Oregon Press, 1970.

Harris, J. *Summary of a Project for Computerized Vocational Information Being Developed at Willowbrook High School, Villa Park, Illinois.* Villa Park, Illinois: Willowbrook High School, 1967. (ED 019 840)

_____ et al. *Toward Guidelines for Computer Involvement in Guidance.* Washington, D.C.: Commission on Computer-Assisted Guidance Systems, National Vocational Guidance Association, 1971.

Harvard University. *Information System for Vocational Decisions. Annual Report 1967-68.* Cambridge, Massachusetts: Graduate School of Education; Newton, Massachusetts: Newton Public School System, September 1968.

Herr, E. L. Implications for State Vocational Guidance Program Development. *Selected Office of Education Supported Conferences, National Conference on Development of State Programs for Vocational Guidance,* January 16, 1968.

_____, and Cramer, S. H. *Vocational Guidance and Career Development in Schools: Toward a Systems Approach.* New York, N.Y.: Houghton-Mifflin Co., 1972.

Hosford, R. E., and Ryan, T. A. Systems Design in the Development of Counseling and Guidance Programs. *Personnel and Guidance Journal,* Vol. 49 (1970), pp. 221-230.

The Industrial Arts Curriculum Project. *The Journal of Industrial Arts Education,* Vol. 29, No. 2 (1969), pp. 10-39.

Kagan, N. Multimedia in Guidance and Counseling. *Personnel and Guidance Journal,* Vol. 49 (1970), pp. 197-204.

Katz, M. R. *System of Interactive Guidance and Information (SIGI).* Princeton, New Jersey: Educational Testing Service, 1970.

Krumboltz, J. D. et al. *Vocational Problem-Solving Experiences for Stimulating Career Exploration and Interest: Phase II.*

Final Report. Stanford, California: School of Education, Stanford University, 1968. (ED 015 517)

Leonard, G. E. *Developmental Career Guidance in Action, The First Year.* Detroit, Michigan: Wayne State University and Detroit Public Schools, 1968. (ED 013 456)

Lifton, W., ed. *Educating for Tomorrow.* New York: Wiley, 1970.

Loughary, J. W. The Computer Is In! *Personnel and Guidance Journal,* Vol. 49 (1970), pp. 185-191.

Marland, S. P., Jr. Career Education Now. Paper presented at National Association of Secondary School Principals Convention, Houston, Texas, January, 1971. (For ED number see June issue of *Research in Education.*)

Martin, A. M. *Multi-Media Approach to Communicating Occupational Information to Noncollege Youth. Interim Technical Report.* Pittsburgh, Pennsylvania: Pittsburgh University, December 1967. (ED 017 005)

Minor, F. J., Myers, R. A., and Super, D. E. An Experimental Computer-Based Educational and Career Exploration System. *Personnel and Guidance Journal,* Vol. 47 (1969), pp. 564-569.

National Advisory Council on Vocational Education. *Vocational Education; The Bridge Between Man and His Work. General Report.* Washington, D.C.: National Advisory Council on Vocational Education, 1968. (ED 028 267)

Oettinger, A. G. *Run, Computer, Run: The Mythology of Educational Innovation.* Cambridge, Massachusetts: Harvard University Press, 1969.

Osipow. S. H. *Theories of Career Development.* New York: Appleton-Century-Crofts, 1973.

Parnell, Dale et al. *Teachers Guide to SUTOE (Self Understanding Through Occupational Exploration).* Salem, Oregon: Division of Community Colleges and Vocational Education, Oregon State Board of Education, 1969. (ED 034 227)

Picou, J. S., and Campbell, R. E. *Career Behavior of Special Groups: Theory, Research, and Practice.* Columbus, Ohio: Charles E. Merrill, 1975.

Riccio, A., and Walz, G. R., eds. Forces for Change in Counselor Education and Supervision. *Counselor Education and Supervision* (Special Issue), Spring, 1967.

Rosen, H. Vocational Guidance—Room for Improvement. *Manpower Magazine,* 1969.

Ryan, T. A. *Commitment to Action in Supervision: Report of A National Survey by ACES Committee on Counselor Effectiveness.* Paper presented at the American Personnel and Guidance Association Convention, Las Vegas, Nevada, March 1969. (ED 034 214)

Shertzer, B., and Stone, S. *Fundamentals of Guidance.* Boston, Massachusetts: Houghton Mifflin Company, 1966.

Stiller, A. *Beacon Lights.* Project BEACON. Rochester, New York: Rochester School District, 1968.

Super, D. E., ed. *Computer-Assisted Counseling.* New York: Teachers College, Columbia University, 1970.

_____ et al. *Floundering and Trial After High School. Career Pattern Study: Monograph IV.* Teachers College, Columbia University, 1967. (ED 032 646)

_____. Vocational Development Theory: Persons, Positions and Processes. *The Counseling Psychologist,* Vol. 1 (1969), pp. 2-9.

Tiedeman, D. V. et al. *Information System for Vocational Decisions. Final Report.* Cambridge, Massachusetts: Harvard University, 1970. (ED 042 046)

_____, and Schmidt, L. D. Technology and Guidance: A Balance. *Personnel and Guidance Journal,* Vol. 49 (1970), pp. 234-241.

U.S. Department of Health, Education and Welfare, Office of Education. *Computer-Based Vocational Guidance Systems.* Washington, D.C.: U.S. Government Printing Office, 1969. (Contact Judith Weinstein, O.E.)

Walz, G. R. Technology in Guidance: A Conceptual Overview. *Personnel and Guidance Journal,* Vol. 49 (1970), pp. 175-182.

Wigtil, J. V., and McCormick, R. D. (Co-directors). *Ohio State Department of Education Project Guidelines for Career Development Programs K-12.* Columbus, Ohio: State Department of Education. Seminar held June 3-8, 1971.

Wilensky, H. L. Jobs, Careers, and Leisure. *Conference on Implementing Career Development Theory and Research Through the Curriculum.* Edited by K. B. Ashcraft. Warrenton, Virginia: APGA, AirLie House, 1966.

93

REVIEW AND SYNTHESIS OF RESEARCH ON OCCUPATIONAL ADAPTABILITY

by Douglas D. Sjogren
Professor of Education
Colorado State University
and
ERIC Clearinghouse on Vocational and Technical Education
The Center for Vocational and Technical Education
The Ohio State University
Columbus, Ohio 43210

This publication was originally published by the ERIC Clearinghouse on Vocational and Technical Education as Information Series No. 42. The material in this publication was prepared pursuant to a contract with the Office of Education, U.S. Department of Health, Education and Welfare. Contractors undertaking such projects under government sponsorship are encouraged to express freely their judgment in professional and technical matters. Points of view or opinions do not, therefore, necessarily represent official Office of Education position or policy.

PROBLEM STATEMENT

Vocational education is at a crisis. Kraft (1970) identified the focal point of the crisis when he wrote:

> For many years educators have ignored technological changes in higher technical education and vocationally oriented training; they have persisted in preparing students for a world viewed from an inherited, often locally oriented outlook. Only recently have educators recognized the need for a positive attitude toward space age technology; thus, constructive ideas have been developed regarding the adjustment of vocational and technical curricula in order to prepare students for their future roles. . . . The system of vocational training and higher technical education must be endowed with a capacity for change and innovation so it can adequately respond to the legitimate pressures and demands of modern society.

We are at a turning point in vocational education—turning from a system that was oriented to a stable society, with stable work-roles, to a system oriented to a dynamic society in which rapid and profound changes are occur-

ring. What are the changes that are occurring and what are their implications?

Foremost are the technological changes that effect obsolescence of jobs and stimulate new jobs (see Tavis and Gerber, 1969). Gannon et al. (1967) indicated that in the long run this is not a problem, if adjustments can be made for retraining and transfer. It is the proviso that is important to the vocational educator. How can vocational education facilitate this retraining and transfer to minimize the negative impact of technological change for the individual and society?

The civil rights revolution is another societal change that has implications for vocational education. For years members of minority groups in our society have been underemployed in dead-end jobs. They will no longer accept a subservient role, and are demanding opportunity to advance. Fine (1967) has pointed out how this requires the creation of new career lines, and how important it is to identify career lines from any job. The emergence and the creation of new careers is not, however, merely a means to placate minority groups. Their legitimate concerns have only demonstrated that any worker should have an opportunity to advance. New careers are emerging in many areas. Can vocational education adapt readily to these new careers and contribute to the identification of additional career lines?

A third force in our society with implications for vocational education is the attitude that educational programs should demonstrate both effectiveness and efficiency. The popular term now is "accountability." This term, however, when translated into practice, means that educational programs should do what is intended at the least cost. Vocational education is not only at a crisis, it is also in a crunch. The demands on vocational education are increasing at a more rapid rate than its support. How can vocational education adequately respond to these two forces?

Vocational Educators have recognized the dilemma they are in, and are attempting to resolve it. Bushnell (1969) pointed this out when he wrote, "Opening up career options and preparing students for their larger role responsibilities became one of the concerns of curriculum researchers, who rallied to the cause of reform following the passage of the Vocational Education Act of 1963." Especially since 1963, vocational educators have been studying and experimenting to develop programs that can satisfy the criteria of being efficient for the individual and society, and also effective in preparing the individual to adapt in the dynamic world of work. Many of these efforts have produced results that are important for the vocational educator. This paper is an attempt to review and synthesize these studies, and some related studies, to determine the implications they might have for program planning, and to identify the questions that are still unresolved.

The common thread through all of the studies reviewed is that they all have some bearing on the concept of occupational adaptability. Consequently, this term, which is used in the title, is the theme of the review.

SOME BASIC CONCEPTS

The idea of occupational adaptability connotes terms

like generalizability, transfer, association, etc. An individual who is adaptable is one who can generalize, transfer, or form associations so that the skills, attitudes, and understandings that have been learned or developed in one context can be readily used in a different context. Thus, the problem of occupational adaptability is an aspect of the general problems of transfer and generalizability that have been studied by psychologists and educators for some time. (A good discussion of this point is in Altman, 1966b.)

It is not our intent to review the vast number of studies that have been done on transfer of training. It is important, however, to realize that there is a strong theoretical base that is relevant to the problem of occupational adaptability. Some of the work that is especially relevant is reviewed briefly in the following paragraphs.

Gagne (1965) has demonstrated a hierarchical nature to learning in some situations. Many cognitive skills can be identified. The hierarchical model that Gagne offers seems to be one that can be applied to occupational adaptability, especially in the career line situation. His work is quite representative of the thinking of the behaviorists on transfer and generalizability. A useful summary of the behaviorist position as it applies to curriculum development has been made by Altman (1967) and Altman (1970).

Thorndike (1931) has long been credited with first demonstrating the relationship between transfer and similarity of content. This finding has been examined in many situations over the last several years. Much of the work has been in the area of studying the formation of verbal associations. A vast literature has developed in this area, and a good introduction to it is in Cofer and Musgrave (1963).

Ausubel and others have performed a series of experiments that are quite important in clarifying the relationship identified by Thorndike. (Rather than cite all of the Ausubel references, the author directs the reader to Ausubel, Stager, and Gaite (1969), the reference list of which contains references to other work.) The experiments have demonstrated that learning and retention of new material is facilitated if the learner has a stable and clear knowledge of a clear set of anchoring ideas. For example, persons with a good knowledge of Christianity learn about Buddhism more readily than those with less knowledge of Christianity. The knowledge of concepts of Christianity provides the set of anchoring ideas for learning the concepts of Buddhism. This series of experiments is quite important for the curriculum developer who is interested in facilitating general learning. Certainly the adaptability of an individual to different situations would be facilitated as he has available a repertoire of anchoring ideas for adapting to the new situation.

In terms of the transfer question as it related to occupational adaptability, the works of Gagne, Ausubel, and many associationists seem to be most relevant as a theoretical base. Many of the job-clustering studies reviewed later in this paper have in fact used one or more of these as their theoretical base.

Another aspect of studying occupational adaptability is the need to identify and classify behaviors at a more abstract level than the behavior specific to a single job.

For example, in examining common mathematical behaviors across occupations it is necessary to consider general mathematical skills rather than those skills specific to one occupation. Guilford (1967) has developed a model of the human intellect that provides a means for identifying and classifying cognitive behaviors. In the psychomotor realm, Fleishman has identified a number of psychomotor factors that could be readily used for classifying such behavior. (Fleishman and his associates have reported a number of relevant studies. We cite just one here, and the reader can go to that study to identify other references: Fleishman and Ellison, 1962). Cratty (1967) is another excellent source to use in work on classifying motor behaviors.

The classification of affective behaviors has not received as much attention as the cognitive and psychomotor behaviors from the learning point of view. Krathwohl, Bloom, and Masia (1964) have made an effort in this regard that is helpful. Theoretical developments in the area of occupational choice and interest are of particular relevance to occupational adaptability, especially in the affective area. Many of the theories emphasize those occupations for which a person might be suited. Three excellent sources for identifying the theoretical work in this area are Borow (1964), Tennyson (1968), and Osipow (1968).

The purpose of this brief overview of related theory is to emphasize that there is a rather extensive rationale for empirical studies and program development in occupational adaptability. The theories are not complete, but they do provide a starting point for considering methodology, procedure, and content of studies and programs. Several of the studies reviewed in the remainder of the paper have derived from, and have contributed to, the theories.

EMPIRICAL STUDIES

The studies in this section of the paper are reviewed under five broad headings: occupational adaptability, job analysis, curriculum-oriented work, work adjustment, and critique.

Occupational Adaptability Studies

There have been surprisingly few studies on the adaptability of workers from one job to another. Weinstein (1969) studied the spillover effects of military training and service to civilian occupations, using a large sample of army and navy veterans. He found that only 16 percent of the army veterans and 28 percent of the navy veterans used their skills learned in the military in their civilian work. Generally, the postservice employment was more related to preservice employment than to the military specialty. He also found that there was no effective mechanism to aid veterans to capitalize on their service experience.

The transferability of defense engineers to commercial work was studied by Rittenhouse (1967). He studied a large number of engineers and managers who had made such a transfer, and found no important job-related barriers. Any training requirements seemed to be provided for with on-the-job and other in-house programs. Defense engineers appeared to be best suited for work in research and development, new design, advanced engineering, and analytical areas in the commercial establishments.

The California State Department of Employment (1968) has conducted an extensive study of the transfer of industrial skills from defense to nondefense industries. A high degree of skill transferability was found, and the problems of transfer were due to limited manpower needs, wage differentials, hiring practices, union regulations, and license requirements.

The writer feels that there must be more studies of persons who have changed jobs, with the purpose of identifying factors related to success in the change, but few were found. There are many studies of mobility, and some of these are reviewed later in this paper. It does seem that some case studies and normative studies of job changers would be useful. Furthermore, such studies could be designed to test hypotheses generated from occupational choice or transfer theories, and thus serve to broaden our theoretical base.

Job Analysis

The literature on job analysis is quite extensive. Marsh (1962) published a *Job Analysis Bibliography* with 1,511 references. In this section, however, only two research programs will be reviewed. These studies have not been concerned with training, but only with studying and classifying jobs. The studies do have relevance for planning for occupational adaptability, however, in that they show results that have relevance in terms of behaviors that are generalizable across jobs.

The 1965 edition of the Dictionary of Occupational Titles (DOT) (Department of Labor, 1965a, 1965b) was the culmination of an extensive research program. The research is reported in a number of studies by Studdiford (1951, 1953); Fine (1955a, 1955b, 1957a); Fine and Heinz (1957, 1958); Newman and Fine (1957); and Trattner, Fine, and Kubis (1955). The result was an occupational classification system with 603 occupational groupings, based on nine occupational categories and 84 occupational divisions, in terms of subject matter, activity, products, services, or areas of work. Also, there is a classification of the jobs, in terms of the level at which the worker must function with respect to each of the general headings of Data, People, and Things. Finally, 114 worker-trait groups were defined, in terms of the common traits and abilities required of the workers.

The work on the 1965 DOT, and the publication, are important advances in resolving the problem of occupational adaptability. The research base of the DOT and the classifications developed are useful for other researchers working in this area. Furthermore, the publication is an important tool for counselors, and for developers of occupational programs who are striving to effect adaptability. An interest survey based on the DOT has been developed by D'Costa (1968). The scale has demonstrated high reliability, and it should be a valuable counseling tool, especially if used with the DOT.

Another extensive program of research on job characteristics has been conducted by McCormick and several associates at Purdue University. The following references provide a good summary of the development of their research program: McCormick, Finn, and Schieps, 1957; Palmer and McCormick, 1961; Gordon and McCormick, 1963; Cunningham and McCormick, 1964; and McCormick, 1964. This research program has evolved from an original emphasis on the job to an emphasis on identifying and classifying the behaviors of workers (McCormick, Jeanneret, and Mecham, 1969). McCormick has developed an instrument for the analysis of jobs called the Position Analysis Questionaire (PAQ). The PAQ contains 189 items grouped into six general areas: information input, mediation processes, work output, interpersonal activities, work situation and job context, and miscellaneous. Each of the items is a possible element of a job and the relevance of the element to the job is rated on an appropriate scale. The PAQ has demonstrated high reliability. A factor analysis of data obtained from an administration of the PAQ revealed five dimensions, that were named as follows: Decision, Communication, and Social Responsibilities; Skilled Activities; Physical Activities and Related Environmental Conditions; Equipment and Vehicle Operation; and Information Processing Activities.

A next step in the research was to obtain ratings of the extent to which some 68 human attributes were necessary to satisfactory performance on each job element. The ratings yielded attribute "profiles" of job elements. The validity of the ratings was established by relating the attribute profiles to the aptitude test scores of people on jobs. The results were encouraging. The methodology and the instruments developed in the program of study were judged to offer "promise of serving certain practical purposes such as job evaluation and the establishment of synthetically-derived attribute requirements of individual jobs (McCormick et al., 1969)."

Curriculum-Oriented Work

The DOT and the McCormick research programs were oriented toward describing jobs and workers without specific regard for implications in terms of training the worker for the job. In the last decade especially, many studies have been conducted that have attempted to identify clusters of occupations. The identified clusters were expected to enable the program developer to design programs that would be both efficient and effective in preparing workers who would be occupationally adaptable. Whether these purposes have been met is still a moot question, but the studies have made a contribution to our understanding of the world of work. The studies reviewed in this section have as their common theme the identification of job or behavior clusters for program planning purposes.

The most common method employed is to conduct a job analysis and then form clusters, on the basis of an arbitrary criterion or on the basis of perceived similarity on the job analysis. There are several excellent references on the methodology of job analysis. Certainly the DOT and McCormick studies have contributed much to the methodology of job or task analysis. Marsh, Madden, and Christal (1961) described the well-researched procedures used in the Air Force. Larson (1969) and Larson and

Blake (1969) described an analysis procedure called zoned analysis. The procedure analyzes jobs in four zones from general characteristics to specific details. Seymour (1966) and Glaser (1966) have described job analysis procedures used by industry for designing training.

The job analysis technique or some adaptation has been used in a variety of ways. Grede *et al.* (1968) and Dillon and Horner (1967) presented studies of jobs analyzed at a general level, and identified groupings such as business occupations, health occupations, service occupations, etc. Most of the studies, however, have been done within one of these broad areas.

Peterson (1962, 1964a, 1964b, 1964c, 1966a, 1966b) did a series of studies designed to suggest techniques for determining courses of study in the technological areas of chemistry and metallurgy, mechanical drafting and design, electronic data processing, civil and highway, mechanical, and electrical and electronic.

A large number of job-analysis-type studies have been done in the agricultural field. Most were done in order to better define the area of agriculturally related occupations. These have generally been statewide studies, and have been done in enough states so that it would appear that a person working in this area could find a study done in a state with characteristics similar to his own. Studies in the agriculture occupations area include Gunderson et al. (1966), Mosley (1966), Morrison (1964), Barwick (1965), Drake and Tom (1968), Loreen (1967), McGee (1965), Heaney (1966), Hensel (1968), Baker (1966), Cushman et al. (1965), Hoover et al. (1966), Curtis and Mondart (1967), Cain and Dillon (1966), Wall et al. (1967), and Baker and Woodin (1966).

Job analysis and judgmental clustering has also been done in home economics (O'Donnell, 1967; Ridley, 1967; Shipley, 1967), business and office (Perkins et al., 1968; Ertel, 1968), public service (Institute for Local Self Government, 1969), justice work (Grant et al., 1969), health occupations (Franklin, 1965; Gilpatrick and Corliss, 1969), and engineering technology (American Society for Engineering Education, 1964). The cited references are representative of what is probably a much larger number of similar kinds of studies that were not identified, or that have never entered the usual dissemination channels.

Most of the job analysis type studies cited above have resulted in the identification of commonalities among jobs. Also, in most of the studies the results were discussed in terms of their implications for curricula. None of the studies cited above, however, has reported the next step of building and testing curricula on the basis of the findings.

A noteworthy study, in which the job analysis approach to the cluster concept was used as the basis for curriculum-building, was done at the University of Maryland (Maley, 1967; Mietus, 1969). In this study five criteria were used for defining three clusters: construction, electromechanical installation and repair, and metal forming and fabrication.

The criteria used for defining the clusters were that the clusters should:

be in the area of vocational industrial education,

include occupations that are related on the basis of either similar processes, materials, products, or human requirements,

be broad enough to include occupations with a wide variety of skills and knowledge,

involve occupations that require no more than two years' training beyond high school, and

provide for the opportunity for geographical and occupational mobility.

Several occupations were then identified, and a task analysis was made of each occupation. The task analysis provided the information for building the curriculum. A field study was made of each curriculum, and the evaluation indicated that the curricula were effective in attaining immediate objectives of specified levels of knowledge and skills. Additional studies are now being conducted to determine the long-range effectiveness of the courses in producing workers with satisfactory entry skills, and who exhibit adaptability for a variety of occupations.

The approach used in the Maryland studies for the clustering of jobs and in curriculum definition seems to have also been used in the Richmond, California, (Asbell, 1967) curriculum projects.

In the studies cited to this point, the clusters have been defined on the basis of perceived similarity, using some arbitrary definition of what constitutes similarity. Although this method seems to lack objectivity, evidence is presented by Grunes (1956), Triandis (1959), Gonyea (1961), and Gonyea and Lunneborg (1963) that job perception is quite stable among people.

There are a number of studies in which a mathematical criterion was used to define the clusters. These studies have typically employed a factor analysis or hierarchical grouping methodology. The analytic techniques give the appearance of objectivity, in that the clustering is accomplished according to some mathematical criterion. This apparent objectivity is somewhat misleading, however, in that the scores that are used are usually obtained by some judgment of a rater or observer. Furthermore, the criterion for defining a cluster or noncluster is usually based on a judgment. The most common analytic method is some type of factor analysis of correlation matrices. The correlations may be between jobs or between scales measuring worker behavior on a job. The DOT and the McCormick work used factor analytic procedures, as did several of the studies reviewed later in the paper.

The factor analysis model is useful, but has certain limitations. One limitation is that the data are not always appropriate for such a procedure. Another limitation is that, although it can be used to identify clusters, it does not provide much information as to what determined the cluster. It is nice to know that ten jobs form some sort of cluster, but the pattern of the cluster is still not apparent.

Another analytic technique has had limited use, but seems to have some promise, especially for identifying the components that are causing the cluster to form. This technique is a clustering model. There seem to be two independent lines of development of such a model.

Silverman (1966, 1970) has described a numerical taxonomy approach to task analysis. A similar approach is described by Ward (1961) and Orr (1960). Johnson (1967) presented a detailed discussion of the mathematics of this approach. The clustering procedure establishes clusters on the basis of predefined criteria, so that it is known what determined the cluster.

The work of the Personnel Research Division of the U.S. Air Force is outstanding in its sophisticated treatment of task measurement and analysis. Christal (1970) summarized the work that has been done. They have developed an occupational survey methodology which defines job characteristics at the work-task level. The data from the surveys can be used to cluster tasks and thus organize course content. They use a hierarchical grouping procedure for clustering. The method also permits the researchers to identify elements of the curriculum that can be eliminated. The extensive work of the Personnel Research Division is a valuable contribution both to the methodology of studying occupations and to the understanding of occupations. Several reports have been issued from this group. The cited reference is a good source for an overview of their work, as well as additional references.

Several studies have been done in which factor-analytic methodology has been used to cluster occupations, ostensibly for curriculum-building. There is no report from any of the studies, however, to indicate that the results were used directly for curricula-building.

Phipps and Fuller (1964) factor analyzed activity and knowledge scores separately for agriculturally related occupations. They identified 12 activity factors and 12 knowledge factors that could be used in classifying agricultural occupations.

A factor analysis of 63 job competencies in 125 job titles of agriculturally related occupations was reported by Stevenson (1965). The analysis yielded the following competency factors: human relations, salesmanship, business management, agricultural business management, plant and soil science, animal science, agricultural machinery, and construction technology.

A number of factor analyses of competencies and activities of agricultural workers have been done at Purdue University by Coster and Courtney (1965), Clouse and Coster (1965), and Coster and Penrod (1965). In the Coster and Courtney study, the data were ratings of each of 148 agriculturally oriented competencies needed by workers in three agriculturally oriented occupations; farmers, farm real estate brokers, and grain elevator operators. The data were collected from 40 persons in each occupation. The factor analysis yielded six interpretable factors. Three of the factors were judged to represent the three occupations, and the other three indicated some commonality among the occupations in terms of agronomy, animal and mechanical knowledges, and competencies.

Love (1966) analyzed data from interviews with job incumbents in the areas of agricultural mechanics, agricultural supplies, food products, forestry and ornamental horticulture. Twelve competency and 12 job title factors were identified. A manager factor was found to be quite general across all of the agricultural occupations.

Data from workers in 47 agricultural and 36 metal fabricating occupations were analyzed by Sjogren et al. (1967). Three clusters were identified in each area: production agriculture, agricultural industry, and agribusiness in agriculture, and skilled, semiskilled, and business in the metal industry occupations.

Several investigators have focused their efforts on the identification of the knowledge and competencies needed by workers for successful performance in an occupation.

Altman (1966a) administered a large number of performance tests to high school students. The analysis indicated six general performance areas: mechanical, electrical, spatial, chemical and biological, symbolic, and "people." The results of this study were used extensively in the Quincy, Massachusetts, project (Morrison, 1966).

The work at Washington State University also tended to focus on knowledge (McCloskey, 1968; Rahmlow, 1969). In this work, the tasks that were performed by a large number of workers were identified and analyzed. From the analysis the investigators then either identified the kinds of knowledge to stress in a particular curriculum (for example, Rahmlow and Kiehn, 1967) or the knowledges that generalized across curricula (Rahmlow and Winchell, 1966).

Moss et al. (1970) reported on a procedure to identify the technical concepts possessed by a worker on the job, and the psychological structure of the concepts. The researchers believe that it is necessary not only to identify the common knowledge across occupations but also to identify whether the organization of the knowledge is also common. They refer to the knowledge and the organization as the "map" of the technical concept. A methodology for forming the maps has been developed and tested with encouraging results. (Moss and Pucel, 1967; Pratzner, 1969; Smith, 1968). Ammerman (1970) also reported an application of the method in a radar maintenance course setting. One very important contribution of this work is that the procedure identifies commonalities of higher-order concepts and the hierarchical structure of the concepts.

It is evident that many approaches have been used to attempt to identify job clusters. Cunningham (1969) has started on a program which will attempt to effect a synthesis of the many approaches. In a personal communication, he has reported that the instrumentation phase of the work is near completion, and that the instrument has been designed to measure the many different job variables that have been of demonstrated importance in other research.

Within the field of occupational education, the typical approach to resolving the problem of developing curricula for occupational adaptability has been that of job analysis—job clustering. The focus has been on identification of common skills, behavior, knowledges, etc., across jobs in order to design curricula that are generalizable, or in effect facilitative of adaptability. There are limitations to this approach, which are discussed in the critique section of this paper.

Occupational adaptability is not just a function of being able to perform a variety of tasks. There are affective dimensions to adaptability that are important. The next section contains a review of some studies in this area.

Work Adjustment

Adaptability to a work situation has several facets. First, there is the aspect of being able to perform satisfactorily in the occupations. This aspect is the one that has been the primary focus of the job-analysis, job-clustering studies reviewed above. Dawis, England, and Lofquist (1964) referred to this aspect as the "satisfactoriness" of the worker in his work environment. They also had a dimension of "satisfaction" of the worker in his work environment. A second aspect of work adaptability, then, is in terms of the satisfaction that the worker derives from the work. A satisfied worker is one that has adapted to the work situation. A third aspect of adaptability is with respect to the general social milieu within which the individual is operating. If the worker adapts well to the neighborhood and the community, then he has made an adjustment that is critical to work adaptability. This section of the paper reviews some studies of relevance to the latter two affective aspects of adaptability.

Ronan (1970) reviewed the literature on variables relating to job satisfaction. He found that in many studies the following dimensions of job satisfaction emerged: "(a) the content of the work, actual tasks performed, and control of work, (b) supervision of the direct sort, (c) the organization and its management, (d) opportunities for advancement, (e) pay and other financial benefits, (f) co-workers, and (g) working conditions. He concluded, however, that the relationships among the variables are complex, and also tend to be specific to a situation rather than generalizable.

The Ronan paper is an excellent source for identifying the work that has been done in the area of job satisfaction. A framework for the study of job satisfaction is also presented, taken from Payne et al. (1967).

Special mention should be made of the work of Herzberg and his associates in the area of worker satisfaction. The work, reported in Herzberg, Mausner, and Snyderman (1959), has stimulated a large amount of research. Grigaliunas and Herzberg (1971) includes references to some of the most recent work in this area. Borgen et al. (1968) reported on a promising line of research on occupational reinforcer patterns.

The extent to which factors in the social environment are related to worker adaptability has not been studied as thoroughly as have factors in the work environment. A number of studies on worker mobility that have been conducted recently do provide some information, however. A number of studies have been made of the voluntary and nonvoluntary mobile person.

Johnson and Johnson (1968) and Johnson and Kiefert (1968) studied migration patterns in North Dakota. Generally the migrants were more educated than the nonmigrants, and the outmigration was related to occupational aspiration. The migrants experienced few adjustment problems. Similar results were obtained by Geschwind and Putton (1961) and Olson (1960). Taves and Coller (1964) found that occupational aspiration and career advancement were related to migration decisions among recent high school graduates in Minnesota, but a study of recent graduates in Appalachia did not obtain this relationship (Schwarzeller, 1964). The voluntary migrant can be and is selective in both the job and the social milieu. Olson (1960) found distinctions between the voluntary and nonvoluntary migrants. The voluntary migrants were more selective in the jobs they took and were better adjusted than the nonvoluntary migrants.

During the 1960s several retraining and relocation programs were conducted as part of the War on Poverty. Evaluations of these programs have provided some evidence on factors associated with successful adjustment of nonvoluntary migrants, which is what a relocated worker essentially is. Factors that were related included availability of adequate housing, financial assistance for relocation, and assistance and counseling for orientation to the new job and community, age, and education level. (Ruesink et al., 1968; Ruesink et al., 1969; Nichols and Abrams, 1968; Tuskegee Institute, 1968; Virginia Employment Commission, 1966; Texas Employment Commission, 1969; Georgia Department of Labor, 1969). Schnitzer (1966), in a cross-cultural study, found these factors to be of common influence in relocation programs in several countries. Stevenson (1968) studied Eskimo relocation, and Ablon (1964) studied American Indian relocation. The same factors were important in relocation of these two groups, but a kinship factor was also of special importance for Eskimos and Indians.

The reports of the relocation efforts indicate considerable success if adequate assistance is provided. Somers (1966) has raised the question, however, of whether the relocation allowances are justified as a social investment. Evidence on the question is not yet available.

The relocation studies do demonstrate that the adaptability of a person to a new work situation is not solely dependent on having work-related skills. The worker must also be able to adapt to the broad social environment.

The studies on job-clustering, job satisfaction, and mobility do bring out the following points.

Jobs can be grouped into meaningful clusters, and a person with the ability to perform acceptably in a specific job has skills that are generalizable to other jobs. Thus, in terms of skill, the worker has an adaptability base.

If satisfaction with a job is necessary for true adaptability, then one's adaptability is related to many factors in the work environment other than the ability requirements of the work.

The satisfactory adaptability of the worker to a new work situation is related to successful adjustment to the broad social environment as well as to the work environment.

A considerable amount of effort has been devoted to studies of jobs and job satisfaction. Although progress has been made in understanding this field, there are certain limitations in the research, as well as some lines of research that have not been developed. In the following section of the paper we have identified some of the limitations and research possibilities.

Critique

Much of the job-clustering research has been predicted on the belief that clusters can be identified that will serve as a basis for building a more powerful curriculum than a curriculum based on teaching for a specific job—powerful in the sense that it would be optimally efficient and effective for preparing the student for the world of work. Morrison (1969) pointed out, however, that it is unlikely that a curriculum based on a cluster would be identifiably dffferent from a curriculum for any one job in the cluster because, by definition, the curriculum must contain the elements required by that job. Thus, there is no assurance that a cluster-based curriculum would be more powerful. On the other hand, it does seem that at least the efficiency criterion might be met through clustering. If common elements across jobs can be identified, then these might be taught more efficiently, since they could be taught to large groups of students, which would tend to reduce instructional costs per student.

Perhaps it would be useful if come empirical studies were designed to test the power of cluster-based versus single job-based curricula, but such studies would probably result in acceptance of the null hypothesis. Rather, the purpose of job-clustering studies should be defined in terms of what they can do. Morrison has indicated some of the potential uses.

One use is in terms of guidance. By identifying for students the various jobs that require certain skills, abilities, and interests, they will have a broad information base for making educational and vocational decisions. Furthermore, it would seem that some meaningful predictions might be made regarding the student's likelihood of success in a number of occupations. Shaycroft (1969) has developed a methodology for computing a job propinquity index that might be used in this way.

Other uses of clustering information pointed out by Morrison were to identify training situations that might optimize transfer, to identify reasonable additions to the curriculum (Christal indicated that possible deletions might be identified), and to select students and staff. Jerome Moss, in a personal communication, pointed out that clustering studies also might be useful in restructuring and redefining jobs.

Hamreus (1969) also commented on the purpose of clustering studies. He suggested that clustering is a tool for obtaining insight about jobs, but that it is one or more steps removed from actually building the curriculum.

The important point made by both Morrison and Hamreus is that it is unrealistic to expect that results of job-clustering studies will be immediately applicable to curriculum-building. Perhaps this is why there are quite a few clustering studies but few that have gotten to the stage of curriculum development.

One of the difficulties encountered in using the results of clustering studies is the criterion problem. Sjogren (1969) and Hamreus commented on this problem. The question essentially is one of no objective criterion for deciding whether a grouping of jobs is a cluster or not. No matter what kind of measurement and analysis techniques are used, the determination of the clusters is to a

great extent decided a priori when the decision is made to study certain jobs and not study others. This is not a critical problem if the investigator realizes the situation and recognizes the arbitrariness of the clusters obtained in a single study. Empirical studies would be desirable, in which the mix of jobs studied would be varied to observe the variation in clusters as related to the varied mix. It is likely that any single job would sort into different clusters, depending on the mix of jobs being studied. Such variation would be interesting and useful information about the job.

Another limitation of clustering studies is that they have been done primarily on a cross-section of jobs at a common skill level. Few studies have attempted to identify commonalities in jobs at hierarchical levels. Clustering should be a viable methodology for defining career lines, but it has not been used extensively in this way.

Hamreus (1969) pointed out that job analysis-job clustering methodology should be applied to defining future job requirements. General worker adaptability would seem to be quite dependent on ability to adapt to a job that is not yet defined, at least for many people. Perhaps clustering methodology can be applied to the problem of predicting future jobs. Pilot studies in this regard would be desired.

Ronan (1970), in his review of variables related to job satisfaction, indicated many of the limitations of this work. He pointed out the familiar measurement problem, although he did indicate a belief that measurement of job satisfaction was quite reliable. The measurement of the variables related to job satisfaction was a problem. Perhaps a more critical problem is that the results of job satisfaction studies tend to be situation-specific. This outcome may be due to the measurement problem, but more likely it is due to studying a limited number of variables in any study. Work environments are complex, and multivariate approaches are needed. When only one variable is examined, its relationship to job satisfaction may be obscured by its interaction with another variable or variables that may be operating in one situation and not in another. Multivariate approaches are necessary to ensure sensitivity. The same consideration is appropriate with respect to studies of mobility.

Another point with respect to job adjustment studies, like those of satisfaction and mobility, is that they are predominantly cross-sectional. Kuvlesky (1966) has stressed the need for longitudinal studies of job adjustment or adaptability. A study in this vein has been started by Parnes et al. (1968). This line of research should be helpful in identifying those individual difference characteristics that are predictive of successful vertical and horizontal mobility.

Noticeable progress has been made in our understanding of the world of work over the past 20 years. Methods for identifying commonalities across jobs have been refined. A body of knowledge is developing on factors related to job satisfaction and successful job mobility. There is increased understanding of the phenomenon of generalization of learning. The knowledge in these areas is still far from complete, however. Furthermore, the application of this knowledge to predicting or providing for worker adaptability and work satisfaction is still not clear.

This review, as is true of any review, leads to two general conclusions. The practitioner has available a considerable amount of accumulated knowledge that can be of help in making curricular and personnel decisions. Often, however, the practitioner will not find the answers to questions directly, but will have to make the "inductive leap" from the research to the specific situation. The second conclusion is that although the research needs are still large, the person with an interest in studying in this area does not have to start at point zero.

It is hoped this review will serve the purpose of helping both the practitioner and the researcher identify sources relevant to their needs.

REFERENCES

Ablon, Joan. Relocated American Indians in the San Francisco Bay Area. *Human Organization, 23*, 4, 1964. ED 031 317

Altman, J. W. *A Behavioral View of Vocational-Technical Education.* Pittsburgh, Pennsylvania: American Institutes for Research, 1967. Paper prepared for a Symposium on Vocational-Technical Education, Boston, Massachusetts, November 1967.

_____. Generalization and Curriculum Development. In Smith, B. B., and Moss, J. Jr., eds. *Process and Techniques of Vocational Curriculum Development.* Minneapolis, Minnesota: Research Coordinating Unit, University of Minnesota, 1970. ED 042 917

_____. *Generalization of Vocational Performance.* Pittsburgh, Pennsylvania: American Institutes for Research, 1966. Paper presented at American Vocational Association Convention, Denver, Colorado, December 1966(b).

_____. *Research on General Vocational Capabilities—Skills And Knowledges.* Pittsburgh, Pennsylvania: American Institutes for Research, 1966(a). ED 013 870

American Society for Engineering Education. *Technician Career Opportunities in Engineering Technology.* Washington, D.C., 1964. ED 024 776

Ammerman, H. L. Systematic Approaches for Identifying and Organizing Content for Training Programs. In Smith, B. B., and Moss, J., Jr., eds., *Process and Techniques of Vocational Curriculum Development.* Minneapolis, Minnesota: Research Coordinating Unit, University of Minnesota, 1970. ED 042 917

Asbell, B. *New Directions in Vocational Education, Case Studies in Change.* Washington, D.C.: U.S. Office of Education, 1967. ED 020 326

Ausubel, D. P., Stager, M., and Gaite, A. J. H. Meaningful Verbal Learning and Retention. *Journal of Educational Psychology, 60:* 59-64, 1969.

Baker, J. K., and Woodin, R. J. *Educational Needs of Animal Science Technicians.* Columbus, Ohio: The Ohio State University, 1966. ED 016 779

Baker, R. A. *A Study of the Educational Needs for Workers Engaged in Occupations in Off-Farm Agricultural Business in Alabama.* Auburn, Alabama: Auburn University, 1966. ED 012 297

Barwick, R. P. *Identification of Off-Farm Agricultural Occupations and Education Needed for Employment in These Occupations in Delaware.* Ann Arbor, Michigan: University Microfilms, Inc., 1965. ED 020 369

Beard, H. G. *National Vocational-Technical Education Seminar on Occupational Mobility and Migration.* Report Number Two. Raleigh, North Carolina: North Carolina State University, Center for Occupational Education, 1966. ED 015 263

Borgen, F. H. et al. *The Measurement of Occupational Reinforcer Patterns.* Minneapolis, Minnesota: Industrial Relations Center,

University of Minnesota, 1968.

Borow, H., ed. *Man in a World at Work.* Boston, Massachusetts: Houghton-Mifflin Co., 1964.

Bushnell, D. S. Preface. In Cunningham, J. W., ed., *The Job-Cluster Concept and its Curricular Implications.* Center Monograph No. 4. Raleigh, North Carolina: Center for Occupational Education, 1969. ED 042 897

Cain, P. S., and Dillon, R. D. *Employment Opportunities and Usable Agricultural Skills in Non-Farm Agricultural Occupations in Appalachia.* Morehead, Kentucky: Morehead State University, 1966. ED 017 623

California State Department of Employment. *The Potential Transfer of Industrial Skills from Defense to Nondefense Industries.* Sacramento, California, 1968. ED 044 484

Christal, R. E. Implications of Air Force Occupational Research for Curriculum Design. In Smith, B. B., and Moss, J. Jr. *Process and Techniques of Vocational Curriculum Development.* Minneapolis, Minnesota: Research Coordinating Unit, University of Minnesota. ED 042 917

Clouse, J. P., and Coster, J. K. Factor Analyses of Activity and Competency Variables and of Workers in Agricultural Occupations in Four Selected Indiana Communities. *Purdue University Studies in Education,* 1965.

Cofer, C. N., and Musgrave, B. S., eds. *Verbal Behavior and Learning: Problems and Processes.* New York, New York: McGraw-Hill, 1963.

Coster, J. K., and Courtney, E. W. Factor Analyses of Agricultural Competencies and Workers in Three Selected Occupations. *Purdue University Studies in Education,* 1965.

_____, and Penrod, W. J. Factor Analyses of Competency Items and Workers in Agricultural Occupations in the Metropolitan School District of Wabash County. *Purdue University Studies in Education,* 1965.

Cratty, B. J. *Movement Behavior and Motor Learning.* Philadelphia, Pennsylvania: Lea-Febiger, 1967. ED 018 037

Cunningham, J. W. A Conceptual Framework for the Study of Job Similarities. In Cunningham, J. W., ed., *The Job-Cluster Concept and its Curricular Implications.* Raleigh, North Carolina: Center for Occupational Education, North Carolina State University, 1969. ED 042 897

_____, and McCormick, E. J. *Factor Analyses of Worker-Oriented Job Variables.* Occupational Research Center, Purdue University, 1964.

Curtis, C. M., and Mondart, C. L. Sr. *Non-Farm Agricultural Employment in Louisiana with Implications for Developing Training Programs.* Baton Rouge, Louisiana: Louisiana State University, 1967. ED 019 478

Cushman, H. R., et al. *A Study of Off-Farm Agricultural Occupations in New York State.* Ithaca, New York: Cornell University, 1965. ED 012 302

Dawis, R. V., England, G. W., and Lofquist, L. H. *A Theory of Work Adjustment.* Minneapolis, Minnesota: Industrial Relations Center, University of Minnesota, 1964. ED 018 590

D'Costa, A. *The Development of the Ohio Vocational Interest Survey.* Columbus, Ohio: The Ohio State University, 1968. ED 031 715

Dillon, R. D., and Horner, J. T. *Occupational Commonalities: A Base for Course Construction.* Lincoln, Nebraska: University of Nebraska. Agricultural Experiment Station, 1967. ED 024 792

Drake, W. E., and Tom, F. K. T. *Entry Occupations in Off-Farm Agriculture: A Survey and Task Analysis of Entry-Level Off-Farm Agricultural Occuations in New York State.* Ithaca, New York: Cornell University, 1968. ED 024 808

Ertel, K. A. *Clusters of Tasks Performed by Merchandising Employees Working in Three Standard Industrial Classifications of Retail Establishments.* Boise, Idaho: Idaho Board of Vocational Education, 1968. ED 023 911

Fine, S. A. A Reexamination of "Transferability of Skills" Part I.

Monthly Labor Review, July-December, 1957(b).

———. A Reexamination of "Transferability of Skills" Part II. *Monthly Labor Review,* July-December, 1957(c).

———. A Structure of Worker Functions. *Personnel and Guidance Journal,* October 1955(b).

———. Functional Job Analysis. *Journal of Personnel Administration and Industrial Relations,* Spring, 1955(a).

———. Matching Job Requirements and Worker Qualifications. *Personnel Journal,* May-June 1958.

———. U.S.E.S. Occupational Classification and Minnesota Occupational Rating Scales. *Journal of Counseling Psychology,* 1957(a).

———, and Heinz, C. A. The Estimate of Worker Trait Requirements for 4,000 Jobs. *Personnel and Guidance Journal,* November 1957.

———. The Functional Occupational Classification Structure. *Personnel and Guidance Journal,* November 1958.

Fleishman, E. A. A Factor Analysis of Fine Manipulative Tests. *Journal of Applied Psychology,* 1962.

Franklin, Zelpha C. *Health Careers Guidebook.* Washington, D.C.: Bureau of Employment Security, 1965. ED 014 542

Gagne, R. M. *The Conditions of Learning.* New York: Holt, Rinehart, and Winston, 1965.

Gannon, C. A. et al. *An Introduction to the Study of Technological Change and its Consequences for Regional and Community Development.* Evanston, Illinois: The Transportation Center at Northwestern University, March, 1967. Cited in Fine, S. A. Guidelines for the Design of New Careers. Staff paper, W. E. Upjohn Institute for Employment Research. Kalamazoo, Michigan, 1967. ED 024 762

Georgia State Department of Labor. *Georgia Labor Mobility Demonstration Project.* Atlanta, Georgia, 1969. ED 031 603

Geschwind, R. D., and Putton, V. W. *Job Mobility and Migration in a Low Income Rural Community.* Lafayette, Indiana: Agricultural Experiment Station, Purdue University, 1961. ED 034 607

Gilpatrick, Eleanor G., and Corliss, P. K. *The Occupational Structure of New York City Municipal Hospitals.* New York, 1969. ED 033 235

Glaser, R. *Training in Industry.* In Gilmer, B. V. et al., ed., *Industrial Psychology.* New York: McGraw-Hill, 1966. ED 018 700

Gonyea, G. G. Dimensions of Job Perceptions. *Journal of Counseling Psychology,* 1961.

———, and Lunneborg, C. E. A Factor Analytic Study of Perceived Occupational Similarity. *Journal of Applied Psychology,* 1963.

Gordon, G. G., and McCormick, E. J. *The Identification, Measurement, and Factor Analyses of "Worker-Oriented" Job Variables.* Occupational Research Center, Purdue University, 1963.

Grant, J. D. et al. *Develop New Career Ladders, with Appropriate Education Components, in the Administration of Justice.* Oakland, California: New Careers Development Organization, 1969. ED 035 754

Grede, J. F. *Survey of Occupational Programs in Illinois Community and Junior Colleges, 1967-68.* Chicago, Illinois: Illinois Association of Community and Junior Colleges, 1968. ED 019 950

Grigaliunas, B. S., and Herzberg, F. Relevancy in the Test of Motivator-Hygiene Theory. *Journal of Applies Psychology,* 1971.

Grunes, Willa F. Looking at Occupations. *Personnel and Guidance Journal,* 1956.

Guilford, J. P. *The Nature of Human Intelligence.* New York: McGraw-Hill, 1967.

Gunderson, O. D. et al. *An Analysis of Occupational Titles and Competencies Needed in Off-Farm Agricultural Supplies Businesses.* University Park, Pennsylvania: Pennsylvania State University, 1966. ED 023 810

Hamreus, D. G. Critique of Papers. In Cunnimgham, J. W. ed., *The Job-Cluster Concept and its Curricular Implications.* Raleigh, North Carolina: Center for Occupational Education, North Carolina State University, 1969. ED 042 897

Heaney, D. S. *Off-Farm Agricultural Occupations in Montana: Employment and Education.* D.Ed. thesis. University Park, Pennsylvania, Pennsylvania State University, 1966. ED 022 878

Hensel, J. W. *A Planning Study to Determine the Feasibility of a Research Project Concerning Employment Opportunities and Training Needs in Farming and Off-Farm Agricultural Business and Industry.* Columbus, Ohio: The Ohio State University, The Center for Vocational and Technical Education, 1968. ED 025 616

Herzberg, F., Mausner, B., and Snyderman, B. *The Motivation to Work.* New York: John Wiley and Sons, 1959.

Hoover, N. K. et al. *Off-Farm Agricultural Occupations in Pennsylvania.* University Park, Pennsylvania: Pennsylvania State University, 1966. ED 012 310

Institute for Local Self Government. *Some Who Dared; Community College Involvement with Public Service Aspects of the Urban Problem in California.* Berkeley, California, 1969. ED 032 873

Johnson, R. L., and Johnson, K. J. *Outmigration from North Dakota: A Comparison Between Male Outmigrants in Four States and Their North Dakota Counterparts.* Grand Forks, North Dakota: North Dakota University, 1968. ED 027 990

———, and Kiefert, J. J. *Factors Involved in the Decision to Migrate and the Impact of Migration Upon the Individual and the Sender and Receiver Community.* Grand Forks, North Dakota: North Dakota University, 1968. ED 025 631

Johnson, S. Hierarchical Clustering Schemes. *Psychometrika, 32:* 241-254, 1967.

Kraft, R. H. P. Manpower Planning and its Role in the Age of Automation. *Review of Educational Research, 40,* 4, 495-511, 1970.

Krathwohl, D. R., Bloom, B. S., and Mosia, B. B. *Taxonomy of Educational Objectives: Affective Domain.* New York: David McKay Co., Inc., 1964.

Kuvlesky, W. P. *The Social-Psychological Dimensions of Occupational Mobility.* Raleigh, North Carolina: Center for Occupational Education, North Carolina State University, 1966. ED 029 949

Larson, M. E. *Review and Synthesis of Research: Analysis for Curriculum Development in Vocational Education.* Columbus, Ohio: The Center for Vocational and Technical Education, 1969. ED 035 746

———, and Blake, D. L. *Institute on Occupational Analysis as a Basis for Curriculum Development.* Fort Collins, Colorado: Colorado State University, 1969. ED 031 592

Loreen, C. O. *Occupational Opportunities and Training Needs for Non-Farm Agricultural Jobs in Washington State.* Pullman, Washington: Washington State University, 1967. ED 022 019

Love, E. L. An Analysis of Job Titles and of Competencies Needed in Off-Farm Agricultural Occupations in Pennsylvania. D.Ed. thesis. Ann Arbor, Michigan: University Microfilms, Inc., 1966 ED 020 374

Maley, D. *The Preparation of Curriculum Materials and the Development of Teachers for an Experimental Application of the Cluster Concept of Vocational Education at the Secondary School Level.* College Park, Maryland: University of Maryland, 1967. (ED 016 841) Other ED numbers for reports on this project are ED 022 965, ED 016 844, ED 016 843, ED 016 842, ED 015 261, ED 014 554, ED 010 301, ED 010 302, ED 010 303, ED 010 304.

Marsh, J. E. *Job Analysis Bibliography.* Technical Documentary Report PRL-TDR-62-2, Lackland Air Force Base, Texas. March 1962. Available from Office of Technical Services, U.S. Department of Commerce.

———, Madden, J. M., and Christal, R. E. *Job Analysis in the*

United States Air Force. Personnel Laboratory, Wright Air Development Division, Air Research and Development Command, USAF, Lackland Air Force Base, Texas. WADD-TR-61-113, 1961. Available from Office of Technical Services, U.S. Department of Commerce, Washington, D.C.

McCloskey, G. *Summary, Evaluation and Long-Range Plans for Related Work.* Pullman, Washington: Washington State University, 1968. ED 024 820

McCormick, E. J. *The Development, Analysis, and Experimental Application of Worker-Oriented Job Variables.* Occupational Research Center, Purdue University, July 1964. VT 001 441; available in VT-ERIC Set ED 039 370

———, Finn, R. H., and Schieps, C. D. Patterns of Job Requirements. *Journal of Applied Psychology,* 1957.

———, Jeanneret, P. R., and Mecham, R. C. *A Study of Job Characteristics and Job Dimensions as Based on the Position Analysis Questionnaire.* Lafayette, Indiana: Occupational Research Center, Purdue University, 1969. Manpower 000 883

McGee, I. C. *The Identification and Analysis of Agricultural Occupations in Seventeen Pennsylvania Counties.* D.Ed. thesis. University Park, Pennsylvania: Pennsylvania State University, 1965. ED 022 872

Mietus, W. S. Development, Implementation, and Field Evaluation of the Cluster Concept Program in Vocational Education at the Secondary School Level. In Cunningham, J. W., ed., *The Job-Cluster Concept and its Curricular Implications.* Raleigh, North Carolina: University of North Carolina Center for Occupational Education, 1969.

Morrison, E. J. *General Vocational Skills and the Secondary Curriculum.* Paper presented at a conference on research in vocational and technical education, University of Wisconsin, 1966.

———. Job-Cluster Concept and its Curricular Implications: Discussion of a Symposium. In Cunningham, J. W., ed., *The Job-Cluster Concept and its Curricular Implications.* Raleigh, North Carolina: Center for Occupational Education, North Carolina State University, 1969.

Morrison, R. G. *Development and Application of Techniques and Procedures for Determining Training Needs and Occupational Opportunities for Students of Vocational Agriculture Within the Baton Rouge Agri-Business Complex.* Ann Arbor, Michigan: University Microfilms, Inc., 1964.

Mosley, P. T. *Curricula Implications for Non-Farm Agricultural Employment in Connecticut.* Hartford, Connecticut: Connecticut State Department of Education, 1966. ED 011 038

Moss, J. Jr. et al. An Empirical Procedure for Identifying the Structure of the Technical Concepts Possessed by Selected Workers. In Smith, B. B., and Moss, J. Jr., eds., *Process and Techniques of Vocational Curriculum Development.* Minneapolis, Minnesota: Research Coordinating Unit, University of Minnesota, 1970.

Moss, J. Jr., and Purcel, D. J. *Using the Free Association Methodology to Determine the Conceptual Structure of Radio and Television Repairmen.* Minneapolis, Minnesota: Research Coordinating Unit, University of Minnesota, 1967.

Newman, J., and Fine, S. A. Validity of Job Descriptions for Physical Requirements and Work Condition Information. *Personnel Psychology,* Summer, 1957.

Nichols, J. L., and Abrams, H. A. *The Relocation of the Hard Core Unemployed.* Minneapolis, Minnesota: Rehabilitation Center, 1968. ED 032 404

O'Donnell, Beatrice. *Worker Requirements and Methods of Entry Into Home and Community Occupations Related to Home Economics.* East Lansing, Michigan: Michigan State University, 1967. ED 023 795

Office of Manpower, Automation, and Training. *The Length of the Working Life of Males.* Report Number Eight. Washington, D.C., 1968. ED 025 596

Olson, P. G. *Job Mobility and Migration in a High Income Rural Community.* Lafayette, Indiana: Agricultural Experiment Station, Purdue University, 1960. ED 034 606

Orr, D. B. A New Method for Clustering Jobs. *Journal of Applied Psychology,* 1960.

Osipow, S. H. *Theories of Career Development: A Comparison of the Theories.* 1968. ED 026 698

Palmer, G. J. Jr., and McCormick, E. J. A Factor Analysis of Job Activities. *Journal of Applied Psychology,* 1961.

Parnes, H. S. et al. *The Pre-Retirement Years: A Longitudinal Study of the Labor Market of the Cohort of Men 45-59 Years of Age.* Columbus, Ohio: Center for Human Resource Research, The Ohio State University, 1968. ED 026 525

Payne, R. L., Hickson, D. J., Inkson, J. H. K., and Pugh, D. S. *Social Behavior in Organizations.* Oxford, England: British Psychological Society, 1967.

Perkins, E. A. Jr. et al. *Clusters of Tasks Associated with Performance of Major Types of Office Work.* Pullman, Washington: Washington State University, 1968. ED 018 665

Peterson, C. E. *Chemical and Metallurgical Technologies.* Washington, D.C.: U.S. Office of Education, 1962. ED 013 316

———. *Civil and Highway Technology.* Washington, D.C.: U.S. Office of Education, 1964(c). ED 013 314

———. *Electrical and Electronic Technologies.* Washington, D.C.: U.S. Office of Education, 1966(b). ED 013 327

———. *Electronic Data Processing in Engineering, Science, and Business.* Washington, D.C.: U.S. Office of Education, 1964(b). ED 013 325

———. *Mechanical Drafting and Design Technology.* Washington, D.C.: U.S. Office of Education, 1964(a). ED 012 321

———. *Mechanical Technology, Design and Production.* Washington, D.C.: U.S. Office of Education, 1966(a). ED 017 661

Phipps, L. J., and Fuller, G. R. Activities of Technicians and of Other Workers Who Need Some Technical Education; and Knowledge Areas in which Identified Technicians and Other Workers Needing Some Vocational Education Must be Competent. Both in Phipps, L. J. et al., *Technical Education in and for Rural Areas.* Urbana, Illinois: University of Illinois, 1964. VT 000 426; available in VT ERIC Set ED 016 876.

Pratzner, F. C. *Testing an Empirical Procedure for Identifying Technical Associative Conceptual Structure.* Unpublished thesis. Minneapolis, Minnesota: University of Minnesota, 1969. ED 034 023

Rahmlow, H. F. Application of Cluster Research to Curriculum Development. In Cunningham, J. W., ed., *The Job-cluster Concept and its Curriculuar Implications.* Raleigh, North Carolina: Center for Occupational Education, North Carolina State University, 1969.

———, and Kiehn, Shirley. *A Research Basis for Child Care Curriculum Development.* Pullman, Washington: Washington State University, 1967. ED 029 950

———, and Winchell, L. P. *Mathematics Clusters in Selected Areas of Vocational Education.* Pullman, Washington: Washington State University, 1968. ED 010 659

Ridley, Agnes F. *Gainful Employment in Home Economics.* Tallahassee, Florida: Florida State University, 1967. ED 035 715

Rittenhouse, C. H. *The Transferability and Retraining of Defense Engineers.* Menlo Park, California: Stanford Research Institute, 1967. ED 030 838

Ronan, W. W. Variables Relating to Job Satisfaction. *Journal of Applied Psychology Monograph,* 1970, *54,* 1, Part 2, pp. 1-31.

Ruesink, D. C. et al. *Dimensions of Research in Rural Sociology.* College Station: Texas A&M University, 1968. ED 027 997

———. *Relocating Mexican-Americans Who Have Been Retrained.* Paper presented at Rural Sociological Society meeting, San Francisco, California, 1969. ED 032 157

Schnitzer, M. *Economic Policies and Practices: Programs for Relocating Workers Used by Governments of Selected Countries.* Washington, D.C.: Joint Economic Committee, U.S. Congress,

1966. ED 026 456

Schwarzeller, H. K. *Career Placement and Economic Life Chances of Young Men from Eastern Kentucky.* Lexington, Kentucky: Agricultural Experiment Station, University of Kentucky, 1964. ED 035 506

Seymour, W. D. *Industrial Skills.* London: Sir Isaac Pitman and Sons, Ltd., 1966. ED 013 383

Shaycroft, Marion F. *A New Multivariate Index for Use in Educational Planning.* Palo Alto, California: American Institutes for Research, 1969. ED 035 026

Shipley, Anna F. *Analysis of Tasks in Three Home Related Occupations.* Ames, Iowa: Iowa State University, 1967. ED 026 484

Silverman, J. *A Computer Technique for Clustering Tasks.* Technical Bulletin STB 66-23. San Diego, California: Naval Personnel Research Activity, 1966. ED 031 572

_____. Structuring Job Content through a Numerical Taxonomy Approach to Task Analysis. In Smith, B. B., and Moss, J. Jr., *Process and Techniques of Vocational Curriculum Development.* Minneapolis, Minnesota: University of Minnesota Research Coordinating Unit, 1970.

Sjogren, D. D. A Functional Approach to Curriculum Development. In Cunningham, J. W., ed., *The Job-Cluster Concept and its Curricular Implications.* Raleigh, North Carolina: Center for Occupational Education, North Carolina State University, 1969.

_____ et al. *The Identification of Common Behavioral Factors as Bases for Pre-Entry Preparation of Workers for Gainful Employment.* Ft. Collins, Colorado: Colorado State University, 1967. ED 019 471

Smith, B. B. *Testing an Empirical Procedure for Identifying Technical Associative Conceptual Structure.* Unpublished thesis. Minneapolis, Minnesota: University of Minnesota, 1968.

Somers, G. G. *Retraining and Migration as Factors in Regional Economic Development.* Madison, Wisconsin: University of Wisconsin, 1966. ED 013 399

Stevenson, D. S. *Problems of Eskimo Relocation for Industrial Employment.* Ottawa, Canada: Canadian Dept. of Indian Affairs and Northern Development, 1968. ED 031 334

Stevenson, W. W. *A Study of Employment Opportunities and Training Needs.* Stillwater, Oklahoma: Oklahoma State University, 1965. ED 012 744

Studdiford, W. S. A Functional System of Occupational Classification. *Occupations,* October 1951.

_____. New Occupational Classification Structure. *Employment Security Review,* September 1953.

Taves, M. J., and Coller, R. M. *In Search of Opportunity: A Study of Post-High School Migration in Minnesota.* Minneapolis, Minnesota: Agricultural Experiment Station, University of Minnesota, 1964. ED 029 123

Taviss, I., and Gerber, W. *Technology and Work.* Research Review Number Two. Cambridge, Massachusetts: Harvard University, 1969. ED 031 580

Tennyson, W. W. Career Development. *Review of Educational Research, 38:* 346-366, 1968.

Texas Employment Commission. *Texas Labor Mobility: Experimental and Demonstration Project.* Austin, Texas, 1969. ED 032 972

Throndike, E. L. *Human Learning.* New York: Appleton-Century-Crofts, 1931.

Trattner, M. H., Fine, S. A., and Kubis, J. F. A Comparison of Worker Requirement Ratings Made by Reading Job Descriptions and by Direct Job Observation. *Personnel Psychology,* 1955.

Travis, H. *Mobility and Worker Adaptation to Economic Change in the United States.* Manpower Research Bulletin Number One. Washington, D.C.: Office of Manpower Policy, Evaluation, and Research, 1963. ED 020 322

Triandis, H. C. Categories of Thought of Managers, Clerks, and Workers About Jobs and People in an Industry. *Journal of Applied Psychology,* 1959.

Tuskegee Institute. *Labor Mobility Demonstration Project.* Tuskegee, Alabama, 1968. ED 032 397

U.S. Department of Labor. *Dictionary of Occupational Titles: Definitions of Titles.* Volume 1, Third Edition. Bureau of Employment Security, Washington, D.C. 1965(a). ED 013 963

_____. *Dictionary of Occupational Titles: Occupational Classification.* Volume 2, Third Edition. Bureau of Employment Security, Washington, D.C., 1965(b). ED 013 964

Virginia Employment Commission. *Virginia Labor Mobility Pilot Project.* Richmond, Virginia, 1966. ED 023 788

Wall, J. E. et al. *Employment Opportunities and Competency Needs in Nonfarm Agricultural Occupations in Mississippi.* State College, Mississippi: Mississippi State University, 1967. ED 014 533

Ward, J. H. Jr. *Hierarchical Grouping to Maximize Payoff.* Personnel Laboratory, Wright Air Development Division, Air Research and Development Command, USAF, Lackland Air Force Base, Texas. WADD-TN-61-29, 1961.

Weinstein, P. A. *Labor Market Activity of Veterans: Some Aspects of Military Spillover.* College Park, Maryland: University of Maryland, 1969. ED 033 308

94

THE ROLE OF CAREER EXPLORATION IN CAREER EDUCATION

by Wesley E. Budke
The Center for Vocational and Technical Education
The Ohio State University
Columbus, Ohio

Career education is a continuous process, which begins in kindergarten or before and extends through the adult years. There is no period of time in this career development process more critical than the junior high school years. This is a transitional time for most students, and a period in which they should be given an opportunity to actively explore work in relation to their individual interests and abilities. Career exploration is the career education component designed to provide these learning experiences.

Before addressing the topic of career exploration directly, learning something of its origin and setting it in perspective with the entire career education program are desirable. Career education came to the forefront in education following U.S. Commissioner of Education Sidney P. Marland's call for "Career Education Now," issued to the National Association of Secondary School Principals in Houston in January, 1971 (Goldhammer and Taylor, 1972). Problems surrounding increasing separation between students and the world of work, poorly prepared graduates, and inflexible educational systems have provided the impetus for recent emphasis on career education.

There are nearly as many definitions of career education as there are educators involved in the concept, and a widely accepted definition of career education is yet to be identified. The controversial nature of the concept makes it doubtful whether more than general agreement will ever be achieved. Career education has been characterized as being

> . . . designed to capacitate individuals for their several life roles: economic, community, home, avocational, religious, and aesthetic. It recognizes the centrality of careers in shaping our lives by determining or limiting where we work, where we live, our associates, and other dimensions that are significant in defining our lifestyles. Designed for all students, career education should be viewed as lifelong and pervasive, permeating the entire school program and even extending beyond it. Career education is a systematic attempt to increase the career options available to individuals, and to facilitate more rational and valid career planning and preparation. Through a wide range of school and community-based resources, young people's career horizons should be broadened. Their self-awareness should be enhanced. (Goldhammer and Taylor, 1972:6)

PROGRAM DEVELOPMENT EFFORTS

Extensive state and local career education program development efforts have been undertaken with monies from Part C (Federally Funded Research and Development Projects in Career Education) and Part D (Federally Funded Exemplary Projects in Vocational Education) of the Vocational Education Amendments of 1968. The efforts have resulted in programs which can be used as exemplars by local schools now directing their attention to career education.

The U.S. Office of Education has made substantial efforts in research and development activities relating to career education. Resources have been concentrated on the development of four career education models which offer alternative conceptualizations or alternative ways of facilitating career education goals. They are the school-based, employer-based, home/community-based, and the rural residential-based models.

CAREER EDUCATION PROGRAM FRAMEWORK

Because career education is a complex, interrelated set of concepts, it is necessary to place career exploration in perspective with other components of the program. Systematic presentation of career options or goals to students may be accomplished through an education program framework consisting of career awareness, orientation, exploration, preparation, and specialization. Although there is some disagreement about the activities within these components, there is general agreement that they exist.

Career awareness occurs in grades K through 6, and is designed to develop in students an awareness of the personal and social significance of work, to teach them the basic skills of learning and social development, to help them become sensitive to social roles, to help them understand the potentialities and limitations in their environment, and to help students know more about themselves (Goldhammer and Taylor, 1972).

Grades 7 and 8 comprise the career orientation stage of the school-based career education program which is generally characterized by the study of occupational clusters across content areas. Career exploration is emphasized in grades 9 and 10, where work simulations and "hands on" experiences which relate to specific occupational clusters are provided. Career preparation begins in grades 11 and 12, where students become involved in cooperative work experiences, specific vocational courses, and preprofessional courses. Career specialization, offering in-depth training and understanding of a specific job, is available in post-secondary vocational and technical schools.

CAREER EXPLORATION

The career exploration component of the career education program usually occurs in the ninth and tenth grades, but depending on the activities and school organization, may extend downward into the seventh grade. Students in junior high school are moving from the general skill acquisition of the elementary school toward the more specific preparation for adult life. Junior high school students are in a period of rapid change, with considerable variation in the individual developmental level within any grade; they are beginning to develop abstract and verbal skills, and experience intense feelings associated with their rapid growth and change.

Hoyt et al. (1972) identify the following objectives of the junior high school occupational exploration program:

> Every junior high school student should be able to explore his occupational interests and aptitudes from among the broadest possible range of occupational areas.

> Every junior high school student should see clearly the relationships between the academic content he is being asked to master and his tentative occupational choices.

> As many junior high school students as possible should acquire some real work experience.

> Junior high school students should be provided with some basic vocational skills which they can use as building blocks in their later career education development.

> Occupational choice options should be kept open for all junior high school students, while each should be simultaneously encouraged to make tentative personal commitments to one or more broad occupational areas at some broad level of competence.

> Junior high school students should be provided with sufficient knowledge about, and experience in, the various vocational education areas open to them at the senior high and post-high school level, so that these students can really choose from among them.

> Those students who express an intention to leave the formal education structure, at least for awhile, near the end of the junior high school years, should

be provided with a set of salable vocational skills that they can use in obtaining employment.

Vocational exploratory programs should be provided in such a way that academic learnings in traditional junior high school areas will be enhanced rather than deemphasized. (p. 88)

A career exploration program must be attuned to the needs of all students, occur in a human learning context, and emphasize action and student involvement. Team teaching is particularly desirable, utilizing resource persons from the community, industry, and business. Realism is important, offering short-term exploration of broad occupational families, and capitalizing on career awareness and career orientation experiences from the elementary level. Students should have an opportunity to learn about the interrelatedness of occupations, in terms of similar kinds of attributes, activities, work roles, levels of ability, services rendered, and products produced.

This can be effectively achieved by organizing occupations into clusters. Classification or clustering systems have been developed by Role (1956), Holland (1966), Super (1957), the U.S. Department of Labor (1965), and the U.S. Office of Education.

Typical career exploration activities include onsite work observation, work experience, hands-on laboratory experience, role playing, and class discussions with resource persons. Simulations in laboratory settings occur in industrial arts, home economics, business education, and general agriculture classes. New Jersey (York, 1972) uses the following career exploration activities:

Career exploration clubs.

Summer career exploration (field trips, role playing, conducting community career-oriented surveys, and operating student businesses).

Use of the video-recorder in career counseling.

Part-time job placement.

Introduction to Vocations—exploratory, manipulative, classroom, shop and laboratory experiences, offered in a wide range of occupational areas and combined with the resources of business and industry, to assist youth in the development of more realistic career plans.

Short term intensive entry skill preparation for students who plan to leave school at the end of grade 9 or 10.

A Career Resource Center.

Actual work experience at the junior high school level is complicated by child labor laws. A more common exploration activity has been to offer six to eight weeks of summer school in which students from the junior high school can spend one week in up to eight vocational education programs normally offered in the senior high school.

To a large extent, the success of career exploration hinges on the effectiveness of the career guidance program. Career exploration needs an integrated, cross-disciplinary guidance program which can help each student explore and understand his interests, abilities, and aptitudes. This developmental, multicontact approach to career guidance requires more counselors having new and diverse methods of helping youngsters. Teachers must be highly involved in the guidance process, and parents and other community resources must be used to help the student explore career alternatives and understand his potential for success.

Several programmed learning career exploration activities have been developed utilizing microfilm and simulations. Vocational Information for Education and Work (VIEW), developed by the Department of Education in San Diego County, California, is one example. This system uses a microfilm aperture card containing four pages of national, regional, and local occupational information. Students or counselors may read the information on a microfilm reader, or make an 8½″ x 11″ printout of the desired pages. The VIEW system has been adopted by several states across the nation.

Computer-assisted career exploration programs are becoming more common as the technology improves. Two of the major advantages of the computer are the considerable storage capacity for information, and the rather easy access and updating possibilities. The following computer programs are fairly representative of present capabilities.

The Educational and Career Exploration System (ECES) allows the student to choose, from a list of several hundred occupations, those he wishes to study. Brief bits of relevant information, such as samples of work, educational requirements, and working conditions, are fed back to the student. The computer asks the student questions about his reactions to the facts, and provides continuous feedback on appropriateness of choices.

The Computerized Vocational Information System (CVIS), in Willowbrook High School, Villa Park, Illinois, utilizes the student's grade point average, test batteries, and the Kuder Vocational Preference Inventory, along with Roe's classification of levels of training and categories of interest. Through a dialogue with the computer, the student is advised if his choice of a vocational classification level seems feasible, or if there seems to be a minor or major discrepancy between his choice and his interests and abilities.

The Occupational Information Access System (OIAS), University of Oregon, uses an interactive process called QUEST, which features a series of questions designed to assist the student in narrowing his field of occupational exploration by identifying areas of interest and capacity. This program utilizes raw data gathered by the employment service for original information files or for update purposes.

EXEMPLARY CAREER EXPLORATION PROGRAMS

Career education programs have been established in every state and at all educational levels. Some schools have chosen to implement career education by components, i.e., only at the elementary, junior high school, or senior high school level. Others have elected to initiate a comprehensive program of career awareness, career orientation, career exploration, and career preparation. The following career, education programs demonstrate the breadth of activities found in the career exploration component.

The Cobb County Public Schools in Georgia have a career-oriented curriculum for all grades designed to provide an orderly means of making career choices. Career exploration in the eighth grade features a state-wide Program of Education and Career Exploration (PECE) organized around work roles, using Roe's occupational classification system. Occupations were divided into six categories of interest, arranged in a continuum from an orientation of working with people to working with objects or ideas. The six major occupational groupings were service, business, organizational, expression of ideas, outdoors, and technology. Ninth graders are enrolled in either industrial arts, human services, business and distribution, band, or art. Tenth grade students have an option of choosing a career exploration class which rotates through six occupational areas in the vocational education department (Morgan et al., 1973).

McTigue School, in Toledo, Ohio, offers a career orientation program in grades 7 and 8, and career exploration in grades 9 and 10. The program provides an opportunity for students to explore occupations related to various school subjects, and integrates career study in each subject area. This allows the individual teacher to integrate the career-related materials into the context of the curriculum at the most effective time. A career coordinator and the instructor cooperate in trying to match career clusters and subject matter areas for the best possible fit. The coordinator and a planning committee, comprised of teachers, guidance counselors, and administrators, have the responsibility for developing a list of careers indicating their relationship to subject matter areas. Unique features of this program include elimination of study halls for students selecting vocational interest classes, placement of tenth graders on at least two jobs of their choice, and adoption of a school by a local business firm (Morgan et al., 1973).

Kershaw County School District, Camden, South Carolina, provides a comprehensive career education program composed of career orientation, career development, career preparation, and remedial activities. Career exploration occurs at the ninth and tenth grades, when students begin some in-depth study in selected occupational areas through prevocational courses and subject. Summer programs are operated at the area vocational center for ninth and tenth grade students. This is an outgrowth of the prevocational program in the sixth through eighth grades, which allows each student to rotate through career areas in several 12-week periods each year (Morgan et al., 1973).

The McKnight School at Renton, Washington, has an "occupation versatility" program. It is an ungraded, student-student-directed program in which all boys and girls rotate by class through the large multipurpose shops, selecting their individual projects, following detailed instructions in print and on film, using power machines and safety equipment, and maintaining complete records of their progress. Instructors act as consultants and maintain a continuing watch over student activities (Morgan et al., 1973).

PROBLEMS AND CONSTRAINTS

Career exploration meets with most of the same problems and constraints as the total career education concept. Adoption of the program relies heavily on a positive attitude by lay people and educators, on legislation to provide a sound and adequate program, on the commitment of key state leadership, and on backing of the local school district. Resistance is commonplace, because people tend to take comfort in adhering to an established routine and view new programs with skepticism. Cost and financing must be carefully considered, and although ongoing programs can serve as a foundation, a substantial amount of additional funding is often required.

Problems with organization and implementation primarily revolve around teacher and counselor attitudes, lack of understanding of the career development needs of youth, shortage of knowledgeable personnel to conduct the program, lack of suitable curriculum and resources, and a rigidity in existing educational curricula.

Although each of these problems is sizable, there is a sound basis for believing that they can be overcome with sound planning and adequate transitional time.

SUMMARY

Career exploration is that component of career education occurring during the junior high school years which allows students to actively explore work in relation to their individual interests and abilities. Career exploration offers the student onsite work observation, work experience, hands-on laboratory experience, role-playing, and discussions with resource persons from the work world. The success of the program relies heavily on an integrated, cross-disciplinary guidance program which can help each student explore and understand his interests, abilities, and aptitudes. Problems commonly associated with a career exploration program revolve around community support, teacher and counselor understanding of the program, staff training, and curriculum development.

REFERENCES

Goldhammer, Keith, and Taylor, Robert E. *Career Education: Perspective and Promise.* Columbus: Charles E. Merrill Publishing Company, 1972.

Holland, John L. *The Psychology of Vocational Choice.* Waltham, Mass:: Blaisdell, 1966.

Hoyt, Kenneth B., Evans, Rupert N., Mackin, Edward F., and Mangum, Garth L. *Career Education: What It Is and How To Do It.* Salt Lake City: Olympus Publishing Company, 1972.

Morgan, Robert L., Shook, Mollie W., and Dane, J. K., eds. *An Anthology of 15 Career Education Programs.* Volume II. Raleigh, N.C.: Center for Occupational Education, North Carolina State University, 1973. (VT 020 747)

Roe, Ann. *The Psychology of Occupations.* New York: John Wiley and Sons, 1956.

Super, Donald E. *The Psychology of Careers: An Introduction to Vocational Development.* New York: Harper and Brothers, 1957.

U.S. Department of Labor. *Dictionary of Occupational Titles, 1965.* Volume II. Occupational Classification and Industry Index. Washington, D.C.: Bureau of Employment Security,

Department of Labor, 1965.

York, Edwin G., ed. *7th, 8th, and 9th Grade Career Exploration.* Special Paper. Trenton, N.J.: Department of Education, May 1972.

ADDITIONAL RESOURCES

Budke, Wesley E. *Review and Synthesis of Information on Occupational Exploration.* Information Series No. 34. Columbus, Ohio: ERIC Clearinghouse on Vocational and Technical Education, The Center for Vocational and Technical Education, The Ohio State University, 1971. ED 056 165

———, Bettis, Glenn E., and Beasley, Gary F. *Career Education Practice.* Information Series No. 65. Columbus, Ohio: ERIC Clearinghouse on Vocational and Technical Education, The Center for Vocational and Technical Education, The Ohio State University. 1972. VT 017 221

Campbell, Robert E., and Vetter, Louise. *Career Guidance: An Overview of Alternative Approaches.* Information Series No. 45. Columbus, Ohio: ERIC Clearinghouse on Vocational and Technical Education, The Center for Vocational and Technical Education, The Ohio State University, 1971. ED 057 183

Center for Vocational and Technical Education. *Abstracts of Instructional Materials in Vocational and Technical Education.* Volume 5, No. 1 through Volume 6, No. 4. Columbus, Ohio: The Ohio State University, 1972-1973.

Drier, Harry N., Jr., and Associates. *K-12 Guide for Integrating Career Development into Local Curriculum.* Worthington, Ohio: Charles A. Jones Publishing Company, 1972.

Hansen, Lorraine S. *Career Guidance Practices in School and Community.* Washington, D.C.: National Vocational Guidance Association, 1970.

Herr, Edwin L. *Review and Synthesis of Foundations for Career Education.* Information Series No. 61. Columbus, Ohio: ERIC Clearinghouse on Vocational and Technical Education, The Center for Vocational and Technical Education, The Ohio State University, 1972. ED 059 402

Moore, Allen B. *Abstracts of Instructional Materials for Career Education.* Bibliography Series No. 15. Columbus, Ohio: The Center for Vocational and Technical Education, The Ohio State University, 1972.

Morgan, Robert L., Moore, Allen B., Shook, Mollie, W., and Sargent, Brenda. *Synopses of Selected Career Education Programs: A National Overview of Career Education.* Volume I. Raleigh, N.C.: National Center for Occupational Education, North Carolina State University, 1972. ED 063 461

Ristan, Robert A. Career Education at the Junior High Educational Level—A Time for Career Exploration Plus. A paper presented to the Fifth Annual Research Conference of the National Association of Business Teacher Educators, Chicago, Ill., February 21, 1973. VT 020 350

95

CREATIVITY DEVELOPMENT

by Sidney J. Parnes
Professor of Creative Studies
State University College at Buffalo
and
President, Creative Education Foundation

Creative behavior may be defined as that which demonstrates both uniqueness and relevance in its product.

The product may be unique and relevant to a group or organization, to society as a whole, or merely to the individual himself. Creativity is thus a function of knowledge, imagination and evaluation.

Without knowledge, there obviously can be no creativity. By way of analogy, we might consider the kaleidoscope, wherein the more pieces we have in the drum the more possible patterns we can produce. Likewise, the greater our knowledge the more patterns, combinations, or ideas we can achieve. However, merely having the knowledge, the bits and pieces in the kaleidoscope, does not guarantee the formation of new patterns. One must "revolve the drum," manipulate the knowledge by combining and rearranging the facts into new patterns. In the mind, these new patterns are ideas.

Data are accumulated in a person from one's total life experience. These data are played upon constantly by the current input through the senses. The person's creativity depends, then, on one's ability to interrelate not only what he or she already has accumulated, as in the kaleidoscope analogy, but also that new data which one is constantly drawing in through the senses.

The effectiveness of creative productivity also depends, of course, on the evaluation and development of embryonic ideas into usable ideas. Without imaginative manipulation, abundant knowledge cannot help us live in a world of change. And without the ability to synthesize, evaluate and develop our ideas, we achieve no effective creativity.

The essence of the concept of creativity might be considered to be the new and relevant association of thoughts, facts, ideas, etc., into a new configuration which pleases—which has meaning beyond the sum of the parts—and which provides a synergistic effect. The new connection may relate elements residing inside our minds and/or within our perceptual field. The new and relevant connection, or new and harmonious connection, often "just happens," accidentally or serendipitously. In earlier days, it was frequently thought that this was the only way it could happen—accidentally—i.e., one had to wait and just let it happen, like the famous "Eureka!" of Archimedes in the bathtub. However, what research of the last 25 years has made increasingly clear is that there are many processes a person can use to help increase the likelihood that the chance connection will take place. Notice that I do not say processes that will *make* the connection happen, but only that will increase the likelihood, or probability, or its occurring.

SCOPE

By the beginning of the 1970s, thousands of courses offering instruction in these processes had been offered—courses in creative problem-solving, creative studies, etc. Just before his death Osborn reported, for example, that in 1965 alone over 200 new courses had been instituted (Osborn, 1965). These courses have been offered in liberal arts colleges, as well as in professional schools, teachers colleges, and evening school programs, and industrial and governmental programs both in the United States and abroad. Special issues of the *Journal of Creative Behavior* (1969) are devoted to foreign developments. A survey of types of courses offered in education, industry, and government by 1967 is given in the Appendix of the *Creative Behavior Guidebook* (Parnes, 1967). One especially significant industrial course, applying creative thinking to cost and value programs, is Value Engineering, which has been offered at over 50 universities and in the majority of major industrial organizations.

Most early courses in creative problem-solving were at the college or adult levels. However, in the late 1960s a number of secondary schools began offering courses. The sixties also saw a sharp increase in the trend toward preparing teachers for a more creative type of teaching—the type of teaching that causes students actually to discover their own creative abilities and to strengthen those creative abilities while mastering subject-matter. Some of the best-known examples of regular formal programs for teachers are the University of Utah workshops held each June, the master's degree program at Seattle Pacific College (along with its special summer offerings), the graduate programs at the University of Georgia, and the regularly scheduled graduate work at Buffalo State University College. As a result of his creative education courses for undergraduates at State University College at Oswego, New York, James Smith produced an entire series of texts on creative teaching of the various subject-matter areas (Smith, 1966). The *Journal of Creative Behavior* will carry a list of schools where courses are currently being offered for teachers or teacher trainees. It covers some 50 institutions (Mohan, in press).

These teacher-education programs have led to greatly increased emphasis on creative education approaches within almost all subject-matter fields. Most disciplines were represented in the 195 regular subjects into which creative principles and procedures had been incorporated by the time of Osborn's last report in 1965. He concluded, "This fact indicates that the teaching of creativity is outstandingly *inter*disciplinary—almost as interdisplinary as our common language."

In addition to full courses on the subject, and to the incorporation of creative approaches and procedures within other subject-matter disciplines, the basics of creative problem-solving have also been taught in increasingly more institutes, conferences, and conventions, and in the orientation of incoming college freshmen. Programs include areas of the arts, education, community services, engineering and science, government and military, the health professions, management and marketing, personnel and training, and other professional fields.

REVIEW OF RECENT LITERATURE OR DEVELOPMENTS

During the 1960s, work at the University of Minnesota, the University of Buffalo, and dozens of other institutions had shown almost overwhelming evidence that creative behavior could be enhanced by instruction and programs deliberately constructed for that purpose. More and more foundation, governmental, and industrial support was applied to the creativity research field. The pioneering series of national conferences on the identification of creative talent was extended to cover the development of such talent (Taylor, 1972).

In 1967 the *Journal of Creative Behavior* was inaugu-

rated by the Creative Education Foundation. Its first two issues described the increasing research evidence that appropriate educational methods can encourage creative behavior. The following excerpt is especially significant:

> Approximately 1,250 bibliographic entries on creativity have appeared in the last year-and-one-half. A rough but dramatic indication of the explosion of literature on creativity is that in sheer bulk the research from January 1965, to June 1966, equals that of the preceding five years, and that again balances the work of the preceding 100 years. The number of relevant doctoral dissertations is a particularly good qualitative barometer of this interest and activity. About 300 such reports existed prior to 1965; in the last year-and-one-half almost 200 new dissertations have been recorded, under diverse headings, in a variety of disciplines (*1*, 1, 52).

In 1967, the Creative Education Foundation published a list of about 1,500 items for 1965-1966, bringing up to date its earlier bibliography of 4,176 items (through 1964). In 1971, the Foundation published, in Volume 5 of its Journal, a cumulative bibliography of all books through the end of 1970; it reports new listings each quarter thereafter in its *Journal of Creative Behavior*.

One of our bibliographic searches uncovered over 40 studies evaluating programs for teaching students to improve their sensitivity, fluency, flexibility, originality, elaboration, and related abilities. These investigations range from the retarded level to the gifted level, and from the first grade through college and adult education. Studies of adults have involved subjects from such diverse groups as military officers, teachers, and industrial personnel. Approximately 90 percent of the total number indicate that subjects' creative-productivity levels were significantly increased by deliberate educational programs. A number of informal and unpublished studies include similar findings (Parnes, 1967).

In 1972, Torrance summarized 142 research studies of programs, materials, and conditions designed to nurture creative behavior. The title of his comprehensive report was, "Can We Teach Children to Think Creatively?" His summary statement was as follows:

> In answer to the question posed by the title of this paper, it does indeed seem possible to teach children to think creatively. The most successful approaches seem to be those that involve both cognitive and emotional functioning, provide adequate structure and motivation, and give opportunities for involvement, practice, and interaction with teachers and other children. Motivating and facilitating conditions certainly make a difference in creative functioning, but differences seem to be greatest and most predictable when deliberate teaching is involved. (Torrance, 1972)

The literature thus seems to provide confirmation of the conviction expressed over 20 years ago by J. P. Guilford: "Like most behavior, creative activity probably represents, to some extent, many learned skills. There may be limitations set on these skills by heredity; but I am convinced that through learning one can extend the skills within those limitations (Guilford, 1952)."

A comprehensive longitudinal investigation was launched at the State University College at Buffalo in 1969. This ongoing study is called the Creative Studies Project. Specific hypotheses tested in the Project were as follows:

Students who complete a four-semester sequence of Creative Studies courses will perform significantly better than otherwise comparable students on: Selected tests of mental ability, problem-solving, and job performance; tests of creative application of academic subject matter; nonacademic achievement in areas calling for creative performance; and certain personality factors associated with creativity.

Further hypotheses for the longitudinal study are currently being formulated.

A very brief capsulization of the results is as follows: (a) The course students show significant differences over comparable controls in ability to cope with real-life situational tests, including not only the production of ideas, but also their evaluation and development. (b) They show significant differences over comparable controls in applying their creative abilities in special tests given in English courses. (c) They perform significantly better than the comparable controls on the semantic and behavioral half of J. P. Guilford's Structure-of-Intellect (S-O-I) Model, including three of five of his mental operations—cognition, divergent production, and convergent production; they show no significant accomplishment over the controls in the symbolic and figural half of Guilford's model, nor in his memory or evaluation operations. (d) Most course students report large gains in their own productive, creative behavior; they rate the program as quite helpful in their other college courses and their everyday lives. In the second year, there is a significant increase in the percentage of students who report large gains in ability to cope with problems and to participate actively in discussions. (e) Test results bear out their significant year-to-year improvement over comparable controls. (f) Course students show a growing tendency (not yet attaining statistical significance) to become more productive than comparable controls in their nonacademic achievement in areas calling for creative performance. (g) The data show consistent positive movement on personality measures by course students compared with their controls, although not significant on any single scale. One coping instrument, as well as the course students' own questionnaire responses, provided further significant evidence of gains in personality dimensions. (h) As to generalizability, it was concluded that, for a group comparable to our total sample of experimentals and controls who started such a two-year program of Creative Studies—and this would very likely include a portion of the student body at most colleges and universities—the gains in the study relative to time spent in courses would be expected for those continuing with the program (Parnes and Noller, 1973).

SPECIFIC PROGRAMS AND/OR APPLICATIONS

By the latter part of the sixties some beginning steps had been taken toward widespread application of the mounting research findings. For example, Paul Torrance and his associates produced and widely disseminated their exercise books and records for the elementary level (Myers and Torrance, 1965-1966; Cunningham and Torrance, 1965-1966). Also, by the end of the decade Torrance was consultant for a series of elementary school

reading books with a consistent creativity strand (Clymer et al., 1969-1971). The stories and artwork teach children the creative problem-solving process and involve them in it. Teacher guides provide additional ideas and exercises for facilitating creative thinking before, during, and after each lesson.

On December 31, 1969, J. P. Guilford published his final report, entitled "A General Summary of Twenty Years of Research on Aptitudes of High-Level Personnel" (Guilford, 1969). The summary lists major books and publications providing full details on his comprehensive research project. Guilford illustrated the impact of his work on the educational developments of the sixties as follows:

> Numerous educators have indicated that they have put SI (Structure-of-the-Intellect) concepts to work in connection with curriculum building and teaching operations. New goals, e.g., teaching for creativity, have become increasingly common, largely as a consequence of the University of Southern California's Aptitudes Research Project findings.

Many devices and programs to stimulate creative behavior are now available. A large variety are summarized by Donald Treffinger and John Gowan (1971). Examples are the diverse exercise programs of Synectics Educational Systems (Gordon and Poze, 1971), the Productive Thinking Program emanating from the extensive work of the research scientists at the Institute for Personality Assessment and Research at the University of California at Berkeley (Olton and Cruthfield, 1969; Olton et al., 1967) and the creativity programs that resulted from the National Schools Project (Williams, 1970, 1972).

CURRENT CHALLENGES

What appears to be the most significant challenge in the field of creativity development is the question of the relative degree of emphasis that needs to be given to the development of cognitive versus affective aspects of the creative personality. There are differences of opinion about the relative emphasis to be placed between the judgment and the imagination, as well as between the open awareness of the environment through all of the senses, and the deep self-searching into layer upon layer of data stored in the memory cells; between the logic and the emotion; between the deliberate creative effort and the incubation; and between the individual working with the group and his working alone. The underlying problem seems to become one of developing a balance between each of these extremes, by strengthening the weaker aspect but not by stunting the stronger side.

Thus, the challenge seems to be to develop both the freedom and the self-discipline in people, as though each were one leg of their bodies. We want both legs to be of even length, and we want both to be full length and strong. The research evidence and the developments of the past 20 years offer strong promise that this is possible. Hence, there appears to be the opportunity for a great surge forward toward positive change, far beyond what we have witnessed today, but in a more directed sense—almost like a guided missile, as against a missile out of control. If we can help people become fully aware of their total potential—both their spontaneity and their self-discipline—it seems fairly certain that we can increase each person's creative productivity, for both his own self-fulfillment and the benefit of society.

REFERENCES

Clymer, T. et al. *Reading 360 Program.* Lexington, Mass.: Ginn, 1969.

Cunningham, B. F., and Torrance, E. P. *Imagi/craft.* Lexington, Mass.: Ginn, 1965.

Gordon, W. J. J., and Poze, T. *The Metaphorical Way of Learning and Knowing.* Cambridge: Porpoise Books, 1971.

Guilford, J. P. Some Recent Findings on Thinking Abilities and Their Implications. *Informational Bulletin,* Training Analysis and Development, TA&D Directorate, Deputy Chief of Staff Operations, Hq. ATRC, Scott AFB, *49,* 1952, Fall (3).

——. *A General Summary of Twenty Years of Research on Aptitudes of High-Level Personnel.* Los Angeles: University of Southern California, Department of Psychology, Aptitudes Research Project. Final Report, December 31, 1969, NR 150-44.

Mohan, M. Is There a Need for a Course in Creativity in Teacher Education? *Journal of Creative Behavior,* 1973, 7(3).

Myers, R. E., and Torrance, E. P. *Invitations to Thinking and Doing.* Lexington, Mass.: Ginn, 1964.

——, and Torrance, E. P. *Can You Imagine?* Lexington, Mass.: Ginn, 1965(a).

——, and Torrance, E. P. *Invitations to Speaking and Writing Creatively.* Lexington, Mass.: Ginn, 1965.

——, and Torrance, E. P. *For Those Who Wonder.* Lexington, Mass.: Ginn, 1966(b).

——, and Torrance, E. P. *Plots, Puzzles and Ploys.* Lexington, Mass.: Ginn, 1966(b).

Olton, R. M., and Crutchfield, R. S. Developing the Skills of Productive Thinking. In Mussen, P., Langer, J., and Covington, M. V., eds., *New Directions in Developmental Psychology.* New York: Holt, 1969.

—— et al. *The Development of Productive Thinking Skills in Fifth-Grade Children.* Technical Report, Research and Development Center for Cognitive Learning, University of Wisconsin, 1967.

Osborn, A. F. *The Creative Trend in Education.* Buffalo: Creative Education Foundation, 1965.

Parnes, S. J. *Creative Behavior Guidebook.* New York: Charles Scribner's Sons, 1967.

—— and Noller, R. B. *Toward Supersanity: Channeled Freedom.* Buffalo: D. O. K. Publishers, Inc., 1973.

Smith, J. A. *Setting Conditions for Creative Teaching in the Elementary School.* Boston: Allyn & Bacon, 1966. (Six additional books in specific subject-matter areas make up a series in creative teaching by the author and his colleagues.)

Taylor, C. W., ed. *Climate for Creativity.* New York: Pergamon, 1972. (Four other compilations on earlier conferences are included below.)

Torrance, E. P. Can We Teach Children to Think Creatively? *Journal of Creative Behavior,* 1972, 6(2).

Treffinger, D. J., and Gowan, J. C. An Updated Representative List of Methods and Educational Programs for Stimulating Creativity. *Journal of Creative Behavior,* 1971, 5(2).

Williams, F. E. (comp.). *Classroom Ideas for Encouraging Thinking and Feeling* (2nd rev. ed.). Buffalo: D. O. K. Publishers, 1970.

——. *A Total Creativity Program for Individualizing and Humanizing the Learning Process; Vol. I—Identifying and Measuring Creative Potential.* Englewood Cliffs, N.J.: Educational Technology Publications, 1972, Spring.

——. *A Total Creativity Program for Individualizing and Humanizing the Learning Process; Vol. II—Encouraging Creative Potential.* Englewood Cliffs, N.J.: Educational Technology Publications, 1972, Spring.

ADDITIONAL RESOURCES

Davis, G., and Scott, J., eds. *Training Creative Thinking.* New York: Holt, 1971.

Guilford, J. P. *Intelligence, Creativity, and Their Educational Implications.* San Diego: Knapp, 1968.

Osborn, A. F. *Applied Imagination* (3rd ed.). New York: Charles Scribner's Sons, 1963.

Otto, H. *Group Methods to Actualize Human Potential: A Handbook.* Beverley Hills: Holistic Press, 1970.

Parnes, S. J., and Harding, H. F., eds. *A Source Book for Creative Thinking.* New York: Charles Scribner's Sons, 1962.

Prince, G. M. *The Practice of Creativity.* New York: Harper, 1970.

Taylor, C. W., ed. *Creativity: Progress and Potential.* New York: McGraw, 1964.

——. *Widening Horizons in Creativity.* New York: Wiley, 1964.

——, and Barron, F., eds. *Scientific Creativity: Its Recognition and Development.* New York: Wiley, 1963.

——, and Williams, F., eds. *Instructional Media and Creativity.* New York: Wiley, 1966.

Torrance, E. P. *Encouraging Creativity in the Classroom.* Dubuque: W. C. Brown, 1970.

MAJOR INTEREST ORGANIZATION

Creative Education Foundation, Inc.
State University College (Buffalo)
1300 Elmwood Avenue—Chase Hall
Buffalo, New York 14222

96

ECONOMIC EDUCATION

by George Dawson
Director
Joint Council on Economic Education
New York, New York

Broadly defined, economic education refers to any effort designed to increase or improve people's understanding of economic facts, concepts, principles, or problems. In a sense, then, the first grade teacher who shows her pupils that their "free" milk actually involves a cost in terms of labor, natural resources, and capital utilized in its production; the college professor teaching "Principles of Economics," the journalist who attempts to explain the significance of the Gross National Product to the layman; and the publisher producing booklets and filmstrips on inflation are all engaged in economic education. Some would prefer to confine the definition to formal instructional programs, such as those offered by schools, colleges, and other interested institutions. (Among the "interested institutions" are such organizations as the American Bankers Association, the AFL-CIO, the National Association of Manufacturers, the Henry George Institution, and various other nonprofit organizations.)

Very often, the term "economic education" refers to the organized movement to increase economic literacy. The Joint Council on Economic Education, which was incorporated in 1949, is generally recognized as the leader of the economic education movement in the United States. The formation of the Council was one of the outcomes of the New York University Workshop on Economic Education, held in 1948 and attended by educators from all over the country. As an independent, nonprofit, and nonpartisan educational organization, the Joint Council is guided by the principle that every citizen should be able to recognize and objectively analyze economic issues essential to his or her own welfare, and to the welfare of the nation. Those involved in the movement point to the fact that some 70 percent of all major legislation in some way deals with economic issues, and that every individual is intimately affected by economic problems.

As of fall 1973, there were 92 college-based Centers for Economic Education and 53 state and regional Councils on Economic Education affiliated with the Joint Council. The state and regional Councils are organized in much the same way as the national Joint Council, with representatives of labor, business, agriculture, government, and education on their governing boards. To join and remain affiliated with the national body, they must adhere strictly to an objective, nonpolitical and nonpartisan approach to economic issues. As with the national Joint Council, the state and regional Councils are community organizations, which derive their support from labor unions, agricultural organizations, banks, business firms, individuals, and foundations. The Centers, on the other hand, are collegiate rather than community institutions, and draw their basic support from the college or university budget. Before being accepted as an affiliate of the Joint Council, a Center must meet certain minimum standards regarding staff, budget, program, and control. Although there is considerable variation throughout the country, the ideal arrangement is seen as one in which there is a single state Council with several affiliated Centers strategically located throughout the state. Each Council is basically responsible for its own fund-raising, and determines its own program. Councils and Centers enjoy a considerable amount of autonomy, although Councils often provide funds to Centers for program purposes and there is a high level of cooperation in terms of activities, geographic area of operation, sharing of resources, and policy-making.

Thanks to numerous studies made by Opinion Research Corporation, various individual researchers, and many of its affiliated Councils and Centers, the Joint Council has acquired a massive amount of evidence indicating that the American public is economically illiterate. It has often been found that high school teachers of social studies or business subjects know little more about economics than do their students. Because these teachers are in a key position to do something about the problem, this fact is particularly distressing. The leaders of the economic education movement, in deciding how to allocate their very scarce resources, have often stressed the training of teachers. One of the Joint Council's surveys revealed that half of the teacher-training programs in the United States did not require economics of social studies teacher-trainees. Another study, made by the noted economists G. L. Bach and Phillip Saunders (1965), showed that the minimum amount taken by those teachers who were exposed to economics instruction in college (usually three or six credits) was not sufficient to provide them with a lasting understanding. In short, the overwhelming majority of teachers do not feel confident in their ability to teach this crucially important subject. A major program of the Joint Council and affiliates, therefore, is the support of workshops, inservice courses, and institutes designed to increase the teacher's economic knowledge, and to provide help in conveying that knowledge to elementary and secondary school pupils. As many as 70 of these workshops have been held in a single summer throughout the country, with up to 3,000 teachers participating. During a single school year as many as 12,000 teachers have participated in economics inservice programs.

Obviously, school administrators are not inclined to incorporate economics into the curriculum unless they feel that their teachers are qualified to handle the subject. Several follow-up studies have shown, then, that these workshops usually increase the teaching of economics in the schools. In 1951 only five percent of the students graduating from high school had had a formal course in economics. Although precise figures are hard to obtain, it is estimated that as many as 32 percent of the high school graduates of the early 1970s had a separate economics course.

In any event, the percentage of secondary school students who have had an economics course nearly doubled between the 1960-1961 and the 1970-1971 academic years. Between 1963 and 1970, 91 percent of the nation's 102 largest school systems added major units in economics, and currently somewhere between 35 and 49 percent of all secondary schools offer this subject. School administrators often state that they would gladly add economics to their curricula, but need additional resources and help. The number of school systems in the Joint Council's Cooperating Schools Program has grown from ten in 1964-1965 to 194 as of the fall of 1973. Let us now briefly examine some of the major programs of the formal economic education movement.

PROGRAMS

Teacher Training

The workshops and other courses for teachers vary considerably in terms of content, format, length, and method. To be co-sponsored by the Joint Council, however, they must meet its standards for objectivity and nonpolitical, nonpartisan approach, and consideration must be given to methods of teaching as well as to economics content. Usually, a college economist and an educator will cooperate in planning and running the program. Outside speakers representing various sectors of the economy are often employed, and field trips are commonly taken. The participants usually receive instruction in basic economics and in methods of teaching the subject in the elementary or secondary schools. Research has shown that, on the average, the participants learn about as much as college students in a one-semester Principles of Economics course. Recent studies made by the Joint Council and its affiliates also show that the pupils of teachers who have received workshop training learn more than similar pupils of similar teachers who have not received such instruction. (In these studies, such variables as pupil intelligence and teacher background have been controlled.)

Although the most common approach in the workshops is to teach the participants economics and then deal with instructional strategies for the elementary or secondary classroom, some interesting new techniques have been tried. In a workshop for elementary teachers in Des Moines in 1972, the teachers first examined the textbook series they would be using with their pupils in the 1972-1973 school year, to identify (with the help of the workshop staff) the economic facts and concepts those materials contained, and were then given instruction in those topics. Here, methods and problems of teaching took priority over economics content. Nevertheless, those teachers performed just as well on a standardized test of economic understanding as did teachers in the more traditional workshops. Another study, made in Arkansas, showed that the mixing of education and economics in a course does not reduce the amount of economics learned by teachers, but actually increases it.

Preservice economic education programs for teachers are practically nonexistent. About half of the college teacher-training programs for social studies majors, and nearly all of those for business teachers, require some economics, but with little or no instruction in how to teach the subject. (Most teachers who have had economics in college state that their preparation is inadequate, and that instruction in methods of teaching economics is imperative if they are to incorporate it in the curriculum.) The probability of getting adequate undergraduate training in economic education is remote.

In addition to the summer workshops, and a few inservice programs and institutes, there are a few universities which offer graduate programs in this field. Doctoral candidates in business education or social studies at the University of Minnesota may concentrate on economic education, and most of those who have done so have served a one- or two-year internship in the Center for Economic Education there. There are masters programs for teachers at the Center for Economic Education in St. Cloud and at the Center at the College of St. Thomas in St. Paul, Minnesota. Some others which have offered some sort of graduate economic education program for teachers are Wright State University in Dayton, Ohio, the University of Illinois at Urbana, the University of Colorado, the University of Nebraska, the State University College of New York at Oneonta, the University of Missouri at Columbia, Samford University in Alabama, Oklahoma State University, Purdue University in Indiana, Clark University in Worcester, Massachusetts, and Ohio University in Athens. The last institution actually as a separate Department of Economic Education.

Given the fact that very few states require economics of social studies teachers, that only about half of the preservice college programs require it of the social studies major, that only about ten percent will take the subject voluntarily, and that even the existing requirements are inadequate, it appears that there will be a great need for more inservice training programs for a long time to come.

Economic Education Materials

Partially because of inadequacies in their own economics backgrounds, and partially because they lack the time to develop their own materials, teachers rely heavily upon textbooks, pamphlets, audiovisual aids, and the like, in their efforts to teach economics. It is not the primary function of the Joint Council or of any of its affiliates to produce materials. Indeed, the Joint Council's policy is to avoid producing anything that is available elsewhere. Nevertheless, because of the absence of some badly needed materials, or because of gross inadequacies in existing items, the Joint Council and its affiliates have been publishing books, pamphlets, teachers' manuals, films, filmstrips, records, cassettes, and the like, in increasing numbers. Not wishing to compete with commercial publishers, the economic education organizations will publish only those items which are not likely to be profitable. The emphasis is usually upon material for the teacher rather than for the students.

Teaching Economics in American History, published in 1973, is an example of a badly needed item which would not be produced by a commercial publisher. Because American history is replete with economic incidents (such as recessions and depressions, inflations and deflations, banking crises, and labor disputes), it cannot be taught properly without some attention to the analytical concepts underlying those events. This manual, then, identifies the economic issues and principles in every period of American history, and provides the teacher with suggested discussion questions, activities, and materials that can be used to teach about them in a more meaningful way.

Economics is important because it affects our current lives. Indeed, there are few issues and problems which do not have an economic dimension. To help teachers and their pupils understand this, the Joint Council's Economic Topic series includes such pamphlets as *The Economics of Crime, The Economics of Pollution, The Economics of Youth Unemployment,* and *The Economics of Poverty and Racial Discrimination.* The texts are written by economists who are authorities on the topic, while experienced educators write a "Teach About" section containing ideas and materials for use in the classroom. Filmstrips with records or cassettes have been produced to accompany many of these topics.

Other available publications are designed to help educators introduce economics into various existing curriculums, to relate economic concepts to the individual consumer and citizen, to develop a basic economics library, to become aware of research in this field, to learn of existing games, simulations, fugitive materials, and audiovisual aids, and so on. The demand for materials produced by the economic education organizations has increased steadily.

Awards Programs for Teachers

With a grant from the Calvin K. Kazanjian Foundation, the Joint Council has been conducting an annual awards program since 1962. Teachers from kindergarten through the university level submit descriptions of their economic education projects. These are judged by a committee of well-known economists and educators. At each of five levels (primary, intermediate, junior high, senior high, and college) prizes are offered. Descriptions of the winning entries are published in a book each year, and the original projects, which can be borrowed, are housed in the Vernon R. Alden Library at Ohio State University in Athens. Recently, several of the state and local Councils and Centers have instituted similar awards programs. The purpose of these programs is to reward outstanding teaching, to disseminate ideas, and to encourage more and better teaching of economics. Research shows that the program has indeed had a "multiplier effect," for more teachers and schools have been induced to include economics in the curriculum. A controlled experiment, completed in 1973, indicated that pupils using these materials learned more economics than similar pupils in similar programs in which the materials were not used. (Other variables, such as teacher's economic background and knowledge, and pupil ability, were held constant.)

Research and Evaluation

Economic education specialists have been forced to fight their way through a morass of skepticism on the part of college economists and others who have doubted that it is possible to teach economics in the elementary and secondary schools. An essential first step, of course, was the construction of valid and reliable tests of economic understanding. Before a test could be written, however, the objectives of economic education had to be defined. To identify the minimum level of economic understanding essential for good citizenship, a National Task Force on Economic Education was created in 1960. The highly respected (perhaps "revered" would be a more appropriate term) American Economic Association appointed the members. After a year of intensive study and discussion, the Task Force (1961) published its report *Economic Education in the Schools.* This became the virtual Bible of the economic education movement. Textbooks and other materials produced since 1961 have drawn heavily upon the report for guidance on the economic concepts to be included. It became clear, however, that schools had no adequate means of measuring the effectiveness of their economics programs.

Responding to the need for an evaluation instrument, the Joint Council appointed a Committee on Measurement of Economic Understanding, made up of outstanding economists and educators. The Committee developed the *Test of Economic Understanding,* which was published in 1964 by Science Research Associates. This test has been widely used, not only with high school students, but in colleges and with adult groups as well. An enor-

mous amount of research has been done using this instrument, and only a very small sample of the findings can be mentioned here. It has been well established, for example, that high school economics courses *are* effective, that students in college economics courses who have had high school economics generally enjoy an advantage over those who are getting their first introduction to the subject, that a variety of strategies can be used to teach economic concepts, and that a significant amount of economic content can be taught by incorporating it in other social studies courses (such as history or problems of democracy).

Although the TEU has been used extensively in colleges, professors often felt uncomfortable with a test that was designed primarily for secondary schools. Consequently, the Joint Council appointed a Committee for a College-Level Test of Economic Understanding, made up of such noted economists as G. L. Bach, Rendigs Fels, Paul Samuelson, and George Stigler. Designed to sample the content of the typical college introductory economics course, this *Test of Understanding in College Economics* (TUCE) quickly gained widespread acceptance among economists. The availability of a nationally normed and valid standardized test, generous grants from several sources, the publication of a new journal (*The Journal of Economic Education*) interested in research papers, and student demands for better courses undoubtedly help to explain the tremendous increase in research and evaluation at the college level. College professors of economics have been busily experimenting with the use of computer-assisted instruction, case studies, games and simulations, programmed texts, problem-solving approaches, field work, behavioral objectives, and various other teaching techniques in their courses. It is hoped that by the development of more interesting and effective courses, more college students will elect to take the subject, and better-prepared citizens and teachers will emerge. Thus, the economic education movement now covers every educational level, from the primary grades through the university. (In the summer of 1973 a workshop was held at Purdue for economics professors who are interested in improving their teaching of the undergraduate courses.)

How Economics is Taught

It is difficult to obtain reliable figures on the extent to which economics is taught in the schools. There are practically no separate economics courses at the elementary level (although separate units in economics are quite common), the teachers usually include their economics lessons in the social studies curriculum—if they include economics at all. Those secondary schools which have separate courses in economics usually offer the subject at the 11th- or 12th-grade level (commonly the latter), but rarely require it. With few exceptions, it is a one-semester course. Economics is most often the responsibility of the social studies department, although it sometimes comes under the jurisdiction of the business department. Consumer education may be taught by social studies, business, or home economics teachers. This course offers opportunities to include some analytical economics, but it is unlikely that many teachers do so.

Most of the consumer education textbooks contain much sound advice on family budgeting, filing an income tax report, buying insurance, etc., but provide little in the way of the analytical tools of economics that would help consumers understand their role in our complex market economy. There is no reliable information on how many schools offer consumer education, or on how many use this course to teach economic reasoning. Most colleges, of course, offer a basic economics program.

Now, if it is hard to ascertain how many schools have economics programs, it is virtually impossible to get quantifiable data on the methods used to teach the subject. Nevertheless, by examining widely used textbooks and other materials, by collecting course outlines and teacher-made projects, and by classroom visits and conferences with teachers at workshops, professional meetings, and the like, economic education specialists have a fairly good idea of what goes on in the classroom. The variety of techniques employed is truly astounding (for example, see the ten volumes of *Economic Education Experiences of Enterprising Teachers*), and only a small sampling can be presented here.

Economics in the Elementary Grades. If teachers rely heavily or solely upon their textbooks, the amount and quality of economics taught will vary considerably. The economics content of elementary social studies materials has increased and improved during the past few years, but most teachers still need additional help. Many of those who go beyond their textbooks develop ingenious ways of conveying economic concepts to young children.

For example, a third-grade class wants to raise money to go on a bus trip, or to buy equipment for their classroom. They decide to go into business, making and selling a product to raise the necessary funds. After surveying their existing resources they find that they can produce either candy or cookies. A poll is taken in the school to see which product would sell, and how much the buyers would be willing to pay. (At this point, of course, the teacher can deal with the law of demand.) To maximize their profits, they will have to produce the cookies, say, at the lowest possible unit cost. They will learn about the various factors of production (natural resources, labor, capital), how each contributes to a firm's output, and what each input will cost. They will learn that they can increase and improve their production if they engage in specialization, as in the formation of an assembly line. By comparing their classroom firm with an actual business in the community, they will augment and deepen their knowledge, and discover that government plays a role through various controls (such as health standards or licenses) and taxation. The children may learn that if they produce too much they will have to lower their prices (law of supply and demand). They may even be confronted with competition from a real life firm or from other classroom enterprises. In a well-run project of this sort, the pupils will discover the *opportunity cost principle* (by producing cookies they sacrifice the opportunity to produce candy with the same resources), the way in which wages and prices are determined, the importance of efficiency and productivity, and many other basic principles. And, in the process, they will have

enjoyed themselves tremendously.

Economics in Secondary Grades. Teachers who are guided largely by existing secondary textbooks may present economics in a fairly conventional manner. Depending upon the instructor's aims, approaches, and materials used, their efforts may result in a descriptive, consumer-oriented course, or in a rigorous, college-type introduction to analytical economics. Creative teachers, however, will devise realistic games and simulations or involve students in practical projects.

As an example of the latter, a teacher might have the students make studies of their chosen occupations. What is the supply and demand situation for workers in this field? How are wages or salaries determined? Is the industry in question affected by the business cycle? In what way, if any, is it affected by government actions? By international economic developments? What is required to prepare for this job? To what extent are the workers protected by union-management contracts? These and many other questions call for a knowledge of the analytical tools of economics, and those tools will be applied to something of immediate interest to the student. Since the students are affected by inflation, since they too pay taxes, and since the unemployment rate is highest among young people, problems of this nature can be examined in the secondary grades. Economic principles, then, can become instruments for the solution of personal problems, and not simply academic abstractions to be foisted upon a captive audience.

Economics in Higher Education. The lecture-discussion method continues to dominate the scene in the colleges, but professors are beginning to bend with the wind. Computerized games and simulations are rapidly gaining in popularity, as is the use of case studies, and the analysis of current problems. Although there is as yet no mass movement on the part of college economists to recognize the existence of elementary and secondary schools, some are beginning to feel that lines of communication ought to be established and maintained.

CONCLUSION

Few economic educators expect to gain instant popularity for their subject, but there is a growing awareness on the part of the public that economic ignorance cannot be tolerated. Increasingly, people are beginning to realize that soaring prices, inequalities in income distribution, dollar devaluations, the ups and downs of the business cycle, changes in interest rates, government efforts at price-wage control, and a host of other current problems do affect them. If they are to understand these problems and give enlightened consideration to the alternative solutions available, their knowledge of economic principles must be expanded. The network of Councils and Centers on Economic Education, probably a unique phenomenon in the educational world, will have to draw upon the resources and coordinate the efforts of schools, from the primary grades through the universities, to meet current and future needs for greater economic literacy and more adequate preparation for citizenship.

REFERENCES

Bach, G. L., and Saunders, Phillip. Economic Education: Aspirations and Achievements. *American Economic Review,* Vol. 55, No1 3, June 1965, 329-356.

Calderwood, James D., Lawrence, John D., and Maher, John E. *Economics in the Curriculum: Developmental Economic Education Program.* New York: John Wiley and Sons, 1970.

Clark, Jere, Guyton, Percy, and Dawson, George G., eds. *Economic Education Experiences of Enterprising Teachers.* 10 vols. New York: Joint Council on Economic Education, 1963-1973.

Dawson, George G., and Symmes, S. Stowell, eds. *Economics in Social Studies Textbooks.* 4 vols. New York: Joint Council on Economic Education, 1973.

_____. Preservice, Inservice and Graduate Programs in Economic Education. *Review of Social Economy.* Vol. 29, No. 1, March 1971, 63-78.

Frankel, M. L. *Economic Education.* New York: The Center for Applied Research in Education, 1965.

Lewis, Darrell R., and Orvis, Charles C. *Research in Economic Education: A Review, Bibliography, and Abstracts.* New York: Joint Council on Economic Education, 1971.

Lumsden, Keith, ed. *Recent Research in Economic Education.* Englewood Cliffs, N.J.: Prentice-Hall, Inc., 1970.

National Task Force on Economic Education. *Economic Education in the Schools: Report of the National Task Force on Economic Education.* New York: Committee for Economic Development, 1961.

Prehn, Edward C. *Teaching High School Economics: The Analytical Approach.* New York: Pitman Publishing Corporation, 1968.

97

ETHNIC STUDIES IN HIGHER EDUCATION

by Winnie Bengelsdorf
U.S. Nuclear Regulatory Commission
Division of Organization and Personnel
Washington, D.C.
formerly:
Office of Urban Programs (1972-1974)
American Association of State Colleges and Universities
Washington, D.C.

Ethnic studies is the systematic study of the culture, history, literature, lifestyle, philosophy, and language of a minority group to stimulate ethnic identity and pride, community commitment and service, and understanding of the distinctiveness, relationships, and interdependence of various groups.

The traumatic birth of black studies on predominantly white campuses, starting about 1968 amid power struggles and student protest, survived an infancy of dissension and confrontation to become an accepted, legitimate academic field of study in American higher education within five years.

Black studies, in turn, provided impetus and inspiration for creating other ethnic studies programs, recognizing positive values of cultural pluralism and enhancing institutional change in colleges and universities.

Competing with more entrenched disciplines for scarce financial support in the mid-seventies, these controversial and newly established ethnic programs may suffer setbacks.

TOPIC SCOPE

Projected from a scientifically representative 1973 survey of all two- and four-year institutions and all universities, 1,584 higher education institutions (61 percent of all institutions) offered at least one course in ethnic studies in fall, 1972 (Dutton, 1973). This includes more than 90 percent of universities, about two-thirds of four-year institutions, and almost half of two-year institutions in the United States. Courses in black studies (including Afro-American studies) rank first, accounting for 55 percent of all ethnic studies courses offered, with Spanish-speaking (including Chicano and Puerto Rican studies) ranking second, with 18.5 percent, and Asian-American (including Chinese and Japanese American) studies ranking third, with 8.5 percent of the total ethnic studies courses. It is estimated that over 10,000 individual courses were offered, with a combined enrollment topping 270,000.

Major programs are estimated at 358 institutions and minor programs at 186 institutions. The survey computes black studies major programs are offered by 182 institutions, Spanish-speaking studies majors by 98 institutions, white ethnic and multiethnic studies majors by 25 institutions each, and Asian American studies majors by 19 institutions. Other ethnic studies major programs, including American Indian programs, account for the remainder. Students graduated between July 1971 and June 1972 with such majors are estimated at over 1,000.

REVIEW OF RECENT LITERATURE AND DEVELOPMENTS

Lombardi (1971) states the emergence of black studies constitutes the most extensive modification of community college curriculum since addition of vocation-technical courses, decades ago. Only ten junior colleges offered black studies before 1965. By 1972, 500 of these institutions were estimated by the American Council on Education (Dutton, 1973) to offer such courses.

Similar increases at four-year colleges and universities are reported for Asian-American, black, Chicano, Indian, Puerto Rican, white ethnic and multiethnic programs (Bengelsdorf, 1972). For example, less than ten Chicano studies programs existed before 1967, whereas about 60 programs were estimated for 1972. Estimates in 1970 were even higher (Sanchez; Ethnic Studies, Intercultural). Colleges are reporting more Jewish studies, as well as Polish American and Italian American courses (Jewish Studies, 1972; Geryk, 1971; Pioneer Course, 1972).

Bengelsdorf provides a comprehensive review of the literature, including summaries of research reports, surveys, books, journal articles, and bibliographies relating to ethnic programs; lists higher education institutions known to offer various ethnic study programs in 1972; and indicates sources for further information.

Black and Chicano studies programs suffered from rapid and uncoordinated proliferation. Many sources relate the history of the problems encountered in focusing on program goals, organizational structures, separatism, faculty shortages, suitable textual material, and financing (Black Studies: Perspective, 1970; Blassingame, 1971; Black Studies Retrospect, 1973; Ethnic Studies, Intercultural, 1970).

However, Smith (1971), surveying over 230 institutions, found that although models differed, objectives in black studies were similar for all institutions, including the learning of contributions, history, and contemporary role of blacks; enhancing self-concept; providing relevant education for work in the black community; defining the black role in America; preparing for vocations; studying relationships; and combating racism.

Cleveland (1969), surveying almost 200 institutions, found that black history and literature were most emphasized. Ford (1973), also studying 200 institutions, noted 15 basic courses, with the three most popular (history, sociology, and literature) accounting for over 56 percent of total offerings.

Similarly, a survey of institutions offering Chicano studies revealed similarities of existing programs, including studying contributions of Chicanos, promoting better understanding among all Americans, disseminating information to professionals, and promoting higher education for Chicanos. A majority of efforts were concentrated in the social sciences (Sanchez, 1970).

Although organizational patterns for black studies programs differ, it is widely documented that most institutions establish an interdepartmental or interdisciplinary program, rather than create a separate department (Gehret, 1969; Black Studies Added, 1970; Colmen, Wheeler, 1970). Ford (1973) found 75 percent of the programs he reviewed were interdisciplinary, with the program director responsible for the administration of the program working with regular departments which provide faculty members for black studies courses.

Factors associated with the likelihood that an institution will offer ethnic programs have been identified. These include an urban location, a large total enrollment, a comparatively large minority enrollment, public sponsorship, support by faculty and administrators, presence of minority faculty, and a high level of selectivity of the institution (Lombardi, 1971; McDaniel, McKee, 1971; Goldstein, Albert, Slaughter, 1972).

Some scholars emphasize that studying black history and culture is not a new phenomenon, since many predominantly black colleges offered such courses 50 years ago (Interview with Franklin, 1971; Ford, 1973). Thus, these black colleges can play a crucial role in assisting predominantly white institutions now offering black studies. Some suggestions include pooling resources, developing model programs, and educating blacks with a sense of identity and for careers (Turner, 1970, Drake, 1971).

Virtually every ethnic group has compiled bibliographies of relevant material. Some examples are a massive directory for black resources (Schatz, 1970); an im-

pressive inventory by Chicanos at California State University, San Diego (Bibliografia de Aztlan, 1971); a Chicano publications clearinghouse (La Causa, 1972); and a bibliography evaluating library materials from the Indian perspective (American Indians, 1970). White ethnics have a publication on ethnicity and ethnic groups (Kolm, 1973), and teachers can refer to a directory of over 200 multicultural programs in teacher education (James, 1971).

Studies indicate geographic patterns for institutions offering ethnic studies. Offerings in Asian-American, Chicano, Indian, and Puerto Rican studies are heaviest in those areas where these minorities reside. Most surveys show the West and North as having the highest level of black or ethnic courses, and all research indicates the South has the fewest programs (Cleveland, 1969; Lombardi, 1971; McDaniel, McKee, 1971; Dutton, 1973). Enrollment in courses is vastly higher in the West, followed by the Northeast, Midwest and South (Dutton, 1973).

Some surveys find enrollment in ethnic studies generally adequate, ranging from one to six percent of total enrollment and including whites (Lombardi, 1971). Ford (1973) states black studies enrollment in most colleges and universities "is increasing so rapidly that there is unprecedented demand for qualified instructors (p. 7)." Wright (1970) reports, "over 60 percent of those enrolled in Black Studies have been white (p. 212)." One survey (Goldstein, Albert, Slaughter, 1972), with almost 1,000 responding institutions, disclosed "Two-thirds to more than four-fifths of the traditionally White colleges have Black Studies courses which have a majority of White students (p. 28)."

However, some institutions report disappointing enrollment. Various press reports cite falling enrollment (Studies in Ethnics, 1972). Enrollment may relate to the quality and stability of specific programs so that no general pattern emerges.

Among the institutional changes fostered by the ethnic movement are a student-centered orientation in curricula planning; increased attention to relevance in education; importance of community service experiences; more flexible academic procedures and requirements; and modification of admissions and credentialing procedures. "Improvements in these areas by the universities benefit not only the black students whose protests often have necessitated them, but all students (College and Cultural, 1971, p. 85)."

The concept of cultural pluralism, which may be regarded as both a cause and a result of ethnic studies, has been endorsed by numerous national organizations, such as the American Association of Colleges for Teacher Education (Multicultural Statement, 1972). Illustrious contributors, representing various ethnic groups, stress "cultural pluralism rather than cultural homogeneity must be recognized and accepted within our educational institutions—not as a necessary evil, but as a strong positive force (Stent, Hazard, Rivlin, 1973, bookjacket)." Among recommendations of a conference of teachers on cultural pluralism: "Strong ethnic studies programs should be established in colleges and universities, with adequate facilities and financial support, and should be so oriented as to serve nonminority students as well as others (Stent, Hazard, Rivlin, 1973, p. 157)."

The upsurge of white ethnic spirit and interest in ethnic studies is evident in testimony on the Education Amendments of 1971, prior to passage of the Ethnic Heritage Program (Education Amendments, 1971). This law was hailed by its sponsor (Schweiker, 1972) as evidence that Congress, for the first time, provided "official national recognition to ethnicity as a positive, constructive force in our society today."

Many factors accounted for, and enhanced higher education interest in, ethnic studies in the climate of the 1960s. Among them were the civil rights movement, increased black militancy to redress past injustices, and upsurges of ethnicity among many minorities claiming the "melting pot" was unworkable and/or undesirable. Federal government policies, practices, and laws served to heighten ethnic awareness with ethnic questionnaires, guidelines, record-keeping requirements, and affirmative action programs. Further, the amendments to the Immigration Act of 1965 increased immigration and formed a new wave of ethnic Americans.

Concurrently and increasingly, state legislatures passed laws requiring or recommending that the contributions of minority groups be included in school curricula. Almost half the states either required or resolved to include ethnic content in elementary and secondary school curricula in 1973. This increased the need for higher education emphasis on training teachers to instruct with multiethnic materials.

California and Wisconsin appeared to be pace-setters in ethnic education in 1972. Conditions have changed. California policy required that ethnic studies be offered by every community college by 1975. However, in 1973, the State Coordinating Council on Higher Education urged decreased spending on ethnic studies, claiming falling enrollment as the reason (Sievert, 1973). Others state enrollments are increasing.

The University of Wisconsin system, by unanimous action of the Board of Regents, in 1971 created an Ethnic and Minority Studies Center, which was abandoned in 1973. Further, support has been withdrawn from the Afro-American and Native American student centers. One reason cited was the Board of Regents' resolution supporting only multicultural and integrated campus programs (U. of Wisconsin, 1973).

Philanthropic organizations, notably the Ford Foundation, contributed millions of dollars for university black studies programs in 1968-1970, and for developing scholarly materials, thus speeding development of ethnic programs. Although Ford now supports generously many other projects to expand minority educational opportunity, most grants for ethnic studies have terminated.

It is expected that some ethnic studies, now pressed as separate programs, will eventually be included in mainstream history for the benefit of both majority and minority students. The true impact of ethnic studies would be the revision of the frame of reference by which all Americans view history and events.

A recent survey of state colleges and universities revealed that almost 70 percent of responding institutions had ongoing or planned programs incorporating multiethnic content in regular courses (Urban Affairs, 1973).

Some ethnic leaders applaud the tendency toward multiethnic education, while others fear that such an emphasis smacks of efforts to assimilate, and threatens the individual ethnic programs. No doubt, both strong separate ethnic studies programs and cross-cultural studies will persist. Separate ethnic programs will be necessary, especially to prepare teachers for ethnic programs at all educational levels, and in recognition that scholarly study of any and all cultures is a valid intellectual pursuit. In the words of John F. Kennedy (1964), "Every ethnic minority, in seeking its own freedom, helped strengthen the fabric of liberty in American life (p. 65)."

SPECIFIC PROGRAMS

Some black studies programs have a cultural emphasis, others a research interest, and a few, such as UCLA's Afro-American Studies and Cornell's Africana Research Center, combine these approaches. In other examples, the University of Pittsburgh has a Department of Black Community Research; Howard University is developing a model program for predominantly black institutions; while University of California campuses formed a consortium (What's the Score, 1972). New York University has an autonomous Institute of Afro-American Affairs, providing for interdisciplinary study, joint professorships, junior and senior fellowships, informal educational activities, special education, and travel and exchange programs (Brown, 1970). New programs emerge each year, with a recent degree program added at Jersey City State College (N.J.), where career placement will be an integral part of the program.

A composite black studies curriculum from 140 institutions responding to a survey is given in 25 subject areas by Smith (1971). Blassingame (1971) presents a model program based on consultations with over 75 scholars. Successful experiences and practices for implementing programs are shown by Lombardi (1971). Another report reviews programs at Atlanta, Duke, Howard, Lincoln, New York, Princeton, Rutgers, Stanford, Vanderbilt, and Yale universities (Black Studies: How, 1971). Ford (1973) reviews seven significant programs at various types of institutions: Wayne County Community College, California State University, San Jose, Morgan State College, Chicago State, Yale, and Atlanta Universities, and the University of Michigan.

El Plan de Santa Barbara (1969) provides several models for developing Chicano studies programs, including core course lists and course outlines. Chicano Studies Institute worked to coordinate standards for their programs (Sanchez, 1970). Well-known programs exist at many California universities, and at the universities of New Mexico, Arizona, Colorado, and Texas. Hostos Community College and El Paso Community College have innovative bilingual-bicultural programs with an ethnic focus.

Among institutions offering Indian studies programs are Arizona State University, Northern Arizona University, the University of California at Berkeley, Adams State College, and the Universities of Minnesota and Southern Mississippi. Problems encountered in program formation are discussed by Buffalohead (1970). Illustrative curricula for Asian-American studies is available (Yoshioka, Hayashi, Lok, Ota, Sakai, Watanabe, 1973).

In the multiethnic sphere, some degree-granting institutions are California State College, Sonoma, Pepperdine University, Adams State College, Governors State University, St. Olaf College, and Northeastern State College (okla.). At Western Washington State College, ethnic studies majors are required to take a minimum of ten credit hours in cross-ethnic culture.

CURRENT CONTROVERSIES

Danforth (Black Studies Retrospect, 1972) states:

> Black studies continues to suffer—as does the nation—from the fact that the integrationist/segregationist question divides blacks as well as whites. . . . *No* institutional program in Black Studies is without its local critics, whether for "irrelevance" or for "Tom-ism," or for over- or under-politicization. (p. 10)

Ethnic studies proponents believe the study by minorities of their own heritages will enhance minority group identity, contribute to racial reconciliation, allow minorities to deal from a position of strength, and lead America to appreciate differences.

Opponents of ethnic studies fear festering group chauvinism could lead to polarization, fragmentation, and conflict. Some claim ethnic studies serves to perpetuate the racism it was designed to remedy (Bloom, 1971). There are objections to programs if the primary commitment is to race rather than to academic principles (Clark, 1969; Furniss, 1969).

Troublesome areas in black studies are identified by Epps (1973), and apply to other ethnic groups. Given the diverse goals and functions sought for black studies, Epps (1973) claims black studies must develop an academic focus, and notes, "A single program cannot adequately serve all of the socio-emotional, political and academic functions desired by students (p. 92)."

Academic standards are an issue, with critics claiming programs fail to achieve traditional performance standards. Advocates claim well-planned programs can be as academically valid as any other discipline, and that programs are needed to counter traditional anti-black bias.

Regarding separatism, some view white participation as interfering with communication among blacks, and feel whites cannot teach black studies effectively. Pragmatism has tempered many ethnic studies advocates into accepting the inevitability and desirability of including whites.

Another conflict focuses on control, with some spokesmen pleading for complete autonomy for programs and others arguing that black studies operate under regulations comparable to other disciplines.

Some minority educators claim ethnic studies are not sufficient preparation for careers, and would prefer that minority students study more job-related skills and professions. Others express confidence that college-educated ethnic studies students, similar to liberal arts majors, will be able to contribute to their communities in numerous fields. Ford (1973) notes the common practice of requiring double majors for ethnic studies, and suggests that ethnic education is an additional benefit

rather than a limiting factor.

Although ethnic educators disagree on many facets of ethnic studies, there is unanimity on the urgent need for training faculty and teachers, since lack of instructors plagues and often imperils programs. Further, all ethnic studies advocates agree that financing for relatively newly established ethnic programs may suffer in competition with the more established disciplines in institutions, due to the financial problems on campuses, concurrent with withdrawal of foundation support and lack of Federal initiatives (U. of Wisconsin, 1973). Other areas of agreement relate to the need to continue efforts to enroll larger numbers of minority students and to increase the quality and quantity of ethnic study materials.

REFERENCES

American Indians: An Annotated Bibliography of Selected Library Resources. Minneapolis: University of Minnesota, 1970.

Bengelsdorf, W. *Ethnic Studies in Higher Education: State of the Art and Bibliography.* Washington, D.C.: American Association of State Colleges and Universities, 1972.

Bibliografía de Aztlan: An Annotated Chicano Bibliography. San Diego: Centro de Estudios Chicanos Publications, 1971.

Black Studies Added. *The Christian Science Monitor,* February 19, 1970, 5.

Black Studies: How it Works at Ten Universities. New York: Academy for Educational Development, 1971.

Black Studies in Retrospect. St. Louis: The Danforth Foundation, 1972.

Black Studies: Perspective 1970. *Danforth News and Notes,* March 1970, 5.

Blassingame, J. W. *New Perspectives on Black Studies.* Urbana: University of Illinois Press, 1971.

Bloom, R. F. House Servant. *Community,* April 15, 1971.

Brown, R. C., Jr. New York University: The Institute of Afro-American Affairs. Black Studies in American Education, Yearbook 39, *The Journal of Negro Education,* 1970, 214-220.

Buffalohead, W. R. Native American Studies Programs: Review and Evaluation. *Indian Voices: The First Convocation of American Indian Scholars.* San Francisco: The Indian Historian Press, 1970, 167-190.

La Causa. *Publications List, 1972-1973.* Santa Barbara, Calif.: La Causa Publications, Inc., 1972.

Clark, K. B. A Charade of Power: Black Students at White Colleges. *Antioch Review,* 1969, *29,* 145-148.

Cleveland, B. Black Studies and Higher Education. *Phi Delta Kappan,* 1969, *51,* 44-46.

The College and Cultural Diversity: The Black Student on Campus. Atlanta: Southern Regional Education Board, 1971.

Colmen, J. G., and Wheeler, B. A. *Human Uses of the University, Planning a Curriculum in Urban and Ethnic Affairs at Columbia University.* New York: Praeger Publishers, 1970.

Drake, St. C. The Black University in the American Social Order. *Daedalus,* 1971, 833-897.

Dutton, J. E. Courses and Enrollment in Ethnic/Racial Studies. *Higher Education Panel Report.* Washington, D.C.: American Council on Education, 1973.

Education Amendments of 1971. Hearings before the Subcommittee on Education of the Committee on Labor and Public Welfare, United States Senate, Part 2. Washington, D.C.: U.S. Government Printing Office, 1971.

Epps, E. G. A Social Scientist Views Afro-American Studies Programs. *Achievement and Promise.* Greensboro, N.C.: Six Institutions' Consortium, 1973.

Ethnic Studies. *Intercultural Education,* 1970, *1,* 9.

Ford, N. A. *Black Studies: Threat or Challenge?* Port Washington, N.Y.: Kennikat Press, 1973.

Furniss, W. T. Black Studies and Civil Rights. American Council on Education *Special Report,* 1969, 9.

Gehret, K. G. Black Studies Gain Status on Campus. *The Christian Science Monitor,* March 6, 1969.

Geryk, R. *Polish Language and Polish Area Course Offerings and Instructors at Colleges and Universities in the United States.* Orchard Lake, Mich.: St. Mary's College, 1971.

Goldstein, R. L., Albert, J., and Slaughter, T. F. Jr. *The Status of Black Studies Programs at American Colleges and Universities.* Mimeo, 1972.

Interview with John Hope Franklin. *The Urban Review,* 1971, 5.

James, R. L. *Directory of Multicultural Programs in Teacher Education.* Washington, D.C.: American Association of Colleges for Teacher Education, 1971.

Jewish Studies in American Colleges and Universities. Washington, D.C.: B'nai B'rith Hillel Foundations, 1972.

Kennedy, J. F. *A Nation of Immigrants.* New York: Harper and Row, 1964.

Kolm, R. *Bibliography of Ethnicity and Ethnic Groups.* Washington, D.C.: U.S. Government Printing Office, 1973.

Lombardi, J. *Black Studies in the Community College.* Los Angeles: ERIC Clearinghouse for Junior Colleges, 1971.

McDaniel, R. R., Jr., and McKee, J. W. *An Evaluation of Higher Education's Response to Black Students.* Bloomington: Indiana University, 1971.

Multicultural Statement. American Association of Colleges for Teacher Education *Bulletin,* November 1972, *25,* 2, 6.

Pioneer course on Italian-Americans at the State University College at Buffalo. *Modern Language Journal,* May 1972, 330.

El Plan de Santa Barbara. Oakland, Calif.: La Causa Publications, 1969.

Sanchez, C. J. A Challenge for Colleges and Universities—Chicano Studies. *Civil Rights Digest,* 1970, 3.

Schatz, W. *Directory of Afro-American Resources.* New York: R. R. Bowker Co., 1970.

Schweiker, R. S. Schweiker Ethnic Studies Bill Passes Congress. Press release, undated, 1972.

Sievert, W. A. Ethnic Studies: Vanishing or Not? *Saturday Review of Education,* January 1973, 54.

Smith, W. D. Black Studies: A Survey of Models and Curricula. *Journal of Black Studies,* 1971, *1,* 259-272.

Stent, M. D., Hazard, W. R., and Rivlin, H. N. *Cultural Pluralism in Education.* New York: Appleton-Century-Crofts, 1973.

Studies in Ethnics Falling Off. *Washington Post,* October 8, 1972, G7.

Turner, D. T. The Center for African Afro-American Studies at North Carolina Agricultural and Technical State University. Black Studies in American Education, Yearbook 39. *The Journal of Negro Education,* 1970, 221-229.

U. of Wisconsin Halts Fiscal Aid to Black and Indian Student Centers. *The New York Times,* August 9, 1973, C19.

Urban Affairs Newsletter, June 1973, *5,* 40.

What's the Score on Black Studies? *Today's Education,* 1972, 62.

Wright, N., Jr. *What Black Educators are Saying.* New York: Hawthorn Books, 1970.

Yoshioka, R. B., Hayashi, P., Lok, K., Ota, A., Sakai, J., and Watanabe, C. *Asian-Americans and Public Higher Education in California.* Sacramento: California Legislature, 1973.

ADDITIONAL RESOURCES

Americans for Indian Opportunity, Inc.
1820 Jefferson Place, N.W.
Washington, D.C. 20036

The Balch Institute
1627 Fidelity Building
123 South Broad Street
Philadelphia, Pa. 19109

Bureau of Indian Affairs
U.S. Department of Interior Office of Educational Programs
1951 Constitution Avenue, N.W.
Washington, D.C. 20006

Center for Migration Studies
209 Flagg Place
Staten Island, N.Y. 10304

Center for the Study of Ethnic Pluralism
University of Chicago
Chicago, Ill. 60637

E. H. Butler Library
State University College at Buffalo
1300 Elmwood Avenue
Buffalo, N.Y. 14222

Martin Luther King Memorial Library
Black Studies Division
901 G Street, N.W.
Washington, D.C. 20001

Schomburg Center
103 West 135th Street
New York, New York 10030

Major Interest Groups, Associations, and Organizations

Afram Associates
National Association for African American Education Clearinghouse
68-72 East 131st Street
New York, N.Y. 10037

American Association of Colleges for Teacher Education
One Dupont Circle, Suite 610
Washington, D.C. 20036

American Association of State Colleges and Universities
One Dupont Circle, Suite 700
Washington, D.C. 20036

Aspira of New York, Inc.
296 Fifth Avenue
New York, N.Y. 10001

Centro de Estudios Chicanos
California State University, San Diego
San Diego, Cal. 92115

Conference on African and African-American Studies
Atlanta University
Atlanta, Ga. 30314

El Congreso Nacional de Asuntos Colegiales
Office of Spanish-Speaking Fomento
American Association of Community and Junior Colleges
One Dupont Circle, Suite 410
Washington, D.C. 20036

National Center for Urban Ethnic Affairs
4408 8th Street, N.E.
Washington, D.C. 20017

National Indian Education Association
1605 Pine Street
Stillwater, Minn. 55022

National Project on Ethnic America
American Jewish Committee
165 East 56th Street
New York, N.Y. 10022

98

THE STRUCTURE AND STATUS OF ENVIRONMENTAL EDUCATION

by Robert E. Roth
Associate Professor, Environmental Education
School of Natural Resources
Ohio State University
Columbus, Ohio

The last few years have seen widespread recognition of the critical role environmental education must play in the nation's educational life if environmental quality is to be effectively pursued. President Nixon emphasized that role on several occasions; in his introduction to the first annual report of the Council on Environmental Quality, in August 1970, he stated,

> The basic causes of our environmental troubles are deeply embedded. . . . It should be obvious that we cannot correct deep-rooted causes overnight. . . . We must seek nothing less than a basic reform in the way society looks at problems and makes decisions. Our educational system has a key role to play in bringing about this reform. It is also vital that our entire society develop a new understanding and a new awareness of man's relation to his environment—what might be called "environmental literacy." This will require the development and teaching of environmental concepts at every point in the educational process.

Similarly, the then Commissioner of Education, Sydney P. Marland, said: "Every educational mechanism and institution in our society is and must be involved in environmental education. . . ." Mr. Marland went on to state that environmental education is "education that cannot wait."

STRUCTURE

Environmental education is concerned with an individual's understanding of himself, his fellow man, the environment, and the interrelationships within and among each of these constellations of concern. A major goal is to encourage the individual to develop the ability to make thoughtful decisions which will create an environment that allows him to live a quality life. Specifically, environmental education is concerned with developing a citizenry that is:

knowledgeable about the biophysical and sociocultural environments of which man is a part;

aware of environmental problems and management alternatives of use in solving those problems; and

motivated to act responsibly in developing diverse environments that are optimum for living a quality life.

(Roth, 1969)

Thus it can be seen that environmental education is concerned with knowledge of the universe, society, and the individual, in that it not only attempts to provide the individual with environmental understandings, but also views him as a potentially creative being and encourages him to accept the responsibility of decision-making which is his by virtue of being human.

Another characteristic of environmental education is that it deals with attitudes, the attitudes people hold about themselves, toward other individuals and groups of individuals and toward their environment. These constellations of ideas greatly affect our level of living and quality of life.

Because environmental education is not just ecology, resource-use, sociology, art appreciation, philosophy, or management, an interdisciplinary focus is required that embraces the social sciences, humanities, science, and technology in like measure for purposes of developing cognitive understanding and belief and attitude change, and providing motivation for behavioral change and action.

A Model for Environmental Management Education

The concepts important to know for purposes of achieving the goals of environmental management education can be grouped into four categories: Biophysical, Socio-cultural, Environmental Management, and Change (Bowman, 1972). Each cluster of concepts exists on a continuum, and the four areas are represented as spheres on the model in Figure 1. The continuum works on the assumption that through increased understanding of the four conceptual schemes and their interrelationships higher-quality environmental decisions are possible. The conceptual core is applied through "Educational and Communication Processes," comprising a range from formal education to nonformal communication. The major goal described on the right side of the model is "Quality of Life," which can be interpreted as the individual's conception of "the good life."

The four conceptual schemes and related concepts are suggested as follows:

I. BIO-PHYSICAL: Living things are interrelated with one another and their environment.
   1. Green plants are the ultimate sources of food, clothing, shelter, and energy in most societies.
   2. An organism is the product of its heredity and environment.
   3. In any environment one component, like space, water, air, or food, may become a limiting factor.
   4. The natural environment is irreplaceable.

II. SOCIO-CULTURAL: The culture of a group is its learned behavior, in the form of customs, habits, atti-

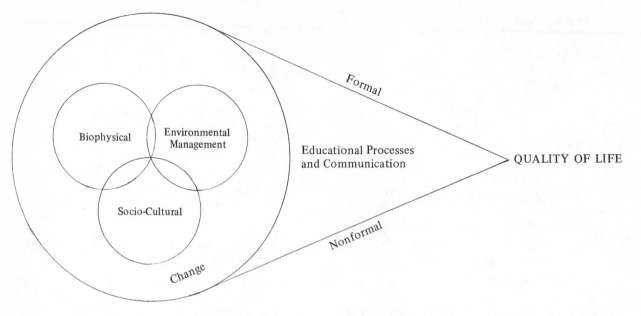

FIGURE 1. Environment Management Education

tudes, institutions, and lifeways that are transmitted to its progeny.

1. The relationships between man and the natural environment are mediated by his culture.
2. Natural resources affect and are affected by the material welfare of a culture, and directly or indirectly by philosophy, religion, government, and the arts.

III. MANAGEMENT: The management of natural resources to meet the needs of successive generations demands long-range planning.

1. Family planning and the limiting of family also are important, if overpopulation is to be avoided and a reasonable standard of living assured for successive generations.
2. Environmental management involves the application of knowledge from many different disciplines.
3. Management is the result of technical and scientific knowledge being applied in a rational direction to achieve a particular objective.

IV. CHANGE: Organisms and environments are in constant change.

1. The rate of change in environment may exceed the rate of organism adaptation.
2. All living things, including man, are continually evolving.
3. Man has been a factor affecting plant and animal succession and environmental processes.
4. Increasing human populations, rising levels of living, and the resultant demands for greater industrial and agricultural productivity promote increasing environmental contamination.

The preceding model is useful as a focus for further discussion and exploration, as a guide in the development

of environmental management education curricula, and as an organizer for continued research. The arrangement of concepts is suggested to be useful as a guide to the development of teaching strategies appropriate for the education of our citizenry in relation to environmental quality. Broadening the scope of understanding contained in the conceptual representation of each area should enable the individual to more knowledgeably select and control the way in which he lives and interacts with "spaceship earth."

STATUS

You ask: "Are we making any progress in the areas of teacher education, and in the development of a generation of environmentally literate citizens?"

The Facts for Teacher Education

Through the ERIC Center for Environmental Education, a questionnaire was sent to 900 four-year teacher education institutions to inventory the extent of environmental education programs and courses extant in the United States in 1973. The returns are coming in at the rate of 50 to 60 per week, with about 400 being returned so far.

Preliminary analysis of data indicates that of the 400 returns thus far processed, about 80 institutions indicated they had a course or program in environmental education. Of those indicating such a course or program, it seems likely that 25 to 30 percent could be categorized as offering only a course. Similarly, it should be pointed out that "outdoor education" was not specified by some that had such a course, but this kind of omission will be double-checked by examination of catalogs from each institution.

It can be concluded from this brief, and as yet incomplete, status survey that there are few programs in environmental education aimed specifically at preservice teacher education.

A second consideration is the status of teacher certification in environmental education. A survey conducted by Dr. Sigmund Abeles, of the Connecticut State Department of Education, inventoried certification in 47 states, and found that one state, Wisconsin, has secondary certification in conservation education, and none has it at the elementary level. In addition, seven states favor certification, while 23 oppose it, with 17 giving "no response" to the question. Three states indicate a separate course in environmental education, or ecology, as a requirement for elementary teachers: Montana, Oregon, and Wisconsin. Two indicate a course requirement at the secondary level, and those are Wisconsin and Oregon. Five states indicate interest in developing a course requirement as "supplemental" or "minor area" certification, and those are Washington, Nebraska, Oklahoma, Maine, and Illinois.

There is not very large acceptance of certification at the elementary or secondary level in environmental education. Many colleges and universities do offer a workshop or special course, on a more or less continuing basis, specifically for teachers. Similarly, NSF Institutes have made contributions to the education of science teachers about environmental science. Yet, in relation to the total number of teachers yet to be reached these efforts are small.

In relation to teacher education one must therefore conclude that we have *not* prepared a generation of teachers equipped to handle the content, attitudes, and skills requisite to developing an environmentally literate citizenry.

The Facts for School and Nonschool Environmental Education and Communication

The level of literacy about environmental issues and alternative management strategies is difficult to measure. Indicators do exist, and following are some that might provide the evidence we seek.

In a study conducted in late 1971 by Helgeson and Helburn, existing environmental education programs in public schools were analyzed. Results of the investigation indicated that there are relatively few operational programs in the United States, compared to either the number of school districts or, more significantly, to the number of school buildings. Programs designed for grades K-12 are few in number, while more programs do exist in either elementary schools or secondary schools.

Materials produced in relation to environmental education are extensive in amount, are available in both print and nonprint form, and are improving in quality. Most, however, do not appear to be interdisciplinary, and often lack concepts related to the social sciences or humanities. Similarly, urban-oriented materials are few in number, and most city schools have not developed materials oriented to their milieu.

Analyses of most programs being developed, and those which have been developed, indicate that a single person often was responsible for initiation of the pro-

gram, and has provided the drive for program continuance. The more successful programs have involved teachers, administrators, and citizens in the community, with some staff time assigned for coordination of the program and for inservice work with teachers.

Another attempt to promote environmental education at the Federal level was enactment of Public Law 91-516, The Environmental Education Act. An "office" was created, and funding was obtained at the levels of $1.7 million for 1971, $3 million in 1972, and an estimated $3.1 million for 1973. With this money 74 project were funded in 1971 and 162 in 1972. However, the amounts originally sought for these three years were $5 million, $15 million, and $25 million. A renewal of the Act was sought with a funding level of about $4 million for 1973-1974. The 1975 attempt is comparable to the levels originally sought.

The mass media continue to produce a mix of good and not-so-good program specials on environmental topics. Reaction seems to be one of general interest, with heightened interest on some topics like National Parks and various crisis issues, e.g., Energy. Similarly, based on preliminary analysis of a National Assessment of environmental concepts and attitudes held by 10th and 12th grade children from a 10 percent sample of students around the country, it would seem that many attitudes are now held that could lead to greater support for environmental improvement. Bowman (1972) measured attitude shift in a large enrollment environmental management course at Ohio State, and found a significant shift toward societal control, controlled use of technology, and population stabilization.

In summary, the "environmental literacy" level is perhaps a bit higher in relation to crisis-oriented issues like population, energy, water, and air pollution, but lower in terms of support when dollars must be spent to solve the problems. The "EQ Index," distributed by the National Wildlife Federation, would seem to support this contention because of some gains in the renewable resource areas and losses in the nonrenewable categories. Overall we are a bit ahead, with much progress still to be achieved.

CONCLUSION

Now the Question: "Are we making any Progress?" A qualified "yes," with:

slow, regressive gains in the areas of curriculum development and balanced program development;

modest gains in teacher education, but much work remaining to be achieved in the form of program development and certification considerations;

considerable progress in materials development, with a strong need for urban-oriented and social science/humanities-related activities;

a wide array of media approaches to environmental issues that generally receive considerable viewer audience; and

impetus from the Environmental Education Act at the

Federal level, but with modest promise of future effectiveness.

Environmental management education is directed at modifying man's attitudes toward his world—both the world of nature, from which he derives and inherits his responses, and the world which he is creating. As his attidues are reflected in informed democratic processes, both in the polling both and in the marketplace, man must recognize that whatever happens or is not permitted to happen to his world can be substantially influenced by a majority vote. Speaking realistically, this "vote" by each individual man, woman, or child is determined by his or her attitudes toward self, toward others, and toward the quality of life for all. This means that we must encourage self-respect, respect for our fellows, and respect for the living earth.

REFERENCES

Abeles, Sigmund. Teacher Certification in the U.S. *ERIC EE Newsletter*, Vol. 3, no. 3.

Bowman, Mary Lynne. *The Development and Field Validation of An Instrument to Assess College Students' Attitudes Toward the Determinants of Environmental Issues.* Unpublished Ph.D. Dissertation, 1972. The Ohio State University, Columbus.

ERIC/Smeac. Analysis of Exemplary Environmental Education Programs and Courses in U.S. Teacher Education Institutions. The Ohio State University. In Progress, 1973-1974.

Roth, Robert E. *Fundamental Concepts for Environmental Management Education (K-16).* Unpublished Ph.D. Dissertation, 1969, University of Wisconsin, Madison.

Environmental Quality. The First Annual Report of the Council on Environmental Quality. U.S. Government Printing Office, 1970.

99

TEACHING ENGLISH AS A SECOND LANGUAGE

by Michael Morrisroe, Jr.
Professor, University of Illinois
Chicago, Illinois
and
Margaret Sue Morrisroe
Teacher, Maine Township High School, West
Des Plaines, Illinois

The phrase "teaching English as a second language" refers to a teaching situation in which English is the language of instruction in the school system but the student is not a native speaker of English. English is presented to a student who speaks his own native language and is learning English as a second language because English is the language of the country in which he is living. The typical situation in the United States is found in the teach-

ing of English to immigrants, citizens of Spanish American origin, and American Indians. But analogous situations might be found in the teaching of English in the Philippines and India. In the Philippines, English is the language of instruction. The native language of the people, however, is not English. In India there are many languages spoken by the natives, but English exists as a common second language among speakers of the various languages.

It is important to understand the distinction between teaching English as a second language and teaching English as a foreign language. English taught as a foreign language is English taught as a school subject, or as an adult learning project, for the purpose of acquainting a student with the language of another country and helping him gain confidence in that language. The confidence which one normally gains in such a teaching situation is the confidence needed to read technical works or literature, or to listen to a radio, or understand motion picture dialogue. Conversation may be taught, but there is no day-to-day communication within the foreign country. Teaching English as a second language is usually defined as the teaching of English within a country in which English is an important language spoken by most or all of the population, and taught to the non-native speaker in order that he may better become acquainted with the country in which he is living. The teaching of English as a second language takes place today throughout the United States and the British Commonwealth in thousands of schools. The level of sophistication in the school systems varies widely, but English as a second language is taught in all grade levels, from the primary grades through graduate schools. The number of students learning English as a second language exceeds 100 million.

In the United States, public awareness of the teaching of English as a second language is a relatively new phenomenon. It was as late as 1961 that the National Council of Teachers of English published *The National Interest and The Teaching of English As A Second Language.* This pamphlet constitutes the first substantial publication to point out clearly the new American involvement with the teaching of English as a second language. Since 1961, a tremendous number of books, pamphlets, and short notes have been published in the general area of teaching English to non-native speakers. Unfortunately, as a recent study shows (Morrisroe, 1972), much of what has been published has not had proper scientific parameters, nor have the authors taken serious account of the scientific method. A critical evaluation of what has been published in the field of teaching English as a second language must include a sharp division between publications which are essentially scientific in their approach and publications which, although at times interesting and helpful, are essentially nonscientific.

The single largest body of research has been in the area of the relationship of reading ability to oral English instruction. Linguists have argued that because speech is primary, children should speak a second language before they begin to learn to read it. This theory has been the basis for a variety of experiments on all grade levels. For example, Naum Dimitrijevec (1965) taught English as a second language to two groups composed of 80 children each. One group received a 12-week oral introduction to English before it began to learn to read. A second group was introduced simultaneously to reading and speaking English. The children learned pronunciation by reading aloud. One disadvantage of learning pronunciation by reading aloud was that the children heard the incorrect pronunciations of their classmates. Also, they neglected the meanings of words in their attempts to correctly pronounce words. To the contrary, the students in the oral-introduction group developed fluency because they were already familiar with pronunciation. All students were tested by taping and evaluating a reading sample. The conclusion of Dimitrijevec's test concurs with the linguistic theory that those who first learn orally will learn more quickly and accurately. The groups in which oral training preceded reading scored higher on the tests than the groups in which speaking and reading were started simultaneously.

The widely held theory that students should be trained intensively in the phonemics and graphemics of English before they study the morphological and syntactical levels was examined in an analogous experiment (Estarellas and Regan, 1966). The study posed the question whether students should learn to read and write only after they have had training in listening and speaking. There were two sections of students: a control group, that learned English by an audio-lingual method, using tapes but no written text, and another group, which used written material coordinated with audiotape recordings. After the learning period the students were given an achievement test, with sections on writing, stress, syllabification, linking, intonation, and reading. Achievement of the experimental group was substantially superior. As the authors pointed out, appropriate materials and appropriate teaching-learning processes, involving intensive instruction of sounds and letters, presented simultaneously, does not hinder the student's progress. To the contrary, it may well accelerate the learning process. Consequently, the fashionable linguistic theory was challenged.

Another interesting study (Cooper, 1964) examined the effects of oral English instruction on first-graders in Guam. It was found that exposing Chamorro-speaking children in four elementary schools to up to a year of conversational English in the first grade was not reflected in their reading skills three years later. There was no reflection of improved reading skill in the fourth grade in those who had been exposed to one year of conversational English in the first grade. The article is interesting. It had, however, several weaknesses, the most glaring of which was the failure of the experimenters to obtain a contrastive analysis of the native language (Chamorro) and English. Such an analysis, which normally pairs English with the native language phonomically, morphomically, and syntactically, was necessary to judge whether or not there were any significant changes in the children's abilities.

Current theory in the field of teaching English as a second language conflicts with the basal-reader approach. One carefully controlled experiment (McCanne, 1966) that must be mentioned was that conducted in 15 state districts in Colorado on 249 Spanish-speaking first-graders. The results of this study show the superiority of a basal-

reader approach. The purposes of the experiment were two. First, researchers wanted to test the hypothesis that there would be no difference in English reading achievement in first grade children who speak Spanish at home and are taught (a) conversational English readiness and a basal-reader approach, (b) a modified teaching English as a second-language approach, or (c) a language-experience approach. Second, researchers wanted to obtain data to determine what specific sequence of skills is appropriate for first grade Spanish-speaking children learning to read English. Further, they wished to identify the appropriate materials and techniques for teaching those skills. Twenty-nine teachers in 21 schools participated. The results of the tests showed nothing unfavorable about the use of a combination of teaching English as a second language and the language-experience approaches at the preschool and kindergarten levels. The authors recommended that these techniques be used at the first-grade levels as supplemental approaches for language skills other than reading.

In the United States, the largest single group of non-native speakers of English is the Spanish-speaking population. Many of the studies done in the field of English as a second language are done in the Southwestern states. One of the most interesting of these was an experiment with Spanish-speaking children on the first-grade level in San Antonio, Texas, under the direction of Thomas D. Horn, of the University of Texas, Austin (1966). As reported elsewhere (Stemmler, 1966), the experiment used materials whose content supposedly did not reflect the value systems of any particular culture or group, and consequently would be equally difficult for children from all social classes or ethnic groups. The researchers chose science as their "culture fair" content. The children were taught English by an audio-lingual technique based on comparative phonology. Seven hundred thirty-five children from 28 first grade sections of nine San Antonio schools were used. Three groups were established: (1) Oral-Aural English, (2) Oral-Aural Spanish, and (3) no Oral-Aural instruction. Each day the students worked with the "culture fair" science materials. One group received instruction in English, one group in Spanish, and one group used the same materials but had no intensive language instruction. The conclusions drawn from the experiment are important. No significant differences between the test scores of the students in each of the three groups were discovered. The need for developing suitable measures for assessing the capabilities, background, cognitive functioning, and language levels of Spanish-speaking children is the most significant implication that can be drawn from the research.

The government of the United States is interested in educational attempts to deal with the Mexican-American reading problem. Government grants have led to many experiments. Unfortunately, most of the experimentation has not been carefully controlled. One experiment (Werner, 1966) relating to the oral teaching of English was conducted in the Shiprock Boarding School on the Navajo reservation in Arizona, New Mexico, Colorado, and Utah. The experiment attempted to determine if the use of the oral-aural approach to teaching English as a second language might prove effective with the Navajo children. The project exemplifies the tremendous difficulty that researchers have in maintaining a controlled situation, especially on a large scale. Reservation boarding schools have highly mobile populations. The children move frequently from school to school.

Another difficulty which the researchers had was that the teachers on the reservations were not particularly interested in new techniques of teaching English as a second language. The students were given oral-aural approach to English. They were tested after their learning experience by the Stanford Achievement examination, and results indicated that the oral-aural approach would benefit the Navajo children. In this particular instance, however, as in so many others, the modes of testing, the statistical reviews of empirical data, the number of uncontrolled variables, and the general lack of control throughout the experiment do not permit any but the most tentative of conclusions.

The whole area of testing in the teaching of English as a second language is open. Very little has been done in a constructive way to either evaluate the teaching of English as a second language or to evaluate the tests which attempt to do these evaluations. At a five-day conference in May 1967, at the University of South Dakota, a list of several primary problems of the field were published (Osborne, 1968). One of the major problems talked about at the conference was the lack of development and lack of validation of diagnostic tests in the areas of speaking and listening behavior. Few steps have been taken to overcome testing problems.

One of the brighter areas within this testing problem is the report given at Indiana University (Arterburn, 1968) from an extremely important experiment. The researchers examined at length the hypothesis that there is such a factor as overall proficiency in a second language, or that such proficiency may be measured by testing a subject's ability to send and receive messages under varying conditions. They examined white noise (such as static) and an interference pattern (which blocked out the voices) to see if they affected the communication of a group of messages. Both native speakers and non-native speakers were subjects. They found that their proficiency test could be used for testing only advanced students. The test was too difficult for students below the intermediate level. It was found that all tricks should be eliminated on tests of this sort, and that there should be an accurate and constant mixing of the signal with the noise. The researchers implemented this last suggestion in other tests, wherein white noise was mixed electronically with English sentences. The test is an efficient way of screening subjects with high and low efficiency.

An attempt to develop tests was also made at the Navajo area agency (Briere, 1968). Under a government grant, a series of short achievement tests was developed to help teachers determine whether their students were learning English (and at what rate). The researchers attempted to devise a test based on the textbook used in the Navajo schools. They determined when vocabulary items were introduced and what the objectives of the textbook were, and then they devised a number of tests. The first test gave, on tape, a Navajo stimulus to which

the children were to respond. The second test gave directions in Navajo and asked questions in English. The third test was a mimicry test (calling for a mechanical parroting of utterances). The results of the tests led the researchers to dismal conclusions. The children responded like robots. This is particularly important insofar as one of the complaints against teaching English as a second language by patterns is that children taught by this method are not able to break out of the patterns in order to speak naturally later. Many of the tests have reflected a feeling of futility about teaching English.

Students of English as a second language in the United States are in a peculiar position. Unlike American students of a foreign language, they hear the second language spoken around them each day. They are often forced to speak it in order to function in society and in school. These facts dictate something about teaching methods and materials. Three questions arise: (1) is formal foreign instruction useful for students living and working in that environment? (2) Is sequential mastery of materials in a language course necessary? (3) Is sequential mastery of materials possible? One study (Upshur, 1968) proposed the hypothesis that English language learning is not related to the amount of instruction given to the students living in an English language environment. It posed the hypothesis that for students living in our country the mastery of course materials is in no way related to mastery of subsequent materials in an English course. One of the startling conclusions was that a group of language learners who had been taught course materials will not perform any better on a test of later course materials than a group who had not been taught the earlier materials. The conclusions of the study are four: (1) Courses in a second language may not be as effective as a means of teaching language as using the language in other activities might be. (2) Presentation and drill of sets of sentences do not teach the underlying structure of sentences. (3) Second language learners should not be expected to produce and interpret sentences in the order the sentences were presented. (4) Second language placement tests using sentences, but not testing the students' knowledge of underlying sentence structure, cannot show the examiners which sentence type has or has not been taught. This constitutes another attack on the teaching of English sentence patterns, and it is similar to that found in the Navajo experiments mentioned above.

The whole problem of whether English should be taught as a second language in a regular classroom or in a special classroom cannot be resolved. One study (Boucher, 1968) examined an unnamed city where 49 percent of the students came from homes where only Spanish was spoken. A group that had no help in learning English and a group that received English as a second language instruction were compared. Groups given special instruction outside or inside the classroom learned more quickly. Groups which had no specific language instruction scored substantially lower than others.

The area of reading is currently receiving the most attention and most serious research in the second language field. This is reasonable, since in Texas in 1963 as high as 80 percent of non-native speakers failed the first grade

(Stemmler, 1966). The Bureau of Indian Affairs reports (Traill, 1968) that by upper elementary or high school Indian students are two to four grades below national norms. Research in the reading area seems more carefully controlled, and is on a broader base, than other research in the English as a second language field. The question arises: How do current texts in English as a second language teach reading?

The following generalizations can be made. Almost all the books use the meaning approach in the teaching of reading. The comprehensive skills taught in the books are at the literal comprehensive level. Vocabulary in each book is carefully controlled, as is grammar and sentence structure. Teachers are given little or no suggestions or instructions in the books about how to teach from the texts. The content in most books is clearly dated, and for the most part boring. One conclusion stands out clearly in the examination of the commonly used texts: there is a need for additional reading materials, and for good teacher guides to accompany them, in the field of English as a second language. One possible suggestion that may resolve the problem of the need of good reading materials is the use of remedial reading materials. Remedial reading texts used for native speakers of English are frequently of good use to teachers of English as a second language. As a discipline, reading is a neglected area in the English as a second language field. The emphasis has been placed on the oral aspects of language. This is an understandable reaction against the years of language teaching where students learned to read but never really learned to communicate in a foreign language. What is now needed is a balance between the oral and written areas. There is a need for materials which are in the middle of the spectrum, where reading, listening, speaking, and writing are taught as part of a balanced curriculum.

Further information on the subject of teaching English as a second language is available from the national organization of Teachers of English to Speakers of Other Languages. Address correspondence to James E. Alatis, Executive Secretary, TESOL, School of Languages and Linguistics, Georgetown University, Washington, D.C.

REFERENCES

Allen, H. B. *Teaching English as a Second Language*. New York: McGraw-Hill, 1965.

Arnold, R. D. English as a Second Language. *The Reading Teacher*, 1968, *21*, 634-639.

Arterburn, C., Sato, M., Sigurd, B., Spolsky, B., and Walker, E. Preliminary Studies in the Development of Techniques for Testing Overall Second Language Proficiency. *Language Learning*, 1968, *18*, 81-96.

Boucher, C. R., and Krear, M. L. A Comparison of Special Programs of Classes in English for Elementary School Pupils. *The Modern Language Journal*, 1967, *51*, 335-337.

Briere, E. J. Testing ESL Among Navajo Children. *Language Learning*, 1968, *18*, 11-21.

Ching, D. C. Methods for the Bilingual Child. *Elementary English*, 1965, *42*, 22-27.

Cooper, J. G. Effects of Different Amounts of First Grade Oral English Instruction Upon Later Reading Progress with Chamorro-Speaking Children. *The Journal of Educational Research*, 1964, *43*, 123-127.

Croft, K. *Readings on English as a Second Language*. Cambridge, Mass.: Winthrop Publ. Inc., 1972.

Dimitrijevec, R. Teaching Reading of English as a Foreign Language. *English Teaching Forum*, 1965, *3*, 16-20.

Dimitroff, L. Small Group Training for Spanish-Speaking Pupils. *Chicago Schools Journal*, 1963, *45*, 65-71.

Estarellas, J., and Regan, T. F., Jr. Effects of Teaching Sounds and Letters Simultaneously at the Very Beginning of a Basic Foreign Language Course. *Language Learning*, 1966, *16*, 173-182.

Gardner, R. C., and Lanbert, W. E. Language Aptitude, Intelligence, and Second Language Achievement. *Journal of Educational Psychology*, 1965, *56*, 191-199.

Horn, T. D. Three Methods of Developing Reading Readiness in Spanish-Speaking Children in First Grade. *The Reading Teacher*, 1966, *20*, 38-42.

Vernon, J. J. Effects of Childhood Bilingualism, I. *Elementary English*, 1962, *39*, 132-143.

_____. Effects of Childhood Bilingualism, II. *Elementary English*, 1963, *39*, 358-366.

Kloss, H. *The American Bilingual Tradition*. Rowley, Mass.: Newbury House Publishers, 1971.

Lane, H. Experimentation in the Language Classroom. *English Teaching Forum, I*, 1963, *1*, 3-8.

Lugton, R. C., ed. *English as a Second Language: Current Issues*. Philadelphia: Center for Curriculum Development, 1971.

McCanne, Roy. Approaches to First Grade English Reading Instruction for Children from Spanish Speaking Homes. *The Reading Teacher*, 1966, *19*, 670-675.

Morrisroe, M., and Morrisroe, S. TESL: A Critical Evaluation of Publications, 1961-1968. *Elementary English*, 1972, *49*, 50-61.

Osborne, L. R. Speech Communication and the American Indian High School Student. *The Speech Teacher*, 1968, *17*, 39-42.

Pimsleur, P., and Quinn, T., eds. *The Psychology of Second Language Learning: Papers from the Second International Congress of Applied Linguistics, Cambridge 1969*. New York: Cambridge University Press, 1971.

Ramsey, R. M., Riegel, K. F., and Riegel, R. M. A Comparison of First and Second Languages of American and Spanish Students. *Journal of Verbal Learning and Verbal Behavior*, 1967, *6*, 536-544.

Smith, P. D. Jr. *Toward a Practical Theory of Second Language Instruction*. Philadelphia: Center for Curriculum Development, 1972.

Stemmler, A. O. An Experimental Approach to Teaching of Oral Language and Reading. *Harvard Educational Review*, 1966, *36*, 42-59.

Thompson, H. Teaching English to Indian Children. *Elementary English*, 1966, *43*, 333-340.

Traill, A. Concerning the Diagnosis and Remedying of Lack of Competence in a Second Language. *Language Learning*, 1968, *18*, 253-258.

Upshur, J. A. Four Experiments on the Relation Between Foreign Language Teaching and Learning. *Language Learning*, 1968. *17*, 111-124.

Werner, R. E. An Oral English Experiment with Navaho Children. *Elementary English*, 1966, *43*, 777-784.

Yoes, D., Jr. Reading Programs for Mexican-American Children of Texas. *The Reading Teacher*, 1967, *20*, 313, 318, 323.

100

NONSTANDARD ENGLISH AND DIALECTS

by Karen M. Hess
Project Director
Innovative Programming Systems, Inc.
Minneapolis, Minnesota

Once upon a time the teaching of English was as traditional and as predictable as the beginning of a fairy tale—and as unrealistic. Students were taught to read and write "good" English. Errors in grammar were cause for correction and even ridicule. Students diagrammed sentences and memorized the parts of speech to "learn" their native language. The dictionary, the grammar book, the English teacher—these were the authorities which prescribed acceptable and proper English. Anything which deviated from this prescription was a corruption of the language.

Times have changed for some students, but not for all.

TOPIC SCOPE

During the past few decades authorities on language (linguists) have adopted a new vantage point: They have become descriptive rather than prescriptive, delineating what occurs in the language rather than what should be occurring. This change in vantage did not go unnoticed or unchallenged, as testified by the reception of Webster's *Third New International Dictionary,* published in 1961, which was clearly descriptive rather than prescriptive. The negative reaction throughout the country was evident in such newspaper headlines as:: "Saying 'Ain't' Ain't Wrong: See Webster," "100,000 Words Become Legal," "The Death of Meaning," "It Ain't Good," "Good English Ain't What We Thought," "A Non-Word Deluge," "Say it Ain't So," "Logomachy—Debased Verbal Currency," "Sabotage in Springfield," and "New Dictionary Cheap, Corrupt" (Sledd and Ebbitt, 1962). Everyone knew there was no such word as "ain't," but suddenly there it was—in the dictionary. The dictionary was no longer the prescriber of what was "pure and good," it was the describer of how people actually were using the language.

The research resulting from this descriptive perspective has revealed that much of what was commonly thought to be true of language is not true. It has led to changes in the way language differences are viewed and the way they are approached in the classroom. It has also led to controversies regarding whether the way an individual speaks should be tampered with, and how and when a standard English should be taught to students.

REVIEW OF THE LITERATURE

Common Misconceptions Dispelled

A common misconception about dialects is that a dialect is a corrupt form of the English language spoken by uneducated or ignorant people. But research has demonstrated that a dialect is simply a variety of a specific language.

Just as everyone who drives a car drives a specific kind of car, say a VW or a Mercedes, everyone who speaks a language speaks a specific variety of that language—a dialect. And, just as an individual can own more than one car, an individual can speak more than one dialect. Further, the way an individual speaks his dialect will set him apart from all other speakers of the dialect (you can identify someone you know simply by hearing him talk). This unique, individualistic way of speaking is called his "idiolect." The idiolect was learned because there was a need for that manner of speaking—a person learns the dialect spoken by those around him. He needs this dialect to communicate with people who are important to him. The dialect he acquires is directly influenced by where he lives and what social groups he belongs to.

A linguist uses three variables to classify dialects: The words used (lexicon), the way they are pronounced (phonology), and the way they are structured into sentences (grammar). Each of these differences must be considered in any program which attempts to teach a standard English dialect to students.

A second common misconception is that there is one "standard" English in the United States. In reality there are several regional standard dialects of American English. The standard dialect of any language is a variety of the language most commonly used by the majority of educated people. What is standard can and does change. (Recall that automatic transmissions became "standard" equipment when they were requested by the majority of car buyers.)

Anyone traveling in the United States would observe the language differences among speakers in the North, the South, and the East. General descriptions of these regional dialects have been reported in Allen and Underwood's *Readings in American Dialectology* (1971), Furbee's *The Study of Dialect* (1969), Shuy's *Discovering American Dialects* (1967), and Reed's *Dialects of American English* (1967). Tapes such as *American Speech Dialects,* or records such as *Americans Speaking,* offer samples of the speech used in different regions. Regional differences in language have become widely accepted, and do not generally carry significant social stigma.

A third misconception is that an individual who does not speak one of the regionally standard dialects of English speaks a corrupt or substandard form of English. The prefix "sub" means "below" or "inferior." A stick-shift is not substandard; it is simply not standard, i.e., nonstandard. Even this term may, unfortunately, carry negative or derogatory overtones, but it is more objective and descriptive than other terms which have been used to label differences from a standard dialect.

A descriptive perspective of language avoids value judgments; it does not declare one dialect as better, or more melodious, or more correct, or more functional, than another dialect. If a dialect does not fall within the parameters of one of the regional standard dialects, it is labeled as nonstandard, with no negative connotations intended.

Closely linked to the misconception that variations from the standard dialects are substandard English is the erroneous belief that speakers of nonstandard dialects are deficient in language skills.

If a speaker of a standard English were to travel to France, it would be unreasonable (and unjust) to call him deficient in language if he could not communicate with an individual speaking French. The traveler is not deficient in language, he merely speaks a *different* language. Technically, he could be described as "deficient" in French, but the negative implications of such a statement would serve no useful purpose. It is truer to say he speaks a different language.

This is also true of a speaker of a nonstandard dialect. He is not deficient in language. He merely speaks a dialect which is different from the standard. Technically, he could be called "deficient" in a standard dialect, but not in language skills. In fact, the speaker of a nonstandard dialect may perceive the speaker of a standard English to be deficient in language:

> A judgment of deficiency can be made only in comparison with another language system. Let's turn the table on Standard English for a moment and look at it from the West African point of view. From this angle, Standard English: (1) is lacking in certain language sounds, (2) has a couple of unnecessary language sounds for which others may serve as good substitutes, (3) doubles and drawls some of its vowel sounds in sequences that are unusual and difficult to imitate, (4) lacks a method of forming an important tense, (5) requires an unnecessary number of ways to indicate tense, plurality and gender, and (6) doesn't mark negatives sufficiently for the result to be a good strong negative statement.
> Now whose language is deficient?
> (Seymour, 1971, p. 178)

In spite of linguistic evidence, the deficiency-versus-difference debate continues. The position which is adopted has direct relevance to when instruction in a standard English begins, as well as to the methods used in teaching it.

Another misconception is that nonstandard dialects are illogical, careless, unsystematic, and nonfunctional. Linguistic investigations, however, have demonstrated that every dialect is a structured, consistent, patterned, well-ordered, valid language system, with its own rules, and the system functions adequately among those who communicate with it (Hess, 1972). Although an individual speaker of a dialect may not consistently use all the rules or patterns of his dialect, just as a speaker of a standard dialect may not, the dialect itself is a valid linguistic system.

Implications

Because standard and nonstandard dialects have been shown to be logical, valid language systems, functional for those who speak them; and because an individual's dialect is an integral part of his personality, and a reflection of his regional and social ties; all dialects should be accepted and respected. Acceptance of and respect for the way an individual speaks is particularly important in the schools. As Dorothy Strickland (1970) notes:

> The school, and particularly the teacher of language arts, must accept the language which the learner brings to school. It is doubtful that these children will accept the language of the school if the school does not accept their language. Teachers must refrain from referring to students' speech as careless or wrong. (p. 17)

The literature on dialects and dialect instruction repeatedly emphasizes the overriding importance of attitudes toward language and the acceptance of language variety.

A Dilemma

Research has provided the basis for accepting and respecting dialects which differ from the standard, but research has also demonstrated that the dialect one speaks is used by others to make judgments about the speaker—a reality which must be acknowledged by educators (Hess, 1972). It is a social reality that some dialects are considered more valuable than others in specific contexts. As Marckwardt (1971) states:

> Those who have urged the establishment of a functional bi-dialectalism as part of the school language program have been charged with hypocrisy and sometimes worse. . . . In general, however, these attacks have been uninformed and naive. Some of them restate positions which any competent student of the language already holds. This is especially true of those who insist that all dialects possess equal value and have an equal right to their existence as media of communication. As far as I know, no linguist has ever called this into question, but no linguist in his right mind could possibly say that all have equal prestige, and there is little point in insisting upon the self-deception that they do. (pp. 33-34)

Additionally, certain dialects are used in the academic, economic, and political affairs of the country, and others are not—another reality which must be acknowledged by educators.

The diversity of dialects spoken by the children in our schools, and the most effective approach to instruction, pose a special challenge to concerned educators. Should speakers of nonstandard dialects learn a standard dialect? Research would indicate that they should, but there are many who contest this. If the decision is reached to teach a standard English, the question "How?" must be addressed.

SPECIFIC PROGRAMS AND APPLICATIONS

Nearly all programs which are effective in teaching a standard English to speakers of nonstandard dialects share certain features:

> They provide evidence of linguistic knowledge about nonstandard dialects.

The tone is objective and nonperjorative.

The intent is to add a standard dialect to the speaker's repertoire, not to correct or replace the nonstandard dialect.

The specific features of the nonstandard dialect which differ from a standard dialect are identified and dealt with contrastively, i.e., the standard and nonstandard ways of saying a word or phrase are shown to be two different ways of expressing the same thing.

The student is provided with ample opportunity to practice the standard forms orally.

Among the materials and programs which have been developed, several are worthy of careful examination by educators seeking to institute a program for teaching a standard English in their schools.

Dialect of the black American. With the assistance of linguist William A. Stewart, Western Electric has prepared a recording which presents general information about black dialects, provides numerous examples of its clarity and communicability, and illustrates the interference which black dialect may cause, especially in a job-interview situation.

English Now. Based on his work in Teaching English as a Second Language (TESOL), Feigenbaum (1970), of the Center for Applied Linguistics, has developed an extensive series of lessons for practicing standard English features. These lessons include tested oral pattern practices and discrimination practice materials for black nonstandard speakers in grades 7 through 12. The self-instructional, self-correcting, workbook-text has 14 programmed lessons, each concentrating on a specific phonological or grammatical feature commonly found in nonstandard speech. The lessons are not intended to correct or eradicate the speech of the nonstandard speaker, but rather to add a second dialect. An accompanying teacher's manual provides a commentary on each lesson, as well as suggested classroom activities.

Developing Language Programs for Young Disadvantaged Children. Yonemura (1969) provides linguistically sound discussions of language and attitudes toward language variations, as well as many workable suggestions for establishing dialect programs. Numerous materials especially suitable for small children are contained. This text is based on two years of research at Abbott House in New York, where Yonemura developed oral language programs applicable to Harlem English, Pidgin English, Creole English, nonstandard forms of Appalachian English, and other varieties of nonstandard language used throughout the country.

Standard Oral English. Cockrell and Johnson (1967), Hernandez (1967), and Wilson (1967) collaborated on an oral language program intended for use with black students who speak a nonstandard English. The program includes guides which present general background information on dialects, motivational materials, pronunciation, and usage lessons, with an analysis of those features which

cause interference, an outline of the main characteristics of black dialect, general teaching suggestions, and a bibliography.

English: Target Series. Robinett and Bell (1968) have written three books for junior-high students which contain information on dialects and a variety of language activities concentrating on important linguistic features, reading, composition, and oral language skills. The intent is to improve the students' ability to use a standard American English dialect in both speaking and writing. The orientation is additive rather than corrective or remedial.

Syracuse Oral Language Development Program. This program attempts to teach the oral communication skill of auditory discrimination, and to provide experiences in language expression and comprehension. The major objective of the program is to develop an awareness of standard English usage as a tool for communicating feelings, ideas, and experience (Lissitz and Cohen, 1970).

The Psycholinguistic Oral Language Program: A Bi-Dialectal Approach. This program, developed by the Board of Education of the City of Chicago under the direction of Leaverton (1968), is intended for Afro-American children in the elementary grades who speak a nonstandard English. The language to be used is described as "School Talk" or "Everyday Talk." The materials are based on the additive approach to dialects, and include many pattern drills, followed by dialogues, written exercises, and other classroom activities.

A comprehensive summary of promising materials and programs for dialect instruction is included in the *Basic Report: Teaching a Standard English to Speakers of Nonstandard Dialects* (Hess, 1972).

CURRENT CONTROVERSIES

Different versus Deficient Language

The debate as to whether nonstandard dialects are different or deficient linguistic systems has been alluded to. Despite research findings to the contrary, numerous references to "language deficient" children can be found in the literature on dialects. This view is most fully articulated by Bereiter and Engelman (n.d.), who view the child as coming to school functionally without language, at least without a language which will suffice for academic learning. Children therefore must be taught a wide range of concepts such as color, spatial relationships (up, down, over), and numerical classifications, as well as such verbal concepts as tense, number, and conditionality.

The majority of linguists and educators, however, contend that speakers of nonstandard dialects are *not* language deficient; they simply speak a different dialect. A forceful statement against the deficiency theory is posited by Labov (1969), who calls the theory wrong and corrupting. He contends that such an approach to language tends to become a self-fulfilling prophecy.

Another straightforward attack on the deficiency

model is contained in "It's Either Brain Damage or No Father: The False Issue of Deficient vs. Difference Models of Afro-American Behavior" (Valentine, 1969). A case study of a black child who was hastily diagnosed and institutionalized as brain damaged, retarded, and psychotic was used to illustrate the point that distorted notions of deficient and different Afro-American subculture have led white psychologists and guidance counselors to incorrectly diagnose behavior in black children based on the dialect they speak.

Wolfram (n.d.) summarizes the arguments on both sides of the issue, and concludes that the literature to date would indicate that nonstandard dialects are different, not deficient, linguistic systems.

Should a Standard English Dialect be Taught?

The "relativistic" view of language, which stresses that all dialects are acceptable and worthy of respect, has presented a dilemma which was alluded to earlier. Several educators and linguists now contend that, based on research results, students should be allowed to use their language, whatever dialect it might be, and that educators should not attempt to teach a standard dialect to individuals who speak nonstandard English. Most vocal on this issue is Sledd (1969), who describes the realities of why bi-dialectalism is difficult:

> The basic assumption of bi-dialectalism is that prejudices of middle-class whites cannot be changed but must be accepted and indeed enforced on lesser breeds. Upward mobility, it is assumed, is the end of education. But white power will deny upward mobility to speakers of Black English, who must therefore be made to talk white English in their contacts with the white world. . . . (p. 1309)

> The bi-dialectalist, of course, would not be so popular with government and the foundations if they spoke openly of the supremacy of white prejudice; but they make it perfectly clear that what they are dealing with deserves no better name. No dialect, they keep repeating, is better than any other—yet poor and ignorant children must change theirs unless they want to stay poor and ignorant. (p. 1310)

The major arguments set forth by those who oppose the teaching of a standard English are: it is morally wrong; it may be psychologically damaging; it may alienate nonstandard speakers from their subculture; it may not result in better jobs or greater social opportunities; and it may be a form of racism, compelling speakers of nonstandard dialects to conform to a standard which is not consistent with the cultural pluralism the United States presumably values. They further contend that it is not really possible to teach students a second dialect, or at least it is not an efficient use of time in school. Efforts directed toward achieving bidialectalism could more profitably be spent on developing the child's capability to use his own dialect and to read in a standard English.

The majority of educators and linguists, however, feel it is imperative that students be provided with the opportunity to learn a standard English as an additional dialect, to use when the need arises (Hess, 1972).

The major arguments which recur in the literature favoring the teaching of a standard English are: standard English is helpful economically; standard English facilitates communication; and learning a standard English is not racist.

One forceful attack on those who advocate not teaching a standard English was presented by McNeil (1969):

> Withholding educational advantages from a disadvantaged child is a subtle form of discrimination and prejudice. Regardless of the terminology used to discuss the rationale for this approach, I perceive that it is a classic example of deluded professional thinking which is condescending, degrading, and particularly damning for disadvantaged youth. (p. 4)

Whether learning a standard English will open doors to the nonstandard speaker is not certain. Nevertheless, the weight of informed opinion, the stated wishes of parents and students, and the appearance of the economic and social situation suggest that there is value in learning a standard English.

How Should a Standard English be Taught?

Should the student learn a standard English in place of his nonstandard dialect or as an addition to his nonstandard dialect? The first approach is to correct, change, replace, or remediate the nonstandard dialect. Advocates of the corrective approach contend that it is extremely difficult to become bidialectal; therefore, it is hypocritical to attempt to provide an alternative language which students can use when needed. Early corrective training in a standard English is more often advocated by those who adhere to the language deficiency theory.

The majority of educators, however, contend that correction, change, replacement, and remediation are not the best approach. Attempting to replace nonstandard English is frequently a contributing cause to alienation of the minority student. The direction indicated by H. Allen (1967), that an additive or bidialectal approach is the most fruitful avenue to follow in teaching a standard English, is representative of several educators and linguists:

> Although there are still those persons who seem to advocate a ruthless replacement of the nonstandard variety by standard, the weight of evidence from psychology and linguistics as well as from the related discipline of teaching of English as a second language, argues rather that standard English should be taught to these people as a second dialect without prejudice to their first dialect. The goal is addition, not substitution. (p. 2)

The additive approach has been described in a variety of terms: Bidialectalism or the second dialect approach, augmentation, alternative dialect, expansion, conservation, bi-loquialism, supplemental dialect, and diglossia. The essence of the additive approach, no matter what it is technically called, is summed up by Troike's (1968) statement that in language learning it must be made clear to the child that the choice of dialect is a matter of social appropriateness and expediency, rather than one of right versus wrong or good versus bad.

A striking example of the need for an additive approach was provided by a black woman who had become bidialectal:

I said to myself, "If this second language is so great, I'm going to use it all the time." So, I went down the street every morning saying, "Good morning. How are you? How are you feeling?"–being very particular about what I was saying and how I was saying it. The neighbors told my husband I was stuck up.

Now, I go down the street saying, "Hi, how you doin'?" and they all love me. I now reserve my second language for office use and for my 2-year-old son. (They talk their way . . ., p. 2)

Although this woman clearly valued her newly learned dialect, she nevertheless needed her nonstandard dialect to fit comfortably into her neighborhood.

When Should Students be Taught a Standard English?

The opinions on this question are varied. Several linguists and educators contend that teachers should begin to teach a standard English as early as possible. Troike (1968) summarizes the major arguments for early instruction:

To the oft-repeated objection that the first-grade child is too innocent of the social world around him to appreciate the significance of dialect differences, I can only reply, "Nonsense." We should not wait until the child is six to begin that training, for by then he will have lost the four most crucial years in the language-learning process, but rather we should start working with children at the ages of two and three, in order to help them achieve the fullest development of their linguistic capabilities. When we realize that most academic casualties are made before the first grade, we can't afford to wait. There is no time to lose. (p. 2)

Others advocate waiting until the upper elementary grades, but starting before adolescence. Malmstrom (1970) suggests that the teaching should be accomplished in the elementary school, since the ability to learn a language "like a native" freezes at adolescence. Lenneberg (1967) presents evidence that primary acquisition of language is predicated upon a developmental stage which is quickly outgrown at the age of puberty: "Between the ages of three and the early teens the possibility for primary acquisition continue to be good . . . after puberty . . . it quickly declines (p. 158)."

Still others contend that teaching a second dialect should not begin until the student enters secondary school, and has the maturity to decide whether he wants or needs to learn a standard English. Feigenbaum (1969) states that it is not until secondary school that students are aware of social appropriateness; if a student is too young to understand appropriateness, teaching a standard English and when to use it will be very difficult, and perhaps fruitless.

The literature on when to teach a standard English is not easily interpreted. There are strong arguments for beginning early; there are equally strong arguments for waiting until at least the upper elementary grades or even the junior high school grades.

WHERE TO FIND MORE INFORMATION

In addition to the references cited at the conclusion of this article, new information on the topic of teaching English as a second dialect is continuously disseminated by three major sources:

The National Council of Teachers of English
1111 Kenyon Road
Urbana, Illinois 61801

The Center for Applied Linguistics
1611 North Kent Street
Arlington, Virginia 22209

The *Florida FL Reporter* (a language education
801 N.E. 177th Street   journal)
North Miami Beach, Florida 33162

A comprehensive synthesis of over 1,500 current documents dealing with the topic of dialect and dialect instruction, including bibliographies in several specific areas, is also available (Hess, 1972).

REFERENCES

Allen, H. B. Expanding Frontiers in Dialect Study. Paper presented at the annual convention of the National Council of Teachers of English, Honolulu, 1967. ED 021 837

____, and Underwood, G. N., eds. *Readings in American Dialectology*. New York: Appleton-Century-Crofts, 1971.

American Speech Dialects. Resource Center, Division of Instructional Media, Texas Education Agency. (Tape)

Americans Speaking. National Council of Teachers of English. (Record)

Bereiter, C., and Engelman, S. Language Learning Activities for the Disadvantaged Child. New York: Anti-Defamation League of B'nai B'rith. ED 020 002

Cockrell, W., and Johnson, K. R. Standard Oral English, Tenth Grade: Instructional Guide C. Report no. LACS-Pub-ESEA-3-4, 1967, Los Angeles City Schools, Division of Secondary Education, California. ED 027 351

Dialect of the Black American. A community relations presentation. Western Electric Company. (Record)

Feigenbaum, I. Using Foreign Language Methodology to Teach Standard English Evaluation and Adaptation. *Florida FL Reporter*, 1969, *7*(1), 116-122, 156-157.

____. *English Now*. New York: New Century, 1970.

Furbee, N. L. The Study of Dialects. In A. L. Davis, ed., *American Dialects for English Teachers*. Urbana: ISCPET, May, 1969.

Hernandez, L. F. Standard Oral English; Seventh Grade: Instructional Guide B. Report no. LACS-Pub-ESEA-3-2, 1967, Los Angeles City Schools, Division of Secondary Education, California. ED 027 354

Hess, K. M. *Basic Report: Teaching a Standard English to Speakers of Nonstandard Dialects*. St. Ann, Missouri: CEMREL Institute, 1972.

Labov, W. The Logic of Non-Standard English. *Florida FL Reporter*, 1969, *7*(1), 60-75, 169.

Leaverton, L. et al. Psycholinguistic Oral Language Program: A Bidialectal Approach. Experimental Edition, Part 1. Chicago: Chicago Board of Education, 1968. ED 034 970

Lenneberg, E. H. *Biological Foundations of Language*. New York: John Wiley and Sons, Inc., 1967. ED 015 480

Lissitz, R. W., and Cohen, S. L. A Brief Description and Evaluation of the Syracuse Oral Language Development Program. *Reading Teacher*, October 1970, *24*(1), 47-50.

Malmstrom, J. Teaching Linguistically in Elementary School. *Florida FL Reporter*, Spring/Fall, 1970, *8*(1 and 2), 31, 48.

Marckwardt, A. H. The Concept of Standard English. In *The Discovery of English*, National Council of Teachers of English Distinguished Lectures. Urbana: National Council of Teachers of

English, 1971.

McNeil, S. Stop the Bad Trips with Language Arts Accountability in the Megalopolis. Paper presented at the National Council of Teachers of English Convention, Washington, D.C., 1969.

Reed, C. *Dialects of American English.* Cleveland: World Publishing, 1967.

Robinett, R. F., and Bell, P. W. *English: Target Series.* New York: Harcourt, Brace and World, 1968.

Seymour, D. Black Children, Black Speech. *Commonweal,* 1971, *95*(8), 175-178.

Shuy, R. W. *Discovering American Dialects.* Urbana: National Council of Teachers of English, 1967.

Sledd, J. Bi-Dialectalism: The Linguistics of White Supremacy. *English Journal,* 1969, *58*(9), 1307-1315.

_____, and Ebbitt, W. *Dictionaries and That Dictionary.* Chicago: Scott, Foresman and Company, 1962.

Strickland, D. S. Black is Beautiful vs. White is Right. Paper presented at the National Council of Teachers of English Convention, Atlanta, 1970.

They Talk Their Way into Jobs. *Manpower* Magazine, April 1969, U.S. Department of Labor, Manpower Administration.

Troike, R. C. Social Dialects and Language Learning: Implications for TESOL. *TESOL Quarterly,* 1968, *2*(3). ED 024 036

Valentine, C. A. It's Either Brain Damage or No Father: The False Issue of Deficit vs. Difference Models of Afro-American Behavior. Paper presented in part at the annual American Psychological Association Convention, Washington, D.C., September 1969. ED 035 707

Wilson, M. Standard Oral English; Seventh Grade: Instructional Guide A. Report no. LACS-Pub-ESEA-3-3, 1967, Los Angeles City Schools, California. ED 027 353

Wolfram, W. An Appraisal of ERIC Documents on the Manner and Extent of Nonstandard Dialect Divergence. (no date) ED 034 991

Yonemura, M. *Developing Language Programs for Young Disadvantaged Children.* New York: Teachers College Press, 1969.

101

BLACK ENGLISH: THE STRUGGLE FOR LEGITIMACY

by Ray C. Rist, Ph.D.
National Institute of Education
Washington, D.C. 20208

It has only been within the last decade that the argument for the distinctiveness of the language used by most black people in the United States has been granted a positive, though tenuous, acceptance. Yet today there are many who argue that the English used by many black people is not distinctive, is not unique, and therefore is not properly categorized as a separate dialect within the family of dialects comprising the English language. The evidence gathered by linguists, sociologists, and anthropologists, however, is increasingly persuasive in substantiating the presence of a distinctive dialect for black Americans.

THE FOCUS OF THE DEBATE

Writing on the circumstances surrounding the emergent study of Black English, Dillard (1972, 6) has noted:

> Significant research on Black English in the United States is almost entirely a product of the 1960's. In this decade a group of linguists, freed of preconceptions about the geographic provenience of American dialects, have shown that Negro Non-Standard English is different in grammar (in syntax) from the Standard American English of the mainstream white culture. They maintain that there are sources for varieties of English elsewhere than in the British regional dialects. Like the West Indian varieties, American Black English can be traced to a creolized version of English based upon a pidgin spoken by slaves; it probably came from the West Coast of Africa—almost certainly not directly from Great Britain. Some dialects of American English, then, did not follow the route of the Mayflower.

It is possible to extend this argument further, by suggesting the examination of Black English has emerged concurrent with the demands of blacks for a reinterpretation of their history, culture, and place in American society. For too long, the perspective of Black America was one created by whites to fit with their own misconceptions; in short, the description of black America first had to be filtered through layers of white racism.

Traditionally, the perspective on Black English has been one in which Black English is described as an incomplete, inadequate, and bastardized form of the standard English spoken by whites. Often, the description of the language of black people was a part of a more general perjorative description of black life in general. Assuming an incomplete, inadequate, and imitating mimic of white culture, the description of the "deficient" culture of blacks became a justification for subjugation at the hands of whites. But as black people have come to challenge vigorously such assertions about the absence of vitality and wholeness in black culture, they have not ignored the traditional descriptions of their language.

Central to an examination of Black English is the ongoing work being done to ascertain the degree to which Black English demonstrates similarities and linkages to languages spoken in Africa and the former slave ports in the Caribbean and South America. The stronger the demonstrated linkages to such languages, the most suspect becomes the argument that Black English is an incomplete or "restricted" version of the English coming from the British Isles. To grant African linkages is to acknowledge the presence of cultural traits possessed by the black independent of what has been "given" by the white. Such an admission of cultural diversity strikes at a central tenet of white racism: that a black person is an incomplete and therefore deficient version of the white.

The cultural origins of Black English appear to have several distinct phases. The first phase results from the experience of slavery. It is well known that slave traders sought to maintain their control by mixing together slaves of different languages, so as to minimize communication and possible collective resistance. This mixing forced slaves to develop a communication system independent of any one specific African language. The developing language (referred to as Pidgin) was able to serve as a means to communicate across various linguistic systems. There emerged several varieties of Pidgin—Portuguese, French, and English. Each developed as a result of peripheral contact with the language of the master. Both the English and French variations of Pidgin were present in the United States, reflecting the differences between, say, Louisiana and South Carolina. Over time, the presence of new generations meant the increased use of the Pidgin and only selective use of African words and phrases. (It should be noted that many of these Pidgin varieties of English are still in use today, as with Louisiana French Creole and Gullah, spoken on the Sea Islands off the coast of Georgia and South Carolina.)

The second developmental stage in Black English emerged as black people began to experience more direct and continuous contact with whites through a variety of settings—economic, political, and social. The significance of these settings was not that blacks and whites were meeting as equals—far from it—but that blacks were conversing with whites and learning portions of the English used by whites. The third and fourth stages of the development of the dialect of English currently spoken by most blacks involved respectively the influence of urbanization and mechanization in the South and the migration and concentration of large numbers of black people in the North. Throughout, the continuity of the developing language was maintained. Words, phrases, concepts were added or discarded as the circumstances changed. But each succeeding stage carried with it significant portions of those preceding stages. As Seymour (1971, 177) has noted:

> Is it really possible for old differences in sound, structure, and vocabulary to persist from the West African languages of slave days into present-day inner-city Black English? Easily. Nothing else really explains such regularity of language habits, most of which persist among black people in various parts of the Western Hemisphere. For a long time, scholars believed that certain speech forms used by Negroes were merely leftovers from archaic English preserved in the speech of early English settlers in America and copied by their slaves. But this theory has been greatly weakened, largely as the result of the work of a black linguist, Dr. Lorenzo Dow Turner, of the University of Chicago. Dr. Turner studied the speech of Gullah Negroes, in the Sea Islands off the Carolina coast, and found so many traces of West African languages that he thoroughly discredited the archaic-English theory.

Such a perspective on the emergence of Black English necessitates the recognition that Black English is not some bizarre or exotic language, but a language that is in use by large numbers of people every day, as are any number of other languages on the earth. It helps to structure perspectives on reality, gives expression to beliefs and values, and provides the means by which culture is transmitted from one generation to the next. These are functions all languages serve. The deprication and unwillingness to recognize the coherence of the language spoken by most black people reflects not on the utility of the language, but on the instance of whites to maintain a cultural hegemony, and thereby define what is appropriate and acceptable for everyone according to cultural standards of whites. What this implies is that not black people alone, but all minority groups (and their cultures) in the United States, have been slighted and categorized as "deficient" when compared to prevailing white normative standards.

BLACK ENGLISH AND THE SCHOOLS

The current debate and controversy surrounding Black English is nowhere more accurate than in relation to its use in schools. A brief outline of the argument on using Black English in the schools will be offered. By focusing on the relation of Black English in the schools, we are deliberately bypassing a discussion of the syntactical structure of Black English (cf. Dillard, 1972; Haskins and Butts, 1973; Labov, 1968; Steward, 1968), as well as a more protracted discussion of the relation of Black English to other English dialects (cf. Dillard, 1972; Engelmann, 1968; Seymour, 1971). What follows draws on the works of Baratz (1970), Baratz and Shuy (1969), Dillard (1972), Inclan (1972), Kobrick (1972), Rist (1972), and Steward (1969, 1970).

Consider the following exchange (quoted from Seymour, 1971):

> "Cmon, man, les git goin'!" called the boy to his companion.
> "Dat bell ringin'. It say, 'Git in rat now'!" He dashed into the school yard.
> "Aw, f'get you," replied the other. "Whe' Richuh? Whe' d' muvvuh? He be goin' to schoo'."
> "He in de' now, man!" was the answer as they went through the door.
> In the classroom they made for their desks and opened their books. The name of the story they tried to read was "Come" It went:
> Come, Bill, come.
> Come with me.
> Come and see this.
> See what is here.
> The first boy poked the second. "Wha' da' wor'?"
> "Da' wor' *is*, you dope."
> "*Is*. Ain't no wor' *is*. You jivin' me? Wha' da' wor' mean?"
> "Ah dunno. Jus' *is*."

This exchange represents one of the profound contradictions inherent in the current pedagogical arrangements of American public education. Children who speak one language are required to learn through another. Where black children who come to school speaking Black American English are not allowed to use that dialect, but instead must function with Standard American English, the stage is set for massive failure at worst, and only slow, grueling learning at best.

The situation of black children who speak Black American English, and are necessarily forced to use Standard American English in the classrooms, does not arise solely from pedagogical ignorance. There are many, black teachers and parents included, who view Black American English as a "bad" language, as "street talk," or as "ghettoese." Many assume Black American English is sloppy, incomplete and inadequate; therefore, it is not to be tolerated in classrooms. (In my own research, I have found black teachers who told the speakers of Black American English, "Shut your mouth until you learn to talk right.") The consequences of this approach can be anticipated. The child may come to feel his language is "bad," while that English primarily identified with whites is viewed as "good"; he may extrapolate to his culture in general, and come to believe black life is unacceptable and white culture is desirable; he may simply withdraw, to avoid the humiliation of being told his language is "deficient"; or he may become defiant, and respond, "F'get d' honky talk."

But if what was argued in the first part of this paper is correct, the approach of denying the legitimacy of Black American English essentially reduces itself to a denial of the viability of a cultural system which is meaningful and utilized by millions of people. Whether the rejection is couched in terms of the "restricted" nature of the culture and language, or in terms of the isolation of the system from the standardized language of the dominant society, or as a product of lower class life, the end result is the same. A value decision is made about what is "good" or what is "bad," and the dialect of Black American English ends up being labeled as "bad." Such a decision is independent of the fact that those who use the dialect find it meaningful and fulfilling of their cultural expressions.

Consider this alternative outlined by Seymour (1971, 178):

> Linguists have made it clear that language systems that are different are not necessarily deficient. A judgment of deficiency can be made only in comparison with another language system. Let's turn the tables on Standard English for a moment and look at it from the West African point of view. From this angle, Standard English (1) is lacking in certain language sounds; (2) has a couple of unnecessary language sounds for which others may serve as good substitutes; (3) doubles and drawls some of its vowel sounds in sequences that are unusual and difficult to imitate; (4) lacks a method of forming an important tense; (5) requires an unnecessary number of ways to indicate tense, plurality, and gender; and (6) doesn't mark negatives sufficiently for the result to be a good strong negative statement.
>
> Now whose language is deficient?

The point is well made. There is an inevitable relativity to all language and cultural systems. Thus, any evaluative statement implies the speaker has a norm against which the language or culture is being measured. Black American English has been judged inferior vis-à-vis Standard American English, and is thus to be avoided. Yet such an evaluation, besides being arrogant, does not solve the situation of thousands of black children in public schools—it only tries to avoid it.

IS THERE A WAY OUT?

If one is willing to accept the dictum, first posited by John Dewey, that the learning experiences of the child in school should mirror as closely as possible those in the home, there is an obvious imperative for change in the current modus operandi of public schools serving black children speaking Black American English. So long as significant groups of black children continue to use Black American English as their mother tongue, the schools must necessarily respond, or perpetuate the current schisms.

An alternative approach, which appears to have a generally favorable consensus among linguists and educators interested in this issue, is that of teaching standard American English. Black American English would be the major communication system within the classroom, and Standard American English would be gradually learned as one would learn any language different from one's own. The Educational Study Center, in Washington, D.C., headed by William Stewart, has sought to carry this proposal to its logical end by not only teaching standard American English as a second language, but also teaching reading to black children who speak Black American English in that same dialect. Thus the children are learning to read their own dialect as well as that of Standard American English. They are becoming bidialectical.

The goal of bidialecticalism is to allow the child the opportunity to use either as he chooses to do so. By building on the dialect he already knows, and then showing him the similarities and differences between his dialect and others, he is able not only to understand his own better, but also to gain the understanding of another. The imperative is to equip the black child with Standard American English without denigrating the vernacular that is his own. The end result would be individuals who could use either dialect equally well—as did Dr. Martin Luther King, for example—depending upon the circumstances in which they find themselves.

Bidialecticalism can give the black child an option not available if he remains only monodialectical. To wit, Standard American English is the lingua franca of the mainstream American society. As Baratz (1970, 417) has noted:

> If the black child is to participate and compete in that mainstream, he must be able to read, write, and speak standard English. If he wishes to opt out of the mainstream and not use these skills, that's his choice; he can make it. If, however, he does not learn these skills, he can not "choose" to opt out. He is automatically excluded.

I would only add a note of caution here. It would be erroneous to conclude from Baratz that the reason black people currently receive so little of the material benefit of this society is because they have all chosen to opt out. I would think it more accurate to say they have been frozen out. Linguistic barriers are not equivalent to racist barriers. Further, simply giving speakers of Black American English the use of a second dialect, standard American English, does not guarantee employment, decent housing, and educational opportunities. It only means that one small obstacle to achieving those goals is removed. The major obstacles to black advancement remain those created by whites.

It may well be asked whether black people will want to learn Standard American English when they see that white racism does not diminish because of a change in black speech patterns. Why should black cultural patterns give way to white ones if there is no payoff for doing so? Dillard (1972, 294) has addressed himself to this issue:

> There always remains the possibility . . . that the Black community, disenchanted with pretenses as desegregation, and with the white man's attempts—futile and weak even on the part of liberals—to bring about social justice, may stop seeking

to adjust itself to mainstream (white) culture. In that case, the teaching of standard English to Black speakers may be rejected no matter what the method. And in that case a new use of Black English as a vehicle of education will become imperative. It seems inescapable that the black community has the right to make its own choice, particularly in view of the white community's poor record of accomplishment in Negro education in the past decade.

Dillard is correct. If whites do not give up their racism, and are only willing to accept "oreo's" into mainstream society, then blacks have a moral and cultural imperative to resist. No people should be forced to strip themselves of their heritage and culture to become acceptable. No other people should be so arrogant as to demand they do so.

RESEARCH AND PROGRESS

With the increased interest in Black English, the amount of research and instructional programs oriented toward coping with its analysis and transmittal has greatly grown. Research is being conducted at the Educational Study Center, in Washington, D.C.; at the Center for Applied Linguistics, in Washington, D.C.; at the Southwest Regional Laboratory, in Austin, Texas; and at the School of Education, Florida State University. Programs seeking to implement research findings and translate them into viable classroom curricular materials are located at School District One, in New York City; the Center for Applied Linguistics, in Washington, D.C.; the Tallahassee, Florida Public School System; the Boston, Massachusetts Public School System; and the Los Angeles Public School System. Other cities and states are working through their departments of education to initiate programs in bilingual education.

REFERENCES

Baratz, J. Should Black Children Learn White Dialect? *Asha,* 1970, *12,* 415-417.

———, and Shuy, R., eds. *Teaching Black Children to Read.* Washington, D.C.: Center for Applied Linguistics, 1969.

Dillard, J. L. *Black English.* New York: Random House, 1972.

Engelmann, H. O. The Problem of Dialect in the American School. *Journal of Human Relations,* 1968, *16,* 524-531.

Haskins, J., and Butts, H. *The Psychology of Black Language.* New York: Barnes and Noble, 1973.

Inclan, R. Can Bilingual-Cultural Education be the Answer? *Educational Horizons,* 1972, *50,* 192-195.

Kubrick, J. The Compelling Case for Bilingual Education. *Saturday Review,* 1972, *55,* 54-58.

Labov, W. The Non-Standard Negro Vernacular: Some Practical Suggestions. In *Position Papers from Language Education for the Disadvantaged.* Report No. 3 of the NDEA National Institute of Advanced Study in Teaching Disadvantaged Youth, June 1968.

Rist, R. C. Black English for Black Schools: A Call for Educational Congruity. In Rist, R., ed., *Restructuring American Education.* New Brunswick, N.J.: Trans-Action Books, 1972.

Seymour, D. Z. Black Children, Black Speech. *Commonweal,* 1971, *19,* 175-178.

Stewart, W. Continuity and Change in American Negro Dialects. *Florida Foreign Language Reporter,* 1968, *6,* 3-14.

———. On the Use of Negro Dialect in the Teaching of Reading. In Baratz, J., and Shuy, R., eds. *Teaching Black Children to Read.* Washington, D.C.: Center for Applied Linguistics, 1969.

———. Current Issues in the Use of Negro Dialect in Beginning Reading Tests. *Florida Foreign Language Reporter,* 1970, *8,* 9-15

102

LISTENING

by Elizabeth Pflaumer
Assistant Professor
Department of Speech Communication
Northern Illinois University
DeKalb, Illinois

DEFINITION OF LISTENING

Listening is the process of using and synthesizing combinations of perceptive sense modalities (interacting) to facilitate communication. Listening involves the total being, not just the ears. The listening "apparatus" includes complicated attitudes, emotions, prejudices, and values.

Since the central nervous system controls the pathways off all sense modalities (optical, audial, tactile, olfactory, and salivary), and since in a living organism all senses are normally functioning interactively, we must synthesize in order to decode, evaluate, and interpret reception.

In normal functional operation, senses can be said to facilitate input sensitivity, rather than inhibit communication, since without these receptor devices communication would certainly be inhibited. These modalities do not necessarily act, except as receptors, and hence are involved in the integral receptive end of the communication event. This is at any given moment of stimulation, rather than as a dimension isolated. In order to have listened, or done any part of the above, that which was heard must have been used.

THE SCOPE OF LISTENING

It is this process of using and synthesizing that is under speculation, rather than the physical mechanisms facilitating the process. It is for this reason that attitudes and desires, degrees of involvement, abstract and organizational ability, reality, alertness, and logicality—versus emotional passivity, perceptivity and introspectiveness, standards of toleration, and satisfaction—are considered integrally in the process of listening.

With this general definition of the process of listening, one can look at much of the listening material available and see that very little attention has been given to more than an assumption of the word's meaning. Rather, many studies are concerned with isolating components of listening, principles of listening, kinds of listening, "good" or "bad" listening, and methods of improving and measuring listening. One can see only a hazy, implied area of consensus on just what is listening.

Listening may have more than one type of system or methodology of listening within it, depending upon the given needs and situation at a particular time. There seems to be an intercommunication system which is used more frequently by some listeners than by others (Pflaumer, 1968, 1970).

What factors and categories distinguish types of listeners? How do listeners become acquainted with intercommunication? Are there inherited tendencies, or is their system developed and adapted? Are there those listeners whose needs are completely met without extended effort? What kinds of people are they? Is their system of education in need of readaptation to better serve the needs of its students? Does intelligence and education vary with kinds of listeners?

How do listeners A and B communicate with each other, and with C? Do they necessarily have to mutually compromise or adjust? Or can they more conveniently balance and counterbalance each other's adaptations? How are time and distance, speed, and availability and qualifications involved? What impressions and attitudes sensorily facilitate this subsystem of listening? How is aid given to the handicapped, or is there anything done? How is feedback improved or inhibited? Are there choices in process of listening? Is listening demonstrable and enforceable? What conditions of climate or atmosphere are conducive to good or effective listening? What reinforcements are there? It seems that there is an infinite number of questions that for the most part are unanswered.

REVIEW OF RECENT LITERATURE AND DEVELOPMENTS

Reviewing the literature reveals many studies and attempts to teach listening, but they generally reveal, upon posttesting, very little significant change in habit or practice of listening over time. Obviously a number of psycho-socio-anthropological studies would need to be conducted to complete the analysis of people in order to program the approach to education and rehabilitation necessary to improve listening.

It is generally known that about four times as much research has been conducted in the area of reading as has been conducted in the area of listening. It can be established that listening, reading, and speaking are related facets of verbal learning. Much time and emphasis are spent in education on the area of reading—somewhat less on "English," or speaking—and very little is devoted to listening. It has been agreed that certain IQ, psychological-emotional readiness, and motivation (or "will to learn") aspects are necessary to accomplish learning. We have "reading readiness tests" and "reading preparation exercises," reading adjustment, and reading instructors—even speed reading. Therefore, could it be posited that there eventually will be developed listening readiness tests, listening preparation and adjustment, listening instructors, and speed listening? Ultimately it will be imperative, in meeting the needs of the future hypertensive

education, activity, social interaction, and competition, in our civilization.

Currently work in the area of compressed speech concurs with previous conclusions that still hold ". . . the barrier to the comprehension of fast rates of speech appears to be within the information processing capacities of the listener, and not in the fidelity of the time compressed signal. In short, the problem is primarily due to human, not equipment, shortcomings (Sticht 1969, 1970)."

While there is a growing accumulation of materials related and useful to the study of listening, there is a strong need to do much more. There is evidence in the research studies of a need for viable measurement devices. Research at this point indicates that there is no single technique that universally gives valid and reliable information.

Theoretical expectancies include the following areas for question and further exploration, at least:

1. Theory: That a listening personality may be modified, at least superficially, to meet the individual's needs in particular areas and times of life, i.e., as a student, or as a trained person on a job, while overall tendencies remain stable. This, at the moment, is still unknown, and would seem only remotely available after training intensely focused on effective listening.

2. Theory: That an individual's listening style may be picked up early in childhood, and change only with obtuse changes in personality life style. This seems possible, but at the moment tests are yet to be constructed to measure over time. Difficulty would seem to arise in predicting those who would sustain obtuse personality changes, should such occur.

3. Theory: That age, education, and station may not be directly influential, or provide any major alterations in the individual's modified and adapted listening personality. It would seem fundamentally contingent to first achieve measurable modified listening personality, but it might also be predicted as having some probable merits.

4. Theory: That physical health and psychic motivation may both be interrelated to the amount of effort and success an individual achieves or directs to listening. Theoretically this would seem to have some probabilities of truth. And it would seem vital in focusing toward a designing of a program of instruction.

5. Theory: That changing an individual's attitudes or self-concept, if possible, may activate major changes in his listening ability.

6. Theory: That an individual's listening habits may be cyclic, and effort exerted only as needed to meet the demands made upon him as a listener in various situations. Davitz (1964) included two studies concerned with possible correlates of the ability to identify vocal expressions of emotional meanings. The first deals with personality variables, the second with perceptual and cognitive variables. This deals in part with demands and motivations, but there is very little on the implications of individual cyclic rhythms correlated to

listening effectiveness. Perhaps *Biofeedback and Self-Control 1972,* an Aldine Annual on the regulation of bodily processes and consciousness, could provide foci for conjecture here.

7. Theory: That one's listening effectiveness may directly relate to his measure of attitude toward himself, or his self-concept and self-respect. In other words, self-expectancy is confirmative.

Having studied the listener and the person in process, one might project a further need to study the "environment" and the "product" (consequent significant fit) in creative, scientific research on listening.

SPECIFIC PROGRAMS AND APPLICATIONS

If little has been said thus far about specific programs and applications, it is due to the infancy, rather than sophistication, of programs in application. A variety of programs have been developed in the past few years. They are cited as examples, rather than as model approaches or programs.

Dr. Belle R. Witkin is directing an Auditory Perception Training Project within the Alameda City School District, Hayward, California (1969). Dr. Arnold Abrams has developed a new student orientation program that includes a listening course at the Thomas Nelson Community College, Hampton, Virginia. A number of instructional programs have been developed using audio tapes. McGraw-Hill has produced a program created by Ella Erway, titled *A Programmed Approach to Listening.* Xerox Corporation has developed a program, *Effective Listening Skills.* Dun-Donnelley, A Dun and Bradstreet subsidiary, has a course developed by Dr. Ralph Nichols titled *A Complete Course in Listening.*

A great deal of a listener's success may depend upon his ability to decode and interpret his system's reporting realistically. There is a dual listening system within the best listeners as coveted ideals. One system is internalized, in that it is developed within the individual and is a personal and introspective code—almost a semi- or subconscious listening system. The other system is externalized. It is consciously outer-directed and deliberative. Clearly the listener is more than just a passive thing, a radar screen to pick up the message to be decoded.

One can readily see a similarity of ideas surrounding a core concept which serves as a relevant foundation of the personality approaches to creative listening. This core concept deals with the aspects of internalization, both by definition of terms and by process of integration. One must consider the person to be the basic definer of auditory dissonance. Every person, by the mere repetition of living, orders the experience(s) into his own system of filing and information retrieval. The accessibility provides multiple mental concepts, potential frames of reference, and contexts upon which he bases future experience.

The context upon which the individual bases future experience also constitutes certain expectations of fulfillment, which are either reinforced or cancelled in further intake. Its implications would seem to relate centrally to the fact of integral contingency involved between personality and listening correlates. Listening and person-

ality must incorporate an allowance, or toleration, for the process and dynamics of change. Provision must be made for such intermediary processes as thinking and feeling, to create change or response (evidence of listening). The correlates of listening and personality must, of necessity, be considered both singly and corporately, and also applied in the process of personalization, to achieve change or response in behavior or learning.

That people are creative as listeners and as individuals is evident by their uniqueness. Perception—the ability to follow the process of release (amputation) inherent in creativity—and intuition are both creatively receptive. Perceptive intuition may be considered a sensitive subsystem of internalized listening, and combined with another, somewhat more externalized, subsystem. Reason will resolve a basic understanding of the process of listening. Listening is thus again defined as the process of using and synthesizing combinations of perceptive sense modalities (interacting) to facilitate communication.

People listen emotionally (often it may be even preverbal perception) and intellectually (critically consciously and analytically evaluative in reason). One cannot say "active" and "passive," since both systems are interactive, and at once both active *and* passive. It is feasible that intelligence is related to the external, outer-directed systems as far as comprehension is measurable (IQ, STEP, Brown-Carlson, etc.). However, intelligence as measured is not referrable to the internalized, subconscious listening subsystem; it is internalized and active, but not always measurable. A great deal of the listener's success may depend upon his ability to decode and interpret this system's reporting realistically. The process of integration necessarily depends upon a certain balance between the two inputs. Integration is an energized process generated toward a goal of productivity (growth), the creative tendency inherent in communication.

Then comes the process of integration, which must surely depend upon a certain balance between the two inputs. This balance is between the ability to decode and the ability to interpret one's system's reporting realistically. To understand the balance in this process of integration, one must consider the nature of the person involved and his personality. The theories of personality presented by John Locke (1956), George Kelly (1955), Carl Rogers (1961), Alfred Adler (1927), and others are particularly relevant for the significance of their theoretical approach to personality, as it appears to be related to the integration of the particular listening subsystems under speculation.

CURRENT CONTROVERSIES

Certain implications gain credence for consideration and points of departure, in making legitimate and systematic advances in this field of knowledge. Listening is certainly more than the opposite of its counterpart, speech.

One clue to the ineffectiveness of instruction problem may be found in a misunderstanding of how to handle what Marshall McLuhan (1964) calls "implosion" and "self amputation," or Gestalt discriminatory insight.

Most instruction is based on an active control, by the

listener, of the excess thought time in utilizing information input to the maximum benefit. This assumes a certain compartmentalizing of input to information storage and retention. McLuhan would have us operating under varying degrees of social-psychological threat to the central nervous system. This system he describes as seeking to maintain an equilibrium, or balance. He sees a

> parallel of response between the patterns of physical and psychic trauma, or shock. . . . Shock induces a generalized numbness, or an increased threshold to all types of perception. . . . Depending on which sense or faculty is extended technologically, or 'autoamputated,' the 'closure,' or equilibrium-seeking among the other senses, is fairly predictable—sensation is always 100 percent—but the ratio among the components in the sensation can differ infinitely. . . . To behold, use, or perceive any extension of ourselves . . . is necessarily to embrace it. To listen . . . is to accept . . . into our personal system and to undergo the 'closure,' or displacement of perception, that follows automatically.

This "acceptance" or "embracing" (in a receptor action), or even "auto amputation," is diametrically opposed to the more commonly accepted idea of actively controlled listening. The two approaches (McLuhan versus convention—as surveyed above) seem to conflict unreconcilably, in that a person may not be open to all input at the threshold level and at once be discriminatory or in control of this input. It is only after the initial reception that he can decide how he will approach the interpretive handling of the input. This is at a higher level of the perceptual-learning process, and involves all sorts of cognitive dissonance/consonance, psycho-physical, socio- and anthropological variability factors.

In studying the phenomena of listening, the literature and data, one might see a framework for proposing a justified rational new perspective emerging, contingent upon the individual's centrality to the issues. No longer can it be assumed that the individual must adjust to the course in listening, but instead hypothesize that the opposite may be necessary: that the course in listening instruction or improvement, to be effective, must adapt to the listener personally. The relatively unexplored field of listening research as yet leaves much to be answered.

REFERENCES

Adler, Alfred. *The Practice and Theory of Individual Psychology.* New York: Harcourt, 1927. Individual Psychology in C. Murchison, ed.

_____. *Psychologies of 1930.* Worcester, Mass.: Clark U. Press, 1930, pp. 395-405.

Barbara, Dominick A. *The Art of Listening.* Springfield, Ill.: Charles C. Thomas, Publisher, 1958.

Davitz, Joel R. *The Communication of Emotional Meaning.* New York: McGraw-Hill Book Company, 1964. Personality, Perceptual, and Cognitive Correlates of Emotional Sensitivity, pp. 57, 59, 60, 68; Auditory Correlates of Vocal Expressions of Emotional Meanings, Chapter 8, pp. 106, 108.

Duker, Sam. *Listening Bibliography.* New York: The Scarecrow Press, Inc., 1964.

_____. *Listening Readings, Vols. 1 and 2.* New York: The Scarecrow Press, Inc., 1966 and 1971.

Fessenden, Seth A. Levels of Listening—A Theory. *Education,* January, 1955, *75,* 288-291.

Furness, Edna Lue, Listening: A Case of Terminological Confusion. *Journal of Education Psychology,* December 1957, *48,* 237-242.

Holtzman, Paul D. Communication Versus Expression in Speaking and Listening. In *Psychological and Psychiatric Aspects of Speech and Hearing,* ed. Dominick A. Barbara. Springfield, Ill.: Charles C. Thomas, 1960, Ch. 1, pp. 5-26.

Kelly, George A. *The Psychology of Personal Constructs.* New York: Norton and Company, 1955.

Locke, John. *Essays Concerning Human Understanding.* Los Angeles: Gateway Editions, Inc., 1956. Chapter 1, Of Knowledge in General; Book IV: Of Knowledge and Probability.

Lundsteen, Sara W. *Listening Its Impact on Reading and the Other Language Arts.* NCTE/ERIC, 1111 Kenyon Rd., Urbana, Ill., 1971.

McLuhan, Marshall. *Understanding Media: The Extensions of Man.* New York: McGraw-Hill Book Company, 1964, pp. 53-55.

Mooney, Ross L. A Conceptual Model for Integrating Four Approaches to the Identification of Creative Talent. A Report from the Bureau of Educational Research, Ohio State University, Columbus, Ohio, 1957, p. 8.

Nichols, Ralph G., Listening Instruction in the Secondary School. *Bulletin of the National Association of Secondary School Principals,* May 1952, *36,* 158-174.

_____, and Lewis, Thomas R. *Listening and Speaking.* Dubuque, Iowa: Wm. C. Brown, 1954.

_____, and Stevens, L. A. You Don't Know How to Listen. *Colliers,* July 25, 1953, pp. 16-19.

_____. Listening is a 10-Part Skill. *Nation's Business,* July 1957, *45*(7), 56-60.

_____, and Stevens, Leonard A. *Are You Listening?* New York: McGraw-Hill, 1957.

_____. Do We Know How to Listen? Practical Helps in a Modern Age. *Speech Teacher,* March 1961, *10,* 118-124.

Petrie, Charles Robert, Jr., *An Experimental Evaluation of Two Methods for Improving Listening Comprehension Abilities.* Doctoral dissertation, Purdue University, Lafayette, Ind., 1961.

Pflaumer, Elizabeth M. *A Definition of Listening.* Masters thesis, The Ohio State University, 1968, pp. 61-65.

_____. *Personality Correlates of Effective Listening.* Doctoral dissertation, The Ohio State University, Columbus, Ohio, 1970.

Rogers, Carl R. *On Becoming a Person.* New York: Houghton-Mifflin Company, 1961, p. 350.

Shapiro, David, Barber, T. X., Dicara, Leo V., Kamiya, Joe, Miller, Neal E., and Stoyva, Johann, eds. *Biofeedback and Self Control, 1972.* Chicago: Aldine Publishing Company, 1973.

Weaver, Carl H. *Human Listening Processes and Behavior.* Bobbs Merrill series in Speech Communication, Bobbs-Merrill Company, Inc., Indianapolis, 1972.

Witkin, B. R. Auditory Perception: Implications for Language Development. *Journal of Research and Development in Education,* Fall, 1969, pp. 53-68.

103

HIGH SCHOOL PHYSICS COURSES

by Raymond E. Thompson
Senior Examiner, Educational Testing Service
Princeton, New Jersey

In this paper I will describe and discuss the nature and purpose of high school physics courses; and the students, teachers, and instructional materials that have been a part of high school physics courses in the United States in the past 15 years.

Physics, like other scientific disciplines, has two inseparable facets. On the one hand, it is the process through which man seeks an understanding of the physical world. On the other hand, it is the product of that process, it is the collection of propositions that have stood the test of time and are generally regarded as true and worth knowing. A physics course can stress one or the other of these two facets of the discipline. The best courses strike a reasonable balance between the two. In the best courses the students have an opportunity to confront some real physical phenomena of interest to them. They formulate hypotheses, devise tests of the hypotheses, do their utmost with their brains and hands, no holds barred, and struggle toward reasonable conclusions. They are exposed to the original works of physicists, and learn of conflicting models, critical experiments, and discarded theories. But it is ineffective and inefficient to place all stress on this facet of physics. The students will clearly not possess the ability, interest, or time to discover everything for themselves. Much information must be presented in finished form, the fruits of physicists pursuing the processes of physics in the past.

There is probably a natural tendency for teachers to stress too much the second facet, to present physics as a finished collection of unassailable propositions laid down from on high. This is because it is easier to do it that way; the teacher is clearly in control, as the one who always knows the answer, and he doesn't have to struggle through the uncertainty and frustration of confronting new and different physical problems. But it is in practicing the processes of physics that the students and teacher are likely to find their greatest exhilarations and motivations to seek more understanding.

For an example of what can be done, witness Rollin Porter's physics classes at Maine Township High School in Illinois. Porter (1972) teaches phenomenological physics, which he describes as "teaching entirely through the use of examples from the real world (p. 194)." He finds to his great delight that the students are learning more physics, they are more active, more involved, and have a greater appreciation of an interest in physics.

If the effectiveness of any physics course is to be evaluated, we need an idea of what the purpose of the course is. In a phrase, the purpose is probably to promote improved understanding of physics. We need to consider now what kind of course is most likely to yield improved understandings. I think the following ten propositions,

set forth by Watson (1971), provide an excellent summary of the learning theory that is most directly pertinent to classroom teaching. We can gauge the effectiveness of a physics course by the degree to which the course is planned and executed to take account of and respond positively to these ten propositions.

Watson's ten propositions are:

1. The primary purpose of schooling is to facilitate certain culturally selected learning.
2. During this schooling the teacher must be learning about the learner and the learning process.
3. Learning occurs individually; the rates and styles differ greatly among learners.
4. Learning occurs internally but can be assessed only through overt behavior.
5. The learner must have a purpose or goal which causes him to commit his attention to the learning task.
6. The learner must experience or anticipate some progress toward goals.
7. The most powerful rewards for learning are internal feelings of growing competence and capability to cope with phenomena of interest.
8. Positive learning rewards are more potent than negative ones.
9. Students learn much from each other.
10. The teacher arranges the environment and defines the task for the learners. (p. 503)

After a consideration of the purpose of physics courses and the pertinent learning theory, we turn attention to the components of a course. The course exists solely for students, so we consider them first. Next come the teachers, and the third component is the course materials.

STUDENTS

The students in a high school physics course are likely to be about 17 years old. Most of them will be seniors. They will already have completed courses in general, introductory, or earth science their first year in high school, biology their second year, and chemistry their third year. They will also have had algebra and geometry, and probably additional mathematics. Most of them will be boys. They will be academically able and bound for college. There are numerous exceptions, of course, to this general description, but it comes close to describing typical physics students.

I will cite the results of two surveys of high school physics courses several times. The first survey by Thompson (1969) was conducted in the 1965-1966 school year. The student sample on which I will report in this chapter was representative of seniors taking the College Board Physics Achievement Test in the mid-60s.

The second survey, by Ivany, Mullaney, Huegel, Faust, and Strassenburg (1973), was done in the 1971–1972 school year. This survey focused on 42 high schools, and the information was based on teacher and student questionnaire and test responses, as well as on data collected during week-long visits to each of the schools. According to Ivany et al. (1973), "the selection of 42 schools was drawn from 11 North Atlantic states and Washington,

D.C. from a list that was initially randomly selected (p. 223)."

Drawing on the Thompson (1969) and the Ivany et al. (1973) surveys, and several other sources, we can document and further expand the description of typical high school physics students given at the beginning of this section. In so doing we should remember that both survey samples are superior in ability to the national population of physics students.

Ivany et al. (1973) report that 21 percent of the seniors in the 42 schools they surveyed were in physics. Data from Simon (1971) indicate that in 1969-1970 only 2.5 percent of all students in public secondary schools (junior high schools, senior high schools, junior/senior high schools, and regular four-year high schools) were enrolled in physics. Less than one-fifth of high school graduates have had physics, and the trend seems to continue downward.

Ivany et al. (1973) write that "with only minor variations the science curriculum sequence available in the sample schools is the traditional biology-chemistry-physics pattern (p. 223)." The appropriateness of this sequence has been questioned. It has been reasoned that a thorough understanding of physics is needed before one can delve effectively into the complexities of chemistry or biology. A living organism is, after all, a complicated physical and chemical system. Dickens (1971) writes that "it is simply not logical for a student to be exposed to modern chemistry and biology without a good background in physics (p. 319)." The explanation for the persistence of this seemingly illogical sequence may be that the study of biology and chemistry are ordinarily not at such a fundamental level as some might hope for. At any rate, the sequence persists.

There have been some recent changes in the first high school science course many students take. In the prefaces of both the 1964 edition of *Modern Physics* and the 1970 edition of *PSSC Physics*, it is stated that because of changes in the earlier science courses that many students take, some of the introductory material included in prior editions of both texts has been deleted. This introductory material from the prior editions dealt with such topics as measurements, functions, scaling, notions about time and space, and the atomic nature of matter in *PSSC Physics;* and with the properties of matter, the mechanics of liquids and gases, and weather in the case of *Modern Physics.*

According to Thompson (1969), "the high school students participating in the field survey of all subject-matter areas, including physics, ranked close to the 75th percentile on the Scholastic Aptitude Test, as compared with a national sample of college entrants; and of the subgroups by subjects, *the physics subgroup was the most able of all* (p. 5)." Ivany et al. (1973) write that "it is true that very few students who are not intending to enter college enroll in physics (p. 293)."

Perhaps more important than any of the descriptions offered so far are data on the changing achievement of students who have studied high school physics. Kruglak (1972) reports that the physics achievement of freshmen entering Western Mighican University in 1958, 1963, and 1968 has been steadily increasing. The achievement

was measured by 45 out of 75 items in the Dunning Physics Test judged by 12 or more physicists as especially important. He reports that boys scored significantly higher than girls in all comparisons, and that *PSSC Physics* students did no better than *Modern Physics* students.

TEACHERS

High school physics teachers are an interesting lot. In some larger and more affluent schools the teacher is responsible for physics only, and he has several physics classes. But as the size and/or affluence of the school decrease the physics teachers' responsibilities spread out to other science courses, mathematics courses, courses of almost any ilk, and to assorted extracurricular duties.

The Panel on the Preparation of Physics Teachers, of the Commission on College Physics, reported in 1968 that the average number of semester hours studied in college by high school physics teachers was only 18. In the past 15 years there have been rather abundant opportunities for physics teachers to strengthen their academic backgrounds through academic year, summer, and inservice institutes at numerous colleges, with the financial support of the National Science Foundation. Ivany et al. (1973) report that in the 42 schools they surveyed "a significant majority of the teachers have enjoyed one or more opportunities to benefit from summer institute courses (p. 294)." The teachers surveyed by Ivany et al. represent an atypically superior group; the average number of semester hours of physics studied by this group was 42. These teachers had an average of about ten years of teaching experience, and two-thirds of them received *The Physics Teacher*, one-half *Scientific American*, one-third *Physics Today*, and one-tenth the *American Journal of Physics*.

Ivany et al. (1973) found that

> the majority of the teachers they surveyed believe that prospective scientists should be taught a physics course which emphasizes experimental work in high school. Indeed most do include laboratory work, but it does not play a dominant role. An even larger majority of teachers believe other kinds of students should study a course which uses an historical-cultural approach, but few have either such students or such courses. Among a variety of stated course objectives, one stood out as a clear first choice: "a verbal and mathematical understanding of the topics covered in physics." (p. 294)

Rothberg, Welch, and Walberg (1966) reported the fascinating finding that "teachers' personalities and value systems are more strongly related to students' changes in physics achievement, attitudes towards physics, and interest in science than are the extent of teachers' preparation in physics, mathematics, and the history and philosophy of science, their knowledge of physics, and their years of physics teaching experience (p. 63)."

To summarize this section, we turn again to Watson (1971), and his observation that the behavior of a physics teacher depends on his orientation toward science, technology, children, and the learning process. These orientations involve value systems evolved through a lifetime, and they are clearly resistant to quick and easy change. Watson (1971) writes,

> in summary, the pedagogical training of physics teachers is a life-long operation in which many of the basic value systems have been well established before the potential teacher enrolls in any pedagogical training. Study of the history of educational ideas and of the theories of learning are desirable. Clinical practice and constructive criticism are essential. But the specifics and emphasis depend on what you physics teachers and your colleagues consider to be important about science to communicate to the next generation. (p. 505)

MATERIALS

It may be helpful to outline the recent history of course material development. In mid-20th century *Modern Physics* by Dull et al., and its companion texts, *Modern Chemistry* and *Modern Biology,* were far and away the most widely used texts in American high school science courses. In 1956 the Physical Science Study Committee (PSSC) has its beginnings. When, in October 1957, the Russians launched Sputnik, there was alarm about American science education, and great impetus was given to PSSC. Several hundred prople, mainly school and college physics teachers, with massive government support through the National Science Foundation, contributed to PSSC. The first hard-bound edition of *PSSC Physics* appeared in 1960. The declining enrollments in physics were only briefly stemmed, and it became clear that although *PSSC Physics* was excellent for the future physicist, it would not appeal to the great numbers of humanistically oriented students who were still missing physics. In the late 60s another large team of physicists, educators, teachers, and others organized, again with substantial government and private foundation support, to develop *Harvard Project Physics.* The first hard-bound edition of *Project Physics* came out in 1970.

Ivany et al. (1973) note that "a striking observation is that the longer specific project course materials are available, the more likely one is to find *some* influence of that project on any particular course he studies, but the less likely he is to find any course which uses those project materials exclusively (p. 294)." Thompson (1969) found in his 1965-1966 survey of 1,312 seniors that 42 percent said *Modern Physics* and 28 percent said *PSSC Physics* was the primary text in their physics course. At five administrations of the College Board Physics Achievement Test in 1971, 1972, and 1973, the examinees identified the principal textbook used in their high school physics course. The percentages using each text were: 30 percent *PSSC Physics,* 9 percent *Project Physics,* 33 percent some other text (mainly *Modern Physics*), and 28 percent uncertain. Ivany et al. (1973) found, in their 1971–1972 survey of 42 schools, that 23 schools used primarily a traditional course, 14 primarily PSSC, and five primarily *Project Physics.* The most widely used text in so-called traditional courses is *Modern Physics.*

One of the clearest distinctions among the three leading textbooks is the greater emphasis on technology in *Modern Physics* and the greater emphasis on pure science in *PSSC Physics.* Equally clear is the emphasis on the history of science and the humanistic side of science in

Project Physics. Modern Physics has many practical engineering applications, whereas *PSSC Physics* tends to approach physics from an abstract and theoretical viewpoint. I believe *PSSC Physics* and *Project Physics* are more intellectually demanding texts than *Modern Physics. PSSC Physics* is no doubt excellent for the future scientist. But the capabilities and interests of the average student who is not destined for a career in science may be better served by *Modern Physics* or *Project Physics.* In terms of content, *Modern Physics* placed more emphasis on heat than the other two texts, and *Project Physics* emphasizes astronomy more than the other two. These three texts are typically studied in high school in first physics courses. The texts, and especially *PSSC Physics* and *Project Physics,* are equally appropriate for college students or adults who have not studied physics and seek a better understanding of the physical world.

It is instructive to contrast the objectives of these three texts. In the preface of *Modern Physics* we read that "the objective in *Modern Physics* has always been to present physics with a directness and simplicity that will enable every student to achieve maximum comprehension. A real understanding of science is always its own best motivation."

In the preface to the first edition of *PSSC Physics,* Killian writes: "This textbook is the heart of the PSSC course, in which physics is presented not as a mere body of facts but basically as a continuing process by which men seek to understand the nature of the physical world."

The purposes of *Project Physics* were to develop a humanistically oriented physics course for high school students, increase enrollments in high school physics, and research factors that influence science learning.

In addition to textbooks, the course materials include laboratory apparatus and guides, films, film loops, transparencies, teacher guides, tests, and auxiliary printed matter.

Ivany et al. (1973) found, in the 42 schools they surveyed, that laboratory experiments are always, or often, a required weekly activity in 75 percent of the schools, but that laboratory experiments result in unresolved debates about concepts and methods of interpretation always or often in only 10 percent of the schools. Ivany et al. (1973) report that PSSC laboratories appear unusually helpful on two counts: teachers do answer questions with questions, and the laboratories are not designed to prove what has already been learned.

Thompson (1969) found substantial differences between PSSC and non-PSSC laboratories. The percentages of PSSC students doing experiments on reflection and interference of water waves, interference of light waves, and conservation of momentum in collisions exceeded the percentages of non-PSSC students doing these experiments by more than 40 points. On the other hand, the percentages of non-PSSC students doing experiments on the coefficient of linear expansion, the mechanical advantage of a lever, specific heat, and coefficient of friction exceeded the percentages of PSSC students doing these experiments by 40 points.

There is an extensive array of excellent 16-millimeter PSSC sound films. There are only a few Project Physics sound films, but there is a large collection of film loops and transparencies in PP.

The PSSC and PP teacher guides are enormously helpful. All three courses have tests available. Project Physics also offers student handbooks, readers containing many informative articles from a variety of sources, and programmed instruction booklets.

There are a great number of other textbooks and accompanying course materials for high school physics courses. A rich lode of high-quality course materials exists. In most cases the materials developed for a single course are much more extensive than a teacher can use in one year. Hence, he is in the enviable and challenging position of being able to pick and choose what will best serve his purposes.

I wish to mention three other programs closely related to high school physics courses. One is the Engineering Concepts Curriculum Project (ECCP). The course developed by ECCP is intended for average college-bound high school students who are not choosing careers in science or engineering. According to ECCP (1973), more than 1,000 teachers were using all or part of the content and approach of *The Man Made World*, the textbook for the course, by September 1972.

The second is Physical Science II, a course designed for students of average ability or above in grades 9 and 10, and in grades 11 and 12 for students who did not take chemistry or physics. The course developers are the same people who prepared the recent edition of PSSC.

The last is the College Board Advanced Placement Program in Physics. Finn, Pasquesi, and Thompson (1972) write that "The Advanced Placement Program provides an opportunity for capable students to study college-level courses while still in high school. The AP Course Descriptions serve as a guide for this course. Through the AP Examinations students may gain college credit for their study and advanced placement in their college sequence of courses (p. 391)."

The discipline of physics is clearly a significant one. The importance of understanding something about physics, especially for persons in a scientific-technological society, is also widely recognized. Yet only a relatively few able students take physics. Expanding this group to include more girls, more humanistically oriented students, and more noncollege-bound students, while retaining the intellectual integrity of physics, is a very difficult task. It requires sustained and dedicated discipline, but it certainly is, I believe, a worthy goal to pursue.

REFERENCES

Dickens, R. S. The Development of a Physics Curriculum at Forrest High School. *The Physics Teacher*, Sept. 1971, *9*, 315-319.

Dull, C. E., Metcalfe, H. C., and Williams, J. E. *Modern Physics*. New York: Holt, Rinehart, and Winston, 1964.

Finn, E. J., Pasquesi, R. J., and Thompson, R. E. The College Board Advanced Placement Physics Program. *The Physics Teacher*, Oct. 1972, *10*, 391-397.

Haber-Schaim, Uri, Cross, J. B., Dodge, J. H., and Walter, J. A. *PSSC Physics*, 3rd Edition. Lexington, Mass.: D. C. Heath and Co., 1971.

Ivany, G., Mullaney, R., Huegel, D., Faust, R., and Strassenburg, A. A. High School Physics Teaching, a Report on Current Practices in the Northeast. *The Physics Teacher*. April and May 1973, *11*, 223-228 and 289-294.

Kruglak, Haym. The Physics Background of College Freshmen Ten Years After Sputnik. *The Physics Teacher*, Sept. 1972, *10*, 331-333.

Panel on Preparation of Physics Teachers. Preparing High School Physics Teachers. Commission on College Physics, 1968, College Park, Maryland.

Potter, R. D. Phenomenological Physics—Maine Township High School Style. *The Physics Teacher*, April 1972, *10*, 193-195.

Rothman, A. I., Welch, W. W., and Walberg, H. J. Physics Teacher Characteristics and Student Learning. *Journal of Research in Science Teaching*, 1966, *6*, 59-63.

Simon, K. A., and Grant, W. V. *Digest of Educational Statistics*, 1971 edition. U.S. Department of Health, Education, and Welfare.

Thompson, R. E. A Survey of the Teaching of Physics in Secondary Schools. *Test Development Report 69-3*. Princeton, N.J.: Educational Testing Service, 1969.

Watson, F. G. Pre-Service Pedagogical Formation of Physics Teachers. *The Physics Teacher*, Dec. 1971, *9*, 501-505.

ADDITIONAL RESOURCES

College Board Advanced Placement Program in Physics

Program Director
College Board Advanced Placement Examinations
Box 977
Princeton, N.J. 08540

Engineering Concepts Curriculum Project

Text Materials: Webster Division of McGraw Hill
Manchester Road
Manchester, Mo. 63011

Laboratory
Materials: AMF Electrical Products, Development Div.
102 North Royal Street
Alexandria, Va. 22314

ERIC—Information Clearninghouse:

ERIC Information Analysis Center for Science, Mathematics, and Environmental Education
1460 West Lane Avenue
Columbus, Ohio 43221

Ivaney et al. Survey—Complete survey results:

American Institute of Physics Information Pool
Box 617
Stony Brook, N.Y. 11790

Physical Science Study Committee—Course materials and information:

D. C. Heath and Co.
125 Spring Street
Lexington, Mass. 02173

Physical Science II—

Course materials: Prentice-Hall, Inc.
Englewood Cliffs, N.J. 07632
Descriptive brochure: Physical Science Group
Newton College of the Sacred Heart
Newton, Mass. 02160

Project Physics—Course materials and information:

Holt, Rinehart, and Winston
383 Madison Avenue
New York, N.Y. 10017

The Physics Teacher – Journal

The American Association of Physics Teachers
335 East 45th St.
New York, N.Y. 10017

Thompson survey – Complete survey results:

Raymond E. Thompson
Educational Testing Service
Rosedale Road
Princeton, N.J. 08540

104

READING PROGRAMS

by Sister Mary Luke Reiland
Director, Reading Center
Loyola University
Los Angeles, California

American education's "moon shot," launched early in this decade, aimed at a totally literate society by the year 1980. As a result, current emphasis on the teaching of reading at all levels in society is unprecedented in the history of this nation. The challenge which continues to confront educators is whether they can provide effective reading instruction that will meet the needs of each unique learner, be he a preschooler, a college student, or an adult illiterate. This goal of the right-to-read effort has spawned the growth of a variety of newly designed programs; stimulated long-range research projects; initiated a tremendous flood of new materials; and given rise to prolific ideas on how reading should be taught.

The enormity of the presumption, in attempting to condense within a few pages the research and the innovative approaches to present-day reading programs, is all but overwhelming. Thus, it must be emphasized that any portrayal of the state of the art, can but highlight the broad spectrum of approaches to reading instruction at each level of the educational ladder.

Definition. In the literature concerned with reading instruction, and in various curriculum guides, the terms "reading programs," "reading methods," and "reading techniques," are used interchangeably. Harris (1969, p. 1090) observed that there was a need for greater uniformity in defining what is meant by "program," "method," and "technique." In this paper, a reading program is understood to take into account the framework, procedures, media, and materials used in the teaching of reading skills.

PREREADING PROGRAMS

Delaying formal reading instruction until a child has reached the mental age of 6.5 years has persisted for more than forty years. The reasons for the continued practice, and some of the serious flaws in the early use and inter-

pretation of "reading readiness," were detailed by Durkin (1972). More recently, dramatic changes in the concept of readiness has emerged. One example can be seen in the enrollment trends of formal programs of instruction below first grade. In the fall of 1971, 40 percent of the nation's children, ages three to five, were attending schools, as compared with 25 percent in 1964 (Brown, 1971).

Major forces influencing the current national trend for providing earlier schooling, as well as a variety of different kinds of programs for three-, four-, and five year-olds, received their impetus from several sources: (1) The research and writings of Bruner (1960), Hunt (1961), Deutsch (1963), and Bloom (1964), all of whom have underscored the learning potential of young children and emphasized the crucial importance of early learning opportunities; (2) the "War on Poverty," which provided funds for Head Start and other programs to equalize educational opportunities; and (3) the cumulative research supporting successful preschool reading experiences (Durkin, 1966; McKee and Brzeinski, 1966; Fowler, 1968; and Cohen, 1969).

Innovative Beginning Reading Programs

Ongoing reading projects in the regional laboratories and the research and development centers across the nation are examples of new programs with extensive field-testing aimed at effective instruction of specific reading behaviors for varied populations. Commercial availability is had only after completion of large-scale field testing with targeted populations. A sampling of these programs, with brief descriptions, will highlight their diversity.

The Southwest Regional Laboratory's work in the development of a preschool and elementary reading and language instructional system is partially completed. The SWRL Program is an integrated instructional approach having two basic systems: The Instructional Concepts Program (ICP) and the Beginning Reading Program (BRP). There are two support systems: The Tutorial Program and the Parent-Assisted Learning (PAL) Program. After extensive field-testing, involving more than 30,000 children in school systems in 12 states over a period of four to six years, the SWRL Kindergarten Program and the Beginning Reading Program have become available through the Ginn Company (1972).

The Wisconsin Research and Development Center for Cognitive Learning has designed a program to expedite individually guided instruction in reading skill development. The Design is divided into four to seven levels, which include six skill areas that roughly correspond to Kindergarten through grade 6. At the time of this writing, only the Word Attack element of the Design was available to schools. Distribution was restricted to those schools who had participated in the special teacher-training sessions. The effectiveness of Word Attack was validated through field-testing in more than 400 schools in some 25 states.

A third example is the Southwestern Cooperative Educational Laboratory's Communication Arts Program, which is designed to equip Chicano and Indian children

(K through first grade) whose first language is not English with the prerequisite skills needed to master reading.

The Pittsburgh Learning Research and Development Center's individually prescribed early reading program is perhaps the nation's first successfully operated systematic program on a step-by-step basis. In the program, the pupil sets his own pace. When he completes a unit of work, he is tested immediately. The teacher offers a series of alternative activities to correct his weaknesses, including special tutoring if such is needed. There are no textbooks. Virtually no lecturing to a group as a whole is done. Some students have performed from three to four grade levels above those which normally would be expected at their ages.

Distinctive features of the programs cited above include parental involvement in the learning activities, both in the home and at school, and inservice training systems for the teachers.

Model Programs

Wide experimentation is concerned with efforts to enhance significant factors in early reading success. Some 34 promising programs on reading and language development have been cited recently as "Model Programs" (National Center for Educational Communication, 1970).

One such program is the DOVACK Program (1970) in Monticello, Florida, which uses a computer-assisted language experience approach. It is designed for children who speak an Afro-American dialect, and for whom traditional approaches to the teaching of reading have had limited success. Children start with the concepts and vocabulary they already know. All of the child's sensory experiences can be used as a background for the stories, which he dictates on dictaphone belts. A computer furnishes print-outs of the stories, helps to identify learning problems and patterns, and prints progress reports. Tape recordings are made so that the child can hear his own stories while reading them. The words which form the acronym DOVACK—differentiated, oral, visual, aural, computerized, kinesthetic—indicate the multisensory approach employed to meet the needs of each child (DOVACK, 1970, p. 2).

Other model programs deserving mention include: New York City's P.S. 76 Interdependent Learner Model, a follow-through program (1970) which is designed to raise reading achievement by encouraging children to learn interdependently (children explain things to one another in small-group arrangements), by employing paraprofessionals, and by a heavy emphasis on decoding skills. Dayton, Ohio's Behavioral Principles Structural Model (1970), a follow-through program, is designed to help disadvantaged children learn basic skills quickly by using programmed materials and continuing teacher reinforcement. San Antonio, Texas' Bilingual Early Childhood Program (1970) attempts to meet the language and other needs of Spanish-speaking Mexican-American children, ages 3 to 5 years, through a high degree of adult-child contact and the use of language as a tool for thought.

Evaluation reports of the model programs indicate progress in achieving major student objectives. Some of the programs report significant gains in IQ scores. Data on long-range effects are not yet available.

DEVELOPMENTAL PROGRAMS

Developmental reading programs recognize learning to read as a continuous and gradual process, which develops sequentially and proceeds to higher and more complex understandings. It is generally wide in scope, beginning reading with three- to four-year-olds and continuing beyond high school.

Basal Reader Programs

For decades, the basal reader and its coordinated workbook has formed the core of American reading instruction. Reasons for its almost universal use include: (1) years of study and research in the development of materials; (2) more than 100 years of trial and error in many types of situations; (3) teacher manuals which offer minutely detailed directions; and (4) state adoptions.

Traditionally, the basal reader series provided a carefully sequenced program of basic skills and continuity of all skills through the grades. Comparisons of different basal systems published by major companies tended to be very much alike, and were often the subject of much criticism.

The ever-rising volume of criticism from a wide variety of sources emphasized the fact that over the years the basal reader series were dull, repetitive, unrealistic, and insipid (Klineberg, 1963; Niemeyer, 1965; Blom et al., 1970). These complaints were summarily implied by Heilman (1972), when he wrote, "Until the mid-60's, the primary difference between competing basals was to be found in the name of the characters who pulled the little red wagons and called to the housebroken doggies (p. 213)." Durkin, (1971) citing yet another criticism stated,

> . . . in the 1960's, it became popular to criticize primary grade basal readers because their illustrations portrayed nothing but Caucasian children in the setting of suburbia. Quickly—or, as quickly as million-dollar investments allow for change—publishers began to use pictures of multi-racial children in surroundings of obviously urban character. (p. 117)

In spite of its many critics, the basal reader has continued to be the means by which most American children learn to read (Barton and Wilder, 1964, p. 378-379; Chall, 1967, p. 188-189).

Research Findings

Recently a carefully organized and coordinated series of studies (Bond and Dykstra, 1967), supported by the U.S. Office of Education and under the direction of 27 investigators, compared two or more reading programs in first-grade classrooms. The comparison programs represented a large variety of instructional approaches and several popular basal reader systems. At the end of one year, the results of this massive effort indicated no overall superiority for any one particular program.

In the summary of the second-year followup, Dykstra (1968) selected 13 projects, from the original 27, for evaluation of five types of instructional methods with the basal reader. The various basal-versus-nonbasal comparisons indicated at the end of grade 2 that linguistic, phonic/linguistic, and initial teaching alphabet programs were generally superior to conventional basal programs in word recognition, spelling, and word meaning. However, in terms of pupil achievement in paragraph comprehension, no one program had demonstrated superiority (p. 49).

Trends in Basal Programs

Major modifications in current editions of basal systems reflect the findings of significant educational and psychological research and the combined talents of many authorities from a variety of fields. Representative major changes include: (1) greater diversity in content of the materials; (2) earlier and stronger phonics instruction; (3) a profusion of books, games, and other materials for high, average, and low achievers; (4) filmstrips, records, and tapes; (5) kits of story cards and boxes of paperbacks; (6) multiracial stories and multiethnic settings; and (7) convenient teacher guides, with reduced facsimilies of pages in student texts, annotated and keyed.

The "sameness" of the old basal systems has been replaced by notable diversity, sophisticated designs, new and exciting illustrations, sensitive photography, and content that challenges and involves the student. Some examples include: Scott, Foresman's *Read Systems* (1970), which is a systems components approach in three teaching sequences for 12 levels covering the first three grades. There are interlocking multisensory components, and auditory, visual, and kinesthetic orientations which provide for different learning modalities to suit different learning styles. Ginn and Company's *Reading 360* (1970) represents a departure from conventionally graded books with 15 levels planned for diverse groups of pupils at each level. The program format includes provision for the junior high level. Harcourt, Brace, Jovanovich's *Bookmark Program,* Second Edition (1973), shows distinctive features represented in change of content and an emphasis on study-type reading, and a variety of expository materials stress "how to learn." And finally, Houghton-Mifflin's *Discoveries* (1972) combines basal features with individualized features of self-selection, self-pacing, self-correction, and free reading.

Language Experience Programs

The interrelationships among listening, speaking, writing, and reading skills are utilized in the language-experience programs. A significant body of research supports the basic tenets of this approach to the teaching of reading. Loban's (1963) extended research of children's language development suggested the need for more opportunities among young children to express their own thoughts in order to develop adequate reading and writing skills. Hahn (1966, p. 590) cites the research of Allen, Ashton-Warner, Downing, Mazurkiewicz, and others who have shown that children who develop writing skills early

in the reading program become avid independent readers. Hahn's own study (1967) in its second year indicated some advantages where children were given opportunities for self-expression in oral and written language.

In the language-experience programs, reading is conceived as but one part of the communication process. Young children have the ability to communicate their experiences and their thoughts. As children talk, their own language is written by the teacher or an aide. Reading skills are taught as they emerge from the story-writing and reading. The unique feature of this program is that each child creates his own reading materials, and gradually gains a personally tailored vocabulary which is said to be in excess of that introduced in the basal-reader programs. Each child shares in listening to, and in reading, the stories which other children create. Library or trade books are introduced at a later point, so that in effect an individualized reading program emerges. Proponents of language-experience programs point out that in the teaching of reading, early success is vital; that this approach accommodates the young child with limited language skills, and the disadvantaged student as well. These children are not pressured to go beyond their language patterns and vocabulary.

On the other hand, the approach has been criticized (Spache, 1969) for the assumption of similarity and ready transfer among the vocabularies in listening, speaking, writing, and reading; for its lack of attention to the transition a child must make from reading his own productions to reading books; and for the incidental approach to the learning of skills (pp. 170-185).

Until recently, implementation of a language experience program was dependent almost entirely upon the teacher's ingenuity. Sources for the teacher were meager. Today, however, there is a steadily growing collection of comprehensive teacher guides, and many resources rich in creative ideas. Some of these include: Durkin (1972), McCracken et al. (1972), Smith (1967), Allen (1966), and Lee and Allen (1963).

The research evidence for Language-Experience programs is not conclusive. Among the 27 USOE First Grade Studies (Bond and Dykstra, 1967), seven projects involved the comparison of Language-Experience with Basal Reader Programs and ITA. In the summary report, no significant differences in terms of reading achievement were found at the end of the first grade. In the follow-up study at the end of the second year, Dykstra (1968) reported, "Achievement after two years of instruction in these quite different programs was very similar (p. 62)."

However, when each of the seven studies was considered individually, conflicting findings were obvious. Vilseck (1968) identified a number of variables that may have influenced these differences. Goodman (1965) and Loban (1968) advocate a language-experience approach to initial reading instruction for children who speak with dialect differences, and in 36 children Kohl (1961) demonstrated dramatic success working with inner-city sixth graders.

Individualized Reading Programs

Seeking, self-selection, and self-pacing are key concepts which distinguish individualized reading programs from others. The concepts are derived from Olsen (1949), who stressed that learning is more effective and more efficient when the learner is allowed to progress at his own pace and to the extent of his capacity.

"Individualized Reading" and "Personalized Reading" are terms which are used in the literature to describe programs that recognize the individual's uniqueness. Barbe (1961) and Duker (1971) stressed the difficulty in attempting to define individualized reading. It is more a way of thinking, or a point of view about reading instruction. "There is no single right way to teach while using this approach (Duker, 1971, p. 259)."

The nature of the program requires student selection of the books he wishes to read and from which skills are taught. A pivotal part of the instructional program is the individual pupil-teacher conference. Skill instruction occurs when the child needs it. Written records of student progress are integral to the conference period. Student sharing of what has been read is important, and leads to the extension of reading interests.

A major factor in the effectiveness of this approach is the accessibility of a large stock of many kinds of books, magazines, newspapers, etc. Leopp (1973) presented a seven-fold plan for implementing individualized reading instruction, and described the environment ". . . which must fit each child, who is as unique as his fingerprints (p. 65)." A second major factor is exceptional teacher competence regarding the instruction of all reading skills, and a high level of teacher effectiveness in classroom management. Sartain (1968) cited eight studies which suggested that the average teacher is not only professionally, but also personally, unaware of important reading principles and skills.

The research evidence concerned with the effectiveness of individualized instruction is inconclusive. Two extensive reviews (Groff, 1963; Duker, 1963) reveal that studies vary greatly from one experiment to the next. Some cautions in viewing the research findings which favor totally individualized reading was cited by Sartain (1967): lack of control groups; serious flaws in research designs; and the halo, or Hawthorne, effect. Further questions were raised as to the effectiveness of individualized reading for children with differing modality preferences for learning; children from deprived areas; and those who are highly anxious or compulsive, and need a considerable amount of structure for learning. Such findings force the conclusion that individualized reading instruction may be appropriate for some children but not for others.

Detailed guidelines and procedures for the organization of individualized reading programs are included in Veatch (1959), Barbe (1961), Hunt (1967), and Duker (1971).

Modified Alphabetic Approaches

Some innovative attempts to resolve inconsistent letter-sound relationships have centered on the use of printed symbols to represent specific sounds, and respelling of English words so that the orthography parallels the speech sounds. Examples of such attempts follow:

Initial Teaching Alphabet (ITA). ITA represents one of the more recent and unique efforts to decrease the many irregularities in the relationship between sound and symbol in English. Briefly, ITA is an augmented Roman alphabet, adapted by Sir James Pitman from one originally created by his grandfather, Sir Isaac Pitman, author of the Pitman shorthand method.

ITA utilizes 44 characters, composed of our lower-case conventional alphabet (excluding q and x), plus 20 new symbols. The intent is to present one symbol for each phoneme, or sound, in English. Thus, the decoding aspect of learning to read is simplified. When the learner has progressed to the point at which he can read fluently in ITA, and with adequate comprehension, he transfers his skills to traditional orthography (TO).

In England, large-scale research started in 1961 under the direction of John Downing. Interim reports (Downing, 1963, 1964) of superior results in reading and spelling warranted objective study of ITA in this country. Mazurkiewicz (1964) reported the first research in the United States (Bethlehem, Pennsylvania) which confirmed the findings in England. Five of the Cooperative First-Grade Studies, sponsored by the United States Office of Education, employed ITA materials in comparison with other approaches. In two summary reports of the research (Dykstra, 1968, pp. 61-62; Ames, 1968, pp. 126-137) ITS was not significantly superior, although significant differences favoring ITA were found on some of the standardized reading subtests (i.e., vocabulary, spelling, and word meaning).

In California, ITA appeared to be more effective than TO in teaching beginning reading to Mexican-American children (Holmes and Rose, 1969). Much of the research, however, with the American version of ITA has been inconclusive or contradictory. Data from various studies have failed to indicate the superiority of ITA. A number of writers point to the important variables which were not controlled in the comparative studies with ITA (Gillooly, 1966; Spache, 1969; Heilman, 1972).

Diacritical Marking System (DMS). Fry's Diacritical Marking System (1964) attempts to regularize orthography for beginning readers by placing diacritical marks on the letters. In one of the 27 First Grade studies (Fry, 1967), a three-year comparative study was conducted with a basal series (TO), with ITA, and the same basal series with DMS. None of the three methods showed major effects at the end of the third grade. Interestingly, Fry (1972) noted that the newer attempts at simplification, by changing the alphabet, differed little from proposals dating back to the 18th century.

Other alphabetic approaches. The 40-letter alphabet, *UNIFON,* which the author (Malone, 1965, 1967) also calls "The New Single-Sound Alphabet," represents another innovative attempt to reform our writing system. The 40 block-like characters were designed for teaching both children and adults. The author proposes that his system of symbols may be easily converted for computer use and storage. It has been used on an experimental basis in Chicago city schools and in the schools of St. Louis.

Frank C. Laubach, well known for his worldwide literacy program, "Each One—Teach One," has developed an adaptation of the alphabet called *Laubach's Alphabet* (1962, 1963). His adaptation utilizes the conventional alphabet, with a slant line following any vowel which has its long sound; other vowel combinations are spelled phonetically, and silent letters are omitted.

Developed by Gattegno (1962), *Words in Color* attempts to solve the unphonetic nature of English by the use of color. In 21 wall charts, 27 consonant sounds and 20 vowel sounds are each represented by a different color. For example, every variation of the long *a* sound (*a, ai, eigh, ay,* etc.) is presented in one color—green. A teacher's guide, with 1,020 word cards, is provided for the eight-week program. Gattegno (1970) holds that reading is a relatively simple process of matching the sound system of a language with its written symbol, and that, helped by color-coded instructional materials, all children can learn to read easily. *Words in Color* has not been subjected to rigorous research. Numerous questions, including the problem of color blindness, have not been answered. Thus, the value of this colorful approach to beginning reading instruction is uncertain.

Special Phonic/Linguistic Systems. When basal reader materials were used almost exclusively, phonics was presented by the inductive, or analytic, approach. After a child had acquired a few sight words, the phonic element was introduced. The learner was taught to generalize from what he already knew.

In contrast, some of the newer programs provide earlier and heavy emphasis on phonics, in an effort to prevent reading failure. The deductive, or synthetic, approach, often called the "decoding" approach, begins with the individual letter and the sound it records. The young learner is taught the sound, then to blend it in a three-letter word. Many of the special phonics systems are designed to be completed by the end of the third grade.

Linguistically based programs differ, in that they begin with an emphasis on both oral and written language patterns. Reading skills are presented sequentially in word patterns, phrases, and then sentence patterns. Two programs that are widely used are The Palo Alto Reading Program (1973), a nongraded primary program in 21 levels; and the Merrill Linguistic Readers (1966), in six levels; these are like the alphabetic approaches, designed for beginning reading instruction.

There are a number of different phonics programs, but all are similar in that they start by teaching generalizations about the letter sounds. For example, Hay and Wingo (1954) presents new phonic elements printed in red; the Carden Method (1953) omits all pictures; McCracken and Walcott (1963) move the learner quickly, with 317 lessons to be completed in 180 days; and Spaulding (1963) teaches phonics closely tied to writing.

An impressive bulk of the research in reading deals with various aspects of phonics instruction (Russell and Fea, 1963, p. 875). Reviews of these studies (Chall, 1967) and (Dykstra, 1968) tend to indicate that basal reading programs may be strengthened by adding a supplemen-

tary phonics program.

Secondary Programs

The expanding growth of secondary reading programs, both at the college level and in the high schools, indicates current recognition of the need for implementing reading instruction beyond the elementary school. Secondary programs differ from school to school in both scope and operation: there are advanced programs designed for the better-than-average students; special remedial programs; and combinations of programs with well-equipped laboratories, reading resource centers, and media centers. Each school must tailor its program to fit the needs of its students.

In a review of more than 180 studies of secondary reading programs, Artley (1968) raised a number of questions which call for further research. Several disturbing factors were noted: (1) There is a decline in reading growth beginning about the age of entrance to junior high school. (2) Although there was evidence of a greater number of junior high programs than senior programs, most of them included only a small segment of the total school population.

A variety of bright new materials, in the form of soft, slick, paperbound books have recently become available. Many begin with readability levels at third or fourth grade. Examples include *The Break Through Series* (Allyn and Bacon, 1972), *Getting It Together* (Science Research Associates, 1973), *Action Libraries* (Scholastic Services, 1971), *The Way It Is* (Xerox, 1973), and *Crossroads* (Noble and Noble, 1970). All have very high appeal for the adolescent reader in content, modern illustrations, and low readability.

SPECIAL REMEDIAL PROGRAMS

The Fernald Approach

Language-experience techniques are incorporated into the Fernald approach, and the student is bombarded with visual, auditory, kinesthetic, and tactile (VAKT) impressions. Various terms are used interchangeably to describe the program developed by Fernald (1943): kinesthetic method, the visual-motor approach, or the training method.

The student dictates his own material or stories, and learns the words he needs through a multisensory approach. The sense of touch is utilized, as the student traces over the word written for him by the teacher. Fernald placed great stress on the need for the student to experience each word he is learning through various modalities. Each word is learned as a whole and immediately placed in a context that is meaningful to the student. There are four stages, which blend one into the other, as the pupil improves his ability to learn words and read them in context. Except in extreme remedial cases, the painstaking nature of the approach and the time it consumes tend to limit extensive use.

The Gillinhham-Stillman Approach

Heavy emphasis is placed on the teaching of letter discrimination (naming the letters) and associating sounds with the printed symbols at the beginning stages of this program. The child is involved by tracing letter forms, saying or blending sounds, and later writing the letters and words from dictation. Gillingham-Stillman (1964) advocate many discrete steps, mastery of each before moving to the next, and a careful sequencing of instruction. Certain materials are an integral part of the program. A child is expected to remain in the program for a minimum of two years (preferably four or five years), and should not be exposed to regular classroom reading instruction outside the tutorial situation.

The Neurological-Impress Method

Heckelman (1969) claimed that simultaneously seeing the printed word and hearing it spoken produced a neurological memory trace. Reading in unison with the teacher, the student slides his finger along the line of words being read. The teacher provides support by increasing the volume and speed of her reading when the student falters. The immediate objective is concerned with reading many pages without long pauses. Gradually, the student begins to take more responsibility for the reading and the teacher's voice quietly fades away. Although not a complete approach in itself, the Neurological Impress Method has been used with success with some seriously disabled readers.

Other Specialized Programs

Some highly specialized programs have attempted to alleviate reading problems by treating aspects of physical development assumed to be basic to the development of reading. Published reports of the research designed to study the relative effectiveness of these approaches are generally not supportive. Three of the more widely publicized programs are discussed briefly:

The Frostig Perception Program. The Frostig Program is concerned with the development of visual perception, and assumes that through proper visual training, major obstacles to the development of reading skills can be removed. *The Developmental Test of Visual Perception* (Frostig, 1964) is composed of five subtests: Eye-motor Coordination; Figure Ground; Form Constancy; Position in Space; and Spatial Relations. The instructional materials (Frostig-Horne, 1964) were designed to train pupils in the five areas covered in the tests, as well as other aspects of perceptual functioning. Attention is focused on figures and patterns, with the expectation that such training will have transfer effects in learning to read. Research studies have shown that gains on the visual perception tests were not reflected in reading growth (Rosen, 1966; Cohen, 1966-1967; Wingert, 1969).

There is a need for more research on the development of the various facets of visual perception, and the possibilities of stimulating their development or compensating for their lack. Goldberg and Schiffman (1972) point to well-documented evidence that visual-perceptual training after the age of 6 is of questionable value in treating

learning disorders.

The Delacato Approach. Delacato (1959, 1963) considered incomplete neurological development to be the cause of specific reading disabilities. A training program, described as neurological "patterning," consists of crawling exercises, certain sleeping postures, and other physical exercises. It is prescribed for the child before remedial reading instruction is started. Research has not supported the Delacato Program (Robbins, 1966a, 1966b). Although it has gained wide publicity in some sections of the country, the Delacato Approach has generally been rejected by the medical profession. Eight major medical and health associations issued a joint report in *The New York Times* (1968) which described the theory as without merit, and charged Delacato and his associates with undocumented claims of cures.

The Kephart Approach. The Kephart Program attempts to develop such basic skills as crawling, hopping, throwing, lifting, etc. Kephart (1960) identified six developmental areas to be of importance in school achievement: posture, laterality, directionality, body image, form perception, and spatial orientation. The training program assumes that higher forms of behavior have their roots in motor learning, and that strengthening weaknesses in perceptual-motor skills will result in improved performance in more complex activities, such as reading.

ADULT PROGRAMS

Adult Reading Improvement

Numerous reading improvement programs for adults, sponsored by universities and private enterprise, involve business executives, professionals, and individuals from various walks of life. Such programs have the express purpose of improving speed of reading, developing vocabulary, and increasing comprehension. Some highly publicized commercial programs make extravagant claims of high rates of speed that cannot be defended by present-day facts made available through eye-movement photography. The problem may be one of definition. A form of skimming or scanning cannot be confused with continuous reading. Aside from the brief recognition of the existence of such programs, no other purpose is intended.

Adult Basic Education and Literacy Training

In adult basic education programs (ABE), reading instruction is considered most basic. Specifically, the ABE Program is aimed at those millions of adults, 16 years and older, who have not attained the equivalent of an eighth-grade education. While the term "functionally illiterate" has not been clearly defined, the label has been applied to that group of Americans who do not possess sufficient "survival" reading skills. In 1970, a survey sponsored by the National Reading Council, and conducted by Louis Harris and Associates, reported that 21 million persons over 16 years of age lacked the reading ability necessary to perform simple, everyday tasks.

Numerous legislative acts in the mid-sixties indicated the Federal government's commitment to the task of helping adults acquire basic skills sufficient to function in today's society. Presently, all 50 of the states are operating Federally sponsored programs; there are special projects, each different in its approach to the problems of adult education.

Until the 1960s, few publishers bothered much with programs designed for teaching illiterate adults. Government funding gave rise to a new impetus in the development of adult programs, and with it more innovative approaches in content and methodology. Selected types of programs include the following varied sampling.

Machine-centered programs. Machine-centered programs are those in which tachistoscopic or other hardware, forms a crucial part of the program. *The EDL Learning 100* (1969) is a well-designed adult program in which all major reading skills are taught. On a smaller scale, computer-assisted instruction has been used with adult illiterates. At present it is expensive, and much more research evidence is required before large-scale use can be justified.

Programmed approaches. Programmed instruction, in both linear and scrambled book form, is a method of instruction that may be used successfully with some adults. Although it has certain drawbacks, its advantageous features allow each person to work at his own rate; skills are presented sequentially, with varied repetition; and feedback and reward are immediate. One example of this approach, *Lessons for Self-Instruction in Basic Skills, Reading Comprehension* (1963), representative of "branching," or the scrambled book. begins with a readability level of four and extends through high school. Another, *Program Reading for Adults* (1966), is a series of workbooks, programmed in linear fashion, which provides a strong word-attack program. Comprehension skills are not developed adequately.

Multilevel program kits. The multilevel kit, or laboratory, made up of individual lessons, provides flexibility and permits the individual to progress at his own rate. Some examples: *Reading Developmental Kits A and B* (1968) are especially designed for illiterate adults. Each kit contains 80 different lesson pamphlets, coded on readability levels of one through six. High-interest passages contain exercises for developing vocabulary and comprehension. *Basic Adult Reading Kit* (1965) is a series of high-interest, low-readability-level booklets designed to appeal to adults. Booklets begin at first grade reading level and extend through fourth grade. *Dimensions in Reading* (1968) contains 300 pamphlets with readability levels of four through eleven. Designed to develop comprehension, emphasis is placed on content and format acceptable to adults.

Traditional basal series. Several other types of programs are modeled on the basal approach. The "total language program" of the *Mott Basic Language Skills Program* (1964) covers readability level one through twelve, and is one example which provides instruction in reading, spelling, and writing.

Adult basic education programs have generally faced a staggering number of problems, with limited resources to solve them. Many programs suffer from a high dropout rate, inadequate inservice training for staffs, and poor counseling services. However, the research has demonstrated that illiterate adults can learn to read. Studies reported from three representative areas—private industry, public education, and the Armed Service (Otto, 1970)—demonstrated that positive results can be obtained when adequate resources are brought to bear.

SUMMARY

This review of selected reading programs sought to present a clear concept of the state of the art. The current attempts to meet the instructional needs of every individual were evident in broadened and revised programs with provisions for multisensory, multilevel, and multimedia teaching techniques. Nationwide, a collage of vast quantities of printed materials, films, records, tapes, kits, and games, converge and undergird the singular goal—a literate society.

However, such a concept may be distorted in the failure to mention the teacher, for a massive bulk of the research on reading has indicated very clearly that the single most important element of any reading program is the teacher. Future efforts, therefore, must focus on teacher training.

REFERENCES

Action Libraries. New York: Scholastic Book Services, 1971.

Allen, R. V., and Allen, C. *Language Experiences in Reading.* Chicago: Encyclopaedia Britannica, 1966.

Ames, W. S. Research Findings Regarding the Use of ITA. In E. C. Vilscek, ed., *A Decade of Innovations: Approaches to Beginning Reading.* Newark, Del.: International Reading Association, 1968, *12*, Part 3, 126-137.

Artley, A. S. *Trends and Practices in Secondary Reading: A Review of the Literature.* Newark, Del.: International Reading Association, 1968.

Austin, M. C., Morrison, C. et al. *The Torch Lighters: Tomorrow's Teachers of Reading.* Cambridge, Mass.: Harvard University Press, 1961.

_____, and Morrison, C. *The First R: The Harvard Report on Reading in the Elementary Schools.* New York: Macmillan, 1963.

Barbe, W. B. *Educator's Guide to Personalized Reading Instruction.* Englewood Cliffs, N.J.: Prentice-Hall, 1961.

Barton, A. H., and Wilder, D. E. Research and Practice in the Teaching of Reading: A Progress Report. In M. B. Miles, ed., *Innovations in Education.* New York: Teachers College, Columbia University, Bureau of Publications, 1964, pp. 361-398.

Basic Adult Reading Kit. Pleasantville, N.Y.: Reader's Digest, 1965.

Behavior Principles Structural Model: Model Programs Childhood Education. Washington, D.C.: U.S. Government Printing Office, Catalog No. HE 5.220:20155, 1970.

Bilingual Early Childhood Program: Model Programs Childhood Education. Washington, D.C.: U.S. Government Printing Office, Catalog No. HE 5.220:20134, 1970.

Blom, G. E., Waite, R. R., and Zimet, S. G. A Motivational Content Analysis of Children's Primers. In H. Levin and H. P. Williams, eds., *Basic Studies on Reading.* New York: Basic Books, 1970, pp. 188-221.

Bloom, B. S. *Stability and Change in Human Characteristics.* New York: Wiley, 1964, pp. 88-89.

_____, Davis, A., and Hess, R. *Compensatory Education for Cultural Deprivation.* New York: Holt, Rinehart & Winston, 1965.

Bond, G. L., and Dykstra, R. The Cooperative Research Programs in First-Grade Reading. *Reading Research Quarterly,* 1967, *2*(4).

The Bookmark Program. (2nd ed.) San Francisco: Harcourt, Brace, Jovanovich, 1973.

Breakthrough Series. Boston: Allyn & Bacon, 1972.

Brown, S., ed. *PEN the Preschool Education Newsletter,* 1971, *3*(2), p. 2.

Bruner, J. S. *The Process of Education.* Cambridge, Mass.: Harvard University Press, 1960.

Carden, M. *The Carden Method.* Glen Rock, N.J.: Mae Carden, Inc., 1953.

Chall, J. *Learning to Read: The Great Debate.* New York: McGraw-Hill, 1967.

Cohen, R. Remedial Training of First Grade Children with Visual Perceptual Retardation. *Educational Horizons,* 1966, *45,* 60-63.

Crossroads. New York: Noble & Noble, 1970.

Delacato, C. H. *The Treatment and Prevention of Reading Problems.* Springfield, Ill.: Thomas, 1959.

_____. *The Diagnosis and Treatment of Speech and Reading Problems.* Springfield, Ill.: Thomas, 1963.

Deutsch, M. The Disadvantaged Child and the Learning Process. In A. H. Passow, ed., *Education in Depressed Areas.* New York: Teachers College, Columbia University, Bureau of Publications, 1963, pp. 163-180.

Dimensions in Reading. Chicago: Science Research Associates, 1968.

Discoveries. Boston: Houghton-Mifflin, 1972.

DOVACK Program: Model Programs Childhood Education. Washington, D.C.: U.S. Government Printing Office, Catalog No. HE 5.200:20141, 1970.

Downing, J. A. The Augmented Roman Alphabet for Learning to Read. *The Reading Teacher,* 1963, *16,* 325-336.

_____. The Nature and Functions of I.T.A. in Beginning Reading. In E. C. Vilscek, ed., *A Decade of Innovations: Approaches to Beginning Reading.* Newark, Del.: International Reading Association, 1968, *12,* Part 3, 149-161.

Duker, S. Master's Studies of Individualized Reading. *Elementary English,* 1963, *40,* 280-282.

_____. *Individualized Reading.* Springfield, Ill.: Thomas, 1971.

Durkin, D. *Children Who Read Early.* New York: Teachers College, Columbia University, Bureau of Publications, 1966, 133-139.

_____. *Teaching Them to Read.* Boston: Allyn & Bacon, 1970.

_____. *Teaching Young Children to Read.* Boston: Allyn & Bacon, 1972.

Dykstra, R. Summary of the Second-Grade Phase of the Cooperative Research Program in Primary Reading Instruction. *Reading Research Quarterly,* 1968, *14*(1), 49-70.

EDL Learning 100. Huntington, N.Y.: Educational Development Laboratories, 1969.

Fernald, G. M. *Remedial Techniques in Basic School Subjects.* New York: McGraw-Hill, 1943.

Fowler, W. The Effects of Early Stimulation. In R. D. Hess and R. M. Bear, eds., *Early Education.* Chicago: Aldin, 1968, pp. 28-29.

Frostig, M. *The Marianne Frostig Developmental Test of Visual Perception.* Palo Alto, Calif.: Consulting Psychologist, 1964.

_____, and Horne, D. *The Frostig Program for the Development of Visual Perception.* Chicago: Follet, 1964.

Fry, E. B. A Diacritical Marking System to Aid Beginning Reading Instruction. *Elementary English,* 1964, *41,* 526-529.

_____. *Comparison of Three Methods of Reading Instruction (ITA, DMS, TO): Results at the End of Third Grade.* USOE Project No. 3050. New Brunswick, N.J.: Rutgers University, 1967.

_____. *Reading Instruction for Classroom and Clinic.* New York: McGraw-Hill, 1972, pp. 389-391.

Gattegno, C. *Words in Color.* Chicago: Encyclopaedia Britannica Press, 1962.

_____. The Problem of Reading is Solved. *Harvard Educational Review,* 1972, *40,* 283-286.

Getting it Together. Chicago: Science Research Associates, 1973.

Gillingham, A., and Stillman, B. *Remedial Training for Children with Specific Disability in Reading, Spelling, and Penmanship.* Cambridge, Mass.: Educators Publishing Service, 1968.

Gillooly, W. B. The Promise of I.T.A. is a Delusion. *Phi Delta Kappan,* 1966, *47,* 545-553.

Goldberg, H. K., and Schiffman, G. B. *Dyslexia, Problems of Reading Disability.* New York: Grune & Stratton, 1972.

Goodman, K. S. Dialect Barriers to Reading Comprehension. *Elementary English,* 1965, *42,* 853-860.

Groff, P. J. Comparison of Individualized and Ability-Grouping Approaches to Reading Achievement. *Elementary English,* 1963, *40,* 258-264, 276.

Hahn, H. T. Three Approaches to Beginning Reading Instruction— ITA, Language Arts, and Basic Readers. *The Reading Teacher,* 1966, *19,* 590-594.

_____. Three Approaches to Beginning Reading Instruction— ITA, Language Experience, and Basic Readers—Extended into Second Grade. *The Reading Teacher,* 1967, *20,* 711-715.

Harris, T. L. Reading. In R. L. Ebel, ed., *Encyclopedia of Educational Research.* (4th ed.) New York: Macmillan, 1969, pp. 1069-1104.

Hay, J., and Wingo, C. E. *Reading with Phonics.* Philadelphia: Lippincott, 1954.

Heckelman, R. G. A Neurological Impress Method of Reading Instruction. *Academic Therapy,* 1969, *4,* 227-282.

Heilman, A. W. *Principles and Practices of Teaching Reading.* (3rd ed.) Columbus, Ohio: Charles E. Merrill, 1972.

Holmes, J. A., and Rose, I. M. Disadvantaged Children and the Effectiveness of ITA. *The Reading Teacher,* 1969, *22,* 350-356.

Hunt, L. C. J., ed. *The Individualized Reading Program: A Guide for Classroom Teaching.* Newark, Del.: International Reading Association, 1967, *11,* Part 3.

Hunt, J. McV. *Intelligence and Experience.* New York: Ronald Press, 1961.

Interdependent Learner Model: Model Programs Childhood Education. Washington, D.C.: U.S. Government Printing Office, Catalog No. HE 5.220:20149, 1970.

Kephart, N. C. *The Slow Learner in the Classroom.* Columbus, Ohio: Charles E. Merrill, 1960.

Klineberg, O. Life is Fun in a Smiling, Fair-Skinned World. *Saturday Review,* 1963, *46,* 75-77, 87.

Kohl, H. *36 Children.* New York: New American Library, 1967.

Laubach, F. C. *Learn English the New Way.* Syracuse, N.Y.: New Readers Press, 1962.

_____. Progress Toward World-Wide Literacy. In R. C. Staiger and C. Y. Melton, eds., *New Developments in Programs, Training Aids, and Procedures for College-Adult Reading.* Milwaukee, Wis.: National Reading Conference, 1963, 87-99.

Lee, D. M., and Allen, R. V. *Learning to Read Through Experience.* (2nd ed.) New York: Appleton-Century-Crofts, 1963.

Lessons for Self-Instruction in Basic Skills. Monterey, Calif.: California Test Bureau, McGraw-Hill, 1963.

Loban, W. D. Teaching Children who Speak Social Class Dialects. *Elementary English,* 1968, *45,* 592-599, 618.

_____. The Language of Elementary School Children. *National Council of Teachers of English, Research Report No. 1.*

Champaign, Ill.: National Council of Teachers of English, 1963.

Loepp, K. V. Individualizing Reading Instruction. In T. C. Barrett and D. D. Johnson, eds., *Views of Elementary Reading Instruction.* Newark, Del.: International Reading Association, 1973, pp. 65-70.

Malone, J. R. The Unifon System. *Wilson Library Bulletin,* 1965, *40,* 63-65.

———. The Larger Aspects of Spelling Reform. In W. K. Durr, ed., *Reading Instruction: Dimensions and Issues.* New York: Houghton-Mifflin, 1967, pp. 60-70.

Mazurkiewics, A. J. Teaching Reading in America Using I/T/A. *Elementary English,* 1964, *41,* 766-772.

McCracken, G., and Walcutt, C. C. *Basic Reading.* Philadelphia: Lippincott, 1963.

McCracken, R. A., and McCracken, M. J. *Reading is Only the Tiger's Tail.* San Rafael, Calif.: Leswing Press, 1972.

McKee, P., and Brzeinski, J. E. *The Effectiveness of Teaching Reading in Kindergarten.* Cooperative Research Project, 5-0371. Denver: Denver Public Schools, 1966.

Merrill Linguistic Readers. Columbus, Ohio: Charles E. Merrill, 1966.

Mott Basic Language Skills Program. Galien, Mich.: Allied Educational Council, 1964.

National Center for Educational Communication. *Model Programs Childhood Education.* Washington, D.C.: U.S. Government Printing Office, 1970.

Niemeyer, J. H. The Bank Street Readers: Support for Movement Toward an Integrated Society. *The Reading Teacher,* 1965, *18,* 542-545.

New York Times, The. A Therapy System for Young Scored. 1968, May 7, *42*:2.

Olsen, W. D. *Child Development.* Boston: Heath, 1949, pp. 402-404.

Otto, W. Reading and ABE: What We Know, What We Need to Know. In W. S. Griffith, and A. P. Mayes, eds., *Adult Basic Education: The State of the Art.* Washington, D.C.: United States Government Printing Office, March 1970, 110-128.

———, McMenemy, R. A., and Smith, R. J. *Corrective and Remedial Teaching.* (2nd ed.) Palo Alto, Calif.: Houghton-Mifflin, 1973.

Palo Alto Reading Program (2nd ed.) San Francisco: Harcourt, Brace, Jovanovich, 1973.

Programmed Reading for Adults. New York: McGraw-Hill, 1966.

Ratz, M. S. Unifon: A Sound Way to Read. In E. C. Vilscek, ed., *A Decade of Innovations: Approaches to Beginning Reading.* Newark, Del.: International Reading Association, 1968, *12,* Part 3, 92-99.

Read Systems. Chicago: Scott, Foresman, 1971.

Reading 360. Boston: Ginn, 1970.

Reading Development Kits A and B. Menlo Park, Calif.: Addison-Wesley, 1968.

Robbins, M. P. Creeping, Laterality, and Reading. *Academic Therapy Quarterly,* 1966, *1,* 200-206. (a)

———. The Delacato Interpretation of Neurological Organization. *Reading Research Quarterly,* 1966, *1,* 57-58. (b)

Rosen, C. An Experimental Study of Visual Perceptual Training and Reading Achievement in First Grade. *Perceptual and Motor Skills,* 1966, *22,* 979-986.

Russell, D. H., and Fea, H. R. Research on Teaching Reading. In N. L. Gage, ed., *Handbook of Research on Teaching.* Chicago: Rand McNally, 1963, 865-928.

Sartain, H. W. Of Stars and Statistics. In L. C. Hunt, ed., *The Individualized Reading Program: A Guide for Classroom Teaching.* Newark, Del.: International Reading Association, 1967, *11,* Part 3, 64-72.

———. Individualized Reading: Conclusions Based on Research Reports. In E. C. Vilscek, ed., *A Decade of Innovations: Approaches to Beginning Reading,* 1968, *12,* Part 3, 45-56.

———. What are the Advantages and Disadvantages of Individualized Instruction? In N. B. Smith, ed., *Current Issues in Reading.* Newark, Del.: International Reading Association, 1969, *13,* Part 2, 328-343.

Smith, J. A. *Creative Teaching of the Language Arts in the Elementary School.* Boston: Allyn & Bacon, 1967.

Smith, N. B. *American Reading Instruction.* Newark, Del.: International Reading Association, 1967.

Spache, G. D., and Spache, E. B. *Reading in the Elementary School* (2nd ed.) Boston: Allyn & Bacon, 1969, pp. 170-185.

Spaulding, R. B., and Spaulding, W. T. *The Writing Road to Reading.* New York: Singer, 1963.

Strickland, R. A. The Language of Elementary School Children: Its Relationship to the Language of Reading Textbooks and the Quality of Reading of Selected Children. *Bulletin of the School of Education,* Indiana University, 1962, *38,* pp. 1-131.

SWRL Beginning Reading Program. Boston: Ginn, 1972.

SWRL Kindergarten Program. Boston: Ginn, 1972.

Veatch, J. *Individualizing Your Reading Program.* New York: Putnam, 1959.

Vilseck, E. C. What Research has Shown about the Language-Experience Program. In E. C. Vilseck, ed., *A Decade of Innovations: Approaches to Beginning Reading.* Newark, Del.: International Reading Association, 1968, 12, Part 3, pp. 9-23.

The Way It Is. Boston: Ginn, 1967.

Wingert, R. C. Evaluation of a Readiness Training Program. *The Reading Teacher,* 1969, *22,* 325-328.

ADDITIONAL RESOURCES

Aids to Media Selection for Students and Teachers. Washington, D.C.: United States Government Printing Office, 1971.

Buros, Oscar K., ed. *Reading Tests and Reviews.* Highland Park, N.J.: Gryphon Press, 1968.

Elementary English and *English Journal.* Champaign, Ill.: National Council of Teachers of English.

ERIC Clearinghouse on Reading. Bloomington, Indiana: Indiana University School of Education.

Center for Applied Linguistics. *Inventory of Projects and Activities in Reading and English.* Washington, D.C.: The Center, 1968.

Journal of Reading. Newark, Del.: International Reading Association.

Journal of Reading Behavior. Athens, Ga.: National Reading Conference.

Journal of Reading Specialist. Rochester, N.Y.: College Reading Association.

Reading Newsreport. New York, N.Y.: Multimedia Education, Inc.

Reading Research Quarterly. Newark, Del.: International Reading Association.

The Reading Teacher. Newark, Del.: International Reading Association.

Right to Read Office. U.S. Office of Education, 400 Maryland Ave., S.W., Washington, D.C.

MAJOR INTEREST GROUPS

American Educational Research Association
1126 Sixteenth Street, N.W.
Washington, D.C. 20036

Association for Supervision and Curriculum Development
1201 Sixteenth Street, N.W.
Washington, D.C. 20036

Committee on Diagnostic Reading Tests, Inc.
Mountain Home, North Carolina 28758

Council for Basic Education
725 Fifteenth Street, N.W.
Washington, D.C. 20003

International Reading Association
Six Tyre Avenue
Newark, Delaware 19711

National Advisory Committee on Adult Basic Education
Department of Health, Education and Welfare
Washington, D.C.

National Advisory Committee on Dyslexia and Related
  Reading Disorders
Office of the Secretary
Department of Health, Education and Welfare
Bethesda, Maryland 20014

National Advisory Committee on the Education of
  Disadvantaged Children
1900 E. Street, N.W.
Washington, D.C. 20415

National Council of Teachers of English
508 South Sixth Street
Champaign, Illinois 61820

Phi Delta Kappa, Inc.
Bloomington, Indiana

Philco-Ford Corporation
Communications and Electronics Division
Willow Grove, Pennsylvania 19090

RCA Instructional Systems
530 University Avenue, Dept. QA
Palo Alto, California 94301

105

EDUCATION FOR SEXUALITY IN THE UNITED STATES

by Mary S. Calderone, M.D., M.P.H.
Sex Information and Education Council of the U.S.
(SIECUS)
New York, New York

Sex education for children and young people is no new thing in the United States. World War I marked the liberalization of many attitudes about sex as well as the beginnings of changes in behavior. Leading individuals here and there advocated "telling the truth" to children. The Child Study Association of America in the 1920s led the way toward an open approach on all topics, including sex. The United Congress of Parent-Teacher Associations and two White House Conferences on Children in the period between the wars recommended sex education programs. Yet, looking back, we have to recognize that what at that time was being called *sex* education was in reality *reproductive* education. The pioneer Sidonie Gruenberg's classic, *The Wonderful Story of How You Were Born,* still a best seller since its appearance in the 1950s, did give the facts of reproductive life for younger

children, but dealt little with the sexual aspects. Thus it and other similar books, good as they were, still permitted parents to think that once the child had been given this information about reproduction, the whole job of education about sex had been done—a point of view that was obviously limited, and certainly does not meet the needs of today's preadolescents, much less those of adolescents.

What marks the 1960s, and especially SIECUS' role, is open acknowledgement and confrontation of truths about *sexuality,* i.e., the totality of the being of any age as male or female—with the multiplicity of variations in forms of expression and feelings of that sexuality at various life stages and in various lifestyles, very few of which, whether in individual or group, having to do with reproduction.

I shall refer later to gender identity, gender behavior, and genitalization, all components of the total sexuality of the individual that today bear on the changing concepts of male and female roles and relationships in a rapidly evolving society. It is this aspect of education for human sexuality in the United States, so necessary for adolescents, that has stirred up the opposition's deepest fears and guilts: being for the most part nonscientists, untrained to distinguish between objective descriptions of phenomena and advocacy, for them discussion of masturbation or homosexuality means to advocate these—indeed, actually to teach them in the classroom! The facts about masturbation as an almost universal and "normal" phenomenon, and about the origins (as we now perceive these) of homosexuality in early childhood, simply could not be assimilated in any realistic way by many members of this society, just as today the facts about human evolution are still being denied by fundamentalist groups in various parts of the world, or for that matter, as was Galileo's fact that the earth revolves around the sun.

Nevertheless, as will be shown, the movement forward since 1971 ensures that the former narrow or false views of human sexuality, and how to teach about it, are not likely again to prevail.

There are many indications of broadening comprehensions and searchings outside of the United States, that are indicative that other countries quite independently are probing and following the same trains of thought to very similar conclusions. Small groups of scientists in Spain, Switzerland, France, Venezuela, and some other Latin American countries are quietly but firmly leading the way. The reason is not hard to find: today the sex education movement is characterized by two factors: (1) broadening recognition that its primary target cannot any longer be youth alone, but the human being of any age; (2) its primary effectors are not a few isolated, pioneering, nonprofessional individuals, but leading members of the major professions who have become aware that training in human sexuality will not merely help them as individuals, but is actually essential to extend their qualifications for the practice of their professions. This has been SIECUS' position since 1964.

It is for these reasons that this paper will not focus only on the sex education of youth in the United States today, but on the far broader scene, for it is the changing climate of awareness by the society and of developing skills in the major professions that can be counted on ultimately to carry the day on behalf of youth.

EFFORTS IN THE PROFESSIONS

Medicine

The first significant professional efforts occurred in the field of medicine, when Lief (1964) and others first began drawing attention to the inadequate and troubled attitudes about sex found among medical students, both on behalf of themselves and of their patients. At that time only three of the 110 medical schools in the United States and Canada included even scanty course work in the field of human sexuality. In that same period, at the 1964 Annual Meeting of the American College of Obstetricians and Gynecologists, the President, Dr. Frank Lock (Professor of Obstetrics at the Bowman Gray School of Medicine in North Carolina) electrified the members by presenting an opening symposium on marital, family, and sexual counseling at which three out of the four presenters were sociologists and marriage counselors, rather than physicians.

Shortly thereafter, Dr. Lock established the Behavioral Science Center within his own Department of Obstetrics and Gynecology, to serve as a teaching center in marital and sexual problems encountered in the practice of medicine. Subsequently Dr. Harold Lief, after coming to the University of Pennsylvania Medical School as Professor of Psychiatry and Director of the Division of Family Studies, established there the Center for the Study of Sex Education in Medicine. This Center has served as a focal point for the training and orientation of physicians, clergymen, and other professionals in the areas of marriage and sex counseling. In particular, it has served as a training center for faculty members of medical schools wishing to initiate curricular offerings in the field of sexuality. Coombs (1968) showed that by 1966, 29 medical schools had begun doing so. As of 1972, approximately 88 of the 110 medical schools, and in 1975 close to 100 percent of them, included sexuality courses, many required rather than elective.

A new and especially interesting development is typified at the University of Minnesota Medical School, where, under the direction of Dr. Richard Chilgren, an Interdisciplinary Division of Human Sexuality was established in 1971 directly under the office of the Dean of the Medical School. Its faculty is drawn from the graduate schools and major departments of the University (medicine, nursing, law, sociology, etc.) and from the American Lutheran Church's National Office and the three theological seminaries based in the Minneapolis area. In addition to the more extensive permanent curricular courses in the medical school, intensive workshops in sexuality are conducted by the medical school not only for medical, nursing, education, law, theological, home economics, sociology, psychology, and other students and their spouses, both undergraduates and graduates, but also to meet the increasing requests from practicing professionals of the local community, such as the clergy, police and other law officers, judges, educators, youth workers, etc. Whereas the course work at medical schools

extends over a period of time, these workshops usually last only two days, and are specifically designed to be totally experiential rather than didactic, in terms of intensive and lengthy exposure to professionally produced, explicit films of all varieties of human sexual behavior. Immediately following each segment there are equally intensive and lengthy (one- to two-hour) small group discussions. The primary goal of these workshops is not to instruct, but to break through the calcified attitudes about human sexual behavior of the participating individuals as quickly as possible, in order to reach their inner and most protected attitudes, prejudices, and feelings. The entire process is one of desensitization and demythologizing, followed by resensitization. Carefully conducted before-and-after attitude testing has demonstrated the value of this saturation approach, for after experiencing the sessions the individual is then apparently freed to move into more didactic work with fewer blocks and a more rational acceptance of human sexuality and sexual behavior than previously. The extended course work in human sexuality of the University of Minnesota Medical School curriculum itself is found to be more productive for those who have first gone through the short and intensive two-day workshop sessions.

Dr. Lief, of Pennsylvania, carries on similar workshops in various parts of the United States for graduate physicians, clergy, and teachers, and at his Center has developed the Sex Knowledge and Attitude Test (SKAT) for use before and after educational experiences. These tests are widely used, and are proving their value in measuring the changes in attitudes during the workshops and courses. Other similar centers are being developed in various parts of the United States.

Additionally, a number of state and county medical societies, as well as specialty groups such as academies of general practice or of pediatrics in the larger cities, have carried out or sponsored half-day or one-day symposia on a broad range of topics relating to human sexual behavior, as did the American Medical Association at its 1975 annual meeting. It can truly be said that the present generation is already showing an understanding and awareness of human sexual behavior and its problems that should prove immensely valuable to them in practice.

Education

One indication of the increasing interest of the education profession is the number of requests coming to the SIECUS Education and Research Department for guidance in framing and selecting materials for doctoral theses in one or another aspect of teaching about or research in human sexual behavior. These requests come primarily from the fields of education, sociology, or psychology, and excellent reference textbooks are being published for use at university undergraduate and graduate levels; and SIECUS' own publication. *The Individual, Sex and Society—a SIECUS Handbook for Teachers and Counselors,* edited by Broderick and Bernard (1969), sociologists who were members of the SIECUS Board, and published by The Johns Hopkins University Press, is regarded as a basic source book.

Sex education courses for college and university students themselves, rather than as professionals, have developed greatly in the past 18 months. Some of the courses have been initiated by faculty, but a number have undoubtedly been stimulated and helped to be developed on the initiative of the students themselves. Several models are followed: a simple course of lectures, given by faculty members or resource people from the community or from other parts of the country; lectures combined with discussion groups, which themselves are usually led by students who have taken the course the previous year; or a series of evening seminars organized and led entirely by students who invite speakers. Some measure of the growing inclusion of this kind of course work at the university level is the growing number of excellent reference textbooks in the field.

A number of counseling guides on sex for college-level students, including information on contraceptive and abortion counseling, have been published, some of them prepared by student committees, and available also on the open market in soft cover.

Religion

Few people outside the United States are aware of the extensive involvement and activities in this field on the part of the major religious communities. Even in the United States, the facts come as a considerable surprise to many individuals. Yet the SIECUS Board has always included Roman Catholic, Protestant and Jewish clergy as strong participants.

The U.S. Catholic Conference of Bishops, through its Family Life Division, in Washington, D.C. (1969), published an outstanding series of booklets on sex education for use by Roman Catholic schools, some for parents and others for teachers. The Committee on Sex Education of the Diocese of Rochester, New York (1971) published teachers' guides for children 6-13 and 14-18, as well as a parents' handbook. The Director of Chicago's Cana Conference, The Reverend Walter Imbiorski (1971), published a series of eight texts with teachers' guides and parents' handbooks designed for children 6-13, a teacher's resource kit with cassette tape and printed materials, and a book of readings for parents and teachers.

Similarly, various Protestant communities (American and Southern Baptist Conventions, the three Lutheran Church groups, the United Methodist Church, the United Presbyterian Church in the U.S.A., and others) have each published their own curricular materials. Unlike the Roman Catholic Church, which is free to use its religiously oriented materials in its own schools, the Protestant denominational materials are necessarily designed to be used in their own church schools.

Likewise, several of the Protestant denominations have issued publications for adults on religion and sex education, and on the relationship between religion and sexuality.

The theological seminaries have become aware of human sexuality as a topic that should be integrated into their curricula later than the medical schools. It has been shown that, with physicians, it is the clergy to whom persons in trouble about sex most often turn.

Behavioral Sciences

It is undoubtedly from the field of behavioral science that our greatest knowledge about human sexuality has developed so that, in turn, educators can approach youth with a better understanding of the sexual stages of development for each age, and the content that might be appropriate for specific cultural or age groups. The Group for the Advancement of Psychiatry (GAP), consisting of nearly 200 of the leading psychiatrists of the United States, has published *Sex and the College Student* (1966) and *Normal Adolescence: Its Dynamics and Impact* (1968). Both of these documents accord full value and attention to the psychosexual development of the young individual, and, coming from such authoritative sources, have helped to dispel a number of crippling mythologies, as did the 1974 statement of the American Psychiatric Association that the state of homosexuality does not per se constitute an illness.

A number of eminent sociologists have carried out studies of profound importance as regards sexual behavior. Reiss (1967), Bell, R. and Chaskes (1970), and Zelnik and Kantner (1971) delineated in their successive studies the changes in attitudes and behaviors observed regarding premarital sex, first among college-age students and now in adolescents. Such carefully documented research provides knowledge that is invaluable to convey to youth, which can then place their own personal behavior in the context of a wider framework, to facilitate more informed judgments for governing their sexual lives.

Closely related is the important research work of Dr. Lawrence Kohlberg and his associate, Dr. Carol Gilligan, at Harvard University (1970). As a graduate student at the University of Chicago, Dr. Kohlberg became interested in children's moral development. For his Ph.D. thesis he interviewed 75 children between the ages of 10 and 16, to investigate social and environmental influences on them. In the years since then, he and his colleagues followed these groups, interviewing them every three years with standardized moral dilemmas. From their responses he identified distinct stages of moral development, and in the seven advanced and less advanced societies in Western Europe, the Far and Near East, and North and South America, he found the same six stages and in the same sequence. Not all individuals progressed through the six, but no individual reached any stage without having passed through all of the previous stages.

The first two, or "preconventional," stages are characteristic of younger children, and are simple cause-and-effect, obedience-and-punishment stages. The second two, or "conventional," stages are reached by the great majority of people, and relate to reasoning based on good behavior or social approval, law and order, and strict rules.

In the last two, or "postconventional," stages there was independent effort to define and choose moral principles, values, and behavior apart from authority and the individual's membership in a group.

Kohlberg states that the higher stages of moral reasoning are not reached by discipline or punishment or training, nor by fiat or preachment. The way to encourage higher-stage moral reasoning is to live in a society that takes moral issues seriously, and allows participation in discussion on them by its members. Thus, exposure of the child to individuals who are in higher stages, so that he becomes involved in discussions and disagreements and perhaps a defense of his own moral stance is, as Kohlberg states, the major determinant of his own advance to higher stages.

The importance of this work to sex education is clear: for the first time it provides religion with solidly based and researched information on the *process* by which individuals arrive at their moral values. SIECUS has taken pains to disseminate information about this research to as many national church bodies as possible, which have responded with interest, for it appears to support a basic position of leading religionists, including the Roman Catholic Church here in the United States. As Meyer (1969), a Roman Catholic, stated:

> [Education] should aim at encouraging the child to grow into an adult who thinks, judges, and acts for himself. It should not aim to turn out an obedient robot relating by heart the wisdom (or lack of wisdom) imparted by its teachers. Sex education is just one aspect of this whole process. It rests on the firm conviction that it is impossible for anyone to attain real maturity unless his sexuality is developed and educated along the way.

With Kohlberg's work in mind, the fears of many religiously oriented parents that in the U.S. public school framework, by which consideration of religion has to be excluded, discussion of sex outside of a religious context will lead to a neglect or deterioration of moral values can be shown to be unfounded. A SIECUS book, *Sexuality and Human Values* (1974), has highlighted these findings.

Other Professional Groups

Other professions are beginning to interest themselves in learning about human sexuality, especially those in contact with children and youth at critical formation times in their development. Teachers, nurses, social workers, youth leaders in various organizations such as the Ys, librarians, officers of the law, family planning workers—all are becoming aware that the time of the birds and the bees is long past, and the time of dealing directly with the great truths of the sexual aspects of human nature is with us and can no longer be put aside. These professions, therefore, are moving at varying rates toward incorporation of study materials in human sexuality in their professional curricula. Obviously this will not happen overnight, but the rate at which it is happening is significant: the decade of 1960-1970 could be called the decade of recognition of human sexuality as an area of scholarship by professionals in many fields.

There are other national organizations, such as the American Association of Sex Educators and Counselors, that are concerning themselves with the sex education of youth. Among these are: the National Council on Family Relations; American Social Health Association; American Association of Marriage and Family Counselors; and the Society for the Scientific Study of Sex.

THE SEXUALIZATION PROCESS

In order for professionals to understand the full meaning of the term "education" for human sexuality, so that they can bring their efforts to bear on this process in the growing individual in an effective way, whatever their profession, it is necessary to sketch in at this point what is meant by the sexualization process. This consists essentially of three components.

One must first reemphasize that reproductive maturation is not one of these components, but stands alone, being automatic in its evolution. Whatever the early influences brought to bear on the individual, that individual will nevertheless, short of anatomical or chromosomal abnormality, or extraordinary physical inanition, eventually ejaculate or menstruate. It is not even necessary for the male to ejaculate to be able to function sexually in the strict sense, he need only erect and experience orgasm, and the female can most certainly function reproductively in the absence of all true sexual functions. Therefore, the reproductive aspect of individual maturation will not be considered here.

The three components of the sexualization process, roughly in order of their chronologies (which of course overlap), are (1) establishment of *core gender identity*, (2) development of *gender role behavior* appropriate to that identity, and (3) *genitalization*.

It is generally accepted by behavioral scientists that the child achieves his *gender identity* at the latest by the age of 3: that is, by then he should be able to say with sureness and accuracy, "I am a boy" or "I am a girl." Most parents have little or no concept of their vital role in the achievement of their child's gender identity, which they quite literally program into him by their own attitudes; so it is those who deal with parents who must begin to educate them on their critical role in this as well as in the other two components of the sexualization process.

The second is the development of *role behavior* appropriate to gender. Here the arena of action expands from the parents primarily, to all adults who come in close contact with the child. Here too, sociology and anthropology can help society and parents to understand that the movement away from the former narrow and stereotyped sexist concepts of what constitutes "appropriate" masculine or feminine role behavior is today marked part of the evolution of the society. It will be some time before stabilization of universally acceptable masculine and feminine roles can take place, if ever, particularly when sexual behavior is so closely bound up with the socioeconomic and educational status of women in all parts of the world. What psychiatrists emphasize, however, is the importance of avoiding conflict between gender identity and self-desired role behavior: a boy who feels stable in his identity as a male, and yet wants to play with dolls or dance ballet, should not be subjected to mockery or criticism, nor any implication that he is in any way not normal. Just as little girls may be given stethoscopes to play with, and told they may become nurses *or* doctors when they grow up, so little boys may be given toys that may more closely relate to their own interests, rather than insistence on mechanical or sporting toys exclusively.

Furthermore, as the consensus grows that homosexuality exists in a wide range, as demonstrated by Kinsey in his 0-6 scale, there is also increased understanding that the estimated 5 percent of males and 2.5 percent of females who are exclusively homosexual can function satisfactorily and responsibly within this wide range, provided society permits them to do so. It needs to be reemphasized that the origins of heterosexuality and of homosexuality are not congenital, glandular, or due to mental illness, but are now considered to be laid down very early within the preschool child's closest family relationships, namely with his or her mother and/or father. In any case, male homosexuals who in adult life choose other males as sex objects almost always identify clearly as males and need have little problem with gender identity except that which society creates for them, and the same is true in female homosexuality.

The third component of the sexualization process is *genitalization,* that is, the development of the capacity to localize sensual feeling at the genital level, eventually culminating in the experience of orgasm. It is this process that people are most afraid of, and is therefore the least understood. I would point out that the development of genital capacity is, to all intents and purposes, automatic in the male: he cannot have pubertal seminal emissions without orgasm. Indeed, Kinsey observed that by the age of one year approximately 30 percent of boy babies had experienced orgasm, and that by the age of 18 practically 100 percent of males have in one way or another achieved it. But the genitalization process in the female, whether for biological or cultural reasons, is apparently different. Kinsey showed that by the age of 18 only about 40 percent of females had achieved it, and there is general consensus that, far from being automatic, as with the male, capacity for orgasm in the female is apt to be learned, either by oneself or from another.

Another major difference in genitalization between the male and the female has been widely observed: apparently in the male, genitalization is just that—sharply and specifically focused in the genitals. In the female, genitalization, when it is accomplished, is more apt to be embedded in a matrix of generalized feelings that affect the entire body—part of a diffuse sensuality, so to speak. Of great importance is the psychiatric consensus that parents must be helped to understand that over-interference by them regarding the toilet-training and sexual activities in their young children is almost undoubtedly one precursor of their later unsuccessful sexual adjustments as adults. In other words, whatever efforts parents make on either of these two counts should be restricted to socialization, that is, to learning how to differentiate between what is acceptable public or private behavior, and parental efforts to socialize should not involve repression, punishment, shame, or guilt. Successful erotic response in later life requires acceptance on the part of adults of the right of the child, not only to sexual privacy—that is, to his own sexual life, including sexual fantasies—but to sexual experiencing at appropriate moments and in appropriate ways. It is obviously the question of appropriateness to which scientists and moral-ists are turning their attention today, but there is general agreement that it is vital to accord recognition and acceptance of the child's body as a legitimate source of pleasure. The balance as to how human beings consider it appropriate to use genitality throughout the life cycle can swing wildly, from the 13-year-old girl who considers it appropriate for herself to have full intercourse to the parent who considers *any* form of body contact totally inappropriate until the wedding night. Both are not only unrealistic, but carry real potentiality for damage. Refinement of this balance requires not moralistic pronouncements, but the combined knowledge, skills, and open warmth of many people.

The challenge for sex education is how to reach our young people before irreparable damage to them continues to occur from irrational attitudes and mythological misinformation. For the most profoundly effective and permanent form of sex education is not that which takes place in the comparative formality of the classroom, in the form of a lecture, a film, or a book. Rather, it is that flood of sex-related and sexual impressions and interpersonal interchanges that flood in on the growing organism from the moment of his birth—and perhaps even before—from the people with whom, and the society in which, he has his being.

In the United States it is at this time not possible to hazard even a wild guess as to how many schools include course work in human sexuality, much less its extent, quality, and effects. The panorama is too vast, and surveys are too difficult and expensive to conduct at this time. One must bear in mind, too, that because of the vocal minority opposition, with its personal persecution of individuals who teach or administer programs, many school programs are undoubtedly quiet and underground. There is clear evidence, however, that professionals *will* construct, and parents accept, the school programs they want for their children. It was toward creating a climate of opinion for deepening and broadening society's concepts of what individuals need at various ages, as regards information and education about human sexuality, that SIECUS was formed and continues to gear its efforts.

PROGNOSIS

It is my personal belief that the 1970s and perhaps the decade through the 80s, will eventually be known as the period in which we finally confronted and began to understand the nature, the importance, and the role of that portion of sexuality which we can call eroticism. Although we can be aware that it is far more than mere genitality, at this moment the comprehension of it is not clear. Certainly many other cultures, in other ages as well as in our own, have assigned varying values to it—from the most negative to the most positive. I do not believe, however, that any society has ever really come to terms with it, if only because, for one thing, up to now eroticism has tended to be male-oriented, with the female being the male's convenient adjunct for its enjoyment. In fact, it is not primarily its enjoyment so much as its existence, its nature, our understanding of it, and what role we will choose to accord it, that it presently at issue.

Obviously the more intellectually or spiritually oriented cultures or individuals have tended to separate the erotic from mere genitality, and to ascribe to it higher values than sheer expression of, and outlet for, sexual tension. Other cultures have worshipped it as a be-all and end-all of living. Still others, including that in the United States and elsewhere today, exploit it for commercial profit.

But the sex drive, so-called, is born to greater or lesser degree in every individual. This being so, we cannot ascribe a value to it as good or bad in and of itself, any more than we can ascribe a value to intellectual capacity; that is how we put to use these inborn faculties, and how they are developed, that can lead to value judgments. Our young people today are recognizing in many ways that eroticism is clearly a part of life, one to be accepted and honored, but along with their repudiation of exploitation of other human attributes by adults, they repudiate our exploitation of eroticism. This is one great advantage we have in education about sex: the drive of today's youth toward a clear-sighted and honest approach to the understanding of the human being as an entity, with all of his weaknesses and his strengths, and all of his capacities, both inborn and acquired. We need to support this drive, for education is and for sexuality is phenomenological: what the child experiences sexually, the child becomes and the adult will be. Only by a positive climate in the society and a massive, planned, positive approach to the sexualization process by the highest leadership elements of the society, will parents and their children be reached and helped in the next two decades to confront, to understand, to accept, to integrate, to honor, to use, the eroticism that is part of being human. Then, perhaps, we might begin to see generations of growing up free of the guilts, mythologies, and distortions about sex that we see today, fully capable of living fulfilled and joyous sexual lives well into old age, in responsible and meaningful relationships that contribute to the well-being not only of those within the relationships and of those surrounding them, but of the society at large.

One thing is sure: in the United States we are no longer playing guessing games, or trading on tradition based on wishful thinking. We are at the beginnings of finding and establishing the scientific truths about this central area of human life.

REFERENCES

Bell, R., and Chaskes, J. Premarital Sexual Experience Among Coeds. *Journal of Marriage and Family,* February 1970.

Broderick, C., and Bernard, J., eds. *The Individual, Sex and Society: A SIECUS Handbook for Teachers and Counselors.* Baltimore: The Johns Hopkins Press, 1969.

Calderone, Mary S., ed. *Sexuality and Human Values.* New York: Association Press, 1974.

Committee on Sex Education, Diocese of Rochester, N.Y. *Education in Love.* New Jersey: The Paulist Press, 1970.

Coombs, R. H. Sex Education in American Medical Colleges. In *Human Sexuality in Medical Education and Practice,* C. Vincent, ed. Springfield, Ill.: Charles C. Thomas, 1968.

Family Life Division. *Guidelines for the Formation of a Program of Sex Education; Sex Education: A Guide for Parents and Educators; Sex Education: A Guide for Teachers.* Washington, D.C.: U.S. Catholic Conference, 1969.

Gilligan, C., Kohlberg, L. et al. Moral Reasoning about Sexual Dilemmas. In *Report of Commission on Obscenity and Pornography.* Washington, D.C.: U.S. Government Printing Office, 1971.

GAP (Group for Advancement of Psychiatry). Committee on Adolescence, *Normal Adolescence.* New York: Charles Scribner's Sons, 1968.

———. Committee on the College Student, *Sex and the College Student.* New York: Antheneum Publishers, 1966.

Imbiorski, W., ed. *Becoming a Person.* New York: Benziger, Inc., 1971.

Katchadourian, Herant A., and Lunde, Donald T. *Fundamentals of Human Sexuality,* second edition. New York: Holt, Rinehart and Winston, 1975.

Kohlberg (see Gilligen).

Lief, H. Orientation of Future Physicians in Psycho-Sexual Attitudes. In *Manual of Contraceptive Practice,* Calderone, M.S., ed. Baltimore: The Williams & Wilkins Co., 1964 (first edition).

Lock, F. *The Challenge of Change.* Obstetrics and Gynecology, September 1964.

McCary, J. *Human Sexuality.* Cincinnati: Van Nostrand-Reinhold, 1967.

Meyer, J. Sex Education and Psychological Readiness. In U.S. Catholic Conference, *Sex Education: A Guide for Teachers.* Washington, D.C., 1969.

Money, John, and Ehrhardt, Anke A. *Man & Woman, Boy and Girl.* Baltimore: The Johns Hopkins University Press, 1972.

Reiss, I. *Premarital Sexual Standards.* SIECUS Study Guide No. 5. New York, SIECUS, 1967.

Yale University, Student Committee on Human Sexuality. *The Student Guide to Sex on Campus.* New York: New American Library, 1971.

Zelnik, M., and Kantner, J. Premarital Sexual Experience in Girls under 19. In *Report of the Presidential Commission on Population Growth and the American Future.*

PART VIII

SOME ALTERNATIVES AND OPTIONS IN EDUCATION

106

OPEN EDUCATION

by George E. Hein
Lesley College
Graduate School of Education
Cambridge, Massachusetts

Open education (or informal education, integrated day, open corridor or Leicestershire plan—the last used briefly and only in the United States) describes an educational philosophy and practice which sees both learning and knowledge as interactive processes between the learner and the thing known. Open education stresses the value of the individual as a person, the need to view the learner as an important member of the learning process, and the necessity to respect schooling as an important part of life, rather than simply as a preparation for life. This set of views places great emphasis on learning through interaction with the world, thus materials and experiences of many kinds are important; it concerns itself with the social processes attendant to education, thus open education adherents talk about the society within schools and the relations between schools and society.

In the United States the movement has grown from a small beginning in the middle sixties to recognizable proportions today. There are major programs supporting and developing open education in a number of cities, towns, and rural districts. The movement is still small, affecting less than 5 percent of the children in school today. Although most recently some interest has been expressed at the middle school and high school level, the majority of open schools are at the elementary level. A number of independent schools, continuing a long tradition dating back to the progressive education movement, and receiving support for teachers through workshops sponsored by National Association of Independent Schools, have developed open education programs. The major activity today, however, is within the public schools.

The stress on work within the public schools distinguishes open education from the "free school" movement—on the whole, a more antiauthoritarian, less intellectual, more middle-class effort concentrated in "alternative schools" (often short-lived), and outside the structure of publicly supported education (Graubard, 1972). The acceptance of schools as an institution of society also separates open education from the deschooling advocates, who argue for the abolition of state-run education (Illich, 1971). The term open education has also been used to refer to the recent trend to build schools without interior walls, i.e., "open plan" or "open structure" schools. Although open education advocates show a concern for "humanizing" schools, a sensitivity towards individuals, and an interest in group interaction, the program can be differentiated from the human potential movement by its concern for the traditional intellectual pursuits in schools and by the strong emphasis on practical, hands-on materials in the curriculum approach. Finally, open education is a movement with a program and philosophy which go far beyond such ideas as individualized instruction, the unit approach, team teaching, interest centers, multi-aged grouping (family grouping, nongradedness) or other catchwords which have invaded the education world at various times.

CONCEPTUAL BASIS

A major foundation for open education programs is the belief in developmental learning theory based on the research of the last 50 years. Although many have contributed to it, and it goes back to earlier observations and conjectures of Rousseau, Froebel, Susan Isaacs, and, in part, Tolstoy and Maria Montessori, the overpowering influence at this time is Jean Piaget (see Beard, 1968; Ripple and Rockcastle, 1964; Isaacs, 1972; Schwebel and Ralph, 1973). His view of learning is an interactive process between the child and the environment, the recognition of stages of development, and the acceptance of each stage in the child's own development for itself, rather than in terms of adult standards, has brought about profound changes in educational views. Piaget stresses that through experience children not only learn, but "learn to learn," and that the process of intelligence is changed through interaction with the environment. Thus there is a stress on experience, materials, "stuff" of the world, as well as concern that children have time and opportunity to assimilate these experiences, and to "work" on them internally so that they increase their capacity to learn, to reason, to think. Piaget has postulated a succession of stages in intellectual development. Children can deal only with immediate experience until the ages of approximately 4 to 7, they are restricted to "concrete" sense-related judgments until approximately 11 to 14, and in favorable conditions they achieve "hypothetical-deductive" thought, or abstract logical thought, somewhere after puberty.

On the one hand, this psychological position is distinct from behaviorism, which views the child as a receptacle for influences of the environment, and the role of educators to monitor these influences and reward the appropriate responses and suppress the unwanted ones. On the other hand, it is also distinct from nativist views, which see the "true" nature of the child unfolding, maturing, or flowering during growth, and urge educators to intervene only to prevent deviations and nurture true growth.

Advocates of open education also believe that knowledge itself results from the interaction of an individual with the environment. This position was most clearly articulated by John Dewey in the doctrine of instrumentalism, and in his insistence that knowledge comes from *doing*, through the interaction of an individual with the surrounding world, both inanimate and social.

This position is distinct both from the view that what is to be learned (the curriculum, or the academic discipline) has a structure and a content which are essentially independent of the learner, and from the belief that knowledge is self-knowledge, something gained by introspection (rational or mystical) which comes from growing self-awareness, and for which experience is essentially secondary. Open education advocates are more likely to describe what children have learned in terms of the work which is the outcome of that learning, be it poems, a construction, or a report, rather than principles which can be enunciated or a point on a standard syllabus which has been reached. (For a clear example, see Clegg, 1971.)

Open education philosophy is concerned with change and development over long periods of time. Learning of particular skills, or turning insights into concepts or unifying principles, happen after repeated interaction between the child and a variety of materials or social situations. Open education also allows for major differences between individuals in their learning styles, interests, and abilities to relate to the world. Thus a wide range of curricula and materials is necessary to accommodate all children. An appropriate model for a classroom is not a lecture hall, an office, or a museum, but rather a kitchen, a studio, or a workshop, a place which is gradually developed through use and in response to growing activity.

A useful distinction between different types of education has been made by Bussis and Chittenden (1971): they describe open education as characterized by high input from *both* teachers and children, as distinct from traditional education with high teacher input and low child input; "laissez-fiare," which has low teacher input and high child input; and, finally, programmed instruction, where the input from both teachers and children is low.

Finally, as is clear in the work of Dewey and Piaget, and is recognized by practitioners of open education, concern with experience as a base for learning must be extended to the social realm. According to Piaget (1948), the only way to understand, that is, really learn, morality is to have to make moral decisions—to be placed in positions where decisions are not determined by higher authorities. Dewey (1916) stresses the need to both teach about democracy in schools and to practice democracy in them. The concepts of the active learner and of the acquisition of knowledge by doing, lead directly to an interrelated view of moral development (Kohlberg, 1972). Advocates of open education also believe that by performing satisfying work of high quality, accomplished both individually and collectively, children will achieve a better self-image, and ultimately become more complete persons. Besides the evidence from practice, the work of Erikson and others in personality theory has been influential. Erikson (1950) relates identity to mastery; that one knows oneself through the results of one's action on the interaction with the world. Again, both the inanimate and social worlds are involved.

HISTORY

The history of open education in this country can be directly traced to the curriculum reform movement starting in the 1950s. Contact between English educators and staff members of Elementary Science Study (part of Education Development Center) began in the early 60s. Later, American reformers, realizing that new curriculum alone was not going to alter schools, began to explore

more drastic modifications in curriculum and classroom practice. Increasing community concern with education, both in inner cities and in some enlightened suburban communities, and the wealth of critical writing about schools which appeared in the late 60s, spurred other efforts. Independent school involvement has already been mentioned. A series of three articles by J. Featherstone (1967) concerning practices in Leicestershire and other parts of England had a profound effect, and the English example has since been studied by a large number of Americans. The publication of *Crisis in the Classroom* (Silberman, 1970), with its stinging attack on American classrooms as "grim and joyless places" and its long chapter on English informal schools, made the movement more widely known.

Major current open education programs are in operation in a number of schools associated with Education Development Center in North Dakota and in Vermont, and in New York City, Philadelphia, Chicago, and other cities. University support is centered at the City University of New York, the Universities of Connecticut and North Dakota, the Bank Street College, and smaller schools in Boston and elsewhere. There are also many smaller, independent efforts; Nyquist and Hawes (1972) contains a list of schools with open education programs.

Much of the work carried on in England, and some of it in the United States, does not claim any formal allegiance to a particular advocate or theoretician, but represents a true "grass roots" effort to change schools. The increasing popularity of open education now provides legitimacy and support for teachers who have discovered these practices through their own observation of children and experimentation. In most instances, the starting points are in work with younger children, with a gradual spread of the methods to older ones.

English educationists are quick to point out their debt to Dewey and the progressive education movement (the term never acquired pejorative connotations in England). They also recognize the influence of Nathan Isaacs' popularization of Piaget, the kindergarten tradition fostered by Froebel, the necessities of the Second World War—during which thousands of children were evacuated to country schools, where nature study and the use of makeshift materials and nonstandard, nontraditional curricula and schedules were necessities, not luxuries—and the tradition of small schools with no national curriculum. Although advocates of open education in the United States often speak as if the movement originated de novo in the last few years, it has, of course, strong ties to a longer tradition. Comeneus (1592-1670) advocated "activity schools" in those days.

THE PRACTICE OF OPEN EDUCATION

Open education is centered on individual children and individual teachers. There is no way to establish it system-wide by fiat; it has to grow from specific examples. A teacher must be sensitive to the particular children's needs and interests and must provide materials, think about room arrangement, and take advantage of occasional situations, such as local events, the seasons, etc.; and generally, through his or her behavior as an alert, interested, stimulating person, provide an example for the children. Many teachers find this way of working difficult and more demanding than traditional teaching, but usually also well worth the effort. A considerable body of literature is available which focuses on the teacher's role. (For example, see Brown and Precious, 1970; Kohl, 1970; Morrow and Morrow, 1971; Sargeant, 1970.)

Curriculum tends to be eclectic and occasional, rather than predetermined. Language arts are usually based on the children's language experience, rather than on carefully graded basal readers. Children are encouraged to express themselves early, and to write about their own experiences in and out of school. This work then becomes part of the reading material for them and their classmates. As a rule, no specific basal reader is followed, and the classrooms are filled with "real" books of a variety of levels, so that children can use books as the need arises. Mathematics is also materials-based, with emphasis on measurement, use of mathematical concepts to solve problems, and integration of mathematics with crafts, science, and sports. Science is phenomenological, starting with the events from which further activities evolve, with the development of concepts as a possible but not necessary consequence. Secondary school programs follow similar lines, but with activities more appropriate for older students. Projects are encouraged, which may combine, for example, social studies, math, art, science, and language arts. In school and out of school (work-study experiences) are appropriate to this approach, as are more inquiry-oriented programs in traditional subject areas. In British schools, especially, a central position is provided for art, movement, and other creative and aesthetic activities. They are seen as valuable both in providing outlets for children to express themselves and as central, integrating activities for the curriculum.

In the United States, the stress on shared responsibility and joint decision-making has involved parents, who often play a crucial part in developing open education programs. Open education advocates often organize parent workshops, encourage parent volunteers in classrooms, and on planning committees, and, especially in Federally funded programs, include parents on the school staffs as classroom aides. A number of parent-organized, community-controlled schools have adopted open education programs after rejecting the traditional school district offerings.

The introduction of open education programs raises difficult problems for school administrations. First, the structure of most American schools and school systems is highly authoritarian and rigid, with little opportunity for teachers, the lowest members of the hierarchy, to contribute significantly to curriculum or budget decisions. Secondly, the higher orders of the system have primarily supervisory and administrative responsibilities, rather than supportive and educational roles. Finally, systems are organized to encourage centralization, "efficiency" through standardized procedures, departmentalization, and interchangeability of personnel. These organizational practices also apply to the children, who are often arranged as homogeneous groups ("tracking"), rather than viewed as individuals.

Evaluation is a major issue in the implementation of open education programs. Standardized tests, because of their obvious socio-economic bias, their limited ability to measure growth and learning, and the harmful effects of their administration (deRivera, 1973), are incompatible with open education programs. Fortunately, there is an increasing awareness of the limitations of the traditional psychometric testing paradigm and of the possible alternatives available for assessing individual growth and programs (Hein, 1975), and of the complex and partly subjective relationships between evaluation methodology and results and decision-making in schools (House, 1973).

The major concerns of open education programs, in addition to the need to make statements about mastery of specific skills, are general growth and development of the child; 'horizontal growth,' that is, the development of various stages and abilities in depth and breadth; the use to which a child puts the skills he or she has learned; and progress in the ability to engage in more complex problem-solving abilities, or "learning to learn." Approaches are being developed to achieve these goals. One powerful method is to maintain longitudinal records of various phases of children's work and activities in order to provide documentary evidence of their growth over time (Carini, 1973). In some instances the results of activity programs have been assessed by engaging the children in activities, rather than by means of paper-and-pencil tests (e.g., Duckworth, 1970). Clinical interviews, used so extensively by Piaget in his research work with children, are also applicable to evaluation activities, as are check lists and observation methods. Although many of these approaches appear to be much more difficult and expensive than standardized tests, they often provide significantly more information about the children or programs evaluated, and can much more easily feed back directly to the education activities to provide ongoing support to the program. The introduction of these measures on a large scale to support open education programs will require a shift in attitudes, large-scale financial support, time, and, most important, the reorganization of testing and evaluation personnel in present systems.

Efforts to implement open education programs are also leading to changes in teacher education. Traditional preservice programs which include little involvement with materials, assign a passive role to students, and provide limited practical experience, must be modified to include activities more similar to those advocated for the open classrooms.

The growth of informal education in England in the last few decades has been accompanied by the development of a support system for this approach. Similar efforts are now under way in the United States. A major new role is that of the advisor. Advisors visit teachers, suggest new materials or ideas, run workshops, talk about difficult children, join in on field trips, distribute experiences, and generally encourage and advise. In some cases they have officially rejected all supervisory duties, and accept only an advisory status. In the United States today there are 40-50 advisories, and a growing body of a few hundred individuals who act as advisors to teachers in a primarily nonsupervisory sense.

Another major English innovation which is being transplanted to this country is the Teacher Center. Teacher centers play a combined social and professional role. Often the home base for advisors and a place for workshops, meetings, and courses, there are a growing number in the United States. One publication, *Scholastic Teacher 1972,* lists 50 Teacher Centers. Most of the centers have a strong interest in hands-on activities, and often include a shop area and a variety of crafts. In addition, there will typically be locally developed materials, as well as equipment, manipulative math and science activities, and books about education and more general topics. The centers in many ways are designed to resemble the classrooms that their advocates help set up. The arrangement of space and the way in which activities are carried out also reflect upon education practices.

The approach to experiences suitable for teachers parallels that advocated for children. Teachers have an opportunity to develop their creative abilities and to improve their skills through individual and group work of their own choice, in the conviction that the increased confidence and sense of identity they will develop by being treated as mature, responsible persons will enable them to provide similar recognition and opportunities for children.

REFERENCES

Beard, R. M. *An Outline of Piaget's Developmental Psychology for Students and Teachers.* New York: Basic Books, 1969.

Brown, M., and Precious, N. *The Integrated Day in the Primary School.* New York: Agathon Press, 1970.

Bussis, A., and Chittenden, T. *An Analysis of an Approach to Open Education.* Princeton, N.J.: Educational Testing Service, 1970.

Carini, P. The Prospect School: Taking Account of Process. *Childhood Education,* 1973, *49,* 350-356.

Clegg, A. *Revolution in the British Primary Schools.* Washington, D.C.: National Education Association, 1971.

deRivera, M. Academic Achievement Tests and the Survival of Open Education. *E.D.C. News,* 1973, *2,* 7-9.

Duckworth, E. Evaluation of the African Primary Science Program. Education Development Center, Newton, Mass., 1970.

Dewey, J. *Democracy and Education.* New York: Macmillan, 1916.

Erikson, E. *Childhood and Society.* New York: W. W. Norton, 1950.

Featherstone, J. The Primary School Revolution in Britain. *The New Republic,* 1967.

Graubard, A. *Free the Children.* New York: Random House, 1960.

Hein, G. E. *An Open Education Perspective on Evaluation.* Grand Forks: University of North Dakota, 1975. See also the other monographs in this series published by the North Dakota Study Group on Evaluation.

House. E. R. *School Evaluation, the Politics and Process.* Berkeley: McKutchen, 1973.

Illich, I. *Deschooling Society.* New York: Harper and Row, 1971.

Isaacs, N. *Piaget for Teachers.* New York: Agathon Press, 1972.

Kolhberg, L., and Mayer, R. Development as the Aim of Education. *Harvard Educational Review,* 1972, *42,* 449-496.

Kohl, H. *The Open Classroom.* New York: Vintage, 1970.

Morrow, L., and Morrow, C. *Children Come First, The Inspired Work of the English Primary Schools.* New York: American Heritage Press, 1971.

Nyquist, E., and Hawes, G. eds. *Open Education, A Sourcebook for Parents and Teachers.* New York: Bantam Books, 1972.

Piaget, J. *The Moral Judgment of the Child.* Glencoe, Illinois: Free Press, 1948.

Ripple, R. E., and Rockcastle, V. N. *Piaget Rediscovered.* Ithaca: Cornell University Press, 1964.

Sargeant, B. *The Integrated Day in an American School.* Boston: National Association of Independent Schools, 1970.

Scholastic Teacher, *Guide to Teacher Centers.* New York: Scholastic Magazines, Inc., 1972.

Schwebel, M., and Ralph, J. *Piaget in the Classroom.* New York: Basic Books, 1972.

Silberman, C. *Crisis in the Classroom.* New York: Random House, 1970.

ADDITIONAL RESOURCES

Barth, R., and Rathbone, C. H. *A Bibliography of Open Education.* Newton, Mass.: Education Development Center, 1971.

———. *Open Education and the American School.* New York: Agathon, 1972.

Blackie, J. *Inside the Primary School.* London: Her Majesty's Stationery Office, 1967.

Devany, K. *Developing Open Education in America.* Washington, D.C.: National Association for the Education of Young Children, 1974.

Informal Schools in Britain Today, a series of pamphlets. New York: Citation Press, 1971.

Perspectives on Open Education. National Elementary Principal, vol. 52, November 1972.

Silberman, C. E., ed., *The Open Classroom Reader.* New York: Vintage, 1973.

Stephens, L. S. *The Teacher's Guide to Open Education.* New York: Holt, Rinehart and Winston, 1974.

The ESS Reader. Newton, Mass.: Education Development Center, 1970.

Weber, L. *The English Infant School and Informal Education.* Englewood Cliffs, N.J.: Prentice-Hall, 1971.

107

NONGRADED SCHOOLS

by Bob F. Steere
Professor of Education
Missouri Southern State College
Joplin, Missouri

Though a commendable amount of humaneness and empathy are practiced by most teachers in organizationally regimented, graded schools, in many instances these schools practice mental cruelties comparable to the physical cruelties Procrustes indulged in when he accommodated travellers to the length of a bed by stretching those too short for it or amputating the limbs of those too long for it. Schools are like this legendary brigand of Eleusis when they fit and pace students to a single curriculum on the basis of the child's chronological age.

Most professional educators (87 percent) and lay people (71 percent) are not content with the Procrustean conditions in our schools, conditions which require all individuals to be the same at a specified age, and to move, lockstepped, through 12-plus years of public schooling (Gallup, 1972). In fact, a small percentage of our schools have become receptive to, and have implemented, the concept that schools can function more effectively without grade levels. This concept of a different type of school organization, nongradedness, proposes the abolition of grade levels and age placement as the principal methods of grouping for instruction. It renounces the chronological age, and therefore the birth date, as being the most important factor in structuring the learning pace and curricula for children.

HISTORICAL PERSPECTIVE

A brief historical synopsis will show that the concept of nongraded schools, in opposing graded schools, is not challenging a divinely inspired educational theory. Rather, a survey will reveal that graded schools were developed to meet the needs of a bygone era.

During the period between 1821 and 1860, the pressure of new subjects made arrangements desirable which would provide for "economy" of both the pupils' and teachers' time. The population growth led to a greatly enlarged enrollment, and a corresponding increase in the number of elementary and secondary schools—both of which remained, for the most part, without formal grades through this period. However, a few schools, such as the English Classical School in Boston, established grade designations. One of the early attempts at adopting a system of grading classes was made by J. D. Philbrick in 1848, in the Quincy Grammar School of Boston.

Guggenheim writes that within two decades after the establishment of the Quincy Grammar School Experiment, almost every elementary school in the country had adopted the graded system. He continues:

> The transition from ungraded class to a system of definitive grouping was accomplished in a remarkably short time. However, it must be recognized that this quick adoption was based more in administrative and organizational convenience than on sound psychological or pedagogical knowledge. (Guggenheim, 1966, p. 181)

The graded structure, which has existed since 1870 in both the elementary and secondary schools, has proven to be an orderly system of classifying the many students who flooded the American schools during the last 100 years; but to some educators the pendulum had swung too far. One historian, William Shearer, interprets the change by stating that "The pendulum has swung from no system to nothing but system (Brown, 1963, p. 28)." Indeed, by 1870 most schools were made up of graded classes, graded textbooks and content, and even graded teachers. "The setting was right for the graded structure, and so schools were graded and remained graded (Goodlad and Anderson, 1963, p. 56)." This "all system" organization has eventually caused some educators to begin questioning the congruency of so much regimentation to individual differences of children (Steere, 1967, pp. 10-11).

Efforts to nongrade schools have included initiators such as the St. Louis Plan (1868), the Pueblo Plan (1888), the Portland Maine Plan (1910), the Batavia Plan (1910), the Winnetka Plan (1920s) and the Dalton Plan (1922). More recent attempts toward nongradedness have periodically been accompanied with evaluative studies. These attempts include, among others, the Western Spring Plan (Illinois-1935), Milwaukee Program (Wisconsin-1952), Appleton Plan (Wisconsin-1956), St. Louis Archdiocesan Schools (1958), Flint Program (Michigan-1969), Chicago's Telsa School (1963), and the Melbourne High School Program (Florida-1966). The evaluative results of several of these programs and other studies can be found in the May 1972 issue of *Educational Leadership* (Steere, 1972).

WHY NONGRADEDNESS

The professional educator may be reluctant to accept a movement which would replace the graded organization of our schools—a structure which has schooled Americans with the expertise to place mankind on the moon. While admitting that consideration of individual differences is desirable, the educator may be skeptical of the ability of the nongraded school to accomplish significant improvement. However, the researcher will find most statistical studies of nongraded schools to reveal significant achievement gains.

The realization of the need to eliminate the compression of individual differences has led more and more schools in the last 20 years to remove grade level designations and to open the total curriculum to all pupils, regardless of their chronological age or years spent in school. The innovators in these efforts, probably influenced by educators and psychologists such as Goodlad and Anderson (1956, p. 59), viewed the limitations of nongradedness. They emphasized that "the nongraded plan is a system of organization and nothing more," and contended that it is "no panacea for problems of curriculum and instruction." Later writers, seeing our educational practices as being almost criminal at the present stage of sophistication of insight on child growth and development, make it clear that nongrading cannot eliminate these "criminal" practices. But they realize that improvement must involve nongradedness. Hillson says, "But let me further indicate that any plan that attempts to do it must essentially be basically without regard for what we term 'grades' or 'grade levels' (Guggenheim, 1966, pp. 206-207)." They find no loss in abandoning the graded system, which has little or no pedagogical support. Jerome Bruner says, "School grading is simply a poor piece of technology for using the resources of the school, one that has to be removed if the next step is to be taken (Brown, 1965, p. xiii)." "It [grade] serves as a comfortable compartment in which school administrators can, and do, catalog youngsters for custodial purposes (Brown, 1963, p. 44)."

The case for ungradedness can probably best be made by encouraging the reader to realize the great differences of the many children assigned to a teacher. Can we expect teachers to individualize learning for each child when we assign to her a group of 25-30 children with so great a disparity of achievement levels? True, some teachers have taken the initiative and have found the time to evaluate each student, develop learning continuums in one or more subjects, and then appropriately place each child on self-pacing curricula, but these energetic professionals are truly super-people. An analysis of Table 1 and Table 2 should make any educator sensitive to the overwhelming task of providing for the achievement differences found in typical graded classroom and schools.

TABLE 1

Student	I.Q.	Read. Comp.	Arith. Fund.	Mech. of English
A	100	3.3	4.3	2.6
B	120	5.5	5.4	4.7
C	104	4.4	5.3	4.5
D	122	5.9	5.4	5.5
E	82	2.9	3.2	2.4
F	92	3.2	4.8	3.3
G	115	6.4	4.7	4.7
H	101	3.5	4.4	3.3
I	108	4.6	3.2	3.2
J	91	3.0	3.2	2.8
K	121	7.4	5.6	8.0
L	124	6.4	4.9	5.6
M	–	4.4	3.9	4.3
N	80	2.4	4.2	2.1

The California Achievement Tests and California Test of Mental Maturity scores of the first 14 "fourth grade" students listed on a randomly selected print-out page of a large (900) elementary school.

Note in Table 1 that fourth grade student "A" is at the 4.3 year level in Arithmetic Fundamentals, but he is at the 2.6 year in Mechanics of English. The disparity between the achievement levels of different children of the same age is equally striking when comparing the reading Comprehension scores of Student "K" and Student "N." Comparable differences are found in our secondary graded classes when one analyzes the scores of Table 2 and finds that the Correctiveness of Expression score of Student "A" is at the 90th percentile, while Students "E" and "I" have respective scores of 47 and 9.

TABLE 2

Student	Social Studies Background	Natural Science	Correctiveness of Expression	Quantitative Thinking	Reading—Social Studies	Reading—Natural Science	Reading—Literature	General Vocabulary	(Composite Scores; Tests 1-8)	Use of Sources of Introduction
A	79	98	90	56	25	75	61	85	78	77
B	74	62	90	86	70	64	89	85	82	90
C	84	74	61	69	78	75	67	75	78	72
D	34	21	81	48	57	64	42	80	55	72
E	79	62	47	56	57	70	55	57	62	67
F	84	94	61	63	25	75	73	75	74	67
G	67	51	81	40	88	80	78	80	78	67
H	40	46	9	40	6	23	1	19	13	12
I	46	62	68	40	25	64	61	63	55	55

Iowa Tests of Educational Development scores of the first nine names in a randomly selected class of a large (1700) graded high school.

THE STRUCTURE OF NONGRADED SCHOOLS

A 1964 survey revealed only 12 of 353 secondary school systems to have nongrading, while a 1971 sampling of 181 secondary schools found 400 to be with nongraded programs (Patterson, 1973). Even though the reader is alerted to the probable excessively high count found in the latter survey, the figures attest to the increasing popularity of nongraded schools at both the secondary and elementary levels.

When one studies either secondary or elementary schools with nongraded programs, recurring themes of philosophy and structure become evident, even though no two programs are identical and all are at various stages of being completely nongraded. Elementary and secondary schools share concepts, structures, and practices when achieving a nongraded status. The following is a list of similarities:

• The personnel of continuous progress (nongraded) schools believe that graded schools were created when little was known about individual differences, that graded schools were geared to the mystical average, and that the graded practice has not been replaced primarily because of tradition and the relative ease of administering the graded school.

• Nongraded schools recognize past achievement, and even interests and work habits, as being more appropriate for placing children than the use of chronological ages.

• Most nongraded schools have modified each subject curriculum into a "learning continuum," each continuum with many steps or levels, and each level with behavioral objectives which, if reached, is indicative of learning. A mastery of the objectives of each level provides the student with the readiness necessary for the next higher (vertical) level, or for a more in-depth study of closely related studies (longitudinal). This description is less appropriate for nongraded secondary schools, in that most are found to provide courses with five levels of varying difficulty. The school's courses, each course with varying achievement levels, and each level of equal credit value, are open to all students, regardless of age or previous grade placement. The practices of appropriate placement and continuous progress are also of prime importance in guiding the instruction and administration of nongraded secondary schools.

• Most nongraded schools had their beginnings by a single teacher or principal, not only accepting the nongraded philosophy of having appropriate placement and continuous progress for each child, but by the individual also serving as a catalyst in both the program's developmental and implemental stages.

• Most staffs, after their wholehearted acceptance of the philosophy of "appropriate placement and continuous progress," work diligently for a minimum of one year preparing curricula, administrative procedures, student movement systems, placement procedures, methods of evaluating and reporting, and working on other related concerns. Faculties consistently agree that a position in a nongraded school requires more energy but is more professionally rewarding.

● School districts preparing to nongrade usually provide inservice training for their teachers, administrators, parents, and news media personnel. The inservicing of professional personnel may be in the form of workshop classes or at frequently scheduled faculty meetings.

● The majority of nongraded schools were not provided with an appreciable increase in funds, but most spent their allotted funds differently, and modified their usage of existing instructional resources.

● A teacher unable to relinquish his graded labels and practices as a teacher of fourth-graders, or a teacher of tenth-grade English, tends to have a detrimental effect on newly implemented nongraded programs. Proponents of nongradedness remind other educators that a child-centered teacher, in either graded or nongraded schools, accepts her "fourth grade" class as being composed of second-, third-, fourth-, fifth-, and sixth-graders in actual levels of achievement. Likely, few more than 50 percent will be on the fourth year level in any one subject, and therefore a teacher expecting all to learn the same material at the same rate is suffering from self-delusion. Teachers of nongraded schools apparently accept this logic, and believe that by working together as a team under an ungraded organization that they can better provide for the differences of children than can isolated teachers working with children of approximately the same birth-dates.

● Nongraded schools stress the appropriate placement of each child in each subject, recognize the appropriateness of independent and self-pacing learning, and maintain flexibility in grouping and regrouping.

● The evaluation standards vary in nongraded schools, but most continue to use letter marks as indicators of progress. But the marks in ungraded schools are evaluations of the individual's progress, and seldom a comparison with others of the same age. Some nongraded schools provide "comparison grades" to insistent parents. Report cards often indicate progress both quantitatively and qualitatively.

● Nongraded schools are defensive toward the issuance of the same grade for varying degrees of academic gains. These schools remind educators that two teachers of the same subject often vary greatly as to their requirements for a specific letter grade; thus, where is the consistency in graded schools?

● Many nongraded schools will attach to the cumulative record or transcript a brief description of the school's learning continuum, the pupil's level attainment, and his evaluative grade for each level. This information is helpful to the receiving teacher, should the student transfer to either a graded or nongraded school.

● When asked about a nongraded student transferring to a graded school when the nongraded student hasn't covered all of the same books normally covered in a graded school, the proponent reminds the questioner that "covering" is not the same as learning. To cover something over the child's head doesn't prepare him for advanced achievement levels, nor does the keeping of a capable child from an academically advanced level facilitate his education or mental health.

Differences in practices exist in nongraded elementary and secondary schools, as the following question and answer series will demonstrate.

QUESTIONS: NONGRADED SECONDARY SCHOOL

Q. What is meant by the term nongrading in your high school?

A. Nongrading at _____ High School refers primarily to educational practices based upon the concepts of appropriate placement (a suitable educational place for each student) and continuous progress (provision for each student to move at his own best rate).

Q. Are grade levels really eliminated from your curriculum?

A. Yes. There are no ninth-, tenth-, eleventh-, or twelfth-grade courses as such—the entire curriculum has been built largely ignoring age and grade levels in order to make all courses available to each student when his interest and need is greatest.

Q. What is mean by phasing?

A. A phase is an achievement level; many courses have five different phases, and some are unphased. This is an attempt to provide placement opportunity for students in each course according to interest, achievement, and ability.

Q. What is the definition (level) of each phase?

A. Phase I. For students who lack the basic skills and require special assistance in smaller classes.

Phase II. For students who need special emphasis on basic concepts and skills.

Phase III. For students of average achievement in the subject.

Phase IV. For students whose achievement is above average and who desire to study the subject in depth.

Phase V. For students with exceptional interests and/or achievement who desire to study the subject in an advanced level.

Q. Should a student select the same phase in all courses?

A. No. We do not "peg" or "track" students as slow, average, or fast and expect them to do equally well in all subjects. A student may be Phase IV in English composition, Phase II in art, Phase V in algebra, or suchlike.

Q. What criteria are used to aid students in their selection of courses and phases best suited to their needs?

A. a. Standardized tests.

   b. Previous school achievement in related subjects.

   c. Teachers' and counselors' evaluations and recommendations.

Q. Do students start at Phase I and stay in a course until they complete all phases assigned to that course?

A. No. The phases are designed to allow students to be initially placed into proper achievement levels; the phases are not necessarily steps in a learning sequence.

Q. May a student move from one phase to another if the movement is in his interest?
A. Certainly, at certain intervals during each semester.

Q. How often may a student move to another phase?
A. There is relatively little movement; however, students are eligible to move at the beginning and middle of each nine-week quarter.

Q. Will a student remain in a phase until he completely masters all the subject matter, even if it takes two or three years?
A. No. Repetition of a course with identical subject matter is of limited value. This is not to say that a student is deprived of this opportunity if it fits his needs. Fewer students fail when they are appropriately placed, and provision is made in the instructional program for individualized learning.

Q. Does each phase of a course carry the same amount of credit?
A. Yes.

Q. Do all phases offer all achievement marks (A, B, C, D, and F);
A. Yes. However, consistently high grades for a student in a low phase, or low grades in a high phase, would suggest consideration of an adjustment in phasing for that student in that course.

Q. Is a "B" in Phase III worth as much as a "B" in Phase V?
A. This can perhaps be answered best by asking if a "B" in general science is equal to a "B" in advanced physics. It depends on whether you're looking at the amount and depth of learning, or whether you are weighing the grades to the student's ability to learn. Whatever the case, the transcript and report card always list the phase and grade of each course taken, plus an interpretation of the meaning of each phase.

Q. How are registration and scheduling accomplished?
A. Prior to registration day each semester, students are oriented to the course offerings as shown in the course catalog, and allowed to make a preliminary choice of subjects and phases. From a compilation of this data a master schedule of courses and phases to be offered is prepared. On registration day each semester students select courses, phases, and teachers from the master schedule, and prepare their own program and schedule.

Q. Won't some students choose the teachers and classes where less effort is required?
A. If there are such students, classes, and teachers, maybe they deserve each other. It is our belief that the student is consistently the best judge of his own interest and ability when properly counseled.

QUESTIONS: NONGRADED ELEMENTARY SCHOOL

Q. I understand that your program is sometimes called a "level plan." Please explain.
A. Our reading program can be used as an example. The staff determined the needed reading skills and levels, then developed behavioral objectives inclusive of the skills, after which we selected evaluative instruments for both placing students and evaluating their progress.

Q. How many levels are in your reading program?
A. Our textbook series was found to be divided already into over 30 progressive stages of learning, and each stage had an accompanying achievement test, reinforcement worksheets, readers, and activities. We found a need to add seven additional levels, making a total of 37 levels, with the 37th level open for unlimited growth of exceptional readers. Many traditional schools' resources are adaptable to nongradedness if staffs will only structurally eliminate their graded practices and then work together as an organizational team in opening the curriculum to all children, regardless of age.

Q. It sounds as if your school was fortunate in having a series which could be so easily adapted—nongradedly.
A. Right! But our teachers still had to make many refinements, and in this developmental process our teachers became truly creative professionals by their adjustment of previously prepared resources and in their development of new curricular materials and methods.

Q. How were students placed?
A. Each student's achievement level was of a primary importance, and was largely determined by an achievement test, his past achievement in the subject, and the recommendations of needs as reported by his previous teacher. But also his chronological age, his peer relationships, and other factors were considered, with the objective being: what is the best placement for this individual? Seldom has it been necessary, or even desirable, to group children who are markedly different in chronological age.

Q. Administratively, how were students placed?
A. A placement committee, composed of one teacher from each grade level and the principal, individually placed each child. Their efforts were facilitated by being armed with pertinent information on each student, a learning continuum composed of many achievement levels, a strong desire to provide an optimum learning opportunity for each child, and a staff willing to be assigned wherever their talents could best be used.

Students were then assigned on a large "continuum board," with individuals being graphically recorded and groups formed as needed. Teachers were then assigned to the pupils. Before the initiation of our nongraded programs, we would first assign teachers and then assign students to them by their ages and years in school. We now diagnose students, prescribe their needs, and then assign teachers.

Q. How large are the groups? Do students remain in the same group?

A. The groupings vary, from independent study to three or four students, and even up to 35 students, in the case of students working at level #37 (the open level beyond the normal sixth-grade curriculum). The size of the group is determined by student needs and our limited personnel resources. Some groups remain fairly intact, but most will vary in composition during a semester. In any case, a student is to progress at his best rate and a flexibility of grouping is maintained in each subject matter area.

Q. Has your staff had many difficulties in developing and implementing your program?

A. You bet we have, but the difficulties also existed under our graded program. With time, we had learned to ignore them. Our program forced us to make decisions based on priority, decisions which usually called for improved instructional conditions but which also required an adjustment in our thinking, practices, and efforts.

Though most nongraded programs are typically either of the level or phase design, nongradedness is showing itself through many organizational variations and instructional products. Textbook and electronic companies are producing individualized resources, series with levels, and equipment which, when appropriate to a school's needs, can save a staff many hours in the development of materials. The education divisions of these companies stand ready and willing to display their individualized program and resources.

The theme of nongradedness is an important thread in personalized programs such as Individually Prescribed Instruction (IPI), Individually Guided Education (IGE), and scores of other programs designed for individualized/nongraded learning. There are hundreds of schools available as study-models for the potential implementor of nongradedness, some of which are provided in the following list. The reader is advised that the listings were accumulated during the last several years, and many of the programs have likely become more or less nongraded with the years, the caliber of leadership, and the program's degree of success.

INSTITUTION AND LOCATION

Primary

Arizona; Phoenix	G. F. Skiff School
Hawaii; Lanikai, Oahu	Lanikai Elementary School
Michigan; River Rouge	River Rouge School District
Minnesota; Edina	Edina Public Schools
New Jersey; Newark	Camden Street Schools

Elementary

California; Berkeley	Columbus-University Laboratory School
California; Los Angeles	University Elementary School of the University of California
Illinois; Lockport	Valley View School District
Kentucky; Lesington	Lansdowne Elementary School
Kentucky; Owensboro	Owensboro City Schools
Maryland; Baltimore	Villa Cresta Elementary School (Parkville)
Maryland; Brunswick	Brunswick Elementary School
Massachusetts; Lexington	Bridge School
Missouri; Columbia	Ridgeway Elementary School
Nevada; Las Vegas	Ruby Thomas School
Nevada; Las Vegas	Will Beckley School
New Jersey; Mt. Lake	Wildwood School
New Jersey; Union City	Roosevelt Elementary School
New York; Wyandanch	Milton Olive Elementary School
Oregon; Ontario	Alameda Elementary School
Pennsylvania; Media	Rose Tree Media School
Pennsylvania; Pittsburgh	Oakleaf Elementary School
Virginia; Hampton	Hampton nongraded Institute Laboratory School
Washington; Kirkland	Lake Washington Special Education Center
Wisconsin; Madison	Wisconsin R&D Center/IGE

Intermediate

New Jersey; Montclair	Montclair Public Schools

Elementary and Secondary

Massachusetts; Newton	Newton Public School System

Elementary and Junior High School

California; San Bruno	Portola School

Kindergarten—Jr. High School

Florida, West Palm Beach	Palm Beach Public Schools

Kindergarten—High School

Alabama; Anniston	Anniston Schools
California; Palo Alto	PLAN, Westinghouse
Florida; Ft. Lauderdale	Nova Schools
Minnesota; Duluth	Duluth Public Schools
Missouri; Kansas City	Loretto School

Jr. High School—High School

Alabama, Theodore	Theodore High School

High School

Florida; Melbourne	Melbourne High School
Florida; Satellite Beach	Satellite High School
Illinois; Norridge	Ridgewood High School

Massachusetts, Amherst	Amherst High School
Minnesota; Duluth	Chester Park School
Nevada; Las Vegas	Western High School
New York; Scottsville	Wheatland Chili Central School

Secondary

Pennsylvania; Oil City	Venango Christian High School

REFERENCES

Bishop, L. K. *Individualizing Educational Systems.* New York: Harper and Row, 1971.

Brown, B. F. *The Nongraded High School.* Englewood Cliffs, New Jersey: Prentice-Hall, 1963.

_____. *The Appropriate Placement School: A Sophisticated Nongraded Curriculum.* West Nyack, New York: Parker Publishing Co., Inc., 1965.

Buffie, G. H. ed. *Curriculum Development in Nongraded Schools: Bold New Venture.* Bloomington: Indiana University Press, 1971.

Gallup, G. H. The Fourth Annual Gallup Poll of Public Attitudes Toward Education. *Phi Delta Kappan,* 1972, *54,* No. 1, pp. 33-46.

Goodlad, J. I. *The Nongraded Elementary School.* New York: Harcourt, Brace and World, Inc., 1963.

Guggenheim, F., ed. *New Frontiers in Education.* New York: Grune and Stratton, 1966.

Henrie, S. N., ed. *A Sourcebook of Elementary Curricula Programs and Projects.* San Francisco: Far West Laboratory for Educational Research and Development, 1972.

Hillson, M. *Continuous-Progress Education: A Practical Approach.* Palo Alto: Science Research Associates, 1971.

Lewis, J. Jr. *A Contemporary Approach to Nongraded Education.* West Nyack, New York: Parker Publishing Co., Inc., 1969.

McCarthy, R. J. *The Ungraded Middle School.* West Nyack, New York: Parker Publishing Co., Inc., 1972.

National Commission on Teacher Education and Professional Standards (TEPS). *The Teacher and His Staff: Selected Demonstration Centers.* St. Paul, Minn.: 3M Education Press, 1967.

Patterson, J. L. Why Has Nongradedness Eluded the High School? *The Clearinghouse,* 1973, No. 7, 47.

Steere, B. F. *A Comparative Study of a Nongraded and Graded Secondary School as to Achievement, Attitude, and Critical Thinking Ability.* USOE Project No. 7-8080. Unpublished doctoral dissertation, Department of Educational Administration, Utah State University, 1967. (ERIC ED08003)

_____. Nongradedness: Relevant Research for Decision Making. *Educational Leadership,* 1972, *29,* 709-711.

Tewksbury, G. L. *Nongrading in the Elementary School.* Columbus, Ohio: Charles E. Merrill Books, Inc., 1967.

108

DESCHOOLING

by Gertrude S. Goldberg
Research Associate
ERIC-IRCD
Teachers College
Columbia University
New York, N.Y.

The term deschooling, which has been invented and most fully elaborated by Ivan Illich, refers to the disestablishment of the public school system, the abolition of compulsory education, and the development instead of education structures which facilitate the learning of one's choice (Illich, 1970, 1971). Deschooling thus involved a negative proposal—disestablishment—and a positive plan for providing people with the resources to learn what they choose. In the case of Illich, but not necessarily all of its proponents, deschooling is education entirely free of social control. It is also a means of bringing about radical changes in society as a result of sweeping changes in the structure of education.

Although a number of writers have favored either total or partial deschooling (Berg, 1971), Illich has been most precise in his definition of terms, most detailed in his proposals for free education structures, and most consistent in his advocacy of both full disestablishment and completely nondirected learning. It is, in fact, not at all clear that some who urge deschooling are distinguishing between free schooling and education that is free of social control. Others may be unaware of the social and political implications of leaving direction with the learners, and still others may not recognize that educational liberty could fail to benefit the disadvantaged, since it implies the differential ability to utilize free resources. And finally, there are those who are perhaps willing to risk anarchy in order to free society of the undesirable controls now imposed by schools. Some of these individuals, however, may have failed to scrutinize the assumption that radical change in education can either precede or effect social revolution.

While remaining aware that most persons who identify with the deschooling movement do not want to go as far in the direction of social or educational revolution as Illich, our discussion of deschooling will deal primarily with his work, because such an approach will make explicit some of the implications of deschooling and will encourage a more precise definition of terms. At the same time, we need to begin by attempting to differentiate the Illich brand of deschooling from a number of educational reforms, critiques, and proposals, notably free schooling, the voucher system, and the inferences of the work of Christopher Jencks and his associates. Following this, we shall examine the implications of freeing education from various forms of social control, and then proceed to analyze the pedagogical issues raised by deschooling. The latter include reference to its benefits for the poor.

DESCHOOLING vs. OTHER EDUCATIONAL ALTERNATIVES

Deschooling is difficult to distinguish from a broad range of educational reforms which have as their goal a freer, less directed form of schooling but which do not necessarily propose the abolition of all schools, or completely nondirected learning. For example, George Dennison, who has been identified with deschooling, would like to see the intimacy and small scale of his experimental First-Street School widely imitated. He favors mini-schools, which would be free of the school's conventional routines, its miliary disciplines, and its punishments and rewards—in short, schools that would give freedom rather than take it away. Illich, however, holds that schools, no matter how free they try to be, are always directed, and he is probably right. As one review of a number of free schools (including the First Street School) concludes, freedom in nondirected schools is not leeway for students to do whatever they please, but freedom to choose from a number of options, e.g., to discover what courses interest them or to work at their own pace.

Whatever the distinction between deschooling and free schooling, the differences are blurred, partly because some who originally advocated free schooling, like John Holt and Paul Goodman, have despaired of reform and have come "to hanker after deschooling society altogether." Holt, who is a great admirer of Dennison's school, favors deschooling, which he takes to mean doing away with compulsory education laws, right-to-work laws, and the entire system of discipline and grading. Goodman, who placed himself in the deschooling camp, nonetheless expressed reservations about deschooling for all groups, notably the socially deprived or psychologically disturbed. Illich, on the other hand, considers deschooling particularly beneficial to the disadvantaged—a contention which will be explored subsequently.

The voucher system is another educational reform which would make possible some freer schools, but it does not propose deschooling in the sense of disestablishment and abrogation of compulsory education laws. Through a system of direct tuition grants to parents, it attempts to develop a number of competing schools systems, and hence a wider range of choices in education. Although vouchers would presumably break up the present monolithic school system, they are not intended to abolish schools. Illich is predictably critical of the voucher plan because it "condemns itself by proposing tuition grants which would have to be spent on schooling (Illich, 1971)." Indeed, given the predilection of many parents for directed learning and highly disciplined classrooms, the voucher system would inevitably lead to some schools which offer more control, as well as others which provide freer learning than our present systems.

It is well to point out that the work of Christopher Jencks and his associates (Jencks, 1972), though potentially quite damaging to the school establishment, is not a plea for deschooling. Rather, these authors have attempted to show that schools do not contribute significantly to the reduction of economic inequality. Unlike Illich, who hopes to effect a cultural revolution through changes in education, the Jencks group has little confidence that school improvements can contribute to the societal improvements they favor, primarily a more equitable distribution of wealth. The Jencks findings, if accepted, could greatly diminish confidence in the ability of the public schools to accomplish the social-mobility goals which have traditionally been imputed to them, and hence could call into question our heavy investment of resources in public education. Although the authors have failed to stress sufficiently that schools may teach children even if they do not equalize educational achievement, they have not proposed deschooling or even any specific educational program. Rather, they have urged that schools become more decent and pleasant places for children. If, as Jencks suggests, schools need not, indeed cannot, carry the burden of social mobility or equality, they may be encouraged to let up—in short, to become freer and less directed.

SOCIETAL IMPLICATIONS OF DESCHOOLING

Like Paul Goodman, Illich is more concerned with mis-education than with the failure of schools to teach (Goodman, 1962). We do not become educated or wise, and we are taught much that is undesirable. All deschooling advocates decry the restrictveness, pettiness, and officiousness of schools. They consider that schooling stifles the pursuit of knowledge and the expression of joy and creativity generally in our social life. They point out that our compulsory education develops a schooled mentality that leads us to confuse credentials with knowledge and skill, to mistake instruction for learning, and to judge ourselves and others by the graded and bogus standards of the classroom rather than by more intrinsic values. Goodman, for example, considers that schools are not so much purveyors of bourgeois, but of a meaner set of petit-bourgeois, norms; they may be a bit worse than society—certainly no ideal small community. Illich is quite eloquent in cataloging the intellectual, social, and moral travesties of the school, but he carries the case against it a bit further, making schooling responsible for most of the societal institutions he considers corrupt.

Illich (1971) holds that we learn a kind of prototypical dependence in school: the need to be taught rather than to learn for ourselves. "Once we have learned to need schools, all our activities tend to take the shape of client relationships to other specialized institutions." Similarly, he writes: "School prepares us for the alienating institutionalization of life by teaching us the need to be taught (p. 47)." We depend on institutional treatment, generally; that is, we learn to be taken care of, rather than to care for ourselves or to be independent. School furthermore teaches us to be modern producers and consumers. We learn to want the wasteful and useless products that the post-industrial society produces and needs to market. Some of us get the credentials which jobs require (not necessarily the skills necessary to perform them), and as a result we aspire to be compulsive consumers of schooling, along with other commodities. Holt expresses the same idea when he comments on the competitive consumption of schooling: "My being able to get ahead of you depends upon my having been able to consume more schooling than you. . . (Holt, 1972)." (This is, of course, a tenet questioned by Jencks, who concludes that more schooling does not necessarily lead to higher incomes or even better jobs.)

MIS-EDUCATION

In addition to mis-education in the economic sphere, Illich decries it in the moral sphere as well. In contrast to an observer like Urie Bronfenbrenner (1970), who considers our educational system deficient in character training, Illich finds our schooling officious. Teachers tell pupils what is right and wrong, in school and out, and impart a kind of paternalistic patriotism by ensuring "that all feel themselves children of the same state (Illich, 1971)." School is, in short, a major cultural bulwark of our social system, and to disestablish it is to strike the first, fatal blow in social revolution.

In its emphasis on education free of moral, technical, or any other type of social control, the Illich brand of deschooling appears to depart most radically from nearly all educational and social theory. For social control is considered intrinsic not only to schooling but to any system of education that is formally established by the community. Anthony F. C. Wallace (1968), an anthropologist, concludes: "There is no human society on the face of the earth which concedes to *any* individual the right to learn anything he chooses."

Illich and some of his colleagues are evidently more concerned with abolishing moral mis-education than with the societal fragmentation implied by complete deschooling. Durkheim, for example, argued that education must assure among the citizenry "a sufficient community of ideas and sentiments, without which any society is impossible (Durkheim, 1956). Furthermore, he held that in order to achieve this cohesion "it is also necessary that education not be completely abandoned to the arbitrariness of private individuals (Durkheim, p. 80)." And, it should be noted, Durkheim had in mind broad cultural values, such as a respect for reason, science, and democratic principles. It might conceivably be argued that the school need not provide this community culture, since we have available in our day, unlike that of Durkheim or Jefferson, other media to convey common ideas and sentiments. Yet, it would seem that these are even less likely than the schools to be free of the post-industrial excesses to which deschooling advocates object.

TECHNICAL MIS-EDUCATION

Deschooling eschews not only community direction of moral education, but of preparation for the labor market as well. This position is based partly on Illich's judgment that people do not need schooling to prepare them for most jobs, but more basically on the opinion that many of the goods and services we think we need are unnecessary. It is argued that we can do without these commodities and hence without many jobs.

Illich holds that educational freedom is possible because modern technology enables man to relinquish the productive role. Producing the necessities of life has ceased to take up his time. Available hours could be filled in producing a limited range of durable and useful goods, and in providing access to institutions which increase potential for human action, for joyous learning, and for leisure. Presumably such action is best promoted by learning which is an end in itself, and which needs no external reinforcement. The learner is under no other control or curriculum than that which the subject of his choice dictates. Although Illich does not specifically make the connection, we may infer that in a society where men are to a great extent free of the labor market, education should encourage free intellectual and cultural development. Such an educational system is not utopian, but functional to the social system. Illich considers that the choice between unemployment and joyful, active leisure, once unthinkable, is "inevitable" for post-industrial man. Thus, free education seems dictated by a particular stage of industrialism, rather than what Illich calls an "inalienable right."

Such an economic analysis is quite similar to that of Robert Theobald (1966) and the Triple Revolution group, although it is primarily concerned with education rather than with guaranteed income. Critiques of the Triple-Revolution position, which are also applicable to this aspect of Illich's work, hold that it is premature in view of the quantity of unmet needs in our society and all others. For example, in 1968 Leonard Lecht, of the National Planning Association, estimated that to achieve 16 modest national goals (e.g., renewal of our cities, adequate medical care for all, etc.) would require more manpower than we have—a labor force of more than 100 million in 1975, or some 10 million more persons than are expected to be available for employment in that year.

PEDAGOGICAL ISSUES

Deschooled education is designed for a "well-motivated student who does not labor under a specific handicap," and who therefore "often needs no further human assistance than can be provided by someone who can demonstrate on demand what the learner wants to learn to do (Illich, 1971, p. 68)." Unlike present teachers who serve as moralists, custodians, and therapists, deschooled educators would keep out of the way, merely helping learners to get what they need in order to learn what they choose to learn. "Opportunity webs" or "networks" would be devised to provide access to the four sets of resources needed by learners: "things," ranging from computers to machines to dismantle and put together; teachers of skills, who demonstrate the skills people want to learn; "peers" or "partners-in-inquiry," with whom to challenge, argue, compete; and "educators-at-large," or "elders," to provide educational leadership akin to that of masters to their disciples. The only professional educators in the system, as distinct from teachers of skills and learned "elders," would be the administrators who devise the networks and counselors who guide students and parents in their use.

SELF-MOTIVATION

Illich assumes that without compulsory schooling, which distorts the natural impulse to learn, individuals will be motivated to seek partners in inquiry and teachers of skills. Illich observes that the ability to inspire others to learn is rarely combined with the capacity to impart a skill. But, since motivation is a given in his view, Illich makes the skills teachers the keystone of deschooled education.

Those who advocate deschooling hold that motivation is no longer problematic when there is no prescribed curriculum. Everyone will want to learn something sooner or later. What many learners lack under the present system is the motivation to learn what school and society force them to learn. While it is true that by definition everyone is motivated to learn what he wants to learn, we may still ask whether nondirected learning leads all children to learn more extensively or intensively than does learning which is less free (leaving aside the important issue of the content of their learning, which deschooling proponents consider unimportant). Generally speaking, we lack sufficient experience with self-motivated learning to be able to answer this question, and hence should be wary of basing an educational system on it.

In all likelihood, some children need no more than the opportunity to pursue their learning interests by being helped to find skills teachers and partners in inquiry. Illich assumes that most are so motivated and that the rest are handicapped. Yet for many children, perhaps the majority, mild direction may optimally serve what is probably moderate motivation. And still others, not necessarily handicapped, may require more forceful schooling.

Illich prefers delayed learning to external motivation or manipulation for those not eager to learn when they are young. He proposes an edu-credit card, so that they can accumulate educational entitlements to be used later in life, a kind of voucher which need not be used on schooling. Yet the problems of motivation may be compounded if we desist from directed learning for the young who do not direct themselves. Jerome Bruner (1969) has observed that if certain basic skills are not mastered first, later more elaborate ones become increasingly out of reach. Some later learners will go through all of the necessary steps, but many of these may be less appealing to them than to the young, even though the latter may not have the motivation to read. The more mature learner must be sufficiently motivated to put up with the discomfort of learning simple skills when he is no longer a child.

THE MEANING OF MOTIVATION

A central issue in this discussion is what we mean by motivation. Is it the desire to learn the history of one's people, to play the piano, to speak a foreign language, to design a building? Or is it the interest in the skills which must be mastered in order to achieve these goals? Is motivation to play the piano enough to sustain the course of study that is dictated not by arbitrary ritual or curriculum, but by the subject matter itself? Perhaps only the very avid and diligent can endure the endless practicing, not of music, but of isolated passages, scales, and arpeggios, without the encouragement, intervention, even prodding, of their teachers. We need to be far clearer about the meaning of motivation and its relationship to educational outcomes before we can wholly urge self-directed learning for all.

DESCHOOLING AND THE DISADVANTAGED

We do not know how many children in any social class fit the model of the well-motivated learner, but Illich (p. 6) seems to think the poor are less likely than the affluent to take advantage of educational opportunities early in life. He observes that they "lack most of the educational opportunities which are casually available to the middle-class child"—conversation and books in the home, vacation travel, and a different sense of oneself. In fact, he proposes the edu-credit card in order to "favor the poor." Evidently the impulse to learn is a natural one that can be easily distorted, not only by an education which is probably more prescriptive in the case of the disadvantaged, but by an environment that does not stimulate it. Or perhaps motivation depends upon such stimulation and cultivation.

Whether less able to be employed or to enjoy life, people will be handicapped so long as they delay their education. Furthermore, given the boundaries of the lives of the adult poor, one is not at all sanguine that their latter experiences will provide them with the "casual advantages" they missed when they were young.

The main beneficiaries of deschooled education would probably be those groups in which self-motivated learning has higher incidence. Indeed, many middle- and upper-class parents would welcome such education for their children. Deschooling would offer the better motivated a tutorial system which would be costly to purchase privately. Free education may thus be like other publicly provided equal opportunities—museums, libraries, cultural centers—that are unequally used. It will resemble these resources in that it will primarily benefit and subsidize the affluent who have developed the capacity to use them (Holt, 1972, pp. 184-216).

CONCLUSION

The deschooling movement will probably not succeed in disestablishing the school, but it may well help to deschool values and to make education freer. Illich and his colleagues help us to recognize how schooled our minds and lives have become, how we limit learning to the narrow confines of the classroom, rather than include the broad scope of experience. They teach us that the subject matter of education is greater than a school curriculum, and in so doing, they have encouraged use of the community as an important learning resource. They are showing us that we substitute instruction for learning, and that we are too often spurred by assignments rather than by the desire to know. All of these insights, forcefully expounded, help us to recapture the intrinsic purposes and benefits of learning, as well as to break the hold of schooling on other aspects of our lives.

Our analysis suggests that deschooling is not only inadvisable for the disadvantaged (as some deschooling advocates have also suggested), but that it may be less than the optimum form of education for learners in other classes and categories as well. We need to define the educational results we are seeking to achieve through freer schooling, and especially to determine what are the effects of nondirected learning on selected groups of people: disadvantaged and privileged, educationally stimulated and apparently unmotivated. We should also study the effects of deschooling at one educational level, e.g., making the secondary school optional rather than compulsory. Above all, we need to be clear about what we mean by deschooling, particularly whether we are seeking freer education or the more radical and probably utopian goal of education free of social control.

REFERENCES

Berg, Leila. Moving Towards Self Government. In *Children's Rights: Toward the Liberation of the Child*. New York: Praeger, 1971.

Dennison, George. *The Lives of Children*. New York: Random House, 1969.

Bronfenbrenner, Urie. *Two Worlds of Childhood: U.S. and U.S.S.R.* New York: Russell Sage Foundation, 1970.

Durkheim, Emile. Education: Its Nature and Role. *Education and Society*, translated and with an introduction by Sherwood D. Fox. Glencoe, Illinois: Free Press, 1956, pp. 79-80.

Gartner, Alan, Greer, Colin, Riessman, Frank, eds. *After Deschooling, What? Ivan Illich, et al.* New York: Harper and Row, 1973.

Gintis, Herbert. Toward a Political Economy of Education: A Radical Critique of Ivan Illich's Deschooling Society. *Harvard Educational Review*, 1972, *42*, 70-96.

Goldberg, Gertrude. Deschooling and the Disadvantaged: Implications of the Illich Proposal. In *Educating the Disadvantaged, 1971-1972*, edited and with an introduction by Erwin Flaxman. New York: AMS Press, 1973, pp. 88-106.

Goodman, Paul. *Compulsory Mis-Education and the Community of Scholars*. New York: Vintage Press, 1962.

Holt, John. *Freedom and Beyond*. E. P. Dutton and Co., 1972.

Illich, Ivan. After Deschooling, What? *Social Policy*, 1971, *2*, 5-13.

_____. *Deschooling Society*. New York: Harper and Row, 1970.

_____. *Celebration of Awareness: A Call for Institutional Revolution*. New York: Doubleday, 1970.

Jencks, Christopher. *Inequality: A Reassessment of Family and Schooling In America*. New York: Basic Books, 1972.

Lecht, Leonard. *Manpower Requirements For National Objectives in the 1970's*. Prepared for the U.S. Department of Labor, Manpower Administration, by the Center for Priority Analysis, National Planning Association. Washington, D.C.: U.S. Government Printing Office, 1968, p. 39.

Neill, A. S. *Summerhill*. New York: Hart Publishing Co., 1960.

Reimer, Everett. *School Is Dead: Alternatives in Education*. New York: Doubleday & Co., Inc., 1971.

Rosen, Sumner M., Jerome, Judson, Greene, Maxine, and Pearl, Arthur. Illich, Pro and Con. *Social Policy*, 1972, *2*, 41-52.

Theobald, Robert, ed. *The Guaranteed Income: Next Step in Economic Evolution?* New York: Doubleday, 1966.

U.S. Department of Health, Education and Welfare, Office of Economic Opportunity. *A Proposed Experiment in Education Vouchers*. OEO Pamphlet 3400-1, January 1971.

Wallace, Anthony F. D. Schools in Revolutionary and Conservative Societies. *Social and Cultural Foundations of Guidance*, edited by Esther M. Lloyd-Jones and Norah Rosenau. New York: Holt, Rinehart, and Winston, 1968, p. 197.

109

ALTERNATIVE SCHOOLS AND THE FREE SCHOOL MOVEMENT

by Bruce S. Cooper
Lecturer
University of Pennsylvania
Philadelphia, Pennsylvania

An alternative, or free, school is an experiment in living and learning that seeks often (a) to reduce the size and impersonality of classroom life; (b) to alter the adult-student relationship by freeing up and empowering students to direct their own activities; (c) to de-emphasize traditional organizational structures and means of pupil control, like grades, promotion, detention, and conduct evaluation; and (d) to promote the value of non-competition, communitarianism, and political awareness, involvement, and change.

Though it would be difficult to put the potpourri of "new schools," "free schools," "community schools," "cooperative schools," "freedom schools," "parents' schools," and "children's schools" (they go by all these names) into the straightjacket of a single definition, we have identified three essential areas of alternative school experimentation. (1) *New learning environments*—some free schools seek primarily to use "open" educational strategies, the individualization of instruction, and informal interpersonal relations, allegedly to free the children to pursue their own interests at their own speed. (2) *New organizational structures*—other alternatives are attempts to be nonbureaucratic, communal/consensual social systems which seek to change education by avoiding the pitfalls of rule-bound organizations. (3) *New societal perspectives*—still others challenge the conventional wisdom concerning the role of schools in society. Rather than supporting the social order, as schools have traditionally been expected to do (Durkheim, 1956), some free schools seek to undercut it, both by turning out a new kind of child—counter-cultural, subversively noncompetitive, etc. (Reich, 1970; Roszak, 1969)—and by being a new model for other schools and organizations. Each new alternative school may embody one or more of these characteristics, depending on its location and constituency.

TOPIC SCOPE

Alternative education is not confined to a particular location or sponsorship. The estimated half-million American children participating in new-wave education may be found in public schools or private ones, in large urban centers like New York, Boston, and the San Francisco Bay area or small rural settings like Putney, Vermont or the mountains of California. We did find, however, that a disproportionate number of free schools seemed clustered in more sophisticated, university towns like Berkeley, Cambridge, and Madison, Wisconsin, for example, or in more politicized Third World communities like Harlem and Roxbury (Boston) which have a history of community organization and civil rights activities (Graubard, 1972b; Cooper, 1971). Originating in the mid-sixties, this movement to change American schools was supported by a very small number of professional educators, writers like Goodman (1960; 1966), Friedenberg (1965), and Holt (1967; 1972), and families from various racial-class groups. These activists, perhaps heartened by the spirit of the early civil rights and peace movements, saw conventional educational systems as authoritarian, racist, class-biased (Katz, 1971) at one extreme, or as boring and a waste of time at the other. Their reactions, as we shall explore, were to leave the system or to stay and fight. In either case, the kinds of new schools these people advocated were indicative of their own personal interests and needs—based in part upon their race, their social class, and their ability to tolerate working within the system.

Currently, the ideas of alternative education (often expressed as "open" education) have gained widespread acceptance among establishment leadership in government and in various communities. The diffusion rate of state-supported alternatives has increased markedly in the last three years, while support from the private sector appears in some areas to be peaking or even declining. For example, the federal government, through efforts like the Experimental Schools Project (ESP), Office of Education, has had a noticeable impact on the growth of alternative public systems. In Berkeley, for example, one of the first ESP districts, an increasing number of students (over a third) are enrolled in a public alternative, while the number of privately supported free schools has diminished during the last two school terms. Perhaps a combination of competition from non-fee-charging public alternatives and intense interpersonal conflict among free school people themselves has led to the gradual demise of new independent schools.

Also, the long-ignored "voucher plan" has taken root in California and New Hampshire, and promises to bring free school education to even more school districts. And even in the usually quite conservative Roman Catholic diocese, we find a surprising number of exciting school alternatives, like St. Mary's Center for Learning, a secondary free school drawing students from Chicago's inner city and suburbs, and the string of community schools started by Catholic organizers in the locations of former parochial schools in Milwaukee.

Who are the founders and supporters of these various alternatives in education? Some are poor and Third World peoples who are dissatisfied with the way their children are treated in public schools. A number of such critics have detailed how the educational system maintains the class and racial biases of American life (Katz, 1971;

Greer, 1970) by convincing black, brown, red, and poor children of their own inferiority, while systematically denying them access to equal educational opportunity (Kozol, 1967; Kohl, 1968; Wilcox, 1969; Friere, 1970). Or, as one group of school children themselves succinctly concluded, the school is the battleground where the state makes war upon the poor (The Schoolboys of Barbiana, 1970).

The response of a very small group of poor and minority parents has been initially to withdraw from public schools altogether, forming their own community-centered, privately-funded alternatives. Religious groups, federal agencies, foundations, and corporations provided the money, since these families could not afford tuition. The results were a series of "street academies" and "storefront schools" like CAM Academy of Chicago (Erickson, 1971, p. IV-72ff; Eash, 1970), sponsored by the Christian Action Ministry's 11 churches, and Harlem Prep (Carpenter and Rogers, 1971), and several "community schools" like the Roxbury Community School, East Harlem Block Schools, the Group School, Cambridge, a white working-class program, and the New Orleans Free School (Cooper, 1972).

These alternatives, though numbering only a couple of dozen, have become models of educational innovation for schools devoted to community-based education for poor children. Many of these new schools offer an intense experience in the culture of the particular ethnic-class groups, as well as basic academic skills. These alternatives tend to be more structured than programs for more affluent families, as Third World and poor parents and teachers seek to help their youngsters catch up academically and "get their thing together." Careful about the rhetoric of personal "freedom" and "spontaneity" as simple answers to the problems of poverty and racial discrimination, community school supporters realize the limitations of romantic slogans as ways of changing anything fundamental to them. Rather, they seek an education away from the racism and class-bias of public schools, and yet capable of providing the survival skills they need.

For the majority of minority and poor families, however, the public schools remain their major point of reference. Attempts at "community control" (and "power to the People") have led in some instances to the creation of organizational sub-units within public school systems, supposedly under the control of the local minority "community," like New York's Ocean Hill-Brownsville (Berube and Gittell, 1969; Mayer, 1968; Rubinstein, 1970) and Chicago's Woodlawn Experimental School District. Short of system-wide reorganization, public school leaders have also opened individual alternative schools for poor and nonwhite groups like Berkeley's United Nations, West School, and "College Prep," or have started new curricular innovations within existing schools, such as courses in black (and brown) culture and history. Whatever the particular alternative may have been, these new programs manifested an increased awareness of the importance of schooling to the efforts of poor and Third World peoples to gain freedom and equality in the United States.

Middle-class white folks, too, have been instrumental

in creating educational alternatives. Since their critique of our social and educational woes differs from their less affluent counterparts, the kinds of reforms they seek and schools they support also differ. Basically, these upper-income families condemn conventional schools as "grim, joyless places . . ., intellectually sterile and esthetically barren (Silberman, 1970, p. 10)." If children were only left alone, the reasoning goes, they would develop on their own, naturally into complete and self-fulfilled human beings (Holt, 1967; Neill, 1960; Goodman, 1960). It is the conventional school, as an agent of a repressive and "up-tight" society, that impinges on the children's sense of order and justice, for the ostensible purpose of preparing youngsters by a process of toughening and conditioning for a life in the cruel world (Jackson, 1968; Dreeben, 1968).

Middle-class free school proponents reject the notion that the "worst" of the industrialized, bureaucratic state should be foisted on the young. Instead, they insist on "opening" the schools, freeing the children to explore and learn on their own. A few thousand such families, like their less affluent counterparts, have opened their own private free schools, sometimes patterned after the 50-year old English experimental school, Summerhill, or after British "informal" educational program (Featherstone, 1971). These new schools number about 500, are extremely small (about 40 students), run on a shoestring budget of about $14,000 yearly, and shun conventional bureaucratic procedures.

Or these middle-class activists concentrate their efforts on changing the local public schools, and with amazing success. Hundreds of public schools across the nation have instituted alternative education, often because of pressure from these families. Currently available in public school systems are a choice of alternatives: "open classrooms," schools with special emphases, and "schools without walls." The demand for parental choice will continue, with school districts working to meet these requests.

Finally, some professional educators have been catalysts in starting alternative school programs. After all, these adults are most continuously and intimately involved with schools, bearing the brunt of the hostility and/or indifference that many students show. Moreover, being inside the system provides these professionals with a unique chance to change the system.

Many have done so within the context of public school systems. In comparison to those creating private alternatives, innovators in public systems are often (1) believers in the worth of public education, (2) agitators for change, without losing their credibility with the superiors and the public, and (3) skillful managers in finding funds, facilities, and equipment to open new programs within existing bureaucracies. John Bremer, for example, started the first "school without walls," the Parkway School, in Philadelphia (1969), a large school district known for its traditional approaches and resistance to change (Cox, 1972; Reznik, 1970). Bremer decided that the entire city would be the classroom, and the city's workers and leaders the staff for his school. "The object is to reconnect the schools with the larger community, not through conventional field trips, but

through some continuing experience (Silberman, 1970, p. 351)." Other "schools without walls" that followed were Chicago's Metro School (Center for New Schools, 1972) and New Orleans' Gateway School (Cooper, 1972). Today we find similar programs nationwide.

Public school teachers and professors of education, too, have taken the lead in starting in-system alternatives. Marcia Perlstein, an experienced San Francisco high school teacher, recognized the needs of inner-city students and started Opportunity I and Opportunity II. Both programs offer work-study, tutoring, counseling, and classes in basic skills in informal settings (the schools are housed in warehouses). Dr. Lillian Weber, professor of education at New York's City College, has assisted scores of public elementary schools in converting their programs and buildings—often using the school corridors—to "informal educational settings (Weber, 1971; Silberman, 1970, pp. 297-306)."

While these "free schools" within the public schools, started by veteran schoolpeople, could be considered more moderate and perhaps more bureaucratic than their nonpublic counterparts, they are useful, effective alternatives that are widely available to larger numbers of families at no personal expense. If the trend toward open education continues—and there is good evidence that it will—the remainder of the seventies should find thousands of public alternatives made available to American families.

A REVIEW OF THE LITERATURE

A diverse body of written materials has been associated with the free school movement. It is neither easily categorized nor internally consistent. Rather, it is all an expression of some form of opposition to prevailing norms about schools and society.

Schools and society. A range of books and articles have appeared treating the political and economic consequences of conventional schooling (Friere, 1970; Kozol, 1972; Illich, 1970; Gintis, 1972; Reimer, 1971; and Graubard, 1972b). While these works primarily attack the traditional role of schools, as presented cogently by writers like Dreeben (1968) and Jackson (1968), other works often discussed by free school people present a set of positive alternatives, albeit utopian and limited though they be. These include writings on Israeli *kibbutzim* (Bettelheim, 1969; Spiro, 1958), communes (Zablocki, 1971; Skinner, 1967), and other kinds of special communities (Yablonski, 1967).

Personal experiences. A growing body of literature tells of personal life in schools. Kozol (1967), Kohl (1968), and Herndon (1969), for example, describe in graphic and often humorous detail their efforts to teach innovatively in the public schools—Kozol and Herndon were fired for their efforts. Other authors have themselves tried doing alternative schools, with mixed results. Dennison (1969) at First Street School, writes probably the best book in this category. Others include works by Neill (1960), Marin (1971), and a group of students, teachers, and parents at the Elizabeth Cleaners

Street School (1972).

Practical hints. a number of educators and journalists have traveled to England, returning with sound advice on how to apply the techniques of the British Infant School (also called the Leicestershire method schools) to the American setting (Weber, 1971; Hertzberg and Stone, 1967), or with engaging descriptions of these new schools (Featherstone, 1971). Even private free schools have produced some practical guides on how to do small cooperative schools (Rasberry, 1970).

Critical evaluation and analysis. The rejection of conventionality within the movement has included a reluctance to scrutinize what free schools do. Thus, little real analysis is available currently. Graubard (1972b) has written the best book on the assumptions and practices of free schools. Sussmann (1971), examined the classroom life in terms of teacher, student, and milieu; and Cooper (1973) developed a theory of how these new schools grow, change, and survive organizationally. But overall, it is too early to gather much substantial information on the effects of the new wave of radical schools.

CURRENT CONTROVERSIES

With a movement as current and diverse as the alternative schools phenomena, there are bound to be issues over which many participants disagree.

How radical is radical? Free school people outside the public schools may accuse the so-called liberal reformers inside the system of taking half-steps and of actually preserving, not changing, the system. Those working in the public schools, on the other hand, may see the other group as escapists, elitists, or just plain extremists (Kozol, 1972). Whichever point of view is extended, the fact remains that one side needs the other. Without proding, goading, and motivating, large public systems will not change; without someone to organize and maintain new innovations, they will never reach the students and their families.

How "free" should an alternative be? This issue is central to any discussion of educational reform. Few would argue against the need for children to learn to be able, self-motivated adults. Rather, the conflict revolves around when controls should be relaxed, and to what extent (*Summerhill: For and Against,* 1970). Free school advocates, perhaps in their haste to change what seems an intolerable situation, may discard all trappings of authority, e.g., titles like teacher and director, and school by-laws. Public school change agents, on the other hand, are understandably more cautious.

How "political" should alternative schools be? Traditionally, schools have claimed to be politically neutral. Radical school members challenge this assumption, explaining that schools support a conservative political and social ideology, both in the curriculum and the way schools are run. These new schools, in turn, attempt at one extreme to be totally apolitical, escaping the evils of the system, while other free schools (particularly the ones for poor and Third World families) have sought to use schools as springboards for political activities in the community. Hence, while most alternative schools realize the political nature of education, they react in very different ways. Even publicly supported experimental schools must "fight for their lives," using whatever clout they have to resist the opponents of change in the schools and the community (Reznik, 1970).

How important is learning? This issue plagues virtually every experimental school. The radical (and upper-middle class) say that formal learning is too constricting; poor and Third World schools promote learning as a tool to social and economic security and power. And some schools seem to strike a balance between individual freedom and classroom structure and learning.

What should schools be doing for the future? Someone raised the question which seems at the heart of the issue: "How long has it been since you knew what was important for children to know?" The point is, we do not know which way our society is moving, or in fact which way we want it to go. Thus, the education of young people cannot proceed with any certainty.

As for the free school movement, we are enthralled, somehow, that a rag-tag group of romantics could appear to influence the monolithic public school Leviathan. But whether the free school phenomenon is really a revolution or even a meaningful change is hard to assess. We can all agree, perhaps, that new-wave alternatives in education are making schooling more humane and interesting. And that is a big step toward change, though its direction and outcome are not as yet clear.

FURTHER INFORMATION

Those interested in information on how to start and maintain free schools should consult the final section of Kozol's *Free School* (1972, pp. 125-146) and issues 24 and 25 of *Ed Centric-Center Peace,* 1973, which may be received by writing Ed Centric, 2115 "S" Street, N.W., Washington, D.C., 20008

For further help in locating alternative schools, finding jobs in these schools, and sharing ideas, write the New Schools Exchange (publishers of the NSE *Newsletter*) at P.O. Box 820, St. Paris, Ohio 43082. Participants in public alternatives are advised of the Center for New Schools, 431 S. Bearborn Street, Chicago, Illinois 60605, which supplies assistance in starting and evaluating in-system experimental schools.

REFERENCES

Barth, Roland. *Open Education and the American School.* New York: Agathon Press, 1972.

Berube, Maurice, and Gittell, Marilyn, eds. *Confrontation at Ocean Hill-Brownsville: The New York Schools Strikes of 1968.* New York: Praeger, 1969.

Bettelheim, Bruno. *Children of the Dream.* New York: Macmillan, 1969.

Bhaerman, Steve, and Denker, Joel. *No Particular Place to Go: The Making of a Free High School.* New York: Simon and

Schuster, 1972.

Carpenter, Anne M., and Rogers, James. Harlem Prep: An Alternative System, New York City. In Ronald Gross and Paul Osterman, eds., *High School.* New York: Simon and Schuster, 1971, 248-262.

Center for New Schools. Strengthening Alternative High Schools. *Harvard Educational Review,* 1972, *42, 313-350.*

Cooper, Bruce S. *Free and Freedom Schools: A National Survey of Alternative Programs.* Washington, D.C.: The President's Commission on School Finance, 1971.

——. Two Schools. In Donald A. Erickson, *Three R's of Nonpublic Education in Louisiana: Race, Religion, and Region.* Washington, D.C.: The President's Commission on School Finance, 1972.

——. Organizational Survival: A Comparative Case Study of Seven American "Free Schools." *Education and Urban Society,* September 1973.

Cox, Donald W. *The City as a Schoolhouse.* New York: Judson, 1972.

Dennison, George. *The Lives of Children: The Story of the First Street School.* New York: Random House, 1969.

Dreeben, Robert. *On What is Learned in School.* Reading, Mass.: Addison-Wesley, 1968.

Durkheim, Emile. *Education and Sociology.* New York: The Free Press, 1956.

Eash, Maurice B. *Abstract: a Comprehensive Curriculum Evaluation of the Christian Action Ministry Academy, 1970.* Chicago: Office of Evaluation Research, University of Illinois of Chicago Circle, 1970.

Elizabeth Cleaners Street School. *Starting Your Own High School.* New York: Random House, 1972.

Erickson, Donald A. *Crisis in Illinois Nonpublic Schools.* A report to the Elementary and Secondary Nonpublic Schools Study Commission. Chicago, Illinois, 1971.

Featherstone, Joseph. *Schools Where Children Learn.* New York: Liveright, 1971.

Friedenberg, Edgar Z. *Coming of Age in America: Growth and Acquiescence.* New York: Random House, 1965.

Friere, Paulo. *Pedagogy of the Oppressed.* New York: Herder and Herder, 1970.

Fuller, R. Buckminster. *Education Automation: Freeing the Scholar to Return to his Studies.* Carbondale, Ill.: Southern Illinois Press, 1964.

Goodman, Paul. *Growing Up Absurd.* New York: Random House, 1960.

——. *Compulsory Mis-Education and the Community of Scholars.* New York: Vintage, 1966.

Gintis, Herbert. Toward a Political Economy of Education: A Radical Critique of Ivan Illich's *Deschooling Society. Harvard Educational Review, 42,* 1972, 70-96.

Graubard, Alan. The Free School Movement. *Harvard Educational Review,* 1972a, *42,* 351-373.

——. *Free the Children: Radical Reform and the Free School Movement.* New York: Pantheon, 1972b.

Greer, Colin. *Cobweb Attitudes: Essays on Education and Cultural Mythology.* New York: Teachers College Press, 1970.

Herndon, James. *The Way It's Spozed to Be.* New York: Bantam Books, 1969.

Hertzberg, Alvin, and Stone, Edward. *Schools are for Children.* New York: Schocken, 1967.

Holt, John. *How Children Learn.* New York: Pitman Publishing Co., 1967.

——. *Freedom and Beyond.* New York: E. P. Dutton, 1972.

Illich, Ivan. *De-Schooling Society.* New York: Harper and Row, 1970.

Jackson, Philip W. *Life in the Classroom.* New York: Holt, Rinehart and Winston, 1968.

Katz, Michael B. *Class, Bureaucracy, and Schools.* New York: Praeger, 1971.

Kohl, Herbert. *36 Children.* New York: Signet Books, 1968.

Kozol, Jonathan. *Death at an Early Age.* Boston: Houghton-Mifflin, 1967.

——. *Free Schools.* Boston: Houghton-Mifflin, 1972.

Marin, Peter. The Open Truth and Fiery Vehemence of Youth. In R. Gross and P. Osterman, eds., *High School.* New York: Simon and Schuster, 1971.

Mayer, Martin. *The Teachers Strike.* New York: Harper and Row, 1968.

Neill, A. S. *Summerhill: A Radical Approach to Childrearing.* New York: Hart Publishing Co., 1960.

Rasberry, Salli, and Greenway, Robert. *Rasberry Exercises: How to Start a School . . . And Make a Book.* Sebastopol, Calif.: Freestone Publishing Co., 1970.

Reimer, Everette. *School is Dead: Alternatives in Education.* Garden City, N.Y.: Doubleday, 1971.

Reich, Charles. *Greening of America.* New York: Random House, 1970.

Resnik, Henry S. *Turning on the System: War in the Philadelphia Public Schools.* New York: Pantheon, 1970.

Roszak, Theodor. *The Making of a Counterculture.* Garden City, N.Y.: Doubleday, 1969.

Rubinstein, Annette, ed. *Schools Against Children: The Case for Community Control.* New York: Monthly Review Press, 1970.

Schoolboys of Barbiana. *Letter to a Teacher.* New York: Random House, 1970.

Silberman, Charles E. *Crisis in the Classroom: The Remaking of American Education.* New York: Vintage, 1970.

Skinner, B. F. *Walden Two.* New York: Macmillan, 1948.

Spiro, M. *Kibbutz: Adventure in Utopia.* New York: Schocken, 1958.

Summerhill: For and Against. New York: Hart Publishing Co., 1970.

Sussmann, Leila. *The Role of the Teacher in Selected Innovative Schools in the United States.* Paris: Organization for Economic Cooperation and Development, December 3, 1971.

Weber, Lillian. *The English Infant School and Informal Education.* Englewood Cliffs, N.J.: Prentice-Hall, Inc., 1971.

Wilcox, Preston. The Community-Centered School. In Beatrice and Ronald Gross, eds., *Radical School Reform.* New York: Simon and Schuster, 1969.

Yablonski, Lewis. *Synanon: The Tunnel Back.* Baltimore: Penguin, 1967.

Zablocki, Benjamin. *The Joyful Community.* Baltimore: Penguin, 1971.

110

THE STOREFRONT SCHOOL AS AN EDUCATIONAL ALTERNATIVE

by William C. Nelsen
Vice President and Dean of the College
Associate Professor of Political Science
and
Myron L. Solid
Assistant Professor of Education
St. Olaf College
Northfield, Minnesota

DEFINITION AND OBJECTIVE

The term "storefront school" normally refers to a smaller school organized outside the traditional public school system as an alternative model to reach students not being served adequately by the larger system. Along with terms such as "street academy," "mini-school," and such broader concepts as "open school" and "alternative school," the "storefront school" has been used to describe a variety of alternative educational institutions, ideas, and models. In the working definition above, the term "smaller" is used to differentiate the storefront school from such larger-scale educational alternatives as the Parkway Plan in Philadelphia. The term "alternative" refers to the fact that such schools normally operate under an educational style and philosophy different from that predominant within the local public school system. The term "model" emphasizes that the leaders of most storefront schools are attempting to demonstrate to others the validity of their own and similar educational ideas. The word "normally" must appear because a tight working definition of "storefront school" is impossible, given the variety of educational alternatives that the term has come to symbolize. Thus, the authors do not regard the term as referring only to a small school for children operating in a specific physical location—namely, a storefront building.

Why has the phenomenon of storefront schools arisen? Presently there seem to be two influences which apply pressure on the public schools to ensure demonstrable learning: the public, in its demand for "accountability," and disillusioned youth, who frequently charge that schools fail to meet their needs. It is the latter group, along with other education critics, that are demanding alternatives to the public school system, and in many communities storefront schools have been created in response to that demand.

Although the educational styles and philosophies vary widely among storefront schools, most share many common concerns. Each demonstrates a belief that there are a number of things radically wrong with the present public system in most cities, that education can and ought to be more relevant to the community and the individual and corporate problems of its residents, that children with the potential to do much better are being overlooked, and that educational change is possible.

In summary, the storefront school serves two major objectives: (1) it provides an alternative approach toward education for youth attracted to its principles, and (2) it serves as an attempt to influence change within the educational program of the public schools.

EXTENT AND VARIETY OF THE STOREFRONT SCHOOL MOVEMENT

In the context of the topic as defined above, storefront schools have directed themselves to a variety of different learner outcomes. Some of the alternative educational institutions concentrate on educating high school dropouts and getting many of them into a college or university, while others provide experiences toward earning only the General Equivalency Degree. Some storefronts represent new schools for dropouts, in an attempt to offer a different kind of learning experience, while still others serve as a supplement to the public school experience by providing individualized tutoring or other special educational programs. An example of this variety of purposes can be found in the Minneapolis-St. Paul area, where alternative schools have been described as existing to meet the following needs: (1) to make it possible for a high school dropout to obtain basic academic skills, and possibly a diploma; (2) to provide dropouts and potential dropouts with meaningful and relevant social and academic experiences; (3) to assist all interested students who possess basic skill deficiencies; (4) to meet special needs of minority race and low-income students (some attempt to serve as models of racial integration, others are created for specific ethnic groups); (5) to provide appropriate educational experiences for students returning from correctional institutions; and (6) to provide opportunities for students in need of the development of self-concept, as well as for multi-cultural enrichment. In the Twin Cities (Minneapolis-St. Paul) area, alternative education schools provide for a range in age level from preschool through post-high school, with over 20 schools available for elementary age children (which includes eight that are K-12), over 30 concentrating on junior high and senior high grade levels, and approximately 18 post-high school programs or colleges (Educational Exploration Center, *Directory*, 1973).

In a similar vein, storefront schools have utilized a variety of educational styles, as illustrated by portions of the names of various schools: Survival School, Open School, Mini-School, Community School, Learning Center, Project, Street Academy, Montessori, Youth Development, Urban Education Center, Urban Arts Program, School Without Walls, Storefront. There are likewise varying philosophies among leaders of the alternatives in terms of curriculum, amount of freedom to be allowed students and teachers, methodology and facilitation of learning experiences, and how much autonomy the school should maintain. Storefront schools also vary in their geographic scope; some schools are created and designed to include only students in a specific neighborhood, while others have no residency limitations.

In the past few years, storefront schools of many different styles have been organized to meet many different needs in nearly every large city in the nation; among the most notable are the Street Academies of the Urban League of New York City. In 1970 Harvey Haber, founder of the New Schools Exchange in Santa Barbara, California, maintained that two or three new "alternative" schools were born every day, although he estimated the average life of a new school as being about 18 months, after which it dies completely, merges with another school, or alters its course so severely it ceases to be a radically innovative institution (Robinson, 1970). But even if most of the storefront schools in the country ultimately disappear, the number and variety of the institutions being created is symptomatic of unfulfilled needs in the nation's public schools, particularly in urban settings.

RECENT DEVELOPMENTS

Currently there appears to be much open interest in alternative education, by educators as well as the general public. In a 1973 article Brownson documented that during the previous two years

> . . . a national consortium on educational alternatives has been established, two national and a series of regional conferences have been held, a number of professional associations have conducted workshops at national meetings on public alternatives, teacher education programs have been adapted, a number of major educational periodicals have included feature articles on alternatives, and the U.S. Office of Education has funded over 12 million dollars for experimentations with alternatives. (p. 299)

Brownson continues by noting that there were then 60 school districts either operating alternatives within their systems or in the process of developing new alternatives, including storefront schools specifically: Seattle with 19, Philadephia with 18, and New York, St. Paul-Minneapolis, Louisville, Tacoma, Grand Rapids, and Ann Arbor with at least one alternative, some with more (pp. 299, 303). An example of the seriousness with which school districts considered alternative modes of education was the March 1973 decision of the Minneapolis School Board to examine the idea of offering alternative styles of education to *all* elementary school pupils in the city by the fall of 1976. The action followed positive assessment of the City's "Southeast Alternatives" experimental program.

CURRENT ISSUES FACING THE STOREFRONT SCHOOL

Several issues surround the attempts of storefront school leaders to reach the dual objectives of serving well those students turned off by the public system and at the same time trying to influence the system to change educationally. These issues can be listed in the following categories: (1) the development of a clearly-stated educational philosophy, (2) funding and survival of the storefront school, (3) the relationship of the storefront school to the public school system, (4) the role of cooperative arrangements with other alternative school models, (5) program cost considerations, (6) evaluation and ac-

countability, and (7) responsible governance arrangements for the storefront school program. (For a more complete discussion of most of these issues see Nelsen, 1971.)

Educational Philosophy

Can alternative education proponents state a well-defined philosophy of education? Storefront school educators are often criticized for offering a strong negative critique of the public system while failing to develop a good positive statement of their own educational philosophy. The situation is reminiscent of Dewey's criticism of the educational reformers of his day:

> There is always the danger in a new movement that in rejecting the aims and methods of that which it would supplant, it may develop its principles negatively rather than positively and constructively. Then it takes a clew in practice from that which it rejected instead of from the constructive development of its own philosophy. (As quoted by Jackson, 1972, p. 22)

Constructive statements of educational philosophy will be helpful to the storefront school in developing its own program, and in stating its case to the general public.

Funding and Survival

How can the storefront school be financially viable? Storefronts often get started with private foundation or business support. However, in times of financial recession this support can be cut back. Also, most private funding agencies do not expect to provide continuing support. Thus the storefront school must be able to get its hands on the public dollar. Some storefronts are now seeking to develop contracts with the public system, or to get the public system to undertake the model itself.

Relationship to the Public School System

Should the storefront school have a good, communicative, working relationship with the public school system? Experience has shown that educational change usually results from some combination of challenge from without and adjustments from within. For example, the "mini-schools" operating within the New York City Public System are generally regarded as having resulted from the models of the Urban League Street Academies. Storefront school personnel ought to be conscious of creating models which can be translated into the public system. A good working relationship with the public system (despite the opposition of some educators to communicating with the "enemy") may be very helpful in bringing about educational change. In certain cases, notably Minneapolis' "Southeast Alternatives" program, storefront schools are being started under the auspices of the public system.

Cooperative Arrangements

Should individual storefront programs link up with other alternative schools? Cooperative arrangements among alternative schools in a number of cities—for example, St. Louis, Boston, New York, Milwaukee, Minneapolis—have resulted in positive advantages both for the programs of the individual schools and for their relationship to the public system. Cooperation has helped in pooling resources, developing joint inservice training programs, sharing educational philosophy and instructional techniques, seeking outside funding, and communicating with and influencing the public system. In St. Louis, for example, a notable achievement was reached when the Chairman of the Educational Confederation (a consortium of alternative models) was elected to the Public School Board.

Program Cost Considerations

Can a storefront school operate at less cost per pupil than the public school? The question is important, for the public school system will not likely adopt or contract with a costly educational model. Thus, the storefront school must give careful attention to per-pupil costs, in order both to be financially viable and to demonstrate to the public system that it can produce better educational results at approximately the same or even less cost.

Evaluation and Accountability

Can the storefront school educate certain students better? In order to answer the question—to its own and the public's satisfaction—it must be able to measure and evaluate its impact on students. Standard educational tests may not work well in the storefront setting, but some comparable method of demonstrating achievement must be devised.

Governance Arrangements for the Storefront School

How should the storefront be governed? In certain cases governance arrangements—election procedures for the Board, the relationship between directors, administrators, and teachers, etc.—have not been carefully defined. If the storefront school is to operate relatively smoothly its own program, and provide new directions for community involvement in educational policy-making, it must give careful scrutiny to its own polity arrangements.

Storefront schools will need to pay close attention to each of these seven issues in order to have any real impact on American education.

What is the future of the storefront school? Educational institutions in this country as well as in other countries often face challenges by new educational "movements." Storefront schools, as one means of providing alternative educational models, could be regarded as a movement that will soon pass. However, that storefronts have pointed toward the need for developing a variety of alternative educational mechanisms and methods to teach a pluralistic student clientele is clear. It is in the judgment of the authors that many storefronts have a good chance for long-term existence, if they pay close attention to the seven issues outlines above. However,

even if they go out of existence as independent institutions, they will continue to serve for some time as an important symbol of the need for educational alternatives within the public school system.

REFERENCES

Brownson, B. Alternative Schools and the Problem of Change: School is a School is a School . . . . *Contemporary Education,* 1973, *44,* 298-303.

Divoky, D. New York's Mini-Schools—Small Miracles, Big Troubles. *Saturday Review,* December 18, 1971, 60-67.

Education Exploration Center, Inc. *Twin City Alternative Education Directory,* Fall, 1973.

———. *Twin City Alternative Schools Catalogue,* Fall, 1973.

Jackson, P. W. Deschooling! No! *Today's Education, NEA Journal, 1972, 61,* 18-22.

Nelsen, W. C. The Storefront School: A Vehicle for Change. *The Journal of Negro Education,* 1971, *40,* 248-254.

O'Gorman, N. *The Storefront.* New York: Harper and Row, 1970.

Robinson, D. W. "Alternative Schools": Challenge to Traditional Education? *Phi Delta Kappan,* 1970, *51,* 374-375.

ADDITIONAL RESOURCES

The National Consortium on Educational Alternatives
Educational Alternatives Project
School of Education, Suite 328
Indiana University
Bloomington, Indiana 47401

> This is an ad hoc group of schools, organizations, and individuals interested in the development of alternatives schools.

The National Alternative Schools Program
School of Education
University of Massachusetts
Amherst, Mass. 01002

> Serves as a resource center and clearinghouse for information and consultant services dealing with alternative schools.

111

RUDOLPH STEINER EDUCATION

by Henry Barnes
Chairman of the Faculty
Rudolph Steiner School
New York, New York

More than 100 coeducational elementary and secondary schools in 18 countries of the free world base their teaching methods and curricula on the educational ideas put forward by Rudolf Steiner (1861-1925), which were first incorporated by him in the school which he founded in 1919 in Stuttgart, Germany, known as the Waldorf School (Die Freie Waldorfschule).

An almost equal number of institutions for the education of children who require some form of special education derive their pedagogical inspiration from Rudolf Steiner's work. In addition, numerous kindergartens work with Steiner's ideas, and individual teachers in many countries apply insights derived from his work in their teaching. The education identified with Rudolf Steiner and with the Waldorf Schools draws its methods of instruction and its curriculum from a comprehensive insight into the nature of man as a being of soul and spirit as well as body. It is unique in the detail with which it relates physiological, psychological and spiritual factors in child development. Its basic premise is that education is an art.

The Waldorf, or Rudolf Steiner, educational movement is growing rapidly, especially in the United States, Germany, Holland, and Switzerland. The demand for teachers trained in these methods, and the demand by young people seeking an alternative to those forms of education which derive their content and curricula from a view of man which ignores the spirit and the psyche and their interaction with the physical organism, have led to the establishment of institutions for the training of teachers in Switzerland, Germany, England, Holland, Sweden, and the United States. It is now possible to obtain an M.A. in Waldorf Education from Adelphi University, and a diploma leading to certification in the state of Michigan from the Waldorf Teacher Training Institute of Mercy College, Detroit. Several other schools offer training programs without official academic credit. Emerson College, Forest Row, England, offers a two-year course of graduate study leading to a certificate in education.

A further significant development within the Steiner, or Waldorf, educational movement is the introduction of a strong program of prevocational and apprentice training in a number of fields within the framework of a broad, general education. One school in particular, the Hybernia Schule, Wanne Eickel, in the Ruhr district of Germany, began as an apprentice program for the chemical industry, and proved so effective that the industries involved supported its expansion into a full 12-year school, which also offers those students who qualify entrance to the universities. The purpose of this new development is twofold: to provide a basic human education for those students who are going to learn a trade, so that their early vocational experience will be part of an all-round educational development, and to offer those students who will go on to universities and technical schools a more practical education than they would otherwise receive.

In the United States, a similar trend has been inaugurated with the establishment of a Farm School in Columbia County, N.Y., which offers city children a regular, ongoing opportunity to experience country life, with work on the farm, in the garden, in the kitchen, etc., as part of their regular education at the Rudolf Steiner School, New York. A day school has also been established on the farm which seeks to integrate rural work experience with academic and artistic learning. Similar opportunities are being developed in a number of Steiner schools in this country. In all instances, the intention is to educate practically as well as theoretically, and to reach the nonintellectual sides of the child's nature as well as the mind.

These developments, although recent in time, reflect a fundamental aspect of Rudolf Steiner's approach to education: the effort to present every subject in such a way that it arouses the active participation of the student and penetrates to his will. Its aim is to educate capacities, rather than impart mere information. To achieve this, several distinctive educational procedures have been developed, all of which, however, lose their educational effectiveness when divorced from the view of child development and of the nature of man from which they originated. Among these procedures, some of the more evident are: the organization of the school day, the organization of the week and year, the relationship with the teacher, and use of artistic experience.

One of the enemies of sound education is the fragmentation of experience typical of schools today, as well as of the media and of life in general. To counteract this, the day in a Steiner school is organized into a long, often two-hour lesson with which the day begins. Each morning, for several weeks at a time, the same subject is studied during this long lesson. In a fifth grade, for instance, this would mean that the following subjects would be studied in "blocks" of time: geography, history, botany, English, math. The teacher would divide these subjects and arrange their rotation in such a way that a humanistic subject alternates with a more objective one, thus creating a natural rhythm. During these "main lesson blocks," the homework revolves around the subject under study, and the children have the opportunity to build up a notebook which they illustrate themselves, serving as a reinforcement of their learning and as a permanent record of what they have learned and achieved. These notebooks largely replace the conventional textbooks, and are frequently consulted in later years by the students themselves when they are reviewing a subject at a higher level. The long "main lesson" is especially well suited for the in-depth introduction of new material, where so often retention is determined by interest and atmosphere rather than by mechanical pressure. The lesson is also long enough that the teacher can introduce a variety of experience, including physical activity, and written or illustrative work, as well as presentation and discussion.

The main lesson is followed by the conventional shorter periods during the later part of the day, which lend themselves to the teaching of foreign languages, the development of skills in English and math, and to artistic and practical subjects. The attempt is made to balance the day so that the more concentrated attention in the early, main lesson is followed by lessons with a more recitational character, and by the bodily active lessons in the afternoon.

One of the consequences of the concentrated blocks of study is the evolution of a spiral curriculum, in which the same subject recurs from year to year at different levels of experience. For example, chemistry is introduced in the seventh grade and recurs each year thereafter through grade 12. The same thing is true for physics (introduced in grade 6) and for biology, as well as history, literature, mathematics, etc. As the individual matures, he is able to experience the same subject in a new way, and the new exposure provides the opportunity for review as well as extension. The spiral curriculum "grows with the child," enhancing each subject's contribution to his total human development. Although a year's course may well be offered as an elective in the upper grades, the emphasis is always on the developmental impact, never during the school years on vocational specialization as such.

The relationship between teacher and pupil constitutes an especially important chapter in Steiner education. In the kindergarten, the essential factor is the character and personality of the teacher herself. Here, the children absorb experience primarily by imitation, they identify with their environment. Who the teacher is, is here far more important than what she teaches. How she handles materials, how she forms the day, what kind of an atmosphere she creates around her are essential tools of her educational influence. In the elementary school, imitation recedes and the faculty of imagination comes to the fore. It is now the teacher's task to so digest her subject matter that she can transform it into a language of pictorial, imaginative experience without in any way sacrificing its factual accuracy. To the extent she succeeds in this, she will stimulate interest and awaken an emotional as well as an intellectual response. This will have a great deal to do with how the children remember what they learn, and how it becomes part of them.

Children at this age have a natural desire to look up to the adult, especially the teacher. Although this desire has been frustrated and deliberately destroyed in many instances, if given the opportunity it asserts itself as one of the natural prerogatives of childhood. In this sense, Steiner placed great importance on establishing a natural, unforced emulation by the pupil in response to a wise, objective and loving authority on the part of the teacher. He went so far as to maintain that without the experience of genuine authority in the middle years of childhood, the individual as an adult will lack the capacity to relate in a natural, democratic, and human way to his fellowmen. Can the problem we encounter on all sides in this sphere today reflect the breakdown of this kind of spontaneous relationship between teachers and children, parents and children, and adults and children in general?

This relationship is supported during the elementary years in a Steiner, or Waldorf, school by having the class teacher accompany his or her class from year to year. This arrangement is not only efficient, as only the teacher who has taught the class one year really knows them when she starts the next, and can build her teaching from step to step, but it creates security through continuity, and educates the capacity for those enduring relationships on which the fabric of social life absolutely depends. The idea of the continuing class teacher often evokes skepticism, and the question is frequently asked: what if my child is stuck with a poor, or even a merely mediocre teacher? Won't this prolonged influence warp my child? Experience answers that the poor teacher either becomes better or quits such a system. If Miss Williams is having trouble with Max she is much more disposed to try to

get to the bottom of the problem and solve it (which almost always requires some growth on the part of the teacher) if she knows she will have Max next year, instead of handing him on to Mrs. Carey. Continuing with the same group of children calls forth the best in every teacher. She has to master new subject matter each year, and cannot get into a rut. She has to grow to keep up with her children. If she teaches in a school where others are going through the same experience, and in a faculty which meets regularly and enjoys discussing children, she will be helped to overcome her limitations and will get fresh insights from her colleagues, who also teach her group in their special subjects.

In high school the relationship is very different. The students outgrow the relation with one class teacher as naturally as they once grew into it. They want to be free to find their own models. The authority of the teacher as a specialist is now more important, and the main lesson subjects are taught by different teachers. A class advisor takes the place of the class teacher.

The role of art in Rudolf Steiner education is by no means exhausted by the fact that virtually all the artistic disciplines are taught and practiced during the course of the 12 school years. It is intended that artistic method shall penetrate the teaching of every subject, and very specially so during the elementary school year. What does this mean?

The method of art has much in common with the art of reading. The letters themselves reveal nothing except their immediate physical properties; they have shape, color, texture, substance, etc. They acquire meaning as symbols only when the reader has the key which unlocks their significance as language. Then they reveal the "story" which they have hitherto concealed. The artist starts from perception and "reads" a meaning through the physical elements of color, shape, tone, gesture, etc. This is also the way of the young child. He experiences the world as percept and divines the story, the meaning through the letters of perception. If a teacher follows an artistic, rather than an intellectual method, and he has the task of introducing acoustics, let us say, to a sixth grade, he will not start with a definition, but will arrange his lesson in such a way that the phenomena speak for themselves. For instance, he may set up a screen in his classroom on the first morning and behind it create a series of sound impressions by rustling paper, striking iron, scraping wood, pouring water, etc. leaving his pupils to guess how each sound is produced. This experience leads of itself to the recognition that every substance reveals something of its nature through the sound it gives forth, and with this, one is at the first of the three qualities of sound, namely tone quality, or timbre. There is then no problem to demonstrate the relationship of length and thickness to height and depth of pitch, or the force with which a sound is evoked to intensity. When one then discusses sound as vibration and sound waves in the air the student brings a different qualitative response to the concepts than if one had begun by defining sound: "sound is vibration which strikes a receptive membrane." Simple as the illustration is, there is a far-reaching methodological principle at stake. The artistic method starts from perception and proceeds finally to concept as a crystallization of experience. Concepts achieved in this way are able to grow with the child. Concepts presented as finished definitions remain undigested and unchanged. Mere factual learning, on the other hand, leads to rote memorization and disconnected information. Artistic method works both with the facts of perception and with process of digestion and transformation which makes of an exterior fact an interior experience and a life possession, and in this difference lies the role of education as distinct from training and conditioning. The educated man responds individually from within; the trained person has conditioned reflexes which respond to stimuli from without.

To characterize an education which was inaugurated over 50 years ago and which, to the author's knowledge, is growing more rapidly than any other independent school movement in the world today, in so brief a space is necessarily sketchy and likely to be misleading. In attempting an understanding of Steiner, or Waldorf, education, it is essential to bear in mind that it is not so much what is done in a Waldorf school that constitutes the education, but the insight into the nature of man and of child development which stands behind it. Steiner's work as an educator stands or falls on the validity of the knowledge on which it is based. This knowledge, Steiner claims, is won with the methods of scientific discipline, and through investigation applied to realms of experience not directly accessible to the senses. It includes a knowledge of man as a spirit and soul being as well as a physical being. To be valid, this knowledge must be tested by each individual, as he would test every other insight which comes his way. This makes of Steiner education not a convenient recipe, but a challenge to the individual to become active, to test his insights, and to allow them, if he so wishes, to become creative capacities in his own teaching.

It might be added that it is generally characteristic of Waldorf schools that they are administered by their teachers on an elected or rotating basis. In this way, those who have direct responsibility for the children also determine policy and deal with administrative problems.

REFERENCES

Barnes, H., and Lyons, N. *Education as an Art*. New York: Rudolf Steiner School, 1967.
Harwood, C. *The Recovery of Man in Childhood*. London: Hodder & Stoughton, 1970.
Heydebrand, C. V. *Childhood*. London: Rudolf Steiner Press, 1970.
Konig, Karl. *The First Three Years of the Child*. New York: Anthroposophic Press, 1969.
Steiner, R. *The Education of the Child*. London: Rudolf Steiner Press, 1965.
_____. *The Essentials of Education*. London: Rudolf Steiner Press, 1968.
_____. *Education as a Social Problem*. New York: Anthroposophic Press, 1969.
_____. *Human Values in Education*. London: Rudolf Steiner Press, 1971.

MAJOR INTEREST GROUPS

Rudolf Steiner School Association
15 East 79th Street
New York, N.Y. 10021

Waldorf School Association of Ontario, Inc.
51 Limcombe Drive
Thorn Hill, Ont., Canada

112

CREDIT BY EXAMINATION: A REVIEW AND ANALYSIS OF THE LITERATURE

by Hannah S. Kreplin
Project Associate
Center for Research and Development in
Higher Education
Berkeley, California

Programs of credit by examination provide the student with an opportunity to complete course requirements by examination only, without completing the usual accoutrements of course work such as mid-term examinations, term papers, and final examinations. Credit by examination may result in placement and/or credit. Although programs of credit by examination have been in existence in the U.S. since the early 1920s, only in the past five or six years have they been taken seriously as alternative models for postsecondary education, spurred in good part by the nontraditional education movement. There is no adequate estimate available of the number of credit by examination programs currently in operation. On the one hand, new programs are springing up every day. On the other hand, many programs, particularly those in traditional institutions, are on paper only.

Until the early 1970s, with few exceptions the research literature on credit by examination was sporadic and unsystematic (Flaugher, Mahoney, and Messing, 1967). Since the turn of the current decade, however, much more comprehensive attention has been paid to the topic. The reader is particularly directed toward the several volumes resulting from the Commission on Non-Traditional Study, especially *Diversity By Design* (1973), edited by Samuel B. Gould and K. Patricia Cross, and *The External Degree* by Cyril O. Houle (1973). In addition, a number of statewide public systems of higher education have addressed the credit by examination issue in working papers and recommendations, most notably New York and Florida.

Historically, credit by examination failed to take hold in the American postsecondary education scene for a variety of reasons. First, credit by examination challenges two traditions unique to the American higher education scene: the unit-credit-hour system and the emphasis on time spent, rather than on knowledge acquired (Gerhard,

1955; Lewis, 1961; Nutting, 1949; Pressey, 1945; Pressey, 1949). Second, such programs have traditionally been directed to nontraditional students (Center for the Study of Liberal Education for Adults, 1961; Stern and Missal, 1960). The current charge of nontraditional education to the forefront of the postsecondary educational scene accounts in good part for the increased attention being paid to credit by examination.

Six major types of credit by examination programs may be identified.

Type 1: *Anticipatory Examinations for Graduating High School Seniors.* The most widely known program of anticipatory examinations for graduating high school seniors is the Advanced Placement (AP) program of the College Entrance Examination Board (CEEB). The AP program offers superior high school students the opportunity to receive advanced standing in college on the basis of college-level work which they have completed in high school. The program is national in scope, and hundreds of thousands of students have been tested, while thousands of high schools and colleges participate in the program. Surveys of participating colleges have revealed that the granting of placement is more likely than the awarding of credit, but policies vary considerably from institution to institution (Casserly, 1965; Casserly, Peterson, and Coffman, 1965; Casserly, 1968, 1968-1969; Cole, 1961; Radcliffe and Hatch, 1961).

Type 2: *Examinations upon College of University Admission to Waive Prerequisites to Advanced Courses for Lower Division Students.* Most colleges and universities in the U.S. allow, and sometimes require, entering freshmen to take examinations in certain basic subject areas, such as English composition, languages, and mathematics. The purpose of such examinations is most frequently placement rather than credit, however, and such examinations will not be detailed here. One of the oldest, most extensive, and most heavily researched programs of credit by examination is that at the University of Buffalo (the program actually represents both Types 1 and 2). The program was initiated in 1932, and explicitly encouraged acceleration. By 1956, 1700 students had taken more than 4000 credit examinations. Buffalo's participation in the AP program has resulted in a reduction in both the size and breadth of the credit by examination program (Barnette, 1957; Jones and Ortner, 1954). Ohio State University and the University of Illinois have also offered fairly extensive programs of credit by examination. For the most part, however, Type 2 programs focus on superior students, and are limited in practice, if not in theory, to a few departments and/or courses.

Type 3: *Examinations for Lower and/or Upper Division Students as an Alternative to the Satisfaction of all Attendance, Papers, Mid-terms, Finals, and Such Requirements of a Regular Credit Course.* Little is known at this writing of the extensiveness of Type 3 programs. Most college and university catalogues contain a provision for credit by examination, but actual institutional practices remain for the most part unknown. The most extensive Type 3 program is currently in operation in New York

State. The New York State College Proficiency Examination Program (CPEP) was introduced in 1963. CPEP examinations are offered in over 20 subject areas. There are no prerequisites for taking the examinations; and anyone may take them, including individuals who are not residents of New York State. As of 1972, over 30,000 examinations had been given and over 40,000 course credits had been granted. Decision as whether or not to grant credit, and how much, is left with individual colleges and universities, although CPEP makes recommendations as to how much credit should be granted for each examination (New York State Education Department, 1971).

One additional Type 3 program deserves mention here. The University of Wisconsin School of Education offered, as of 1959, a program of teacher certification by examination for undergraduate and graduate students. Students could satisfy all or a portion of the requirements of the undergraduate programs in the School of Education by examination, without classroom attendance.

Type 4: *Examinations to Demonstrate the College-Level Ability of Nontraditional Students (Military, Adults, Foreign Students, Transfer Students).* In 1945 the American Council on Education established the Commission on Accreditation of Service Experiences (CASE), to assist educational institutions in evaluating military experiences. Since 1945 CASE, in conjunction with the U.S. Armed Forces Institute (USAFI), developed instructional materials and examinations to provide high school and college credit for all military personnel. Although the Comprehensive College Testing Program (CCT) provided general examinations and subject examinations at the college level, the tests were apparently used primarily for purposes of evaluation within the military services (Committee on Evaluation of Tyler Fact-Finding Study of the American Council on Education, 1956; Commission on Accreditation of Service Experiences, American Council on Education, 1965). Recently the Office on Educational Credit of the American Council on Education took over the work of CASE.

The current nontraditional education movement, focusing primarily on the adult student, has resulted in a dramatic increase in Type 4 programs. A 1972 study of opportunities and programs for nontraditional education in 1,185 traditional colleges and universities reported that at two-thirds of the institutions surveyed, students could earn some credit toward a degree, and reduce the length of their program, by scoring acceptably on one or another examination (Cross, Valley, and Associates, 1973).

The most extensive Type 4 program currently in operation is the College-Level Examination Program (CLEP), initiated by the CEEB on a nationwide scale in 1966. The CLEP program is explicitly focused on persons whose learning experiences have taken place primarily outside formal college classrooms. Two types of examinations are offered: the general examinations, focusing on five basic general education areas, and the subject examinations. Over 25 subject tests are available. The aforementioned study of nontraditional education revealed that 64 percent of the institutions surveyed award course credit to undergraduates on the basis of the CLEP tests (Cross, Valley, and Associates, 1973). Many of the newly emerging nontraditionãl education programs across the country are using the CLEP examinations.

Type 5: *Examinations Covering More than One Course and Degree by Examination Only.* Comprehensive examination programs (examinations covering subject-matter greater in scope than a single course) have never caught on in the U.S. Undoubtedly the best-known program of comprehensive examinations, which encouraged acceleration and challenged the traditional credit-hour scheme, has been that at the University of Chicago. The Chicago College Plan, initiated in 1931, explicitly separated the instructional and examination functions of undergraduate education. Students could take the required comprehensive examinations whenever they felt prepared, regardless of classroom attendance, and performance in the classroom had no influence on the final grades. A number of changes have been made at Chicago over the past 40 years, generally resulting in a closer linking of the instructional and examination functions and a more traditional undergraduate curriculum (Bell, 1966; Boucher, 1935; 1940; Gray, 1931; University of Chicago, 1931; University of Chicago, 1950). Michigan State College, the General College program at the University of Minnesota, and Antioch College have in the past emphasized comprehensive examinations in their curricula (Dressel, 1958; Eckert, 1943; Jones, 1933; Sweet, 1954).

The oldest, and one of the few programs of degree by examination has been offered through the University of London for 135 years. Degrees are awarded to External Students at the Bachelor's, Master's, and Doctoral levels. Candidates for the B.A. General Degree, for example, must take written examinations on the same occasion in three of 59 subjects. External Students need not be enrolled in any institution of higher education while working on the degrees, nor be British citizens or residents (University of London, 1970, 1970-1971).

The only major degree by examination program in the U.S. is currently offered in New York State. Started in 1971, the Regents' External Degree Program enables qualified individuals to earn undergraduate degrees by means of independent study. On-campus residence or classroom attendance is not required. Regents' External Degrees are available to all who qualify, without regard for such considerations as age or residence. The following degrees are offered as of 1974: Associate in Arts, Associate in Science, Associate in Applied Science in Nursing, Bachelor of Science in Business Administration, and a Bachelor of Arts or of Science in Liberal Studies or selected concentrations. Credit by examination programs such as the CPEP and CLEP represent a major means of earning credit toward the degree. As of early 1975, over 2,000 individuals had been granted an AA degree, and large numbers of persons were involved in the nursing, business administration, and bachelors degree programs, with some degrees already awarded in each program.

Under the auspices of the CEEB and the Educational Testing Service, Jack Arbolino and John Valley in 1970 prepared a proposal for a National University which would,

among other things, award degrees based solely on examinations in its own name, and award credits and certificates on the basis of established credit by examination programs such as the CLEP. However, in 1973 the Commission on Non-Traditional Study declined to recommend the establishment of a national university (Commission on Non-Traditional Study, 1973).

Type 6: *Examinations, Generally for Graduate Students, to Satisfy Noncredit Competence Requirements Such as Language or Mathematics.* Examinations to satisfy noncredit competence requirements are sufficiently familiar to require little elaboration. Since such examinations result in neither placement nor credit, they are of only indirect relevance to credit by examination, and will not be detailed here.

The major issues surrounding programs of credit by examination include the following: the appropriateness of various subject-matter areas to credit by examination; acceleration vs. enrichment; faculty attitudes about credit by examination; results of credit by examination for students; financial costs and benefits of credit by examination; and patterns of examination design and administration.

The most frequent applications of credit by examination schemes are in those subject areas where there is considerable overlap between high school and college offerings—in skill subjects such as languages and mathematics. However, the CLEP program offers over 20 individual subject area examinations, and the University of London offers over 30 disciplinary areas (excluding the many languages) for the B.A. General and B.Sc. examinations, suggesting that extensive use of credit by examination is possible.

Programs of credit by examination have traditionally emphasized enrichment (providing a fuller, rather than a shorter or cheaper, educational experience) rather than acceleration (progress through an educational program at rates faster, or ages younger, than conventional) (Pressey, 1949). Currently, the nongraditional education movement is strongly emphasizing acceleration. Certain potential advantages of credit by examination may only be realized if programs place an emphasis on acceleration. The major potential benefits of credit by examination alone include:

1) Greater flexibility in individual institutional curricula, requirements, and suchlike.
2) A variety of possibilities for educational enrichment: spending the equivalent of two senior years; taking graduate work during the senior year; broadening the undergraduate experience in general.
3) The provision of a measure of achievement rather than of time spent, thus enabling students to avoid repetition of materials already covered.
4) Recognition of diversity in students' experiences, abilities, potentials, and objectives.
5) Upgrading of the college or university curriculum.
6) The attraction of superior students.
7) Better articulation between high school and college curricula.

When credit by examination emphasizes acceleration, all of the above potential benefits except (2), "enrichment," may be realized, plus: a saving of time and money for students and a possible saving of faculty time and university resources.

The major obstacle to programs of credit by examination appears to be the negative attitudes of faculty members. The primary faculty objections relate to questions of quality-control and student maturity. It is clear that to ensure faculty cooperation in such programs new incentive structures are required, especially in the areas of work loads or salaries. Information on the results of credit by examination for students strongly challenges the aforementioned faculty objections. In general, the available studies indicate that students awarded course credit by examination, whether or not they accelerate, are likely to have the following characteristics (Casserly, 1968, 1968-1969; Flesher and Pressey, 1955; Jones and Ortner, 1954; Wagner, 1952):

Low attrition rates
High GPAs
High likelihood of graduating with honors
High likelihood of continuing to graduate or professional school
Average extracurricular participation

In addition, studies of students who have accelerated through programs of credit by examination indicate that such students suffer few, if any, academic or personal-social disadvantages; indeed, they are more likely to be above average both academically and in terms of personal-social adjustment (Chapman, 1961; Fund for the Advancement of Education, 1957; Haak, 1953; Pressey, 1949).

The available literature provides very little information on the financial costs and benefits of credit by examination programs. It has been suggested, however, that an extensive program of credit by examination requires that the basis for financial support be the credits earned, not the processing time.

With reference to examination design, the examinations for most of the programs reviewed here do not differ from regular course examinations in terms of format or time required. A variety of policy issues surround programs of credit by examination. Since nothing approaching general agreement on these issues has been reached, they will be merely listed here as a reminder of potential areas of disagreement:

Administrative level at which program is initiated and operated
Emphasis on enrichment vs. acceleration
Administrative level at which examinations are designed, administered, and graded
Administrative level at which approval is given to take examinations
Regulations concerning which students may take examinations
Standards for grading examinations
Subject-matter areas appropriate to credit by examination
Recording of examination results on transcript

Registration requirements
Regulations on numbers of hours of credit to be applied toward degree
Level of study at which examinations are to be provided
Regulations concerning repetition of examinations
Facilities for counseling students on examinations
Strategies for handling problems of interinstitutional communication

REFERENCES

Barnette, W. L. Jr. Advanced Credit for the Superior High School Student. *Journal of Higher Education,* 1957, *28,* 15-21.

Bell, D. *The Reforming of General Education.* New York: Trustees of Columbia University, 1966.

Boucher, C. S. *The Chicago College Plan.* Chicago: University of Chicago Press, 1935.

Casserly, P. *College Decisions on Advanced Placement: I. A Follow-Up of Advanced Placement Candidates of 1963.* Research and Development Report 64-5, No. 15. Princeton: Educational Testing Service, 1965.

_____, R. E. Peterson, and W. E. Coffman. *College Decisions on Advanced Placement: II. An Interview Survey of Advanced Placement Policies and Practices at Sixty-Three Colleges.* Research and Development Report 65-6, No. 4 and Research Bulletin 65-41. Princeton: Educational Testing Service, 1965.

_____. What College Students Say About Advanced Placement. *College Board Review,* 1968, 6-10, 28-34; 1968-1969, 18-22.

Center for the Study of Liberal Education for Adults. *College Without Classes: Credit Through Examination in University Adult Education.* Chicago: Center for the Study of Liberal Education for Adults, 1961.

Chapman, G. O. The Effect of Acceleration on Social and Academic Achievement. *Journal of Higher Education,* 1961, *32,* 143-148.

Cole, C. C. Jr. *Flexibility in the Undergraduate Curriculum.* Washington, D.C.: U.S. Department of Health, Education and Welfare, Office of Education, 1961.

College Entrance Examination Board. *Advanced Placement News.* Princeton, 1969.

_____. *CLEP: Bulletin of Information for Candidates.* Princeton, 1970.

_____. *CLEP: What Is It.* Princeton, 1970.

_____. *College Credit by Examination Through the College-Level Examination Program.* Princeton, 1970.

_____. *A Guide to the Advanced Placement Program.* Princeton, 1969-1970.

Commission on Non-Traditional Study. *Diversity by Design.* San Francisco: Jossey-Bass, 1973.

Committee on Evaluation of Tyler Fact-Finding Study of the American Council on Education. *Conclusions and Recommendations on a Study of the General Educational Development Testing Program.* Washington, D.C.: American Council on Education, 1956.

Commission on Accreditation of Service Experiences, American Council on Education. Opportunities for Educational and Vocational Advancement: GED Testing Program, Comprehensive College Testing Program, USAFI Courses and Tests. *The Bulletin,* No. 10, Third Edition, June 1965.

Cross, K. P., Valley, J. R., and Associates. *Planning Non-Traditional Programs: An Analysis of the Issues.* See especially J. Ruyle, L. A. Geiselman, and J. B. L. Hefferlin, Nontraditional Education: Opportunities and Programs in Traditional Colleges and Universities 1972. San Francisco: Jossey-Bass, 1973.

Dressel, P. L., ed. *Evaluation in the Basic College at Michigan State University.* New York: Harper and Brothers, 1958.

Eckert, R. E. *Outcomes of General Education: An Appraisal of the General College Program*. Minneapolis: University of Minnesota Press, 1943.

Flaugher, R. L., Mahoney, M. H., and Messing, R. B. *Credit by Examination for College-Level Studies: An Annotated Bibliography*. Princeton: College Entrance Examination Board, 1967.

Flesher, M. A., and Pressey, S. War-Time Accelerates Ten Years After. *Journal of Educational Psychology*, 1955, *46*, 228-238.

Fund for the Advancement of Education. *They Went to College Early*. Evaluation Report No. 2. New York: Fund for the Advancement of Education, 1957.

Gerhard, D. Emergence of the Credit System in American Education Considered as a Problem of Social and Intellectual History. *American Association of University Professors Bulletin*, 1955, *41*, 647-668.

Gray, W. S., ed. *Recent Trends in American College Education*, Vol. III. Proceedings of the Institute for Administrative Officers of Higher Education, 1931. Chicago: University of Chicago Press, 1931.

Haak, L. A. Acceleration by Examination. *College and University*, 1953, 39-52.

Houle, C. O. *The External Degree*. San Francisco: Jossey-Bass, 1973.

Jones, E. S. *Comprehensive Examinations in American Colleges*. New York: The Macmillan Co., 1933.

_____, and G. K. Ortner. *College Credit by Examination: An Evaluation of the University of Buffalo Program*. The University of Buffalo Studies, Vol. 21, No. 3, January 1954. Buffalo: University of Buffalo Press, 1954.

Lewis, L. *The Credit System in Colleges and Universities*. Washington, D.C.: U.S. Department of Health, Education and Welfare, Office of Education, 1961.

New York State Education Department. *College Proficiency Examination Program*. New York: The University of the State of New York, 1971.

_____. *College Credit for What You Know: College Proficiency Exams*. New York: The University of the State of New York, 1971.

Nutting, W. D. College: Assembly Line or Community? Evaluating Intellectual Attainment by the Course-With-Credit Method. *Commonweal*, 1949, *50*, 382-384.

Pressey, S. L. *Educational Acceleration: Appraisals and Basic Problems*. Columbus, Ohio: Ohio State University Press, 1949.

_____. Credit by Examination: Present Use and Future Need. *Journal of Educational Research*, 1945, *38*, 596-605.

Radcliffe, S. A., and Hatch, W. R. *Advanced Standing*. Washington, D.C.: U.S. Department of Health, Education and Welfare, Office of Education, 1961.

Stern, B. H., and Missal, E. *Adult Experience and College Degrees: A Report of the Experimental Degree Project for Adults at Brooklyn College, 1954-58*. Cleveland: Western Reserve University Press, 1960.

Sweet, R. L. *A Study of Acceleration by Examination in the Basic College at Michigan State College*. Unpublished Ed.D. dissertation, Michigan State College, 1954.

University of Chicago. *The New College Plan*. Chicago: University of Chicago Press, 1931.

_____. *The Idea and Practice of General Education: An Account of the College of the University of Chicago*. Chicago: University of Chicago Press, 1950.

University of the State of New York. *The Regents External Degree. Handbook of Information for Candidates*. New York: University of the State of New York, 1972.

University of London. *General Information for External Students*. London: University of London, Senate House, 1970.

_____. *Regulations for External Students, 1970-71*. London: University of London, Senate House, 1970.

_____. *Regulations Relating to University Entrance Requirements*. London: University of London, Senate House, 1970.

Wagner, M. E. *Anticipatory Examinations for College Credit: Twenty Years Experience at the University of Buffalo*. University of Buffalo Studies Vol. 20, No. 3, December 1952. Buffalo: University of Buffalo Press, 1952.

113

INDEPENDENT STUDY

by Charles A. Wedemeyer
The William H. Lighty Professor of Education
The University of Wisconsin, Madison and Extension
Madison, Wisconsin

Independent Study in the United States exists in two contexts, each of which was influenced by the British tutorial and extension movements of the 19th and early 20th centuries. The two streams of American independent study appeared in different institutional contexts, and were defined accordingly. Definitions of independent study differed according to whether learners were perceived as internal to the institution's environment or external to it. Recently a single inclusive definition was proposed (Wedemeyer, 1971), because "independent study programs, whether for internal or external students, have much to contribute to each other, share to a considerable extent a common philosophical base, and employ similar techniques. They belong in a common category . . . because in important ways they are more similar than different (p. 550)."

INDEPENDENT STUDY FOR INTERNAL LEARNERS

Earlier called Honors Programs (Aydelotte, 1923), independent study referred to special honors-type programs for on-campus, usually superior learners in American colleges and universities. In this context, independent study was an early alternative to conventional classroom instruction for learners within the college's or university's regular programs and environment.

These programs had their origin in the experiences of members of the American Expeditionary Forces stationed in England during World War I who came under the influence of the tutorial and extension opportunities at Oxford and Cambridge. College and university honors programs were generally called independent study after 1925 (Bonthius, David, and Drushal, 1957).

INDEPENDENT STUDY FOR EXTERNAL LEARNERS

In the mid-19th century, the English university extension movement influenced the extension of education in the United States (Shannon and Schoenfeld, 1965).

The extension movement in the U.S. became a formal part of private higher education in 1891, with the founding of John D. Rockefeller's University of Chicago under President William Rainey Harper. Harper's plan for the University of Chicago included a Division of University Extension. In 1906 the University of Wisconsin established the first Extension Division in a state university, and William H. Lighty became Secretary of an extension program which, along with Harper's at Chicago, brought to external students an alternative opportunity for higher education (Axford, 1961). The task of Extension was "to carry the best knowledge and the best methods to the people . . . [to] meet the countless and complex needs of 20th-century civilization (Votaw, 1915)."

The alternative method used by Harper and Lighty to reach external learners at a distance from campus and faculty was correspondence study. In 1967, however, the University of Wisconsin changed the name of its correspondence instruction program to independent study, in recognition of the basic learning characteristics of this form of study. Not long thereafter, this change of name had swept through most of the institutions which belong to the National University Extension Association, and became NUEA's official designation for such external programs (Wedemeyer, 1971).

Thus, what had been perceived as two separate programs, begun at different times, set in different contexts, and serving somewhat different consumers of American higher education, were perceived as related in theory and purpose, although the "set" respecting the location of the learner continued to maintain definitions which were exclusive until recently. The definitions of independent study supplied by Bonthius, David, and Drushal (1957), "teaching and learning which focuses on the individual instead of the group, which emphasizes the person-to-person relationship between teacher and student (p. 3)," and "the pursuit of special topics or projects by individual students under the guidance of faculty advisers apart from organized courses (p. 8)," posit a tutorial teacher-student relationship in an implied campus contest for "special" work.

Gleason (1967) broadened the definition by observing that independent study is composed of instructional systems which "make it possible for the learner to pursue the study of personally significant areas in an independent manner—freed of bonds of time, space, and prescription usually imposed by conventional instruction (p.v.)." Dubin and Taveggia (1968) recognized two kinds of independent study, one including teacher-direction and guidance in the learning process, and the other emphasizing the learner, in recognition that learning can take place in the absence of the teacher.

INDEPENDENT STUDY

The inclusive definition suggested by Wedemeyer (1971) stated:

> Independent Study consists of various forms of teacher-learning arrangements in which teachers and learners carry out their essential tasks and responsibilities apart from one another, communicating in a variety of ways, for the purposes of freeing internal learners from inappropriate class

pacings or patterns, or providing external learners opportunity to continue learning in their own environments, and developing in all learners the capacity to carry on self-directed learning, the ultimate maturity required of the educated person. Independent Study programs offer learners varying degrees of freedom in the self-determination of goals and activities, and in starting, stopping, and pacing individualized learning programs which are carried on to the greatest extent possible at the convenience of the learners. (p. 550)

In 1973, definitions of independent study began to take on the broader, more inclusive perceptions first noted in 1967 and 1971. Clark (1973), following Verner's (1964) dichotomy of learning in the instructional setting and learning in "the natural societal setting," observed that "in an independent learning situation the leaner is responsible for his own learning and functions autonomously. He is independent of the guidance and influence of others as he identifies his own learning needs and selects the appropriate sequence of learning tasks needed to achieve his objectives (p. 7)." Both Clark and Verner have suggested that the learner engaged in independent study has to function in two roles: that of the proficient learner and that of the competent instructor.

In a commentary on the Wedemeyer (1971) definition, Moore (1973) finds four characteristics essential to independent study: (1) independent study is concerned with both teaching and learning; (2) independent study is concerned with the capacity of learners to be self-directing; (3) independent study is found both within educational establishments and external to them; (4) independent study teachers and learners carry out their tasks separately from one another. Moore notes that in independent study "teaching is, paradoxically, both responsive and anticipatory (p. 37)," and asks what the independent learner is independent of?

> He is independent, first, of other-direction; he is autonomous. Second, he is independent of the space-time bondage made necessary only by a tradition of dependent or "other-directed" teaching. The greater his autonomy, the more "distance" he can tolerate, and therefore the more he is independent. (p. 38)

Dressel and Thompson (1973) comment that "Independent study, interpreted as a capacity to be developed, comes close to being, if it is not, indeed, the major goal of all education (p. vii)," and they define independent study as "the student's self-directed pursuit of academic competence in as autonomous a manner as he is able to exercise at any particular time (p. 1)." While Dressel and Thompson seem to be writing mainly in the context of internal independent study programs, their definition is inclusive, because they note elsewhere that "independent study can meet the student need for off-campus experiences (p. 10)." In Europe, the term "distance education" has recently become widely accepted to describe what in the U.S. is called external independent study (Wedemeyer, 1974; Ljoså, 1975).

While no single definition of independent study is likely at this time to be satisfactory to all definers or practitioners, nevertheless recent definitions indicate increasing congruence and inclusivity. Independent study, it is clear, is concerned with the provision of opportunities that develop the learner's capacity for self-direction and autonomy, whatever the institutional context, whatever the method, and wherever the learner may be.

SCOPE

The scope of independent study is presently only partly known. The element of self-selection in independent study (one of the freedoms implied in this method) makes it difficult to anticipate enrollments and teaching loads, and contributes to the conventional view of independent study as a deviation from the regular work of the schools. Hence, independent study within regular schools is largely carried on without special budgeting, and without standard measures for providing statistical summaries; nor are reports of this activity required in county, state or federal summaries.

Outside of conventional institutions independent study statistics are more carefully recorded, because the institutions providing programs (at first private and/or proprietary) were organized specifically for independent study, and needed enrollment data for their own internal planning and operating purposes. The data yielded up by such institutions, however, were for a long time ignored, because independent study data did not fit established reporting categories.

Institutions which had a mission to provide both independent study and regular forms of instruction (such as University Extension) kept records of each. But again, because educational statistics were so rigidly categorized according to the needs of regular schools, the data were not assimilated, were often misclassified, and generally ended up in separate, incomplete, and rather misleading summaries.

Consequently, there are today no accurate figures of scope of participation in independent study. Parker's "College and University Enrollments in America, 1972-3" provides no statistical information on independent study, although he notes that an increase in the use of independent study is a suspected factor in the diminished enrollment growth rate at the entering freshmen level, and in the "stopping out" of enrolled students.

The broad definition of independent study suggested earlier includes programs and learners which are often reported separately: honors and independent study students in regular school-college-university programs, most "open" learning programs, correspondence students, and those in radio, television, telephone, computer, programmed instruction and satellite-mediated programs, except where such programs are restricted.

Although the definitions in the preceding section were chiefly derived from writers concerned with alternate programs of higher education, independent study is a recognized alternative in elementary, secondary and postsecondary continuing education (Congreve, 1963, 1965; Beggs and Buffie, 1965; Marion, 1967; Empey, 1968; Wedemeyer, 1968).

The scope of independent study is only suggested by the statistics available. In the United States it is estimated that about five million persons were enrolled in external independent study programs in 1971 (the last year for which reasonably reliable statistics are available). This estimate does not show much change from 1967, but includes only those learners reported by the National Home Study Council, colleges and universities reporting through the National University Extension Association, federal and military schools, religious institutions, and business and industry programs. The estimate does not include all types of external independent learners, and is therefore a serious underestimate of the actual number of learners engaged in external independent study.

Statistics regarding internal independent study learners in the U.S. are even less complete. Dressel and Thompson's (1973) survey of independent study in one-third of the 1,126 liberal arts colleges and universities in the U.S. did not report numbers of students, although the authors indicate that 69 percent of the institutions surveyed have independent study programs in all departments, and 24 percent of the institutions involve all students in independent study experiences. The National Collegiate Honors Council has not reported the number of students involved in honors type independent study on a national basis, although it has statistics on individual institutions.

On a world basis, scope is no more readily determined. While independent study, internal and external, is found throughout the world, neither UNESCO, nor the International Council of Correspondence Education, nor the International Council of Adult Education, at present compile such statistics.

However, with regard to external independent study in the correspondence mode, several studies have been started which may lay the basis for a comprehensive system of reporting. UNESCO is supporting two research studies under the direction of ICCE, which will gather and assess information on a world-wide basis respecting developmental processes leading to the establishment of independent study institutions in different countries, and the needs of educators for upgrading in current trend development where such institutions are already established. Eventually, the information network thus established should yield more complete and reliable information respecting scope and impact. The West German Federal Institute for Research on Vocational Education and Training is undertaking a global assessment of distance education, and the International Extension College of Cambridge, England, has been compiling information on independent study programs in Africa. The number of Ph.D. dissertations on independent study, world-wide, is increasing.

Outside the United States independent study is a part of the educational offerings of many countries at nearly all levels. However, such is the appeal of independent study as an alternative, and its capacity for ready adaptation in a variety of situations, that the rationale for independent study will vary from country to country. Indeed, as is the case with the classroom format, independent study may be employed in different settings for quite different reasons.

In one country independent study will be viewed as an alternative to the bigness and rigidity of a highly structured educational system. In another it will be the means of ameliorating the effects of elitism in higher education. In another it will be perceived as a necessity because the conventional school-college hierarchy is incapable of rapid expansion to meet the requirements of industrialization. In another it may be the only viable solution to the practical problems of extending educational opportunity to a population thinly dispersed over vast areas. In still another it may be a means of individualizing learning in the impacted areas of cities which have reached the limits of wholesome growth and are in disarray, in part because the conventional educational system is out of phase with the culturally altered societies it is intended to serve.

The scope of independent study in the world today, and its persistence within societies which differ greatly from each other, suggests that this alternative method of teaching and learning is not the narrow, parochial, and inconsequential variant of conventional instruction that it is often assumed to be. Independent study seems to be so broad in its appeal, so capable of adaptation to widely different teaching-learning needs, and so persistent in the face of minimal support and recognition (or even occasional outright hostility) from established educational hierarchies, that it may be more accurate to acknowledge independent study not as a variant of conventional instruction, but as its true alternative, in the classic sense of the mutually exclusive opposite.

While the size of the total independent study programs in the U.S. or throughout the world is not precisely known, there is little doubt that the number of learners engaged in such programs is significant and growing. New institutional formats employing independent study are being developed (such as the Open University of Britain, the University of Mid-America, the Free University or Iran, and the Open University of West Germany), while existing programs (such as the Instituto Nacionál Cooperativa Educacion of Venezuela) are expanding. It is a pity that the world scope and significance of independent study as an alternate to conventional education cannot be ascertained in statistical terms. One can only note that if independent study throughout the world were suddenly withdrawn, the consequences would be dramatic. Conventional reporting systems have largely overlooked and under-reported the numbers of learners engaged in independent study.

REVIEW OF LITERATURE

Because independent study has developed in two streams, the literature is also divided. When *Independent Study, Bold New Venture* (Beggs and Buffie, 1965) was published, some practitioners of external independent study referred to the programs described as neither bold nor new. A more recent book on internal independent study (Dressel and Thompson, 1973) does not reference works concerned with external independent study, although current literature regarding alternatives to conventional education are cited. Similarly, writers concerned solely with correspondence, radio, television, programmed instruction, computer-assisted learning, telephone learning networks, and the use of the satellite generally do not perceive the relationship of their endeavors to internal

independent study, although they do cite generally similar literature on learning alternatives (Dressel and Thompson, 1973; Edstrom, Erdos, and Prosser, 1970; Mathiesen, 1971).

Faculty members who work in independent programs, as pointed out by Wedemeyer and Najem (1969), are themselves no freer of narrow vision than are their colleagues in more conventional programs. It is noteworthy, therefore, that Coyne and Hebert (1972), former Peace Corps workers writing as dissenters from the corporate educational establishment, and seeing independent study from the learner's point of view rather than from an institutional "set," stress the true alternative view:

> You don't need a college to get a higher education anymore. That has changed. If you are on the edge of college, unsure if you want to go, or have already dropped out, consider an independent education, on your own. It may be more valuable to you and your country.

Coyne and Hebert feel that a new student has appeared. "This student must contrive an education in the environment, which has become a learning environment. It is this new kind of education we call Independent Study (p. 3)."

The literature concerned with educational options and alternatives expresses those needs and forces which are fueling the pressure for change. Here one finds (Gould and Cross, 1972; Carnegie Commission, 1971; Liveright and DeCrow, 1963) an acceptance of need for change, a fascination with the varied proposals and programs-in-being to provide alternatives, and an acceptance of the concept of independent study. There is, however, little interest in, or awareness of, the development of educational theory to underpin ventures which depart from the conventional.

The exception was Gleason (1967) who, as Chairman of the 1965 Articulated Instructional Media Conference at Wisconsin, collected the viewpoints of McDonald, Gagne, Sears, Lee, and Jourard, to provide one of the earliest theoretical frameworks for independent learning as an alternative. In addition, Allen Tough (1971) provided one of the most comprehensive views of adult independent learning.

The innovations of the 1960s, employing many aspects of independent study, were undertaken apparently by innovators acting under motivations similar to those of Dr. Walter Perry, Vice Chancellor of the Open University in Britain, who pointed out (Wedemeyer, 1972), "I did not see myself as a philosopher or educational theorist. I was a problem-solver. I simply had to create an institution and make it work." Once into the game, however, innovators find that the evolving theories of independent study have immediate application in new and sometimes radical institutional programs.

The Kellogg Invitational Conference on Independent Learning, at the University of British Columbia (1973), had as its purposes "1) to explore basic concepts and assumptions related to independent study, and 2) to discuss the implications of independent learning for continuing education in the health sciences." A number of innovative programs in medical, nursing, pharmacy, and other health sciences were discussed against background papers in independent learning by Clark, Moore, Johns, and Wedemeyer. The conference summary by McCreary concludes,

> We have all learned that people in their natural state undertake independent learning in some way. The unnatural state is the dependent learning which our logical but rigid educational system forces us into. Some concept of dependent learning is an essential to see clearly the opposite characteristics of independent learning. In dependent learning we have goals set by others—not by the individual concerned. We have methods of learning dictated by others and, most important, we have evaluation—the knowledge that we have achieved or failed to achieve these dictated goals—decided by others. In other words we face an organized, systematic program of instruction totally under the direction of someone else. (p. 77)

On the other hand, McCreary pointed out,

> Independent learning occurs when an individual sets his own goals, selects his own assistance whether it may be the opinions of others, a library, a tape or whatever, and decides for himself whether or not he has reached that goal. It is a highly personal process, and when it is successful it is extremely rewarding. (p. 79)

If independent study is the opposite of conventional classroom instruction, then its deviation from conventional educational theory and practices are not serious drawbacks, but are essential, must stand on their own, and be grounded on the study of learners in the independent mode. The acceptance of this view would greatly assist independent study teachers and learners to shed the guilt or uncertainty they sometimes feel as deviants from the conventional. It would further motivate workers in this field to loose their tethers to conventional theory and systems so that they can work more openly and effectively, especially in the development of theory and practice relevant to independent study as a true alternative.

While the discontent which has fueled innovation has come from the social and political issues of the times, as well as the glacial slowness of educational institutions to develop flexible responses to changed contexts, the roots of the various alternative approaches which have appeared are in independent study.

PROGRAMS AND APPLICATIONS

Dressel and Thompson (1973) supply a comprehensive description of internal independent study in their chapters on Current Practices and Case Studies. Their critique of Ford Foundation-sponsored programs (Operation Opportunity, Independent Study Program, Program II, and Ford Independent Study Program) is insightful. Independent study programs, because of the freedoms inherent in the concept, exist in great variation. An exceptional student described by Dressel and Thompson engaged in "self-directed interdisciplinary work during an independent study term. Not only did he construct a program of original work in psychology and sociology, but he suggested and outlined the evaluative process by which faculty from both disciplines might determine the extent to which he succeeded in his proposal (p. 48)."

External independent study programs also show wide variation. However, because learners are at a greater distance from faculty and resources, external programs exhibit a wider concern with communications, and require (in Moore's terminology) both anticipatory and responsive techniques. These techniques are sometimes applied in a highly structured format to meet learners' needs, as described by the College Entrance Examination Board (1972):

> Some people are supremely confident of their ability to guide their own learning effectively. They have successfully directed some of their own educational experiences in the past.... But many people are very unsure of their ability to do something they have experienced previously only in a structured situation—that is, a school where teachers assumed most of the directive responsibility.... Most people fall somewhere between the two extremes, sometimes feeling confident, sometimes not quite as much so. (p. 38)

The communications medium employed frequently gives the name to the learning experience—a radio course, or a television course. However, the learner is an independent learner, engaged in independent study, and to some extent (this is one of the variables) exercising freedoms not ordinarily found in conventional instruction. Perry (1972) pinpoints the concern with communications of the British Open University because of the sense of isolation experienced by distant learners, who are not a part of a conventional information network.

> The national character of the University, with students scattered all over the United Kingdom, makes the problem of keeping students informed of matters that concern them particularly difficult. Whereas notice boards and drawing pins subsume this function in a conventional university, the Open University has to find a national notice-board. (p. 105)

Anticipatory and responsive instruction must be diffused through a communications network. The network usually includes print, and may also employ telecommunications. the AUEC–NUEA description of a correspondence course (1971-1972) emphasizes the importance of communications in this form of independent study: "A program, involving a continuing exchange between instructor and student, conducted primarily by written communication (p. 1)."

In the independent study program of the University of Illinois College of Medicine (Johns, 1973), the learner is offered "1) an individualized pace for learning, and 2) the opportunity and mandate to gain a higher than usual competence in a self-selected area of medicine (p. 45)." Since this program operates on campus, there is no need to create an external communications network, although (as noted by Johns, and Dressel and Thompson) the informal campus communications channels are often put under great strain in meeting the needs of independent learners.

CURRENT ISSUES

No doubt the definition of independent study is itself a current issue. Dressel and Thompson (1973) point out that "Programmed materials and mechanical equipment provide possibilities for *individual* study which can be highly structured in advance. In some ways it is more dependent than the average lecture-and-text-centered classroom (p. 67)." The use of highly structured anticipatory and response mechanisms may diminish the exercise of independence in learning. This is a variable, however, that is probably not qualitatively different from that other variable, the nature of the teacher who conducts independent study within a conventional institutional set. Dressel and Thompson (1973) identify the teacher and institutional set as two hazards to independent study, with a third being the students themselves. The variables of structured materials (in external programs) and teacher characteristics (in internal programs) seem to be closely related in their impact on the independence exercised by independent learners. What is needed is a typology by which independent learning experiences can be classified according to a scale of dependence-independence, taking into account numerous variables. Such a typology would be useful in an analysis of all forms of instruction, as a means of assessing the extent to which organized education helps or impedes the achievement of that ancient goal, the self-sufficient learner.

Other issues which require investigation have been listed by authors. For example (Wedemeyer, 1971):

Are the schools' social interaction motives compatible with the individualism that has been traditional in this country, and that finds expression in independent study?

What methods and techniques in independent study succeed best, cause least disruption of conventionally structured schools, and meet the economic cost-benefit ratios that society is willing to support?

What skills, attitudes, and other characteristics must the independent study student possess to succeed? Can these be measured? Can they be taught with predictive success?

What are the root causes of academic hostility or indifference to the need for and values of independent study? How can academic support equal to the need and significance of independent study be strengthened?

Are any changes in academic structure, teacher education, school administration, and finance needed to enable independent study to achieve its purposes and potential?

How can the educational media, largely applied from a "mass" consumer concept, be utilized for the individualization of teaching and learning?

What is self-motivation? How does alteration of the learner's environment lead to goal acceptance or selection?

What new safeguards must be built into American education to lay an affirmative basis for the broad accreditation of independent study curricula, courses and programs? (p. 557)

The recommendations of Dressel and Thompson (1973) imply some further issues:

Clear objectives for independent study must be developed.

An environment must be created which encourages independent study and which is not bound by credits or grades.

A regular curricular review should be made so that departmental innovations such as independent study may be based on common institutional objectives, evaluated by common criteria, and considered in terms of financial investment.

Faculty should be encouraged to sponsor independent study, stimulate the apathetic and fearful to engage in it, and allow a maximum of freedom to those prepared to do it.

Faculty, who often come from a lecture-oriented background, must be taught how to guide students to increasing self-direction.

Studies of student self-evaluation are needed to determine the extent to which it can supplant present grading systems.

Independent study must be distinguished from the one-to-one teacher-student relationship or tutorials.

Research is needed on the application of individual and group techniques to different ability groups.

Evaluation must be designed so that the degree of success is not misrepresented by participants who are not prepared for self-direction; it also must be designed to measure the success of the self-direction rather than the amount of accumulated information.

For college students to achieve a high degree of self-direction, secondary education, or even lower levels of learning, must begin the process of developing independence.

The cost of independent study must be investigated, especially the cost and success of patterns which require less faculty time than the prevalent tutorial systems.

The role of pass/fail grading, interim programs, and field work in developing self-direction should be studied. (pp. 144-150)

Perhaps the greatest issue at stake in the development of independent study has to do with broadening opportunity to learn—not only to achieve economic mobility, but also to attain human dignity. Bereday (1973) notes that

In an industrial society there is simply no avoiding the social significance of educational aspirations. . . . It is not a crime for even the stupid to seek high levels of education, and social customs which reject such aspirations can hardly be repositories of ultimate human wisdom. . . . The lesson for all nations . . . is that they must move faster and faster into the age of mass education. (pp. 141-145)

Paradoxically, independent study, with its stress on self-development through the exercise of freedoms and responsibilities in learning, may be an important methodology in mass education, though the terms seem contradictory.

REFERENCES

AUEC-NUEA. *Programs and Registrations, 1971-2,* Gayle Childs, ed. AUEC-NUEA, Washington, 1972.

Axford, Roger W. *William H. Lighty–Adult Education Pioneer,* Unpublished doctoral dissertation, The University of Chicago, 1961.

Aydelotte, F. Honors Courses in American Colleges and Universities. *Bulletin of The National Research Council,* 1924, *7,* Part 4 (40), 9-18.

Beggs, David W., and Buffie, E. G. *Independent Study, Bold New Venture.* Bloomington: Indiana University Press, 1965.

Bereday, George G. *Universities for All.* San Francisco: Jossey-Bass, 1973.

Bonthius, Robert H., David, F. Jones, and Drushal, J. Garber. *The Independent Study Program in the U.S.* New York: Columbia University Press, 1957.

Carnegie Commission on Higher Education. *Less Time, More Options.* New York: McGraw-Hill, 1971.

Clark, Kathie. Independent Learning, A Concept Analysis. A paper presented at the *Kellogg Seminar on Independent Learning in the Health Sciences,* The University of British Columbia, Vancouver, June 1973.

College Entrance Examination Board. *Guide to Continuing Education in America,* Thomson, Frances Coombs, ed. New York: Quadrangle Books, 1972.

Congreve, Willard J. Toward Independent Learning. *The North Central Association Quarterly,* Spring 1963, 248-302.

_____. "Independent Learning," *The North Central Association Quarterly,* Fall, 1965, 40(2): 222-228.

Coyne, John, and Hebert, Tom. *This Way Out.* New York: E. P. Dutton and Co., 1972.

Dressel, Paul L., and Thompson, Mary Magdala. *Independent Study.* San Francisco: Jossey-Bass, 1973, 1.

Driscoll, William J. *A Rationale and Role for Independent Study in Higher Education.* Unpublished doctoral dissertation, Indiana University, Bloomington, Indiana, 1970.

Dubin, Robert, and Taveggia, T. C. *The Teaching-Learning Paradox: A Comparative Analysis of College Teaching Methods.* Center for the Advanced Study of Educational Administration, University of Oregon, Eugene, 1968, 29-30.

Edstrom, Lars-Olaf, Erdos, Renée, and Prosser, Roy. *Mass Education.* Dag Hammarskjold Foundation, Stockholm, 1970.

Empey, Donald W. What Is Independent Study All About; *Journal of Secondary Education,* March 1968, *43*(3), 104-108.

Gagne, Robert M. Learning Research and its Implications for Independent Learning. *The Theory and Nature of Independent Learning,* Gleason, ed. Scranton: International Textbook Co., 1967.

Gleason, Gerald T., ed. *The Theory and Nature of Independent Learning.* Scranton: International Textbook Co., 1967.

_____. Technological Developments Related to Independent Learning. *The Theory and Nature of Independent Learning.* Scranton: International Textbook Co., 1967.

Gould, Samuel B., and Cross, Patricia. *Explorations in Non-Traditional Study.* San Francisco: Jossey-Bass, 1972.

Johns, Charles E. The Independent Study Student in a Medical School. *Proceedings of a Conference on Independent Learning,* The University of British Columbia, Vancouver, 1973.

Jourard, Sidney M. A Phenomenological Perspective on Independent Learning. *The Theory and Nature of Independent Learning.* Scranton: International Textbook Co., 1967.

Kellogg Invitational Conference on Independent Learning. *Proceedings of a Conference on Independent Learning,* Adult Education Research Centre and Division of Continuing Education in the Health Sciences, The University of British Columbia, Vancouver, 1973.

Lee, Dorothy. A Socio-Anthropological View of Independent Learning. *The Theory and Nature of Independent Learning.* Scranton: International Textbook Co., 1967.

Liveright, A. A., and DeCrow, Roger. *New Directions in Degree Programs Especially for Adults.* The Center for the Study of Liberal Education for Adults, Chicago, 1963.

Ljoså, Erling. *The System of Distance Education.* Papers of the 11th World Conference of ICCE. Hermods, Malmö, 1975.

MacDonald, James B. Independent Learning. The Theme of the Conference. *The Theory and Nature of Independent Learning.* Scranton: International Textbook Co., 1967.

Marion, Marjorie A. Independent Study: A First Attempt. *English Journal,* February 1967, *56*(2), 235-244.

Mathiesen, David E. *Correspondence Study, A Summary of the Research and Development Literature.* Syracuse: ERIC Clearinghouse on Adult Education and the National Home Study Council, 1971.

McCreary, John F., and Baumgart, Alice. Conference Summation. *Proceedings of a Conference on Independent Learning,* The University of British Columbia, Vancouver, 1973.

Moore, Michael. Some Speculation on a Definition of Independent Study. Proceedings of the *Kellogg Seminar on Independent Learning in the Health Sciences,* The University of British Columbia, Vancouver, June 1973.

Parker, Garland G. College and University Enrollments in America, 1972-73. *Intellect,* February, 1973, *101*(2347), 314-337.

Perry, Walter. *The Early Development of the Open University.* Milton Keynes, The Open University, 1972.

Sears, Pauline S. Implications of Motivation Theory for Independent Learning. *The Theory and Nature of Independent Learning.* Scranton: International Textbook Co., 1967.

Shannon, Theodore J., and Shoenfeld, Clarence A. *University Extension.* New York: The Library of Education, The Center for Applied Research in Education, Inc., 1965, 8.

Tough, Allen, *The Adult's Learning Projects.* Ontario Institute for the Study of Education, Toronto, 1971.

Verner, Coolie. Definition of Terms. In Jensen, Liveright, and Hallenbeck, eds., *Adult Education: Outlines of An Emerging Field of Study.* Adult Education Association of the U.S.A., 1964.

Votaw, Clyde W. *Proceedings.* First National University Extension Conference, Madison, Wisconsin, 1915, 314.

Wedemeyer, Charles A. With Whom Will You Dance? The New Educational Technology. *The Journal of the American Dietetic Association,* October 1968, *53*(4), 325-328.

_____, and Najem, Robert. *From Concept to Reality.* Syracuse: Syracuse University Publications in Continuing Education, 1969.

_____. Independent Study. *The Encyclopedia of Education.* New York: The Macmillan Co. and the Free Press, 1971, *4,* 548-557.

_____, Perry, Walter, and James, Walter. *Conversations,* a Video Tape on the Open University. BBC and the U.S. Endowment for the Humanities, London, 1972.

_____. Independent Learning and the Distant Independent Learner. *Proceedings of a Conference on Independent Learning,* The University of British Columbia, Vancouver, 1973.

_____, Sims, Ripley A., Ghatala, M. Habeeb, and Singh, Bakhshish. *Current Issues and Approaches in Distance Education.* The Proceedings of the 10th World Conference of ICCE, Patiala, India, 1974.

ADDITIONAL RESOURCES

African Association for Correspondence Study
P.O. Box 30688
Nairobi, Kenya
    Peter E. Kinyanjui, Chairman

Carnegie Corporation of New York
437 Madison Avenue
New York, New York 10022
    Alan Pifer, President

Educational Media Council
1346 Connecticut Avenue, N.W.
Washington, D.C. 20036
    Harriet Lundgaard, Executive Director

European Home Study Council
Hermods
Slottsgatan 24, 205 10
Malmö, Sweden

Institute for Educational Development
888 7th Avenue
New York, N.Y. 10019
    Dr. Samuel Gould, President

International Council for Adult Education
The Ontario Institute for Studies in Education
252 Bloor Street West
Toronto, Canada
    J. R. Kidd, Secretary-General

International Council on Correspondence Education
The Rapid Results College
Tuition House
London SW19 4DS, England
    Mr. David Young, President

Japan Council on Correspondence Education
Tezukayama Gakuin University
Sayamacho Osaka 589, Japan
    Dr. Mitoji Nishimoto, President

National Association of Education Broadcasters
1346 Connecticut Avenue, N.W.
Washington, D.C. 20036
    Dr. James A. Fellows, Office of Research and Development, Director

National Collegiate Honors Council
1205 W. Oregon
University of Illinois
Urbana, Illinois
    Dr. Jean Phillips, Executive Secretary

National Home Study Council
1601 - 18th Street, N.W.
Washington, D.C. 20009
    Mr. William A. Fowler, Executive Director

National University Extension Association
1 DuPont Circle, Suite 360
Washington, D.C. 20036
    Dr. Robert J. Pitchell, Executive Director

Organization for Economic Cooperation and Development
Chateau de la Muette
2 rue Andre Pascal
Paris 16, France

Pädagogiches Zentrum
Weinheim, Berlin
    Materialien zur Diskussion einer neuen Unterrichtsform.

United Nations Education, Scientific and Cultural Organization
Division of Higher Education and Division of Methods and
    Techniques
Place de Fontenoy
75 Paris-7ᵉ, France

FURTHER INFORMATION

Information on independent study may be obtained directly from sources which focus on independent study itself, and obliquely from sources which deal with the conditions which seem to be impelling independent study into a more prominent position, i.e., from learning theory, economic studies of education, manpower studies, evaluations of teaching strategies, comparative studies, educational technology and the literature of innovation in education. For example,

Arnesey, James W., and Dahl, Norman C. *An Inquiry into the Uses of Instructional Technology.* New York: A Ford Foundation Report, 1973.
Committee on Institutional Cooperation. *Development and Experiment in College Teaching.* Ann Arbor, 1973.
Gould, Samuel B. *Diversity by Design.* Commission on Non-Traditional Study. San Francisco: Jossey-Bass, 1973.
Hasburgh, Theodore M., Miller, Paul A., and Wharton, Clifton R. Jr. *Patterns for Lifelong Learning.* San Francisco: Jossey-Bass, 1973.
Houle, Cyril. *The External Degree.* San Francisco: Jossey-Bass, 1973.
Milton, Ohmer. *Alternatives to the Traditional.* San Francisco: Jossey-Bass, 1973.
Ritterbush, Philip C., ed. *Let the Entire Community Become our University.* Washington, D.C.: Acropolis Books, 1972.
Simpson, J. A. *Today and Tomorrow in European Adult Education.* Strasburg: Council of Europe, 1972.
Symonds, Percival M. *What Education Has to Learn from Psychology.* New York: Teachers College Press, 1965.
Taylor, Harold. *Students Without Teachers.* New York: McGraw-Hill, 1969.
Wedell, E. G., and Perraton, H. D. *Teaching at a Distance.* London: National Institute of Adult Education, 1968.
Wedemeyer, Charles A., and Childs, Gayle B. *New Perspectives in University Correspondence Study.* Chicago: Center for the Study of Liberal Education of Adults, 1961.
Wolff, Robert Paul. *The Ideal of the University.* Boston: Beacon Press, 1969.

114

COOPERATIVE EDUCATION AND INTERNSHIPS—COLLEGE

by Stewart B. Collins, Director
Department of Cooperative Education
Drexel University
Philadelphia, Pennsylvania

To point the lens of a camera at the panorama of cooperative education, and its various forms as it exists in the United States and Canada today, is to attempt to take a snapshot of an automobile race with a box camera. The subject is moving at such a fast pace, it is difficult to assess at any one moment just what is happening.

This form of experiential education was introduced in 1906 by Dean Herman Schneider at the University of Cincinnati. It exhibited very slow growth in the United States until after World War II. Until that time only 20 institutions embraced the concept. Between the years 1943 and 1962, 50 new institutions joined the movement. From 1963 until the year 1972 a phenomenal 300 new institutions started cooperative programs, for a total of 370. A count of students with at least one period of employment that year was 68,000 (Director of Cooperative Education, Cooperative Education Association, 1973). At the time of this writing (early 1975), there are between 600 and 700 institutions either actively practicing or planning to begin programs, and it is likely that close to 120,000 students will have active participation during the year (Cooperative Education, Directory, 1975).

The cooperative education plan has many definitions, depending on the viewpoints of the persons doing the defining. One typical definition which is acceptable to a majority is as follows: Cooperative Education may be defined as the integration of classroom theory with practical experience, under which students have specific periods of attendance at the college alternated with specific periods of employment. The following factors should be adhered to as closely as possible:

1. The student's work should be related to his field of study and individual interest within the field.

2. The employment must be considered a regular, continuing, and essential element in the educational process. Some minimum amount of employment and minimum standard of performance must be included for the credit or unit to be granted.

3. The working experience will ideally increase in difficulty and responsibility as the student progresses through the academic curriculum, and, in general, shall parallel the student's progress through the academic phases.

With the above being used as a definition of an ideal cooperative education plan, in practice it may be difficult to completely meet the theoretical ideal. Ultimately, what becomes most important is just what a particular student will derive from his employment, his receptivity to what he discovers, his attitudes, and his ability to get along with his coworkers.

As each new college undertakes to start its own program, they coin their own title for the alternating working and studying program. Such titles as "Internship," "Field Experience," "Off-Campus Period," "Professional Practice Program," "Extramural Term," "Interval," and "Interlude" are some of the better-known ones.

In the colleges practicing cooperative education, it is not likely that any two of them operate exactly similar programs. Each institution adapts those ingredients which it best values. Motivations for participation are many. While all programs are student-centered, in that it is expected that the student will be the main bene-

ficiary of the related work experience prior to graduation, there are many side benefits to the participating college. Having a cooperative education program reduces the "isolationism" of the institution, makes better use of the college's physical plant, creates a rapport with the local community, provides real-life experiences for the classroom, acts as a stimulus to student recruiting, provides employer with facilities and equipment which the college cannot afford (as laboratory equipment), provides a background of experience for the student which will make him more employable upon graduation, and assists the college in its fund-raising activities by providing linkages with potential donors.

The advantages to students who are enrolled in cooperative education programs are rather obvious, although documentation supporting this was unknown until 1958, when a study was undertaken directed by Dr. Ralph Tyler, Director, Center of Advanced Study in the Behavioral Sciences. Data were collected on a national level from faculty members, students, administrators of cooperative programs, and employer representatives. The results of this comprehensive research were published in a book entitled *Work-Study College Programs*, authored by Wilson and Lyons, 1961. Its voluminous detail verified the values claimed for cooperative education, and from this study has evolved a listing of acknowledged differences between cooperative and noncooperative education.

EDUCATIONAL ADVANTAGES TO THE STUDENT

Some educational advantages to students include the following:

By coordinating work experience with the campus education program, theory and practice are more closely integrated, and students find greater meaning in their studies.

This coordinating of work and study increases student motivation. As students see connections between the jobs they hold and the things they are learning on the campus, greater interest in academic work develops.

For many students, work experience contributes to a greater sense of responsibility for their own efforts, greater dependence on their own judgments, and a corresponding development of maturity.

Because the work experiences involve the students in relations with coworkers who come from a variety of backgrounds, and because success in these jobs requires constructive relationships with colleagues, most students in cooperative education develop greater understanding of other people and greater skills in human relations. It is particularly valuable for those students to work with adults as a bridge between their years of schooling—living almost entirely with their own contemporaries—and their own adult life among mixed age groups.

Cooperative education helps markedly to orient college students to the world of work. In cooperative education programs, students have opportunities for exploring their own abilities in connection with real jobs, and they find a direct means of gaining vocational information and guidance—not only in the occupations in which they are employed, but in a number of related fields as well. They have a chance to test their own aptitudes more fully than is normally possible on the campus. Furthermore, students are able to understand and appreciate more fully the meaning of work to the individual and the function of occupations in providing the wide range of goods and services characteristic of our economy.

Other assumed advantages to the student:

The student's earnings contribute to financing his own education, leading to self-dependence and independence, and contributing to his self-esteem and confidence.

Since the student is carried as a productive employe, with an attendant rating of his performance, he usually develops good work habits.

His role as a team member in a real and productive working environment inculcates a seriousness of life and purpose which is often denied the traditional college graduate.

As a result of this alternation between the college and the cooperative position, the student tends to appreciate better the role of each environment.

A smoother transition into full-time employment awaits the graduate of the cooperative program because of his undergraduate experience. Often the length of apprenticeships and training programs upon graduation are reduced or even eliminated for him because of his cooperative experience.

ADVANTAGES TO THE COOPERATING ORGANIZATION

Organizations may benefit in the following ways:

The student can be thoroughly grounded in established employer practices and organization while he is still at a formative level.

The program is an excellent source of temporary and potentially permanent manpower.

The infusion of bright young people, fresh from an educational environment, into an organization can provide new ideas and viewpoints which can be refreshing and stimulating.

Most cooperative programs are developed in a way that allows continuous job coverage, so the employer usually does not have to be concerned about job continuity.

The cooperative student serves as a "goodwill" ambassador" for his cooperating organization with faculty and other students, upon returning to campus.

A mutually important industry-college relationship is enhanced.

The cooperative program provides the company with a low-cost training program, since the cooperative student generally earns a salary which is below the average salary paid to a graduate; he more nearly "earns" his salary at the beginning stages of professional employment.

TYPES OF PROGRAMS

The extent to which the cooperative education is part of the total educational process in any particular college varies a great deal. The best description of the type and extent of involvement can be classified as Mandatory, Optional, and Selective. A recent survey indicates that only 10 percent of the senior colleges offering cooperative education programs and only 9 percent of the junior colleges have Mandatory Programs. Optional Programs are operated in 51 percent of the baccalaureate degree-granting institutions and 58 percent of the two-year colleges. In the remaining institutions, programs are Selective. (Knowles, A. S., *Handbook of Cooperative Education*, 1971, Chapter III, p. 31). An explanation of each type follows:

Mandatory Programs

Some colleges and universities have adopted cooperative education as the keystone of their educational thrust. This means that all, or virtually all, of the students must pursue the plan if they enroll. These institutions are said to have mandatory programs. Examples of institutions wholly commited to mandatory programs are Antioch College, Drexel University, Northeastern University, and Wilberforce University. Examples of those with mandatory programs in some of the colleges within the university are the University of Cincinnati, University of Detroit, and Rochester Institute of Technology. Students enrolled in mandatory programs are expected to satisfactorily complete prescribed periods of off-campus work as part of the total requirements for the degree. These institutions hold a strong belief in the values of off-campus experience for their students.

Optional Programs

Some colleges offer cooperative programs as a choice to the student, in that the student may attend college in the traditional manner, with no work experience required, or he may choose the work experience. Students who wish to follow the cooperative plan are accepted or rejected on the basis of their qualifications, their interest in the program, and the availability of job openings. Some colleges and universities require that the student have his own job or off-campus experience determined and available before entering the program. Optional programs may involve only a small number of students in very large institutions and may be limited to particular departments of colleges or individual colleges within a university.

Selective Programs

Colleges and universities with selective programs usually enroll cooperative students on the basis of academic performance. Customarily, students are required to maintain a specified grade-point average to qualify for, and perhaps remain in, the cooperative program. Those who wish to pursue the cooperative plan apply and are offered the opportunity by appropriate selection criteria or committee. Under such arrangements, the college or department offers a traditional plan of study with the cooperative program as an alternative.

LEVELS OF EDUCATION

The use of the cooperative plan of education is not restricted to the traditional four-year baccalaureate degree institution. It can be, and is, used effectively at all levels of education. Cooperative education is now found at the junior and community college level, as well as in masters and doctoral programs. However, the latter is quite limited.

Differing objectives may be found between the different educational levels and disciplines. Cooperative programs which are found on the junior or community college level usually emphasize a heavy vocational relationship between academic course work and the cooperative employment. This same relationship will be found at the baccalaureate degree-granting institution in the professional courses, such as engineering and business administration. However, for students majoring in philosophy, history, etc., the type of cooperative employment can vary widely, as values are sought which are not necessarily directly related to the student's major course of study. Rather, emphasis might be placed on concepts of "social involvement" or "experience in living" in broadening the student's total education.

Progressing to the master's degree, most cooperative education programs are in professional areas of science, engineering, and business administration. Again, such programs will emphasize a high level of job specialization, but will stress research, development, and pursuit of individual projects.

The few schools presenting cooperative education at the doctoral level are mostly engineering-oriented. The employment of such students usually is tied in with the academic side, and includes close faculty supervision.

CONDUCT OF PROGRAMS

The conduct of the cooperative education program usually lies in the hands of a professional person or staff, if the program is of any appreciable size. These staff members are usually known as coordinators. The personality and make-up of a coordinator, to be successful, should combine all the attributes of the all-American boy or girl. He or she should have an interest in young people and want to help them in all respects. He should be resourceful and thrive on the challenge of solving problems. This individual must be salesminded and able to influence others, both to secure job openings from employers and also to influence the outlook of the students under his or her jurisdiction. Qualifications must include the capacities or organization and detail, and the ability to apportion time to those things which are most important to the overall execution of the position. Weakness in any one of the above attributes will result in a less than excellent performance.

The coordinator has many responsibilities in carrying out the program. In institutions with an optional program, he must recruit students for the program by pointing out the advantages of departing from the traditional patterns. In every case, the coordinator must know which students are to be placed well in advance of placement, and, if appropriate employment is not available, he must have an ongoing program of job development to secure the necessary openings to serve the student. He must be something of a vocational counselor to the student, and be able to present a good description of the various openings. This ensures, at the end of the placement process, a good fit between what the employment presents and the student's interest. It is a complicated procedure, and variables will exist which might interfere with the process. Such items as the student's home location and the inability or lack of interest in relocating for the employment is one of the greatest deterents. Lack of a student-owned automobile may prevent certain placements, as the employer may not be served by public transportation. These are just a few of the myriad problems which can and will arise, and which must be solved for successful placement.

Most programs will require the student to write a report on his experiences while working, and the coordinator must read and approve it. Many also request the employer to evaluate the student while on assignment. When the student returns to college, it is the coordinator's responsibility to review the evaluation with him. In this way the student may be aware of his progress on the job. If any shortcomings exist, it is important that the student know of them so he might improve himself in the next period of employment. One critical point of contact with the student occurs when the student has returned from his employment and his viewpoint is obtained. It is at this time that the student is prone to be most critical of his employment, and he may have a negative view of returning to the same employer. If the employer is counting on the student's return at a later period, complications may arise. The coordinator must know how to handle such a situation, as there is a possible risk of losing a valued employer if the student does not return.

Part of a coordinator's time is usually spent in actual visitation with the employer, where, face to face, they can discuss all aspects of the working locations and the students which are involved. This is desirable, as the rating form which is submitted by the employer usually does not indicate the whole story on an individual student. Also, the assessment by the college coordinator of the working location can be important in determining if it should remain as appropriate in serving the needs of the student.

ACADEMIC CREDIT

Until recent years it was unusual for academic credit

to be granted as a reward for the successful completion of the cooperative education period. Rather, it was more common to require "cooperative credit" for graduation. With the tremendous growth of experiential education there has come growing recognition of the value of such experience, and the subsequent granting of full academic credit by many schools. At the time of this writing, 79 percent of the colleges offering cooperative education experience do grant such credit (Directory of Cooperative Education, 1975), and most of them grant it not as "add-on" credit but as part of the normal academic load. Academic credit for cooperative education experience has been recommended by the Joint Committee on Academic Credit (Cooperative Education Association and Cooperative Education Division of American Society for Engineering Education), in recognition of the true value of employment experience.

ADMINISTRATIVE REQUIREMENTS

For cooperative education to succeed in a particular college it is important to inform all parties as to the philosophy and objectives of such a venture, to ensure every chance of success. It is wise to recognize that those in the college community (students, faculty, and administration) will have many individual viewpoints and feelings about it. These viewpoints are not all sympathetic to the idea, and indeed may actively be in opposition.

Initially, there must be one or two persons of influence from the faculty or administration who will accept this philosophy without reservation. They must also be willing to spearhead its investigation and development. Beyond this, there must be a willingness to consider major changes in the institution as a result of the adoption of the cooperative education program. The academic calendar, the mechanics of operation, and the curricula must all be designed in terms of what is best for the cooperative students. Many academic subjects are sequential, so the curricula should be arranged in such a way that the cooperative student is not handicapped by his periods of absence from the campus. Cooperative education programs which grow to appreciable size usually require that a slate of subjects be presented for two consecutive terms, so that the dual student body, one at work while the other is in college, will have equal exposure to alternating periods.

NEW AND INNOVATIVE PROGRAMS

It would be impossible to describe all of the variations in practice and philosophy of the different programs within the confines of this chapter, but note should be made of those which are notably different or innovative. Considering that cooperative education had its initial start largely in the field of engineering, and it is still thriving in that area, other variations in disciplines and practices bear an interesting contrast.

Most innovative cooperative education is found at the liberal arts college, probably a natural setting for experimentation. Factors influencing this would be the seeking of different objectives for their students. As it is some-

times difficult to find that employment which would directly relate to the students' major course of study (examples: history and philosophy) they seek to find employment which will serve broader educational purposes. Much of their employment is centered in areas of social concern, urban problems, and involving the student firsthand in the betterment of mankind. Many are employed in government agencies, educational institutions, physical and mental health institutions, as well as the more normal outlets in business and industry which involve the more pragmatic student.

One departure from tradition is practiced by Antioch College, which has a significant number of students placed in foreign countries, taking advantage of what other cultures have to offer as an influence on their students. While a number of colleges maintain foreign placement, Antioch is unique, as it maintains at least one coordinator abroad to effect placements.

A large company-based program is operated by the General Motors Corporation, which conducts five-year cooperative programs in engineering and industrial administration. The students alternate six-week periods, rotating with the various plants and the General Motors Institute, which is located in Flint, Michigan, a degree-granting institution.

Additional program variations include senior cooperative colleges which offer a two- or three-year cooperative program equivalent to the junior and senior years at a traditional college. Examples are the University of Michigan (Dearborn Campus) and the new Universities of North and West Florida, which depend on transfers from other institutions. The University of Tennessee at Knoxville, and its junior branch at Martin, have an arrangement whereby the junior institution at Martin transfers the student to the senior college at Knoxville. The cooperative student maintains the same affiliation with the employer throughout his tenure at both schools. Broward Community College, Fort Lauderdale, Florida also has linking programs with senior colleges based on cooperative program arrangements. A "one employer" university, the University of West Virginia, has employment arrangements with the West Virginia Roads Commission, which serves as its sole source of cooperative work.

At least one consortium arrangement exists at present. Lees Junior College and Alice Lloyd College, both in Kentucky, have one overall cooperative director with individual coordinators on each campus. North Carolina A&T University operates a consortium of cooperative colleges predominating in black enrollment.

These examples are just a few of the great variety of cooperative programs existent, and further prove the diversity of American education in the desire to consider new and hopefully advanced practices.

FUTURE OF COOPERATIVE EDUCATION

Present information indicates that the future of cooperative education appears to be most promising. The increasing demand from the students for actual life experiences, a willingness and satisfaction on the part of employers to have such students in their organizations, and, finally, a growing recognition and overcoming of inertia on the part of the colleges seem to ensure further growth. The economic factors alone, both for the individual student in helping to finance his own education, and the direct financial benefits to the college which has a sizable program, are also important considerations for such an optimistic oulook.

Other than its own vitality, the financial support of the Office of Education of the Department of Health, Education and Welfare to aid individual colleges in starting their own cooperative programs has been a tremendously important factor. Also, the efforts of the National Commission for Cooperative Education have stimulated much interest in the college community.

After 69 years, it can truly be said that this important break with the lockstep of traditional education is gaining the full recognition it deserves in providing students with a more serviceable and informed education.

REFERENCES

Academic Credit, Joint Committee, Cooperative Education Association and Cooperative Education Division. ASEE, Report, 1971.

Cooperative Education Association. Cooperative Education Division of the American Society for Engineering Education joint brochures, *How to Start a Cooperative Program at the College* and *How to Start a Cooperative Program at the Employer,* 1970.

Director of Cooperative Education, Cooperative Education Association, 1973.

Knowles, Asa S. and Associates. *Handbook of Cooperative Education,* 1971, pp. 31, 32, 33, 34, 80, 231-234.

National Commission for Cooperative Education. Undergraduate Programs of Cooperative Education in the United States and Canada, 1973.

Wilson, J. W., and Lyons, E. H. *Work-Study College Programs.* Summary of the Study, 1961, 9-11.

115

THREE-YEAR BACCALAUREATE PROGRAMS

by Edward L. Allen
Assistant Dean
College of Commerce and Business Administration
University of Illinois
Urbana, Illinois

Three-year baccalaureate programs are those programs which allow undergraduates to complete their studies within a three-year, rather than the traditional four-year, time frame. Employing a strict definition, the curriculum for such programs is not merely an acceleration of conventional four-year programs. The three-year curriculum is designed specifically to meet the needs of a particular student clientele, and has its own unique mission and design. Three-year programs represent an attempt to re-

vitalize the undergraduate educational experience by introducing structural and curricular changes compatible with the efficient and imaginative use of institutional resources productive of instructional innovation.

Traditional baccalaureate programs are defined in terms of credit hours, courses, and years—in terms of procedures rather than objectives, effort rather than work accomplished or knowledge gained. Three-year programs alter the time frame and the means of measuring a degree, restating it in terms of achievement. Such programs stress mastery of educational content more than steady progress within a fixed time span. The emphasis in three-year programs is, in general, an integrated rather than discrete learning experience, and encourages wide options in teaching methods and learning experiences.

By April 1973, there were 34 colleges and universities offering three-year baccalaureate programs in the United States. These are listed at the end of this paper. Further, there were an additional 21 colleges and universities in the process of developing three-year programs and/or studying the feasibility of such programs.

THE RATIONALE

The underlying rationale for three-year programs is based on several assumptions. First, college-age students today are not only physiologically and intellectually more advanced when they begin college than their counterparts of a generation earlier, but they are also better prepared academically upon completion of secondary school. They have also been exposed, through television and wider opportunities for travel, to a greater number of culturally enriching experiences than previous generations of college freshmen. Second, most entering freshmen are well enough advanced in general education to make it possible to reduce substantially the amount of time devoted to the undergraduate curriculum to general education. Third, increasingly greater numbers of high school students are completing the legally required number of credits for high school graduation at the end of their junior year, or by the end of the first semester of their senior year. This trend indicates a higher level of maturity for today's high school youngsters, and suggests that a larger percent of general education courses now taught in colleges might be taught in the secondary schools. Fourth, consciously designed three-year baccalaureate programs, based upon a reexamination of the meaning of the undergraduate experience in terms of today's social and educational environment, are likely to be more coherent and responsive to society's needs for the last quarter of the twentieth century than the traditional four-year programs. Fifth, the three-year baccalaureate makes a more efficient use of human, fiscal, and physical resources. It results not only in a savings of dollars for students and their parents, and more efficient utilization of institutional resources, but it also saves students valuable time in reaching that point in their lives when they can begin to seriously pursue a chosen career.

THE MODELS

There are four conventional routes to three-year programs. For the purpose of clarification, they may be designated as the *compression* model, the *early-admission* model, the *credit-by-examination* model, and the *restructuring* model.

The *compression* model is an old device, used for years to shorten the length of the baccalaureate. It simply involves encouraging students to carry a heavier academic load than the norm during the school year, and/or to attend summer sessions. In short, the student completes all graduation requirements in three years by compressing the content of a four-year program into a shorter time frame.

The *early-admission* model provides the student an opportunity for concurrent enrolment in high school and college. This procedure involves a prearranged agreement between the college and the secondary school by which a specifically identified program or set of courses are designed as college level courses. Satisfactory completion of such courses—which may be taught at a local high school or on a campus—earns college credit for the student prior to matriculation at a college or university. In some programs, students skip their senior year of high school entirely. The high school diploma is then awarded upon satisfactory completion of the first year of college.

Through the use of the *credit-by-examination* approach, students can earn academic credit by demonstrating mastery of a given subject matter at a predetermined level, whether they master the material in high school or on their own. This approach permits students to be given advanced placement or credit toward graduation for knowledge and skills gained prior to college matriculation. Placement is generally awarded through the use of Advanced Placement Tests designed either by the Educational Testing Service or internally by the institution's own staff. The College Level Examination Program (CLEP) examinations are offered to entering freshmen classes, and substantial numbers are able to shorten their bachelor's degree program by one year. Both general and subject-matter examinations are administered under this program.

The *restructuring* model involves a reduction in degree requirements. Some institutions have completely eliminated one-fourth of the total number of hours required for the bachelor's degree. Others have developed an entirely new curriculum designed to provide an undergraduate experience in three years. Such specially structured programs are designed to be as rigorous and valid as the tradition-bound four-year undergraduate curriculum.

APPLIED MODELS

Each of the four models is employed singly or in combination with the others at institutions throughout the United States. Compression has been widely used over the years by those students who chose to take intensified course loads and could afford financially to continue their studies on a year-round basis. This route to the three-year degree has been most readily available at those institutions which are able to offer a strong summer school program, employ the quarter system, or, more recently, adopt a trimester calendar.

An example of a program which employs the compression model is that offered at the State University of New York, College of Ceramics, at Alfred University. Alfred's accelerated program in Ceramic Science is designed to attract and "challenge students of exceptional scientific capability—a veritable call to excellence in engineering, science and education." Alfred students must be in the upper ten percent of their high school graduating class. Students are required to maintain a "B" average, and a failure to do so requires them to "drop back to the normal bachelor's program." The program requires 120 hours.

Other institutions which use the compression model are Ripon College in Wisconsin and Muskingum College, New Concord, Ohio. The Muskingum plan is designed to permit the student to complete all the requirements for graduation in three consecutive years by attending summer classes for eight weeks each summer. In addition to the compression model Muskingum has a contract arrangement. At the time of second semester registration, in early February, a freshman student wishing to take advantage of the accelerated education opportunity receives a contract and confers with his advisor.

At Ripon there are no special entrance requirements or fees. Secondary school students apply for admission in the usual manner. Students take 112 credit hours, with no summer work. The program, however, is designed for the above average student. Among the advantages of the program to the student listed by Ripon College are possibilities to: (1) save $4,000 without summer school or summer research projects; (2) get a jump on the job market, and an increased earning power of $8,000 for one year; (3) enter graduate or professional school one year early; and (4) free one year of "prime time" for travel or outside study.

Among those institutions which use the credit-by-examination model extensively are: Florida Atlantic University; George Washington University—Columbian College; Shimer College; St. Louis University; and Utica College. The Florida Atlantic program employs primarily the College Level Examination Program. The "New Plan" at George Washington University is designed to provide the student greater responsibility for determining his own program, to permit greater flexibility of programming, to associate the student with his major field earlier than heretofore, and in general to establish a pattern of less time and more options. The students are permitted to earn credit or waive requirements through the use of examinations. The program at George Washington University also includes a special "90-hour degree program." This is designed for the exceptionally able student, and leads to the regular Columbian College degree. This program makes possible graduation in three normal academic years with a total of 90 semester hours credit, of the standard 120. A student who fails to maintain the required academic performance while studying toward the 90-hour degree simply continues for the standard 120-hour degree. The programs at St. Louis University and Utica College of Syracuse University both employ CLEP examinations.

Among those institutions which use the early-admission and coordinate programs with high schools are Appalachian State University at Boone, North Carolina, the State University College of New York at Fredonia, the State University of New York at Albany, and the combined program of the State University College of New York at Plattsburg with Hudson Valley Community College and Shaker High School, Albany.

The SUNY program at the State University College at Buffalo employs a plan for early admission in which students who have completed their junior years in secondary school, and who show high promise of success in college, are permitted to enter the State University College. The Buffalo program also permits unusually capable students who, in many cases, will not be satisfied with standard modes and formats for instruction, to plan their degree by contract. This program for shortening the time to earn the bachelor's degree is based on the assumption that some of the work required of a student in any given course has only marginal relevance to his needs.

The program at the State University College of New York at Fredonia is called the 3-1-3 Program. The title stands for three years of high school, one year which is cooperatively taught by both the high school and the college, and three years of college. This 3-1-3 pattern is designed to enable students to earn the high school diploma after four years, while the combined high school and college degree sequence can be completed in a total of seven, rather than the traditional eight years. During the transitional, cooperative year the student will take two courses at his high school and three at the college. The high school will accept the college work as credit toward the diploma, and the college will accept certain designated high school courses toward the degree.

The State University of New York at Albany has a program of acceleration at their James E. Allen Jr. Collegiate Center. The program is a four-year program but one which provides for acceleration, in that students are allowed to enter the college program after their 11th year of school.

The "experimental time-shortened degree program" of the State University College at Plattsburg, Hudson Valley Community College, and Shaker High School of Albany, New York, is a special program which is designed by agreement, and calls for the establishment of a curriculum offering the opportunity to complete a program similar to, and compatible with, the first year of academic work offered at Hudson Valley Community College and the State University College at Plattsburg.

At Appalachian State University, the three-year or accelerated program is called the Admissions Partnership Program. It is so named because part of the program calls for cooperation between Appalachian State University and neighboring public schools in shortening the time it takes for a student to complete the baccalaureate. By combining the senior year of high school with the freshman year of College, the redundancy that often exists between those two levels, especially for the better students, is eliminated.

There are five institutions whose programs are illustrative of the restructuring approach. Among them are Manhattanville College, at Purchase, New York and the New College of California, at Sausalito, California. At Manhattanville College a special program which scraps the

credit system has been established. The college has replaced the traditional transcript and credit requirements for graduation with what it calls a "portfolio system." Under this system each student will present evidence of academic and extracurricular achievement to a special faculty board, which will have the power to grant a degree at any time after two years of residence at the college. The "portfolio," or three-year degree, candidates must demonstrate the fulfillment of a program comparable in quality, depth, and breadth to that of four-year candidates. It is also assumed that the students in the three-year program will pursue a course of study more intensive and more highly structured than students in the four-year program.

The New College of California offers only three-year bachelor's degrees. The program requires a minimum of 123 semester hours for its degree, completed in three years. Other institutions which employ three-year programs based upon curricular revision are New College, at Sarasota, Florida and Ferris State College, at Big Rapid, Michigan. The "University Without Walls" program offered at Central Michigan University, under the sponsorship of the U.S. Department of Housing and Urban Development, is another example of programs developed around the curricular revision concept.

THE DEBATE: OPPONENTS

There are several objections to the three-year baccalaureate raised by skeptics and opponents. Briefly, their arguments are as follows: (1) Recognizing that an established route to a three-year bachelor's degree is already available through compression, there is no need for any changes in the existing system. (2) Colleges and universities should not give college-level credit for high school work. (3) Confronted by a "knowledge explosion" in all fields, the college curriculum should be lengthened, rather than shortened. (4) Students benefit by a fourth year of college, because it provides a beneficial environment for socialization and maturation. (5) Three-year programs will result in a diluted or cheapened undergraduate degree. (6) Three-year programs will not be accepted as reputable degrees by graduate institutions and the public at large.

THE DEBATE: ADVOCATES

Those arguments most central to the case made by advocates of three-year programs were presented above in the discussion of rationale. To review, they are that entering freshmen today compared with previous generations are: more mature; better prepared academically; have a better background in general education; and are completing high school earlier. Further, three-year programs are more appropriately in tune with contemporary social and educational conditions. Finally, three-year programs represent a more efficient use of physical, fiscal, and human resources.

In refuting the points raised by critics of such programs, advocates argue: (1) The compression model results in a bogus three-year degree. In actuality, they point out, it is a four-year program disguised in the mantle of a three-year degree. In addition, because of the added psychological, monetary, and time burdens it places upon students, it is a curricular alternative available only to a select few. (2) Colleges and universities should give recognition to any demonstrated knowledge and skills which can be legitimately converted to academic currency, regardless of how and where the youngster has acquired the knowledge and skills. Degree certification should be based upon competencies, not time served or hours accumulated in residence. Students should not be forced to repeat in college what they have learned elsewhere. (3) The logical conclusion of any policy which would extend the undergraduate curriculum in direct proportion to the increase in mankind's accumulated knowledge is that the undergraduate curriculum should be lengthened with each succeeding generation. What is required is that we establish a set of meaningful criteria as a measure of the baccalaureate which reflects an identifiable level of academic attainment and performance, as certified by colleges and universities. (4) Students enter college with wide ranges of maturity and widely varying levels of need for the collegiate socialization process. For those who are physically, intellectually, socially, and psychologically mature, and know what career goals they wish to pursue, colleges and universities have an obligation to provide an alternative to the four-year curriculum. (5) The thesis that three-year programs are, or will result in, a diluted baccalaureate has absolutely no basis in fact, and is purely an unfounded assumption. Studies done on three-year programs around the country show that students enrolled in three-year baccalaureate programs have gone through a course of study equal to, and in many cases more rigorous than, the standard curriculum for four-year students. Historically, the same point can be made about the time-shortened programs at the University of Chicago during the 1930s and 1940s, as well as the numerous three-year degree programs offered at major universities across the country between 1880 and 1910. (6) The claim that three-year baccalaureates will be looked upon as second-class degrees by graduate schools and the general public is also an unsubstantiated assumption. Graduate schools are more likely to be more interested in how a prospective student scores on the Graduate Record Examination, and his overall grade point average, than the number of years he spent in residence.

CONCLUSION

The debate regarding the question of time and the measure of the baccalaureate degree will bring the need for the establishment of a new consensus regarding the purposes of a college education to the fore, in light of social and economic conditions peculiar to the last quarter of the twentieth century.

The educational goal of time-shortened degree programs is not essentially different from that of four-year programs. Ultimately, the test of any three-year baccalaureate must be to ensure intellectual growth and learning, as well as cultivate habits of inquiry and reasoning which will serve the individual long after his undergraduate years. The quality of the three-year program

which provides that intellectual growth, as well as the cultivation of skills and habits of reasoned inquiry, must be equal to that of the traditional four-year programs. Quality must be preserved, but new ways of measuring, delivering and certifying the level of intellectual growth in a more equitable and accurate manner must be found.

Three-year programs go beyond the purposes and goals established for four-year programs at the turn of the century. They also stress the importance of ensuring the efficient use of the student's time, the institution's instructional man-hours, and the parents' investment in their children's education.

When one searches for a single term which most accurately sums up the essence of the three-year degree, one word comes to mind: efficiency. The purpose of the three-year degree is simple. It is not to destroy or displace the four-year tradition. It is to do away with the wasteful use of energy and resources built into that system. It is to find a more accurate means of measuring what a college education is, and in the process make more efficient use of fiscal and, most importantly, human resources.

INSTITUTIONS OFFERING THREE-YEAR PROGRAMS

Alfred University, State University College of Ceramics
Appalachian State University
Bowling Green State University
California State College—Dominguez Hills
Central Michigan University
Claremont Men's College
College of St. Francis (Illinois)
Concordia Senior College
Florida Atlantic University
George Washington University
Goucher College
Manhattanville College
(College of) Mount St. Vincent
Muskingum College
New College (California)
Northwestern University
Ripon College
St. Louis University
Shimer College
Southern Methodist University
SUNY, Albany
SUNY, Binghamton
SUNY, State University College at Brockport
SUNY, State University College at Buffalo
SUNY, State University College at Fredonia
SUNY, State University College at Geneseo
SUNY, State University College at Plattsburgh—Hudson
    Valley Community College-Shaker H.S.
University of Illinois, Urbana
The University of the Pacific, Raymond College
Utica College
Webster College

INSTITUTIONS AND SYSTEMS DEVELOPING OR CONSIDERING THREE-YEAR PROGRAMS

DePauw University
Eastern Illinois University
Florida State University System
Franklin College
Harvard University
Hobart and William Smith Colleges
The Johns Hopkins University
Long Island University, C. W. Post College
University of Iowa
University of Massachusetts
Moorhead State College (Minnesota)
University of North Dakota
Ohio State University
Princeton University
Stephens College
University of Utah State System
University of Vermont
Weber State College (Logan, Utah)
Yale University

REFERENCES

Bloom, Benjamin S. *The Relationship Between Educational Objectives and Examinations Designed to Measure Achievement in General Education Courses at the College Level.* Chicago: University of Chicago Press, 1946.

Dressel, Paul L., and DeLisle, Frances H. *Undergraduate Curriculum Trends.* Washington, D.C.: American Council on Education, 1969.

Eells, Walter C. *Degrees in Higher Education.* New York: The Center for Research in Education, 1963.

Hawkins, Hugh. *Between Harvard and America.* New York: Oxford University Press, 1972.

Hungate, Thad L., and McGrath, Earl J. *A New Trimester Three-Year Degree Program.* New York: Teachers College, Columbia University, 1963.

Hutchins, Robert Maynard. *Five College Plans.* New York: Columbia University Press, 1931.

McGrath, E. J. *Are Liberal Arts Colleges Becoming Professional Schools?* New York: Teachers College, Columbia University, 1958.

_____. *The Graduate School and the Decline of Liberal Education.* New York: Teachers College, Columbia University, 1959.

Slosson, Edwin E. *Great American Universities.* New York: The Macmillan Company, 1910.

Spurr, Stephen. *Academic Degree Structures: Innovative Approaches.* New York: McGraw-Hill Book Company, 1970.

Storr, Richard J. *Harper's University.* Chicago: University of Chicago Press, 1966.

Veysey, Lawrence R. *The Emergence of the American University.* Chicago: University of Chicago Press, 1970.

Woodring, Paul. *The Higher Learning in America: A Reassessment.* New York: McGraw-Hill Book Company, 1968.

BIBLIOGRAPHIC

"Abbreviated Baccalaureate Programs." *School and Society,* Vol. 100 (Summer, 1972), p. 100.

Adams, Walter. The Undergraduate Experience. *Change,* Vol. 4 (November 1972), pp. 14, 61-62.

Allen, Edward L. The Three-Year Baccalaureate. *Journal of General Education,* Vol. 25 (April 1973), pp. 61-76.

Anderson, G. Lester. Academic Degree Structures: A Point of View. *College and University,* Vol. 47 (Spring, 1972), pp. 194-200.

Andrews, E. B. Time and Age in Relation to the College Curriculum. *Educational Review,* Vol. 1 (1891), pp. 135-136.

Astin, Alexander. Challenge to the Credentialing Process. *Liberal Education,* Vol. 63 (May 1972), pp. 183-188.

Barlett, S. C. Shortening the College Course. *Education,* Vol. 11 (June 1891), pp. 585-590.

Conklin, Kenneth R. The Three-Year B.S.: Boon or Bust? *AAUP Bulletin,* Vol. 58 (March 1972), pp. 35-39.

Early College. *Newsweek,* April 24, 1972, p. 82.

Erhich, Thomas L. As Costs and Learning Climb, Many Colleges Consider Three-Year Degree. *Wall Street Journal,* August 25, 1971, p. 13.

Growth of the Three-Year College. *U.S. News and World Report,* Vol. 72 (January 1972), pp. 21-23.

Haak, Leo. Acceleration by Examination. *College and University,* Vol. 29 (October 1953), pp. 39-52.

Harris, John. Baccalaureate Requirements: Attainments or Exposure? *Educational Record,* Vol. 53 (Winter, 1972), pp. 59-65.

Innovations, Part I: Three-Year Degrees, New Flexibility. *College Management,* Vol. 6 (October 1971), pp. 20-22.

Less Time. *Chronicle of Higher Education,* April 3, 1972, p. 3.

Lieberman, Bernhardt, and Wycoff, Deborah. National Baccalaureate Examinations. *Education,* Vol. 91 (September 1970), pp. 76-83.

Lunneborg, C. E., and Lunneborg, P. W. Relation of Delayed Entrance to College Achievement. *Journal of Counseling Psychology,* Vol. 14 (July 1967), pp. 390-391

Nyquist, E. B. Society's Emphasis on Credentials Suggests College Degree Equivalency Program. *College and University Journal,* Vol. 10 (January 1971), p. 23.

Palfrey, J. Is Acceleration a Threat to the Liberal Arts College? *Newsletter of the Inter-university Committee on the Superior Student,* Vol. 3 (October 1960), pp. 14-16.

Princeton Eyes Three-Year Degree. *College and University Bulletin,* Vol. 24 (December 15, 1971), p. 8.

Sandeen, C. Arthur. The Meaning of a Bachelor's Degree. *School and Society,* Vol. 96 (February 17, 1968), pp. 101-102.

Society's Emphasis on Credentials Suggests College Degree Equivalency Program. *College and University Journal,* Vol. 10 (January 1971), p. 23.

Sorenson, Parry D. Earn your Degree . . . In Three Quarter Time. *National Observer,* July 1, 1972, p. 1.

Three-Year Degree. *Newsweek,* January 17, 1972, p. 74.

Three-Year Degree Gains Favor. *Phi Delta Kappan,* Vol. 53 (April 1972), p. 526.

Three-Year Degree Urged by Yale Faculty Unit. *Chronicle of Higher Education,* April 17, 1972, p. 3.

Weldlein, Edward R. Medical Degree in Three Years Gaining Favor. *Chronicle of Higher Education,* March 27, 1972, p. 1.

Whitaker, Urban. A Case Study of CLEP: Credit by Examination at San Francisco State. *College Board Review,* No. 83 (Spring, 1972), pp. 12-16.

Whitla, Dean K. The Three-Year B.A.—A Proposal for Harvard. *Liberal Education,* Vol. 63 (May 1972), pp. 247-257.

Works, George A. Arguments in Favor of Granting a Bachelor's Degree at the End of the Junior College Period. *Current Issues in Higher Education,* Vol. 9 (1937), pp. 3-13.

ADDITIONAL RESOURCES

Allen, Edward L. The Three-Year Baccalaureate: Some Preliminary Observations and Findings of a Study of its Form, Geographical Distribution and Rationale. Urbana, Illinois: Three-year Baccalaureate Programs National Survey Office, October 1972. (Mimeographed)

_____. Time and the Baccalaureate: An Analysis of the Three-Year Undergraduate Degree Concept in the American College and University. Unpublished doctoral dissertation, University of Illinois, 1973.

Dumke, Glenn S. A New Approach to Higher Education . . . for the California State Colleges. Remarks delivered to a Committee of the Board of Trustees, January 26, 1971. (Xeroxed)

Evans, Charles M. Experimental Time-shortened Degree Programs. A Cooperative Effort of Shaker High School, Hudson Valley Community College, State University College at Plattsburgh, State University of New York and Central Administration. Albany, New York: State University of New York, Office of the Provost, December 1, 1972. (Mimeographed)

Frost, James A. A Paper Prepared for the Rensselaerville Conference on the Three-year Bachelor's Degree, June 21-25, 1971. Albany, New York: State University of New York, 1971. (Mimeographed)

Stark, Joan S. The Three-Year B.A.: Who Will Choose It? Who Will Benefit? Paper presented at the AERA Meeting, New Orleans, Louisiana, 1973. (Mimeographed)

Waller, Robert A. Position Paper on the Three-Year Baccalaureate. Urbana, Illinois: University of Illinois, College of Liberal Arts and Sciences, December 1971. (Mimeographed)

116

CLUSTER COLLEGES

by Warren Bryan Martin
Vice President
The Danforth Foundation
St. Louis, Missouri

CONTEXT

The past 25 years have been a profoundly significant period for American higher education. It was a time of unparalleled numerical, fiscal, and spatial growth, especially during the 50s and early 60s. It was also a time of unprecedented challenges to the philosophical assumptions and organizational provisions of most colleges and universities, as evidenced by the student dissatisfaction which seemed in the mid- to late-60s to be nothing less than a student revolution. A related development of the 60s and early 70s has been the emergence of uncertainty concerning the adequacy of traditional modes of teaching and learning, of testing and grading procedures, of the organization of knowledge by subject matter specialization, and of the ideational dominance of graduate and professional schools featuring research. The conventional roles of institutions of higher education within American society—as agents of socialization and certification—have also been challenged. The current reassertion of traditional functions simply emphasizes the magnitude of the division among educators and the confusion in the general citizenry concerning the legitimacy of these roles.

Over this span of 20 or 25 years, given growth, change, and the problems of higher education, numerous ideas have been brought forward as means of meeting some or all of these challenges confronting colleges and universi-

ties in the moden society. The concept of cluster colleges has been one among many "answers" to these complex problems.

DEFINITION

Cluster colleges cannot be explained by any simple definition. The term is applied to federated colleges, where several institutions are geographically contiguous but organizationally separate. Such colleges usually share some services and facilities—counseling and health services, the athletic program, auditoriums, the library—while carefully guarding their essential independence. The cluster college rubric also is used to cover the establishment of new semi-autonomous subunits within established universities, where the cluster components have a degree of instructional autonomy but little or no fiscal authority. Another use of the concept is in connection with the creation of an experimental "college" within a college or university. The purpose is to set up a program which can accommodate innovations unlikely to be accepted elsewhere. Finally, "clustering" may signify a grouping of students and faculty by subject matter specializations, or by curricular problems and themes deemed appropriate for study, or by some pedagogical or methodological arrangement that is thought to justify setting up a special administrative unit which is then called a "college."

There are certain issues, problems, and themes which are recurring, and consequently, help to provide a justification for the cluster college movement. How to be small while getting large? This is one question for which cluster colleges have been seen as an answer. In that period of unprecedented growth for American colleges and universities, the 50s and 60s, it became apparent that while there were fiscal and organizational advantages in large size, these quantitative gains were being offset by qualitative disadvantages. Students complained about mounting impersonality and tendencies to dehumanization. Faculty joined students in objecting to bureaucratic rigidities which seem to be the consequences of large size. What could be done, perceptive educators asked, to encourage humane environments for teaching and learning while institutions of higher education grew bigger and bigger?

These concerns were joined with others. Despite claims to diversity, there was persuasive evidence that colleges and universities were becoming more and more alike. The general tendency was toward conformity or uniformity, with the institutional model being the complex university and the professor's model being that of the autonomous research scholar. Could the lockstep be broken? How to safeguard diversity? Was there a way to assure pluralism? Institutional distinctiveness became a goal, and cluster colleges were seen as a means of achieving it.

A related concern had to do with making a place for educational innovations for people who wanted to try unusual modes of pedagogy, or new ways of testing and grading, or a different level or quality of student-faculty interaction. Would established institutions find a place for such faculty and students, or would these people be forced out? Was there a way for innovations to be tested and leadership for change to be developed without disrupting the traditional programs and their conventional leaders? The concept of cluster colleges seemed promising in this connection.

There was also the issue of community on campus. While postsecondary institutions were becoming more uniform, thus providing a basis for "the community of scholars," there was often no ideational concensus on a given campus, no essential rationale for the existence of a particular college or university, nothing that set it apart from all the others. Certain groups of students and faculty might be joined together by subject matter specialization and departmental structures, or by commitment to some methodological distinction, i.e., behaviorism, experimentalism, etc., but too often there seemed to be a lack of shared assumptions about the purposes of education. Indeed, more modestly, there seemed to be no way to set those people free who had some sort of procedural preference that they wanted to exercise. Was it at all significant, educators asked, that most places were communities of convenience, held together by shared libraries, labs, and other services, while at least a few places were more nearly communities of conviction, characterized by distinct philosophies of education or other ideational commitments? And was there a provision that would make it possible, on a single campus, to have both? Maybe, some leaders thought, the cluster college concept provided a way to work it out.

VARIATIONS

Cluster colleges emerged about 1960 as, in some cases, a means for colleges and universities to retain the advantages of smallness even while they became larger and larger. In the complex, multi-campus system called the University of California, Clark Kerr and other administrators made plans for two new campuses—Santa Cruz and San Diego—to be organized by colleges, with smaller units at Santa Cruz and larger ones at San Diego. The organizing principle would be the semi-autonomous college. In each of the colleges certain faculties and students would be based, do most of their work, establish friendships, and create a special relationship. The cluster college concept was a response to the problem of size.

The University of the Pacific was one of the smaller private universities where the cluster idea was seen as a way to encourage institutional distinctiveness. In the competition for students in a state with a comprehensive public educational system, what could UOP do to secure its place? Cluster colleges were seen as one answer. Cluster units would be small, approximately 250 students each, and they would be characterized by educational philosophies or pedagogical methodologies likely to set them apart from each other and from colleges elsewhere. At a time of increasing conformity, the cluster colleges at UOP would offer alternatives.

Michigan State University, like the University of California, was concerned about becoming a huge, impersonal institution. State also wanted diversity in programs and in modes of teaching and learning. In this University, as elsewhere, there were creative faculty eager to test cherished ideas; there were students who wanted unusual educational experiences; and there were faculty and students ready for the privileges and responsibilities of a unique academic community. Cluster colleges, three in number, were State's response to these challenges.

The antecedents and precedents for these and other kindred developments of the 60s were based on the centuries-old experience of the Oxford and Cambridge colleges and the venerable "house plans" of Harvard and Yale. Edward S. Harkness provided Harvard in 1928 with its House system and Yale, in 1930, with its system of colleges. These arrangements were intended to encourage social graces and moral behavior in students who were increasingly removed from old-fashioned collegiate values by the transformation of Harvard and Yale into complex universities. Other forerunners of the cluster college movement were, first, the establishment of the essentially autonomous but federated colleges at the Claremont Colleges in California and, second, the relationships of Morehouse, Spelman, Clark, Brown, and the Interdenominational Theological Center, which, taken together, comprise the Atlanta (Georgia) cluster of institutions.

Other influences on clustering were certain highly innovative or radically experimental colleges of the 30s and after—Swarthmore, Black Mountain, Reed, St. John, Bard, Shimer, and the University of Chicago. Equally influential were certain audacious educational thinkers—Dewey, Meiklejohn, Hutchins, Taylor, Riesman. To illustrate, almost every innovative scheme devised for the cluster colleges of the 60s was a part of Swarthmore's instructional program of the 30s, as Harold Taylor has faithfully pointed out.

By the early 70s the cluster college concept had become an established feature, albeit with limited application, throughout the United States. Several major state-wide systems tried the idea—State University of New York, at Old Westbury and Buffalo; Michigan State University, at East Lansing and Oakland; and the University of California, at campuses already mentioned. The California State University and Colleges had a variation on the concept in effect at Sonoma. Western Washington State College, Bellingham, set up three subunits. Other colleges and universities developed a single innovative or experimental unit—Wayne State (Montieth), University of Michigan (the Residential College), Rutgers University (Livingston), University of Alabama (New College), and University of Redlands (Johnston College). Variations on the house plan, as affected by clustering notions, were installed at Florida State, University of Kansas, Michigan State and elsewhere.

Other related developments include the so-called "free universities" (there must have been, usually for short life spans, about 200 of them in the late 60s), plus various learning centers and other variations on what was a growing commitment to experiential education and field experience.

ADVANTAGES

The cluster college concept has now been in use at enough places and with differing people long enough to make possible some general conclusions. First, with reference to contributions, it is appropriate to assert that these colleges do make a difference, that is, they do serve to intensify the interaction of participating faculty and students, with the result that some faculty teach better than they otherwise would have done and some students learn more than would otherwise have been the case. It is also true that for many participants there is a heightened sense of involvement in policy formulation and institutional governance; people seem to care more and work harder.

An additional benefit that can be drawn from the cluster idea is essentially economic in nature. While it costs many millions of dollars at today's prices to plan, build, and launch a free-standing liberal arts college, costs are greatly reduced if the new college is located within an established university, and provision is made for the students and faculty of this college to use the libraries, labs, playing fields, health facilities, and other services of the sponsoring institution. Start-up costs for any educational enterprise are high, but in this way they can be made lower.

Another "service" of cluster colleges is as testing grounds for innovation and experimentation. It is a time-honored procedure in American colleges and universities to spin off new units as settings where novel ideas can be tested. Then, if these ideas prove worthwhile, they are shifted over or co-opted by the more conventional segments. Cluster colleges can be seen, negatively, as incinerators useful in burning off ill-placed enthusiasm and ill-fitting ideas, or, positively, as baking ovens where new fare is developed for wider consumption.

The reference to baking ovens introduces still another way cluster colleges contribute to a sponsoring university. There is sometimes a leavening effect, in that what is done in the cluster school alerts elements of the older, established programs to a range of possibilities they might not otherwise have considered. Furthermore, competition may be stirred on individual and institutional levels, competition which may have positive rather than negative consequences. A new cluster college can get attention locally or even nationally to such an extent that older elements of the institution are put on notice that they need to change their programs in order to keep pace.

This organizational arrangement—the cluster college—does in fact contribute to institutional distinctiveness. In 1972, the Educational Testing Service administered the Institutional Goals Inventory to 116 colleges and universities in California. The two institutions that stood out, on scale after scale, were the Santa Cruz campus of the University of California and the Sonoma campus of the California State University and Colleges. Both are campuses featuring the cluster concept. While it would be inappropriate to claim that clustering explains the difference between these campuses and others, it is certainly true that this way of organizing curricular and extracurricular life contributed to their measurable distinctiveness.

For the American setting, which emphasizes diversity and pluralism, the cluster college concept is especially compatible. It is a way of acting out a revered American admonition: when in doubt, multiply the options. At a time of doubt about the best way to educate, the best we can do is to provide a variety of ways.

DISADVANTAGES

While cluster colleges are important positive influences for many students and faculty, and are consistent with certain educational and societal values, it is equally true that ten years of experience with this concept have exposed serious problems.

First, there is always tension between the new college and the sponsoring body. The cluster program usually authenticates its existence by claiming to be different, and perhaps better. This claim is sure to be offensive to people involved in those programs against which the comparison is made. Also, while the cluster school draws selectively from the tradition out of which it comes, it is usually dependent for resources on that very source. So, by biting the hand that feeds it, trouble is assured. The old is in the new, but the new seldom acknowledges that indebtedness, at least to the satisfaction of the old.

Within a very few years, divisions are likely to appear within a cluster school. The first planners will be challenged by people who come later, by those who do not understand the reasons for the college's main features, by those who conclude that those features are not wearing well, or by those who want to give priority to other considerations. Thus, very soon a split develops between "old guard" and "young Turks." There is the problem of instant tradition.

A related difficulty has to do with the succession to leadership of the second generation. Cluster colleges are often extensions of the personalities who founded them. Before long, this coterie of initiators burns out, moves along, or sags down. A transfer of authority becomes necessary, yet it threatens continuity and is often resisted. This problem, of course, is not confined to cluster colleges.

Then there is the inevitable discrepancy between expectations and practice, between ideals and reality. This problem hits faculty as well as students. When a program is described to prospective faculty or students, there is an element of unintended misrepresentation in the presentation, plus a tendency on the part of the listeners to hear only what they want to. Later, charges will fly. This prospect is intensified because of the desire on the part of the planners to set their program apart, and to persuade people into it. Another factor, of course, is the evolving nature of all such programs. They seldom become what they were expected to be, and they never remain as they begin. Parenthetically, subsequent changes are almost always back toward the status quo. The innovative college will probably never be as radical as it was on the day it opened.

Most cluster colleges have all of the problems associated with a community of true believers. There is the apocalyptic element, or those persons living in the expectation of disaster. There are the legalists, determined to hold to every jot and tittle of the "contract." There are camp followers, who never identify with the work to be done but only with its benefits. There are the revisionists, who want to make the effort into something it was not intended to be. There are the false prophets and the true (but which is which?), the heretics and the saints. And internal insecurity is always matched by external threats.

Evaluation or assessment is another serious problem for cluster college participants. If the college is part of a complex institutional system, faculty in other programs, even those on the same campus, will in all probability want to hold the new cluster endeavor to criteria or standards that are thought to apply to older units. Whether or not established programs have in fact been measured by the norms these faculty would apply to others, it is a certainty that people in the innovative college will regard any standards imposed on them as inappropriate, given the special or innovative character of their venture.

In the competition for funds and other resources, it is crucial to decide the basis for comparison. Yet, alas, even as the old ways of measuring success are often useless for the new ventures, so these new programs often find that they are able to devise defensible ways of evaluating their work. They seem, therefore, to ask for support carte blanche.

A final problem has to do with the "contribution" of cluster colleges as tracking mechanisms for distinguishing between or discriminating among students. Few cluster colleges are avowedly honor programs, but many do set up courses of study that require unusual skills or special aptitudes. All this may be well and good, except as it violates the desire of most educators to mix students of differing interest and abilities. Cluster college environments, as viewed by social egalitarians, can be seen as elitist, unrealistic, precious. But from another perspective, one which is critical of the formlessness or indecisiveness of so many established educational programs now, cluster colleges provide an important corrective, to the extent that they offer clearly delineated, purposeful alternatives.

PROSPECTS

As for the future, the present tendency on the part of students and faculty to return to traditional forms of higher education, having concluded that these programs are the best means for achieving the expected outcome of the educational experience, i.e., jobs and social status,[1] means that cluster colleges dedicated to the liberal arts, and to being centers of innovation and change, may find the going very hard. On the other hand, the effects of the educational counterculture could prove to be sufficiently strong that a sizable minority of students will continue to be interested in programs that are unapologetically different in mood and form and outcomes.

There will be pressure from many sources, especially in view of the aforementioned tendency, to keep experimentation in the 70s modest, to limit it to procedural changes rather than to more substantive ones. Cluster colleges will be seen as new means to establish ends. They will not be favored if they try to be places offering new means to new or unknown ends. They will not be allowed to become significant change agents, but only agents of small change.

Even if the intention is modest, and cluster colleges are thought of as administrative conveniences for locating certain people and programs, it will be important in the future to see that these efforts remain flexible and capable of change. There is always the possibility that new entities, having come into being through change, will then become so concerned for their continuation that they proceed to institutionalize themselves, and to encourage definitions, procedures, and regulations that lead eventually to bureaucratic rigidities. Although the product of change, they become the enemy of subsequent change. Cluster colleges in the future could become centers of academic traditionalism. With the interest today in career education and practical, realistic, vocationally-oriented programs, cluster schools might react and become havens for advocates of theoretical, idealistic liberal education, dedicated to students and faculty who have the time, resources, and disposition for theory and abstraction. These colleges could turn out to be defenders of those aspects of traditional postsecondary education that the traditional college and universities are more and more forsaking.

Another prospect, however, is that at least some cluster colleges of the future will see it as their business to design and put into effect new approaches to liberal education. An example might be a program worked out in conjunction with career education themes, and featuring liberal learning reached via career training. Or, there may be new cluster colleges for new clientele: for older adults who come to the campus on week-ends only, or in the evenings, or during summer sessions. There could be cluster programs arranged to improve the transition from high school to college, picking up certain youth at about the junior year of high school and moving them along into work normally done in the first year or two of college. Such intermediate programs are compatible with the organizational provisions of the cluster college concept.

Clustering is here to stay. Efficiency and economy demand it. It is an appropriate way of meeting the call for community. Institutional subunits are good places for testing innovation. And, as stated earlier, on the basis of the evidence accumulated thus far it can be stated that these colleges and this concept make a difference—with faculty, for students, and on the sponsoring institution. There is reason, then, for this concept, these colleges, and the people who work in them to stay around.

NOTES

[1] More than one-half of the entering freshmen at Harvard in the fall of 1974, declared themselves interested in becoming premedical students.

REFERENCES

Gaff, J. G., and Associates. *The Cluster College.* San Francisco: Jossey-Bass, 1970.

Kells, H. R., and Stewart, C. T. The Conference on the Cluster College Concept: Summary of the Working Sessions. *Journal of Higher Education,* April 1968.

Martin, W. B. *Alternative to Irrelevance.* Nashville: Arlington, 1968.

_____. *Conformity: Standards and Change in Higher Education.* San Francisco: Jossey-Bass, 1969.

McHenry, D. E. Small College Program for a Large University. *College and University Business,* July 1964, pp. 31-33.

Taylor, Harold. *Students Without Teachers: The Crisis in the University.* New York: McGraw-Hill, 1969.

Tussman, J. *Experiment at Berkeley.* New York: Oxford, 1969.

Whitehead, A. N. *The Aims of Education.* New York: Macmillan, 1959.

APPENDIX

Representative Clustering Institutions (Colleges and Universities with subunits)

Claremont Colleges
    Pomona College
    Scripps College
    Claremont Men's College
    Harvey Mudd College
    Pitzer College
    Claremont Graduate School and University Center

Atlanta University Center for Higher Education
    Morehouse College
    Spelman College
    Morris Brown College
    Clark College
    Interdenominational Theological Center

University of California
    Santa Cruz campus
    Cowell College
    Stevenson College
    Crown College
    Merrill College
    Kreage College
    Oakes College

Michigan State University
    Justin Morrill College
    Lyman Briggs College
    James Madison College

University of the Pacific
    Raymond College
    Covell College
    Callison College

Wayne State University
    Monteith College

Rutgers—the State University of New Jersey
    Livingston College

University of Redlands
    Johnston College

St. Olaf College
    The Paracollege

California State College, Sonoma
    School of Arts and Sciences
    Hutchins School
    School of Expressive Arts
    Environmental Studies School

University of Nebraska
    Centennial Education Program

University of Vermont
    Experimental Program

———

117

EXTERNAL DEGREE PROGRAMS

by John R. Valley
Co-Director, Office of New Degree Programs
College Entrance Examination Board
New York, New York

In the early 1970s several patterns of higher education emerged in the United States which can be grouped under the rubric of *external degree programs.* Higher educational institutions, other agencies, and individuals have been fairly inventive in designing programs that are not centered on traditional patterns of residential study. From 1970 to 1973, within state public educational systems alone, approximately 25 systems had either established such programs or had appointed planning groups to see to their implementation. This author, writing in 1972, had identified six models of external degrees (Valley, 1972). The term itself is curious. While educators have used it extensively, and occasionally it appears in the title of a program, little attention has been given to its definition. In the single recent, comprehensive, and scholarly analysis of external degrees by Houle (1973), the following definition is offered: ". . . one awarded to an individual on the basis of some program of preparation (devised either by himself or by an educational institution) which is not centered on traditional patterns of residential collegiate or university study (pp. 14-15)." Houle's definition, in its most all-inclusive sense, would permit extension degrees, special degree programs for adults, and adult evening college degree programs to be included as external degrees. With such activities recognized as external degrees, the programs number in the hundreds. In 1972-1973 there were 181 institutional members of the Association of University Evening Colleges alone (Association of University Evening Colleges, 1972).

This article will focus on broad external degree developments, particularly since 1970. The reader is referred elsewhere for detailed information regarding specific programs. The bibliography offers several suggestions where information may be obtained. The year 1970 was indeed a landmark year. While Open University in England had not yet admitted its first students, its plans were known, and found to be sufficiently attractive to American educators that the trek to visit and study Open University had begun. While in England, visitors also had the opportunity to become familiar with two other variations of external degrees, namely the University of London and the National Council For Academic Awards. In the United

States, in an address at the annual meeting of the College Entrance Examination Board in October 1970, Alan Pifer, President of the Carnegie Corporation, asked if the time had not come for an external degree in America. At about the same time, Ewald B. Nyquist, the Commissioner of Education of the State of New York, indicated his support for a degree to be based largely on examinations to be offered by the New York Regents. Chancellor Boyer, of the State University of New York, announced the establishment of Empire State College, and in California both The University and The State University and Colleges systems announced their intentions to move ahead. And professional educators and potential students alike were trying to understand another program with a disarming name, the University Without Walls.

External degree programs develop either in response to restriction on access to residential collegiate and university study, or from the belief that residential study is not necessarily the best or most effective form of postsecondary education for all individuals. Three categories of techniques have been used, singly or in combination, in the design of the external degree program: technological, administrative, and educational. Technological techniques would include educational television, audio and visual cassettes, computer-assisted instruction, radio, tele-lectures, etc. Educational techniques would include the development of special curricula or new courses, programmed instruction, auto-tutorials, credit by examination, independent or self-directed study, practicums, internships, etc. Administrative techniques would include modifications of traditional academic calendars and schedules, week-end classes, intensive courses, revisions of academic regulations, etc. A further example of an administrative technique is the extension of degree-granting authority to institutions or agencies whose major function is not teaching or instruction.

There are two additional points to be made regarding the term "external degree." First, apparently the term has been imported into the American higher educational lexicon from England. However, at the University of London, where supposedly the external degree system originated (in theory, at least), no external degrees are awarded. London distinguishes not between internal and external degrees, but only between internal and external students. Internal students are those preparing for degree-qualifying examinations by attending institutions which are admitted as schools of The University. External students are those who are preparing elsewhere for the examinations. The distinction, by the way, is also not between full-time and part-time students (Logan, 1971). The University of London's external student population numbered 35,000 in 1971.

Second, "external degree" is used relatively infrequently in the title of programs by the institution under whose auspices they are offered. Other names for such programs are open universities, universities without walls, extended universities, or special adult degree programs. In instances such as Thomas Edison College all degree programs are external, yet the institution's name does not convey this information. Among the complications introduced by the use of different names for external degree programs is the difficulty of taking a census of such programs and the problem of compiling directories and guides to them.

SIGNIFICANT RECENT DEVELOPMENTS

Two major general themes in higher education provide a framework into which to cast recent developments pertaining specifically to external degrees. The first theme is the emerging support, almost world-wide, for the concept of lifelong learning: the view that education is an integral and continuous aspect of living, rather than something to be completed in preparation for life. The second theme is the emergence of "competence" as a rally word around which new program designs have begun to cluster.

The theme of lifelong learning is expressed in numerous local, national and international studies and reports (University of the State of New York, 1972; the Commission on Post-Secondary Education in Ontario, 1972; Commission on Non-Traditional Study, 1973; Faure, 1972). Various developments regarding external degree programs can be seen as each contributing, in its own way, to increasing lifelong learning opportunities. Five external degree developments are cited by way of illustration.

The Extension of Degree-Granting Authority

Prior to the 1970s, with some exceptions, authority to grant degrees in the United States was limited to teaching institutions of higher education. Typically a degree was an award made by a college or university, a teaching institution. Additional types of organizations or agencies have now acquired degree-granting authority. Two patterns can be discerned. First, organizations whose primary mission is not teaching have organized an instructional program and have secured or have requested degree-granting authority from the states in which they are headquartered. Examples are Arthur D. Little, Inc. in Massachusetts and the Rand Corporation in California.

The second pattern is the exercise of degree-granting authority by organizations and agencies which do not provide instruction. In Illinois, New Jersey, and New York, external degrees are now offered by agencies responsible for coordinating state educational systems. The Illinois Board of Governors Bachelor of Arts degree, the New York Regents Degree, and Thomas A. Edison College are the program titles under which this authority is exercised. Further, the Ohio Board of Regents extended degree-granting authority to a consortium of public and private colleges most of which are not located in Ohio. The Union For Experimenting Colleges and Universites, the sponsoring consortium of the University Without Walls, now has authority to grant degrees. The Union also has been admitted to correspondent accreditation status by the North Central Association. Finally, in Connecticut in 1973 a bill to create a Board For State Academic Awards was under consideration by the General Assembly. The Board, which would not be a teaching body, would have authority to award undergraduate degrees and course credit based on examinations.

The Geographic Extension of Institutional Operations

The removal of place as a restriction on student learning opportunities has been a major feature of external degree programs. The early 1970s saw dramatic geographic extensions of institutional operations. At least five newly established institutions have neither a campus nor permanent central educational facilities: Minnesota Metropolitan State College is an upper-division institution that services the greater St. Paul area; Whatcom Community College in Washington serves a county and has no campus; Wayne County Community College, in Michigan, has 26 instructional centers in the county and serves 13,000 students, most of whom are part-time; Vermont Community College operates anywhere in the state, supplying courses needed by the state's rural poor; the Empire State College, that offers a full baccalaureate program, operates out of centers located in New York State's several educational regions.

Much more extensive than the above is geographic extension of Northern Colorado University, which by 1972 was offering both baccalaureate and masters degree programs in 16 locations in Arizona, California, Colorado, District of Columbia, Florida, Indiana, Kansas, South Dakota, Virginia, and Wyoming. Similarly, Nova University, headquartered in Fort Lauderdale, Florida, offers instruction to students seeking the degree of Doctor of Education in four locations in Florida and in six other states. While for many years students from Antioch College, in Yellow Springs, Ohio have dispersed throughout the land to study under the college's cooperative education plan, more recently Antioch has established a network of educational centers ranging from Columbia, Maryland to San Francisco, California. Included in the network are some centers whose long-range aspirations are to be independent institutions.

Various technologies are also being used by colleges and universities to bring programs of degree courses to students at off-campus locations. The approaches range from classes conducted in specially outfitted New York commuter railroad cars, to courses televised, to special classroom facilities located in business and industrial plants and offices. The latter arrangements permit employees to take courses at their place of business, eliminating commuting to campus, parking problems, travel costs, etc. A new institution that merits continued attention is the State University of Negraska (S-U-N) that plans a state-wide educational television network, correspondence study, regional study centers, etc., to service students throughout the state (State University of Nebraska, 1973).

The point to be stressed in the above examples is that classroom instruction is being brought to students at locations far afield from the college's normal teaching base. A byproduct of these efforts is a reexamination of the meaning of residence and a restudy of residence requirement for degree awards.

The Use of the Community As an Educational Resource

The definition of external degree offered earlier indicated that such programs operated outside the framework of resident campus instruction. A question arises as to where indeed the student does learn. In external as well as conventional degree programs, increasingly the community is being seen as an educational resource. Consequently communities are being approached systematically, and efforts are being made to organize their resources to increase their availability for learning. The task, not an easy one, includes inventories of facilities, personnel, and equipment, as well as developing procedures to make these resources available and functional for students who need them. The following examples illustrate different approaches, as well as some of the dimensions of the problem:

The New York City Regional Center For Life-Long Learning operates under the auspices of the Regents Regional Coordinating Council For Post-Secondary Education in New York City. The Center's mission is to further their educational goals. The project has inventoried postsecondary and continuing education programs at both collegiate and noncollegiate postsecondary institutions. The next phase will be to operate a center for adults to match their interests and needs to the available programs. The long-range plans include a clearinghouse for the dissemination of information about continuing educational opportunities, guidance, and referral services, with the center functioning as a catalyst for the development of cooperative regional adult education programs.

The Community Involvement Program was designed to establish a Community Involvement Center (CIC) on each community college campus in the State of Washington, together with a State Coordinating Office. The CICs function as agencies to direct students to projects in the community, as well as the contact through which the community can draw upon the resources of the college.

The centers provide faculty orientation and training, supervise and evaluate community projects, develop policies and procedures for awarding academic credits, provide information about the community, maintain a catalog of student placements, assist students in relating their skills and interests to projects, and maintain student records. The project was completed in 1972, and steps have been taken to incorporate its recommendations into community college academic regulations and budgets (Werner, 1973).

As an outgrowth of The External Degree Study (Policy Institute of Syracuse University Research Corporation, 1971), the Regional Learning Service of Central New York was established to develop and operate a guidance system for people unable or unwilling to study at traditional institutions. The Service operates counseling centers. It also helps students to locate learning resources, and to meet other students for mutual psychological support. The Service refers to its third function as "validation": working through panels drawn from faculties of schools and colleges, the Service judges the worth of study materials, learning modules, learner experiences, etc.

The Office of Library Independent Study and Guidance Projects, established in 1972 by the College Board, assists public libraries to become organizing forces for nontraditional approaches to higher education. The Office reflects the growing interest among libraries in assisting individuals in self-directed study. The project provides national leadership and support for activities which had been explored earlier in various local efforts (Brooks, 1973 and Denver Public Library, 1973). Of related interest is the cooperative arrangement between Ohio University and the Cleveland Public Library, which served as a learning center for the University's Extended Learning Program (Extended Learning Program, 1973).

University Year For Action began in 1971 at ten colleges and universities, and by 1973, 55 institutions were participants in the program. ACTION, the federal volunteer service agency, enters into partnership with educational institutions and low-income community groups to create year-long full-time community service projects for students. Each participating college awards full academic credit to students for full-time work in the community, enabling normal progress toward a degree to be maintained.

The Development and Expansion of Supporting Services

External degrees have created a demand for services that facilitate or support such programs. The kinds of services being provided are quite varied, and only a few that are national in scope are cited as illustrations. Note that these services are not restricted to external degrees. However, it is suggested that services such as the following have a facilitative or supportive role that is particularly pertinent for external degrees.

Some services are offered directly to students. Examples are the Courses By Newspapers Project and the College-Level Examination Program. The former provides college courses distributed via newspapers. A pilot course, *America and The Future of Man,* will consist of twenty 1400-word units, each written by a distinguished teacher. Those who pursue the course for credit meet for two sessions of three hours each, held in the evening on campus at a cooperating college. Midterm and final exams are required. The College-Level Examination Program (CLEP), recognizing that individuals have diverse opportunities to learn, offers a national program of examinations for college credit. The use of CLEP is perhaps the single most common element characterizing recently established external degree programs.

Other supporting services serve institutions or professional workers in the field. Two examples of the latter are the Society For Field Experience Education and the National Center For Public Service Internship Programs. Examples of the former are the Office of New Degree Programs, the Instructional Systems Clearinghouse, and the Institute for Off-Campus Experience and Cooperative Education. The parallel emergence of these services with external degree programs since 1970 is striking. For further information about such services see the list of agency addresses at the end of this article.

National Commissions—The Elusive Consensus

In the early 1970s a series of reports emanated from various national educational commissions or task forces. A question arises whether their findings reflect consensus or divergence of opinion on matters relating to the external degree. The reader is urged to examine the reports issued by the Assembly on University Goals and Governance (The Academy of Arts and Sciences, 1971), the Carnegie Commission on Higher Education (1971), the Newman Task Force (1971), and the Commission on Non-Traditional Study (1973). Within the two-year period covered by these reports, the recommendations shifted from suggestions that certain matters be studied to suggestions for specific structures and arrangements for awarding external degrees. Although the concept of an examining university was not expanded in the Newman Report, a year later at least one state was apparently pursuing the idea in earnest. The New York Regents (University of the State of New York, 1972) urged that ". . . the possibilities of establishing an interstate regional examining center to evaluate postsecondary learning experiences and to award credit for appropriate collegiate learning be explored (p. 38)." The Regents report also pointed out, "As a first step toward establishing a regional examining center, the State Education Department has entered into cooperative arrangements with the Department of Higher Education of the State of New Jersey, which established Thomas A. Edison as an external degree-granting institution (p. 37)." Subsequently these two activities decided to go their separate ways, however.

The Commission on Non-Traditional Study, chaired by Samuel B. Gould, (as would be expected given its particular mission) directed more attention than have the other study groups to the external degree. Space does not permit even a listing of The Commission's pertinent recommendations here. Nonetheless, it can be said that four major study groups, working from a national perspective at approximately the same period of time, offer some recommendations in which they are in apparent agreement. However they also offered different advice and counsel on particular issues. Thus there is room for further discussion, exploration, investigation, and debate.

The second major higher educational theme of the 1970s that undergirded developments related to the external degree was the focus on competence as the organizing basis for degree programs (Morris, 1972). At a variety of institutions, including several stressing external degrees, baccalaureate degree requirements were being converted from the conventional 120 semester hours to statements of specific competencies expected of students. Degree requirements expressed as competencies afforded freedoms and opportunities for programs to be shaped as external degrees. That is, if a degree could be awarded whenever the candidate demonstrated he had met the institution's competency expectations, where, when, or how he was taught lost its significance. Learning independent of, or external to, the college counted. Expressions of the theme of competency can be seen in three developments related to external degrees: the increased need for varied techniques and service for assessing learning, the contract learning system, and protection of the public interest.

If external degrees encourage learning outside traditional patterns of residential study, such programs increase the need for techniques and services for assessing learning, whenever or wherever it may have occurred. Four major approaches have received attention: credit by examination, course evaluation, individual assessment, and validation model degree programs. Two national programs and a state program of credit by examination have expanded in support of external degree opportunities. They are the College-Level Examination Program and the Advanced Placement Program, both sponsored by College Entrance Examination Board, and the College Proficiency Examination Program of New York. The course evaluation approach is illustrated by the recommendations offered by the American Council on Education for crediting military training (Turner, 1968). A new edition of the ACE guide, offering credit recommendations to junior and community colleges, is in preparation (CASE, 1973). Two other projects parallel the efforts of ACE, but these are directed to crediting courses offered to employes by business and industry (Chaminade College, 1973 and Anderson, 1973). Individual assessment procedures have developed slowly and somewhat haphazardly, and the need for improvement is keenly felt. Several proposals were addressed to the Fund For The Improvement of Post-Secondary Education and to private foundations in 1973 to support work on the problem. In September 1973, Educational Testing Service (ETS), in association with the College Entrance Examination Board, convened a conference of major programs, for the purpose of determining what kind of a cooperative major research and development effort would be needed over the next three to five years. In the spring of 1974 ETS, in cooperation with nine colleges and universities (and later joined by a tenth institution), launched the Cooperative Assessment of Experiential Learning (CAEL) project. Finally validation model degree programs have now emerged, and are represented operationally by institutions like the New York Regents Degree and Thomas A. Edison College. Both of these programs lead not to just course credit, but also to the award of associate and baccalaureate-level degrees. Despite the recency of their establishment, both programs had awarded Associate in Arts degrees to several hundred candidates by the fall of 1973.

Certain models of external degrees have the potential for individualizing the processes whereby the student moves from enrollment to degree completion. These models require new approaches to the administration and management of instruction, as well as the supervision and assessment of the student. Given flexible or variable degree requirements, systematic and organized means for defining the interactive roles, responsibilities, and expectations of student and institution are needed. Several external degree programs, for example—Empire State College, Minnesota Metropolitan State College, and the Florida State University System External Degree—have incorporated contract learning. A contract typically will cover the student's objectives, how the student proposes to obtain his objectives, the educational resources required, and how and when they will be used. Further, a contract indicates the bases on which the student's performance is to be evaluated; i.e., the evidence to be submitted to demonstrate that the learning goals have been attained. It is this aspect of the contract learning system, together with its stress on behavioral statements of learning objectives, that helps to relate external degree programs to the theme of competence.

Finally the theme of competence also winds its way into concerns for program standards and the protection of the public interest. Accrediting agencies have taken note of external degree developments. The Southern Association of Schools and Colleges, having completed a study of nontraditional programs, issued Standard IX, which revised criteria for the evaluation of such programs (Southern Association of Colleges and Schools, 1973). Similarly, in 1973 the Federation of Regional Accrediting Commissions of Higher Education announced the development of new guidelines for nontraditional study programs. These guidelines are intended to assist both regional accrediting commissions and their constituent institutions to work within the framework of accrediting without impeding experimentation and innovation. In 1972, the North Central Association accepted the Union For Experimenting Colleges and Universities' "University Without Walls" program as a candidate for accreditation. The general thrust of actions such as these is encouraging to the development of new programs.

However, as external degree programs set aside as not applicable those conventions by which the legitimacy of educational programs have been assessed in the past, the public is left more exposed to degree mills and other forms of fraudulent enterprise. Attention has been given to the matter by the Educational Commission of the States. In 1973 a task force report offered model state legislation for the approval of postsecondary educational institutions and authorization to grant degrees. The report was endorsed by the Federal Trades Commission and referred to each of the states for consideration (Education Commission of the States, 1973).

CURRENT ISSUES

Space limitations preclude extended discussion of even the major issues surrounding external degree programs. At best only the general nature of some of the major issues can be suggested under the following headings.

Economic. Economic issues are among the most commonly voiced concerns. How much do external degree programs cost, in comparison to traditional educational programs? Is it true, for example, that external degree programs offer cost advantages? Should external degree program clientele be expected to pay for their full cost (or perhaps more?)? In times when educational financing is especially tight, what priority should be given to external degree programs in competition with other programs? The reader is reminded that several models of external degree programs exist. Therefore, questions of the economics of external degree programs need to be explored, accompanied by clear conceptualization of the kind of programs under analysis.

Political. Significant educational political issues are involved in external degree programs. Under whose auspices will programs be offered? Will they be controlled by the traditional educational establishment or by forces and agents outside the establishment? Certainly many of the new external degree programs have been offered at the state level; how do, or should, these move to relate to the private educational sector?

Educational. How can we be assured regarding questions of academic standards? For what should academic credit be awarded if different standards are appropriate; what are these standards, how will they be formulated and monitored, and by whom?

Social. What is the appropriate role of public vs. private educators in external degree programs? (For example, fees charged by certain public external degree programs are so low as to preclude the entry of private educational programs into the field.) What steps need to be taken to make the opportunities more equitably available, in terms of geography, social class, ethnic group, etc.?

SUMMARY

Many external degree programs developed in the early 1970s differed substantially from earlier attempts to serve special student clientele. The new models have yet to go through a substantial shake-down period before a fair appraisal of their success can be made. Collectively the programs are sufficiently innovative that they deserve the chance to demonstrate their potential. It will be interesting to observe which programs succeed, which ones fail, which ones will be absorbed into the traditional institutional fabric so as to loose their claim to externality, and which ones will become centers around which will emerge a thrust sufficiently strong to significantly change higher education in the future.

REFERENCES

The American Academy of Arts and Sciences. *A First Report: The Assembly on University Goals and Governance.* Cambridge, Massachusetts: The American Academy of Arts and Sciences, January 1971.

Anderson, Arthur W. *Educational Programs in Business and Industry and Implications for Receiving Credit Toward the External Degree.* East Lansing, Michigan: University of Michigan, Office of Institutional Research, undated.

Association of University Evening Colleges, 1972-73 Directory. Norman, Oklahoma.

Brooks, Jean. Report to the National Interest Council. Dallas, Texas: Dallas Library Independent Study Project, March 8, 1973. Mimeographed.

Carnegie Commission on Higher Education. *Less Time, More Options: Education Beyond High School.* New York: McGraw-Hill, 1971.

CASE. *Newsletter,* No. 39, May 1973. Washington, D.C.: Commission on Accreditation of Service Experience, American Council on Education, May 1973.

Chaminade College. Non-Traditional Education Evaluation Study (NON-TRAD). Honolulu, Hawaii: Office of Special Programs, July 1973, Vol. I-V. Mimeographed.

Commission on Non-Traditional Study. *Diversity By Design.*

San Francisco: Jossey-Bass, 1973.

The Commission on Post-Secondary Education in Ontario. *The Learning Society.* Toronto: Ministry of Government Services, 1972.

Denver Public Library. *On Your Own Newsletter.* Denver, Colorado: February, April, and May 1973.

Education Commission of the States. *Model State Legislation, Report No. 39.* Denver, Colorado: Education Commission of the States, June 1973.

Extended Learning Program. *A Report to the Ohio Board of Regents.* Athens, Ohio: Ohil University, June 1973. Mimeographed.

Houle, Cyril O. *The External Degree.* San Francisco: Jossey-Bass, 1973.

Logan, Sir Douglas. *The University of London, An Introduction.* London: The Athlone Press, 1971.

Morris, J. et al. *A Proposal For a Proficiency Based Degree Program.* Hamilton, New York: Colgate University, September 1972. Mimeographed.

Newman, F. *Report on Higher Education.* Washington, D.C.: U.S. Department of Health, Education and Welfare, March 1971.

Policy Institute of Syracuse University Research Corporation. *Newsletter: External Degree Program.* Syracuse, New York: Syracuse University, July 1971 and monthly thereafter.

Southern Association of Colleges and Schools. *Accreditation In Adult and Continuing Education Programs.* Atlanta, Georgia, 1973.

State University of Nebraska. *NEWS.* Lincoln, Nebraska: S-U-N Program, Vol. II, Nos. 1, 2, 3, and 4, 1973.

Turner, Cornelius P., ed. *A Guide to the Evaluation of Educational Experiences in the Armed Services.* Washington, D.C.: American Council on Education, 1968.

University of the State of New York. *Education Beyond High School.* Albany, New York: The State Education Department, September 1972.

Valley, John R. External Degree Programs. In *Explorations in Non-Traditional Study,* Gould, Samuel B., and Cross, K. Patricia, eds. San Francisco: Jossey-Bass, 1972.

Werner, Kathie. "Community Involvement Program Status Report," *Washington Involvement.* Olympia, Washington: Vol. 2, No. 3, July 1973.

ADDITIONAL RESOURCES

Cross, K. Patricia, and Valley, J. R. *Planning Non-Traditional Programs: An Analysis of the Issues.* San Francisco: Jossey-Bass, 1974.

Davis, Charles, ed. *The 1000 Mile Campus: The California State University and Colleges.* Los Angeles: Office of the Chancellor, California State University and Colleges, April 1972.

Gould, Samuel B., and Cross, K. Patricia, eds. *Explorations in Non-Traditional Study.* San Francisco: Jossey-Bass, 1972.

Journal of Higher Education, Vol. 44, No. 6, June 1973. Special Issue containing the following:

Houle, Cyril O. The Potential Audience for the External Degree.

Vickers, Donn F. The Learning Consultant: A Response to the External Degree Learner.

Mickey, Barbara H. Designing the External Degree Program.

Warren, Jonathan R. External Degrees, Coping with Problems of Credit.

Bowen, Howard R. Financing the External Degree.

Marien, Michael. Space-Free/Time-Free Higher Learning: New Programs, New Institutions, and New Questions. *Notes on the Future of Education,* Vol. III, No. 1, Winter, 1972. Syracuse, New York: Syracuse University, 1972.

Ritterbush, Philip C., ed. *Let the Entire Community Become Our University.* Washington, D.C.: Acropolis Books Ltd., 1972.

Shulman, Carol Hernstadt. A Look at External Degree Structures. *Research Currents.* Washington, D.C.: ERIC Clearinghouse on Higher Education, American Association for Higher Education, November 1, 1972.

Troutt, Roy. *Special Degree Programs for Adults: Exploring Non-Traditional Degree Programs in Higher Education.* Iowa City: American College Testing Program, 1971.

Valley, John R. *Increasing the Options.* Princeton, New Jersey: Office of New Degree Programs, 1972.

Vermilye, D. W., ed. *The Expanded Campus: Current Issues in Higher Education.* San Francisco: Jossey-Bass, 1972.

Walkup, Betsy S. *External Study for Post Secondary Students.* New York: Office of New Degree Programs, CEEB, Feb. 1972, and Aug. 1972 Supplement.

MAJOR INTEREST GROUPS, ASSOCIATIONS AND ORGANIZATIONS

American Council on Education
Committee on Higher Adult Education of the Commission on Academic Affairs
One Dupont Circle, N.W.
Washington, D.C. 20036
(202) 833-4720
W. Todd Furniss, Director

Association of University Evening Colleges
1700 Asp Avenue
Norman, Oklahoma 73069
(405) 325-1021, 1022
Dr. Howell W. McGee, Executive Secretary

Center for Research and Development in Higher Education
Tolman Hall
University of California
Berkeley, California 94720
(415) 642-5769
Dr. L. L. Medsker

College Entrance Examination Board
888 Seventh Avenue
New York, New York 10019
(212) 582-6210
George A. Hanford, Executive Vice President

Educational Testing Service
Princeton, New Jersey 08540
(609) 921-9000
Mr. William W. Turnbull, President

National Advisory Council on Extension and Continuing Education
1325 "G" Street, N.W., Suite 710
Washington, D.C. 20005
(202) 382-7985
Edward A. Kielock, Executive Director

National Center for Public Service Internship Programs
1735 Eye Street, N.W., Suite 601
Washington, D.C. 20036
Richard Ungerer, Executive Director

National University Extension Association
One Dupont Circle, N.W., Suite 360
Washington, D.C. 20036
(202) 659-3220
(Executive Director not appointed as of this writing)

The Office of New Degree Programs
c/o College Entrance Examination Board
888 Seventh Avenue
New York, New York 10019
(212) 582-6210
Director, John R. Valley

Panel on Alternative Approaches to Graduate Education
Box 2607
Princeton, New Jersey 08540
I. Bruce Hamilton, Executive Secretary

Society for Field Experience Education
John Duley
Justin Morrill College
Michigan State University
East Lansing, Michigan 48824

118

A STUDENT VOLUNTEER SERVICES BUREAU

by Leslie Purdy
ERIC Clearinghouse for Junior Colleges
Graduate School of Education
and the University Library
University of California
Los Angeles, California

Previously published as an ERIC Clearinghouse for Junior Colleges Topical Paper, University of California, Los Angeles, September, 1971.

Universal higher education is gradually becoming accepted as a widespread, if not national, commitment of American society today. It is seen as one viable—and tenable—solution to social problems, an answer to the demands of minority groups for equal opportunity, and an attempt to put into action our concept of democracy. While of recent vintage, the ideal is being fairly rapidly realized. In 1959, California made a commitment to provide higher education opportunities for all its high school graduates. More recently, the City University of New York opened its doors to all city residents, regardless of previous school records. Some 15 states have adopted hierarchical higher education systems. Because they have lower entrance requirements and fees than the other schools, community colleges are the keystones to these systems. Approximately 40 percent of all first-year college students in the country are in community junior colleges. This figure is growing annually as more junior colleges open their doors and as entrance to four-year colleges and universities becomes more difficult. The junior colleges, pressured to accept the responsibility for educating more students, and to educate them in a greater number of ways, will thus be the first to consider whether 14 years of schooling, rather than 12, is universally desirable and/or possible.

This expansion of institutions and students alike is not without problems. The public may accept the ideal of universal higher education on theoretical grounds, but it is showing less and less inclination to provide financial support for the goal. This clash between the demand for what higher education offers—skills, status, and adolescent community centers—and the resources available for higher education, makes it necessary to reconsider the desirability of such mass education and to begin studying some alternatives.

The disenchantment evident in society's resistance to support for higher education is matched by the general dissatisfaction of students with the schooling they presently receive. The various demands and complaints of students suggest, in part, that organized schooling beyond the twelfth year is serving an increasingly apathetic or even resisting audience. Going on to college has become almost as automatic as attending elementary and secondary school, an expectation implying a lack of autonomy that breeds dissatisfaction. Cohen and Brawer summarize the current debate over the involuntariness of attending college by saying:

> The argument that the college is an instrument of social mobility loses much of its force when a majority of the high school graduates go on to college because they have nowhere else to go. Dropping out of the mainstream of schooling is not easy. Van Hoffman (1970) speaks of "a vast social conspiracy to force a kid onto welfare, into the Army or back to school!" And Jerome (1969) points out that "college education has become, de facto, compulsory." Why are they there? Where else can a young person go? (p. 99)

It is not only from the student's point of view that further schooling at the end of high school may be undesirable. Administrators and teachers complain about the lack of preparation and maturity of the young people who demand entrance into college. Not all of these vociferous students are ready to undertake serious academic study immediately upon high school graduation. Others do not necessarily want further schooling, yet college is their most attractive, if not their only, option because they want to be with others of their same age, want to put off making what may possibly be permanently binding decisions about vocations, like the social opportunities of the college campus, and don't want to be drafted.

Thus, higher education is caught in a situation of conflicting expectations and inadequate resources. At a time when universal higher education is seen as a panacea to social problems, critics of current higher education say that it is not only impossible financially, but may also have such undesirable consequences as failing to recognize the needs of many young people for socially acceptable alternatives. What, then, are available options? What are the alternatives for high school graduates? Which adolescent characteristics make alternatives necessary?

THE NEED FOR OPTIONS

Many writers have noted the contrast between the interests of youth and the conditions of college attendance. They observe that young people are often intensely idealistic, want opportunities for involvement in solutions to social problems, seek relationships with other people, and demand immediate results from their activities. In contrast, college requires deferred gratification of goals and ideals, whether personal or vocational,

aims to develop cognitive rather than affective skills, and provides little opportunity for the student to test his ability to take responsibility. Katz notes that students press for extracurricular activities that provide an opportunity for them to show their social concerns, to help the underprivileged, or to further campaigns for civil rights and ecology. Keniston says that students want time to try out their solutions to these problems without academic penalty, even if not for academic credit. Accordingly, students on campuses all over the country have tried to bend the curriculum and the extracurriculum to permit expression of social awareness.

Other observers suggest that students need a kind of "year off" after high school, an indefinite time to assess opportunities and to gain experiences to help them make decisions about their future. If they subsequently decide to go to college, they will be more mature and purposeful students.

The creation of alternatives to schooling for the high school graduate has been recommended by such prestigious groups as the Carnegie Commission, the Assembly on University Goals and Governance, and the Report on Higher Education (Newman Report). This proposal is scarcely realistic at present because few socially sanctioned opportunities for education and experience exist other than within the colleges and universities. Society has given the schools, including the junior colleges, the total responsibility for job training, general education, custody until adulthood, any necessary counseling, and even entertainment, yet now we hear the recommendation that "upon completion of secondary school, the young should have a great variety of interesting alternatives available to them, of which immediate entry into college would be only one (Faltermayer, 1970, p. 98). What could some of these "alternatives" be?

One solution to the problem of involuntary college attendance would be to increase such options as credit by examination, adult education opportunities, credit for education while in military service, and improved extension programs. At least two agencies have reviewed these possibilities in depth: the College Entrance Examination Board report on "Credit by Examination for College Level Studies" and the ERIC Clearinghouse on Higher Education report, "College Credit for Off-Campus Study." Increasing the ways one can earn the BA or BS degree at any time in his life might reduce the "now or never" pressure on high school graduates to go directly on to college, but they do not begin to solve the problem of serving various adolescent needs. Some of these, such as the desire for active social involvement, seem actually antithetical to the educational purposes of colleges.

This paper will explore the idea of a year off as an option for young people. A new, community-based agency is proposed to provide opportunities for fulfilling at least one of the expressed needs of young people today—that of desire to help others and, in the process, explore their own personality and skills. Considering that there is little in present society in the way of meaningful work or experiences for young people, unless some viable alternatives are created we have little reason to encourage students to postpone entrance into college.

Furthermore, while it may be desirable for colleges to continue offering many services for youth, it should not be necessary for all young people to continue in school to profit from them. In other words, the trend should be away from making the junior college the societal clearinghouse for all 17-year-olds, counseling and preparing them for jobs, further academic work, or home and marriage.

A VOLUNTEER BUREAU

The proposal offered here is that a volunteer bureau or agency provide an outlet for youthful idealism. Though it would be affiliated with a junior college, it would not itself grant degrees. This agency would be, in effect, a clearinghouse for all types of available volunteer work, both in the local community and in the nation. Not only would it keep an up-to-date listing of opportunities, but agency staff would also handle some of the necessary training for the work, whether a simple, one-day orientation for teachers' aides, or the three-month, in-depth training for VISTA or Peace Corps. Staff from the agency would supervise and counsel volunteers and write a brief description of their work when the job was completed or the volunteers resigned. The agency would also work with employers using volunteers and with the local community to work on community projects.

Volunteer agencies already exist in our larger cities. Some are managed by highly experienced personnel, others are small offices with limited activities and staff. Along with a growing literature on volunteer work, social scientists predict a growing need for, and use of, volunteer services. The problem is that these agencies typically attract few young people; volunteers often are white, middle-class women, engaging in society-page charity work. Agencies engaged in the more controversial work that appeals to the young are too small or underfunded to attract and handle many of them.

Consequently, some colleges have tended to establish their own volunteer centers under the leadership of the student personnel staff and student government, rather than to encourage students to use the local community volunteer center. Many of these college volunteer organizations have become quite extensive. Student personnel administrators help find work for students off campus, and counsel and supervise them. UCLA, for example, has a Community Service Commission, modeled after a similar program at Harvard, which has found positions for several hundred students a year. The UCLA Commission published a catalog of service opportunities listing approximately 300 agencies that can use volunteers. Some participants in these extracurricular activities receive credit for part of the work, but most do not. Junior Colleges, such as Golden West in Huntington Beach, California, and Staten Island in New York, have also set up extensive extracurricular programs that involve students in social work in the local communities. Students have been helped to find summer volunteer work through such listings of jobs as *Invest Yourself,* a manual published by the Commission on Voluntary Service and Action.

Other opportunities for student social work are provided with the curriculum of certain new and experimental colleges and programs. Eberly gives an account of three well-developed programs: schools where students are given independent study credit for off-campus work; colleges such as Franconia College in New Hampshire that require off-campus study for one or two of the four years; and cooperative regional efforts to provide governmental summer internships. Other radical experiments, where the students' experience and work in the field are part of the curriculum, are being conducted at Friends World College and the Columbia, Maryland, campus of Antioch College.

By far the majority of students in higher education institutions, however, neither find such experiences included in their studies nor have the time to participate in them in the extracurriculum. Many educators question whether providing "real life" experiences for adolescents is the responsibility of colleges. However, the pressure from students for more "relevance" in their education is bound to continue. Young people whose major educational sources have been schools and television are pressing for the opportunity to experience other things for themselves, and, as long as most of the high school graduates enter college without such experience, they will put pressure on the schools to permit it, whether for credit or not.

The Volunteers

A volunteer agency, located near a local community college, could combine and extend volunteer work presently handled by local volunteer agencies and college student personnel workers. Young people who came to this agency could be:

1. enrolled full-time or part-time in the junior college, seeking part-time volunteer work for their own fulfillment. The work might, though not necessarily so, relate to the students' vocational interests.
2. not enrolled—perhaps junior college dropouts. They could be employed full- or part-time in the community or be interested in some kind of volunteer work that provided basic subsistence pay, as does VISTA or the planned California Conservation Corps.
3. already in a paraprofessional or preprofessional "human service" program of the junior college, which has an internship or practicum as part of its degree requirements.

Thus, all young people, whether students or not, would have the opportunity to try out a wide variety of work and experience presently available only in a limited way. Let us now deal with some of the practical details of staffing, organization, and funding of this proposed agency.

Community Relations

The size of the community would determine the size of the volunteer center. Ideally, the agency would have its own building on the periphery of a community college, with director and staff offices, where volunteers could gather for orientation sessions, news and announcements, group and individual counseling, and just for relaxation and informal discussion. The prospective volunteer would come here for information on openings. He would then fill out an application, giving previous experience (tutoring, political precinct work, newsboy, etc.), skills (typing, knowledge of a foreign language, life guard), type of work desired, times available, and such other details as need for transportation. If an opening existed and the person had never been a volunteer before, he would receive a general orientation. Specific training could occur in the center, on the job, or even in mini-classes on the campus, taught by either college faculty or community resource people. Should no openings exist of interest to the volunteer, the staff and the volunteer might work together to see if a new position could be created.

The community's social-economic conditions would also affect the types of volunteers and the types of work. The EPIC (Educational Participation in Communities) program at California State College at Los Angeles and Los Angeles City College has placed many of its students in positions dealing with urban problems, such as Head Start, ethnic community centers, family planning centers, and welfare agencies. A volunteer center located in a region with agriculture as its economic base, on the other hand, might want volunteers for English tutoring for Mexican-Americans, running day-care centers for children of migrant workers, or aiding livestock inspection teams. Thus, the types of work done by volunteers would necessarily be influenced by the problems facing the community where the center is located.

Staff

The staff members could come from any number of backgrounds: existing volunteer bureau staff, college student personnel workers with relevant experience, social workers, Peace Corps returnees with experience in community organizing, and faculty members (perhaps on a part-time basis) experienced in setting up and supervising work study and field work training.

Training and placing volunteers is a complex job, and requires varied personnel. At least one staff member must work in the community, finding openings for volunteers, working with agencies who use volunteers, and reviewing the volunteer positions in use. Part of this job is public relations, but part must also serve to ensure that volunteers are being used effectively in a given position. Other staff handles registration, placement, and advising volunteers. A new volunteer might need encouragement, transportation, specific skills, or perhaps even a transfer to another position. The volunteer's interests, abilities, and previous experiences must be carefully matched with the demands of the assignment if the work is to be useful to the volunteer and to the agency. Thus, to function successfully the center must have a full-time paid professional director and staff members. It also needs a secretarial staff, either paid or volunteer, for maintaining job descriptions and handling volunteer applications and records. Resource people to help with the inservice training could be faculty volunteers or community people familiar both with the neighborhood where the volunteer

would work and with techniques helpful for the job.

Staley has written an excellent summary of the steps involved in placing volunteer teacher aides in the public schools in Oregon and Washington; his observations on staff responsibility apply to any volunteer work. His survey indicated that little thought had been given to the legal and professional problems arising from the use of volunteer aides. Not knowing how best to use aides, teachers often gave them menial chores merely to keep them busy. He recommended that teachers who request aides be given short workshops to learn what services aides can perform. A blanket administrative edict to use volunteer aides will irritate teachers or any other professionals, and that irritation may be turned on the volunteer. Thus, Staley suggests that the staff must be sensitive to the dynamics of the interactions among employers, professionals, paraprofessionals, and volunteers.

Organization

A Board of Directors would provide overall leadership and direction in the volunteer agency, and would also carry full fiscal responsibility. Members of the board would serve on a rotating basis, and be broadly representative of the community. For example, it seems necessary that they represent local service agencies such as welfare, the schools, recreation, churches and synagogues, as well as the community college administration and faculty.

Funding

The financial support for most existing volunteer bureaus comes mainly from United Way or Community Chest organizations, and is supplemented by donations, special drives, local charity clubs, and occasionally from a city council budget. The educational work of the new agency would make it eligible for funds from state and federal agencies. Some money would have to come from the local community, of course, because the agency would primarily serve its needs. If a community college wanted to help establish a volunteer bureau in a town without one, aid, in the form of staff and funds, might be secured from the local churches and synagogues, the YMCA and YWCA, as well as from the Washington office of Volunteers of America, Inc.

A related problem facing a volunteer agency centers on how young people, who usually have little financial security, could afford to be volunteers. Some will be able to support themselves through part-time work, and others will be allowed to live at home for a year or so after high school while trying out options through the volunteer services (even though parents willing to support a son or daughter through college might not feel the same toward volunteer work). To attract those from less well-to-do homes, however, the volunteer bureau ideally should be able to pay a subsistence wage for full-time work, as is already being done for VISTA work and for the alternate service performed by conscientious objectors in the military. California is now starting a conservation corps for conscientious objectors that pays room, board, and $15 a month. This will be extended to interested volunteers as soon as enough camps can be established.

If more such programs were established, many young people would be willing to commit themselves for the sake of the experience and travel they could not otherwise afford.

ADVANTAGES AND DISADVANTAGES

For Youth

The most obvious advantage for young people is the chance to try out some part- or full-time work, not blindly, but with supervision and counseling. The work would be tied to their interest and appropriate to their maturity and previous experience. For some young people, working as a nurse's aide might be stimulating and meaningful because of the close supervision and chance to be with other young volunteers. Others, who might want more independence and responsibility, could act as researchers, for example, for conservation groups seeking data on voting records of congressmen, or as workers with minority groups in community centers. A young person could take several assignments of increasing complexity over a one-year period, be committed to a one-year assignment away from home, or come and go for short periods of time alternating with attendance at school.

Some clues to the advantages of volunteer work for young people come from the research on college student volunteers. Some data exist that distinguish student social activists from both nonactivists and political radicals. Campagna's research indicates that students who do involve themselves in some kind of service work report greater satisfaction with both their studies and themselves. University of Minnesota community volunteers tended to be upperclassmen who had above-average GPAs. A high percentage of them lived close to campus, were enrolled in social science majors, and had families that emphasized "helping" values. In other words, research indicates that students who do volunteer work usually have a firm commitment to it. This is demonstrated by the fact that they make time to tutor while keeping up good grades.

The question that arises from studying these data is whether the volunteer experiences actually help them become better students, or whether better and more mature students volunteer for community work. If an opportunity for community service existed, would junior college students or high school graduates who were unsure of their academic goals take advantage of it? Present data on college students indicate that only a small percentage of all of them actually volunteers. In one study, however, many supported such work verbally, and indicated that if they had had the time and the knowledge of how to join, they too would have volunteered.

It is logical that only the most highly motivated and organized students have felt they could take time off from school to do social service. Only the most innovative campuses presently give academic or community recognition of or reward for a student's extracurricular work. The new or weak or unsure student could not afford to take the risk of extracurricular work because it would compete with his academic work. And dropping

out to travel or work has been seen as tantamount to failure for a girl and an invitation to the draft for a young man. If more significant support and guidance came from college administrators, parents, and high school staff for a young person to leave "the system" for a time, it is likely that we would see a type of youthful volunteer quite different from those reported in the literature thus far. But the research suggests that only when solidly structured and well-designed options exist, ones that do not detract from a young person's future chances, will there be volunteers from the group that presently enters the community college en masse. This leads us to look at the advantages and disadvantages of the volunteer agency for the community and for the junior college and its faculty.

For The Community

The major advantage of a volunteer agency would be that it could work on solutions to community social problems. The creation of paraprofessional programs for human service occupations in the junior college demonstrates a recognition of the great shortage of trained manpower in these fields. By 1975, some 3.5 million persons will be fully employed in service fields in this country, and many more will be involved on a volunteer or part-time basis. The figure is expected to grow as the nation directs more and more of its attention to domestic problems. It will be impossible to fill these jobs with paid, college-trained personnel, partly because not enough are available and partly because the need is much greater than the funds available.

Most social planners recognize that a significant part of the manpower deficit in service occupations will have to be filled with volunteers. Being a volunteer, however, does not mean the person is untrained or ill-prepared to do the job. Many volunteers have the knowledge of a paraprofessional, received through training on the job and through years of experience, but choose not to take a position as a full-time, paid employee.

Whether a young person tried volunteer work as part of a specific training program, as part of his leisure-time activities for self-development, or as a way to learn about the kind of service work he wanted to specialize in, the experience would help acquaint him with the growing and complex field of human service work. At the same time, it would help to alleviate a tremendous manpower shortage.

Are there presently enough volunteer jobs available for large numbers of young people to take advantage of this option? This question may reflect the fact that few people are aware of the many health, welfare, and recreational services that already exist. The Los Angeles County *Director of Health, Welfare, Vocational and Recreational Services,* for example, lists them under 64 different headings. Volunteers could be placed in any of the agencies, commissions, departments, and bureaus under these headings:

Adoption
Adult Education
Services for the Aged (housing, recreation centers, etc.)

Alcoholism
Apprentice and vocational training, placement
The handicapped—deaf, blind, physically disabled, etc.
Community Action groups
Community centers and settlements
Consumer education and protection
Correctional facilities
Family counseling, casework, etc.
Services for the foreign-born, immigration,
   naturalization
Health education
Hospitals, clinics, etc.—for mentally ill, maternity,
   drugs, crisis intervention, children, retardation
Housing—emergency
Industrial relations and labor law enforcement
Juvenile delinquency control and prevention
Law enforcement
Public health service and communicable disease
   control—venereal diseases
Race relations and intercultural groups
Recreation
Legal aid and lawyer's reference services
Missing persons
Sex education—homes for unwed mothers, abortion
   counseling, planned parenthood
Servicemen and women, veterans organizations and
   services
Small business development
Tutorial services
Urban renewal
Youth services—Big Brothers, clubs, Head Start, etc.

This list shows that city, county, state, and federal government, as well as religious groups, special interest groups, and private businesses, are in the human service business. It also shows that these services are not offered for any one particular class, race, or subgroup; everyone at some time will use a public service. But these are not the only areas where volunteers could be used; there are at least two other broad areas that will need personnel of all kinds—communications (libraries, cable TV, and other media), and environmental protection (legal aides, naturalists). Thus, the problem is not whether volunteers are needed, but how to get employers and service agencies to use them.

Besides gaining help in solving community problems and filling shortages in service personnel, the volunteer center has more nebulous advantages for the community. The ancient "town-gown" tensions could be reduced, or at least differences more clearly seen, as youths and city residents work together on common problems. Conceivably, the alienation and dissatisfaction of young people would lessen if they too were allowed a stake in the community's attempts to deal with its problems. Those who have worked as volunteers report a greater feeling of involvement and purpose than those who have no outlets for their concerns.

For The Community College And Its Faculty

Having this agency near the campus would offer several advantages for the junior college. First, the scope of the on-campus student personnel programs could be reduced to those services related directly to students, such as financial aids, academic counseling, and student organizations and publications. Time presently spent in telling a student about vocational options and in giving him vocational tests might be better used in allowing the student to experience various jobs and discover for himself where his skills lie.

Second, the volunteer work done through the agency could fulfill the "experience" requirements for the new paraprofessional human service programs that are a growing segment of junior college curricula. These include two-year programs in Child Day-Care and Homemaking, Communications and Transportation, Education (teachers' aides, etc.), Environmental Services, Fire Prevention and Safety, Government Service, Law Enforcement and Corrections, Medicine (nurse, dental assistant), Recreation and Parks, and Social Work. Not all of these programs, of course, require internships or practicums, but even there, young men and women could still use the volunteer work as an opportunity to find out more about the field before completing the theoretical and academic preparation. Setting up a good practicum or internship, when part of a college program, has consumed much faculty time and effort in the past. An agency with staff trained in placement, supervision, and counseling of volunteers in a wide range of service experiences could free faculty from work for which they have little preparation and less time.

Third and last, the volunteer agency would be specific arm of the junior college's "Community Service" commitment without consuming budget and staff time.

QUESTIONS ABOUT THE PROPOSAL FOR A VOLUNTEER AGENCY

In addition to describing the advantages and disadvantages of a student volunteer agency, another way to understand the implications of the agency is to answer the following four questions:

1. If some kind of service experience is necessary for the aware and mature adult in this society, why not make it a required part of the junior college general education curriculum?

Put another way, why should the volunteer agency be outside the junior college curriculum and structure? If such experiences in the community have educational benefit for all young people, should not such work be considered part of their formal education while in school? Stanton presents a case for adopting student internships under junior college general education. Most courses presently taught under the general education rubric, he argues, are sterile, and fail to accomplish their purpose, helping young people gain understanding of themselves and their world.

While the idea of broadening the general education concept to include adolescent service experience may be a desirable long-range goal, it would not only be difficult to establish, but would also have several other drawbacks. The difficulty would come partly from faculty resistance to the idea of making general education courses more practical. Many faculty still assume that only vocational courses should be practical and tied to concrete experience, and these they consider nonintellectual. Instructors who have themselves learned by the textbook, formal-lecture method see little reason for new teaching methods and content. While this bias against the practical, specific, and concrete is breaking down, it may be many years before faculty will accept student internships as a vehicle of instruction in general education courses.

A second drawback to incorporating student service work into general education courses immediately is that nonstudents will continue to be denied such educational experiences. The assumption behind the proposal to expand the curriculum to serve ever more people is that education should continue to occur on campus and in the classroom. By building the volunteer agency off campus and opening it to students and nonstudents alike, youth could take advantage of this educational experience without enrolling in a course.

Last is a fundamental contradiction between volunteer service and required service as part of course work. Part of the effectiveness of such efforts at community development comes from the fact that they are voluntary. To make such work part of a required general education curriculum before all young people are willing to volunteer would destroy the educational and social benefits of the experience.

By making the voluntary agency independent of the junior college, both students and faculty could profit from the agency's work without the drawbacks of a required curriculum. The agency could become a place where faculty and volunteer staff formulated and tested educational objectives for internships before incorporating them into course work. Research could be done to improve our understanding of the kind of learning that results from service work. The need for volunteer work in our society is clear, but our knowledge of the educational processes that go on during such work is insufficient for us to require such experiences as part of all students' general education. Thus, the opportunities for research and for trial runs of internships could make the agency a workshop for new curricula and teaching methods for community colleges.

2. Are young people mature enough to handle the responsibility?

This question assumes that students are children, an idea that has kept colleges in the business of providing custodial care. The irony is that students are told they are immature and irresponsible, but are also advised to stay in school until they are ready to take on adult responsibilities, usually synonymous with a paying job. The situation is similar to a colonial government prohibiting self-government for the natives until they demonstrate they are ready for it, but denying them the opportunity to learn it. Similarly, keeping young men or women in school until they have made decisions about vocational plans and interests denies them the experiences necessary for making those decisions.

Many colleges have long functioned in loco parentis, justifying the practice on the assumption that students were not yet adults either legally or physically. Now, of course, the 26th amendment has changed the legal status of students. Keniston gives us new perspectives on the psychological and physiological age of youth:

> Since the turn of the century, the average amount of education received by each student group has increased by approximately one year per decade. Also, the average age for the onset of puberty has decreased by approximately one-fifth of a year per decade. Finally, the average student of any given age today appears to score approximately one standard deviation above the average student of the same age a generation ago on most standardized measures of intellectual performance. . . .
>
> Translated into individual terms, this means that the average 16-year-old of today, compared with the 16-year-old of 1920, would probably have reached puberty one year earlier, have received approximately five years more education, and be performing intellectually at the same age level as a 17- or 18-year-old in 1920. Today's high school and college students are about a year more mature physiologically and a year more developed intellectually than their parents were at the same age, but on the other hand, they must defer adult responsibilities, rights, and prerogatives five years longer. (p. 118)

The segregation of college students from the adult world thus puts an understandable pressure on them if they wish to gain immediate experience and to take on responsibilities before going on for college work.

3. If young people leave school and fail to enroll directly after high school graduation, will they ever receive a college degree?

This question is prompted by the idea that once a youth leaves school he will not likely return. At a recent regional conference of junior college deans of instruction, a question arose about the possible effect on junior college admissions of the abolition of the twelfth grade, a proposal put forth by the California Superintendent of Public Instruction in 1971. One dean felt that college should encourage the eleventh graders to start college classes part-time so that "we can keep them in the system," but it is no longer true that youth will never return to school if they take time off. Patterns of college attendance are changing rapidly, tending toward continuing education and periods of retraining throughout adult life. One study has concluded that the students who succeed in college have most often been between the ages of 21 and 25; been out of high school between two and five years; learned how to work; and had some idea of what kind of work they want to do. There should be less concern with "getting them right after high school" and more for encouraging older people to return to school.

To break the lockstep of students from high school to college, however, will require some educators to change their perspectives. High schools will have to prepare the students to live and work better in society, as well as to profit from any schooling they might undertake in the indefinite future. Higher education institutions will have to increase the number of criteria for admissions to include students' experiences after high school, rather than depend so much on high school grades and dated test scores as predictors of success in college.

4. Isn't encouraging youth to participate in social-help programs just allowing them to postpone adulthood still longer?

This question implies that participating in volunteer services merely provides another institution to keep young people off the streets or out of the job market. On the contrary, its purpose is to give them a chance to learn about their community while contributing their time and skills to its development.

Thus, the provision of service opportunities for youth assumes a new view of the value and purpose of social services in general. We must give up the old myths about those who take and provide social service, namely, that "social programs" of any kind are merely handouts for prisoners, alcoholics, and others who are somehow too weak to make good on their own. As noted earlier, the social services now performed in our society, where volunteers could contribute the most, are available to, and often taken for granted by, every member of the society. From birth to the grave, we use public schools, public libraries, hospitals, and community centers. Rather than revealing weaknesses by using public services, a person shows he is aware of more options, and thus feels greater personal freedom. As Hubert C. Noble, of the National Council of Churches, has commented, the community must ". . . recognize that our society is no longer individual, open, and free, and that individual autonomy is only possible as we develop programs and structures within the structures that encourage it." If the purpose of social services is to encourage individual autonomy, personal growth, and fulfillment, whoever participates in them, either as a volunteer or a paid employe, is contributing to these goals for himself as well as for others.

Providing an opportunity for everyone—young, middle-aged, or elderly—to contribute in some way to the betterment of his community might do much to alleviate the feeling of estrangement and alienation between individuals and society, for the volunteer then becomes a participant in the process of improving the community, rather than a passive receiver of its services. It is important that we start now to establish these opportunities for young people so that they too can begin to feel a part of a community effort and relate their education more closely to the needs of the world in which they live.

REFERENCES

American Academy of Arts and Sciences, the Assembly on University Goals and Governance. First report, written by Martin Meyerson and Stephen Graubard. Reprinted in the *Chronicle of Higher Education,* Jan. 18, 1971.

Block, J. H., Haan, N., and Smith, M. B. Activism and Apathy in Contemporary Adolescents. In J. F. Adams, ed., *Contributions to the Understanding of Adolescents.* Boston: Allyn and Bacon, 1967.

Burns, Martha A. New Careers in Human Service: A Challenge to the Two-Year College. A Preliminary Report. Center for the Study of Higher Education, Report No. 9, Pennsylvania State University, University Park, Pa., March 1971. (ED 049 732)

Brewster, Kingman, Jr. The Involuntary Campus and the Manipulated Society. *Educational Record, 51:*2 (Spring 1970), pp. 101-105.

Campagna, Dennis. Non-Academic Aspects of College Experience. Paper presented at the Annual Meeding of the American Educational Research Association, Los Angeles, Feb. 5-8, 1969.

Carnegie Commission on Higher Education. *Less Time, More Options: Education Beyond High School.* New York: McGraw-Hill, 1970.

Clements, William H. Research on Who Should Go to College, and When. Paper presented at the Wisconsin Personnel and Guidance Association Convention, Nov. 5-6, 1970. (ED 044 737)

Cohen, Arthur M. *Dateline '79: Heretical Concepts for the Community College.* Beverly Hills: Glencoe Press, 1969.

———. Stretching Pre-College Education. *Social Policy, 2:*1 (May-June 1971), pp. 5-9.

———. and Brawer, Florence B. *Confronting Identity: The Community College Instructor.* New York: Prentice-Hall, 1972.

Directory of Health, Welfare, Vocational and Recreational Services in Los Angeles County. Los Angeles, California: Welfare Information Service, Inc., 1969.

Eberly, Donald J. Service Experience and Educational Growth. *Educational Record, 49* (Spring 1968), pp. 197-205.

Faltermayer, Edmund K. Let's Break the Go-to-College Lockstep. *Fortune, 82:*5 (Nov. 1970), pp. 98-103, 144, 147.

Flaugher, Ronald L., Mahoney, Margaret H., and Messing, Rita B. *Credit by Examination for College-Level Studies; An Annotated Bibliography.* New York: College Entrance Examination Board, 1967.

Gelineau, V. A., and Kantor, D. Pro-Social Commitment Among College Students. *Journal of Social Issues, 20* (1964), pp. 112-130.

Goldman, Leroy H. New Approach to Community Services Through Community Involvement. Unpublished seminar paper, 1969. (ED 035 414)

Illich, Ivan. Schooling: The Ritual of Progress. *New York Review of Books,* Dec. 3, 1970. (First of a two-part series)

———. Education Without School: How It Can Be Done. *New York Review of Books,* Jan. 7, 1971. (Second of a two-part series)

Invest Yourself: A Catalogue of Service Opportunities, 1970. New York: The Commission on Voluntary Service and Action, 475 Riverside Drive, 1970.

Jerome, Judson. *Culture Out of Anarchy; The Reconstruction of American Higher Learning.* New York: Herder and Herder, 1970.

Katz, Joseph et al. *No Time for Youth: Growth and Constraint in College Students.* San Francisco: Jossey-Bass, 1968.

Keniston, Kenneth. What's Bugging the Students? *Educational Record, 51:*2 (Spring 1970), pp. 116-129.

———. *Young Radicals; Notes on Committed Youth.* New York: Harcourt, Brace and World, Inc., 1968.

———. *The Uncommitted: Alienated Youth in American Society.* New York: Harcourt, Brace and World, Inc., 1965.

McNeer, Lenore W. Something Special in Friendship. *Junior College Journal, 40:*8 (May 1970), pp. 38-39.

Neale, Daniel C., and Johnson, David W. College Student Parcipation in Social Action Projects. Washington, D.C.: American Education Researh Association, 1969. (ED 028 469)

New Work for CO's. *Saturday Review,* July 3, 1971.

Reimer, Everett. *An Essay in Alternatives in Education.* Cuernavaca, Mexico: Center for Intercultural Documentation, 1970.

Report on Higher Education. Frank Newman, Chairman. U.S. Department of Health, Education, and Welfare, March 1971.

Schindler-Rainman, Eva, and Lippitt, Ronald. *The Volunteer Community: Creative Uses of Human Resources.* Washington, D.C.: Center for a Voluntary Society, 1971.

Sharon, Amiel T. *College Credit for Off-Campus Study.* Washington, D.C.: ERIC Clearinghouse on Higher Education, Report No. 8, March 1971.

Staley, Gerald J. Volunteer Aides in Public Schools. Policies and Procedures in Oregon and Washington. Eugene: Oregon

University, Bureau of Educational Research, March 1970. (ED 041 862)

Stanton, Charles M. Community Service and the Need for a Human Resources Center. Unpublished report, September 1970. (ED 046 378)

Taylor, Harold. *Students Without Teachers; The Crisis in the University.* New York: McGraw-Hill, 1969.

Toward a More Relevant Curriculum; An Occasional Paper. Report of a National Seminar Jointly Sponsored by the Danforth Foundation, Institute for the Development of Educational Activities, Inc., and the National Association of Secondary

School Principles. St. Louis, n.d.

Ullrich, Mary. A Human Service Career Conference. *Junior College Journal, 41:4* (Dec.-Jan., 1970-71), pp. 23-28.

Volunteer Opportunities in L.A. County. Prepared by ASUCLA Programs Office, Community Service Commission, Kerckhoff Hall, UCLA, June 1969.

von Hoffman, Nicholas. Dropouts—Are They Just Tired? *Chicago Sun-Times,* Section 3, p. 4, Jan. 11, 1970.

Willingham, Warren W. Educational Opportunity and the Organization of Higher Education. Palo Alto, California: College Entrance Examination Board, June 1970. (ED 043 276)

KEY-WORD INDEX

Numbers refer to article numbers, *not* page numbers;
article titles and numbers are printed at the upper right
corner of each right-hand page in the book, before the
page number.

AUTHOR INDEX

Numbers refer to article numbers, *not* page numbers; article titles and numbers are printed at the upper right corner of each right-hand page in the book, before the page number.